LAW AND LANGUAGE
Current Legal Issues 2011

VOLUME 15

Law and Language

Current Legal Issues 2011

VOLUME 15

Edited by
MICHAEL FREEMAN FBA
Emeritus Professor of English Law
University College London
and
FIONA SMITH
Senior Lecturer, Faculty of Laws
University College London

OXFORD
UNIVERSITY PRESS

Great Clarendon Street, Oxford, OX2 6DP,
United Kingdom

Oxford University Press is a department of the University of Oxford.
It furthers the University's objective of excellence in research, scholarship,
and education by publishing worldwide. Oxford is a registered trade mark of
Oxford University Press in the UK and in certain other countries

© The several contributors 2013

The moral rights of the authors have been asserted

First Edition published in 2013

Impression: 1

All rights reserved. No part of this publication may be reproduced, stored in
a retrieval system, or transmitted, in any form or by any means, without the
prior permission in writing of Oxford University Press, or as expressly permitted
by law, by licence, or under terms agreed with the appropriate reprographics
rights organization. Enquiries concerning reproduction outside the scope of the
above should be sent to the Rights Department, Oxford University Press, at the
address above

You must not circulate this work in any other form
and you must impose this same condition on any acquirer

Crown copyright material is reproduced under Class Licence
Number C01P0000148 with the permission of OPSI
and the Queen's Printer for Scotland

British Library Cataloguing in Publication Data

Data available

ISBN 978–0–19–967366–7

Printed in Great Britain by
CPI Group (UK) Ltd, Croydon, CR0 4YY

Links to third party websites are provided by Oxford in good faith and
for information only. Oxford disclaims any responsibility for the materials
contained in any third party website referenced in this work.

Preface

Putting law and language together seems so natural that it is surprising we waited until the fifteenth colloquium to pair them.

This book contains the revised papers from that colloquium held in July 2011. Like previous colloquia and books in the series, the theme is the relationship between two or more disciplines. The colloquia began in 1997 with Law and Science and will continue in 2012 with Law and Global Health. Future colloquia are projected on Law and Gender Studies, Law and Order, and Law and the City.

As ever, the Law and Language colloquium raised a multiplicity of issues, ranging from interpretation to translation and literature, and to the deaf. This book reflects that diversity. The colloquium attracted participants from around the world and from a variety of disciplines.

We believe that the papers will not only contribute to scholarship but also prove valuable teaching material.

The book is edited by the joint convenors of the colloquium. I wish to place on record that the bulk of the work was done by Dr Fiona Smith, and to express my gratitude to her for her hard work, initiative, and commitment to the project throughout.

The colloquium benefited from financial support from UCL's Grand Challenge on Intercultural Exchange and from the UCL Faculty of Laws. We are both grateful for this support which enabled us to hold such a rich and diverse conversation on law and language.

We both wish to thank UCL's Events Manager, Lisa Penfold and her team, and Jacqui Bennett for their administrative skills, without which there would not have been a colloquium or this book.

Professor Michael Freeman FBA
March 2012

Contents

List of Contributors   xi

1. Law and Language: An Introduction   1
   Michael Freeman and Fiona Smith

2. Legal Texts and Canons of Construction: A View from Current Pragmatic Theory   8
   Robyn Carston

3. Linguistic Meaning and Legal Truth   34
   Brian H. Bix

4. Truth in Law   45
   Andrei Marmor

5. Language, Truth, and Law   62
   Andrew Halpin

6. Claims of Legal Authorities and 'Expressions of Intention': The Limits of Philosophy of Language   79
   Veronica Rodriguez-Blanco

7. Legal Pluralism: A Systems Theory Approach to Language, Translation, and Communication   100
   Richard Nobles and David Schiff

8. Frame Semantics and the 'Internal Point of View'   115
   Steven L. Winter

9. Hart as Contextualist? Theories of Interpretation in Language and the Law   128
   Ross Charnock

10. On Goodness and Genre: Talking about Virtue in Law and Literature   151
    Jan-Melissa Schramm

11. The Grin's Cat: Language, Law, and Literature   164
    Sebastian McEvoy

12. Reading and Writing the Law: Macaulay in India   187
    Michael Hancher

13. 'Where be his quiddities now'? Law and Language in *Hamlet*   201
    Eric Heinze

14. Stories in Law: Providing Space for 'Oppositionists'?   221
    Steven Cammiss

15. Literal Interpretation and English Precedent in 246
    Joe Ma's *Lawyer, Lawyer*
    Marco Wan

16. Toward a Cognitive Science of Legal Interpretation 259
    Benjamin Shaer

17. Do You Kick a Dog when it's Down? Considering the Use of 292
    Children's Video-Recorded Testimonies in Court
    June Luchjenbroers and Michelle Aldridge-Waddon

18. The Power of Naming: Surnames, Children, and Spouses 310
    Jonathan Herring

19. The Role of Language in Legal Contexts: A Forensic 328
    Cross-Linguistic Viewpoint
    Luna Filipović

20. Vagueness and Power Delegation in Law: A Reply to Sorensen 344
    Hrafn Asgeirsson

21. Plato's Fertility Clinic: Status and Identity Rhetoric in 356
    Parenthood Disputes
    David Gurnham

22. Silence, Speech, and the Paradox of the Right to Remain 371
    Silent in American Police Interrogation
    Janet Ainsworth

23. The Consumption of Legal Language: Consuming the Law 386
    Anthony Amatrudo

24. (Language + Law)^2 = ? 400
    Catrin Fflur Huws

25. MMORPGing, Law, and Lingo 417
    Kim Barker

26. Construing Commercial Contracts: No Need for Violence 434
    Paul S. Davies

27. Why Are Non-US Contracts Written in US Legalese? Some 457
    Preliminary Thoughts and a Research Agenda
    Claire A. Hill

28. The Role of Parliamentary Rhetoric in Facilitating the Racial Effect 466
    of the Stop and Search Powers in Section 44 of the Terrorism Act 2000
    Rachel Herron

29. Precedent at the Court of Justice of the European Union: The 483
    Linguistic Aspect
    Karen McAuliffe

30. Law and Language(s) at the Heart of the European Project: 493
    Educating Different Kinds of Lawyers
    Bénédicte Sage-Fuller, Ferdinand Prinz zur Lippe, and Seán Ó Conaill

31. Foreign Law in Translation: If Truth Be Told… 513
    Simone Glanert and Pierre Legrand

32. First-Person Perspectives in Legal Decisions 533
    Lorenz Kaehler

33. Deaf People at the Old Bailey From the 18th Century Onwards 557
    Bencie Woll and Christopher Stone

34. Rule of the Root: Proto-Indo-European Domination 571
    of Legal Language
    Gary Watt

35. Necessary Violence? Inscribing the Subject of Law 590
    Penelope Pether

Subject Index 619

Name Index 623

List of Contributors

Janet Ainsworth, John D. Eshelman Professor of Law at Seattle University.

Michelle Aldridge-Waddon, Senior Lecturer, Centre for Language and Communication, Cardiff University.

Anthony Amatrudo, Reader in Criminology at Middlesex University.

Hrafn Asgeirsson, Postdoctoral Research Fellow at Monash University, Faculty of Law.

Kim Barker, PhD candidate, Aberystwyth University, Fellow at the University of Birmingham.

Brian H. Bix, Frederick W. Thomas Professor of Law and Philosophy, University of Minnesota.

Steven Cammiss, Lecturer in Law, School of Law, University of Leicester.

Robyn Carston, Professor of Linguistics, University College London and CSMN, Oslo.

Ross Charnock, MCF, Univ Paris-Dauphine, CRCL/CREA.

Paul S. Davies, Fellow of Gonville and Caius College, University of Cambridge.

Luna Filipović, Senior Lecturer in Applied Translation, University of East Anglia.

Michael Freeman FBA, Emeritus Professor of English Law, University College London.

Simone Glanert, Senior Lecturer in French and European Comparative Law, University of Kent (Canterbury).

David Gurnham, Reader, School of Law, University of Southampton.

Andrew Halpin, Professor of Law, Faculty of Law, National University of Singapore.

Michael Hancher, Professor of English, University of Minnesota.

Eric Heinze, Professor of Law, Department of Law, Queen Mary, University of London.

Jonathan Herring, Fellow in Law at Exeter College, University of Oxford.

Rachel Herron, PhD candidate, Law School, University of Durham.

Claire A. Hill, Professor and James L. Krusemark Chair in Law and Director, Institute for Law and Rationality, University of Minnesota Law School.

Catrin Fflur Huws, Lecturer, Department of Law and Criminology, and Director of the Centre for Welsh Legal Affairs, Aberystwyth University.

Lorenz Kaehler, Professor, Faculty of Law, University of Bremen.

Pierre Legrand, Professor of Law, Sorbonne (Paris).

June Luchjenbroers, Senior Lecturer, Department of Linguistics and English Language, Bangor University.

Andrei Marmor, Professor of Philosophy and Law, and Maurice Jones Jr Professor of Law, University of Southern California.

Karen McAuliffe, Senior Lecturer, School of Law, University of Exeter.

Sebastian McEvoy, UPOND (University of Paris Ouest Nanterre La Défense).

Richard Nobles, Professor of Law, Queen Mary, University of London.

Seán Ó Conaill, Law and Irish Lecturer, Faculty of Law, University College Cork.

Penelope Pether, Professor of Law, Villanova University School of Law.

Ferdinand Prinz zur Lippe, Law School, Trinity College Dublin.

Veronica Rodriguez-Blanco, Senior Lecturer, University of Birmingham, School of Law.

Bénédicte Sage-Fuller, Faculty of Law, University College Cork.

David Schiff, Professor of Law, Queen Mary, University of London.

Jan-Melissa Schramm, University Lecturer in English and Fellow of Trinity Hall, University of Cambridge.

Benjamin Shaer, Adjunct Research Professor, Department of Law and Legal Studies and School of Linguistics and Language Studies, Carleton University.

Fiona Smith, Senior Lecturer in Laws and Director, WTO Scholars Forum, Faculty of Laws, University College London.

Christopher Stone, Interpreter and Coordinator, Deafness Cognition and Language Research Centre, University College London.

Marco Wan, Assistant Professor of Law and Honorary Assistant Professor of English, University of Hong Kong.

Gary Watt, Professor of Law, University of Warwick.

Steven L. Winter, Walter S. Gibbs Professor of Constitutional Law at Wayne State University Law School.

Bencie Woll, Professor, Institute of Cognitive Neuroscience, University College London.

1
Law and Language: An Introduction

*Michael Freeman and Fiona Smith**

Robert Cover's classic essay 'Violence and the Word' opens:

Legal interpretation takes place in a field of pain and death. This is true in several senses. Legal interpretive acts signal and occasion the imposition of violence upon others: A judge articulates his understanding of a text, and, as a result, somebody loses his freedom, his property, his children, even his life. Interpretations in law also constitute justifications for violence which has already occurred or which is about to occur. When interpreters have finished their work they frequently leave behind victims whose lives have been torn apart by these organized, social practices of violence. Neither legal interpretation nor the violence it occasions may be properly understood apart from one another.[1]

Although he does not do so, Cover could have traced this association back to the mists of history, to the 'story' of the Tower of Babel.[2] According to the book of Genesis, a multiplicity of languages was the result of disobedience of the law. But it may be much more interesting than that. The reference in Genesis (in the chapter before the Babel story) to 'maritime peoples spread[ing] out into the lands in their clans within their nation, each with its own language'[3] may be to what we now know as historical fact. It was the imperial practice of the neo-Assyrians to impose their language on peoples they conquered. An inscription of the time records that Ashurbanipal II 'made the totality of all peoples speak one speech'. A cylinder inscription of Sargon II says: 'Populations of the four quarters of the world with strange tongues and incompatible speech...whom I had taken as booty at the Command of Ashur my Lord by the might of my spectre, I caused to accept a single voice'. The neo-Assyrians asserted their supremacy by insisting that their language was the only one to be used by populations they had defeated. Is 'Babel' then an early critique of imperialism?

As a discipline 'law and language' has barely 40 years of scholarship.[4] But there are discussions of the relationship well before current critical thinking emerged. Bentham was a conscious innovator both of legal language ('Codification', 'international law') and of new forms of enquiry into the structure of law. With his ultimate goal the erection of

---

* The authors would like to thank the editorial team at Oxford University Press who contributed to the preparation of this volume.

[1] (1985–1986) 95 *Yale Law Journal* 1601.

[2] *Genesis* 11: 1–9. Scholars agree that the edifice referred to was a *ziggurat*, a Mesopotamian temple tower. George Steiner in *After Babel* (Oxford: Oxford University Press, 1975) does not address this, which is rather a pity.

[3] *Genesis* 10: 31.

[4] David Mellinkoff, *The Language of The Law* (Boston: Little, Brown & Co., 1963) is an early example. It addresses the historical development of legal language. See also Peter Tiersma, 'What is Language and the Law? Does Anyone Care?' in Frances Olsen. Alexander Lorz, and Dieter Stein (eds), *Law and Language: Theory and Society* (Loyola L.A. Legal Studies Paper No. 2009–11, 2009). And more fully Peter Tiersma, *Legal Language* (Chicago: University of Chicago Press, 1999). See also A. Phillips, *Lawyers' Language* (London: Routledge, 2003).

a structure within which law reform would take place, Bentham was prepared to 'fix the meaning of terms',[5] so as not to be restricted by contemporary patterns. Bentham also developed what we call deontic logic.[6]

H.L.A. Hart, the father of modern positivist jurisprudence, was also sensitive to the relationship between law and language. In the Preface to *The Concept of Law*[7] he quotes the philosopher J.L. Austin to the effect that 'a sharpened awareness of words' can 'sharpen our awareness of phenomena'.[8]

The Scandinavian Realists have also contributed to our understanding of the relationship between law and language.[9] Thus Axel Hägerström,[10] who wanted to establish a real legal science, needed to liberate legal science from mythology, theology, and metaphysics. Legal thinking and language is permeated with such concepts. His study of Roman law is particularly instructive. He saw the *ius civile* as a system of rules for the acquisition and exercise of supernatural powers. Equally, he saw in modern law ritualistic exercises: the Coronation ceremony, the black cap placed on a judge's head before he pronounced the death penalty, the wedding ring. The influence of Hägerström is apparent in Karl Olivecrona's analysis of legal language, in his discussion of what he calls 'performativs', legal words which are used to produce certain desired results, usually a change in legal relationships.[11] Thus, 'I do', said during a marriage ceremony, influences people to regard a man and a woman (or now man and man or two women) in a different light from the way they treated them prior to the ceremony. As Olivecrona puts it: 'it is the language of magic.'[12]

A more recent intervention into the debate about law and language, still within the philosophical tradition, is Brian Bix's *Law, Language and Legal Determinacy*.[13] Bix argues that philosophers of language cannot generate philosophies of law because of law's normative and political dimensions. Another recent example within this tradition of scholarship is found in Frederick Schauer's edited collection, *Law and Language*.[14] He sees law and language as united in their distinctive institutional generality and also in the future that language plays in dispute resolution.

The centre of gravity of law and language no longer occupies this analytical system. There is now an overlap with law and literature.[15] Thus James Boyd White[16] and Richard

---

[5] On Bentham and language see R. Harrison, *Bentham* (London: Routledge and Kegan Paul, 1983).
[6] See D. Lyons, *In the Interests of The Governed* (Oxford: Oxford University Press, 1973), ch.6.
[7] H.L.A. Hart, *The Concept of Law* (Oxford: Oxford University Press, 1961, 2nd edn, Oxford, 1994).
[8] Hart, *The Concept of Law* (cited in n.7), vii.
[9] See the discussion in M.D.A. Freeman, *Lloyd's Introduction To Jurisprudence* (London: Sweet & Maxwell, 2008), ch.11.
[10] See Patricia Mindus, *A Real Mind: The Life and Work of Axel Hägerström* (Dordrecht: Springer, 2007). See also N. Simmonds (1976) *Judicial Review* 210.
[11] Karl Olivecrona, 'Legal Language and Reality' in R.A. Newman (ed.), *Essays In Jurisprudence In Honor of Roscoe Pound* (Indianapolis, Ind.: The Bobbs-Merrill Co. Inc., 1964), 151. See also Karl Olivecrona, *Law As Fact* (2nd edn) (London: Stevens & Sons, 1971), chs 8 and 9.
[12] Olivecrona, 'Legal Language and Reality' (cited in n.11), 175.
[13] B. Bix, *Law, Language and Legal Determinacy* (Oxford: Clarendon Press, 1993).
[14] F. Schauer, *Law and Language* (New York: Longman, 1993).
[15] See a previous volume in this series: M. Freeman and A. Lewis (eds), *Law and Literature* (Oxford: Oxford University Press, 1999). For a collection of essays on Shakespeare see P. Raffield and G. Watt, *Shakespeare and the Law* (Oxford: Hart Publishing, 2008).
[16] J.B. White, *The Legal Imagination* (Boston: Little, Brown & Co., 1973); *When Words Lose Their Meaning* (Chicago, 1984); 'What Can a Lawyer Learn From Literature?' (1989) 102 *Harvard Law Review* 2014–47; *The Edge of Meaning* (Chicago: University of Chicago Press, 2001); *Living Speech* (Princeton, N.J.: Princeton University Press, 2006).

Weisberg[17] straddle both disciplines. In *Poethics*,[18] Weisberg claims that law and literature are 'our culture's most celebrated narrative endeavours'.[19] In *Vichy Law and the Holocaust in France*[20] Weisberg offers perhaps the best case study of Cover's thesis in 'Violence and the Word'.[21] Weisberg puts much of the blame for the persecution of the Jews under the Vichy regime on to legal texts (statements, judicial decisions, academic writing). The lawyers who produced this material sparked a legal 'exclusionary discourse'. He indicts also the French 'Catholic method of reading legal texts'.[22] The influence of Cover is found also in the work of Austin Sarat[23] and Robin West.[24]

For Sarat, violence, as 'both a linguistic and physical phenomenon, as fact and metaphor, is integral to the constitution of modern law'.[25] So, the 'courtroom and the discourse of the trial provide one particularly important site to observe the way violence and pain enter language'.[26] West's concern is with the absence of a political state shaped by law that gives rise to 'the subjugation of others, through fratricidal, infantile violence'.[27] The rule of law is not there to 'frustrate politics, but to enable it'.[28] And politics is 'the means by which communities and individuals create meaning.'[29]

Another strand in contemporary law and language scholarship is represented by the work of Peter Goodrich.[30] His *Reading The Law*[31] contains, inter alia, a history of legal discourse that questions orthodox modes of reading, writing, laying down, interpreting, and understanding law that do not register, or acknowledge, or accept that to understand law's effective social meaning and practice, its history and empirical readings entails an understanding that the 'process of reading is an inherently social and political activity'. This 'selects and privileges meanings and accents'.[32] In *Languages of Law*,[33] Goodrich understands 'the religious life of the law, of the institution, as an historical ruin, as the legible surface or marked text of a lived world'.[34] He wishes to deconstruct, reinhabit, read and change law.[35] An analysis of the material forms through which law has been 'memorised' and 'presenced' entails an analysis of language.[36] This is because

---

[17] R. Weisberg, *The Failure of The Word: The Lawyer As Protagonist in Modern Fiction* (New Haven, Conn.: Yale University Press, 1984).
[18] R. Weisberg, *Poethics And Other Strategies of Law and Literature* (New York: Columbia University Press, 1992).
[19] Weisberg, *Poethics* (cited in n.18), xiv.
[20] R. Weisberg, *Vichy Law and the Holocaust in France* (New York: New York University. Press, 1996).
[21] Cover, 'Violence and the Word' (cited in n.1).
[22] Weisberg, *Vichy Law and the Holocaust in France* (cited in n.20), 428–9.
[23] A. Sarat, 'Speaking of Death: Narratives of Violence in Capital Trials' in A. Sarat and R. Kearns (eds), *The Rhetoric of Law* (Ann Arbor, Mich.: University of Michigan Press, 1994).
[24] R. West, *Re-Imagining Justice* (Aldershot: Ashgate, 2003).
[25] Sarat, 'Speaking of Death' (cited in n.23), 136.
[26] Per E. Scarry, *The Body in Pain* (New York: Oxford University Press, 1985), 10.
[27] West, *Re-Imagining Justice* (cited in n.24), 9.
[28] West, *Re-Imagining Justice* (cited in n.24), 9.
[29] West, *Re-Imagining Justice* (cited in n.24), 9.
[30] Peter Goodrich, 'Silent Speech' in Peter Goodrich, *Legal Emblems* (Cambridge: Cambridge University Press, forthcoming 2013).
[31] P. Goodrich, *Reading The Law: A Critical Introduction To Legal Method and Techniques* (Oxford: Blackwell, 1986).
[32] Goodrich, *Reading The Law* (cited in n.31), x.
[33] P. Goodrich, *Languages of Law: From Logics of Memory To Nomadic Masks* (London: Weidenfeld & Nicholson, 1990).
[34] Goodrich, *Languages of Law* (cited in n.33), viii.
[35] Goodrich, *Languages of Law* (cited in n.33), viii.
[36] Goodrich, *Languages of Law* (cited in n.33), viii.

It is language in the end which remembers, it is language which bears tradition and it is through language...that we remember not simply the appearance of the past but also its discourse...In discourse we read language to recollect not simply what was said but the context of what was said, a copious linguistic context.[37]

In *Law In The Courts of Love*,[38] sub-titled 'Literature and other Minor Jurisprudence', Goodrich offers us a history of literacy and legal texts that constitute 'minor jurisprudences'.[39] These represent 'the strangeness of language and so the possibilities of interpretation as also of plural forms of knowledge',[40] all to reconnect law with 'subject, person,...emotion', thus enabling 'the dialogue or the attention to singularity which justice or ethics requires'.[41] He goes on to argue for using the 'literary genre of law to reinstate the uncertainty and the undecidability of the writing of law'. He elaborates:

The reason and value of such suspension...in relation to judgment is a question of justice...Suspension of judgment opens up the possibility to reorganize and...account for the desires of the subject that writes and of the subject judged. That subjectivities motivate both judgment and the writing of law as a theme closer to literature than to legal doctrine.[42]

In *The Laws of Love*[43] Goodrich constructs an alternative jurisprudence, what he calls a 'case law of love'.[44] Pether describes this as a 'scholarly guerrilla assault on and satirical mirror for the common law'.[45] It is, she says, 'closed, detached from bodies and from history, from ethics and others'.[46]

Much work on the relationship between law and language today is undertaken by linguists and other social scientists (linguistic anthropologists, psychologists, sociologists). That linguistics has taken a strong foothold in the intellectual world is uncontentious. It is also clear that language is a social phenomenon and that its use is instrumental. Through language social institutions are established, including legal ones. Linguistic knowledge can facilitate our understanding of the substance of law. Thus Janet Ainsworth some 20 years ago explained why interrogating police officers were sometimes allowed to ignore requests by suspects for the assistance of a lawyer during the interrogation.[47] Lawrence Solan and Peter Tiersma in *Speaking of Crime: The Language of Criminal Justice*[48] identified critical sites for the operation of semantics and hermeneutics in the criminal procedural arena. Another area where language and linguistics have played a role is constitutional law. A significant example occurs in the USA, where freedom of 'speech' is constitutionally protected[49]: But what is 'speech'?[50] Can it include non-verbal

---

[37] Goodrich, *Languages of Law* (cited in n.33), viii.
[38] P. Goodrich, *Law In The Courts of Love* (London: Routledge, 1996).
[39] Goodrich, *Law In The Courts of Love* (cited in n.38), 2.
[40] Goodrich, *Law In The Courts of Love* (cited in n.38), 2.
[41] Goodrich, *Law In The Courts of Love* (cited in n.38), 2.
[42] Goodrich, *Law In The Courts of Love* (cited in n.38), vii.
[43] P. Goodrich, *The Laws of Love: A Brief Historical and Practical Manual* (Basingstoke: Palgrave Macmillan, 2006), 8.
[44] Goodrich, *The Laws of Love* (cited in n.43).
[45] Penelope Pether, 'Language' in A. Sarat, M. Anderson, and C. Frank (eds), *Law and the Humanities: An Introduction* (New York: Cambridge University Press, 2010), 331.
[46] Pether, 'Language' (cited in n.45).
[47] J. Ainsworth, 'In a Different Register: The Pragmatics of Powerlessness in Police Interrogation' (1993) 103 *Yale Law Journal* 259.
[48] L. Solan and P. Tiersma, *Speaking of Crime: The Language of Criminal Justice* (Chicago: University of Chicago Press, 2005).
[49] By the first Amendment, and see *Spence v Washington* 418 U.S. 405, 409–11 (1974). The classic source is J.S. Mill, *On Liberty*, ch.2.
[50] See S.J. Brison (2004) 6 *Legal Theory* 261.

acts that communicate in some way? Is hateful speech 'conduct' rather than speech, and so not protected?[51] Some of the considerable literature on this issue makes use of the tools of speech act theory and the philosophy of language.[52]

The area where knowledge of language and linguistics has made its greatest impact is legal interpretation, especially the interpretation of statutes. This was at its apogee when the literal rule dominated.[53] This rule (or canon of construction) requires judges to determine the meaning of a text acontextually.[54] To assist they developed maxims of interpretation: examples include *eiusdem generis*[55] and *expressio unius, exclusio alterius*.[56] Judges in the UK are now more committed to purposive interpretation of statutory material.[57] These canons of interpretations have, unsurprisingly, been subjected to considerable criticism in recent times. Nevertheless, Sinclair[58] and Miller,[59] using the tools of linguistic pragmatics, in particular Grice's notion of conversational implicature,[60] have shown that the canons referred to are linguistically-based generalizations about language.

The plain meaning rule (the literal rule) and the canons had less impact in the USA. However, the Supreme Court Justice, Antonin Scalia, has waged a campaign in the last two decades to emphasize their importance.[61] This has not been without controversy. Of course, the very notion of 'plain meaning' is problematic.[62] Insights into legal interpretation may also be found in cognitive linguistics.[63]

It is coming to be recognized that linguistics has a role to play in understanding legal interpretation. However, there is little evidence that legal scholars are developing the skills to make use of linguistic skills. This is surprising given the contrast with the way in which they have embraced the fundamentals of economics.[64]

There is considerably more interest in language and law in other parts of the academy: linguistics, communications, literature, sociology, anthropology. But because these are discrete disciplines, the field is somewhat 'fractured'.[65] A couple of examples will illustrate this. Discourse analysis and sociolinguistics more generally is being used to throw light on the legal system. There were several studies of the discourse strategies found in trials. Well-known examples are Janet Cotterill's study of the O.J. Simpson murder

---

[51] See C.W. Collier (2001) 7 *Legal Theory* 203.
[52] See K. Greenawalt, *Speech, Crime and the Uses of Language* (Oxford: Oxford University Press, 1989); Franklyn Haiman, *Speech Acts and the First Amendment* (Chicago: University of Chicago Press, 1993).
[53] During the period from about 1830 to 1970.
[54] See Lord Simon in *Maunsell v Olins* [1975] AC 373, 391.
[55] See Lord Diplock in *Quazi v Quazi* [1976] 3 WLR 833, 839.
[56] See *R v Palfrey and Sadler* [1970] 2 All ER 12, 16.
[57] And thus more willing to consider *travaux préparatoires* in coming to an understanding of what a statute entails. See *Pepper v Hart* [1993] AC 593. And see Lord Steyn (2001) 21 *Oxford Journal of Legal Studies* 39.
[58] M.B.W. Sinclair, 'Law and Language: The Role of Pragmatics in Statutory Interpretation' (1985) 45 *University of Pittsburgh Law Review* 373.
[59] G.P. Miller, 'Pragmatics and the Maxims of Interpretation' (1990) *Wisconsin Law Review* 1179.
[60] H.P. Grice, *Logic and Conversation: Studies in the Way of Words* (Cambridge, Mass.: Harvard University Press, 1989).
[61] An example is *Zedner v United States* 547 U.S. 489 (2006), in which he stated, 'The use of legislative history is illegitimate and ill-advised in the interpretation of any statute'.
[62] See L. Solan, *The Language of Judges* (Chicago: University of Chicago Press, 1993).
[63] See S. Winter, *A Clearing In the Forest: Law, Life and Mind* (Chicago: University of Chicago Press, 2001).
[64] Where the thinking of Pareto has been particularly influential.
[65] Per Peter Tiersma.

trial,[66] Greg Matoesian's study of the William Kennedy Smith rape trial,[67] and Susan Ehrlich's account of a rape case (the rape having taken place on a university campus).[68] Another example is the ethnographic study by Conley and O'Barr of discourse in small claims courts.[69] Semiotics has also focused on law. The leading scholar in the English-speaking world is Bernard Jackson.[70] But the discipline is more firmly embedded in continental Europe: it is particularly associated with Greimas[71] and Lacan,[72] and many less well-known European scholars.

The relationship between law and philosophy is explored both by legal academics (mainly jurists) and by philosophers. Most relevant to language and law is speech act theory: a notable example is the work of Dennis Kurzon.[73] A central question, which should interest both jurists and philosophers—but does so less now than once was the case—is what kind of a speech act is the law. Is it 'an assemblage of signs declarative of a volition', as Bentham postulated?[74] A command?[75] A rule?[76] A statement to judges telling them how to decide cases? A prediction of how the courts will rule?[77]

There is also increasing interest in forensic linguistics. Linguistic analysis has, for example, been used to challenge whether some written confessions used in British criminal cases are authentic or not.[78] It has also been used to identify a person's national origins. But Diana Eades[79] has questioned how accurate this is. So have Solan and Tiersma.[80] Do we know how reliable the results of forensic linguistics are? This is a crucial barrier to surmount if such analysis is going to be used as evidence in courts.

This has been a brief and necessarily selective introduction to law and language. Much of what has been ignored or glossed over is taken up in essays in this compendious volume. But the relationship between law and language remains relatively unexplored in the British legal academy. How many courses are there in British universities which specifically address the issues explored here? It has always been one of the goals of this series of colloquia, and the books that result, to open up new areas of scholarship and to encourage expansions in the law school syllabus. Most of the encounters that we have

---

[66] J. Cotterill, *Language and Power in Court: A Linguistic Analysis of the O.J. Simpson Trial* (Basingstoke: Palgrave Macmillan, 2003).

[67] G. Matoesian, *Law and The Language of Identity: Discourse in the William Kennedy Smith Rape Trial* (Oxford: Oxford University Press, 2001).

[68] S. Ehrlich, *Representing Rape: Language and Sexual Consent* (London: Routledge, 2001).

[69] J.M. Conley and W.M. O'Barr, *Rules versus Relationships: The Ethnography of Legal Discourse* (Chicago: University of Chicago Press, 1990).

[70] B. Jackson, *Semiotics and Legal Theory* (London: Routledge & Kegan Paul, 1985). See also his *Law, Fact and Narrative Coherence* (Liverpool: Deborah Charles Publications, 1988).

[71] A.J. Greimas, *Structural Semantics* ((Lincoln: University of Nebraska Press, 1983).

[72] J. Lacan, *Ecrits: A Selection* (A. Sheridan ed.) (New York: W.W. Norton & Co., 1977).

[73] D. Kurzon, *It Is Hereby Performed: Legal Speech Acts* (Amsterdam: John Benjamins Publishing Co., 1986).

[74] In J. Bentham, *Of Laws in General* (Oxford: Clarendon Press, 1970).

[75] John Austin's view: see his *The Province of Jurisprudence Determined* (London: Weidenfeld & Nicolson, 1954). And see W.P. MacNeill, *Novel Judgements* (Abingdon: Routledge, 2012), ch.2 (a comparison with Jane Austen).

[76] As argued by Hart in *The Concept of Law* (cited in n.7).

[77] O.W. Holmes view: see 'The Path of The Law' (1897) 10 *Harvard Law Review* 457 (the 'internationally-cited goblin-painting of realism' according to Karl Llewellyn).

[78] An example is Malcolm Coulthard, 'Whose Voice Is It? Invented and Concealed Dialogue in Written Records of Verbal Evidence Produced by the Police' in Janet Cotterill (ed.), *Language in the Legal Process* (Basingstoke: Palgrave Macmillan, 2002), 19.

[79] Diana Eades, 'Applied Linguistics and Language Analysis in Asylum Seeker Claims' (2005) 26 *Applied Linguistics* 503.

[80] Solan and Tiersma, *Speaking of Crime* (cited in n.48).

with the law are language events: meetings and interactions with lawyers, confrontations with the police, appearances in court. Yet, until recently, we tended to ignore the insights that linguistics can turn on these events. This collection will be invaluable to those who feel they would understand the law and its processes better if they were able to appreciate the insights of another discipline.

2

Legal Texts and Canons of Construction: A View from Current Pragmatic Theory

Robyn Carston

1. Introduction

The perspective of this paper is that of a linguist working on communication theory and the semantics/pragmatics distinction, who has an interest in whether and how well general theories of linguistic communication and comprehension apply to the specific case of legal language. On reading some of the legal interpretive debates I have been struck by similarities between some of the interpretive heuristics used in legal interpretation (known as 'canons of construction') and some dominant principles in current neo-Gricean pragmatics. My first objective in this paper is to demonstrate this convergence of heuristics and highlight certain limitations that they share, including the propensity of any such system of maxims or heuristics to yield directly contradictory results. My second aim is to look at the extent to which a pragmatic theory based more directly on principles of human cognition, that is, relevance theory, may shed some light on the processes of legal interpretation and, conversely, the extent to which the legal domain presents a special case that does not readily fall within the reach of any general pragmatic theory.

In the course of this discussion, other important issues will inevitably crop up but will not be engaged with in detail: the debate between *textualist* and *intentionalist* approaches to interpretation, the debate between *literalist* (or minimalist) and *contextualist* views in semantics (especially word meaning), and the distinction between the correct *interpretation* of a legal text (such as a statute) and its proper *application* in specific cases.

The paper is structured as follows: in section 2, I say a brief word about the nature of pragmatics and give a list of (some of the) kinds of meaning phenomena that fall within its domain; next, in section 3, two central maxims of communication posited in current neo-Gricean pragmatics are set out, with examples of how they work and a discussion of the problems they face; in section 4, I turn to the interpretation of legal language and the role of canons of construction, which is exemplified by a discussion of some famous cases of disputes over the correct interpretation of a word or phrase in a legal document; in section 5, I look at the textualist/intentionalist debate in legal interpretation and the way that alleged textualist uses of canons or maxims of interpretation appear to require a kind of intentionalism. The real issue here, I suggest, is that of the nature of the appropriate 'context' for interpretation, especially when that context seems to include consideration of intentions that are not textually expressed. Finally, in section 6, I briefly survey the basic precepts of the relevance-theoretic account of pragmatic interpretation and consider its possible application to issues that arise in legal interpretation.

2. Pragmatics

The modern-day discipline of pragmatics has its origins in the *philosophy of language*, in particular, the work of Paul Grice, who made a key distinction between what a speaker said and what she meant by saying it.[1] Understanding what a speaker has said is largely a matter of knowing the conventional linguistic meaning of the phrase or sentence used, but in order to grasp what she meant, when this goes beyond what she said, a pragmatic inferential derivation is required, taking as premises what was said, certain aspects of the context of utterance and the presumption that the speaker is observing principles of rational communicative behaviour (Grice's famous 'maxims of conversation'). Pragmatics also has a place within the field of *linguistics*, where it is distinguished from semantics: while semantics is concerned with the meaning encoded in the formal components of a language (its words and syntax), pragmatics focuses on the way those forms with those meanings are used in particular contexts to express or communicate a range of different concepts or thoughts. More recently, pragmatics has become situated within *cognitive science*, and with this has come a greater emphasis on the actual processes of interpretation, the constraints on those processes due to limits on addressees' cognitive resources, and the mental representations that an addressee forms of a speaker's intended meaning.

The domain of pragmatics then is speaker meaning (that is, communicatively intended content)[2] and the goal of a pragmatic theory is to account for how hearers/readers bridge the gap between linguistically encoded meaning and what the speaker means. The most obvious way in which a speaker's meaning can differ from the meaning linguistically encoded in the sentence she utters is when she implicates a proposition, as in the following well-known cases:

1. a. Utterance: Some of our students will fail the qualifying exam.
   Implicature: Not all of them will fail the qualifying exam.
   b. Utterance: There's a petrol station round the corner.
   Implicature: The petrol station is open, has supplies of petrol and is selling it.

In (1a), the meaning derived from the encoded content of the uttered sentence is perfectly compatible with the proposition that *all* the students will fail. However, in many contexts, the speaker of such an utterance will be taken to be implicating that *not all* of them will fail, because if she thought that they will all fail her utterance would be underinformative and so would not comply with a general presumption that speakers are as

---

[1] The central text is H. P. Grice, 'Logic and conversation' in P. Cole and J. Morgan (eds), *Syntax and Semantics* vol. 3 (New York: Academic Press, 1975), 4. This paper was reprinted (together with many others by Grice on language and meaning) in H. P. Grice, *Studies in the Way of Words* (Cambridge, Mass.: Harvard University Press, 1989).

[2] A speaker's meaning is a complex mental state made up of several layered intentions, that is, roughly, a higher-order intention that a lower-order intention to have a particular effect on an addressee be fulfilled, at least in part, by the addressee's recognition of the speaker's lower-order intention (see Grice 1989, ch.5 'Utterer's meaning and intentions' (cited in n.1), 86). D. Sperber and D. Wilson discuss this Gricean 'm-intention' in some detail and replace it with the concept of a 'communicative intention' which is an intention on the part of the speaker that her first-order informative intention be mutually manifest (to speaker and hearer). See D. Sperber and D. Wilson, *Relevance: Communication and Cognition* (Oxford: Blackwell, 1986, 2nd edn 1995). While there are some important differences between the two accounts, these can be bypassed for the purposes of this paper, as the significance here of both Grice's m-intention and Sperber and Wilson's communicative intention is their common concern to capture the open and overt nature (the mutual manifestness) of the intention involved in this kind of human interaction.

informative as they relevantly and truthfully can be. In (1b), the proposition expressed by the uttered sentence is compatible with the petrol station being closed or out of petrol, but in many contexts, it would only be appropriately relevant if taken to implicate that the station is in fact open and selling petrol.

Less obvious perhaps, but hugely prevalent, are cases where there is a disparity between the linguistically encoded meaning of an utterance (or what was actually 'said' by the speaker) and what is asserted (the proposition the speaker explicitly communicates). There are many varieties of this phenomenon:

2. Cases of propositional incompleteness:
'She is ready,' 'He has arrived,' 'I've had enough,' 'Tom's too short,'
'It's raining/hot/dark'....

These are all syntactically complete sentences of English, but they don't express complete thoughts or propositions without some kind of pragmatic process that supplies a necessary component of content: 'She is ready [to have dinner/to sit her exam/to get married/...],' 'Tom's too short [to reach the top shelf/to be a good basketball player/...],' 'It's hot [in Seville/outside/in a particular room/...].' And there are cases of conceptually incomplete phrases too, such as the so-called possessive construction, e.g. 'John's gun,' which could be meant and understood in numerous different ways, depending on context: 'the gun John owns,' 'the gun John wants to buy,' 'the gun that is John's favourite,' 'the gun that John thinks was used in the murder (as opposed to the one that *Tom* thinks was used)' and so on.

A second kind of case is the productive process of forming a compound by putting two nouns together:

3. battle fatigue, snake poison, silkworm, apple cake, bird sanctuary, dishwater, fertility pills, headache pills, heart pills...

Here there is no bit of linguistic form at all indicating anything about the relation between the two objects or phenomena picked out by the nouns, and the range of relations that may be understood seems to be as various as the ways in which the world works: 'fatigue *caused by taking part in* battles,' 'poison *produced by* snakes,' 'worms *that produce* silk,' 'cake *made from* apples,'.... Note that 'fertility pills' and 'headache pills' are understood as having the opposite relation from each other, though in a particular (strange) context these relations could be reversed. The general point is that the intended relation between the two entities denoted by the two nouns is not linguistically encoded, but has had to be pragmatically inferred.

A more circumscribed part of the vocabulary is number terms (and certain other scalar terms) which can be understood in the following three distinct ways, depending on both linguistic and extra-linguistic context.

4. a. You can take *three* hours to complete the exam. [at most 3]
   b. Anyone with *three* kids is eligible for the extra benefit. [at least 3]
   c. Mrs Smith has *three* children under five. [exactly 3]

An interesting sort of case is what is known as restrictions on the domain of a quantifier, where quantifiers are expressions like 'everyone,' 'most students,' 'some lecturers,' 'nothing' and, according to many, definite descriptions, like 'the women.' The point is that very often the class of entities which is being quantified is not linguistically expressed, as in the following examples:

5. a. Exam invigilator: '*Everyone* must stop writing now.'
   b. Commentator: '*The Russian* has voted for *the Russian*.'

In (5a), patently, the invigilator is not delivering an order to everyone in the world but just to everyone in the particular room who is doing the particular exam. In (5b), an attested example, the commentator (on a gymnastics competition) does not mean that someone voted for herself but rather that the Russian judge voted for the Russian competitor.

Another class of cases involves operators like 'not,' 'almost,' and 'too'/'also,' whose 'scope' can vary across different portions of the rest of the sentence:

6. a. The king of France was *not* interviewed by CNN.
   b. Fonzy *almost* robbed a bank.
   c. Mary wrote a novel *too/also*.

Consider what the 'almost' in (6b) applies to. There seem to be (at least) the following possibilities, so the intended interpretation on any particular occasion of use is something that an addressee has to infer pragmatically:

Fonzy tried and nearly succeeded in robbing a bank.
He barely stopped himself from robbing a bank.
He was intent on robbing something, but decided on something other than a bank.
He didn't rob a bank, but ended up doing something to it other than robbing it.

Similar points can be made about the scope of the negation in (6a) and 'too' or 'also' in (6c).

Yet another kind of case (one much discussed in the pragmatics literature) is that of connectives like 'and,' 'or,' and 'if,' whose linguistic meaning often underdetermines their meaning in context. Take the simple case of 'and,' which is widely claimed to be semantically equivalent to the logical connective '&' and so symmetric, that is, sentences of the form 'P and Q' have the same meaning as sentences of the form 'Q and P.' But the asserted content of particular 'P and Q' utterances is often asymmetric. It seems unlikely, for instance, that the following would be accepted as a sound line of reasoning in most contexts, including in a court of law:

7. If John stopped his car in an illegal position and Bill ran into John, then John is liable for damages.
   Bill ran into John and John stopped his car in an illegal position.
   _____
   John is liable for damages.

Even more striking perhaps is the asymmetry of the currently standard interpretations of the notices 'Pay and display!' and 'Display and pay!' The considerable difference between their interpretations is in part due to the fact they are semantically incomplete: 'Pay what for what? Display what (to whom)?' The first one has been for some time a standard notice in car parks and is understood as, roughly, 'pay for a parking ticket and display that ticket in your car window.' The second, in which the only surface difference from the first is the reversal of order, began appearing more recently in car parks and means, roughly, 'if you display your possessions (i.e. leave them visible inside your car) you may pay by being robbed of them.' In both cases, what is meant far outstrips what is encoded by the linguistic expressions used.

Finally, there are many linguists and philosophers of language who maintain that the meaning of words is often adjusted or modulated in context and so may be different from one occasion of use to another. This phenomenon is to be distinguished from lexical ambiguity (homonymy) when, through sociohistorical accident or a long forgotten etymological route, a lexical form is mapped onto two unrelated meanings, as is the case for 'bank,' 'coach,' and 'pen,' each of which is the outer form of (at least) two distinct words (e.g. 'coach' meaning bus and 'coach' meaning instructor). Word meaning adjustment or modulation involves a single word, hence a single encoded linguistic meaning, but one that may manifest a range of different, albeit related, meanings in different contexts. Here is a well-known example from the philosopher John Searle:[3]

8. a. Jane opened the window.
   b. Open your mouth, please.
   c. Sally opened her book to page 36.
   d. The child opened the package.
   e. A fox has opened the bags of garbage.
   f. The surgeon opened the wound.

Searle's point is that the verb 'open' is not ambiguous and is not being used in any special non-literal way in these sentences and yet the action understood (the concept expressed by the use of 'open') is different in each case. In other words, the contribution that the univocal verb 'open' makes to the proposition expressed by quite literal utterances varies with the sentential context it occurs in. This is dependent on a background of assumptions concerning what is typically involved in a particular subject opening a particular object (e.g. a person opening her mouth, a fox opening a garbage bag). Furthermore, the specific nonlinguistic context on an occasion of utterance may outweigh such standard assumptions so that the verb is understood as expressing yet another concept (for instance, if someone's mouth has been stitched closed for some reason, the process of opening it would be different from the usual one).

Assuming the verb 'open' has a single general encoded linguistic meaning,[4] what happens with the examples in (8) is that the meaning is made more specific, narrowed down to a concept of a particular action with a particular outcome. Arguably, there are cases where the process of adjusting lexical meaning has the opposite effect, that is, the concept expressed in context is broader or more general than the encoded lexical meaning:

9. a. She was asleep when he called.
   b. Leave me alone—I'm asleep.
   c. Nadal was asleep during the second set.

In contrast with the literal use (probably) in (9a), the other two instances of 'asleep' are loose or hyperbolic uses: the speaker of (9b) is not strictly asleep, although she may be very drowsy and intent on sleeping, and in (9c), the commentator describing the highly physically energetic tennis-player, Nadal, uses the word 'asleep' to express a concept along the lines of 'less than optimally alert, swift, and brilliantly athletic.' Although these cases of broadening of a lexical meaning are less widely agreed on than the cases of narrowing in (8), they too can be seen as instances of pragmatics contributing to the proposition expressed by the speaker.[5]

---

[3] J. Searle, *Intentionality* (Cambridge: Cambridge University Press, 1983), 145.
[4] The precise nature of encoded or conventional word meaning is a topic of considerable debate, with positions ranging from word meanings being fully contentful, to their being abstract or schematic (hence always requiring pragmatic enrichment when used communicatively), to the view that there are no word meanings as such but just a stored history of uses (for discussion, see F. Recanati, *Literal Meaning* (Cambridge: Cambridge University Press, 2004), ch.9). For the purposes of this paper, I am assuming (without ultimate commitment) that most descriptive words (nouns, verbs, adjectives, adverbs) encode a concept, hence may sometimes be used to express that very concept, although pragmatic meaning adjustment is a very common occurrence.
[5] For arguments in support of this view, see R. Carston, *Thoughts and Utterances: The Pragmatics of Explicit Communication* (Oxford: Blackwell, 2002); Recanati 2004 (cited in n.4); D. Wilson and R. Carston, 'A unitary approach to lexical pragmatics: Relevance, inference and *ad hoc* concepts' in N. Burton-Roberts (ed.), *Pragmatics* (Basingstoke: Palgrave, 2007), 230.

The collective label for the kind of process employed to recover or ascertain the meaning in cases (2)–(9) is 'pragmatic enrichment or adjustment.' The label reflects the fact that the process is not one of inferring a whole distinct proposition (as with implicatures), but rather of the fleshing out, developing, or adjusting of the meaning template that is provided by the decoded linguistic meaning. This is just a very small sample of cases where there is a disparity between linguistic meaning and proposition expressed.[6] It has been argued that it is an inherent property of language systems that the sentences they generate do not (cannot) fully determine the meaning expressed or communicated by a speaker; this is known as the 'linguistic underdeterminacy' hypothesis.[7]

3. Pragmatic maxims/heuristics

What the examples in the previous section indicate is that utterance comprehension (or interpretation) is achieved by means of (defeasible) inferential processes, which are constrained, but not determined, by the linguistic evidence. These interpretive inferences are taken to be guided by certain pragmatic principles concerning standards of communicative behavior that we are entitled to expect from rational agents. These have been formulated as a set of conversational maxims or norms by Grice[8] and others (in particular Laurence Horn and Stephen Levinson),[9] and, more fundamentally, as cognitive interpretive principles by Dan Sperber and Deirdre Wilson.[10] I focus on the first approach here and turn to the second in section 6.

Current neo-Gricean (as opposed to Gricean) pragmatics is dominated by two apparently complementary pragmatic maxims that the speaker is taken to follow (together with their corresponding interpretive heuristics employed by the addressee). Each is based on Grice's original two maxims of quantity (informativeness):[11]

[A] Grice's first maxim of quantity: Make your contribution as informative as is required (for the current purposes of the exchange).[12]

Q-principle: Say as much as you (truthfully and relevantly) can.[13]

---

[6] For further examples and discussion, see K. Bach, 'Conversational impliciture' (1994) 9 *Mind and Language* 124; Carston 2002 (cited in n.5); Recanati 2004 (cited in n. 4).

[7] For discussion of the linguistic underdeterminacy hypothesis, see F. Recanati, 'Contextualism and anti-contextualism in the philosophy of language' in S. Tsohatzidis (ed.), *Foundations of Speech Act Theory* (London: Routledge, 1994), 156; Sperber and Wilson 1986 (cited in n.2); Carston 2002 (cited in n.5).

[8] Grice 1975 (cited in n.1).

[9] L. Horn, 'Towards a new taxonomy for pragmatic inference: Q-based and R-based implicature' in D. Schiffrin (ed.), *Meaning, Form and Use in Context: Linguistic Application* (Washington: Georgetown University Press, 1984), 11; L. Horn, 'Vehicles of meaning: Unconventional semantics and unbearable interpretations' (1995) 73 *Washington University Law Quarterly* 1145; S. Levinson, *Presumptive Meanings: The Theory of Generalised Conversational Implicature* (Cambridge, Mass.: MIT Press, 2000).

[10] Sperber and Wilson 1986/95 (cited in n.2); see also Carston 2002 (cited in n.5).

[11] L. Horn and S. Levinson are two of the earliest and most prominent neo-Gricean theorists. Both have set out systems of pragmatic principles or heuristics, which give a central place to these two maxims concerning quantity of information. There are small differences in the way they formulate their heuristics and certain other more substantial differences in their outlook (Levinson believes in 'default' interpretations, Horn does not), but none of these differences is significant for the points I want to make in this paper.

[12] Grice 1975 (cited in n.1), 45.

[13] Horn 1995 (cited in n.9), 1151.

The hearer presumes that the speaker is abiding by prevailing communicative norms and interprets her utterances accordingly, so the interpretive correlative here is that if the speaker didn't say something which she is in a position to know and which would be relevant to the current exchange then that must be because she doesn't think it is the case. This is sometimes put in the following rather sloganistic way:

> Interpretive heuristic (Q): What isn't said, isn't the case.[14]

Among the most often cited examples that fall under this maxim/heuristic are cases of scalar pragmatic inference, such as example (1a), discussed earlier, where the speaker of 'Some of our students...' is taken to mean (implicate) 'Not all of our students....' Other examples that work in the same way are the following:

> 10. a. Please buy me a croissant or a muffin.
>   Implicates: Don't buy me both a croissant and a muffin.
>   b. He has a good background in linguistics.
>   Implicates: He doesn't have an excellent/outstanding background in linguistics.

What governs the line of reasoning here is that, given a scale of salient and relevant alternatives, e.g. <some, most, all>, <or, and>, <good, excellent, outstanding>, if the speaker chooses to make a statement employing a weaker item on the scale when she is in a position to know whether any of the stronger items hold, then we can infer that she means that the stronger proposition doesn't hold. Of course, as with all pragmatic reasoning this is a defeasible inference and will not go through in all contexts.

The second of the main neo-Gricean maxims appears to be an amalgam of the second of Grice's quantity (informativeness) maxims and his maxim of relevance:

> [B] Grice's second maxim of quantity: Do not make your contribution more informative than is required.
> Grice's maxim of relation: Be relevant.[15]

The modern formulations are various, but the following are representative:

> I-principle: Say no more than you must.[16]
> Interpretive heuristic (I): What is simply/briefly described is the stereotypical or normal (default) instance.[17]

Underlying the I-principle is the reasonable idea that what can be taken for granted need not be said. Among the cases often discussed in the literature as subject to this maxim are the following:

> 11. a. John will give you £10 if you mow his lawn.
>   Implicates: He'll give you £10 only if you mow his lawn.
> [If you don't, he won't.]
>   b. Mary turned the key and the motor started.
>   Implicates: Mary's turning of the key caused the motor to start.

Here, we are licensed to infer that the speaker intends the default or stereotypical situation, the one that immediately comes to mind, in the absence of any indications to the contrary. Of course, it's perfectly compatible with what was actually said in (11a) that John will give the hearer £10 whether he mows the lawn or not, and with what was said

---

[14] Levinson 2000 (cited in n.9), 31.
[15] Grice 1975 (cited in n.1), 45, 46.
[16] Horn 1995 (cited in n.9), 1151.
[17] Levinson 2000 (cited in n.9), 37.

in (11b) that Mary's turning of a certain key was a distinct event unconnected to the distinct event of the motor starting, but considerations of relevance mediate against that. For her part, the speaker can assume that her use of a brief/simple formulation ('if' rather than 'if and only if,' 'P and Q' rather than 'P and this caused Q') will be pragmatically enriched to the more specific stereotypical interpretation.

The adequacy of these two principles/heuristics (the Q and the I)[18] is highly debatable and there is considerable discussion in the theoretical pragmatics literature about them.[19] An immediate point is that they are potentially in conflict with each other and give opposite results in some cases. So, for instance, if the Q-principle, enjoining a speaker to say as much as she can on the topic at issue, were applied to the examples in (11), we would get the opposite result (the wrong result):

12. a. It's not the case that if and only if you mow John's lawn he'll give you £10.
    b. It's not the case that Mary's turning of the key caused the motor to start.

With regard to (12a), the reasoning would be that she could have said the stronger 'Q if and only if P' but she chose instead the weaker 'Q if P,' therefore she must think that the stronger proposition does not hold. Clearly, something has to prevent this maxim from applying and ensure that the I-maxim does apply.

An interesting illustration of how the maxims may drive interpretation in opposite directions is provided by the pragmatics of indefinite nouns of the form 'an X.' Consider some examples:

13. I've lost an earring/a contact lens.
    Implicates: It's one of my own earrings/contact lenses.

Here the indefinite is enriched to a definite involving personal ownership and seems to fit the prediction of the I-principle: the speaker is seen as having used a semantically minimal expression, 'an X,' and so to mean more than she said, hence a stereotypical relation (of ownership) can be assumed to hold between the speaker and the earring/contact lens. Application of the Q-principle, based on a salient semantic scale of alternatives <an X, my X>, would give the opposite (and wrong) result ('not my X'). However, the situation seems to be reversed in the next case:

14. I've found an earring/a wallet.
    Implicates: It's not one of my own earrings/wallets.

This time it is the Q-heuristic which gives what, in the absence of any more specific contextual information, seems to be the right result. Then again, an utterance of 'I've found a contact lens' might communicate either just the minimal encoded meaning ('a' contact lens, without any ownership implications) or, in the appropriate context, one or other of the more specific meanings. The speaker could communicate that it's one of her own (suppose we know she's prone to dropping and losing her lenses at night when she takes them out, and then one day, while cleaning her bathroom, she utters (14)),

---

[18] There are other maxims in the neo-Gricean arsenal, including versions of Grice's original maxims of quality (truthfulness) and of manner, but it is the two discussed here that have been given the most attention, especially with regard to scalar implicatures and other (alleged) generalized conversational implicatures.

[19] See, for instance, J. F. Richardson and A. W. Richardson, 'On predicting pragmatic relations' (1990) *Proceedings of the 16th Annual Meeting of the Berkeley Linguistics Society: Parasession on the Legacy of Grice* 498; M. Green, 'Quantity, volubility, and some varieties of discourse' (1995) 18 *Linguistics and Philosophy* 83; R. Carston, 'Informativeness, relevance and scalar implicature' in R. Carston and S. Uchida (eds), *Relevance Theory: Applications and Implications* (Amsterdam: John Benjamins, 1998), 179.

or that it's someone else's (suppose she comes into a lecture theatre she's never been in before and sitting at one of the seats, about to put her notebook on the table, she utters (14)). It looks, then, as if the correct application of the two maxims/heuristics is a highly context-sensitive matter.

Consider now what these two maxims/heuristics predict with regard to the phenomenon of lexical adjustment discussed in the previous section. Note first that neither seems to have anything to say about cases where the encoded lexical meaning is broadened (as in the 'asleep' examples in (9), discussed earlier) since both are formulated so as to encourage a more specific interpretation than the linguistic meaning itself provides: we go from 'some Fs' to 'some but not all Fs,' from 'Q if P' to 'Q if and only if P,' from 'P and Q' to 'P and as a result Q,' from 'an X' to 'my X' or 'someone else's X.' Focusing then on lexical narrowing cases, it looks as if the I-maxim/heuristic (enrich to the stereotypic/default instance) could account for the standard interpretations of the various uses of 'open' in (8), discussed earlier, while the Q-maxim would not enter the picture. But consider the word 'vehicle' in the following example:

15. There's a vehicle blocking the driveway.

Again, the two interpretive heuristics seem to give different (and opposing) predictions about the correct interpretation: according to the I-heuristic, it should be narrowed down to a stereotypical construal, so probably to a motor car; according to the Q-heuristic, on the other hand, given the salient semantic entailment scale <vehicle, car> and the fact that the speaker has chosen to use the semantically weaker word, we can infer that (as far as the speaker knows) it is not a car.[20]

So the pressing question is: what determines which of the two maxims/heuristics applies when? It seems that there must be certain constraints/conditions on their application and/or some ordering on their application.[21] From a different perspective, though, these context-sensitive maxims/heuristics, while they both reflect certain recurrent patterns of pragmatic inference, can be seen as somewhat superficial manifestations of some other deeper or more general principle underlying all pragmatic inferences. I would maintain that a properly developed concept of communicative 'relevance' is required, a concept which will play a key role in accounting for why it is sometimes right to infer a stereotypical/default interpretation and at other times right to infer that, because a speaker didn't say something, she means to imply that it is not the case. I will discuss this idea in section 6. Before that, I want to look at how interpretive tools very like these Q and I heuristics are employed in legal interpretation, sometimes explicitly, sometimes implicitly.

4. Interpretation of legal language and canons of construction

In a recent paper on the pragmatics of legal language, Andrei Marmor says that it is unlikely that Gricean maxims apply to legal language because they are formulated so as

---

[20] There is, in fact, a third possibility here on Levinson's account which is that, according to another heuristic, which concerns 'manner' of expression, the speaker's use of 'vehicle' in (15) communicates an M-implicature that 'there's something special or unusual about the entity referred to': perhaps it is a car but it's not a typical one (for that speaker/hearer)—it may be a dilapidated old jalopy or a brand-new expensive sports car. In any case, the speaker wants to draw some sort of extra attention to it that would not be afforded by using the very frequent, unmarked expression 'a car.' For discussion, see Levinson 2000 (cited in n.9), 38–39, 135–153.

[21] See Levinson 2000 (cited in n.9), 39.

to apply to 'cooperative exchanges of information' and 'the enactment of a law is not a cooperative exchange of information' but rather 'legislation is typically a form of strategic behaviour.'[22]

While it would be foolish to deny that legal language has some special properties, including its strategic nature, I think it's much less clear that the Gricean maxims do not apply to it. It is true that Grice says that his maxims are instantiations of a broader Cooperative Principle, according to which we are to 'make our conversational contributions in accordance with the accepted purpose or direction of the talk exchange we are engaged in.'[23] However, he hedges this with a *ceteris paribus* clause and gives every impression that he intends his 'logic of conversation' to apply to the full range of talk exchanges which are but one 'variety of purposive, indeed rational, behaviour.' He goes on to say that he wants his maxims to cover not just maximally effective informational exchange but also 'such general purposes as influencing or directing the actions of others,' and to apply to such non-cooperative exchanges as 'quarrelling and letter writing.' It seems to me that there is a *thin* notion of cooperative, purposive activity that might cover all these kinds of linguistic communication, including legal language: the producer of the language wants to get a certain meaning across to an audience and the audience wants to grasp that meaning. There is then a joint cooperative activity here—in a perhaps somewhat attenuated sense.[24]

In any case, as a matter of interpretive practice, at least some of the 'canons of construction' (or interpretation) that are actually used by judges and other interpreters of the law are instantiations of Gricean maxims.[25] Consider the canon formulated as *Expressio unius est exclusio alterius*, that is, 'Expression of the one is exclusion of the other,'[26] which has been widely discussed as applying to the following notice at a local swimming pool:

16. 'Children under ten get in free'
    Inference: Children ten or over do not get in free

What is explicitly expressed here is the age 'under ten' rather than any higher age ('under eleven,' 'under twelve,' etc.), so we are entitled to infer that (children at) the higher ages are excluded (from getting in free). As Gary Ostertag has pointed out, the inference involved looks like an instantiation of the Q-heuristic ('What isn't said is not the case'),[27] the speaker having followed the Q-principle ('Say as much as you relevantly and truthfully can'). However, according to Stephen Neale, this particular

---

[22] See A. Marmor, 'The pragmatics of legal interpretation' (2008) 21(4) *Ratio Juris* 423.

[23] Grice 1975 (cited in n.1), 45.

[24] It has been pointed out to me by Lucia Morra (who cites Marco Ricciardi) that another reason for doubting that Grice intended his maxims of conversation to apply only to prototypically harmonious cooperative exchanges is his contact in Oxford with the eminent legal theorist H. L. A. Hart. Hart discusses joint practices of a rule-governed sort in which the participants, although competing with one another, must cooperate in following the rules that constitute the practice or otherwise the practice could not be maintained. In other words, cooperation and competition/strategy are not necessarily at odds. See H. L. A. Hart, 'Are there any natural rights?' (1955) 64(2) *The Philosophical Review* 175.

[25] I will confine my attention here to 'textual canons,' those whose assumed utility is specifically directed to the understanding or interpretation of the language comprising legal texts. There is also a set of 'substantive canons,' which instruct courts to favour interpretations that promote certain values or policies, such as the Rule of Lenity, according to which an ambiguous criminal statute is to be resolved in favour of the defendant. This would seem to come into force only when the textual canons fail to deliver a single (agreed on) interpretation.

[26] For some legal cases in which this canon has been explicitly called on in arguing for a particular interpretation of a statute, see K. Llewellyn, 'Remarks on the theory of appellate decision and the rules or canons about how statutes are to be construed' (1950) 3 *Vanderbilt Law Review* 395.

[27] G. Ostertag, 'The pragmatics of textualism,' talk presented at the *Language and Law* Conference, CSMN, Oslo, June 2008.

example is an instance of conditional perfection,[28] a case of which was discussed as (11a) in the previous section. It is, after all, equivalent to an utterance of 'If a child is under ten, then he/she gets in free' and so should fall under the I-principle and accompanying heuristic ('Say no more than you must,' 'Enrich to the stereotypical/normal case'). Interestingly, in this case the two maxims converge on the same interpretation and the canon of *Expressio unius* could be seen as a subclause of both of them. This looks like further evidence that the two pragmatic maxims (and the '*Expressio unius*' canon) are surface manifestations of some deeper underlying principle, as mooted in the previous section. However, my main point in this section is that the interpretive canons/heuristics called upon by official interpreters of legal texts (including legally binding public notices) are very closely related to the principles/heuristics formulated by theorists of pragmatics for communication and interpretation quite generally.

Here is another canon subscribed to by theorists of legal interpretation and used by those involved in applying laws: *Eiusdem generis*, (literally: 'Of the same kind'), that is, 'The meaning of a general term applies to things of the same sort (as those that are explicitly mentioned).' Here is a (slightly adapted) example to which this rule has been applied:[29]

> 17. 'Exceptions to the prohibition (on employment of foreign workers) are professional actors, singers, artists, lecturers [and others].'

Based on the canon, we can infer that the exceptions to the prohibition include violinists, dancers, and stand-up comedians, that is, all (temporarily visiting) entertainers or performers, and that the exceptions do not include manual labourers, doctors, nurses, or lawyers (among others). This looks like an instantiation of the second pragmatic maxim/heuristic discussed in section 3, the I-principle ('Say no more than you must'), which licenses the interpreter to enrich in a stereotypical, uncontroversial sort of way. Of course, the previous canon, *Expressio unius*, would yield a different result if it were applied, as it well might be, especially when the phrase 'and others' or 'and the like' is not explicitly given in the statute: it would exclude (from the exceptions to the prohibition) any employment category not explicitly mentioned in the text. Such divergent predictions come as no surprise, given the similarity of the canons to the neo-Gricean maxims discussed in the previous section. As noted by some discussants of the utility of

---

[28] S. Neale, *Textualism with Intent*. Paper for discussion at Oxford University Law Faculty, November 2008, 45. Available at <http://www.ucl.ac.uk/laws/jurisprudence/docs/2008/08_coll_neale.pdf>.

[29] The 1885 US federal law on which this example is roughly based prohibited 'the importation and migration of foreigners and aliens under contract or agreement to perform labor or service of any kind in the United States...' but listed exceptions, namely, 'professional actors, artists, lecturers, singers and domestic servants.' A much discussed case, *Church of the Holy Trinity v United States*, 143 U.S. 457 (1892), concerned whether or not an employment contract between the Church of the Holy Trinity, New York and an English clergyman was legal. Given that clergy were not listed among the exceptions to the prohibition, there seems to be a role here for either the canon of *Expressio unius* or, if it could be established that there was an implicit 'and others' expressed, the canon of *Eiusdem generis*, giving opposite results. For discussion, see Marmor 2008 (cited in n.22), 427–428.

Another interesting application of this canon is discussed by R. Charnock, 'Lexical indeterminacy, contextualism and rule-following in common law adjudication' in A. Wagner, W. Wouter, and D. Cao (eds), *Interpretation, Law and the Construction of Meaning* (Dordrecht: Springer, 2007), 21. In this case, an English court had to decide in 1980 whether the category of articles (described as sound and picture recordings) referred to in the Obscene Publications Act 1959 could be said to include video-cassettes, which, as a relatively modern invention at the time, were not explicitly mentioned in the Act. Here, as in the *Holy Trinity* case, the interpretive dispute was not easily resolved by *Eiusdem generis* but moved to a debate on what is involved in being 'of the *same* kind' as the listed items.

the canons,³⁰ there is an antecedent decision to be made about whether the appropriate conditions for applying any given canon are met. In this case, the presence of a list of items whose common property is apparent and which is followed by the explicit phrase 'and others' is a fairly clear indication that *Eiusdem generis* is applicable.

The most general of all of these interpretive canons is the *Plain Meaning* rule which says: The meaning of a statute is to be understood as the ordinary (plain) meaning of the language of the statute (except when it makes explicit that a word is a technical term or provides a special legal definition). Sometimes this rule is extended (or perhaps there is a distinct associated rule) as follows: when the meaning of the text is plain and unambiguous, that is the end of the matter and the plain meaning must be given effect. In other words, the assumption is that, unless explicitly indicated to the contrary, the framers of the law are to be taken as having used words in their ordinary literal senses.³¹ This rule could be argued to bear considerable similarity to some of Grice's maxims concerned with manner of expression (brevity, orderliness, clarity) and to the neo-Gricean I-principle and its heuristic, which licenses hearers to interpret unmarked linguistic expressions in an ordinary stereotypical way, although it is more general than any of these. It takes precedence over the other canons which only come into play if it doesn't deliver a clear unambiguous interpretation. The problem, of course, is that all too often it doesn't and legal interpretive disputes are often precisely over what the plain meaning of a word or a phrase is, as the cases to be discussed below will illustrate. In particular, it is not at all clear whether the plain meaning of a word/phrase is to be equated with the literal, encoded meaning of a word/phrase or with the usual, most familiar interpretation of the word/phrase (for this distinction, recall discussion of uses of the word 'open' in section 2).

The general point that I've been trying to highlight here is that pragmatic maxims/heuristics that apply to linguistic comprehension quite generally seem also to come into play in the interpretation of legal language and that certain explicitly formulated legal interpretive precepts (or rules of thumb) bear a strong resemblance to these general maxims.

However, legal texts clearly do have some special properties, distinguishing them from other kinds of communication or linguistic expression: they have a prescriptive or normative content rather than a descriptive content, and that content has to carry over to times, places, and conditions distant from the time/place/conditions of origin. This combination of properties might well make for certain tendencies in the linguistic formulation of legal documents. We might expect a much higher degree of verbal explicitness than is typical (or necessary) in face-to-face speech, due to a less rich or clearly shared context in which to interpret the language, and, as a result, few, if any, implicatures and fewer cases requiring pragmatic enrichment than in ordinary communication.³² This seems to be the view of Marmor, who says, 'You may think that there

---

³⁰ For instance, M. Sinclair, '"Only a sith thinks like that": Llewellyn's "duelling canons", one to seven' (2005–2006) 50 *New York Law School Law Review* 919.

³¹ Of course, if the law was framed some centuries or even just decades ago, the 'ordinary' meaning of some words may have changed and, clearly, it is that earlier ordinary sense that is essential for correct interpretation. This point is a central component of 'semantic originalism,' as opposed to 'expectation originalism,' for discussion of which, see R. Dworkin, 'Comment' in A. Scalia, *A Matter of Interpretation* (Princeton, N.J.: Princeton University Press, 1997), 119.

³² On the other hand, we might also expect, at certain points in a legal text, a judicious use of linguistic indeterminacy and/or vagueness, even beyond that which is inherent to language itself, where law-makers have recognized that they cannot envisage the full range of possible future situations that a law might need to be applied to. They may deliberately choose linguistic expression which will leave open to future judicial decision whether or not the law is to be applied in particular cases. See T. Endicott, *Vagueness in Law* (Oxford: Oxford University Press, 2000) and papers in A. Marmor and S. Soames (eds), *Philosophical Foundations of Language in the Law* (Oxford: Oxford University Press, 2011).

must be some cases in which it is quite obvious that the content the legislature prescribes is not exactly what it says. Perhaps there are, we cannot rule such things out, but I think that such cases would be very rare.'[33] Given the way language works and the quite extensive role that pragmatics plays in verbal comprehension (see section 2), I doubt that they are so rare. In any case, there are several much-discussed cases in the literature, two of which I would like to look at next, primarily to highlight the role of canons of construction and/or neo-Gricean maxims (though, of course, the latter, unlike the former, are not explicitly invoked by judges in support of their interpretations). The first is a debate about the meaning of a particular occurrence of the word 'vehicle' and the second about the correct interpretation of the phrase 'use a firearm.'

In describing his concept of the 'open texture' of law,[34] H. L. A. Hart discusses the uncertainties of legislative communication due to the inherent limitations of language, in particular with regard to general terms such as 'vehicle.' He says, 'If anything is a vehicle a motor-car is one' and this is a consequence of the recurrent usage of the word, in similar contexts, in which its denotation includes cars, but when, for instance, there is a notice prohibiting 'vehicles' in a certain public park, its meaning is no longer obvious. Does it apply to bicycles, skate-boards, toy trains, a sculpture of an historic airplane, a motor-bike used as a prop in a theatrical production taking place in the park, and so on? A question along these lines arose in the case of *Garner v Burr*.[35] The legislature had made it an offence to use a 'vehicle' without pneumatic tyres on a public road. Lawrence Burr, a farmer, fitted iron wheels to his chicken coop, attached it to his tractor, and pulled it down a stretch of public road adjacent to his property. He was prosecuted under the statute, but the magistrate acquitted him on the grounds that a chicken coop (on wheels) is not a 'vehicle' so the law did not cover his action. Which of the possible meanings of 'vehicle,' a term which is arguably both ambiguous and vague, did the magistrate take to be the one expressed in the statute in question? It sounds as if he was (implicitly) guided by the interpretive heuristic that licenses enrichment to the stereotype or default (the I-principle), which narrows the meaning to a concept of motorized wheeled vehicles typically used on public roads for the carriage of people or goods (hence including in its denotation cars, vans, buses, lorries, and not much else—perhaps tractors). However, the decision was reversed by the appeal court judge who rejected the narrow (stereotypical) construal of the meaning of 'vehicle' and apparently broadened it to a concept of anything (above a certain size and weight) which is on wheels and is run (on those wheels) along a public road, whether motorized itself or drawn by a motorized vehicle. This concept of vehicle includes in its denotation chicken coops on wheels, and a great many other atypical things on wheels (grass-mowers, grand pianos, fridge-freezers, large sculptures, fairground ride structures, trampolines...). The judge's argument here did not include an appeal to any textual canons or a concern for 'plain meaning,' but rather to the manifest *purpose of the statute* which was, clearly, to prevent damage to public road surfaces. So, whether or not the object on wheels running along the

---

[33] Marmor 2008 (cited in n.22), 429.

[34] H. L. A. Hart, *The Concept of Law* (Oxford: Clarendon, 1961, 2nd edn 1994), 126. Hart's understanding of the term 'open texture' is not clearly the same as that of F. Waismann who coined it; see F. Waismann, 'Verifiability,' in A. Flew (ed.), *Logic and Language* (1st series) (Oxford: Blackwell, 1951), 119. For discussion of the two usages, see R. Charnock, 'Meaning and reference: a linguistic approach to general terms and definite descriptions in legal interpretations,' Lecture to the Statute Law Society, Institute for Advanced Legal Studies, University of London, October 2007. Available at: <http://sites.google.com/site/celluledelinguistique/Accueil-CRL/membres/ross-charnock>.

[35] *Garner v Burr* [1951] 1 KB 31.

public road was a typical road-using vehicle or was being used to transport people or goods, were not relevant factors, however prominent they may be in the ordinary concept of a vehicle.

In his discussion of this example, Timothy Endicott[36] talks of a clash of *legal* principles (rather than interpretive ones): the importance of giving effect to the statutory purpose versus the importance of protecting people from a criminal liability that has not been unequivocally imposed. He maintains that anyone addressing the problem of the application of the term 'vehicle' in *Garner v Burr* has to make evaluative judgements on the normative question of how these two principles are to be respected. In section 6, I will try to argue that the issue here is, at base, still a matter of utterance interpretation and that considerations of 'purpose,' when they fall within the communicative relevance (yet to be defined) of a word's use, can reasonably be recruited in the pragmatic inferential process that results in the broad meaning for 'vehicle' in this case.

The second case I want to look at concerns the interpretation of the phrase 'use a firearm,' again an issue of how narrowly or broadly it is to be construed, focusing on the recently much discussed interpretive dispute that arose in *Smith v United States* (1993).[37] The issue was whether a man's exchanging a machine gun for narcotics constituted his 'use' of a firearm 'during and in relation to...a drug trafficking crime' within the meaning of Statute 18 U.S.C. s. 924(c)(1) (hereafter referred to as Stat-18). The statute imposes an additional five-year prison term when a gun is used and if the weapon is a machine gun the mandatory sentence is 30 years.[38] The defendant, John Angus Smith, offered to trade a MAC-10 machine gun to an undercover federal agent for two ounces of cocaine. He was convicted of conspiracy to possess and distribute cocaine, and of 'using' the machine gun in relation to the conspiracy in violation of Stat-18. On appeal, Smith argued that trading a gun was not among the 'uses' of a firearm defined by the statute. He lost his appeal.

According to Justice Sandra Day O'Connor, speaking for the majority, Smith's action fell within the meaning of the statute, while Justice Antonin Scalia, speaking for the dissent, maintained that Smith did not 'use a firearm' in the relevant sense. O'Connor and Scalia are both *textualists*, that is, both profess to be concerned only with the 'plain meaning' of the statute and not with the intentions of the legislature. As Scalia puts it: 'It is the law that governs, not the intent of the lawgiver...men may intend what they will;

---

[36] T. Endicott, 'Law and Language' in *Stanford Encyclopedia of Philosophy* (2010). Available at: <http://plato.stanford.edu/entries/law-language/>.

[37] *Smith v United States*, 508 U.S. 223 (1993). Among the many discussions of the debate over the correct interpretation of 'use a firearm' in the statute are: J. Polich, 'The ambiguity of plain meaning: *Smith v. United States* and the new textualism' (1994) 68(1) *Californian Law Review* 259; Scalia 1997 (cited in n.31); S. Neale, 'On location' in M. O'Rourke and C. Washington (eds), *Situating Semantics: Essays in Honor of John Perry* (Cambridge, Mass.: MIT Press, 2007), 251; Neale 2008 (cited in n.28); L. Morra, 'Normative implicatures in normative texts' in A. Capone (ed.), *Perspectives on Pragmatics and Philosophy* (Dordrecht: Springer, 2012).

[38] Here is the full text of the relevant part of the statute:

> Whoever, during and in relation to any crime of violence or drug trafficking crime (including a crime of violence or drug trafficking crime which provides for an enhanced punishment if committed by the use of a deadly or dangerous weapon or device) for which he may be prosecuted in a court of the United States, uses or carries a firearm, shall, in addition to the punishment provided for such crime of violence or drug trafficking crime, be sentenced to imprisonment for five years, and if the firearm is a short-barrelled rifle, or a short-barrelled shotgun, to imprisonment for ten years, and if the firearm is a machinegun, or a destructive device, or is equipped with a firearm silencer or firearm muffler, to imprisonment for thirty years.

but it is only the laws that they enact which bind us.'[39] The one very general interpretive rule that they both claim to observe is the *Plain Meaning* rule, discussed earlier: the legislature intends to use ordinary English words in their ordinary senses (and statutes should be construed accordingly). As already noted, the problem with this is that, all too often, what the 'ordinary meaning' is in particular instances is an issue.[40]

O'Connor's view was that the phrase 'use a firearm' as its occurs in the relevant statute should be interpreted as including the use Smith made of the firearm in his crime, that is, as an instrument of barter (for drugs). Scalia's view was that the phrase is to be interpreted more narrowly, as the employment of a firearm for its primary purpose (its raison d'être), that is, as a weapon, and so does not apply to Smith's action. Both attempted to provide argument and evidence for their favored interpretation, including appeals to interpretive canons or pragmatic maxims, albeit for the most part implicitly.

For O'Connor, the ordinary meaning of 'use a firearm' includes actions in which a gun is 'employed' or 'put into service' to further some end and she cites as evidence for this several dictionary definitions of the word 'use.' Her approach, then, is to pin down a meaning for the word 'use' and then to compose it semantically with the more or less clear meaning (not disputed by either party here) of 'firearm.' She further argued that Congress never said that the statute did *not* apply to gun-for-drugs swaps, adding that, 'Had Congress intended the narrow construction that petitioner urges, it could have so indicated,' a line of reasoning which seems to invoke an application of Levinson's Q-heuristic: What isn't said isn't the case (they didn't say that it does not apply to gun trade so it does apply to gun trade).

Scalia maintains that the meaning of the *phrase* 'use a firearm' should be considered as a whole and depends on the context in which the term appears and that, by consulting definitions of the word 'use' in dictionaries, O'Connor has artificially isolated the word from its immediate context, i.e. its collocation with 'a firearm.' In its occurrence in the key section of Stat-18, where it appears unmodified by any qualifying terms, the phrase has its 'ordinary' meaning, the meaning that, in his opinion, any 'reasonable' person would take it to have: that of using a firearm as a weapon (that is, shooting with it or threatening to do so). He supports his position with the following analogy: 'To use an instrument ordinarily means to use it for its intended purpose. When someone asks "Do you use a cane?" he is not enquiring whether you have your grandfather's antique walking-stick on display in the hall; he wants to know whether you *walk* with a cane.'[41] So Scalia's line of reasoning is very much in line with the I-principle ('Say no more than you must') which licenses the hearer to enrich a simple unmarked phrase in a stereotypical/normal/default way: S said 'use a firearm,' S has used a brief, unmarked mode of expression indicating that they intend the standard unmarked (stereotypical) meaning of the phrase. Hence S meant 'use a firearm *as a weapon*.' A further line of argument here (not used by Scalia) would be that if the statute's authors had chosen, instead of 'use a firearm,' a longer, more complex phrase such as 'make some use of a firearm' or 'involving a firearm in some way,' the interpretive inference to the stereotypical use—as a weapon—would not take place. The prolix phrasing would be taken as a signal that the usual, stereotypical meaning is not in force.[42] Thus, the Gricean

---

[39] Scalia 1997 (cited in n.31), 17.
[40] In *Watson v United States*, 128 S.Ct. 697 (2007), the court decided that a transaction in the opposite direction does not violate the same statute (i.e. while in *Smith* it was held that one 'uses' a gun by *giving* it in exchange for drugs, in *Watson* it was held that one does *not* 'use' a gun by *receiving* it in exchange for drugs).
[41] Scalia 1997 (cited in n.31), 23–24.
[42] Discussed in n.20.

maxims (or, at least, the two *neo*-Gricean maxims of quantity or informativeness) appear to be alive and well in the interpretation of legal language by legal practitioners, but they are not particularly helpful since, unsurprisingly, they may deliver contradictory results.

I note a final point of interest in O'Connor's argument: she concedes that the use of a firearm as a weapon is the use that comes to mind first, but insists that we cannot conclude on that basis that other uses are excluded: 'It is one thing to say that the ordinary meaning of "uses a firearm" includes using a firearm as a weapon, since that is the intended purpose of a firearm and the example of "use" that most immediately comes to mind. But it is quite another to conclude that, as a result, the phrase also excludes any other use.'[43] Her presumption is that we shouldn't accept the first construal that comes to mind, that is, jump to an easy quick conclusion, but should rather think more carefully and reflectively in order to discern the correct meaning. Despite the apparent reasonableness of this stance, I will suggest in section 6 that, in fact, the first interpretation that occurs to a hearer/reader does have a special status—it's not always correct, but it very often is and for good reason.

In the next section, I want briefly to survey some wider issues that have been (inevitably) seeping into the discussion; in particular, two apparently divergent views on interpretation, namely 'textualism' and 'intentionalism,' and the role (and extent) of the context of interpretation.

5. Textualism, contextualism, intentionalism, and the problem of 'context'

In his essay on legal interpretation, Scalia presents himself as a textualist and he makes frequent remarks of an anti-intentionalist sort: 'We do not enquire what the legislature meant; we only ask what the statute means', 'The text is the law, and it is the text that must be observed'[44] and, in a discussion of the *Plain Meaning* rule, he says that its widespread acceptance and use makes no sense 'if what the legislature *intended*, rather than what it *said*, is the object of our inquiry'.[45] However, he eschews a narrow kind of textualism: 'Textualism should not be confused with so-called strict constructionism, a degraded form of textualism that brings the whole philosophy into disrepute, ... the good textualist is not a literalist.'[46] He explicitly advocates the use of interpretive canons in aid of getting at the 'plain meaning' of the text, but also insists that any canon is 'simply *one indication* of meaning, and if there are more contrary indications (perhaps supported by other canons), it must yield.'[47] As far as I know, O'Connor hasn't presented a philosophy of interpretation, but on the basis of her mode of argument in *Smith v United States*, she appears to be more narrowly textualist, perhaps what Scalia means by a 'constructionist,' adhering to 'what is said' *by the words in the text*, this being recovered by a process of syntactic composition of the inherent meanings of the basic parts (the individual words) with little, if any, intervention of pragmatic considerations. In short, she is a 'literalist,' while Scalia veers more in the 'contextualist' direction, allowing that the literal meaning(s) of a word in the abstract may alter when it is contextualised and that

---

[43] Available at <http://bulk.resource.org/courts.gov/c/US/508/508.US.223.91–8674.html>.
[44] Scalia 1997 (cited in n.31), 23.
[45] Scalia 1997 (cited in n.31), 16.
[46] Scalia 1997 (cited in n.31), 23–24.
[47] Scalia 1997 (cited in n.31), 27.

some phrasal meanings are not strictly compositional.[48] He recognizes (to some extent, at least) that encoded linguistic meaning falls short of determining what an utterance (or text) means, thereby holding a (limited) version of the linguistic underdeterminacy view discussed in section 2.

Although textualism and intentionalism are often presented as opposed interpretive doctrines, it seems to me that textualism with its various interpretive aids and rules, as advocated by Scalia, is not at all at odds with the goal of recovering speaker meaning (a particular kind of intentionalism). Quoting him again: 'The focus should be upon what the text would reasonably be understood to mean, rather than upon what it was intended to mean,'[49] but what the text is *reasonably understood to mean* and what the legislature intended (properly construed) are but two sides of a single communicative coin, two sides that do not, however, always perfectly coincide. All communication takes place at a risk: speakers want to convey certain thoughts to their addressees; addressees do not have, and cannot be given, direct access to those thoughts; speakers do what they can to provide sufficient evidence (linguistic, contextual), on the basis of which addressees, using their pragmatic interpretive capacities, all going well, can infer those thoughts, or thoughts similar enough to them that the ongoing interaction may proceed without disruption. The interpreter's 'reasonable understanding' of a text, inferred from the evidence the speaker has set before him, just is his rationally warranted grasp of the speaker's (intended) meaning.

Pragmatic principles or maxims (and by extrapolation, canons of construction) are prevailing constraints on both speaker and hearer. Grice's maxims are framed as injunctions to the speaker to produce utterances which meet certain standards of informativeness, relevance, truthfulness, and orderliness, and, with certain provisos,[50] hearers presume that speakers are observing these standards and this presumption plays a key role in their derivation of the speaker's meaning. In other words, the raison d'être of the maxims/heuristics is to facilitate successful communication: for the speaker's part, they constrain her to produce an overt behavior (certain sounds, gestures, or marks) which (together with other accessible contextual evidence) can enable an addressee to grasp the thought(s) she wants him to grasp; for the addressee's part, they guide him in the process of inferring the speaker's meaning, her m-intention. The m-intention is a special kind of fully overt intention which, roughly, consists of a higher-order intention that a lower-order intention to provide a certain content or information is made evident to the addressee.[51] When producing an utterance, a speaker will often have several intentions; for instance, an utterance of the sentence 'I hope you will' in a particular context, may come with (at least) the following intentions: that the addressee should recognize that the speaker intends him to think that she hopes that he will win a certain contest, that the addressee should feel supported and encouraged by her, that he should think the speaker is a good friend to him, that he should confide in her, and perhaps more. But only the first of these intentions has the overtness of an m-intention and a correct interpretation of the utterance will consist in recovery of the content of just this intention.

Correlatively, in the interpretation of legal language, whether a contract, a will, a statute, or a constitution, the only intention that is of interest is the m-intention. The legislators who enacted a statute that adds a heavy penalty for a drugs-related crime involving

---

[48] See Recanati 2004 (cited in n.4), for discussion of literalism and (several varieties of) contextualism.
[49] Scalia 1997 (cited in n.31), 144.
[50] Grice 1975 (cited in n.1), 49 discusses a number of ways in which speakers may fail to fulfil a maxim, some of which will be evident to hearers.
[51] Discussed in n.2.

the 'use of a firearm' might have intended, expected, or hoped that the statute would reduce the occurrence of certain crimes, that it would lead to tighter control of gun licenses, that it would improve the safety of children, and so on, but it is not the recovery of these intentions that is the goal of the interpretive process, the process of ascertaining the meaning of the text. If it is these kinds of intention that Scalia dismisses, no pragmatic intentionalist would argue with him, but then his apparent anti-intentionalism would not be at odds with those views according to which what we are doing when we interpret an utterance is trying to uncover the content of a speaker's m-intention.[52] Scalia is not entirely explicit about the range of kinds of intention he wants to ban from consideration, but what is explicit is his opposition to delving into the history of the making of the statute, including in particular the concerns that preoccupied the original framers, hence their intentions, expectations, or hopes about what the statute might achieve, what or who it would be applied to. It is far from clear that he eschews m-intentions.

Still, one might wonder in what sense there is an m-intention to be recovered for a great many legal texts; after all, statutes are seldom, if ever, the product of a single mind, they go through multiple redraftings by different people, particular clauses are amended or added to mollify certain parties, and it may be that there is no single person who authors or oversees the final text. However, none of this interferes with the following claim from Stephen Neale: 'A statute is treated—not by choice, but because there is no alternative if the concept of a statute is to be intelligible—*as if it were a purposive statement made by a person or a group of persons.*'[53] There is, of course, a big conceptual issue about how adequately to characterize the notion of a joint or collective intention (specifically, a collective m-intention), a notion that is needed when we move from single authorship to multiple authorship, but that problem is not to be solved by denying its existence.[54] Sometimes this (or something very like it) seems to be what Scalia himself is getting at: 'we do not really look for subjective legislative intent. We look for a sort of "objectified" intent—the intent that a reasonable person would gather from the text of the law, placed alongside the remainder of the *corpus juris*.'[55] It looks, then, as if the goal of this non-literalist textualism is no different from the goal of any communication intentionalist, i.e. the recovery of the author(s)' m-intention.[56]

---

[52] R. Charnock 2007 (cited in n.34) notes that in the case of the interpretation of wills, it has long been accepted that 'the judge may place himself in the testator's armchair and consider the surrounding circumstance in order to discover his intention.' Of course, wills are an easier kind of legal text with regard to the recovery of speaker meaning (m-intention), as they are usually the utterance of a single individual whose purpose is very circumscribed and the temporal-spatial distance between formulation, on the one hand, and interpretation and application, on the other, is usually much shorter than that of statutes (or constitutions). Nevertheless, each of these dimensions is surely a continuum, so there isn't any clear cut-off point between legal texts for which recovery of an 'm-intention' is the goal and legal texts for which it is not.

[53] This quotation is from S. Neale, *Textualism with Intent* (cited in n.28), which is a sustained and powerful argument that textualism, which is essentially an interpretive methodology, cannot but have as its objective the recovery of speaker meaning (i.e. communicatively intended content). The excerpt is available at: <http://www.ucl.ac.uk/laws/jurisprudence/docs/2008/08_coll_neale.pdf>.

[54] There is a further interesting issue that arises in the case of contracts: the signatories to a contract may come to find that they have a genuine disagreement about its correct interpretation. It seems, then, that, contrary to what was assumed at the time of signing, they must have had different m-intentions (there was no collective m-intention). This raises a host of questions, including the following: how can one or other of the divergent interpretations be judged the correct one when both parties signed up in good faith to a text that they each took to be concrete evidence of their own m-intention? Did they each, in fact, unwittingly, sign different contracts?

[55] Scalia 1997 (cited in n.31), 17.

[56] In somewhat similar vein, in his commentary on Scalia's essay, Dworkin (cited in n.31), 117) says Scalia's textualism is not really anti-intentionalist: it's a question of *which intention* of the law-makers

The real issue seems to concern context. Scalia says: 'In textual interpretation, context is everything,'[57] by which I take it he means that small differences of context can have a powerful effect on the interpretation of linguistic forms in a text. This is all well and good, but the hard question is: what is the relevant contextual information in any given instance of interpretation? Without a doubt, the immediate linguistic context is one important aspect of it. In this regard, one of the interpretive canons that Scalia discusses (approvingly) is *Noscitur a sociis* (The meaning of a term is known by its companions). This is context as *co-text* (or immediate linguistic context), and the often-cited sort of illustrative example is that of an ambiguous linguistic form like 'bank' which may be disambiguated by words in its immediate vicinity ('its companions') in the utterance or text:

18. a. John put his money in the bank.
    b. John pulled his boat onto the bank.

The canon is, of course, of limited value since it can be easily overridden by some aspect of salient extra-linguistic context or by background set up earlier in the text: e.g. John lives on a barge on a river, has little to do with conventional social institutions and stashes all his valuables in (holes in) the bank. While co-text (neighboring words/phrases) surely can and often does play an important role in how we interpret a given word or phrase, noting this doesn't take us very far into the context issue and it's not clear that we would want such a specific interpretive rule.

In the case of *Smith v United States*, O'Connor turned to wider textual context (and an implicit appeal to textual coherence) to support her position. A later and related section of the same statute concerns the seizure and forfeiture of any 'firearm and ammunitions intended to be used' in any of several crimes, explicitly including illegal interstate transfer and trade of firearms. O'Connor's reasoning is that since the 'use' of firearms here clearly includes their employment as instruments of barter, Congress must have intended 'use a firearm' in Stat-18 to include this kind of use as well as their employment as weapons. However, drawing on the salient differences in the immediately surrounding linguistic context within the two sections of the Act, Scalia argued that the two occurrences of the phrase had different meanings despite occurring in the same statute, the one restricted to using a firearm as a weapon, the other (explicitly) including the selling and trading of firearms.[58]

As textualists, what neither of them called on as contextual evidence for their interpretations was the legislative history of the statute, that is, committee reports, floor speeches, statements from lobbyists and other nonlegislators, related legislation, and a host of other archived documentation. It is Scalia's deep aversion to the use of this kind of 'contextual evidence' by judges in interpreting a statute that lies behind his apparent opposition to considerations of legislative intention. The relevant aspect of legislative history turns out to be the record of intentions expressed by members of the legislature

matters and the intention that Scalia respects is the 'semantic intention' with which the words were produced, not any intentions or expectations that the legislators might have had about how the legal language might be *applied* in different circumstances or what its consequences might have been. This is pointing in the right direction—the original semantic intention is surely relevant (that is, the intention to use certain words with certain meanings) but is subsumed by the more expansive m-intention which is the real object of interpretation. In his response to Dworkin, Scalia 1997 (cited in n.31) 144 endorses the distinction Dworkin has made but says he would prefer the term 'import' to 'semantic intention.' One could take this as another indication that he has no issue with the view that the goal of textualist interpretation is the recovery of m-intended content.

[57] Scalia 1997 (cited in n.31), 37.
[58] For discussion, see Polich 1994 (cited in n.37).

about particular statutes in the making and their desired or expected consequences and applications. For Scalia, the real problem with legislative history (and its alleged evidence of legislative intent) is that, as 'selectively' used by judges, it provides them with a concealed means of furthering their own political agendas and/or prejudices. As John Polich says, 'it permits judges to claim that their own policy preferences are really the unexpressed will of Congress.'[59]

The pressing question remains: What is the proper context of interpretation of legal texts? Clearly, the immediate linguistic co-text is a relevant component, but what beyond that? Is it the whole statute, or just the section at issue? Other related statutes? The whole body of law? Some, or as much as possible, of the legislative history of the statute (committee reports, floor speeches, records of lobby group interests, etc.)? What, if any, are the constraints on the relevant contextual evidence? There are strong echoes here of the 'frame problem' in cognitive science, that is, the problem of how it is that, when we are engaged in processes of *rational belief fixation*, we know when to stop gathering and considering evidence that might have a bearing on the belief or decision at issue. For the legal interpretation situation, the general question is whether there are any principles or heuristics for constraining these processes or it is an arbitrary and opportunistic matter: you stop when you run out of time, money, energy.[60] Neither the canons of construction nor neo-Gricean maxims seem to provide any guidance on this.

In the next section, I move to a brief consideration of a different kind of pragmatic theory from the systems of maxims discussed so far. This is relevance theory, which endorses Grice's claims that (i) an essential feature of human communication is the expression and recognition of a certain kind of overt intention, and (ii) addressees bring to the inferential process of utterance interpretation certain warranted expectations about the nature of communicated information. It is not, however, *neo*-Gricean in that it does not set out a system of interacting (or conflicting) maxims or interpretive heuristics but grounds addressees' pragmatic expectations in a single principle of communicative relevance.

6. Relevance theory and the interpretive bedrock

The account of the pragmatics of communication and interpretation developed within Relevance Theory (RT) is grounded in a general property of human cognitive systems; that is, their evolved orientation towards achieving as many improvements to their representational contents as possible, while ensuring that the cost to their energy resources is kept as low as reasonably possible. At the centre of the theory is a technically defined notion of *relevance*, where relevance is a potential property of any input to any perceptual or cognitive process. An input may deliver a variety of different types of *cognitive effects* to the system, one of which, *contextual implications*, is of most interest here: these are implications which follow (inferentially) from the new input in combination with a *context*

---

[59] Polich 1994 (cited in n.37), 288. According to Polich, however, textualism serves much the same function: 'only it replaces the fiction of Congressional intent with other fictions about the legislative process and the meaning of language.' (cited in n.37), 288.

[60] For discussion of the frame problem, see Z. Pylyshyn (ed.), *The Robots Dilemma: The Frame Problem in Artificial Intelligence* (Norwood, N.J.: Ablex, 1987), in particular, the very different perspectives on the problem presented in the chapters by P. J. Hayes and J. A. Fodor. For an attempt to answer Fodor's important question 'What is a nonarbitrary strategy for delimiting the evidence that should be searched in rational belief fixation?', see D. Sperber and D. Wilson, 'Fodor's frame problem and relevance theory' (1996) 19(3) *Behavioral and Brain Sciences* 530.

of existing assumptions, but not from either alone. That is, new information is only relevant if it connects up productively with contextual information. The other key factor affecting the degree of relevance of an input is the *processing effort* it consumes: deriving contextual implications and other cognitive effects from any given input requires a mobilization of cognitive resources, including attention, memory, and various processing algorithms and heuristics. Thus, the relevance of any input is a trade-off between the (positive) cognitive effects it yields and the processing effort it requires: the greater the ratio of effects to effort the greater the relevance of the input. The basic claim of the framework is that human cognition is oriented towards maximizing relevance (known as the *Cognitive Principle of Relevance*).

Verbal utterances (and other acts of ostensive communication) are a special kind of input in that they raise specific expectations of relevance in their addressees, that is, expectations about the cognitive effects they will yield and the mental effort they will cost. Quite generally, an utterance comes with a presumption of its own *optimal relevance*; that is, there is an implicit guarantee that the utterance is the most relevant one the speaker could have produced, given her abilities and her preferences, and that it is at least relevant enough to be worth processing. This is known as the *Communicative Principle of Relevance* and it follows from the *Cognitive Principle of Relevance* in conjunction with the overtness of the intention that accompanies an utterance: the speaker openly requires effort (attention and processing) from her addressee who is thereby entitled to expect a certain quality of information and no gratuitous expenditure of effort. The fact that utterances carry this presumption licenses a particular comprehension procedure, which, in successful communication, reduces the many logically possible interpretations to a single warranted interpretation:

Relevance-theoretic comprehension procedure
a. Follow a path of least effort in computing cognitive effects (contextual implications):
Test interpretive hypotheses (disambiguations, reference resolutions, lexical adjustments, implicatures, etc.) in order of accessibility.
b. Stop when your expectations of relevance are satisfied.

It is claimed that this procedure is automatically applied in the online processing of verbal utterances: taking the schematic decoded linguistic meaning as input, processes of pragmatic completion and enrichment at the explicit level occur in parallel with the derivation of the contextual implications of the utterance.[61]

Central to the working of the procedure is a subprocess of *mutual parallel adjustment* of explicit content and intended contextual implications, a process guided and constrained by expectations of relevance. Here is a brief example involving the adjustment of explicit content in response to expected implications and where the outcome is a narrowing down of a lexically encoded meaning:

19. Bill: I'm doing the 20-km circuit run this afternoon. Would you like to come?
Sue: No thanks, I'm *resting* today.

The verb 'rest' encodes a rather general concept, rest, which can cover any degree of inactivity (physical or mental), from sleeping, to staying awake but not moving much, to performing a range of not very strenuous tasks (with many more possibilities in between).

---

[61] For the original detailed account of the theory, see D. Sperber and D. Wilson, *Relevance: Communication and Cognition* (Oxford: Blackwell, 1986/95); for an updated account, see D. Wilson and D. Sperber, 'Relevance theory,' in L. Horn and G. Ward (eds), *The Handbook of Pragmatics* (Oxford: Blackwell, 2004), 607; for a recent short overview, see R. Carston, 'Relevance theory,' in G. Russell and D. Graff Fara (eds), *Routledge Companion to the Philosophy of Language* (London: Routledge, 2012), 163.

Suppose that Bill knows that Sue is a very athletic person, who exercises rigorously and regularly, so when she talks of resting in response to his question, the most highly activated information among the wide range associated with his general lexical concept REST is propositions such as the following: athletes need to schedule rest days in their training programs; they do not take long runs on their rest days; they are nevertheless likely to be up and about doing less physically demanding things; this gives their muscles time to recover; it is important for their health, and so on. Other assumptions associated with resting, such as that people often lie down when resting, people should not be disturbed when resting, and so on, are much less highly activated in this exchange. These items of general knowledge about resting are deployed by Bill, in their order of accessibility, as contextual assumptions, on the basis of which he derives contextual implications, along the lines of: Sue cannot take a long run today; her body needs some recovery time; she will probably be available for a walk and some socializing today, and so on. As a part of the process of mutual parallel adjustment of the components of the interpretation, the concept of resting, which is a constituent of the proposition Sue has expressed, is narrowed from the general encoded concept REST to a concept of a specific kind of resting. This adjusted propositional content and the contextual assumptions function together as premises that ground the contextual implications of the utterance, which in turn satisfy its expected relevance.[62]

As should be evident from the discussion of this example, the operative notion of 'context' in this account is of a set of (highly activated or accessible) mentally represented assumptions or propositions. For Sperber and Wilson, the interpretation that is speaker-meant includes not only the proposition expressed but also the *intended* contextual assumptions and implications, which together form an inferentially sound interpretation. The first interpretation thus derived which is consistent with the presumption of optimal relevance is the 'correct' interpretation, that is, the one that the hearer/reader is rationally justified in accepting as what the speaker meant. Of course, sometimes this interpretation is not in fact the one intended and so there is some degree of miscommunication, which may or may not be serious for the ongoing interaction of the interlocutors.

I hope this very brief overview at least indicates the distinctively cognitive nature of this pragmatic theory, including its emphasis on how minimizing cognitive costs plays a role in our interpretive activities albeit relativized to our expectations of cognitive effects (the greater the expected gain, the more effort we are prepared to make). In this respect, among others, it is very different from the Gricean and neo-Gricean maxims and interpretive heuristics. Recall that the I- and Q-maxims/heuristics reviewed in section 3 sometimes converge on the same interpretation but at other times give contradictory predictions, indicating that there may be a deeper underlying principle from which they follow as more specific heuristics whose application is limited to particular subdomains of linguistic interpretation. I suggest that the communicative principle of relevance is that deeper principle.

Whether this is right or not (and it needs a lot more investigation),[63] one might well wonder what bearing any of this has on the issues of legal interpretation already

---

[62] In different circumstances—for instance, as a response to the question, 'Would you like to walk to the corner shop with me?'—the concept of resting would be narrowed down much further to a concept which denotes a much lower level of activity. For a more detailed account (and a range of worked-through examples) of the relevance-based processes of word meaning adjustment—which may result in a narrowing or a *broadening* of the lexical concept—see Wilson and Carston 2007 (cited in n.5).

[63] See Carston 1998 (cited in n.19) where I attempt to show that the correct predictions of the Q-principle (which generates scalar implicatures) and of the I-principle (which generates stereotypical enrichments), as well as other pragmatic inferences that neither predicts, can all be accounted for by relevance theory.

discussed, in particular, the cases of divergent interpretations and the debates that have ensued. After all, RT is an account of automatic online processes of interpretation which occur (for the most part) at an unconscious 'subpersonal' level, while the explicit marshaling of (alleged) contextual evidence and the reconstructions of lines of reasoning that go on in the disputed interpretations of statutes, as in *Smith v USA* and *Garner v Burr*, are obviously conscious, highly reflective, 'person' level activities. I do believe that an understanding of the underlying cognitive processes of interpretation should (ultimately) be helpful in providing some better grounded explicit guidance in (at least some) cases of disputed interpretation, but this is a very big issue and I cannot hope to begin to do it justice in this short section. All I will do here is pick up certain details of the relevance-theoretic account as they relate to some of the cases of legal interpretation discussed earlier.

Note first that, according to the RT account, interpreters are justified in following a path of *least effort* because the speaker/author is expected (within the limits of her abilities and preferences) to make her utterance as relevant as possible, and hence as easy as possible to understand (since relevance and processing effort vary inversely). As Sperber and Wilson put it: 'the plausibility of a particular hypothesis about the speaker's meaning depends not only on its content but also on its accessibility. In the absence of other evidence, the very fact that an interpretation is the first to come to mind lends it an initial degree of plausibility.'[64] Recall O'Connor's concession, mentioned in section 4, that the first interpretation of 'use a firearm' to come to mind in Stat-18 is that of the use for which firearms were designed, that is, as weapons. Arguably, this would not be the first interpretation to come to mind if the established topic of Stat-18 concerned the buying and selling of firearms, or it was this that was being explicitly discussed in the immediately surrounding text, thus making their use as instruments of trade highly cognitively accessible in interpreting the phrase at issue, but this is not the case in Stat-18. Assuming that the first interpretation to come to mind (that is, 'use as a weapon') is sufficiently relevant (has enough implications), the theory maintains that this is the 'correct' interpretation, that is, the one that is rationally justified. The subsequent search for other uses of the phrase in other parts of the statute is then, arguably, not warranted.

Recall now the contended interpretation of 'vehicle' in *Garner v Burr* and the very broad interpretation that eventually prevailed, with a meaning roughly paraphraseable as 'heavy thing on wheels which is run along a public road,' thus including in its denotation chicken coops on wheels. What the relevant section of the Road Traffic Act 1930 says is: 'Any vehicle travelling on a public highway must be fitted with pneumatic tyres.' Recall that the judge who arrived at this broad interpretation of 'vehicle' based it on the manifest purpose of the statute which was to prevent damage to public road surfaces. This might look like an instance of the kind of move that textualists, like Scalia, would find abhorrent, involving, they might say, an appeal to 'unexpressed intent.' However, the judge here did not have to undertake research into the legislative history of the Road Traffic Act in order to discern the intentions of the makers of this law; he didn't have to work his way through other sections of the Act, or consult other statutes to support his interpretation. He found it directly, one might say, in the relevance of the statute, calling on nothing more than his general knowledge about road surfaces and about iron wheels versus pneumatic tyres. This strikes me as a case where the relevant contextual assumptions are available to all ordinary mentally able citizens and would be immediately activated by the text itself: public roads are used by many people; keeping the roads in good

---

[64] D. Sperber and D. Wilson, 'Pragmatics, modularity and theory of mind' (2002) 17(1/2) *Mind and Language* 18–19.

order benefits all road users; it also helps save on unnecessary expenditure of public funds; running heavy structures on iron wheels may damage a road's surface; fitting such structures with pneumatic tyres greatly reduces the likelihood of damage. The kind of contextual implication that follows from the text of the statute together with these assumptions is obvious: Heavy structures on wheels should be fitted with pneumatic tyres in order to avoid damage to the road surface and thereby further general public welfare. Thus, it accords with the RT mutual adjustment process discussed earlier that, by a process of backwards inference, the concept encoded by 'vehicle' is broadened so as to support these conclusions which are drawn in establishing the relevance of the text.

A similar sort of case, discussed by Andrei Marmor[65] (and many others), concerns a (fictional, but highly plausible) enactment which stipulates that 'It shall be a misdemeanor...to sleep in any railway station.' The word whose interpretation is at issue is 'sleep,' a word which is surely among the least ambiguous or vague words in the language. Consider now the case of a passenger who, while sitting waiting for a delayed train at 3.00 a.m., falls asleep for a few minutes; does he, thereby, commit a misdemeanor? Marmor considers the possibility that while what the law literally *says* is that it is an offence 'to sleep' in the railway station, the prescriptive *content* of the law is, roughly, to prohibit attempts to *use the railway station as a place to sleep in*. However, he dismisses this interpretation as not having sufficient foundation, as being too much of 'a stretch.' This suggested content, or something very similar to it, seems to me to be the right interpretation. No (rational) policeman who noticed the briefly dozing passenger would feel impelled to bring the force of the law down on him. On the other hand, the policeman might well take the law to apply to a man who throws a blanket onto the station platform, lies down on it, and stares up at the ceiling, showing no signs of intending to move on, but who does not in fact sleep. Again, my interpretation of 'sleep' here, as being both narrower in denotation than its literal encoded meaning (it excludes the briefly dozing passenger) and also broader (it includes the awake man on the blanket), can be explained in RT terms: the relevance (or purpose) of the law lies with obvious contextual implications concerning preventing people from treating a railway station as a place to spend the night or set up home in, and this, in turn, by mutual parallel adjustment, leads to an adjustment of the meaning of the word 'sleep'.

As already noted, Sperber and Wilson's claim that utterances (and other communicative acts) come with a presumption of their own *optimal relevance* unpacks as an implicit guarantee that the speaker/author has been as relevant as possible (to the addressees) within the parameters of her *abilities and preferences*. This proviso is interesting as it seems to mesh with interpretive practices sometimes made explicit in legal interpretation. Charnock mentions the case of a will, executed by the testator the day before his death, which said simply: 'All for mother.' The testator's mother was, however, long dead. The court accepted evidence that the testator habitually used the word 'mother' to refer to his wife and the occurrence of 'mother' in the will was duly interpreted (in accordance with its author's naming preference) as meaning his widow.[66]

Recognition of the linguistic, socio-political or other preferences of the author(s) of a legal document and the impact of those preferences on the linguistic expression of intended meaning hasn't been confined to wills. In a discussion of *Church of Holy Trinity v United States*,[67] Marmor mentions a likely preference of Congress which influenced

---

[65] Marmor 2008 (cited in n.22), 428–429.
[66] Charnock 2007 (cited in n.34), 18.
[67] Cited in n.29.

their phrasing of the law which is at the center of this case. In formulating the prohibition on the importation of 'labor or service of any kind,' followed by a list of exceptions (singers, actors, lecturers), it seems that the phrase 'manual labor' had been considered, but Congress preferred not to use it, even though they wanted the Act to put a stop to the influx of cheap unskilled labor. As Marmor puts it: 'It would have been politically rather inconvenient to explicitly declare that the law targets the importation of cheap manual labor.'[68] However, that this particular preference should be accommodated by the interpreter is far less compelling than in the case of the will just mentioned. First, it is based on information that only became available after investigation into legislative history during the interpretive debate occasioned by the case of the Church of Holy Trinity's employment of a foreign clergyman and, second, it is difficult to see any kind of grounding for a narrowing of the phrase 'labor or service of any kind' to 'manual labor or service of any kind,' especially given the explicit list of exceptions, which any such narrowing would render redundant (hence irrelevant).[69] Not all speaker/author preferences are transparent to the interpreter, or intended to be. When there is a sufficiently relevant interpretation derivable without seeking them out, that is the warranted interpretation.[70]

Without doubt, the question of whether the RT account of ordinary everyday utterance interpretation can, perhaps with certain provisos and/or modifications, be carried over to the case of legal interpretation needs much more consideration than I've given it here. It should be that the first-pass reading of any legal document does fall quite straightforwardly within the general pragmatic story. However, one of the ways in which legal interpretation is special is in the kind of conscious effortful scrutiny a legal text may be subjected to in a bid to find an interpretation which may benefit a particular individual's case in a situation where the stakes are very high for that individual. To extrapolate validly from the one kind of interpretive process to the other and to provide cognitively grounded reasons for favoring a particular interpretation in the case of an explicit interpretive dispute is an important challenge for relevance theory.

7. Conclusion: any role for canons of construction?

In this paper, I have tended to focus on cases of legal interpretation where the canons of construction haven't been very helpful, where doubt about the correct interpretation of a phrase in the text of a statute has not been resolved by the canons, but has moved to a debate about whether one or another canon is properly applied to the phrase, or even about what the correct interpretation of a canon is (e.g. what does it mean to be 'of the same kind' in *Eiusdem generis*?). However, given their longevity and stability, the canons have presumably been useful guides over the centuries in a great many instances where the language of a legal text has left an interpretive gap. In a balanced discussion of

---

[68] Marmor 2008 (cited in n.22), 427.

[69] The result of the original trial by a circuit judge was to find the church guilty of breaking the law, but the verdict was overturned on appeal by the Supreme Court, the judges there interpreting 'labor or service of any kind' as 'manual labor or service of any kind,' using the piece of legislative history mentioned. See Scalia 1997 (cited in n.31), 18–23 for scathing criticism of this interpretation based, as he puts it, on 'unexpressed intent.'

[70] There are no doubt interesting ways in which the 'abilities' component of speaker/author 'abilities and preferences' could enter into the legal interpretive process. Setting aside 'scrivener's errors,' which must be accommodated when recognized, it may be that law-makers' manifest epistemic limits should also impact on the interpretation; for example, when a current context includes social and technological conditions they could not possibly have anticipated. I suspect this raises a host of thorny issues, which I cannot pursue here.

their role, Michael Sinclair describes them as 'wise saws backed by experience and intuition... not law, not universally binding, but of greater significance than mere clichés,'[71] and, he says, 'Given their durability and apparent usefulness to decision-makers, one would expect some foundational principles of general applicability could be found to underlie canons.'[72]

Nevertheless, few would disagree with John Polich's conclusion that the bare text of statutes together with the canons (and even boosted with evidence from legislative history) cannot solve all issues of statutory interpretation, and there must be ongoing effort to develop an interpretive methodology that 'enables courts to apply statutes as objectively as possible.'[73] It remains something of an article of faith on my part that this effort would be enhanced by paying close attention to an account of the cognitive processes of and the constraints on ordinary utterance comprehension, such as that offered by relevance theory. Ultimately, though, even if the situation can be improved and judges come to interpret from a position of deeper understanding of language and communication, genuine disagreements about the correct interpretation of a legal text are inevitable, given the nature of language, that is, its underdeterminacy of the propositions it is used to express, and the defeasibility of the pragmatic inferences employed to fill the interpretive gaps.

---

[71] Sinclair 2005–2006 (cited in n.30), 921.
[72] Sinclair 2005–2006 (cited in n.30), 920.
[73] Polich 1994 (cited in n.37), 288.

3
Linguistic Meaning and Legal Truth

Brian H. Bix*

1. Introduction

Augustine wrote of 'time', that it is something we all know, until we have to explain it.[1] One might make a similar observation about truth—and even more so about truth in law.[2] While philosophers have trouble giving a clear explanation of 'truth'[3]—and, I will show, special problems apply to that same concept in the legal context—this does not mean that general or legal discourse is in general chaos.[4] For most purposes, we have no trouble identifying true (empirical) propositions and true propositions of law. However, underneath the general smooth operation are difficult questions, which tend (in law) only to arise at the margin or for the most hotly disputed questions.

This article will explore the issues of legal truth distinctive to legal systems in general, and common law legal systems in particular, focusing on different factors, including the role of linguistic meaning in legal truth and the problem of legal error. In what follows, the first two sections consider preliminary questions—of motivation and subject matter. Then follow three sections on complications to legal truth: the dual nature of law, common law reasoning, and legal mistake. The article then concludes with sections on the role of linguistic meaning in legal truth and on the connection between debates on legal truth and other jurisprudential debates.

2. Preliminaries: motivation

Following Michael Moore,[5] I will begin the discussion of legal truth by considering the possible motivations for the inquiry. Moore here refers to H. L. A. Hart, who had responded to the traditional jurisprudential inquiry, 'What is law?', not by offering a new answer to the question, but by insisting that we consider what concerns (e.g., regarding the relationship of law and rules, and law and morality) motivate the inquiry.[6] One might similarly wonder what outside concerns might motivate the present inquiry.

---

* An earlier version of this article was presented at the Current Legal Issues Colloquium 2011, 'Law and Language', and an earlier version of some portions of this article was submitted to the 'Law and Truth' Conference organized by the Instituto Tecnologico Autonomo de Mexico. I am grateful for the comments and suggestions of Dennis Patterson and Xiaohuan Qi.

[1] Augustine of Hippo, *Confessions*, lib xi, cap xiv, sec 17 (ca. 400 CE).
[2] Ronald Dworkin makes a similar observation in Ronald Dworkin, 'Law as Interpretation' (1982) 60 *Texas Law Review* 527 at 527–8.
[3] See, e.g., Simon Blackburn, *Truth: A Guide* (Oxford: Oxford University Press, 2005).
[4] A point nicely emphasized to me in comments by Dennis Patterson.
[5] Michael S. Moore, 'The Plain Truth about Legal Truth' (2003) 26 *Harvard Journal of Law & Public Policy*, 23, 23–4.
[6] H. L. A. Hart, *The Concept of Law* (2nd edn, Oxford: Clarendon Press, 1994), 1–17.

Some of the purposes motivating the current inquiry into law and truth (and my past ones[7] as well) relate in part to certain disputes that affect both theoretical and practical debates about law. For example: Is the law (never, sometimes, frequently, or always) indeterminate? And do judicial decisions (always, frequently, sometimes, or never) create new law?

The question of truth-aptness for many propositions about law can be re-characterized as questions about which norms 'exist',[8] and when or how they came into being. When, if ever,[9] do legal norms exist (that is, when are the norms already valid norms of that particular legal system) prior to their promulgation by legislatures, judges, or other legal officials? A related controversy: When judges claim that they are merely 'discovering the law' (in the process of announcing a legal rule that appears to add to or differ from previously promulgated law) rather than legislating anew, can that be 'true'? This has been a claim of Anglo-American judges for centuries, but has been met with increasing scepticism.

Whether there is a truth of the matter about what the law requires prior to judges' making their decisions in individual cases, has obvious implications, not merely for how commentators characterize judicial actions, but, more importantly, for how judges (and lawyers) should approach hard cases. This was a persistent theme of Ronald Dworkin's early work: that whether it was thought that there was a right answer to be found in all (or nearly all) legal disputes would affect the way that judges and lawyers would approach many cases.[10] One uses different sorts of arguments for advocating that an outcome reflects existing law compared to the arguments one would use for urging that one outcome would be the best *new* law on the subject.

Other aspects of legal truth, however, are not directly connected to these debates about legal validity and promulgation (social sources). Instead, as should become clearer, discussions of legal truth can reflect other concerns: e.g., they can be efforts to clarify the relative roles of will (choice or promulgation) and reason (coherence or interpretation) in determining the current status of legal norms, or the relative role of semantic meaning and other factors in determining what the law (does or should) require.

---

[7] Brian H. Bix, 'Global Error and Legal Truth' (2009) 29 *Oxford Journal of Legal Studies* 535; Brian H. Bix, 'Will versus Reason: Truth in Natural Law, Positive Law, and Legal Theory' in *Truth: Studies of a Robust Presence*, Kurt Pritzl, ed. (Washington, D.C.: Catholic University of America, 2010), 208.

[8] The Scandinavian legal realists famously argued that talk of legal norms and legal concepts was metaphysically ungrounded, and generally nonsensical: Brian H. Bix, 'The American and Scandinavian Legal Realists on the Nature of Norms' (2009) *De Lege* (Uppsala: Iustus Förlag,), 85.

[9] Hans Kelsen famously asserted that any application of a general norm within adjudication to particular parties, however uncontroversial the application, was the creation of a new legal norm: Hans Kelsen, *Introduction to the Problems of Legal Theory*, Bonnie Litschewski Paulson and Stanley L. Paulson, trans. (Oxford: Clarendon Press, 1992), 67–8.

[10] See Ronald Dworkin, *Taking Rights Seriously* (Cambridge, Mass.: Harvard University Press, 1977), 81–130; Ronald Dworkin, *A Matter of Principle* (Cambridge, Mass.: Harvard University Press, 1985), 199–245. However, as Mark Tushnet has argued, the fact that a right answer might exist, accessible to a hypothetical super-judge, like Dworkin's 'Hercules', is, at best, an 'ontological' point, that there exists a right answer, regardless of whether we can ever find it, whether we can know whether we have found it, and whether we can ever all agree among ourselves that we have found it. Tushnet asserts that the world in which we live is one in which able lawyers and judges can (at least over the medium term) make determinate questions look indeterminate, and vice versa: Mark Tushnet, 'Defending the Indeterminacy Thesis' (1996) 16 *QLR [Quinnipiac Law Review]* 339.

3. Preliminaries: subject matter

In talking about truth in law, there are threshold questions regarding what the proper focus should be: legal norms, norm propositions, generalizations about areas of law, etc., with each alternative raising different sets of difficulties.

Legal rules tend to have contents like 'all As are prohibited from doing X'—or, more commonly in legislation, something like: 'if an A does X, A will be guilty of a Grade 2 Felony' and 'those guilty of a Grade 2 Felony must serve between 5 and 10 years in prison'. Standard legal or moral norms state directly that something should or should not be done, or give the same message indirectly, by adding a sanction to violation of the directive. These norms, as directives (in John Austin's terms, commands [of the sovereign][11]), cannot be true or false. What could make them true or false? Complying with a directive does not make it true; failing to comply does not make it false.[12] For legal norms, the ascription is characteristically in terms of 'validity' rather than truth.[13]

However, even if 'one ought not murder' does not seem truth-apt, propositions like 'murder is illegal [in this country now[14]]' and 'X is guilty of murder' do seem to be truth-apt, though, as we shall see, the second example carries further complications. This reflects the distinction, made salient by Georg Henrik von Wright, between norms, norm formulations, and norm propositions.[15]

Propositions of, or within, law come at different levels of generality.[16] As propositions, they may come with a certain presumption that, at a minimum, they are 'truth-apt' (that is, they can be true or false). First, there are relatively narrow ascriptions of legal qualities to a person or action: 'X is guilty of burglary [under the laws of this country]'; 'A is contractually bound to pay B $100'; and 'C has no legal obligation to pay child support to D'. Secondly, there are purported legal rules, relatively specific, but abstracted from the first category's ascription to individuals of legal rights and duties: e.g. '[in this country,] a will must have two witnesses to be legally valid'; and 'drivers must not exceed 75 miles per hour on the highway'. This level of generality includes interpretations of legally authoritative texts (statutes, constitutional provisions, and the like).

At a higher level of generality are broad statements about types of transactions or whole doctrinal areas. These are sometimes descriptive observations offered by practitioners, and sometimes 'theories of' particular areas of law (e.g., theories of contact law,[17] theories of tort law,[18] etc.). There remains some question about which observations or

---

[11] John Austin, *The Province of Jurisprudence Determined* (Wilfrid E. Rumble, ed.) (Cambridge: Cambridge University Press, 1995).
[12] Consider American legal realist Karl Llewellyn's insight that people too often conclude from the existence of a legal rule either that citizens always follow the rule in their actions, or that judges are always guided by the rule when it is relevant to their decisions, while the reality is that both conclusions are often far from the truth: Karl N. Llewellyn, 'A Realistic Jurisprudence—The Next Step' (1930) 30 *Columbia Law Review* 431, 439.
[13] Carlos E. Alchourrón and Eugenio Bulygin, *Normative Systems* (Vienna: Springer, 1971), 172–5.
[14] As Andrei Marmor reminds us, legal propositions have truth value only relative to a particular legal system and time period: Andrei Marmor, 'Truth in Law', USC Legal Studies Research Paper No. 11–3 (2011), available at <ssrn.com/abstract=1760053>.
[15] e.g., G. H. von Wright, 'Deontic Logic' (1951) 60 *Mind* 1; G. H. von Wright, *Norm and Action* (New York: Routledge & Kegan Paul, 1963).
[16] cf. Moore, 'The Plain Truth About Legal Truth' (cited in n.5), 24–5.
[17] e.g. Charles Fried, *Contract as Promise* (Cambridge, Mass.: Harvard University Press, 1981).
[18] e.g. Gerald J. Postema (ed.), *Philosophy and the Law of Torts* (Cambridge: Cambridge University Press, 2001).

theories at this level are or should be trying to explain: should it be legal doctrines or individual case outcomes?[19] And certainly claims of 'truth' or 'falsity' at the level of such abstract theories are not as straightforward as comparable claims for the narrower and more concrete propositions discussed above.

4. First complication: the double-life of law

The first complication for truth in law is what John Finnis has called law's double nature: that law is simultaneously a social/historical fact and a normative system.[20] Law as a social-historical fact is constituted by the actions of officials within a particular legal system from its beginning to the present. There are propositions about law which are primarily summaries of what decisions legislatures and judges, and perhaps also administrative agencies and executive/enforcement officials, have made over time. Such claims are made by social scientists and other academics, as well as by legal practitioners and judges.

The perspective of the judge (in a common law legal system) is distinctive, as the judge is required to use the legal materials to resolve disputes brought to the court, and the judge (at least in a common law system) is authorized to modify the law or, to a limited extent, legislate new norms, as part of the process of resolving the legal dispute. How much the judge is constrained (by legal or moral 'right answers') in this process is strongly disputed.

Often, when claims are made about the law, there is some ambiguity regarding whether the claims are descriptive/historical, regarding what actions were actually taken by officials in the past, or whether there some element of modifying, re-characterizing, or reforming the rules to make the current (or future) cases better. And when theories are offered of areas of law, the detailed case outcomes are built into generalizations in ways that reflect a conscious bias towards making the overall picture more just or at least more coherent. This is sometimes described as 'rational reconstruction'.[21]

Since the proper use of legal sources within the form of practical reasoning that is adjudication sometimes involves the modification of existing norms or the creation of new norms, what the law 'is' at the point when the case is being considered by the court seems uncertain: it is the law that has not yet been changed, and yet also the law that will be after the changes are effected.

5. Second complication: common law reasoning

The second complication for truth in law derives from the distinctive form of decision-making in common law legal systems. The complication of common law reasoning has obvious connections with the previous topic, the complication of the 'double-life' of law, as common law reasoning focuses on that second 'life', the use of

---

[19] Jody S. Kraus, 'Philosophy of Contract Law' in Jules L. Coleman and Scott Shapiro (eds), *The Oxford Handbook of Jurisprudence and Philosophy of Law* (Oxford: Oxford University Press, 2002), 687, 691–4.
[20] e.g. John Finnis, 'The Fairy Tale's Moral' (1999) 115 *Law Quarterly Review* 170, 170; John Finnis, 'On the Incoherence of Legal Positivism' (2000) 75 *Notre Dame Law Review* 1597, 1602–6.
[21] Rational reconstruction is comparable to what Ronald Dworkin has called 'constructive interpretation': Ronald Dworkin, *Law's Empire* (Cambridge, Mass.: Harvard University Press, 1986), 49–53.

law by judges as part of their practical reasoning in resolving legal disputes. However, in discussing common law reasoning, there are distinctive intricacies for discussions of legal truth that arise from the way precedent operates in common law systems.

Under common law precedent systems, (1) judicial resolutions of individual cases add to the law; (2) earlier decisions by courts higher in the hierarchy and (usually) the same level in the hierarchy bind later courts; but (3) all that binds is the decision on the facts, not the prior court's stated justification for the decision or its limits, or even the prior court's analysis of which facts are relevant and which are not; it is open to a later court to re-characterize what grounded the prior decision, and (thus) what the limits of that case's rule are. In general, a later court has broad powers to 'distinguish' prior cases that would otherwise bind the later court. Additionally, some courts (usually the highest court in the system) reserve to themselves the right, in appropriate circumstances, to overrule prior decisions.[22] All of these aspects of precedent complicate efforts to characterize what the law is in a common law legal system, and what courts are doing when they restate, modify, or overrule prior decisions.

The practices involved in precedent and common law decision-making create uncertainty about the state of the law at any given time. Today's case may be overruled tomorrow, or its holding narrowed, or its basic point re-construed.[23] Of course, in part this just reflects a basic point of law, but one that is not especially complicated or paradoxical: that the truth values of propositions of law are relative not only to a particular legal system, but to a particular point in time. A recently enacted statute goes into effect, changing the law; some years later, it is amended or repealed, changing the law again. So it is with legislatures' legislation, and judicial legislation can be seen as roughly similar. However, the situation with precedent and common law reasoning is in fact much more complex. Most basically, when legislatures change the law, they often do so on the basis that the prior law was mistaken as a matter of morality or policy, but reversals and reconsiderations by courts go a step further, stating (or at least implying) that the prior court decision was mistaken *as to what the law was*.

In legal systems in general, but particularly in common law legal systems, what the law is, is built on a mixture of what classical philosophy would have called 'will' and 'reason'.[24] Law is a reflection of 'will' in the sense that the choices of legislators and judges add to or change the law, regardless of whether those choices can otherwise be justified. Among the major competing theories about the nature of law, none deny that such choices are important components of what the law is[25]; the disagreements tend to come regarding the role of the other component, 'reason'.

---

[22] e.g., Neil Duxbury, *The Nature and Authority of Precedent* (Cambridge: Cambridge University Press, 2008); Frederick Schauer, 'Precedent' (1987) 39 *Stanford Law Review* 571.

[23] Comparable changes are possible, just based on either the availability of judicial review of legislation or the possibility of appeal: e.g., a statute may be invalidated by the court (because of a purported conflict between the statute and a constitutional provision), but that invalidation could be reversed by an intermediate appellate court, and that decision might in turn be reversed by the highest court in the jurisdiction.

[24] On will in classical philosophy, see Vernon J. Bourke, *Will in Western Thought: An Historico-Critical Survey* (New York: Sheed & Ward, 1964); Albrecht Dihle, *The Theory of Will in Classical Antiquity* (Berkeley, Calif.: California University Press, 1982); Charles H. Kahn, 'Discovering the Will: From Aristotle to Augustine' in *The Question of 'Eclecticism': Studies in Later Greek Philosophy* (Berkeley, Calif.: California University Press, 1988), 234–59. On will and reason in law, see Lon L. Fuller, 'Reason and Fiat in Case Law' (1946) 59 *Harvard Law Review* 376; Bix, 'Will versus Reason' (cited in n.7), 208.

[25] Even Mark Greenberg, who characterizes his own position, and Dworkin's, as denying that legislation directly creates new legal norms, accepts that the enactments of legislatures can change the law indirectly (by affecting an interpretive or all-things-considered moral judgment). Mark Greenberg, 'The Standard Picture and Its Discontents' (2011) 1 *Oxford Studies in the Philosophy of Law* (Leslie Green & Brian Leiter, eds.) 39.

In particular, the question is whether law's aspiration to coherence,[26] and to justice, justifies an interpretation of the legal materials that will either add norms to the list of other (social-source-based) valid legal norms, or remove some (social-source-based) norms from the list of valid norms. To restate the point more clearly, there are views both that a norm can fail to be valid in the legal system, even if it otherwise meets all the formal and procedural requirements of the legal system; and that a norm can be valid in the legal system, even if has not been promulgated according to the formal and procedural rules of the legal systems. The first view (norms not legally valid even if they meet all formal and procedural requirements) is exemplified by the well-known 'Radbruch Formula', which states that a sufficiently unjust rule loses its status as a valid legal norm.[27] The second view (norms legally valid even if they are not promulgated according to the system's formal and procedural rules) is connected with the idea that certain moral norms have a legal status in all legal systems, regardless of the social sources. Here is John Finnis justifying the outcome of the Nuremberg Trials:

> [T]he moral rules applied were also rules of the 'higher law' applicable in all times and places ... as a source of argumentation and judgment 'according to law' when the social-fact sources which are the normally dominant and quasi-exclusive source of law are, in justice, inadequate and insufficient guides to fulfilling obligations such as the judicial obligation to do justice according to law, or everyone's obligation to behave with elemental humanity.[28]

It should be noted that the views of Radbruch and Finnis are controversial, and rejected by many scholars. There are less radical, and less controversial, views regarding how 'reason' contributes to the content of law, and in ways that appear to modify the products of 'will'. For example, judges will frequently interpret one statute in a way that makes it more consistent with other statutes or earlier case law, even if that interpretation of the statute may be in conflict with the plain meaning of the statutory language the law-makers chose, or with the intentions with which the law-makers acted.

The connection with truth in law is that there is unsettledness and controversy regarding which norms are and are not valid norms in the legal system at a particular time, either because there is controversy as to whether considerations of justice can invalidate an otherwise valid norm or add to the list of social-source-based norms; or because there are justice- or coherence-based changes to social-source-based norms that judges can make or, in some sense, should[29] make, but have not yet made.

6. Third complication: legal mistake

A discussion of truth in law needs also to be able to respond to the problem of legal mistake: the fact that courts can reach decisions that are wrong (or, if one prefers a more

---

[26] Which Dworkin re-characterized under his rubric of 'Integrity': Dworkin, *Law's Empire* (cited in n.21), 225–58.

[27] Gustav Radbruch, 'Statutory Lawlessness and Supra-Statutory Law (1946)', Bonnie Litschewski Paulson and Stanley L. Paulson, trans. (2006) 26 *Oxford Journal of Legal Studies* 1.

[28] John Finnis, 'Natural Law Theories' in Edward N. Zalta (ed.), *Stanford Encyclopedia of Philosophy* (Stanford, Calif.: Stanford University, 2007), available at <http://plato.stanford.edu/entries/natural-law-theories/>, sec. 3.1.1.

[29] One can understand this 'should' either as a moral or legal 'should'—that is, one can argue that judges in some legal systems may have a legal obligation to change the law in the ways indicated. Or one could argue that this obligation is not one imposed by the legal system, but is part of the general moral obligation for all officials in all legal systems to make the law more moral when it is within their power to do so.

cautious phrasing, that most other competent practitioners consider to be wrong). Such 'wrong' decisions might be reversed later by the same court, or by a higher court, but they also might *not* be overturned, and become part of the settled law of the system.

Legal officials are to act according to the law: to apply statutes and administrative regulations in line with their content, within the constraints set by the constitution or other basic laws. However, as legal officials are human—subject to error through ignorance, corruption, or simple imperfection—they sometimes make mistakes in their application of legal norms to facts. First, this can create a paradox in the case in which the error occurs. X breached her contract with Y, but the court came to the erroneous conclusion that there had not been a breach. There are then grounds for stating both 'X breached the contract' and 'X did not breach the contract'. And it is the same for situations where a court mis-interprets and mis-applies a statute or constitutional provision, and so on.

Secondly, and more generally, a legal system creates standards for decisions, but also grants legal officials power to make authoritative decisions, which bind citizens and other officials, whether they are correct or incorrect (and even when they seem to be blatantly incorrect).[30] Thus, when courts make decisions (and create legal norms) that are (or that observers consider to be) incorrect, there is a sense in which that new decision *does* state the current law (because an authoritative official has spoken) and a sense in which it *does not* (because the decision was contrary to applicable norm(s), and because there is a chance that the 'mistake' will be corrected on appeal or by a later decision of the same court).

This initial consideration of legal mistake connects to two further, related questions: (1) does it make sense to speak of global error in law, of all legal officials being mistaken about what the law is in a given legal system?[31] And (2) in particular, are there (as some natural law theorists claim) *a priori* or universal sufficient or necessary conditions for legal validity such that certain norms might be norms that *are* part of a legal system (or are *not* part of the legal system) contrary to the clear beliefs of all legal officials (a question touched upon in section 5)?

The basic problem is this: legal truths, or at least some significant portion of legal truths, appear to be conventional, in much the way that language or the rules of games are conventional.[32] And with conventional matters, it is the shared beliefs of participants that make propositions true or false. Therefore, there is something paradoxical about speaking of global error in such cases.

Consider the analogous case of language: words mean whatever we—the users of the language (in the present case, English)—collectively choose for them to mean. At least, that is true as a rough first approximation. It is sometimes more complicated than that. For example, with some terms, the connection between the term and a person, object, or category may be conventional, but after that the extension of the term is set by the way the world is, not our views about the world. This phenomenon is known as 'natural kind' terms, or 'Kripke-Putnam reference'.[33] 'Gold' is considered a paradigmatic 'natural kind

---

[30] cf. Stanley L. Paulson, 'Material and Formal Authorisation in Kelsen's Pure Theory' (1980) 39 *Cambridge Law Journal* 172. This authorization is usually thought to extend to cases where the official's error is that he or she is acting beyond his or her authority (even where the decision might otherwise be substantively unexceptionable).

[31] Matthew Kramer, 'Is Law's Conventionality Consistent with Law's Objectivity?' (2008) 14 *Res Publica* 241; Brian H. Bix, 'Global Error and Legal Truth' (cited in n.7).

[32] On the conventional nature of law, see, e.g., Andrei Marmor, *Social Conventions: From Language to Law* (Princeton, N.J.: Princeton University Press, 2009), 155–75.

[33] Saul Kripke, *Naming and Necessity* (Cambridge, Mass.: Harvard University Press, 1972); Hilary Putnam, 'The Meaning of "Meaning"' in *Mind, Language and Reality* (Cambridge: Cambridge University Press, 1975), 215.

term'; we cannot all be mistaken that 'gold' refers to a kind of solid yellowish metal, but we *can* all be mistaken about the properties of that metal (e.g., its chemical composition, atomic structure, etc.), and whether it is the same thing or a different thing from what we call 'pyrite' (also known as 'fool's gold'). The extension of 'gold' is given by the nature of gold (or scientists' current best understanding of that nature), not by general beliefs about gold.

The question is whether there are aspects of law which are like natural kind terms: terms whose meaning is determined by the way the world is, rather than by our beliefs.[34] If so, then propositions about those aspects of law would allow for global errors. Additionally, in legal systems that tie the meaning of statutory or constitutional norms to the original intentions of the law-makers (or, for constitutions, also the ratifiers), it could make sense to say that at some time every legal official or scholar was mistaken about the meaning of a norm, because they could all be mistaken about the historical facts of the relevant parties' intentions.[35] (We will return to the connections between linguistic meaning and legal truth in section 8.)

There also might be a similar possibility of global error if a legal norm incorporated a natural kind term or a moral term (for those who believe that moral terms are truth-apt[36]). For example, the application of a statute that affects the right to catch 'fish' may turn on whether dolphins and whales are in fact 'fish',[37] just as the application of a constitutional provision forbidding 'cruel and unusual punishment' may turn on whether the death penalty is in fact a 'cruel' punishment.

However, legal systems will contain other norms which are not so clearly linked to purportedly external facts (like the historical intentions of law-makers, the proper extension of natural kind terms, or the objective meaning of moral terms). And for those norms, the law must be some function of what the legal officials say—and cannot be contrary to what *all* legal officials say (over the long term).[38] In different terminology, the criteria for validity of legal norms is conventionalist,[39] and it is officials who establish, maintain, or change those conventional criteria, so officials cannot (by definition) all be wrong.

Of course, the conventional (or 'social sources'[40]) aspect of law is not accepted by all theorists. As discussed in section 5, some natural law theorists (e.g. John Finnis and Gustav Radbruch, in his later works) argue that there are norms that are part of law even if never promulgated by legal officials, and other norms that fail to be (to become) valid norms in the legal system, despite their meeting all procedural and formal requirements, because they are too unjust. If these theorists are correct, norms can be valid norms in

---

[34] Or, at least, terms where we are inclined to defer to 'experts' regarding the 'real nature' of some object or category. This is an alternative characterization of what is going on in the case of natural kind terms. See Jules Coleman and Ori Simchen, '"Law"' (2003) 3 *Legal Theory* 1. For an argument that something like natural kind terms is central to law, see Nicos Stavropoulos, *Objectivity in Law* (Oxford: Clarendon Press, 1996).

[35] There are numerous problems with originalist views, regarding which intentions should count, whose intentions should count, and whether such intentions should be given significant moral or political weight, but these are questions well beyond the scope of the present article.

[36] Though this would be consistent with a belief that moral truth is relative to a particular society and a particular time.

[37] Michael S. Moore, 'A Natural Law Theory of Interpretation' (1985) 58 *Southern California Law Review* 277, 322–38.

[38] Brian H. Bix, 'Global Error and Legal Truth' (cited in n.7).

[39] Alchourrón and Bulygin, *Normative Systems* (cited in n.13), 174.

[40] On social sources and law, see, e.g., Joseph Raz, *The Authority of Law*, 2nd edn (Oxford: Oxford University Press, 2009), 37–52.

a legal system, even if all current legal officials claim that they are not, and norms can fail to be valid norms in a legal system, even if all legal officials claim that they are valid norms in the system. For these natural law theorists, truth about which norms are valid in a legal system is not always or entirely a matter of convention, and validity will often turn on the truth of moral propositions.

7. Controversy

What should have become clear from the preceding parts of this article is that the analysis of truth relating to legal systems in general, and common law systems in particular, both reveals and reflects disagreements about the nature of law and legal reasoning. Controversies throughout the philosophy of law have counterparts in disagreements about truth in law.

When a court announces a new rule in a common law case, the court and some commentators may claim that this rule had been law even before it was announced, while other commentators will deny that the result can be accurately characterized as anything other than judicial legislation, the creation of new law. Issues about truth in law also appear in controversies about the legal validity of extremely unjust rules, the legality of prosecutions for actions seemingly valid under the ruling system's laws, the legal status of norms created by erroneous judicial decisions, the proper interpretation of statutes and constitutional provisions, etc.

Jurisprudence in general, and theories about truth in law in particular, create unique challenges. This is not one of those areas where everyone agrees on the best understanding of what goes on in the practice, or what should go on in the practice, and one need only figure out the best philosophical characterization of the practice in terms of truth. Disputes about truth in law are tied to, and motivated by, other significant jurisprudential debates. The debates about truth in law are not likely to be resolved until those other debates are.

8. The role of linguistic meaning

Earlier sections, in particular section 6 on legal error and the discussion of the possibility of global errors in law, touched on the role of linguistic meaning in legal truth. In general, there are two basic questions to ask regarding the role of linguistic meaning in questions of law and truth. First, is linguistic meaning sufficiently determinate to ground simple bivalence in legal propositions (that is, the propositions being either true or false, with no third option)? Secondly, are there factors specific to legal process or legal interpretation that would modify or override linguistic meaning, including, but not limited to, making indeterminate linguistic meaning determinate?

In *The Concept of Law*, H. L. A. Hart argued that the application of legal rules was sometimes indeterminate because language itself was sometimes indeterminate. This was his well-known discussion of the 'open texture' of language—that even commonplace terms can have fuzzy edges. His example was the rule, 'no vehicles in the park', with the question of whether things like bicycles or roller skates would constitute 'vehicles' for the purpose of the rule.[41]

It was perhaps not surprising that Hart's discussions of 'open texture' moved quickly from the open texture of terms to the open texture of rules: where certainty

---

[41] Hart (cited in n.6), 124–32.

in the application of rules was equated with determinate intentions on the part of the rule-maker(s), and the rule-maker(s) having not considered some possibility was equated with the application being left to the discretion of the court.[42]

On the question of whether the vagueness of terms could leave the legal truth of legal propositions uncertain, Ronald Dworkin once argued that any indeterminacy deriving from vague terms could be easily overcome through legal presumptions—e.g., the principle of lenity, that in case of doubt a criminal law should be interpreted in favour of the citizen, in favour of making an action non-criminal.[43] In response, Joseph Raz emphasized that the problem of vagueness could not be so easily solved, for with vague terms, it is not only the boundary between clear application and clear non-application which is unsure, but also the boundary between clear application and uncertain application; therefore a mere presumption will not create determinacy in all cases.[44]

The discussions from Hart, Dworkin, and Raz exemplify the basic structure of analysis. Linguistic meaning can be determinate or indeterminate, but the operation of other processes of legal reasoning can modify the initial linguistic meaning, making it more or less unsettled, and sometimes overriding the linguistic meaning entirely.

There are ongoing debates in many legal systems regarding the proper approach to interpreting and applying wills, trusts, contracts, statutes, constitutional provisions, and other legal texts.[45] Often these debates pit those who emphasize the intentions of the drafters (or ratifiers) against those who emphasize the 'plain' or 'objective' meaning of the words used.[46] It is not necessary for present purposes to resolve that debate, or even to offer views on whether there is one necessary, best, or proper answer for all legal systems, or whether the decision is one that different legal systems might make for contingent or arbitrary reasons. It is sufficient to note that whatever the legal system treats as the initial or presumptive ('semantic') meaning of legal texts is subject to revision in response to other concerns.

First, in many legal systems, courts will act contrary to their current best understanding of a legal text's meaning in the interest of following precedent. Secondly, in many jurisdictions courts have an express, or at least accepted, power to interpret statutes in a way which avoids the absurdity or injustice that would come if the statutes were given their clear meaning.[47]

---

[42] Hart (cited in n.6), 128–9.
[43] Ronald Dworkin, 'No Right Answer?' in P. M. S. Hacker and J. Raz (eds), *Law, Morality and Society: Essays in Honour of H.L.A. Hart* (Oxford: Clarendon Press, 1977), 58, 67–9; see also Dworkin, *A Matter of Principle* (cited in n.10), at 128–31.
[44] Raz, *The Authority of Law* (cited in n.40), 73–4.
[45] e.g., Kent Greenawalt, *Legal Interpretation: Perspectives from Other Disciplines and Private Texts* (Oxford: Oxford University Press, 2010).
[46] In some jurisdictions courts are authorized or obligated (or at least see themselves as authorized or obligated) to read statutes and constitutional provisions according to the law-makers' original intentions or the original public meaning of the terms, even when those intentions and public meanings are inconsistent with the (current or 'real') meaning of the norm's terms. In other places, such possibilities have been discussed in terms of legislators who though that 'fish' included whales and that 'marriage' excluded same-sex couples. See Moore, 'A Natural Law Theory of Interpretation' (cited in n.37), 322–38; Brian H. Bix, *Law, Language, and Legal Determinacy* (Oxford: Clarendon Press, 1993), 140–57; Brian H. Bix, 'Can Theories of Meaning and Reference Solve the Problem of Legal Determinacy?' (2003) 16 *Ratio Juris* 281, 286–92.
[47] For what it is worth, I do not think that any of the above outcomes derive from necessary truths about language and meaning, on one hand, or about law, on the other hand. These are contingent choices made, on moral or policy grounds, by individual legal systems: Bix, 'Can Theories of Meaning' (cited in n.46); Bix, 'Will versus Reason' (cited in n.7), 208.

Thus, in general one can see that the determinacy or objectivity of linguistic meaning certainly plays a role in the determinacy or objectivity of legal propositions, but the (in)determinacy of the first does not guarantee the (in)determinacy of the second.

9. Conclusion

The topic of truth in law resists easy analysis, and raises problems in a number of distinct ways. First, there is the problem that legal rules, as norms, do not seem to be truth-apt. Even once one moves to *propositions about* (legal) norms questions about the appropriateness of conventional logic and truth-relations remain. Second, law has different aspects, which are often in tension: law as a series of historical official actions, and the efforts of judges and commentators to impose coherence and structure on those decisions, and law as a process of dispute resolution, a process that may require or result in the (intended or unintended) modification of existing rules.

Third, within common law systems, there is the paradoxical practice of common law reasoning and precedent, which entails that the meaning or significance of a case cannot be known with confidence even by the judge who decided it, or by commentators at the time of decision. All decisions are subject to narrowing, expansion, or re-characterization by later decision-makers. Fourth, officials often are both guided by legal standards and have the authority to have their decisions become law even when those decisions are contrary to the applicable legal standards.

Fifth, the truth of legal propositions is usually a function of the meaning of the terms of relevant legal texts, though this is, in turn, complicated by the presumptions and processes that can modify or override semantic meaning, sometimes transforming uncertain semantic meaning into determinate legal propositions, but at least as often working in the opposite direction.

Finally, views about truth in law are often closely connected to positions about other controversial jurisprudential claims, so claims about the objectivity or determinacy of law can become the subsidiary conclusions of larger debates regarding the nature of law.

4

Truth in Law

*Andrei Marmor**

It is the regular business of lawyers and judges to draw legal inferences. Many of those inferences look like an ordinary syllogism, whereby a conclusion is derived from some premises about the normative content of the law and statements describing facts or events. Are such syllogisms valid, do they yield conclusions which can be said to be true or false? Can we ascribe truth-value to the content of legal norms? These are the questions I want to examine in this essay. Notice, however, that I will not discuss here the question of what makes it true that a given norm is legally valid. I will assume that the legality of the relevant norms is established. My topic here concerns the question of whether we can ascribe truth-value to what the law says, and what it takes to do so. As we will see, there are two separate issues involved here. The immediate and most obvious concern is about whether legal prescriptions can be assigned truth-value at all. A solution to this problem forms the content of the first part of the paper (sections 1–3). In the last part (section 4), I will explore some structural aspects of legal syllogism, suggesting that there is an interesting analogy between truth in law and truth in fiction.

1. Propositional content of exhortatives

An inference is valid only if the truth of its premises guarantees the truth of its conclusion. Therefore, no question of validity about an inference can arise if the premises consist of sentences or linguistic expressions that do not express a propositional viz, truth-evaluable, content. On the face of it, however, linguistic expressions of particular legal contents, that is, the content of constitutional and statutory prescriptions, judicial decisions, agency regulations, and the like, are not propositions. Laws do not purport to describe an aspect of the world, they do not tell us how things are, or are not; they tell us, roughly, what to do, or what not to do. Thus, the question is whether prescriptive content of the kind we find in legal provisions is the kind of content that is truth-evaluable at all. And if it is not, then no inferences taking such prescriptions as premises can be valid.[1]

Before we proceed, it is important to clarify what is at stake here. I am not suggesting that in order to provide the logical framework for legal inferences, we must confine ourselves to standard propositional calculus. Logicians have long developed systems of deontic logic allowing us to formalize the logical relations between propositions that contain deontic operators, such as obligation, permission, etc. But deontic logic, or any other axiomatic system we could devise to deal with such expressions, is not the solution

---

* I am grateful to Scott Soames, Gideon Yaffe, Mark Schroeder, Joseph Raz, Ron Garet, and the participants in the Analytical Philosophy Conference (San Diego, April 2011) for very helpful comments on earlier drafts.

[1] An early proponent of such a view was H. Kelsen, *General Theory of Norms*.

to our problem, only a tool we can use later. Deontic logic offers us a formalized system to deal with prescriptive sentences, *assuming* that there is some sense in which they can be true (or false).[2] These logical tools do not give us an interpretation of what makes prescriptions or deontic statements truth-evaluable, they assume that such an interpretation is available. But it is precisely the availability of such an interpretation that is being challenged here. In other words, the challenge is to show how legal prescriptions can have truth-evaluable content; once we have such an interpretation, we can then employ deontic logic to evaluate the logical relations between the relevant statements. So let me turn to this now.

The main plausibility of a skeptical position here can be seen by looking at statements expressed in the imperative mood. Imperative utterances, such as "Close the door!", "Stand over there!", etc, are not the kind of utterances that describe anything, their function is to motivate conduct, and they would seem to have no truth-evaluable content. I am not suggesting, of course, that legal norms are typically formulated as imperatives. But their linguistic or communicative function is very similar. And they are similar in two ways: first, laws prescribe modes of behavior, they do not describe how things are (or are not). There is, of course, an enormous variety of ways in which laws are formulated. Very few legal regulations are formulated as standard imperatives. Laws grant rights of various kinds, impose obligations, grant various agents, private and public, powers to introduce normative changes in the law, and so on. The unifying element, however, is conduct guidance. In one way or another, legal norms and legal decisions purport to guide conduct.[3]

Secondly, when the law requires you to do something, say, that you "ought to do φ in circumstance C," it purports to say that you ought to do φ, *and* that you ought to do it *because* the law says so. Legal requirements do not simply point out to their subjects reasons for actions that apply to them. They purport to create or impose those reasons by expressing the relevant requirement. You ought to do it because the law says so. And again, in this laws are very similar to standard imperatives. Consider, for example, the difference between the following two statements:

(1) S saying to H: "You ought to give Sarah $100."
(2) S saying to H: "Give Sarah $100!"

Statements of type (1) are normally expressed to point out a reason for action that applies to H, that is, regardless of S's saying so. By expressing (1), S would normally understood to have pointed out to H, or reminded him, as it were, that there is something that he ought to do, that is, give Sarah $100 (say, because he promised to do it or such). The speech act itself does not purport to make any difference to H's reasons for action (or, if you like, to the truth-value of (1)). The reason is claimed or assumed to be there, as it were, regardless of S's utterance or speech act. On the other hand, imperative expressions like (2) necessarily imply an expectation that H regard the expression of S's imperative as a reason for action. The fact that S had uttered (2) purports to make a difference to H's reasons for action.

Speech act theorists have long recognized that there is a wide range of performative speech acts which are normally expressed in order to induce the hearer to perform a

---

[2] See Jorgensen, "Imperatives and Logic."
[3] It is possible, of course, for some legal enactments to have no prescriptive content. Legislatures sometimes enact various declarative laws which have no conduct guidance element in them, such as declaring a certain bird as the official "state bird," or something like that. Such laws, however, are pretty rare, and in any case, quite tangential to law's main functions in society.

certain action (or refrain from action of course), and by way of recognizing the speech act itself as a reason to do as ordered, requested, etc. These include commands, orders, requests, pleadings, invitations, questions, and many others.[4] Following Austin (with a slight modification) I will call these kinds of performatives *exhortative speech acts* or *exhortatives*.[5] Such speech acts purport to motivate conduct on the part of the hearer by the very act of expressing the relevant utterance, expecting the hearer to recognize the utterance as a reason for action. As with other performatives, there might be some background conditions that are needed to secure the felicity conditions, or the success, of the speech act in question. Sometimes these background conditions consist of social conventions or rules of an institution, but I do not assume that this is necessarily the case.[6]

Legal instructions are typically exhortatives. In fact, they are probably paradigmatic examples of exhortatives. The enactment of a legal requirement, or the official expression of a legal ruling (say, by a court or an administrative agency) are the kind of speech acts that purport to motivate conduct on the part of the addressees by way of recognizing the speech act as providing them with reasons for action. It doesn't mean that all legal prescriptions are formulated in an imperative mood, of course, or even that they are formulated prescriptively. An expression might be an exhortative even if formulated as a simple descriptive statement. Saying, for example, "It is very cold in here" might well be a request from someone to close the window, depending, of course, on the conversational background and mutual knowledge of the relevant circumstances. Similarly, a legal descriptive statement such as "It is a misdemeanour to φ in circumstances C" is not a description of how things are in the world, but rather, a prescription that one ought not to φ in C. And again, when the law says that you ought not to φ, it invariably implies that you ought not to φ, at least in part, because the law says so.

Now, assuming that laws are typically exhortative speech acts, the relevant question here is whether exhortatives have truth-values? One may doubt that there is a problem here. For inferential purposes, it might be thought, we can just stipulate an operator, such as "*imperative that* __", followed by the content of the relevant exhortative. Thus, for example, consider an imperative statement:

(3) (S to H): "Close the door."

Now, the idea is that we can assign truth-value to (3) by the formula:

imperative that {H closes the door}

Notice that the truth-value is not assigned to the content in brackets, since it would entail that the imperative is true if H closes the door and false if H doesn't, which is not what we are after; the truth-value of an imperative cannot depend on compliance with it. Furthermore, notice that something like an "ought" operator will not do, because an imperative might be true (if there is a sense in which it is), as such, even if it is false that one ought to do as instructed. Thus, the idea is that we assign truth-value to "*imperative*

---

[4] For a very useful taxonomy of such speech acts see Bach and Harnish, *Linguistic Communication and Speech Acts*, 47–55.

[5] Austin called them "exercitive" (*How to Do Things With Words*, 151) while Bach and Harnish labeled them, more sensibly perhaps, as "directives" (see their *Linguistic Communication and Speech Acts*, 47). I refrain from using Bach and Harnish's terminology because "directive" has become the standard way of referring to authoritative speech acts, and I want to keep to the broader category that includes speech acts which are not necessarily authoritative.

[6] On the question of whether performative speech acts necessarily rely on a conventional setting there is an ongoing debate in the literature. I have weighed in on this debate in my *Social Conventions* (118–130). In any case, not all performative speech acts are exhortatives.

that ___" such that it is true if an imperative with the content that follows the operator has been issued or expressed, and false if not. For logical-inferential purposes, this should work. But we would still need some interpretation of what makes it the case that the relevant propositions are true (or false). Is it simply the fact that the imperative has been expressed? Maybe it is, but we need some explanation for why it is the case and under what conditions. In other words, we need an interpretation of the truth-*conditions* of such statements. The fact that we can translate imperative statements and, presumably, other types of exhortatives, to some truth-evaluable statements by stipulating some operator which can be assigned a truth-value does not answer our question. We need to know what it is that *warrants* ascribing truth (or falsehood) to exhortatives of various kinds.

For the sake of simplicity, I will henceforth focus on some simple exhortatives, like orders or commands expressed in the imperative mood. The assumption here is that if we can provide an interpretation of ascribing truth-values to imperatives, with suitable modifications other types of exhortatives could be treated similarly. Now, a natural way to interpret the propositional content of imperatives is to suggest that such content is self-referential. When S says to H: "Close the door!" the propositional content expressed is about the wishes of S; it expresses something about the mental state of the speaker, such as "S wants/wishes H to close the door and wants/wishes H to recognize the expression of this wish as a reason for H to comply." This is undoubtedly a propositional content, of the standard descriptive kind. The proposition refers to the speaker's state of mind. In other words, when people express a request or an order or such, they normally express a wish or desire that something happen and the expectation that the addressee sees the expression of the request or the order for what it is, namely, as a motivational reason to act in a certain way.[7] That is, at least in standard cases. I will deal with some non-standard examples shortly.

To be sure, I am not suggesting that the self-referential content is what the imperative *means*; an imperative statement means what it states, namely, "close the door," or "pass me the salt," etc. In other words, imperative sentences are not semantically reducible to their self-referential propositional contents. The propositional content in play is what makes an imperative true, or false, as the case may be. But can it be false? If an imperative expresses self-referential propositional content, then every *sincere* expression of an imperative would constitute a true proposition. If by saying "close the door" I express the proposition that I want you to close the door (and I want you to recognize my expression of this order as a reason for you to do so), how can such propositional content turn out to be false? Presumably, under normal conversational assumptions and given some conditions of sincerity, it cannot. But this is not a serious worry. There are similar phenomena (identified by Lemmon and others[8]), of sentences rendered true by their expression alone, such as "I'm talking to you right now" or, more interestingly, the expression of a promise. When a speaker says, under normal conditions, "I promise to φ," the speaker has made a statement that is true, and it is true in virtue of the fact that it has been uttered. It cannot turn out to be false, even if the speaker did not really intend to keep the promise. By saying "I promise to φ" (in a standard conversational context), the

---

[7] The main difference between an order and a request consists in the difference in the kind of reasons for action the expression is expected to generate. Orders purport to generate protected reasons for action (or obligations), whereas requests would normally be regarded as generating a regular reason for action. The details are not easy to work out, but they do not affect the present argument.

[8] See Lemmon, "On Sentences Verifiable by their Use," and Bach and Harnish, "How Performatives Really Work?"

speaker expressed the fact that she undertook a commitment and it is the undertaking of a commitment in virtue of expressing it, hence true.[9]

I am not suggesting that there is no room for failure. An expression of an imperative may fail to convey a propositional content in the circumstances of its utterance. The order to close the door, for instance, presupposes that there is a door in the vicinity to be closed; if the presupposition is obviously false (say, I ask you to close the door while taking a walk in the meadows, with no door anywhere around), then it is quite possible that the utterance fails to convey a meaningful propositional content. I think that this is typically a pragmatic failure; we know what the sentence means, and what it would take for it to be true; the failure consists in lack of relevance. The speaker uttered something that is not relevant to the conversational situation. But perhaps there are other ways to explain what kind of failure is involved here. I will not insist on this.

To sum up so far, the suggestion is that in standard cases, an imperative statement expresses some propositional content about the speaker's intentions, wishes, or desires, which is typically rendered true by its expression alone. With some appropriate modifications, this is true of exhortatives in general. Exhortatives are the kinds of speech acts by which the speaker intends to motivate some action (or inaction, of course) on the part of the hearer by way of recognizing the expression as a motivating reason for action. It is a crucially important feature of exhortatives that the first person pronoun is always implicit in the expression of the exhortative; it always makes a difference who the speaker is, so to speak. When I make a request, for example, it is an essential feature of the expression that it is my request, that it expresses my wishes, intentions, or such.[10] Though rarely made explicit, the first person pronoun is what the exhortative is about, as it were; it makes a quasi-descriptive statement about the speaker's state of mind. Evidence of this we can see by juxtaposing an exhortative with the negation of its conveyed propositional content. Thus consider the following pairs of statements:

(a) "Close the door" *and* "It is not true that I want you to close the door."
(b) "Please lend me $10" *and* "It is not true that I have a wish/desire to borrow $10 from you."
(c) "You may leave the room now" *and* "It is not true that I have an intention to have/let you leave the room now."

As these pairs of conjunctions show, the juxtaposition of an exhortative with the negation of its conveyed propositional content, referring to the speaker's state of mind, makes no sense. The conjunctions are incoherent or, at best, perplexing. The expression of an exhortative conveys a certain propositional content that cannot be contradicted without assuming that the exhortative has not been expressed sincerely. When you express an exhortative, *under normal circumstances and sincerely*, you have expressed some propositional content that is rendered true by its expression alone. Once again, I am not suggesting that exhortatives are semantically reducible to the propositional content they express. The suggestion is that such content follows from the kind of speech act that exhortatives are and their communicative function. The whole point of an exhortative is to get the hearer to recognize the speaker's state of mind and thereby motivate the hearer to act in certain ways. Exhortatives differ, of course, in the ways in which the speaker's

---

[9] I have explained this in greater detail in my *Social Conventions*, 120 ff.
[10] There are cases, of course, when one can express the exhortative of another; I may have been ordered to order you to φ. I don't think that such cases pose any particular problems. Typically, the second order is a description of the first; the utterance serves as a means of conveying somebody else's wishes, etc.

intentions or wishes, etc. are taken to be reasons for action and the kind of reasons they are.[11]

All this is true in standard cases, where exhortatives are expressed sincerely and the speaker means what she says. But this is not always the case. There are some non-standard cases where the content communicated by an exhortative speech act implicates (or aims to implicate) something different from what it says. Consider, for example, Susan telling her husband Bob, "Sure, you can go to the football game tonight, I don't mind." Let us assume, however, that Susan does mind, actually, and would much prefer Bob to stay at home with her. There are two ways to deal with such cases, depending on the nuances of the conversational context and similar pragmatic factors. One possibility here is that the condition of sincerity is not fulfilled. Susan's expression was not made sincerely. She expressed a permissive speech act but without the requisite sincerity. Another possibility, however, is that in the context of this conversation, given background knowledge of the parties concerned, the expression conveys a different (actually the opposite) content from what the sentence literally means. And this is not unique to exhortative speech acts. There are many instances in which people intend to assert something different from what they literally say, and often this intention is easily recognized by the hearer. A familiar example is the case when, say, Susan asks Bob, "Have you eaten breakfast?" Under normal circumstances, we would not have thought that Susan wants to know whether Bob has ever eaten breakfast, but whether he had breakfast that morning, or such. In short, as with other forms of linguistic expression, the assertive content may be affected by various pragmatic features of the conversational situation and in ways which make the content asserted by the utterance different from what it literally states.[12]

Admittedly, there are more complicated cases as well. Suppose, in our example above, that Susan's permission to let Bob go to the football game does assert what she literally says, and thus, it does convey an intention to let Bob go to the football game, but in fact, Susan also hopes (perhaps against all odds) that Bob will not go.[13] Can we say that Susan's permissive speech act expresses her wish or intention that Bob go to the game? That might seem incorrect, because we assume that she actually entertains the wish or the hope that he not go. This is a tricky case, but I think the plausible solution here is to maintain that Susan's communication intentions are in conflict with her hopes or desires. In other words, I think that Susan's exhortative speech act does express the propositional content that she intends to let Bob go to the game, though she hopes that the opposite will happen. And this is not totally irrational, or unique to exhortatives. A similar problem is familiar from cases in which an agent tries to do something that he knows that he cannot do, or tries to do something because he was told to do it and hopes to show that he cannot. For those who hold the view that trying to do something necessarily involves intending to do it, a similar type of conflict is present in such cases. The intention is in conflict with a hope or an expectation or such. Needless to say, this is not the place to deal with intentions to try and how to accommodate these counterexamples.[14] My point is that it is not necessarily irrational to express a wish or intention that is in conflict with

---

[11] In fact, they may differ in other respects as well. For example, some exhortative speech acts, such as a command or a prohibition, typically presuppose some particular standing of the speaker *vis a vis* the hearer, such as an authoritative position, while others may not require/presuppose any particular standing. See Bach & Harnish *Linguistic Communication and Speech Acts,* at 47–55.

[12] Elsewhere I tried to explain in some detail why this does not often happen in the law. See "The Pragmatics of Legal Language".

[13] Or, here is a similar example: I tell you, "Go ahead, punch me in the nose!" hoping, of course, that you will not do so.

[14] See, e.g., Yaffe, *Attempts,* ch. 2.

a hope or desire; and some exhortative speech acts may involve such conflicts. People can intend to convey one thing and hope that the opposite happens. The propositional content, however, is not determined by hopes or desires that accompany the expression. The fact that the speaker entertains hopes or expectations that differ from what she asserts does not, by itself, affect the truth-evaluable propositional content she conveys.

2. Truth-evaluable content of laws

Let us now return to the legal context. When I ask you to close the door, I express a complex wish: I express my wish that you close the door and my wish that you recognize my expression of this wish as a reason to do so. The suggestion so far has been that the propositional content of exhortative utterances consists in the appropriate description of this complex state of mind. Now suppose that the context is slightly different. There is a sign on the entrance door to our department's main office saying: "No entrance after 6 p.m." Let us regard this sign as a kind of legal or quasi-legal instruction. Well, what makes it a kind of legal instruction? Presumably, the fact that whoever put up that sign was authorized to do so. Suppose it is the department chair. In terms of the propositional content of the instruction, there is no difference between the chair's instruction conveyed by the sign on the door, and his instruction expressed orally, to each one of us one by one. Imagine that instead of putting up the sign, the department chair stood there and issued the same instruction to each of us orally. The propositional content would be exactly the same. It is, of course, just much more efficient to convey that content by putting up the sign.

Now, it is possible, of course, that personally, the department chair could not care less whether anyone is allowed to enter the office after 6 p.m. or not. The instruction reflects his official wish, not necessarily his personal one. There is nothing unusual about that; people often express a certain content in their official roles, which may not reflect anything they personally believe or wish. And this phenomenon is not unique to exhortatives or authoritative roles. For example, customer representatives you call up would often tell you that they thank you for your call and appreciate your business. They don't mean to speak for themselves, but for the company they represent. And of course, you would be terribly mistaken to assume otherwise. The same holds about legal and other official authorities. They don't necessarily speak for themselves, personally, that is. Official exhortatives reflect, as they should, the wishes and intentions of persons in their official roles, qua officials, and this is normally how we understand such locutions.[15]

Let us take this one step further. Suppose that for some reason the issue is somewhat controversial in the department. Thus the department chair holds a department meeting about this little controversy, and after some back and forth, a resolution is reached not to allow people to enter the office after 6 p.m. And thus the sign is put up. Would this make any difference with respect to the propositional content of the instruction? Whether the instruction expresses the view of a single "legislator," so to speak, or a collective decision of a multitude, should not make a difference to what the propositional content of it is. But what if different members of the department meant slightly different things when they voted for the resolution? Perhaps some of them thought that the instruction only applies to students, while others assumed that it applies to faculty members as well. These are two different contents, both (let us assume) consistent with an ordinary understanding of the instruction under the relevant circumstances. Which one is it? Can we tell?

---

[15] This is nicely explained by Dan-Cohen in "Interpreting Official Speech."

Here's what we can say: exhortatives, just like any ordinary proposition, would have some propositional content that is determined by the relevant expression in the context of its utterance, and some content left undetermined or unspecified. Suppose, for example, that somebody points to a particular door and says

(4) "That door cannot be opened."

Clearly, this is a descriptive sentence with some propositional content, which is true or false. But the utterance also leaves some content undetermined; does it mean that the door is locked, or is it jammed? The proposition is consistent with both of these options and, by itself, it does not pick out either. (Unless, of course, the context of the utterance clarifies which option it is; for example, the utterance might have formed part of a conversation about the poor maintenance of the building, suggesting in this case that the proposition asserts that door is jammed, not that it is locked.) And this is true of most utterances expressed in an ordinary conversation, whether the utterance is a straightforward proposition, an imperative, or some other kind of expression. Typically, some content is determined by the expression in the context of its utterance and some content may be left unspecified.[16]

But we have not yet answered the question. And the question is about the relevance of the intentions of the speakers. What we have in the case of the departmental decision is a form of a collective speech, whereby different participants have somewhat different communication intentions about the content of the collective expression. The question is whether these different states of mind affect the propositional content of the collective utterance or not. And here is where we might get in some trouble. In the case of an ordinary propositional statement, the propositional content expressed is typically determined by a combination of the meaning of the words (and syntax) uttered, and some pragmatic determinants in play, such as common knowledge of the relevant contextual background, presuppositions, the maxims governing the conversation, etc. The speaker's intention or state of mind, *by itself*, does not determine what he said. In our example of (4), the speaker may have intended to say that the door is locked. But it is not necessarily what he said. (Unless, of course, some particular contextual background makes it clear that it is what the speaker asserted.)[17]

It might seem, however, that the case with exhortatives is different. If the propositional content of an exhortative is, as I suggest, self-referential, describing the speaker's state of mind, then one might have to conclude that the relevant state of mind is what *determines* the propositional content asserted. And this would be a problematic result. For example, it would entail that in the example of the collective speech, where different participants have somewhat different intentions, wishes, etc., the propositional content would vary with the particular participants involved; that seems like a mess.

The conclusion does not follow, however. Just as people can fail to express the exact content of their communication intentions in the case of a regular propositional statement, so they can also fail to express the content they had wished to express in the case of exhortatives. The truth-evaluable propositional content consists in what *is said or asserted* by a speaker in a given context, not by what the speaker intended to say. I am not suggesting that communication intentions are irrelevant; far from it. Under normal

[16] For a much more detailed analysis see, e.g., Soames, *Philosophical Essays*, Vol. 1, ch. 10. Note that I focus here on assertive content, and for simplicity's sake, do not discuss the kind of content that is implicated, though not quite asserted. On the ways in which implications work in the legal context I have elaborated in my "Can The Law Imply More than It Says?"

[17] Following fairly standard nomenclature, I use the terms "what is said" and "what is asserted" as synonyms, referring to the truth-evaluable content of an expression in a given context.

circumstances, in an ordinary conversational context, it is precisely the communication intentions of the speaker that we try to grasp by figuring out what is said (and perhaps implicated, etc). But speakers can fail to convey all that they had intended to convey. The speaker's intention, by itself, does not constitute what has been said or asserted. The assertive content of an utterance is determined by what *a reasonable hearer*, knowing the relevant conversational background and context, would infer about the speaker's communication intentions from the words or sentences uttered in that context. A purely subjectivist view about assertive content, namely, that it is fully determined by the communication intentions of the speaker, would entail that one can never be quite sure what has been asserted by an utterance; after all, we can never be quite sure what the speaker may have intended to convey. This sounds implausible. Any plausible conception of what assertive content is must make room for the possibility that a speaker can fail to assert by her utterance all that she intended to convey.[18]

Now the question is whether this is different with exhortatives: if the propositional content of an exhortative consists in the appropriate description of the speaker's state of mind, does it mean that the speaker's overall intentions in expressing the exhortative statement are constitutive of the content asserted by it in the particular context of the utterance? The answer is negative. Some intentions are constitutive, of course, but not all. Suppose, for example, that a student walks into my office and I say to him, "Please close the door behind you." It would be surprising if the student concluded that my request was that he lock the door, even if, for some strange reason, it is precisely what I intended to ask. If I had that intention, I simply failed to convey it. The expression of an exhortative is not an invitation for the hearer to guess what the speaker intended. It is an expression of a wish, and just like any other expression, it can fail to convey the full content intended by the speaker.

So now you can see where I am heading: the same goes for collective speech. Not all the intentions participants to a collective speech might entertain with respect to its content are determinants of the content asserted by the collective expression, whether the expression is an exhortative or not. Collective speech, just like an individual's expression, can leave some relevant content unspecified. In this respect, exhortative speech acts are not different from straightforward utterances of propositions.[19]

Let me add an important clarification: the discussion above is confined to the question of what is the asserted, truth-evaluable content of exhortatives. It does not have any direct bearing on the question of how to interpret such expressions when some doubts arise about their contents or application to some problematic case. The latter crucially depends on the hearer's relevant interests or, more precisely, the reasons to pay attention to the utterance. It is quite possible that a hearer would be interested in, or have reasons to figure out, the speaker's intentions, hopes, or expectations, etc., even if they were not quite asserted—or even implicated—by the speaker in the context of the utterance. We often want to know more than what the speaker said or asserted (or implicated).

---

[18] See, e.g., Soames, *Philosophical Essays*, Vol. 1, chs 10 and 11.

[19] One might think that collective speech is different, because we might have cases in which the collective expression does not actually reflect anyone's intentions or preferences. Suppose, for example, that the participants in the faculty meeting had different views, some preferring that nobody be allowed in after 4 p.m., others only after 8 p.m., etc., and the final resolution is a compromise that does not reflect any particular person's wishes or preferences. But these kinds of example are very misleading. Once a proposition is put to a vote, and gains majority support then, at the very least, it gains the collective intention of the majority that it be adopted, which is to say, there is a collective communication intention expressed by the resolution voted on. The fact that each one of the voters would rather have voted on a different resolution is beside the point.

And even in the legal context, such knowledge might be quite relevant to the correct interpretation of the law. But these issues go beyond the focus of this essay. I do not propose a theory of legal interpretation here. My only concern is to provide an account of legal speech acts that would allow us to ascribe truth-values to the contents expressed by them. How to complete such content when it is unspecified by the relevant utterance is a separate and much broader issue, involving many considerations that will not be discussed here.

3. Imperatives without imperator?

Many legal philosophers and legal scholars reject the view that the content of the law is determined by the intentions of the law-makers. There are many variants of such views, and some of them are clearly not relevant to our present discussion. In particular, the age-old debate about the potential relevance of legislative intent in statutory and constitutional interpretation is not about the question of what constitutes the propositional content of legal norms. It is a debate about how to interpret the law, that is, complete it, when some relevant issue is left underdetermined or unspecified by the pertinent legal norm in question. As I said in the concluding remarks of the previous section, this is a debate that is not affected by the issues under consideration in this essay.

The relevant objection to the thesis suggested here concerns the question of what it is that constitutes the truth-evaluable content of legal regulations. Some legal philosophers claim that even when the content of a legal norm is clear enough, it is not clear because we know what the law-makers intended to convey. The content of the law, they claim, is not determined by the communication intentions of its law-makers. But again, it is important to distinguish between two very different, almost diametrically opposed, types of claims here. Some argue that law's overall content is not confined to norms that result from authoritative speech acts; norms or requirements can be legally valid, form part of the law, even if no authority has ever issued them (a view famously advocated by R.M. Dworkin). Others, however, concede that law is always a result of authoritative proclamations, but they deny that the content of those proclamations is determined by the communication intentions of the law-makers. Both of these views, if correct, would raise some problems for the thesis I suggested in sections 2 and 3. So let me take them up, although in reverse order.

Textualism is taken to be the view holding that the content of a law is determined by what the law means, and not by what the law-makers intended to say. I have already indicated that in one sense this is true, but in another, quite implausible. Let me clarify. Textualists sometimes give the impression that it is their view that one can understand what the law requires simply by knowing the literal or lexical meaning (and presumably the syntax) of the words and sentences in question. But of course, from a philosophical perspective, this makes very little sense. The content determined by the literal meaning of words and sentences in a natural language is rarely sufficient for grasping what was actually said on an occasion of speech. Such semantic content is, of course, an essential vehicle for conveying communicative content, but the content conveyed is often pragmatically completed, and/or enriched, by various contextual and other factors. Textualists, however, may be willing to take a further necessary step. Justice Scalia, for example, often talks about legal content as determined by what "words mean in the context."[20] In other

---

[20] Scalia, *A Matter of Interpretation*, 23–25.

words, textualists seem to admit that the same sentence or expression may mean different things, that is, assert different content, in different contextual settings.

But then one should wonder why context would make any difference, if not for the purpose of determining the communication intentions of the relevant legal authority. Normally we employ contextual knowledge and other pragmatic determinates in order to grasp what is the content that the speaker intended to convey under the specific circumstances of the utterance. The assumption that we can somehow account for the assertive content of a linguistic expression without paying any attention to the speaker's communication intentions makes very little sense. On the other hand, I think that textualists are right to assume (if they do) that intentions, by themselves, do not determine what the expression actually asserts. As I mentioned earlier, a purely subjectivist view about assertive content is equally implausible.

So here is where I think we stand: textualism cannot be plausibly interpreted to maintain that the assertive content of a legal text is detachable from the communication intentions of the authority who issued the regulation. Generally speaking, understanding what someone said is precisely the attempt to understand what he or she intended to communicate. Textualists would be quite right to maintain, however, that assertive content is partly determined by some objective features of the conversational situation. What is said by an utterance consists in the kind of content that a reasonable hearer, sharing the relevant background knowledge, etc., can infer from the utterance in the context of its expression. In other words, textualists are quite right to assume that a speaker can fail to convey all that she wanted to convey, and we must always make room for that.

The main import of textualism, however, is not about the question of what constitutes assertive content or what makes legal prescriptions true. Textualism's main point is about the ways in which legal content can be legitimately completed (by judges) when the relevant expression is incomplete or otherwise leaves some content unspecified. As I said earlier, this is a separate issue that I will not consider here.

Now, at the other end of this debate, we find the view that denies, on general jurisprudential grounds, that law is confined to norms and regulations issued by legal authorities. According to Dworkin, for example, a certain normative content may form part of the law even if it does not emerge from an authoritative proclamation. Needless to say, this is not the place to present the full complexities of Dworkin's views about the nature of law and subject them to scrutiny. I have argued elsewhere, on grounds which have nothing to do with the questions we discussed here, that it is implausible to maintain that norms can gain legal validity without being authoritatively enacted as such. Only authoritative decisions make law.[21] However, for the purposes of the present discussion, it may be worthwhile to examine some aspects of this debate regardless of the wider jurisprudential issues involved. In other words, the question is whether we can have an exhortative content that does not express anyone's views about what ought to be done; are there imperatives without an imperator?

It might be tempting to think that the answer must be affirmative; after all, we do not think of moral norms or moral requirements as the kind of prescriptions that express anyone's wishes about what ought to be done. Or, at least, many philosophers think that this is the case, and I have no argument with that. So here is one way to see the difficulty. Take a certain prescriptive content, say

(5) "A is required to φ in circumstances C",

---

[21] See, e.g., Dworkin *Law's Empire*, and my response in *Philosophy of Law*, ch. 4.

and assume that it is both a legal requirement and a moral one. In other words, assume that the exact same conduct is both morally required and prescribed by a legal authority in a given legal system. Let's call them (5M) and (5L), respectively. Shouldn't one expect that the truth-evaluable propositional content of these two prescriptions, the moral and the legal, are to be exactly the same? After all, the conduct required by (5M) and (5L) is, ex hypothesi, identical.

The answer has to be negative; the propositional content of moral prescriptions is, essentially, different from that of legal prescriptions, even if the two prescriptions in question prescribe exactly the same kind of conduct. The truth of a moral requirement, I take it, has nothing to do with the views, intentions, or wishes of the person who expresses the requirement.[22] In saying that A is required to (or should, etc.) φ, one is typically pointing to the fact that A has reasons to φ, to some facts that count in favor of φ-ing, or such. But this cannot be the case with respect to the truth-evaluable content of a legal requirement. As we noted earlier, the expression of exhortatives is crucially different, in that it always invokes, albeit implicitly, the first person pronoun; it matters who the speaker is. Whenever the law tells you to do something, it also tells you that you should do it because *the law* says so. And this is the sense in which legal prescriptions are paradigmatic examples of exhortative speech acts.

For another way to think about this, suppose, for example, that (5M) is true, and suppose that (5L) is the counterpart legal norm in a legal system S1, but not in a different legal system S2. Whatever else is the case, we should be able to explain in what sense (5L) is true if S1 governs and false if S2 governs, despite the fact that (5M) is true in both cases. In other words, whatever it is that would make (5M) true has nothing to do with the speaker who expresses it; whereas it is impossible to say whether (5L) is true or not, without knowing who ordered (5L), in what context, etc.

Needless to say, this is not the place to suggest an analysis of the truth conditions or moral prescriptions. My only point here is that it is impossible to account for the truth-evaluable content of legal norms without reference to the origin or character of the norm as a legal one, namely, without taking into account that the same prescriptive content might be true in one legal system and/or at a given time and place, but not another. Law is one of those domains in which the *saying so* (by the appropriate agent under the appropriate circumstances) *makes it so*. In the next section I explore another aspect of this phenomenon, with relation to a structural aspect of legal syllogisms.

4. The Lewis fallacy

Let me begin with an analogy from truth in fiction. Sherlock Holmes, we are told in the Arthur Conan Doyle mysteries, lived at 221B Baker Street in London. Let us assume, therefore, that there is some sense in which (6) is true:

(6) Sherlock Holmes lived at 221B Baker Street, London.

David Lewis tells us that the building at 221B Baker Street in London at the time was a bank.[23] Let us therefore assume that at the relevant times, (7) is true:

(7) The building at 221B Baker Street, London, is a bank.

---

[22] Of course, some philosophers deny this; I am not arguing against expressivisim here, just assuming that the objection comes from non-expressivists. Expressivism, or any similar view about the nature of morality, would have no quarrel with the views I defend here.

[23] Or, as Lewis, says, there may not have been a building there at all. See "Truth in Fiction", 262.

The inference from (6) and (7) would seem to be:

(8) Sherlock Holmes lived in a bank.

But of course (8) is clearly false. What has gone wrong here? Lewis tells us that we made the mistake of moving from a *prefixed* to an *un-prefixed* context. (6) is true only if it is prefixed by an operator such as "In the fiction *F*..."; whereas (7) is true only if taken as un-prefixed (in the real world, as it were). Thus, unless (7) is prefixed by the same operator "in fiction *F*...", you cannot conclude that (8) is true in the fiction; and because (6) is true only if it is prefixed, you cannot conclude that (8) is true in an un-prefixed sense. Surely, this is quite right (and I will refer to this problem as the *Lewis fallacy*).[24] But now consider a legal example:

(6*) It is a misdemeanor, punishable by a fine of up to $100, to use a wireless telephone while driving a motor vehicle without a hands-free device.
(7*) John was talking on his wireless telephone, without a hands-free device, while driving his car.

The inference from (6*) and (7*) is:

(8*) John committed a misdemeanor punishable by a fine up to $100.

Now of course, the legal expression used in (6*), "it is a misdemeanor to φ..." should be construed here as an exhortative, actually expressing the prescriptive content that one ought not to φ, or something along those lines. Even so, the inference seems to be perfectly valid. In fact, it is the kind of inference that is characteristic of countless legal syllogisms. But, on the face it, we have committed here the Lewis fallacy of moving from a prefixed to an un-prefixed context: (6*) must be prefixed by an operator such as "In the legal system *L*... (at time t, location x, etc.)...", whereas (7*) would seem to be un-prefixed, it is a straightforward description of an event that happened in the world. So how can we correctly infer (8*)? Notice that it doesn't help to construe (8*) itself as prefixed or contained under "In legal system *L* ...", which is probably the right way to interpret the conclusion. Sherlock Holmes did not live in a bank either prefixed "in Fiction *F*..." or un-prefixed. So if the inference about Holmes's lodging is unwarranted, so should be the inference about legal results such as (8*), whether the conclusion is understood as prefixed or not.[25]

Why should we think that (6*) must be taken to be prefixed? Although not expressed in these terms, the idea that sentences expressing the content of a legal norm refer to something that is true, if it is, only from a certain point of view, that is, from the perspective of a given legal system, has been widely accepted in jurisprudence, if not earlier, at

---

[24] See "Truth in Fiction" at 262. A number of publications criticized Lewis's suggestions in this paper, though not on this particular point. See, for example, Byrne, "Truth in Fiction: The Story Continued". Some philosophers are inclined to deny that fiction has any straightforward propositional content. An alternative view (e.g. Kendal Walton's, 1990) regards fictional texts as invitation for the hearer to pretend that they believe what is said, or something along those lines. I am not claiming or assuming that these views are wrong. To account for what counts as propositional content of fiction, we would need to tell a much more complicated story. None of this, however, affects my arguments here. I am only using truth in fiction as an example of a prefixed context.

[25] It is tempting to think that the problem here is easily avoidable if we formulate the legal inference in conditional terms. We can reformulate (6*) as saying that "If X does φ, X is punishable..."; then (7*) can be construed as a statement to the effect that the antecedent obtains, and (8*) would thus follow as a valid conclusion. The problem is that this move avoids the problem only if (6*) is construed as a predictive statement and (8*) as a factual-predictive conclusion; otherwise, we are back to the same problem of mixing a prefixed conditional with an un-prefixed antecedent. Either way, as we shall see, the antecedent has to be incorporated into the prefixed context.

least since Kelsen brought this to our attention.[26] In other words, a sentence like (6*) expresses a particular legal requirement or prescription which must be a requirement or prescription of a particular legal system in place. When people say that "X is the law", they necessarily mean to say that X is the law of some legal system or other at a given time and place. A given norm is a legal one if it forms part of a particular legal system and only as part of that system, at the time and place where it applies. Therefore any statement that expresses the content of a particular legal requirement conforms to a formula that must be prefaced by "*According to the law in S at time t . . .* ". It makes no sense to talk about particular legal requirements or legal contents unless they are taken to be prefixed. Now, of course, there are many other ways to formulate this simple idea, without using Lewis's terminology. We can speak in terms of "true *in* S at time t . . ." or "it is the law in S at time t", or any other formulation which would express the same idea, namely, that the truth about the content of legal norms is necessarily relative to some system or other. This is what I mean by suggesting that legal statements are necessarily prefixed.

Now, you might think that there are prefixes which create a Lewis-type fallacy, and others which don't. And that is quite right. Let me call them *closed* and *open* prefixes, respectively. Open prefixes are such that they can occur in valid arguments with un-prefixed statements to yield valid conclusions. For example, "According to the laws of nature . . .".[27] So what is it about closed prefixes that they create the Lewis fallacy? One suggestion might be to look at the semantics of the prefix. It is probably implicit in the semantics of scientific prefixes—"According to the laws of nature . . ."—that they range over un-prefixed statements to yield valid conclusions. Whereas it is part of the meaning of a prefix such as "according to fiction *F* . . . " that it ties the truth-value of the statement to be contained within a world demarcated by the prefix, that is, the world of fiction *F*. This is probably true, but it may not be enough. Still, you may wonder, what makes it the case that some prefixes are closed? My suggestion is that at least in some central cases prefixes are such that they designate a *constitutive relation* to the truth-values of the statements prefixed by them. A statement is true in a fiction, if it is, because the fiction states it. The saying so makes it true, so to speak. If a fictional text says that "the moon is green" then it is true, *in that fiction*, that the moon is green, and it is true *because the text says so*. Similarly, a prefix of a game, say, "according to [the rules of] chess it is the case that p", makes it the case that p, or that p is true, within the game. And of course, p is true in chess (if it is) because its truth is constituted by the rules of the game.

In short, closed prefixes are those (but probably not only those) in which a constitutive relation obtains between certain essential features of the world/context designated by the prefix, and the truths of the statements expressed about that world/context. So now I hope we can see why it would make sense to assume that the legal prefix is also closed. A certain legal content is true, if it is, in a given legal system S, (at time t, etc.), because the law in *S says so*. A legal prefix, in other words, is closed because it ties the truth-values of statements prefixed by it to the world designated by the prefix itself. In this respect, law is very much like fiction, or structured games; saying so, in the appropriate ways, makes it so in the relevant context.

---

[26] Kelsen, of course, expressed this idea in terms of the necessity of presupposing the Basic Norm. See, e.g., Kelsen, *The Pure Theory of Law*. Joseph Raz endorsed a similar view, expressed by his notion of "statements from a legal point of view"; see his *The Authority of Law* 153–157. And see my *Philosophy of Law* ch. 1 where I explain this in much greater detail.

[27] According to some meta-ethical views, the same holds for "according to morality . . .". But of course, this is highly controversial in meta-ethics. Modal operators, such as "it is necessarily the case that . . . " might be another example of open prefixes.

A natural solution to the Lewis fallacy in the legal case would be to maintain that the entire inference—(6*) to (8*)—is contained within the prefixed context, which is what makes the inference valid. The idea is that the minor premise, (7*), is also prefixed. In other words, (8*) follows as a valid conclusion only if (7*) is understood as prefixed by the operator "According to the law in $S\ldots$". If and only if the action committed by John amounts to "using a wireless telephone while driving" *from a legal point of view*, or *in the eyes of the law*, or such, then (8*) follows.

Before I try to explain this in greater detail, let us return to Sherlock Holmes for a moment. Consider the following inference:

(9) Sherlock Holmes lived in London.
(10) London is a city in the United Kingdom.
(11) Sherlock Holmes lived in the United Kingdom.

We have the same structure here as in (6) to (8), but a very different result. (9) is clearly prefixed by "In the fiction $F\ldots$", whereas (10) seems to be un-prefixed, it is just a fact in the real world that London is in the UK. The conclusion, however, is quite right. Any sensible reader of the Conan Doyle mysteries would have assumed, and rightly so, that Sherlock Holmes's escapades take place in the UK.[28] And, crucially, this would be the case even if the United Kingdom (or England, or Great Britain) is never explicitly mentioned in the text. So what is it that makes the inference of (9) to (11) valid, as opposed to that of (6) to (8), which is not?

The solution has to be this: although (10) seems to be an un-prefixed proposition, in the context of this inference it is not; (10) is incorporated in the fiction by implication. The assumption here is that fictions typically incorporate by implication an indefinite, though limited, number of facts (or factual assumptions) about the world, at least those that are relevant, and can be assumed to be salient and well known to potential readers. Every reasonable reader of the Sherlock Holmes mysteries can be expected to know that London is a city in the UK, and thus, even if the text does not mention this explicitly, it can be regarded as incorporating it by implication (assuming, of course, that there is nothing in the text to suggest otherwise). Thus we avoid the Lewis fallacy; the entire inference of (9) to (11) should be regarded as contained within the prefixed context. Similarly, even if the mysteries never refer to Sherlock Holmes's nose, we can assume that he had one (and only one), in virtue of the stated fictional fact that he is a man. These kinds of unmentioned facts can be said to be incorporated in the fiction by implication and thus, for inferential purposes, they can be regarded as prefixed statements.

Now let us return to the legal case. Can we similarly say that the inference from (6*) to (8*) is valid because (7*) is incorporated into the legal context by implication, and thus the inference as a whole is contained within the prefixed context? The problem with this solution is that it would require us to assume that all the facts in the world are incorporated into the law by implication and contained within its prefixed context. Since any fact or event in the world might be relevant to some legal inference or other, there cannot be a limit to the kind of facts that are contained within the prefixed context of the law. Notice that this is definitely not the case with fiction. There are countless inferences that would not be warranted about Sherlock Holmes, even if they rely on true facts (for

---

[28] To be sure, I am not suggesting that it is impossible to offer an interpretation of the Holmes stories according to which they take place in a parallel universe, or on planet Krypton, etc., where London is not in the UK. I am suggesting, however, that those of us who assume that the Holmes mysteries take place in England would not be making any obvious mistake. And that's all we need for now. If you have doubts about the example, others can be thought of, e.g. that Sherlock Holmes had a nose, or a brain, etc.

example, consider our first example about the bank on Baker Street.) In the case of fiction, we are willing to attribute some factual assumptions to be incorporated within the fictional world, as it were, only under certain conditions; such as certain assumptions of common knowledge, salience, relevance, lack of any contrary indication in the text, etc.[29] In the legal case, however, there seems to be no room for such constraints. This, again, would seem to suggest that we must assume that the law incorporates by implication all the actual facts in the world.

Now, there is a sense in which that is true, but to make it plausible, we must note a crucial constraint: facts have to be incorporated into the law by some stipulation or other. To be sure, I am not suggesting that every legal inference has to incorporate the facts it relies upon to be prefixed by an explicit statement to that effect; that usually happens when the legal classification of the relevant facts is controversial. Otherwise, the stipulation is mostly implicit or presupposed.[30] Notice, however, that even if the legal classification of the relevant facts is not contested or controversial, such classifications are always *contestable*. In principle, it is always possible to contest the incorporation of an alleged fact into the legal syllogism by claiming that in the eyes of the relevant law, E [the action or event in the world] does not *count as* X [the fact as required by the law]. Either way, the stipulation is constitutive. In other words, whenever we have a legal argument of the form—

(a) According to the law in S (at time t, etc.) {if X [fact] then Y [legal result]}.
(b) X
(c) According to the law in S, {Y}.

—the minor premise, (b.), is also prefixed. Typically, we just assume that to be the case, we often take it for granted in the relevant conversational context. But the presupposition is essential. In other words, the complete inference here has another premise, often hidden (viz, presupposed), that the act or event in the world (un-prefixed) *counts as* X, legally speaking. Thus the complete inference looks like this:

(a) According to the law in S (at time t, etc.) {if X [fact] then Y [legal result]}.
(b1) E [something that happened in the world],
(b2) According to the law in S, E counts as X,
 therefore, X.
(c) According to the law in S, {Y}.

An objection comes to mind here. Consider the case of John using his mobile phone while driving. One is very tempted to say that, given the legal requirement of (6*), John committed a misdemeanor whether it is authoritatively determined that he did, or not. After all, we want to say that he committed the offense even if he is never caught; he violated the law. Quite right. Nothing in what I suggest here, however, prevents us from

---

[29] These conditions can be controversial, of course. For example, in one of the Holmes stories, *The Adventure of the Speckled Band*, the culprit is a snake, a Russell's viper, that has climbed a rope to kill his victim. As it happens, the Russell's viper is not a constrictor and cannot climb ropes. Does it matter? Is this the kind of fact readers of Holmes mysteries are supposed to know? Also, note that the extent to which unstated facts are incorporated in a fiction by implication is partly genre-dependent. Some fictional genres, such as realistic novels or detective stories, etc., are such that they tend to be rather generous with implicit incorporation of unstated facts, while other genres, such as surreal fiction, probably less so.

[30] Lawyers often talk about this issue in terms of "finding of facts"; they recognize that legal inferences have to rely on a legal finding of facts, that is, facts legally established for the purposes of the relevant inference. However, this notion of an authoritative finding of fact is ambiguous between the finding that something actually happened in the world, and the finding that it conforms to the relevant legal categorization of it. My discussion in the text concerns the latter issue.

alleging that John committed an offense even if he is never caught. The only point to bear in mind is that when we make such a claim, we presuppose that the minor premise is incorporated into the legal context; that is, we presuppose that in the eyes of the law or, from a legal point of view, he used a mobile phone while driving (and thus has committed an offense).[31] In other words, the inference from (6*) and the relevant facts entails (8*) only if (7*) is legally stipulated, that is, incorporated within the prefixed context. Not unlike in fiction, saying so in the law makes it so. If we regard legal prescriptions as a type of exhortatives, this is not all that surprising.

References

Austin, John L., *How to Do Things With Words* (Cambridge, Mass.: Harvard University Press, 1962).
Bach, Kent and Harnish Robert, *Linguistic Communication and Speech Acts* (Cambridge, Mass.: MIT Press, 1982).
—— "How Performatives Really Work?" (1992) 15 Linguistics and Philosophy 93.
Byrne, Alex, "Truth in Fiction: The Story Continued" (1993) 71 Australian Journal of Philosophy 24.
Dan-Cohen, Meir, "Interpreting Official Speech" in Andrei Marmor (ed.), *Law & Interpretation: essays in legal philosophy* (Oxford: Hart Publishing, 1995), 433.
Dworkin, Ronald, *Law's Empire* (London: Fontana, 1986).
Jorgensen, Jorgen, "Imperatives and Logic" (1937) 7 Erkenntnis 288–296.
Kelsen, Hans, *General Theory of Norms*, M Hartney, trans. (Oxford: Oxford University Press, 1991).
—— *Pure Theory of Law*, 2nd edn, M Knight, trans. 1960, (Berkeley, Calif.: University of California Press, 1967).
Lemmon, E. J., "On Sentences Verifiable by their Use" (1962) 22 Analysis 86.
Llewellyn, Karl, *Jurisprudence: Realism in Theory and Practice* (New Brunswick: Transaction Publishers, 2008).
Lewis, David, "Truth in Fiction", *Philosophical Papers*, Vol. 1 (Oxford: Oxford University Press, 1983), 261.
Marmor, Andrei, *Philosophy of Law* (Princeton, N.J.: Princeton University Press, 2011).
—— "Can The Law Imply More than It Says?" in Andrei Marmor and Scott Soames (eds), *The Philosophical Foundations of Language in the Law*, (Oxford: Oxford University Press, 2011).
—— *Social Conventions: from language to law* (Princeton, N.J.: Princeton University Press, 2009).
—— "The Pragmatics of Legal Language" (2008) 21 Ratio Juris (2008) 423.
Raz, Joseph, *The Authority of Law* (Oxford: Clarendon Press, 1979).
Scalia, Antonin, *A Matter of Interpretation* (Princeton, N.J.: Princeton University Press, 1997).
Soames, Scott, *Philosophical Essays*, Vol. 1 (Princeton, N.J.: Princeton University Press, 2009).
Walton, Kendal, *Mimesis as Make-Believe* (Cambridge, Mass.: Harvard University Press, 1990).
Yaffe, Gideon, *Attempts: Philosophy of Action and Criminal Law* (Oxford: Oxford University Press, 2011).

---

[31] Suppose, e.g., that John talked on his mobile phone using the phone's built-in speaker, thus not holding it up to his ears; surely he can contest the stipulation of the minor premise here, arguing that what he did does not count as violating the law. And a court may need to decide on that.

5
Language, Truth, and Law

Andrew Halpin*

1. Introduction

The three elements of the title above may suggest an expansive ambition for the present contribution to a volume on Law and Language. As though the coupling of law and language was not enough to stimulate debate and engender controversy, the addition of truth to the triad portentously anticipates dissatisfaction with any discussion of the issues that does not grapple with fundamentals, and threatens a process of deeper contestation that makes it less likely to bring immediate illumination to the subject.

This would be a misreading of the title, or, at least, a failure of the title to convey the character of this essay. Although I shall attempt to deal with fundamentals regarding the interrelationships between language, truth, and law, this will be more with the aim of ascertaining what is basic rather than with the ambition of engaging in the profound. Indeed, the drive towards a basic understanding of these matters signals a limited ambition. I shall endeavour to take a path that progresses through observations on the subject that can be stated uncontroversially, and there will be no final position constructed here that might compete with an elaborate view of how our understandings of language, truth, and law should be combined to promote a comprehensive account of human life and social existence. The most that can be hoped for from the present investigation is that it should provide an indication of what is required from projects expressing greater ambitions, if they are to enhance our understanding of language and law.

Once we have allowed the three elements into the title, an obvious exercise suggests itself. We can consider the different ways in which the elements are prioritized in their interrelationship, within attempts to shed light on the way language operates in the law. Language is certainly used as a medium to convey truths about law, and to communicate what might be regarded in some sense as true legal propositions. One ordering of these elements would relate them so as to emphasize a technical understanding of language in deriving a true understanding of law, such as in providing a linguistic understanding of vagueness through which to understand the operation of vague terms in the law;[1] or in

---

* I am grateful to Michael Freeman, Fiona Smith, and the participants at the Current Legal Issues Colloquium on Law and Language held at UCL in July 2011 for much stimulating discussion. Some of the material in this essay was previously aired at a Language and Law Roundtable held at the Center for the Study of Mind in Nature, University of Oslo, June 2008, and at the Spring Legal Theory Workshops in the School of Law, Edinburgh University, May 2009. I am also grateful to the organizers and participants on these occasions for earlier opportunities to shape the ideas presented here.

[1] See Timothy Endicott, *Vagueness in Law* (Oxford: Oxford University Press, 2000); Ólafur Páll Jónsson, 'Vagueness, Interpretation, and the Law' (2009) 15 *Legal Theory* 193; Hrafn Asgeirsson, 'Vagueness and Power-Delegation in Law: A Reply to Sorensen', this volume; also essays by Endicott, Soames, and Waldron in Andrei Marmor and Scott Soames (eds), *Philosophical Foundations of Language in the Law* (Oxford: Oxford University Press, 2011).

embracing the insights of Gricean implicatures as a means of illuminating the meaning of legal texts.[2]

A different ordering of the elements would prioritize the significance of law. An understanding of the particular features of law and its practice would be taken to shape the acceptable meaning that can be conveyed by language in the legal context, and hence establish the basis for any true legal meaning. This alternative ordering can be located in a Wittgensteinian framework but is not limited to that particular view of the relationship between language and practice.[3]

These two configurations of the elements, with a priority on law or language, are capable of raising doubts about the role of truth in the relationship. Should we regard truth as a secondary ornamentation, a rhetorical flourish, on the primary relationship between language and law? We might then conclude that truth is an otiose member of the triad, or even a misleading distraction.[4] There are, nevertheless, serious attempts to establish the importance of truth in the relationship, prioritizing truth in its governing of acceptable understandings of law.[5]

Although all of the configurations of language, truth, and law mentioned, with their different priorities, will be considered in the discussion that follows, the strategy for working through them will be more oblique. Instead of systematically addressing the different permutations of the elements, I shall seek to examine different possible relationships between language, truth, and law as they emerge in a number of scenarios involving the putative operation of legal texts in practice. In addition to clarifying the relationships between the three elements in the particular scenario under consideration, I also consider the assumptions in adopting that scenario for our understanding of law and legal propositions. If the set of scenarios chosen is sufficiently representative of the different ways in which legal texts are regarded as operating, there should be a prospect of reaching one or more general conclusions about language, truth, and law.

2. Preliminaries: law, legal propositions, and the basic characteristic of legal language

Before commencing the substance of the discussion, it will be helpful to provide an explanation of my use of some of the principal terms recurring in this essay. First, I use *law* to refer broadly to the practice of law, encompassing officials, institutions, processes, and materials.

---

[2] See Andrei Marmor, 'Can the Law Imply More Than It Says? On Some Pragmatic Aspects of Strategic Speech' in Marmor and Soames (cited in n.1); Robyn Carston, 'Legal Texts and Canons of Construction: A View from Current Pragmatic Theory', this volume.

[3] Dennis Patterson, *Law and Truth* (New York: Oxford University Press, 1996) adopts a Wittgensteinian approach. For discussion of that, see my 'Or, Even, What the Law Can Teach the Philosophy of Language: A Response to Green's *Dworkin's Fallacy*' (2005) 91 *Virginia Law Review* 175. An alternative approach still emphasizing the command of legal practice over linguistic form can be found in systems theory with its focus on the application of the legal/illegal code—see Richard Nobles and David Schiff, 'Legal Pluralism: A Systems Theory Approach to Language, Translation, and Communication', this volume.

[4] See Anna Pintore, *Law without Truth* (Liverpool: Deborah Charles Publications, 2000).

[5] The obvious champion of the cause is Ronald Dworkin, in two key works in particular. His stand taken in 'Objectivity and Truth: You'd Better Believe It' (1996) 25 *Philosophy and Public Affairs* 87 is portrayed sympathetically by Stephen Guest, *Ronald Dworkin*, 2nd edn (Edinburgh: Edinburgh University Press, 1997), 124–32. Dworkin's more recent treatment of the subject in *Justice for Hedgehogs* (Cambridge, Mass.: Harvard University Press, 2011) receives friendly criticism from Benjamin Zipursky, 'Two Takes on Truth in Normative Discourse' (2010) 90 *Boston University Law Review* 525. A priority for truth is also found in John Finnis's approach to Natural Law: *Natural Law and Natural Rights*, 2nd edn (Oxford: Oxford University Press, 2011), 59–60; and 'Reason, Revelation, Universality and Particularity in Ethics' (2008) 53 *American Journal of Jurisprudence* 23.

A *legal proposition* is used narrowly to cover a statement of what conduct is required by the law of a particular person or group of persons. It will be necessary to expand a little upon this use of 'proposition' to cover what amount to legal norms, in order to deal with some technical issues relating to the designation of such legal propositions as true or false. However, first we will continue with the task of setting out the principal terms of the discussion.

I take it for granted that any useful understanding of law will also provide an understanding of legal propositions, and hence in the exploration of possible relationships between language and truth, on the one hand, and law, on the other hand, the law side has this dual aspect. That is not to say that I assume a particular form in which these two aspects are to be found. It could be the case that we understand law in general in such a way that no legal proposition can be identified other than the statement of what conduct is required of a party to a dispute at the point of a judge resolving the dispute. Such seemed to be the situation in ancient Rome, so as to provoke the plebeian revolt that culminated in establishing the written law of the Twelve Tables, erected in the Forum for all to see. Even with the availability of a wealth of legal materials purporting to provide prior legal regulation of conduct, a radical perspective on contemporary law may recast our understanding of law to insist that only at the point of judicial resolution of cases can we be sure of a determinate legal proposition.

Of course, if we do recognize legal propositions occurring not simply in the specific process of dispute resolution but in a prior form, providing guidance as to what is required so as to avoid disputes, a richer understanding of law and legal propositions is possible. This more sophisticated understanding of law and legal propositions will inevitably produce more interesting possibilities in law's relationships with language and truth. Nevertheless, I include the cruder more limited form of legal proposition so as to avoid controversies as to where exactly (or whether) the more sophisticated form is to be found, and, hopefully, so as to gain widespread acceptance of the *basic characteristic of legal language*, which embraces both forms and any mixture of them.[6]

Without embarking on any technical understanding of language, I claim it is possible to identify a particular characteristic of legal language, which is so trivial that it is really impossible not to accept it, and yet significant. Its significance lies in establishing a threshold which any understanding of *legal language* must cross, and at the same time in providing a potentially distinguishing mark for legal language, which can make understanding of other uses of language irrelevant to the understanding of the relationship between language and law.

So, the basic characteristic of legal language found in both the crude and sophisticated forms of legal propositions is that it expresses a requirement of conduct from a person. It tells people what to do. With some degree of authority. Identifying this basic characteristic of legal language immediately sets apart the language of legal texts (and the way we understand it) from the language of other types of texts, which do not display this characteristic. The language of law is not the language of a novel. Or a newspaper, or a letter, or a conversation.[7]

---

[6] The occurrence of a mixture of crude and sophisticated legal propositions is discussed more fully in section 3.

[7] This simple and obvious point is easily overlooked when efforts are made to bring insights from the use of language in other contexts to assist in understanding the use of language in law. Andrei Marmor (cited in n.2) does recognize the importance of distinguishing legal language from conversational language in his discussion of Gricean implicatures. However, the key characteristic on which he bases the distinction is that of 'strategic speech' which deliberately introduces some element of non-cooperation in the communication to leave room for the speaker to advance his own agenda that is not fully communicated. Significantly, Marmor locates this characteristic in speech during the process of legislation as occurring primarily between legislators, and the speech is only then transmitted onwards to courts and legal subjects. Marmor's characteristic of legal language is, accordingly, first contingent upon the existence of modern Western processes of legislation within a deliberative democracy, and secondly

Identifying the basic characteristic of legal language with the property of authoritatively telling people what to do has other implications. First, it implies that one person holds the position to require conduct of another, in telling that person what to do. If that is the case, then the person in that position has the upper hand over the person being told what to do. This means not simply that X gets to tell Y what to do, but also that X retains the power to establish what it is that is required of Y. Otherwise, for every required conduct communicated by X to Y, Y could respond by performing whatever conduct is desirable to Y and assert he is thereby complying with X's requirement.

This feature of legal language is well described as exhibiting the heteronomy of law, to use Neil MacCormick's expression.[8] The law can tell us to do things we do not wish to do and things we personally do not consider it appropriate to do. This comes together most fully at the point of judgment. For the crude form of legal propositions occurring as the formal outcome of dispute resolution, there is usually not much more to it than that. For the sophisticated form occurring prior to the resolution of disputes with the aim of providing guidance as to what is required so as to avoid disputes, the point of judgment still performs an essential default role in establishing exactly what it is that is required by the law in the guidance it has given, should that itself become a matter for dispute. This role is performed by 'the law' in the broad sense already provided, through judges sitting in courts ruling on points of law.

Before completing this preliminary section, we must engage in the technical digression mentioned earlier, on the use of proposition. Proposition can be used in a broad sense to convey anything that is stated, and I employ this broad sense when speaking of legal propositions in the current essay: what the law states in requiring conduct. However, within philosophy the use of proposition has been restricted to conveying the content of a statement which is capable of being found to be true or false. The exact nature of a proposition and its relationship to a specific utterance (or to two different utterances purporting to have the same content) are enduring problems in philosophy.[9] For present purposes we can simplify matters by regarding the technical philosophical use to be restricted to statements of fact. This excludes the use of proposition for the content of a normative statement, such as where the law states what ought to occur. An associated problem arises when we want to talk about the truth of normative statements (legal propositions), if only statements of fact can be regarded as true. One way out of this is to contrive a way of substituting statements of fact for normative statements.[10] An alternative solution is to seek a different idea of truth that can be used for dealing with normative statements, or values.[11]

One suggestion that might avoid the need to become too bogged down in these technicalities for present purposes is to acknowledge that the nature of a legal proposition as a statement does not in itself create problems about the truth of legal propositions unless we face

---

focused upon the horizontal need for (apparent) agreement between legislators rather than the vertical relationship of authority between legislator and subject. For these reasons, despite the illumination it brings, it cannot be regarded as a *basic* characteristic of legal language.

[8] Neil MacCormick, 'The Relative Heteronomy of Law' (1995) 3 *European Journal of Philosophy* 69; *Institutions of Law: An Essay in Legal Theory* (Oxford: Oxford University Press, 2007), 255–61; *Practical Reason in Law and Morality* (Oxford: Oxford University Press, 2008), 92, 198–9.

[9] Matthew McGrath, 'Propositions' in Edward Zalta (ed.), *The Stanford Encyclopedia of Philosophy* (Fall 2011 edition), available at: <http://plato.stanford.edu/archives/fall2011/entries/propositions/>.

[10] A further motivation for this is provided by the desire to explain how normative statements can be employed in drawing logical inferences that depends on assigning truth values to them. See Andrei Marmor, 'Truth in Law', this volume. For discussion of a different device used to extricate factual statements from normative ones, see Lars Lindahl, 'Stig Kanger's Theory of Rights' in Ghita Holmström-Hintikka, Sten Lindström, and Rysiek Sliwinski (eds), *Collected Papers of Stig Kanger with Essays on his Life and Work*, vol. II (Dordrecht: Kluwer, 2001), 151, 163–4.

[11] This is the approach taken, in very different ways, by Dworkin and by Finnis (cited in n.5).

the need to inquire into the 'truth' of the content of such a statement. This is quite distinct from any need there might be to inquire into the existence of such a statement, accompanying inquiries into the truth of a statement that the legal proposition exists. Here it is not relevant that the subject matter, or content, of the statement whose truth we are assessing itself includes a statement, any more than it would be relevant that it included Socrates or a white rabbit. My strategy will be to clearly indicate below when discussions of truth are concerned with the legal proposition only in this secondary manner, and to demonstrate that the truth of the content of a legal proposition never seriously arises for discussion.

3. Complications in communicating the required conduct

Legal propositions (crude and sophisticated) are constituted by a text whose role is to tell us what conduct is required. Particularly in the sophisticated form, but by no means limited to this form,[12] there may be complications in deriving an understanding of what is required from the legal text. The meaning of the language may not be clear. We need to examine how the introduction of uncertainty within the language of the law may affect the process of establishing what the law requires, and specifically what this might tell us about different possible relationships between language, truth, and law. Since the aim is to avoid controversy, the investigation will not commence by putting forward a contested understanding of the nature of law and legal propositions, but rather will leave open the possibility of different viewpoints being taken into consideration. The implications of each viewpoint will be followed through as it impacts upon the issues of interest to us.

The key to a successful investigation is then to identify at a very rudimentary level the different ways in which the language of the law is regarded as becoming unclear and the corresponding views on how that uncertainty is resolved. I will undertake this by proposing a number of models for the range of scenarios extending over the variables just mentioned. Before these models are introduced, it may be helpful to provide some further clarification on how these variables (the causes of uncertainty and the responses to uncertainty) are to be approached.

I want to suggest that different viewpoints on these matters in fact range across two dimensions. The first can be introduced as involving a matter of disagreement over how determinate legal materials are. The extreme positions may be taken theoretically that all legal materials are determinate or that all legal materials are indeterminate in settling what conduct is required by the law prior to the point of an authoritative judgment in a particular case. Let us signify the one extreme as adopting a determinacy thesis and the other as adopting an indeterminacy thesis. A corollary of adopting the indeterminacy thesis is that legal propositions (as we have explained them) are only encountered in the crude form: due to the indeterminacy of legal materials, no legal proposition can be identified until the point at which a judge resolving the dispute provides the statement of what conduct is required of the party to the dispute.

Outside of theoretical extremes, most experiential accounts of the law would suggest that in practice there is encountered a mixture of determinate and indeterminate legal materials, and accordingly a mixture of sophisticated and crude legal propositions. However, that is not to say that it will be possible to classify with confidence every instance into one case or the other. For example, it may well be that it is only when circumstances arise to provide motivation to challenge a stable understanding of the

---

[12] For example, where a crude-form legal proposition amounts to a judgment order requiring the payment of a sum of money by Y to X, there may still be need for X to return to the court to seek enforcement of the order, and the particular mode and timing of payment sought by X may be contested by Y.

law[13] that the possibility of indeterminacy is considered in a particular instance; and the plausibility of regarding that area of law as indeterminate may itself remain unclear until the legal argument has run its course. On other occasions, there may be from the outset conflicting opinions on whether an area of law could be regarded as determinate or indeterminate. The conflict may remain latent if it is in nobody's interest to bring litigation to test the matter, and determinacy may prevail through acquiescence. It would, accordingly, be more accurate to represent the mixture of determinate and indeterminate legal materials (sophisticated and crude legal propositions) as existing in a state of tension which may be resolved or await resolution in different ways, rather than as a jumble of clear-cut cases of determinate or indeterminate legal materials.

The tension between determinacy and indeterminacy in legal materials relates to, but should not be confused with, another conflict over how legal materials should be approached: as a source of legal doctrine or a venue for social critique. This provides our second dimension. We can label the parties to this conflict as the doctrinalists and the social critics. Even if one takes an extreme doctrinalist position in this latter conflict, considering that legal materials should only be understood from a strict doctrinal perspective, that does not rule out the possibility of embracing the indeterminacy thesis. The resulting viewpoint is that legal texts give rise to opposing doctrinal understandings of what conduct is required by the law.

Conversely, it is possible to move to the other extreme as a social critic, in regarding social critique as the only appropriate response to legal materials, and yet adopt the determinacy thesis. The resulting viewpoint is that legal texts, once approached through the appropriate understanding of what, broadly speaking, we may call the political objective that law is performing in society, will yield a determinate view of what conduct is required by the law.[14] Again, in experiential accounts of the use of legal materials, there may be observed a mixture of, or tension between, legal doctrine and social critique rather than a polarized concentration of one or the other.[15]

The task facing us is not to model the actual practice of the law so as to be able to identify on every occasion which combination of positions on the determinacy/indeterminacy dimension and the doctrine/social-critique dimension will yield a particular understanding of the legal proposition requiring conduct in the case in question. Nor does our interest lie in plotting the different characteristics of theoretical understandings of law against these two axes, so as to produce a definitive survey of variations in theories of law. The point of the exercise is to produce models that are capable of illustrating each of the constituent elements that might surface in any practical encounter with the language of the law, or might feature in any theoretical account of it.

---

[13] The prospect of significant financial gain is the obvious illustration of such circumstances.

[14] Both Ronald Dworkin and Duncan Kennedy view law as politics, albeit in very different ways (law as a result of a philosophically sophisticated political theory, or law as a product of political commitment), and hence both qualify as social critics in the sense used here. However, Dworkin embraces the determinacy thesis and Kennedy the indeterminacy thesis. Contrast Dworkin's *A Matter of Principle* (Cambridge, Mass.: Harvard University Press, 1985) and *Law's Empire* (London: Collins, 1986), with Kennedy's *A Critique of Adjudication* (Cambridge, Mass.: Harvard University Press, 1997). It might be objected that this categorization overlooks the breadth of Dworkin's theory in which the requirement of 'fit' demonstrates an additional doctrinalist strand to his thinking. The need to reconcile doctrinalism with social critique poses a deep quandary for Dworkin (for a succinct sketch of the difficulty, see Roger Shiner's review of *A Matter of Principle* (1986) 45 *Cambridge Law Journal* 511, 515), which will not be examined in detail here. However, the subsequent discussion will suggest that as soon as a mixture of doctrinalism and social critique (political understanding of law) is encountered, it is the latter that will prevail in resolving any uncertainty in the law.

[15] For broader discussion, see 'The Use of Legal Materials', ch. 1 of my *Definition in the Criminal Law* (Oxford: Hart Publishing, 2004).

The models proposed below seek to exhibit the elementary scenarios of acknowledging and dealing with uncertainty in legal language, focusing on the basic characteristic of legal language: expressing a requirement of conduct from a person. After this basic characteristic has been stated as a preamble, Model (A) and Model (B) distinguish between scenarios of legal texts with a clear meaning and scenarios of legal texts capable of more than one meaning. Additional models then differentiate between responses to multiple meanings based on a narrow doctrinal approach, Model (B1), or on a broader social/political approach, Model (B2). These models will form the basis for further discussion of the interrelationships between language, truth, and law.

The Operation of Legal Texts

In general,

LEGAL TEXT
↓
requires conduct

SIMPLE MODEL (A): One clear meaning conveyed by language

THE meaning of
↓
LEGAL TEXT
↓
tells us what conduct is required

COMPLEX MODEL (B): Number of possible meanings conveyed by language

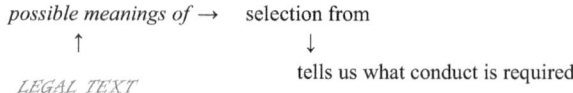

possible meanings of → selection from
↑ ↓
LEGAL TEXT tells us what conduct is required

COMPLEX MODEL (B1): Narrow doctrinal approach to multiple meanings

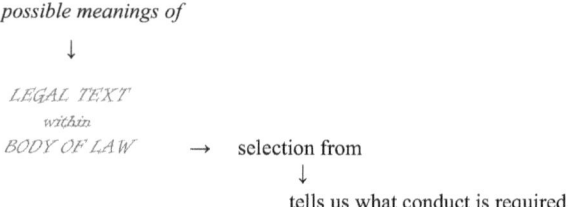

possible meanings of
↓
LEGAL TEXT
within
BODY OF LAW → selection from
↓
tells us what conduct is required

COMPLEX MODEL (B2): Broader social/political approach to multiple meanings

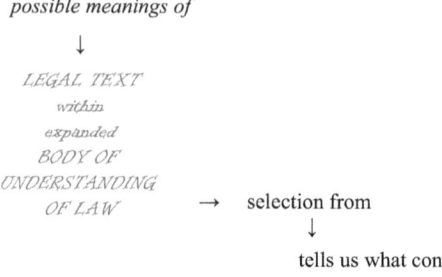

possible meanings of
↓
LEGAL TEXT
within
expanded
BODY OF
UNDERSTANDING
OF LAW → selection from
↓
tells us what conduct is required

4. Models (A) and (B): clear meaning or multiple meanings conveyed by legal language

The scenario in Model (A) provides very little of interest. If the language of the legal text is effective in conveying one clear meaning from which it is evident what conduct is required, technical studies of the nature of language may have their intrinsic appeal but are not needed here. A better understanding of language is unnecessary because the legal language in this case has already performed its role in stating what conduct is required.

Nevertheless, it could be argued that learning more deeply about how language operates in the clear cases might assist us to avoid unnecessary complications, perhaps brought about by the misuse of language, in the difficult cases. The hope is that some cases of Model (B) could be avoided and replaced by cases of Model (A) if only our use of language were informed by a more accurate technical grasp of its qualities. This argument will be addressed in the course of discussing Models (B), (B1), and (B2).

As for the role of truth in Model (A), at a primary level it is redundant. There is a legal proposition. The text of the legal proposition conveys a clear meaning of what is required. To talk of a true legal proposition, or of the true meaning of the text, adds nothing except possibly confusion.

At a secondary narrative level, it is possible to say that S (the statement X is putting forward in saying what the law is) is a true legal proposition, but here the truth relates to X's claim to be representing a legal proposition, not to the law itself. It connotes nothing more than the accuracy of what X put forward: S is an accurate statement of a legal proposition, or not.

If all legal propositions fell under Model (A), the implications for the nature of law would be immense. In particular, the communication of conduct required by the law and the processes attendant upon that requirement could be performed as isolated exercises in respect of discrete norms, with no reflection on general legal doctrine or background community values. The legal machine would become a finely tuned bureaucracy.

Model (B) portrays a scenario where a number of possible meanings arise out of the text itself. This might raise the suggestion aired earlier that the source of multiple meanings is the nature of language (or its misuse), and, accordingly, it might be thought that a better technical understanding of language could assist in the avoidance of unnecessary multiple meanings, or in the selection of an appropriate meaning from the variety on offer.

We need to examine the scenario in Model (B) more carefully so as to discern a number of factors that might be at play here in bringing about the multiple meanings. The first contender is linguistic incompetence: ambiguities and confusions have been produced by a failure to use language effectively and precisely. Such a failing is not the sole preserve of legal draftsmen and judges. It is a potential problem wherever language is employed as a means of communication through human agency. The solution to this source of the problem lies in greater competence in linguistic skills that are readily attainable, not in acquiring a more specialist technical understanding of language.

The second factor that might be at play here is an inherent quality of language. Even when used competently, language as a medium of communication is at times prone to ambiguity and imprecision. One obvious manifestation of this factor occurs when language is employed at a level of abstractness or generalization such that further refinement at more concrete levels is required before a determinate meaning can be provided. Given that law in its particular role of requiring conduct of persons often naturally addresses its requirements at a general or abstract level, this is a factor that is easily traced in the use of legal language. The remedy for this factor lies in a continuing process of refining the meaning of the language employed as more concrete situations are encountered—a familiar process in courts faced with resolving the application of general terms or abstract provisions to concrete disputes.

It might be suggested that a third factor generating a number of possible meanings out of the text could be identified with a failure to appreciate a specialist technical understanding of language (as opposed to common incompetence, or an intrinsic quality of language), and that acquiring such a specialist understanding would dispel the multitude of meanings so as to reach a determinate meaning. There are reasons for doubting that this could prove to be a fruitful line of inquiry.

Fundamentally, the deeper technical understanding is an understanding of the existing practice of language, shedding further light on how language operates so as to produce determinate meaning or to hinder it. Outside of the factors of common incompetence or intrinsic qualities that are present in existing practice, the deeper technical understanding is unlikely to identify an additional source of multiple meanings which it can then provide a novel means of resolving. In this respect, acquiring greater understanding within this discipline differs radically from advances in other disciplines dealing with a practical subject matter, which are free to reinvent the approach to be taken, alter the conventional practice, and produce benefits to those engaged in the practice.

Examination of the applications of a deeper technical understanding of language supports this view. A technical understanding of how a pragmatic rather than a semantic resolution of texts is possible through the working of Gricean implicatures informs us how meaning *is* transferred by non-semantic means in certain contexts among particular linguistic communities.[16] Appreciating the working of Gricean implicatures does not in itself produce meaning, or produce determinate meaning where too many possible meanings accompany the reception of the text. Nor can Gricean implicatures discovered as an effective means employed for the pragmatic resolution of texts in one (non-legal) context be summoned to resolve texts in another (legal) context.[17] In short, if the pragmatic implications of the text operate, they operate, whether we understand the difference between pragmatic and semantic, and whether we are familiar with the theory of Gricean implicatures—or not.

As another example, consider how a theory of vagueness in language, providing a deeper technical understanding, might shed light on how the existing practice of language fails to deliver determinate meaning. As illuminating as this might be on the subject of vagueness in language, it would not thus dispel vagueness from language, as can be seen in Timothy Endicott's sophisticated attempt to explain vagueness as an outworking of the sorites paradox.[18] Again, to put it briefly, one could rely on common competence to avoid vague terms, or admit to the intrinsic quality of certain vague terms and rely on a continuing process of refining the meaning of the vague term in particular instantiations, without benefiting at all from a deeper technical understanding of vagueness in language.[19]

Suppose, contrary to the argument being advanced here, that we were to allow the significance of a deeper technical understanding of language as a distinct third factor.

---

[16] See n.2 of this chapter, and accompanying text.
[17] See n.7 of this chapter, and accompanying text.
[18] Endicott, *Vagueness in Law* (cited in n.1). Significantly, Asgeirsson, this volume, and the three essays on vagueness in Marmor and Soames (cited in n.1) major on discussing the *value* of vagueness in the law.
[19] To be less brief, one would need to deal with an argument for a deeper technical understanding of vagueness which proposes that a proper theoretical understanding of vagueness would lead to the realization that the scope for vagueness is much less than commonly perceived (Scott Soames runs a version of this in his contribution to Marmor and Soames (cited in n.1)). If common language usage caught up

Its absence, alongside the presence of common incompetence and the intrinsic qualities of language, would, hypothetically, contribute to multiple meanings in legal language which would not have otherwise occurred with such technical understanding being present. Once the multiple meanings have occurred, however, the problem to be faced is not how a requirement of conduct would have been made with the benefit of such deeper technical understanding—or, similarly, with better linguistic competence, or guided by a clearer appreciation of the intrinsic qualities of language. The problem requiring resolution with the legal language under consideration is what conduct is required by the law in the face of the multiple meanings that have arisen.

The next stage of our investigation is to turn to different ways in which the law may be regarded as clarifying what conduct is required in the face of a number of possible meanings for the legal text.

5. Models (B1) and (B2): approaching multiple possible meanings

The problem of multiple meanings as depicted in Model (B) can be regarded as being caused by the use of language: the text throws up a number of possible meanings. However, we concluded the previous section with the observation that the solution to the problem is not primarily a matter of language but a matter of law. We need to understand how it is that the law goes about the process of selection from the multiple meanings available so as to specify the precise conduct that is required.

How we regard 'the law' as approaching and solving this problem will be coloured by our general understanding of law. Without endeavouring to take up a particular position in that debate, I use Models (B1) and (B2) to represent what I consider to be the two basic elements that underlie the different positions that are adopted in the debate, as affecting the issue concerning us. Both these models locate the text within a broader understanding of law. At one extreme, that understanding is narrowly doctrinal such that the text is viewed as part of a network of legal doctrines. At the other extreme, that understanding is more extensive in treating the text as contributing to a social or political vision of how law works to organize and regulate relations between citizens. Any particular understanding of the working of doctrine or of the political (which I use broadly to include moral) character of law can be fed into these models, and it remains open for a general understanding of law to combine together specific understandings of these two elements.[20]

---

with this theoretical insight due to its being universally acclaimed, then there simply would be no cases of vagueness in ordinary usage outside the parameters that had been (initially) theoretically set. On the other hand, if the theoretical insight were theoretically contested (or, at least, at variance with common usage), the same number of multiple meanings attributable to vagueness (as prior to the insight being delivered) would remain. Those in favour of some meanings and opposed to others (that the insight would exclude) might well invoke the insight in support of their case, but they could not rely on this to exclude the other contenders, nor to determinately establish their favoured meaning. To think otherwise is to pose a third variant of the complex model, (B3), where a theoretical/philosophical approach to multiple meanings is taken, *and* to posit a uniquely correct theoretically informed meaning—as opposed to multiple theoretically informed meanings (see the parallel discussion of Model (B1) in the main text in section 5). Even to contemplate the possibility of a Model (B3) in a footnote might seem unduly fanciful, but for the seriously framed suggestions that have been made that judges should take on the mantle of theorist (albeit political theorist rather than philosopher of language). For a response to a recent instance, see my review in [2011] *Public Law* 816 of David Robertson's *The Judge as Political Theorist: Contemporary Constitutional Review* (Princeton, N.J.: Princeton University Press, 2010).

[20] See n.14 of this chapter.

Locating the legal text within a narrow body of law or within an expanded body of understanding of law will not only afford a venue in which the selection of an appropriate meaning from those available can be made, but also exert a prior influence on which meanings are regarded as available. The possible meanings of a bare text differ from the possible meanings of that text regarded as part of a body of doctrine, or of that text regarded as part of a particular vision of law's political purpose. The range of possible meanings will then be filtered by the respective approach, as well as competing to form part of it.

At this point, with either Model (B1) or Model (B2), there seems to be an opportunity to reinstate a significant role for truth. If a doctrinal understanding of the existing body of law is capable of discriminating between the available meanings of the text so as to determine the selection of one meaning, can we not assess a suggested legal proposition by this criterion as being true or false? A similar suggestion could be made regarding a political understanding of how law works to regulate relations between citizens. In both cases it appears that an external metric has been provided by which to assess the truth of the possible legal propositions emerging out of the multiple meanings of the legal text.

On closer reflection, however, things are not quite so simple. Suppose in Model (B1) there is indeed a uniquely correct meaning for the text based on an understanding of existing legal doctrine. If so, the appearance of multiple meanings to the uneducated, or inadequately educated, turns out to be illusory. For those who have mastered legal doctrine, there is only one possible meaning, and so we are back dealing with a case under Model (A), albeit the case is now one of a technical doctrinal meaning of the text: Model $(A)_d$. Furthermore, we are also back with a redundant notion of truth, as explained in the previous section, in relation to what is now understood as a Model (A) legal proposition. There is a legal proposition whose text conveys a clear doctrinal meaning of what is required. That is it. Truth adds nothing here.

As for the other meanings that the ordinary language of the text was capable of conveying to those less skilled in the mastery of legal doctrine, could not one of these have been put forward as a purported legal proposition by an ordinary citizen, or an incompetent lawyer, and then upon expert pronouncement have been found to be false? Certainly, but the falsehood of the purported legal proposition occurs at the secondary narrative level. It is the ordinary citizen's statement (or the incompetent lawyer's statement) that S is a legal proposition that turns out to be false. As has already been explained, this amounts to an assessment of the accuracy of the speaker's statement. The ordinary citizen and the incompetent lawyer were inaccurate in describing S as a legal proposition. They got it wrong. Truth and falsehood have no more substantive impact to make here than in assessing the qualities of the answer given to a mathematical calculation. It is either correct or wrong.

There are two concerns that may be something of a distraction here, although in an appropriate context they raise serious issues. The first of these concerns is over the ability to tell the difference between an expert lawyer and an incompetent one. If there really is a uniquely correct doctrinal meaning for the text, then there must also be a way of telling who is capable of pronouncing the correct doctrinal meaning: who is the master of the doctrine. It may be easy enough to reach a consensus on the difference between the incompetent rogue fleecing his clients and a learned expert providing sound advice. The problem comes when two learned experts provide sound but conflicting advice. This is indeed a problem that any view of the law which proposes the possibility of a uniquely correct doctrinal meaning has to deal with.[21] A failing here will lead to a failure of that viewpoint,

---

[21] The same problem arises when the expertise is over practical reason and thought to reside in a mature person of sound experience, Aristotle's *ho spoudaios*, discussed by Finnis, *Natural Law and Natural Rights* (cited in n.5), 31–32. How exactly do we tell the difference when two *hoi spoudaioi*

and the recognition that we are actually dealing with a case of multiple doctrinal meanings for the legal text. However, our task is not to take up this argument, on either side, but to ensure that the models provided are capable of accommodating all viewpoints.

After all the argument is done, be convinced that a uniquely correct doctrinal meaning is possible, and move to Model $(A)_d$. Remain sceptical, and stick with Model (B1).

The second concern is that of taking an approach of an expert lawyer rather than of an ordinary citizen to the legal text. We may feel uncomfortable with the meaning of legal texts depending upon technical expertise rather than being accessible to the citizens whose conduct they are regulating. Such unease may launch campaigns for 'plain English' in the law, which may succeed to some extent in reducing the number of legal texts unintelligible to the ordinary citizen, but success here does not automatically eliminate occasions for Model (B1) being called into play. For having the law stated in plain English does not preclude the possibility that competing understandings of that plain English will arise. And as these are competing understandings of a legal text, a plausible move for resolving the conflict is to seek a doctrinal understanding of the text, as discussed earlier.

Even where there is not a single established doctrinal understanding readily available to resolve the conflict within ordinary usage, it is difficult to imagine a move towards doctrinal understanding not being made when the ordinary English of a legal text is capable of generating multiple meanings. This is, first, because any legal text that is challenged as to its meaning will be considered not in isolation but as part of a body of law and, given the mass and complexity of modern systems of law, a specialist doctrinal understanding of that becomes inevitable. Secondly, once it has been recognized that the ordinary use of language generates more than one meaning, it is no longer possible to rely on the ordinary use of language to resolve what conduct it is that is required by the law.[22] Since the law must nevertheless go on to resolve that matter, a more specialist, doctrinal, usage will emerge from that process. More than that, the competing ordinary meanings must now be regarded not merely as ordinary meanings, for on that basis each is equal and so none can compete. Each must be regarded as a prospective doctrinal meaning, since it is only on being selected as such that a winner can be proclaimed. This suggests that alongside the straightforward doctrinal meanings, where the specialist use of legal language obviously differentiates itself from ordinary usage, there is a less obvious set of doctrinal meanings which impose themselves upon multiple meanings in ordinary usage by a process of competition for a recognized legal meaning.

---

confront us? Significantly, Finnis does not explore that problem, but concentrates on the way that the qualities of a suitably mature person distinguish him from the immature so as to be receptive to the principles of practical reason. In the same way, Dworkin's common assertion that a learned judge would obviously regard his statement of the law as being true (how could he regard it as false?) is never juxtaposed with the 'obviously true' statement of the other learned judge who has just delivered a dissenting judgment—works cited in n.5 of this chapter.

[22] Hence no Model (B0) (an ordinary language approach to multiple meanings) is proposed. Nevertheless, it has to be acknowledged that judicial appeals to 'ordinary language' can be found in cases where the meaning of the legal text is contested; or, in a more refined version, appeals to the dictionary meaning. For discussion of the disastrous appeal to the dictionary meaning of recklessness in the English criminal law, see Halpin (cited in n.15), 78–81. The general flaw is to select one from a number of ordinary or dictionary meanings and to use its status as a member of the group to justify its selection when it is that status (a member of the *group*) that causes the problem necessitating selection. The flaw is concealed by overlooking, at the stage at which the selection is made, the plurality of ordinary or dictionary meanings. Thus the judicially preferred solution is passed off as the discovery of an objectively determined meaning.

It can, accordingly, be seen that success in the concern to avoid legal technicalities is dependent not simply upon the choice of ordinary, or plain, language, but is premised upon the availablity of ordinary language to convey one clear meaning of what conduct is required. Only then is a case of Model (A) ordinary language meaning possible. Failing that, multiple ordinary language meanings either will give way to an established Model (A)$_d$ uniquely correct doctrinal meaning, or will compete as multiple doctrinal meanings under Model (B1). Unease over the use of lawyers does not serve to eradicate the problem of language and multiple meanings.

The course we have charted from multiple ordinary language meanings in Model (B) to a doctrinal response in Model (B1) would be reduced considerably if the position we adopted at the outset was that the multiple meanings encountered at Model (B) could only be viewed as doctrinal meanings—given a particular understanding of the nature of law, or of the state of the law governing the subject in question. We would then move simply and straightforwardly to Model (B1). However, if we start with multiple doctrinal meanings we stay at Model (B1). There is no prospect of stepping back to a case of Model (A)$_d$ from this position as there was from the position of accepting multiple ordinary language meanings at Model (B). In the same way as one cannot escape a conflict of ordinary language by appealing to ordinary language, one cannot escape a conflict of doctrine by appealing to doctrine. This still leaves open to the avid doctrinalist another opportunity for postulating a case of Model (A)$_d$, in those circumstances where others would only notice an ordinary language case of Model (A).

The qualification to a technical doctrinal meaning as the one clear meaning of the text, in Model (A)$_d$, follows through into the associated picture of the nature of law for Model (A), provided in the previous section. In contrast to the picture provided there, the communication of conduct required by the law and the processes attendant upon that requirement can now only be performed as exercises relating to a network of legal doctrines. However, given the reliance on a unique doctrinal meaning, there will still be no reflection on background community values, and no critical reflection on general legal doctrine: engagement with doctrine will be expository in an uncontested manner. The legal machine here changes slightly, to a finely tuned *techno*-bureaucracy.

We now need to make room for the view that multiple meanings of legal texts are not resolved as a matter of narrow legal doctrine but through a political understanding of the law. The various stages of the previous discussion involving Model (B1) can be rerun by substituting Model (B2), taking a political understanding to supplant a narrow doctrinal understanding in overcoming (or replacing) ordinary language understanding.[23]

In considering Model (B2), we might similarly suppose that there is a uniquely correct meaning for the text based on a political (in the broad sense introduced above) understanding of how law works to regulate relations between citizens. We will arrive at a different modification of Model (A), (A)$_p$, with all the implications that brings, ending with the legal machine as a finely tuned *ideological*-bureaucracy: still no reflection

---

[23] I leave it open as to whether the theoretical viewpoint adopted sees the mastery of political understanding as residing in a particular class (a version of *ho spoudaios*, n.21 of this chapter, perhaps) or open to all. The point is that the use of a political understanding to approach legal texts is specialist in the sense that it differs from an ordinary understanding of language with which other texts would be approached.

on background community values but a dogmatic exposition of their received meaning. Again, the falsehood of purported legal propositions that fail to grasp the uniquely correct political meaning[24] of the text in Model $(A)_p$ occurs only at the secondary narrative level. Truth plays no substantive role. Also, where multiple political meanings are recognized at Model (B2) (either directly by Model (B) taking us in a straightforward manner to Model (B2), or as a means of resolving multiple ordinary language meanings found at Model (B) and leading ultimately to Model (B2) through the unavailability of a Model $(A)_p$ unique political meaning), there seems occasion for a further application of the principle applied earlier to multiple ordinary language and multiple doctrinal meanings: one cannot escape a conflict of political meanings by appealing to political meaning.

We have accordingly reached the position, at this stage of the investigation, where we have modified Model (A) with two qualifications, in Models $(A)_d$ and $(A)_p$, but whichever clear meaning is denoted (ordinary language, legal doctrinal, or political), *if* a uniquely correct meaning is established it has to be demonstrated and recognized as such. There is no room for some sort of internal criterion of truth to be involved in this task: truth is redundant. At a secondary narrative level, it is possible to describe statements about legal propositions as true or false, but this is a loose notion of truth that refers to nothing more than the accuracy of statements about law.

Moreover, if in employing Models (B1) and (B2) we seek to use Models $(A)_d$ and $(A)_p$ as external criteria of truthfulness in order to resolve the conflict between multiple ordinary language meanings, it transpires that the invocation of truth operates only at a secondary narrative level again, in relation to the 'false' statements made about legal propositions—and here true and false are poor substitutes for the more incisive descriptors, correct and wrong. Truth is inappropriate.

If, on the other hand, we fail to establish unique doctrinal or political meanings so as to reach Models $(A)_d$ or $(A)_p$, we are left with multiple meanings in Models (B1) or (B2) for which there seems no readily available resolution. If truth is redundant, or inappropriate, when considering the application of Models (A), $(A)_d$, and $(A)_p$, it appears at best evasive when considering the residual condition of multiple meanings in Models (B1) and (B2). If we are now in a position of being faced with multiple meanings within the classification we are dealing with (doctrinal or political), how can we call on truth to discriminate and choose between them—on what would the criterion supplied by truth be based? If the criterion is internal to the practice, then we cannot get from that beyond the multiple meanings; if we are seeking something external to the practice, there is no obvious place left to look.

While reaffirming that the purpose of the present essay is not to advance a particular theoretical understanding of law, it is hardly partisan to point out that the evidence available is overwhelmingly against an exclusive reliance on Models (A), $(A)_d$, or $(A)_p$ in proposing that there is always a uniquely correct linguistic, doctrinal, or political meaning for every legal text. Ordinary language, doctrinal, and political understandings remain

---

[24] The prospect of finding cases with a unique political meaning, $(A)_p$, seems more remote than the prospect of finding cases of $(A)_d$. In liberal democracies, there is not a professional guild to advance such claims for political understandings of law as there is for doctrinal understandings. Somewhat ironically, those promoting a political understanding of law do not have the confidence to entrust this role to professional political scientists but seek to recruit judges to perform the task—this is discussed in my review of Robertson (cited in n.19). And in totalitarian regimes, where it might be expected that some sort of ideology exerts a strong grip upon the law, even the most hardline ideology suffers from splinter groups and revisionists.

highly contested, even among the learned. Furthermore, the understandings of law that accompany these models, variations on unreflective bureaucratic exposition, lack a convincing fit to the experience of law in practice. So until this enormous evidential mountain is overcome, we have to take seriously the likelihood that the residual condition of multiple meanings in Models (B1) and (B2) does represent a significant part of the practical operation of legal texts. Yet whichever model (or whichever combination of the two) we favour, such multiple meanings are resolved in practice to provide a legal determination of the case through the process of judgment. Does this leave open no role for truth?

6. Concluding reflections

There is certainly room for something. If a mere reliance on language in Model (A) is insufficient; and if, as suggested in section 4, a deeper technical understanding of language cannot resolve multiple meanings; and if Model (B) breaks down into Models (B1) and (B2); and if Models (B1) and (B2) cannot be wholly reduced back to more intricate modifications of Model (A), $(A)_d$ and $(A)_p$, then something is needed on which to base the selection which is still required in dealing with the residual condition of multiple meanings in Models (B1) and (B2).

One step which would simplify things a little would be to argue that Model (B1) always eventually transforms into Model (B2). Accept that the legal text is read initially within a narrow doctrinal body of law, and that this may filter the possible meanings to be associated with the text, but if we are left with at least two possible meanings from this process, then we must look for something beyond existing doctrine with which to make the choice between them. And looking to a broader political understanding of how to regulate relations between citizens would be a way of providing what is needed.

There is an additional reason why we should expect Model (B2) to end up with work passed on from Model (B1). A purely doctrinal meaning of a legal text is always subject to processes of qualification and exception, and even to processes of exceptions to qualifications, and qualifications on exceptions, as Jeremy Bentham pointed out.[25] So, if we have a case where we are seeking to impose an established doctrinal meaning on the legal text in question (to move from Model (B) to Model (B1) to Model $(A)_d$), for this to be unchallengeable we have to be sure that there is no qualification or exception that might be advanced so as to distinguish an understanding of the problematic legal text with multiple meanings from the established doctrine. Yet given that the text was problematic, there is an extremely high chance of finding some basis for suggesting a qualification or exception. Whether a qualification or exception should be allowed to established doctrine cannot itself be a matter of legal doctrine. Again, we have a need to move out to a broader political understanding, an engagement in social critique, to consider whether the regulation of relations between citizens established in one set of circumstances should be distinguished from how to regulate those relations in circumstances that might be viewed slightly differently.

---

[25] Jeremy Bentham, *Of the Limits of the Penal Branch of Jurisprudence*, Philip Schofield (ed.) (Oxford: Clarendon Press, 2010), 123–34.

A move from Model (B1) to Model (B2) may also appear attractive because it seems to liberate the process of selection from the grip of imposed doctrine, which by its nature artificially restricts the options available, to a wider reflection on social relations. Precisely how liberal this move proves to be will of course depend upon the particular theoretical viewpoint or practical standpoint that governs the specific political understanding of law with which we are dealing. It will at the very least be a political understanding *of law* that is being considered, rather than an invitation to construct social values on a blank canvas; and, more to the point, our concern is with the political understanding of a particular legal text. However liberal or restrictive the process in Model (B2) turns out to be is not the problem. The problem is that we cannot always presume to rely on a uniquely correct meaning for the text based on a political understanding in Model (B2). We still have a gap for something on which to base the selection required in dealing with the residual condition of multiple meanings in Model (B2). So, what about truth now as a candidate for the gap?

Certainly, an invocation of some sort of higher truth may be made at this point, to adorn the process of practical reasoning that remains, but whatever the professed nature of that truth, it falls down for being aspirational. Its aspirational quality can be seen from the fact that we are still dealing with a case of multiple meanings premised on there being different opinions of the learned. So each of the learned can at best be aspiring with his or her own effort to reach the truth. If the truth of the way in which human relations should be conducted had been acquired, the multiple meanings would have faded away some time ago, with progression to Model $(A)_p$. However lofty or profound the aspiration, it falls down in a failure to convince. The failure is not a failure to convince that *this* is a plausible claim for truth about human social relations. Many such claims are plausible. The failure lies in the inability to demonstrate that *all competing claims* are false, are not plausible.[26]

The judgment that is made by the law to resolve the multiple meanings remaining might still be represented as a search for truth, but even so, the credentials of the judgment are not provided by truth but by the law in appointing the judge to make judgment. There is nothing in this setting to require that the judge appointed by the law should embark upon a grand quest for truth, nor to suggest that the judge should reinvent his or her role as a political theorist. The most that is required is that the judge should determine what meaning to select for the legal text, with a view to requiring the conduct that seems to the judge appropriate in settling the human/social/commercial relations that are at issue in the case.

So law gains precedence over truth. Still, the role of law in truncating the search for truth, or more prosaically the exploration of political understanding, leaves the law in an unstable tension with other possibilities that, given the incomplete doctrinal enterprise of law, may still flow back in on other occasions of legal propositions with multiple meanings.

As for law and language, the exploration of their relationship undertaken here does not vindicate the suggestion at the beginning of section 4 that considering the clear cases might shed light on the complex ones. Quite the reverse. For if the determination of the

---

[26] This takes us back to the failing of Finnis and Dworkin noted in n.21 of this chapter. It makes no difference to the present point that Finnis's idea of truth relies on the existence of external values to which the legal proposition corresponds while Dworkin posits an alternative idea of interpretive truth. If anything, Dworkin's move underlines the aspirational quality of his approach.

meaning of legal propositions, as has been suggested in looking at Models (B), (B1), and (B2), is a matter of the use of doctrine and social critique as seems appropriate to the judge allocated the task by the law, then general understandings of language must defer to these determinants, even to the point that what might otherwise have been considered a clear case for Model (A) under ordinary understandings of language,[27] falls to be regarded as a complex case due to the vagaries of doctrine or judicial outlook.[28] Legal language follows the practice of law.

---

[27] Steven Winter, 'Frame Semantics and the "Internal Point of View"', this volume, points out that the impossibility of relying on a stable simple case from which to anchor the discussion of more complex cases makes Herbert Hart's central case theory of meaning (whereby the simple cases dictate the core meaning of terms that may then be adapted for penumbral cases) unviable. For further discussion, see Winter's *A Clearing in the Forest* (Chicago, Ill.: University of Chicago Press, 2001), 197–206, 303–4, 316–17.

Hart applied his central or standard case methodology not merely to the meaning of the language of a legal rule but also to the process of identifying the appropriate subject matter for a concept of law: the clear standard case of the municipal law of a modern (Western) state, and what are taken to be its central set of elements. See H. L. A. Hart, *The Concept of Law*, 1st edn (Oxford: Clarendon Press, 1961), 3, 16–17, 210. Winter in his contribution to this volume rightly advises against adopting a simplistic one-dimensional representation of law which obscures the multiple orientations we may take towards it. The criticism found in two recent books that have sought to modify Hart's concept of law to deal with transnational or global legal phenomena goes further. Each of these books has rejected Hart's standard case analysis as arbitrary and reflecting the theorist's own evaluation of what should be regarded as important. See Keith Culver and Michael Giudice, *Legality's Borders: An Essay in General Jurisprudence* (Oxford: Oxford University Press, 2010), xxviii–xxix, 126; and, Detlef von Daniels, *The Concept of Law from a Transnational Perspective* (Farnham: Ashgate, 2010), 83–6, 131.

Whereas the meaning attributed to words in legal language (legal rules) relates to the task of establishing what conduct the law requires, the meaning given to law as the subject of theoretical investigation or conceptual analysis relates to theoretical purpose and value (Hart, *The Concept of Law*, 17, 204–5, 207). This introduces other complications, some of which I address in 'Conceptual Collisions' (2011) 2 *Jurisprudence* 507. I am grateful to Steven Winter for helpful discussion of issues considered here.

[28] A startling illustration of judicial transformation of the simple into the complex, in the context of interpreting contractual provisions, is provided by Paul S. Davies, 'Construing Commercial Contracts: No Need for Violence', this volume.

6

Claims of Legal Authorities and 'Expressions of Intention': The Limits of Philosophy of Language

Veronica Rodriguez-Blanco

1. Introduction

Legal authoritative directives and legal rules should be interpreted as expressions of intentions on the part of the authority; an intention aimed at ensuring that citizens perform specified actions. This is not controversial.[1] It is implicit in the notion of command. Thus, I command or order you to ϕ entails that it is my intention that you ϕ. This view is not far from the idea expressed by Aquinas in the analogy of a builder or architect who knows what the building will look like.[2] Let us say that an architect orders the plumber, the mason, and the electrician to perform different tasks, and his orders are expressions of his intention that they perform the actions as he dictates. These are his intentions, namely he has an idea of what the building will look like and why. Similarly, legal authorities know, so to speak, what the successive steps of a directive or rule might look like and why the directive or rule should be followed.

Let us illustrate this point with the following example. In English tort law, an employee can recover from psychiatric injury that he has suffered during the course of his employment if the psychiatric illness that he has suffered was reasonably foreseeable.[3] Through his decision the judge expresses his intention that employers should compensate employees for any psychiatric injury that they suffer during the course of employment if certain conditions are fulfilled. Like an architect building a house, the judges know what their decision entails and how employers should follow their decision. But the judges also know why the decision should be followed. It is found in the justification of the decision, namely that an employer owes a duty of care to an employee who suffers reasonably foreseeable psychiatric illness during the course of employment; the judge avows the view that it is a good sort of thing for the individual

---

[1] For example, Raz points out: "How can actions communicating intentions to create reasons or obligations (for ourselves or others) do so just because they communicate these intentions?": Raz, J., "The Problem of Authority"(2006) *Minnesota Law Review* 1003–1044, 1013 (reprinted in Raz, J., *Between Authority and Interpretation* (Oxford: Oxford University Press, 2009)); Raz, J., "Authorities tell us what to intend, with the aim of achieving whatever goals they pursue through commanding our will": Raz, "The Problem of Authority" 1012. See also Green, Leslie, *The Authority of the State* (Oxford: Oxford University Press, 1998), 60.
[2] St Thomas Aquinas, *Summa Theologiæ*, I–II Q 12, Art.1, ad (trans. Gilby, T.) (1969) XVII *Blackfriars*, London. See also Finnis, J., "Foundations of Practical Reason Revisited" (2005) *American Journal of Jurisprudence* 109–131 and Anscombe, G. E. M., *Intention* (Oxford: Blackwell, 1957).
[3] *Hatton v Sutherland* [2002] 2 All ER 1.

victim and for our society in general that employers assume responsibility for psychiatric injury caused by negligence. In the case of legal rules, the justification is not always as explicit as in the decisions of the courts. I have argued elsewhere,[4] however, that, in paradigmatic cases, if citizens follow legal rules or authoritative directives intentionally, the citizens need to follow such rules because they have reasons for actions as good-making characteristics.

Thus, the idea that the claims of legal authorities represent expressions of intention is, in many ways, uncontroversial. However, what remains unclear is what exactly we mean by "expressions of intention" and the potential repercussions of this understanding. How should we interpret "expressions of intention" when thinking about the claims of legal authorities? Can philosophy of language, e.g. speech act theory, illuminate the nature and character of legal authoritative claims as "expressions of intention?" This article argues that an explanation in terms of speech act theory[5] can only provide a limited explanation of the nature of authoritative claims and that we should look for a deeper understanding of the phenomenon. Speech act theory has the merit of emphasizing the relationship between rule-governed behavior and intentions. However, speech act theorists understand intentions as mental states, which provide a limited and not always sound explanation of the character and nature of authoritative claims as a complete explanation. The hypothesis of this article is that authorities' claims of legitimate authority and moral correctness are expressions of their intentions as to how a legal action will be performed. If the hypothesis is sound and authorities' claims are expressions of intention[6] about how an action will be performed, then the analysis of authorities' claims can be reduced neither to their true propositional content nor to a linguistic characterization such as "speech acts." Furthermore, I argue that authorities' claims as expressions of intention entail practical knowledge. They do not involve actual facts (*facta*) but, rather they encompass the idea that something will be brought about (*facienda*).[7] Authoritative claims express a direction of fit from mind to the world, but this direction of fit is more complex than the one described by speech act theories.

What is the distinction between practical and theoretical knowledge? The assertion that intentions cannot be known by observation tends to be exaggerated. The key issue is whether we can primarily rely on observation only and this is the point that Elisabeth Anscombe[8] was trying to advance. You know primarily the position of your own body not by observation, but it is somehow transparent to you (see section 4 for a discussion of the "transparency condition"). More controversially, in this article, I argue that when legal authorities claim legitimate authority and correctness, they express an intention to perform their actions and commands (intentions) in a specific

---

[4] Rodriguez-Blanco, V., "The Moral Puzzle of Legal Authority" in Pavlakos, G., and Bertea, S. (eds), *Normativity in Morality and Law* (Oxford: Hart Publishing, 2011) and Rodriguez-Blanco, V., "Social and Justified Normativity: Unlocking the Mystery of a Relationship" (2012) *Ratio Juris* 409–433.

[5] For a defence of speech act analysis as the basis for understanding the function of legal norms, see Marmor, A., "Truth in Law" in this volume. This article is an indirect criticism of Marmor's proposal.

[6] The analysis of "expressions of intentions" as involving performance and commitment to act does not mean that expressions of intentions are performative speech acts dependent on conventional means. The analysis follows rather Anscombe's use of "expressions of intentions."

[7] See Velleman, D., "The Guise of the Good" in Velleman, D., *The Possibility of Practical Reason* (Oxford: Oxford University Press, 2000), 109–118.

[8] Anscombe, *Intention* (cited in n.2).

way, i.e. through norms, rules, decisions. If the expressions are genuine, they will, most of the time, succeed in their intentions.[9] The steps of my argument are as follows:

(a) The directives, rules, and norms of legal authorities are partly expressions of intentions that citizens or specific groups should perform an action;

(b) the claims of legal authorities involve practical knowledge;

(c) legal authorities have intentions and most of the time, if the claims are genuine, they succeed in performing them;

(d) legal authorities also express their intentions about how their actions will be performed and this takes the form of claims about moral correctness and moral authority. It might also include expressions of intentions about following most, or all, of the eight desiderata of the Rule of Law.[10] Again, most of the time and if authorities are genuine about their claims, they succeed in performing their actions in the way conceived by their intentions. These claims involve practical knowledge.

Before I analyze these arguments, I will discuss in section 2 the thesis on the nature of "claims of correctness and legitimate authority" as discussed in recent literature; in section 3 I will try then to give the most plausible reconstruction of these claims in terms of speech acts, and I will subsequently show the limits of this reconstruction. Furthermore, I will demonstrate that the account provided by speech acts is parasitic on what I call a "unitary account" of (i) expressions of intention, (ii) intentional action, and (iii) intention in action. Finally, in sections 4 and 5 I will argue that the claims of legal authorities should be understood as expressions of intentions that involve practical knowledge.

2. The character of authorities' claims

Raz develops his theory of legal authority on the premise of a "conceptual claim." In his view, the notion of authority and the claims of legitimate authority by officials play an important role in the understanding of our concept of law and in shaping our attitude towards law. In *The Morality of Freedom*[11] Raz imagines a society where the authorities do not claim legitimate authority, namely authorities do not claim that the population has a duty to obey nor do the authorities claim that they have a right to rule:

We are to imagine courts imprisoning people without finding them guilty of any offence; damages are ordered, but no one has a duty to pay them. The legislature never claims to impose duties of care or of contribution to common services. It merely pronounces that people who behave in certain ways will be made to suffer. And it is not merely ordinary people who are not subjected to duties by the legislature: courts, policemen, civil servants and other public officials are not subjected by it to any duties in the exercise of their official functions either.

The claims of authorities are always present in the context of commands, rules, or norms. They are also present in judicial decisions, in statutes, and in the parliamentary discussions of legislation. But there is something puzzling and absurd about this imaginary scenario.

---

[9] Anscombe points out: "Surprising as it may seem, the failure to execute intentions is necessarily the rare exception. This seems surprising because the failure to achieve what one would finally like to achieve is common; and in particular the attainment of something falling under the desirability characterization in the first premise. It often happens for people to do things for pleasure and perhaps get none or little, or for health without success, or for virtue or freedom with complete failure; and these failures interest us." (*Intention* (cited in n. 2), §§47–48).

[10] Fuller, L. L., *The Morality of Law*, 2nd edn (New Haven: Yale University Press, 1969).

[11] Raz, J., *The Morality of Freedom* (Oxford: Clarendon Press, 1986), 27.

We find two puzzling features. First, the authorities do not need to communicate to their citizens what they ought to do and punishment follows from breach of the rules. Consequently, the population is arbitrarily punished. Secondly, authorities do not express the intention to perform their actions and decisions in a way that will or try to create a right to rule and a duty to obey. Expressions of intention about what to do and expressions of intentions that officials will perform their roles in a correct and legitimate way involve the idea that orders are guided by reasons. Expressions of intentions do not merely play a linguistic function, but show that the authority is exercising its faculty of practical reasoning.

Raz connects authorities' claims on moral legitimacy to two key concepts: capacity and action.[12] Concerning the connection between authorities' claims and capacities, Raz points out that trees cannot have authority over people[13] and if I say that trees do have authority over people, then you can infer that I do not understand our concept of authority. Raz adds "since the law claims to have authority it is capable of having it." Furthermore, the possibility of a mistake or insincere claim is not the paradigmatic case.

How should we interpret this connection between authorities' claims and capacities? For example, we know that birds have the capacity to fly because they have wings, human beings have the capacity to walk because they have feet. Can we infer that authorities have a capacity to exercise legitimate authority because they communicate and give orders to others and, furthermore, because they can claim to do so? Can legitimate authorities act legitimately because they express their intention to do so? The difference between officials and trees is that the former are agents who can act intentionally and express their intentions whereas the latter cannot communicate their intentional actions and what they intend to do. There is a strong conceptual connection between our communicative capacities when we use terms such as "I intend," "I will," and our capacity to act.

According to Raz, there are two kinds of reasons for the failure to exercise legitimate authority. First, the moral conditions of the authorities' directives are not present. Secondly, the non-moral conditions, such as the ability of the authority to communicate its orders, are not present. Raz argues that in order to identify authorities' claims, the population will only need to heed the non-moral conditions of the claim.[14] In other words, the population needs only to understand the linguistic utterance of the authority.[15] In this essay I intend to focus on showing that the claims of legal authorities are expressions of intentions as to how they will perform their legal actions.

As already noted, Raz also connects authorities' claims to the concept of action. Raz considers that the "court's very utterance of its opinion is claimed by it to be a reason for following it, whereas my utterance of my opinion is not claimed to be a reason for following it. At best it amounts to informing the persons concerned of the existence of reasons which are themselves quite independent of my utterance."[16] In other passages, Raz asserts that authorities' claims on legitimate authority are exclusionary reasons for action[17] and that we judge them by their claims. "We look to see whether their actions are such as to justify their own claims to general authority."[18] Other authors who discuss authorities' claims, such as Green, establish the connection between authorities' claims and actions: "authority

---

[12] See also Green, *The Authority of the State* (cited in n.1), 60 who establishes the connection between the agent who performs the action and authorities' claims as follows.
[13] Raz, J., *Ethics in the Public Domain* (Oxford: Oxford University Press, 1995), 217.
[14] Raz, *Ethics* (cited in n.13), 218.
[15] For a criticism of Raz's conditions see Dworkin, R., "Thirty Years On" (2002) *Harvard Law Review* 1655–1665.
[16] Raz, *Ethics* (cited in n.13), 205.
[17] Raz, J., *The Authority of Law* (Oxford: Clarendon Press, 1979), 30.
[18] Raz, *The Morality of Freedom* (cited in n. 11), 4–5.

is to be identified from the point of view of those who participate in it and for whom the relation has a special meaning. Someone claims authority when he makes requirements of another which he intends to be taken as binding, content-independent reasons for action."[19] Gardner also points out that "the official claims as she acts."[20]

Authorities' claims communicate the character of their acts, i.e. the legitimacy or the moral correctness of their acts, to the addressee and the effect is that the addressee takes the act as partly binding because of the authorities' claims.

3. Authorities' claims as speech acts: the limits of philosophy of language

Can we reduce authorities' claims to their true propositional content (actual facts)? Can they be assertions about the future that can be verified or falsified? I will raise three arguments in favour of the view that they should not be reduced to mere true propositions or actual facts. First, authorities' claims involve the idea that the performance will take place in the future and involve endurance and continuity of action. By contrast, if the analysis of authorities' claims is reduced to its true propositional content, the idea of an action and a capacity that will unfold and persist in the future is lost. When an official claims legitimate authority or a judge claims moral correctness in deciding a legal case, he or she claims legitimate authority or moral correctness in relation to his or her actions in the future and in relation to all the successive steps taken to achieve the application of a rule, the decision, or other legal outcome. The claims of legitimate authority and moral correctness concern facts about things that will be done in the future, i.e., the fact that the judge will decide according to moral correctness or the fact that the official will exercise authority in a legitimate way. However, this is not a prediction. Authorities' claims are about something that will be brought about (*facienda*) as opposed to actual facts (*facta*). This point is clearly shown when we look closely at authorities' claims from the first-person point of view. These claims are the salient ones in the context of practical authorities and entail consequences in terms of actions that authorities' claims from the third-person perspective do not possess. Let me illustrate this. You wish to get married in a boat on the high seas and the captain of the boat claims, "I have legitimate authority to marry you." This situation is different if a passenger in the boat claims, with no purpose of giving advice, but merely describing actual facts, "The captain of the boat has legitimate authority to marry you." In the latter case, the proposition can be true or false, but it does not say much about the legal action to be performed by the captain whereas in the former case, the captain's claim from the first-person perspective aims to convey his intention to perform a legal act and to have the legitimate power to perform it. These two sentences are not interchangeable and they remain asymmetrical.

Secondly, the contexts in which authorities make claims become unintelligible if claims are reduced to their propositional content. Officials claim legal authority or moral correctness in the context of giving rules and directives with the intention that the addressees perform actions according to the rules or directives. Officials aim at a goal; i.e., that the addressees perform the action. If claims are reduced to their true propositional content, then the directiveness towards the addressees' actions is lost. Authorities' claims have a practical stance, they cannot be reduced to a property that the authority possesses that can be verified as true or false, nor are they about a theoretical stance that the authority takes

---

[19] Green, *Authority of State* (cited in n.1), 60.
[20] Gardner, J., "How Law Claims, What Law Claims" in Klatt, M. (ed.), *Institutional Reason: The Jurisprudence of Robert Alexy* (Oxford: Oxford University Press, 2010), 29–44.

towards its own actions, i.e., decisions, enactments of statutes, application of rules, and so on. The authority does not state, "Look at me, observe that I have legitimate authority" or "Observe and verify that I decide according to moral correctness." Authorities' claims entail practical[21] knowledge (for a full explanation of practical knowledge see section 4).

In our ordinary life we use similar expressions to convey our intentions about how we perform actions. Let us think about the following examples: to friends who are having a barbecue, I say, "I will cook the lamb to perfection" and to the mother and child to whom I will give a lift, I say, "I intend to drive well." I should emphasize that I am not referring to the linguistic phenomenon, but rather to the deliberative or practical character of intentional statements, to the special "direction of fit" of expressions of intentions.

Thirdly, a textual analysis of some passages in Raz's work shows that when he discusses authorities' claims he does not have in mind the consideration of their propositional content. Raz tells us that the population acknowledges authorities' claims, but that they can be mistaken about this acknowledgement. But if authorities' claims can be reduced to their propositional content, why does Raz refer to acknowledgement rather than to the possibility of establishing whether they are true or false? Raz tells us: "since the law claims authority should its claims be acknowledged? Is it justified?"[22] It is clear that for Raz orders and commands are expressions of intentions, but he also thinks that only those who claim authority can command.[23] If authorities' claims were reducible to their true propositional content, then this latter feature would be unintelligible. Suppose that as an authority I claim: "I am the captain of this boat and therefore have legitimate authority over you at sea." If the proposition is true, I can command you but if the proposition is false I cannot command you. If the propositional interpretation is sound, then Raz's statement should say, "Only those who claim authority and whose claim is true can command." Raz, however, does not make the point in this way. On the contrary, Raz tells us that authorities' claims are evident from the language they adopt.[24] Finally, Raz points out that authorities' claims can be sincere or insincere.[25] If they were reducible to propositions, he should say "authorities' claims can be true or false."

Alexy also argues that authorities make claims and, more specifically, claims of moral correctness.[26] He begins with the example of a senseless order of individuals where the

---

[21] For an analysis of the practical character of authorities' claims along Kantian lines see Bertea, S., *Normative Claim of Law* (Oxford: Hart Publishing, 2009). For an examination of the importance of social and historical practices of law's normative claims, see Delacroix, S., *The Genealogy of Legal Normativity* (Oxford: Hart, 2006). For a discussion on pathological cases of theoretical stances of ourselves see Moran, R., *Authority and Estrangement* (Princeton, N.J.: Princeton University Press, 2001), 170–182.
[22] Raz, *The Authority of Law* (cited in n.17), 33.
[23] Raz, *The Morality of Freedom* (cited in n.11), 37
[24] Raz, *Ethics* (cited in n.13), 217.
[25] Raz, *Ethics* (cited in n.13), 217.
[26] For a comparative analysis of Alexy's and Raz's views on authoritative claims, see Gardner, "How Law Claims" (cited in n.20). Gardner argues that judges do not claim moral correctness and he illustrates his point with the example of an extract from Lord Goff's speech in *Elliott v C* [1983] 2 All ER 1005 at 1010 and 1012. Here Lord Goff tells us about his struggle to find an interpretation that will enable him to reach a decision that will depart from the principles established in precedent cases, which he does not find satisfactory. However, to his dissatisfaction, he is obliged to follow the precedent as any other interpretation will be an illegitimate departure from the principles established in previous cases. Gardner is right in pointing out that Lord Goff is not saying that the law is morally correct, but on the other hand, Lord Goff is expressing his intention to decide according to moral correctness. It will be illegitimate and not morally correct to depart from the precedent. Lord Goff recognizes that Lord Diplock's solution is not the best one; however, he does not think that Diplock's rule is morally incorrect. Lord Goff considers that under the circumstances of the case, he cannot change the precedent. It is morally correct, he argues, to follow the precedent, in spite of its not being the best law.

purposes of the ruler or rules are not discernible. It is a rapacious and predatory order. But the predatory order proves not to be expedient and the bandits strive for legitimacy. They transform the predatory order into a governor system. They have a rules-driven practice that serves a higher purpose, the development of the people, for instance. The system is still unjust, but the governors claim correctness. This claim to correctness changes the order into a legal system.[27] Two examples illustrate Alexy's point on correctness: (a) "X is a sovereign, federal and unjust republic" and (b) "The accused is sentenced to life imprisonment, which is an incorrect interpretation of prevailing law." In the latter case, Alexy tells us, "the judge gives rise to a performative contradiction."[28] Why is this a performative contradiction? It is practically contradictory to make the following statements from the first-person perspective: (1) "I will decide according to what is morally correct", (2) "I will not interpret correctly the law," and (3) "In my view, not to interpret the law correctly is morally incorrect". It is also practically contradictory to say: (1') "I will draft a Constitution for the State in a morally correct way" and (2') "X is a sovereign, federal, and unjust republic." An exemplary analogy might illustrate the point. It is paradoxical to say from the first-person perspective: "I intend to make coffee" and "I will stop myself from making coffee." The "direction of fit" in cases of practical knowledge is to bring something about (*facienda*) and the contradictory is to stop the action. The "direction of fit" in cases of theoretical knowledge is to establish whether the proposition is true or false. The contradictory statement to "it is raining" is "it is not raining." If authorities' claims of correctness are interpreted as expressions of intentions about how they will perform their actions, then the practically contradictory character of the previous statements ((1), (2), and (3); (1') and (2')) becomes apparent. This is the point that we will now show in sections 4 and 5, where I will argue that authorities' claims should be interpreted as expressions of intentions about how they will perform their actions.

I should emphasize that I am not claiming that Raz's and Alexy's arguments purport to show that authorities' claims are expressions of such intentions. My interpretive point is that Raz's and Alexy's arguments about authorities' claims should be reconstructed as expressions of such intentions. This interpretation enables us to have a better grasp of the core features and roles of authorities' claims in both our actions and understanding of the concept of law.

Having gone so far, the temptation is to understand "expressions of intention" as speech acts. Speech acts theories emphasize the possible separation between the force of a sentence from its propositional content. Thus, the following sentences have different forces, but the same propositional content:

(a) "Shut the door!"
(b) "Eleanor has shut the door."
(c) "When I persuaded her to shut the door, she went to shut the door."

Concerning the force, according to J. L. Austin,[29] the first sentence (a) has an "illocutionary" force, the second (b) has a "locutionary" force, and the third (c) has a "perlocutionary" force.[30] However, they all have the same propositional content. A sentence has an illocutionary force if the utterer is warning, undertaking, ordering, etc. and it needs a conventional background. A sentence has a locutionary force if the sentence is uttered

---

[27] Alexy, R., *The Argument from Injustice* (trans. Paulson, S., and Litschewski Paulson, B.) (Oxford: Oxford University Press, 2002), 33–35.
[28] Alexy, *The Argument from Injustice*, (cited in n.27), 39.
[29] Austin, J. L., *How to do Things with Words* (Oxford: Oxford University Press, 1962), 1, 3, 47, and 55.
[30] Austin, *How to do Things with Words* (cited in n.29), 99–108.

with a sense and a reference.[31] If the speaker brings about an effect or consequence by saying something such as convincing, persuading, deterring, etc., then the sentence has a perlocutionary force.[32]

The attractiveness of speech acts theories in terms of a sound explanation of the phenomenology of legal authoritative claims can be grounded on three main reasons. First, they emphasize the performance of an act or force rather than the propositional content of a sentence. Austin tells us that performative acts, i.e. illocutionary and perlocutionary acts, have conditions of felicity rather than truth-conditions.[33] Austin establishes six rules that ensure that the speech act will not be "infelicitous." Four of these rules stress the importance of a conventional background and two of these rules highlight the role of intentions as mental states, feelings, and thoughts. The first four are the following: (1) there must exist an accepted conventional procedure having a certain conventional effect, the procedure to include the uttering of certain words by certain persons in certain circumstances;[34] (2) the particular person and circumstances in a given case must be appropriate for the invocation of the particular procedure invoked;[35] (3) the procedure must be executed by all participants correctly:[36] and (4) the procedure must be executed by all participants completely.[37] The latter are labelled Γ.1 and Γ.2 by Austin who describes them as follows:

Γ.1: where, as often, the procedure is designed for use by persons having certain thoughts, feelings or intentions, or for the inauguration of certain consequential conduct on the part of any participant, then a person participating in and so invoking the procedure must in fact have those thoughts, feelings and intentions and the participants must intend so to conduct themselves. Γ.2: and the participants must so conduct themselves subsequently.[38]

Secondly, Austin also brings to our attention the fact that there is an asymmetry between sentences spoken in the first person and those spoken in the third person. Disappointingly, however, his explanation of this asymmetry does not go to the heart of the problem—which is related to practical knowledge and the transparency condition (discussed in section 4). Austin explains the asymmetry by the obvious fact that if we accept the premise that "by saying something, we are doing something," then we also need to accept that actions can only be performed by persons and that the utterer must be the performer.[39] Thirdly, Austin and Searle connect saying and doing. For Austin performative acts, i.e. actions performed by saying words, are the key to unlocking the mystery of speech acts, and for Searle "speaking a language is engaging in a (high complex) rule-governed form of behaviour."[40] Fourthly, Austin emphasizes the difference in direction of fit between a sentence that describes a state of affairs and a sentence that has either illocutionary or perlocutionary force. The former establishes a connection from world to mind, by contrast the latter purports to establish a connection from mind to world. But the distinctive direction of the latter is not explained.

---

[31] Austin, *How to do Things with Words* (cited in n.29), 94–98 and 109.
[32] Austin, *How to do Things with Words* (cited in n.29), 105–109.
[33] Austin, *How to do Things with Words* (cited in n.29), 1–3 and ch. II.
[34] Austin, *How to do Things with Words* (cited in n.29), 26.
[35] Austin, *How to do Things with Words* (cited in n.29), 34.
[36] Austin, *How to do Things with Words* (cited in n.29), 36.
[37] Austin, *How to do Things with Words* (cited in n.29), 36.
[38] Austin, *How to do Things with Words* (cited in n.29), 39.
[39] Austin, *How to do Things with Words* (cited in n.29), 60.
[40] Searle, J., *Speech Acts: An Essay in the Philosophy of Language* (Cambridge: Cambridge University Press, 1969).

Despite the apparent attractiveness of speech act theories, we should resist the temptation to explain legal authoritative claims in term of such theories. The core objection proposed in this essay to speech act theories is that the idea that "by saying something we are doing something" does not explain how the process of saying causes the doing. The theory lacks any explanatory power and it is rather a re-description of the phenomenology. In other words, it merely establishes a correlation between the speaker's utterances and the speaker's performative acts. The role of the agent, who utters sentences with the intention of "doing something," is neither explained nor unpacked. We can charitably put the objection thus: the notion of "speech acts" is only a partial explanation of a much more complex phenomenon that involves practical reasoning and practical knowledge. A critic might argue that both Austin and Searle recognize the importance of the speakers' intentions and it is implicit that they play the key explanatory role in terms of agency. Furthermore, the critic might continue, Searle develops in his book *Intentionality*[41] an entire theory of how intentions should be understood. He asserts that what underlies speech act theory is a theory of intentionality and in his earlier work he recognizes that a theory of language is part of a theory of action.[42]

My response to these comments is as follows. It is true that Austin recognizes the importance of intentional acts, but he does not engage with an explanation of how the agent's intention is connected to his or her "expressions of intention" and performative acts. It is also true that Searle develops a theory of intention that might complement his speech act theory. However, according to Searle, intentions are mental states that are mirrored in the agent's speech acts.[43] I have argued elsewhere against this psychological account of intentional actions and have shown that it faces insurmountable difficulties.[44] In this essay, however, I will concentrate on a more positive task. In section 4, I will adumbrate an account of intentional action that presents "expressions of intention," intentional action, and intention to act in a "unitary" or "organic" way, and will show that claims of legal authorities should be understood as "expressions of intention" in "unitary" terms.

My interpretive point is that speech act theories have confused the part for the whole. The "expression of intention" is only part of the whole phenomenon of intentional action connected to practical reasoning and practical knowledge. We need, therefore, an explanation of how saying has the effect of producing what we are saying.

Richard Moran and Martin Stone provide us with an interesting account of the intellectual development of this confusion from the 1950s until our days. In 1957 Anscombe published *Intention* and began the book by stating that the subject of the book should be studied under three headings: expression of an intention, intentional action, and intention in acting, and that all these should be understood as interdependent. Thus, an expression of an intention cannot be understood as a prediction about my future acts nor as an introspective explanation of an intention such as desires, wants, etc. Anscombe tells us, however, that people formulate expressions of intention that are about the future and that they turn out to be correct.[45] How is

---

[41] Searle, J. *Intentionality: An Essay in the Philosophy of Mind* (Cambridge: Cambridge University Press, 1983).
[42] Searle, *Speech Acts*, (cited in n.40), 17.
[43] Searle puts this as follows: "Whenever there is a psychological state specified in the sincerity condition, the performance of the act counts as an expression of that psychological state" (*Speech Acts* (cited in n.40), 65).
[44] Rodriguez-Blanco, "The Moral Puzzle of Legal Authority" (cited in n.4).
[45] Anscombe, *Intention* (cited in n.2), §§3–4.

this possible? In order to answer this question, she tries to understand how we can identify intentional actions and demarcate them from non-intentional actions. The logical step is to understand what it means to say that "I have acted with an intention." Anscombe identifies acting intentionally with acting for a reason or "reasons for actions" and such acting involves the view that the question "why" applies.[46] In other words, when we act for reasons, we act intentionally and therefore we are sensitive and responsive to a justificatory framework. If we perform an action ϕ and the answers are genuine, for example, either of the following: "I did not know I was doing ϕ," or "I was not aware I was doing ϕ," then we have neither an intentional action, nor an action performed and guided by reasons; we might have a voluntary action, but not an intentional one.[47] But if the response has, for example, either of the forms: "in order to ϕ," or "because ϕ," then we might have a prima facie case for an intentional action or an action done for reasons. In other words, reasons, so to speak, show themselves in intentional action and indicate, by "showing themselves," how they are able to operate and be part of the agent's practical reasoning. Moran and Stone in "Anscombe on Expression of Intention" explain the transformation of these three headings in the post-*Intention* literature. They say that most authors ignore the heading "expression of an intention" and conflate the other two subheadings: intentional action and the intention with which the action was committed. Consequently, intention becomes a mental state:

Given the possibility of "pure" intending, it becomes hard to see how this category could fail to designate a mental state, attitude or disposition of some kind. So the divisions of "intentions"' now take shape around the philosophical polestar of the division between mind and world: two notions of intentions find purchase only where there is behaviour causing things to happen; a third refers to a mental state, attitude or disposition which, though in some way is present in such behaviour, is also abstractable from it and capable of existing on its own.[48]

We can expand on Moran and Stone's point and assert that the consequence of a strict understanding of (a) "expressions of intention," (b) intentional actions, and (c) the intention with which we perform an action has been to bring about a division of philosophical labor. Thus, philosophy of language began to engage with a study of the force of linguistic utterances and philosophy of mind began to engage with a reflection on intentional actions, whilst moral psychologists and ethicists carried out an elucidation of the notion of "intention with which an action is performed." I will now demonstrate that if we wish to make sense of these three notions and obtain a complete explanation of their interaction then they should be understood in a "unitary" form.

4. Expressions of intentions as involving practical knowledge

In section 2 I argued in favour of the view that (a) the directives, rules, and norms of legal authorities are partly expressions of intentions that citizens or specific groups should perform an action and (b) the claims of legal authorities involve practical knowledge. In this section and section 5, I will concentrate on the following two

---

[46] Anscombe, *Intention* (cited in n.2), §§4–6. This will be called the why-question methodology.
[47] Anscombe, *Intention* (cited in n.2), §17.
[48] Moran, R., and Stone, M., "Anscombe on 'Expressions of Intentions'" in Sandis, C. (ed.), *New Essays on the Explanation of Action* (Basingstoke: Palgrave MacMillan, 2010), 132–168, at 137.

premises: (c) legal authorities have intentions and, if the claims are genuine, they will succeed most of the time in performing them; (d) legal authorities also express their intentions about how their actions will be performed and these take the form of claims of moral correctness and moral authority. They might also include expressions of intentions about following most or all of the eight desiderata of the Rule of Law. Again, most of the time and if authorities are genuine about their claims, they succeed in performing their actions in the way expressed by their intentions. These claims involve practical knowledge.

What is practical knowledge? Let us take a modified version of the example provided by Anscombe in *Intention*.[49] A man is asked by his wife to go to the supermarket with a list of products to buy. A detective is following him and makes notes of his actions. The man reads in the list "butter," but chooses margarine. The detective writes in his report that the man has bought margarine. The detective gives an account of the man's actions in terms of the evidence he himself has. By contrast, the man gives an account of his actions in terms of the reasons for actions that he *himself* has. However, the man knows his intentions or reasons for actions not on the basis of evidence that he has *of* himself. His reasons for actions or intentions are self-intimating or self-verifying. He acts from the deliberative or first-person perspective. There is an action according to reasons or an intention *in doing* something if there is an answer to the question *why*. It is in terms of his own description of his action that we can grasp the reasons for the man's actions. In reply to the question, "*Why* did you buy margarine instead of butter?," the man might answer that he did so because it is better for his health. This answer, following Aristotle's theory of action[50] and its contemporary interpretations advanced by Anscombe, provides a reason for action as a desirability or good-making characteristic. According to Anscombe, the answer is intelligible to us and inquiries as to *why* the action has been committed stops. However, in the case of the detective, when we ask *why* did you write in the report that the man bought margarine, the answer is that it is the truth about the man's actions. In the case of the detective, the knowledge is theoretical, the detective reports the man's actions in terms of the evidence he has of it. In the case of the man, the knowledge is practical. The reasons for action are self-verifying for the agent. He or she does not need to have evidence of his or her own reasons for actions. This self-intimating or self-verifying understanding of our own actions from the deliberative or practical viewpoint is part of the general condition of access

---

[49] Anscombe, *Intention* (cited in n.2), §32.
[50] Aristotle, *Nichomachean Ethics* I. i. 2; III. v. 18–21 (trans. Rackham, H.) (Cambridge, Mass.: Harvard University Press, 1934). See Aquinas, *Summa Theologiæ* (cited at n.2), I–II, Q. 6–17. See also Kenny, A., *Aristotle's Theory of the Will* (London: Duckworth, 1979); Passnau, R., *Thomas Aquinas on Human Nature* (Cambridge: Cambridge University Press, 2002); Finnis, J., *Aquinas* (Oxford: Oxford University Press, 1998), 62–71 and 79–90. For contemporary formulations of the Aristotelian theory of intentional action see Raz, J., "Agency, Reason and the Good" in Raz, J., *Engaging Reason: On the Theory of Value and Action* (Oxford: Oxford University Press, 2002); Quinn, W., "Putting Rationality in Its Place" in Quinn, W., *Morality and Action* (Cambridge: Cambridge University Press, 1993), 228–255; Korsgaard, C., "Acting for a Reason" in Korsgaard, C., *The Constitution of Agency: Essays on Practical Reason and Moral Psychology* (New York: Oxford University Press, 2008), 207–229; Moran, R., and Stone, M., "Anscombe on 'Expressions of Intentions'" (cited in n.48); Thompson, M., *Life and Action* (Cambridge, Mass.: Harvard University Press, 2008). For the connection between the teleological view and the "guise of the good" model see Hanser, M., "Intention and Teleology" (1998) 107 *Mind* 381–401; and Boyle, M., and Lavin, D., "Goodness and Desire" in Tenenbaum, S. (ed.), *Desire, Practical Reason, and the Good* (Oxford: Oxford University Press, 2010).

to our own mental states that is called the "transparency condition."⁵¹ Its application to reasons for action can be formulated as follows:

- *(TC for reasons for actions)* "I can report on my own reasons for actions, not by considering my own mental states or theoretical evidence about them, but by considering the reasons themselves which I am immediately aware of".⁵²

The direction of fit in theoretical and practical knowledge is different. In the former case, my assertions need to fit the world whereas in the latter, the world needs to fit my assertions. The detective needs to give an account of what the world looks like, including human actions in the world. He relies on the observational evidence he has. The detective's description of the action is tested against the tribunal of empirical evidence. If he reports that the man bought butter instead of margarine, then his description is false. The man, by contrast, might say that he intended to buy butter and instead bought margarine. He changed his mind and asserts that margarine is healthier. There is no mistake here.

The agent knows the reasons for his actions without observation. This means that the reasons for his actions are transparent to the agent. The phenomenon of transparency is clear from the example of the man who goes shopping for butter. An expression of an intention, according to Anscombe, is not mainly from the third-person perspective.⁵³ The knowledge that we have about our body's position is not known mainly by observation; it might be aided by observation, but I do not need to take a theoretical or observational stance to know that my legs are crossed whilst I sit typing on my laptop. Anscombe tells us that intentional action is a sub-class of non-observational knowledge.⁵⁴

Gareth Evans in *The Varieties of Reference* refers to the phenomenon of "transparency" that characterizes beliefs:

In making a self-description of belief, one's eyes are, so to speak, or occasionally literally, directed outward—upon the world. If someone asks me "Do you think there is going to be a Third World War?", I must attend, in answering him, to precisely the same outward phenomena as I would

---

⁵¹ See Evans, G., *The Varieties of Reference* (Oxford: Oxford University Press, 1982), 225; Edgeley, R., *Reason in Theory and Practice* (London: Hutchinson and Co., 1969). The most extensive and careful contemporary treatment of the "transparency condition" is in Moran, *Authority and Estrangement* (cited in n.21). For discussions on Moran's notion of transparency, reflection, and self-knowledge see Reginster, B., "Self-Knowledge, Responsibility and the Third Person" (2004) LXIX *Philosophy and Phenomenological Research* 433–439; Wilson, G., "Comments on Authority and Estrangement" (2004) LXIX *Philosophy and Phenomenological Research* 440–447; Heal, J., "Moran's Authority and Estrangement" (2004) LXIX *Philosophy and Phenomenological Research* 427–432; Lear, J., "Avowal and Unfreedom" (2004) LXIX *Philosophy and Phenomenological Research* 448–454; Moran, R., "Replies to Heal, Reginster, Wilson and Lear" (2004) LXIX *Philosophy and Phenomenological Research* 455–472; Shoemaker, S., "Moran on Self-Knowledge" (2003) *European Journal of Philosophy* 391–401; O'Brien, L., "Moran on Self-Knowledge" (2003) *European Journal of Philosophy* 375–390; Moran, R., "Responses to O'Brien and Shoemaker"(2003) *European Journal of Philosophy* 402–419; Moya, C., "Moran on Self-Knowledge, Agency and Responsibility" (2006) 114 *Critica. Revista Hispanoamericana de Filosofía* 3–26; Carman, T., "First Persons; On Richard Moran's Authority and Estrangement" (2003) *Inquiry* 395–408. For a critical view on the transparency condition see Gertler, B., "Do We Determine What We Believe By Looking Outward?" in Hatzimoysis, A. (ed.), *Self-Knowledge* (Oxford: Oxford University Press, 2008).

⁵² This outward-looking approach is also present in Aquinas, *Summa Theologiæ* (cited in n.2), I–II, Q. 87 Art. 2 ad. 2: "Dispositions are present in our intellect not as the objects of intellect, but as the things by which the intellect cognizes. For the object of our intellect, in its state of life at present, is the nature of a material thing."

⁵³ Anscombe, *Intention* (cited in n.2), §§2–3.

⁵⁴ Anscombe, *Intention* (cited in n.2), §8.

attend to if I were answering the question "Will there be a Third World War"? I get myself in a position to answer the question whether I believe that p by putting into operation whatever procedure I have for answering the question whether p.[55]

Wittgenstein asserts:

477 What does it mean to assert that "I believe p" says roughly the same as "p"? We react in roughly the same way when anyone says the first and when he says the second; if I said the first and someone didn't understand the words "I believe", I should repeat the sentence in the second form, and so on.

478 Moore's paradox may be expressed like this: "I believe p" says roughly the same as "p"; but "Suppose I believe that p..." does not say the same as "Suppose p..." ...

490 The paradox is this: the supposition may be expressed as follows: "Suppose this went inside me and that outside"; but the assertion that this is going on inside me asserts: this is going on outside me. As suppositions the two propositions about the inside and the outside are quite independent, but not as assertions.[56]

For both Evans and Wittgenstein answers about whether I "believe p" are outward-looking. I cannot answer the question whether I believe that it is raining, for example, without looking through the window, or reading the weather forecast. To answer such a question in terms of my introspective states seems absurd. We do not need to look inward at our states of mind to know whether or not it is raining.

Moran also advocates the "transparency condition" but goes a step further in arguing that when I answer a question from a deliberative standpoint I need to "make up my mind" and this entails self-constitution. Following in the steps of Evans and Wittgenstein, Moran explains transparency as follows:

With respect of belief, the claim of transparency is that from within the first-person perspective, I treat the question of my belief about P as equivalent to the question of the truth of P. What I think we can see now is that the basis for this equivalence hinges on the role of deliberative considerations about one's attitudes. For what the "logical" claim of transparency requires is the deferral of the theoretical question "What do I believe?" to the deliberative question "What am I to believe?" And in the case of the attitude of belief, answering a deliberative question is a matter of determining what is true. When we unpack the idea in this way, we see that the vehicle of transparency in each case lies in the requirement that I address myself to the question of my state of mind in a deliberative spirit, deciding and declaring myself on the matter, and not confront the question as a purely psychological one about the beliefs of someone who happens also to be me.[57]

For the purposes of this essay we do not need to engage with this dispute about the connection between self-knowledge and self-constitution.[58] We can take the idea of transparency and see how it applies to reasons for actions. If I act intentionally I act according to reasons for actions, therefore I believe[59] that I am acting intentionally for reasons as good-making characteristics, but if the transparency condition is sound, I do

---

[55] Evans, *The Varieties of Reference* (cited in n.51), 225. See also Edgeley, *Reason in Theory and Practice* (cited in n.51).

[56] Wittgenstein, L., *Remarks on the Philosophy of Psychology* (trans. Anscombe, E.) (Oxford: Blackwell, 1980).

[57] Moran, *Authority and Estrangement*, (cited in n.21), 62–63.

[58] On this debate see Shoemaker, S., "Self-knowledge and inner-sense" (1994) *Philosophy and Phenomenological Research* 249–314 and Shoemaker, S., *The First Person Perspective and Other Essays* (Cambridge: Cambridge University Press, 1996); Boghossian, P., "Content and Self-Knowledge" (1989) 17 *Philosophical Topics* 5–26; Byrne, A., "Introspection" (2005) 33 *Philosophical Topics* 79–104.

[59] Setiya defines the connection between belief and acting intentionally as follows: "When someone is acting intentionally, there must be something he is doing intentionally, not merely trying to do, in the belief that he is doing it": Setiya, K., *Reasons Without Rationalism* (Princeton, N.J.: Princeton University Press, 2007), 41.

not need to look at my mental state to know whether I have the belief in my intentional action for reasons that for me are good-making characteristics, I just look outward to the facts, objects, and state of affairs of the world. In this way, my belief that I am acting intentionally and that I have reasons for acting as good-making characteristics is transparent.

Let us go back to the example provided by Anscombe, where a man goes shopping and a detective is following him. The detective makes a description of the man's actions and his statements are true or false in terms of what the man is doing whereas if the man fails to do what he intends to do, we do not say that the proposition "he intends to ϕ-ing" is false, rather we say that there is a mistake in performance. This is what Anscombe calls the Theophrastus Principle,[60] which states that in intentional action the mistake is not in judgement but in performance. Anscombe puts this as follows:

> As when I say to myself "Now I press button A"—pressing button B—a thing which can certainly happen. This I will call the direct falsification of what I say. And here, to use Theophrastus' expression again, the mistake is not one of judgement but of performance. That is, we do not say: What you said was a mistake, because it was supposed to describe what you did and did not describe it, but: What you did was a mistake, because it was not in accordance with what you said.[61]

Thus, when I say that I intend to get up at six o'clock in the morning tomorrow to drive you to the train station because you are my friend and one should always help friends even in little ways, I know that I intend to act for such reasons. I do not need to look at my mental state to know that I have such reasons, I look outward to the world, my car, your presence in my house and the fact that it takes ten minutes to drive to the train station from my house. I have groundless knowledge of my reasons for action. It is not incorrigible.[62] Let us suppose that I discover that you are not truly my friend and that, therefore, my reason of driving you to the station because you are my friend is a mistaken one. However, the way I attain knowledge of my reasons for action does not depend on an inference from my observations or other data about myself. This entails that we have certain capacities, not only conceptual, but also practical. In the case of rules, we can say that we learn rules and their grounding reasons for actions simultaneously. Our practical and conceptual capacities enable us to learn rules in the context of grounding reasons as good-making characteristics.

I am also able to exercise control over my actions because I can direct myself towards the end of my action as described by the reasons for actions as good-making characteristics and I can change the movements of my body if I discover, aided by observation, that I am not doing what I intended to do (Theophrastus Principle). Thus, let us suppose that I am making an espresso and mistakenly I find myself about to pour milk into the cup, then I do not say, "I am not making an espresso after all, I am actually making a latte, that's all right." On the contrary, I change my movements and stop my action of pouring the milk into the cup. The world fits my intentions, I transform the state of affairs through my actions to fit what I intend and am committed to perform, whereas in

---

[60] See Teichman, R., *The Philosophy of Elizabeth Anscombe* (Oxford: Oxford University Press, 2009), 22–26 and also Alvarez, M., *Kinds of Reasons* (Oxford: Oxford University Press, 2010), 70–71.
[61] Anscombe, *Intention* (cited in n.2), §§32–33.
[62] Donnelan, K. S., "Knowing what I am doing" (1963) *Journal of Philosophy* 401–409 at 403 argues that there is a difference between our knowledge of having a headache, being angry, or in pain and practical knowledge that is non-observational. In the latter case, the knowledge is corrigible whereas the former is not. We revise the statements of our intentions and we can make mistakes about them. However, observation is not the basis of our knowledge; we cannot infer our intentions from our observations. What we correct is the result or purpose of our intentions.

theoretical knowledge my beliefs fit the world. In this way, I do not need observational knowledge to know that I intend to make an espresso, but I can be aided by observation to know the results of my intention.

Groundless knowledge of our reasons entails not only the capacity to act for reasons, but also includes knowing how to act intentionally according to reasons for actions in the specific context. Following legal rules entails having know-how about how to follow the legal rules because of their grounding reasons. But this does not mean that this groundless knowledge is not factive. On the contrary, it is knowledge about the world. Anscombe put this as follows:

> Say I go over to the window and open it. Someone who hears me moving calls out: What are you doing making that noise? I reply "Opening the window". I have called such a statement knowledge all along; and precisely because in such a case what I say is true—I do open the window; and that means that the window is getting opened by the movements of the body out of whose mouth those words come. But I don't say the words like this: "Let me see, what is this body bringing about? Ah yes! the opening of the window".[63]

Our practical knowledge is also factual. When I intend to open the window and make the necessary movements with my hands, I know that I am opening the window and that I am actually opening the window.

Can we understand what we are doing because we observe what we are doing? If we take a theoretical stance towards our own actions, then we might argue that there is a kind of alienation concerning the identity of ourselves and our actions;[64] in one sense the action is lost, because we do not look at the goal or object towards which our actions are directed, but we look at ourselves doing the action. We do not look outwards, but inwards and we lose the object or goal that we aim to bring about. Imagine that I am making an espresso and begin to reflect on the movements of my hands; the way the coffee flows into the cup, I see myself putting the coffee beans into the espresso machine and smile at the thought of a fresh coffee. At some point it seems that I will lose the action of "making an espresso." It is impossible to be Narcissus. O'Shaughnessy asks whether this impossibility is really about the impossibility of doing two things at the same time, rather than a matter of the character of practical knowledge because if this is the case, then it is a quantitative matter and trivial. O'Shaugnessy argues that it is a matter of logic: "Just as I cannot be going north and south at the same time, so I cannot be reading a book and playing tennis at the same time."[65] Thus, pathological cases are explained as the separation of the acting and the observing self.[66]

It is common to distinguish between (i) knowledge about the future known by evidence or known empirically and justified by some rule of inference, and (ii) knowledge about the future that is non-observational. In the former case, the knowledge is mainly propositional and I can verify or falsify its propositional content. In this way, I exercise my theoretical reasoning. For example, if I ask whether David Cameron will win the general election and you reply, "Yes, he will as he is winning in the polls," then I can now

---

[63] Anscombe, *Intention*, (cited in n.2), §§28–29.
[64] Moran, R., in *Authority and Estrangement* explores the nature of this theoretical stance towards our deliberative understanding of our actions. He makes an important connection between the Sartrean notion of "bad faith" and the theoretical stance that we might take towards our actions (cited in n.21), 77–83.
[65] O'Shaughnessy, B., "Observation and the Will" (1963) *The Journal of Philosophy* 67–392, at 380.
[66] See Bortolotti, L., and Broome, M. R., "Delusional Beliefs and Reason-Giving" (2008) 21(6) *Philosophical Psychology* 821–841.

say that I have evidence, i.e. your testimony about the polls, that David Cameron will win the general election. It is a mere prediction, one might say, of what will happen in the future. By contrast, let us suppose that John asks me whether I will come to the party tomorrow and I deliberate as to whether I should go or not. I evaluate my options. I then reach a decision and express my intention to John: "Yes, I will come to the party tomorrow." I have expressed my intention to come to the party and there is certainty about my action. Hampshire and Hart call this certainty a certainty based on reasons as opposed to certainty based on evidence and induction.[67] In this case, I exercise my practical reasoning rather than my theoretical reasoning. If someone asks me how I know that I will come to the party tomorrow, I will reply "Because I intend to." My knowledge is practical and non-observational.[68] But is this a proposition that can be verified? The response is negative. We can say about propositions that they are true or false whilst we say about intentions that they are "satisfied" or "non-satisfied." If I do not come to the party and if the expression of my intention was genuine, we will not say that the proposition "I intend to come to the party" is false. You would rather say that I have failed to come to the party as I did not act according to the expression of my intention. There was a failure in performance and you will think that some happening has taken place which has impacted on my attendance, for example, that I had an accident on my way to the party, or that a policemen fined me for speeding on the motorway and that this put me in a bad mood and made me change my mind about the party. We are in the world as agents and planners. We structure our lives around our expressions of intentions which, most of the time, are carried out successfully.

Let us imagine a person whose name is Sham and who, most of the time, fails to perform the actions that she expresses as intentions. Thus, Sham intends to wake up at six in the morning to read a chapter of a book before taking her daughter to school, she then intends to meet a friend at nine for breakfast and to work in the library until four in the afternoon and then she will leave the library to collect her daughter from school at half past four. Sham then intends to take her daughter to a music lesson and to have dinner with her husband at seven in the evening. However, Sham fails to wake up at six and wakes up at eight instead, consequently it is too late to take her daughter to school and she now has to stay at home. She has to change her initial intentions. Sham intends to ask the babysitter to look after her daughter whilst she goes to the library, but she fails to make the phone call to the babysitter. Her friend is waiting for her to have breakfast, but Sham also fails to answer her mobile phone. She now needs to make up her mind about another plan: she intends to make lunch for her daughter, but she also fails to make lunch. They both are starving and her daughter is crying in despair and hunger. This happens almost every day of her life. Sham's life is a sham. She has no control over her actions and we doubt whether she is truly an agent in the full sense. This is, however, not

---

[67] Hampshire, S., and Hart, H. L. A., "Decision, Intention and Certainty" (1958) *Mind* 1–12, at 5. They explain this practical certainty as follows: "The characteristic termination of the practical inquiry is the settled frame of mind when we are no longer undecided what to do. We have made up our mind and are both certain what to do and certain what we will try to do. In describing this termination of deliberation, we cannot separate the temporal reference to the future from the solution of the practical question. We have decided what to do, and that we shall at least try to do it. We cannot have this form of confident belief about our future voluntary action without this form of practical certainty about what to do" (at 12).

[68] For further discussion on the distinction between theoretical and practical knowledge, see Hampshire, S., and Morgenbesser, S., "Reply to Walsh on Thought and Action" (1963) *The Journal of Philosophy* 410–424.

the normal case of agency. Most of the time we succeed in performing the expressions of our intentions.

When I talk about deliberation, I do not mean that for every decision or intention to act there is a prior process of deliberation. The idea, rather, is that we can reconstruct the reasons for the decision and this is the objective of the why-question methodology.[69]

I have presupposed that expressions of intentions are genuine and non self-deceptive. Of course, many expressions of intentions are not genuine and this becomes obvious, in most occasions, through the the agent's performance of other actions and, sometimes, the disingenuity of such intentions is clear by their trivial formulation[70] together with the context and the knowledge of the character or role of the agent.[71] For example, you might say, "I will give up smoking," but I know that you "gave it up" just three months ago and that you took it up again last week.

I will argue not only that we succeed in performing our intentions, which I think is not a controversial point, but also that we have intentions about how to perform our intentions and that we succeed on this most of the time. Let us go back to our previous example. Sham has a twin sister whose name is Exito. Let us suppose that Exito also intends to do exactly the same actions as Sham, i.e. to wake up at six in the morning to read a book before taking her daughter to school and so on. Exito, however, is always successful in performing her intentions; she has, in addition, intentions about how she will perform her actions. She intends to wake up at six in the morning but with a fresh mind. This means that the night before she intends not to drink alcohol and not to go to bed too late. She intends to read a book, but she also intends to read it thoroughly and thoughtfully. She intends to have breakfast with her friend at nine, but she also intends to have a delicious breakfast and be kind, entertaining, and polite to her friend. Exito intends to go to the library and do research, but also to concentrate on a specific question and focus on material relating only to that question, and so on. In other words, we have intentions about how we will perform our actions and, most of the time, if we do not act under incontinence (akrasia) or depression, dominated by some pathological condition, we somehow succeed in performing them. We are, then, focusing on the paradigmatic case of intentional action.

If our intentions are conceived within the model of practical reasoning this enables us not only to plan our lives, but also to coordinate our activities with others. If you express your intention to come to my house for supper tonight, I know that most of the time you will succeed in your intention. I can then rely on your action and invite other friends, go to the market and buy vegetables and meat, clean the house, and prepare supper. If intentions play this function, then intentions cannot only be a matter of reasons for actions in terms of the two-components model.[72] According to this latter model, intentions are just mental states that cause our actions. If intentions are only mental states that cause my actions, then the causal chain can be broken and I cannot rely on the performance of intentions by agents. Let us suppose that you say, "I plan to come to your house for supper tonight with my car." This is your mental state that will cause the action. If your car breaks down you will need to formulate another intention and put yourself in another mental state to be able to come for supper at my house. Then you say to yourself, "I will go to Veronica's house for supper by bus." Let us suppose that you miss the bus to my house.

---

[69] The why-question methodology is discussed in the text at n.46.
[70] Hampshire, S., *Thought and Action* (London: Chatto and Windus, 1960).
[71] Anscombe, *Intention* (cited in n.2), §25.
[72] Thomas Pink argues, in my view correctly, that the function of intentions as coordinators show that intentions cannot be mental states. See Pink, T., "Purpose Intending" (1991) *Mind* 343–359. I will rather say that they are not primarily mental states.

You now need another intention to be able to come to my house. Of course, all this can be avoided if you say to me from the beginning, "I plan to come to your house for supper tonight using whatever transportation is available." But still, it might happen that there is no way to get to my house either by car or by bus, and that you might need to walk. How can this account help us to understand intentions as coordinators? How many intentions do you need to perform an action when you need to continually control and adjust your conduct to the contingencies? If intentions belong to the domain of practical reasoning and are better explained by the "guise of the good" model[73] then you can say to me: "I intend to come to your house for supper tonight by car because it is good to be with good friends like you." Let us suppose that your car breaks down and that you need to readjust your conduct to the contingencies as you still intend to come for supper at my house. You will not come by car, but you will come; you do not need to form another intention. Thus, you will take the bus, arrange a taxi, or walk since your will is directed to the goal of coming to my house because you have a reason as a good-making characteristics, i.e. it is good to be with friends. If intentions are understood as merely mental states it is unclear how your earlier mental states can control your later mental states and actions. In other words, we might say, your intention is not playing any controlling role.[74]

We need to distinguish between the purpose of an action on the one hand, and the intention with which I perform the intentional action and the expression of an intention on the other. The purpose of the action can be assessed observationally whereas my knowledge of the intentions with which I perform the action and the expression of the action, we have learned from Anscombe, are practical and non-observational. Let us suppose that you express the intention to disconnect a bomb and say, "I will disconnect this bomb." You take out all your tools from the tool box, you find the manual, "How to

---

[73] Plato in *The Republic* asserts, "Every soul pursues the good and does whatever it does for its sake" (505e37).
Aristotle in *The Nichomachean Ethics* states:

> Absolutely and in truth the good is the object of volition; but for each person what appears to him good. That which is in truth the object of volition is the object of the good man's volition... the good man judges each class of things rightly, and the truth is what appears true to him. Each state of character differs in what it finds noble and pleasant, and perhaps the most important difference between the good man and others is that he sees the truth in each class of things, being as it were the standard and measure for each of them (1113a25–33).

Aristotle in *De Anima* points out, "it is always the object of desire which produces movement, [and] this is either good or the apparent good" (433a27–29), and in the *Eudemian Ethics* he establishes:

> The end is by nature always a good and one about which people deliberate in particular, as a doctor may deliberate whether he is to give a drug, or the general where he is to pitch his camp; in these there is a good, an end, which is the best without qualification; but contrary to nature, and by perversion, not the good but only an apparent good may be the end (1227a19–22).

How can values actualized in particulars provide reasons for actions? When we begin to deliberate about what to do, we begin with judging whether something, i.e. an object, state of affairs, or an event is good or not. We engage in valuing and we start to desire that this something obtains. Values are instantiated by the good-making characteristics of objects and states of affairs and they become reasons for actions. Pure desires, by contrast, are passive and do not engage in valuations. Pure desires are a pure state of the mind without object. For example, the pure desire for pleasure does not aim at a specific object, but at its own satisfaction or fulfillment, but also at eliminating itself. When making valuations, we aim at the object and the satisfaction of attaining the object. Desires are mute on the question of what is good.

[74] A number of authors have criticized the belief/desire model because it fails to account for the idea that full intentional agency, in its paradigmatic form, is something that the agent does rather than that something just happens to him or her. The agent is at the centre of the action and this is why we want to learn why the agent has done so and so. See Hornsby, J., "Agency and Action" in Steward, H., and Hyman, J. (eds), *Agency and Action* (Cambridge: Cambridge University Press, 2004), 1–23.

disconnect a bomb," and you begin to cut the red wire as instructed by your manual. You say, "I intend to disconnect this bomb" and, if you were pushed to reflect in response to the question, "Why?" your answer might be, "Because it is good to disconnect bombs to save my life and the lives of others." Mistakenly, however, you cut the black wire and the bomb explodes. We know by observation that you have failed in your purpose. There is propositional knowledge concerning the purpose of an action and thus it is either true or false. We will say, "It is not true that you disconnected the bomb." Our knowledge of the purpose of the action might be known empirically. However, the knowledge of your intentions is non-observational. If your expression of intention and the intention with which you act are genuine, you cannot systematically be mistaken about your intention. It is, one might say, groundless, though not incorrigible.

5. Authorities' claims as expressions of intention

We have explained that intentions are non-observational and entail practical knowledge. However, we might be aided by observation in terms of the results or purposes of our intentions. Let us think again about the example of a person making an espresso and realizing that he was about to pour in some milk, but stops in his actions because he is committed to carrying out his intentions of making an espresso. He does not change his mind, rather he changes his bodily movements and transforms the world to fit his intentions. But to carry out our intentions, we need to be sensitive to the world and some observation might enable us to carry out our intentions. We can be aided by perception, but we do not base our practical knowledge on the observation of our actions. Practical knowledge involves instead practical and conceptual capacities.

Thus a judge who claims to have legitimate authority to decide according to moral correctness, needs to master concepts such as "legitimacy," "authority," "justice," "correctness," and so on. However, these conceptual capacities alone will not suffice; he would also need the know-how to make a legitimate and valid command, rule, or order following the precepts of the Rule of Law; the know-how to correct and revise legal and moral principles; the know-how to apply precedents and interpret statutes, and so on. As in the case of the man making the espresso, he can identify mistakes and make self-corrections to adjust the state of affairs to his intentions. He needs to be sensitive to differences and discriminations made by past legal decisions, he needs also to be able to envisage new ways of doing things using his practical imagination and following the grounding reasons as (hypothetical) good-making characteristics of legal rules. Of course, he can fail in his performance or he might be mistaken about either his beliefs or evaluations about the state of affairs, objects, or events, and this is what the idea that authorities' claims as expressions of intentions enables us to explain. We will examine his decisions in the light of his intentions and the results he has obtained. We find, subsequently, the main following possibilities, which should not be considered exhaustive:

(a) The legal authority successfully performs the intention to act and might have sound intentions as to how the act should be performed, but the legal authority has mistaken beliefs about the grounding reasons as good-making characteristics of the legal rule. Suppose that a legal authority makes permissible the murder of disabled children because these children are believed to debase the national race. The authorities claim legitimate authority and moral correctness and, as I have argued, their claims—if they are genuine—should be understood as expressions of intentions about how legal actions will be performed. However, the authorities' beliefs about the grounding reasons as the good-making characteristics of rules are mistaken. They believe, for example, that moral correctness is about the maximization of overall well-being even at the cost of the violation of fundamental human rights, such as the right to life. The authorities will engage in moral and political arguments to show that their solution is the morally correct and legitimate one.[75] They will perform their intentions successfully, but their beliefs about the grounding reasons as the good-making characteristics of a rule that makes permissible the murder of disabled children are false. Nor are there reasons to create a presumption of the authoritative moral force of the authorities' legal decisions. A caveat should be put forward. We have said that the legal authority might have a sound understanding about how to perform the action but that this is, however, unlikely. Arguably, their mistaken beliefs about the grounding reasons as the good-making characteristics of the legal rule will most likely affect their beliefs about how to perform the action. If my beliefs about the grounding reasons of legal rules are mistaken, how can my procedural views on how to make law be sound? Correct law-making procedures involve a commitment to fairness, reciprocity, right expectations, and so on. In other words, if a legal authority cannot acquire sound substantive reasons in the legal decision-making process, how can they acquire sound procedures for the legal decision-making process? This is an alternative reading of Simmonds's point[76] about the impossibility of having an unjust regime that fully complies with the eight desiderata of the Rule of Law. In the above example, the authority's intentions to perform the legal action in an excellent way, i.e., following the desiderata of the Rule of Law, is undermined by its substantively wrong beliefs about the good-making characteristics of legal rules. There is a clear conflict between "having morally wrong beliefs about the grounding reasons of rules" and "knowing how to make rules with (procedural) good-making characteristics."

(b) The legal authority has correct beliefs about the grounding reasons as good-making characteristics of the legal rule, but mistaken beliefs about how the legal act should be carried out. However, there is successful performance of the mistaken intention on how to perform the legal act. Authorities can also have mistaken beliefs about how to perform their actions, namely how to apply and create legal rules. They might believe, for example, that legal rules should not be made public and should apply retroactively. In spite of this, their beliefs about the grounding reasons as good-making characteristics of the legal rule in question might be sound. For example, they think that the value of life is the grounding reason for the road traffic rules, but they apply and create them privately and retroactively. What has failed is their understanding about how rules should be applied and be created. In other words, they have failed on the issue of how to perform their intentions. Let us examine the following example. My aim is to spend more time talking to you because you are my friend and, in my view, to spend time with friends is a good sort of thing. My belief about the good-making characteristics of the reason for the action, i.e., friendship, is sound. However, I have mistaken beliefs about what good quality time with friends means. I become nosey and treat you very impolitely. I did carry out my intention and there was performance, but the purpose or outcome was a failure. You are now able to evaluate the purpose or outcome of my action. Similarly, in the case of legal authorities, we can evaluate the purpose or outcome of the authorities' expressions of intentions about how they have performed their actions and

---

[75] In this kind of system, we can say that there is an inversion of values, see Pauer-Studert, H., and Velleman, D., "Distortions of Normativity" (2011) *Ethical Theory and Moral Practice* 329–56.

[76] Simmonds, N., *Law as a Moral Idea* (Oxford: Oxford University Press, 2007); Finnis, J., *Natural Law and Natural Rights* (Oxford: Oxford University Press, 1980); Fuller, *The Morality of Law*, (cited in n.10). cf. Kramer, M., "Big Bad Wolf: Legal Positivism and its Detractors" (2004) *American Journal of Jurisprudence* 1–10.

see whether the action is a failure or not. For example, retroactive and private road traffic legal rules create complete chaos. Legal authorities claim legitimate authority and moral correctness but because they have mistaken beliefs about how to create and apply rules, the outcome of the performance is a failure. To succeed in a claim of legitimate authority and moral correctness, to succeed in an expression of an intention of performing actions, such as the creation or application of a rule in a legitimate and morally correct way, the officials, judges, and legislators need not only to engage with the grounding reasons as good-making characteristics of legal rules, and with the differences and discriminations of the particulars and the general principles that are part of the precedent cases and statutes, but also to engage with how one should create and apply legal rules, and this know-how is provided, in part, by complying with the eight desiderata of the Rule of Law.

(c) The legal authority has correct beliefs about the grounding reasons as good-making characteristics of the legal rules and sound intentions about how to perform their legal acts, but they fail in performing the latter. In this scenario, authorities fail in their intentions on how to perform the legal act, in spite of having the correct beliefs about how to perform the act. For example, a judge believes that a good rule should be public, coherent, and non-retroactive but nevertheless the judge fails to apply or create a legal rule that is coherent and non-retroactive because she lacks the adequate skills to do so. Her failure is in terms of her intentions about how to perform the legal act. As regards the previous example, I have sound beliefs about how to be entertaining and polite, but I fail in my performance that afternoon, contrary to my intentions because, for example, I lack the required social skills. In the case of the law, judges and legal authorities might lack the required legal and intellectual skills to bring about their good intentions.

In general terms, there cannot be a complete and general disconnection between authorities' expressions of intention of legitimate authority and moral correctness and their performance. There cannot be a total failure of practical knowledge. Evil and less-than-perfect legal systems are possible precisely because any or some of the previous alternatives are possible.

6. Conclusions

This essay has aimed to show the importance of authorities' claims in shaping and creating the law according to the "guise of the good" model. It has also shown that an investigation into philosophy of language such as speech act theories presents only a partial portrait of the intricate relationship between "expressions of intentions" and "intentional actions." The complete story that emerges is a complex one where expressions of intentions, intentional actions, failure and success in performance, and the concept of the good as good-making characteristics are all intertwined.

The idea of authoritative claims, including claims about compliance with the eight desiderata of the Rule of Law, as expressions of intention enables us to create this complex picture where practical knowledge and its possible failure is involved. It is now apparent that (a) expressions of intention, (b) intentional actions and (c) the intentions with which an act is performed can only make sense and be completely understood if they are considered in a unitary or "organic" way.

7

Legal Pluralism: A Systems Theory Approach to Language, Translation, and Communication

Richard Nobles and David Schiff

Most hypotheses about legal pluralism raise difficult problems not only for the conception of law in general but also for its translation from one language into another. These two issues are interrelated. If one has no agreed conception of law, then the different linguistic forms that might be used in different languages to represent law become ever more confused. Legal pluralism seeks to extend the study of law beyond state and inter-state legal orders to include non-state sourced forms of law.[1] In so doing, it raises the spectre that law ceases to be identifiable as a separate social formation, as the border between the legal and the social is dissolved. Phrases such as 'law from below',[2] or 'an oppositional postmodern understanding of law',[3] or 'law between the global and the local',[4] or 'legal hybridization'[5] tend to reverse the hierarchical assumptions implicit in much legal practice and scholarship, and phrases such as those applying the distinction between 'law as one' and 'law as many',[6] or 'the more the merrier'[7] imply that law can only be captured in a combination of conceptions rather than a single conception, and in a range of linguistic forms rather than any

---

[1] Early motivation for such extension reflected criticism of the exclusion of forms of law from the 'imperialism' of Western state-centred approaches (for background see S.E. Merry, 'Legal Pluralism' (1988) 22 *Law & Society Review* 869; P. Fitzpatrick, 'Law and Societies' (1984) 22 *Osgoode Hall Law Journal* 115; M. Chiba, 'Legal Pluralism in Sri Lankan Society: Toward a General Theory of Non-Western Law'(1993) 30 *Journal of Legal Pluralism and Unofficial Law* 197), while recent motivation also reflects the need for inclusion of forms of law that processes of 'digitalisation, privatisation and globalisation' seem to entail (see G. Teubner, 'Societal Constitutionalism: Alternatives to State-Centred Constitutional Theory' in Christian Joerges, Inger-Johanne Sand, and Gunther Teubner (eds), *Transnational Governance and Constitutionalism* (Oxford: Hart Publishing, 2004), 3). For an earlier statement of this more recent motivation, concentrating on *lex mercatoria*, see G. Teubner, 'Global Bukowina: Legal Pluralism in the World Society' in Gunther Teubner (ed.), *Global Law without a State* (Aldershot: Dartmouth, 1997), 3.
[2] S.E. Merry et al., 'Law From Below: Women's Human Rights and Social Movements in New York City' (2010) 44 *Law & Society Review* 101.
[3] Boaventura de Sousa Santos, *Toward a New Legal Common Sense: Law, Globalisation and Emancipation*, 2nd edn (London: Butterworths, 2002).
[4] M. Goodale, 'Locating rights, envisioning law between the global and the local' in Mark Goodale and Sally Engle Merry (eds), *The Practice of Human Rights: Tracking Law Between the Global and the Local* (New York: Cambridge University Press, 2007), 1.
[5] B. de Sousa Santos, 'The Heterogeneous State and Legal Pluralism in Mozambique' (2006) 40 *Law & Society Review* 39.
[6] M. Davies, 'The Ethos of Pluralism' (2005) 27 *Sydney Law Review* 87.
[7] E. Melissaris, 'The More the Merrier: A New Take on Legal Pluralism?' (2004) 13 *Social and Legal Studies* 57.

single form. A concept of law unencumbered by its associations with the nation state and the activities of legal officials can easily lose the ability to understand and thereby study law as a separate formation (as occurs when law is identified with multiple social norms, general accounts of social control, strongly held commitments, etc.). Indeed, once one moves beyond the study of law as state law, what prevents each observer from identifying different criteria for what constitutes law, according to their own observational standpoints and research objectives? The problem that then arises, which appears to be a feature of studies of legal orders motivated by concerns about legal pluralism, is that these studies tend not to build into anything like a coherent and integrated body of knowledge.[8]

In his essay 'Two Faces of Janus: Re-thinking Legal Pluralism'[9] Gunther Teubner claimed that modern systems theory could be used to inform our understanding of legal pluralism including non-state forms of law,[10] without suffering from the problems identified above. But, as he admitted himself, this is a surprising claim to make. The features which systems theory attributes to the legal system—that it is autonomous, reflexive, and self-productive—have some instructive plausibility when one accepts that law is restricted to state legal systems; but the one tenet which unites those who argue for legal pluralism is the insistence that state law is not the only form of, or model from which one can establish, legality. However, Teubner recognized this, and was directly seeking to address the slippery slope which faces legal pluralists when they insist that law is not limited to state law. It is difficult enough to construct an account of the relationship between law and the rest of society when one starts from the assumption that law is indeed limited to state law, or even that state law is the paradigmatic example of law, but once one abandons this position legal pluralism has additional difficulty in identifying any criteria for the legal which can distinguish what is legal from what is not within society, or as others

---

[8] Thus, for example, Griffiths' classic statement of what pluralism is, disputes all of the general definitions (those of M.B. Hooker, J. Gilissen, and J. Vanderlinden) and theoretical understandings from those who had engaged in substantive analysis (L. Pospisil, M.G. Smith, E. Ehrlich, and S.F. Moore) that appear to have been motivated by concerns about legal pluralism: see J. Griffiths, 'What is Legal Pluralism?' (1986) 24 *Journal of Legal Pluralism and Unofficial Law* 1. There is certainly neither one concept of legal pluralism, nor wide agreement about its value, or the value of the 'legal pluralists project', or how the empirical studies that it is engaged with are linked to a common theoretical understanding. For a full discussion of these background debates, see F. von Benda-Beckmann, 'Who's Afraid of Legal Pluralism?' (2002) 47 *Journal of Legal Pluralism and Unofficial Law* 37; and for an introduction to the collection of papers by the 'Project Group Legal Pluralism' that try to move this linking forward, see F. von Benda-Beckmann and K. von Benda-Beckmann, 'The Dynamics of Change and Continuity in Plural Legal Orders' (2006) 53–4 *Journal of Legal Pluralism and Unofficial Law* 1.

[9] G. Teubner, 'The Two Faces of Janus: Rethinking Legal Pluralism' (1991–92) 13 *Cardozo Law Review* 1443.

[10] For an earlier formulation described by Teubner as 'social law' see his 'Autopoiesis and Steering: how politics profit from the normative surplus of capital' in Roeland In'T Veld et al. (eds), *Autopoiesis and Configuration Theory: New Approaches to Societal Steering* (Dordrecht: Kluwer, 1991), ch.11, 138–9. Teubner has more recently offered a number of alternative formulations that reconceptualize legal pluralism issues: for example, 'Breaking Frames: Economic Globalisation and the Emergence of *lex mercatoria*' (2002) 5 *European Journal of Social Theory* 199; (with A. Fischer-Lescano), 'Cannibalizing Epistemes: Will Modern Law Protect Traditional Cultural Expressions?' in Christoph B. Graber and Mira Burri-Nenova (eds), *Traditional Cultural Expressions in a Digital Environment* (Cheltenham: Edward Elgar, 2008), 17; 'Self-Constitutionalizing Transnational Corporations? On the Linkage of "Private" and "Public" Corporate Codes of Conduct' to be published in Gralf-Peter Calliess (ed.), *Governing Transnational Corporations: Public and Private Perspectives* (2012) 19 *Indiana Journal of Global Legal Studies*; (with P. Korth) 'Two Kinds of Legal Pluralism: Collision of Transnational Regimes in the Double Fragmentation of World Society' to be published in Margaret A. Young (ed.), *Regime Interaction in International Law* (Cambridge: Cambridge University Press, 2012).

might argue, from studying society as such, rather than law.[11] And seeking to identify law by reference to its functions (social control, dispute resolution, ordering social relations, etc.) or its structures (institutions, personnel, norms, rules, etc.) has not proved satisfactory.[12] Even where there is consensus on the criteria which should be applied, there is little accord on what follows from their application.

To address these problems, Teubner offered systems theory, which abandons structure or function as the explanation of how society might organize itself to include a distinctly legal subsystem, in favour of communicative codes. This version of systems theory, sometimes referred to as neo-systems or autopoiesis theory, views law as one of modern society's functionally differentiated subsystems with each social subsystem characterized as operating through differentiated codes.[13] In common with society's other subsystems, law generates and maintains its separate identity through the application of a unique code: legal/illegal. The economy, the political system, the science system, the mass media, and the legal system are distinguished from each other by the different binary codes each is applying. The code of law is legal/illegal;[14] that of the mass media is information/non information;[15] for science it is true/false; for the economy payment/non-payment; and for politics government/opposition.[16] Teubner claimed that this approach 'delineates clearly the "legal" from other types of social action'.

Legal pluralism is then defined no longer as a set of conflicting social norms in a given social field but as a multiplicity of diverse communications processes that observe social action under the binary code of legal/illegal.... It is the—implicit or explicit—invocation of the legal code which constitutes [the] phenomenon of legal pluralism, ranging from the official law of the state to the unofficial laws of markets and Mafias.[17]

In this chapter, we explore the nature of the legal code, and how it can be used to study state, inter-state, and non-state legal orders. Further, we hope to illustrate how codes can resolve or reduce problems of translation, and thereby generate a discussion of the nature of codes, and how they operate within language, and across languages, with a view to forming an opinion on Teubner's assertion that systems theory could both clearly

---

[11] This is explicitly stated, for example, as Kelsen's criticism of Ehrlich's notion of 'living law': Hans Kelsen, *General Theory of Law and State* (New York: Russell & Russell, 1945/1961), 28.

[12] This critique is fully developed in Tamanaha's non-essentialist legal pluralism: Brian Tamanaha, *A General Jurisprudence of Law and Society* (New York: Oxford University Press, 2001); and, for a shorter account, 'A Non-Essentialist Version of Legal Pluralism' (2000) 27 *Journal of Law and Society* 296.

[13] Crucially for this version of systems theory, differentiated codes are what maintain subsystems' separate identity, not their functions. Function arises only at the level of society as a system, as a modern differentiated society depends on separate subsystems carrying out their respective functions in order for that society to maintain itself. Whilst a subsystem will include an internal reference within the system to society as an encompassing system, and its role within society, this will not maintain its separate identity. In the case of law, its function at the level of society is the generation of normative expectations (see Niklas Luhmann, *Law as a Social System* (Oxford: Oxford University Press, 2004), ch.3), in the sense that this is what modern society needs from law in order to maintain its differentiation and current levels of complexity. But this does not mean that law is the only system that generates normative expectations, or that an internal reference to this function would maintain law's identity. On the difference between function, performance, and (self-) reflection, see N. Luhmann, 'Differentiation of Society' (1977) 2 *Canadian Journal of Sociology*, 29.

[14] See N. Luhmann, 'The Coding of the Legal System' in Gunther Teubner and Alberto Febbrajo (eds), *State, Law, and Economy as Autopoietic Systems: Regulation and Autonomy in a New Perspective* (Milan: Giuffre, 1992), 145.

[15] See Niklas Luhmann, *The Reality of the Mass Media* (Oxford: Polity Press, 2000).

[16] For a short account of the coding of each of these systems respectively, see Niklas Luhmann, *Ecological Communication* (Chicago: University of Chicago Press, 1989), chs 12, 10, and 13.

[17] Teubner, 'The Two Faces of Janus' (cited in n.9), 1451.

delineate the legal from the non-legal within society, and engage with what motivates legal pluralism studies.

1. How does one identify a subsystem code?

Especially when dealing with state law, within an English-speaking jurisdiction, it seems fairly easy to identify legal coding. The recognition that there are circumstances, actions, or situations that are legal or illegal is something that is present throughout society, as is the general idea that everything that is not illegal is legal, and everything that is illegal, not legal. But despite this Luhmann insists that this code, which is represented in the binary distinction legal/illegal, is not 'logically deduced', neither 'did it [the legal system] come into being because it can be deduced from logical axioms', but rather 'the strict and unyielding distinction between legal and illegal is exceptional and not self-evident'.[18] That said, one finds plenty of communications that refer to things as 'legal' or 'illegal' and this can make the claim that law identifies itself through the application of its binary code of legal/illegal something that seems plausible and relatively unproblematic.

Problems however arise when one considers how codes operate,[19] and what distinguishes them from programmes. The presence of a communication which takes the form 'this is illegal' does not mean that we are in the presence of the legal system, a system that codes in terms of the legal code. References to something being legal or illegal regularly occur in the mass media, in politics, and in the economy. But in these systems, these references will operate as programmes and not as code. What is the difference? With code one is looking for the primary distinction of the system—its basal distinction. Communications within a system generate meaning by accounting for the application of their primary distinction. Communications which account for the application of a code are observations upon coding, called, within the theory, secondary observation.[20] These communications (observations on the application of coding) build into ever more complex programmes which account for the application of the code in the past and its current application, and indicate how the code will be applied in the future. Systems other than law will utilize the distinction legal/illegal, but rather than as code, only as programme. So, for example, the economy will utilize the distinction between what is legal and illegal, and even the semantic 'illegal' or 'legal', but it will not code legal/illegal. Economic communications will not address their secondary observations toward the question of whether this legality is actually illegal, or this illegality rather legal. Indeed, rather than these concerns, whereby the legal system builds ever more complicated programmes, the illegality of some proposed action within the economy represents a cost, which in turn affects the ability to make a payment, as here the basal distinction or

---

[18] Luhmann, *Law as a Social System* (cited in n.13), 177, and see further 173–80.
[19] To appreciate the character of a code and its operation as understood in systems theory, see the example of Luhmann's analysis of the code of art in *Art as a Social System* (Stanford: Stanford University Press, 2000), 185–96.
[20] To engage with Luhmann's analysis, one needs to appreciate the character of second-order observation and its difference from and similarity to first-order observation. This is no simple task since it relies on a range of supporting (or self-supporting) arguments. A clear statement that represents well the form and logic of this analysis, is presented by N. Akerstrom Anderson, 'Luhmann as Analytical Strategist' in Rene John, Anna Henkel, and Jana Ruckert-John (eds), *Die Methodologien des Systems* (Wiesbaden: Westdeutscher Verlag, 2010), 97. For Luhmann's own account of the difference between constructivist second-order observation and deconstruction, see 'Deconstruction as Second-Order Observing' in Niklas Luhmann, *Theories of Distinction: Redescribing the Descriptions of Modernity* (Stanford: Stanford University Press, 2002), 94.

code is payment/non-payment. The trajectory of the communication of the legality of a proposed action is toward the cost of the action, and the distinction between what is legal and illegal as it is operating represents a programme within the economy indicating what might be more costly, and not as code, as it does within the legal system.[21] So, one does not take a single communication, whatever distinction that communication might include, and allocate it to a system; one has to observe which system a communication belongs to by examining its trajectory within systems: what communications this communication is linked to in the past, and in the future, and what code is being applied by the system of which it forms a part. Only if the communication forms part of a social subsystem of communications, which is repeatedly applying the distinction legal/illegal, are we in the presence of the legal system.

To develop the sense of what we are looking for, let us take another example, namely one which might be particularly important for understanding legal pluralism: that of morals. We can ask whether the moral norms that operate for a given community are 'legal', and such a question is implicated in many studies of legal pluralism (as of course it is for many other aspects of jurisprudential discussion). But, for systems theory, one has to ask what the code of the moral is, and how that coding might operate within society. One asks this question knowing that the language of morals operates with distinctions: good/bad, good/evil, right/wrong, but that these distinctions will also operate in legal communication as they do in other communications.

Luhmann has concluded that the code of the moral in modern differentiated societies 'has become contingent', namely that it has lost its ability to organize itself systematically through a basal distinction, even though it still adopts binary distinctions such as good/bad, good/evil and right/wrong.[22] For these purposes, Luhmann argues that moral coding is 'always coding of communication. There are, in other words, no good or bad people, but only the possibility of indicating people as good or bad'.[23] Luhmann describes how the development of the 'interiorization' of the moral,[24] from the Middle Ages, has complicated the possibility of operating with communications that sharply divide themselves around a basal distinction, such as that of legal/illegal for the legal system. Under the conditions of modern differentiated societies, an order develops which reduces the functional operative capacity of the moral code.

This order does not permit code values of function systems to be identified with moral values—neither with good/bad nor with good/evil. The government is not morally better than the opposition (but also not morally worse). The power holder is not morally better than his public. Whoever determines truths is not morally superior to whoever determines untruths.... Moral sinners, as well as the morally justified, must reckon with surprises, when on Judgment Day the true meaning of the code, 'transcendent/immanent,' will become manifest.[25]

---

[21] Teubner expresses the same argument informatively: 'the economy reconstructs the same course of events with its own fictitious distinctions and indications. If legal norms appear on the screen of the economy at all, then they are treated not as normatively valid, but as entries in economic calculations. Economic communication builds an economic fiction of the law and uses it to condition its self-regulating programmes, for instance, those of cost minimization.... Where jurists get infuriated over violations and circumventions of the law, economists praise what they see as efficient economic behaviour—something which is admirably summed up in the notion of "efficient breach of contract"' (G. Teubner, 'Regulatory Law: Chronicle of a Death Foretold' (1992) 1 *Social & Legal Studies* 451, at 466).

[22] N. Luhmann, 'The Code of the Moral' (1992–93) 14 *Cardozo Law Review* 995, at 1009.

[23] Luhmann, 'The Code of the Moral' (cited in n.22), 1000.

[24] This refers to the construction of what is good or bad about an action by reference to the subject's intention, or interior state.

[25] Luhmann, 'The Code of the Moral' (cited in n.22), 1004–5.

Luhmann's account of the code of the moral can, as he recognizes himself, be described as that of the cynic. His analysis is not aimed at decrying the application of the binary distinctions that form the basis of moral discourse and ethics. But he seriously questions whether such distinctions can be studied sociologically in the modern world as providing any primary distinction that organizes the operations, programmes, and communications of a functional subsystem, as opposed to the selection of communications that can be used to commend or criticize the character of actions, behaviour, and thoughts.

2. The problems of translation

How does Teubner's assertion that one can use a systems theory approach to overcome the problems of legal pluralism—to identify non-state law without losing a basis for distinguishing the legal from the rest of society—deal with problems of translation? This is most apparent when one considers the kinds of societies which have been the focus of legal anthropology. Defining law in terms of the understandings of officials, or the presence of a separate staff to enforce sanctions—definitions which are generalizations of the state—have tended to exclude claims that these societies have or had 'law'. And in post-colonial situations, the same criteria will prioritize the law of the central state, and allocate such phenomena as, for example, Hindu 'law' as practised by millions to the status of customs and mores.[26] Functionalist theories—for example those which identify law with dispute resolution—bring such examples back into the definition of law, but at the cost of dissolving the difference between the legal and the social. But what happens with codes? How does one tell whether the Hindu tradition or that of the Yap people[27] or, to take Teubner's own example, the Mafia are applying the legal code?

If we assume that legal/illegal is a semantic distinction, that these terms or their equivalent have to be used, then the code operates as a form of conventionalism. One is looking for communications that apply the code legal/illegal within a network of inter-connected communications that are also applying this distinction, rather than another. This is not conventionalism in the sense that the use of these terms by particular actors would be determinative of that issue. So there are already important differences from the conventionalist approach to legal pluralism offered by Brian Tamanaha, who would treat as 'law' whatever a significant number of actors would call 'law'.[28] For systems theory, it is not the fact that actors use the terms legal/illegal, however frequently, which makes communications part of the legal system. One is looking for communications that form part of a system, and the usage of the code within that system is what is crucial, not a headcount of the humans who make particular kinds of communications. If the system constructs itself through the repeated application of a legal code, such that all of the rest of the communications in the system form networks which lead towards

---

[26] See Werner Menski, *Hindu Law: Beyond Tradition and Modernity* (New Delhi: Oxford University Press, 2003), 3–29.
[27] We choose this example because it is the subject of a leading theorist's research and writing which explores issues of legal pluralism in depth in the context of conflicts of 'legal norms' in societies operating with a range of languages. See Brian Tamanaha, *Understanding Law in Micronesia: An Interpretive Approach to Transplanted Law* (Leiden: E.J. Brill, 1993).
[28] '*if sufficient people with sufficient conviction consider something to be "law", and act pursuant to this belief, in ways that have an influence in the social arena*' (Tamanaha, *A General Jurisprudence of Law and Society* (cited in n.12), 167, italics in original).

and away from the application of this distinction, then we have a legal system. But how is this to be observed?

Unlike the term law, which has an enormous number of alternatives in other languages, the terms legal/illegal operate in a large number of languages. So whereas law has to be translated in French to at least *loi* or *droit*, and in German *recth* or *gesetz*, the terms legal/illegal operate in the German, and French, but also Dutch, Italian, and even Hungarian, using very similar, simple phrasing. In other languages a similar term is not applied, though translations of the term are offered. Can we rely on these translations to identify the legal code? Indeed, can we identify the legal code even where the terms legal/illegal are not being used? A useful starting point, particularly in response to Teubner's suggestion that the legal code could be used to observe the Mafia, is to start with Italian. The Italian state legal system can be described as a system which codes in terms of the opposition of *legale/illegale*, but what of the Mafia? The Mafia operates through codes,[29] such as the code of silence, the *omerta*, but is the Mafia a legal system, or part of the legal system? The *omerta* is only part of what constructs the Mafia. If there is a basic distinction around which all other Mafia communications are orientated it would probably be that of honour/dishonour. But if this is the case, does this lead us to judge that the Mafia is actually not part of the legal system, because it operates a different code from the Italian state system? Is the Mafia actually like the honour system in Gabriel Garcia Marquez's book *Chronicle of a Death Foretold*, in which the dishonour resulting from a girl being rejected by her husband for not being a virgin can only be expunged by the murder of her lover? In his article discussing this book,[30] Teubner described the conflict between the state law of murder and the villagers' honour code as a conflict of 'legal and social norms'. Only the state law involves legal norms. To quote Teubner: 'The logic of redeeming family honour through killing the disgraced party cannot except on the pain of self-denial be subordinated to the contingency of the binary code legal/illegal'[31] or, since Colombians speak Spanish, the code *legales/illegales*.

The fact that so many languages include the words legal/illegal and apply them as a binary distinction does not mean that translation is not a problem. What are we to make of the Serbian and Thai translations,[32] which do not share the same etymology? And how are we to know what leads a translator to the conclusion that these words are an appropriate translation for legal/illegal? What allows us to say that a term used in one language has equivalence in another?[33] Since at least Saussure, we have become aware that signs generate meanings within language through their relationship to each other; and since at least Wittgenstein, that these relationships are established by use, rather than by rules. Thus there is never an exact translation of the terms of one language into another, as the respective terms will always have different possibilities of connection within one language than those they would have within another.[34] The

---

[29] Recent examples suggest that these have taken a written form and mirror religious and other codes, for example the Mafia's 'Ten Commandments' (available at: <http://news.bbc.co.uk/1/hi/7086716.stm>).

[30] Teubner, 'Regulatory Law' (cited in n.21).

[31] Teubner, 'Regulatory Law' (cited in n.21), 456–7.

[32] Respectively: правни/незаконит; ตามกฎหมาย/ที่ผิดกฎหมาย.

[33] For an informative introduction to these questions, as well as an introduction to the further papers in the volume which deals with these issues, see A.-J. Arnaud, 'We Are All E.T.'s' (1998) 41 *Journal of Legal Pluralism and Unofficial Law* 1.

[34] See, for recognition of this, M. Chiba, 'The Intermediate Variable of Legal Concepts' (1998) 41 *Journal of Legal Pluralism and Unofficial Law* 131, and his suggested solution to problems of 'cultural relativism'.

problem is 'doubled' within systems theory by the claim that meanings created by communications are a consequence of the connections between communications within subsystems, so that the meanings of even identical terms within identical sentences as interpreted by different subsystems cannot be the same. Systems theory, which offers code as a substitute for function or structure removes the tools whereby the translation of the legal code, legal/illegal, might be disciplined. One cannot look to common function, or essential forms (or translations of function, and essential forms) to justify the use of words equivalent to 'legal/illegal' in another language. One needs to look to the code to observe the system establishing itself. A system's structures, with the sole exception of its code, are contingent.[35] Functions[36] are a by-product of the application of a system's code, and not what determines the possibilities of coding.

Even where the legal code shares the same etymology one finds difficulties. 'Legal' is probably a mid-15th century word that seems to come from the Latin *'legalis'*, which may be translated as 'pertaining to law'. But if what is legal is that which pertains to law, and that which is not legal is that which does not pertain to law, then the code legal/illegal might be more appropriately translated as 'law/not law' as indeed, in some potential misconceptions of systems theory observations, it has been.[37]

---

[35] And this contingency is prevalent in so many modern observations, for many reasons. One of the standard reasons is set out by Luhmann: 'In the modern world, more and more is attributed to the observer, at least in many cases. This could be a symptom of the fact that all world experiences are contingent. Beyond the ever-present question of whether someone else will characterize something correctly or incorrectly, one can use the observation of one's own observation to observe, characterize, and understand the other observer. A tendency toward attribution to the observed observer is especially prevalent when the second-order observation aims at latent structures and functions, that is, when it works with the schema manifest/latent (psycho-analytically, ideology-critically, science-sociologically, or even in the process of the now-common everyday observations). The fact that an observer *cannot see* something, or even that he *cannot see*, cannot be explained by an absence of information but can only be accounted for in terms of the observer himself' (Luhmann, 'Contingency as Defining Attribute' in Luhmann, *Observations on Modernity* (Stanford: Stanford University Press, 1998), 48–9).

[36] Within systems theory one would have to distinguish between performance and function. Performance is what one system provides to another, e.g. law provides a legal structure for corporations, which facilitates the identification of corporations as actors within the economy. Functions operate at the level of society itself—the encompassing system for all other social subsystems, interactions, and institutions. There is relevant discussion of this in n.13 in this chapter.

[37] For examples of how easily systems theory's observations on society can be misunderstood, see M. King, 'The Construction and Demolition of the Luhmann Heresy' in Jiri Priban and David Nelken (eds), *Law's New Boundaries: the consequences of legal autopoiesis* (Aldershot: Ashgate, 2001), 123. However, the expression of the legal code as law/not law might not be a misconception. Consider Ziegert's expression of this which appropriately distinguishes an external and internal representation of the legal code: 'Generally, when looking from outside in, this puts the focus on *system boundaries* and specifically the boundaries of the legal system. When looking from inside out this is the question as to what constitutes *the unity of legal operations*. Legal operations can refer to ('interpret') the operations in other social systems. But they do not have a key to operate the operations of other functional systems. Therefore, references are typically to the operations of the referring system, here the legal system, and not of the referenced system—such as reading reports, interpreting decisions, establishing facts. The communication that drives *all* legal operations, and thus forms the boundary of their unity, is the 'quaestio juris'—what is law and legal and what is not? This is *the binary distinction* between law and non-law and its encryption as the code for all legal operations. In this way, all communications that relate to legal communication carry the 'law DNA' and can be distinguished from all other, non-law operations. It is, then, the function of the binary code to guide the selection and confirmation of those norms in society, which are deemed to be legal norms and which can be expected to prevail over non-legal norms' (K.A. Ziegert, 'Systems Theory and Qualitative Socio-Legal Research' in Reza Banakar and Max Travers (eds), *Theory and Method in Socio-Legal Research* (Oxford: Hart Publishing, 2005), 60–1).

3. Back to systems theory

Gunther Teubner's suggestion that systems theory could be used to observe legal pluralism is not a version of conventionalism, in which we seek to identify a system that is establishing itself through the use of particular terms: legal/illegal. This is because we are not looking for a particular semantic. We can see this more clearly if we move our focus from the system with which we, as legal academics, are most familiar, the legal system, to consider the codes utilized by other systems. The claim that the code of law is legal/illegal is persuasive because, at least in the English-speaking world, these words are frequently used in the operations of the legal system. But one needs to understand how codes, as a theory of society, operate in each social subsystem, not just the legal system. And this may in turn increase our understanding of the nature of the legal code.

If we consider the mass media, the code identified by Luhmann is information/not information, a code which unifies the mass media as a system which includes advertising, news, and entertainment.[38] But if one contemplated what words represent this distinction within daily newspapers it might be 'news/not news' or 'story/no story', in that one can imagine the rejection of a submitted article in terms of the statement 'This is not news' and a journalist arriving at a location asking: 'What is the story here?' One can apply a similar analysis to the manner in which scientific communications link together. The claim that science codes in terms of true/not true (false) makes sense as a description of a code which links scientific communications together, and makes them a system and not a random set of communications which have no relationship to each other, without the participants having to use the words true, or false, within their communications. Similarly, one can understand that the medical system is not identical with the science system, and that the positive/negative coding that makes possible the connection of medical communications, and thus (since connection is what generates meaning) makes them meaningful, is itself understandable as therapeutic/non-therapeutic without these words being applied on each occasion when the medical system uses communications that apply negative or positive values. Thus attempts to articulate these codes can only partially be explained by conventionalism, if conventionalism is based on the semantics of the participants. Teubner refers to the implicit or explicit invocation of the legal code. Codes can be 'implicit' because they are abstractions. If one had regard only to the 'news' industry, and sought the code that linked all 'news' items, one might describe it as 'news/not news'. But 'the news' is only part of the mass media. If one sought to describe and identify the 'implicit' code that allows communications to connect from advertising, news, and entertainment it would not be 'news/not news' but 'information/not information'. Thus, to return to law, the fact that the conviction of a defendant makes that person's continued detention legal is not a statement that any person needs to make at the time of the conviction, or thereafter. Similarly, within the economy, redeeming a mortgage creates the conditions for further transactions; no one has to utter the word 'payment'.

The issue is whether one can, first, identify the codes through which communications can be interconnected and then generate system-specific meanings. A person undertaking such an exercise is looking for a way of describing how a particular system applies a negative or positive value throughout all of its operations. One might do this in the English-speaking world, using the codes payment/non-payment, legal/

---

[38] Discussed in Luhmann, *The Reality of the Mass Media* (cited in n.15).

illegal, true/not true, information/not information, government/opposition, etc. One does this accepting that a modern society has an economy, law, science, mass media, political system, etc., and that these are in some way differentiated from each other. Looking for codes, and applying the distinction programme/code, is systems theory's answer or methodology for seeking to identify and describe this process of differentiation, and the nature of the relationships that are possible between these different parts of society.

With this understanding of codes one does not simply go to translators and ask them what word they might substitute for 'legal', 'information', 'true', etc. One starts, with systems theory, seeking to identify how law, mass media, science, religion, politics, or economy, etc. are differentiated and interrelate within a national territory, in a region, or globally. The fact that the observed local participants do not speak English would not prevent a person who undertook this exercise and sought to describe it to an English-speaking audience from using English versions of the codes. A person who did this and sought to describe the results to a non-English-speaking audience might choose words from that audience's language to describe the different codes which make it possible for an economy to be separate from a political system, etc. The actual language used by the participants observed when coding these systems is not necessary to the presentation of differentiation. Systems theory starts with the observation that the differentiation of law, economy, politics, mass media, religion, etc., is a feature of modern society (and that includes just about all societies), and then it seeks to identify how that differentiation operates, and translate the results. Michael King offers a useful example of how this process occurs in practice:

A family in a remote village in Botswana watching the O.J. Simpson trial on a television set understand that what they are seeing is law and that this makes it different in nature to health, religion, politics or any other kind of communicative event.... one does not need to go back very far to arrive at a time when the notion of legal as being quite distinct from other meanings would have been incomprehensible.[39]

King's example does not depend on the family speaking English. What will make any discussion of the trial by this family an observation on law and not religion, or even dispute resolution, is their participation in a society in which the differentiation between law, religion, science, etc. is also present.

The codes we are seeking to describe cannot be separated from, or at least need to be understood as part of, the larger theory, which is a theory about the structure of modern society. Systems theory's analysis of law is the application to law of a theory that understands modern society as consisting of functionally differentiated social systems. In searching for the legal code one presumes that society contains differentiated social subsystems, which in turn presume that subsystem functional differentiation has replaced classes and estates (stratification) and tribal membership (segmentation) as society's primary basis for differentiation.[40] Functional differentiation has to be contrasted with non-differentiation. There is little point in looking for the legal code within a society that does not exhibit functional differentiation—a society which does not differentiate the legal, political, economic, religious, and science systems from

---

[39] M. King, 'Comparing Legal Cultures in the Quest for Law's Identity' in David Nelken (ed.), *Comparing Legal Cultures* (Aldershot: Dartmouth, 1997), 123.
[40] For a general explanation of this principal characteristic of modern society, see Luhmann's interview with Eva Knodt, 'Answering the Question: What is Modernity?' in William Rasch, *Niklas Luhmann's Modernity: The Paradoxes of Differentiation* (Stanford: Stanford University Press, 2000), 195.

each other.[41] In describing such a society, using a systems theory analysis, it would be appropriate to say that there was no legal code, legal/illegal, and no legal system. This is because what we are looking for, and seeking to describe, is a legal system in **contradistinction** to an economy, religious system, political system, etc. This is not an arbitrary classification scheme. We seek to describe the legal system, in a modern society, utilizing these other distinctions because these contrasting phenomena actually exist—or at least exist within organized communication networks—one can meaningfully distinguish law from science, politics, religion, etc. because law, in a modern society, manages to distinguish itself from these other phenomena, and vice versa.

If codes presume functionally differentiated social subsystems it is equally correct to say that social subsystems presume codes. The insistence that the code of law, as with any social subsystem, must be binary is not because alternatives are impossible—codes with a third value, or ones which operated like spectrums of colours—but because of the difficulty of joining together all the diverse communications of a subsystem with anything more complex than a binary distinction. Having only two sides to the code allows for an easy move from one side of the code to the other. For example, a state of affairs that has been coded legal, such as a lawful arrest, can be revisited. This might result in the arrest being recoded as illegal, or some part of it being coded illegal (the arrest was lawful, but the amount of force used to achieve it was not). Compare the simplicity of this operation with an attempt to add even one further distinction to a code, such as would occur if one combined legal/illegal with good/bad. Then any coding of a state of affairs would involve four possible states. If one developed programmes to determine what was good from bad which operated independently from those which distinguished legal from illegal, one could manage the complexity, but that would be because two separate codes were being applied, not a combined code with four sides. A genuine four-sided legal code would require programmes which could distinguish the legal good from the illegal good, legal bad, and illegal bad without a separate assessment of legality and morality. Whilst this might be possible in particular situations, would it be possible to develop the ever more refined distinctions between the four states which can occur with a binary code? A binary code allows the crossing over from one side of the code to the other to become ever easier, in the sense that the system can become extremely refined in terms of what can make something legal, rather than illegal. This allows a system to become ever more sensitive to its environment, as it is stimulated to develop its programmes to prevent the switch of coding being arbitrary.[42] The claim for the necessity of a binary code is that this process of ever greater refinement ('technicalization') cannot be achieved with anything like the same

---

[41] Thus modern systems theory has to plead guilty to the charge of 'parochialism' (see, e.g., S. Roberts, 'After Government? On Representing Law without the State' (2005) 68 *Modern Law Review* 1 at 20), in that it principally addresses the forms of law that exist within societies that exhibit functional differentiation. But how much is given away by this concession to parochialism depends on how much of existing societies continue to generate meanings without reference to functional differentiation, i.e. without using communications whose meanings include the understanding that economics, religion, law, science, politics, and the mass media are different entities.

[42] There is a significant difference between considering whether the switching of coding is arbitrary and whether, at its source, it is paradoxical or not based on a plausible foundation. Systems theory adopts the latter explanation and thus accounts for law's binary code of legal/illegal as paradoxical, but not thereby arbitrary. Many of the various issues concerning paradox (including its productive capacity) in law are explored in the essays in Oren Perez and Gunther Teubner (eds), *Paradoxes and Inconsistencies in the Law* (Oxford: Hart Publishing, 2006); see also our review of this book, (2007) 70 *Modern Law Review* 139.

ease, with anything more than a binary code.[43] Luhmann distinguished the meaning of code for linguists from the meaning of code within systems theory, calling the latter 'a special case'. For linguists, codes are symbolic instructions for the encoding of messages, i.e. rules for the proper use of language. With this more complex understanding of codes, the issue for communication becomes whether the sender and receiver of messages are employing the same codes.[44] But whilst codes for linguists determine the appropriate semantics for a particular meaning, codes within systems theory operate without a definite semantic.

The absence of a definite semantic for the code is a consequence of what a code represents: it is a distinction with a positive side and a negative side. The distinction has no inherent meaning.[45] What is legal is simply not illegal, and vice versa. What is true is simply not false, and vice versa. At one level one might say that all social system codes are simply +/– (positive/negative). But to maintain the separation of social systems this positive/negative coding has to be distinguishable, which requires the programmes and codes of subsystems to have a symbiotic relationship to each other. Application of the positive/negative code of the science system is driven forward, but not determined, by the previous history of the application of this code within the science subsystem. As is the positive/negative code of law. And it is secondary observation, or at its most general level self-description, that generates a description of the science code as one of true/not true (false), and the legal code as one of legal/illegal. Thus it is as much the programmes that generate the code, as the code that generates the programmes.

When it comes to identifying whether a society has a legal system, one first observes at a macro level. Is there a system operating that distinguishes what is legal from what is religious, etc.? Here one is operating at a particularly high level of abstraction. One would not look for a code in isolation from the programmes that accompany it. Only by observing the system as a system—as a code being applied by reference to programmes—could one identify what, in English, would be a legal rather than a science system, etc. But once one has identified the presence of such a system, the focus thereafter on coding, rather than programmes, allows one to take account of the contingent nature of programmes compared with codes. The programmes which accompany the application of the legal code differ at the national, regional, international, and transnational levels, and these programmes are always evolving. One must have regard to programmes to identify the presence of functionally differentiated systems—programmes which make it sensible to claim, in English, that this system is applying a legal rather than a moral code, etc. But one should not identify a system with the presence of a particular programme, or group of programmes, whatever the claims made within that system as to their fundamental status.

---

[43] Luhmann, 'The Code of the Moral' (cited in n.22), 998–9.
[44] Luhmann, 'The Code of the Moral' (cited in n.22), 998. For this understanding of codes for linguists, Luhmann refers to Roman Jakobson and Morris Halle, *Fundamentals of Language* (The Hague: Mouton, 1956); they explain: 'If the listener receives a message in a language he knows, he correlates it with the code at hand. This code includes all the distinctive features to be manipulated, all their admissible combinations into bundles of concurrent features termed PHONEMES, and all the rules of concatenating phonemes into SEQUENCES—briefly, all the distinctive vehicles serving primarily to differentiate morphones and whole words' (2nd revised edn, Berlin, 1971, 16).
[45] 'The code values serve as both universal and specific binary schemes that help identify a functions system but are also applicable to the self-referential as well as the extra-referential, the system as well as its environment. Even in this case the unity of the code remains an imagination incapable of operations. The application of the code to itself leads to paradoxes' (N. Luhmann, 'Modernity in Contemporary Society' in Luhmann, *Observations on Modernity* (cited in n.35), 11).

4. Back to legal pluralism

Because system codes are only positive and negative distinctions, the application of these codes can only be stabilized by their structures (programmes) and not determined by them. It is this which allows us to say, with confidence, that the legal system cannot be equated with state law. State law represents a stage in the evolution of the legal system within modern societies, but not its end state. The prevalence and central role played by national legislation within modern legal systems generates a self-description of law, or jurisprudence, which is an abstract and more general representation of these kinds of legal communication: sovereignty, national constitutions, etc. But systems theory does not require us to accept either that the communications generated within the legal system at any moment in its evolution, including those whereby the legal system describes itself to itself as a totality, are essential, or that they determine the future possibilities of what can be coded as positive or negative (legal/illegal) within that system. Any attempt to insist that all law is state law denies the presence of law within pre-modern society, but it also dis-applies this label to the ever-expanding world of transnational legal communications.[46]

How do we know that these transnational communications are legal, and not scientific or medical, or mass media, or economic? One cannot simply look for a particular semantic—legal/illegal—and conclude that we are thereby in the presence of a legal system. One observes them as a system, evolving and developing, through the application of coding—a negative and positive distinction; and thus we ask ourselves: What code is operating here? If we define one of the characteristics of prior programmes as crucial—such as the involvement of a state or a national constitution—we will conclude that they are not. But if we take a broader view, and observe that they are utilizing communications that have previously structured the application of the legal code (legality) and that they are not a continuation of science, mass media, or the economy (that they are not coding true/false, or information/non-information, or payment/non-payment, etc.), then we can conclude that they are continuations of the legal system.

Systems theory provides a sociological understanding of the difficulties of having a common referent, 'law', for both state law in modern societies and non-state law in pre-modern ones. But what of non-state law within a nation state territory?[47] Here there has been an important shift in one of the central assumptions that informed many of the classic case studies in legal pluralism: the tendency to treat the studies' communities, typically villages, as closed societies. It is now accepted that local communities, even in some of the most remote places in the world, are interpenetrated by elements of the

---

[46] As Andreas Fischer-Lescano and Gunther Teubner have aptly demonstrated: see their 'Regime-Collisions: The Vain Search for Legal Unity in the Fragmentation of Global Law' (2004) 25 *Michigan Journal of International Law*, 999. In focusing on transnational legal communications (moving from legal pluralism to legal globalization concerns), by utilizing the methodological approach raised in this chapter, scholars are now exploring other substantial issues, in particular social constitutionalism (see G. Teubner, 'A Constitutional Moment? The Logics of "Hit the Bottom"' in Poul Kjaer, Gunther Teubner and Alberto Febbrajo (eds), *The Financial Crisis in Constitutional Perspective: The Dark Side of Functional Differentiation* (Oxford: Hart Publishing, 2011), 3) and networks (see G. Teubner, '*Coincidentia Oppositorum*: Hybrid Networks Beyond Contract and Organisation' in Marc Amstutz and Gunther Teubner (eds), *Networks: Legal Issues of Multilateral Co-operation* (Oxford: Hart Publishing, 2009), 3).

[47] For an alternative discussion, not informed by systems theory, see William Twining, *General Jurisprudence: Understanding Law from a Global Perspective* (New York: Cambridge University Press, 2009), ch.12 'The significance of non-state law'.

wider societies which surround them.[48] More recent studies acknowledge and explore the manner in which these outside elements, which typically include state laws, impact upon the norms and negotiations of these local communities.[49] This change of assumption informs, for example, Moore's concept of semi-autonomous fields,[50] and Santos's idea of 'interlegality'.[51] But this recognition also diminishes the strength of any argument that a social theory developed in order to explain the nature of modern society has no application to the kinds of societies and case studies that form the subject of much legal pluralism. Participation within a wider modern society requires the members of a local group who may have identified themselves by reference to a common religion or ethnic heritage to engage with social systems. They become patients within the health system, pupils within the education system, voters within the political system, consumers and entrepreneurs within the economy, and litigants or defendants within the legal system. In particular, what pluralists might call religious or customary law becomes only one part of a life that is also experienced through these other systems.

This process has implications for the practice of comparing the strongly held commitments of local communities with the rules and practices of a state legal system. The threat to such local commitments is not limited to how state law might threaten the ability of a particular religious or ethnic group to continue to live according to its own norms. The ability of these particular communities to exist within a modern society, whilst still retaining a strong and widely distributed sense of a customary 'way of life', is premised upon the ability to maintain these features within a wider society that exhibits functional differentiation. The economy, the political system, the science system, the medical system, and the education system all pose problems for this form of social life. And systems theory can orientate our observation of these problems. When studying these communities we do not need to approach them on the basis that only a state legal system can generate legality. In seeking a legal code, we will be looking for a form of law that is a manifestation of functional subsystem differentiation. State law is certainly not the only form of law which systems theory can help us to see clearly, rather systems theory can recognize as 'law' whatever communications link together through the positive/negative code of legal/illegal as it operates locally, nationally, regionally, transnationally, and internationally.

5. Conclusion

In enabling recognition of the plural types and sources of law, and offering a means of their observation and exploration by utilizing a legal code rather than a definite semantic, systems theory engages with the manner in which legal systems, within differentiated societies, distinguish themselves from other social subsystems. It avoids the legal becoming inseparable from the social, not through the use of definitions or conceptions,

---

[48] 'Since the mid-1970's, anthropologists have placed greater emphasis on economic factors, social inequality and forms of domination. Especially in research on brokerage, pluralism and legal change, they have also recognised that the village is not generally an appropriate unit of study' (F. Snyder, 'Law and Anthropology' in P. Thomas (ed.), *Legal Frontiers* (Aldershot: Dartmouth, 1996), 140).

[49] See, e.g., F. von Benda-Beckmann and K. von Benda-Beckmann, 'Changing One Is Changing All: Dynamics In The Adat-Islam-State Triangle' (2006) 53/54 *Journal of Legal Pluralism and Unofficial Law* 239.

[50] Sally Falk Moore, *Law as Process* (London: Routledge & Kegan Paul, 1978), ch.2, 'Law and social change: the semi-autonomous social field as an appropriate subject of study'.

[51] Santos, *Toward a New Legal Common Sense* (cited in n.3), 437.

which can vary between researchers and across societies, but through the observation of the process of coding which links a system's communications. The separation of social subsystems is a feature of modern society; attempts to reduce law to the study of rules, norms, or commitments, whilst they may broaden the scope of what is observed as law, lose the ability to describe law in contradistinction to other social formations.[52] Attempts to account for the distinctions between these different formations in terms of what they do (performance or function) or what values accompany their operations, suffer both from the overlap between systems of whatever is attributed to them, and from the difficulties of explaining examples which contradict these attributions. Systems theory shifts the focus from all of these apparently fundamental and 'necessary' attributes of systems, by recognizing them as programmes which orientate and stabilize but cannot determine the application of a system's code. With this shift of emphasis from programme to code, we have a basis for studying law which does not presume that law can only exist as state law, or that state law provides a paradigmatic example of law to which all non-state forms of law can only approximate.[53] Alongside these benefits, we also have a means to overcome the problems of language and translation. There are no determinative rules for translation, just as there are no determinative rules for the use of language. The codes which allow for the transmission of information through language depend on context, in that successful communication depends on the common de-coding of the context in order to produce a common meaning between the person transmitting and receiving.[54] Thus, in the end, this means that language is both embedded within, and a manifestation of, culture. Translation is an attempt to re-create the meanings of one culture using the language of another. This poses significant problems for the translation of words like 'law', which, within language, provides a symbolic reference to all of the conditional programmes that orientate a particular legal system's application of the legal code, and can include the conditional programmes of other systems that refer to the legal system in the course of applying their codes. By identifying the legal system as a system whose communications link through the application of a common code which is not economic, scientific, religious, or moral, but still manages to produce normative expectations, one identifies a legal system at a level of abstraction that does not rely on a common culture. With this starting point, one can then focus on the actual application of this code, and the programmes which are generated through its secondary observations, and thus describe its operations. This approach may well not satisfy all of those who are motivated to address issues of legal pluralism, but it does offer the possibility of what such motivation has not yet produced—a common theoretical endeavour, not based on a common conception of law, but a sociologically informed understanding.

---

[52] And thereby to fail to study the phenomena associated with legal pluralism through 'the acausal parallel processing of different distinctions' (Teubner, 'Regulatory Law' (cited in n.21), 466) which, as we have argued here, is an appropriate precondition for their adequate linking and potential theorisation.

[53] Of course, much of the criticism of legal theory by legal pluralists is directed at their state-centred focus. However, at the same time, much of the criticism of studies motivated by legal pluralism is also directed at the 'state-centred' character of such research, and the inability of researchers to break from a state-centred orientation (see Griffiths, 'What is Legal Pluralism?' (cited in n.8). Systems theory, with its focus on codes and programmes, offers a different set of criticisms and a different orientation. Rather than focus on what is wrong with 'state-centred approaches', systems theory suggests that the main deficiency which undermines much specific research and its availability for theory building is, as Teubner suggests, approaches that are overly concerned with the linked ideas of 'norm-obedience-deviance-sanction' rather than 'the linguistic diversity in which legal norms are read' (Teubner, 'Regulatory Law' (cited in n.21), 470). What these linked ideas do is detract from an adequate pluralistic understanding.

[54] This idea is discussed further in Luhmann, 'The Code of the Moral' (see n.44).

8
Frame Semantics and the 'Internal Point of View'

*Steven L. Winter**

1. The fundamental problem

The fundamental problem of 'law and language' is what we might characterize as 'the illusion of transparency'. We use language continuously and, except when there is a misunderstanding, are unaware of the complexities that lurk beneath the surface of our comprehension. The illusion of transparency is particularly acute in legal language, both because the stakes are so high and because law is precisely that practice where the ambiguities and uncertainties that arise from language's complexity are constantly tested.

The illusion's power is conspicuous in formalist and textualist approaches to law. An extreme example is the way in which some United States Supreme Court Justices use the dictionary to interpret complex federal statutes. In his plurality opinion in *Rapanos v United States* (2006), Justice Scalia sought to determine the scope of federal regulatory power over wetlands under the Clean Water Act (1972) not by reference to the statute's stated goal of maintaining 'the chemical, physical, and biological integrity of the Nation's waters' (§1251(a)), but rather by reference to the definition of 'waters' found in the version of *Webster's New International Dictionary* published in 1954. Instead of considering whether conditions in the relevant wetlands could affect the Great Lakes system just one mile away, the plurality opinion offered an exegesis of such common hydrological terms as 'streams', 'oceans', 'rivers', 'lakes', 'bodies of water', 'ditches', 'channels', and 'moats'—the latter of obvious concern to a 20th-century statute seeking to prevent water pollution (*Rapanos*, pp. 732–6).

But the fundamental problem of mistaken linguistic transparency afflicts the work of ostensibly more sophisticated legal theorists. This is apparent in H.L.A. Hart's 'core and periphery' distinction, which merely hypostatizes the phenomenon of prototype effects. Thus, Hart (p. 123) claims that 'in the case of everything which we are prepared to call a rule it is possible to distinguish clear central cases'. These 'plain' cases which 'seem to need no interpretation'—that is, where comprehension 'seems unproblematic' or 'automatic'—are, for him, 'just the familiar ones, constantly recurring in similar contexts' (p. 126). Yet, as I have documented elsewhere, the prototype effects that Hart mistakes for the 'plain cases' are the product of complex processes of cognition and categorization—that is, of neural architecture and category structure (Winter, pp. 76–85). The prototypical instances may 'seem' plain, but both the 'core of certainty'

---

* I am grateful to my colleagues Vince Wellman and Tony Dillof for invaluable assistance, criticisms, and suggestions.

and 'penumbra of doubt' are constructed by the same purpose- and context-based cognitive models (Winter, pp. 197–206).

So, too, with Hart's 'internal point of view' and Dworkin's 'internal perspective'—each of which takes a certain discourse as epitomizing what law really 'is'. The 'internal point of view' was first introduced by Hart (pp. 56–57, 88–91) as an analytic precondition for legal rules. The internal aspect of rules is, for Hart, a prerequisite for the intelligibility and semantics of legal statements understood as obligations. It is 'the way in which rules function as rules in the lives of those who... use them as the basis for claims, demands, admissions, criticism, or punishment' (p. 90). The internal point of view thus supports his positivist account of law in terms of socially established rules of recognition (pp. 102–3); but it also serves as the lynchpin of his refutation of sanction- and prediction-based accounts of law (pp. 88–91).[1] Ronald Dworkin (pp. 13–15), in contrast, invokes the 'internal perspective' to sustain his account of law as an interpretive practice centring on substantive moral and political values that derive from but nevertheless stand outside and transcend that practice. For Dworkin, the key to understanding the nature of law is to recognize the 'argumentative character of our legal practice' (p. 14) in which disagreements are not semantic, but theoretical and interpretive ones over the 'rightness' of the principles to be derived from the authoritative legal materials.

One might marvel that the internal point of view thus supports two diametrically opposed accounts of law. The principal flaw of both views is that each invokes an unvarnished, matter-of-fact approach to linguistic behaviour to sustain an otherwise mistaken view of legal practices. For Hart, it is the linguistic behaviour that accompanies the practice of rule following that matters; for Dworkin, it is the linguistic behaviour that comprises legal argument that is exemplary. The common error is that both indulge a one-dimensional understanding of language: it is what the people in each domain *say* that matters, and what they say is taken transparently—that is, as Dworkin says (p. 20), 'at face value'.

If we take J. L. Austin's (1962) distinction between constative and performative utterances together with Jürgen Habermas's (1984) distinction between communicative and strategic action, we could say that Hart and Dworkin both take language as constative and communicative. Yet experience and common sense both tell us that legal language is often performative and highly strategic. One of the salient rituals of the trial courts in the United States, for example, is the exaggerated deference with which the judges are treated. It is not just all the 'Your Honors', etc., but the entire gamut of language and body language and the practically fawning way in which lawyers interact with the judge: 'You're so right, Your Honor. Couldn't have said it better myself', etc. No one seriously thinks that we should take *those* statements at face value; no one thinks that the 'internal perspective' of the practice of law is one in which lawyers actually feel that way about the judges before whom they appear.

Once one understands the complex ways in which language works, it is absurd to think that one could take a one-dimensional view of *any* aspect of legal discourse and infer from that an entire theory of law. The result is likely to be much like the fable of the five blind men and the elephant in which each grabs a different part of the animal and proclaims that an elephant is like a pillar, a rope, a tree branch, a hand fan, and a wall, respectively. To make sense of the phenomenon of law, one must bring to bear sophisticated understandings of language, meaning, history, and culture. This paper focuses on the first two of those concerns. It uses the frame semantics of Charles Fillmore

---

[1] As Shapiro (pp. 1168–70) explains, the internal point of view also serves to naturalize rule following to human behaviour without any assumptions of metaphysical validity.

and the more recent work of Gilles Fauconnier and Mark Turner on conceptual blending to illuminate the complexities and sophistication of the cognitive mechanisms that simultaneously explain and transcend the 'internal point of view'. The upshot is an understanding of law that goes beyond the sterile positivist/natural law debate to reveal the richly human nature of legal practice.

2. A matter of mind, not words

The one-dimensional view of language parallels (or, perhaps, merely duplicates) the fundamental and conventional tendency to hypostatize and fetishize meaning—that is, to assume that meaning is 'in' the words we use and, then, to endow those words with causal efficacy. But meaning is not 'in' the words; meaning is in the mind. Words are at best tokens or stimuli that activate the mental processes that constitute and create meaning.

Consider what happens when, as a member of the audience, you watch a speaker pause in his or her delivery, pick up a cup of water, and bring it to his or her lips. Your visual cortices respond to the colour, shape, and position of the cup. The mirror neurons in your arm fire to simulate the movement of the speaker's hand and arm, though at a level below that needed to stimulate your muscles to action.[2] Your somatosensory cortices use these kinesthetic sensations to register the shape the hand assumes as it grasps the cup and the movement of the hand and arm as they bring the cup to the lips. All these neural, perceptual, and mental processes will be integrated and appear in consciousness as a unitary and 'simple' perception: 'The speaker just took a sip of water.' But the underlying processes are both complex and distributed across anatomically different portions of the neural system.

One might object that this account of meaning as embodied in an individual's neural system elides the important modern insight that meaning is a social phenomenon—that is, that meaning is something that can occur only within a linguistic community. This modern insight is thoroughly, though not entirely correct. For, on the one hand, the brain is a highly social organ. But, on the other, even a purely social meaning must still be processed by and instantiated in the axons, dendrites, mirror neurons, topological mappings, and re-entrant pathways of actual human brains. We might say, more precisely, that meaning lies in patterns of neural firings and these patterns of neural firings are themselves largely forged in social experiences and interactions.

The social dimension of these mental processes of meaning-making is nicely captured by Charles Fillmore's concept of frame semantics. Without going into the neural architecture, we can say that the basic idea is that words are understood only in terms of meaningful experiential gestalts. For example, the words 'buy', 'sell', 'cost', 'goods', 'advertise', 'credit', etc. make sense only in terms of a frame (also referred to as a script, schema, or cognitive model) of a commercial transaction that relates them together as a meaningful, social activity. Any one of these words activates the entire network of buyer, seller, goods, medium of exchange, etc. As Fillmore (1982a, p. 112) says 'words represent categorizations of experience, and each of these categories is underlain by a motivating situation occurring against a background of knowledge and experience'.

---

[2] 'In the real world,... neither the monkey nor the human can observe someone else picking up the apple without also invoking in the brain the motor plans necessary to snatch that apple themselves (mirror neuron activation). Likewise, neither the monkey nor the human can even look at an apple without also invoking the motor plans necessary to grab it (canonical neuron activation)' (Iacobini, p. 14).

Frames not only explain how we understand and communicate but, as noted earlier, also constitute what we experience as both the 'core' and 'periphery' of any word category. Take the concept 'bachelor'. Because he takes for granted that concepts can be specified in necessary and sufficient conditions, Dworkin (p. 72) observes that 'bachelorhood holds of unmarried men'. But natural language does not, in fact, observe this all-or-nothing rule. Rather, it displays unmistakable prototype effects: George Clooney is clearly a bachelor. But is the Pope? On the one hand, the Pope is unmarried; on the other, the Pope—having taken a vow of celibacy—is not *supposed* to get married. These intuitions are expressed by the following statements, either of which would be deemed correct by an ordinary English speaker.

(1) '*Technically*, the Pope is a bachelor.'
(2) 'The Pope may not be married, but he isn't *really* a bachelor.'

In the first statement, 'technically' signals that we are speaking not with respect to the conventional conception of 'bachelor' but, instead, in some specialized domain—in this case the domain of formalized meaning or analytic philosophy. In the second statement, 'really' signals that the Pope stands outside the social expectations regarding marriage and sexuality that characterize the conventional conception of 'bachelor'.[3] As Fillmore (1982b, p. 34) explains, the category 'bachelor' makes sense 'only in the context of a human society in which certain expectations about marriage and marriageable age obtain'.

Note, moreover, that meaning is a matter of the framing and not the specific words used. Thus, one can flip the expressions in a way that reverses the meaning of 'technically' but preserves the point about framing. Suppose a friend is organizing a dinner party and she asks me if I could bring along an unmarried male friend to balance out the table. Recognizing her intention, I say, 'I could bring Father Mike, but he's not technically a bachelor'. Here, 'technically' signals—but no better than 'really' or 'strictly speaking'—that, though unmarried, Father Mike is not 'an unmarried friend' with respect to the *dinner-party* frame. Yet another alternative would be the statement 'The Pope is technically *not* a bachelor'.[4] In this example, the hedge signals that, with respect to the alternative frame of Catholic doctrine, the Pope is not a bachelor because he is married to the Church.

Even so, frames underspecify meaning. To function as categorizations of experience, the frame's constituent elements must be relatively abstract. Fauconnier and Turner (pp. 25–6) give the example of a child on a beach playing in the sand with a shovel. One might ask, variously: 'Is the shovel safe?', 'Is the child safe?', 'Is the beach safe?' Each of these questions inquires after the safety of the child. But there is no fixed, one-dimensional property that the term 'safe' assigns or applies to the shovel, the child, and the beach. Each question inquires into a different potential danger. The first question asks whether the child might be harmed by the shovel, the second whether the child requires supervision, and the third whether the beach is one marked by sudden, dramatic tides. In all of these statements, the word 'safe' prompts the addressee to invoke a *danger* frame with abstract roles and relations such as agent, instrument, patient, and consequent harm. But in each case, the addressee fills out those abstract elements with different contextual components.

---

[3] Lakoff (pp. 122–4) identifies several other hedges such as 'strictly speaking', 'loosely speaking', and 'regular' that similarly signal shifts in framing.
[4] This example was suggested to me by Gary Watts.

In the context of the first question, the sharp edge of the shovel is the agent or instrument capable of inflicting harm on the child (the patient) by cutting him or her. Even this could be reversed, however, in a different context. Suppose I own an archaeological relic similar to the Bethsaida incense shovel (a 1st-century, 8-inch bronze shovel discovered in 1996 on the site of an ancient Roman temple). My nephew has found it and I turn to my brother and ask, 'Is the shovel safe?' In this case, the *danger* frame is exactly the same. But it is the child who is the potential agent of harm and the fragile, antique shovel that is the patient at risk of injury. In this scenario, we see once again that the meaning is not in the words. Rather, meaning can only be in the minds of interpreters who understand those words in light of mental frames activated in particular contexts.

A significant part of human communication involves the telegraphing of frames so that the audience is able to reconstruct the speaker's intended meaning. Consider the text of the Second Amendment to the US Constitution, which provides: 'A well regulated Militia, being necessary to the security of a free State, the right of the people to keep and bear Arms, shall not be infringed.'[5] In *District of Columbia v Heller* (2008), Justice Scalia (pp. 577–8) first parsed the amendment into an 'operative clause' (prohibiting the infringement of 'the right of the people to keep and bear Arms') and a prefatory clause (asserting that a well-regulated militia is 'necessary to the security of a free State'); read the operative clause to refer to the right to own and carry firearms for the purpose of self-defence; and, then, concluded that—because 'a prefatory clause does not limit or expand the scope of the operative clause'—the court need only check 'the prefatory clause to ensure that our reading of the operative clause is consistent with the announced purpose'. The intended result, of course, was to disassociate the former from the latter in order to extend the right to bear arms beyond the historical context of citizen-manned militias to the modern context of private gun ownership in the home.

This convoluted rhetorical strategy depends both on the illusion of transparency (that 'the right to bear arms' has a literal meaning of 'carry weapons' and not a technical meaning of 'serving in the armed forces') and on a studied ignorance of modern semantics.[6] To see the latter point, suppose I said to you, 'We're having some people over tonight and we would appreciate if you could bring an extra chair'. You have a rocking chair, a beanbag chair, and a particularly decrepit-looking, but still functional folding chair. Which do you bring? The answer is that you do not know; it depends on the purpose of the gathering. If we are hosting a dinner party, the rocking and beanbag chairs will not do. But, if we are having a discussion group such as a book club, you would definitely choose the rocking or beanbag chair over the folding chair. Suppose, instead, that I said to you, 'A comfortable audience being necessary to success of a good book club, please bring a chair tonight'. In that event, awkward syntax aside, you would know precisely what kind of chair to bring because the prefatory clause had told you exactly which frame to invoke. In other words, the meaning of a clause such as 'the right to keep and bear arms'

---

[5] As Pocock (p. 528) notes, 'the Second Amendment to the Constitution, apparently drafted to reassure men's minds against the fact that the federal government would maintain something in the nature of a professional army, affirms the relation between a popular militia and popular freedom in language directly descended from that of Machiavelli'.

[6] Thus, Scalia (*Heller*, p. 584) observed not only that 'At the time of the founding, as now, to "bear" meant to "carry"', but also that this is its 'natural meaning'. Of course, the opinion did go on to discuss the historical background of the provision. But its tendentious account of the history is built on the platform of its belligerent literalism: 'A purposive qualifying phrase that contradicts the word or phrase it modifies is unknown this side of the looking glass (except, apparently, in some courses on Linguistics)' (p. 589). A frame semantics approach, in contrast, brings the language and the history together in a way that confirms the historical evidence detailed by the dissent (pp. 652–70).

is not a transparent, context-independent statement deducible from the bare words of the text. The words alone do not tell us what kinds of guns for what kinds of purposes under what kinds of conditions are meant to be included. Rather, the meaning of the clause is frame-dependent and can be inferred only through a more complex process of imaginative reconstruction (albeit one that, here, is telegraphed by the opening clause of the constitutional provision).

So far, we have considered only relatively simple statements understood in light of a single frame that provides the semantics of a given speech act. Human reasoning, however, encompasses the sophisticated manipulation of several frames simultaneously. Fauconnier and Turner (p. 18) call this process 'conceptual blending'. They illustrate the process with two particularly interesting examples: the riddle of the Buddhist monk and the disturbing cultural phenomenon of the 'image club' (pp. 27–50).

The riddle of the Buddhist monk. A Buddhist monk decides to hike up the mountain to meditate. There is a single trail up the mountain. He sets out at dawn and reaches the summit at sunset. After a night's rest, he meditates for three days. At dawn on the next day, he hikes back down the mountain arriving home at sunset. Without making any assumptions about the monk's speed on either trip—indeed, one can assume that he travels at different rates in each direction (for example, taking more breaks to admire the scenery on the way down)—is there any place along the trail at which he will be at exactly the same point at exactly the same time of day on each trip?

This riddle cannot be solved with the sort of algebraic equation one once used at school. We do not know his rate of ascent or descent and, so, cannot calculate distance-divided-by-speed for each trip to work out the precise point of intersection. Nevertheless, the answer to the riddle is an obvious 'yes'. We can demonstrate this with a simple mental exercise. Picture the monk making both trips on the same day. At some point along the trail, the ascending monk will necessarily encounter the descending monk. That is the point at which he is at exactly the same point at exactly the same time of day on each trip.

The proof depends on a counterfactual. The monk cannot actually ascend and descend the mountain at the same time, so he cannot in real-life 'meet himself'. Yet, it is a counterfactual that we have no problem imagining. In one mental space or frame, we can see the monk hiking up the mountain. In a second mental space, we can picture him walking down the same mountain. We can (without even thinking about it) map the two mental spaces onto each other such that we can see the monk hiking in both directions at the same time and 'meeting himself'. (One can conceive of this as a 'third' mental space binding together the ascending and descending frames. Presumedly, what is occurring in the brain is that the ascending and descending frames are being coordinated via dynamic topographic mappings across the two mental spaces. But not much turns on whether the particular neural mechanisms of integration are topographic mappings, neural bindings, or some other as-yet unspecified neurochemical process of integration.)

This imaginative capacity to simultaneously 'run' two frames in a conceptual blend is a common and familiar experience. We use it in everyday counterfactual statements of the type 'If I were you, I wouldn't wear the double-breasted suit'. Of course, I am not you (and double-breasted jackets actually suit me). In a conceptual blending of this sort, the speaker is projecting himself into an alternate mental frame in which he takes the place of the addressee, assumes the addressee's circumstances and physical attributes, but retains his own sense of taste. Logically impossible, of course. But we do it all the time.

The image club. When the *New York Times* columnist Nicholas Kristof (1997) was in the *Times* Tokyo bureau in the 1990s, he filed a troubling report on the growing Japanese obsession with schoolgirls as sexual objects. Part of that trend included a proliferation of 'image clubs'—brothels with specialized rooms designed to cater to the clients' sexual fantasies about schoolgirls. The rooms included a fully equipped classroom, a changing room of a school gym, and a room designed to duplicate a commuter train carriage—complete with a roaring sound track—in which men could molest straphangers dressed in school uniforms. For $150 an hour, for example, a Japanese man could play 'teacher' and act out his sexual fantasy with a youthful-looking, adult prostitute dressed up as a schoolgirl.

Fauconnier and Turner explore the predictable, but nonetheless fascinating construction of meaning in this scenario. 'Why', they ask (p. 28), 'should this make-believe have any power or attraction at all?' The customer undeniably knows that, however skilful her acting, the prostitute isn't really a schoolgirl. In order to maintain the erotic charge that he seeks, the 'John' (in US slang) or 'punter' must inhabit multiple mental spaces simultaneously. In one frame, he is an ordinary customer engaged in a sordid commercial transaction with a professional sex worker. In a second mental frame, he is an adult man with a fantasy that centres on an unattainable, innocent teenage girl. In a third mental space—the 'blend'—he is a teacher having sex with that unattainable schoolgirl. In order to work, the blend requires systematic, but selective mappings from the other mental spaces: The high-school student is projected from the fantasy frame into the blend, 'while the actual sex act...is imported from the material reality linked to the mental space with the prostitute' (Fauconnier and Turner, p. 29). The result is that the blend retains the erotic charge carried over from the fantasy mental space (notwithstanding the emotional neutrality of the *commercial transaction* frame that is also a part of the blend). At the same time, the process of projection selectively leaves out those elements of the fantasy frame that would interfere with the desired result. Thus, although the 'teacher' is also a projection from the fantasy frame, it carries over none of the structure of that role: as Fauconnier and Turner (p. 29) wryly note, 'The customer is not supposed to demand that the prostitute learn how to factor polynomials.'

We are now nearly in position to see why the concept of the 'internal point of view' is too one-dimensional to be of much use in understanding law. Consider Hart's paradigmatic expressions of the internal and external points of view: 'It is the law that X' is the quintessential idiom of the internal point of view, while 'In England, they recognize as law whatever the Queen in Parliament enacts' is the archetypal expression of the external perspective. But what would Hart make of the statement that 'In England, *it is the law that* X'? Perhaps he would take it as a poorly framed articulation of the external point of view. Perhaps he would consider it a misstatement that confuses two mutually exclusive points of view. Thus, Hart (p. 90) insists that, 'What the external point of view cannot reproduce...is the way in which the rules function as rules in the lives of those who normally are the majority of society.... For them the violation of a rule is not merely the basis for a prediction that a hostile reaction will follow but a *reason* for hostility.'

We, however, can recognize this sentence as representing a blend that comfortably combines two analytically inconsistent points of view. The purpose of the blend is, precisely, to convey the insider's sense of the obligatory quality of the rule (that is, as a reason for claims, demands, or condemnation)—but as observed from the external point of view. Consider how this blend works.

First, unlike the Buddhist monk who cannot walk up and down the mountain at the same time, a person 'running' the blend *can* take the internal and external perspective simultaneously. It is not just a matter of being able to go back and forth between the two points of view. Rather, the blend expresses the observer's understanding that for those who live by it the rule has a normative quality that one violates at one's peril ('If I were you, I wouldn't go to court without my powdered wig').[7]

Secondly, just as the blend helps us solve the puzzle of the Buddhist monk case, this legal blend has functional value in matters of practical reason. As a tourist, I am quite aware that in the United Kingdom, it is the rule that one drives on the left side of the road. It seems strange to me as an outsider; I noticed while walking along the Thames on a Sunday afternoon that, though the English drive on the left, they mostly walk on the right. Nevertheless, when I pick up my hire car I will need to observe the rule as if I were an insider. I may do so primarily for safety's sake or simply as a Holmesian 'bad man' (Holmes, p. 459). But, even when the road is clear and no police are nearby, I am not going to drive on the right in the same way that I would not at home go through a red light at 4 a.m. In much the same way, an advocate or a lower-court judge deciding a case may invoke a precedent even though she believes that precedent to be profoundly wrong in some way (say, unconstitutional or in plain conflict with a governing statute). Thus, one can argue that 'in this jurisdiction, it is the rule that X'—expressing a dual understanding in which the rule is obligatory but not necessarily one that the speaker approves of, thinks correct, or would follow anywhere else.

Thirdly, just as in the case of the 'image club' where the blend imbues an otherwise sordid commercial interaction with sexually charged meaning, an external/internal blend of this sort conveys the intensity of the normative imperative. When, for example, the judge says, 'In this jurisdiction, it is the rule that X,' she is conveying that—though you may not like or accept it—here the rule is sacrosanct. Thus, an observer would say that 'In the Episcopal Church, they have a rule that men must remove their hats'. But if one of my colleagues were about to attend his first Orthodox Jewish bar mitzvah, I would tell him, 'In synagogue, it is the rule that men must cover their heads at all times'. My point would be that, however much he may think himself outside the rule, in synagogue he *will* be expected to wear a skullcap and that the people there will make sure he knows there are no exceptions.

3. Six frames for law

We can now consider the complexities that the internal perspective—like the five blind men who mistake the nature of the elephant—so conspicuously obscures. We can describe at least six different semantic frames that characterize our conventional understanding of 'law'. Each of these frames is always available to legal actors as they negotiate or participate in the system, and each of these frames can be blended with the others in

---

[7] It was a sport among senior civil rights lawyers in the early 1960s that, when a new Justice Department lawyer went down to Alabama to appear before the great Frank Johnson, they would not tell him that the judge had a rule in his courtroom that lawyers had to wear a white shirt. These young lawyers would eagerly appear before the great man wearing their conservative, Brooks Brothers suits with their blue, button-down Oxford shirts. Judge Johnson would excoriate them—'How dare you appear in this court not properly dressed!'—and send them to the local haberdasher on Main Street to 'come back in one hour properly attired.'

What the veterans should have told the new lawyers was: 'In Judge Johnson's court, it is the rule that you must wear a white shirt'. Consider the extra information that this formulation conveys. If I told you just that 'In Frank Johnson's court, there is a rule that you must wear a white shirt' you would as a pragmatic Holmesian actor comply with this idiosyncratic rule. But, if I warn you in the language of the blend, you would know something more: that for Frank Johnson, this rule has an emotional, normative dimension above and beyond what one would expect of ordinary rules about courtroom decorum—i.e., that he will take it as both a personal affront and a moral failing of some sort. You would still choose the white shirt—and might do so for purely pragmatic reasons—but, if you were contemplating an outlandish tie or an odd footwear choice in addition, you would probably reassess your entire wardrobe choice to make sure you did not spark his ire.

various ways. These frames, moreover, are evident both in ordinary language and in more sophisticated academic treatments of law. They are:

1) *Law as authority.* The first and, in many ways, most basic frame is an authoritarian one in which 'law' is the command of a sovereign backed up by some sort of social sanction. The prototype is criminal law. In jurisprudence, it is John Austin's (2000) command theory of law. The *law-as-authority* frame, however, is commonly held not just by lay people, but also by sophisticated professionals. In the 1980s, I attended a conference on prison reform litigation. One of the panellists was a well-respected appellate judge on a federal court of appeals. When pressed why, given his comments, his rulings were not more sympathetic to prisoner cases, he replied, 'I might be, but I feel the hot breath of the Supreme Court on the back of my neck'.

2) *Law as social obligation.* The second frame need not detain us because it is the familiar positivistic concept of law elucidated by Hart. It is what we employ whenever we invoke a rule (whether legal, institutional, or bureaucratic) as the ground for an action or demand—e.g., 'I am sorry I cannot fulfil your request, but it is prohibited by the rules'.

3) *Law as moral imperative.* This third, normative frame conceives of law in moral terms such as justice and fairness. It is reflected in the natural law tradition. In its more sophisticated jurisprudential form, it is Dworkin's conception of law as an interpretive practice of argument over the meaning of values (concepts) and what they require in particular circumstances (conceptions). But it is also the frame of every litigant who argues 'It's only fair, Your Honor'.[8]

4) *Law as social mechanism.* This fourth frame is instrumentalist. It understands law as a device of conscious social management to achieve particular societal goals or values. In its prototypical form, it assumes there is a direct, linear relation between legal demand and social response. This frame is what is invoked by the popular view that we should 'get tough on crime'. In its sophisticated form, this is the view of Holmes and the Legal Realists. It is also the dominant view of late modernity—in which law is seen as an autonomous set of practices that functions 'as instrument or strategy within a field of social power'—that Constable critiques under the rubric of 'sociolegal positivism' (pp. 10–11).

5) *Law as strategic tool.* In this frame, law is merely a tool to accomplish particular concrete ends or realize certain values—whether the client's, the advocate's, or judicial ideologue's. It is close to the view of the Holmesian 'bad man, who cares only for the material consequences which such knowledge enables him to predict' (Holmes, p. 459). It is reflected in the popular—and quite sensible—view that, when one is in trouble, one wants a lawyer who knows how to 'work the system'. It is, ironically, also the popular view of the law as corrupt and of lawyers as 'liars' or 'manipulators' of the system. It is, too, the cynical view that sees law as nothing more than the manipulation of the powerful.

6) *Law as social identity.* This last frame conceives of law in cultural terms—though it can also be characterized as historical, anthropological, or sociological—as that which constitutes the group. In legal theory, this view is most closely associated with James Boyd White's (1986) account of law as an ongoing social and literary practice of common constitution and coordination.

---

[8] The first three frames share a common metaphorical structure of a projected 'other' to whom one owes obedience (Winter, pp. 333–40).

Each of these different frames can be viewed from a participant's (internal) or observer's (external) perspective. Consider two of the more counter-intuitive variants. While the second, *law-as-social-obligation* frame is synonymous with Hart's 'internal point of view', Hart's legal theory is itself an external, theoretical description or account of what law 'is'. Conversely, while the sixth, *law-as-social-identity* frame seems inherently descriptive and 'external', it can be held 'internally' by participants even if they do not themselves accept the law as obligatory. The internal aspect of law-as-social-identity is generally true of common law systems, which take the 'rule of law' value as constitutive of who they are. (Although in the context of the so-called 'War on Terror', this sense of ourselves seems to have been substantially undermined.) The more dramatic examples are the cases of the professional baseball players Hank Greenberg in the 1934 American League pennant race and Sandy Koufax in the 1965 World Series, who refused to play on the High Holy Days—not because they were themselves observant, but rather because each felt simply that it was not something he could do 'as a Jew'.

The distinction between the internal and external points of view fails to capture the rich semantics of our orientations to 'law'. It is not that Hart's account of the internal point of view is wrong; on the contrary, it perfectly encapsulates the second, *law-as-obligation* frame. But it is—as suggested at the outset—hopelessly partial, missing the breadth of our attitudes and behaviour toward law. (Or, to put it more pointedly, it fails to provide a truly *general* theory of law.) Few people take the internal point of view all of the time about every law: some laws we internalize as obligatory; others we hold more firmly as constitutive of who we are. Some laws—the right to due process, free speech, or equal treatment—we view as moral imperatives. Some we merely tolerate; others we condemn as intolerable. We orient ourselves to some laws, such as the speed limit, as a proverbial Holmesian 'bad man'. Still others—say, the drug laws in my country—many people honour consistently only in the breach.

True, for Hart (pp. 114–16) it does not matter if lay people take any or all of these attitudes toward law as long as they generally obey it. But Hart's account is nonetheless incomplete in two significant ways. With respect to lay people, he recognizes only obedience (frame 1) and fear of consequences (frame 5) as reasons for compliance (p. 114). With respect to officials, he recognizes *only* the internal point of view accepting the rules as standards for official action—insisting that it is a necessary condition that must be satisfied (pp. 116–17) by officials. Yet, as we have seen (and shall explore further in a moment), lawyers and judges routinely operate in terms of each of the frames that characterize our conventional understanding of 'law'.

Thus, an argument such as Dworkin's that attempts to discover the nature of law on the basis of a one-dimensional, face-value approach to how lawyers and judges talk about it is bound to be—in Dworkin's own words—'impoverished and defective' (p. 14). Consider the very limited role that Dworkin accords historical argument. It is sometimes essential, he says, for the participant's point of view to take in the external, historical point of view—as when a question of the meaning of the US Constitution turns on the intent of the Framers (pp. 13–14). Now imagine an advocate (or, for that matter, a judge) who thinks she has a good historical theory of the causal relation between social circumstances and the substantive content of the law (Llewellyn 1934). Does anyone think she would fail to use it in crafting a persuasive argument? When she does so, does she cease to act from the internal perspective as a participant? Is she acting in 'bad faith', or in any way failing to make the law 'the best that it can be'? Dworkin's understanding of the role of history is as narrowly one-dimensional (and rigidly propositional) as the rest of his theoretical tool kit.

Just as the six frames offer a broader account of our attitudes and behaviour as subjects of law, they also provide a more extensive set of tools with which to unpack judicial behaviour. Imagine the case of a judge imposing 'rule of law' values on an Administration engaged in extra-legal detention of suspected terrorists. She can decide to do so for any (or all) of the reasons suggested above. She can do so because she believes the precedents command it or the social compact requires it. She can do so because she thinks the Administration's policy does not accord with the principle of equal dignity and respect for all persons. She can do so because she is convinced that it is bad social policy. Or she can do so because she thinks it violates the 'rule of law' values that make us who we are. Once she has reached her decision, she can justify it in terms of any (or all) of the frames considered above. Indeed, a persuasive judicial opinion will often invoke multiple frames in support of the outcome because doing so conveys the impression that the result is not just objective, but over-determined.

More importantly, the judge can decide the case for any of these reasons and justify her decision in terms of any of the other frames. We needn't work through all the permutations. But consider one of the more extreme possibilities. Suppose the judge is a member of the opposition party and decides the case in order to embarrass the Administration before the next election. She would never say so, of course, but might instead justify the decision by reference to the requirement of the rule of law or as making the law 'the best it can be' in light of our commitment to the principle of equal dignity and respect for all persons.

Much the same is true for forensic argument more generally. When the lawyer says 'Your Honor, the Court's holding in *Miranda v Arizona* requires that...' we cannot simply take that at face value.[9] The lawyer may mean that he thinks the judge is required—in some sense of duty—to do what *Miranda* says. But it may be that the lawyer is acting strategically just as much as when he fawns over the judge. Perhaps the internal perspective really is not 'Your Honor is bound by precedent to...', but rather 'Smarter, more powerful judges than Your Honor have said that...' or just 'Your Honor risks reversal and embarrassment if...'. In short, the discourse of the judicial system is like the discourse of the 'image club'. The participants are playing a part, and they speak the language of the blend that suits their purpose. Except that, in the actual legal practice of the courtroom, who is the prostitute and who the 'punter' or 'John' is never quite clear.

Dworkin would object that we have no justification for taking judicial opinions at anything less than face value. 'In fact', he says, 'there is no positive evidence of any kind that when lawyers and judges seem to be disagreeing about the law they are really keeping their fingers crossed' (p. 39). He argues, moreover, that such a pretence would never work because it would be easily exposed by the losing side (pp. 37–8).

Perhaps there was no such evidence when Dworkin wrote those words. But his bold claim has since been contradicted by no less than the Supreme Court of the United States. In *Planned Parenthood v Casey* (1992), the plurality opinion offers a paean to decision according to principle. 'Our contemporary understanding is such that a decision without principled justification would be no judicial act at all' (p. 865). But, rather than demonstrating that its decision is 'grounded truly in principle', the plurality explains

---

[9] Dworkin could rightfully object that none of the arguments suggested in the text aptly characterize *our* 'argumentative social practice' (p. 14) because none concerns a substantive moral and political value. The problem, however, is that the arguments in the text reflect the 'face value' arguments that lawyers and judges actually *do* make in such cases. Thus, while *Miranda* refers to the values of human dignity and respect for the inviolability of the individual personality a dozen times, Chief Justice Rehnquist's opinion affirming *Miranda* in *Dickerson v United States* refers to these concerns *not once*.

that it 'must take care to speak and act in ways that allow people to accept its decisions on the terms the Court claims for them'. Thus, the plurality concludes, 'the Court's legitimacy depends on making legally principled decisions under circumstances in which their principled character is sufficiently *plausible* to be accepted by the Nation' (pp. 865–66; emphasis added).

If the plurality so explicitly admits that it has its fingers crossed, one would think that the dissent would surely call them out on it as Dworkin suggested. And Justice Scalia *does* charge that the plurality's 'reasoned judgment' is 'nothing but philosophical predilection and moral intuition' (p. 1000). Yet he reveals in the very next paragraph that he, too, plays the same finger-crossing game. 'As long as this Court thought (and the people thought) that we Justices were doing essentially lawyers' work up here', he laments, 'the public pretty much left us alone'. And what is that lawyers' work according to Justice Scalia? Nothing more than 'reading text and discerning our society's traditional understanding of that text'. 'Texts and traditions', he disingenuously declares, are merely 'facts to study' (p. 1000).

Both sides in the judicial debate over abortion struggle with the recognition that, in the mind of the public, 'law' is synonymous with the objective determination of disputed cases. The two sides disagree only in offering a different sleight-of-hand to distract the public from what is actually going on.[10] For the plurality, it is a claim of 'principle' artfully articulated so as to be sufficiently plausible to be accepted as such. For Justice Scalia, it is the disclaimer that, in reading text and discerning tradition, he engages in no interpretive work whatsoever. Like Sergeant Joe Friday in the 1950s TV series *Dragnet*, it's 'just the facts, ma'am'.

Once we have outgrown the naive illusion of transparency, we can begin to grapple with the elephant in the room. Instead of talking about how language functions in law, we can talk instead about how law functions *as* language. It may enlighten; but it can also deceive. It can persuade; but it may also mislead. With the right framing, a legal proposition can be made to say several different things. The question is not what *language* does, but what *we* do with language.

Twining (p. 116) reports that Llewellyn was fond of saying: 'Doctrine brittle and neat is the tool of tender minds in pursuit of policy that can be embraced without using one's intellect.' Llewellyn, of course, was skewering doctrinal formalists and legal positivists, such as Hart, who think that when the judge is applying the rule's 'core' he or she is somehow avoiding making a judgment of policy. Llewellyn was right; this, indeed, was the point I made earlier about the core and periphery being structured by the same processes. But the converse of Llewellyn's dictum is also true: One can do policy—or normative argument, strategic manipulation, social integration, or any other thing—by speaking doctrine that, because meaning is in the mind, is—like any other bit of language—not brittle and neat but supple and multivalent.

References

Austin, J. L. (1962) *How to Do Things with Words*. Oxford: Clarendon Press.
Austin, John (2000) *The Province of Jurisprudence Determined*. New York: Prometheus Books.
Constable, Marianne (2005) *Just Silences*. Princeton and Oxford: Princeton University Press.
Dworkin, Ronald (1986) *Law's Empire*. Cambridge: Belknap Press.

---

[10] For a comprehensive theory and explanation of the predicament facing the Court in *Casey* that produced this revealing exchange, see Winter (pp. 317–29).

Fauconnier, Gilles, and Turner, Mark (2002) *The Way We Think: Conceptual Blending and the Mind's Hidden Complexities*. New York: Basic Books.
Fillmore, Charles J. (1982a) 'Frame Semantics' in The Linguistic Society of Korea (eds), *Linguistics in the Morning Calm*, pp. 111–37, Seoul: Hanshin, reprinted in (2006) *Cognitive Linguistics: Basic Readings*, Dirk Geeraets (ed.), pp. 393–400. The Hague: Mouton de Gruyter.
Fillmore, Charles J. (1982b) 'Toward a Descriptive Framework for Spatial Deixis' in R. J. Jarvella and W. Klein (eds), *Speech, Place, and Action*, pp. 31–59. London: John Wiley.
Habermas, Jürgen (1984) *The Theory of Communicative Action, Volume I: Reason and the Rationalization of Society*. Boston: Beacon Press.
Hart, H. L. A. (1994) *The Concept of Law*, 2nd edn. Oxford: Oxford University Press.
Holmes, Oliver Wendell Jr. (1897) 'The Path of the Law' 10 Harvard Law Review, pp. 457–78.
Iacoboni, Marco (2008) *Mirroring People: The Science of Empathy and How We Connect with Others*. New York: Farrar, Straus and Giroux.
Kristof, Nicholas D. (1997) 'Tokyo Journal: A Plain School Uniform as the Latest Aphrodisiac', *New York Times*, 2 April 1997, p. A4.
Lakoff, George (1987) *Women, Fire, and Dangerous Things: What Categories Reveal about the Mind*. Chicago: University of Chicago Press.
Llewellyn, Karl N. (1934) 'On Philosophy in American Law' 82 University of Pennsylvania Law Review, pp. 205–12.
Pocock, J. G. A. (1975) *The Machiavellian Moment: Florentine Political Thought and the Atlantic Republican Tradition*. Princeton: Princeton University Press.
Shapiro, Scott (2006) 'What Is the Internal Point of View?' 75 Fordham Law Review, pp. 1157–70.
Twining, William (1973) *Karl Llewellyn and the Realist Movement*. London: Weidenfeld & Nicolson.
White, James Boyd (1986) *When Words Lose Their Meaning: Constitutions and Reconstitutions of Language, Character, and Community*. Chicago: University of Chicago Press.
Winter, Steven L. (2001) *A Clearing in the Forest: Law, Life, and Mind*. Chicago: University of Chicago Press.

Legislation and Cases

US Constitution, Amendment II.
The Clean Water Act, 33 U.S.C. §1251 et seq. (1972).
Dickerson v United States, 530 U.S. 428 (2000).
District of Columbia v Heller, 554 U.S. 570 (2008).
Miranda v Arizona, 384 U.S. 436 (1966).
Planned Parenthood of Southeastern Pennsylvania v Casey, 505 U.S. 833 (1992).
Rapanos v United States, 547 U.S. 715 (2006).

9

Hart as Contextualist? Theories of Interpretation in Language and the Law

Ross Charnock

Legal adjudication clearly involves linguistic interpretation. However, although linguists are frequently consulted on questions of language (and occasionally appear as expert witnesses), they are rarely called upon for advice on the semantics of the law.[1] In jurisprudence, meaning is a matter for the judge, and his objectives do not correspond to those of linguists. Indeed, judges are obliged to resolve a case, by deciding which of two interpretations is correct, and by implication which is mistaken. To this end, they often speak of what they call the 'true and correct' legal meaning. Linguists, on the other hand, see the different possible meanings, not prescriptively as right or wrong, but as data to be explained. They hope to provide a unified description of the various possible meanings and of the relations which may hold between them, as well as a coherent explanation for the apparent variety of linguistic behaviour observed.

Further, the different metalanguages used in the two fields sometimes makes it difficult to see the extent to which the approaches of lawyers and linguists are nevertheless complementary insofar as they are confronted with similar problems. Knowledge of both jurisprudence and philosophy of language is therefore valuable in the search for mutual enlightenment. H. L. A. Hart was the first and the most significant of researchers qualified in both fields.

One of the fundamental problems debated in parallel in the two disciplines is that of the 'alleged priority' of literal interpretation.[2] In the law, there is a clear preference for what is called, vaguely, literal meaning. In general, although judges often see their role as giving effect to the intention of the legislator or of the parties, jurists tend to avoid where possible reliance on the 'slippery' concept of legislative intention,[3] and prefer to rely on what is variously called the ordinary, clear, natural or even 'grammatical' meaning.

In linguistics, the nature of literal meaning is the subject of an ongoing debate opposing the so-called 'literalists' and the 'contextualists'. In outline, although the literalists admit that no observable utterance occurs without a context and that literal, acontextual meaning can be no more than an unobservable theoretical concept, they nevertheless assume the existence of an abstract literal meaning as a necessary starting point for interpretation in context. The contextualists, on the other hand, inspired by Austin's celebrated slogan 'meaning is use', prefer to assume that words take their meaning directly

---

[1] See, however, *Quality Inns v McDonalds* (1988) 695 F.Supp 198 (the *McSleep* case) on whether the McDonalds trademark included exclusive rights to the prefix.

[2] Recanati, François, 'The alleged priority of literal interpretation' (1995) 19(2) *Cognitive Science* 207–32.

[3] *Salomon v Salomon & Co* [1897] AC 22.

from the context, and that 'literal meaning' therefore plays no genuine role in understanding. If this approach is on the right lines, the consequences would be important in legal interpretation.

As both the literalist and the contextualist approaches raise formidable theoretical difficulties, it would be unrealistic to attempt to demonstrate the objective truth or falsity of either theory. Each has its own advantages and disadvantages relative to particular linguistic problems. The more modest contention expressed here is that, in spite of the commonly stated preference for 'true and correct' meanings in the interpretation of statutory expressions, legal practice (as opposed to theory) tends, contrary to expectation, to corroborate the contextualist view. Even though the contextualist approach to semantic interpretation directly contradicts his theory of open texture on many points, Hart is therefore unlikely to have rejected it out of hand.

1. The meaning of general terms

The interpretation of general terms has been considered problematic in the law since at least *Heydon's case*.[4] In the structuralist linguistic tradition, mundane concepts like chairs, for example, are commonly distinguished by elements of contrast and opposition from armchairs or stools, through the presence or absence of backs and arms. Although other semantic models may be presented differently, they usually preserve a reliance on fixed critera. Problems therefore arise whenever it is necessary to (attempt to) predict the features which may or may not be relevant.

Jurists also traditionally assume the existence of jointly sufficient and severally necessary criteria governing the application of terms. Like the structuralists, they continue to define terms by opposition, and speak in this context of definition *per genus et differentiam*. This approach appears well adapted to the law, particularly as regards *eiusdem generis* interpretation. Indeed, as the list of semantic criteria associated with any general term is indefinite, it is usually easy to find one feature which any two general terms have in common. However, because the results obtained are sometimes counter-intuitive, that is not usually the end of the matter. Famously, in *R v Payne*,[5] Pollock CB considered, surprisingly, that a crowbar was included under the words 'mask, dress, or other disguise, or any letter, or any other article or thing'. More recently, in *Flack v Baldry*,[6] Lord Ackner dubiously affirmed, contrary to elementary science, that electricity could be included under the words 'any noxious liquid, gas or other thing' so that the word weapon in the Firearms Act[7] therefore included a 'stun gun'.

In *Donoghue v Stevenson*,[8] Lord Atkin expressly asserted the existence of a feature common to all the various forms of legal negligence.[9] Although this idea seems initially plausible, it is logically mistaken. Because the number of possible semantic features involved in family resemblances is infinite, no member of a family can be expected to

---

[4] *Heydon's case*, 76 ER 637 (1584).
[5] *R v Payne* LR1 CC, 27 (1866).
[6] *Flack v Baldry* [1988] 1 WLR 394.
[7] Firearms Act 1968 s.5(1)(b).
[8] *Donoghue v Stevenson* [1932] AC 562.
[9] *Donoghue v Stevenson* (per Lord Atkin): 'And yet the duty which is common to all cases where liability is established must logically be based upon some element common to the cases where it is found to exist.'

possess them all. It follows that no feature will necessarily be shared by all members. This problem was clearly stated by Wittgenstein:

> Consider for example the proceedings that we call games I mean board-games, card-games, ball-games, Olympic games, and so on.... if you look at them you will not see something that is common to all, but similarities, relationships, and a whole series of them at that.[10]

Wittgenstein described as naive the assumption that different games have in common the disjunction of their common properties. This corresponds well with Lord Macmillan's prescient warning in *Donoghue*,[11] 'The categories of negligence are never closed'.

It is now generally accepted that criterial definitions cannot exhaust the meaning of any given expression. Different expressions referring to identical sets would otherwise be synonymous. In this context, Frege[12] famously affirmed a difference in meaning between the morning star and the evening star even though both expressions are used to refer to the planet Venus. Quine[13] gave the example of a 'creature with a heart' which, although it has the same extension as 'creature with a kidney', cannot be said to have the same meaning. This shows that there must be a fundamental distinction between meaning and reference.

In his account of the difficulties observed in the legal interpretation of ordinary language words, Hart suggested, correctly, that semantic imprecision was a feature of natural language, to be explained in terms of open texture.

> There will indeed be plain cases constantly recurring in similar contexts to which general expressions are clearly applicable (if anything is a vehicle a motor-car is one), but there will also be cases where it is not clear whether they apply or not. (Does 'vehicle' used here include bicycles, airplanes, roller-skates?)[14]

Although he subsequently refers to open texture as an established linguistic theory and as a sufficient explanation for linguistic indeterminacy, the remark itself corresponds merely to the (trite) observation that people may hesitate about the application of terms in particular circumstances, even where they agree on the basic meaning. It would require some generosity to dignify it as a theory of semantics at all, especially as Hart makes little further use of ordinary language analysis.

Although he is largely inspired by Austin's[15] analysis, Hart makes no attempt to take account of all the subtleties of meaning. As a jurist, he is naturally more concerned with extension than with intension. He thus assumes the existence of a generally accepted core meaning, and relegates cases of unclear application to the penumbra of the term. Yet in his celebrated end-notes, he attributes the theory of open texture to Waismann,[16] who had attempted on the contrary to demonstrate that all meaning was indeterminate and provisional. In this way, Hart eludes a debate which is fundamental both in linguistics and in the law. His true sympathies remain unclear.

As presented by Hart, the theory of open texture is reminiscent of the theory of prototypes developed by Rosch[17] some years later in cognitive linguistics.

---

[10] Wittgenstein, Ludwig, *Philosophical Investigations* (Oxford: Blackwell, 1953), §66.
[11] *Donoghue v Stevenson* (cited in n.8).
[12] Frege, Gottlob, *Foundations of Arithmetic* (Oxford: Blackwell and Mott, 1950) (trans. J.L. Austin) [= *Die Grundlagen der Arithmetik* (1884)], 57.
[13] Quine, Willard van, 'Two dogmas of empiricism' (1951) 60 *The Philosophical Review* 20–43.
[14] Hart, H. L. A., *The Concept of Law* (Oxford: Clarendon Press, 1961, 2nd edn, 1994), 126.
[15] Austin, John L., *How to do Things with Words* (Oxford: Oxford University Press, 1962).
[16] Waismann, Frederick, 'Verifiability' in Flew, Anthony (ed.), *Logic and Language* (1st series) (Oxford: Blackwell, 1951), 119–23.
[17] Rosch, Eleanor, 'Prototype classification and logical classification: the two systems', in Scholnick E. (ed.), *New trends in cognitive representation* (Hillsdale, N.J.: Erlbaum, 1983), 111–44.

Hart's open texture and prototype theory in the law

In prototype theory, as originally presented, meaning is given not by definition but by example. This approach has the advantage of allowing for variation at the periphery, in the application of words, whilst preserving the idea of a clear, central meaning. As speakers have shared ideas of best instances, a sparrow, for example, may serve as a prototypical example of a bird, or an apple as a fruit, just as for Hart a car was the best example of vehicle. Conversely, an ostrich would be a more unlikely example of a bird, or an aubergine of a fruit. Ordinary usage predominates, to the extent that it may contradict accepted scientific truths. Thus, in prototype theory, a 'whale' may be considered a peripheral fish or a tomato a particular kind of vegetable.

In his presentation of open texture Hart used the term 'penumbra' to refer to what in prototype theory is called the periphery. In this he followed a tradition found in American jurisprudence (see *Olmstead v US*[18] and *Griswold v Connecticut*, 1965).[19] He thus presents roller skates (among other things) as penumbral instances of vehicles. Even more unlikely examples have been envisaged in both English and American cases. In *Garner v Burr*,[20] a poultry shed was accepted as a vehicle, while in *McBoyle v US*[21] (per Justice Holmes) an aircraft was not.

In an earlier American case, *Nix v Heddon*,[22] it was held that tomatoes could and should be seen as vegetables. The US Tariff Act (1883) imposed a duty on the importation of vegetables at ten per centum ad valorem. Justice Gray held that, notwithstanding the technical definition, the duty was payable on tomatoes, because that was how the term was normally understood in ordinary language:

> In the common language of the people...all these are vegetables, which are...like potatoes, carrots, parsnips,...usually served at dinner with the fish or meats..., and not, like fruits generally, as dessert.

In so holding, he was relying on the authority of *Robertson v Salomon*,[23] in which it was decided for similar reasons that beans should be be classified not as seeds but as vegetables because that was how they were referred to in 'common parlance'.

Waismann's open texture

In presenting his theory of open texture, Hart refers explicitly to Waismann's theory of open texture[24] (originally 'Porosität der Begriffe'). However, Hart's approach, intended to restrict judicial discretion to peripheral cases, is in direct contrast with Waismann's theory, which appears uncompromisingly sceptical.

---

[18] *Olmstead v US* 277 U.S. 438 (1928). Russell had used the same term in his earlier discussion of ambiguity (Russell, Bernard, 'Vagueness' in *The Collected Papers of Bertrand Russell* (London: Routledge, 1992), 147–54. Originally published in (1923) 1 *The Australasian Journal of Psychology and Philosophy* 84–92).

[19] *Griswold v Connecticut* 381 U.S. 479 (1965).

[20] *Garner v Burr* [1951] 1 KB 31.

[21] *McBoyle v United States* 283 U.S. 25 (1931). *Garner* figured on Hart's reading list for his first class when he became professor of law at Oxford. However, if it was *McBoyle* which inspired his famous 'vehicles in the park' example, this would account for his surprising use of the US spelling for 'airplane' which contrasts bizarrely with the British 'motor-car' in the same sentence.

[22] *Nix v Heddon* 149 U.S. 304 (1893).

[23] *Robertson v Salomon* 130 U.S. 412 (1889).

[24] Waismann, 'Verifiability' (cited in n.16), 119–23.

Waismann points out that because no definition can be complete, meaning is not just under-determined in certain, rare cases, but remains perpetually indeterminate in the sense that we can never have certain knowledge of what we are talking about, even in the central cases. He insisted that doubts remain not just regarding the periphery or penumbra of the concept, but also concerning our understanding of the concept itself. This problem goes beyond mere vagueness:

> Vagueness should be distinguished from open texture.... Open texture, then, is something like the possibility of vagueness. Vagueness can be remedied by giving more accurate rules, open texture cannot.[25]

Waismann's view here appears to be that although vagueness is theoretically ineliminable, the problem can be avoided on a practical level by giving more precise details as necessary, just as differential equations can be used in mathematics to reach ever closer approximations to the true figure. In this way, a legal draftsman can introduce more precision as necessary in order to reduce statutory vagueness as necessary, although he can never eliminate the theoretical problem altogether. Open texture cannot be remedied in the same way, as no definition can be definitive. To demonstrate this, he uses a variety of extreme and implausible examples:

> Suppose I have to verify a statement such as 'There is a cat next door'; suppose I go over to the next room, open the door, look into it and actually see a cat. Is this enough to prove my statement?... What, for instance, should I say when that creature later on grew to a gigantic size? Or if it showed some queer behaviour usually not to be found with cats, say, if, under certain conditions, it could be revived from death whereas normal cats could not? Shall I, in such a case, say that a new species has come into being? Or that it was a cat with extraordinary properties? Again, suppose I say 'There is my friend over there'. What if on drawing closer in order to shake hands with him he suddenly disappeared?[26]

Or:

> The notion of gold seems to be defined with absolute precision, say by the spectrum of gold with its characteristic lines. Now what would you say if a substance was discovered that looked like gold, satisfied all the chemical tests for gold, whilst it emitted a new sort of radiation?[27]

He readily admits that these examples are unreal but insists that they are not logically impossible:

> But such things do not happen Quite so; but they might happen, and that is enough to show that we can never exclude altogether the possibility of some unforeseen situation arising in which we shall have to modify our definition. Try as we may, no concept is limited in such a way that there is no room for any doubt.[28]

Thus, it is claimed, the mere fact that such problems cannot be logically excluded is enough to demonstrate the inadequacy of theories of definition based on necessary properties. From this point of view, given the limits of our knowledge, the problem of indeterminacy is inescapable.

> Every definition stretches into an open horizon. Can you foresee all the facts which would turn a putative fact into a delusion?[29]

---

[25] Waismann, 'Verifiability' (cited in n.16), 120.
[26] Waismann, 'Verifiability' (cited in n.16), 119.
[27] Waismann, 'Verifiability' (cited in n.16), 120.
[28] Waismann, 'Verifiability' (cited in n.16), 120.
[29] Waismann, 'Verifiability' (cited in n.16), 123.

For Waismann, therefore, open texture is omnipresent and inescapable. Hence the title of his concluding section: 'Lasciate ogni speranza'.

Nevertheless, while Waismann's theory is uncompromisingly sceptical, it is not nihilist. He nowhere denies the possibility of linguistic communication. He is concerned merely to point out the impossibility of omniscience and thus to demonstrate the inadequacy of the classic theories of definition based on necessary properties. In this way he is able to show that we have no reliable understanding of how successful communication works. His solution is essentially contextualist, insofar as 'every sort of statement has its own sort of logic'.[30]

Waismann's open texture is therefore in direct contradiction with Hart's, in that it brings into doubt not just peripheral uses, but our understanding of the central concept itself. Yet Hart cannot simply have misunderstood the theory on which he relies. He knew his former colleague Waismann well, having worked in the same (philosophy) department and was naturally familiar with developments in linguistic theory.

It should be noted that prototype theory is agnostic regarding the question of the invariance of the basic concept, relative to which the peripheral examples are understood. Although, contrary to Waismann, it assumes an unproblematic central meaning, it nevertheless admits the possibility of geographic variation regarding speakers' reports of best examples. While, for example, a sparrow may be accepted in England as the best instance of a 'bird', in the United States a robin may be preferred. Inhabitants of Antarctica may think first of a penguin. Presumably the theory could also be adapted to admit historical variation and thus to account for etymological development. Because meanings vary according to the community, it should also allow for variation between different professional fields. An 'operation', for example, may refer to different concepts in a medical, a military, or a mathematical context. Similarly 'equity' has different meanings in the law and in finance. This variability of understanding is theorized in Putnam's theory of stereotypes.[31]

Stereotypes

Putnam showed, through a celebrated series of thought-experiments, that no one can mean something of which they are not aware. He supposes a twin earth (Twearth), exactly like Earth except that water is not H_2O but XYZ. A spaceship from Earth will report: 'On Twearth the word "water" means "XYZ"'. Conversely, a Twearthian spaceship will report: 'On Earth, "water" means H_2O'. So far this is just a question of ambiguity, the word having one extension on Earth and another on Twearth. However, if communications with Twearth had taken place at a time when there was no knowledge of chemistry on either planet, then no one would have known that the word 'water' was ambiguous. Yet the extensions of the two concepts were in fact different, as we now know.

Concerning contemporary usage, Putnam gives the example of pots and pans made out of molybdenum rather than aluminium. For non-experts, there is no difference between these two metals, yet the extensions of the terms are in fact different. On the individual level, he famously claimed that he himself did not know the precise difference between an elm and a beech tree, and that he habitually used these words (wrongly) to

---

[30] Waismann, 'Verifiability' (cited in n.16), 129.
[31] Putnam, Hilary, *Mind, language and reality* (Philosophical papers 2) (Cambridge: Cambridge University Press, 1975).

mean much the same thing. His conclusion is that meaning cannot be fixed by description but must vary according to the knowledge and beliefs of the speaker.

In his theory of Stereotypes, Putnam proposed to define natural kinds by reference to a loose-knit group of features, known to speakers, enough of which suffice to validate the use of the word but none of which are necessary. These are the 'stereotypical' features. This approach allows for deficient examples (tigers with only three legs, gold which is not yellow, or water which is not pure H_2O). It also allows for disagreement over the use of a word in cases where speakers disagree over which are the most important among the stereotypical features. Some may claim, for example, that limited overs cricket is not really 'cricket' or that the use of tie-breaks means that the game played at Wimbledon is no longer 'really' tennis. A similar question was debated by the USSC in *PGA Tour v Casey Martin*[32] where the question arose as to whether 'golf with mechanised transport' was really 'golf'. From this point of view, semantics becomes an empirical question, depending on observations of actual usage.

More generally, the theory of stereotypes allows Putnam[33] to conclude, contrary to the classical approach, that there are no fixed, semantic criteria:

> To say that something is a lemon is to say that it belongs to a natural kind whose normal members have certain properties; but not to say that it necessarily has those properties itself.... There are no analytic truths of the form "every lemon has *p*".

Further, following this approach to definition, words may be seen as cooperative tools, their meaning depending not just on personal knowledge, but also on agreement and consensus within the appropriate linguistic community.

> There are two sorts of tools in the world: there are tools like a hammer or a screw-driver which can be used by one person; and there are tools like a steam-ship which requires the cooperative activity of a number of persons to use. Words have been thought of too much on the model of the first sort of tool.[34]

From this point of view, the stereotypical approach, based on consensus among speakers, is antithetic to the very idea of a 'literal meaning'.

In the law, although common law judges have traditionally preferred to base their decisions on a literal meaning they have occasionally adopted a stereotypical approach to interpretation, as in *Mandla v Dowell Lee*.[35] The question to be decided in this case was whether Sikhs (believers in the Sikh religion) could be classed as a race or as members of an 'ethnic group' for the purposes of the Race Relations Act.[36] The Court of Appeal had considered unanimously that, as its name implies, the Race Relations Act did not protect members of religious groups, Lord Denning famously deciding his interpretation by reference to the *Concise Oxford Dictionary*, 1934.[37] The following year, however, the House of Lords, adopting a novel, stereotypical approach, unanimously reversed the decision of the Court of Appeal. Lord Templeman held that it was enough for 'some' of

---

[32] *PGA Tour v Casey Martin* 532 U.S. 661 (2001).
[33] Putnam, Hilary, 'Is semantics possible?' (1970) 1(3) *Metaphilosophy* 187–201.
[34] Putnam, *Mind, language and reality* (cited in n.31), 229.
[35] *Mandla v Dowell Lee* [1983] 2 AC 548 (HL).
[36] Race Relations Act 1976.
[37] *Mandla v Dowell Lee* CA [1982] 3 WLR 932. 'But in 1934 in the Concise Oxford Dictionary it was given an entirely different meaning. It was given as: "Pertaining to race, ethnological" and "ethnological" was given as meaning: "Corresponding to a division of races". That is the meaning which I—acquiring my vocabulary in 1934—have always myself attached to the word "ethnic". It is, to my mind, the correct meaning. It means "pertaining to race"' (per Denning LJ).

the characteristics (or stereotypical features) of a race to be present or at least partially fulfilled:

'[A] group of persons defined by reference to ethnic origins must possess some of the characteristics of a race.... The evidence shows that the Sikhs satisfy these tests. They are more than a religious sect, they are almost a race and almost a nation.[38]

For Lord Fraser, even outsiders who joined the group through marriage or religious conversion could thereby become valid members:

A group defined by reference to enough of these characteristics would be capable of including converts, for example, persons who marry into the group, and of excluding apostates. Provided a person who joins the group feels himself or herself to be a member of it, and is accepted by other members, then he is, for the purposes of the Act, a member.[39]

This decision was recently approved by the (new) UK Supreme Court in *R Ex p. E v JFS*,[40] which referred not to fixed 'orthodox criteria' but to *Mandla* criteria which were held in the new case to suffice for membership of the Jewish community.

In what amounts to a discreet theoretical revolution, Stavropoulos[41] proposes a similar notion, by the simple device of adjusting the meaning of the word 'criterion' so that it no longer refers to a fixed feature. He prefers to define 'criteria' as conditions which are normally necessary and sufficient, but which remain defeasible in special circumstances, so that a term may apply even though some of the criteria are not satisfied and vice versa. This corresponds closely to Putnam's definition of stereotypical features.

It should be noted that, although the theories of prototypes and of stereotypes have different origins and were devised to account for different semantic problems, there is no hermetic distinction between prototypical and stereotypical interpretation. As the two models provide alternative descriptions of the same reality they are often combined in legal argument. In *United Biscuits v Customs and Excise*,[42] the question raised, whether Jaffa cakes were really cakes or biscuits, appeared at first sight to be a prototypical question. However it was argued in terms of stereotypical features. Jaffa cakes are similar to biscuits in size, for example, and they are placed on the biscuit shelf in supermarkets. However, most consumers were unaware of the fact that biscuits go soft when stale whereas cakes go hard. The final decision therefore depended on what, for most speakers, and indeed for most supermarket clients, was a new, unsuspected quality, as suggested in Waismann's account of open texture. At the VAT Tribunal, in language closely corresponding to Putnam's classic presentation of semantic stereotypes, Potter QC was able to hold that 'Jaffa cakes have sufficient characteristics of cakes to qualify as cakes within the meaning of item number 1 in group 1 of the fifth schedule. If it be relevant, I also determine that the Jaffa Cakes are not biscuits.'

It is a feature of natural language that words, far from having a fixed meaning, have an indefinite number of possible senses, which will depend not merely on the speaker's understanding of the relevant concept, but also on the propositional context in which the word is used. An 'arrest' for murder, for example, has little in common with a 'cardiac arrest'. The verb 'to throw' has different meanings according to whether the object thrown

---

[38] *Mandla v Dowell Lee*, per Lord Templeman (cited in n.35).
[39] *Mandla v Dowell Lee*, per Lord Fraser of Tullybelton (cited in n.35).
[40] *R Ex p. E v JFS* [2009] UKSC 15.
[41] Stavropoulos, Nicos, 'Hart's semantics' in Coleman, J. (ed), *Hart's Postscript* (Oxford: Oxford University Press, 2001), 59–98, 65.
[42] *United Biscuits v Customs and Excise* VAT Tribunal 91/160 (1991).

is a stone, a javelin, or a discus. Different movements are involved which may conceivably be relevant in legal proceedings (as is certainly the case in the 'laws' of cricket). The verb is also used in other contexts, in which the semantic relations are even less clear, as in 'to throw a party' or 'to throw a hissy fit'. Although some of these expressions may safely be ignored in the law, and consigned to oblivion as 'non-statutory' language, linguists have no such luxury. All interpretation, not just of lexical items but also of propositional utterances, must therefore be conditioned by the contexts in which they occur.

2. Propositional meaning: contextual and literal interpretation

In the ongoing linguistic debate, semantic contextualism is opposed to the literalist or inferentialist account of understanding. There are of course many aspects to this debate. One of the most basic points is, briefly, that literalists tend to consider that the propositional meaning can be derived from the meanings of the words of which the proposition is composed, and the meaning thus obtained functions as a necessary starting point for interpretation. The pragmatic meaning may subsequently be established as a result of an interaction between this purely linguistic meaning and the relevant contextual features. In contrast, in the strongest version of their theory, contextualists consider the communicative intention as primary and deny any genuine role for abstract literal meaning in natural language understanding.

Literalists thus tend to take a modular view of linguistic competence, and assume that 'what is said' can be established by the application of purely linguistic knowledge. This requires a process of 'enrichment' (or 'saturation') triggered by lexically content-sensitive expressions in the sentence itself. The context trivially supplies the referents for pronouns and other deictic expressions as well as the information necessary for disambiguation. Thus the truth value of, for example, 'He is the presiding judge' depends on who is referred to by the pronoun 'He'. Similarly, 'It is raining' is said to be true or false according to the time and place of utterance. The process is rule-governed and therefore predictable.

On this view, 'what is said' is therefore a basic semantic concept. Once established, it may serve as a basis for pragmatic inference, so that 'It's warm in here' may be understood in certain contexts as meaning, 'Please close the window'. One of the well-known difficulties associated with this view, however, is that it predicts a complex process of implicature, inaccessible to the speaker, which may even involve a form of cognitive backtracking in cases where it is not realized at the outset that the utterance, taken literally, is ambivalent or that the logical meaning does not correspond to the commonly accepted understanding. Carston[43] discusses the example 'I have had breakfast', which is usually interpreted relative to a very restricted time range and not as referring to the indefinite past. Similarly for 'I have had a lovely evening', in which the machinery of implicature is supposedly necessary to avoid the unwanted interpretation 'but this was not it', or, 'I have drunk one glass of wine', which should remain logically true even where the speaker has single-handedly drunk a whole bottle.

The idea of a 'conventional' meaning may serve to avoid this objection to some extent by reducing the number of alternatives available. A commonly accepted and institutionally defined default understanding may thus be taken as the starting point for interpretation rather than a truly literal meaning. 'Could you pass the salt?' may then be understood directly not as a potential question but as a conventional request.

---

[43] Carston, Robyn, *Thought and utterances: the pragmatics of explicit communication* (Oxford: Blackwell, 2002), 253.

In the contextualist model of understanding, on the other hand, communication depends on shared knowledge of the background context. In place of a reliance on purely inferential reasoning, this model allows a greater role for association and common contextual assumptions. In consequence, the starting point for interpretation, or 'what is said', is no longer seen as purely semantic. It can no longer be established by purely linguistic reasoning because it is at least partially pragmatic. The truth values of many perfectly ordinary utterances may thus vary according to the context, even in cases where the same words refer to the same things.

To take a variant on one among many examples proposed by Travis,[44] a simple affirmative sentence like 'The water's blue today' would be interpreted differently by a holidaymaker about to go swimming in the lake and by an inspector measuring pollution levels. In neither case does the so-called literal meaning come into play. Given that it is well known that water is not blue but transparent, such an utterance could only be literally understood as a contradiction in terms. Only after 'what is said' has been established in the particular context can it function as a basis for inferential understanding. Here, in one sense, it could be used to suggest a family picnic by the lake. On the other reading, it could on the contrary pragmatically suggest that bathing should be forbidden.[45]

Many philosophers of language, including for example Searle,[46] have established independently the importance of a background context for the interpretation of utterances. As in Waismann's theory of open texture, this background may be hidden, or not noticed until a new situation presents itself. Once it is admitted that 'what is said' is not independent of pragmatic features at any level of abstraction, this approach brings into doubt the existence of a definite propositional meaning, supposedly established independently of the context. The contextualists may therefore be said to take seriously Austin's celebrated slogan, 'meaning is use'.

Hart himself admitted that:

> The plain case, where the general terms seem to need no interpretation and where the recognition of instances seems unproblematic or 'automatic' are only the familiar ones, constantly recurring in similar contexts, where there is general agreement in judgments as to the application of the classifying terms.[47]

This statement appears to contradict the compromise solution often favoured in the law, and often apparently by Hart himself, in which the judge is supposed to adopt the literal sense of the words as far as possible, and to appeal to contextual meaning only in cases of doubt, or where strict literal interpretation would lead to absurdity or injustice. Hart appears here to be pointing out, on the contrary, that the fact that a particular context is familiar does not imply that it has no role to play. Indeed, it is only the familiarity of the context that gives the mistaken impression that the words themselves have clear meanings.

There are many examples in legal practice of such a contextualist approach.

---

[44] Travis, Charles, 'Annals of analysis' (review of Grice 1989) (1991) 398 *Mind* 237–64.
[45] For a more general defence of the contextualist view see Travis, 'Annals of analysis' (cited in n.44).
[46] Searle, John R., 'Literal meaning' in Searle, John R., *Expression and Meaning* (Cambridge: Cambridge University Press, 1979).
[47] Hart, *The Concept of Law* (cited in n.14), 126.

Literalism and contextualism in the law

In elementary textbooks it is suggested that, as a general rule, the lawyer should adopt the literal meaning of the words wherever possible, and avoid searching for pragmatic intention. 'Intentional meaning' is avoided because it can only be apprehended in particular contexts. English judges traditionally claim, therefore, to respect the ideal of literal interpretation in cases where the context is unlikely to make much difference, and to restrict recourse to contextual understanding to 'hard cases'. Unfortunately, this position is no more coherent than the suggestion that, in the absence of abnormal meteorological conditions, there is no weather. It is always necessary to consider the context, if only to conclude that the situation is 'normal'.

It is well known that attempts to impose a single, constant meaning in different contexts, through a strict application of the so-called 'literal rule', can lead to absurdity. For this reason, the rule is rarely mentioned in judgments, except in cases where the judges are unable to find any satisfactory solution at all. Even the celebrated 'golden rule' fails to avoid the difficulties that it was intended to solve (see Lord Wensleydale in *Grey v Pearson*[48] and Lord Blackburn in *River Wear Commissioners v Adamson*[49]). If, as the contextualists claim, 'what is said' is itself a pragmatic concept, and there is therefore no such thing as purely literal meaning, then the ideal of literal interpretation amounts to no more than wishful thinking.

Faced with the difficulties associated with strict literal interpretation, many judges have proposed a notion of 'literal meaning in context'. However, this apparent oxymoron may correspond to the contextualist notion of 'what is said'.

In certain areas of law, the so-called literal meaning is explicitly taken as a basis for interpretation. The most important of these is that of perjury in US law, the leading case being *Bronston v US*.[50] The accused was found not guilty because, although what he said was deliberately misleading, it was nevertheless logically true. This definition of literal meaning is problematic insofar as it contrasts with the natural, clear meaning which is supposed to predominate in the law. In the footnotes to their judicial opinions, the US Supreme Court therefore imposed limits reminiscent of the problems encountered by exponents of the Gricean conversational theory:

> [I]f it is material to ascertain how many times a person has entered a store on a given day and that person responds to such a question by saying five times when in fact he knows that he entered the store 50 times that day, that person may be guilty of perjury even though it is technically true that he entered the store five times.... Whether an answer is true must be determined with reference to the question it purports to answer, not in isolation.[51]

In procedural appeals depending on whether the accused requested counsel before or during police interrogation (as in *Davis v US*[52]), whatever the words used by the suspect ('Maybe I should ask for a lawyer'), American judges commonly reject the appeal because, as predicted by the contextualist theory, they are unable to find any clear literal meaning at all. On the other hand, when the appeal depends on whether, prior to his arrest, the suspect voluntarily gave permission to the police to search his property (as in *Schneckloth v Bustamonte*[53]), the judges are more likely to adopt a contextual approach,

---

[48] *Grey v Pearson* [1857] 6 AC 61 (HL).
[49] *River Wear Commissioners v Adamson* [1877] 2 AC 743 (HL).
[50] *Bronston v US* 409 U.S. 352 (1973).
[51] *Bronston v US*, per Burger J, n.3 (cited in n.50).
[52] *Davis v US* 512 U.S. 452 (1994).
[53] *Schneckloth v Bustamonte* 412 U.S. 218 (1972).

so that whatever the words used by the police ('Does the trunk open?'), the communicated meaning is taken to be clear. In both types of case, therefore, appeals are usually doomed to failure.

In certain legal fields, at least in English law, interpretation is explicitly contextual. In probate, for example, at least since *Boyes v Cook*,[54] the judge is expected to interpret the will from the point of view of the testator:

> [W]hen it is said that surrounding circumstances may be looked at, that only means that the circumstances existing at the time when the testator made his will may be looked at. You may place yourself, so to speak, in his arm-chair, and consider the circumstances by which he was surrounded when he made his will to assist you in arriving at his intention.[55]

It is even permissible to interpret words in a 'peculiar' manner, if it appears that that is how they were intended at the time:

> Again, the testator may have habitually called certain persons or things by peculiar names, by which they were not commonly known. If these names should occur in his will, they could only be explained and construed by the aid of evidence to shew the sense in which he used them, in like manner as if his will were written in cypher, or in a foreign language.[56]

Attempts to impose a fixed, legal meaning, for example for the term 'money' in wills, are doomed to failure:

> I protest against the idea that, in interpreting the language of a will, there can be some fixed meaning of the word 'money' which the courts must adopt as being the 'legal' meaning as opposed to the 'popular' meaning.... It is far more important to promote the correct construction of future wills in this respect than to preserve consistency in misinterpretation.[57]

The interpretation of the shortest (three-word) will ever accepted as valid ('All for mother') was problematic because the mother had died before the testator and indeed before the will was made. The word 'mother' was therefore interpreted as meaning 'wife'.[58] This meaning was presented, not as a pragmatic inference but precisely as 'what was said', a semantic interpretation corresponding to the default meaning of the word in that context.

In contract law, judicial interpretation depends frequently on the background context. In *Prenn v Simonds*,[59] Wilberforce LJ considered that this factual background, based on shared knowledge among the participants could be admitted as part of what he called the surrounding circumstances:

> [E]vidence of the factual background known to the parties at or before the date of the contract, including evidence of the 'genesis' and objectively the 'aim' of the transaction.[60]

The theoretical problem is considered more explicitly by Lord Hoffmann, who used a particularly contextualist form of words in observing, in *Kirin-Amgen v Hoechst*,[61] that all utterances are made in some context:

> No one has ever made an acontextual statement. There is always some context to any utterance, however meagre. 'Acontextual meaning' can refer only to the conventional rules for the use of

---

[54] *Boyes v Cook* (1880) 28 WR 754.
[55] *Boyes v Cook*, per James LJ (cited in n.54).
[56] *Doe d. Hiscocks v Hiscocks* (1839) 5 M&R 363, per Lord Abinger.
[57] *Perrin v Morgan* [1943] 1 All ER 187 (HL), per Viscount Simon.
[58] *Thorn v Dickens* [1905] Probate WN 54.
[59] *Prenn v Simmonds* [1971] 3 All ER 237 (HL).
[60] *Prenn v Simmonds*, per Lord Wilberforce (cited in n.59).
[61] *Kirin-Amgen Inc v Hoechst Marion Roussel* [2004] UKHL 46.

language, such as one finds in a dictionary or grammar. But then, to compare acontextual meaning in that sense with contextual meaning is to compare apples with pears.[62]

In the same case, he pointed out the danger of assuming that words are exchanged with meanings attached to them:

[T]he attempt to treat the words of the claim as having meanings 'in themselves' and without regard to the context in which or the purpose for which they were used was always a highly artificial exercise.[63]

Lord Hoffmann therefore rejects the literal rule, expressing doubt as to whether it had ever been strictly observed, allowing only that such principles 'used' to be applied in legal interpretation (at any rate in theory). In its place, he appears to advocate a view of 'what is said' which is:

...highly sensitive to the context of and background to the particular utterance. It depends not only upon the words the author has chosen but also upon the identity of the audience he is taken to have been addressing and the knowledge and assumptions which one attributes to that audience.[64]

On this view, therefore, 'what is said' must be a pragmatic concept. However, in English law, for procedural reasons, judges are frequently obliged to 'declare an ambiguity' in order to grant themselves the right to take account of contextual features. In *DPP v Gomez*,[65] Lord Lowry went so far as to declare an ambiguity even while affirming that the phrase in question was not ambiguous at all:

So clear is this conclusion to my mind that, notwithstanding anything which has been said in other cases, I would be very slow to concede that the word 'appropriates' in section 1(1) is in its context ambiguous. But...the Crown case requires that there must be ambiguity.... Therefore, my Lords, I am willing for the purpose of argument to treat the word 'appropriates' as ambiguous in its context.[66]

American judges also have also adopted a largely contextualist approach in statute construction. In *Smith v US*,[67] Justice O'Connor attempted to discover the literal meaning of 'use' of a gun in a drugs-related offence. While admitting that the natural interpretation would normally evoke an image of 'use' for shooting, she considered the definitions given in a number of dictionaries, including *Webster's* ('to convert to one's service' or 'to employ'), and concluded that these other uses could not be excluded. In her opinion, the literal meaning therefore included all the senses mentioned. She thus held, counter-intuitively, that the notion of 'use for barter' corresponded to legislative intention as expressed in the phrase 'use or carry'. Justice Scalia (dissenting) insisted on the contrary that the plain meaning of a word must depend on the context of use:

[T]he meaning of a word cannot be determined in isolation, but must be drawn from the context in which it is used.... To be sure, one can 'use' a firearm in a number of ways, including as an article of exchange, just as one can 'use' a cane as a hall decoration—but that is not the ordinary meaning of 'using' the one or the other.... The Court does not appear to grasp the distinction between how

---

[62] *Kirin-Amgen v Hoechst*, per Lord Hoffmann (cited in n.61).
[63] *Kirin-Amgen v Hoechst*, per Lord Hoffmann (cited in n.61).
[64] *Kirin-Amgen v Hoechst*, per Lord Hoffmann (cited in n.61).
[65] *DPP v Gomez* [1993] AC 442.
[66] *DPP v Gomez*, per Lord Lowry (cited in n.65).
[67] *Smith v US* 508 U.S. 223 (1993).

a word can be used and how it ordinarily is used.... the plain meaning of the word must be drawn from the context in which it is used.[68]

Smith v US is a case in which inferentialist theories based on Gricean principles have little relevance. Justice Scalia was not attempting to discover what may have been the pragmatic intention of the legislature but to establish the basic sense of the language used in that particular context.

In *Bailey v United States*,[69] in which a similar problem arose, the literal definition adopted by the majority in the earlier case was rejected in favour of Justice Scalia's contextualist interpretation. The court was clearly influenced by an article published by a Berkeley professor of linguistics.[70] Although Professor Fillmore was not named in the opinions given, his example sentence was quoted to show that the word could take different senses, even in the same utterance ('I use a gun to protect my house, but I've never had to use it'). Later, in *Muscarello v US*,[71] the court preferred to rely on the alternative word provided in the statutory phrase, and considered instead whether the accused was merely guilty of 'carrying' a gun. However, this new development did not suffice to avoid the need for reliance on the context. The question in this case was whether the gun could be said to be 'carried' when it was not in the hand of the accused, nor on his person, but in the glove compartment of his car. Justice Breyer, in holding that the word 'carry' did indeed apply to a gun transported in the glove compartment of a car, partly based his decision on his analysis of linguistic corpora including databases of the *New York Times* and the *US News*.[72]

In his extended discussion of the debate between the 'literalists' and 'contextualists', Recanati[73] proposes a form of what he calls 'meaning Eliminativism'. In place of literal meaning, he suggests according a 'semantic potential' to expressions, to be activated in particular contexts. A similar notion is evoked in *Julius v Oxford (Bishop)*,[74] in which the House of Lords had to decide the meaning of the deontic 'may' (and similar power-conferring expressions like 'it shall be lawful'). It was held that such expressions could be interpreted as referring not just to a power or a right, but also to a duty, equivalent to 'must'. Rather than considering the word 'may' as ambiguous, however, the court simply held that the true meaning of the word was wide enough to include both senses. The sense of power-conferring expressions was thus declared to be the same 'whether there is or is not a duty or obligation to use the powers which they confer'. Like Recanati, Lord Selbourne described the different possible meanings, including here the coercive meaning, as merely 'potential'.

To the extent that jurists appear in practice to accept the contextualist approach, they would appear to be committed to a similar view of rule-following.

---

[68] *Smith v US*, per Justice Scalia (cited in n.67). Justice Scalia favoured the opposite point of view in *US v Heller* 554 U.S. 570 (2008). He may therefore be guilty of selecting his linguistic theory according to the conclusion he wishes to reach.
[69] *Bailey v United States* 516 U.S. 137 (1995).
[70] Cunningham, Clark D. and Fillmore, Charles J., 'Using Common Sense: A Linguistic Perspective on Judicial Interpretation of "Use a Firearm"' (1995) 73 Wash. ULQ 1159.
[71] *Muscarello v US* 524 U.S. 125 (1998).
[72] In further justification, he also mentions a number of Biblical quotations including: '[H]is servants carried him in a chariot to Jerusalem' (2 Kings 9:28) and '[T]hey will carry their riches on the shoulders of young asses' (Isaiah 30:6).
[73] Recanati, François, *Literal meaning* (Cambridge: Cambridge University Press, 2004), 146.
[74] *Julius v Oxford (Bishop)* [1880] 5 AC 214.

Rule-following

As the Wittgensteinian rule-following considerations are usually presented, agreement on the correct response in a particular case depends on social consensus regarding the interpretation of the rule. A single individual with no awareness of the community would therefore have no reliable intuition concerning his own understanding of the content of the given rule. As Kripke[75] explicates it, the argument is based on the possibility of divergent understandings, which appear whenever rules are interpreted in new contexts. His conclusion is that rule-following requires active decision-making based on assumed social agreement. On this view, no rule can be so clear and simple as to be self-explanatory. Even the simplest and most obvious instructions, like the arrows which appear on signs guiding traffic on the motorway, must be interpreted. Even though these arrows often point vertically downwards, in the given context they are usually taken to mean 'straight ahead'. This interpretation is not a feature of the rule itself but rather a collective interpretative decision taken in the appropriate circumstance. It follows that, contrary to popular assumptions, rules do not constrain behaviour.

It is often objected that some rules appear to admit of no alternative interpretation. This is said to be the case, for example, for the permitted moves in chess or for the application of a simple arithmetical rule. However, in such cases, the general agreement does not depend on a putative literal meaning, but is rather a consequence of the closed nature of a system in which new situations are unlikely to arise. Problems in the interpretation of the rules of chess will therefore only be expected to occur during the process of learning the game. Wittgenstein[76] illustrated the point in the context of elementary arithmetic by imagining a pupil being asked to follow the teacher's example in continuing a series, adding 2 to each number. The pupil successfully continues the series up to 1,000, but then writes: 1000, 1004, 1008, 1012... whilst still claiming to be going on as before. He may have understood the rule as something like: 'Add 2 up to 1000, 4 up to 2000, 6 up to 3000 and so on'. As this interpretation was compatible with all the examples given, the anomaly did not become apparent until he reached four figures.

Similarly, a series 1, 3, 5, 7... may be continued in various ways. If it is assumed that these are odd numbers, one correct answer may be, 11, 13. Yet if instead the series is thought to consist of prime numbers, another valid answer may be 1, 13, 17. Leibniz[77] supplied a mathematical proof to show that more complex interpretations can be imagined to justify any other answer. Wittgenstein[78] describes this situation as paradoxical: 'This was our paradox: no course of action could be determined by a rule, because every course of action can be made to accord with the rule.'

Kripke[79] imagines a 'bizarre sceptic' who insists when anomalies arise that he is simply going on as before, and that it is the other members of the community who have changed their interpretation of the rule. It turns out that it is impossible to prove the sceptic wrong, whether by appeal to previous usage, to introspection, or to natural disposition. His hypothesis may seem bizarre but it is not a priori impossible. More worryingly, as the sceptic himself had never previously considered the problem which now arises, it is enough to imagine that same individual in the future to realize that he or she has no

---

[75] Kripke, Saul, *Wittgenstein—to follow a rule* (Oxford: Blackwell, 1982).
[76] Wittgenstein, *Philosophical Investigations* (cited in n.10), §85.
[77] Leibniz, G. W., *Discourse on Metaphysics* (trans. Martin/Brown) (Manchester: University of Manchester Press, 1988) ([1686], VI: 304).
[78] Wittgenstein, *Philosophical Investigations* (cited in n.10), §201.
[79] Kripke, *Wittgenstein—to follow a rule* (cited in n.75), 9.

knowledge of the content of the rule as presently understood. When contemplating this result, Kripke himself admits to having 'something of an eerie feeling'.[80]

The problem cannot be avoided by introducing more complex rules, first because misunderstandings are inherently unpredictable and secondly because the new rule would itself require interpretation.

Hart famously denounced rule-scepticism as 'incoherent'.

> Yet, 'rule-scepticism' or the claim that talk of rules is a myth, cloaking the truth that law consists simply of decisions of courts and the prediction of them, can make a powerful appeal to a lawyer's candour. Stated in an unqualified general form, so as to embrace both secondary and primary rules, it is indeed quite incoherent; for the assertion that there are decisions of courts cannot consistently be combined with the denial that there are any rules at all.[81]

However, it remains a matter of conjecture whether he would have been convinced by Kripke's exegesis of Wittgenstein. His rejection of scepticism does not in itself amount to a rejection of the Wittgensteinian rule-following considerations. Indeed, although Kripke's[82] (1982) formulation of the problem is often mistakenly equated with nihilism, the possibility of common understanding of rules is nowhere denied. As it is clear that rules cannot function as 'rails to infinity', the problem is rather, in the terms of Wright,[83] to understand the nature of an instruction supposedly able to determine the correct response, in advance, in an infinite range of new unenvisaged contexts, given that all prior experience is compatible with an indeterminate number of other solutions.

Nevertheless, the 'Kripgenstein' model has frequently been denounced, often without argument, as unacceptable in legal theory. Marmor[84] rejects it as absurd. Smith[85] presents Kripke's solution as implausible. Endicott[86] denies the possibility of a consensual solution: 'That sceptical view of the social nature of rules cannot be right', and simply affirms[87] that '[t]here is indeterminacy (if any) only in borderline cases'. Bix[88] rejects the consensual view of rule-following on the grounds that 'there are ample reasons to believe that we cannot simply apply directly Wittgenstein's ideas meant for easy cases, to hard cases'. Yet Wittgenstein's consistent strategy was to argue a fortiori. Thus, if even the simplest rules in easy cases stand in need of interpretation, then this must be true of all rules, especially in hard cases.

Whether speaking as a jurist or as a philosopher of language, it is unlikely that Hart would have been satisfied with such simplistic, purported refutations, based on spurious distinctions between understanding and interpretation, on suggestions that the problem can be avoided by writing it down, or on *ad verecundiam* appeals to received wisdom. On the contrary, he may have recognized that the consensualist theory appears to correspond in many ways to legal practice.

---

[80] Kripke, *Wittgenstein—to follow a rule* (cited in n.75), 21.
[81] Hart, *The Concept of Law* (cited in n.14), 136.
[82] Kripke, *Wittgenstein—to follow a rule* (cited in n.75).
[83] Wright, Crispin, 'Rule-following, objectivity and the theory of meaning' in Holtzman, S. and Leich, C. (eds), *Wittgenstein: to follow a rule* (London: Routledge, 1981), 99–117.
[84] Marmor, Andrei, 'No easy cases?' in Patterson, Dennis M. (ed.), *Wittgenstein and legal theory* (Boulder, Col.: Westview, 1992), 189–232, 189 n.46.
[85] Smith, Gene Anne, 'Wittgenstein and the sceptical fallacy' in Patterson, *Wittgenstein and legal theory* (cited in n.84), 157–88, 180.
[86] Endicott, Timothy, *Vagueness in Law* (Oxford: Oxford University Press, 2000), 25.
[87] Endicott, Timothy, 'Herbert Hart and the semantic sting' in Coleman, J. (ed.), *Hart's Postscript* (cited in n.41), 39–58.
[88] Bix, Brian, 'The application (and mis-application) of Wittgenstein's rule-following considerations to legal theory' in Patterson (ed.), *Wittgenstein and legal theory* (cited in n.84), 209–23, 217.

Rule-following in the law

It is a fundamental feature of the common law system that judges recognize the importance of the judicial institution for the development of the law. As regards questions of linguistic understanding, they recognize the importance of general agreement, or consensus, in a given discourse situation. Yet they are perhaps more likely than others to remain convinced that their decisions are determined by the applicable law rather than by agreement in the (legal) community regarding the appropriate interpretation. They frequently state explicitly that they have come reluctantly to a regrettable, unjust, or unfair decision, and that such unfortunate results can only be avoided in the future through the intervention of the legislature.

Nevertheless, this judicial intuition of being constrained by fixed rules is not incompatible with the Wittgensteinian view. Wittgenstein's stated aim[89] was simply to give a coherent account of what actually happens when rules are obeyed: 'This merely shews what goes to make up what we call "obeying a rule" in everyday life.' On this view, the content of the rule is not necessarily the source of judicial constraint and certainty. On the contrary, the perception of constraint may rather be the result of clear agreement among qualified persons.

It may be observed that legal practice regarding the interpretation of the law corresponds closely to the Wittgensteinian rule-following considerations in several ways, relating to the impossibility of self-explanatory rules, to the application of the rule of precedent, to the practice of 'distinguishing' different applications of a rule, and to the possibility of overruling. First, the courts are frequently required to apply the law in circumstances which were not originally envisaged by the legislature. They sometimes make use of secondary rules of interpretation, introduced to clarify the content of the given rule. However, as predicted by the theory, questions then arise as to the correct application of these new rules. Hart[90] accepted that 'canons of interpretation', whether developed in the common law or as consolidated in the Interpretation Act,[91] necessarily require interpretation themselves:

> Canons of 'interpretation' cannot eliminate, though they can diminish these uncertainties... They cannot, any more than other rules, provide for their own interpretation.

Secondly, just as linguistic understanding depends on shared knowledge of previous usage, legal adjudication in the common law system depends on decisions made in earlier cases, thought to be sufficiently similar to the old. However, in the same way as the meanings of words are unclear when they appear in new contexts, the rule of precedent is often problematic. The contextualist principle proposed in semantics by Recanati corresponds closely to the generally accepted definition of the common law system of *stare decisis*:

> The applicability of a term to novel situations depends on its similarity to the source situations. The target situation must be similar to the source situations not only with respect to the 'explicit' definition of the term, but also with respect to the hidden background. If the two situations diverge, it will be unclear whether the term will be applicable.[92]

---

[89] Wittgenstein, *Philosophical Investigations* (cited in n.10), §235.
[90] Hart, *The Concept of Law* (cited in n.14), 126.
[91] Interpretation Act 1978.
[92] Recanati, *Literal meaning* (cited in n.73), 143.

Thirdly, as in semantics, the practice of 'distinguishing' precedents depends precisely on the discovery of new, previously unnoticed, background features. Much discussion on the applicability of precedents explicitly mentions different possible interpretations. The question in *Perrin v Morgan*,[93] for example, was:

> [W]hether the rule, as applied by the courts in the decisions referred to, is a wrong rule altogether, or is a sound rule, which has been wrongly applied.... With this understanding I do not see why the rule, properly applied, should fail to work justice. The blot, if any, is not the rule, but its misapplication.

Similarly, in *Kleinwort Benson v Lincoln*:

> What is in issue at the heart of this case is the continued existence of a long standing rule of law, which has been maintained in existence for nearly two centuries in what has been seen to be the public interest. It is therefore incumbent on your Lordships to consider whether it is indeed in the public interest that the rule should be maintained, or alternatively that it should be abrogated altogether or reformulated.[94]

But to change the interpretation of the rule is in practice to change its content, that is, simply to substitute one rule for another.

Finally, when overruling, English judges frequently behave exactly like Kripke's 'bizarre sceptic', insofar as they regularly claim to be going on as before whereas they are in fact departing from the existing rule. Numerous examples are available in which, even while rejecting generally accepted, sometimes long-standing interpretations of the law, judges claim to be following the law as, properly understood, it has always been. Alternative views, which may have been dominant for several centuries are thus rejected as misunderstandings or as mere fiction. *R v R* is only one of the most celebrated examples. This case was concerned with the status of Hale's venerable rule on marital rape. Lane CJ, well aware that this rule had been followed for centuries in the highest courts, rejected it, claiming counterfactually that it had never actually existed:

> This is not the creation of a new offence, it is the removal of a common law fiction which has become anachronistic and offensive and we consider that it is our duty having reached that conclusion to act upon it.[95]

Curiously, judges rarely make such counterfactual statements extra-judicially. They are naturally reluctant explicitly to assume a legislative function or to admit to modifying existing law. Indeed, although they frequently point out that a given rule has been overruled in an earlier case, they rarely use the word themselves in its performative sense, even when the act of overruling is clearly justified. In consequence, contrary to expectation, as pointed out by Charnock,[96] the more important the case, the more equivocal the language used.

The problem may also be linked to judicial respect for the 'declarative theory' of law, according to which the common law is assumed to have always been as it is now stated to be. This apparently counterfactual theory continues to play a significant role even though it has been described extra-judicially by Lord Reid as a 'fairy-tale'. Lord

---

[93] *Perrin v Morgan* [1943] 1 All ER 187 (HL), per Lord Thankerton (cited in n.57).
[94] *Kleinwort Benson v Lincoln CC* [1998] 4 All ER 513 (HL), per Lord Goff.
[95] *R v R (Marital Exemption)* [1991] 4 All ER 481 (CA), per Lane CJ.
[96] Charnock, Ross, 'Overruling as a speech act: performativity and normative discourse' (2009) 41 *Journal of Pragmatics* 401–26.

Reid's view has since been cited in numerous judgments, especially in cases involving 'prospective' overruling.[97]

On his postscript, Hart[98] suggests, in discussing the common judicial claim that the law is certain when it clearly is not, that this kind of language is a matter of mere ritual, and may safely be ignored.[99]

3. Parallel objections

It is not surprising that linguists and jurists should be confronted with similar problems regarding the notion of literal meaning. Nor is it surprising that the theories proposed to account for these problems should correspond both to pre-theoretical linguistic intuitions and to common legal practice. It is, however, interesting to note that these theories, as presented in the two disciplines, are susceptible to similar objections, both in linguistics and in the law.

One obvious theoretical difficulty with the contextualist approach is that there is no agreement on how the background context, used to establish 'what is said', is to be distinguished from the foreground contextual features, used to determine the pragmatic intentional meaning. Similar problems are exemplified in the law. In *Prenn v Simmonds*,[100] for example, Lord Wilberforce raised the problem of the delimitation of what he called the 'surrounding circumstances'.

Both the contextualist theory of semantics and the Wittgensteinian rule-following considerations appear to bring into question a number of fundamental methodological assumptions, whether in linguistics or in jurisprudence. These concern the nature of linguistic intention, the function of linguistic intuition, the establishment of the necessary but ever-changing social consensus, the assumption of compositionality and the problem of reflexivity.

The nature of intention is fundamental to statute construction, as the aim of the court is often said to be to give effect to the 'intention of the legislature'. Yet, according to conventional definitions, collectivities cannot have intentions at all. Even when rephrased as corresponding to the intention of a (singular) draftsman, the judicial ideal remains impossible, given that, in principle, neither the intentions nor the feelings of an individual can be shared by others.

The function of linguistic intuition is particularly important in the study of language, as, in principle, speakers' intuitions form the data to be explained. However, on the contextualist view, meaning no longer corresponds to the intentions of the individual speaker but to what he or she expects the interlocutor to understand. Conversely, contextual understanding corresponds to what the interlocutor supposes the speaker meant. This problem is recognized by judges, who commonly refer to 'general understanding' or to 'common parlance' in order to avoid reliance on their own, personal interpretations. The intuitions of judges or of native speaker informants no longer appear as personal knowledge but as mere predictions of what other speakers in the community may say. The Chomskian view of language ability as an individual human cognitive faculty is thus made to appear decidedly solipsist.

---

[97] For example *Kleinwort Benson v Lincoln CC* (cited in n.94) or *R v Governor HM Prison Brockway Ex p. Evans* [2000] 3 WLR 843, in which, following a change in the law, a prison governor was successfully prosecuted for wrongful imprisonment.

[98] Hart, *The Concept of Law* (cited in n.14), 274.

[99] But see the somewhat different account proposed by David Schiff and Richard Nobles, 'Why do judges talk the way they do?' (2009) *International Journal of Law in Context* 25–47.

[100] *Prenn v Simmonds* [1971] 3 All ER 237 (HL) (cited in n.59).

In consequence, understanding, whether in linguistics or in the law, comes to appear as a form of mind-reading. Sperber and Wilson[101] go so far as to present inferential comprehension as 'ultimately a meta-psychological process involving the construction and evaluation of a hypothesis about the communicator's meaning'. This view of understanding as a metalinguistic activity may initially appear unhelpful. However, as speakers are often uncertain about what the interlocutor meant, and sometimes explicitly request confirmation, the mind-reading approach may nevertheless correspond with pre-theoretical observations. On this level, it seems that there can be no clear distinction between understanding and misunderstanding, because otherwise there would be no misunderstanding to explain. Impressions of clear meaning, requiring no interpretation, may therefore be misleading. Indeed, misunderstanding may be more common than understanding, to the extent that it may be considered as the normal case, at least as regards the communication of personal sentiments and opinions. Any rare examples of genuine, complete understanding would then be classed as exceptions.

The establishment of the linguistic consensus is fundamental, on the contextualist view, to common understanding among speakers in a particular context. However, because previous utterances are by definition part of the linguistic context, this implies that the consensus must be created anew for each new occurrence. At first sight, this idea seems too complex to be useful as an explanation of the phenomenon under investigation. However, it is not in itself absurd. Lewis[102] provides a plausible though simplified account of how the consensus can evolve, by means of a baseball metaphor, showing how new senses can be created or destroyed in the course of a conversation.

A further difficulty concerns compositionality. Much research in semantics depends on the assumption that the meaning of a sentence can be derived from the meaning of the words of which it is composed. This is also a basic principle of statute construction, in which much legal argument explicitly concerns the relevant lexical definitions. In order to simplify this debate, most statutes include 'meanings clauses', supposedly intended to clarify the intended definitions. It is, however, noticeable that, when problems arise, these simplistic definitions are rarely helpful. One obvious explanation is that the meaning depends on the context of utterance. However, this raises a further problem, that of reflexivity.

It is generally accepted that because words only occur in continuous discourse, knowledge of their meaning can only be acquired through the analysis of the sentences (or statutes) in which they occur. This corresponds to Frege's semantic principle, in which the overall sense of the sentence, rather than the meanings of the individual words, is primary.[103]

However, although the understanding of the sentence depends on the meaning of the words, knowledge of these meanings depends at the same time on the sense of the complete sentence. The linguist is therefore faced with an infinite regression, which appears to destroy the basis of compositional analysis. In such a situation it is difficult to see how speakers manage to understand each other at all.[104]

---

[101] Sperber, Dan and Wilson, Deirdre, 'Pragmatics, modularity and mind-reading' (2002) 17 *Mind and Language* 3–23, 7.
[102] Lewis, David, 'Scorekeeping in a language game' (1976) 8(1) *Journal of Philosophical Logic* 339–59, 347.
[103] Frege, *Foundations of Arithmetic* (cited in n.12), xii: 'In the enquiry that follows, I have kept to three fundamental principles:... [b] never to ask for the meaning of a word in isolation, but always in the context of a proposition.'
[104] See however Recanati, François, *Truth Conditional Pragmatics* (Oxford: Oxford University Press, 2010), 48–9, who uses the notion of 'semantic flexibility' in attempting to show that contextual modulation is nevertheless compatible with a 'suitably weak' form of compositionality.

Nevertheless, although the problem of reflexivity may be fatal for a purely logical system, it does not seem to prevent either legal adjudication or linguistic communication. Z. Harris[105] demonstrated the logical impossibility of 'discovery procedures', pointing out that, at the most elementary level of linguistic analysis, while morphemes can only be identified through speakers' awareness of phonemes, these same phonemes can only be distinguished from noise through prior knowledge of the relevant morphemes. Yet this problem does not prevent language acquisition by human subjects.

A similar idea may apply to speakers' awareness of the linguistic consensus. The problem may be expressed in a simpler form by reference to the stock market. Individual investors make their decisions based on the market prices, which express the general consensus. Yet at the same time, these prices are determined by the aggregate behaviour of the individual dealers. In the same way, according to the private language argument, in the absence of consensual awareness, an individual would be unable to define his own linguistic intentions. In order to clarify his understanding, even of his own thoughts, he therefore needs some form of access to the intuitions of others. But it is then unclear how the linguistic consensus could be established in the first place, given that it must depend precisely on the aggregate of the (supposedly unknown) individual intentions.

As a partial explanation, it may be suggested that, just as the whole may be greater than the sum of its parts, the linguistic consensus may not be identical with the aggregate of individual intentions. Thus a chair is not to be identified with the pieces of wood of which it is composed, and a ship is distinct from 'mere congeries of planks'.[106]

A further problem is that agreement on the stock market figures does not necessarily lead to similar investment behaviour. Similarly, in linguistics, shared knowledge does not guarantee agreement about the use of words. One way of accounting for failure to agree on semantic definitions, whilst nevertheless preserving the essential intuition of the communitarian solution, is to suggest that the linguistic consensus is not necessarily unique or hegemonic, but may itself be context-dependent. All speakers are members of various linguistic communities, on the professional, familial, or social levels, for example, all of which use words differently. It follows that one linguistic consensus may be substituted for another.

In the law, even where the notion of institutional consensus appears to ensure agreement about the content of rules, there need be no agreement in adjudication. Indeed, legal decision-making depends not just on the semantics of the law but also on ideas of morality and justice, which cannot be decided by majority agreement. Numerous views relating to almost any social issue, once generally accepted, are now decisively rejected. Yet such views were thought to be right in the past, and may still be accepted in other jurisdictions, where different circumstances prevail. Because history teaches us that the majority can be and often is disastrously mistaken regarding ethical decisions, these cannot be justified by reference to general consensus. There is therefore a need for a higher authority (a consensus of consensuses) to decide which among the established views is correct. This problem manifests itself in the law in the need for recourse to a superior court with the requisite authority to decide such questions. However, it may more properly be said to be the object of moral philosophy.

---

[105] Harris, Zelig, *Methods in structural linguistics* (Chicago: University of Chicago Press, 1951).
[106] *River Wear Commissioners v Adamson*, per Lord Blackburn (cited in n.49).

4. Conclusion

For different reasons, Hart's semantics has been variously described as 'Unambitious',[107] or as falling victim to the so-called 'semantic sting'.[108] Yet he does not seem to have adopted any particular semantic theory or indeed to have attempted to defend one theory against another. He nowhere expresses a clear preference either for the literalist or for the contextualist view. On the contrary, he was reluctant to accept either formalism or rule-scepticism, presenting them as the 'Scylla and Charibdis of juristic theory',[109] whilst nevertheless emphasizing that they could both be seen as salutary where they correct each other. It may plausibly be suggested that rather than use provocative language to defend either theory, he may have preferred to adapt his discourse to his audience of jurists, in an attempt to reconcile opposing views by proposing a compromise solution, acceptable to all. If so, in his endeavour to provide a synthesis of disparate approaches, his own personal views would naturally appear sometimes equivocal.

In the Introduction to his major work, Hart[110] presents Austin's approach to ordinary language analysis, modestly, as providing 'a sharpened awareness' of words to sharpen our perception of the phenomena. However, as his title suggests, Hart was less concerned with ordinary language than with the analysis of fundamental technical terms, like legal 'rights' and 'duties', the nature of a 'corporation' or of a 'contract' as well as the 'concept of law' itself. The Austinian approach, although it makes a major contribution to our understanding of everyday language use, is less helpful for the analysis of empirical facts or indeed for clarification of technical (legal) concepts, normally defined by fiat. Austin's analysis of the corresponding terms could not be expected in itself to guarantee a heightened knowledge of the true nature of what may not even qualify in the strict sense as actual 'phenomena' at all.

Neither contextualist semantics nor the consensualist view of rule-following are universally accepted. Many linguists remain naturally reluctant to accept the idea that words have no (fixed) meaning in themselves. Such an idea seems to be in contradiction with the classic methodology of truth-conditional semantics. For jurists, it goes against the accepted view of traditional legal interpretation, in which the priority of literal meaning is explicitly affirmed. Neither group is likely to be comfortable with the idea that rules, interpreted acontextually, fail to constrain behaviour.

As a jurist, Hart is equally unlikely to have abandoned the literalist assumptions. However, many of his remarks show that he nevertheless accepted many of the principles underlying contextual interpretation. In his 'Postscript' to *The Concept of Law*,[111] he went so far as to define the law in Wittgensteinian terms as a 'practice', depending on a consensus established within the judicial institution. His fundamental 'rule of recognition' may also be seen as an essentially social theory of law, in which the correct interpretation is decided by the relevant community of authorized persons. Presumably for similar reasons, in his 1970 lecture on Djering,[112] he considered Austin and Wittgenstein

---

[107] Stavropoulos, 'Hart's semantics' (cited in n.41), 59–98; Rodriguez-Blanco, Veronica, 'A defence of Hart's semantics as nonambitious conceptual analysis' (2003) 9 *Legal Theory* 99–124.
[108] Dworkin, Ronald, *Law's Empire* (London: Fontana, 1986), 45.
[109] Hart, *The Concept of Law* (cited in n.14), 147.
[110] Hart, *The Concept of Law* (cited in n.14), iv.
[111] Hart, *The Concept of Law* (cited in n.14), 254.
[112] Hart, H. L. A., 'Jehring's "Heaven of Concepts" and modern analytic jurisprudence', in Hart, H. L. A., *Essays in Jurisprudence and Philosophy* (Oxford: Clarendon Press, 1983), 265.

as the most important figures in modern legal interpretation. This suggests a certain sympathy both for the idea of 'meaning as use' and for the Wittgensteinian rule-following considerations.

However, although semantic contextualism may have far-reaching consequences in the law, it remains a linguistic theory, whose status depends primarily on semantic rather than legal arguments.

10
On Goodness and Genre: Talking about Virtue in Law and Literature

Jan-Melissa Schramm

The English realist novel in the eighteenth and nineteenth centuries often illustrated the social and ethical education of its protagonists: thus by extension it sought to undertake a similar education of its readers. In its close attention to the often vexed relationship between an individual and the society to which he or she should conform, the novel interrogated the moral choices which best promoted personal flourishing and civil cohesion (whilst simultaneously demonstrating that occasionally one of these goals could only be obtained at the expense of the other). In *Human Rights, Inc.: The World Novel, Narrative Form, and International Law*, Joseph Slaughter describes the novel (and particularly, though not exclusively, the *Bildungsroman*), as a powerful vehicle for the work of culture in the individual: in their 'social tutorial effect' Slaughter writes, novels 'perform...transitive work as literary machines for producing subjectivity, machines designed to construct "centred subjects"'[1]—thus articulating the process by which historically marginal subjects become national citizens, self-regulating and obedient to the rule of law. As Slaughter notes, the *Bildungsroman* may narrate either successful or unsuccessful 'claims for inclusion in a regime of rights and responsibilities'[2]: much rests on the fate assigned to the protagonists at the point of narrative closure. Novelistic endings carry great ethical and political weight, and authorial choices as to which laws should govern the protagonist's 'deserts' shape the very telling of the tale.

Victorian authors such as Charles Dickens and George Eliot were well aware of the significance of narrative endings and Eliot in particular positioned her fictional work within the wider debates of the period about where authority and guidance for ethical decision-making was to be found. In *The Mill on the Floss* (1860), for example, she represents with poignancy and compassion the maturation of her suffering protagonist, Maggie Tulliver, who seeks to learn virtue from the imitation of various models. But she is constantly disappointed to find that there are few templates for good, flourishing female experience in an age of provincial prejudice. As she grows up, Maggie copies her parents, her brother, and finally Thomas à Kempis's exposition of the *imitatio Christi*—though none can satisfy her fully. Eliot's narrator cautions us that 'moral judgments must remain false and hollow, unless they are checked and enlightened by a perpetual reference to the special characteristics that mark the individual lot': we must beware of those who judge

---

[1] Joseph Slaughter, *Human Rights, Inc.: The World Novel, Narrative Form, and International Law* (New York: Fordham University Press, 2007), p. 117.

[2] Slaughter (cited in n.1), p. 27.

humankind in the abstract and are unable to respond with sympathy to the particular plight of suffering individuals:

All people of broad, strong sense have an instinctive repugnance to the men of maxims; because such people early discern that the mysterious complexity of our life is not to be embraced by maxims, and that to lace ourselves up in formulas of that sort is to repress all the divine promptings and inspirations that spring from growing insight and sympathy. And the man of maxims is the popular representative of the minds that are guided in their moral judgment solely by general rules, thinking that these will lead them to justice by a ready-made patent method, without the trouble of exerting patience, discrimination, impartiality, without any care to assure themselves whether they have the insight that comes from a hardly-earned estimate of temptation, or from a life vivid and intense enough to have created a wide fellow-feeling with all that is human.[3]

Whilst Eliot offers this observation in a fictional context, it nevertheless gestures with precision towards the wider pedagogic agenda of the Victorian novel—individual, singular experience is foundational for understanding the human condition: our responsibility to our neighbour predates our responsibility to the wider polis: the novel should encourage, through reading, the education of our sympathies, the development of our 'wide fellow-feeling with all that is human' through the practice of imaginative identification. According to Adam Smith, in his influential *Theory of Moral Sentiments*, this is the very definition of 'imagination'—the capacity by which we 'change places in fancy with another',[4] and extend thereby our capacity for compassion. In her correspondence with the positivist lawyer, Frederic Harrison, Eliot manifests a nuanced awareness of the issues at stake:

I think aesthetic teaching is the highest of all teaching because it deals with life in its highest complexity. But if it ceases to be purely aesthetic—if it lapses anywhere from the picture to the diagram—it becomes the most offensive of all teaching. Avowed Utopias are not offensive, because they are understood to have a scientific and expository character: they do not pretend to work on the emotions, or couldn't do it if they did pretend.

In her own words, her methodology involved 'the severe effort of trying to make certain ideas thoroughly incarnate, as if they had revealed themselves to me first in the flesh and not in the spirit'.[5] 'Incarnation' for Eliot implies a particular claim to the 'work [of] the emotions' and the value of affect, which, throughout the corpus of her writing, she suggests constitutes a form of knowledge—that is, *scientia*, rather than simply opinion. And for Eliot, affect is elicited by attention to particularity: form and content cooperate to generate the required readerly response. But even as she purports to prefer the complicated lived experience of singular individuals, she praises the Ten Commandments and the golden rule of ethics ('do as you would be done by'), and her own novels are punctuated by epigraphs and lapidary generalizations which question the extent to which biographical amplification of virtue is necessary for its communication. Although Eliot tells Harrison that she 'shrink[s] from "deliverances" on momentous subjects',[6] Leah Price notes that she allowed at least one edition of the anthologization of her own proverbs and epigraphs (the *Wise, Witty, and Tender Sayings in Prose and Verse Selected from the Works of*

---

[3] George Eliot, *The Mill on the Floss* [1860] (Harmondsworth: Penguin, 1985), p. 628.
[4] Adam Smith, *The Theory of Moral Sentiments* [1759], Knud Haakonssen (ed.) (Cambridge: Cambridge University Press, 2002; repr. 2007), pp. 11–12.
[5] George Eliot to Frederic Harrison, 15th August 1866, in *George Eliot: Selected Essays, Poems, and Other Writings*, A. S. Byatt and Nicholas Warren (eds) (Harmondsworth: Penguin, 1990), pp. 248–9.
[6] Eliot to Frederic Harrison, 15th January 1870, in *Selected Essays* (cited in n.5), p. 256.

George Eliot (1872)), thereby suggesting that narrative detail was expendable in the quest for a more easily digestible form of 'wisdom'.[7]

What then is the relationship between 'wisdom' and the narrative form required to 'illustrate' it?[8] More specifically, how much attention to individual particularity is required to model for readers the acquisition of goodness? Victorian literature offers us a range of competing examples—moral reformation is effected by sitting up late at night reading the Bible (in Elizabeth Gaskell's *Mary Barton*), or by studying the example of admirable human beings (in most novels by Dickens or Eliot), but even the lives of virtuous neighbours have to be compared to the Scriptures to give force to their example. Mid-Victorian writers ponder repeatedly the required 'amplitude' of efficacious parables of wisdom, from unglossed Scriptural quotation, to the extraction of material from Biblical tracts, to the extraordinary descriptive length of the prose works themselves which, Deirdre Lynch suggests, showcased the complexities of an emergent moral psychology and thus promoted the genre as *the* art-form of a progressive age.[9] Dickens and Gaskell periodically quote without elaboration from the Bible, yet all mid-Victorian writers tended to regard the Biblical Tract, circulated freely by the Bible Society, and containing short case studies of sin and repentance, as completely devoid of any ability to teach goodness or the path to salvation. As Charles Reade explains in *It is Never too Late to Mend* (1856), Bible verses 'learned-by-heart' can only take us so far, for 'many a scoundrel has a good memory':[10] a 'searching sermon' might work if 'each sinner takes it to himself... [and] fit[s] the cap on';[11] but it is the 'writing of lives' and the sharing of 'biography'[12] which, in Reade's portraits of Victorian prisons, promotes sympathy and communication amongst the inmates, and it is the voluntary assumption of mutual suffering by the chaplains which softens the hardened men to penitence.

Transmission of a moral message, then, is inseparable from the language which is chosen to communicate it: its truth resides not simply in what we might call narrowly 'content' but also in the vehicle in which that content is transmitted (as various as Dickens's *Hard Times*, Charles Kingsley's *The Water Babies*, and Eliot's *Middlemarch*). To return to George Eliot's incarnational metaphor, how much flesh do the dry bones need in order for the moral message to live? A whole life—the domestic epic of *Middlemarch* or *Little Dorrit*? A short but memorable fable or parable—like *Hard Times* or *Silas Marner*? An epitaph in which the peaceful death of a good man is summarized? And how do formal choices—of rhetoric, of the means of representation—determine the wider moral judgments a reader makes in response to a work? Whilst Jacques Derrida in 'The Law of Genre' suggested that what lay at the heart of generic division was in fact a 'law of impurity or a principle of contamination',[13] the relationship between formal choices and the moral function of a work has more recently been understood as a question of exclusion, and literary criticism has called for renewed attention to be given to that material which is shut out of a work in order to give its representation of lived experience a coherence relative to its frame of reference (arriving at a verdict in a court of law:

---

[7] Leah Price, *The Anthology and the Rise of the Novel* (Cambridge: Cambridge University Press, 2000), pp. 119–28.
[8] For a more extensive treatment of this topic, see Jan-Melissa Schramm, *Atonement and Self-Sacrifice in Nineteenth-Century Narrative* (Cambridge: Cambridge University Press, 2012), pp. 6–20.
[9] Deirdre S. Lynch, *The Economy of Character: Novels, Market Culture, and the Business of Inner Meaning* (Chicago: Chicago University Press, 1988), pp. 251–5.
[10] Charles Reade, *It is Never too Late to Mend* [1856] (London: Collins, n.d.), p. 387.
[11] Reade (cited in n.10), p. 277.
[12] Reade (cited in n.10), p. 385.
[13] Jacques Derrida, 'The Law of Genre' (1980) 7(1) *Critical Enquiry* 55–81 at 57.

persuading one's readers to assent to a work of fiction). In *Testimony and Advocacy in Victorian Law, Literature, and Theology*, I argued that Victorian authors like Dickens and Eliot grounded their critique of legal positivism in their assessment of the value of the potential evidentiary material which is not put to the jury—the testimony that could not be received, the voices which could not be heard in a courtroom all found the opportunity for expression in the more capacious (because less verdict-driven) fictional text. The result was simultaneously the literary appropriation of legal methodologies (to enhance a narrative's claims to verisimilitude) and a condemnation of legal judgment (to promote by implication the cultural value and significance of poetic justice).[14] In his *Anatomy of Criticism*, Northrop Frye had noted that the rhetoric of comedy shares certain salient affinities with the rhetoric of jurisprudence (both imply confidence in human powers of reason, and an optimism that despite the occasional temporal crisis, all will be well in the end): in *A Power to do Justice*, Bradin Cormack suggested that any potential conflict of literary and legal genres can be understood as analogous to the question of jurisdiction.[15] In his recent study *Poetic Justice and Legal Fictions*, Jonathan Kertzer draws on the work of both Cormack and Frye to argue that the conventions expressed in our understanding of how genre works are closely tied to the idea of justice which a text is seeking to articulate—for example, we trust that comedy will produce a good end, and we possess a foreknowledge that tragedy will end badly because it is already and in advance committed to the generation of pity and fear aroused by the spectacle of suffering. In Kertzer's analysis, '[d]eath is a poetically just ending in tragedy, not because it is what the hero deserves, but because it fulfills a pattern imposed internally by the plot, and externally by the laws governing tragedy'.[16] This *telos* towards a given end in turn determines wider questions of narrative shape and direction. If the quest for a verdict closes down the information available to decision-makers in the process of adjudication—*interest reipublicae ut sit finis litium* (there has to be an end to litigation), after all—the Victorian novel prefers instead amplitude, digression, the closest replication possible of lived experience. And the more a reader knows about a life, and the reasons for a seemingly transgressive action, the more likely he or she is to respond with what John Rawls called the superogatory virtues[17] of love or forgiveness (that is, virtues in excess of simple obedience to the law—an abundance of altruism in which the fictional art of the period was so invested).[18]

In the mid-Victorian period, re-writings and reinterpretations of the fall of Camelot exerted a powerful traction on understandings not only of English national origins but of the ways in which apparently straightforward moral truths are complicated by the aesthetic form in which the artist chooses to represent them. In the early anonymous medieval French romance about the fall of Camelot, *La Mort le Roi Artu*, when Lancelot and Guinevere are ambushed in the act of adultery, Artu seeks revenge: 'I intend that

---

[14] Jan-Melissa Schramm, *Testimony and Advocacy in Victorian Law, Literature, and Theology* (Cambridge: Cambridge University Press, 2000), pp. 1–23 and pp. 101–44.
[15] See Bradin Cormack, *A Power to do Justice: Jurisdiction, English Literature, and the Rise of the Common Law, 1509–1625* (Chicago: Chicago University Press, 2007), and Northrop Frye, *The Anatomy of Criticism: Four Essays* (Princeton, N.J.: Princeton University Press, 1957).
[16] Jonathan Kertzer, *Poetic Justice and Legal Fictions* (Cambridge: Cambridge University Press, 2010), pp. 6–18 (quote at p. 10).
[17] John Rawls, *A Theory of Justice*, rev. edn (Cambridge, Mass.: Harvard University Press, 1971, repr. 1999), p. 167.
[18] See Stefan Collini, *Public Moralists: Political Thought and Intellectual Life in Britain 1859–1930* (Oxford: Clarendon Press, 1991), pp. 65–6, and Schramm, *Atonement* (cited in n.8), pp. 1–37, and pp. 216–36.

severe justice should be taken on her for this crime she has committed'. He seeks the advice of his barons:

'My Lords, what must we do with the queen according to true justice?' The barons drew aside and discussed the matter... They said it was their judgment that justice called for her to be put to a shameful death, because she had committed great treachery by sleeping with another knight in place of such a noble man as the king... The king commanded his sergeants to light a great and dreadful fire in the jousting-field of Camelot, in which the Queen would be burnt, because a queen who was guilty of treachery could die in no other way, given that she was sacred.[19]

For this writer (or perhaps more accurately, in this tradition), the issue at stake is the authority of the King and the cultural value of masculine heroism: little access is offered to the speech of Guinevere herself, let alone her interior deliberations. This imbalance of narrative attention persists in Thomas Malory's more famous *Morte D'Arthur*, a fifteenth-century English epic which drew on an amalgam of French sources. Malory states that when Arthur consigns Guinevere to the flames, his strongest sense of loss is homosocial:

'My heart was never so heavy as it now. And much more am I sorrier for my good knights' loss than for the loss of my fair queen; for queens I might have enough, but such a fellowship of good knights shall never be together in no company'.[20]

The representation of Guinevere's voice is excluded at this point, although Malory does go so far as to assure his readers of her subsequent repentance: after Arthur's death, 'never creature could make her merry, but [she] lived in fastings, prayers, and alms-deeds, that all manner of people marveled how virtuously she was changed'.[21] But, again, the account of her transformation is offered to the reader in the third person.

By the mid-Victorian period, however, traditional narrative interest in the performance of heroic action had been displaced onto the figure of the chastely virtuous heroine, who advocates mercy, sympathy, and fellow-feeling, and whose love provides the incentive for otherwise undisciplined men to reform and live wisely. The ideology of domestic sentiment (of private 'goodness' rather than classical, republican virtue) located political as well as ethical significance in marriage; as Andrew Miller has observed, the Victorian novel places particular emphasis on the marital union as the means by which claims based on intimacy and claims based on contract might be reconciled[22]—in other words, the trajectory of a narrative towards marriage models for the attentive reader the processes by which wider social reconciliation (between classes as well as genders) might occur. Women's vulnerability to sexual temptation was thus politically freighted, yet as numerous critics have noted, literature nevertheless treated the plights of fallen women with considerable sympathy (for example, Dickens's Lady Dedlock, and Gaskell's Ruth are both the objects of readerly pity even as they are cast out of their communities by death at narrative's end). But the fate of Guinevere refracted this crisis of political thought at mid-century in particularly compelling ways because (in the popular interpretation of medieval law) her adulterous love for Lancelot also constituted evidence of the crime of treason. Consequently, any attempt to narrate their growing affection for one another

---

[19] Anon, *La Mort le Roi Artu*, trans. James Cable (Harmondsworth: Penguin, 1971; repr. 1988), pp. 119–20.
[20] Thomas Malory, *Le Morte D'Arthur*, Helen Cooper (ed.) (Oxford: Oxford University Press, 1998; repr. 2008), pp. 481–2.
[21] Malory, *Le Morte D'Arthur* (cited in n.20), p. 517.
[22] Andrew H. Miller, *The Burdens of Perfection: On Ethics and Reading in Nineteenth-Century British Literature* (Ithaca, N.Y.: Cornell University Press, 2008), p. 25.

also had to acknowledge the responsibility they bore for the destruction of an admirable and indeed ideal political polity, the Fellowship of the Round Table—thus placing great pressure on any attempt to harmonize justice and mercy, revenge and forgiveness in the narrative arc of their story. The mid-Victorian generation had experienced at first hand the profound class conflict of the 1840s and the Chartist protests of 1848: literary art in the following decade went to great lengths to prioritize reconciliation. Guinevere's alleged transgressions and their ineluctable consequences (both ethical and political) thus provided a particularly compelling challenge to claims for the political efficacy of sympathy.

Despite all the ways in which we might then expect Victorian writers to treat this material conservatively and cautiously, the two most famous re-tellings of the tale at mid-century were both first-person accounts, in poetic form, of the dilemma of choice narrated from Guinevere's point of view. In his 'Defence of Guenevere' [sic] (1858), William Morris offers us a portrait of a vital, suffering but defiant woman, neither repentant nor as yet condemned to death: he manages this by capturing a momentary exchange between Guenevere and her accusers and he refuses to narrate her end. Morris's Guenevere asserts in defiant, first-person speech the falsity of the accusation of adultery made against her, though her defence turns less on her substantive innocence and more on the authenticity of her love for Lancelot; she also suggests that, in any event, the contours of the moral choice with which she was presented were not clear. Her plight, she argues, could only be apprehended in metaphorical terms—as if a 'great God's angel' had offered her a choice between coloured samples of cloth, devoid of any more legible moral signification:

> And one of these strange choosing cloths was blue,
> Wavy and long, and one cut short and red;
> No man could tell the better of the two.
>
> After shivering half-hour you said:
> 'God help! Heaven's colour, the blue;' and he said: 'hell.'
> Perhaps you then would roll upon your bed,
>
> And cry to all good men what loved you well,
> Ah Christ! If only I had known, known, known...[23]

But it was Alfred, Lord Tennyson, who undertook the more sustained analysis of conscience and the operation of remorse, and for Tennyson, too, the female voice was clearly central to the genesis of his wider project: his poem 'Guinevere' appeared as one of the first four *Idylls of the King* (along with 'Enid', 'Vivien', and 'Elaine') in 1859. (The close chronology of the two poems is a coincidence in that neither man had read the other's work,[24] but they were responding to the same seething cauldron of political and theological ferment as England recovered from the Crimean War and the Anglican church was convulsed by controversy concerning the role of sacrifice and forgiveness in the process of man's reconciliation with God.)[25] Tennyson depended heavily upon Malory for the dry narrative bones of his own poetic project, but his treatment of Guinevere's plight marks perhaps his greatest departure from the earlier sources.[26] For unlike Morris,

---

[23] William Morris, 'The Defence of Guenevere' [1858] in Peter Faulkner (ed.), *William Morris: Selected Poems* (Manchester: Carcanet, 1992, repr. 2002), pp. 22–3.

[24] Christopher Ricks, 'Introduction' to 'Guinevere', in *Tennyson: A Selected Edition* (Harlow: Pearson, 1969, rev. edn. 2007), p. 941.

[25] For a discussion of the theological context of the 1850s, see Schramm, *Atonement* (cited in n.8), pp. 140–80.

[26] See David Staines, *Tennyson's Camelot: The Idylls of the King and its Medieval Sources* (Waterloo: Wilfrid Laurier University Press, 1982), pp. 42–54.

Tennyson chose to offer us in his 'Idyll' a portrait of Guinevere as moral exemplar, and the result is a particularly sustained engagement with the theology and jurisprudence of the 1850s.

In 'Guinevere', the Queen knows that her liaison with Lancelot has effected the ruination of the wider polity, and she renounces her sensual memories accordingly: she has sworn 'not even in inmost thought to think again/the sins that made the past so pleasant to us'[27] and has fled to a nunnery to escape the war that has been brought to the land. For Tennyson's Arthur, the Order of the Round Table was an attempt to formulate a coherent political system based on a fusion of private morality and public benevolence: his Knights had to swear 'to reverence the King, as if he were/their conscience, and their conscience as their King' (l. 464). He had been seeking to systematize ethical and political action, calling his colleagues and brethren to subscribe to a charter of duties which descended from the evangelical to the marital: that if they obeyed Christ and the law, then all else would follow accordingly. But instead Guinevere and Lancelot, through secrecy and betrayal, have initiated 'the breaking up of laws' (l. 419).

In depicting the dissolution of the Fellowship of the Round Table, Tennyson returns to the template of Milton's *Paradise Lost*, offering us a portrait of Arthur as God-like in the compassion he extends to his errant wife: in their final meeting, he does not call for her death, but instead he declares,

> And all is past, the sin is sinned, and I
> Lo! I forgive thee, as Eternal God
> Forgives: do thou for thine own soul the rest (ll. 540–2).

Arthur speaks in the figure of the Christ of the Unitarians, or of Broad Churchmen like Benjamin Jowett and Frederick Denison Maurice who shared much common ground with the Unitarians at mid-century:[28] he is a human figure, the embodiment of a good man: he identifies with her shame, and feels for her a 'vast pity'. Arthur is suggesting here that the work of forgiving oneself is difficult—that it involves mental labour to appropriate the forgiveness offered by another. The sin is not effaced miraculously or instantaneously by the eruption of grace and the work appointed her is to '*do* thou for thine own soul the rest'. Initially, Guinevere cannot even respond: like Milton's Eve ('with tears that ceased not flowing,/and tresses all disordered, at his feet/Fell humble, and embracing them, besought/His peace'),[29] she can only collapse at Arthur's feet. But unlike Eve, she can articulate no appeal for clemency: whilst Morris's Guenevere offers resistance and defiance, Tennyson's Guinevere is at this point passive:

> And he forgave me, and I could not speak.
> Farewell? I should have answered his farewell.
> His mercy choked me (ll. 609–11).

---

[27] Alfred, Lord Tennyson, 'Guinevere' in *The Idylls of the King*, Ricks (ed.), *Tennyson: A Selected Edition* (cited in n.24), pp. 941–59 at ll. 372–3. Other references to this edition are by line and are included in the body of the text.

[28] Tennyson was particularly close friends with F. D. Maurice (who was, in fact, godfather to Tennyson's son Hallam): see Robert M. Ryan, 'The Genealogy of Honest Doubt: F. D. Maurice and In Memoriam', in David Jasper and T. R. Wright (eds), *The Critical Spirit and the Will to Believe: Essays in Nineteenth-Century Literature and Religion* (Basingstoke: Macmillan, 1989), pp. 120–30, and also Tennyson's poem 'To the Rev. F. D. Maurice' in Ricks (ed.), *Tennyson: A Selected Edition* (cited in n.24), pp. 505–8.

[29] John Milton, *Paradise Lost* [1667] (New York: Norton, 1975), Book X, ll. 911–13.

If Tennyson means to imply only that she is silenced by his largesse, the final image here is a disturbingly violent one, with 'choking' an allusion to the deaths by strangulation inflicted upon those condemned for capital crime (the context in which appeals for mercy impacted most powerfully upon the Victorian public imagination).[30] Guinevere dies, momentarily, for her sin, before being re-born to her new appreciation of Arthur's moral stature and his irreplaceable singularity:

> Ah my God
> What might I not have made of thy fair world,
> Had I but loved thy highest creature here?
> It was my duty to have loved the highest:
> It surely was my profit had I known:
> It would have been my pleasure had I seen.
> We needs must love the highest when we see it,
> Not Lancelot, nor another (ll. 649–55).

Alongside her spiritual renewal, Guinevere can confess to a recovery of her (private) love for Arthur and a recognition of its value and potential impact at the ethico-political level had she been able to sustain it. That utopian vision has been lost but personal redemption remains available to her if she chooses to pursue it—and his love for her gives her the incentive to do so: 'I must not scorn myself; he loves me still' (l. 667). Yet Guinevere is nevertheless denied any form of reconciliation that would heal the broken marital bond: the politics of her redemption are expressed in her vows of chastity and penitential servitude offered up to the Sisterhood at the Convent to which she retreats (ll. 669–80). She acknowledges her fault for that 'voluptuous day,/Which wrought the ruin of my lord the King' (ll. 682–3): her final reference to Arthur here is expressed in terms of hierarchical deference not second-person intimacy. In *Deceit, Desire and the Novel: Self and Other in Literary Structure*, René Girard identified precisely this renunciation of sensual pride as the standard trajectory of the great pan-European nineteenth-century narratives from Stendhal to Dostoevsky: Guinevere thus undertakes the journey of the age as she assumes responsibility for her sins and stands chastened before her God. For Girard, such narrative conversion is always commensurate with religious experience, 'engender[ing for the protagonist] a new relationship to others and to oneself'.[31] Tennyson assures us that Guinevere's final destination is heavenwards: 'for her good deeds and her pure life,/And for the power of ministration in her', she is ultimately permitted to pass to 'where beyond these voices there is peace' (ll. 687–92). Just as Milton's Eve is reassured that her seed will redeem mankind, so too in 'Guinevere' the agent by whom ruin has come models for the reader the path of penitence. Guinevere remains for the reader both guilty scapegoat for the dissolution of the wider polis (after all, various Knights of the Round Table failed to obey their vows as well), and at the same time the template that the reader has to follow if he or she accepts Tennyson's argument that social progress must be predicated upon personal transformation.

Perhaps the tale continues to exert such a hold over the English literary imagination because it apprehends and articulates some of the ways in which equally important but incommensurable values may be brought into dialogue with one another. Guinevere's plight—as accused before the law and yet cherished companion of the sovereign—brings

---

[30] See V. A. C. Gatrell, *The Hanging Tree: Execution and the English People, 1785–1868* (Oxford: Clarendon Press, 1994), pp. 520–2.

[31] René Girard, *Deceit, Desire, and the Novel: Self and Other in Literary Structure*, trans. Yvonne Freccero (Baltimore, Md: Johns Hopkins University Press, 1961), p. 294.

justice and mercy into conflict in ways that cannot easily be reconciled. As Gillian Rose notes in her poignant intellectual autobiography, *Love's Work*:

> King Arthur explained his dream of Camelot to Guinevere, his beloved wife. He would end the feuds and warfare between the barons and knights, not by becoming a tyrant or despot, but by becoming a just king, who would maintain the rule of law. He would give straight judgments to foreigners and to his own people, so that they would prosper and enjoy peace, not war. They would have plentiful harvests, not famine or blight or plague, and the women would bear children. In answer to Guinevere's doubts about the likely stability of this new regime of peace, King Arthur proposed to enlist the participation of the knights. He built a Round Table, emblem of equality, and sent out criers for the best knights to join the debate.
>
> Launcelot, afar in France, heard of this vision of Camelot, and like other warriors and wise men, he was eager to join the Fellowship of the Round Table. Launcelot hoped that the new kingdom would create the perfect realm, whereas King Arthur's aim was to guarantee a knowable and reliable law, which would serve the people and their customs as they were. Guinevere and the other knights warned Arthur that Launcelot cared more for ideals than for others. However, they were all convinced of Launcelot's human heart when, in a jousting tournament, he wept as he slew a knight. So Launcelot became a Knight of the Round Table.
>
> Launcelot and Guinevere fall in love. For some time, every one except the King knows of their illicit passion. When the King finds out about it too, should he continue to pretend not to know what has happened, so as to preserve the vision of Camelot? This would destroy the authority of the Round Table and the law. Should he banish Launcelot and condemn Guinevere to die, according to the law, which they have all sworn impartially to uphold? If he enforces the law, against his desire, he will lose his beloved wife, who has betrayed him, and his beloved best friend, Launcelot. The King carries out the law: Launcelot is banished and Guinevere is condemned to death. Launcelot saves Guinevere, who enters a convent, and he wages war against Arthur. King Arthur wins the war, but he loses Guinevere, Launcelot, and the vision of Camelot.
>
> Whatever King Arthur chooses, whether to overlook the betrayal or to prosecute the crime, the choice is not the issue. For, one way or the other, the King must now be sad. Betrayed or avenged, sadness is the condition of the King. Whether action is taken in the spirit of the law, or whether its requirements are ignored, the law will rebound itself against his human weakness so as to disqualify itself. Either its authority will be eroded by the deliberate oversight of the King, or, if executed, it will be overthrown by Launcelot's revenge.

For Rose, this 'medieval tale' represents the quintessential problem of Aristotelian metaphysics: how to negotiate between the general and the particular, from the 'law of the concept to the peculiarity of each instance':

> If metaphysics is the *aporia*, the perception of the difficulty of the law, the difficult way, then ethics is the development of it, the *diaporia*, being at a loss yet exploring various routes, different ways towards the good enough justice, which recognizes the intrinsic and the contingent limitations in its exercise. Earthly human sadness is the divine comedy—the ineluctable discrepancy between our worthy intentions and the ever-surprising outcomes of our actions. This comic condition is *euporia*: the always missing, yet prodigiously imaginable, easy way.[32]

Rose's insight here is a crucial one, although her reading of the tale (despite its consciously archaic cadences) is inflected by Victorian re-tellings of the dilemma (in the earlier romances, Guinevere in herself is rarely seen as an object worthy of compassion). As I noted previously, for the mid-Victorian generation, the conflict between justice and mercy had particular resonance as the country sought reconciliation between working-class and elite interests in the light of the Chartist protests of the previous decade.

---

[32] Gillian Rose, *Love's Work* (London: Chatto & Windus, 1995), pp. 113–16.

And there was another context too, in which tensions between positivist approaches to the law and the need for equitable 'correction' can be understood—in the attempts to coordinate (and ultimately integrate) the complementary procedures of the common law courts and the Court of Chancery. As Simon Petch has observed,

> in the 1850s, when ['Guinevere'] w[as] written, the reform of Chancery that would lead to the procedural fusion of Law and Equity was taking legislative shape. During this decade Law and Equity were brought closer together by legislation transferring power between the jurisdictions, a process of reform that culminated in the Judicature Acts of 1873 and 1875.[33]

According to Petch, 'Tennyson... responded to the mid-Victorian reorganization of his country's traditions and institutions by examining the national conscience'; he does not 'engage directly with the legal debate', but 'put[s his] various configurations of law and conscience in relationship to a sense of justice which is unconstrained by the machinery of the law'.[34] Ultimately, as Petch notes, Tennyson is part of a larger conversation in the period about the origins of our moral sense—whether it is an innate faculty which speaks of man's association with angels, or something socially constructed over time, which speaks only to our descent from beasts.[35]

The law of Equity derived initially from the royal Prerogative of Grace, exercised according to the conscience of the King in the Court of Chancery: Petch traces the ways in which Equity cases and precedents 'formalized conscience' as '*civilis* and *politica*'— that is, not a private but an institutionalized faculty deployed for procedural purposes.[36] On the one hand, such clarification was necessary to avoid accusations of inconsistency and unpredictability in the exercise of 'conscience'—it had to be seen to be governed by uniform principles—but on the other hand this might result in an ossification of the sympathetic impulse. Once Equity jurisprudence was reduced to Chancery practice, its flexible principles of corrective justice were discarded and the only solution was seen to lie in a fusion of the two jurisdictions. After intense debate, the age-old maxim that 'equity follows the law' was in fact displaced by the Judicature Act 1873 s.25(11) which provided that in cases of conflict, the rules of Equity should prevail: as Petch notes, this serves somewhat unexpectedly to 'enshrine... the precedence of Equity procedures in the very legislation by which the chief institution of Equity was dissolved and its procedures absorbed into those of the Common Law'.[37]

For Deiter Paul Polloczek in his study *Literature and Legal Discourse: Equity and Ethics from Sterne to Conrad*, the petrification of Equity procedure and its subsequent dissolution as a separate jurisdiction can be mapped alongside modern literature's ethical preoccupation with fulfilling Equity's traditional role: he locates Equity's displaced survival in the forms of social and sentimental benevolence promoted by the novel—charitable activity, the development of the our sympathy for our neighbours, the capacity of art to explore and then insist upon the ethical value of irreducible singularity.[38] But, as Gary Watt observes in *Equity Stirring: The Story of Justice Beyond the Law*, it can also be argued that 'the jurisprudential distinction between equity and law does not depend

---

[33] Simon Petch, 'Law, Equity, and Conscience in Victorian England' (1997) 25(1) *Victorian Literature and Culture* 123–39 at 134.
[34] Petch, 'Law, Equity, and Conscience in Victorian England' (cited in n.33), pp. 133–6.
[35] Petch, 'Law, Equity, and Conscience in Victorian England' (cited in n.33), p. 139.
[36] Petch, 'Law, Equity, and Conscience in Victorian England' (cited in n.33), p. 124.
[37] Petch, 'Law, Equity, and Conscience in Victorian England' (cited in n.33), pp. 134–5.
[38] Dieter Paul Polloczek, *Literature and Legal Discourse: Equity and Ethics from Sterne to Conrad* (Cambridge: Cambridge University Press, 1999), p. 244.

for principled justification on the jurisdictional divide between the chancery and the common law courts,'[39] and Watt's account raises a number of problems for Polloczek's otherwise suggestive hypothesis. First, Watt insists, rightly, that literature has expressed a commitment to equitable principles from Aristotle onwards (equitable thinking makes its presence felt with particular force in Shakespeare's plays, for example)[40] and it cannot be seen to do so in any qualitatively different way after the enactment of the Judicature Acts. Secondly, Watt notes that Equity in fact failed to thrive for a generation after 1875,[41] (in other words, we might infer that literature could not automatically fill the vacuum left by Chancery's demise). And finally, but relatedly, what Tennyson represents in the wider corpus of the *Idylls* is in one sense the fallibility of Equity: the attempt to extend a rule of law based on the work of conscience—on conformity with such standards as honesty and good faith—fails to survive at the level of the *polis*. For sin and weakness—on the part of all, rather than simply Guinevere—undermine the vision of a Kingdom based on voluntary subscription to an ethical code. But mercy can still be extended to those whose all too human failings have played their part in the destruction of the community and it is the practice of this mercy which affords the poem's only vision of redemption.

How, then, does mercy differ from the institutionalized practices of Equity? If justice is the principle which insists that like cases are treated alike, then there is obviously some overlap between mercy and Equity—both are corrective principles, which call for attention to the particular rather than the general, in Aristotelian terms, and which ask for mitigating factors to be taken into account in deviating from the distribution of proportional punishment or 'just deserts'.[42] But mercy always works to ameliorate the severity of a penalty whereas Aristotle felt that equitable correction of a general principle could potentially work towards the exacerbation of punishment if required.[43] This distinction, traced so effectively by John Tasioulas in his work on current understandings of the operation of mercy in criminal trial procedure,[44] offers an important clue to what Tennyson is seeking to achieve in 'Guinevere'. Tasioulas notes that it is easy to dismiss mercy as a private virtue—an economy of forgiveness that operates only between friends and neighbours—but there is great value in trying to assert for mercy a valid role in public life. Even as Tennyson concedes that the Fellowship of the Round Table must fail, he seems to insist that forgiveness should be a part of public discourse, that it should play some role in the reconciliation of those parties to wrongs in which, in Tasioulas's terms, state or third-party interests are also at stake.[45] Like his contemporaries, Dickens, Gaskell, and Eliot,[46] Tennyson strives to maintain mercy's visibility in the public sphere. Tasioulas claims a public role for mercy by undertaking a careful clarification of the purpose of punishment: if retributive theories prioritize punishment proportional to the gravity of the offence, then Tasioulas 'makes room for mercy' by suggesting that

---

[39] Gary Watt, *Equity Stirring: The Story of Justice Beyond the Law* (Oxford: Hart Publishing, 2009), p. 47.
[40] Watt, *Equity Stirring* (cited in n.39), pp. 195–225.
[41] Watt, *Equity Stirring* (cited in n.39), pp. 79–80.
[42] Aristotle, *The Nichomachean Ethics*, trans. David Ross (Oxford: Oxford University Press, 2009), V. 10 (1137b), p. 99.
[43] Aristotle, *The Nichomachean Ethics* (cited in n.42). See also Watt, *Equity Stirring* (cited in n.39), p. 39.
[44] John Tasioulas, 'Mercy' (2003) 103 *Proceedings of the Aristotelian Society* (NS) 101–32.
[45] Tasioulas, 'Mercy' (cited in n.44), p. 105.
[46] On the novel and mercy in the period, see Schramm, *Atonement* (cited in n.8), pp. 25–32, and pp. 227–32.

even the hallowed principle of 'just deserts' is only 'one value amongst many' in our account of justified punishment. Alternative models such as the communicative theory of punishment (the idea that the essential point of punishment is to declare society's emphatic condemnation of criminal wrongdoing, thereby encouraging the offender's repentance and reformation) valorize other aims, such as communal reconciliation.[47] In this way, Tasioulas argues that mercy may be acknowledged as a distinct value with a role to play in the public administration of criminal justice: 'considerations of mercy highlight the potential excessiveness of the just punishment in the light of a further range of considerations that bear on the offender's character and the vicissitudes of life'[48] and 'the institution of legal punishment is thereby equipped to communicate its censure in a more nuanced and humane vocabulary'.[49] The merciful person thus expresses 'hope in the human capacity for redemption and trust in the good faith of others who have powerful incentives to deceive him',[50] and Victorian literature, in its capacious treatment of character and intention, claims the inculcation of that hope in its readers as its ethico-political agenda.

In 'Guinevere', Tennyson demonstrates Arthur's retreat from *lex talionis*, or even 'just deserts', to an emphasis on the morally educative impact of a hard-won and very human understanding of the work of mercy and repentance. When Malory offered Tennyson a template with which to privilege severe justice and strict accounting, Tennyson chose to articulate a more generous view of New Testament values. Despite his own doubts about some tenets of Anglican belief and his consequent sympathy for Unitarianism, Tennyson remains profoundly committed to literature as a form of theological expression: Christ-like mercy can succeed where other forms of equitable correction will fail. For Tennyson, recourse to Christian symbolism is aesthetically compelling—in the terms of Girard's analysis, the narrative arc of sin, suffering, and redemption is neither 'purely decorative' nor 'purely apologetic': it 'gives form' to the experience of the particular in history in the course of the nineteenth century.[51] In Tennyson's assurance that Guinevere is not condemned to hell after her death, he offers the reader what little comfort he or she can find in a world where conscience and good faith are not enough to sustain political cohesion: Equity remains an important ideal, but, as Watt notes, even for Aristotle, equitable thought 'was concerned with the practical reform of individual character rather than reform of the law'[52] and consequently 'one cannot legislate for equity'.[53] Tennyson's suggestion is that the hard work of forgiveness might succeed where even the suppleness of Equity is vulnerable to failure. In Matthew 18: 21–22, Peter asks Christ, 'How oft shall my brother sin against me, and I forgive him? Till seven times? Jesus saith unto him, I say not unto thee seven times; but until seventy times seven'.[54] Tennyson's hope is that through such personal commitments, offered freely and without concern for self-interest, the wider life of the *polis* might be transformed in turn. In the composition of his 'Idyll', Tennyson felt the most compelling vehicle for such a message was the poetic form and the first-person female voice, marginalized before the law and disenfranchised by the unreformed Constitution, and yet a powerful conduit for the gospel of forgiveness

---

[47] Tasioulas, 'Mercy' (cited in n.44), p. 114.
[48] Tasioulas, 'Mercy' (cited in n.44), p. 115.
[49] Tasioulas, 'Mercy' (cited in n.44), p. 123.
[50] Tasioulas, 'Mercy' (cited in n.44), p. 128.
[51] Girard, *Desire, Deceit, and the Novel* (cited in n.31), pp. 309–10.
[52] Watt, *Equity Stirring* (cited in n.39), p. 28.
[53] Watt, *Equity Stirring* (cited in n.39), p. 35.
[54] This reference is to the King James Version of the Bible.

which poetry is particularly well suited to explore. Tennyson's choice of form and genre directs his audience to new and potent definitions of 'goodness'. The nation torn by Chartist violence at home and the Crimean War abroad was in search of the tools of reconciliation, and Tennyson's vision shares points of contact with Girard's: violence must be renounced, for '[t]he time has come for us to forgive one another. If we wait any longer there will not be time enough'.[55]

---

[55] René Girard, *The Scapegoat*, trans. Yvonne Freccero (Baltimore, Md: Johns Hopkins University Press, 1986), p. 212.

11

The Grin's Cat: Language, Law, and Literature

Sebastian McEvoy

The title of this paper was not intended to allude to Chris Marker's film *The Grin without a Cat*, and one of its interpretations, according to which international socialism gradually became ineffectual 'like a spearhead without a spear' once it lost the Soviet Union and the Communist Party as reference points.[1] The allusion, however, would not have been absolutely irrelevant, because the issue around which this paper revolves is whether, reacting to 'the slings and arrows of outrageous fortune' etc., literature, as such, can target, not characters, but persons, 'legal' or 'juristic' and so-called 'natural', or must attempt to modify the social order, if at all, otherwise, for instance through a stylistic re-education of perception, which M. H. Abrams claimed the radical romantics sought to achieve, and Victor Chklovski, specifying that the re-education should free perception from automatism, advocated as the purpose of art and, particularly, literature.[2] Moreover, both titles allude to Lewis Carroll's *Alice's Adventures in Wonderland* and one of its characters, the Cheshire cat, about whom Alice says that she has often seen a cat without a grin but never a grin without a cat.

Alice's remark is taken here to raise the issue of the relation between predicates and subjects. The grin stands for any predicate and the cat for any subject. The word 'cat', however, is not perfect, because it does more than refer to a subject: like the word 'person', it encapsulates a number of predicates. Why 'grin' for 'predicate'? Because a predicate often, if not always, does not cover up the individual thing it is attributed to. Thus, one has talked of the *Mona Lisa*'s 'grin' and even her 'mysterious grin', rather than her 'smile'. In the language of this paper, the painting, arguably epitomizing an aspect of the Renaissance, the promotion of individuality, suggests what an individual might be: that which escapes predication.[3]

Can predicates and subjects exist separately? Is there such a thing as an un-predicated subject? Does a proper name not only stand for a subject, but already predicate something of its bearer? Those questions have been endlessly debated. In this paper, the issue

---

[1] David Sterritt, 'A Grin Without a Cat' (2009) XXXIV (4) *Cineaste*, available at <http://www.cineaste.com/articles/ema-grin-without-a-catem>, accessed 27 October 2011. The original title of the film, released in French in 1977, was apparently more optimistic, but ironic: *Le fond de l'air est rouge*.

[2] M. H. Abrams, *Natural Supernaturalism: Tradition and Revolution in Romantic Literature* (New York: Norton, 1973). Victor Chklovski, 'L'art comme procédé de singularisation', in Tzvetan Todorov (ed.), *Théorie de la littérature: Textes des formalistes russes* (Paris: Seuil, 1965), 76–97.

[3] The individual, indeed, is sometimes thought of as complex, and the best way to represent him to be to add predications on predications. One can then speak of a 'more or less' individual being. However, the multiplication of conflicting predicates may well result in nothing more than a mess, as in Honoré de Balzac's *Le chef-d'oeuvre inconnu* (Paris, 1831), a painter's perfectionism. The short story is available at <http://www.beq.ebooksgratuits.com/balzac/Balzac_70_Le_chef_doeuvre_inconnu.pdf>.

is: in literature, can (in the deontic senses of 'can') the subject be not only a literary fiction, a character, but also a legal fiction, say a person, and beyond that, a real thing, that is, in the language of this paper, an individual thing?[4]

'The real world' or 'reality', in the language of this paper, means a fictional world distinct from other fictional worlds, a world distinct in particular from the linguistic world and two of its subworlds, the worlds that law and literature create with ordinary language.[5] Whereas the latter are populated with predicated or predicable subjects, the former is populated with individuals, about whom, as such, nothing can be predicated.[6] The real world, as defined here, is a fictional world where categories are irrelevant. It is an anti-Aristotelian world or rather a world complementary to the Aristotelian world, because Aristotle repeatedly says there is no science or art about the individual (*hekaston*)[7] and, in general, Western thinking has followed, but he suggests thereby that the individual does exist and there is, at least, that minimal science about individuals.[8] For expository purposes, the real world or reality will be presented metaphorically as situated *below* the other fictional worlds. Thus an individual may be '*sub*sumed' under a legal concept or category.

More precisely, then, the issue is: if from the real world (a fictional world populated with individuals, that is un-predicable subjects), one distinguishes three other fictional worlds, populated with predicable subjects, the linguistic world and two of its subworlds, the legal and the literary worlds, is it permissible in the legal world for a linguistic fiction, say 'X' or 'cat', used in literature (in the restrictive sense[9]), to have a reference, not

---

[4] The paper, in other words, does not focus on the theory of possible worlds in relation to literature, although it does refer to that epistemic theory, in particular as presented and developed by Thomas Pavel, in *Fictional Worlds* (Cambridge, Mass.: Harvard University Press, 1986).

[5] Fictional worlds are countless. Others will be alluded to: political worlds, moral worlds. They also include scientific worlds, for instance mathematically constructed worlds, such as the geocentric world, but they are not immediately relevant here. 'Fiction', one may note here, comes from the Latin 'fingere' and the Indo-European 'dheigh-', meaning 'model in clay'. In Genesis 2:7, God shaped the first man, Adam, thus, out of 'adamah' (meaning earth) and breathed into his nostrils the breath of life.

[6] The real world can be imagined differently, for instance as an amorphous, indivisible whole. Such a world is suggested by the community responsibility system. Thomas Pavel, *Fictional Worlds* (cited in n.4), 115, recalls that Ferdinand Saussure's theory of linguistic signs incorporated not only a theory common since at least Aristotle, according to which the relation between the two sides of a linguistic sign is arbitrary, not causal, but also Wilhem von Humboldt's romantic view that each language expresses the vision of its users, which isolates objects out of the (hypothetical) indistinct continuum of nature.

[7] For instance, *Rhetoric*, I, 2, xi, 1356b. References to Plato and Aristotle follow respectively Henri Estienne's and August Immanuel Bekker's editions, available with translations at <http://www.perseus.tufts.edu>, accessed June 2011. The final numbered and lettered indications refer for Plato's texts to the page and section of the page and for Aristotle's to the page and column (here, '1356b' refers to page 1356, column b). Occasionally, for Aristotle's texts, the paper adds the line number. Other indications, here 'I, 2, xi', refer respectively to parts, chapters, and sections.

[8] The individual is here defined as what predication cannot cover: a hypothetical left-over or rest of predication. The statement suggests that the real world, apart from that rest, corresponds to usual perceptions. Aldous Huxley's texts on his mescaline experiences, *The Doors of Perception* (London: Chatto & Windus, 1954) and *Heaven and Hell* (London: Chatto & Windus, 1956), like Henri Michaux's, for instance *L'infini turbulent* (Paris: Mercure de France, 1957), show that one can escape those perceptions and that they are dependent on a particular biochemical combination, which a drop of what the law calls 'a dangerous drug' can alter. Yet, they also show that ordinary language can describe the hallucinatory worlds, which are therefore linguistic sub-worlds.

[9] Wherever possible, 'literature' replaces Plato's or Aristotle's word for 'poetry' ('poiesis'), but includes genres, for instance the novel and lyrical poetry, which neither Plato nor Aristotle considers. 'Literary author' and 'literary text' are used accordingly. For the issue of this paper with literature in the broad sense (as meaning any document) and in relation to the USA, see George Pring and Penelope Canan, *SLAPPS: Getting Sued for Speaking Out* (Philadelphia: Temple University Press, 1996), SLAPPs being 'strategic lawsuits against public participation' in government, which the authors consider to be violations of the First Amendment Petition Clause.

only in the literary world, populated with characters (human or non-human, animate or inanimate), but also in the legal world that parliament and the courts, which are themselves instituted by laws, populate through laws with legal fictions (persons, natural or juristic, and non-persons)?

The purpose of research is arguably to make paradoxical questions non-paradoxical or, at least, to add weight to one of the answers to a non-paradoxical question, that is, a question that can be discussed, because opinion still accepts several answers. Law and literature are generally considered to be different, except in the narrow circle of law and literature researchers, more exactly some of its members, since others, on the contrary, stress the difference between the two genres. In this paper, law and literature will first be argued to be similar in their relation to the real world. Then, one obvious difference between the two will be acknowledged, but paradoxically questioned, especially as creating imbalance between them in relation to referential access to the real world.

Law and literature are similar, not identical, in being required by principle or theory to be universal, not to deal with the individual, and so to be referentially vacuous in respect of the real world (section 1). However, law and literature differ in that the law is intended to be applicable to actual persons and in the process to real individuals, but withholds literature, despite the latter's sources, simulations, and effects, within a referential vacuum from the real world (section 2). Having argued those two points, the paper concludes by noting that the law has tended to restore the balance between law and literature, but submits paradoxically and then rejects the proposition (a) that full force should be acknowledged to paratextual disclaimers that a literary text is fiction and to theories that deny truth to literary predications and (b) that all predications of real individuals should be subjected to similar invalidation. In this paper, 'law', unless otherwise stated, means English law, but references to literature and literary theory, as is usual in the latter, are not limited to English authors.

1. The universality of fiction

The terms 'universal' and 'general', which may not be synonymous, can be defined negatively: the universal or general is neither the particular nor the individual. In one sense, universality is a matter of quantification: if a predicate can be attributed to 'all' subjects, especially a priori, not as an empirical collection, the proposition is universal; if only to 'some', it is particular; if only, say, to Socrates or Alcibiades, it is 'individual'. Law and literature are similar, not identical, in being required by principle or theory to be universal or general, not to predicate of individuals, and so to be referentially vacuous in relation to the real world.

Two theories are considered here: the theory of constancy, according to which law and literature remain or should remain always the same stylistically whatever their fictional world and their real world context (subsection 1.1) and the schematic theory, under which law and literature do not or should not refer to the real world (subsection 1.2). The consideration of those two theories does not imply adherence to them.

If law and literature are imagined to be mirrors, then they are distinct from whatever they reflect for two reasons: under the theory of constancy, because they are always the selfsame mirrors, universally, that is, whatever they mirror; under the schematic theory, because they mirror, not the individuals that appear before them, but types, which are more universal or general than individuals, indeed quite foreign to the latter, and which they exhibit in themselves as mere possibilities.

1.1. The theory of constancy

There is a persistent theory that a literary author has or should have a constant manner of writing in all his works whatever subject he speaks about and whatever he predicates of it and that, in so doing, he upholds or should uphold values that are or should be acknowledged by all and that are, in that sense, universal, most obviously the value of constancy. Constancy is also manifest in the drafting of statutes, which suggests that it complies with the theory of constancy. The theory of constancy does not exclude the possibility for law and literature to refer to subjects (real or not) and predicate of them, but it does make the manner in which they do so prevail over the reference and predication themselves and excludes the imitation of subjects and predicates.

The first exponent of the literary theory is Plato. In *Republic*, book III, it is argued that literature must imitate nothing, except virtues that are required of Plato's fictional City's guardians, among which are constancy, discipline, or self-mastery. Literature should imitate neither characters or passions, for example women (if the author is a man), slaves in their servility, craftsmen (who are not guardians of the City), the unhappy, the sick, those who weep at the death of someone, those who insult, drunkards, madmen (395d–396b), and impassioned lovers (396d) nor the physical world, for instance 'neighing horses and lowing bulls, and the noise of rivers and the roar of the sea and the thunder and everything of that kind' (396b, repeated more or less at 397a). The prohibition affects not only content, but also form and especially rhythm. 'The right speaker, Socrates says, speaks… [all through his text] almost on the same note and in one cadence' (397b). The sound, that is to say, should never be an echo of the sense.[10] Literature, according to Plato, should be rather like the 'starlit or moonlit dome', in William B. Yeats' 'Byzantium' (lines 5–8), [that] 'disdains' [or better here: stands apart from]/'All that man is/All mere complexities/The fury and mire of human veins'.[11] Moreover, as Stephen Dedalus, in James Joyce's *A Portrait of the Artist as a Young Man*,[12] says of art in general, literature should not provoke passions and desires in its readers. *Republic* does not discuss the aesthetic state that, perhaps like Yeats in 'Byzantium', Dedalus advocates. It is concerned only that literature should manifest and foster those virtues that the fictional City, universally, requires of its guardians, among which are constancy, discipline, and self-mastery.

In English poetry, Plato's requirement was satisfied for several centuries while the accentual-syllabic model of versification, especially the iambic pentameter, with its cosmological, political, and ethical implications,[13] was the norm under which most poets accepted to write. It is not known who, if anyone, imposed the norm, but several of its early exponents and practitioners were associated with government, that is the guardians of the kingdom: Roger Ascham, George Puttenham (Sir Thomas Eliot's nephew), Thomas Sackville, and Thomas Norton (Thomas Cranmer's son-in-law). The norm, which was admittedly flexible enough to allow period and individual differences, as required by modernism, was at the same time rigid enough to enable one to subsume under 'such a plain and simple

---

[10] Alexander Pope's *An Essay on Criticism* (1711) declares exactly the opposite (line 326). Unless otherwise stated, the texts of the poets quoted are all available at <http://www.bartleby.com/verse/>.

[11] William Butler Yeats, *Collected Poems*, 2nd edn (London: Macmillan, 1950), 280.

[12] James Joyce, *A Portrait of the Artist as a Young Man* (London: The Egoist, 1917).

[13] For a summary presentation of those implications, see Sebastian McEvoy, 'The Argumentative and Legalistic Analysis of Versification', in F.H. van Eemeren, B.J. Garssen, D. Godden, and G. Mitchell (eds), *Proceedings of the 7th Conference of the International Society for the Study of Argumentation* (Amsterdam: SicSat, 2011), ch. 122.

manner of writing', as George Gascoigne[14] described it, most poetry written for two or three centuries, with the effect that English versification appears to have been relatively, not absolutely, indifferent to its varied predications and possible references. The model has been abandoned. However, modernism has required and still requires each poet and in general each artist to have developed a new manner of his own identifiable in all his works and whatever he speaks about. In so doing, an author upholds not only constancy as a value, but also individuation, individuality,[15] and consequently newness.

In its former relative constancy, English poetry has been similar to English statutory discourse, which does not alter either where it alteration finds, but is similar in style however much its provisions differ. (One could argue the same point about modern law reports, which also have a recognizable format.) There is arguably no stylistic difference between for instance the Protection of Birds Act 1954, the Terrorism Act 2000, the Constitutional Reform Act 2005 and the Marriage (Wales) Act 2010. Thus, just as one can oppose what have been the English and French norms of versification, one can oppose the English and Continental or French statutory styles.[16] Legal drafting, like verse, might be subjected to rhythmic analysis, but one cannot limit to rhythm its constant features, no more than poetry's. Indeed, even the rhythmic analysis of verse involves other features: punctuation, syntax, and semantics. One recurrent feature of English, as opposed to French, statutory drafting is the interpretation or definition section, by which the meaning of ordinary words is altered for the purposes of a statute; another feature is long, analytical sentences. Statutory definitions are often complex in the sense that each term of the initial definition of a term is then itself defined. Complex definitions are a regular feature of statutory drafting, but admittedly can be found elsewhere than in statutes and, indeed, not only in legal writings. An early instance is to be found, not in a statute, but in Sir Edward Coke's *Institutes*, book III, chapter 7, with the definition of murder. There is, beyond Coke's complex definition of murder, Aristotle's complex definition of tragedy in *Poetics*, 6, 49b, which the greater part of the treatise then glosses. It is not the originality of the feature, but its regularity that matters. Among countless statutory examples, one can cite the definitions of theft (Theft Act 1968 s.1) and the degree of force in public and private defence (the Criminal Justice and Immigration Act 2008 s.76). The two statutes exhibit a third feature of English statutory drafting: analytical layout with numbered sections, broken down into indented numbered subsections with indented lettered sub-subsections, as in the Theft Act 1968 s.2, and sometimes, as in the Criminal Justice and Immigration Act 2008 s.76, even indented sub-sub-subsections with roman numerals. Statutory drafting, as Plato required of literature, remains relatively constant and recognizable whatever its subject matter and thereby the drafters manifest a virtue, constancy, which the City, according to Plato, should foster in all its guardians. Highlighting the inevitable difference between the linguistic and the real worlds, there is thus, in statutory drafting and there has been in verse and still is in a more individualistic manner, a deliberate generic demarcation between texts, content, and the context within which they are produced.

Statutory discourse and literary discourse, when it complies with the theory of constancy, consider endearing wild birds, tempests, terrorist actions, weddings or whatever and are never affected. It is the constancy of manner, the discipline, or the self-mastery that matters

---

[14] George Gascoigne (1575), *Certain Notes of Instruction*, in Gavin Alexander (ed.), *Sidney's The Defence of Poetry and Other Renaissance Literary Criticism* (London: Penguin, 2004), 240.

[15] Note that if individuality is a modernist value, Gerald Manley Hopkins, in upholding it, referred to a medieval philosopher, Duns Scotus.

[16] Michael Zander, in *The Law-Making Process*, 6th edn (Cambridge: Cambridge University Press, 2004), 25–36, quotes passages from several essays on the English statutory drafting style, some of which are comparative.

most, not whatever the texts speak about. Thus, under the theory of constancy, one can argue that Racine is to be preferred to Shakespeare,[17] Shakespeare's sonnet 116 ('Let me not...') to sonnet 129 ('Th'expense of spirit...'), and the iambic pentameter to Hopkins' prosodic system which, however rule-bound, self-mastered, and individualistic, adapts excessively to subject matter, for instance in 'That Nature is a Heraclitean Fire and the Comfort of the Resurrection' and even in 'The Windhover'. Or, indeed, to that of Shakespeare or Donne the verse of the Augustan Age, which John Keats ridiculed in *Sleep and Poetry* (ll. 186–7), saying, 'They sway'd upon a rocking horse/And thought it a Pegasus'. Had poets, even under the accentual-syllabic system, abided fully by the theory of constancy, their works would indeed be unbearably monotonous: some might say, as statutes are.

The mention of the sonnet, which is rule-bound, in whichever of its forms, so that those forms remain constant whatever the subject, leads one to the second theory of universality. Contrary to the theory of constancy, which only excludes the possibility for laws and literary texts to imitate the predicates they attribute to subjects, but not to refer to the latter and predicate of them, this second theory presents literature and law as estranged from the real world by their own internal organizational requirements and limits them to the creation of worlds of their own.

1.2. The schematic theory

Among the several theories that Thomas Pavel calls 'segregationist', because they deny truth value to literature,[18] there is one, which he calls 'conventionalism', and in relation to narratives 'mythocentriscm',[19] here referred to as the 'schematic theory', according to which literary authors observe or should observe the (hypothetical) universal requirements of literature and its generic subdivisions, for instance the novel, the short story, the sonnet, or the tragedy, with the effect that literature, as such under that theory, does not or should not primarily, if at all, mirror the real world. For a different reason, the principle of the rule of law, laws do not refer to specific persons either nor a fortiori to individuals.

Under the schematic theory, neither literature nor law mirrors the real world and its individuals, but exhibits subjects and predicates as types and possibilities. In relation to law especially, this disconnection from the real world has often served as an argument for disparagement. Rightly or not, it has been understood as justifying the development of equity, in the broad, philosophical or narrow, originally English sense. The law, it is said, is too general, provides slots or categories that are inadequate, into which individual data do not really fit, but in respect of which adjudication, bound to apply the law, must follow a pragmatic approach or else resort to an (inequitable) equitable suiting of the law to the facts of cases.[20] Thus, Lord Wilberforce, in *New Zealand Shipping Co Ltd v A M Satterhwaite & Co Ltd*:

English law, having committed itself to a rather technical and *schematic* doctrine of contract, in application takes a practical approach, often *at the cost of forcing the facts to fit uneasily into the marked slots* of offer, acceptance and consideration.[21]

---

[17] One reason is that Shakespeare's plays, unlike Racine's, combine verse and prose and do so for various imitative purposes, for instance, but not only, to distinguish noble and other characters.
[18] Pavel, *Fictional Worlds* (cited in n.4), 11.
[19] Pavel, *Fictional Worlds* (cited in n.4), 114 ('conventionalism'), 4 ('mythocentrism').
[20] John Bentham, in *Truth versus Ashhurst* (London, 1792), may be read as criticizing case law, which he there called 'dog law', one might say for being 'made to measure', to suit litigants as individuals, and contrary to the rule of law, and in that sense 'inequitably', rather than 'ready-made', 'off the peg', or 'ready to wear' law.
[21] [1975] AC 154, HL at 167 (emphasis added). Judges have also used words other than 'slot' to mean the same thing.

The earliest exponent of the literary theory is Aristotle. His dialectical purpose in *Poetics* is to refute Plato's arguments in *Republic* to ban literature from the City. Most of the work concerns tragedy. One of Aristotle's claims against Plato is that literature is, not opposed, but similar to philosophy in aspiring to the universal or general. Four of his arguments to uphold that claim are relevant here. The first three arguments, I–III, are stated in chapter 9,[22] the fourth in chapter 17[23]:

I) Literature, as opposed to histories or chronicles, speaks about the possible, that is to say what could have happened, in accordance with likelihood or necessity,[24] not what has happened, the former being more general or less individual than the latter.

II) Literature, as opposed to histories or chronicles, speaks about types of men and the types of things they are likely to or necessarily do, which is general (*katholou*), not individual (*hekaston*),[25] unlike Alcibiades and others and the individual things they do or have done, even though literature does name its characters.

III) Literature, especially tragedy, often uses pre-existing stories[26] that are believed to be true, only because what is believed to be true is believed to be possible, but it would be ridiculous to require literature to use such stories, because readers who do not know a story to be true can enjoy it as much as those readers who know it is true.[27]

IV) The literary author should first consider the story 'in general' (*katholou*), and add the names of the characters after and presumably also the location in time and space.

Following Dupont-Roc and Lallot's French translation for the 'general' outline of the story,[28] this theory (which Thomas Pavel, as said above, calls 'conventionalism' or, more specifically, 'mythocentricism') is here called the 'schematic' theory of literature. The most productive modern exponents of the theory have been the structuralists in the 1960s and 1970s (for instance, Roland Barthes, Umberto Ecco, or Tzvetan Todorov), who purposed to institute a science of literature,[29] and their formalist or other forerunners (for example, Joseph Bédier, Victor Chklovski, or Vladimir Propp) in their works on narratology.[30] Under the schematic theory, a play or narrative must be considered

---

[22] Aristotle, *Poetics*, 9, 1451a36–1451b26.

[23] Aristotle, *Poetics*, 17, 1455a34–1455b12.

[24] Pavel, *Fictional Worlds* (cited in n.4), 46, translates the relevant passage as follows: 'what is possible according to possibility and necessity' and interprets it in Leibnizian terms as meaning that literary authors make propositions that are possible, because true in at least one possible world, or necessary, because true in all possible worlds. In other words, he assimilates likelihood (or verisimilitude) and possibility, which Aristotle distinguishes when he says that an author must prefer what is not possible but likely to what is possible but unlikely (*Poetics*, 24, 1460a26).

[25] In their edition of *Poetics* (Paris: Seuil, 1980), Roselyn Dupont-Roc and Jean Lallot translate 'hekaston' by 'particulier', which is confusing, since Aristotle distinguishes the particular and the individual. However, it does agree with the theory of this paper that the individual escapes predication. Alcibiades is arguably not a universal type, but whatever can be said about him does not make him an individual either.

[26] Pavel, *Fictional Worlds* (cited in n.4), 46, refers to this part of the passage in his comparison of possible worlds and fictional worlds to support the claim that characters may be thought possible. He does not give Aristotle's reason for saying why tragedy often uses pre-existing stories and his dismissive comment on that reason.

[27] Note that *Poetics*, unlike *Rhetoric* (cited in n.7), II, xx, 1391a, does not analyse those pre-existing stories as relating individual facts about individuals. The question is then: why are the characters of existing stories types; or how do they become types?

[28] Dupont-Roc and Lallot, *Poetics* (cited in n.25), 65.

[29] A science in the Aristotelian sense, under which there is no knowledge of the individual, as discussed in text to n.7.

[30] Roland Barthes, 'L'analyse structurale du récit' (1966) 8 *Communications* 1–27; Joseph Bédier, *Les Fabliaux* (Paris: Champion, 1893); Victor Chklovski, 'La construction de la nouvelle et du roman' in

first, and perhaps exclusively, as manifesting more or less universal generic features that make the text a play or narrative or more specifically, for instance a tragedy, a novel, a short story, a *Decameron* tale or a James Bond novel, etc.[31] Non-textual reality, as Roland Barthes argued in 'L'effet de réel', is at most only a textual effect achieved through elements that appear to have no narrative function.[32]

The schematic theory, in the structuralist version, is more extreme than in Aristotle's version, in its segregation from the real world. For Aristotle, characters and stories were not disconnected from the real or individual world: they were types and possibilities, which actual individuals might instance, without being reducible to them. Literature, despite Plato's claim, was therefore similar to philosophy, in moving the mind from the individual to the universal. In the structuralist version of the schematic theory, characters are not necessarily types of which instances may be recognized in the legal and the real worlds. The variation is understandable, because modern literature, in contrast with a frequent simplistic view of earlier literature, has made characters complex. Complexity in characterization can be understood as an attempt at representing the individual and may have shaped the perception of what an individual is. For structuralist narratology, a character, however, is merely a cluster of predicates.[33] Moreover, whereas some authors equate verisimilitude and possibility,[34] structuralist narratology, emphasizing the gap between literature and reality, has preferred to disconnect verisimilitude, understood as being primarily opinion-based, and possibility, understood as distinct from opinion. In the structuralist version of the schematic theory, characters and stories are not constructed as types and possibilities which the real world may instance, although they may inform and, like ideology, pervert the experience of the real world. Thus, Aristotle requires stories to have a beginning, a middle, and an end,[35] but the real world cannot be chopped up to fit into those categories.

Notwithstanding those differences between the Aristotelian and structuralist versions, literature, under the schematic theory, can be argued to be similar to law, as it has been in subsection 1.1 under the theory of constancy. The governing principle in law-making is arguably the principle of the rule of law. Statute law, in the Constitutional

---

Tzvetan Todorov (ed.), *Théorie de la littérature* (cited in n.2), 170–95; Umberto Ecco, 'James Bond: une combinatoire narrative' (1966) 8 *Communications* 77–93; Vladimir Propp, *Morphology of the Folktale* [1928] (Austin, Tex.: University of Texas Press, 1968); Tzvetan Todorov, *Grammaire du 'Décaméron'* (Hague–Paris: Mouton, 1969), *Introduction à la littérature fantastique* (Paris: Seuil, 1970), and *Qu'est-ce que le structuralisme? la poétique* (Paris: Seuil, 1977).

[31] Just as there has been a collective system of versification whereas now each poet arguably must find his own, individual system, so there are, according to the narratologists, narrative structures that are common to all narratives, but also narrative structures that are common to narratives of a given genre or of a given author. Pavel, in *Fictional Worlds* (cited in n.4), 2, remarks that the quest for a work's structure is illusionary, because structure requires interpretation, which is by definition infinite and subject to debate. One can add that the theory that universal structures are at work in individual works is also questionable, if the theory allows, as it does, a structure to be more or less actualized in a work. Thus, if one postulates, as does Todorov, in *Qu'est-ce que le structuralisme?* (cited in n.30), that a narrative sequence comprises five propositions (equilibrium, disruptive factor, disequilibrium, restorative factor, equilibrium), one may argue that a particular text focuses only on a few and leaves the others in absentia, without declaring that the text contradicts the theory.

[32] 'L'effet de réel' (1968) 11 *Communications* 84–9.

[33] Todorov, *Qu'est-ce que le structuralisme?* (cited in n.30), adopts the theory that a name, strictly speaking, refers to an unpredicated subject (in the language of this paper, an 'individual'), but it is the support of all the predications attached to it.

[34] This view is discussed in n.24, referring to Pavel, *Fictional Worlds* (cited in n.4), 46.

[35] Aristotle, *Poetics* (cited in n.22), 7, 1450b26. A similar remark can be made upon the concept of cause and the need, often expressed in adjudication, to avoid a *regressum ad infinitum*.

Reform Act 2005 s.1, has acknowledged the rule of law as an 'existing constitutional principle'.[36] The Act does not define the principle, which Lord Goldsmith and Lord Bingham have set out to do in their lectures after the enactment.[37] Lord Bingham has proposed eight sub-rules, which it seems could be further broken down into sub-sub-rules. Sub-rules I, which includes predictability, and III, which includes general applicability, were arguably at work already in 1215, in the first version of Magna Carta, clauses 39 and 61. The latter, in making the king answerable for a breach of the Charter, implies that all, even the monarch, are equally under the law. The former, in requiring that all freemen be tried according to the law of the land ('per legem terrem'), suggests that law cannot be retroactive. The latter aspect of the rule of law is operative especially in criminal law. In accordance with the constitutional rule of law principle, understood as requiring that law should be proactive and should apply to all persons whatever their individual characteristics, one can hold that:

A) a law, as such, does not refer to what has happened, but to what may happen.
B) a law, as such, speaks about types (or clusters of predicates), not individuals.

Propositions A and B, which concern law-making, are comparable respectively to Aristotle's propositions I and III, on the one hand, and his proposition II, on the other, that relate to the making of literature, except that law, unlike literature, does not name its subjects, but naming, under the schematic theory, is contingent (see proposition IV).

Setting aside private Acts and personal Acts, which are relatively rare, statutes are comparable to the schema of the story that a literary author, according to Aristotle, should conceive clearly before naming the characters. They do not refer to individuals, past or present. They do not even name actual legal or natural persons. Typically, they speak about types; they speak about 'a' + common noun (for instance 'a company', 'a person'); the indefinite pronoun, amounting to a universal quantifier, means that whatever is said about a type is universally true of all its argued occurrences or instances in the real world. Contrary to its misleading name, case law operates in the same manner. It is true that for instance *Donoghue v Stevenson*[38] has its origin in an extra-textual series of events that occurred in a given spatio-temporal context with named persons, to which individuals corresponded in the real world, but its two *ratios* are formulated in general terms with no reference to the events and the individuals which occasioned their formulation. Typically also, both statute law and, in its *ratios*, case law, as Aristotle requires of literature, do not speak about what has happened, but about what may happen. Thus, their frequent use of 'if' clauses, as in the Theft Act 1968 s.1(1): 'a person is guilty of theft if he dishonestly appropriates property belonging to another with the intention of permanently depriving the other of it; and "thief" and "steal" shall be construed accordingly'. Case law, it is true, has been reproached for creating rules of law to suit the case, as in *Donoghue v Stevenson* or *R v R*,[39] but the judgments themselves, arguably not to breach

---

[36] In other statutes, the expression 'rule of law' means 'legal rule', like the French 'règle de droit'.
[37] Lord Bingham of Cornhill, 'The Rule of Law', 6th Sir David Williams Lecture, Centre for Public Law, the Cambridge Faculty of Law, 2006, available at: <http://www.cpl.law.cam.ac.uk/past_activities/the_rt_hon_lord_bingham_the_rule_of_law.php>. Lord Goldsmith, 'Government and the Rule of Law in the Modern Age', LSE Law Department and Clifford Chance Lecture Series on Rule of Law, 22 February 2006, available at: <http://www2.lse.ac.uk/publicEvents/pdf/20060222-Goldsmith.pdf>, both accessed 24 June 2011.
[38] [1932] UKHL 100.
[39] [1991] UKHL 12, 3 WLR 767, [1992] 1 AC 599.

the principle of the separation of powers overtly, state that the relevant law has always been such or never otherwise and they merely declare it.[40]

Literature, under the schematic theory, and law, under the principle of the rule of law, are objects and are partly recognizable as such in their 'segregation' from the real world and the individuals who participated in their making. Under the schematic theory of literature and the principle of the rule of law, attempts at discovering the contextual origins of literary texts and laws are equally vain, because irrelevant. Richard Ellman's and George Painter's biographies of respectively William Butler Yeats or James Joyce and Marcel Proust, however interesting, just miss the point, if they are intended to be explanatory.[41] The lives of literary authors, according to the schematic theory, are genetically unrelated to their works, which are governed by the internal requirements of literary fiction, and are irrelevant for their understanding. Similarly, under the principle of the rule of law, the decision in *Pepper v Hart*[42] appears misguided in having relaxed the rule that absolutely no reference should be made for the interpretation of laws to the statements of those involved in their making and, whereas a statute is attributed only to an arguably fictional set of authorial authorities in the enactment formula,[43] one can question the relevance of even naming those who, through their opinions, have arguably, but often self-deniably, authored case law.

Notwithstanding these and the former propositions on the similarities between literature and law, which may well be paradoxical and which are stated here without any implication as to adherence, there is an all-important and obvious difference, to which it is time to turn: laws are usually enacted to regulate the real world and enable the courts to apply them to arguably actual occurrences of its types and beyond that, contingently, to individuals, but, among the laws, there are provisions to prevent literature, unlike law, from breaking out of its referential vacuum and from referring to individuals, when the latter are persons, despite the frequent origin of literature in both the legal and the real worlds and also its frequent simulation of those worlds.

2. Fiction's access to reality

Setting aside for a moment their hypothetical universality, one could, in reading law and literature, just marvel at their creativeness, their ability to construct, usually through ordinary language, fictional worlds, for instance the United Kingdom of Great Britain and Ireland, Denmark, Scotland, Cyprus, and Narnia, constellated with fictional heavenly bodies, towns, and villages, say the sun, London, Dublin, Venice, Balbec, and Cambrai, peopled with fictional citizens, for example the people of the United States of America,

---

[40] A similar issue arises in poetics or rhetoric. For instance, did Aristotle create what tragedy should be, with the effect that some already existing tragedies do not fit the definition perfectly, or declare what it is from some, not all, existing tragedies?

[41] Richard Ellman, *Yeats: the Man and the Masks* (London: Faber, 1948) and *James Joyce* (Oxford: Oxford University Press, 1984); George Painter, *Marcel Proust* (London: Chatto & Windus, 1959–1965).

[42] [1992] UKHL 3. The allowance has not been resorted to frequently. For the interpretation of contracts, *Chartbrook Ltd v Persimmon Homes Ltd* [2009] UKHL 38 refined the purposive approach, but reaffirmed the exclusionary rule regarding pre-contractual negotiations and the parties' declarations as to their subjective intentions as opposed to their objectively constructed intentions. Similarly, literature, for many literary critics, must be interpreted objectively, notwithstanding the authors' declared intentions. The possibility of objective interpretation is equally questionable for law and literature.

[43] The monarch and the two houses of Parliament do not actually author statutes, but authorize or enact them: in the case of the monarch and, for public bills, the Lords, more or less automatically.

Hamlet, Othello, Leopold Bloom, with fictional rights and duties, who can be subject to fictional states, thoughts, feelings, and emotions, McNaghten insanity, infancy or minority, ambition, envy, jealousy, provocation, and whatnot, perform fictional acts, such as murder, theft, and defamation, and create fictional rights and obligations among themselves, for instance through contracts.

One can and one does, especially in the academic world, read law and literature without relating them to the real world and considering them as true or false in that respect, delighting for instance, at their inner complexity and coherence or, on the contrary, pointing at their shallow simplicity and complicated incoherence, as if complexity and coherence were relevant criteria of qualitative assessment and, indeed, as if whatever the criteria, qualitative assessment were relevant. Case law is arguably attractive because, like literature, it abounds with stories, but is one primarily concerned with their truthfulness? Are they not primarily related as examples or illustrations of how the law has been applied in like cases and of how cases have been distinguished to justify differing judgments? Do not fictional or moot examples serve the same purpose for examinations?

Besides, if a reader approaches a text as being literary, the text's use of names to designate its subjects that are also used to designate subjects in the legal world has the immediate effect of peeling off the literary subjects from their homonyms in the legal world, because his approach to the text as literary prepares him for the possibility that the subjects thus named may not be predicated of in the text as they are usually in that other world. Indeed, despite Pavel's suggestion,[44] one need not and perhaps does not experience in reading a literary text any difference between, for example, the phrases 'the sun' and 'Mr Pickwick'. 'The sun' may well turn out to refer to a purely fictional thing that actually does turn around the earth and 'Mr Pickwick', upon verification, the name of a person in the legal world and below that an individual in the real one.

One might well consider that literature, whether or not it uses names from the legal world, creates worlds that are disconnected or 'segregated' from the legal world and should therefore not be subjected to the rules of the legal world. The same applies when a literary text uses pronouns. Thus, when a literary author writes, for example, 'I wonder by my troth what thou and I/Did till we loved', as John Donne did in 'The Good-morrow', he constructs a fictional world that has a past and a present, with a character, who says 'I', and addresses another as 'thou', and where the two love (one another). Some readers think that, in the legal and the real world, the two characters were John Donne himself, born in 1572, and Anne More, the Lord Keeper's and his employer's niece, whom he married secretly in 1601, when she was 17. Others consider such hypotheses irrelevant. Similar in this to Donne himself, who manifested an interest in the theory of the plurality of worlds, they take the poem as creating a world distinct from Donne's biographical, anecdotal world, but likewise populated with predicated and so de-individuated subjects.

In its structuralist versions, the schematic theory holds that literature, regulated by its own constraints or conventions, is utterly estranged from the legal and the real worlds. Under the schematic theories of law and, in that version, of literature, law and literature are identical. Law and literature not only stand apart, under the theory of constancy, from the real world, but also, under the schematic theory, do not refer to the real world. As sub-worlds of the linguistic world, they are constructed with components that have a general meaning, but no reference to individuals in the real world. The words 'iambic' and 'tree' mean types of things, which might well, like unicorns, have no existence but

---

[44] Pavel, *Fictional Worlds* (cited in n.4), 11.

mental. Neither of those words refers to any individual thing; similarly, the legal words 'company' or 'person'. Likewise, literature, under the schematic theory, constructs, or should construct, types or clusters of predicates. It has peopled its worlds with, for example, 'hubristic', 'vengeful', 'ambitious', etc. characters. It has given them names, for instance 'Agamemnon', 'Faustus', 'Hamlet'. However, even under the Aristotelian version of the schematic theory, those names, even if historical, do not refer or are not used to refer to actual persons or individuals.

The linguistic world and its sub-worlds, under the schematic theory, may comprise several occurrences of their subjects, to which internal reference may be made; but those subjects, under the schematic theory, do not or should not refer to the legal or the real worlds, from which however they can be talked about. Those occurrences, co-textually, intertextually, and in metatextual discourse, can be nominally, anaphorically, or otherwise referred to. Within the literary world, characters can appear several times, in a single text or in several (Faust is an example). They can also refer to one another. In the legal and the real world, persons and individuals can talk about them. They can even say that, here or there, a subject has been represented incoherently or combines several types; indeed, they can marvel at the 'individuality' of the type. However, if names, by definition, refer to individuals, those names, Agamemnon etc., are not really names, but clusters of predicates, like the word 'cat', beyond which there is nothing. Indeed, in the literary world, under the schematic theory, even the deictic 'I' is used either by a character to refer to himself or by the narrator, a type also, not the person and the individual who has authored the text in respectively the legal and the real world.

There is, however, a major difference between the linguistic and the legal worlds, on the one hand, and the literary world, on the other: the former are not barred from referring to the real world whereas the legal world, in accordance with the schematic theory, prevents the latter from doing so except under certain conditions. The types of both the linguistic and the legal worlds are regularly used with reference to real individuals and actual persons whereas the law imposes upon literature a disconnection from the real world. For instance, the word 'iambic' can be used as meaning an unstressed syllable followed by a stressed syllable to rightly or wrongly describe a real occurrence of the phrase 'a tree' (as when an individual utters it) and the legal word 'theft' can be used, for instance in a law report, to describe what a person and individual has done; but if a literary text uses the word 'Macbeth' to describe a living person or individual not so called or predicates of a living person or individual as Shakespeare has of Macbeth, the author, under certain conditions, can be sued.

This section focuses on the difference on this point between law and literature. Law and literature, whether or not they can truly be likened as argued in section 1, differ in that laws define types and associated possibilities, but are usually intended to be applicable, normally in the future, to individuals described as persons and when they are so applied have contingent effects on the corresponding individuals (subsection 2.1) whereas there are laws which, as though in accordance with the schematic theory of literature, enable literary authors and those who publish their texts to be sued or prosecuted for certain predications of individuals that are actual persons in the legal world and thus to be withheld within a referential vacuum from both the legal and the real worlds (subsection 2.2).

2.1. The law's public judicial application

In general and excepting private Acts and personal Acts, if a law were to speak of 'a man' with reference, overt or covert, to an actual person, it would breach the rule of law, as defined earlier (in subsection 1.2). There are laws that may be deemed successful because they have provided for possibilities of which, following the enactments, there have been no occurrences, but they are exceptional. Some, one could call 'scarecrow laws'. David Ormerod[45] mentions the Children and Young Persons (Harmful Publications) Act 1955, which was deemed completely successful as long as there had been no prosecution under it. There are also laws or provisions, for which no commencement date has been appointed. However, most laws, be they criminal or civil, are applied, with the effect that, not only persons (instances of a legal type), but consequently and inevitably individuals, are brought within narrower legal types or slots.[46]

The Theft Act 1968 s.1(1) provides that 'a person is guilty of theft if he dishonestly appropriates property belonging to another with the intention of permanently depriving the other of it'. The same Act, in s.7 as amended, provides that 'a person guilty of theft shall on conviction on indictment be liable to imprisonment for a term not exceeding seven years'. Other provisions, in the Act, in other Acts, and in court rules, are required to understand exactly what those two provisions mean. However, on the basis of those two provisions, one can say that:

1) if an individual X (of the real world) is a person (in the legal world) and
2) if X is convicted on indictment of having dishonestly appropriated property belonging to another with the intention of permanently depriving the other of it, then
3) X is liable to imprisonment for a term not exceeding seven years.

The Theft Act 1968, that is to say, reaches, under the types ('thief', 'theft') it defines, not only actual persons, but also the corresponding individuals of the real world. 'Condemn the fault, and not th'actor of it?' Angelo asks in *Measure in Measure*, in act 2, scene ii. It is not only the actor of the fault whom the law condemns. It is the individual, who is more than the actor of a particular offence, but whom the court will not and, under the principle of the rule of law, should not take into consideration except as fitting the slot of the offence and, in order to fix the sentence on the provided scale of seven years, the relevant slots of aggravating and extenuating circumstances.

Before the Murder (Abolition of Death Penalty) Act 1965 or rather when offenders were actually executed, as they still are in different parts of the world, there were laws that enabled the courts to terminate the existence, not only of a person as such, by depriving him of that legal status, but of the individual who had benefited from it. The Theft Act 1968, like many other criminal laws, only provides that a thief should be liable to a limited term of imprisonment, but in so doing it is an individual as a whole who can be affected, in all his activities day and night. Indeed, the law allows a person's rights to be restricted, even if he is only suspected of an offence.[47]

The legal world reaches down from the universal and its types towards the individuals of the real world and hooks them back up within its sphere of predication to make

---

[45] David Ormerod, *Smith and Hogan Criminal Law* (Oxford: Oxford University Press, 2008), 3.
[46] One hypothesis to account for the subsumption of individuals under legal or other fictional slots is that it is achieved through arguments. As arguments are by definition refutable, the subsumption requires authority. In the case of legal fictions, it is through court hierarchy and the majority rule that a final, irreversible decision is reached.
[47] The case of S, an acquitted 11-year-old suspect, had to be brought before the ECHR for his right of privacy over his fingerprints and DNA samples to be acknowledged: *S and Marper v UK* [2008] ECHR 1581. The judgment of the ECHR has also been required for the privacy rights of visitors to prisoners to be recognized: *Wainwright v UK* [2006] ECHR 807.

their individuality meaningless. Punishment is particular to offences, but the effects of judgments under civil law also effect, not only persons, but individuals. The distinction, in that respect, is artificial. Although common to common law and civilian systems, it is perhaps, as J. H. Baker[48] and others have suggested, a historical accident. In their application, laws, which create fictional entities, in the sense that no individual thing can be reduced ontologically to its types, not only are fictional, but strike at the real world itself and its individuals.

The principle of open justice, which is a safeguard against breaches of the principle of the rule of law, more precisely unequal treatment of like cases, requires that judicial predications of individuals as persons should be public; but publication is not limited to the audience at the trial. The requirement, also under the principle of the rule of law, that the law should be knowable, the fact that, in the English legal system, as in all common law systems, all law is ultimately case law, because statutes are subject to judicial interpretations, and the fact that it is part of case law's self-representation to be rooted in the real world, often result in amplification of publication, since cases which, for one reason or another, are deemed important are reported with their individual (often legally irrelevant) details and the reports are available to the world at large, through newspapers and other media.[49]

Indeed, under the Law of Libel Amendment Act 1888 s.3, 'a fair and accurate report of proceedings publicly heard before any court exercising judicial authority shall, if published contemporaneously with such proceedings, be privileged...'. Completing that section, there is a restriction to the privilege, which is that 'nothing in this section shall authorise the publication of any blasphemous or indecent matter'. The Defamation Act 1996 s.16, Sch.2, has repealed the section[50] and replaced it in s.14(1) of the Act with an absolute privilege. Subject to the right of postponement in s.14, which relates to the law of contempt, absolute privilege means that the exercise of the privilege cannot be denied on any ground, not even malice.

Moreover, the Judicial Proceedings (Regulation of Reports) Act 1926 s.1(1) is still in force. It enables the restriction of reporting, with the sanction under s.1(2) of the Attorney-General, but does not apply, according to s.1(4), to publications, unlike newspapers, consisting solely of law reports. Consequently, unlike, for example, newspaper reports, such reports, under s.1(1)(a) can include 'any indecent matter or any indecent medical, surgical or psychological details being matter or details the publication of which would be calculated to injure public morals'.

Furthermore, the Rehabilitation of Offenders Act 1974, which purposes to rehabilitate 'an individual' convicted for an offence once that conviction is 'spent', provides in s.4(2) that such an individual has the right not to acknowledge the spent conviction, but that right is limited. Indeed, not only are there several exceptions to that rule, but s.8(3) provides that the defendant in an action for libel or slander for having published

---

[48] J. H. Baker, *An Introduction to English Legal History* (London: Butterworth & Co., 1979), 411–12.

[49] In *Guardian News and Media Ltd & Ors v Ahmed & Ors* [2010] UKSC 1 [63], Lord Rogers, arguing against the development of anonymity in judicial proceedings, said that freedom of the press should outweigh the right to privacy and that the former depended on commercial viability, which itself required the use of appropriated means, such as naming and providing 'individual' details, to appeal to 'human nature' and so attract enough readers. The legally irrelevant or immaterial details, which are found, not only in newspapers, but in the law reports, might be said to produce what Barthes (cited in n.30) called 'l'effet de réel'.

[50] 'From a day to be appointed', say Patrick Milmo and W. V. H. Rogers (eds), *Gatley on Libel and Slander*, 11th edn (London: Sweet & Maxwell, 2008), 1370, n.9.

that a person 'has committed or been charged with or prosecuted for or convicted for an offence which was the subject of a spent conviction' can rely 'on any defence of justification (i.e. truth) or fair comment or of absolute or qualified privilege'. If the case has been reported, the report supports the justification.

The effect of law reporting, which used to be left to natural persons and is the work of the Incorporated Council of Legal Reporting (ICLR) since 1865 and divers other juristic persons (for instance, News Corporation, which owns *The Times*, or BAILII, a charity like the ICLR) is that individuals are for ever and before the world at large immobilized and exhibited at instants or in aspects of their lives which the law has foreseen as possibilities in general terms under its multiple types, but which the reports have the privilege of describing in their more or less individual details and, in the case of publications that include only reports, however indecent or likely to injure public morals.

If his case is reported, whoever is tried for an offence is thus exposed to two forms of punishment: the punishment provided for by the relevant law; and permanent stigma during his lifetime and forever. Crime alone is said to stigmatize the offender. However, in holding a party liable to another in damages, for example for breach of contract or defamation, a civil court affects not only a person and an individual's monetary property, but also his reputation and, if the case is reported, does so forever. The individual will remain in history, for instance, as a contract breacher or a defamer. No matter the category of the case, a defendant is reduced synecdochically to the legally relevant predicates, and whatever other predicates he may have instanced in his lifetime will most likely be forgotten.

Those who uphold personal liability and reject rehabilitation may see nothing wrong in this, but one need not have a systemic approach to breaches of the law and social disorder to question the justice of immortalizing litigants whom the courts decide have not breached the law at all. Indeed, many reported cases decide a question of law. Often, the facts of the case have already been admitted or proven. Where the court resolves the question of law in such a way that the alleged offender, tortfeasor, or contract breacher has committed no offence, no tort or breach, the report nevertheless immortalizes him with the predications that have occasioned the proceedings.

That is the case also where, notwithstanding a judge's decision, upon a motion to the contrary, that there is a case to answer, the jury returns a verdict of not guilty. Thus, in *Clarke*,[51] on a motion to quash the first count (rape), Byrne, J., citing Hale's authoritative statement on marital rape, created an exception to the exemption, according to which a separation order could cancel a wife's marital consent. James Clarke pleaded not guilty. The judge therefore put the factual question to the jury whether the defendant had or had not raped his wife. Apparently nullifying the exception, arguably in breach of its institutional jurisdiction, the jury found the defendant not guilty. The case remains important historically because it was the first case to have begun to demolish the exemption, which was finally abolished only in *R v R*.[52] Notwithstanding his acquittal and, from a systemic point of view, the legal context in which he was raised and that persisted for several decades, including probably in statutory form, in the Sexual Offences (Amendment) Act 1976 s.1(1)(a), James Clarke remains and will remain (morally) guilty of marital rape

---

[51] *R v Clarke* (1949) 33 Cr. App. R. 216. In *R v Clarence* (1889) LR 22 QBD 23, a few of the 13 judges had questioned the immunity, but *obiter* with no effect on the judgment.
[52] *R v R* (cited in n.39).

for the modern, re-educated reader of the report, for whom marital rape is a possible offence.[53]

There again, one may say fair enough, but what of the victims? If the path to remedy for the wrong they have suffered were made too easy for victims of malicious prosecutions and persons suspected but found not guilty, the administration of justice would be rendered even more difficult than it is: such is the uncertainty of laws and facts that nobody would ever start an action. But what of the victims of other offences, which the reports immortalize, as they do offenders and alleged offenders, in more or less individual situations that they might well wish to forget or at least not have the public remember? For instance, the victims in *Caswell* (1983) and *Kowalski* (1988),[54] who will be remembered forever as having been subjected to debasing conduct, for which the jury acquitted their husbands, notwithstanding in the second case the judge's declaration or creation of a new exception to the marital exemption and the unusually detailed account of the facts (probably to justify it). The question can be asked about countless cases, which relate the acts that persons and individuals have undergone, unwillingly or, as in *R v Brown*,[55] consensually. Perhaps publication has therapeutic virtues, but then should not victims be at least given the choice of going through the therapy? Certainly, many victims, it is said, prefer not to start proceedings, for fear of moving out of their private individual worlds into the public legal world.

The fear is not ill-founded. Under the principle of the rule of law and its sub-principles, open justice and the knowability of the law, all the parties, not only offenders and alleged lawbreakers, but also their victims, lose, in starting an action, their right over their public representation, in the reports series (and indeed in the media at large). A judicial action, one might say, has the effect of striking all the parties dead. Indeed, a party can no more correct his image as portrayed in a report than a person can bring an action for the defamation of a deceased person or a third party obtain a declaration to restore a deceased relative's reputation (unless the defamatory words reflect upon his own reputation). Be he the offender or the victim, he is condemned to be identified with an image that has as it were replaced him and that will certainly outlive him.

The old common law maxim *actio personalis moritur cum persona* is still operative only in the law of defamation,[56] which will be considered in subsection 2.2 in relation to literature, but it is not exactly that maxim which accounts for the effect of litigation on persons and individuals. The relevant proposition shifts the terms of the maxim around. It is not 'a personal action dies with the person', but 'a person dies with a personal (and indeed any) action'. Once an individual, under his rights and obligation in the legal world, is involved in litigation, he loses his personal right to his representation and, in

---

[53] Conversely, in *Dudgeon v UK* [1981] ECHR 5, Jeffrey Dudgeon, who was arrested for a suspected drugs offence, was questioned on and convicted for his sexual conduct. He remains not only exposed publicly in his privacy, which he brought an action to defend (although he is sometimes described as a gay activist), but also, for those who do not accept the present law in respect of homosexuality, branded as a homosexual.

[54] *R v Caswell* (1983) Crim. L.R., 111. *R v Kowalski* (1988) 86 Cr. App. R. 339.

[55] *R v Brown* [1992] UKHL 7, [1993] 2 WLR 556, [1994] 1 AC 212. The fully named victims, in that sadomasochism case, were also offenders. Here again, in *Kowalski*, the description of the facts exceed the needs of their legal description, but the excess appears justified by the legal difficulty of the decision: in *Kowalski*, a new exception; here, a limitation of the maxim *volenti non fit injuria*, that is of consent as a defence. In *Donovan* [1934] 2 KB 498, CCA, however, there does not appear to be any such justification for naming the (possibly consenting) 17-year-old victim, Norah Eileen Harrison, who is sometimes referred to as a prostitute, although the report does not use the word.

[56] Milmo and Rogers, *Gatley on Libel and Slander* (cited in n.50), 235.

that restricted sense, legally dies. To acknowledge changes in the law, qualifications to that statement will be made in the conclusion. It is time now, in contrast with the law's, to consider literature's access to the real world and its legal restriction.

2.2. The law's restriction of literary referentiality

The theory of constancy, which would have manner prevail over matter and reference, and the schematic theory, which denies the relevance of reference, have the effect of containing literary fiction within a referential vacuum apart from the real world. As though supported by those theories, law includes several provisions to keep literature within that vacuum. Yet literature has, on the one hand, often drawn from the legal and the real worlds and, on the other, more generally, simulated those worlds; besides, most readers no doubt react more or less consciously to manner and schema, but are more interested in the literary worlds that literature constructs, to which they refer as though they were part of the legal or real worlds.

Literature, first, has developed fictions from historical facts and with judicial method.[57] Daniel Defoe's *Moll Flanders* (1722) derives from the Old Bailey proceedings and, thus or otherwise titled, *The Ordinary of Newgate's Accounts of the Behaviour, Confession and Dying Words of Malefactors*, the first of which was compiled in 1676. On the other side of the Channel, there are several instances of that same relationship between literature, history, and law reports. Stendhal's *Le Rouge et le Noir* (1830) was developed from two cases, *Lafargue* and *Antoine Berthet*, the latter of which had been reported in the *Gazette des Tribunaux de Grenoble*. Gustave Flaubert's *Madame Bovary* (1857) is another famous example. To such examples of literary worlds that have their sources in the legal world, biographers, such as Richard Ellman, and other literary historians have added countless instances of hypothetical sources of literary worlds in the personal and individual lives of the authors.

Literature also includes texts, sometimes called 'factions', which more or less truthfully claim to be true accounts of historical facts or can be read as such. Truman Capote's *In Cold Blood* (1966) is an example.[58] Such texts differ from the novels mentioned above, in that their claim that, while being literature, they provide a 'true account' (Capote's subtitle) of historical facts is, at least partly, true, blurring the categorical opposition between literary fiction and history, biography, or journalism. In France, Régis Jauffret achieved a similar categorical confusion in *Sévère* (2010).[59] In 2009, he had reported for *Le nouvel observateur* on Cécile Brossard's trial for the murder of Edouard Stern. Also influenced by the case, Olivier Assayas, in his film *Boarding Gate* (2007), departs from it and presents quite another story, especially continuing on after the murder. Without ever naming the protagonists (except indirectly in the title), Jauffret, writing *Sévère* as though he were Cécile Brossard, at a time when auto(biography)fiction had been the vogue for more than a decade, mostly represents the facts of the case, and, abandoning his usual minimalist manner in that respect, locates them with relative precision in time and space. Notwithstanding variations and the author's claim, in the preamble, that 'no

---

[57] Ian Watt, *The Rise of the Novel: Studies in Defoe, Richardson and Fielding*, 1st edn 1957 (Berkeley and Los Angeles: University of California Press, 2001).
[58] Truman Capote, *In Cold Blood* (New York: Random House, 1966).
[59] Régis Jauffret, *Sévère* (Paris: Seuil, 2010).

one [personne]' exists in a novel, 'characters being dolls made of words', the story, from beginning to end, is recognizably Edouard Stern's and Cécile Brossard's.[60]

Secondly, many, not all, literary authors simulate the legal and real worlds and might be said to insert their fictional worlds within them. Many, not all, literary authors locate their fictional worlds within legal time and legal space, some referring to historical events. *Madame Bovary*'s Yonville is a literary place or a literary renaming of a legal place, like Marcel Proust's Norman Balbec, but not Paris, which is also named in those works.[61] Not only do many literary authors draw from and simulate the legal and the real worlds, but readers have in certain cases believed their stories to be true: an extreme case is *Gulliver's Travels* (1721) which, at the time of its first publication, many readers considered a true account.

Readers' interest in the characters and their stories prevails, as Thomas Pavel[62] has remarked in his criticism of structuralism, over their interest in an author's manner and a genre's structural constraints; the result is that university teachers who refuse to accept this state of affairs attempt to drill their students out of a psychological approach to characters, which is based, according to such teachers, on the fallacy of taking characters for actual persons or real individuals. Furthermore, whereas only universal types, according to the Aristotelian version of the schematic theory, should populate the literary worlds, it is perhaps partly through some, not all, literary texts and their complex predications that readers conceive what the real world might be. Literary characters, as Thomas Pavel suggests,[63] may have grown out of *exempla*, the characters of which were arguably no more complex than the moral purpose required, but the construction of some characters, not only in modern literature, but already in Antiquity, can attain such a degree of complexity that they escape predication like the hypothetical individuals of the real world.[64] Even psychoanalytical encapsulations, for instance of Hamlet, have failed to be final.

Notwithstanding literature's frequent sources and simulations of the legal and the real worlds and readers' approaches to characters as persons or individuals, the law, like the theory of constancy and the schematic theory, participates in containing literature within a referential vacuum. The situation can be summarized as follows. In a biography, considered as history, not literature, 'Caesar' is the name of a person of the legal world and refers to that person and, beyond that, to the corresponding individual of the real world. In Shakespeare's *Julius Caesar*, he is, according to the schematic theory, only the name of a possible type or cluster of predicates and his story only a possibility. According to Aristotle, history may well confirm the type and the story as possibilities, but the confirmation is superfluous. Law further limits literature within the world of mere possibility by making confirmation in present history actionable. If Julius Caesar is a living person (and especially under US law, not a public figure), the author should be careful in his predications of him and even if he does not name him.

---

[60] At the end of *Sévère*, the heroine-narrator says to her husband: 'It is as if this story had happened to someone else.' Then, she reformulates the statement: 'It is as if it had not happened at all.'
[61] Pavel's summary of Alexis Meinong's ontology and Terence Parsons' related theory of non-existent objects distinguishes several possible relationships between what are here called the literary, legal, and real worlds: Pavel, *Fictional Worlds* (cited in n.4), 27–31.
[62] Pavel, *Fictional Worlds* (cited in n.4), 146.
[63] Pavel, *Fictional Worlds* (cited in n.4), 145.
[64] This point is discussed at n.3.

The range of predications that cannot be made of a person without the author of the predications being exposed to proceedings for defamation or malicious falsehood is considerable; and the available defences are few. The Official Secrets Acts 1911–1989[65] and the law of privacy broaden the range. Other limitations to what an author can say could be considered. Under the law of France, 16 other European countries and Israel, but not the UK directly, holocaust denial is an offence. In France, during Florence Rey's trial (1998), it was rumoured that a law would make it an offence for an author to have conceived a fiction that was later enacted in the real world, because Oliver Stone's *Natural Born Killers* (1994) had allegedly influenced Audrey Maupin, an undergraduate philosophy student at Nanterre, and the defendant, his girlfriend. If such a law were to be enacted, a literary author would be liable for having predicated of a character what a court later predicated of an individual as a person. The rest of this subsection focuses on the law of defamation.

Under the law of defamation, a person has a right of action for any (linguistic or other) predication that:

I) lowers him in the estimation of right-thinking members of society generally,

II) tends to cause others to shun or avoid him, or

III) tends to expose him to hatred, contempt, or ridicule.[66]

Lady Colin Campbell v Lily Safra[67] is noteworthy here, although the action failed for lack of proof, in showing that an allegation of defamation can itself be defamatory. In that case, the claimant brought an action for libel and inducement to breach of contract, alleging that the defendant, who had without proceedings obtained the withdrawal of the claimant's novel from the publisher for defamation, had published an article accusing her of defamation.

Furthermore, the *melior sensu* rule having been abandoned since 1807, the interpretation of the predication at issue has no other limit than the understanding of a fictional 'ordinary man', injected for 'true innuendos' with the knowledge of the required extrinsic signifying facts. Indeed, where the predication is verbal, it is to be assessed on the basis of:

1) the natural and ordinary meaning of the words and

2) as part of that meaning, their implications and inferences ('false innuendo') and

---

[65] The Act has been used on a few occasions against literary fiction: an attempt was made to ban Peter Wright's *Spycatcher* and David Shayler, who was later convicted for disclosing classified information to the *Mail on Sunday* in *R v Shayler* [2002] UKHL 11, was required to obtain Home Office permission to publish his novel, *The Organisation*, of which excerpts were then published in *The Guardian* in 2000.

[66] The list is adapted from Milmo and Rogers, *Gatley on Libel and Slander* (cited in n.50), 12. There is, it will be noted, no action for 'defamation' that has the opposite effects: in other words, that makes a person unduly esteemed, befriended, loved, or taken seriously. The exception is tortious negligent misstatement, as when a person who owed a duty of care to another provides the latter with an inaccurately good report on a third party: *Hedley Byrne & Co Ltd v Heller & Partners* [1964] AC 465. The law on the use of false documents, for instance academic diplomas, would also need to be considered. In the case of goods and services, consumer protection legislation and contract law can make persons liable for breach of conditions, warranties, collateral contracts, unrepresentative descriptions or samples, misrepresentation, but not advertising puff.

[67] [2006] EWHC 819 (QB).

3) their rhetoric (as when laudatory words are ironical)[68] and

4) the meaning that may result from extrinsic facts ('true innuendo').[69]

The defences available to a literary author are few, fewer than those available to, for example, a journalist or a historian:

A) Unlike for instance, the law reporter, he has no privilege, absolute or qualified.

B) He may of course justify[70] his predications, by proving that the facts are true, that his suspicion that they are true is reasonable, or that his opinion of them, if stated, is correct, whatever his (malicious) intentions in publishing the facts, suspicion, or opinion. The law of privacy, which is developing in the UK, has qualified this defence as it has in the USA, so that it may be or may become actionable to publish the truth.[71] Likewise, under the Official Secrets Acts 1911–1989, truth is not a defence. The defence, in any case, is bizarre, if the author has presented his text as fiction.

C) The same remark applies to his other available defence: fair comment, which requires the matter commented on to be of public interest and the comment or predication to express an honest (i.e. non-malicious) belief on averred facts. Indeed, if he has paratextually disclaimed his work as fiction, how can an author plead his comment expresses even a belief?[72]

With the qualification that not all persons are protected from predications that have the effects of (I), (II), or (III), and that not all who are so protected can exercise their right of action, or wish to, one cannot but conclude from this outline of the law of defamation that, even when he only makes laudatory predications, which might be interpreted as ironical, an author should be very, very careful, all the more so since there are few legal and real subjects whom the law deprives of a right of action for defamation. Even if he intends to target literary fictions, his predicative arrows may, under what may be called 'the referential rule', hit a legal fiction which the law empowers to retaliate with legal proceedings against him, with real effect.

There are legal or real subjects that the law of defamation does not protect from predications of any sort: God, the dead, the Crown, government bodies, classes of persons (Catholics, lawyers, etc.), animals, and things; but even that preliminary statement must

---

[68] The expression 'laudatory predication', in one sense of the latter word, is pleonastic. Modern, feminist criticism has denounced poetry that overtly puts women on a supra-human pedestal as denying them their humanity just as much as theological fictions that have deprived them of a soul.

[69] For a detailed account see Milmo and Rogers, *Gatley on Libel and Slander* (cited in n.50), I, 3, 3, 101–37.

[70] The name of this defence, 'justification', is 'unfortunate', Milmo and Rogers (*Gatley on Libel and Slander* (cited in n.50), 309), remark, because the publication of truth, they say, requires no good reason and is not actionable, except under the Rehabilitation of Offenders Act 1974.

[71] Following *von Hannover v Germany* [2005] 40 EHRR 1, see *Murray v Big Pictures (UK) Ltd* 2008 EWCA Civ 446. Note, however, that according to *P, Q, R v Quigley* [2008] EWHC 1051 (QB), the question of truth, in an action for invasion of privacy, is perhaps irrelevant. In that case, the defendant had threatened to publish a novella on the Internet, in which 'P and Q would appear, thinly disguised, as partaking in various unsavoury and fictitious sexual activities'.

[72] Note that public interest or interest of the State is a defence neither under the Official Secrets Acts 1911–1989 nor for direct action, on the ground that 'the interest of the State' means 'the interests of the State according to its recognised organs of government and the policies as expounded by the particular Government of the day': *R v Ponting* [1985] Crim. L.R. 318. For a detailed account of defences see Milmo and Rogers, *Gatley on Libel and Slander* (cited in n.50), II, 307–661.

be qualified. The Criminal Justice and Immigration Act 2008 s.79[73] provides for the abolition of the offence of blasphemy. However, under the Racial and Religious Hatred Act 2006, to speak of God and religion with the intent of provoking religious hatred is actionable. The freedom of predication of the dead has already been stated (in subsection 2.1). Tragedies, Aristotle notes, often use stories that have happened. The Medieval 'Mirrors', a form of *exempla*, did the same. The reason, says Aristotle of tragedy, is that such stories are instances of the possible. The law provides another, perhaps anachronistic, explanation: the dead cannot sue for defamation. Interestingly, the authors of 'Mirrors', through the fictitious ghosts' real stories, indirectly targeted (possibly defamed) their own contemporaries. The Crown cannot sue either.[74] Nor can government bodies or local authorities (since *Derbyshire CC v Times Newspapers*).[75] However, members of either type of organization can do so; likewise, agencies with transferred governmental powers;[76] likewise, members of a class of persons (even other than racial or religious), if they can establish they were referred to. Even animals and things are not wholly unprotected, since corporations and firms can sue for defamation and for malicious falsehood and do so in respect of whatever they deal in.[77]

There are then few legal or real subjects that the law of defamation does not protect from defamatory predications. Therefore an author who does not wish to limit his writing to unquestionable eulogy would be well advised to predicate only within the literary world; but even that, under the law of defamation, would not save him from actions against him: unless he also chose to predicate of nothing, to predicate a grin of nothing, rather than a cat. Different situations come to mind:

(i) Braving the law of defamation, especially seeing the ill-famed target, an author, presenting his text as fiction, may choose to use the name of a known person and predicate of him freely. Such was Mathieu Lindon's option for his novel, *Le procès de Jean-Marie Le Pen* (1998). The Paris Criminal Court fined the author and his publisher in 1999. The ECHR[78] largely upheld the judgment.

(ii) 'Inspired' by the legal and the real worlds, a literary author may wish somehow to connect his literary world to its source in the legal and the real worlds while at the same time departing from them. He may opt for the *roman-à-clés* or some similar device. Like Patrick Modiano, in *La rue des boutiques obscures* (1978), he may take the legal first and last names of the legal and real protagonists and remix them. In this case, most, if not all, were dead at the time of publication. Another possibility is to do as Régis Jauffret did: for *Sévère*, he used the legal name of the (deceased) protagonist (Stern) for his title, but translated it into French as though it were an English adjective.

(iii) Make-believe is a literary author's stock-in-trade. Wary of the law of defamation, he may choose a name, say Hulton, that sounds like a legal name, but which he believes is either not a legal name or a rare one, unlike, for example, Jones. He believes therefore

---

[73] Ormerod, *Smith and Hogan Criminal Law* (cited in n.45), 31, said the commencement date had not yet been appointed.
[74] Milmo and Rogers, *Gatley on Libel and Slander* (cited in n.50), 229. For a detailed account of parties who may sue see Milmo and Rogers, *Gatley on Libel and Slander* (cited in n.50), I, 8, 227–60.
[75] [1993] A.C. 534.
[76] An explanation is provided in n.9, where there is also reference to SLAPPs. SLAPPs are alleged to take advantage of those distinctions between governmental bodies and authorities, which are unprotected against defamation, and agencies with transferred powers and natural persons who are members of the former.
[77] Notice that the mere photographing of things can be actionable, for instance under the Official Secrets Acts 1911–1989.
[78] [2007] ECHR 836.

that it will not be associated with a particular person or individual, especially since he also domiciles him at a literary, non-legal address. See option (v).

(iv) Understandably, a literary author, submitting to the injunction that he should stay within a referential vacuum, might have difficulty in losing his habit acquired in the linguistic world of predicating of subjects, for instance as isolated by proper names. In deciding to predicate of proper names, he may well, to avoid legal action against him, fabricate a fantastic name. Such was the practice of satirists in the reign of Elizabeth I.[79]

(v) He may even call his character 'X'. Unfortunately for him, under the rule in *Hulton v Jones*,[80] even that option will not save him. Should a set of people reasonably believe that he was referring to an actual legal person, the latter has a right of action against him, if it is decided that the predications have one of the effects (I), (II), or (III).

Even if one considers only the law of defamation, setting aside the law of malicious falsehood, the law of privacy, and the Official Secrets Acts 1911–1989, the law is too flexibly rigid to account for the fact that countless literary books are published without actions being brought against their authors and publishers. Whatever a literary author does, he must just hope that, in his case, the application of the law will remain a mere possibility and that, for fear of further publicity[81] or for lack of means, nobody will attempt to use the sword that the law offers him against the author of the words and all those involved in their publication. (Note that in the past such actions were available for periods ranging from three to six years but the limit is now one year.)[82]

3. Conclusion

This paper has argued that literature, under the theory of constancy, has or should share stylistic characteristics with law, which uphold certain values (constancy, discipline, self-mastery) over whatever they speak about and that literature, under the schematic theory, and law, under the principle of the rule of law, speaks or should speak about universals and possibilities, not the real world and its individuals.

It has then acknowledged and developed a difference between the two, which is that law is usually intended to apply beyond the legal world to the real world and its individuals and, when applied through judicial predications, affects them directly for a time and,

---

[79] Some of their works nevertheless fell under the Bishops' Ban 1599. The Stationers' Register never provides justifications for censorship, with the effect in that case that historians of literature have argued several possibilities. See, for instance, Cyndia Susan Clegg, *Press Censorship in Elizabethan England* (Cambridge: Cambridge University Press, 1997).

[80] [1910] AC 20. For a detailed account of reference in the law of defamation see Milmo and Rogers, *Gatley on Libel and Slander* (cited in n.50), I, 7, 211–26 and also *O'Shea v MGN Ltd* [2001] EMLR 40.

[81] Legal proceedings, being public, generate publicity, as demonstrated in subsection 2.1. In the case of Régis Jauffret's *Sévère*, it has been said that Edouard Stern's family brought an action for invasion of privacy, less to have the book banned than to prevent the making of a film, based on the novel, with two popular actors (Benoît Poelvoorde and Laetitia Casta). Ten French writers signed a petition to defend the author, among them Bernard-Henri Lévy and Michel Houellebecq. Interestingly, there has been no action against Airy Routier's *Le fils du Serpent: vie et mort du banquier Stern* (Paris: Albin Michel, 2005), a documentary account of the case.

[82] Formerly, under the Limitation Act 1980, the time limit for actions founded on tort was six years from the date when the action accrued, but for actions for libel and slander and for slander of title, slander of goods, and malicious falsehood, the Administration of Justice Act 1985 s.57 reduced the limit to three years and the Defamation Act 1996 s.5 has further reduced it to one year. After that time has passed, a person loses his right of action as though he had died.

in the case of reported cases, permanently before the world at large, whereas it withholds literature within a referential vacuum, in the case of comparable predications.

The balance between law and literature, admittedly, has perhaps begun to be restored through the above-mentioned amendments to the Limitation Act 1980 and the development of procedural anonymity, but at the cost of open justice and, according to Lord Rodger, remarks from the media that dockets read like 'alphabetical soup';[83] possibly also through the uncertain qualification of the referential rule in *O'Shea v MGN Ltd*.[84]

One could advocate that all authors of predications should benefit from the law of defamation in respect of the alleged defamation by or of the dead, the alleged defamation of third parties between husbands and wives, or the usual judgment in respect of alleged defamation by children (but possibly not mentally disordered or drunken persons) that their authors 'lack the requisite mental capacity for malice'.

Preferably, it is submitted that, with the support of what Thomas Pavel calls segregationist theories, full force should be granted to paratextual indications that a text is fiction. Indeed, whichever world they are proffered in, all predications, be they privileged or not, including teachers', employers', colleagues' and police reports, should be subjected to similar qualifications, which would result in freeing individuals from the straitjacketing effect of predication and delivering them back into the real world.

Constantine Cavafy, in *Ithaca* (1911), envisages that, upon reaching one's destination, one may realize that what has mattered was the journey, not its end.[85] So it is sometimes with conclusions: the quest for arguments is more interesting than whatever direct and indirect, perhaps initially unintended, conclusions they have led to. In the present case, the submissions in the last two paragraphs are paradoxical and possibly undesirable.

The human world, which includes all its fictions, cannot do without predications and it has always allowed some to be proffered and others not. It is a virtue to be admired in literary authors as such that, despite 'the slings and arrows of outrageous fortune', they have the constancy and the self-mastery to operate within the narrow, usual definition of fiction and to abstain from predicating of living persons and individuals, in accordance with the law, and at best only to simulate predication, within their worlds: to predicate, however abundantly, of no one and nothing (or of subjects that the law does not protect from literary, as opposed to journalistic or other, predication).

---

[83] *Guardian News and Media Ltd v Ahmed* [2010] UKSC 1.
[84] Cited in n.80.
[85] Text available at <http://www.cavafy.com/poems/content.asp?id=74&cat=1>.

12

Reading and Writing the Law: Macaulay in India

*Michael Hancher**

Parliamentum voluisse quod dicit lex. (Parliament is deemed to have wanted what the law says.)

Ejus est interpretari cujus est condere. (He who writes the law gets to interpret it.)

It really is very difficult to understand what they mean sometimes. I always look at Hansard, I always look at the Blue Books, I always look at everything I can in order to see what is meant. —Quintin Hogg, Lord Chancellor; 26 March 1981.[1]

1. Introduction and overview

On 5 February 1835, Thomas Babington Macaulay prepared a memorandum or 'minute' for the governor general of India, Lord William Bentinck, in which he interpreted aspects of 53 Geo. III c. 155 (1813), known as the East India Act or Charter Act. That Act was one of the series of statutes that at twenty-year intervals revised and renewed the charter of the East India Company, which administered British interests in India.

Macaulay advised Bentinck that it would be within the meaning of the statute to stop subsidizing advanced instruction and scholarship in Arabic and Sanskrit and to subsidize advanced instruction in English literature instead. He gave that advice as the fourth ordinary member of the Council of India (the so-called 'law member'), who advised the council on legal questions. He was also president of the General Committee of Public Instruction (GCPI), the body that administered the funds in question. He had held both appointments for only a few months.

In a family memoir composed later in the century Henry Thoby Prinsep (1836–1914) objected that Macaulay's legal opinion in the matter had been 'irregular' and 'premature': he should have reserved judgement until a question was brought to him regarding (new) legislation. Prinsep was the son of Henry Thoby Prinsep (1792–1878), secretary to the British government in India and an antagonist of both Bentinck and Macaulay; the son's technical objection to Macaulay's intervention probably reflects his father's feelings in the matter.[2] Indeed the proper responsibilities of the law member of the council

---

* I thank three units of the University of Minnesota for supporting this research: the Graduate School, the College of Liberal Arts, and the Office of International Programs. Special thanks are due to Justin Biel for his expert advice on many aspects of this project. Thanks also to George Sheets for advice on particular points.

[1] H. L. Debs. 26 March 1981, vol. 418, col. 1346, as quoted by Stephen D. Girvin, 'Hansard and the Interpretation of Statutes' (1993) 22 *Anglo-American Law Review* 475, 477.

[2] Henry Thoby Prinsep, 'Three Generations in India', BL APAC MSS Eur C97/1–3: 178, 179.

were a matter of continuing dispute from 1834, when Macaulay sought to have them clarified or revised, until as late as 1850, long after Macaulay had returned to London; and the elder Prinsep was a party to that dispute. (For his objections to the method and substance of Macaulay's construction of the statute, see section 3.) When Macaulay asked to have his duties clarified, he complained that otherwise he would be taking the risk that he would either 'be intermeddling in what does not concern me' or be neglecting his duties.[3] The younger Prinsep suggests that in offering his legal opinion on the interpretation of the Charter Act, Macaulay was indeed intermeddling in what did not concern him.

Macaulay's intervention, which later would become famous and, even later, infamous as 'Macaulay's Minute on Indian Education', provided Bentinck with a rationale for issuing a resolution on 7 March 1835, which settled the long-disputed question in favour of English. Macaulay himself drafted that resolution[4]—which Bentinck revised, signed, and published. Macaulay's minute and Bentinck's resolution together mark a critical moment in the establishment of English as an influential language in India and as the leading global language.

It has often been said that Macaulay decided the question in favour of English;[5] and it has also been said that he merely put the finishing touches on a change of policy that would have been undertaken, sooner or later, even if he had never reached India.[6] Also, later actions of the government in India moderated the reforms that Macaulay advocated by partially renewing financial support for Oriental studies.[7] But whether Macaulay's minute was instrumental or mere window dressing, and whether its impact was decisive or gradual, its bold rhetorical gestures have fascinated readers since the 1830s, and continue to do so. It has become the symbol, if not the cause, of English in India.

Dismissing arguments prepared by some of his colleagues on the council and on the GCPI, arguments insisting that the Charter Act specifically authorized subsidizing Arabic and Sanskrit education, Macaulay remarked near the start of his minute, '[i]t does not appear to me that the Act of parliament can by any art of construction be made to bear the meaning which has been assigned to it'.[8] He did not pause to examine any method of construction that might lead to the conclusion he opposed.

This paper develops one ground for construing the statute so as to uphold the 'Orientalist' position (as it was called) favouring Arabic and Sanskrit, against the

---

[3] *First Report from of the Select Committee on Indian Territories* (1853), Appendix 10, 516–45; 521 (Macaulay's letter of 27 June 1834).

[4] Macaulay, *Letters*, ed. Thomas Pinney, 6 vols (Cambridge: Cambridge University Press, 1996), 3: 138–9.

[5] For example, W. Nassau Lees, *Indian Musalmáns* (London: Williams and Norgate, 1871), 61; W. F. B. Lurie, *Sketches of some Distinguished Anglo-Indians, Second Series* (London: W. H. Allen & Co., 1888), 184; Natalie Robinson Sirkin and Gerald Sirkin, 'The Battle of Indian Education: Macaulay's Opening Salvo Newly Discovered' (1971) 14 *Victorian Studies* 407; Robert Phillipson, *Linguistic Imperialism* (Oxford: Oxford University Press, 1992), 110.

[6] For example, Arthur Mayhew, *The Education of India* (London: Faber and Gwyer, 1926), 26–7; Percival Spear, 'Bentinck and Education' (1938) 6 *Cambridge Historical Journal* 85; Stephen Evans, 'Macaulay's Minute Revisited: Colonial Language Policy in Nineteenth-Century India' (2002) 23 *Journal of Multilingual and Multicultural Development* 260–81.

[7] For the compromise struck in this regard by George Eden, earl of Auckland, who succeeded Bentinck as governor general, see Lynn Zastoupil and Martin Moir (eds), *The Great Indian Education Debate: Documents Relating to the Orientalist-Anglicist Controversy, 1781–1843* (Richmond, UK: Curzon, 1999), 304–31. This useful volume is cited below as ZM.

[8] ZM 163 (cited in n.7). It is convenient to quote from Zastoupil and Moir's scholarly edition of Macaulay's minute, which they based on an official manuscript copy. Macaulay himself never published the minute, but it has often been extensively quoted or published in full from at least 1838 onwards.

'Anglicist' position that Macaulay advocated. That ground is the legislative history of the relevant sections of the East India Act, a history that has been slighted since the nineteenth century.

In dismissing the Orientalist reading of the statute Macaulay might plausibly have relied upon the emergent tradition, stemming from the celebrated copyright case *Millar v Taylor* (1769), which excluded as irrelevant to the construction of a statute any consideration of its legislative history. Thus Judge Willes in that case: 'The sense and meaning of an act of parliament must be collected from what it says when passed into a law, and not from the history of changes it underwent in the house when it took its rise. That history is not known to the other house, or to the sovereign'.[9] In Macaulay's day that dictum was becoming settled law. He would not have anticipated the many objections that it would attract later in the nineteenth century and on into the twenty-first, objections that eventually would mitigate if not entirely cancel its force.[10] Such concerns lend moral if not jurisprudential support to an inquiry into the legislative history of the statute.

It happens that there is a personal aspect to that legislative history, tangential to but not irrelevant to the main question. It is well known that Macaulay's father, the evangelical reformer Zachary Macaulay, helped to introduce language into the Charter Act of 1813 that sanctioned the sending of Christian missionaries to India. Previously the East India Company had excluded them as disruptive to trade. A particular statutory phrase that the father sponsored, 'useful knowledge', figures as a touchstone in the son's general construction of the Act, though he uses the trope casually and does not cite the relevant passage in the statute. Thomas Babington Macaulay was not a disinterested interpreter of the legislative document that Zachary Macaulay influenced. It will become apparent, however, that his interest was not quite the same as his father's.

Additional language introduced by others in a late stage of drafting the statute drew Macaulay's explicit attention, though he ignored the occasion of that language. Discovering its history will show that Macaulay interpreted that section against the grain of its purpose and intended meaning.

This chapter will close by noticing Macaulay's stated concerns about the freedom of judicial construction, a freedom that he sought to limit as he drafted the penal code for India. As he observed, 'The power of construing the law in cases in which there is any real reason to doubt what the law is amounts to the power of making the law'. This remark well characterizes Macaulay's construction of the Charter Act of 1813.

2. The language of section 43

The Charter Act 1813 s.43 reads in part as follows:

And be it further enacted, that it shall be lawful for the Governor-general in Council to direct, that out of any surplus which may remain of the rents, revenues, and profits, arising from the said territorial acquisitions, after defraying the expenses of the military, civil, and commercial

---

[9] Quoted by Theodore F. T. Plucknett, *A Concise History of the Common Law* (5th edn., Boston: Little, Brown and Co., 1956), 335. Plucknett casts a critical eye on this old tradition. Robert G. Natelson notes that the rule was inconsistently observed, even in *Millar v Taylor*; and he finds that it was not hardened until 1840, when Chief Justice Denman stated it in *Q v Capel*: Natelson, 'The Founder's Hermeneutic: The Real Original Understanding of Original Intent' (2007) 68 *Ohio State Law Journal* 1239 (re *Millar v Taylor*), 1268 (re *Q v Capel*).

[10] The leading case is *Pepper v Hart* (1992), in which the House of Lords authorized judicial reference to the parliamentary record in certain instances. See Girvin (cited in n.1), 475–6.

establishments, and paying the interest of the debt, in manner herein-after provided, a sum of not less than one lack of rupees in each year shall be set apart and applied to *the revival and improvement of literature, and the encouragement of the learned natives of India, and for the introduction and promotion of a knowledge of the sciences among the inhabitants of the British territories in India*[.][11]

A *lack* (also *lac* or *lakh*) of rupees was 100,000 rupees: about £10,000 sterling—a substantial income for the hero of *Pride and Prejudice*, which was published the same year as the Charter Act; but not a great deal of money to pay for the education of Indian scholars.

It is conventional among historians of this text to see in the phrase here italicized a divided purpose: first, the 'revival' of learning in the classical literatures of India, specifically Sanskrit and Arabic; secondly, the 'introduction and promotion' of something more modern: 'a knowledge of the sciences'. John Clive, who wrote the chief twentieth-century biography of Macaulay, emphasized the division in these terms: 'The intention of this provision seemed to be to accomplish two different aims at one and the same time: to foster both Oriental learning and Western science. The precise meaning of the provision was to become the subject of intense dispute and, indeed, the main subject matter of Macaulay's Education Minute of 1835'.[12] Lynn Zastoupil and Martin Moir put the matter more pointedly: the ambivalent phrasing 'was manifestly the result of a compromise between two competing visions of empire' (*ZM* 7). In fact three competing visions of empire entered into the history of this phrase, and compromise proved a useful strategy at more than one stage of negotiation. The three visions of empire can be simply, if reductively, named: Orientalism (that is, the study of the classical learning and cultures of India); evangelical Christianity; and Science. In his minute Macaulay preferred the third, eschewed the second, and ridiculed the first.

3. Macaulay versus Prinsep

As has already been noted, Macaulay addressed the legal question as such near the start of his minute. His main strategy was to quibble on the epithet 'learned' and to scoff at the pretensions to learning of scholars of classical Arabic and Sanskrit texts:

It does not appear to me that the Act of parliament can by any art of construction be made to bear the meaning which has been assigned to it. It contains nothing about the particular languages or sciences which are to be studied. A sum is set apart 'for the revival and promotion of literature, and the encouragement of the learned natives of India, and for the introduction and promotion of a knowledge of the Sciences among the inhabitants of the British Territories.' It is argued, or rather taken for granted, that by literature the parliament can have meant only Arabic and Sanscrit literature; that they never would have given the Honorable appellation of a 'learned native' to a native who was familiar with the poetry of Milton, the metaphysics of Locke, and the Physics of Newton, but that they meant to designate by that name only such persons as might have studied in the sacred books of the Hindoos all the uses of Cusa-Grass,[13] and all the mysteries of absorption into the Deity. This does not appear to be a very satisfactory interpretation. To take a parallel case:—Suppose that the Pacha[14] of Egypt,—a country once superior in knowledge to the nations of Europe, but now sunk far below them,—were to appropriate a sum for the purpose of 'reviving

---

[11] *ZM* 91; emphasis added.
[12] John Clive, *Macaulay: The Shaping of the Historian* (New York: Alfred A. Knopf, 1973), 346.
[13] A common grass used as a cleansing agent and medicine, associated with Hindu ritual.
[14] The Pacha (or Pasha) of Egypt held chief administrative power in that country under the Ottoman Empire.

and promoting literature, and encouraging learned natives of Egypt,' would any body infer that he meant the youth of his Pachalik to give years to the study of hieroglyphics, to search into all the doctrines disguised under the fable of Osiris, and to ascertain with all possible accuracy the ritual with which cats and onions were anciently adored[?] Would he be justly charged with inconsistency if, instead of employing his young subjects in decyphering obelisks, he were to order them to be instructed in the English and French languages, and in all the sciences to which those languages are the chief keys?

The words on which the supporters of the old system rely do not bear them out, and other words follow which seem to be quite decisive on the other side. This lac of rupees is set apart not only for 'reviving literature in India,' the phrase on which their whole interpretation is founded, but also 'for the introduction and promotion of a knowledge of the sciences among the inhabitants of the British territories'—words which are alone sufficient to authorize all the changes for which I contend. (*ZM* 163)

Macaulay's analysis prompted a detailed rebuttal from Henry Thoby Prinsep (the elder), one of the most outspoken defenders of the Orientalist position on the GCPI and secretary to the government of India. Prinsep turned first to 'the legal question':

It is submitted that the Act 53 Geo III must be construed with special reference to the intention of the Legislature *of that day*. So construed there cannot be a doubt in the mind of any person that by 'the revival and promotion of literature and the encouragement of *learned natives*' the legislature *did not* mean to refer to any other literature than native literature nor to any other learned natives than such as were eminent by their proficiency in that literature. These were the persons *then* intended to be produced and encouraged and it is surely forcing the words out of their natural construction when it is argued that the revival of native literature can best be effected by abolishing all institutions for teaching the literature that then existed and that had existed for ages before and by communicating instruction only in English. (*ZM* 175–6)

Insisting on the relevance of 'the intention of the Legislature *of that day*', Prinsep tried to reject, as anachronistic, Macaulay's ebullient construction of the phrase 'learned natives' as covering scholars of English literature. Against this passage, in the margin of Prinsep's manuscript, Macaulay wrote, '[o]n the legal question I have had the opinion of Sir E. Ryan' (Edward Ryan was chief justice of Bengal and a sympathetic colleague on the GCPI). 'He pronounces that there is not the shadow of a reason for Mr. Prinsep's construction'. Prinsep, in turn, added his retort: 'I do not feel overwhelmed by this authority'. (It happened that two years later Ryan would co-edit a report of *Fauntleroy's Case* [1824], in which counsel had asserted, citing precedents, that 'every statute ought to be construed, not according to the letter, but according to the intent of the parliament', and that '[t]he preamble and occasion of passing a statute must therefore be looked to, in order to collect the intention of the legislature'.)[15]

Soon afterwards the debate was renewed in the Asiatic Society of Bengal, to which the government offered to offload some of its previous responsibilities for Oriental scholarship. Ryan, as president of the society, introduced a draft of a statement prepared by a special committee that had been appointed to respond to the government's action, a committee of which he was a member. Prinsep moved an amendment that implicitly called into question the government's construction of the statutory phrase 'for the revival and improvement of literature, and for the encouragement of learned natives of India'.

---

[15] William Moody (ed.), *Crown Cases Reserved for Consideration; and Decided by the Judges of England from the Year 1824 to the Year 1837*, 2 vols (London: Saunders and Benning, 1837), 1: 60, 61. For Ryan see 1: iii.

Ryan, though in the chair, objected to the amendment, 'because it appeared to entertain a doubt of the legality of the course pursued'. During discussion,

Mr. H. T. Prinsep quoted the words of the act, which he believed had been grounded on a minute of Mr. H. Colebrooke's, specially pointed to the literature and learned natives of the country. He thought there could be no doubt as to the meaning of the clause, and if such were entertained by any present, he should not hesitate to take the votes of members as to the construction to be put upon the words.... He was quite sure it was the general feeling, that the grant was made by Parliament to the literature of India, which ought not to be robbed of the provision so made to it.

Prinsep's amendment passed.[16]

4. 'Useful knowledge': father and son

In a later section of the minute, after he has gone beyond considerations of 'the form of proceeding', Macaulay takes up a broader question, which resonates nonetheless with the complex legislative history of the Act, and his own father's role in its formulation:

It is said that the Sanscrit and Arabic are the languages in which the sacred books of a hundred millions of people are written, and that they are on that account entitled to peculiar encouragement. Assuredly it is the duty of the British Government in India to be not only tolerant, but neutral on all religious questions.[17] But to encourage the study of a literature, admitted to be of small intrinsic value, only because that literature inculcates the most serious errors on the most important subjects, is a course hardly reconcilable with reason, with morality, or even with that very neutrality which ought, as we all agree, to be sacredly preserved. It is confessed that a language is barren of *useful knowledge* [emphasis added]. We are to teach it because it is fruitful of monstrous superstitions.[18] We are to teach false history, false astronomy, false medicine, because we find them in Company with a false religion. We abstain, and I trust shall always abstain, from giving any public encouragement to those who are engaged in the work of converting the natives to Christianity. And while we act thus[,] can we reasonably or decently bribe men, out of the revenues of the state, to waste their youth in learning how they are to purify themselves after touching an Ass, or what texts of the Vedas they are to repeat to expiate the crime of killing a goat[?] (*ZM* 170)

The pivotal phrase in this paragraph is 'useful knowledge'. For Macaulay, useful knowledge is the goal of education, and it is not to be found in the classical and sacred literatures of India.

By 1835 'useful knowledge' had become identified with the utilitarian educational theories of Jeremy Bentham and Lord Brougham. The Society for the Diffusion of Useful Knowledge (which spanned two decades, from 1826 to 1846) was the vivid engine of modernity, founded as a fresh alternative to the much older Society for Promoting Christian Knowledge, which since 1698 had supported missionary work in Britain and abroad.

In the paragraph quoted above Macaulay rehearses the traditional neutrality and tolerance of the British government as regards religion in India. Originally, as has already

---

[16] Minutes of the meeting of 3 June 1835, (1835) 4 *Journal of the Asiatic Society of Bengal* 287–94.

[17] In a dispatch of 29 May 1807 the East India Company had restated its long-standing policy of neutrality in matters of religion. *Papers Relating to East India Affairs*, Parliamentary Papers 1813: 4.

[18] Here Macaulay caricatures an argument of John Tytler's; see Sirkin and Sirkin (cited in n.5), 424–5.

been noted, that tolerance did not extend to the enterprise of Christian missionaries, which the East India Company positively discouraged as a nuisance. By 1835 the government's posture had shifted towards a more inclusive neutrality, tolerating though not officially encouraging Christian missionary work. And that adjustment had been brought about in section 33 of the Charter Act of 1813, in a 'whereas' clause that deploys the phrase 'useful knowledge' in a complicated way:

> XXXIII. And whereas it is the Duty of this Country to promote the Interest and Happiness of the Native Inhabitants of the *British* Dominions in *India*; and such Measures ought to be adopted as may tend to the Introduction among them of useful Knowledge, and of religious and moral Improvement; and in furtherance of the above Objects, sufficient Facilities ought to be afforded by Law to Persons desirous of going to and remaining in *India*, for the Purpose of accomplishing those benevolent Designs....[19]

Here 'the introduction of... useful knowledge' is explicitly allied to 'religious and moral improvement', as a partial justification for authorizing and accommodating 'persons desirous of going to and remaining in India, for the purpose of accomplishing those benevolent designs'—that is, Christian missionaries.

The bracketing notions of 'useful knowledge' and 'moral improvement' were ideas that Thomas Babington Macaulay could and did embrace emphatically—but not the central idea of 'religious... improvement':

> The claims of our own language [i.e., English] it is hardly necessary to recapitulate. It stands pre-eminent even among the languages of the west. It abounds with works of imagination not inferior to the noblest which Greece has bequeathed to us,[—]with models of every species of eloquence, with historical compositions which, considered merely as narratives, have seldom been surpassed, and which, considered as vehicles of ethical and political instruction, have never been equaled,[—]with just and lively representations of human life and human nature,—with the most profound speculations on metaphysics, *morals*, Government, jurisprudence, trade, with full and correct information[20] respecting every experimental science which tends to preserve the health, to increase the comfort, or to expand the intellect of man. Whoever knows that language has ready access to all the vast intellectual wealth which all the wisest nations of the earth have created and hoarded in the course of ninety generations. (*ZM* 165–66; emphasis added)

Also, morality stands at the heart of one of the most notorious pronouncements of Macaulay's minute: 'We must at present do our best to form a class who may be interpreters between us and the millions whom we govern[—]a class of persons Indian in blood and colour, but English in tastes, in opinions, *in morals* and in intellect' (*ZM* 171; emphasis added).

Useful knowledge, certainly ('full and correct information respecting every experimental science', etc.); moral improvement, yes; but religion, not particularly: in this last respect Macaulay stood apart from the text and the legislative history of section 33 of the Act. The full history of that important section, known at the time as a 'Pious clause', has not yet been written. Suffice it here to say that Macaulay's father, Zachary, had been instrumental in securing its adoption in 1813—thereby succeeding in a cause that he had supported in 1793, when the Charter had last been under legislative review; and,

---

[19] *The Statutes of the United Kingdom of Great Britain and Ireland, 53 George III, 1813* (London: J. Butterworth and Son, 1813), 694.

[20] 'Full and correct information' had been a standard commendatory formula in journalistic use since the late eighteenth century; it probably derived from the legal formulas 'full and correct representation' and 'full and correct declaration'. Here it stands as a synonym for 'useful knowledge'.

also, that the concept of 'useful knowledge' had been associated with moral improvement by Christian divines since the seventeenth century.[21] In 1835 Thomas Babington Macaulay was being unconventionally modern in detaching useful knowledge from questions of religion. In that respect he was not his father's son.[22]

5. Henry Colebrooke and Lord Minto

Although the 'useful knowledge' phrase of section 33 does figure in Macaulay's minute, stripped of its religious associations, standing there as a proxy for Science and the language of Science (that is, English), most of Macaulay's attention is focused on the equivocations of section 43—which, in a tour de force, he manages to find unequivocal.

Macaulay would have known that an ambition to encourage 'the revival' of Oriental learning had been expressed as long ago as 1811 by Gilbert Elliot, Lord Minto, then governor general, in a minute that he prepared with the assistance of Henry Colebrooke, a colleague on the Council of India who was skilled in Sanskrit.[23] In 1832 that minute was published in full and also abstracted for the benefit of the Select Committee on the Affairs of the East India Company, of which Macaulay was a member. The minute opens with a general complaint about the decay of classical learning in India, and by a call for its 'revival':

It is a common remark, that science and literature are in a progressive state of decay among the natives of India. From every inquiry which I have been enabled to make on this interesting subject, that remark appears to me but too well founded. The number of the learned is not only diminished, but the circle of learning, even among those who still devote themselves to it, appears to be considerably contracted. The abstract sciences are abandoned, polite literature neglected, and no branch of learning cultivated but what is connected with the peculiar religious doctrines of the people. The immediate consequence of this state of things is, the disuse, and even actual loss, of many valuable books; and it is to be apprehended, that unless Government interpose with a fostering hand, the revival of letters may shortly become hopeless, from a want of books, or of persons capable of explaining them.[24]

Minto understands this decline to follow from the loss of literary patronage previously afforded by the rulers of India, and he recommends that the British government should, as a remedy for this loss, 'extend its fostering care to the literature of the Hindoos', and establish several Hindu colleges for 'the restoration of learning'. He further proposes that, after securing 'the restoration of Hindoo science and literature', similar patronage might be extended to accomplish 'the revival of letters among our Mahomedan subjects' (1: 485).

---

[21] For example, Francis Bampfield, *All in One* ([London]: n.p., 1677), 47. See also *Hymns for Children* ([London]: Henry Haslop, 1797), 96. 'Useful knowledge' was a watchword in the second paragraph of the prospectus of the *Christian Observer*, the evangelical journal that Zachary Macaulay edited; (1803) 2, [iii].
[22] Robert E. Sullivan, Macaulay's most recent biographer, blames Zachary Macaulay's overbearing manner for his son's retreat from religion: 'it was Zachary's heedlessness and hectoring that worked to turn his heir against him and away from the God for which he claimed to speak'. *Macaulay: The Tragedy of Power* (Cambridge, Mass.: The Belknap Press, 2009), 29–30.
[23] T. E. Colebrooke, *The Life of H. T. Colebrooke* (London: Trübner and Son, 1873), 283.
[24] *Minutes of Evidence Taken before the Select Committee on the Affairs of the East India Company*, 6 vols (London: printed at the command of Parliament, 1832), 1: 484; closely abstracted by Thomas Fisher at 1: 399–400.

6. Hansard: Robert Percy ('Bobus') Smith

Hansard gives a record of discussion of the education clause as it was first introduced in Parliament. So far as I know, that record has been consulted only once before to shed light on the meaning of the statute.[25] On 2 July 1813 Mr Robert Percy Smith, who had entered Parliament the previous year, indicated that it was 'his intention to propose several clauses...to lay aside a *modicum* for founding schools for the literature of the natives, wherein they should be themselves the teachers; and for communicating the sciences to them through the medium of Europeans'.[26] After a brief interval, 'Mr. *R. Smith* then proposed two or three clauses relative to the appropriation of a sum of money for the promotion of native literature in the East, for the encouragement of sciences among the natives, and for the establishment of a native college or colleges'. Charles Grant, a close ally of Zachary Macaulay and advocate of Christian education in India, immediately objected that 'it was going too far to establish a college for the continuation of native prejudices and errors; in fact, to institute a Mahometan college for the Mahometan religion'.[27] It is evident from Grant's response that the money was to be assigned at least in part to what Minto called 'the revival of letters'.

Smith knew Minto: when he was advocate general in India and Minto was governor general, he paid him a visit, which Minto reported with pleasure to his family:

I have lately had a most agreeable visit from Mr. Smith, 'Bobus', the Advocate General. Though he is not exactly my contemporary, he has a great deal of excellent conversation that is a feast for all ages. We think alike too on European politics, which is rare here; and for that reason, as well as from a sense of propriety, I abstain entirely from that topic; but it is not unpleasant to be agreed with once in a way when one gets into good company.[28]

Sir James Mackintosh, on assuming a legal appointment in Bombay in 1804, had remarked, 'I have heard a good deal of Bobus. His fame is greater than that of any pundit since the time of Manu'.[29]

In 1999 Zastoupil and Moir noted that some of Macaulay's antagonists in the Anglicist-Orientalist controversy 'believed that Minto's ideas were reflected in the act's provisions, along with those of Henry Colebrooke'; but they were uncertain whether, given the slow pace of international communication, Minto's minute would have reached 'those involved in the preparation of the act during the first half of 1813'. They found the question 'an intriguing one, which requires further detailed research' (*ZM* 91). Minto's minute was dated 6 March 1811. Whether or not it reached London within a year, which seems probable, Bobus Smith concluded his appointment as advocate general in Bengal that same month,[30] and he may be presumed to have kept it in mind

---

[25] The exception is the very helpful paper by Justin Biel, 'Inventing the Empire of Opinion: History, Active Forgetting, and the Legacy of the British Imperialists' (University of Minnesota, 2008), 5–9. Heretofore credit for the clause has been assigned to Zachary Macaulay and other evangelicals, as by Clive, *Macaulay* (cited in n.12), 345.

[26] H. L. Debs. 2 July 1813, vol. 26, cols 1097–8.

[27] H. L. Debs. 2 July 1813, vol. 26, col. 1099.

[28] Emma Minto (ed.), *Lord Minto in India: Life and Letters of Gilbert Elliot, First Earl of Minto* (London: Longmans, Green, and Co., 1880), 88. Smith acquired the nickname 'Bobus' as a student at Eton—maybe because he was unusually skilled in Latin.

[29] James Mackintosh, *Memoirs of the Life of the Right Honourable Sir James Mackintosh*, R. J. Mackintosh (ed.) (London: Edward Moxon, 1835), 208.

[30] *The English Reports* (London: Stevens & Sons; Edinburgh: W. Green & Son, 1900–1930), 37: 219.

when he entered Parliament the following year. Certainly the clause that Smith introduced into the Charter Act of 1813 expresses the concerns and echoes the phrasing of that document.

The obituary notice for Smith in the *Gentleman's Magazine* mentioned that in Parliament 'he rendered...really eminent services as a most diligent and pains-taking member of committees',[31] but not that he addressed the East India question. In the revised entry for Smith in the second edition of the *Oxford Dictionary of National Biography* (1994), Katherine Prior remarks that '[h]e was anti-evangelical and in the debates over the renewal of the East India Company's charter he opposed the entry of Christian missions to British India and advocated the education of Indians in their own cultural tradition'. M. H. Port and R. G. Thorne provide a more detailed account in *The House of Commons 1790–1820*, observing that Smith 'had several contributions to make (as a select committeeman) to the debates on the renewal of the East India Company charter in 1813: he was hostile to Christian missions to India and wished provisions to be made for the education of Indians in their own cultural tradition; but he was ignored'.[32] Actually, he was not ignored.

Smith's crucial role in shaping part of the Charter Act, although not specially remarked then or since, justifies such objections to Macaulay's construction of it as the one made by Horace Hayman Wilson—a protégé of Colebrooke's in India in 1811 (he was appointed secretary of the Asiatic Society of Bengal upon Colebrooke's recommendation) and, from 1833, Boden professor of Sanskrit at Oxford:

Learned natives assuredly implied 'persons cultivating Oriental literature',—their own literature; and this is further intimated by the expressions 'revival and improvement': *revival* could not apply to English, which had never formed any branch of native literature, and it would be a strange, though not, perhaps, a wholly unparalleled, interpretation of the term *improvement*, to argue that it signified 'annihilation'. Adverting, also, to the authors of the measure,—to the Government of India at the time, with Lord Minto, a liberal patron of Oriental literature, at its head, and that eminent scholar, Mr. Colebrooke, a member of council,—there can be no doubt of the spirit of the provision; there can be no doubt that the bounty was intended to rescue the native scholars and professors of Hindustan from the state of destitution into which they had been plunged by foreign rule, and to afford them means and inducements to prosecute, with renovated vigour and hope, the cultivation of their own languages and their own literature. It was not designed to elevate upon their downfall a new race and new studies.[33]

In a word, Macaulay was 'wrong' in his reading of the statute.[34] Nonetheless, his reading carried the day.

7. Macaulay the civilian: authentic interpretation

Only a few months after Macaulay prepared his minute on Indian education in his capacity as law member of the Council of India, he accepted an additional appointment,

---

[31] 'Robert Percy Smith, Esq.' (1845) n.s. 23 *Gentleman's Magazine* 440, 441.
[32] R. G. Thorne (ed.), *The House of Commons 1790–1820*, 5 vols (London: Secker & Warburg, 1986), 5: 203. I have not been able to confirm that Smith served on the Select Committee on the Affairs of the East India Company, which issued a series of reports from 1808 (before Smith entered Parliament) until 1812.
[33] H. H. Wilson, 'Education of the Natives of India' (1836) n.s. 19 *Asiatic Journal and Monthly Register* 1, 5.
[34] Lees (cited in n.5), 64. Similarly Percival Spear, 'Bentinck and Education' (1938) 6 *Cambridge Historical Journal* 78, 84.

which he had sought, as president of the India Law Commission. That entity had been created by the Charter Act of 1833—at Macaulay's own instigation, when he was a member of Parliament. In his speech on the India Act Macaulay faulted the palimpsested multiplicity and unreliability of the systems of law in play in India: 'Hindoo law, Mahometan law, Parsee law, English law, perpetually mingling with each other and disturbing each other, varying with the person, varying with the place'.[35] Such uncertainty gave a convenient opening to the caprice of judges: 'The consequence is that in practice the decisions of the tribunals are altogether arbitrary. What is administered is not law, but a kind of rude and capricious equity'—'a mere lottery'. What resulted in India was a kind of parody of the 'judge-made law' that Jeremy Bentham had excoriated at home.[36] Macaulay could tolerate the English version of that injustice, but not the Indian one:

> Even in this country, we have had complaints of judge-made law; even in this country, where the standard of morality is higher than in almost any other part of the world; where, during several generations, not one depositary of our legal traditions has incurred the suspicion of personal corruption; where there are popular institutions; where every decision is watched by a shrewd and learned audience; where there is an intelligent and observant public; where every remarkable case is fully reported in a hundred newspapers; where, in short, there is everything which can mitigate the evils of such a system. But judge-made law, where there is an absolute government and a lax morality, where there is no bar and no public, is a curse and a scandal not to be endured. It is time that the magistrate should know what law he is to administer, that the subject should know under what law he is to live.[37]

A code for England (such as Bentham wanted) might be well enough, but 'India stands more in need of a code than any other country in the world'.

On 4 June 1835, three days after he was appointed chair of the Law Commission, Macaulay recommended such a code to the council, in crisply Benthamite terms:

> I would instruct [the commissioners] to frame a complete Criminal Code for all Parts of the Indian Empire. This Code should not be a mere Digest of existing Usages and Regulations, but should comprise all the Reforms which the Commission may think desirable. It should be framed on Two great Principles;—the Principle of suppressing Crime with the smallest possible Infliction of Suffering, and the Principle of ascertaining Truth at the smallest possible Cost of Time and Money.[38]

This proposal was approved, and Macaulay managed the task almost single-handedly (his colleagues on the Law Commission were frequently indisposed). He completed the work in May 1836, and it was published the following year.[39] Actual implementation was delayed until 1862, after some revision. It remains a force even today.

---

[35] Thomas Babington Macaulay, *Speeches of Lord Macaulay* (London: Longman, Green, Longman, and Roberts, 1860), 158–9.
[36] Jeremy Bentham, *Justice and Codification Petitions* (London: Robert Heward, 1829).
[37] Macaulay, *Speeches* (cited in n.35), 158–9.
[38] Macaulay, minute of 4 June 1835, in *Returns and Papers Presented to the House of Lords... in Session 1852, Relative to the Affairs of the East India Company* (London, 1852), 21. Regarding Bentham's general influence on Macaulay's ambitions for penal reform in India see Eric Stokes, *The English Utilitarians and India* (Oxford: Clarendon Press, 1959), 51–2, 219–24.
[39] *A Penal Code Prepared by the Indian Law Commissioners, and Published by Command of the Governor General of India in Council* (Calcutta: printed by G. H. Huttmann at the Bengal Military Orphan Press, 1837).

8. Illustrations

In his preface Macaulay drew attention to an unusual feature of the code: its inclusion of many terse, exemplary cases, designed to illustrate typical applications of a provision. For example:

> 331. Whoever wrongfully restrains any person in such a manner as to prevent that person from proceeding beyond certain circumscribing limits, is said 'wrongfully to confine' that person.
>
> (a) A causes Z to go within a walled space, and locks Z in. Z is thus prevented from proceeding in any direction beyond the circumscribing line of wall. A wrongfully confines Z.
>
> (b) In the last illustration, if there is in some nook of the walled space a door which is not secured, but which may easily escape observation, as A had voluntarily caused it to appear impossible to proceed beyond the line of wall, A has wrongfully confined Z.
>
> (c) A places men with fire arms at the outlets of a building, and tells Z that they will fire at Z, if Z attempts to leave the building. A wrongfully confines Z. (*Penal Code* 86)

Such illustrations, supposed to 'make nothing law which would not be law without them', are also supposed to make clear the *legislator's* intention: 'they are cases decided not by the judges but by the legislature, by those who make the law, and who must know more certainly than any judge can know what the law is which they mean to make' (*Penal Code* 7).

John Stuart Mill was charmed by this innovation. Reviewing the *Penal Code* not as regards its content but for the interest of its reform-minded structure, he wrote:

> What first strikes the eye... is the happy invention of appending authoritative examples by way of Illustration, to all those enactments of the code which require them: an idea by which the advantages of general language, and those which English statutes vainly seek to attain by an enumeration of particulars, are happily blended; and which, besides the greater certainty and distinctness given to the legislator's meaning, solves the difficult problem of making the body of the laws a popular book, at once intelligible and interesting to the general reader. Simple as this contrivance is, it escaped the sagacity of Bentham, so fertile in ingenious combinations of detail.[40]

When the penal code for India was finally adopted, so were this method of illustration, Macaulay's rationale for it, and many of his illustrations—often verbatim.[41]

Later in the century Frederick Pollock praised in high terms 'Macaulay's invention'— Benthamite in spirit, perhaps, but Macaulay's contrivance: 'It is an instrument of new constructive power, enabling the legislator to combine the good points of statute-law and case-law... while avoiding almost all their respective drawbacks'.[42] He adopted the method for his own treatise, as have the authors of some Indian treatises. Bijay Kisor Acharyya commended the method in *Codification in British India* as 'the greatest specific advance that has been made in modern times in... "the mechanics of law-making"'.[43]

---

[40] Unsigned review (1838) 29 *London and Westminster Review* 393, 402. Sullivan, *Macaulay: The Tragedy of Power* (cited in n.22) identifies Mill as the author (148). The argument-from-popularity expresses Mill's lighter side; he ignores or takes for granted the supposed function of the illustrations to prevent judge-made law.

[41] Walter Morgan and A. G. Macpherson, *The Indian Penal Code* (Calcutta: G. C. Hay and Co., 1861).

[42] Frederick Pollock, *A Digest of the Law of Partnership* (London: Stevens & Sons, 1877), iv.

[43] Bijay Kisor Acharyya, *Codification in British India* (Calcutta: S. K. Banerji & Sons, 1914), 139. However, he does sketch the misgivings of one justice (140–1).

Pollock later regretted that Parliament had not taken up Macaulay's example.[44] Sanford H. Kadish has pointed out that Macaulay was not in fact the first to use such illustrations: Macaulay acknowledged consulting 'the valuable code of Louisiana, prepared by Mr. Livingston' (*Penal Code* 6), and that code does contain occasional illustrations.[45] Livingston's Benthamite rationale for the innovation is similar to Macaulay's: in illustrating the code '[t]he lawgiver takes upon himself that part of his duty which has heretofore been improperly devolved upon the judge'.[46]

Whatever the precedents or practical merits of the illustrative method, Macaulay's rationale for it is remarkable. He, too, would use it to pre-empt interpretation, and for that he cites the authority of Justinian:

> *The power of construing the law in cases in which there is any real reason to doubt what the law is amounts to the power of making the law.* On this ground the Roman jurists maintained that the office of interpreting the law in doubtful matters necessarily belonged to the legislature. The contrary opinion was censured by them with great force of reason, though in language perhaps too bitter and sarcastic for the gravity of a Code. 'Eorum vanam subtilitatem tam risimus quam corrigendam esse censuimus. Si enim in praesenti leges condere soli imperatori concessum est, et leges interpretari solo dignum imperio esse oportet Quis legum aenigmata solvere et omnibus aperire idoneus esse videbitur nisi is cui legislatorem esse concessum est? Explosis itaque his ridiculosis ambiguitatibus tam conditor quam interpres legum solus imperator juste existimabitur. (*Penal Code* 7–8; emphasis added)

Macaulay here quotes elliptically from the emperor, who, in a letter to the praetorian prefect Demosthenes, had belittled those who doubted his hermeneutic authority:

> [W]e have both laughed at this foolish subtlety and have deemed it proper to correct it.... For if at the present time it is conceded only to the emperor to make laws, it should be befitting only the imperial power to interpret them. For why do the nobles run to us for advice when a doubt arises in lawsuits and they do not trust themselves to give a decision, and why are ambiguities which are apt to be found in laws referred to us, if true interpretation does not proceed from us?[47]

Macaulay applies the same logic to his situation: 'The publication of this collection of cases decided by legislative authority will, we hope, greatly limit the power which the Courts of Justice possess of putting their own sense on the laws' (*Penal Code* 8).

In renewing Justinian's precautions, including the publication of exemplary and supposedly determinative judgments, Macaulay displays several anxieties about legislative interpretation. He knows, from his own recent experience as an interpreter of the Charter Act of 1813, that '[t]he power of construing the law in cases in which there is any real reason to doubt what the law is amounts to the power of making the law'. He may have remembered the caution of Hobbes:

> For it is not the letter, but the intendment, or 'Meaning'; that is to say, the *authentique interpretation* of the law (which is the sense of the legislator,) in which the nature of the law consisteth; And therefore the Interpretation of all Laws dependeth on the Authority Sovereign; and the Interpreters can be none but those, which the Sovereign (to whom only the subject oweth obedience) shall

---

[44] Pollock, *Digest*, (11th edn, London: Stevens & Sons, 1920) [v]. For the influence of these illustrations see George C. Rankin, *Background to Indian Law* (Cambridge: Cambridge University Press, 1946), 203; and M. C. Setalvad, *The Common Law in India* (London: Stevens & Sons, 1960), 129–30.

[45] Sanford H. Kadish, 'Codifiers of the Criminal Law: Wechsler's Predecessors' (1978) 78 *Columbia Law Review* 1098, 1133.

[46] Edward Livingston, *A System of Penal Law for the State of Louisiana* (Philadelphia: James Kay, Jun. and Co., 1833), 109.

[47] Fred H. Blume, *Annotated Justinian Code*, Timothy Kearley (ed.) (2nd edn), available at: <http://uwacadweb.uwyo.edu/blume&justinian> 1.14.12: 2, 3, 4, 5, accessed June 2011.

appoint. For else, by the craft of an interpreter, the law may be made to beare a sense, contrary to that of the sovereign; by which means the interpreter becomes the legislator.[48]

Etymologically *authentique* or *authentic* derives from the Greek 'αὐθεντία 'original authority', and αὐθέντης 'one who does a thing himself, a principal, a master, an autocrat', 'αὐτ(ο- self...[ )]'.[49] The word is not related to *author*, but it might as well be: authentic interpretation is authorial—authorized—interpretation.

As the imperial author now of a criminal code Macaulay would resist unauthorized interpretation, hedging it as best he could with illustrative examples to pre-empt judge-made law. Macaulay does not entertain the further anxiety that such illustrations themselves must be interpreted. But he does acknowledge that questions will arise despite his best efforts—and so he goes on to set out, in paragraphs not quoted here, an elaborate procedure for revising the code from time to time. The task of laying down the law is unending.

It may appear that in framing the two chief documents of his celebrated Indian career Macaulay was guilty of gross inconsistency. When it suited him, as in the case of the Charter Act, he exercised the licence of an interpreter, averting his eyes from the purpose of the text and the traces of that purpose in the text. But as legislator it suited him to use every means to restrict the licence of the interpreter; even to preclude interpretation as such, if that were possible. How to reconcile these practices—if not just as betraying the interested disinterest of the skilled lawyer?

The simplest explanation is that in crafting his minute on Indian education and his criminal code for India Macaulay adhered to standard practices of distinct branches of the law: the common law and the civil law. The contradiction is not merely his but expresses the difference between the two systems. Although it is a commonplace of statutory construction in the common law that the intention of the legislature should be fulfilled, a countervailing and prevalent commonplace holds that the intention of the legislature is inherent in the statute, and that the interpreter need go no farther than the words of the statute to find it. Such a premise will indulge great latitude for the interpreter of the text, of which Macaulay took his advantage. But as the author of the law he would have the last word. Bentham sought to prune 'the overgrowth of *judge-made* law', preferring, as more reliable, '*legislature-made* law'.[50] So did Macaulay the legislator.

Writers, as writers, may generally be civilians, jealous of their authority and zealous to control the reading of their words.[51] Readers, as readers, may value the greater freedom afforded by such professional mysteries as the common law. In each role, as a reader and as a writer, Macaulay models the ideal.

---

[48] Thomas Hobbes, *Leviathan* 2.26 (emphasis added), here quoted from Gary L. McDowell, *The Language of Law and the Foundations of American Constitutionalism* (Chicago: University of Chicago Press, 2010), 78.

[49] *Oxford English Dictionary* (2nd edn, 1989) online version accessed June 2011.

[50] Bentham, *Justice and Codification Petitions* (cited in n.36), 184. Apparently Bentham coined both terms.

[51] Michael Hancher, 'Dead Letters: Wills and Poems', (1982) 60 *Texas Law Review* 507.

13

'Where be his quiddities now'? Law and Language in *Hamlet*

*Eric Heinze**

> *[T]o die: to sleep—*
> *No more, and by a sleep to say we end*
> *The heartache and the thousand natural shocks*
> *That flesh is heir to: tis a consummation*
> *Devoutly to be wished. [...]For who would bear the whips and scorns of time,*
> *Th'oppressor's wrong, the proud man's contumely,*
> *The pangs of despised love, the law's delay,*
> *The insolence of office and the spurns*
> *That patient merit of th'unworthy takes,*
> *When he himself might his quietus make*
> *With a bare bodkin? (Ham. 3.1.59–63, 65–75)*

In world literature's most famous speech, 'To be or not to be' (*Ham.* 3.1.55–87), Hamlet ponders whether suicide would cure what he calls the 'natural', as well as the social ills that grieve us. He never itemizes the natural ones. Their afflictions are too obvious and too numerous. Whether they be a 'gout', or a 'pox,' or an 'ague', pain is pain. Suffice it to hate collectively those 'thousand natural shocks/That flesh is heir to'[1] (*Ham.* 3.1.61–2).

Hamlet has no such equivocal view of the indignities caused by humans. He enumerates six,

(1) '[t]h'oppressor's wrong',

(2) 'the proud man's contumely',

---

* Unless otherwise indicated, citations to *Hamlet* are to the Arden Shakespeare Third Series edition (gen. eds Richard Proudfoot et al.) [hereafter ARD3]. Other textual references, when not otherwise indicated, are to The Oxford Shakespeare (gen. ed. Stanley Wells) (individual plays) [OXF4]. The other editions cited are *New Cambridge Shakespeare*, Philip Brockbank et al., eds, 1984– [CAM4]; *Revised Arden Shakespeare*, U. Ellis-Fermor et al., gen. eds, 1951– [ARD2]; *New Penguin Shakespeare*, T.J.B.Spencer, gen. ed., from 1967 [PEN2]; and *The Norton Shakespeare*, Stephen Greenblatt et al., eds. (New York, NY: Norton & Co., 2nd edn, 2008) [NOR2]. Abbreviations of Shakespeare titles and editions follow Modern Language Association, *Shakespeare Variorum Handbook* (Richard Knowles, ed., 2nd edn, web publication, 2003). I would like to thank Paul Raffield and Leif Dahlberg for their comments, as well as Michael Freeman, Fiona Smith, Emma Brady, and all other UCL and OUP staff for their generous support. I would also like to thank Elspeth Graham for inviting me to present a version of this chapter at the Liverpool John Moores University School of Humanities & Social Science in December 2012.

[1] Given Hamlet's troubled sexuality (e.g., *Ham.* 2.2.274–80), notably in relation to Ophelia (e.g., *Ham.* 3.1.114–27), those 'shocks' might certainly include sexual urges. (Note also his questionable belief that such urges reach their 'heyday' in youth (*Ham.* 3.4.66–8)). If that is the case, then the entire arena of 'problematical sexuality' (whose isn't?) reminds us of that the division between 'natural' and 'social' afflictions remains fluid, as suggested also by the third of the social ills Hamlet mentions.

(3) '[t]he pangs of despised love',

(4) 'the law's delay',

(5) '[t]he insolence of office',

(6) 'the spurns/That patient merit of th'unworthy takes'.

One puzzling item on that list is 'the law's delay'. Does sheer 'delay' really equate with, say, the 'oppressor's wrong'? Or even with 'the proud man's contumely'? Might it not betoken justice itself—the care and attention with which all sides of a dispute are heard, all facts investigated, and hasty results avoided? Shakespeare never tires of exposing abuses of power by kings, aristocrats, churchmen, or merchants. Law is merely another face, or tool, of that power structure. And yet Shakespeare's depictions of law's abuses, throughout the corpus, retain a distinct quality.

During the famous *memento mori* in the graveyard, Hamlet picks up the first skull, imagining it to have belonged either to a 'politician' (*Ham.* 5.1.74), not in the more recent sense of candidate or holder of government office, but in the earlier sense of 'schemer, intriguer, plotter'[2]; or to a 'courtier' (*Ham.* 5.1.77), whose use of language scarcely surpasses flattery. Yet, having tossed out some stock remarks about such persons, remarks familiar elsewhere in the corpus, he has little more to say about them. By contrast, turning to a second one, wondering 'may not that be the skull of a lawyer?' (*Ham.* 5.1.93–4), Hamlet launches into a curious tirade against law and its practitioners,

'Where be his quiddities now, his quillets, his cases, his tenures, and his tricks? Why does he suffer this rude knave now to knock him about the sconce with a dirty shovel, and will not tell him of his action of battery? Hum! This fellow might be in's time a great buyer of land, with his statutes, his recognizances, his fines, his double vouchers, his recoveries. Is this the fine of his fines, and the recovery of his recoveries, to have his fine pate full of fine dirt? Will his vouchers vouch him no more of his purchases, and double ones too, than the length and breadth of a pair of indentures? The very conveyances of his lands will hardly lie in this box; and must the inheritor himself have no more, ha? (*Ham.* 5.1.94–106 [OXF4])

Why anyone would find a lawyer more irksome than a politician or a court mandarin is a puzzle. But more so in Hamlet's case. Certainly, the hints about manipulated land law remind us that Claudius has removed Hamlet from any prospect of direct succession from Hamlet's father[3] (*Ham.* 3.2.331). In so doing, however, Claudius had played far more the 'politician' than anything like a practitioner of ordinary land law. More generally, it would seem at first glance that, for a prince, the web of palace officials like Polonius or Osric would prove more irksome than the machinery of everyday, common law, which remains more burdensome for subjects than for an otherwise comfortable prince. At most, it would seem, law no more embodies power than do monarchy, aristocracy, the church, or the emerging bourgeoisie. What is it about law that prompts Hamlet to single it out for singular treatment?

In this article, I shall suggest that, in *Hamlet*, law's oppressive character emerges largely through its linguistic qualities. *Hamlet* represents Shakespeare's most original statement on legal language as the essence of all that is manipulative and duplicitous in

---

[2] 'Here, as always in Shakespeare, the word carries a pejorative sense—unprincipled schemer.' (OXF4, p. 324; cf. PEN2, p. 294). See David Crystal and Ben Crystal, *Shakespeare's Words* (London: Penguin, 2002), p. 337.

[3] Whilst the Danish monarchy is elective (*Ham.* 5.2.339–40; cf. 4.5.102–8), much suggests that Hamlet would have enjoyed popular support for succession (*Ham.* 4.3.4; cf. 3.1.150–3). In that case, Claudius has effectively cut off both father and son (cf., ironically, *Ham.* 1.2.64, 109–12, 117), a reality incessantly reinforced by the shared name of 'Hamlet'.

law's norms, institutions, guardians, and practitioners—a culmination of insights progressively developed earlier in the corpus. Before returning to *Hamlet*, I shall begin, in section 1, by examining law and language in one of Shakespeare's early works, the history play *Henry VI, Part Two*, which partly anticipates, but partly also diverges from *Hamlet*'s portrayal of law. That play's famous peasant rebellion includes a mock trial of the leading jurist Lord Saye, whose humanist view of law is challenged precisely on grounds of law's propensity to manipulate power through language.

I then, in section 2, examine *Hamlet*'s broader political context. Even more overtly than the nominally medieval setting of the early history plays, *Hamlet*'s world anticipates the modern surveillance state, in which the 'literacy' of power—far from overcoming the sheer, brute force correlated to the Renaissance stereotype of medieval law—merely dresses it in that same manipulable language which is put on trial in the *Henry VI* trilogy. In section 3, I argue that law in *Hamlet* is distinct not in the sense of existing separately from other forms of power, but because, again through its linguistic element, it becomes the paradigm for the oppressive tendencies of power generally as exercised within the modern state.

1. What does the law Saye?

'The first thing we do, let's kill all the lawyers.' Few passages in Shakespeare so predictably stoke giggles, even among lawyers who lack any clue about where or why the quip is uttered. Hearing it in performance, proclaimed by a cohort of the rebel leader Jack Cade in *Henry VI, Part Two* (*2H6*, 4.2.71), the viewer might feel perplexed. The play's peasants and workers certainly rail against class privilege (*2H6*, 4.2.7–20). But why particularly that slur against lawyers? Why not against the monarchy, or the nobility, or a corrupted Church, or the emerging merchant class? Those socio-political actors will certainly face scrutiny elsewhere in Shakespeare.

As it happens, the rebel leader scarcely hates monarchy. Class hostility may motivate some of the Kentish rebels, but Cade tells us in an aside that he has 'invented' (*2H6*, 4.2.145) his far-fetched lineal claim to the crown (*2H6*, 4.2.37–46, 126–36). He aims not to abolish, but to seize monarchical power (*2H6*, 4.2.64–5). His drive to destroy the legal profession, with its penchant for rules, records, and procedures, suggests that this demagogue actually hungers to be a monarch more absolute, less constrained by law (e.g., *2H6*, 4.7.13–14, 112–15), than any king England has known before: 'The proudest peer in the realm shall not wear a head on his shoulders, unless he pay me tribute.' (*2H6*, 4.7.112–13) Cade pledges even to retain the *droit de seigneur* (*2H6*, 4.7.113–17).

That appetite cannot come as a complete surprise. In Shakespeare's day, British and European monarchies are charging down the absolutist road.[4] Nor does nobility as such annoy Cade. His first step to the throne takes the form of his own, inadvertently farcical self-knighting[5] (*2H6*, 4.2.108–9; cf. 4.7.4). It is not institutionalized power as such, it is not government as such, that most irks the rebels, but rather something specific about the exercise of power through the methods and procedures of law. What they abhor is law's linguistic expression—ostensibly more peaceful, yet also subtler and less overt than the brandished sword of crude, unadorned power politics. Critical Legal Theorists

---

[4] See, e.g., Leonard Tennenhouse, *Power on Display: The Politics of Shakespeare's Genres* (New York: Methuen, 1986).

[5] That charade apes the more calculated strategy of the factious Richard Plantagenet, whose recovery of the Dukedom of York (*1H6*, 3.1.152–80), lost when his father was hanged for treason against Henry V (*1H6*, 2.5; *3H6*, 1.1; *H5*, 2.2), ends up merely as his first step towards toppling the House of Lancaster and asserting his own royal claim.

would not be surprised to learn that, for Jack Cade, it is through language that law serves not to overcome brute power struggles, but merely to paint those struggles with the veneer of justice, in the interests of the prevailing order.

Emblematic of the counter-brutality that will arise even from the workers' legitimate gripes is their pseudo-trial of the jurist Lord Saye—drawn from the historical James Fiennes Saye, Lord Chamberlain and Treasurer of England[6]—whose sheer surname (in some editions it appears as 'Say') pre-figures the distinct qualities that the rebels will scorn in law and lawyers. It is because of what this jurist can say, and how he can say it, it is because of the peremptory and elusive power of language in a steadily bureaucratizing world, that Saye will perish. With the pseudo-ceremony of a proceeding that simultaneously enacts and mocks a criminal trial—its own feigned authority raising questions about what, exactly, legitimates 'duly' constituted legal authority—Cade includes among the 'charges' against Saye: '[T]hou hast built a paper-mill. It will be proved to thy face that thou hast men about thee that usually talk of a noun and a verb and such abominable words...' (*2H6*, 4.7.34–8). What is on trial is not merely a government official, not merely an officer of law, but law as such, and its quintessential medium of language. If language is a tool of power, then grammatical, i.e., meta-linguistic talk of 'a noun and a verb' betokens a special, privileged mastery of and access to that tool. Language at least symbolically distinguishes law from other exercises of authority, certainly in the English histories' nominally late medieval world, but also in Shakespeare's early modern England,[7] where matters of politics and government may still be settled at the point of a sword. It is that distinctly modern exercise of power, whereby words become more potent but also less fathomable than swords, that the Kentish rebels detest.

From Shakespeare's Renaissance-humanist perspective, the power-mongering of the English plays is the hallmark of corrupted politics in the Middle Ages. Yet is not a regime based on reason and accountability, a regime whose emblem is precise and enlightened language, central to justice and to civic freedom? Does not the rationally uttered word always excel the brandished sword? Do not literacy and education count among civilization's greatest goods?[8] The Renaissance-humanist world of letters may boast Shakespeare as its star creation; however, the poet seems already to anticipate anti-Enlightenment, indeed Foucauldian and Derridian suspicions about language as the pernicious tool of manipulation and subordination, all too handily dressed in the mantle of peace-making neutrality, objectivity, or universality. Language's deceptively benign power becomes all the more lethal when it assumes the guise of cultivated, specialist knowledge and professionalized technique.[9]

Saye has his chance to dodge the rebels, but chooses to confront them (*2H6*, 4.4.42–7, 56–60), trusting that his enlightened humanism will speak for itself, that his ethos of law for the common good, for the benefit of rich and poor alike, will be manifest. It is in that vein

---

[6] See, e.g., OXF4, p. 109; ARD3, p. 148.

[7] In leading studies on Shakespeare's histories, particularly since the advent of the New Historicist movement, we witness greater attention to Shakespeare's recent Tudor context than to his medieval sources. See, e.g., Tennenhouse (cited in n.4); Graham Holderness, *Shakespeare: The Histories* (New York, NY: St. Martins Press, 2000); Paola Pugliatti, *Shakespeare The Historian* (New York, NY: Palgrave Macmillan, 1996); Phyllis Rackin, *Stages of History: Shakespeare's English Chronicles* (Ithaca, NY: Cornell University Press, 1990).

[8] '[T]he main hope of getting a good prince hangs on his proper education': Erasmus, *The Education of a Christian Prince*, Neil M. Cheshire and Michael J. Heath trans., Lisa Jardine, ed. (Cambridge,: Cambridge University Press, 1997), p. 5. cf., e.g., Holderness (cited in n.7), pp. 67–73 (discussing humanist ideals in *Hamlet*).

[9] Foucault famously represents the proliferation of specialized discourses in modernity, under the watch of professionalized elites, as a technique of social control: Michel Foucault, *Histoire de la sexualité*, vol. 1 (Paris: Gallimard, 1994).

of nascent Western liberalism that he defends himself. Saye embraces the ideals of the rule of law and of justice tempered by mercy: 'Justice with favour have I always done,/Prayers and tears have moved me, gifts could never.' (*2H6*, 4.7.63–4) With those words, Saye aims not just to save his skin. He sincerely views his erudition—which, in the curious Shakespearean lexicon, he will call in the following speech his 'book'[10]—as the very embodiment of justice through law, as the safeguard of justice against arbitrariness and brute force. He declares as much in a proto-Enlightenment paean to law and the techniques of knowledge,

Because my book preferred me to the King,
And seeing ignorance is the curse of God,
Knowledge the wing wherewith we fly to heaven,
Unless you be possessed with devilish spirits,
You cannot but forbear to murder me. (*2H6*, 4.7.68–72)

Yet one feature of oppression in Marxist as well as Foucauldian or Derridian analyses is that the powerful may participate in regimes of arbitrary class difference, whilst sincerely believing in the justice of the system, as they translate their class-based self-interest into universal good.[11] Saye invokes the classical humanist imagery of sacrifice of his own welfare or gain, to the point of illness, for the sake of the greater good. The rebels, however, hear only the devious language of class privilege,

SAYE These cheeks are pale for watching for your good—
CADE Give him a box o' the ear and that will make 'em red again.
SAYE Long sitting to determine poor men's causes Hath made me full of sickness
    and diseases. [. . .]
DICK Why dost thou quiver, man?
SAYE The palsy, and not fear, provokes me.
CADE Nay, he nods at us as who should say, 'I'll be even with you'. I'll see if his
    head will stand steadier on a pole, or no. Take him away, and behead him.
SAYE Tell me wherein have I offended most?
    Have I affected wealth or honour? Speak.
    Are my chests filled up with extorted gold?
    Is my apparel sumptuous to behold?
    Whom have I injured, that ye seek my death?
    These hands are free from guiltless bloodshedding,
    This breast from harbouring foul deceitful thoughts.
    O, let me live! (*2H6*, 4.7.79–97)

Where Saye says law's tools achieve justice, Cade's men hear cunning eloquence, a strategy of exclusion and privilege,

BUTCHER What say you of Kent?
SAYE Nothing but this: 'tis *bona terra, mala gens*.
CADE Away with him, away with him! He speaks Latin. (*2H6*, 4.7.52–4; cf. *2H6*,
    4.2.156)

---

[10] See OXF4, p. 254.
[11] Brecht's quest for constructive estrangement (*Verfremdung*) of the audience from the artwork, assumes, among its audience, not merely the working classes, for whom such alienation merely recapitulates the familiar, but also the more privileged, generally educated classes, who will already believe themselves in possession of a legitimate, coherent, generally applicable moral code, which the artwork ought not to confirm, but to challenge. See Berthold Brecht, *Schriften zum Theater: Über eine nicht-aristotelische Dramatik* (Frankfurt a.M.: Suhrkamp, 1957).

The First Quarto variant, adopted in some current editions, underscores that element of Saye's speech which, confounding the illiterate peasants, mockingly betokens their alienation from the world of literate power,

> **SAYE** ...'tis bona terra, mala gens.
> **CADE** *Bonum terrum*—zounds, what's that?
> **BUTCHER** He speaks French,
> **FIRST REBEL** No, 'tis Dutch.
> **SECOND REBEL** No, 'tis Out-talian. I know it well enough. (Norton 2, *2H6*, 4.7.47–52)

So distant, even otherworldly, is the jurist's language that it seems demonic, 'Away with him, he has a familiar under his tongue.' (*2H6*, 4.7.101; cf. 4.7.73) Such corporal references to the tongue or the mouth recur, focusing the iconography of power not merely upon language, but literally on the crudeness of the body part that produces it. The reduction, and often debasement, of humanity to body parts is familiar enough in Shakespeare. Law is traced to language, and language traced to the dark pit of the oral cavity, locus of bestial mastication, which indifferently utters words as it chews, bellows, or belches. Merely by opening his mouth, or flexing his tongue, the powerful can dictate fundamental power relations.[12] Henry Bolingbroke observes as much, in *Richard II*, marvelling at the power that issues from 'the breath of kings' (*R2*,1.3.215; cf. 1.3.152–3; 3.2.56–7). *Measure for Measure*'s corrupted deputy Angelo will boast of being 'the voice of the recorded law' (*MM* 2.4.61), in a passage in which he condemns an innocent to death (*MM* 2.4.33–8; cf. 2.2.34–55) for a trespass trivial in comparison to his own abuses.

Hamlet rebukes Rosenkrantz and Guildenstern for allowing the King and Queen to manipulate *them* into manipulating *him*,

> Why, look you now, how unworthy a thing you make of me: you would play upon me! You would seem to know my stops, you would pluck out the heart of my mystery, you would sound me from my lowest note to the top of my compass. And there is much music, excellent voice, in this little organ. Yet cannot you make it speak. 'Sblood! Do you think I am easier to be played on than a pipe? (*Ham.* 3.2.355–62)

Pipe playing, Hamlet insists, 'is as easy as *lying*. Govern these ventages with your fingers and thumb, give it breath with your mouth, and it will discourse most eloquent music' (*Ham.* 3.2.351–3, emphasis added). Unsurprisingly, Claudius constructs an analogy, whereby 'The head is not more native to the heart,/The hand more instrumental to the mouth,/Than is the throne of Denmark' to the duplicitous Polonius (*Ham.* 1.2.47–9). In contrast to Hamlet, the ambitious Fortinbras handily musters an army and scorns, 'makes mouths at...death and danger' (*Ham.* 4.4.49–51). Finally, in the graveyard scene, the 'politician', 'courtier', or 'lawyer' possess no longer a mouth, but only a skull and jawbone, bereft of speech, therefore of power (*Ham.* 5.1.71–105).

It is Saye's mouth that will be humiliated after he and his son-in-law are executed. When their heads are brought in on poles, Cade commands, 'Let them kiss one another, for they loved well when they were alive' (*2H6*, 4.7.122–3), followed by the Q1 stage direction '*The two heads are made to kiss*' (*2H6*, 4.7.123.1 SD), and by Cade's further insistence, 'at every corner have them kiss' (*2H6*, 4.7.127–8). Cade seeks absolute power for himself, signified through the incarnated authority of the mouth,

> **BUTCHER** I have a suit unto your lordship. [...]
> Only that the laws of England may come out of your mouth. [...]

---

[12] See Charles R. Forker, 'Introduction', *in R2*, ARD3, pp. 1–169, at pp. 65–6.

CADE I have thought upon it, it shall be so. Away, burn all the records of the
realm: my mouth shall be the parliament of England. (*2H6*, 4.7.3–14)

Jane Howell's class-conscious, Brechtian[13] staging places a ritualistic burning of 'all the records' at the riot's centre. Camera close-ups show the flames devouring legal tomes.[14] Again, it is not power per se, rather it is law per se, manifesting as an intricately linguistic enterprise, that the rebels assail. Saye's linguistic virtuosity in mounting his own defence seals his fate. Cade disposes of Saye, commanding, 'He shall die an it be but for pleading so well for his life.' (*2H6*, 4.7.100) To the rebels' ears, legal language recites neither clarity nor transparency, but rather, as Marx and then Brecht would have it, obfuscation and *Entfremdung* ('alienation').[15] Saye's pride in the power of law as justice becomes, for the rebels, a sinister, suspicious, ubiquitous force—an exercise of violence not openly, like a 'blow in the field', but covertly, donning the mantle of justice and fairness,

SAYE This tongue hath parleyed unto foreign kings
For your behoof—
CADE Tut, when struck'st thou one blow in the field?
SAYE Great men have reaching hands. Oft have I struck
Those that I never saw, and struck them dead.
BEVIS O monstrous coward! What, to come behind folks? (*2H6*, 4.7.73–8)

If the workers' revolt will degenerate into mindless rowdiness, it is nevertheless motivated by a justified sense of oppression. Coupled with the 'charge' that Saye talks 'of a noun and a verb' are also some weightier accusations. Literacy betokens not merely benign privilege, but the iniquity whereby criminal punishments inflicted upon the poor and illiterate are harsher than those imposed upon the educated classes,[16]

Thou hast appointed justices of peace, to call poor men before them about matters they were not able to answer. Moreover, thou hast put them in prison, and because they could not read, thou hast hanged them, when indeed only for that cause they have been most worthy to live. (*2H6*, 4.7.38–43)

Throughout Shakespeare's early history plays, powerful nobles flamboyantly place themselves above law[17] (e.g., *1H6*, 2.4.7–9). If the fundamental tension is class-based after all, the question remains, why do the rebels not inveigh against the nobles, or indeed against the king, emblem of the legal order, directly? In addition to some reasons already suggested, we must also observe that, far more than any monarch in Shakespeare, Henry VI adheres scrupulously to the rule of law. It is the nobles surrounding him who scorn formal, legal channels of dispute resolution.[18] What emerges from those nobles is as much Shakespeare's early modern world as any medieval one narrated in the chronicles. We witness a Foucauldian world of institutionally disseminated power,

---

[13] See, e.g., Graham Holderness, 'Radical Potentiality and Institutional Closure', in *Political Shakespeare: Essays on Cultural Materialism*, Jonathan Dollimore and Alan Sinfield, eds. (Manchester: Manchester University Press, 2nd edn, 1994), pp. 206–25, at pp. 221–3.
[14] *Henry VI, Part Two* (Julia Howell, dir., BBC TV Shakespeare edn (1983)).
[15] See generally Brecht (cited in n.11).
[16] See, e.g., Pugliatti (cited in n.7), ch. 9; Alexander Leggatt, *Shakespeare's Political Drama* (London: Routledge, 1988), pp. 16–22; Ian Ward, *Shakespeare and the Legal Imagination* (London: Butterworths, 1999), pp. 138–40.
[17] See Leggatt (cited in n.16), chs 1–2. See also, e.g., Eric Heinze, 'Power Politics and the Rule of Law: Shakespeare's First Historical Tetralogy and Law's "Foundations"', (2009) 29 *Oxford Journal of Legal Studies*, pp. 230–63.
[18] See generally Heinze (cited in n.17).

always everywhere, yet never anywhere in particular, simultaneously perpetuated by, yet altogether consuming even those powerful figures appointed to serve as law's stewards. The nobles' fates arguably end up as bleak as the peasants' in Shakespeare's early English histories. The powerful may sincerely protest the righteousness of the existing order— Saye protests, 'Justice with favour have I always done' (*2H6*, 4.7.63)—yet they inevitably serve to perpetuate, to 'maintain' that selfsame order. Saye asks, 'When have I aught exacted at your hands,/But to maintain the king, the realm and you?' (*2H6*, 4.7.65–6), which effectively means: to maintain you within the realm *as constituted*.

The disempowered are no static class in Shakespeare. From the earliest plays, we witness the poor as a class being actively created by powerful and wealthy interests, as the class divide in England accelerates. Crucial to that shift is the emerging crisis of land enclosures, whereby aristocrats increasingly appropriate, and fence off, erstwhile public commons, reducing the quality and quantity of arable land left for the peasants. A landless, increasingly indigent, and sometimes also itinerant segment, so-called 'masterless men', is generated, with a vast increase in crime, and, concomitantly, in the brutality of punishments. Such men are hinted at in *Two Gentlemen of Verona* and *As You Like It*.[19] But the problem is displayed in its origins in *Henry VI, Part Two*, as a labourer vainly attempts a petition '[a]gainst the Duke of Suffolk, for enclosing the commons of Melford.' (*2H6*, 1.3.22–3)

Law, would-be bastion of justice, far from resisting that socio-economic shift, progressively accommodates it, securing individual, privileged commercial interests above the public good[20] (a pervasively commercial role for law that will be pushed to a simultaneously comic and harrowing extreme in a legal order fully abandoned to commercial interests, in *The Merchant of Venice*[21]). Law's complicity in that injustice, and the sense that law camouflages such a role through linguistic force, is nowhere more poignantly suggested than when law is portrayed as a Christ-killing enemy of justice: 'Is not this a lamentable thing, that of the skin of an innocent lamb should be made parchment; that parchment, being scribbled o'er, should undo a man?' (*2H6*, 4.2.72–5) The theme of alienation resurges in existential terms. Having only once ventured to access the machinery of legal language, 'sealing' to a legal instrument, Cade finds himself only further bound into personal and civic disempowerment: 'Some say the bee stings, but I say, 'tis the bee's wax; for I did but seal once to a thing, and I was never mine own man since.' (*2H6*, 4.2.75–7)

2. The emerging surveillance state

Among the elements Hamlet recites in his famous soliloquy, law is cast in de-personalized terms, as an abstract force or system. Insidious is not merely the judge's, or lawyer's delay, which would mirror the passage's other personified signifiers of debasement, but rather the workings of a disembodied law, like a machine beyond the human's abilities to control. Reviling '[t]he oppressor's wrong', Hamlet condemns a broader social dynamic steeped in hierarchy. It is as abuse and as disempowerment that '[t]he insolence of office' or 'the spurns/That patient merit of th'unworthy takes' become intolerable. In Shakespeare, even '[t]he pangs of despised love' seethe with political content (*Ham.*

---

[19] See Richard Wilson, *Will Power: Essays on Shakespearean Authority* (Detroit, Ill.: Wayne State University Press, 1993), pp. 63–82.
[20] See, e.g., Ward (cited in n.16), ch. 5.
[21] cf. Eric Heinze, *The Concept of Injustice* (London: Routledge, 2013), pp. 114–44.

2.2.138; *2H4*, 2.1.116–19; *TN* 5.1.322–3; *MM* 3.1.210–32, 4.1.13; *AW* 1.1.80–87[22]). The 'proud man's contumely' may seem limited in its political content, since a pauper can prate as proudly as a prince.[23] However, haughty underlings in Shakespeare are rarely 'whips and scorns'. Like Malvolio, indeed like Polonius for Hamlet, they are figures of fun or scorn. It is the arrogance of the elevated and powerful that devalues us—of Coriolanus, of Richard III, of Angelo in *Measure for Measure*, of Leontes in *A Winter's Tale*, of the Duke of Suffolk in *Henry VI, Part Two*, of Saturninus in *Titus Andronicus*, or of Orlando's or the 'good' Duke's brothers in *As You Like It*.

For Hamlet, the only response of the aggrieved, who may be a prince as easily as a pauper, is either suffering or suicide. Yet Shakespeare had already staged eight English history plays in which well-born nobles, in response to the 'contumely' or 'insolence' of an actual or perceived 'oppressor', and more like Laertes or Fortinbras, keenly 'take up arms', killing all and sundry—anyone but *themselves*.

In the rare case in which one of their rank, like Henry VI (arguably Hamlet's first precursor in the corpus) finds himself at an existential impasse (e.g., *3H6*, 2.5), he pales as a ridiculed anomaly. Meanwhile, that greatest of all political dramas, *Julius Caesar*, hovers conspicuously in *Hamlet*'s background (*Ham.* 1.1.112–19; 3.2.99–102; 5.1.201) as yet another reminder of a world in which, even if they fail, politically minded men act decisively to affirm themselves by overthrowing the oppressor's wrong and the proud man's contumely.

Hamlet's famous indecision is not a purely psychological impediment within a world in which he would otherwise enjoy freedom to act.[24] Rather, unlike in Rome, the faceless operation of law in the early modern surveillance state has disarmed him. If Laertes deploys an autonomy that Hamlet lacks (e.g., *Ham.* 1.2.62–3, 112–17), it is because he, despite being watched by his father, does not immediately present that degree of danger to the state which keeps Hamlet's every word and deed so tightly monitored (e.g., *Ham.* 4.1.13–19; 4.3.1–2). It is with inadvertent irony that Polonius sees Hamlet's political rank, in wholly conventional terms, as allowing the prince 'a larger tether' (*Ham.* 1.3.124), since Hamlet is the most monitored Dane of all. Only too late can Laertes grasp what Hamlet perceives early on: 'Denmark's a prison'[25] (*Ham.* 2.2.235.5[26]). If an unmistakably Foucauldian strand peeks out even from the notionally medieval trappings of Shakespeare's fifteenth-century histories, it comes to the fore in *Hamlet*'s Denmark, more conspicuously styled in the garb of modernity.

---

[22] Whilst 'despised' here means 'shunned', several critical editions (ARD2, CAM4, OXF4) prefer the Folio's 'disprized', meaning 'un- or undervalued', arguably widening the sentence's scope, to include such politically weighty examples as *KL* sc.1.77–271; *WT* 2.1.56–199, 3.2.10–241, or, on a feminist reading, *CE* 2.1.30–7, 88–9; *2H4*, 2.1; *Ado* 4.1; *Oth.* 5.2 or *Cym.* 3.4.18–100. Later in the 17th century, disprized love will often have political content, as in, for example, Jean Racine's *Andromaque* (1667) or *Phèdre* (1677).

[23] Contrary to the Q2 passage appearing in most scholarly editions, the Folio in fact uses 'poor man's contumely'. See *Hamlet: The Texts of 1603 and 1623*, ARD3, p. 256.

[24] That fierce psychological focus enjoyed a heyday in the mid-20th century. Freudian psychoanalytic theories were reaching popular audiences, as witnessed, for example, in Ernest Jones, *Hamlet and Oedipus* (New York: Doubleday, 1949). That trend was immortalized in Laurence Olivier's film version, featuring a voiceover to introduce the 'tragedy of a man who could not make up his mind': *Hamlet* (dir. Laurence Olivier, 1948). As many directors have done, Olivier eliminates the Fortinbras theme, diminishing the political dimension to emphasize the private and familial. cf. Harold Jenkins, 'Introduction', in ARD2, pp. 136–40.

[25] The inevitable reference is, of course, Michel Foucault, *Surveiller et punir: Naissance de la prison* (Paris: Gallimard, 1975).

[26] A 'Folio-Only' passage, ARD3, p. 466, generally included in the leading critical ('conflated') editions.

Crucial to Tudor rule is the consolidation of power in the monarchy,[27] at the expense of the Roman Church, but also at the expense of a nobility progressively transforming from the recalcitrant, quasi-autonomous *noblesse d'épée* to the co-opted (if they are to avoid being altogether sidelined) *noblesse de robe*. Centralized power will increasingly bureaucratize, with an emerging class of professional administrators, drawn from the aristocracy where possible—where loyalty and obedience to the Crown seem secure— or from the bourgeoisie where convenient.[28] If the deceased King Hamlet is depicted as the old-style, medieval warrior king, his brother's political acts consist of nothing but 'writing' (*Ham.* 1.2.27–8) and plotting (*Ham.* 4.3.56–63; 4.7.59–66; 5.2.18–26), always sanitarily sequestered within the palace walls. It is not merely a king, but an entire socio-political order that Claudius replaces; even his name recalls the post-heroic, bureaucratically imperial Rome, in contrast to the tribally Nordic King 'Hamlet'.

In our own day, we tend to think of democracy and monarchy as opposites, the former having overthrown the latter. In Graeco-Roman thought, however, as revived in the Renaissance, and commonplace in Shakespeare's day, the relationship is more complex. Masses can raise up or pull down rulers, as displayed in *Julius Caesar* or *Coriolanus*.[29] Denmark's strongly centralized, yet nevertheless elective monarchy[30] draws it close to the modern state. Controlling opinion and information become decisive political skills, through astute permutations of surveillance and propaganda.[31] Crucial to the synthesis of conformity through language is sheer habituation—the acceptance of a belief not because of, but regardless of, its truth: 'that monster Custom' (*Ham.* 3.4.159) as witnessed, for example, in Gertrude's 'common' philosophy of death (*Ham.* 1.2.70–3), which conveniently recapitulates the king's (*Ham.* 1.2.87–106). 'Custom hath made it…a property of easiness' (*Ham.* 5.1.53–4).

That element of the emerging surveillance state provides a crucial background, now to be more closely examined, before I return, in section 3, to the role of legal language. Only through that broader insight into the machinery of state can we appreciate how law and language pervade seemingly unpolitical elements of the drama. Knowledge, modernity's technique of power through expertise, supersedes the more openly coercive relations of brute force associated with the Middle Ages; *nota bene:* not more coercive, just more manifestly so, more ostentatiously so. In early modernity, the word does not so much eliminate as dissemble the sword. Coercive enforcement remains, yet less visibly, overtly retreating to the fringes. Everyday legal life is about power exercised through registration and regulation. The more efficiently it works, the less one perceives it as an exercise of power. Unsurprisingly, *Hamlet* is as political as any drama in Shakespeare, yet does not always seem so—and, traditionally, has never led the pack as the English or Roman histories have done[32]—precisely because its machinery is so efficiently designed, to deflect attention away from the techniques of power, to give the impression, so dominant among the old-style humanist critics, that the drama 'just happens' within 'life'. It gives the famous impression of a 'universal', 'human' predicament, not specifically generated by its politics. The technique clearly works: generations of skilled readers have spilled ink about *Hamlet*, collapsing it into a purely personal—and only in that apolitical

---

[27] See generally Tennenhouse (cited in n.4).
[28] See, e.g., Holderness (cited in n.7), ch. 1.
[29] That complex relationship between popular will and monarchical rule will remain central to early modern thought, as witnessed in Pierre Corneille's *Cinna* (1641), or Jean Racine's *Bérénice* (1670).
[30] Referred to in n.3.
[31] See, e.g., Holderness (cited in n.7), chs 1–2.
[32] Leggatt, for example, does not include it. See Leggatt (cited in n.16).

sense, 'universal'—tragedy, often scarcely noticing its pervasively political structure.[33] Political and legal power work most effectively, they most disempower us, precisely when they have us viewing their pernicious effects fatalistically, as 'just the way things are' and 'just the way life is', indeed 'universally'.

Polonius passes effortlessly from father monitoring his children to government official monitoring Hamlet, using the selfsame ways and means. Ophelia does not merely submit to that network of control, but loves its agent, her father. Having been raised in her role as obedient daughter (*Ham* 2.2.106), that function, too, ends up being natural to her, as she scarcely sees herself as an object of calculated, state control. When Polonius uses the machine of surveillance to trap her, all the audience can see, within the terms of conventionally classical literary humanism, is her 'personal' dilemma, oblivious to the fact that the technique determines not merely a family dynamic, but a total political world—which has so utterly pervaded the private sphere as to seem purely private, with no real political content.

In Kenneth Branagh's 1996 film version, Polonius and Claudius spy on the Prince and Ophelia not merely behind an arras, but through the updated technology of a one-way mirrored hall. In Michael Grandage's 2009 stage production, Ron Cook departs from the tradition of playing Polonius as the dotty, blundering *senex*, underscoring instead the character's bureaucratic managerialism, in which nothing and no one escape his KGB-esque oversight. Jude Law's Hamlet echoes him in that performance, avoiding excessive displays of the Prince's episodic madness. After all, we expect a madman to be easily tripped up. By instead emphasizing Hamlet's lucidity and intelligence, Law portrays a modern figure whom no amount of purely personal insight or integrity can save from the machinery of state—a Winston Smith, whom Orwellian state technologies of power can always defeat, a mouse who can always be trapped (*Ham.* 3.2.231) within a political machine that 'runs by itself'.[34]

Gregory Doran's 2009 RSC performance, starring David Tennant, draws these elements to their logical, or at least post-industrial, conclusion, showing the entire action captured on a network of security cameras.[35] Like Soviet psychiatry, Big Brother prevails not merely by subduing Smith, but by converting any resistance he may manifest into a purely personal problem—'I have found/The very cause of Hamlet's lunacy' (*Ham.* 2.2.48–9)—to be overcome through coercion as therapy. *Hamlet* unsurprisingly transforms any of Hamlet's or Ophelia's leanings towards political resistance into either the personal reality, or the strategic appearance, of mental illness: Hamlet resists the political-legal machine's 'valves' and 'stops' (*Ham.* 3.2.355–63) by affecting his 'antic disposition' (*Ham.* 1.5.170), but overcomes it only in death.

Knowledge through surveillance will become the instrument of a new kind of power that is simultaneously consolidated and, as the very technique of its consolidation, diffused. Decisive for the trial of Mary, Queen of Scots had been the elaborate network of covert intelligence, notably the interception of private communications.[36] In several plays, authority figures demand that their subordinates—indeed their own children,

---

[33] As discussed in n.24.

[34] See Roger Cotterrell, *The Politics of Jurisprudence* (London: Butterworths, 2nd edn, 2003), p. 107 (citing Carl Schmitt).

[35] I am grateful to István Zöld for pointing out that the technique obliterates the traditional illusion of utterances made in confidence, either between characters, or as asides to the audience. Even Hamlet's seemingly private soliloquoys are shown to be picked up on a security camera—precisely as, in the original, Hamlet's 'To be or not to be' can be espied by Claudius and Polonius behind an arras.

[36] See, e.g., Holderness, (cited in n.7), pp. 31–2.

albeit in politically sensitive contexts—disclose secret writings to them (*R2*, 5.2.56–72; *KL* sc.2.25–44; cf. *TGV* 1.3.51–55), not unlike Polonius hectoring Ophelia, as to Hamlet, 'What is between you? Give me up the truth' (*Ham*. 1.3.97).

Under Foucault's influence, that element of diffused power has become central to readings of Shakespeare. For example, *Measure for Measure* will present a duke very different from his peripheral, ineffectual counterparts in *The Merchant of Venice* or *Romeo and Juliet*. Vincentio ostensibly suspends his power, whilst in fact expanding it by diffusing it everywhere, turning himself into a living and breathing security camera, always safely concealed beneath a cloak of piety.[37] The England of *Henry VI, Part II* is not yet a surveillance state in that sense. Lord Saye's pseudo-trial still only hints at the new face of power as bureaucracy. It is power more clearly exercised by one class upon another. A revolt of the poor against the rich comes as no surprise. The rebels in particular attack that exponent of power which signally symbolizes their alienation. By contrast, in *Hamlet*, looking towards the modern state, it is no longer a distinctly disempowered class, so much as an entire realm that falls within the state's grip, which even the one 'most immediate to [the] throne' and 'chiefest courtier' (*Ham.* 1.2.109, 117) cannot escape. Hamlet will be played 'like a pipe', not by the state's highest officers, but by his sometime friends. Rosencrantz and Guildenstern remain far inferior to Hamlet in socio-legal rank, yet become instruments of a state power that even their prince can decry, but can never shake off, except through their deaths (*Ham.* 4.2.13–19, 5.2.355).

3. Language, performance, existence

Legal transactions in the conventional sense of contracts, lawsuits, or trials play little role in Shakespearean tragedy. Full-blown trial scenes instead occur in the comedies (*CE* 1.1., *MV* 4.1, *Ado* 4.2, *MM* 5.1, *WT* 3.2); an exception proving the rule would be the bleakly comic fool's court in *KL* sc.13. Trials occur also in the English histories (*1H6*, 5.5; *2H6*, 2.3, cf. 4.7; *R2*, 1.1, 1.3, 4.1; *H5*, 2.2.76–7). Law in the tragedies, by contrast, although closer to the histories, tends to highlight cardinal matters of state, such as treason, political murder, or war. In *Hamlet*, the suspicion of a fratricidal and regicidal murder appears early on, but conspicuously lacking any conventional legal elements. The discourse hearkens back to the feudal-heroic vocabulary of honour and revenge, not to any juridical lexicon of *actus reus* or *mens rea*. Similarly, armed conflict with Norway, more of a sub-plot (although rightly elevated in Branagh's version), is discussed solely in political terms, with nothing like the famous exposition (or rather, invention) of a *causa belli* that inaugurates *Henry V*. It is all the more remarkable when, in one of *Hamlet*'s dramatic high points, that eerie amalgam of comedy and introspection in the graveyard, Hamlet speculates that one of the skulls might be that of a lawyer (*Ham.* 5.1.93–4). That thought arises, it would seem, out of the blue; it seems true only in the trivial sense that it could be *anyone*'s skull, and might therefore be a lawyer's.

In a drama otherwise so different from *Henry VI, Part Two*, lawyers are again singled out in a sarcastic, arguably unexpected way. When the gravedigger throws up the second skull (*Ham.* 5.1.92.1 SD), it is, once again, the linguistic element, more intricate than

---

[37] See, e.g., Wilson (cited in n.19), pp. 126–31; Jonathan Dollimore, 'Transgression and Surveillance in *Measure for Measure*' in *Political Shakespeare: Essays on Cultural Materialism*, Jonathan Dollimore and Alan Sinfield, eds (Manchester: Manchester University Press, 2nd edn, 1994), ch. 4; cf. Paul Raffield, *Shakespeare's Imaginary Constitution: Late Elizabethan Politics and the Theatre of Law* (Oxford: Hart Publishing, 2010), pp. 191–204 (discussing parallel themes in *Measure for Measure*).

the politician's plots or the courtier's niceties, which becomes law's paramount feature, not, this time, in the eyes of peasants, who have stood powerless before mighty judges, but in the eyes of one near to the throne, yet no more able to control the machinations of power, 'Where be his quiddities now, his quillets, his cases, his tenures, and his tricks?' (*Ham.* 5.1.94–5 [OXF4]).

That passage's verbal torrent, its Sayesque echoes of English mixed with Latin, parodies lawyerly loquacity, overpowering not with depth, but with sheer, patter-song speed. Archetypical of Shakespeare's depictions of legal language, the passage employs a layering of rhetorical devices, notably *erotema*, *congeries*, *bathos*, and *irony*. Why would that compression of so many rhetorical strategies emerge here? It is the equivocating, dissimulating character of legal discourse that Hamlet mimetically mocks. Taking the form of a rhetorical question (*erotema*), the obvious reply would be 'They're nowhere. I'm dead, and, moreover, I can't even hear your question.' Accordingly, as with any erotema, the question is, what other point, aside from that obvious one, does that rhetorical strategy aim to convey?

The erotema, in turn, employs *congeries*, a clustering of terms for cumulative effect,[38] and further marries that technique to *bathos* (a calculated anti-climax, in contrast to the anticipated climax of the more typical *auxesis* or *gradatio*[39]), whereby the lawyer's seeming high-blown skills collapse into mere 'tricks'. That synthesis of congeries with bathos further yields the rhetorical device of irony. Were the sequence not to anti-climax with 'tricks', the passage would retain a more contemplative, less sarcastic tone. It would be musing about the death of a lawyer whose various attributes are named, though not necessarily with disdain. Even 'quillets', meaning mere quibbles,[40] can sound, on first hearing, like more of a lawyerly quirk—a playful, but not necessarily derisive description of lawyerly precision—than anything so manifestly pernicious as a 'trick'. It is only that final word 'trick' which retroleptically casts its four predecessors as patently sinister. 'Quiddities', referring to a thing's 'essential nature' in scholastic philosophy,[41] becomes grimly elided with the rest of these underhanded 'tricks', mirroring the play's simultaneously poignant and sardonic treatment of ontology and existence. Hamlet utters the statement as if cross-examining the imaginary lawyer, using legal ploys against law's agent. The graveyard scene is altogether remarkable in its re-enactments of the things that are being parodied. Precisely at that point in which law, as a tool of oppressive power, is at issue, Horatio, departing from the ease with which he generally addresses his social superior, suddenly performs the role of obsequious subject (cf., e.g., *Ham.* 2.1.66–70), mechanically agreeing with each of Hamlet's whimsies: 'It might, my lord' (*Ham.* 5.1.76), 'Ay, my lord' (*Ham.* 5.1.82), 'Not a jot more, my lord' (*Ham.* 5.1.106) (cf. *Ham.* 3.2.367–73).

As with Lord Saye, what may appear, from the perspective of the powerful jurist, to be the very soul of legitimacy, law's articulated rationality, appears, from the perspective of the disempowered, who can even be a prince, to be a tool of deception. The point is made through parody, as the gravedigger's 'equivocation' mocks lawyerly hairsplitting,[42]

HAMLET Whose grave's this, sirrah?
GRAVEDIGGER Mine, sir. [...]
HAMLET I think it be thine, indeed; for thou liest in't.
GRAVEDIGGER You lie out on't, sir, and therefore it is not yours. For my part, I
   do not lie in't, and yet it is mine.

---

[38] cf., e.g., 'thou Dromio, thou snail, thou slug, thou sot!' (*CE* 2.2.197).
[39] e.g., Julius Caesar's progressively climactic 'Veni, vidi, vici' ('I came, I saw, I conquered').
[40] OXF4, p. 325.
[41] See OXF4, p. 325.
[42] See ARD3, p. 419.

> **HAMLET** Thou dost lie in't, to be in't and say it is thine. 'Tis for the dead, not for the quick. Therefore thou liest.
> **GRAVEDIGGER** 'Tis a quick lie, sir, 'twill away gain, from me to you.
> **HAMLET** What man dost thou dig it for?
> **GRAVEDIGGER** For no man, sir.
> **HAMLET** What woman, then?
> **GRAVEDIGGER** For none, neither.
> **HAMLET** Who is to be buried in't?
> **GRAVEDIGGER** One that was a woman, sir, but, rest her soul she's dead.
> **HAMLET** [*to Horatio*] How absolute the knave is! We must speak by the card or equivocation will undo us. (*Ham.* 5.1.110–30)

That parody on law's dialectics recalls a conspicuous counterpart in the corpus, the other royal sounding-out of commoner subjects incognito in *Henry V*. If Henry, supreme Shakespearean architect of the surveillance state, uses the technique to further consolidate power,[43] the disempowered Hamlet is in precisely the opposite position. A lowly gravedigger can trip Hamlet up by invoking that language of disembodied law which can trip up *anyone* who falls within its grip, great or small. A moment later, Hamlet will curse the language of law whilst contemplating the supposed lawyer's skull.

Equivocation is not the gravedigger's alone. Throughout the play, it is Hamlet's salient style. It is typical of Hamlet to condemn those things which most characterize him; he can never—one can never—step out of the system, but can only revile those very elements of it which he himself constantly recapitulates: its faceless inhumanity, its covert aggression, its machineries of surveillance and duplicity. The linguistic manipulation of law, coupled with the technique of power deployed through the surveillance state, embodies Shakespeare's depiction of law in *Hamlet*, and the culmination of his vision of law progressively developed in the corpus. As in *Henry VI, Part Two*, law's literacy is again evoked through the image of innocent beings sacrificed to make parchment ('sheep and calves' being glossed as 'simpletons'[44]),

> **HAMLET** Is not parchment made of sheepskins?
> **HORATIO** Ay, my lord, and of calves' skins too.
> **HAMLET** They are sheep and calves which seek out assurance in that.[45] (*Ham.* 5.1.107–10)

If we return once again to the early English history plays, we find elsewhere another of the canon's more remarkable explorations of law, in the Temple Garden scene of *Henry VI, Part One*. A group of aristocrats and lawyers have had to leave the Temple hall, at the Inns of Court, because their debate was turning to aggression, becoming 'too loud' (*1H6*, 2.4.3). Although the substance of their dispute is not yet clear,[46] what is striking is how the nobles, whom we would expect to be vigilant guardians of law, bask in their contempt for it, scarcely discouraged by the lawyers. The Duke of Suffolk, joining privilege to machismo, boasts of his breaches of law,

---

[43] See, e.g., Pugliatti (cited in n.7), ch. 8; Stephen Greenblatt, 'Invisible Bullets: Renaissance Authority and Its Subversion, *Henry IV* and *Henry V*' in Dollimore and Sinfield (cited in n.13), ch. 2.
[44] See OXF4, p. 326; PEN2, p. 296.
[45] Glossed as 'people who trust such documents are fools', ARD3, p. 418.
[46] It presumably concerns Richard's claim to the Dukedom of York, referred to in n.5.

Faith, I have been a truant in the law,
And never yet could frame my will to it,
And therefore frame the law unto my will. (*1H6*, 2.4.7–9)

The Earl of Warwick, having boasted of his prowess in sport, arms, and sex (*1H6*, 2.4.11–15), and whose house will nevertheless prove adept at law when it serves their cause (*2H6*, 3.2.153–94; *3H6*, 1.1.132–45), not merely dismisses, but proudly and boastfully derides 'these nice sharp quillets of the law' (*1H6*, 2.4.17).

Warwick's contrast of law with such masculine affairs as armed, athletic, or sexual conquest casts law as that which uses language not as a superior alternative to violence, but merely as the wily, manipulative, 'women's' weapon of words (e.g., *TS* 2.1.137). And nothing plagues Hamlet more than either impotence (his immobility being perhaps the play's most famous theme[47] (e.g., *Ham.* 3.4.106–7; 4.4.38–45)) or femininity (his misogyny is notorious[48] (e.g., *Ham.* 1.2.146; 3.1.142–4)). 'Masculine', armed conflict may be brutal, but is at least overt; law purporting to overcome sheer powermongering, but merely adorning it in the 'feminine' guise of peaceful and humanist discourse, rendering it, like a torrent of legal argument, both overwhelming and opaque, turns the abuse of power into something beyond one's ability to oppose or to subvert. The simultaneously covert and loquacious quality of the surveillance state takes the form of a feminization of the outward display of power, as Hamlet's impotence within the power structure witnesses his emerging misogyny. If Hamlet is paralysed, it is because killing Claudius, far from achieving some idealized notion of justice in the manner of the old-style revenge tragedy,[49] is, in a brave new modern world, futile and beside the point. Claudius sits atop the machine that runs by itself, and which is not destroyed simply by toppling its public face. The problem is not so much that Hamlet 'cannot' kill Claudius, but that, unlike the conspirators against Caesar, the ineffable power dynamics of the Foucauldian state no longer offer any alternative, nor, then, any obvious grounds for doing so. The plausible Let-Caesar-die-so-Rome-may-live has turned implausible in early modernity. Freud broached the age-old problem of Hamlet's delay[50] by depicting a Hamlet immobilized because his nemesis had in fact expressed the prince's own Oedipal wish.[51] A Foucauldian construction, by contrast, can view Hamlet as immobilized because the omnipresent political-legal machine eviscerates the sheer possibility of meaningful political action.

Another of the plays most amenable to Foucauldian theories of power is *Henry V*. Where Henry was once taken at face value as Shakespeare's vision of the model monarch, more recent scholars, taking their cues from the propagandizing function of official iconography in the Tudor period, have emphasized the ways in which Henry masters the techniques of power deployment in the modern state, through means of surveillance—e.g., in the entrapment of the conspirators plotting to kill him (*H5*, 2.2.76–7) or the covert sounding-out of foot soldiers (*H5*, 4.1.–)—but more importantly in emerging as a charismatic figure in the Weberian sense,[52] mastering popular psychology through recourse to language.[53]

---

[47] See Jenkins (cited in n.24), pp. 136–40.
[48] See, e.g., Jacqueline Rose, 'Sexuality in the Reading of Shakespeare' in *Alternative Shakespeares*, 2nd edn, John Drakakis, ed. (London: Routledge, 2002), ch. 5.
[49] See Jenkins (cited in n.24), pp. 82–103.
[50] cf., e.g., Jenkins (cited in n.24), pp. 136–40.
[51] See Sigmund Freud, *Die Traumdeutung* (Leipzig und Wien: Franz Deuticke, 1900); cf. Jones (cited in n.24).
[52] Max Weber, *Wirtschaft und Gesellschaft* II.ix.5 (Tübingen: Mohr, 1976), pp. 654–87.
[53] See, e.g., Pugliatti (cited in n.7), ch. 8; Greenblatt (cited in n.43); Stephen Greenblatt, *Shakespearean Negotiations* (Oxford: Oxford University Press), pp. 56–65.

In *Hamlet*, Claudius lends himself to a similar analysis. As late as the 1980s, before Foucauldian analysis had become widespread, scholars sometimes praised Claudius as a competent ruler—despite the glaring fact, for which one hardly needs Foucault, that Claudius fatuously allows the enemy (*Ham.* 1.2.17–25) Fortinbras passage of his legions through the realm (*Ham.* 2.2.72–82), supposedly to invade a 'little patch of ground' in Poland (*Ham.* 4.4.17), yet conspicuously clearing the path to power in Denmark (*Ham.* 5.2.334–40, 373–4). A question arises about how viewers might find overall competence in a king, like Claudius, who delivers Denmark to an invader, even believing he has done the opposite, and spends much of the rest of his time either 'wassailing' (*Ham.* 1.4.9), or plotting against his nephew (*Ham.* 4.3.56–63; 4.7.59–66; 5.2.18–26), and otherwise manipulating law (*Ham.* 3.3.36–64; 5.1.217). In the same vein, we can ask why so many audiences have seen, and continue to see Henry V as Shakespeare's ideal monarch, despite his manipulation of both positive and divine law to justify an imperial invasion of France (*H5*, 1.2), and the summary trials and executions of the conspirators with little due process (*H5*, 2.2).

In both plays, the traps Shakespeare had set centuries ago seem still to work into our own day. Like the Tudors, who disseminated iconographic images of monarchical power,[54] these new-style monarchs orchestrate power through the manipulation of language and symbols—through the verbal dissemination of the iconography of power. Arguably, 'model' monarch would be a better phrase than 'ideal' monarch for describing such figures, in the sense that Shakespeare is not, in fact, endorsing them as exemplars of justice, so much as simply using them to explore the degree to which Machiavellianism can be honed to a high art form. Whilst the dead King Hamlet, *noblesse d'épée*, never praised for making speeches, had taken up arms to defeat Norway on the battlefield, his successor, *noblesse de robe*, need merely write letters, but then announce it with pomp and fanfare (*Ham.* 1.2.27–8). Hamlet flounders between those two models. If Claudius, in those same triumphant tones, feigns liberality by allowing Laertes to leave Denmark (*Ham.* 1.2.44–6, 62–3), that display serves only to mask the tighter grip to be placed on the more important person of Hamlet (*Ham.* 1.2.112–17). Claudius 'may smile, and smile, and be a villain' (*Ham.* 1.5.108).

In the play's broader context, there is nothing surprising about Claudius's recourse to verbal performance as a technique of power. *Hamlet*'s entire world is structured as a series of performances orchestrated for the deployment of power. Polonius, 'accounted a good actor' (*Ham.* 3.2.96–7), coaches Reynaldo to perform deceitful and potentially damaging tricks on Laertes for the purpose of gathering information, 'by indirections' to 'find directions out' (*Ham.* 2.1.63). Claudius marshals Rosencrantz and Guildenstern to stage similar performances, to 'draw' Hamlet 'on to pleasures' (*Ham.* 2.2.15), for similar purposes of espying Hamlet's reactions. Polonius and Claudius collaborate to have Ophelia perform the reading of a religious text, again to monitor secretly Hamlet's behaviour (*Ham.* 3.1.29–45). Hamlet, immersed in this culture of deceptive words and practices, first turns himself into a performer, planning to deploy his 'antic disposition' in order to test others' reactions; then to stage the play's most famous performance, the play-within-the-play, whereby Hamlet and Horatio monitor the king to establish Claudius's criminal guilt (*Ham.* 2.2.523–40; 3.2.71–85).

That play-within-the-play is called *The Murder of Gonzago* (*Ham.* 2.2.474). When Claudius asks Hamlet the title, however, Hamlet calls it *The Mousetrap* (*Ham.* 3.2.231), symbol of the device constructed to ensnare base, unwitting vermin. The play, like much of Shakespeare, is obsessed with the differences between man and beast (e.g., *Ham.* 1.2.150–1; 4.4.32–4). Its political world of traps and tricks defeats Saye's classical humanist ideal of a noble, dignified human existence depending merely upon one's will

---

[54] See generally Tennenhouse (cited in n.4).

to achieve it, when one exists within a political-legal machine that systematically disarms, deflates, and disempowers the human (cf. *Ham.* 2.2.262–75). The play-within-the-play becomes not an exotic episode, but a model for all human relations in *Hamlet*. Words having been emptied of reliable meaning, they instead serve only for any one set of characters to contrive situations within which human behaviours—personalities—are actively generated for purposes of being recorded.

That engineering function of language pervades the play, yet always traces back to law as the paradigm human institution of manipulated language deployed with the effects of mechanical control and the resulting individual alienation. Legal language becomes the premier tool for re-manufacturing humans as mice. Amidst the perpetual doubt about when Hamlet is mad, when he is only affecting that 'antic disposition', and when he is perhaps a mix of both—a question highly dependent upon the actor and performance—the prince's compulsive prolixity (e.g., *Ham.* 2.2.190–201) intentionally or inadvertently parodies language as the outstandingly malleable and manipulated medium of political power and human existence—all to be more bleakly parodied in the garbled tongue of Ophelia's madness (*Ham.* 4.5.160–92).

Immediately before Hamlet's encounter with the skulls, a more improvized play-within-the-play is staged by the gravediggers, or 'clowns', long a source of wonderment in view of the bleak events so late in the play. The only thing resembling a full-blown, conventional legal argument in *Hamlet* is, as we have seen, the parody of one with the gravedigger. If Hamlet's dilemma concerned subjective deliberation as between existence and non-existence, the one surrounding Ophelia concerns an equally unstable, objective determination of that question,

> **GRAVEDIGGER** Is she to be buried in Christian burial, when she wilfully seeks her own salvation?
> **2 MAN** I tell thee she is. Therefore make her grave straight. The crowner [coroner—EH] hath sat on her and finds it Christian burial.
> **GRAVEDIGGER** How can that be unless she drowned herself in her own defence?

Law operates not according to any discernable reason, but merely by *fiat*,

> **2 MAN** Why, 'tis found so. (*Ham.* 5.1.1–8)

The familiar Shakespearean mangling of arcane legal language, in the mouths of lowly illiterates, alienated from power within a regime which keeps them disempowered[55] (cf. *Ado* 3.3, 4.2; *MM* 2.1; cf. also *2H6*(Fol.) 1.3.33.0–2), and precisely on the ethical and ontological status of the dead Ophelia, again manifests in malapropisms of the erudite Latin *se defendendo*[56] ('*se offendendo*') or *ergo*[57] ('*argal*'), followed by a spoof of casuistic distinctions drawn between active and passive, reminiscent of medieval-scholastic disputes on metaphysical questions, whereby Ophelia's bleak end dissolves into pseudo-legal sophisms,[58]

> **GRAVEDIGGER** It must be *se offendendo*. It cannot be else. For here lies the point: if I drown myself wittingly, it argues an act, and an act hath three branches—it is to act, to do, to perform. Argal, she drowned herself wittingly. (*Ham.* 5.1.9–13)

---

[55] cf. generally Eric Heinze, '"Were it not against our laws": Oppression and Resistance in Shakespeare's *Comedy of Errors*', (2009) 29 *Legal Studies* pp. 230–63.
[56] See OXF4 321; cf. ARD3, p. 410.
[57] See OXF4 321; cf. ARD3, p. 410.
[58] See Raffield (cited in n.37), p. 93 (linking the legal questions surrounding Ophelia's suicide to the 1562 case of *Hales v Petit*).

Immediately following that spoof on the abstractions of legal logic, comes a spoof of forensic argument, again eliciting (not least through the water imagery) the arbitrariness and concomitant instability of ethical problems beholden to legal language,

> **2 MAN** Nay, but hear you, goodman delver.
> **GRAVEDIGGER** Give me leave. Here lies the water—good. Here stands the man—good. If the man go to this water and drown himself, it is, willy-nilly, he goes. Mark you that. But if the water come to him and drown him, he drowns not himself. Argal, he that is not guilty of his own death shortens not his own life.
> **2 MAN** But is this law?
> **GRAVEDIGGER** Ay, marry, is't. Crowner's 'quest law. (*Ham.* 5.1.14–22)

The sequence of skulls from politician/courtier, then to lawyer, next progresses to the supposed skull of the court jester Yorick (*Ham.* 5.1.174–84), to whom Hamlet puts a question parallel to that for the lawyer, yet with none of the biting acrimony. Again through the rhetorical technique of congeries, Hamlet now asks if that clown—court jesters, as in *Lear*, being well known for speaking inconvenient truths—had been the worthier figure: 'Where be your gibes now—your gambols, your songs, your flashes of merriment, that were wont to set the table on a roar?' (*Ham.* 5.1.179–82). In one of the play's rare uses of the word 'truth',[59] the gravedigger returns to the theme of law being used to benefit powerful interests, reminiscent of the deeper examinations of class difference in *Henry VI, Part Two* and other English or Roman political dramas,

> **2 MAN** Will you ha' the truth on't? If this had not been a gentlewoman, she should have been buried out o' Christian burial.
> **GRAVEDIGGER** Why, there thou sayst, and the more pity that great folk should have countenance in this world to drown or hang themselves more than their even-Christen [fellow Chrisitans—EH]. (*Ham.* 5.1.23–9)

The legal manipulation is easily overlooked, since we may grieve for Ophelia and wish her a dignified burial. The question of her death remains unresolved, and, even if she did kill herself, we, like Laertes (5.1.227–31), might find any lesser rites to reek of hypocrisy. But manipulation it is, to save the face of power: 'great command o'ersways the order' (*Ham.* 5.1.217). Law leaves us, then, with a tasteless dilemma. We cannot side with the church pronouncement, which, as Laertes shows, is cynically sanctimonious, albeit wrapped in the language of divinely ordained law. Nor can we side with the trumping of it through state decree, through the king's secular prerogative, which merely piles the hypocrisy of class privilege, and some politically opportunist face-saving (the king needs Ophelia dispatched with as little trouble as possible from Laertes, who has already challenged the throne (*Ham.* 4.5.88–134)), atop the church's sinister law. The gravediggers have spoofed the procedure, and the presumption, whereby state law, incorporating canon law, would pass final ethical judgment on Ophelia's life and its end: 'Her death was doubtful; [. . .] She should in ground unsanctified have lodged/Till the last trumpet' (*Ham.* 5.1.216–19). Divine law is invoked not to challenge, but to maintain, and to lend authority to, the machinations

---

[59] The others are revealing. Polonius uses it in the context of gathering information about his children (*Ham.* 1.3.97). Hamlet uses it in a love poem, to drop a hint about much of the play: 'Doubt truth to be a liar' (*Ham.* 2.2.116).

of Denmark's law. In a cosy circle, each legal regime draws legitimacy by justifying the other.

The role of legal language to mask deployments of power becomes an exemplar of the schism between appearance and reality that dominates *Hamlet* and much of the corpus (e.g., *Ham.* 1.2.76–86). From the outset, language is used by the head of state to conceal breaches not only of the law against murder, but of the law against treason, as Claudius describes the death of King Hamlet as nothing more than nature's 'common theme' (*Ham.* 1.2.103; cf. 1.2.74), which, for the prince to challenge through 'obstinate condolement' (*Ham.* 1.2.93) would make not Claudius, but Hamlet himself the criminal, perpetrator of 'a fault to heaven,/A fault against the dead, a fault to nature' (*Ham.* 1.2.101–2). Ophelia is pressed into that same state-managed mendacity (already deployed by Polonius to have Reynaldo spy on Laertes (*Ham.* 2.1.1–71)), as she is duped into lying to Hamlet about vows that had passed between them,

> My lord, I have remembrances of yours
> That I have longèd long to redeliver.
> I pray you now receive them. (*Ham.* 3.1.92–4)

Curiously, Hamlet does not merely refuse to take them back. Rather, he denies having given them in the first place (*Ham.* 3.1.95)—very possibly his first outright lie in the play, precisely as it is becoming clearer to him that truth and lie are scarcely to be distinguished (*Ham.* 2.2.175–6, 232–4). That moment raises a problem for modern audiences, for whom oaths have acquired a more marginal, pro forma status in law. If Hamlet and Ophelia had earlier exchanged vows, kept secret in view of their differing stations[60] (*Ham.* 2.2.138), then Ophelia's renunciation of them, Hamlet not knowing that she is coerced to do so, becomes the breach of a sacred bond, for which the 'remembrances' serve as formal consideration (comparable to the more usual rings for betrothals, which, worn for public view, involve no such problems of social rank, as witnessed in the ring exchange themes of *Two Gentlemen of Verona* or *The Merchant of Venice*). By denying having given such tokens in consideration, countering a lie with a lie, Hamlet revives a status quo ante, in which Ophelia is precluded by *fiat* from committing any such breach, because a new past has been created in which no vows had in fact been exchanged. Hamlet from that point forward mirrors his world, using the deceptions of language to fabricate realities which Denmark's political and legal world have been engineered to conceal. Hamlet thenceforth distrusts all appearances, not only the appearances of words.

Thinking Ophelia's disavowal sincere, he launches into misogyny, a tirade against all women, inveighing against deceptive appearances: 'God has given you one face, and you make yourselves another: you jig, you amble, and you lisp' (*Ham.* 3.1.142–4). Included in that rant is the charge that women 'nickname God's creatures', i.e., give them fond or frivolous names, strikingly recalling the problem of language's disaggregation from realities, paradigmatic in law, yet now suffered or sensed by Hamlet everywhere. Even

---

[60] Shakespeare leaves teasingly obscure the question as to whether Ophelia had reciprocated Hamlet's vows. Such a supposition, however, is hardly far-fetched. Assuming that she is not quite as 'green' (*Ham.* 1.3.100) as Polonius and Laertes believe—she certainly grasps sexual double standards (*Ham.* 1.3.45–49)—she will have known perfectly well that Hamlet, in terms of conventional socio-political rank, 'with a larger tether may...walk' (*Ham.* 1.3.124), and that she must therefore keep her actions and intentions discreet; and Hamlet would have grasped that need for caution. In subsequently denying his vows, he by *fiat* annuls any that she might have made in reciprocation, so that they, by definition, cannot be broken, and her honesty is maintained.

discovering lies lends Hamlet no way out of the manipulations of the broader power structure. He knows perfectly well that Rosencrantz and Guildenstern are in the King's service, merely performing the words of friendship in order to monitor Hamlet (*Ham.* 2.2.235–57), but that insight scarcely advances him.

4. Conclusion

Hamlet's emerging modernist world of arcane machinations, intertwining and blurring word and deed, seems far removed from the world of power imposed, clearly, directly, unabashedly by the sword. In one sense, those techniques of power also seem far removed from the more conventional legal and linguistic world of statutes, writs, and trials for which Saye was attacked. What unites them are the ways in which linguistic manipulation within more conventional legal settings emerges as a model for the dissemination and manipulation of power generally. Words become tools of oppression precisely as manipulation of them empties them of any reliable meanings. Words simultaneously become trivial and impenetrable. It is their Orwellian proliferation and dissemination which work as a simultaneously overwhelming and inscrutable torrent of 'Words, words, words' (*Ham.* 2.2.189).

That radical disaggregation of words from meanings has a twofold significance. First, it brings us nearer to a sense of how law is being portrayed. Law exists by no means distinct from other loci of power. Rather, law, through its characteristic uses of language, becomes archetypical for the specific modes of power and control in modernity. Secondly, that disjunction between signifier and signified leads to the heart of existential turmoil in *Hamlet*. Some traditional readings might be content to see in Polonius little more than an overprotective father, and in Claudius little more than a flawed king. Yet their recourse to lies, whilst insisting that others tell truth, their perpetration of appearances calculated to conceal realities, are never secondary or episodic. Those techniques become the pervasive mode of existence in the Danish court. Linguistic dysfunction becomes a hallmark of discourse throughout the play, yet not in a sense which would render its status, as component of existential anxiety, somehow distinctly personal, divorced from politics. On the contrary, the extermination of meaning for the characters, the play's creeping nihilism—not so much distinct to Hamlet, as distinctly perceived by him yet common to all—follows as a direct result from a world in which quillets and quiddities, earmarks of legal discourse, come to denote the absence of any reliable meanings in the sphere of politics, ethics, justice, or human relations.

In the final scene, Fortinbras assumes control. Horatio certainly promises truth telling, but scarcely promises to wield more influence than he had done before. Rather, that truth will emerge within the framework of the same kind of tightly orchestrated power structure that has preceded. Fortinbras's final commandment revives appearance and decorum as the watchword: 'Take up the bodies. Such a sight as this/Becomes the field, but here shows much amiss' (*Ham.* 5.2.385–6). The signifiers of mayhem strut political glory in battle, but reek of excess in the palace, in which signifiers of order, precisely as Claudius had so well contrived, must dominate. Decisive is not the truth that Horatio has to tell, but the managerial state within which that truth will be harnessed, directed, and controlled.

14

Stories in Law: Providing Space for 'Oppositionists'?

*Steven Cammiss**

Stories, parables, chronicles, and narratives are powerful means for destroying mindset... [1]

In the introduction to a special issue of the *Michigan Law Review* on 'Legal Storytelling', Scheppele asks, '[w]hy is there such a rush to storytelling?'[2] Defining and getting across one's story is now said to be the key to advertising and politics, and a number of other disparate fields.[3] While this broad movement is of interest, and the growth of law and narrative scholarship is in all probability linked to this wider movement, I don't want to dwell too much on what could be described as the narrative turn. Rather, the focus here is upon the claims made in the *Michigan Law Review* special issue, and elsewhere, on the benefits of storytelling in law: the claim that storytelling provides space for voices that have traditionally been excluded from legal discourse.

It is usually customary at this stage to define one's terms. For instance, Binder and Weisberg define a story as 'a sequence of events happening to a human or anthropomorphized subject over time', while narrative can be distinguished from story as narratives consist of 'the conjunction of a story and a teller'.[4] Alternatively, Labov adopts a slightly different definition of narrative as a chronological sequence of at least two events.[5] I propose to suggest a rather loose definition of narrative and story based upon Labov's, but proposing that the sequence of events does not have to be in strict chronological sequence, as was suggested by Labov (flashbacks, for instance, can play a part in the constructions of narrative).[6] Additionally, we do not need to reflect on the distinction between narrative and story (although the distinction suggested by Binder and Weisberg seems appropriate and, as they acknowledge, is borrowed from

---

* I would like to thank the conference participants for comments on the oral paper, particularly Steven L. Winter who also generously provided detailed comments on an earlier draft. The usual caveats really do apply. I also would like to thank the University of Leicester for generously providing a period of study leave so as to enable completion of this paper.

[1] Richard Delgado, 'Storytelling for Oppositionists and Others: a Plea for Narrative' (1989) 87 *Michigan Law Review* 2411, 2413.
[2] Kim Lane Scheppele, 'Foreword: Telling Stories' (1989) 87 *Michigan Law Review* 2073, 2073.
[3] Christian Salmon, *Storytelling: Bewitching the Modern Mind* (London: Verso, 2010).
[4] Guyora Binder and Robert Weisberg, *Literary Criticisms of Law* (Princeton, N.J.: Princeton University Press, 2000), 209.
[5] William Labov, *Language in the Inner City: Studies in the Black English Vernacular* (Oxford: Blackwell, 1977).
[6] Anthony G. Amsterdam and Jerome Bruner, *Minding The Law: How Courts Rely on Storytelling, and How Their Stories Change the Way We Understand the Law—and Ourselves* (Cambridge, Mass.: Harvard University Press, 2000).

literary studies). I suggest that for present purposes, no further elaboration of the terms used in this paper is necessary. Most of the studies explored here fail to fully define the terms used, with narrative and story frequently used interchangeably.[7] While one could attempt to inspect these studies for implicit descriptions, this would be largely unnecessary as the terms narrative and story are really used as proxy for 'experience'; what these studies suggest is that understanding the experience of others will improve the law. As we are therefore engaged in the recounting of experience, narrative and story are thereby used in their everyday sense, rather than as technical literary terms.

Further comment is, however, needed on the sources explored in this paper. The main focus is upon claims made by authors such as Delgado, in the epigraph, that stories provide a space for silenced voices to be heard in the law. However, so as to analyse these claims fully, reference will be made to works in the domain of law and literature and law and the image. These studies are pertinent as they also make claims for the importance of 'experience' in countering what is regarded as problematic in legal discourse; the abstract and universalizing nature of law. Furthermore, in critiquing these approaches, reference will be made to psychological and ethnomethodological approaches that explore the construction and interpretation of narrative and the situating of narratives within interaction.

1. Telling stories

The cure is storytelling (or as I shall sometimes call it, counterstorytelling)[8]

Scarry suggests that those who advocate the telling of stories in law rely upon three oppositions: the universality of law is opposed by the individuality of the simple story; the abstract of law is opposed by the lived reality of the story; and the rationality of law is opposed by the emotional impact and empathy inducing aspects of the story.[9] We can see here an explicit vision of law that is frequently implicit in the law and narrative school and this is a vision that regards law as inherently problematic. Abstract cold reason is thought to operate in a manner that excludes, and those excluded are citizens who are not versed in the language of law. Law, legal rationality, and legal bureaucracy are said to operate through the application of abstract rules that deny the reality of those who come to legal processes. Law presupposes an image of man as a rational and autonomous agent and legal subjects are constructed in this image so that 'concrete social relationships and real (social) people are transmogrified into the abstractly free and equal legal subjects of the legal code'.[10] Furthermore, law's clients must bend to this image. To make a successful legal claim, one must fit one's story into the language of law:

[T]o be clients of the legal system, people have to operate within the system. They have to be aware of a legal problem; have to define their situation accordingly and have to commit themselves to advance legal claims or at least to communicate them.[11]

---

[7] Jane B. Baron and Julia Epstein, 'Is Law Narrative?' (1997) 45 *Buffalo Law Review* 141.
[8] Delgado (cited in n. 1), 2414.
[9] Elaine Scarry, 'Speech Acts in Criminal Cases' in (eds), Peter Brooks and Paul Gewirtz, *Law's Stories: Narrative and Rhetoric in the Law* (New Haven, Ct.: Yale University Press, 1996), 165.
[10] Peter Goodrich, *Legal Discourse: Studies in Linguistics, Rhetoric and Legal Analysis* (Basingstoke: Macmillan, 1987), 167.
[11] Niklas Luhmann, 'The Self Reproduction of Law and its Limits' in (ed.), Gunther Teubner, *Dilemmas of Law in the Welfare State* (New York: Walter de Gruyter, 1988), 111.

As a result, the application of legal rules works to silence those who do not speak the language of law.[12]

So, if the law is abstract, stories are particular. If the law is reason, the story is emotion. If the law is universal, the story is singular experience. The claim of legal storytelling is therefore a call to context;[13] a call to draw the language of the law back to the lives of the citizens who live the reality of legal, social, and political oppression. We can see this reflected in the numerous assertions advanced to promote the use of stories in law:

[S]torytelling serves to convey meanings excluded or marginalised by mainstream legal thinking and rhetoric.[14]

I see in the mode of storytelling the possibility of enacting and expressing insights about the particularly of any individual's viewpoint, as well as the hope that we can come to imagine the viewpoint and experiences of others.[15]

[N]arrative may be a particularly powerful means of facilitating empathetic understanding: a concrete story comes closest to actual experience and so may evoke our empathic distress response more readily than abstract theory.[16]

Narrative enquiry is proposed as a means to exhuming and rediscovering these hidden human remains.[17]

Stories are the oldest, most primordial meeting ground in human experience. Their allure will often provide the most effective means of overcoming otherness, of forming a new collectivity based on the shared story.[18]

While many stories are themselves hegemonic, helping to sustain the legitimacy of the taken-for-granted world, resistant stories are a potent means through which individual lives and experiences are able to transcend the immediate and personal in such a way as to become socially meaningful and potentially transformative.[19]

Rather than rely upon a single quote or reference to evidence this point, I have provided a range of quotations so as to illustrate the convergence of justifications of the call to narrative. The proponents of legal storytelling are drawing upon familiar images of the shared story in informal contexts; the story in conversation, in the home, workplace, and elsewhere, is used to reinforce social bonds. Storytelling, therefore, in both its form and its context, is a cultural activity with which we are all familiar and which we mostly enjoy and endorse as a humanizing practice. Stories are good, so how could one deny, therefore, the role of storytelling in law?

I would suggest that because storytelling is recognized as a solidarity-building activity, is near-universal in culture, and concerns the particularities of lived events, most proponents of storytelling in law seem not to question how stories in law will achieve the goals claimed for legal storytelling. For many, no more need be said beyond the assertion that stories can provide a voice for others whose stories have traditionally been excluded

---

[12] John M. Conley and William M. O'Barr, *Rules versus Relationships: The Ethnography of Legal Discourse* (Chicago, Ill.: University of Chicago Press, 1990) and Lucie E. White, 'Subordination, Rhetorical Survival Skills, and Sunday Shoes: Notes on the Hearing of Mrs. G.' (1990) 38(1) *Buffalo Law Review* 1.

[13] Toni M. Massaro, 'Empathy, Legal Storytelling, and the Rule of Law: New Words, Old Wounds?' (1989) 87 *Michigan Law Review* 2099.

[14] Peter Brooks, 'The Law as Narrative and Rhetoric' in (eds), Brooks and Gewirtz, *Law's Stories* (cited in n.9), 16.

[15] Martha Minow, 'Stories in Law' in (eds), Brooks and Gewirtz, *Law's Stories* (cited in n.9), 34.

[16] Massaro, 'Empathy, Legal Storytelling, and the Rule of Law' (cited in n.13), 2105.

[17] Dawn Watkins, 'Exhuming Human Remains from Case Law: the Role of Narrative Research in Legal Education' (2009) 3 *Web JCLI*.

[18] Delgado, 'Storytelling for Oppositionists and Others' (cited in n.1), 2438.

[19] Patricia Ewick and Susan Silbey, *The Common Place of Law: Stories From Everyday Life* (Chicago, Ill.: University of Chicago Press, 1998), 241.

from legal reasoning. Faced with the real, lived experience of others, one is forced to reconsider one's analytical and reasoned position; there is an implicit understanding here that we make sense of the world through evidence. We interpret the world around us so as to create understandings of the world; raw experience is necessary to shake our preconceptions in a way that abstract reasoning cannot. Nonetheless, this remains a rather abstract notion of how stories work and assumes that stories are necessarily humanizing and will more likely be interpreted as such. As we will see later, this optimism may well be misplaced.

Before we move to assess these broad claims, we need to explore more practical problems with storytelling in the law. These are not problems such as how to ensure that stories are representative and not aberrations[20] or questions concerning the appropriate place of emotion in the law.[21] While these are pertinent questions to ask, presumably proponents of legal storytelling would respond that their critics have simply missed the point. Rather, the problems below concern matters of how legal storytelling could work, not if it is appropriate.

We have explored why proponents of legal storytelling advocate such an approach, and noted that there is only a modest emphasis on how stories will work. However, if we playfully evaluate their claims as a meta-narrative, we can apply narrative analysis to their grand story. Labov, in his evaluation model, suggests a framework for the analysis of stories, from simple to complex.[22] To simplify somewhat, Labov suggests that narratives contain a number of sections: abstract, orientation, complicating action, evaluation, result, and coda. Not all sections are necessary (for instance, we need not provide an abstract at the opening of a story and we need not deliver a coda to formally indicate the cessation of the storytelling phase of the interaction), but we can use the model to analyse the content and form of a narrative. So, in the orientation the parties are introduced and in the complicating action we get the events or plot. The evaluation explains the point of the story, or how it is to be interpreted, while the result is what finally happened. For Labov, each section is constructed so as to address potential questions on the narrative such as: who? what? why? when? where? how? and so what? Applying this model to the meta-narrative of the legal storyteller's 'story' we are left with many questions.[23] We are told *why* stories matter; they allow for silenced voices to be heard.[24] Also, in addressing the 'who?' we are told that marginalized groups are to tell stories, but to *whom*? We are likewise given little guidance on *which* stories are to be told, and how to choose among competing stories.[25] Similarly, little is said on *how* stories are to be told, but most importantly, nothing is said on the 'when?' and 'where?' of storytelling. We can see, therefore, that there is a major silence from those who advocate the telling of stories in the law. These are important omissions that call into question the possibilities for stories in law.

Where are stories to be to be told and to *whom* are they addressed? Law is not a single-site enterprise; legal processes and interactions take place in a variety of contexts,

---

[20] Daniel A. Farber and Suzanna Sherry, 'Legal Storytelling and Constitutional Law: The Medium and the Message' in (eds), Brooks and Gewirtz, *Law's Stories* (cited in n.9).
[21] Paul Gerwirtz, 'Victims and Voyeurs: Two Narrative Problems at the Criminal Trial' in (eds), Brooks and Gewirtz, *Law's Stories* (cited in n.9).
[22] Labov, *Language in the Inner City* (cited in n.5).
[23] It is acknowledged that this is only playful, as the claims that legal storytellers make cannot, using Labov's criteria, be classified as narrative. However, the analysis does illuminate some difficult questions for the movement.
[24] Delgado, 'Storytelling for Oppositionists and Others' (cited in n.1) also suggests the telling of one's story is a form of therapy.
[25] Minow, 'Stories in Law' (cited in n.15).

such as on the street, in a police interview room, in a lawyer's office, in the legislature, in administrative bureaucracies, in courts (whether they be first instance or appellate courts), etc. Within these encounters when are stories to be told? For some contexts, the answer is deceptively simple as there are predetermined spaces for the telling of stories. Nevertheless, these differing contexts all need differing storytelling practices and they need to be adopted at different times, if at all. To put it bluntly, when faced with oppression on the street by police officers, say in the face of an arbitrary and racially profiled stop and search, should the suspect tell a story about minority oppression? These are important questions, because, as Twining points out, even when stories are eminently appropriate in legal processes, such as in advocacy, different types of stories are required and 'it cannot be assumed that their role in each context is identical'.[26] According to Twining, stories in the trial will be different from stories in an appeal which are different again from stories in mitigation. So as to fully advance the claims made, legal storytellers need to be clear on how these differing contexts should influence the stories to be told.

Thinking of *how* stories are to be told, the proponents of legal storytelling largely ignore a body of work influenced by ethnomethodology and conversation analysis that looks to how social interaction is achieved in situ. So, O'Barr suggests that narrative evidence is more persuasive than fragmented evidence in testimony.[27] On the face of it, this is supportive of the legal storytelling movement; we should all be telling stories in court. But as Harris points out, witnesses in court do not have free rein to construct their utterances in a manner of their choosing; rather, their evidence is elicited through questioning by advocates.[28] Furthermore, the opportunity for storytelling by witnesses in the courtroom is not evenly distributed; cross-examination, for instance, is more tightly controlled by advocates than examination in chief. Advocates, unsurprisingly, are more likely to allow 'friendly' witnesses more scope and leeway in the presentation of their testimony. Furthermore, as advocates are attempting to construct an overall narrative for the case,[29] even friendly witnesses have to be controlled to some extent so as to ensure that witnesses speak to this overarching narrative, thereby resulting in an inevitable degree of fragmentation to their testimony. As Jackson reminds us, in addition to the story *in* the trial, we can apply a narrative model to the story *of* the trial.[30] That is, while the advocates are proposing a particular narrative of the events in issue, there is the wider narrative of how each advocate is strategically building a case that is pitted against the other side with other actors in the setting (judge, jury, etc.) playing a part in how the 'drama' unfolds. In short, even in those spaces where storytelling seems most applicable to legal processes, the setting of the interaction works in a manner that inhibits, to varying degrees, the telling of stories.

While not within the ethnomethodological tradition, Hall, in advocating the role of victims' stories within the criminal justice system, recognizes that there are practical limitations with telling the victim's story. So, witness statements are constructed by

---

[26] William Twining, *Rethinking Evidence* (Evanston, Ill.: Northwestern University Press, 1994), 228.
[27] William M. O'Barr, *Linguistic Evidence: Language, Power and Strategy in the Courtroom* (London: Academic Press, 1982).
[28] Sandra Harris, 'Fragmented Narratives and Multiple Tellers: Witness and Defendant Accounts in Trials' (2001) 3(1) *Discourse Studies* 53. Also see Atkinson and Drew on the role of the question/answer adjacency pair in courtroom interaction: John Maxwell Atkinson and Paul Drew, *Order in Court: The Organisation of Verbal Interaction in Judicial Settings* (London: Macmillan, 1979).
[29] See W. Lance Bennett and Martha S. Feldman, *Reconstructing Reality in the Courtroom* (London: Tavistock, 1981).
[30] Bernard S. Jackson, *Fact, Law and Narrative Coherence* (Liverpool: Deborah Charles, 1988).

police officers rather than by the victim. Similarly, Victim Impact Statements are read out in court by prosecutors, who may 'emphasise different aspects of it than the victim would'.[31] Indeed, victims in the criminal justice system are 'not there to tell stories, but to answer questions'.[32]

Nevertheless, these are all, to some extent, practical problems that a more fully worked up theory of legal storytelling may well be able to address. However, problems of a more theoretical nature remain to be considered.

2. Interpreting stories, investing events with meaning

The whole idea of matching descriptions against the world is misleading, because it assumes there is only one perspective, only one point of view, only one ideology... [33]

Narrative often starts at the end.[34]

The oppositions that Scarry proposes as central to the storytelling movement[35] are a somewhat false duality. To categorize law as merely 'abstract' and the story as mere 'emotion' somehow misses important features of both enterprises. In a moment, I want to spend some time exploring the rationality and, some may say, ideology inherent in the simple narratives that we use to explain our world. In short, the story is much more than mere 'emotion' or experience.[36] But I want to start this section by exploring the categorization of law as 'universalizing', 'abstract', and 'rational'. When we teach law, we do so in a way that emphasizes these characterizations. So, in the use of the problem question, we ask our students to apply abstract knowledge to particular 'facts'; we teach our students to apply abstract reasoning to legal problems so as to come to a legally acceptable answer. To relate to law in this way, however, reinforces 'a fairly conventional vision of law as a domain empty of anything other than rules, inhabited solely by unimaginative rule technicians'.[37] As Jackson shows, the operation of legal rationality could be best viewed under a narrative model, with the general legal rule understood as a typical or paradigmatic narrative, and we decide whether an incident falls within a legal rule by comparing that incident for 'fit' with our paradigm example of the rule.[38] Legal adjudication is, therefore, more of a comparison of stories than an application of abstract rule to fact. Similarly, Winter states that 'standard legal scholarship is just a special case of storytelling.'[39] All of this is not to say that the experience of emotion within law does not undergo some process of 'translation'. One needs only to think of cases such as *Re A*,[40]

---

[31] Matthew Hall, *Victims of Crime: Policy and Practice in Criminal Justice* (Cullompton: Willan, 2009), 108.

[32] Hall, *Victims of Crime* (cited in n.31), 110.

[33] Kim Lane Scheppele, 'Practices of Truth-Finding in a Court of Law: The Case of Revised Stories' in (eds), Theodore R. Sarbin and John I. Kitsuse, *Constructing the Social* (London: Sage, 1994), 94.

[34] Alan M. Dershowitz, 'Life is Not a Dramatic Narrative' in (eds), Brooks and Gewirtz, *Law's Stories* (cited in n.9), 101.

[35] Discussed in n.9 and associated text.

[36] Baron and Epstein, 'Is Law Narrative?' (cited in n.7).

[37] Jane B. Baron, 'Law, Literature, and the Problems of Interdisciplinarity' (1999) 108 *Yale Law Journal* 1059, 1079. Also see Steven L. Winter 'Law, Culture, Humility' in (eds), Austin Sarat, Matthew Anderson, and Catherine O. Frank, *Law and the Humanities: An Introduction* (Cambridge: Cambridge University Press, 2010).

[38] Jackson, *Fact, Law and Narrative Coherence* (cited in n.30).

[39] Steven L. Winter, *A Clearing in the Forest: Law, Life and Mind* (Chicago, Ill.: University of Chicago Press, 2001), 106. It was both a delight and somewhat disconcerting to have Winter read a previous draft of this article and apply a similar analysis to that which he uses in chapter 5 of *A Clearing in the Forest*.

[40] *Re A (children) (conjoined twins)* [2000] 4 All ER 961.

where the emotion involved in the decision whether to perform a separation operation on conjoined twins was translated into technical criminal law questions such as whether the operation would inevitably be undertaken with 'murderous intent'.[41] Rather, that law is not the wholly monolithic abstract beast suggested in Scarry's oppositions.

In order to fully investigate the role of rationality and ideology in narrative, we need to explore the importance of narrative in legal and non-legal culture and attempt to understand narrative structure, transmission, and reception. As a starting point, one does not necessarily need to agree with Reissman that storytelling is a universal cultural act, to appreciate it is an important activity.[42] We tell stories to our children from an early age and the delight that children take in hearing these stories stretches into adult life, whether this be low or high culture (if such a distinction is indeed meaningful). Our culture is saturated with stories and narrative, whether fictional or real (again, if such a distinction is meaningful). Cinema, literary fiction, the confessional, the talk show, the soap opera, and television drama are all important stories in the lives of many. Furthermore, within face-to-face interaction stories are an important means by which we express agreement or disagreement with others and engage in solidarity-building social interaction, whether this is in the home, the workplace, or elsewhere. We tell stories about ourselves, other friends, relatives, and colleagues, and mundane and important events (whether in our immediate experience or the wider world). In this context, we can agree with the legal storytelling movement that stories are important because they are influential in identity formation, whether individual or group (in-group or out-group).[43] But understanding their importance does not mean that we should just rush to storytelling. Rather, we need to understand how stories work so as to better appreciate their effects.

To adopt the evaluation model briefly explained above,[44] narratives are structured in a manner that addresses presumed questions such as 'who?' 'where?' 'when?' 'how?' and 'so what?' While Labov describes narratives at the most basic level as simply the description of at least two events, with a temporal dimension,[45] the evaluation model is particularly useful for understanding more complex narratives. The importance of the evaluation model is that it illuminates a rather trite fact; stories usually have a point! Storytelling is not a random activity, but rather the events in the story are to be evaluated so as to explain the point of the story. According to Labov's model, the evaluation can take place within a distinct section of the narrative, or evaluation clauses can be placed within the body of the complicating action so as to explain the significance of events as the story is being told. Furthermore, such evaluation clauses can be explicit or implicit, but their purpose is the same.

We can see in this discussion the seeds of a view that regards narrative as socially constructed. Our narratives, because they have a point, are formed with this in mind. If we turn to Cortazzi's view of narrative, he explains how narrative is not simply a retelling of events, but is rather a (re)construction of events with implications for the correspondence of the narrative with the world 'out there'. Each telling is both a retelling and a new performance of the narrative, with an eye to the new setting. So, when we tell stories

---

[41] Furthermore, the deeply religious views of the parents were reduced to a simple question as to the appropriate place of the views of parents, with mere lip service paid to these views. For a similar analysis of the removal of emotion from a legal story see Jane B. Baron, 'Storytelling and Legal Legitimacy' (1998) 25(1) *College Literature* 63.
[42] Catherine Kohler Riessman, *Narrative Analysis* (London: Sage, 1993).
[43] Delgado, 'Storytelling for Oppositionists and Others' (cited in n.1).
[44] At n.22, and associated text.
[45] Labov, *Language in the Inner City* (cited in n.5).

we omit details, underplay others, highlight some, and distort others; what Cortazzi describes as 'flattening', 'sharpening', and 'rationalisation'.[46] As a result:

> Informants' stories do not mirror a world 'out there'. They are constructed, creatively authored, rhetorical, replete with assumptions, and interpretive.[47]

Furthermore, this (re)construction works through the uptake of schema by the narrator so as to plot the events within the chosen schema.[48] Schemas are 'an active organisation of past reactions and past experiences which organises elements of recall into structured wholes'.[49] Schemas allow us to organize complex events into narratives with events slotted into convenient places within the schema, and they allow us to fill in the gaps when important details are omitted. A significant point to understand about schema is that they perform a dual role; they are implicated in both the construction and the reception of narrative. When we tell stories we do so by drawing upon these prior understandings. Similarly, when we listen to stories we also draw upon schema to interpret the events described. My favourite description of the role of schema (although not described as such) can be found in Barthes' *Mythologies*:

> Each sign in wrestling is therefore endowed with an absolute clarity, since one must always understand everything on the spot. As soon as the adversaries are in the ring, the public is overwhelmed with the obviousness of the roles. As in the theatre, each physical type expresses to excess the part which has been assigned to the contestant.[50]

Wrestling, for Barthes, is not a sport, but is theatre, and each character is assigned a role, a role that is clear to the audience. Similarly, in *S/Z*, Barthes notes that, 'the author first conceives the signified (or the generality) and then finds for it... "good" signifiers, probative examples'.[51] While wrestling presents a rather simple narrative with clearly defined roles, and a good story is never as obvious as this, we can see the importance of schema here in sense-making.

Why does this matter to our 'story'? To recap, storytelling is not a neutral activity; rather, we do so to make a point, and the point of the story is embedded within the narrative. Indeed, this is the attraction of narrative to the legal storytelling movement; law, when confronted with the narratives of others, is encouraged to 'get the point' and accept this new perspective. But it is just this 'perspective' inherent in narrative that diminishes the impact of some stories when compared to others. There are numerous approaches that could be adopted to illuminate the importance of standpoint within narratives. Returning to schemas, for instance, I argue that schemas are adopted not only in the construction of narratives by tellers, but also in the interpretation of narratives by recipients. In short, narratives are not interpreted neutrally, but are instead interpreted into already existing schema, and in that interpretive activity the same processes of 'flattening', 'sharpening' and 'rationalisation' will be adopted.[52] Rather than take up the terminology of schema, we could instead think of frames and scripts as important sense-construction devices.[53]

---

[46] Martin Cortazzi, *Narrative Analysis* (London: Falmer, 1993), 61.
[47] Riessman, *Narrative Analysis* (cited in n.42), 4–5.
[48] Cortazzi, *Narrative Analysis* (cited in n.46).
[49] Cortazzi, *Narrative Analysis* (cited in n.46), 61.
[50] Roland Barthes, *Mythologies* (London: Vintage, 1972), 16–17.
[51] Roland Barthes, *S/Z* (Oxford: Blackwell, 1990), 173.
[52] Cortazzi, *Narrative Analysis* (cited in n.46), 61.
[53] Friedrich Ungerer and Hans-Jörg Schmid, *An Introduction to Cognitive Linguistics* (London: Longman, 1996) and Amsterdam and Bruner, *Minding The Law* (cited in n.6).

The point, therefore, is that narratives are reinterpreted in a manner that accords with our world view. Van Roermund makes this point in a sophisticated analysis of the construction and interpretation of narratives.[54] He examines the hierarchy between event and interpretation, and a positivistic approach to narrative construction would view event as prior to interpretation. In other words, the interpretation of narratives results from the events told. The events are prior and of primary importance in making sense of the narrative. However, we could posit that interpretation takes priority over the events within the narrative:

According to this presupposition, the narrative can only be understood if one acknowledges that the 'events' referred to are not independent of and prior to the Interpretation, but are rather the products of discursive forces, restrictions and requirements.[55]

According to this hierarchy of interpretation/event, we make sense of the world via our interpretations, theories, rationalities, and discourses. Events are not, therefore, neutrally selected but are instead implicated in the very interpretations that we adopt in sense making.

As a result:

[o]ur epistemic claims are not picturing reality, it is rather the other way round: reality is a picture of our epistemic claims (to be disguised as power claims rather than truth claims).[56]

Narratives are 'constituted' in the telling and '[t]he act of constructing a narrative, moreover, is considerably more than "selecting" events either from real life, from memory or from fantasy and then placing them in an appropriate order'.[57]

Van Roermund suggests that neither event nor interpretation should take priority in this way; rather, narrative construction is both a top-down and bottom-up process.[58] Such a view allows for, in the mould of legal storytellers, a degree of resistance to dominant narratives, although the extent of this resistance is limited, because of the importance of already existing interpretations in the construction and reception of narratives. Narratives that are outside the dominant may be either rejected as fanciful, unbelievable, or implausible, or reinterpreted in a manner consistent with dominant interpretations.[59] Elsewhere, Bennett and Feldman suggest that bias in the criminal justice process can be traced to just this misunderstanding of marginal narratives and explanations for events. They also claim that jury decision-making revolves around judgments as to the coherence of the stories presented at trial, and their correspondence with the world view of jurors:

If legal facts are reconstructed as stories whose plausibility depends on understandings drawn from experience, then jurors who come from differing social worlds may disagree about the meaning and plausibility of the same stories.[60]

---

[54] Bert van Roermund, *Law, Narrative and Reality: An Essay in Intercepting Politics* (London: Kluwer, 1997).
[55] van Roermund, *Law, Narrative and Reality* (cited in n.54), 24.
[56] van Roermund, *Law, Narrative and Reality* (cited in n.54), 32.
[57] Jerome Bruner, 'The Narrative Construction of Reality' (1991) 18(1) *Critical Inquiry* 1, 8.
[58] Cortazzi, *Narrative Analysis* (cited in n.46) makes similar claims for the importance of schema in the construction of narratives.
[59] Jane B. Baron and Julia Epstein, 'Language and The Law: Literature, Narrative, and Legal Theory' in (ed.), David Kairys, *The Politics of Law: A Progressive Critique* (3rd edn) (New York: Basic Books, 1998) and Jane B. Baron, 'The Many Promises of Storytelling in Law: An Essay Review of *Narrative and the Legal Discourse: A Reader in Storytelling and the Law*' (1991) 23 *Rutgers Law Journal* 79.
[60] Bennett and Feldman, *Reconstructing Reality in the Courtroom* (cited in n.29), 171.

Adopting a view that interpretation is a top-down, or both a bottom-up and top-down, enterprise inevitably leads one to question whether stories can significantly change world view, as world views are inevitably implicated in the selection of the events used to construct and interpret the narrative. Events that do not fit with this world view will therefore risk being either rejected or reinterpreted.

Hayden White, in an analysis of the importance of narrative in the writing of history, makes a number of arguments on the formation of narrative that support this thesis. He tells us, for instance, that facts 'are not so much found as constructed by the kinds of questions which the investigator asks of the phenomena before him'.[61] Echoing the importance of schema above, in the construction of narratives from these facts, the story is made by 'the suppression or subordination' of some facts and 'the highlighting of others'.[62] White also points to the reader of the historical narrative as getting the point of the story when she recognizes the type of story being told. The result is that:

[N]arrative is not simply a recording of 'what happened' in the transition from one state to affairs to another, but a progressive *redescription* of sets of events in such a way as to dismantle a structure encoded in one verbal mode in the beginning so as to justify a recoding of it in another mode at the end.[63]

For White, recognizing that historical narratives are constructed in this way helps us to 'identify the ideological';[64] identifying ideology behind narratives allows for a deconstruction of those narratives.

Turning to a different perspective evidences the importance of interpretation in narrative (re)production practices. Drawing upon work influenced by ethnomethodology and conversation analysis, we can see how in legal settings and elsewhere stories are not freestanding, but are instead elicited in specific contexts, and the context and shape of any interaction influences the formation of narratives in situ. For instance, Ryave shows how within an interaction speakers frame their stories in conversation so as to attend to what previously occurred, whether this is to offer support for a previous statement or to challenge such a statement. Conversationalists do not randomly deliver stories, but instead skilfully shape their stories so as to continue an interaction:

The meaning and relevance of a description, as exhibited in the form of a story, is not a pregiven matter to be analytically determined solely by inspecting the particulars of some recounting, but is itself best conceived as a social activity that is interactionally negotiated and managed in and through the emerging particulars of a situation.[65]

Providing support for this situated view of narrative within interaction, Jefferson, writing in the same volume, provides an example of a narrative that 'is treated as utterly irrelevant to the ongoing talk and is subsequently deleted'.[66] In everyday conversation we make our stories meaningful for the interaction in which they are situated. Also in the ethnomethodological tradition, Linell and Jönsson examine the elicitation of stories in police interviews in Sweden. Utilizing what they describe as perspective, they note how in the police interview, while broader narratives of the defendant's position may

---

[61] Hayden White, *Tropics of Discourse: Essays in Cultural Criticism* (Baltimore, Md.: John Hopkins University Press, 1978), 43.
[62] White, *Tropics of Discourse* (cited in n.61), 84.
[63] White, *Tropics of Discourse* (cited in n.61), 98.
[64] White, *Tropics of Discourse* (cited in n.61), 99.
[65] Alan L. Ryave, 'On the Achievement of a Series of Stories' in (ed.), Jim Schenkein, *Studies in the Organization of Conversational Interaction* (London: Academic Press, 1978), 130.
[66] Gail Jefferson, 'Sequential Aspects of Storytelling' in (ed.), Schenkein, *Studies in the Organization of Conversational Interaction* (cited in n.65), 229.

be offered, these are routinely rejected or reframed into police-focused narratives of the case.⁶⁷

We have explored above a rather general and abstract picture of narrative construction in order to enquire into the claims of stories in law proponents. So as to flesh out the bones of the argument we should now turn to examples that help us make sense of legal interpretation of stories. The first set of examples that we will explore shares much with the storytelling movement, in that it is an approach that is largely optimistic on the question of whether the stories of clients are able to be heard by the legal system. This approach can be classified as 'lawyers as translators', and has been adopted by writers such as White,⁶⁸ Cunningham,⁶⁹ and Gilkerson.⁷⁰ This approach views lawyers and clients as largely speaking different languages and the transmission of statements from one language to another is akin to the act of translating. The role of the lawyer, therefore, is to act as an effective translator, taking the language of the client and fitting this to the code of the legal system. While there is an acknowledgment of the difficulty of this task, there remains optimism that translation is possible. White, for instance, recognizes that translation cannot be performed faithfully and effectively to the extent that the language of a speaker can be fully reconstructed in a different language:

The common mistaken expectation about translation—that 'what is said' in one language can be 'said' in another—is itself I think the result of the defective view of language more generally... that language is a 'code' into which 'messages' are encoded, or perhaps a system of 'signifiers' that derives its ultimate meaning from the real or imaginary things 'signified'.⁷¹

Rather, translating from one language to another is problematic as each language does not refer to an external world 'out there', but rather that world is constituted through our language:

[O]ur experience is linguistic at every stage: our languages shape what we say and what we mean, what we see and what we experience; we are always talking in inner or outer speech; there can be no 'content' without language; and language is neither a 'code' nor a system of signification that points to things external to it.⁷²

It is therefore meaningless to talk of a literal translation from one system to another as each act of description is remaking the world afresh. This is linked to our discussion above on the importance of our interpretations in making sense of events. If our world view differs, and this is constructed through the language we use, when we speak different languages we cannot hope to translate faithfully from one to the other. Rather, there will always be an absence, a gap, or a transformation of experience. Nevertheless, White

---

⁶⁷ Per Linell and Linda Jönsson, 'Suspect Stories: Perspective-Setting in an Asymmetrical Situation' in (eds), Ivana Marková and Klaus Foppa, *Asymmetries in Dialogue* (Hemel Hempstead: Harvester Wheatsheaf, 1991). Mehan draws similar conclusions from an analysis of a psychiatric examination and describes how the participants talked past each other. However, the professionals are able to come to a definitive definition of the situation: Hugh Mehan, 'Oracular Reasoning in a Psychiatric Exam: The Resolution of Conflict in Language' in (ed.), Allen D. Grimshaw, *Conflict Talk: Sociolinguistic Investigations of Arguments in Conversations* (Cambridge: Cambridge University Press, 1990).
⁶⁸ James Boyd White, *Justice as Translation: An Essay in Cultural and Legal Criticism* (Chicago, Ill.: University of Chicago Press, 1990).
⁶⁹ Clark D. Cunningham, 'The Lawyer as Translator, Representation as Text: Towards an Ethnography of Legal Discourse' (1992) 77 *Cornell Law Review* 1298 and 'A Tale of Two Clients: Thinking About Law as Language' (1989) 87 *Michigan Law Review* 2459.
⁷⁰ Christopher P. Gilkerson, 'Poverty Law Narratives: The Critical Practice and Theory of Receiving and Translating Client Stories' (1992) 43 *Hastings Law Journal* 861.
⁷¹ White, *Justice as Translation* (cited in n.68), 253.
⁷² White, *Justice as Translation* (cited in n.68), 254.

still talks of managing a successful translation—'translation can of course "succeed" and do so in ways beyond number'[73]—but this is not the same as faithful reproduction. Rather, matters such as 'coherence', 'fidelity' to the original text, and 'the ethical and cultural meaning it performs as a gesture of its own' are the criteria to be adopted in the evaluation of translations.[74]

There are two interlinked reasons to doubt the possibility of translation. The first is the importance of interpretation in making sense of events; can lawyers simply jettison or suspend their interpretations of the world so as to achieve a more successful translation? Of course, lawyers do not only speak the language of the law, as they live and talk in different cultural realms. Nevertheless, lawyers judge success by the winning of cases so, from their perspective, what matters is a good translation, not in the sense of more or less corresponding to the client's story, but rather more or less effective as a legal claim. We could argue that this would be the case for a lawyer who took the goals of translation, as defined by White, seriously. For instance, Garfinkel describes how, even in a setting where research is taken seriously, patient records are not constructed in a manner that assists with external auditing or research, but are instead what he describes as 'contractual' accounts, whereby the imperatives of medico-legal practice are more influential in the construction of records.[75] In other words, organizational culture and the prime function of an organization influence the manner in which tasks are conceived. In this context, while research was regarded as important, the primary task was patient care and records were constructed so as to account for activities with this in mind. To return to lawyers as translators, while we could convince lawyers that translation is important, it must, from their perspective, inevitably take a back seat to the winning of cases, in the absence of a fundamental reappraisal of the goals of legal practice.

This links to the second problem with the optimism expressed by White: what the client wants. We could make a case that a client's primary motivation is not success, but rather the desire to be heard.[76] But, if the client sees being heard as more important than winning, an ethical translation may decrease the chances of a successful legal outcome. Indeed, if our analysis above is correct, failing to prioritize the legal elements of translation, that is, not placing the client's narrative into a stock legal narrative, increases the chances of the client's story being ignored or transformed by the legal audience. In short, ethical translation may decrease the chances of clients winning their cases. This leads to a number of questions that therefore need to be addressed: what is and should be the primary concern of lawyers? If lawyers do not win cases but instead simply retell the stories of clients, do we need lawyers? Does a move toward ethical translation falsely raise a client's hopes that he or she will be heard, when the reality is that legal processes will fail to hear non-legal stories? While to some extent these questions attack a straw-man version of the 'lawyers as translators' case—in that they would argue that cases can be translated into effective legal cases and be examples of ethical translation[77]—I would argue that the material above on the reception of narrative illuminates the importance of *legal* translation in the winning of cases, whatever this means for the narratives of clients.

---

[73] White, *Justice as Translation* (cited in n.68), 256.
[74] White, *Justice as Translation* (cited in n.68), 256.
[75] Harold Garfinkel, *Studies in Ethnomethodology* (Englewood Cliffs, N.J.: Prentice Hall, 1967), ch. 6.
[76] Cunningham, 'The Lawyer as Translator' (cited in n.69). Gilkerson (in 'Poverty Law Narratives' (cited in n.70), 916) also asserts this as of importance in translation. Baron questions whether all clients want to be heard, and whether some are just interested in legal outcomes: Baron, 'The Many Promises of Storytelling in Law' (cited in n.59).
[77] This is the task of legal translators according to Gilkerson, 'Poverty Law Narratives' (cited in n.70), 915.

Our second examination of the limitations of legal storytelling begins with the proponents themselves. In the special issue of the *Michigan Law Review*[78] and other publications where storytelling is encouraged, such as *Law's Stories*,[79] advocates of storytelling, and others who engage with the concept sympathetically, acknowledge the limitations that we are exploring here. Scheppele, for instance, notes that stories may clash, even as 'self-believed descriptions', because they come 'from different points of view informed by different background assumptions about how to make sense of events'.[80] This is an acknowledgment of the situated nature of narratives and the importance of interpretation. Similarly, she later encapsulates the nature of law and its description of events as focused upon legally relevant details:

> The traditional strategy of story-beginning looks to when 'the trouble' began, and fans out in the direction of legally relevant facts.[81]

Legal case construction, therefore, is not simply a rendering of the facts in a particular setting, but rather cases are constructed with legal requirements in mind. So, in the criminal law, for instance, the stories constructed start from 'the trouble', the alleged crime, and the events and facts are constructed around that trouble. Criminal lawyers, therefore, are not necessarily interested in any wider narrative that may or may not illuminate socially causative events in describing the trouble (unless such facts help answer legally relevant questions such as intention, via an explanation of motive, for instance); rather, the case is constructed around the legal requirements of *actus reus*, *mens rea*, and lack of defence.[82]

Winter, when engaging with the law and storytelling movement, makes similar claims about the constructed nature of our narratives and he also explores the implications of this for legal storytelling.[83] Drawing upon an approach similar to schema theory, he notes that:

> Central to the intellectual process is the construction and sharing within a culture of idealized cognitive models ('ICMS') to structure and make meaningful regular aspects of our daily experiences. These are like 'stock stories' or 'folk theories' by which humans in a given culture organize the diverse inputs of daily life into meaningful gestalts that relate that which is 'relevant' and ignore that which is not.[84]

I would prefer the term scripts or schema rather than ICMS but their meaning is similar. Winter later describes how narratives are not, therefore, simply descriptive of a world out there, but are instead constructions rendered meaningful with 'preexisting cultural ICMS'.[85] Furthermore, as argued above, ICMS are also implicated in the reinterpretation of narratives so that hearing is also influenced by our already existing perspectives on the world. It is this freedom in interpretation that Winter uses to claim that '[c]ommunication is possible, but there are no guarantees'.[86] As reinterpretation is a creative process, 'the reader remains free to invoke alternative ICMs not intended by or not shared

---

[78] Discussed in n.2 and associated text.
[79] Brooks and Gewirtz (eds), *Law's Stories* (cited in n.9).
[80] Scheppele, 'Foreword: Telling Stories' (cited in n.2), 2082.
[81] Scheppele, 'Foreword: Telling Stories' (cited in n.2), 2094–5.
[82] Steven Cammiss, '"He Goes Off and I Think He Took the Child": Narrative (Re)Production in the Courtroom' (2006) 17(1) *Kings College Law Journal* 71.
[83] Steven L. Winter, 'The Cognitive Dimension of the Agon Between Legal Power and Narrative Meaning' (1989) 87 *Michigan Law Review* 2225.
[84] Winter, 'The Cognitive Dimension of the Agon' (cited in n.83), 2233.
[85] Winter, 'The Cognitive Dimension of the Agon' (cited in n.83), 2252.
[86] Winter, 'The Cognitive Dimension of the Agon' (cited in n.83), 2252–3.

with the author and, therefore, to construct alternative meanings'.[87] Outsider stories, as argued throughout this paper, are more likely to be reinterpreted in this way, resulting in violence to their discourse, as these stories do not fit with dominant cultural understandings. That being so, they are more likely to 'founder in the face of social discord, overt defiance, or failed communication'.[88] Baldwin provides a specific example of this, in his analysis of *P, C & S v UK*[89] where the dominant schema of Munchausen syndrome by proxy was adopted so that alternative understandings of the case 'were either ignored or recuperated into the schema'.[90]

Also writing in the same special issue of the *Michigan Law Review*, Sherwin explores the importance of accepted ways of thinking on understanding narrative.[91] He discusses, as an example, the discourse of criminal law and how this shapes the narratives of participants in the criminal justice process. Whatever the chosen goal of the criminal justice system, according to Sherwin, whether this be deterrence, rehabilitation, incapacitation or retribution, legal subjects and narratives are conceived in the shadow of the goal. The conceptions thereby adopted have their own method of constructing stories so that 'selecting a goal gives a particular structure and coherence to the legal stories told by those involved.'[92]

One would not expect Delgado, as a proponent of the legal storytelling movement, to acknowledge the situated nature of legal storytelling. Nevertheless, in his call to storytelling, Delgado notes that 'ingroup' stories are constitutive of identity and operate so as to give the group 'a form of shared reality in which its own superior position is seen as natural'.[93] Similarly, he notes that narratives 'shape what we see and that to which we aspire'.[94] Despite this, he fails to fully draw the conclusion that narratives are therefore limited in their role of challenging authority.

I want now to turn to practical examples of storytelling in *legal* settings, starting with jury understanding of narratives. We have already explored Bennett and Feldman's assertion that narrative interpretation by juries is based upon coherence and correspondence with already existing experience.[95] Further studies underscore both the importance of schema and the nature of legal adjudication as focused upon legal rather than everyday narratives. Meyer asserts that juries understand narratives through a particular script; the Hollywood movie script. He provides a convincing analysis of an individual case[96] to show how advocates constructed the case to accord with this schema. In so doing, the advocates simply reflected the everyday reality of sense-making by jurors:

[W]e exist in a post-literate storytelling culture and the dominant and most influential form of storytelling is, I believe, that of the popular cinema. Jurors, and attorneys, are products of this culture and their ways of understanding and meaning making are deeply rooted in the folk psychology

---

[87] Winter, 'The Cognitive Dimension of the Agon' (cited in n.83), 2253.
[88] Winter, 'The Cognitive Dimension of the Agon' (cited in n.83), 2270.
[89] ECHR (2002) App No 56547/00 (ECtHR, 16 July 2002).
[90] Clive Baldwin, 'Who Needs Fact When You've Got Narrative? The Case of P, C & S vs United Kingdom' (2005) 18 *International Journal for the Semiotics of Law* 217, 236.
[91] Richard K. Sherwin, 'A Matter of Voice and Plot: Belief and Suspicion in Legal Storytelling' (1988) 87 *Michigan Law Review* 543.
[92] Sherwin, 'A Matter of Voice and Plot' (cited in n.91), 593.
[93] Delgado, 'Storytelling for Oppositionists and Others' (cited in n.1), 2412.
[94] Delgado, 'Storytelling for Oppositionists and Others' (cited in n.1), 2416.
[95] There is discussion of such ideas in n.60 and associated text.
[96] *United States v Bianco* 998 F 2d 1112 (1993).

and schematic patterns of the popular cinema, as well as in the specifics and cultural vocabulary created by the cinematic stories themselves.[97]

Our narrative reproduction practices, therefore, are based upon stock stories and shared means of understanding the world. Nevertheless, Manzo claims that the stories that jurors tell in deliberation are still *legal* stories.[98] Jurors, in interpreting events, retain a degree of fidelity to the legal task in hand, and thereby construct a story of the case that addresses legally relevant questions. This therefore accords with the statement above that to make a legal claim necessarily requires a submission to legal language.[99]

This focus upon *legal* narratives is also to be found in plea bargaining hearings in Maynard's study. Maynard tells us that advocates construct stories around an 'upshot', with the result that narratives 'do not neutrally render what happened but aim toward the teller's ultimate bargaining stance'.[100] Events are, therefore, selected with a focus upon the bargaining position of the advocates rather than upon the telling of a faithful story. Interpretation here is prior to event. Furthermore, Maynard points out that, in routine cases, narratives can be dispensed with altogether, if the parties to the discussion do not perceive a need to explore the facts of a case.[101] On the need to construct legal narratives within the courtroom, O'Barr and Conley argue that some litigants in small claims cases lose, despite narrating the events, due to a failure 'to include a full theory of the case that links an *agent* with an *action* that caused harm to the plaintiff'.[102] In short, a good story is not enough and the stories told were not complete *legal* stories. Mitchell, similarly, in an analysis of *Shogun Finance Ltd v Hudson*,[103] explains how the story of 'an innocent third-party purchaser' is ignored in the judgment of the court: he 'remains a rather shadowy and silent figure in the judgment' because of 'a stark unwillingness to listen to stories, or at least certain *kinds* of stories', that is, stories that are 'simply irrelevant to the way the legal rules work'.[104]

Further evidence of legally irrelevant stories being ignored can be found in the work of Moorhead, who examined the conduct of proceedings with litigants in person. He comments that litigants who dismiss their lawyers, so as to be able to present a narrative to court that their lawyer deemed irrelevant, were frowned upon by other court users. While litigants asserted their right to be heard, others thought such tactics 'misguided, wasteful of scarce judicial resources, upsetting to opponents' and their narrative was 'ultimately rejected'.[105] Gilkerson similarly comments that lawyers do not necessarily want to engage with client stories that are regarded as legally irrelevant as to engage 'is perceived as too costly in terms of time and energy, outside the lawyer's role, and an impediment to the lawyer's job'.[106]

---

[97] Phil Meyer, 'Why a Jury Trial is More Like a Movie Than a Novel' (2001) 28(1) *Journal of Law and Society* 133, 134.
[98] John F. Manzo, 'Jurors' Narratives of Personal Experience in Deliberation Talk' (1993) 13(2) *Text* 267.
[99] These ideas are discussed in n.11 and associated text.
[100] Douglas W. Maynard, 'Narratives and Narrative Structure in Plea Bargaining' (1988) 22(3) *Law and Society Review* 449, 454.
[101] See Cammiss, '"He Goes Off and I Think He Took the Child"' (cited in n.82) for similar comments in routine mode of trial hearings.
[102] William M. O'Barr and John M. Conley, 'Litigant Satisfaction Versus Legal Adequacy in Small Claims Court Narratives' (1985) 19(4) *Law and Society Review* 661, 698. Emphasis in original.
[103] [2003] UKHL 62, [2004] 1 AC 919.
[104] Catherine Mitchell, 'Narrativising Contract Law' (2009) 29 *Legal Studies* 19, 29.
[105] Richard Moorhead, 'The Passive Arbiter: Litigants in Person and the Challenge to Neutrality' (2007) 16 *Social and Legal Studies* 405, 421.
[106] Gilkerson, 'Poverty Law Narratives' (cited in n.70), 894.

So, we have explored the claims of the storytelling in law movement through an examination of theoretical approaches to narrative construction and interpretation and we have then looked to specific studies for examples of the claims made. I would like to conclude this section by exploring a handful of studies that resonate with the storytelling in law movement in different ways; these are based upon law and literature and law and the image. Exploring this literature serves two purposes; it allows for an examination of the claims of this paper in different fields, but it also serves the purpose of stepping back somewhat, retreating from the pessimistic vision elaborated in this paper so as to conclude this section by exploring whether dominant stories can be questioned in subtle ways.

I start with Aristodemou[107]: while she advocates literary practices so as to enable the telling of a different story, this, as I also assert, must come after deconstruction of dominant narratives. The need for deconstruction emerges when one understands the manner in which dominant narratives are ideological constructions that hide their constructed and political nature. Amsterdam and Bruner suggest that in order to 'replace or reconstruct the familiar world, you must first defamiliarize what you would replace—make what was familiar or obvious seem strange again'.[108] Similarly, Haaken, exploring 'stock stories' of domestic violence—'stories of bondage, stories of deliverance and stories of struggle and reparation'[109]—notes that while resistance to ideological dominant narratives is possible, through the telling of alternative stories, effectiveness is limited because stories of resistance are based on 'the stock script of virtuous (white) maidens and smarmy villains' so that 'too many plots and subplots are left behind'.[110] Turning to law and the image, in a semiotic study of law in film and television, Valverde notes how television dramas such as *Law and Order* mirror and reinforce political trends. So, in this drama criminal justice is represented in a two-part format that focuses initially upon the police, and then upon the prosecution. There is no equivalent space for defence practices and these appear in the drama at the margins, reflecting a societal focus on victims and crime control. Similarly, while prison films may well provide stories of resistance, such as the prison escape, there is no ideological questioning of the prison-industrial complex. Furthermore, the protagonists in such dramas are able to engage the sympathy of the audience, only because the hero 'was wrongfully convicted or otherwise subject to unjust punishment'.[111] Gurnham has explored images of the family in *The Kids Are All Right* and noted that the film, on the face of it, carries a radical message on the construction of the lesbian family. However, the closure of the narrative suggests support for 'the family in its traditional nuclear form in which parenthood is identified with a sexual relationship' and 'the homonormative order of things is re-established by the enforcement of monogamy as the law of the family'.[112] Drawing conclusions akin to Gurnham,[113] Campbell explores representations of Islam in film and, while a film such as *The Siege* appears to espouse a radical view by adopting a sympathetic line, particularly through the use of a

---

[107] Maria Aristodemou, *Law and Literature: Journeys From Her to Eternity* (Oxford: Oxford University Press, 2000).
[108] Amsterdam and Bruner, *Minding The Law* (cited in n.6), 237.
[109] Janice Haaken, *Hard Knocks: Domestic Violence and the Psychology of Storytelling* (Abingdon: Routledge, 2010), 79.
[110] Haaken, *Hard Knocks* (cited in n.109), 101.
[111] Mariana Valverde, *Law and Order: Images, Meanings Myths* (New Brunswick, N.J.: Rutgers University Press, 2006), 41.
[112] David Gurnham, '*The Kids Are All Right*... Really? Parenthood and the Sexual Family in Law and Culture' (SLSA Conference, Brighton, April 2011).
[113] Gurnham, '*The Kids Are All Right*... Really?' (cited in n.112).

Muslim lead character, the dominant narrative of Islam as Other remains. For instance, the lead character is westernized, while for others 'the Muslim is not rendered through frames which humanize: we are presented with no story of suffering, no biography, no family, no history. Instead, the film's iconography connects in a seamless way Muslim practice and violence.'[114]

The law and literature and law and image studies do, however, make an important point about the nature of interpretation that in some way militates against the full force of the claims made in this paper. Young, for instance, in *Framing Crime*, acknowledges that the image is constructed around a 'preferred reading', but 'the spectator may well interpret the image against the grain of its preferred reading, but, as with any act of resistance or differentiation, such an interpretive gesture operates both to generate a new reading and to affirm the unstated norm.'[115] We could, however, take a more radical view:

[F]inding coherent and clear structures of meaning in film text is well nigh impossible, as there is an inherent instability in the process of communication and interpretation, a kind of 'shifting sand' which does not allow us to discern a stable set of codes, ideas or beliefs from any given movie.[116]

Yar rejects such a radical postmodern view but both quotations point towards the notion of the 'death of the author' and flexibility in interpretation.[117] This insight is central to the thesis of this paper; if interpretation is flexible, then outsider narratives can be interpreted in legal processes in a manner consistent with dominant ideological readings. Yet, the converse can also take place; dominant ideological readings can be interpreted in a subversive manner:

The same language that promises closure, fullness and resolution is the vehicle through which new stories, new interpretations, and new resolutions will be negotiated and contested.[118]

In short, resistance is possible. Yet, the point is that, within legal settings, the cultural strength of the dominant model, and its perceived natural character, is such that subversive readings are likely to be rejected. Something more than simply telling subversive stories is needed: 'theory or analysis must play *some* role if storytelling scholarship is meant to induce reflection on the part of those caught up in a practice'.[119]

3. Telling stories (reprise)

They were quick to dismiss him as an extremist, a demagogue, a hothead…[120]

Now that we have looked in detail at reasons for doubting the claims of the legal storytelling movement, we should return to those claims to explore whether these criticisms are effectively tackled by the movement's proponents. As we have seen in the last section,

---

[114] Alexandra Campbell, 'Imagining the War on Terror: Fiction, Film and Framing' in (eds), Keith J. Hayward and Mike Presdee, *Framing Crime: Cultural Criminology and the Image* (Abingdon: Routledge, 2010), 103.
[115] Alison Young, 'The Scene of the Crime: Is there such a thing as "Just Looking"?' in (eds), Hayward and Presdee, *Framing Crime* (cited in n.114), 86.
[116] Majid Yar, 'Screening Crime: Cultural Criminology to the Movies' in (eds), Hayward and Presdee, *Framing Crime* (cited in n.114), 79.
[117] As discussed in Aristodemou, *Law and Literature* (cited in n.107), 82 and in Valverde, *Law and Order* (cited in n.111), 38–9.
[118] Aristodemou, *Law and Literature* (cited in n.107), 228.
[119] Binder and Weisberg, *Literary Criticisms of Law* (cited in n.4), 235.
[120] Delgado, 'Storytelling for Oppositionists and Others' (cited in n.1), 2431.

there is an explicit acknowledgment of discrete parts of the argument made above, without a wholesale understanding of what this means for legal storytelling. Delgado, for instance, notes the importance of narrative, and I would add narrative schema, in shaping our perceptions of the world and of the importance of narrative in the construction and maintenance of group identity.[121] However, in telling and analysing his story, a story that is designed to make the point that stories matter, he illuminates the problem with legal storytelling.

Delgado tells a story of institutional racism in the recruitment of academic lawyers in a US law school. His protagonist is John Henry, a black candidate rejected for a job at school X. The story is told from different perspectives; the 'stock story', John Henry's story, the legal complaint, and two counter-stories. The stock story came from a tenured professor, told to a student on the 'student advisory appointments committee', explaining why Henry was not appointed. John Henry's story about the process was told to a junior colleague. The story of the legal complaint and its outcome was told as a story of the subsequent legal proceedings after Henry initiated a legal action; he did so upon hearing from faculty members that disparaging comments were made about him, concerning his qualifications and likely role as an agitator. The counter-stories were both from student perspectives. The first, from Al-Hammar, consisted of an angry outburst at the front of the school in which he described the faculty as an 'all white club'[122] and made accusations of 'institutional if not garden-variety racism'.[123] The second counterstory told of an anonymous leaflet, distributed within the faculty and elsewhere, that criticized the 'special committee' formed after the controversy broke. This leaflet was an analysis of the impoverished response of the faculty, constructed as 'a caricature of the Dean's memo'[124] that announced the formation of the committee, and the story outlined current hiring practices and explained why these were problematic. At the conclusion of each story, Delgado explores that story so as to encapsulate its features and effects. So, for the stock story, 'the dominant fact about this first story...is its seeming neutrality'[125] and this is contrasted with how this must appear for Henry as his 'story shows, among other things, how different "neutrality" can feel from the perspective of an outsider'.[126] The nub of the problem to be addressed by Delgado can be found in his analysis of the legal story:

> Putting the facts in the linguistic code required by the court sterilized them. The interview was abstracted from its context, squeezed into a prescribed mold that stripped it of the features that gave it meaning for Henry. It lost its power to outrage.[127]

For our purposes, it is important to explore Delgado's analysis of the counter-stories, as he claims that it is through counter-stories that we are able to confront authority with the reality of Henry's claims. Yet, Al-Hammar's counter-story did not work, as he was regarded as 'an extremist, a demagogue, a hothead'.[128] He was angry, but 'anger is out of bounds in legal discourse, even as a response to discrimination'.[129] As a result, his claims were not heard. This is surely the problem that we have been identifying: to make legal claims necessitates subjecting oneself to the discourse of law, to surrender to its

---

[121] There is related discussion in text at n.93.
[122] Delgado, 'Storytelling for Oppositionists and Others' (cited in n.1), 2430.
[123] Delgado, 'Storytelling for Oppositionists and Others' (cited in n.1), 2429–30.
[124] Delgado, 'Storytelling for Oppositionists and Others' (cited in n.1), 2431.
[125] Delgado, 'Storytelling for Oppositionists and Others' (cited in n.1), 2422.
[126] Delgado, 'Storytelling for Oppositionists and Others' (cited in n.1), 2425.
[127] Delgado, 'Storytelling for Oppositionists and Others' (cited in n.1), 2428.
[128] Delgado, 'Storytelling for Oppositionists and Others' (cited in n.1), 2431.
[129] Delgado, 'Storytelling for Oppositionists and Others' (cited in n.1), 2430.

rationality, and to conform to accepted methods of argumentation. Delgado can see this, yet continues to call for stories, but stories of a particular kind. The second counter-story, for instance, worked because it addressed:

> [T]he faculty less frontally in some respects—for example it does not focus on the fate of any particular black candidate, such as Henry, but attacks a general mindset. It employs several devices including narrative and careful observation—the latter to build credibility... the former to beguile the reader and get him or her to suspend judgment.[130]

But was this a story of an *oppositionist*? The narrative of the injured party was, as Delgado acknowledges, erased from the script. Furthermore, is this a *story*? Delgado tells of the distribution of the leaflet as a story, of events which he invests with meaning, but the leaflet itself is more satire and analysis than narrative. The 'story' it tells is of the recruitment process, how the faculty is looking for a 'mythic figure'[131] at the start of the recruitment search, and at this moment the faculty believes itself to be 'colorblind'.[132] However, when the net has to be cast wider, as no 'mythic figures' have been found, the usual network of personal recommendations is relied upon to fill the post, resulting in institutional discrimination:

> Persons hired in this fashion are almost always white, male and straight. The reason: We rarely know blacks, Hispanics, women, and gays. Moreover, when we hire the white male, the known but less-than-mythic quantity, late in February, *it does not seem to us like we are making an exception.* Yet we are.[133]

When we explored the claims of legal storytellers, we noted how storytelling was designed to foster empathy, to expressing an individual's viewpoint, and that 'what is asserted is the right to be heard and not merely the right to a hearing'.[134] The story purported to confront the problem does not allow Henry to be heard, as Delgado acknowledges. It fails to call on our empathy and makes no claim to understand an individual's viewpoint. Rather, it is a somewhat conventional analysis of the institutional practices made to look like a story. It is none the worse for that, but to call it legal storytelling is a mistake.

Other studies suggest that even when narratives are successful, dominant ways of seeing are reasserted.[135] Bruner tells how he was involved in the proffering of stories that were influential in the seismic decision of *Brown v Board of Education*.[136] Bruner, and others, told stories of the effect of racial segregation on school children, stories that laid the ground for the decision in *Brown*. However, the progress lauded in *Brown* was met with resistance, and a new narrative emerged to counter the claims for equal treatment:

> The inward turn of literary narrative about race went a long way toward changing the legal interpretation of equal protection when it was given a subjective dimension in *Brown*, and that opinion was widely hailed as a great and humane step forward. But no culture is about just one story. A dialectically contrary one quickly arose: the story of the black being given 'unfair advantages'.[137]

---

[130] Delgado, 'Storytelling for Oppositionists and Others' (cited in n.1), 2434.
[131] Delgado, 'Storytelling for Oppositionists and Others' (cited in n.1), 2432.
[132] Delgado, 'Storytelling for Oppositionists and Others' (cited in n.1), 2432.
[133] Delgado, 'Storytelling for Oppositionists and Others' (cited in n.1), 2432. Emphasis in original.
[134] Gilkerson, 'Poverty Law Narratives' (cited in n.70), 925.
[135] Jerome Bruner, *Making Stories: Law, Literature, Life* (Cambridge, Mass.: Harvard University Press, 2002).
[136] 347 US 483 (1954).
[137] Bruner, *Making Stories* (cited in n.135), 57.

Within the *Michigan Law Review* special issue one paper explores how a story told to others actually works to persuade. Singer describes a story that he tells to his students so as to illuminate the issues around the closing of factories and the impact this has upon workers and their families.[138] Before the storytelling, Singer notes how his students were resistant to his analysis of this being 'a story of betrayal', with the students instead seeing the events as an example of 'the efficient restructuring of production through the invisible hand of the free market'.[139] So as to try and persuade his students of his position, Singer developed a story that he thought would engage his students and illuminate the plight of workers. The story is one of change in the faculty; so as to improve the skills and competence of practising lawyers, the faculty, with immediate effect, intends to fail all first-year students in the bottom third of the class, rather than the usual 2 to 3 per cent. Those students would then have their courses terminated. Unsurprisingly, Singer's students are disturbed by this story. Furthermore, the students know he is role playing but they 'are not playing a role', rather, '[t]hey want to win the argument'.[140] In arguing, they assert their rights: to consultation; to have their needs considered; to not be subjected to retrospective law. Singer responds that the market for legal professionals will be improved and that their 'contract' with the faculty allows for such a change. The students complain that they did not read the small print, to which Singer responds that they should have been more careful. The story worked in that the students saw 'that there was something to the arguments they had at first rejected out of hand'.[141] This was not merely self-interest, but that 'it encouraged the students to try to empathize with the victimised workers' and that 'it taught the students something about themselves and their own beliefs of which they had been unaware'.[142] His analysis of the story suggests an example of storytelling attacking mindset. His students came to acknowledge analytical arguments made by Singer only through the story.

The central thesis of this paper is that narratives are interpreted in accordance with schema, scripts, and frames. As a result, stories will only be interpreted in a manner consistent with the schema of the interpreter. Singer was able to utilize a story that relied upon a frame of reference that his students could understand—a script of relationships and fair dealing—to challenge a schema that students learn in law school—the script of the primacy of legal rules and analysis. A contractual approach is thereby critiqued so as to illuminate the power imbalance inherent in the worker's position. To me, this is reminiscent of Conley and O'Barr's analysis of legal discourse.[143] They show that litigants in small claims courts adopt either a rule or a relational discourse. Rule-orientated litigants claim the primacy of the written or oral agreement, literal interpretation of the terms, and strict legal adjudication. Relational litigants, however, claim a primacy for ethical dealing, the situated nature of legal exchanges, and a prior notion of substantive justice. For Conley and O'Barr, rule discourse is the discourse of the powerful; of men, of business, and of lawyers. A rule-orientated judge does not hear the claims of relational litigants, as their claims do not accord with the discourse of law. To adopt the translation metaphor, relational litigants fail to translate their grievance into effective legal claims. To transpose this analysis to Singer's students, the students initially interpret the plant closure in rule terms; they look to the terms of workers' contracts to explore if the actions

---

[138] Joseph William Singer, 'Persuasion' (1989) 87 *Michigan Law Review* 2442.
[139] Singer, 'Persuasion' (cited in n.138), 2445.
[140] Singer, 'Persuasion' (cited in n.138), 2450.
[141] Singer, 'Persuasion' (cited in n.138), 2453.
[142] Singer, 'Persuasion' (cited in n.138), 2453.
[143] Conley and O'Barr, *Rules versus Relationships* (cited in n.12).

of the firm are legally justified and then adopt the language of the powerful to further justify closures through the take-up of free market ideology. Singer, via his story, manages to persuade the students to adopt a relational approach, one where substantive justice, fair play, and equity are of prime importance. If one accepts Conley and O'Barr's claim that lawyers adopt rule-orientated language, then one wonders if the story would be successful in different contexts. Students are being trained in the discourse of rules; all of us who teach law will recognize occasions when we ask students to not simply tell us the facts of the case, but instead quiz those facts for legally relevant details. The wider picture is only important if it illuminates a legal point; if not, the context is to be jettisoned. We don't want the facts, we want the *ratio*.[144] It is no surprise, therefore, that students can be persuaded to switch to a prior relational view and jettison the, as yet, partially formed rule-orientated approach. Whether this could work with those steeped in the language of the law remains to be seen.

Work that engages students in storytelling practices has been undertaken in the UK by Dawn Watkins.[145] Her work is designed to encourage students learning Equity and Trusts by utilizing an approach that requires them to engage in creative writing exercises so as to illuminate the human aspect of legal decision-making. Watkins sees this approach as consistent with a view of law teaching as part of a wider liberal arts education. While I am supportive[146] I argue that her work supports my claim that storytelling in law has severe limitations. On reporting her findings, Watkins notes that a substantial majority of the students who completed the project were female.[147] To return to Conley and O'Barr, they assert that women are more likely to adopt relational discourse. Storytelling, and the promotion of empathy, could be said, therefore, to be attractive to those who do not speak the language of law. Conversely, those who withdrew from Watkins' project did so because they 'didn't understand the relevance of what we were doing' or were unsure as to 'what I was meant to be learning or what I was working towards'.[148] Watkins puts such withdrawals down to being uncomfortable with public speaking (the students had to read out their stories) or 'a lack of a defined outcome'.[149] It could be said, however, that these students were sufficiently well versed in the language of law that they did not see the relevance of an approach that challenged that language and perspective.[150] Watkins also reports that within their creative writing project, 'a number lapsed into "lawyer-speak"'.[151] Nevertheless, the students who completed the task largely responded in feedback that they were able to appreciate the human aspects of the cases that they read.[152] All the same, this success was rather shallow: 'there being no evidence of empathy, no conscious awareness of the grief or hope or despair that might have been experienced by the human characters'.[153]

Singer's and Watkin's papers both suggest a role for storytelling. I have questioned whether this approach would be successful with those fully versed in legal discourse, but

---

[144] Watkins, 'Exhuming Human Remains from Case Law' (cited in n.17).
[145] Dawn Watkins, 'The Role of Narrative in Legal Education' (2011) 32(2) *Liverpool Law Review* 113.
[146] As a colleague and friend, and with the aims of the project.
[147] Dawn Watkins, 'Exhuming Human Remains from Case Law: A Report on the First Dig' (Learning in Law Annual Conference, University of Warwick, January 2010). The full text of the paper can be found at: <http://www.ukcle.ac.uk/resources/teaching-and-learning-practices/watkins09/>.
[148] Watkins, 'Exhuming Human Remains from Case Law' (cited in n.147), 4.
[149] Watkins, 'Exhuming Human Remains from Case Law' (cited in n.147), 5.
[150] They were all final year law students.
[151] Watkins, 'The Role of Narrative in Legal Education' (cited in n.145), 127.
[152] Watkins, 'The Role of Narrative in Legal Education' (cited in n.145), 127.
[153] Watkins, 'The Role of Narrative in Legal Education' (cited in n.144), 129.

their findings nonetheless provide at least some support to the legal storytelling movement. I have argued that this is due to students' position as mere trainees, not yet fully versed in the law. Their work does, therefore, place the content of legal training front of stage. If one accepts the problems inherent in law, as described by the legal storytelling movement, then the manner in which the next generation of lawyers is schooled becomes, following Watkins and Singer, of prime importance.

Writing in the law and literature school, Aristodemou shares some of the concerns of the legal storytelling proponents, while not necessarily calling for storytelling in law.[154] Rather, the law and literature approach, for Aristodemou, is a means by which we can understand legal processes and legal reasoning. She shares a conception of law as one whereby law adopts an illusion of objectivity in a manner that masks its origin and power, and claims that literature is able to throw light on this process:

Legal language tends to abstract and detach itself from everyday experience once it has spoken; literature on the other hand may reveal what law obscures by reopening the gaps and ambiguities that law necessarily distanced itself from in its insistence on speaking univocally, and forever.[155]

However, for Aristodemou, while law denies this, the poetic in law, as language, remains and can be uncovered by a literary analysis. Aristodemou uses literary techniques to explore and expose the law's patriarchy, so as to rewrite the law in a feminist image. Much of this excellent book purports to tell a story hitherto silenced, but unlike the proponents of legal storytelling, she achieves this through the deconstruction of the dominant story of law so as to make space for an alternative vision:

[M]yths are more important and influential than state laws in educating, unifying, and perpetuating a society and its cultural conventions and expectations. Indeed, the question whether such myths are true, false, or constitute a systemic unity... are not as interesting as the question of what purposes and whose interests they have served... Furthermore, if myths are, as Freud thought by analogy to dreams, expressions of a society's rather than an individual's unconscious, then they are also, like dreams, over determined, loaded with a variety of meanings and uses, and thus open to reinterpretation and appropriation by interested parties, including feminists.[156]

We can see here that while literary methods are useful and important in the deconstruction of the myths of law and society, so as to make space for new retellings, the retellings are only able to occur after an analysis of the myths so as to find the weak spots, the contradictions, and spaces of resistance. Furthermore, this over-determination and ambiguity in myth that allows for retellings is always, as we have argued above, ripe to be reinterpreted by the reader when we perform the retelling:

[T]he freedom and responsibility for finding alternative stories and alternative ideologies rest with the reader's engagement with the text, not the writer's prescriptions.[157]

Finally, Aristodemou also acknowledges that more is needed than simply deconstructing and retelling legal stories for the advancement of women's position, but also that 'changes in legal, social, and economic conditions are necessary' accompaniments to a 'transformation in language'.[158]

---

[154] Aristodemou, *Law and Literature: Journeys From Her to Eternity* (cited in n.107).
[155] Aristodemou, *Law and Literature: Journeys From Her to Eternity* (cited in n.107), 24–5.
[156] Aristodemou, *Law and Literature: Journeys From Her to Eternity* (cited in n.107), 62.
[157] Aristodemou, *Law and Literature: Journeys From Her to Eternity* (cited in n.107), 176.
[158] Aristodemou, *Law and Literature: Journeys From Her to Eternity* (cited in n.107), 176.

4. Resistance is futile?

> *[S]uspicion—and the critical interpretive practice that makes it possible—emerges as a necessary safeguard against the risk of rhetorical domination.*[159]
>
> *Dominant narratives are not called stories. They are called reality.*[160]

In section 3, we explored in detail a number of studies that claim that storytelling in law works so as to provide space for alternative voices that are usually silenced by dominant legal discourse. I concluded by suggesting that what is really effective is not storytelling in isolation, but storytelling linked to analysis such as deconstruction. It is on this last point that I want to explore whether, outside of storytelling, there is really any space for opposition to dominant legal discourse.

In many respects I concede that the message in this paper is largely a counsel of despair; by acknowledging the power of narrative in the construction of individual and group identity, and the strength of narrative in reinforcing that identity in the face of outsider narratives, the message seems to be one of 'resistance is futile'. Outsider stories are either reintegrated into dominant discourse, and thereby captured, or rejected as fanciful, meaningless, or unintelligible. Yet such a message is surely unduly pessimistic; social change does occur[161] (although not necessarily at the pace that outsider groups would like[162]) so we need to consider how this is possible. I would argue that this is achieved in a number of different ways, although all suggest that change is a slow and ongoing political, social, and legal process. The thoughts below are not fully elaborated, as the focus of this paper is upon the claims for legal storytelling, but it is not enough to simply critique the legal storytelling movement without at least sketching out an alternative vision of effecting social change.

I have already outlined in section 3 the work of Watkins that links to a wider movement that attempts to humanize legal education and tie legal training to the liberal arts. As explained therein, I see much merit in this approach as it takes students who are yet to be fully immersed in the language of law and emphasizes a different approach.[163] However, if this is to be successful, I argue that what is needed is widespread curriculum reform, rather than a tinkering at the edges with specialist modules such as those in the field of law and literature (as worthwhile as these may be). It is still largely the case, no matter how we advertise our degree programmes and modules to our existing and potential students, that doctrinal legal research dominates legal education. While 'law in context', or 'socio-legal' approaches are much more prevalent now than a couple of decades ago, one need only consider that the dominant mode of assessment, both formative, summative, and informal, remains the legal problem question. Recognizing legal issues and applying law to 'the facts' is a staple of most law modules, in exams, written assessments, and tutorial teaching. We may expect long essays that call on analytical and reasoning skills, but if my students are in any way representative, the problem question is still preferred as the best means of achieving that all-important Upper Second Class degree. This is a problem if we accept the starting point of the legal storytelling

---

[159] Sherwin, 'A Matter of Voice and Plot' (cited in n.91), 592.
[160] Catharine A. MacKinnon, 'Law's Stories as Reality and Politics' in (eds), Brooks and Gewirtz, *Law's Stories* (cited in n.9), 235.
[161] Winter, 'The Cognitive Dimension of the Agon' (cited in n.83) and Amsterdam and Bruner, *Minding The Law* (cited in n.6).
[162] Derrick Bell, 'The Final Report: Harvard's Affirmative Action Allegory' (1989) 97 *Michigan Law Review* 2382.
[163] Watkins, 'The Role of Narrative in Legal Education' (cited in n.145) and text at n.145.

movement; the construction of legal discourse is problematic for the way it is universal, individualizing, and abstract. The problem question teaches our students to ignore the wider narrative, to listen to legal stories only to extract the 'relevant' facts and to turn clients into legal constructions.

However, as I have claimed in section 3, storytelling on its own is insufficient; stories, I have suggested, are only able to advance claims outside of dominant narratives if those dominant narratives have at first been deconstructed. Or as Sherwin states, we need to interpret dominant narratives with 'suspicion' while engaging in a 'critical interpretive practice'.[164] The narratives of law need to be exposed for what they are: ideological constructions that hide their ideological nature:

Ideological readings of stories require that we uncover the role of social power in this narrative work of the ending and how ruling modes of story production may foreclose on the range of alternative resolutions.[165]

In applying the evaluation model to the legal storyteller's 'story' above, I showed that many questions remain unanswered; such as 'who? 'when?' and 'where?'[166] These same questions need to be addressed if we are asserting that stories need to follow deconstruction; where should we engage in deconstructive practices before storytelling? I do not propose to address these questions in any depth here, but my comments above should make it clear that this is not an easy issue to address. To borrow from the example above, would one attempt to deconstruct the concept of police authority when faced with an arbitrary and racially profiled stop and search? Deconstructive practices, followed by the telling of new stories, seem to be better suited to some arenas than to others. Engaging in political and social action, on such issues, offers better scope for challenging dominant narratives. Public engagement arenas are better venues for storytelling because, as the quotation from Aristodemou that concludes section 3 makes clear, storytelling has to operate alongside actions that impact upon social, political, and legal conditions. Indeed, such political and social activity suits the cause of the proponents of legal storytelling. The causes that the legal storytellers wish to advance are the causes of outsider groups; given that the complaint is that law individualizes and that its abstract nature works to decontextualize the narratives of outsiders, storytelling in this individuated arena could well be a mistake in that the narratives of groups will be decontextualized into the narrative of an individual grievance. If, as asserted above, coming to the law means submission to law's categories, coming to the law means submission to the language of individual conflict rather than societal struggle. Political and societal action, on the other hand, is collective and collaborative and, therefore, more appropriate for the formation of long-lasting outsider groups able to continue with their struggle.

Throughout our discussion of narrative, a sometimes expressed sub-text to the paper is that narrative, like all language, is constitutive of the social world. As language is constitutive, we remake the social world in each new performance. The structures of law are made real in their performance, whether those performances are liberating or oppressive. Understanding social structures as made real via performance allows us to be perhaps a little more optimistic about the possibilities of resistance and struggle:

The enactment of collective understandings is variable, locally shaped and situated, involving improvisation and invention as well as appropriation and replication. We understand consciousness

---

[164] Sherwin, 'A Matter of Voice and Plot (cited in n.91), 592.
[165] Haaken, *Hard Knocks* (cited in n.109), 5.
[166] Labov, *Language in the Inner City* (cited in n.22) and text at n.22.

to be formed within and changed by social action. It is 'less a matter of disembodied mental attitude than a broader set of practices and repertoires,' inventories that are available for creative and banal uses.[167]

On this view, social structures are not monolithic already existing reifications that are imposed on interaction in situ, but are rather (re)produced in performance, and as each (re)performance produces and reproduces (hence the bracketing of re), individual struggle and resistance is made possible in the remaking of law:

> The stories people tell do not merely reflect existing schemas and resources. They are not merely inserted into the consciousness-raising group, the prison, the family dinner, the neighbourhood poker group or the interview situation. Rather, the interaction is constructed in part by the stories told there. Storytelling is thus part of the constitution of its context.[168]

However, as social structures feel real for members of society, institutional workers, and their clients, there is a limited extent to which each re-rendering of social structures can differ from previous performances. The world, via storytelling, cannot be changed at a stroke. But resistance in these spaces of interaction may allow for the seeds of change to be sown.

---

[167] Ewick and Silbey, *The Common Place of Law* (cited in n.19), 46, with footnotes excluded.
[168] Ewick and Silbey, *The Common Place of Law* (cited in n.19), 244.

15

Literal Interpretation and English Precedent in Joe Ma's *Lawyer, Lawyer*

*Marco Wan**

Joe Ma's *Lawyer, Lawyer* revolves around a court case in late nineteenth-century Hong Kong. A man is framed for murder and is sentenced to death by the colonial court. At the eleventh hour, his lawyer saves him by arguing that, on the true interpretation of the provision on the death penalty in the Qing Penal Code, the man should be freed. This moment of interpretation forms the subject of this paper, which will situate the film in the context of Hong Kong's legal history and argue that the scene of interpretation can be read as a response to anxieties about the use of English legal authority at the time of the film's appearance. *Lawyer, Lawyer* appeared at a pivotal moment in Hong Kong's legal and political history: 1997, the year of the city's retrocession from Britain to the People's Republic of China. One of the major debates in the years leading up to the handover concerned the place of English precedent in the Hong Kong courts after the colonial period: what status or authority should English cases have, and how should they be cited? This paper posits that the film provides one answer to these questions.

The argument is divided into three parts. The first part gives the basic narrative arc of *Lawyer, Lawyer*. The film is well known amongst cinemagoers in Asia and amongst film studies scholars, but it is relatively little known to cultural-legal scholars, perhaps in part because of the dominance of Western texts in the area of 'law and humanities'. That being so, a brief plot summary is called for. This paper is part of a larger, longer-term project of introducing non-Western texts to socio-cultural legal studies, and it is hoped that it will contribute towards the expansion of the canon in law and film, law and literature, and law and humanities more broadly.[1]

The second part of the paper examines the debate about the place of English precedent in Hong Kong law after the handover. It highlights the different views on the desirability of continued reliance on English cases after 1997, and underscores the anxiety and uncertainty about the impact of the impending political changes to the legal system.

The final part discusses the scene of interpretation in *Lawyer, Lawyer* in relation to this debate. It argues that Chan's interpretative move in the film trial is in fact premised on another fictional case, the one brought by Shylock against Antonio in William Shakespeare's *The Merchant of Venice*. The outcome of Foon's murder trial is in fact determined by a clever and unexpected use of an English precedent case in a Hong Kong court. The chapter concludes by positing that when situated in the context of Hong

---

* I would like to thank Andrew Counter and Cora Chan for their comments on the paper.
[1] See M. Wan, 'Law and Humour in Johnnie To's *Justice, My Foot!*' (2010) 31 *Cardozo Law Review* 1313 and Marco Wan, 'Law and Film in Hong Kong' in Esther Cheung, Gina Marchetti, and Esther Yau (eds), *Blackwell Companion to Hong Kong Cinema* (forthcoming).

Kong's legal history, Chan's use of Shylock's case can be read as a comment on the place that English precedent should occupy in the courts of postcolonial Hong Kong.

The choice of film as a genre for thinking about legal issues, and of Joe Ma's film in particular, is of course not arbitrary. As one film scholar has noted, films are culturally and historically situated products; they should be 'read in relation to the specific circumstances in which they were first produced and circulated' because they 'grew out of, and responded to, the social, economic and cultural circumstances' of a period.[2] This paper will show that placing *Lawyer, Lawyer* in its historical-legal context can enhance our appreciation of the film itself and also allow us to use the film text as a way of deepening our understanding of a particular moment in Hong Kong's legal development. Moreover, local viewers seemed aware that *Lawyer, Lawyer* could be read as an intervention into the debates about Hong Kong's legal system when it first appeared. As film critic Paul Fonoroff wrote in the *South China Morning Post*, the film came out 'as the new judicial process' was coming under 'critical scrutiny', and could be regarded as 'an attack on pre-July 1 [1997] notions of justice'.[3] Fonoroff's comment underscores the link between Ma's film and the legal debates of the time, and the fact that East Asia's leading English-language newspaper made the editorial decision to publish an opinion piece on a Chinese-language film—a rare occurrence— testifies to the importance of *Lawyer, Lawyer* to scholars who are seeking to further their understanding of both Hong Kong cinema and Hong Kong's legal and political history.

1. The narrative arc of *Lawyer, Lawyer*

The film opens in the southern Chinese province of Guangdong, where the viewers are introduced to Chan Mong-Kut, a man both revered and feared by the local inhabitants for his intelligence, and his servant Foon. After a comical quarrel between master and servant, Foon abandons Chan and leaves China for the British colony of Hong Kong. Things take an unfortunate turn in Hong Kong, and Foon is framed for murder. When Chan's wife reads about the upcoming murder trial in the newspaper, she and her husband rush to Hong Kong to rescue Foon, and Chan is employed as his defence counsel.

The colonial court in *Lawyer, Lawyer* is portrayed in a negative light: its rules are arcane and convoluted, the (Caucasian) judge is arrogant and unsympathetic, and the witnesses are corrupt. Worst of all, the court privileges procedure over justice; the judge instructs the jury to disregard Chan's defence because he had spoken at the wrong time during the trial and had not followed the rules and protocols of the courtroom. According to the judge, the rules of procedure must be followed to the letter. Moreover, it transpires in the course of the proceedings that the barrister on the opposing side is in fact the real murderer, yet the judge instructs the jury to disregard the relevant evidence, again because it was not presented according to proper procedure. Despite overwhelming evidence of Foon's innocence, the court refuses to deviate from its strict adherence to procedural rules; it finds him guilty of murder and sentences him to death by hanging. Chan can hardly bring himself to believe that English justice could allow such an outcome: 'Your Honour, surely we don't need to follow the rules so closely?' he exclaims.

The camera then cuts from the courtroom to the scene of the execution. A guard leads Foon up to the execution stand and puts the rope around his neck. All seems lost for

---

[2] John Hill, *British Cinema in the 1980s* (Clarendon Press, Oxford, 1999), xi. For a stronger argument about how film can function as both a 'source' and an 'agent' of history, see Marc Ferro, *Cinema and History*, Naomi Greene, trans. (Wayne State University Press, Detroit, 1988).

[3] Paul Fonoroff, 'Nothing Funny About Lawyers', *South China Morning Post* (SCMP) (Hong Kong, 15 August 1997).

Foon, but Chan saves the day at the last moment. He does so through an act of interpretation, arguing that on a proper construction of the provision on the death penalty in the Chinese Penal Code Foon's death did not in fact constitute the necessary outcome of the sentence. His argument is as follows: the Chinese term for death by hanging is 'wuan sao ji ying' (環首之刑), which literally means 'a sentence whereby a hoop is placed around one's neck' (wuan (環) = hoop or circle, sao (首) = neck, ji (之) = of, ying (刑) = punishment or penalty). Chan argues that since the rope had already been placed around Foon's neck, the sentence had already been carried out to the full according to the strict letter of the sentence; nothing in the expression 'wuan sao ji ying' (環首之刑) stipulates that the hoop needs to be tightened. Chan's legal interpretation is perversely literal, but the judge cannot deny Chan the force of his argument given that he himself had insisted that the rules of procedure in the courtroom be followed to the letter in a similarly literal fashion. Foon is therefore released. The film ends with a brief scene that takes place one year after the trial; Chan and his wife pose for a second wedding photo to celebrate the overcoming of differences between them which had formed the subplot, and the audience is told that Foon has married the woman he loves.

2. Anxieties and uncertainties about English precedent in Hong Kong, circa 1997

To understand the legal-historical significance of this scene of interpretation, it is necessary to place *Lawyer, Lawyer* in the context of Hong Kong's legal history. The film appeared in the year of the handover. This was a time of intense concern about the place English precedent cases would have in the courts of post-1997 Hong Kong, both within the legal community and within society more widely. Hong Kong has always prided itself on the rule of law and on the high quality of its judiciary; the city's common law system differentiated it from the socialist legal system of Mainland China and formed the basis of its development as an international financial centre. There was therefore much at stake in the maintenance of the hallowed common law beyond the handover. Daniel Fung, the city's first Solicitor General, summed up the mood when he acknowledged that 'whilst Hong Kong enjoyed a robust and liberal legal and independent judicial system', there were fears that 'all that would disappear down some juridical black hole after China resumed her sovereignty', thereby spelling the demise of Hong Kong.[4] A glance at the headlines in the press of the period suffices to give a sense of the concerns about the survival of the common law after 1997: people worried about the rise of corruption and bribery in the courts, they fretted over the replacement of the English language by Chinese as the medium of judicial proceedings, they resisted attempts to politicize the selection of judges, and they questioned the place which English cases ought to occupy in Hong Kong's legal corpus after the handover.[5] The final concern was a particularly complex one. On the one hand, it was obvious that continued reliance on English case law was crucial to maintaining the credibility of the legal system; English precedent was pivotal in maintaining the rule of law. On the other hand, as Hong Kong transformed

---

[4] Daniel R. Fung, 'Paradoxes of Hong Kong's Reversion: The Legal Dimension' in James C. Hsiung (ed.), *Hong Kong and the Super Paradox: Life After Return to China* (Macmillan, Basingstoke, 2000), 107.
[5] See, for example, Niall Fraser, 'Graft-busters Gird for New Battle', SCMP (Hong Kong, 1 July 1997); Linda Choy, 'Court Decision Sparks Fury on Short Notice', SCMP (Hong Kong, 24 July 1997); Greg Manuel, 'Translation of Attempted Rape Annoys Lawyers', SCMP (Hong Kong, 3 June 1997).

itself from a British colony to a Special Administrative Region of the People's Republic of China, there was a strong argument for it to develop its own, indigenous, case law and to move away from a reliance on cases that were decided based on socio-cultural conditions vastly different from its own.

Prior to the handover, local judges in the Hong Kong courts were bound by the decisions of the Privy Council and traditionally regarded themselves bound by decisions of the House of Lords; the former was the colony's court of final appeal, and the latter was 'the supreme tribunal for the identification of English law'.[6] Hong Kong's judges were not formally bound to the English Court of Appeal or to the other English courts, but they generally followed their decisions, on the basis that it was desirable for the common law not to diverge amongst countries in which it operated, that the English courts provided a greater range of decisions for the guidance of the local lawyers, and that adherence to English law would promote certainty.[7] The transfer of sovereignty introduced complications to this relatively straightforward schema. The status of English law in post-handover Hong Kong is governed by Article 8 of the Basic Law, Hong Kong's mini-constitution. It states that 'laws previously in force [i.e. during the colonial period] in Hong Kong' including 'the common law, rules of equity, ordinances, subordinate legislation and customary law shall be maintained' unless they contravene the Basic Law itself or are subsequently amended by Hong Kong's legislature. However, even though Article 8 deals with the common law and equity as they existed at the time of the handover, it is silent on their place after the transition. This silence created much uncertainty and debate, and different views were posited on the desirability of maintaining Hong Kong's fidelity to English case law.

Peter Wesley-Smith, a former Dean of the Faculty of Law at the University of Hong Kong, has pointed out that while institutional factors such as the vast holdings of common law reports in local universities and the scarcity of textbooks on local law would mean that English law would still continue to be cited, it would be 'unnecessary, anachronistic and undesirable' for the Hong Kong courts to remain strictly bound by English precedent cases.[8] In a similar vein, Solicitor General Fung described abandoning the notion of binding English law as a move which would enable Hong Kong to cut its 'constitutional umbilicus from the United Kingdom' and which would free it 'from an earlier culture of relying for judicial inspiration on predominantly English case law'.[9]

While Wesley-Smith and Fung regarded a move away from English precedent as a positive one, there were many who did not share their views and were concerned that such a move would represent a significant erosion of the common law system. One of the most cited works on legal precedent was edited in Hong Kong during the colonial period, and in his introduction the editor noted that while 'democracy (of a sort) exists here, and the English system of common law prevails', concurrently 'a body of opinion says that neither of these institutions is desirable'.[10] The volume was published in 1987, just three years after the signing of the Sino-British Joint Declaration, the document which forms the modern legal basis for the retrocession. That one of the seminal works

---

[6] Peter Wesley-Smith, *An Introduction to the Hong Kong Legal System*, (3rd edn, Oxford University Press, Hong Kong, 1998), 84.
[7] Wesley-Smith, *An Introduction to the Hong Kong Legal System* (cited in n.6), 85.
[8] Peter Wesley-Smith, 'The Common Law of England in the Special Administrative Region' in Raymond Wacks (ed.), *Hong Kong, China and 1997: Essays in Legal Theory* (Hong Kong University Press, Hong Kong, 1993), 39.
[9] Fung, 'Paradoxes of Hong Kong's Reversion' (cited in n.4), 109.
[10] Lawrence Goldstein, 'Introduction' in Lawrence Goldstein (ed.), *Precedent in Law* (Clarendon Press, Oxford, 1987), 1.

on legal precedent begins with a note about the uncertain survival of the common law in Hong Kong after the transfer of sovereignty shows that anxieties about colonial precedent were born almost at the same time as the moment when it was decided that Hong Kong would once again become part of China. Such anxieties intensified as the years passed, and reached a climax around the time of the actual transfer of sovereignty. In an article published on the day of the handover, the legal correspondent of the *South China Morning Post* notes that 'when lawyers discuss the future of Hong Kong's criminal law they often sound like environmentalists concerned with preserving an endangered species'.[11] The criminal law is arguably the area that saw the greatest localization, and the desire to protect and reserve what remained of the English cases attests to the fears about their eventual abandonment after 1997. A law lecturer hoped that a legal profession 'steeped in common law tradition would provide protection' against corruption. Another lecturer notes that in the area of commercial law there would likely be 'a strong move towards local precedent' and predicts that 'the courts and advocates will distance themselves from British jurisprudence'.[12] However, in the same article the Chairman of the American Chamber of Commerce warned that the business community would be wary of too much change in the law: 'The assumption is that the legal system will stay the same. If there is significant tinkering it could affect business confidence.' There were also concerns about the possible updating of Hong Kong's Companies Ordinance from an English model to one which would incorporate American, Canadian, New Zealand, and Australian traditions. One lawyer suggested that the move away from the English model could be 'politically driven by a desire to sever ties with Hong Kong's colonial past' rather than by any genuine desire to improve the city's company law.[13] While the debate over the Companies Ordinance is more concerned with the place of English legislation than with case law, it points more generally towards anxieties about moving away from the English common law after 1997; such moves were often regarded as a lamentable wearing away of the common law. Article 8 of the Basic Law did little to clarify the status and use of English precedent in post-handover Hong Kong, and the debate continued.

Lawyer, Lawyer thus appeared at a time of uncertainty about the future of English authorities in the Hong Kong courts. There were fears that deviations from such English precedent would undermine Hong Kong's legal edifice, yet there were also strong voices for freeing the Hong Kong courts from the shackles of colonial cases and developing local case law. In light of such hopes, fears, and unease, how could Hong Kong proceed so as to maintain a balance between preserving the common law system that has served Hong Kong well and escaping from the ideological shackles of colonial law? The next two sections will argue that Chan's interpretative move in the film could be read as a response to the debate over this question.

3. *Shylock v Antonio* as English precedent in *Lawyer, Lawyer*

To return to the scene of legal interpretation with which this chapter began, Chan's argument is premised on a strictly literal interpretation of the law: he posits that on a true reading of the wording of the sentence, 'wuan sao ji ying' (a sentence whereby a hoop is placed around one's neck) only stipulates that a hoop is to be placed around the

---

[11] Cliff Buddle, 'Common Law Will Defend Itself', *SCMP* (Hong Kong, 1 July 1997).
[12] Patricia Young, 'Companies Put Confidence in Judicial System', *SCMP* (Hong Kong, 27 June 1997).
[13] Sheel Kohli, 'Doubts Increase Over Rule of Law', *SCMP* (Hong Kong, 2 June 1997).

defendant's neck, and that there is no requirement that the hoop be tightened. Foon's sentence had therefore been carried out to the full the moment the hoop was placed around his neck. This argument seems strange in part because of its strict literality, and in part because it is so unanticipated by the audience. It makes one wonder about its genesis: how did Chan come up with this interpretative strategy at the last moment? There are multiple answers to this question. One view is that it is derived from observation: Chan's first encounter with English law through his interaction with the judge and the barrister in Foon's trial taught him that English lawyers stick closely to the letter of the law, and with his intelligence he quickly learned from his opponents and turned their way of reading to his own advantage.

However, there is another possible view, which is that Chan learned this mode of literal interpretation not from Foon's case, but from another, less obvious, source. I would suggest that there is in fact another court case which Chan is relying on here, one which is not named explicitly in the film but whose presence can be detected by the careful viewer. This is a fictional case, which is appropriate given that we are concerned with a film trial. The case which Chan relies on here is the case of *Shylock v Antonio* in Shakespeare's *The Merchant of Venice*, in which Portia traps Shylock through a perversely literal reading of his bond. In that case, Shylock the Jew lends money to Antonio the merchant, and it is stipulated in the bond that should Antonio fail to repay his debt, Shylock will be entitled to a pound of his flesh: 'Three thousand ducats for three months, and Antonio bound.'[14] Antonio agrees to the bond in order to give his friend financial backing to woo Portia. In the trial scene in Act IV Scene 1 of the play, Shylock insists on the pound of flesh to which he is entitled. Portia intervenes in the case disguised as Balthazar, a learned doctor from Rome. Much to Shylock's delight, she initially agrees that he is entitled to a pound of flesh from Antonio, but her agreement is in fact a trap: she notes that the bond entitled Shylock to nothing more and nothing less than a pound of flesh, which means that (i) he cannot draw any blood while cutting the flesh (as blood is not explicitly stipulated in the bond), and (ii) he must perform the impossible task of cutting exactly one pound of flesh. Her perversely literal reading of the term of 'a pound of flesh' in the bond uses the very law which Shylock relies upon to deny what he seeks; sticking strictly to the term means that it becomes impossible for him to obtain the pound of flesh he is entitled to.[15]

The interpretative strategy at work in Shakespeare's play and in Ma's film creates a set of intertextual relations between them; at the core of both texts is a mode of legal interpretation which many people would regard as perversely literal. When we consider the multiple parallels between Portia's argument in Shylock's case and Chan's argument in Foon's case, it becomes possible to argue that the former informs and directs the latter.

First of all, there is a parallel in the way Shylock and the judge initially insist on an absolute fidelity to the wording of the law because they believe their own understanding of the wording to be the only possible one. In the trial scene of *The Merchant of Venice*, Shylock insists on a pound of Antonio's flesh according to the strict letter of his entitlement because he does not believe that it can be denied according to the wording of the bond. Similarly, in *Lawyer, Lawyer* the judge insists upon an unswerving adherence to

---

[14] William Shakespeare, *The Merchant of Venice* (first published 1598, Signet Classic 2004), I.3.9–10.
[15] For recent discussions of *The Merchant of Venice* in the frame of 'Law and Literature', see Lord Millett, *Villainy in Venice* (University of Hong Kong Occasional Publication, Hong Kong, 2005); Paul Raffield and Gary Watt (eds), *Shakespeare and the Law* (Hart Publishing, Oxford, 2008), 235–99; Gary Watt, *Equity Stirring* (Hart Publishing, Oxford, 2009), 214–18; Kenji Yoshino, *A Thousand Times More Fair* (HarperCollins, New York, 2011), 29–59.

the strict letter of the rules of procedure because he sees them as the means to establish order in an otherwise unruly colony. 'I crave the law' says Shylock, and this craving arguably also reflects the judge's desire for absolute obedience to the rules of colonial law.[16] Neither of them understood that literality is a sword that cuts both ways.

Secondly, the very perversity of the reading allows the interpretative act to form the narrative climax in both texts. Legal realism is sacrificed in favour of a dramatic or cinematic denouement. In Shakespeare's play, Shylock is trapped by a singularly unconvincing interpretation of the terms of his bond; in a real court of law such a reading would not have carried weight. As Terry Eagleton points out, Portia's reading of the bond is '"true to the text" but therefore lamentably false to its meaning... Her interpretation is *too* true, too crassly literal, and so ironically a flagrant distortion'.[17] Yet it is precisely this perversity which lends the reading its dramatic force; the fact that Shylock is punished by the very law he relies on constitutes the irony and hence the tragedy of the scene. Similarly, the judge in *Lawyer, Lawyer* is trapped by an overly literal interpretation of the sentence: he had previously insisted on a literal reading of the law, so he must now agree to Chan's literal interpretation of the sentence. Parodying the judge's own logic, Chan insists that 'the law is the law, and not a single word or punctuation can be changed'; it is the perversely literal quality of the interpretation which constitutes its cinematic force because the judge is now trapped in his own interpretative framework and has no choice but to allow Foon to walk free. Like Portia's argument, Chan's interpretation is 'aberrant because too faithful' and as such would not have been accepted in a real-life court room, but it is precisely for this reason that it provides an appropriately comic denouement to an otherwise tense execution scene.[18]

Thirdly, there are parallels in the way Chan and Portia capitalize on the consequences of their literal interpretation. In Shakespeare's play, Portia does not merely deny Shylock the terms of the bond, but actively takes away what he already owns independent of the bond. It is a ruthless interpretation, and critics have argued that such ruthlessness can be understood as premised on anti-Semitic sentiments.[19] In *The Merchant of Venice*, the law is clear that dire consequences await a Jew who dares to shed Christian blood. Portia tells Shylock that if he takes the flesh and draws blood from Antonio, he will lose all his possessions:

Take then thy bond, take thou thy pound of flesh,
But in the cutting it, if thou dost shed
One drop of Christian blood, thy lands and goods
Are (by the laws of Venice) confiscate
Unto the state of Venice.[20]

She also tells him that even if he refrains from taking Antonio's flesh, the fact that he, as a Jew and hence a non-citizen, attempted to do so would mean that he would still lose his possessions, and possibly his life:

It is enacted in the laws of Venice,
If it proved against an alien,
That by direct, or indirect attempts

---

[16] Shakespeare, *The Merchant of Venice* (cited in n.14), IV.1.205.
[17] Terry Eagleton, *William Shakespeare* (Blackwell, Oxford, 1986), 37.
[18] Eagleton, *William Shakespeare* (cited in n.17), 37.
[19] See, for example, James Shapiro, *Shakespeare and the Jews* (Columbia University Press, New York, 1996); and Harold Bloom, *Shakespeare: the Invention of the Human* (Riverhead Books, New York, 1998), 171–92.
[20] Shakespeare, *The Merchant of Venice* (cited in n.14), IV.1.307–11.

He seek the life of any citizen,
The party 'gainst the which he doth contrive,
Shall seize one half his goods, the other half
Comes to the privy coffer of the state,
And the offender's life lies in the mercy
Of the Duke only, 'gainst all other voice.[21]

The two passages above underscore the ruthlessness of Portia's literal interpretation: its consequence is not only that Shylock loses his case, but he loses all: 'You take my house, when you do take the prop/That doth sustain my house: you take my life/When you do take the means whereby I live'.[22] Portia's interpretative strategy reduces Shylock to abjection. Moreover, it changes the power balance between appellant and defendant so that Shylock is turned from someone who seeks the protection of the law into a criminal himself.

Chan draws on Portia's example and refuses to stop at winning his case; he goes further and uses the very law on which the judge relies as the means of trapping him. Portia says to Shylock: 'For as thou urgest justice, be assur'd/Thou shalt have justice more than thou desir'st'; Chan learns from his predecessor that this excess justice produced by an unswerving reliance on the law can itself be a form of power.[23] As the judge hesitates over how to respond to Chan's argument, Chan says, 'Think before you speak, [if you insist on killing Foon]... I'll also sue you for murder!' In other words, he redirects the force of the law away from Foon and towards the judge. Like Portia, Chan reverses the power balance, so that the judge becomes a potential criminal, and the man originally branded as a criminal regains his freedom.

Beyond the structural parallels between Shakespeare's play and Chan's argument, there is a further point bolstering the view that Chan is following Shylock's case, in which there is an explicit reference to Shakespeare in *Lawyer, Lawyer*. It appears in the final five minutes of the film, and it is strategically placed near the end so that it would be more likely to remain in the mind of the viewer. In the penultimate sequence of the film, the events of which take place one year after the trial, Foon tells Chan that his wife has gone to England to study:

> Chan: Really? What is she studying?
> Foon: English literature.
> Chan: Ah right, as in Shakespeare...
> Foon: Yes! Wow you're good, you even know Shakespeare?
> Chan: The study of Shakespeare is suitable for her. Yes, you can ask me anything about Shakespeare...

The scene then fades into another one, and as it does we see Chan continuing to expound upon Shakespeare. At first sight, this scene seems incongruous with the rest of the film; why is there a reference to Shakespeare in the final five minutes of the story, when the playwright had not been mentioned before? However, the scene no longer seems incongruous if we read it in the context of the trial: as a man known for his intelligence and his knowledge, Chan is very worldly and very well read. The scene shows the audience that he is not only familiar with Shakespeare, but that he has an in-depth knowledge of his work; it is likely that he is familiar with *The Merchant of Venice* specifically, given that it

---

[21] Shakespeare, *The Merchant of Venice* (cited in n.14), IV.1.347–55.
[22] Shakespeare, *The Merchant of Venice* (cited in n.14), IV.1.374–6.
[23] Shakespeare, *The Merchant of Venice* (cited in n.14), IV.1.314–15.

contains the most famous trial scene in the entire Shakespearean canon. The function of the final sequence is therefore to reveal the inspiration of Chan's interpretative strategy.

This section has so far suggested that the trial scene in *The Merchant of Venice* informs and directs Chan's argument in Foon's trial. To put the idea in slightly different terms, it posits that Shylock's case functions as a precedent on which Chan relies to build his argument. Neil Duxbury has argued in a recent book that the doctrine of precedent is not, as conventionally understood, premised on the idea that cases bind, but on the more nuanced requirement that 'past events be respected as guides for present action' in the common law courtroom.[24] It is precisely in this capacity that Chan draws upon Shylock's case in *Lawyer, Lawyer*: the reasoning and the outcome of that case from the past guide the present argument, and it is arguably because Chan sticks to the philosophy of that case so closely that the judge has no choice but to concede to his conclusion. By relying on *Antonio v Shylock*, Chan can be said to be following an English precedent: Shylock's case functions as a (fictional) precedent which guides and informs his legal argumentation in the (film) trial set in late nineteenth-century Hong Kong. The principle that the law should be given a literal interpretation is derived directly from Shylock's case, and is here applied to Foon's advantage by his lawyer. One can also say that by citing Shylock's case in this way, Chan is also being true to Shakespeare's text, for Portia herself is aware of the value of the play's trial scene as judicial precedent: she notes that the correct judgment must be rendered and the right principle laid down in Shylock's case because 'Twill be recorded for a precedent', and if wrongly decided 'many an error by the same example/ Will rush into the state'.[25]

4. Citing Shakespeare in court, or the place of English precedent in post-handover Hong Kong

The scene of interpretation in the film takes on legal-historical significance when analysed in the context of the debates about the place of English precedent in the postcolonial courts in Hong Kong at the time of its release. Following the film scholars' argument that the film both reflects and participates in the cultural and political climate of its time, and taking our cue from Fonoroff's recognition that the film can be regarded as a critique of the law in Hong Kong around the time of the handover, it is possible to think of the scene as a response to the debate. Chan's use of Shylock's case as English precedent in his argument in the execution scene can be read as a comment on the proper place of English precedent in the Hong Kong courts after the handover.

Chan draws on an English case in order to save his servant. This continued use of an English precedent in the film can be understood as a response to local critics with strong nationalist sentiments who regarded the common law system as a mode of domination and who advocated its outright rejection. These critics often regarded English law's rigidity as favouring procedural justice over substantive justice; they were sceptical of the ability of equity to offset such rigidity and favoured a Chinese system which emphasized humanity and morality over the strict application of rules.[26] Through Chan, *Lawyer,*

---

[24] Neil Duxbury, *The Nature and Authority of Precedent* (Cambridge University Press, Cambridge, 2008), 183.
[25] Shakespeare, *The Merchant of Venice* (cited in n.14), IV.1.219–21.
[26] This view of Chinese law is premised on the Confucian notion of *li*. See Phillip M. Chen, *Law and Justice: The Legal System in China, 2400BC to 1960 AD* (Dunellen Publishing Company, New York and London, 1973), 34–40.

Lawyer suggests that it is possible for a Chinese lawyer to cite an English precedent and still achieve justice: Chan's wit lies precisely in showing how procedural justice can lead to substantive justice in the common law, and hence shows that there are parts of the English system that are worth keeping. Chan's reliance on Shylock's case therefore seems to suggest that it would be unwise to discontinue the use of English precedent entirely; English case law has served Hong Kong well in the past and is likely to do so in the foreseeable future. It would be rash to jettison English cases in the name of a pro-China nationalist politics.

However, despite Chan's continued use of English precedent, it would be a mistake to see the film as indicative of an attitude of uncritical or deferential reliance on English cases. This is so for three reasons. First of all, Chan is by no means uncritical of the English presence in Hong Kong. At the beginning of the film, Chan proposes a truce with his enemies in China: 'The nation is under threat because Hong Kong, Kowloon and the New Territories have fallen into the hands of Westerners. We should put aside our differences and join forces against the foreigners.' Moreover, when Foon first decides to move from China to the British colony, Chan urges him to stay by saying that 'Hong Kong is a colony. It is not for the habitation of real people, it is only for the habitation of Western people.' Finally, during the trial he becomes irritated by the judge and the opposing counsel in the Hong Kong court: 'Will they shut up about their great British Empire! Have they forgotten that they only borrowed Hong Kong from us, and that they need to return it in the future!' This is an explicit reference to the handover of 1997. Chan's impatience with the British presence in Hong Kong, his criticism of English attitudes, and his at times overtly racist remarks betray his deep suspicion of English law and indicate that he would be unlikely to make use of English cases passively or deferentially.

Secondly, even though Chan relies on the logic of Portia's argument, he in fact makes use of Shylock's case in a highly unconventional way. The normal procedure for citing precedent in the courtroom would of course require the lawyer to name the case and to remind all relevant parties of the facts and how they apply to the circumstances at hand. In this instance, however, *The Merchant of Venice* guides and structures Chan's legal argument, but it is never explicitly cited in court. The advantage of this method of introducing precedent in one's argument is that the inspiration for the argument is never revealed, so that it would be much harder for the lawyer on the opposing side to try to set aside Chan's argument through the traditional means of distinguishing a case based on its facts. Given the vast differences between the context of Shakespeare's play in Renaissance Italy and the context of Foon's trial in late nineteenth-century Hong Kong, one can easily imagine the opposing lawyer seeking to distinguish *The Merchant of Venice* as authority by underscoring the circumstantial differences between them. However, since Chan relies on the case without explicitly naming it, the other lawyer must confront the logic and principle of the case in their purest form, without the trappings of the specific facts giving rise to them. He cannot seek to parry the force of Chan's argument by seeking to distinguish Shylock's case on the facts. Chan is citing Shylock's case, but he does so in an entirely original way that allows him to capitalize on its core principle of literal interpretation and bypasses the potential problem of having the case distinguished on its facts.[27]

---

[27] Interestingly, this use of cases without direct citation is echoed by the use of comparative jurisprudence in some overseas courts, in which judges at times adopt a legal principle without citing the case. See C. McCrudden, 'A Common Law of Human Rights? Transnational Judicial Conversations on Constitutional Rights' (2000) 20 *Oxford Journal of Legal Studies* 499, especially 510–12.

Chan's method of using the precedent case is also unconventional for jurisprudential reasons, because when he introduces Shylock's case he is not merely making a legal argument in defence of Foon, but taking on the colonial legal system itself and undermining it from within. When Portia traps Shylock through her perversely literal reading of the bond, she is bolstering the legal edifice in the play: the legal system is one which is biased against Shylock the Jew in favour of the Christians, and by advancing the interest of the Duke, Bassanio, and the other Christians she is on the side of the law. Chan's literal reading, however, is nothing short of a postcolonial strategy of resistance because it draws on an English case to challenge the English colonial legal system. In other words, Chan is using a core element of the system—English precedent—to undermine the system from within. If the judge finds Foon guilty, he would have to contradict his own premise that the letter of the law must be interpreted literally, and this would imply an unjustifiable deviation from past practice and would hence expose an inconsistent judicial attitude at the heart of colonial law. 'Your judgment will bring your great British Empire to shame through your own inconsistency' Chan tells the judge, and urges him to do justice and release Foon from the execution stand. Chan therefore uses English precedent not only to advance his own argument, but to strike at the very rigidity and nepotism in the heart of the colonial legal project.

The final indication that the film does not advocate a deferential attitude towards English precedent lies in the way Chan refers to Shakespeare in the last scene. Foon has just told Chan that his wife is studying English literature in England, and Chan has revealed his knowledge of Shakespeare to Foon. The entire conversation takes place in Cantonese, and contains a pun. The Cantonese term for Shakespeare is 'Sa Si Bei Ah' (莎士比亞), a transliteration of the English word. Within this transliteration, the meanings of the four characters which make up the Chinese word for Shakespeare are purely onomatopoeic; their normal meanings are set aside so that this particular combination of the four characters refers to the playwright and to nothing else. Yet when Chan refers to Shakespeare, he comically—some might say facetiously—changes the last two characters, so that 'Sa Si Bei AH' (莎士比亞) becomes 'Sa Si Bei LA' (莎士脾罅). 'Bei La' (脾罅) in Cantonese refers to the area between one's crotch and one's leg, that narrow area of the body that is usually overlooked and is not regarded as particularly appealing. The effect of this pun, then, is to transform the greatest playwright in English literary history into a random body part, and not a particularly elegant part either.

Such word play is an integral part of the comedy of this film, a form of comedy known both in popular culture and in the more rarefied discourse of film studies as 'Moleitau' humour, which roughly translates as non-sense humour or nonsensical humour. Film scholars have pointed out the subversive potential of such humour, and have argued that it represents an undoing of dominant structures of thought and cinematic conventions.[28] In this light, the reduction of Shakespeare to an overlooked body part can be seen as a way of undermining the canonicity and the authority of the playwright, a mocking gesture which takes him down from the pedestal of great English literature and places him amongst the silly, the mundane, and the everyday. Chan's appellation of Shakespeare, his transformation of 'Sa Si Bei AH'(莎士比亞) to 'Sa Si Bei LA' (莎士脾罅) can be interpreted as an indication of how he conceives of Shakespeare: not as an unalterable authority or a great figure to be revered or deferred to, but as an entity which can be linguistically transformed, remoulded, even mocked in a Chinese

---

[28] See, for example, Linda Chiu-Han Lai, 'Nostalgia and Nonsense: Two Instances of Commemorative Practices in Hong Kong in the Early 1990s' in Law Kar and Stephen Teo (eds), *Fifty Years of Electric Shadows* (Urban Council, Hong Kong, 1997), 95.

context. Through translation into a different linguistic and cultural frame, the name 'Shakespeare' can become funny in ways which Shakespeare himself would not have understood. This treatment of Shakespeare's name can, by extension, give us an indication of the way Chan is prepared to read and cite his plays in general, and Shylock's case in particular: not with great deference or reverence, as if it were an absolute authority which must be strictly followed, but with creativity, lateral thinking, playfulness, even a certain degree of disdain. He is capable of using his plays creatively to suit the new cultural and legal contexts in which he finds himself.

In short, Chan's use of Shylock's case does not suggest an attitude of continued deference to English case law in the Hong Kong courts. His attitude towards English precedent is not one of colonial awe, and he certainly does not regard Shylock's case as being in any way binding on himself or on the judge in Foon's trial. Rather, it is merely a guide or an inspiration for his argument. In Chan's mind, English precedent is one form of argument amongst many rather than an absolute binding authority which he cannot set aside. Unlike some of the lawyers cited in the *South China Morning Post* in the first section of this chapter, Chan does not rarefy English law by regarding it as an endangered species which needs to be protected after the handover, nor does he place it on a pedestal and regard it as having any more force or legitimacy than other laws in the land.

Not outright rejection, and not uncritical reliance: the film seems to present a third way of using English cases in the postcolonial period through Chan's act of interpretation. It suggests that English cases should be retained, but adapted in such a way as to be useful to Hong Kong's postcolonial situation as it confronts new legal scenarios after the retrocession. Chan draws on Shakespeare but evokes his name in a way which is irreverent and even daring, by turning him into a body part, and he cites Shylock's case in a way which departs from the traditional mode of introducing cases in court. In a similar mode, Hong Kong lawyers could continue citing English precedent, but be bold enough to do so in new, creative, and even unorthodox ways to enable the legal system in Hong Kong to face the challenges which lie ahead. 'Legal case-history is not just a record of past "applications" of the law, but a tradition of continuous interpretation of it which bears in forcibly on any current act of legal judgement',[29] and the ability to draw on English precedent in new and creative ways is part of this process of 'continuous interpretation' which is especially necessary at a time when there is a change of sovereignty. The scene of interpretation in the film seems to suggest that instead of rejecting or deferring to the colonial past, Hong Kong should take what we have inherited from English law, but always be ready to change it, to treat it with irreverence, to adapt it to the local context, to the local language, and to the local culture in the postcolonial period.

Some examples of such an attitude could already be found in the law at the time of the handover. Article 84 of the Basic Law is a case in point. The provision explicitly allows Hong Kong courts to refer to precedents from common law jurisdictions other than England. As Solicitor General Fung pointed out, after the handover:

Hong Kong courts... regularly cite and follow, by way of precedent, decisions of the House of Lords, the Privy Council, the High Court of Australia, the New Zealand Court of Appeal, the Indian Supreme Court, the South African Supreme Court, the Supreme Court of Canada and last, but by no means least, decisions of the U.S. Supreme Court and the U.S. Federal District Court.[30]

---

[29] Eagleton, *William Shakespeare* (cited in n.17), 36.
[30] Fung, 'Paradoxes of Hong Kong's Reversion' (cited in n.4), 109.

The drafters of Article 84 and the judges who have interpreted this provision arguably epitomize the creativity and boldness in the treatment of English precedent in the film: Hong Kong lawyers continue to cite English cases in the courts but no longer treat them as inherently more authoritative or persuasive than cases from other common law jurisdictions, and by following a much wider and much more international range of precedents they creatively modify the use of case law to make it suit the new global order in which Hong Kong found itself, resulting in a more cosmopolitan and more fertile legal system. As Sir Yang Ti-liang, the first Chinese person to serve as Hong Kong's Chief Justice, once noted, the common law in Hong Kong must adapt and evolve: there 'must be transformation—a process by which the spirit of the legal system is so mingled with the culture and ethos of the new society that a new system emerges, still largely based on the ancestry whence it came, but evidencing a metamorphosis which has eradicated its foreignness'.[31] *Lawyer, Lawyer* can be read as a filmic depiction of how such a transformation can take place: significantly, Chan's creative use of English precedent means that he is able to achieve a just outcome in a way which no English lawyer without knowledge of the Chinese language could have done, because he brings Portia's literal interpretation to bear on the *Chinese* phrase for 'death by hanging' in the Penal Code. Chan's use of English precedent reflects Yang's vision of Hong Kong law which retains 'the ancestry whence it came', but which also undergoes 'a metamorphosis' that makes it distinctly local. In the context of the debates about the place and status of English precedent in post-handover Hong Kong, Chan's strategy seems to suggest that Hong Kong lawyers should continue to make use of English case law, but they must not be afraid to allow them to be reworked, recontextualized, and reinterpreted, so that they can evolve together with Hong Kong as the city moves into a new era.

---

[31] Cited in Lau Chi Kuen, *Hong Kong's Colonial Legacy* (Chinese University Press, Hong Kong, 1997), 131.

16
Toward a Cognitive Science of Legal Interpretation

Benjamin Shaer*

Introduction

This paper has a simple goal, which it shares with many other studies of legal interpretation. This is to make sense of the character of this form of interpretation and to assess some of the many claims about how legal interpretation does or should proceed. What I believe will distinguish my effort from others is its goal of sketching a cognitively realistic approach to legal interpretation, which seeks to understand such interpretation as a 'triadic' process that relates a text to its author or authors, on the one hand, and its interpreter or interpreters, on the other; and which reveals the cognitive tasks that legal interpreters perform in arriving at conclusions about a legal text in the legal context. The theory of communication that I shall be appealing to is one couched in terms of Relevance Theory, a framework for the study of cognition that, I believe, is particularly well suited to the task of elucidating legal interpretation—something that I hope this paper will show.

To be sure, there has been ample recognition that legal interpretation involves 'a process by which meaning is divined'—and that '[t]he invocation of "plain meaning"', meaning that is clear and unambiguous, 'just sweeps [this process] under the rug'.[1] There have also been attempts to understand such interpretation in terms of—arguably rather unrealistic—'decoding' models of human communication.[2] And legal scholarship is hardly unfamiliar with appeals to linguistic theory, cognitive psychology, and other branches of cognitive science, which have figured in the legal academy's efforts at 'ransacking the social science and the humanities for insights and approaches with which to enrich our understanding of the legal system'.[3] Yet, to my knowledge, there have been few, if any, attempts to construct an overarching account of legal interpretation couched in cognitive-scientific terms, which takes as its starting point the recognition of legal interpretation as a process and permits scrutiny of the various components of this process, and the claims made about legal interpretation, in these terms.

---

* I wish to thank Nicholas Allott, Hrafn Asgeirsson, Dwight Barnaby, Liam McHugh-Russell, and the audience of the Law and Language Colloquium for very helpful comments and references. The usual disclaimers apply.

[1] Frank H Easterbrook, 'Statutes' Domains' (1983) 50 *U Chi L Rev* 533; see also e.g. Jonathan R Siegel, 'The Inexorable Radicalization of Textualism' (2009) 158 *U Pa L Rev* 117, 135: 'some process must be used to discern the meaning of the text'.

[2] See e.g. Cheryl Boudreau, Arthur Lupia, Mathew D McCubbins, and Daniel B Rodriguez, 'What Statutes Mean: Interpretive Lessons from Positive Theories of Communication and Legislation' (2007) 44 *San Diego L Rev* 957, 966–7.

[3] Richard A Posner, 'Law and Literature: A Relation Reargued' (1986) 72 *Va L Rev* 1351, 1351.

One reason for this dearth might be the scepticism often expressed about the relevance to legal interpretation of the 'triad' of author, text, and interpreter and a more general scepticism of analyses couched in any terms other than those provided by the law itself or the institutions in which it operates. For example, jurists as various as Ronald Dworkin, William Eskridge, and Justice Antonin Scalia have rejected the idea of legal interpretation as a form of communication between makers and interpreters of law.[4] And Adrian Vermeule has claimed that 'the decisive considerations in choosing methods of constitutional interpretation are necessarily institutional'[5] and that 'the high-level premises commonly brought to bear on interpretation... —premises about democracy, or constitutionalism, or the nature of law, of statutes, or of language—are fatally abstract' and 'typically lack the cutting power to resolve operational controversies at the ground level about what interpretive rules judges ought to follow'.[6] Even Kent Greenawalt, someone far more sympathetic to the application of non-legal methods to legal analysis, has argued that '[g]eneral theoretical considerations about the nature of language and interpretation can be very illuminating, but they do not determine how courts do, or should, interpret texts that have legal force. On issues about which people can disagree, resolution depends heavily on normative assessments about how a legal system should work.'[7] Thus, 'other disciplines and general theories about language and interpretation provide limited positive guidance for judges deciding what perspectives to employ'.[8]

Of course, an appeal to cognitive-scientific (or other theoretical) considerations cannot *determine* how judges should go about interpreting legal texts. Yet, such considerations, I shall suggest, can be more than merely illuminating: they can provide powerful tools for assessing the plausibility of claims about legal interpretation. This is because, as I shall argue, legal interpretation is irreducibly an act of verbal communication. It is, however, one with very distinctive features, arising from the principles, practices, and background information in which it is embedded; and these principles, practices, and background information form a web dense enough that it is reasonable to see them as constituting a 'culture of law', as Paul Kahn describes it.[9] Indeed, it is difficult to understand legal interpretation without recognizing that the 'culture of law' includes procedures known by authors and interpreters of legal texts alike that are unique to the law and thus foreign to other forms of communication. This last fact highlights the need to investigate such procedures within the purview of the 'culture of law', rather than seeing them as 'incoherent' or 'idiosyncratic', as some commentators have claimed.[10]

All of this is to say that it is possible to agree with Vermeule that questions about how judges should interpret are 'systemic all the way down' while still rejecting his claim that considerations of 'the nature of language' can play no significant role in deciding how judges should interpret. This is because such decisions should be compatible with what we know about the process of interpretation if they are not to buttress unsustainable

---

[4] See e.g. Ronald Dworkin, *Law's Empire* (Cambridge, Mass.: Harvard University Press, 1986); William N Eskridge Jr, *Dynamic Statutory Interpretation* (Cambridge, Mass.: Harvard University Press, 1994); Antonin Scalia, *A Matter of Interpretation: Federal Courts and the Law* (Princeton: Princeton University Press, 1997).
[5] Adrian Vermeule, *Judging Under Uncertainty* (Cambridge, Mass.: Harvard University Press, 2006) 33.
[6] Vermeule, *Judging Under Uncertainty* (cited in n.5) 63.
[7] Kent Greenawalt, *Legal Interpretation: Perspectives from Other Disciplines and Private Texts* (New York: Oxford University Press, 2010) 14.
[8] Greenawalt, *Legal Interpretation* (cited in n.7) 17.
[9] Paul W Kahn, *The Cultural Study of Law: Reconstructing Legal Scholarship* (Chicago: University of Chicago Press, 1999).
[10] Lawrence M Solan, *The Language of Judges* (Chicago: University of Chicago Press, 1993) 1.

fictions about this process. Thus, what I shall be claiming is that legal interpretation is as much cognitive as it is institutional 'all the way down'—that it is a particular kind of linguistic activity, carried out as part of the culture of law. This indicates that a plausible account of it must ultimately meld institutional and cognitive analyses, showing how the latter perspective is compatible with, and can actually elucidate, the former.

The key to this melding, I shall argue, is to recognize that the culture of law is instrumental in structuring various kinds of verbal 'activity types',[11] including legal interpretation. This recognition allows us to enrich the basic picture of communication provided by Relevance Theory with an approach, due originally to Wittgenstein and later developed by the linguist and anthropologist Stephen Levinson, which highlights the role of 'activity types' in verbal communication. Such an approach, I believe, has the potential to bridge the divide between highly abstract considerations of legal interpretation and its functioning on the ground, a divide to which Vermeule's work in particular has drawn attention. Thus, what also distinguishes my effort to understand legal interpretation from many others is its claim that a 'cognitive turn' in analysing legal interpretation is broadly consistent with the 'institutional turn' that Vermeule has advocated.[12]

Worth emphasizing about this effort is that, unlike those that are essentially attempts to analogize between legal and other forms of interpretation, this one does not take legal interpretation to be *like* verbal communication, drawing out various commonalities from this analogy. Rather, it takes such interpretation to *be* verbal communication, albeit a very particular variety of this and one subject to its own complex principles. The goal, then, is to draw on a detailed theory of communication to construct a theory of legal interpretation that permits us to isolate the basic components of any process of communication and the distinctive features of different forms, including the specific restrictions placed on them. This, in turn, will permit us to address certain persistent questions in much theorizing about legal interpretation. Among these are the nature of 'legislative intent' and 'original meaning' and their relevance to the interpretation of statutory and constitutional law and the proper use of evidence beyond enacted laws themselves. By addressing such questions within the framework of a theory of communication, we can gain a clearer sense of which claims are consistent with what is known about the workings of interpretation generally, which ones are consistent with the distinctive features of legal interpretation and the culture of law, and which ones are not compatible with either and represent more controversial positions on legal interpretation that require a different kind of defence.

It might be felt that the questions just outlined are largely intramural ones, which have exercised American jurists but few others. While these questions have indeed received a great deal of attention in the United States, they are by no means confined to it.[13] Moreover, these questions remain fundamental to legal interpretation and are likely to attract increasing attention in other jurisdictions, as the migration of legal ideas continues. In Canada, for example, where these interpretative questions have been quiescent for many years, the rise of neo-conservative politics and its disdain for 'judicial

---

[11] Stephen C Levinson, 'Activity Types and Language' (1979) 17 *Linguistics* 365.
[12] Although not with Vermeule's institutional proposals themselves, which have faced significant criticism; see e.g. Jonathan R Siegel, 'Judicial Interpretation in the Cost-Benefit Crucible' (2007) 92 *Minn L Rev* 387.
[13] See e.g. Peter W Hogg, 'The Charter of Rights and American Theories of Interpretation' (1987) 25 *Osgoode Hall LJ* 87; *Pepper v Hart*, [1993] AC 593 (HL) (appeal taken from Eng.); Francis Bennion, *Understanding Common Law Legislation: Drafting and Interpretation* (Oxford/New York: Oxford University Press, 2001).

activism'[14] signal the likelihood that such questions will be revisited—hence the desirability of developing more robust answers to them.

To foreshadow the discussion somewhat, I see at least two key results emerging from my 'cognitive-scientific' sketch of legal interpretation. One is a highlighting of the role of 'author's meaning', which—notwithstanding claims to the contrary—is revealed to be as integral to the analysis of such interpretation as contextual information is acknowledged to be. Another is a demonstration that determining even the explicit content of legal and other texts is a far less mechanical process than acknowledged by those who favour a greater hewing to the 'surface text', involving considerable 'enrichment' of the text by the interpreter—a conclusion that undermines the idea that interpreters can avoid 'making' law.

The rest of this paper is organized as follows. In section 1, I spell out the problems that the paper will tackle: the gap between high-level principles and decisions on the ground, as observed by Vermeule, and the lack of any clear articulation of how legal interpretation actually works at the level of cognitive process. In section 2, I spell out the Relevance Theory framework and some of its implications for legal interpretation. In section 3, I explore the features of legal interpretation by briefly comparing them to those of 'ordinary' communication and literary interpretation, and then return to some of the problems in legal interpretation touched on earlier. Section 4 ends the paper with some brief conclusions about the approach to legal interpretation that the paper has offered.

1. Some live issues in legal interpretation

As suggested above, the basic goal of this paper is to examine certain issues in legal interpretation through the lens of a cognitive-scientific theory of communication. The claim is that doing so might help to clarify these issues and to assess various claims that have been made about how legal interpretation does or should proceed.

Arguably, there remains a pressing need for new analytical tools to examine legal interpretation in general and statutory interpretation in particular. If we accept Justice Antonin Scalia's assessment of 'the state of the science of statutory interpretation in American law', it is that 'American judges have no intelligible theory of what we do most', and 'the American bar and American legal education, by and large, are unconcerned with the fact that we have no intelligible theory'.[15] One reflection of this, as already noted, is the co-existence of 'high-level premises...brought to bear on interpretation'[16] with the actual practices of legal interpretation, yet no way to 'move directly' from one to the other[17] or to 'resolve operational controversies at the ground level'.[18]

At least some of those interested in the workings of legal interpretation might take Vermeule's mention of its 'ground level' to refer to the things that judges and others actually do with the words of legal texts. However, Vermeule's view of legal interpretation (the key questions for which are 'systemic all the way down', as already noted) clearly takes the 'ground level' to be institutional rather than cognitive; and he gives

---

[14] See e.g. Dan Gardner, 'Judges and the Inscrutable Prime Minister' *Ottawa Citizen* (6 May 2011) <http://www.dangardner.ca/index.php/books/item/132-will-harper-politicize-the-judiciary>, accessed 30 September 2012.
[15] Scalia, *A Matter of Interpretation* (cited in n.4) 14.
[16] Vermeule, *Judging Under Uncertainty* (cited in n.5) 63.
[17] Vermeule, *Judging Under Uncertainty* (cited in n.5) 71.
[18] Vermeule, *Judging Under Uncertainty* (cited in n.5) 63.

scant attention to legal interpretation's 'ground level' in the latter sense. Yet, there is good reason to believe that greater attention to the latter 'ground level' would assist in our understanding of legal interpretation and to assess the various claims made about it—including claims about the alleged similarities and differences between competing theories of interpretation.

That additional tools may well be needed to make these assessments is suggested, for example, by recent discussion of the interpretative theory known as 'textualism' and one of its rivals, 'intentionalism'. These theories are commonly understood to involve the goals of 'identify[ing] the objective meaning of statutory text without regard to what any legislator intended that text to mean' and of 'implement[ing] the intent of the legislature', respectively.[19] What is noteworthy for our purposes is that a key point of disagreement in recent discussion is whether these theories do or do not take statutory interpretation to have the same basic goal.

Caleb Nelson, one textualist scholar, suggests that statutory interpretation can be understood to have one or more of three broad goals. These are related to (i) fulfilling the author's intent; (ii) fulfilling the 'reader's understanding'; and (iii) purposes independent of communication between author and reader, 'such as promoting sound policy, making our legal system as coherent as possible, or keeping the costs of the interpretive process within manageable bounds'.[20] Intentionalists 'commonly associate themselves with the first set of goals' and 'call upon courts to try to enforce the directives that members of the enacting legislature understood themselves to be adopting'.[21] By contrast, textualists 'commonly associate themselves with the second' and 'suggest that interpretation should focus "upon what the text would reasonably be understood to mean, rather than upon what it was intended to mean"'.[22] Nelson argues that while '[s]tandard formulations of the distinction' between these theories focus on a putative difference in their goals, close examination of recent Supreme Court cases indicates that 'prevalent styles of judging do not really track these categories.'[23] Although Nelson does not deny that differences exist between the two theories, he nevertheless insists that each of them 'give[s] every indication of caring *both* about the meaning intended by the enacting legislature *and* about the need for readers to have fair notice of that meaning, as well as about some additional policy-oriented goals'.[24]

This characterization of the two theories has been emphatically rejected by Jonathan Siegel, who sees textualism as tending inexorably toward an 'unworkable' radicalization[25] as 'textualist doctrine work[s] itself pure'[26] through judge-made law. Siegel argues that the essence of textualism is the 'formalist axiom' that '[t]he text is the law, and it is the text that must be observed'.[27] More specifically, '[t]extualists believe that the constitutional process of enactment imbues statutory text with legal force, regardless of what any legislator *understood* or *intended* the text to mean'.[28] This view of statutory interpretation is deeply at odds with that of intentionalism, which sees statutory interpretation as serving to 'discern and implement the intent of the legislature'—a view that entails neither

---

[19] Siegel, 'The Inexorable Radicalization of Textualism' (cited in n.1) 118–19.
[20] Caleb Nelson, 'What Is Textualism?' (2005) 91 *Va L Rev* 347–418, 351.
[21] Nelson, 'What Is Textualism?' (cited in n.20) 351–52.
[22] Nelson, 'What Is Textualism?' (cited in n.20) 352.
[23] Nelson, 'What Is Textualism?' (cited in n.20) 352.
[24] Nelson, 'What Is Textualism?' (cited in n.20) 353.
[25] Siegel, 'The Inexorable Radicalization of Textualism' (cited in n.1) 178, 150.
[26] Siegel, 'The Inexorable Radicalization of Textualism' (cited in n.1) 150.
[27] Scalia, *A Matter of Interpretation* (cited in n.4) 22; quoted in Siegel, 'The Inexorable Radicalization of Textualism' (cited in n.1) 131.
[28] Siegel, 'The Inexorable Radicalization of Textualism' (cited in n.1) 123 (emphases in original).

'ignor[ing] statutory text' nor 'regard[ing] the text as simply being the law, independent of the intent behind it'.[29] Thus, 'the intentionalist regards legislative intent, not statutory text, as the ultimate determinant of the law'.[30] For Siegel, this must mean that the two theories are fundamentally irreconcilable.

Yet, Siegel's characterization has in turn been rejected by other scholars. Lawrence Solan, for example, points out that, notwithstanding textualist rhetoric, 'it is virtually impossible to be a true textualist on the ground.... [W]hen it comes to real cases, most judges will often enough subordinate their bent toward formalism in favor of what they believe to be a result more consistent with the legislative will, the purpose of the statute (whether they mention it or not), their own political beliefs, other public law values, or some combination of the above.'[31] We might take this stark difference of opinion between Siegel, on the one hand, and Nelson, Solan, and others, on the other, regarding the nature of textualism to reflect, at least in part, the gulf between what textualism promises and what it actually delivers—a gulf recognized by friends and foes of textualism alike—as well as a certain amount of sloganeering and overstatement, which is not obviously to be taken at face value.[32] It might be worth dwelling on these divergences between theory and practice, rhetoric and reality, since they can help to uncover substantial issues facing theories of legal interpretation.

As it happens, these divergences emerge very clearly in claims and counterclaims about key textualist assertions, including the principle that 'the text is the law', as just described; the rejection of both 'legislative intent' and legislative history in determining statutory meaning;[33] and the claim that the meaning of statutes is constituted in their 'original meaning'. What we find among these assertions are not only claims that most jurists, both textualists and non-textualists, would probably assent to but also those that are at odds with the statements and practices of textualists themselves, including Justice Scalia.

We have already noted Justice Scalia's assertion of the 'text is the law' principle. Despite the apparent centrality of this principle in textualist thinking, it is qualified even by many staunch textualists, who have recognized that the text itself must be understood in context. Justice Scalia himself concedes that it is 'not contrary to sound principles of interpretation' for a judge to qualify the 'text is the law' principle by 'giv[ing] the totality of context precedence over a single word'[34]—as he did in *Green v Bock Laundry Mach. Co.*[35] in acknowledging a 'scrivener's error' in a statute that referred to '"defendant" when "criminal defendant ma[de] sense.'[36] However, much broader qualifications of the principle have been offered—for example, by the textualist Judge Frank Easterbrook, who makes the following observations about 'plain meaning':[37]

An unadorned 'plain meaning' approach to interpretation supposes that words have meanings divorced from their contexts—linguistic, structural, functional, social, historical. Language is a

---

[29] Siegel, 'The Inexorable Radicalization of Textualism' (cited in n.1) 123.
[30] Siegel, 'The Inexorable Radicalization of Textualism' (cited in n.1) 123.
[31] Lawrence Solan, 'Opportunistic Textualism' 158 *U Pa L Rev* 225, 228.
[32] Elliott M Davis, 'The Newer Textualism: Justice Alito's Statutory Interpretation' (2006–7) 30 *Harv JL & Pub Pol'y* 983, 984.
[33] It is worth noting that the frequent appeal to legislative history in American courts distinguishes them from Commonwealth jurisdictions. In Canada, for example, as Hogg, 'The Charter of Rights and American Theories of Interpretation' (cited in n.13) 97 notes, '[l]egislative history, although...admissible, is to be used with great caution and given little weight'.
[34] Scalia, *A Matter of Interpretation* (cited in n.4) 20–21.
[35] 490 US 504 (1989).
[36] Scalia, *A Matter of Interpretation* (cited in n.4) 20.
[37] *In re Sinclair*, 870 F2d 1340, 1342 (7th Cir 1989) (Easterbrook, J) (internal citations omitted).

process of communication that works only when authors and readers share a set of rules and meanings. What 'clearly' means one thing to a reader unacquainted with the circumstances of the utterance—including social conventions prevailing at the time of drafting—may mean something else to a reader with a different background. Legislation speaks across the decades, during which legal institutions and linguistic conventions change. To decode words one must frequently reconstruct the legal and political culture of the drafters.

What these qualifications of the 'text is the law' principle suggest, then, is that the relationship between the actual 'words of the law' and the meaning that they are recognized to have in context is not a simple one.

Similar comments apply to the rejection by Justice Scalia and other textualists of the use of legislative history. Arguably, this rejection understates both the considerable acceptance among jurists of some limits on the use of legislative history and the difficulty of justifying a total ban. Consider Justice Scalia's assertion that legislative history 'should not be used as an authoritative indication of a statute's meaning',[38] and 'is much more likely to produce a false or contrived legislative intent than a genuine one'.[39] Despite his provocative tone, Justice Scalia's basic point is conceded by many commentators. For example, Laurence Tribe, certainly no textualist, agrees that 'when we ask what a *legal text* means ... we ought *not* to be inquiring (except perhaps very peripherally) into the ideas, intentions, or expectations subjectively held by whatever persons were, as a historical matter, involved in drafting, promulgating, or ratifying the text in question'.[40] And, as Caleb Nelson observes, in the past non-textualist judges may have seemed at times 'willing to enforce statements in committee reports without regard to whether they bore on the intended meaning of anything in the actual statutory text', but '[n]owadays ... it is hard to find anyone who advocates such untethered use of legislative history'.[41]

Granting widespread agreement on 'untethered' uses of legislative history, there seems little to recommend Justice Scalia's and others' blanket rejection of its use or the 'kitchen sink' arguments[42] for this rejection. As many commentators have noted, two basic weaknesses emerge in the textualist critique of the use of legislative history, both related to the idea that such materials serve as 'authoritative sources of statutory meaning'.[43] It is well established that these materials, in 'represent[ing] unenacted legislative intent', cannot be treated as authoritative 'without offending the bicameralism and presentment requirements prescribed by Article I, Section 7'.[44] But as Elliott Davis points out, this critique addresses only the use of 'legislative history as an *authoritative* source of congressional intent' rather than simply 'as a *persuasive* source of context';[45] and it has long been recognized even among textualists that '[l]egislative history may be invaluable in revealing the setting of the enactment and the assumptions its authors entertained about how their words would be understood'.[46] Moreover, '[a]ll modern textualists ... rely on extra-statutory sources to provide context' and none of them would claim that these are subject to the same constitutional requirements.[47] This is not to deny that doubts as

---

[38] Scalia, *A Matter of Interpretation* (cited in n.4) 29–30.
[39] Scalia, *A Matter of Interpretation* (cited in n.4) 32.
[40] Laurence H Tribe, 'Comment' in Scalia, *A Matter of Interpretation* (cited in n.4) 65 (emphases in original).
[41] Nelson, 'What Is Textualism?' (cited in n.20) 364.
[42] On these, see e.g. Nelson, 'What Is Textualism?' (cited in n.20) 362–8.
[43] John F Manning, 'Textualism as a Nondelegation Doctrine' (1997) 97 *Colum L Rev* 673, 696–7.
[44] Manning, 'Textualism as a Nondelegation Doctrine' (cited in n.43) 696–7.
[45] Davis, 'The Newer Textualism' (cited in n.32) 1001 (emphases in original).
[46] *In re Sinclair* (cited in n.37), quoted in Davis, 'The Newer Textualism' (cited in n.32) 997.
[47] Davis, 'The Newer Textualism' (cited in n.32) 1001.

to the ultimate utility of legislative history deserve to be taken seriously—as do claims like Vermeule's that 'fallible judges will do better by ignoring legislative history than by using it',[48] given that 'further increments of information, complexity, and flexibility produce definite costs for only speculative gains'.[49] However, even these 'operational' doubts about legislative history provide more justification for minimizing recourse to those forms of it that do not constitute 'credible sources for legislative rationale'[50] than for an outright ban on its use.

Similar remarks apply to the search for legislative intent, although this is a far more complex matter, as we shall see presently. On this matter, Justice Scalia asserts that '[i]t is the law that governs, not the intent of the lawgiver',[51] rejecting the idea that 'what the legislature intended, rather than what it said, is the object of our inquiry'[52] and quoting with approval Justice Oliver Wendell Holmes's dictum 'We do not inquire what the legislature meant; we ask only what the statute means.'[53] Justice Scalia asserts further that 'despite frequent statements to the contrary, we do not really look for subjective legislative intent', the intent that the legislature actually had in enacting a statute, but rather 'for a sort of "objectified" intent—the intent that a reasonable person would gather from the text of the law, placed alongside the remainder of the *corpus juris*'.[54] As Justice Scalia understands it, then, a court's search for 'the intent of the legislature' amounts to its making decisions 'not on the basis of what the legislature said, but on the basis of what it *meant*', with 'there [being] no necessary connection between the two';[55] and moreover 'being bound by genuine but unexpressed legislative intent rather than the law'.[56]

Despite the apparent cogency of this rejection of legislative intent, closer inspection suggests that it presents us with various false dichotomies. These include the implication that an inquiry into legislative intent must be contradistinguished from, rather than seen as consistent with, an inquiry into statutory meaning. Surely what gives purchase to the search for legislative intent is that such intent is seen to inform statutory meaning rather than substitute for it. These false dichotomies also include the implication that the search for legislative intent is a search for what the legislature meant but did not express, rather than for what it meant by what it *did* express—whether in the statute itself or in the documents understood to constitute legislative history. This false dichotomy suggests a third, namely, that between a search for 'subjective' legislative intent, which Justice Scalia takes to be illegitimate, and one for 'objectified' intent, which he supports. Examination of Justice Scalia's formulation of this dichotomy, as given above, reveals at least two reasons to see it as artificial. One is that it simply overstates the difference between these two kinds of intent, given how each is actually determined. As Nelson points out, even those who affirm the legitimacy of the search for subjective intent in fact 'seek only what someone who was drawing upon an artificially restricted information base—from which

---

[48] Vermeule, *Judging Under Uncertainty* (cited in n.5) 11.
[49] Vermeule, *Judging Under Uncertainty* (cited in n.5) 5.
[50] Hrafn Asgeirsson, 'On Restricting Appeal to Legislative Purpose in Hard Cases' (ms., University of Southern California, 2011) §3; for related discussion, see Boudreau et al., 'What Statutes Mean' (cited in n.2), on which Asgeirsson's analysis is based.
[51] Scalia, *A Matter of Interpretation* (cited in n.4) 17.
[52] Scalia, *A Matter of Interpretation* (cited in n.4) 16.
[53] Oliver Wendell Holmes, *Collected Legal Papers* (New York: Harcourt, Brace and Howe, 1920) 207; quoted in Scalia, *A Matter of Interpretation* (cited in n.4) 23.
[54] Scalia, *A Matter of Interpretation* (cited in n.4) 17.
[55] Scalia, *A Matter of Interpretation* (cited in n.4) 18.
[56] Scalia, *A Matter of Interpretation* (cited in n.4) 17.

information has been excluded for reasons other than unreliability—would *believe* to be the legislature's actual intent'.[57] Another reason is that Justice Scalia's formulation of 'objectified' legislative intent encompasses only what 'a reasonable person would gather' from a statute and the rest of the *corpus juris* but not from other materials—the latter of which a 'reasonable person' could likewise use to determine legislative intent but for Justice Scalia's rejection of them.

It is worth noting that the view underwriting the rejection of legislative intent— namely, that 'any "purpose" attributed to a statute may be a mere construct',[58] particularly given the multi-member composition of legislatures and individual legislators' divergent purposes—is far from unique to Justice Scalia and other textualists. Rather, it figures in various approaches to statutory interpretation, such as that of Ronald Dworkin's theory of 'law as integrity', which takes 'propositions of law [to be] true if they figure in or follow from the principles of justice, fairness, and due process that provide the best constructive interpretation of the community's legal practice';[59] and William Eskridge's theory of 'dynamic statutory interpretation', according to which a statute 'takes on new meaning in light of subsequent formal, social, and ideological development'.[60] On both of these theories, the legislative 'author' of a statute plays no explanatory role in the process of interpretation, which involves the construction of meaning by the interpreter. For Dworkin, statutory interpretation is 'constructive' rather than 'conversational', fundamentally concerned with the purposes 'not...of some author but of the interpreter'.[61] For Eskridge, 'statutory interpretation...involves interaction between interpreter and text that creates new and perhaps unexpected meaning over time'.[62]

Yet, many commentators have argued that recognition of a legislature's intent does not import the difficulties that these and other theories have attributed to it. Solan, for example, suggests that the parallel between legal and 'ordinary' language interpretation is a robust one, and cannot be easily dismissed. In particular, just as the latter involves both a hearer's 'striving to understand the intent of the speaker' and a speaker's 'effort to facilitate [a] hearer's efforts to understand [a] message',[63] so too can 'our laws...be no more than efforts at communication based on the intention of the drafters',[64] intent that we glean 'from both the words of a statute and the circumstances surrounding its enactment'.[65] And just as 'we routinely attribute beliefs and intentions to groups of people as if they were a single individual',[66] so too do judges make such attributions '[w]hen [they] attribute intent to the legislature as though it were a single individual with a mind of its own'.[67]

Moreover, as Richard Ekins argues, the doubts famously expressed by Dworkin about the intelligibility of such attributions rest on a reduction of 'what the *legislature* intended' to 'what the *legislators* intended',[68] with the former characterized as 'a compendious

---

[57] Nelson, 'What Is Textualism?' (cited in n.20) 360 (emphasis in original).
[58] Siegel, 'The Inexorable Radicalization of Textualism' (cited in n.1, above,) 126.
[59] Dworkin, *Law's Empire* (cited in n.4) 225.
[60] Eskridge, *Dynamic Statutory Interpretation* (cited in n.4) 11.
[61] Dworkin, *Law's Empire* (cited in n.4) 52.
[62] Eskridge, *Dynamic Statutory Interpretation* (cited in n.4) 62.
[63] Lawrence M Solan, *The Language of Statutes: Laws and Their Interpretation* (Chicago: University of Chicago Press, 2010) 87–8.
[64] Solan, *The Language of Statutes* (cited in n.63) 88.
[65] Solan, *The Language of Statutes* (cited in n.63) 95.
[66] Solan, *The Language of Statutes* (cited in n.63) 88.
[67] Solan, *The Language of Statutes* (cited in n.63) 98.
[68] Richard Ekins, 'Legislative Intent in *Law's Empire*' (2011) 24 *Ratio Juris* 435, 438 (emphases in original).

statement of the discrete intentions of particular actual people'.[69] For Dworkin, this can only be 'a theoretical construction',[70] given that 'institutions do not have minds'[71] and thus cannot have mental states. But this view of legislative intent overlooks the very plausible possibility that '[t]he legislature is a complex purposive group—an institution—that forms and acts on intentions...not reducible to the intentions of the members of the group (the individual legislators)'.[72] On this understanding, group intention, far from 'involv[ing] spooky group mental states', as Dworkin has claimed, is simply 'the plan of action that...members [of the group] adopt, and hold in common, to structure how they are to act in order to achieve some end'.[73] Accordingly, 'legislative intent arises only when the institution of the legislature acts'; and it is only the legislators, those with the 'authority to legislate...whose intentional action may constitute the act of lawmaking', not the private individuals, lobbyists, and various other persons who 'participate in the legislative process'.[74] And it is the intentions of both minority and majority legislators that 'are relevant because and to the extent that they interlock and enable the legislators to act jointly as the legislature'.[75]

Thus, as Solan points out, speaking of 'the intent of the legislature' does not entail a commitment to the claim 'that every legislator shares the intent that we attribute to the entity'.[76] In other words, each member of the legislature need not 'have the same reasons for supporting a bill, as long as there is general recognition that those who ushered the bill through the process did so with particular subplans that deserve to be honored.'[77] By the same token, investigation of intent cannot reasonably rely on 'stray remarks from individual legislators', which are not reflective of even the intent of the subgroup that guided a piece of legislation through the law-making process 'and are most often not probative of much of anything'.[78]

These considerations make it possible to reject the contention of some commentators 'that the complex bargaining necessary to the enactment of statutes may produce a statute that implements multiple, conflicting intentions'.[79] Such a contention can accordingly be attributed to a confusion between intention, 'the state that explains how and for what [one] act[s]' and 'what one hopes or expects to follow from, or to be caused by, one's act',[80] which we might refer to as 'motive', borrowing a term from criminal law.[81] Once we discount the latter understanding of 'legislative intent', other helpful distinctions fall into place. For example, Ekins distinguishes 'secondary (standing) intentions' and 'primary (particular) intentions', which are 'plans to form and adopt other plans' and 'plans that directly concern how the group is to act on this or that occasion', respectively. Similarly, Elliott Davis distinguishes what might be described as 'thick' and 'thin' notions of legislative intent, which are, respectively, 'the overarching intent of Congress'

---

[69] Dworkin, *Law's Empire* (cited in n.4) 315.
[70] Dworkin, *Law's Empire* (cited in n.4) 315.
[71] Dworkin, *Law's Empire* (cited in n.4) 336.
[72] Ekins, 'Legislative Intent in *Law's Empire*' (cited in n.68) 440.
[73] Ekins, 'Legislative Intent in *Law's Empire*' (cited in n.68) 440.
[74] Ekins, 'Legislative Intent in *Law's Empire*' (cited in n.68) 443.
[75] Ekins, 'Legislative Intent in *Law's Empire*' (cited in n.68) 444–5.
[76] Solan, *The Language of Statutes* (cited in n.63) 90.
[77] Solan, *The Language of Statutes* (cited in n.63) 96.
[78] Solan, *The Language of Statutes* (cited in n.63) 97.
[79] Siegel, 'The Inexorable Radicalization of Textualism' (cited in n.1) 175.
[80] Ekins, 'Legislative Intent in *Law's Empire*' (cited in n.68) 447.
[81] The distinction made in criminal law is one between 'intent' and 'motive', where the former refers to 'the exercise of a free will to use particular means to produce a particular result', while the latter refers to 'that which precedes and induces the exercise of the will' (*R. v Lewis* (1979) 47 CCC (2d) 24 (SCC) 33).

and 'what Congress meant by using [a particular] phrase'.[82] And commentators such as Andrei Marmor and Hrafn Asgeirsson, in seeking to determine the appropriate use of legislative history, have distinguished general and specific legislative aims.[83] Arguably, each of these distinctions is better described in terms of legislative intent than in terms of legislators' motives.

Clearing away various inapposite conflations and distinctions that inhabit discussions of legislative intent, we can finally see that the claims and counterclaims about this notion boil down to the following questions. These are (i) whether the goal of statutory interpretation is to determine what a statute means or what a legislature has meant in enacting the statute, and thus (ii) whether it is legislative intent that provides evidence of what a statute means or the statute that provides evidence of what the legislature meant. Inextricably linked to these two questions are (iii) whether it is plausible to appeal to legislative intent in determining statutory meaning, and if so, (iv) whether it is legitimate to do so; and (v) whether it is proper in interpreting a statute to depart from its plain meaning on the basis of the legislature's likely intent in enacting the statute.

At least the last question would seem to have a straightforward answer, given an observation by Solan and others. This is that an appeal to intent is crucial for a court to be able to decide 'that the legislature has made a mistake',[84] whether the mistake consists of a 'scrivener's error' or a provision that leads to an absurd result. This is because the mistake may emerge only through consideration of the likely intent of a provision, which may well be perfectly grammatical and capable of receiving a coherent interpretation. Solan points out that textualists such as John Manning have sought to reconstruct the 'absurd-results doctrine' in non-intentional terms,[85] appealing to the idea of a 'linguistic sub-community' that, in the context of a particular statute, would typically not use an expression in a particular way. Manning applies this non-intentional version of the doctrine to the famous case of *United States v Granderson*,[86] which involved a provision in the *United States Code* that required the court, on finding that a defendant had 'violate[d] a condition of probation', to 'revoke the sentence of probation and sentence the defendant to not less than one-third of the original sentence'.[87] This provision, if interpreted according to its 'plain meaning', would lead to the absurd result of a more lenient sentence arising from a violation of probation conditions. Solan argues that Manning's account of the absurd result here fails in not acknowledging that the expression 'one-third of the original sentence' in the statute cannot reasonably mean 'one-third of the original period of probation' simply because it is implausible to conclude that those in Congress responsible for drafting this language intended 'to reduce the sentences of probation violators'.[88] In other words, 'it is intent that makes a mistake a mistake'.[89]

The other questions just enumerated appear to be more difficult, engaging much weightier issues about the nature of legal interpretation. As Solan points out, '[i]f statutes have meaning on their own without inquiry into the intent of their makers, then decision makers need only read the statute to determine when it should apply. But if determining intent is a necessary element of interpretation, then statutory language can be no more

---

[82] Davis, 'The Newer Textualism' (cited in n.32) 995.
[83] See e.g. Andrei Marmor, *Interpretation and Legal Theory* (2nd edn, Oxford: Hart, 2005) 126–32; and Asgeirsson, 'On Restricting Appeal to Legislative Purpose in Hard Cases' (cited in n.50).
[84] Solan, *The Language of Statutes* (cited in n.63) 104.
[85] John F Manning, 'The Absurdity Doctrine' (2003) 116 *Harv L Rev* 2388.
[86] 511 US 39 (1994).
[87] 18 USC §3565 (1990).
[88] Solan, *The Language of Statutes* (cited in n.63) 105–6.
[89] Solan, *The Language of Statutes* (cited in n.63) 107.

than evidence of intent';[90] and '[t]he need to look beyond a statute's language...means that constitutional procedures for enacting laws are not enough to determine the rights and obligations of the citizenry in a significant set of circumstances'.[91] It is this difficulty with intent that 'the textualists recognized...long ago' and that has driven their desire 'to eliminate intent as part of the interpretive enterprise'.[92] Yet, as Solan observes, it is, as a matter of human cognition, 'almost impossible to avoid thinking in the intentionalist terms that [Justice Scalia] would outlaw'.[93] Solan's observation thus leaves us with a dilemma: can we recognize intent as integral to legal interpretation, just as it is recognized to be in human communication, or is such an understanding of legal interpretation fundamentally at odds with constitutional principles?

A final principle of textualism worth investigating is its assertion of the primacy of 'original meaning' and rejection of 'dynamic' approaches to statutory and constitutional interpretation. According to Justice Scalia, '[t]o be a textualist in good standing, one need not be too dull to perceive the broader social purposes that a statute is designed, or could be designed, to serve; or too hide-bound to realize that new times require new laws. One need only hold the belief that judges have no authority to pursue those broader purposes or to write those new laws'.[94] As with the other textualist principles discussed here, this one, in Justice Scalia's hands, takes on a blunt form that demands some qualification in the light of other considerations. Moreover, the principle itself appears to sit rather uncomfortably with the textualist rejection of legislative intent, as just described.

If we consider the arguments advanced in favour of originalism, perhaps one of the strongest is that offered by Steven Smith.[95] According to Smith, 'the statute is not just a collection of words, but rather the expression of a collective decision: a decision made by the established political authority and expressed in a form recognized as conferring legal force and validity upon the decision'.[96] Yet, 'dynamic' approaches to interpretation 'reject or resist a view which understands statutes primarily as the expression of particular decisions made by specific, temporally situated political officials'.[97] This means that on the latter view, 'be[ing] bound by the statute does *not* entail being bound by the actual human understanding or collective decision that brought the statute into being',[98] which 'effectively separates the statute from the source of its authority'.[99] Of course, this defence of originalism assigns far more prominence to the actual intent of particular political officials than Justice Scalia and other textualists seem willing to countenance. If, however, Smith's argument is a forceful one, it derives its force from its creation of a link between what the statute means and what the legislators who drafted it intended it to mean.

The foregoing considerations do, therefore, offer some support for originalism, albeit at the cost of some inconsistency with textualism's rejection of legislative intent. Despite this support, originalism encounters significant conceptual and empirical problems, particularly in the constitutional context. These are, of course, in addition to the dismal practical consequences of this principle—which, as Peter Hogg notes, include the

---

[90] Solan, *The Language of Statutes* (cited in n.63) 110.
[91] Solan, *The Language of Statutes* (cited in n.63) 111.
[92] Solan, *The Language of Statutes* (cited in n.63) 111.
[93] Solan, *The Language of Statutes* (cited in n.63) 104.
[94] Scalia, *A Matter of Interpretation* (cited in n.4) 23.
[95] Steven D Smith, 'Law Without Mind' (1989) 88 *Mich L Rev* 104.
[96] Smith, 'Law Without Mind' (cited in n.95) 111.
[97] Smith, 'Law Without Mind' (cited in n.95) 111.
[98] Smith, 'Law Without Mind' (cited in n.95) 111 (emphasis in original).
[99] Smith, 'Law Without Mind' (cited in n.95) 111.

impossibility of allowing 'the elimination of racial segregation [to] be administered by the courts because the group of men who framed the Fourteenth Amendment after the Civil War...did not contemplate its use for that purpose', something that does not 'fire the imagination'.[100] One key problem facing originalism, as Eskridge points out, is a straightforwardly empirical one: this is that no originalist theory 'accurately describes what American agencies and courts do when they interpret statutes'.[101] Another is the difficulty of squaring it with *stare decisis*, a doctrine that fosters the evolution of constitutional principles. That Justice Scalia accepts this doctrine as 'a pragmatic exception to' rather than a '*part* of' his textualism[102] does little to counter the fact that one of the most basic tools of judicial decision-making in the common law world is at odds with originalism.

Originalism is likewise at odds with the 'transtemporal' enactment of the American Constitution (among other constitutional documents).[103] As Laurence Tribe points out, 'much of the Constitution simply cannot be understood as a law enacted by a particular body of persons on a specific date but must instead be comprehended as law promulgated in the name of a "people" who span the generations'.[104] This emerges, for example, in the interpretation of the First Amendment: most of the cases related to the freedoms of speech, press, and religion captured in this amendment 'enforce those freedoms against the states and necessarily rest on the Fourteenth Amendment, ratified seventy-seven years later in 1868'.[105] This means that 'understandings or meanings frozen circa 1791 can[not] possibly serve as the definitive limits to these freedoms as enforced today, particularly against the states through a provision that became law in 1868'.[106] It is thus necessary to recognize that 'constitutional provisions sometimes acquire new meanings by the very process of formal amendment to other parts of the Constitution'—and that 'what we understand as "the Constitution" speaks across the generations, projecting a set of messages undergoing episodic revisions that reverberate backward as well as forward in time'.[107]

This 'transtemporality' of the American Constitution poses a second challenge to an originalist understanding of meaning, related to originalism's view of meaning as 'frozen' at the time of enactment. This challenge has been described by Hogg as follows:[108]

> The originalist's assumption is that the framers had clear views about the meaning of the words they were adopting and intended that these meanings should be forever conclusive. However, it is at least equally plausible to attribute a quite different 'interpretive intent' to the framers. They undoubtedly intended their handiwork to last for a long time. They knew that there would be great changes in society in the succeeding decades and centuries. They knew that amendment would be difficult. It is at least possible, therefore, that the framers did not desire that their text be frozen in the sense that it bore at its origin; that they were content to leave the detailed application of the constitution to the courts of the future; and that they were content that the process of adjudication would apply the text in ways that could not be anticipated at the time of the drafting. In other

---

[100] Hogg, 'The Charter of Rights and American Theories of Interpretation' (cited in n.13) 95.
[101] Eskridge, *Dynamic Statutory Interpretation* (cited in n.4) 13.
[102] Scalia, *A Matter of Interpretation* (cited in n.4) 82.
[103] Tribe, in Scalia, *A Matter of Interpretation* (cited in n.4) 83.
[104] Tribe, in Scalia, *A Matter of Interpretation* (cited in n.4) 84; these remarks echo those of Jed Rubenfeld, 'Reading the Constitution as Spoken' (1995) 104 *Yale LJ* 1119, 1178–9.
[105] Tribe, in Scalia, *A Matter of Interpretation* (cited in n.4) 84.
[106] Tribe, in Scalia, *A Matter of Interpretation* (cited in n.4) 85–6.
[107] Tribe, in Scalia, *A Matter of Interpretation* (cited in n.4) 87.
[108] Hogg, 'The Charter of Rights and American Theories of Interpretation' (cited in n.13) 96.

words, the principle of 'progressive interpretation' is not necessarily antagonistic to the 'original understanding' or the intention of the framers.

While Hogg's understanding of 'original intent' is a compelling one, the alternative that he offers to a reliance on 'frozen meaning' is rather less compelling. What Hogg proposes is to have 'the words of the text ... given a meaning that seems natural to contemporary eyes, not a meaning that has been distilled from historical records extrinsic to the actual text'.[109] Unfortunately, it is not at all clear how such an approach would work. If taken at face value, it would involve simply imposing modern meanings on the words of a legal text, ignoring both how the author of the text actually used these words and what he or she intended to communicate with them. To see the difficulties that arise in doing so, consider these lines from Shakespeare's Sonnet LIII:

> Describe Adonis, and the counterfeit
> Is poorly imitated after you;
> On Helen's cheek all art of beauty set,
> And you in Grecian tires are painted new

Surely we would not try to interpret these lines by, for example, taking the words 'counterfeit' and 'tires' to have their modern meanings. Rather, we would seek out meanings for these words 'distilled from historical records extrinsic to the actual text', contrary to Hogg's suggestion, engaging precisely in what Alexander Aleinikoff refers to dismissively as 'archaeology'.[110] (Of course, the insight here—namely, that language has a 'propensity ... to change', so that 'understanding past speech recorded in texts requires a "historical" dictionary'[111]—is a commonplace in literary scholarship.) It seems, then, that the 'updating' of an older legal text must involve a process far more complex than commentators such as Hogg and Aleinikoff acknowledge, which somehow traces even a text's 'updated' meaning to the meaning that its author intended to convey. What we might therefore conclude from the foregoing discussion is that originalism, though hobbled by serious conceptual and empirical problems, nevertheless points to a role in statutory interpretation of both authorial intention and the original meaning of statutory texts that is greater than many commentators have recognized.

Consideration of this and the other debates about legal interpretation described earlier thus leaves us with a host of open questions. One is whether the divergences between textualist and non-textualist approaches to legal interpretation reflect fundamentally different options for legal interpretation or more of a 'blind men and the elephant' situation—that is, different perspectives or emphases on the same process. If the latter, then we have essentially the difficulty that H L A Hart described, where these different approaches 'throw a light which makes us see much in law that lay hidden; but the light is so bright that it blinds us to the remainder and so leaves us still without a clear view of the whole'.[112]

This question can be seen to encompass many others. Among them are whether the 'text is the law' principle reflects a cognitively realistic account of legal interpretation or is more of a slogan; whether appealing to legislative intent or taking a statute as evidence of this intent is illegitimate or inevitable, either in theory or in practice; whether an outright ban on the use of legislative history represents a plausible or implausible restriction on evidence; and finally whether granting an explanatory role to original meaning or

---

[109] Hogg, 'The Charter of Rights and American Theories of Interpretation' (cited in n.13) 101–2.
[110] T Alexander Aleinikoff, 'Updating Statutory Interpretation' (1988) 87 *Mich LR* 20, 23.
[111] Sanford Levinson, 'Law as Literature' 60 *Tex L Rev* 373, 376.
[112] H L A Hart, *The Concept of Law* (2nd edn, Oxford: Oxford University Press, 1994) 2.

original intent is ultimately compatible with a 'dynamic' approach to legal interpretation or commits one to a 'frozen meaning' conception of interpretation.

What I shall be suggesting is that satisfying answers to these questions require appeal to a cognitively realistic understanding of what interpreters do when they interpret legal texts. Such an understanding will allow us to determine whether the various claims about legal interpretation that they reflect can be seen as cognitively, and not just legally, plausible; and can thus truly underwrite a theory of legal interpretation built 'from the ground up'. I lay out the basic tools to achieve such an understanding of legal interpretation in the next section.

2. Relevance Theory and some characteristics of interpretation

As already noted, the key problem that this study seeks to address is the absence in legal theorizing of an empirically grounded framework in which to understand, and to assess various contentious claims about, the actual process of legal interpretation. Intuitively speaking, it is clear,[113] as Solan notes, that '[w]hen I say something to you, I expect that you will understand it more or less as I would if you said it to me. Similarly, when you say something to me, I expect that you intended to express more or less what I understood you to have said.... When we communicate, all we have are intentions and some confidence that our language faculties are more or less the same.'[114] However, we can give considerable flesh to these bones by making use of a detailed cognitive-scientific theory of communication to do so. In this section, I shall suggest that Relevance Theory, a framework first developed by Dan Sperber and Deirdre Wilson, provides the basis for such a theory, and shall demonstrate this by spelling out the basic features of this framework and applying them to the problems of legal interpretation sketched in section 1. Along the way I shall also introduce some useful vocabulary that, while not specific to Relevance Theory, can help to clarify some of the issues raised in this study.

Relevance Theory in a nutshell

Relevance Theory is 'a framework for the study of cognition, proposed primarily in order to provide a psychologically realistic account of communication'.[115] It takes utterance interpretation to be a cognitive process, and thus amenable to explanation in cognitive psychological terms.[116] It can accordingly be seen as a contribution to cognitive science, the scientific study of the mind, in having 'testable consequences' and being 'open to confirmation, disconfirmation or fine-tuning in the light of experimental evidence', even if 'its most general claims can be tested only indirectly'.[117]

Relevance Theory's point of departure is the claim, deriving from the work of H Paul Grice, 'that an essential feature of most human communication, both verbal and

---

[113] At least if we admit some important exceptions, such as our expectations when communicating with children or non-native speakers. Thanks to Nicholas Allott for reminding me of these complications.
[114] *The Language of Statutes* (cited in n.63) 111.
[115] Nicholas Allott, 'Relevance Theory' in Alessandro Capone, Franco Lo Piparo, and Marco Carapezza (eds), *Perspectives on Pragmatics and Philosophy* (Berlin/New York: Springer, forthcoming).
[116] Deirdre Wilson and Dan Sperber, 'Relevance Theory' in Laurence R Horn and Gregory Ward (eds), *The Handbook of Pragmatics* (Malden, Mass.: Blackwell, 2004) 607, 625.
[117] Wilson and Sperber, 'Relevance Theory' (cited in n.116) 625.

non-verbal, is the expression and recognition of intentions'.[118] In other words, '[w]e are all speakers and hearers. As speakers, we intend our hearers to recognise our intentions to inform them of some state of affairs. As hearers, we try to recognise what it is that the speaker intends to inform us of. Hearers are interested in the meaning of the sentence uttered only insofar as it provides evidence about what the speaker means. Communication is successful not when hearers recognise the linguistic meaning of the utterance, but when they infer the speaker's "meaning" from it'.[119]

What this analysis reflects, then, in taking 'the expression and recognition of intentions' as basic, is a view of comprehension as involving 'the ability to attribute mental states to others in order to explain and predict behavior',[120] an ability recognized as 'a characteristic feature of human cognition and interaction. Humans typically conceptualise human and animal behaviour, not in terms of its physical features, but in terms of its underlying intentions'.[121] We might get a clearer picture of this kind of attribution, which the philosopher Daniel Dennett calls the 'intentional stance', from his description of it: 'first you decide to treat the object whose behavior is to be predicted as a rational agent; then you figure out what beliefs that agent ought to have, given its place in the world and its purpose. Then you figure out what desires it ought to have, on the same considerations, and finally you predict that this rational agent will act to further its goals in the light of its beliefs'.[122] On this (Gricean) understanding of communication, 'sentence meaning is a vehicle for conveying a speaker's meaning, where a speaker's meaning is an overtly expressed intention that is fulfilled by being recognized'.[123]

Significantly, however, Relevance Theory moves beyond Grice's view of communication in its explicit consideration of an addressee's attention to a speaker's meaning. That is, on a Relevance Theory view, communication crucially requires a speaker first to capture and then to hold the addressee's attention. 'If attention tends automatically to go to what is most relevant at the time, then the success of communication depends on the addressee taking the utterance to be relevant enough to be worthy of his or her attention. Thus, a speaker, by the very act of communicating, indicates that the addressee is intended to see the utterance as relevant enough to be worth processing.'[124]

Such claims about communication represent an alternative to the 'classical code model', according to which 'a communicator encodes her intended message into a signal, which is decoded by the audience using an identical copy of the code'.[125] On Relevance Theory's 'inferential model', by contrast, 'a communicator provides evidence of her intention to convey a certain meaning, which is inferred by the audience on the basis of the evidence provided'.[126] While verbal comprehension certainly 'involves an element of decoding', given that '[a]n utterance is...a linguistically coded piece of evidence', 'the linguistic meaning recovered by decoding is just one of the inputs' to an

---

[118] Wilson and Sperber, 'Relevance Theory' (cited in n.116) 607.
[119] Dan Sperber and Deirdre Wilson, *Relevance: Communication and Cognition* (Cambridge, Mass.: Harvard University Press, 1986) 23. Note that while I use various terms—communicator, author and speaker, interpreter and hearer—to denote the participants in particular forms of communication, I use the more technical terms 'speaker's meaning' and 'sentence meaning' regardless of the kind of communication.
[120] Wilson and Sperber, 'Relevance Theory' (cited in n.116) 623.
[121] Sperber and Wilson, *Relevance: Communication and Cognition* (cited in n.119) 23–4.
[122] Daniel C Dennett, *The Intentional Stance* (Cambridge, Mass.: MIT Press, 1987) 17.
[123] Deirdre Wilson, 'Relevance Theory', *Routledge Pragmatics Encyclopedia* (London: Routledge, 2009) 393 (emphasis omitted).
[124] Wilson, 'Relevance Theory' (cited in n.123) 396.
[125] Wilson and Sperber, 'Relevance Theory' (cited in n.116) 607.
[126] Wilson and Sperber, 'Relevance Theory' (cited in n.116) 607.

inference process that 'yields an interpretation of the speaker's meaning'.[127] Accordingly, the theory 'makes a fundamental distinction between two types of processes: the decoding process of the language system and the pragmatic inferential process'.[128]

Relevance Theory's central claim, again drawing on Grice, is that a speaker's utterance creates expectations in a hearer of this utterance's relevance to him or her—an expectation that the theory takes as basic to human cognition.[129] Moreover, such expectations 'are precise and predictable enough to guide the hearer toward the speaker's meaning'.[130] The goal of the theory, then, is 'to explain in cognitively realistic terms what these expectations of relevance amount to, and how they might contribute to an empirically plausible account of comprehension'.[131]

The theory offers a technical definition of 'relevance' intended to capture the intuition that utterances and other inputs are relevant to individuals when they can be related to available background information 'to yield conclusions that matter to [them]'.[132] The idea is that 'an input is relevant to an individual when its processing in a context of available assumptions yields a POSITIVE COGNITIVE EFFECT', understood as 'a worthwhile difference to the individual's representation of the world'.[133] The most important of such effects is what is called a 'contextual implication', which is 'a conclusion deducible from the input and the context together, but from neither input nor context alone'.[134] Background information, or 'background assumptions',[135] in John Searle's terms, is the dense network of assumptions that each of us has about the social and natural world around us, related to 'how things are' and to 'how to do things'[136]—including assumptions generally so basic to our conception of the world that it would never occur to us to make them explicit. The notion of 'context' as understood here encompasses these and many other assumptions. As Sperber and Wilson describe it, 'context' is '[t]he set of premises used in interpreting an utterance', which constitute 'a subset of the hearer's assumptions about the world'.[137] This set of premises includes not only 'information about the immediate physical environment or the immediately preceding utterances', but also 'expectations about the future, scientific hypotheses or religious beliefs, anecdotal memories, general cultural assumptions, [and] beliefs about the mental state of the speaker', which 'may all play a role in interpretation'.[138]

Significantly, the 'relevance' of an input is 'a matter of degree', involving a trade-off between cognitive effects and processing effort. In other words, an input will be worth attending to because 'it is *more* relevant than any alternative input available to us at that time', so that 'other things being equal, the greater the positive cognitive effects achieved

---

[127] Wilson and Sperber, 'Relevance Theory' (cited in n.116) 607.

[128] Robyn Carston, 'Explicature and Pragmatics' in Steven Davis and Brendan S Gillon (eds), *Semantics: A Reader* (New York: Oxford University Press, 2004) 817, 820.

[129] This claim echoes Daniel Dennett's point in *The Intentional Stance* (cited in n.122) 18 that 'what we come to know, normally, are only all the *relevant* truths our sensory histories avail us. I do not typically come to know the ratio of spectacle-wearing people to trousered people in a room I inhabit, though if this interested me, it would be readily learnable... [M]any perfectly detectable, graspable, memorable facts are of no interest to me and hence do not come to be believed by me.'

[130] Wilson and Sperber, 'Relevance Theory' (cited in n.116) 607.

[131] Wilson and Sperber, 'Relevance Theory' (cited in n.116) 608.

[132] Wilson and Sperber, 'Relevance Theory' (cited in n.116) 608.

[133] Wilson and Sperber, 'Relevance Theory' (cited in n.116) 608.

[134] Wilson and Sperber, 'Relevance Theory' (cited in n.116) 608.

[135] John Searle, 'The Background' in *Intentionality: An Essay in the Philosophy of Mind* (Cambridge/New York: Cambridge University Press, 1983) 141.

[136] Searle, 'The Background' (cited in n.135) 144.

[137] Sperber and Wilson, *Relevance: Communication and Cognition* (cited in n.119) 15.

[138] Sperber and Wilson, *Relevance: Communication and Cognition* (cited in n.119) 15–16.

by processing an input, the greater its relevance will be'.[139] Contrariwise, 'the greater the effort of perception, memory and inference required, the less rewarding the input will be to process, and hence the less deserving of our attention', so that 'other things being equal, the greater the PROCESSING EFFORT required, the less relevant the input will be'.[140] The idea, then, is that 'humans... have an automatic tendency to maximize relevance' given 'the way our cognitive systems have evolved.'[141]

Relevance Theory takes the concept of 'relevance', then, to be central to the process of communication. However, this concept reflects only one side—namely, the hearer's side—of the communicative exchange. Another key part of this picture of communication reflects the speaker's side of the exchange. This is what Relevance Theory calls 'ostensive-inferential communication', which 'involves an extra layer of intention', consisting of two distinct kinds of intention.[142] These are the 'informative intention', which is '[t]he intention to inform an audience of something'; and the 'communicative intention', or '[t]he intention to inform the audience of one's informative intention'[143] On this picture of communication, '[u]nderstanding is achieved when the communicative intention is fulfilled—that is, when the audience recognises the informative intention'.[144]

What will turn out to be significant for our purposes is that 'ostensive-inferential communication' exploits 'an ostensive stimulus'—that is, a stimulus 'designed to attract an audience's attention and focus it on the communicator's meaning' and the use of which, by hypothesis, 'may create precise and predictable expectations of relevance not raised by other stimuli'.[145] Since 'an audience will only pay attention to an input that seems relevant enough', the communicator's production of an ostensive stimulus 'encourages her audience to presume that it is relevant enough to be worth processing'.[146] This presumption is the basis of another key principle in Relevance Theory, that '[e]very ostensive stimulus conveys a presumption of its own optimal relevance'.[147] Like the concept of 'relevance' itself, the presumption of 'optimal relevance' to an audience also involves a trade-off between 'effort and effect': an audience 'is entitled to expect' that an ostensive stimulus 'is relevant enough to be worth the audience's processing effort' and that '[i]t is the most relevant one compatible with [the] communicator's abilities and preferences'.[148] Note that the qualification regarding communicators' 'abilities and preferences' is meant to acknowledge certain limits on communicators' contributions. In particular, communicators may have 'relevant information that they are unable or unwilling to provide'; and may in principle be able to produce 'ostensive stimuli that would convey their intentions more economically, but that they are unwilling to produce, or unable to think of at the time.'[149]

---

[139] Wilson and Sperber, 'Relevance Theory' (cited in n.116) 609 (emphasis in original).
[140] Wilson and Sperber, 'Relevance Theory' (cited in n.116) 609.
[141] Wilson and Sperber, 'Relevance Theory' (cited in n.116) 610.
[142] Wilson and Sperber, 'Relevance Theory' (cited in n.116) 610.
[143] Wilson and Sperber, 'Relevance Theory' (cited in n.116) 611. This distinction between kinds of intention is based on one found in Grice's notion of 'speaker's meaning'. For some discussion of this notion in the context of Relevance Theory, see e.g. Wilson and Sperber, 'Relevance Theory' (cited in n.116) 53–54; and Allott, 'Relevance Theory' (cited in n.115) §3.1.
[144] Wilson and Sperber, 'Relevance Theory' (cited in n.116) 611.
[145] Wilson and Sperber, 'Relevance Theory' (cited in n.116) 611.
[146] Wilson and Sperber, 'Relevance Theory' (cited in n.116) 611.
[147] Wilson and Sperber, 'Relevance Theory' (cited in n.116) 612.
[148] Wilson and Sperber, 'Relevance Theory' (cited in n.116) 612.
[149] Wilson and Sperber, 'Relevance Theory' (cited in n.116) 612.

The principle that ostensive stimuli convey a presumption of their own 'optimal relevance' and the presumption of 'optimal relevance' itself 'ground [a] practical heuristic for inferring the speaker's meaning.'[150] This involves hearers following a 'least effort' principle in inferring this meaning, and 'stop[ping] when [their] expectations of relevance are satisfied (or abandoned)'.[151] As Wilson and Sperber explain, it is reasonable for hearers to follow such a principle, given their expectation that speakers will 'make [their utterances] as easy as possible to understand'; and for them 'to stop at the first interpretation that satisfies [their] expectations of relevance, because there should never be more than one'.[152] Moreover, '[a]n utterance is most likely to be understood when it simplifies the hearer's task by demanding as little effort from him or her as possible, and encourages the hearer to pay it due attention by offering him or her as much effect as possible. It is therefore manifestly in the speaker's interest for the addressee to expect not merely relevance enough, but as much relevance as is compatible with the speaker's abilities and preferences'.[153] Thus, when a hearer arrives at such an interpretation, it is, 'in the absence of contrary evidence... the most plausible hypothesis about the speaker's meaning', even though it 'may well be false' given the 'least effort' principle that the hearer has followed.[154]

This general heuristic can also be seen to underlie the various sub-tasks of which the hearer's overall comprehension task consists. One such sub-task involves forming a hypothesis about an utterance's 'explicit content'. This includes a process of linguistic 'decoding' that results in the recovery of the 'logical form' of an utterance, which may be thought of as its conceptual representation or skeletal meaning. It is the fact that utterances encode such logical forms, which the speaker 'has manifestly chosen to provide as input to the hearer's inferential comprehension process', that ultimately allows the hearer 'to recognise the speaker's informative intention'.[155]

It should be noted, however, that the linguistic expression that the hearer decodes into a 'logical form' 'need only provide the addressee with skeletal evidence of the speaker's intended meaning'.[156] The sub-task of deriving explicit content also includes such inferential processes as the disambiguation of ambiguous expressions, the fixing of the reference of context-dependent expressions, and other processes that serve to 'enrich' logical forms. A second sub-task involves forming a hypothesis about 'contextual premises', the assumptions that the speaker has intended the hearer to infer from the context. A final sub-task involves forming a hypothesis about 'contextual implications',[157] which 'follow logically from the [explicit content] of the utterance and the context".[158] To see the process of deriving explicit content from a 'logical form', consider an utterance by Peter of 'I'll get it ready in time', used to express the content 'Peter will get the car ready for the trip to the seaside in time to set off early enough to get there by noon.' The kinds of 'fleshing out' of the 'logical form' involved in this example include inferring that the pronouns 'I' and 'it' refer respectively to Peter and the car, and enriching 'ready' to yield

---

[150] Wilson, 'Relevance Theory' (cited in n.123) 396 (emphasis omitted).
[151] Wilson and Sperber, 'Relevance Theory' (cited in n.116) 613.
[152] Wilson and Sperber, 'Relevance Theory' (cited in n.116) 613–14.
[153] Wilson, 'Relevance Theory' (cited in n.123) 396.
[154] Wilson and Sperber, 'Relevance Theory' (cited in n.116) 614.
[155] Wilson and Sperber, 'Relevance Theory' (cited in n.116) 614.
[156] Robyn Carston, 'Relevance Theory and the Saying/Implicating Distinction' in Laurence R Horn and Gregory Ward (eds), *Handbook of Pragmatics* (Malden, Mass.: Blackwell, 2004) 633, 643.
[157] Wilson and Sperber, 'Relevance Theory' (cited in n.116) 615.
[158] Wilson and Sperber, 'Relevance Theory' (cited in n.116) 617.

'ready for the trip to the seaside' and 'in time' to yield 'in time to set off early enough to get there by noon'.[159]

This example also serves to highlight certain key aspects of Relevance Theory's conception of these sub-tasks. One is that 'the explicitly communicated content of an utterance goes well beyond what is linguistically encoded', even if 'the decoded logical form of an utterance is an important clue to the speaker's intentions'.[160] In other words, 'a speaker's meaning cannot be simply perceived or decoded, but has to be inferred from his or her behaviour, together with background information'.[161] A second, closely related, point is that the process of recovering explicit content is as inferential, and as much guided by the Communicative Principle of Relevance, as the process of recovering implicit content. This is notwithstanding a view, common in the pragmatics literature (and also reflected in much legal theorizing), that a significant asymmetry exists between these two processes as regards the role of inference[162] and the admitted role of decoding, an automatic, non-inferential process, in the recovery of explicit content. A final point (taken up in section 3) concerns the processes of 'narrowing' and 'broadening', whereby the use of an expression in a particular context serves to describe a more specific and a more general concept, respectively, than that linguistically encoded by this expression.[163] Relevance Theory invokes these processes to explain the way in which content words such as nouns, verbs, and adjectives, even when 'linguistically unambiguous, may communicate a range of distinct (though related) meanings in different contexts'.[164] Thus, a 'narrowing' of lexically encoded meaning is, by hypothesis, the source of the range of interpretations that we find, for example, with the verb 'open', whose meaning in 'Pat opened the curtains' is rather different from its meaning in 'Bill opened his mouth'.[165] Similarly, a 'broadening' of meaning is taken to be the source of the different meanings of, for example, the adjective 'flat' in sentences like 'The back garden is flat' and 'He had a flat face and sad eyes', where these meanings reflect different 'departure[s] from true flatness' according to context.[166]

Significantly, Relevance Theory treats 'narrowing' and 'broadening' as kinds of pragmatic enrichment processes involving the same search for relevance as other sub-tasks that help to derive the speaker's meaning.[167] Moreover, such processes are implicated in 'fine-tun[ing] the interpretation of virtually every word' in an utterance.[168] As we shall see, these concepts of 'narrowing' and 'broadening' can play an important role in making sense of debates about the proper meaning of terms in statutes and other legal texts.

---

[159] Allott, 'Relevance Theory' (cited in n.115) §3.5.
[160] Wilson and Sperber, 'Relevance Theory' (cited in n.116) 614–15.
[161] Wilson, 'Relevance Theory' (cited in n.123) 393.
[162] Wilson and Sperber, 'Relevance Theory' (cited in n.116) 615.
[163] Robyn Carston and George Powell, 'Relevance Theory—New Directions and Developments' (2005) 17 *UCL Working Papers in Linguistics* 279, 283.
[164] Carston and Powell, 'Relevance Theory—New Directions and Developments' (cited in n.163) 181–2.
[165] Carston and Powell, 'Relevance Theory—New Directions and Developments' (cited in n.163) 182 (emphasis omitted).
[166] Carston and Powell, 'Relevance Theory—New Directions and Developments' (cited in n.163) 182 (emphasis omitted).
[167] Wilson and Sperber, 'Relevance Theory' (cited in n.116) 617.
[168] Carston and Powell, 'Relevance Theory—New Directions and Developments' (cited in n.163) 183.

A further refinement: 'activity types'

A further direction in which to take the Relevance Theory account of communication described in the previous subsection—and to allow it to capture Vermeule's insight about the institutional character of legal interpretation—is to extend it to encompass what are sometimes referred to as 'institutional speech acts'. Although proponents of Relevance Theory have sometimes seen the analysis of such speech acts as falling outside the study of verbal communication proper,[169] it seems straightforward to incorporate them into a Relevance Theory account by taking them to be part of the 'higher-level' content of an utterance, which embeds the utterance's 'basic-level' content. This is similar to the Relevance Theory analysis of, for example, an utterance of 'I never paid enough attention to my teachers' that is intended to express regret. The 'higher-level' content communicated by this utterance would be 'John regrets that he never paid enough attention to his teachers.' In a similar fashion, an 'institutional speech act' such as bidding two no trumps during a bridge game would communicate the higher-level content 'the speaker bids two no trumps as a turn in a bridge game'.

One way in which the idea of 'institutional speech acts' has been cashed out is in terms of what Stephen Levinson calls an 'activity type'. Levinson defines this as a 'category whose focal members are goal-defined, socially constituted, bounded events with constraints on participants, setting, and so on, but above all on the kind of allowable contributions'.[170] 'Paradigm examples' of these include 'teaching, a job interview, a jural interrogation, a football game, a task in a workshop, a dinner party and so on'.[171] (These would also include the 'institutional speech act' given above.) The intuition behind the identification of such 'activity types' is that 'having a grasp of the meaning of utterances... involves knowing the nature of the activity in which the utterances play a role'.[172] Moreover, 'the knowledge required to make the appropriate inferences' for such activity types 'seems to be a distinct and further kind of structural expectation that lies behind inference in discourse'—in other words, one that 'is much more specific'[173] than that described earlier in terms of Relevance Theory. Levinson's claim is that it is the structure of particular activities themselves that drives the kinds of inferences appropriate to them, which are accordingly 'activity-specific'.[174] That is, 'there are strict constraints on contributions to any particular activity', which create 'corresponding strong expectations about the functions that an utterance at a certain point in the proceedings can be fulfilling'.[175] Thus, understanding the meaning of the verbal exchanges that figure in a given activity 'rests on our knowledge of the kind of activity'[176] that is involved—a perspective that also highlights the fact that talk of 'ordinary' communication often obscures significant differences between kinds of daily communication. Moreover, in many cases—such as that of a cross-examination, which Levinson analyses in some detail—the understanding of verbal exchanges also involves 'reference to the underlying strategies or plans employed

---

[169] On this, see e.g. Sperber and Wilson, *Relevance: Communication and Cognition* (cited in n.119), 244–5; Mikhail Kissine, 'Illocutionary Forces and What Is Said' (2009) 24 *Mind & Language* 122, 123.
[170] Levinson, 'Activity Types and Language' (cited in n.11) 368 (emphasis omitted).
[171] Levinson, 'Activity Types and Language' (cited in n.11) 368.
[172] Levinson, 'Activity Types and Language' (cited in n.11) 365.
[173] Levinson, 'Activity Types and Language' (cited in n.11) 373.
[174] Levinson, 'Activity Types and Language' (cited in n.11) 393 (emphasis omitted).
[175] Levinson, 'Activity Types and Language' (cited in n.11) 377.
[176] Levinson, 'Activity Types and Language' (cited in n.11) 382.

by both parties, which in turn are derived from the nature of the activity and the goals that it assigns the various participants'.[177]

What attention to 'activity types' ultimately suggests, then, is that '[a] very good idea of the kind of language usage likely to be found within a given activity can...be predicted simply by knowing what the main function of the activity is seen to be by participants'.[178] This idea that the goals of a given activity shape language usage—and thus the way that this language is understood during the course of this activity—has clear relevance to legal interpretation, as we shall see.

Implications for legal interpretation

Relevance Theory, as just described, offers a detailed and empirically grounded picture of verbal communication—and, equally important, one that supports a plausible understanding of legal interpretation as a variety of such communication. In particular, it spells out the basic components of any kind of verbal communication and provides some analytical tools to investigate legal interpretation in these terms.

One consequence of such a perspective is that legal interpretation, like other varieties of verbal communication, emerges as having an irreducibly triadic character, encompassing an author, the legislature; an interpreter, the judiciary; and an 'ostensive stimulus', the text that the author has produced. This is, of course, notwithstanding the rejection of this characterization by textualist and other theories of interpretation, as noted in section 1. Recall that Justice Scalia claims that '[w]e look for a sort of "objectified" intent—the intent that a reasonable person would gather from the text of the law';[179] and that Dworkin and Eskridge both see legal interpretation as essentially involving the judicial interpreter's construction of meaning through creative engagement with the statutory text, with the legislative 'author' having no privileged role in this process. For Dworkin, in particular, legal interpretation is 'constructive' rather than 'conversational'; in other words, it is unlike ordinary communication, 'in which the interpreter aims to discover the intentions or meanings of another person'.[180] Recall too, though, that Ekins has raised substantial doubts about the cogency of Dworkin's rejection of the role of a legislative 'author' and authorial intent in legal interpretation, which in turn casts doubt on Dworkin's conception of legal interpretation as 'constructive' and not 'conversational'. Among the significant difficulties that this conception faces is that it offers no plausible account of 'what the legislature or legislators do'.[181] That is, on Dworkin's account, the legislature appears to be 'incapable of decision or communication', and 'just enacts a text, which will be found to mean whatever the judge decides it should mean'.[182] Yet, this would mean that 'legislators do not act to make law, but instead just provide new interpretive material'.[183] A Relevance Theory understanding of communication suggests another reason to doubt the plausibility of conceptions of legal interpretation that deny a role for a legislative 'author': this is their failure to recognize both the gap between 'sentence meaning' and 'communicated meaning' and the recovery of 'speaker's meaning' as a key component of such interpretation. (Admittedly, the legal domain presents a far

---

[177] Levinson, 'Activity Types and Language' (cited in n.11) 383.
[178] Levinson, 'Activity Types and Language' (cited in n.11) 394.
[179] Scalia, *A Matter of Interpretation* (cited in n.4) 17.
[180] Dworkin, *Law's Empire* (cited in n.4) 54–5.
[181] Ekins, 'Legislative Intent in *Law's Empire*' (cited in n.68) 454.
[182] Ekins, 'Legislative Intent in *Law's Empire*' (cited in n.68) 456.
[183] Ekins, 'Legislative Intent in *Law's Empire*' (cited in n.68) 456.

more complex picture here than 'ordinary' verbal communication does; we shall return to this matter in section 3.)

What also emerges from a Relevance Theory perspective on legal interpretation is a view of the author as having an intention to communicate through the vehicle of his or her text and of the interpreter as having an expectation that the author intends to communicate relevant information to him or her through this text. On this view of communication, an author's intention to communicate to an interpreter is not unexpressed; rather, a meaning is conveyed precisely because 'sentence meaning is a vehicle for conveying a speaker's meaning', where the latter form of meaning 'is an overtly expressed intention that is fulfilled by being recognized'.[184] What also emerges is that a speaker's motives are irrelevant to the hearer's task.

Another consequence of this Relevance Theory perspective is a view of legal interpretation as necessarily involving (at least) two distinct cognitive processes: linguistic decoding, on the one hand, which produces a skeletal 'logical form' or 'sentence meaning'; and an inferential process, on the other, which draws on relevant evidence to enrich this skeletal meaning in various ways. Crucially, the recovery of 'speaker's meaning' is basic to the latter process and encompasses even what is understood as the utterance's explicit content. Moreover, the notion of 'speaker's meaning' informs this process in myriad ways, including the 'fine-tuning' of word meanings, as noted earlier. As such, 'speaker's meaning'—and thus speaker's intent—is not plausibly understood as a notion that interpreters resort to only '[o]nce we encounter...controversy or uncertainty', as Solan has suggested.[185] Nor can approaches that take the determination of some 'surface meaning' to be a reasonable goal of legal interpretation do justice to the richness of the inferential process involved in determining 'speaker's meaning'. This is simply because this process appears to bridge a significant gap between a 'decoded' legal text and the meaning ultimately derived from it.

The idea that a key goal of legal interpretation is to recover the meaning that the author of a legal text has sought to convey through this text is also consistent with our earlier conclusions about an interpreter's ability to identify 'scrivener's errors' in or absurd consequences of statutes, which we took to implicate the interpreter's recognition of what the author likely intended. This conclusion follows naturally from a Relevance Theory understanding of 'ordinary' verbal communication, on which hearers 'generally discount the wrong meaning' when they 'realise that the speaker has misused a word or made a slip of the tongue', even if the rejected meaning is not 'ill-formed or undecodable'.[186] What makes the meaning 'wrong', then, is only that 'it provides misleading evidence about the speaker's intentions'.[187]

Admittedly, a Relevance Theory understanding of legal interpretation—crucially involving 'speaker's meaning' and taking 'the meaning of the sentence' to be relevant to interpreters 'only insofar as it provides evidence about what the speaker means'[188]—must

---

[184] Wilson, 'Relevance Theory' (cited in n.123) 393 (emphasis omitted). On such a view, the distinction between 'speaker's meaning' and 'sentence meaning' does not 'disappear on close analysis', as Lawrence Solan, in *The Language of Statutes* (cited in n.63) 112, has claimed. Although Solan suggests that this distinction is 'a matter of whether we focus on the individual intent of the speaker or on the intent of the speaker as a member of a group with shared knowledge', it is more plausible to see the latter as independent of a speaker's intent, being instead the vehicle through which the speaker expresses an intent.

[185] Solan, *The Language of Statutes* (cited in n.63) 114.
[186] Sperber and Wilson, *Relevance: Communication and Cognition* (cited in n.119) 23.
[187] Sperber and Wilson, *Relevance: Communication and Cognition* (cited in n.119) 23.
[188] Sperber and Wilson, *Relevance: Communication and Cognition* (cited in n.119) 23.

still confront the two worries expressed by Solan, as described earlier. These are that this view of legal interpretation makes 'statutory language... no more than evidence of intent'[189] and that it makes this language and the 'constitutional procedures for enacting laws' insufficient 'to determine the rights and obligations of the citizenry in a significant set of circumstances'.[190] Relevance Theory, however, offers a cogent response to these worries. First, statutory language is not merely one form of evidence among many for legislative intent, but a privileged form of evidence—in Relevance Theory terms, the 'ostensive stimulus', which, we might recall, 'is designed to attract an audience's attention and focus it on the communicator's meaning'[191] and which carries 'a presumption of its own optimal relevance'[192] to its intended audience. Since on this view the authority of statutory language as an indication of intent is much greater than that of any other form of evidence, Solan's first worry seems to be adequately addressed. As regards his second worry, it seems to lose much of its force given the admission even by textualists that statutory texts are not 'self-interpreting' and can be understood only in context. Thus, the conclusion that statutory language and law-making procedures cannot by themselves fully determine rights and obligations follows on any reasonable view of interpretation. In sum, while Solan might be right that these worries about intent have driven textualists 'to eliminate intent as part of the interpretive enterprise',[193] there is good reason to see their efforts as ill-conceived.

Moreover, as we have already seen, textualist efforts to remove intent from legal interpretation by reconstructing intent in other terms have been far from successful. And, as Solan argues, though textualists like Justice Scalia take the ordinary meanings of statutes and canons of construction as proxies for legislative intent, 'the ordinary-meaning approach' can do no more than 'provid[e] a useful rule of thumb as to how a word was most likely used';[194] and canons of construction are, similarly, 'best seen as default rules for assessing the likely intent'[195] and as such cannot truly substitute for the consideration of intent.

Relevance Theory's view of speaker's intent as integral to interpretation is thus very much at odds with the outright rejection of legislative intent by some textualists. Yet, the theory's recognition of the key role of 'ostensive stimuli' in communication appears to place it equally at odds with the view of intentionalists that '[t]he actual words used by the legislature may be strong evidence of its intent, but they are merely windows on the legislative intent (or purpose) that is the law', so that 'a thing may be within the letter of the statute and yet not within the statute, because not within its spirit, nor within the intention of its makers'.[196] Such a view of statutory text seems difficult to square with Relevance Theory, which takes 'sentence meaning' not to be a mere 'window' on 'speaker's meaning', but rather the basic vehicle for communicating it.

It is worth noting also that a Relevance Theory perspective on legal interpretation can give us some insight into the vexed question of whether appeal to certain kinds of evidence—in particular, legislative history—is appropriate. The basic conclusion that emerges from Relevance Theory is that the evidence drawn on during the course

---

[189] Solan, *The Language of Statutes* (cited in n.63) 110.
[190] Solan, *The Language of Statutes* (cited in n.63) 111.
[191] Wilson and Sperber, 'Relevance Theory' (cited in n.116) 611.
[192] Wilson, 'Relevance Theory' (cited in n.123) 396.
[193] Solan, *The Language of Statutes* (cited in n.63) 111.
[194] Solan, *The Language of Statutes* (cited in n.63) 68.
[195] Solan, *The Language of Statutes* (cited in n.63) 104.
[196] Aleinikoff, 'Updating Statutory Interpretation' (cited in n.110) 23–4.

of interpretation is whatever evidence is 'relevant', where this is defined as a trade-off between effort and effect. This conclusion seems broadly consistent with the liberal position on evidence reflected in Justice Byron White's remark that 'common sense suggests that inquiry benefits from reviewing additional information rather than ignoring it'[197] and in Chief Justice Marshall's famous dictum that 'where the mind labours to discover the design of the legislature, it seizes every thing from which aid can be derived'.[198] Of course, what counts as 'relevant' to legal interpretation is arguably rather different from what counts in face-to-face communication, as we shall see shortly. Moreover, because 'relevance', as just noted, entails a trade-off in any case between effort and effect, the search for 'every thing from which aid can be derived' would of necessity be subject to practical limits.

Granting these qualifications, we can still conclude that an interpreter's determination of the relevance of evidence is highly dependent on context. This suggests a clear answer to the question of whether, 'in the aggregate...judges [will] reach more accurate assessments of intended meaning if they try to gauge the reliability of legislative history on a case-by-case basis or if they apply a more categorical presumption against its usefulness'.[199] This is that the former will more likely result in more accurate assessments. This answer comes, however, with an important proviso, as suggested by our discussion earlier in section 2: namely, that not all legislative history is of equal value in determining legislative rationale and that certain kinds of talk are likely to be more credible than other kinds.[200] Of course, this answer does not preclude a categorical rejection, based on legal or policy considerations alone, of the use of legislative history to obtain additional evidence of legislative intent. But such a rejection would seem to require strong arguments to overcome the objection that reliance on legislative history could indeed 'make the law easier to interpret in a given case'.[201] And, as suggested earlier, constitutional arguments about 'unenacted legislative intent' are not obviously sufficient to deny a role for legislative history as additional, rather than authoritative, evidence of intent. Nor are the highly speculative claims that some commentators have made about judges' institutional inability to assess the reliability of legislative history from a position 'at some remove from the legislative process'.[202] This seems particularly doubtful given that '[j]udges make reliability determinations as a matter of course'.[203]

3. Some remaining issues in legal interpretation

In section 2, I sought to show that a cognitively realistic approach to communication like that of Relevance Theory offers a way to address a number of persistent questions for the theory and practice of legal interpretation. This involved focusing on basic aspects of interpretation that are shared by legal interpretation and 'ordinary' verbal communication, highlighting a common observation that 'legal interpretation is not a kind of isolated island [but] resembles in many respects forms of interpretation that reach'

---

[197] *Wisconsin Public Intervenor v Mortier*, 501 US 597, 610 n.4; quoted in Solan, *The Language of Statutes* (cited in n.63) 87.
[198] *United States v Fisher*, 6 US (2 Cranch) 358, 366 (1805); quoted in Solan, *The Language of Statutes* (cited in n.63) 87.
[199] Vermeule, *Judging Under Uncertainty* (cited in n.5) 363.
[200] See Asgeirsson, 'On Restricting Appeal to Legislative Purpose in Hard Cases' (cited in n.50).
[201] Siegel, 'Judicial Interpretation in the Cost-Benefit Crucible' (cited in n.12) n.193.
[202] Vermeule, *Judging Under Uncertainty* (cited in n.5) 363.
[203] Davis, 'The Newer Textualism' (cited in n.32) 1000.

other aspects of the rich variety of human life'.[204] In this section, I shall extend the reach of the Relevance Theory approach to legal interpretation by using it to isolate certain features of legal interpretation that are unique to it or that it shares either with 'ordinary' communication or with another form of interpretation, namely, literary interpretation, analogies to which are commonplace in legal scholarship. In this way, I hope to show how this approach can be pressed into service to address other perplexing questions about legal interpretation—including those already singled out for closer examination in section 2.

'Ordinary', literary, and legal interpretation

As already suggested, there are many features that legal interpretation shares with 'ordinary' verbal communication (granting that the latter category is best thought of as encompassing a number of distinguishable kinds of communication), making it plausible to elucidate legal interpretation in terms of Relevance Theory. But it is also worth asking in what ways legal interpretation resembles or differs from 'ordinary' communication, on the one hand, and literary interpretation, on the other, given the compelling analogies that commentators have drawn to each.

In section 2, I introduced the notion of an 'activity type' as a way of incorporating the institutional dimension of legal interpretation into a Relevance Theory account of this form of interpretation. The practices of law-making and legal interpretation present a range of legal 'activity types', including legal interpretation itself. Given the legal character of these activities, the linguistic practices that figure in them are plausibly seen as shaped not merely by the structure of a particular activity itself, but also by the overarching institution of law in which the activity is embedded. As noted earlier, this institution is so rich in ritual and procedure and has such a dense network of meanings that it has been productive to analyse it, as Paul Kahn has advocated, as a cultural phenomenon, 'a distinct way of understanding and perceiving meaning in the events of our political and social life'.[205]

Brief reflection on legal interpretation should be sufficient to convince us that many of its key differences from other forms of interpretation can be attributed to the distinctive organizing principles of such a 'legal culture', which constrain legal interpretation in various ways and can be thought of as constituting a 'pragmatics of law'. These principles include, among many others, those governing the admissibility of evidence. Crucially, such principles of evidence cannot be understood simply in terms of a Relevance Theory trade-off between cognitive effort and effect, but engage broader institutional goals. Consider, for example, 'the near-total ban on testimony about legislators' private understandings'.[206] While puzzling from the perspective of 'ordinary' face-to-face communication—where the ability to immediately confirm or disconfirm the speaker's meaning in the event of confusion is generally taken for granted—this restriction must be understood in terms of such concerns as 'the need for citizens and their lawyers to have fair notice of the law's requirements and for voters to be able to understand what their elected representatives are up to'.[207] Moreover, the concession that a hearer's hypothesis about a speaker's meaning 'may well be false; but it is the best a rational hearer can do'[208]

---

[204] Greenawalt, *Legal Interpretation* (cited in n.7) 3.
[205] Kahn, *The Cultural Study of Law* (cited in n.9) 1.
[206] Nelson, 'What Is Textualism?' (cited in n.20) 359.
[207] Nelson, 'What Is Textualism?' (cited in n.20) 359.
[208] Wilson and Sperber, 'Relevance Theory' (cited in n.116) 614.

is arguably far less acceptable in the legal context than it is in the context of 'ordinary' verbal communication. This is because the commonly adversarial nature of the former means not only that interpretations are highly contested, but also that only one of them can 'win'; and this in turn means that the consequences for a party's interests of arriving at an incorrect interpretation can be severe. In other words, the considerable stakes often at play in the legal context motivate a treatment of evidence rather different from that governing 'ordinary' communication: one that may impose higher standards of evidence, even as it restricts access to certain kinds of evidence.

Given these considerations about legal interpretation, we can see the various debates described in this study as largely reflective of institutional choices about how to reconcile competing goals in legal culture. These choices are related to the achievement of authoritative interpretative results that are nevertheless compatible with constitutional and rule of law principles. The basic choice, then, as Solan suggests, 'is between insisting upon a standard set of methodologies, sensible enough most of the time but sure to result in errors, even on its own terms, and living with a more relaxed set of evidentiary standards, less able to constrain judicial discretion but better able to head off results that are likely at odds with what an enacting legislature intended its law to accomplish'.[209]

Note that specifically legal principles also include those that guide the process of interpretation itself. Among these are the principle of *stare decisis* and substantive canons of construction, such as the rule of lenity ('penal laws are to be construed strictly'),[210] and textual canons such as '*eiusdem generis*' and '*Expressio unius est exclusio alterius*' (prescribing, respectively, that the meaning of general terms be restricted to the same class as the specific terms that precede them in a list; and that the absence of items on the list be presumed to indicate that they are not covered by the statute). These and many other standard principles, recognized by drafters and interpreters alike,[211] serve to restrict available interpretations.

What, of course, equally distinguishes legal interpretation from other varieties is the distinctive 'activity types' involved in this form of interpretation. Recall Levinson's definition of 'activity types' as 'goal-defined, socially constituted, bounded events with constraints on participants, setting, and so on, but above all on the kind of allowable contributions'.[212] With this definition in mind, we can see that the features of legal interpretation make it very much an 'activity type' (itself complex, given the various activities, both inside and outside a court, that fall under the rubric of 'legal interpretation') that complements the (also complex) 'activity type' of 'law-making'. Both are, notably, goal-defined in very clear senses: the latter is directed both at ordering a particular legal domain in a particular way through law and at communicating the enacted law to those subject to it; while the former tracks these goals by determining both the content of the enacted law and its application to the case before the court that has occasioned this interpretative activity. Contrast these goals with those of 'ordinary' communication: there we typically find only 'informative' and 'communicative' intentions; and any further goals that a speaker might have would best be seen as ulterior motives or as a signal that

---

[209] Solan, *The Language of Statutes* (cited in n.63) 80.
[210] *United States v Wiltberger*, 18 US (5 Wheat.) 76, 95 (1820); see e.g. Solan, *The Language of Statutes* (cited in n.63), 41–7 for a discussion of this rule.
[211] However, as noted by Ruth Sullivan, *Statutory Interpretation* (Toronto: Irwin Law, 2007) 14–65, while courts rely on assumptions about 'the knowledge and competence of the legislature, its use of language, and its fidelity to the conventions of legislative structure and style' in interpreting statutes, in practice 'the pressures of the job and the limitations of language' mean that 'drafters of legislation are unlikely to achieve' the competence, clarity, and consistency 'attributed to them'.
[212] Levinson, 'Activity Types and Language' (cited in n.11) 368.

the participants in the conversation are engaging in an overarching 'activity type' that structures this conversation.

Although the features of legal interpretation just described clearly set it apart from other forms of verbal communication, there are nevertheless many other features that are not unique to it. Certain ones it shares with literary interpretation, which set both off sharply from 'ordinary' communication. One such shared feature is the possibility—and frequent occurrence—of a significant displacement both in space and time between the creation of a text and its interpretation. This gives rise to a second shared feature: in contrast to 'ordinary' communication, which is addressed to a specific and immediate audience, the communicative intention informing both legal and literary texts is directed at a broader and often temporally and spatially dispersed audience—members of which may live in circumstances very different from those known or contemplated by the author, as is commonly acknowledged by constitutional scholars especially.

One key effect of a displacement in time between the creation and interpretation of legal and literary texts is related to the breadth of evidence considered 'relevant' in determining 'speaker's meaning'. As Sperber and Wilson observe in contrasting 'ordinary' communication with yet another kind of cognitive process, that of scientific theorizing: '[O]rdinary utterance comprehension is almost instantaneous, and however much evidence *might* have been taken into account, however many hypotheses *might* have been considered, in practice the only evidence and hypotheses considered are those that are immediately accessible.'[213] By contrast, 'the construction and evaluation of a scientific theory may take all the time in the world' and 'the range of hypotheses that can be considered, and the range of evidence that can be taken into account, can be enormous'.[214] Similarly, the process of inferring meaning in legal and literary interpretation, while arguably still guided by a general trade-off between effort and effect, just as scientific theorizing is, involves a trade-off that is not between cognitive so much as professional or institutional effort and effect.

The displacement in time between author and interpreter in the case of both legal and literary interpretation and 'the propensity of language to change'[215] mean that both the decoding and the inferential processes associated with older texts will inevitably require an 'archaeological' investigation of meanings in order to translate an older idiom into a modern one, as noted earlier. This is true even if we subscribe to an explicitly 'dynamic' approach to legal interpretation: since an author uses 'sentence meaning' as a vehicle for conveying 'speaker's meaning', the 'sentence meaning' that an interpreter decodes from the text must be the one that the author actually encoded in the first place. If it is not, then the interpreter has abandoned the task of interpreting and 'updating' *that* text, and is simply substituting a modern text for the original one. This is the same problem that I described earlier in rejecting the possibility of substituting modern meanings for older ones in seeking to interpret a Shakespearean sonnet.

Given these striking parallels between legal and literary interpretation, it seems fair to ask whether 'law is, in some meaningful sense, a branch of literature',[216] as some commentators have suggested; and thus whether the principles and processes of literary interpretation serve as a plausible model for legal interpretation. Despite the compelling analogy that literary interpretation does offer for legal interpretation, it also obscures

---

[213] Sperber and Wilson, *Relevance: Communication and Cognition* (cited in n.119) 66 (emphases in original).
[214] Sperber and Wilson, *Relevance: Communication and Cognition* (cited in n.119) 66.
[215] Levinson, 'Law as Literature' (cited in n.111) 376.
[216] Levinson, 'Law as Literature' (cited in n.111) 376.

important differences—differences that turn out to make literary interpretation resemble legal interpretation less in certain important respects than 'ordinary' communication does.

Of course, one uncontroversial difference between legal and literary intepretation is that only the latter concerns texts whose universe is a fictional rather than a 'real-world' one. More controversial, though, is the question of whether it is fruitful to describe either variety of interpretation as conforming to the traditional view of literary interpretation defended by M H Abrams and others. On this view, 'the reader sets himself to make out what the author has designed and signified through putting into play a linguistic and literary expertise that he shares with the author. By approximating what the author understood to signify the reader understands what the language of the work means.'[217] Railing against this position are those like Stanley Fish, for whom '[i]nterpretation is not the art of construing but the art of constructing. Interpreters do not decode poems; they make then.'[218]

In fact, consideration of this debate among literary scholars allows us to see that legal and literary interpretation evince a real difference as regards the role of authorial intention. Granting significant differences of opinion on this matter, it remains reasonable to see the meanings of a literary text as extending far beyond the conscious control of the author—hence 'the commonplace observation that an author's text usually says much more than the author herself thinks it does'.[219] Moreover, this 'open-ended' quality of a literary text is generally seen as a desirable one, since it is basic to an author's ability to give readers the latitude to 'construct' a text's meaning.[220] By contrast, it is far less reasonable to efface authorial intent as a source of meaning for legal interpretation. This is simply for reasons already noted in section 1: namely, that doing so obscures an understanding of statutes 'primarily as the expression of particular decisions made by specific, temporally situated political officials'.[221] What this means is that the parallel between legal and literary interpretation as regards authorial intention is far less robust than that between legal interpretation and 'ordinary' communication. After all, it is as implausible with 'ordinary' communication as it is with legal interpretation to contend that a speaker's contribution to a verbal exchange includes unexpressed thoughts that he or she may have revealed unintentionally; indeed, in the former case doing so might well lead a speaker to respond that the hearer has 'put words in my mouth'.

What these considerations suggest, then, is that seeing 'law as literature' can take us only so far in our efforts to understand the process of legal interpretation—and that some other means must be found to account for the 'dynamism' of legal interpretation. The next subsection will explore some possibilities for doing so.

Interpreting across time: word meanings, 'archaeology', and change

In the previous subsection, we explored certain features of legal interpretation by highlighting their similarities to and differences from those of literary interpretation and

---

[217] M H Abrams, 'How to Do Things with Texts' (1979) 46 *Partisan Rev* 566, quoted in Levinson, 'Law as Literature' (cited in n.111) 376.
[218] Stanley Fish, *Is There a Text in This Class?* (Cambridge, Mass.: Harvard University Press, 1980) 327; quoted in Levinson, 'Law as Literature' (cited in n.111) 381.
[219] Eskridge, *Dynamic Statutory Interpretation* (cited in n.4) 58.
[220] For a discussion of this point in Relevance Theory terms, see e.g. Billy Clark, 'Stylistic Analysis and Relevance Theory' (1996) 5 *Language and Literature* 168.
[221] Smith, 'Law Without Mind' (cited in n.95) 111.

'ordinary' communication. What we saw, however, was only a basic picture of legal interpretation, which still leaves us with a significant problem for it, both in theory and in practice. This is how to reconcile a crucial role for authorial intent with the possibility of interpreting older legal texts in such a way that they can speak meaningfully to current situations, even those not contemplated by the authors of these texts.

In fact, our previous discussion of the principle of *stare decisis*, and of the 'transtemporal' nature of constitutional interpretation especially, already provides us with two means to capture 'dynamism' in legal interpretation. We observed in the previous subsection that the communicative intention informing legal interpretation is best understood as directed at the 'transtemporal' (and 'transspatial') character of a legal text's audience, whose members may live in circumstances very different from those contemplated by the author. This suggests that the communicative intention itself must permit communication with an indefinite number of audiences over an indefinite period of time and thus convey a general enough 'speaker's meaning' for interpreters to apply it in, and to, a broad range of circumstances. Significantly, by conceiving the process of legal interpretation as assigning a crucial role to the author of the legal text—rather than substituting for the author a temporally situated 'reasonable person' seeking to gather [intent] from the text of the law',[222] as Justice Scalia suggests—we can capture the temporal specificity of a legal text's creation without this specificity dictating a strictly 'original understanding' of this text.

The principle of *stare decisis* lends further support to this 'transtemporal' picture of legal interpretation, since it necessarily involves an accretion of interpretations of a legal text. While this accretion of interpretations has suggested to some commentators that '[i]nterpretation is a contemporary interpreter's dialogue with the text and the tradition that surrounds it',[223] it is just as plausible to see the interpreter's dialogue as occurring not with the text but rather with the author of the original text and with subsequent interpreters, who have themselves authored persuasive or binding interpretations of this text. As it happens, this picture of legal interpretation has been adumbrated in two analogies prominent in the literature, those of Aleinikoff and Dworkin, respectively. According to the former, a legal text is like a ship, which 'Congress builds' and whose 'initial course' it 'charts', but whose 'ports-of-call, safe harbors and ultimate destination may be a product of the ship's captain, the weather, and other factors not identified at the time the ship sets sail'.[224] According to the latter, legal interpretation is like writing a chain novel, in which 'each novelist in the chain interprets the chapters he has been given in order to write a new chapter, which is then added to what the next novelist receives, and so on'.[225] A more precise, if perhaps less colourful, picture of legal interpretation than either of these is one in which this kind of interpretation involves an exegetical tradition in which an interpreter considers the communicative intention not only of the original author but of each of the interpreters who have preceded him or her, adding thereby to the text that must be understood and applied anew.

Now, if we revisit the claim made earlier that the 'speaker's meaning' of a 'transtemporally' applied statute must be general enough for the statute to apply to a variety of circumstances, we can see some reflection in this claim of the Relevance Theory idea that 'sentence meaning' is highly underspecified with respect to 'speaker's meaning'. Applying

---

[222] Scalia, *A Matter of Interpretation* (cited in n.4) 17.
[223] William N Eskridge Jr, 'Dynamic Statutory Interpretation' (1986–1987) 135 *U Pa L Rev* 1479, 1509.
[224] Aleinikoff, 'Updating Statutory Interpretation' (cited in n.110) 21.
[225] Dworkin, *Law's Empire* (cited in n.4) 229.

this idea to the legal domain, we can arrive at the observation that the 'sentence meaning' of a statute might be compatible with several distinct 'speaker's meanings', which arise from distinct reinterpretations of the original text over time. One way to give greater concreteness to this observation is in terms of the processes of 'narrowing' and 'broadening' described in section 2, which Relevance Theory makes use of to account for the frequent restriction and extension of an expression's linguistically encoded meaning in particular contexts. As it happens, many prominent legal cases have turned on the reasonableness of just such a narrowing or broadening of the meaning that a legislature likely intended for an expression. These Relevance Theory notions of 'narrowing' and 'broadening' can thus offer a means not only to capture the problem posed by such 'evolving' meanings but also to reconcile progressive readings of older legal texts with the words of the texts themselves. One illustration of the relevance of 'narrowing' to legal interpretation is its applicability to the definitional conundrum at the heart of the famous 'Persons' case, a Canadian case ultimately decided by the Judicial Committee of the Privy Council.[226] At issue in this case was whether women were considered to be 'qualified Persons' for the purpose of appointment to the Senate of Canada according to the terms of the British North America Act 1867 s.24.[227] At the time the case was decided, women were widely recognized to have a general incapacity under the common law to 'exercis[e] public functions'.[228] Interestingly, however, the textual evidence from the British North America Act itself—which included a distinction between 'persons' and 'males' made in a number of the Act's provisions and the fact that the 'qualifications' for Senate appointment specified in the section of the Act immediately preceding s.24 did not include any clearly related to gender[229]—arguably favoured an interpretation of 'qualified persons' as including qualified women. From a Relevance Theory perspective, the central question in this case can be framed as follows. This was whether the 'narrowing' of the linguistically encoded meaning of 'qualified Persons' whereby this phrase referred only to men should have been the controlling one, particularly given that Parliament would have been fully aware of women's ineligibility for public office at the time that the British North America Act became law; or whether an interpretation that involved no such 'narrowing', and was in fact more consistent with the text of the British North American Act itself, should have prevailed. As it happens, the Privy Council decided that women were indeed 'persons' for Senate appointment—a decision seen by the Canadian legal establishment at the time as a radical one.[230] For our purposes, what is relevant about this decision is its illustration of the tension between the most plausible 'speaker's meaning' of the expression at issue and its obvious linguistically encoded meaning. What is also relevant is the possibility that this decision suggests of an appeal to linguistically encoded meaning to arrive at an understanding of a provision different from its original understanding, particularly when the latter reflects a 'narrowing' of linguistically encoded meaning that is not necessary for a reasonable interpretation of a provision.

Similar comments apply to the process of 'broadening', whose utility can be seen in another, very contentious, provision in a statute, discussed by Aleinikoff,[231] Steven

---

[226] *Edwards v Attorney General for Canada*, [1929] JCJ No. 2, [1930] AC 124, [1930] 1 DLR 98, [1929] 3 WWR 479. This case is the subject of work in preparation.
[227] 30 & 31 Victoria, c.3 (UK), s.24.
[228] *Edwards v Attorney General for Canada*, [1929] JCJ No. 2, [1930] AC 124, [1930] 1 DLR 98, [1929] 3 WWR 479 (cited in n.226) para.12.
[229] 30 & 31 Victoria, c.3 (UK) s.23.
[230] See e.g. Robert J Sharpe and Patricia McMahon, *The Persons Case: The Origins and Legacy of the Fight for Legal Personhood* (Toronto: University of Toronto Press, 2007), 257–9 for some discussion of this.
[231] Aleinikoff, 'Updating Statutory Interpretation' (cited in n.110).

Smith,[232] and others. This is the provision in a 1952 American immigration law that excludes, among other persons, '[a]liens afflicted with psychopathic personality, epilepsy, or a mental defect'.[233] Given that the statute when originally enacted was undoubtedly intended by Congress to cover gay and lesbian individuals, a basic question that it has raised is whether an interpretation of the statute that 'declines to apply' it to these groups truly violates the 'expressed intent of the enacting legislators'.[234] Again appealing to Relevance Theory, we can frame this question in terms of the 'broadening' of the linguistically encoded meaning of 'mental defect' evinced here, which, as in the 'narrowing' of 'qualified Persons' reflected in the 'Persons' case, is not necessary for a reasonable interpretation of the provision. We might then go further and argue that the 'broadening' of the expression 'mental defect' to include gays and lesbians, given both the provision's likely purpose—namely, to prevent those with infirmities and addictions from creating burdens on the state or other ills—and the absence of the term 'homosexual' or the like in the statute itself, was in retrospect simply in error. This case of 'broadening' might be akin, then, to other errors recognized as within the power of judges to correct—such as the putative error in *United States v Granderson*[235] analysed by Manning, Solan, and others, as discussed in section 1—rather than to basic legislative purposes that courts must honour. If so, then it might be possible to reconcile a progressive interpretation of the provision in question both with its actual language and with (at least a 'thick' notion of) legislative intent.

4. Conclusion

In this study, I suggested that certain open questions in legal interpretation could be productively treated in terms of a cognitively realistic theory of communication, which was able to describe legal interpretation 'on the ground' as a special variety of communication.

One key virtue of this approach to legal interpretation that I spelled out is its highlighting of the 'triadic' nature of legal interpretation, which necessarily involves an author, a text serving as a vehicle for the author to communicate a 'speaker's meaning', and an interpreter seeking to recover this 'speaker's meaning' by decoding the text and drawing further inferences about 'speaker's meaning' from it. Another is the distinction that it makes between 'decoding' and inferential processes, which both play a key role in legal interpretation and highlight an 'originalist' component of even 'dynamic' approaches to interpretation. A third is the notion of 'relevance', clearly at the core of Relevance Theory, which provides a useful way of thinking about the appropriateness of various restrictions on evidence in the law.

A comparison of legal interpretation with both literary interpretation and 'ordinary' communication brought out some important similarities and differences between legal interpretation and these other varieties of communication. Important similarities between legal and literary interpretation included the 'transtemporal' nature of the relationship between author and interpreter in each and the absence in each of a specific, temporally restricted audience. An important difference between them, however, concerned the possibility of a search for meaning plausibly extending beyond 'speaker's meaning' itself. This possibility did seem to be a real one for literary interpretation but

---

[232] Smith, 'Law Without Mind' (cited in n.95).
[233] 66 Stat 163, 182 (1952).
[234] Aleinikoff, 'Updating Statutory Interpretation' (cited in n.110) 51.
[235] *Granderson* (cited in n.86).

neither for legal interpretation nor for 'ordinary' communication. This suggested that drawing on literary interpretation in order to understand legal interpretation had certain real limits.

Finally, the paper revisited the thorny question of whether a 'triadic' understanding of legal interpretation that took 'speaker's meaning' seriously could be reconciled with a 'dynamic' approach to interpretation. I suggested three ways in which this reconciliation could be achieved: by recognizing the 'transtemporal' legislative intent behind legal, and particularly constitutional, interpretation; by seeing the operation of *stare decisis* as involving a relationship between an interpreter and previous interpreters as well as the original author of a legal text; and by exploring the possibility that 'original' understandings of expressions in legal texts should be seen as involving concepts whose scope can be broadened or narrowed—a claim that I sought to cash out in terms of the Relevance Theory notions of 'broadening' and 'narrowing'.

Inevitably, this study could only touch on a number of important issues in the theory and practice of legal interpretation, and was able to offer only limited empirical support for its assertions from the case law. Despite these limitations, I hope to have shown that the exploration of legal interpretation as a cognitive process holds some promise for the investigation of this phenomenon.

17

Do You Kick a Dog when it's Down? Considering the Use of Children's Video-Recorded Testimonies in Court

June Luchjenbroers and Michelle Aldridge-Waddon

Introduction

The title of this paper is deliberately provocative, because it takes issue with the procedural amendments made in the England and Wales legal system regarding how children need to be treated by the police and in court, referred to in the *Memorandum of Good Practice* (1992),[1] and the subsequent replacements: *Achieving Best Evidence* (2002, 2004, 2007 and 2011).[2] The primary objective of the policy changes has been to enhance justice for all, without terrorizing those most vulnerable to the inquisitorial process (e.g., children). However, while the amendments have arguably been successful in minimizing the terror experienced by children in the legal process, resulting in more detailed and reliable testimonies, it is also arguable that justice is still likely to be out of reach for these vulnerable witnesses, as they do not have the linguistic skills needed to utilize appropriately the invitation to 'tell their own story', and they don't always have the social skills necessary to comprehend what is being said to them.

Others working in this field have long observed that children's free narrative contributions in an evidentiary setting are often internally contradictory and structurally incoherent. Narrative is a developmental linguistic skill, and children often cannot structure their narrated contributions appropriately to facilitate comprehension (such as temporal ordering of narrative components; making full use of all story components; and/or using the appropriate causal connectives to facilitate hearer comprehension).[3] In this paper we offer a detailed consideration of children's evidentiary experience and performance, as well as the nature and content of police questioning that can also be harmful to their case. Children generally do not have either the linguistic or social experience necessary

---

[1] Home Office/Department of Health, *Memorandum of Good Practice on Video Recorded interviews with Child Witnesses for Criminal Proceedings* (London: HMSO, 1992).

[2] Home Office, *Achieving Best Evidence in Criminal Proceedings: Guidance for Vulnerable or Intimidated Witnesses, including Children* (ABE 2002) (London: Communication Directorate, 2002, draft); Welsh Assembly Government, *Achieving Best Evidence in Criminal Proceedings: Guidance for Vulnerable or Intimidated Witnesses, including Children: A Training Pack* (ABE 2004) (Cardiff: Welsh Assembly Government, 2004); National Policing Improvement Agency, *Achieving Best Evidence in Criminal Proceedings: Guidance for Vulnerable or Intimidated Witnesses, including Children* (ABE 2007) (London, revised 2007). Ministry of Justice, *Achieving Best Evidence in Criminal Proceedings: Guidance on interviewing victims and witnesses, and guidance on using special measures* (ABE 2011) (London, revised 2011).

[3] For a full discussion of the body of cross-disciplinary literature dealing with these areas, see M. Aldridge and J. Wood, 'Telling it how it was: a comparative analysis of children's evidential and non-evidential narrative accounts' (1999) 9(2) *Narrative Inquiry* 1–21.

to recognize the semantic ramifications of the lexical choices they or the police make in their testimonies, and if they do, they would be powerless to correct any unfavourable semantic associations hearers (such as jurors) are likely to make. It is finally our argument that the initial interview by the police should not be used in court as the victim's Evidence-in-Chief, because the police function of collecting evidence is not consistent with the chief prosecutor's role of putting the victim's 'best foot forward' in court. In effect, the current situation requires those recognized by the legal process as 'vulnerable' (i.e., dogs who are 'down') to build their own case, which even those not recognized as vulnerable would be hard pressed to do appropriately or successfully.

1. Legal procedure and 'vulnerable' witnesses

The Criminal Justice Acts in England and Wales (1988 and 1991) advocate that children be recognized as requiring support in the established legal process, with regard to how they are initially questioned and how their credibility can be attacked by the defence counsel. Such witnesses are now referred to as 'vulnerable' in the legal process, a term meant to capture those who are so traumatized by the legal process that it inhibits their ability to give clear and/or reliable evidence.[4] It is accepted in England and Wales that this class of witnesses will include children, rape and intimidated victims (in general), and those with learning difficulties. A full range of strategies is now in place to offer these witnesses better access to the law, including the use of screens in court; cross-examination by TV-link; the use of intermediaries and communicative aids to facilitate witness comprehension; and the use of the (first) video-recorded police interview in court as the witness's Evidence-in-Chief.

The questioning in that interview is thus the domain of the police, but it must serve two distinct and equally important functions: it must (i) first inform the prosecutors of the Crown Prosecution Service (CPS) so that they can determine how to proceed with the case; and (ii) be presented in court as that witness's Evidence-in-Chief.[5] We must expect that awareness of the likely impact of this second function will also be used to inform the first. Police officers are given specific training to interview vulnerable witnesses in ways that are designed to give those witnesses the opportunity to provide their best (i.e., reliable) evidence. However, further scrutiny of the questioning methods used by the police, as well as the practice of using the police interview as the witness's Evidence-in-Chief, is warranted by the very fact that so few of these police interviews make it to trial.

The Social Services Inspectorate reported in 1994 that in the year ending October 1993, 14,000 video interviews had been conducted with children in the UK but only 6 per cent reached court.[6] This statistic provides an important motivation to consider whether making changes to enable children to best articulate 'what has happened' to

---

[4] For a more in-depth discussion on research and definitions of 'vulnerable witnesses' see R. Bull, 'The investigative interviewing of children and other vulnerable witnesses: Psychological research and working/professional practice' (2010) 15 *Legal and Criminological Psychology* 5–23.

[5] The most recent ABE report, that for 2011 (cited in n.2), allows for the videoed police interview to not be used in court, but it is clear that using the police interview remains the expected outcome. ABE 2011 also allows the CPS to not require children to be in court for their case ('if they believe they can secure a conviction without it' §2.11), but again a child's presence is expected and it is up to the presiding judge whether to approve an alternative Evidence-in-Chief or an opt-out request.

[6] We have requested more recent statistics from the Home Office and CPS, but have been informed that 'It is not possible to identify from centrally held data whether a child was required to attend court in any proceedings or a videoed police interview was used during the trial'. The earlier inspectorate appears to no longer exist, having moved in 2004 to the Care Quality Commission which now appears to focus on health-care issues. Further requests to other organizations such as the police have so far been unsuccessful.

them (i.e., improving the quality of their evidence) is the most profitable strategy if offering better access to the legal process is the true motivation. Even though child rape cases can now proceed to court without the child's participation (should the CPS believe it can build its case without it), and it is hard to imagine that since the first implementation of the ABE reports,[7] more children's cases have made it to trial or have resulted in convictions than was the case before video-recorded police interviews, however noble the intention of the introduced changes to child questioning procedures.

The concerns we will discuss in this paper deal primarily with how fundamental social philosophies about children and rape permeate the legal process and undermine children's ability to achieve justice in the legal process. These philosophies include the view that 'children lie'/'cannot be relied upon to tell truth instead of fiction', and the now well-understood rape myth,[8] as well as the as-yet new, but related 'autonomous testosterone' myth.[9] Each of these is discussed in the sections below, with the testimony examples that make them evident.

2. The data

The data discussed in this paper are from videoed police interview transcripts and court transcripts taken from trials that involve the physical and/or sexual abuse of children. All names in our data have been removed to protect the people involved. Our examples are selective in the sense that we did not catalogue every instance of the target features across the entire data set; instead, the examples offered in this paper have been chosen to illustrate the relevant myths (stereotypes) that can influence how the claimant's case would be heard and/or understood in court. An understanding of these biases and their expected influence is important in that they would affect whether a claimant's case would even get to court. The CPS would need to be sensitive to the social biases it would expect juries to have, and so an understanding of those influences would also affect the decisions of the CPS regarding how to proceed with a case, in that it would not proceed with a case if it felt there was little chance of court success.

3. Social myth no. 1: children make stuff up

The field of research dealing with child testimonies has focused on how best to enable children (as young as possible) to provide an account of the events that have befallen them, in the clearest and most accurate way. The concept of 'accuracy' here centres on gleaning testimony that is 'closest to the truth', for better or for worse. While accuracy should be paramount in police investigations, and for the CPS to determine how best to proceed, the wording in children's testimonies dealing with this need is a very sensitive matter as the actual words will be heard in court should the child's testimony be used.

The first relevant issue raised in the police interview is the need to balance the need to assess whether the child can comprehend the gravity of 'lying' or 'making things up' with the more immediate need of encouraging the child to participate at all. The police

---

[7] ABE reports (2002, 2007, 2011), cited in n.2.
[8] Susan Ehrlich, *Representing Rape: Language and Sexual Consent* (London: Routledge, 2001); J. Luchjenbroers and M. Aldridge, 'Conceptual manipulation with Metaphors and Frames: Dealing with rape victims in legal discourse' (2007) 27(3) *Text & Talk* 339–59.
[9] M. Aldridge and J. Luchjenbroers, 'Reasoning with Conceptual Frames and Mental Spaces in legal contexts dealing with child rape', paper presented at Cognitive Linguistics Conference, Leiden, Netherlands, 2008.

interview is a highly stressful situation for the child that can often cause her to 'shut down'.[10] Research in the field has offered the view that encouraging 'free narrative' in children's testimonies is the interviewer's best means of gaining an accurate account, as this is when children are likely to be less suggestible to the potential contamination of other forms of information derived from adult questioning'.[11] However, before free narratives are likely at all, the police interviewer must successfully encourage the child to relax and to see him (the interviewer) as being helpful to both her and her case. The interview needs to follow a four-part process designed to best encourage children to verbally participate in the investigative process as well as to offer space for free narrative.[12]

The recorded police interview begins with (i) rapport building, in which the officer sets out to relax the witness and encourage her to open up to him.[13] After the child is deemed sufficiently relaxed with the interviewing officer and the interviewing context, she is invited to (ii) openly narrate what has happened to her, during which account the officer must not interrupt her. When the child has finished narrating, the police officer will then (iii) ask specific questions relating to the case to expand on information provided in the narrative or to flesh out matters that the police officer deems relevant but which the witness has not mentioned.[14] The final phase of this procedure is (iv) closure, where the interviewing police officer will leave the room to negotiate with others elsewhere (who have viewed the interview in progress), to ensure all information has been adequately obtained, and if not, he will ask a number of follow-up questions. When finished, the police officer will close the interview.

As mentioned above, the police interviewer needs to balance how to best encourage the child to verbally participate with the need to assess whether she can comprehend the gravity of 'lying' or 'making things up'. Across police-child transcribed testimonies however, we have noted remarkable variation, in both how this concept is discussed with the child, and where in the child's testimony this discussion occurs—see Examples (1) and (2) below.

(1) Police officer, start of phase 2 (witness = boy 11 years, rape allegation)

Good. Before we start really talking [name], it's very important that when we're talking in this special room, we tell the truth.
Child: Yeah
Yeah. Do you know the difference between telling the truth and not telling the truth?
Child: [nods]
Could you, could you tell me like a little example?
Child: When you tell the truth sometimes you, it's naughty to tell the truth [sic]
That's right. So, what if I had a pencil in my hand here and I broke it in half and I did it and I went outside and I said to the policeman 'look at what [name] has just done, he's broken my pencil'. So, what would that be?

---

[10] For ease of description, we will use the conventions 'he' and 'him' when referring to the interviewing officer, and 'she' and 'her' in reference to the interviewed witness. This is not to convey any expectation on our part that these are the customary genders of these different roles.
[11] Aldridge and Wood, 'Telling it how it was' (cited in n.3).
[12] This process follows research suggestions made by (among others) Ray Bull, 'Good practice for video recorded interviews with child witnesses for use in criminal proceedings'. In G. Davies, S. Lloyd-Bostock, M. McMurran, and C. Wilson (eds), *Psychology, law and criminal justice* (Berlin: Walter de Gruyter, 1996).
[13] Although the child's interview is meant to be shown in court, unedited and uninterrupted, recent practice has cut out the rapport stage before the videoed interview is shown in court.
[14] In many of the interview transcripts analysed, phases 2 and 3 seem to coalesce, as young children in particular need a lot of encouragement to narrate at all.

Child: Lie
That's right because I broke it, didn't I?
Child: Yeah
And how do you think you would feel if I did that?
Child: Sad
Yes so it's not good is it, to tell lies?
Child: No
It's very important to tell the truth. Does he normally tell the truth?
Mother: Yeah

(2) Police officer, start of phase 1 (witness = girl 14 years, rape allegation)

OK, I don't want you to make anything up. I just want the truth from how you remember it. I'm not interested in what you've heard people say about what happened last night.

In many ways, the police interviewer in Example (1) deals sensitively with the issue of whether the child understands what it means to tell the truth and the gravity of the situation. Anyone witnessing this exchange would be left with the minimal view that 'this child understands', and the optimal, preliminary view that 'this child can be believed'. In stark contrast, however, the example given in (2) occurred in the opening contribution[15] by the interviewing police officer, to a 14-year-old girl alleging rape, and is a context-free instruction. The interviewing police officer does not discuss or assess the witness's understanding of 'lies' or the gravity of the situation, but instead (because there is no prior discourse) he presupposes that lying would be her natural inclination and she's not to do so on this occasion.

Examples (1) and (2) thus show the scale of variation in how a child's understanding or inclination to fabricate may be dealt with in police interviews. There is, however, also meaningful variation regarding where in the child's testimony the issue is dealt with at all. As shown, the example offered in (2) occurred in the opening, interviewer contribution, but other transcripts reveal that this discussion/advice or instruction typically occurs much later in the 'rapport'-building phase (even at the very end, as in Example 1). The general tendency seems to be that this advice occurs later with younger children and where there are allegations of physical assault rather than rape.

We have found a total of three important parameters with regard to how Phase 1 (rapport) is conducted across witness types. These include: (i) whether the child is probed as to whether she understands what it is to lie and then advised of the importance of 'not lying', or just instructed/warned to 'not lie'; (ii) when in the rapport-building phase this discussion/warning occurs; and (iii) how much discourse time the interviewing officer devotes to the rapport phase. For example, in the testimony of an 11-year-old boy (alleging physical assault), the rapport-building phase contains approximately 100 contributions by the questioning police officer (with some instances of banter) and the witness is asked if he knows what it means to tell a lie in the final quarter of that phase. Similarly a 12-year-old girl alleging sexual assault is also asked if she understands what it means to tell a lie, but her rapport-building phase was only 45 contributions in length and she is asked about her understanding of lies after 16 contributions. The 14-year-old girl (in Example 2) was offered a rapport-building phase of only 26 contributions and she was instructed to 'not lie' in the opening contribution.

---

[15] 'Contributions' here are measured by interviewer, speaker turns.

While it is true that these results may be a function of interviewer experience, it is similarly possible that they correlate with either the age and/or gender of the witness, or the officer's attitude toward the type of allegations made. In effect, the practice of dealing with whether the witness understands the gravity of the process and the need to be entirely truthful can also reveal the degree of interviewer empathy with the complainant—i.e., whether the interviewer queries the witness or makes an instruction; and whether this advice/instruction is offered early or later in the interview can signal the investigator's inclination whether or not to believe the witness.[16]

While gaining evidence of this suspicion requires further investigation that goes beyond the bounds of this paper, there is nevertheless a body of psychological evidence that shows that suggestions made early in discourse will stay with hearers, and will colour their memory and interpretation of subsequent discourse. Consider, for example, 'there is no pink elephant in this paper'.[17] This seemingly irrelevant assertion follows research in psychology that has shown that saying to someone 'don't think X' will ensure that s/he will 'think X', and similarly, saying to someone 'don't lie' will ensure that hearers will see that person as a (potential) liar. In effect, the hearer/reader cannot ignore the semantic fallout from how the police 'advice' is phrased or when in the testimony it occurs, and they will interpret subsequent contributions within that frame offered by the police interviewer.

'Frame'-based reasoning and hearer assumptions

The power of frame-based reasoning has been explored in earlier works dealing with children as vulnerable witnesses in the judicial system of England and Wales, in terms of the semantic fallout from the lexical choices of police and barristers—which can have profound effects on how the child and her case will be understood.[18] How frame-based reasoning works is illustrated in Example (3) below. In order for readers/hearers to comprehend this contribution (and what information the police interviewer was hoping to glean from the child when asking it) requires them to access (adult) world knowledge about sexual practices. Without that world knowledge, the child would not be able to guess what a grown man might be doing with one hand, while rubbing a girl's vulva with the other.

(3) Police officer, phase 3 (witness = girl 12 years, rape allegation)

You said he was kneeling down and one hand was doing what you described, what was his other hand doing?

Examples such as (3) give a clear illustration of how hearers need to draw on additional knowledge to what is said (in general as well as in court) to fully determine a speaker's

---

[16] Even though the rapport stage is no longer shown in court, the dynamics of these testimonies may still be relevant to whether a child's case makes it to court (i.e., in persuading the police and/or CPS), and also how the child is likely to respond to the interviewing officer. Children can often sense whether the interviewer is 'on their side' (whether or not the child's assumptions are actually correct), and if a child should sense that the interviewer is 'against' them (from the outset) it is hard to imagine that the rapport phase will have been successfully completed.

[17] For works in this area, see D.M. Wegner, D.J. Schneider, S.R. Carter, and T.L. White, 'Paradoxical effects of thought suppression' (1987) 53(1) *Journal of Personality and Social Psychology* 5–13; E. Geraerts, H. Merckelbach, M. Jelicic, and E. Smeets, 'Long term consequences of suppression of intrusive anxious thoughts and repressive coping' (2006) 44(10) *Behaviour Research and Therapy* 1451–60.

[18] M. Aldridge and J. Luchjenbroers, 'Linguistic manipulations in legal discourse: Framing questions and "smuggling" information' (2007) 14(1) *Journal of Speech, Language and the Law* 339–59.

meaning.[19] The body of research into frame-based reasoning (from linguistics, psychology, and IT)[20] has evidenced how the use of frame-based associations drawn from context and the hearer's world knowledge is part of a fundamental process for comprehension purposes and is not just employed in cases where the full informational import is not provided in speech. For example, if you were to hear someone say, 'They're shooting at the chemist', mention of the word 'shoot' would likely trigger a crime frame, generating images of bullets flying and possible fatalities. From that frame, additional components become available to the cognitive processing of information, such as that there would be a gun (tool); a villain (protagonist) to do the shooting; and a reason (or goal, such as robbery). If you were to then hear the speaker say, 'Let's just hope they get a bundle for this', assumptions can then be drawn about the relationship between the 'villains' and the speaker, as well as confirm that the robber's goal would be robbery, and that the chemist must have large sums of money on site. If that second assertion were then followed with, 'Lord knows, movie companies make enough money from these films!' all previous assumptions would immediately be scrapped in favour of new semantic associations to be drawn from the replacement frame of reference, 'making movies', which involves actors, locations, budgets, movie plots, etc. Very important here is the fact that until new, contradictory information is received to lead the hearer to abandon an initial frame of reference, that frame will be the lens through which subsequent information will be processed.

In effect, discourse comprehension always involves accessing particular frames of reference that are the natural product of a person's growing experience of the world and are consequently utilized to help hearers make sense of new, incoming experiences and linguistic information. So the child in Example (3) could not answer the police investigator's question and probably did not understand what the investigator was alluding to, but adult hearers (first the police/CPS but later the judge, barristers, and jurors if this case was heard in court) would presumably have the relevant world knowledge to make the necessary associations.

Once the importance of frame-based reasoning is accepted, it is easy to see the possible ramifications of triggering an adverse frame, such as the 'don't make anything up' instruction in Example (2). Essentially the relevant frame draws on the social view (stereotype) that 'children lie'/'make stuff up'/'can't always tell truth from fiction' and the strength of this general view is evident in the frequency with which it is relayed to hearers throughout the entire legal proceedings, not just in the cross-examination. A range of cross-examination, questioning strategies already known to be used in child and rape testimonies include (i) repeated questions,[21] (ii) questions to test or challenge the witness's memory, such as 'Are you sure?' and (iii) repeating the barrister's own propositions as though the witness has agreed. These questioning strategies are illustrated in Example (4) below. This example also dwells on the use of 'hearsay' to discredit a witness's testimony (and memory).

(4) Lawyer during cross-examination (witness = girl 10 years, witness to abuse)

Was it your mum who told you that XXX had hit [your sister]?

---

[19] Theorists in cognitive semantics have long argued that speech under-represents speaker meaning—cf. Gilles Fauconnier, *Mental Spaces* (Cambridge, Mass.: MIT Press, 1985).

[20] M. Marvin, *A Framework for Representing Knowledge*. MIT-AI Laboratory Memo 306, June 1974. Available at: <http://web.media.mit.edu/~minsky/papers/Frames/frames.html>; Vyvyan Evans and Melanie Green, *Cognitive Linguistics: an introduction* (Oxford: Oxford University Press, 2006).

[21] Chris Lane referred to this practice as 'recycling' topics, which lawyers tend to do until they get the desired response: Chris Lane, 'Miscommunication in Cross-Examinations'. In J.B. Pride (ed.), *Cross-Cultural Encounters Communication & Miscommunciation* (Melbourne, 1985), 196–211.

Child: No because I seen all of that in my mum's room.
Are you sure?
Child: Yes
Has Nicola said to you 'Well, XXX hit me'?
Child: No, I have tried to ask her things about it, but she says that she didn't want to talk about it.
I see. Because XXX didn't hit (your sister), did he?
Child: When?
When you told us that he did hit her, he didn't really hit her, did he?
Child: He did
And he didn't hit you either, did he?
Child: Yes[22]

Even though Example (4) illustrates a number of questioning procedures considered typical of cross-examinations, Examples (5) to (7) illustrate that these strategies are also found in police interviews with children—i.e., the use of question types that challenge the child's testimony, such as 'Are you sure?', as well as the practice of rephrasing the child's testimony as her 'story' instead of the 'facts' as related by the child. This creates a chasm between 'the truth' and the child's testimony that would resonate with the 'children lie' stereotype.

(5) Police officer, phase 2 (witness = girl 14 years, rape allegation)

So, you went back to his flat, did you?
Child: No, I didn't go into his flat.
Are you sure about that?

(6) Police officer, phases 2–3 (witness = boy 11 years, attempted rape)

OK, so what was he doing when you said you were trying to get him off you?
Child: Well, he's trying to get hold of me and he's, well, he had his pants down already and he's tried to put his willy into me.
Right, I'm sorry I've got to keep on asking you all these questions but I need to get it right, alright?
Child: Yeah
So you're telling me now XXX's bed's in the middle and you're in bed and then he gets into bed and you're looking that way to start with.
Child: Yeah
OK and then you're telling me that he pulls down his pants.

(7) Police officer, phase 3 (witness = boy 11 years, rape allegation)

So, what could you see?
Child: Like him pulling his pants down.
OK so what did he do then?
Child: He tried to do it again.
And you're telling me, when you say he tried to do it, what exactly was he trying to do?

---

[22] This example also illustrates another feature of testimonies in general and certainly relevant in children's testimonies, and that is the ambiguity of Yes/No answers. We suspect that the child's second answer 'Yes' in the final line of this excerpt is short for, 'Yes, he did', but because the child did not include the sentence nucleus ('he did') her answer can be mistaken for agreement with the barrister's assertions which she was otherwise rejecting.

Child: Trying to put his willy in me and that's it.
...
What else could you see?
Child: I could see his willy and that's it coz I turned round then dead quick then went.
So, you're telling me it touched you?
Child: Yeah
...
And you're telling me [alleged abuser] has got his pants down to there?
Child: Yeah about there
...
OK, so when you're telling me that he tried to put his willy in your bum—those were your words, weren't they?
Child: Yeah
So, you could feel it, could you?

The examples given in (4) to (7) are indicative of a frequent questioning strategy seen across the legal process for children, that captures elements of disbelief of the child's case and brings into doubt the child's ability to remember facts clearly. The challenging question, 'Are you sure?' amplifies the stereotype that 'children can't be relied upon to tell the truth', while the interviewer's frequent transposing of the child's testimony as 'their' story, and even worse, 'their story now', captures not only how the police officer distances himself from the content of the child's testimony, but also how the constant repetition of the interviewer's questions can reinforce the suggestion of disbelief to hearers.

These examples also illustrate how police officers in police interviews can be seen to use questioning strategies considered typical of court cross-examinations, which furthers our argument that the police interview should not be used in court, as 'normal' (i.e., not 'vulnerable') witnesses would never be questioned by the prosecuting barrister in such a way. Hence, the challenging nature of the investigation procedure is not consistent with outlining the witness's case to the court.

In this section we have offered a number of examples that capture the frequent and typical questioning strategies with child witnesses throughout the legal process that either actively involve the 'children lie' frame, or draw on it indirectly. The consistency in the use of these questioning strategies in children's testimonies as well as the legal process in general, evidences a social bias that holds that children can't reliably differentiate fact from fiction. Although we can expect the police process to exercise caution in pursuit of the truth, playing these videoed interviews (which include elements of scepticism and doubt) in court would surely alert others in the legal process to the view that 'children can't (always) be believed', thereby offering the Defence the 'any reasonable doubt' defence before the child's case is considered at all.

The inclination to disbelieve has also been raised in the Home Office report into rape case attrition.[23] Even though this report focuses on rape cases in general (across all age bands), the authors recommend that the CPS needs to make a shift in focus from a culture of discrediting rape complaints toward enhancing evidence gathering and case building. This is especially true for child witnesses where cultural stereotypes are already stacked against the child complainant.

---

[23] Liz Kelly, Jo Lovett, and Linda Regan, *A gap or a chasm? Attrition in reported rape cases*. Home Office Research Study 293 (London, 2005).

This 'inclination to disbelieve' will be further explored in the next section, which deals with the types of questions found in child testimonies, which we argue are sanctioned by the enduring 'rape myth'.

4. Social myth no. 2: the rape myth

It is clear from a number of public websites that the existence of the 'rape myth' is already well understood, including how the social stereotype of what constitutes a 'true rape victim' deviates from those claiming rape. For example the Rape & Incest Crisis Centre of Northamptonshire reports the key components of this social stereotype to include: rape is only committed by a stranger, on a dark street, late at night; good girls don't get raped; and rape is only committed by a maniac or pervert who is in the grip of an uncontrollable sexual urge.[24] Full characterizations of the rape myth have dealt more with details of the victim, including that she is a decent, young woman (preferably with no sexual history), who provided no advances or provocation whatever, and has wounds to evidence her resistance (see Estrich 1987).[25] The breadth of academic research into this myth[26] has apparently been successful in revealing to the general public how this stereotype is manifestly evident in the questioning procedures during police interviews and rape trials (in general) and is presumed to be chiefly responsible for the high attrition rate in pursuing rape cases. However, what is possibly less well understood is the extent to which this stereotype is also manifest in the questions put to children in the videoed police interviews.

Statistical evidence over the years has revealed that the social stereotype of the rape victim is far removed from the actual reports of rape made by alleged victims, such as the finding that less than 10 per cent of all rapes are carried out by someone unknown to the victim,[27] and women from all cross-sections of society (not just good girls) have been victims of rape. A critical argument in the face of a rape allegation has for some time been the issue of consent, and past sexual experiences have traditionally been employed as evidence to counter claims of rape. Recent laws in the UK, such as the Sexual Offences Act 2003, now rule against allowing witnesses to be questioned about their past sexual experiences, and the CPS guidelines also make comparable restrictions on what questions may be put to witnesses by their own counsel, the prosecution. These guidelines state:

When presenting cases it is vital to ensure that you are aware of section 41(5) so that evidence is not unintentionally adduced by the prosecution that will allow the defence the opportunity to seek to adduce evidence of sexual behaviour of the victim in rebuttal of that prosecution evidence.[28]

---

[24] <http://www.nricc.com/en/support/myths.asp>.
[25] Susan Estrich, *Real Rape* (Cambridge, Mass.: Harvard University Press, 1987).
[26] Susan Ehrlich, *Representing Rape: language and sexual consent* (Routledge, 2001); Gregory Matoesian, *Reproducing Rape: domination through talk in the courtroom* (Chicago, 1993); Luchjenbroers and Aldridge, 'Conceptual manipulation with Metaphors and Frames' (cited in n.8).
[27] Australian Bureau of Statistics, *Women's Safety* (Canberra, 1996); D. Brereton, 'How different are rape trials? A comparison of the Cross-Examination of complainants in rape and assault trials' (1997) 37(2) *British Journal of Criminology* 242–61. N. Marhia in the UK reports between 8 and 17%: *Just representation? Press reporting and the reality of rape. The Lilith Project* (Eaves, 2008), available at <http://i1.cmsfiles.com/eaves/2012/04/Just-Representation_press_reporting_the_reality_of_rape-d81249.pdf>, accessed 8 October 2012. The range in the UK results may reflect differences in how 'strangers' are defined.
[28] <http://www.cps.gov.uk/legal/s_to_u/sexual_offences_rape/#Procedure_for_application_to>, accessed October 2011.

While these guidelines must be followed in adult court procedures, children in the videoed police interviews are asked very explicit questions about prior sexual experience. See Examples (11a) to (11f) below.

(11) Police officer, phases 2–4 (witness = girl 14 years, rape allegation)

(a) Child: so I did and em and he started kissing me, started biting me again then he started ... [silence]
When it was happening, was the boat dark?
Child: Em there was one little light on it
Can you tell me what you were wearing last night?
Child: I was wearing my cream Reebok jumper and my check shirt and my blue jeans and my trainers
OK, did you have anything on underneath your shirt?
...
Yeah OK, what was he wearing?

(b) Child: Yeah and then I was screaming
Had he ever done that before?
Child: No
Have you ever done anything like that with anyone else before?
Child: No
Has anyone ever fingered you before?
Child: No
So that was your first sexual encounter was it?
Child: Yeah

(c) *Have you ever fancied [accused]?*
Child: No, he's 35
I have to ask these things. Have you ever sort of wanted to have a sort of a kiss or a cuddle with him?

(d) *OK so what are your injuries as a result of last night?*

(e) *Have you ever had sex before?*
Child: No
Have you ever had any boyfriend fondling you or anything like that down below?

(f) *Going back to when you were on the boat, how much of the brandy did you think you had?*
Child: Just half a mouthful
What about cigarettes? Did you have a cigarette on the boat?
Child: He gave me one drag on one of his
OK has he ever said to you anything along the lines of he loves you?

The string of police contributions given in Example (11 a–f) illustrate various aspects of the rape myth that currently prevails in the judicial system in England and Wales, not just to women in general but clearly also to children. The police questions cover each of the rape myth components in turn, regarding the girl's attire, her wounds to evidence unwanted attention, and importantly her sexual history. The excerpt given in (11a) shows the police questions to jump straight from description of the assault to her choice of clothing that night and whether she wore undergarments on that occasion. Any rational hearer would assume a logical link between these questions, such as a causal consequence although this is not asserted. The only relevance of the questions about her state of dress is to measure her likely consent and/or whether she had in any way provoked the alleged rape.

The focus on attire is also apparent in police interviews with children under 13, as in Example (12) below.

(12) Police officer, phases 2–3 (witness = boy 11 years, attempted rape)

Alright OK. So it's a normal double bed is it?
Child: [nods]
What were you wearing?
Child: My pyjamas

The questions in Examples (11b) and (11e) illustrate how the police interview goes into great depth about this girl's prior sexual experience, not just with this man, but with anyone before this alleged event. Even though such questioning is ruled out in normal adult court, we can assume that collecting this information is an important part of the police investigation (at one point the interviewer apologizes for needing to ask these questions).

The remaining questions of Example (11) also deal with known aspects of the rape myth, such as whether the child may have had feelings for the alleged abuser (which he may have recognized and which may have enticed him to presume consent)—in (11c); whether she had fought off her attacker, thus being able to show wounds—in (11d); and whether alcohol or drugs were involved that may have influenced the reported events—in (11f). The relevance of a child's usage of alcohol or cigarettes is that it may serve as a measure of the child's social proclivities. This was remarked upon in the Stern Review, which reports that '26–29% (male and female respondents) feel that a woman is at least partially responsible for her own rape if she had been drunk or was behaving in a flirtatious manner (2005)'.[29]

The focus on these other facets of the 'true victim' stereotype is also evident in the police interviews with children under 13, such as Examples (13) and (14) below. In Example (13), the 12-year-old girl, like the 14-year-old girl in Example (11), is asked to describe her outer and undergarments, if any.

(13) Police officer, phases 2–3 (witness = girl 12 years, rape allegation)

Right, and when that was happening, what were you wearing? [page 4]
Child: My nightie
Would you have anything on under your nightie, your knickers or anything?
Child: No
So when he was touching you down there, was that under your clothing or over your clothing?
Child: Under
So was that on your skin then?
Child: Yeah
– – –
Right, so when he started touching you, where was that? [page 8]
Child: Down below…
Again, was that underneath or over your clothes?
Child: Underneath my clothes
Underneath OK. One thing I wanted to ask as well, what do you have on your bed? What bed covers do you have on?

---

[29] Baroness Vivien Stern, *The Stern Review* (London: UK Home Office: Government Equalities Office, 2010); HM Government, *The Response to the Stern Review* (London: Cabinet Office, 2011).

*Right OK, I've forgotten now. **You said** that was under your nightie?* [page 9]

Although the questions to the 14-year-old about over and under attire were not made relevant, in any way, to discussions of the alleged crime during the testimony, the preoccupation with the nature of the 12-year-old child's garments may be seen as an attempt to properly catalogue the full extent of the alleged crime. However, Example (13) also reveals that the interviewer recycled this matter throughout the 12-year-old's interview (on page 4, phase 2; page 8, phase 3; and page 9, phase 4).

This recycling suggests the interviewer is not convinced by the child's earlier answers, further exacerbated by the final rephrasing, 'you said...' (as discussed above). Whereas Example (13) deals with the claimant's clothing, and Example (14) deals with the alleged victim's resistance to the approach, both examples involve recycling of the subject matter in the child's testimony in a way that indirectly suggests a key relevance of these issues to those who view the interview. Example (14) also reveals how 'resistance' is relevant whatever the age of the child complainant and presupposes that adult decisions would be an appropriate measure for what children might feel able to do or decide.

(14) Police officer, phases 2–3 (witness = girl 12 years, rape allegation)

Right, during that time, do you do anything or say anything? [page 5]
Child: No
Is there any reason that you don't do anything or say anything to him?
Child: Coz he said to me it's mine and your little secret coz I heard his voice. And he
    said, if I do say anything to anybody he'll just deny it.
...
When that's happening do you just lie still or. [page 6]
Child: I just lie still
You just lie there. Has anybody else been in the room when this happens?

Examples (13) and (14) effectively illustrate what a very fine line there may be between establishing the facts of a case and prompting information that may serve to 'blame the victim' due to the fundamental associations made possible by the rape myth—if someone dresses inappropriately, and doesn't fight off the approach, then maybe this wasn't a rape but a matter of consent? This factor is also relevant to our argument that the police interview should not be shown in court and should not be the victim's Evidence-in-Chief.

If we examine the questions put to the 14-year-old (alleged) victim in Example (11), it might be tempting to assume that it is a positive outcome for her that these questions were asked because she is able to refute them. However, any discussion of sexual activity between children and adults 'normalizes' sex with and among minors. Even in the negative, questions that deal with a child's past sexual experience fail to emphasize the child's youth with regard to consent. The child is framed in the adult world of decisions, instead of the interviewer's questions reminding all hearers that as this was an illegal act, any pre-history is evidence of ongoing abuse.[30]

At this point in our examination of the police interview process, it is evident that it has two flaws: (i) the apparent inconsistency in applying the laws of evidence, and (ii) what

---

[30] Some may wish to argue that this argument ignores consenting, non-rape, sexual activity among those currently under the legal age of consent (16). Our argument is that it is inconsistent to argue both that children under 16 cannot consent, and that consent is a mitigating factor for sexual activity with any child, including those under 13 years of age (see CPS website, <http://www.cps.gov.uk/legal/s_to_u/sentencing_manual/s5_rape_of_child_under_13/>).

prior sexual history among minors really proves. The Sexual Offences Act 2003 has ruled out questions about the victim's past sexual history, consistent with the rape myth that holds that although prior sexual history may suggest sexual readiness, it does not evidence consent. These questions are, however, asked of children in the videoed police interviews, and (if a case were to proceed to court) the child's sexual history would be open to cross-examination. Hence the operation of the laws of evidence regarding what questions can be heard in court apparently does not extend to those deemed 'vulnerable' in the legal process.

Furthermore, what is possibly more important is the question of what information can be derived from a child's prior sexual history. Within a context (as in the UK) where sex with children under 16 is criminal, any sexual history must (logically) evidence prior abuse. We have not seen any evidence in the testimonies or police interviews analysed to date that would support the expectation that prior sexual history is interpreted in this light. Instead, as with adults, prior sexual history appears to count against the child complainant. Hence, a child who has to report prior sexual experiences would likely be seen as less of a victim than one who does not.

Given the current age of consent for sex, asking any child questions about her prior sexual history should be ruled out, both in the investigative stage and in court, unless that prior sexual contact is also seen as part of the crime under investigation. By asking questions regarding the victim's prior sexual experience at any stage of the legal process, as a measure of 'consent' or 'inducement', the legal process is essentially guilty of accepting the underlying assumption that it is not so bad to abuse those who have been abused before.

In this section we have focused on different issues relating to the rape myth, as evident in the questions asked, in particular those that relate to prior sexual history, whether asked directly or 'smuggled' into the questions asked through semantic associations.[31] Questions that focus on prior sexual activity—as well as potentially significant factors for a sex event, such as *what was she wearing, where did this happen, how often has this happened*—all serve to normalize sex with minors. Such representations of children also affect the legal treatment of these persons (i.e., children) as they are treated as potentially 'complicit' in any proved sex event instead of as just children who by definition can't be trusted to make sensible decisions and therefore cannot consent to sex.

The range of examples given in Examples (11) to (14) also serve to provide evidence of the third significant myth relevant to rape cases in general and vulnerable children in particular: the 'autonomous testosterone' myth, which is dealt with in the next section.

5. Social myth no. 3: the 'autonomous testosterone' myth

The 'autonomous testosterone' myth essentially holds that once a man is aroused, he cannot resist the sexual encounter he is exposed to: his testosterone will overpower him and move him to carry out the sex act without regard to consequences. Even though the rape myth has a reasonably complex set of defining features that describe the kind of man involved in a rape and the kind of female who can be a victim, the 'autonomous testosterone' myth has only two features, and these would fit any man: arousal leading to penetration. However, within this myth, the portrayal of the man changes: rather than being an aggressor, he is a person who is a victim of his own sexuality and who, when 'brought' into the state of arousal, is no longer capable of 'sound mind' decisions. The responsibility then falls to others (i.e., women and children) to not put him into this potentially dangerous situation.

---

[31] Aldridge and Luchjenbroers, 'Linguistic manipulations in legal discourse' (cited in n.18).

This myth explains the police questions about prior sexual history, because without the 'autonomous testosterone' myth there is no logical connection between a victim's personal history and a measure of (likely or possible) 'consent'. Only within a frame where recognition of a person's 'sexual readiness' can be seen as a predictable way to arouse a man (even to the point where that man's testosterone autonomously directs his actions), and signs of sexual readiness are viewed as deliberate signals of consent, can the victim be seen as at least partly, if not fully, responsible for the sex event, regardless of his or her age.

In particular, Example (11) has illustrated how characteristics of the child that may be interpreted as signs of 'sexual readiness' are catalogued in the police interview, ranging from prior sexual encounters; the nature of any prior sexual encounters; possible sexual curiosity and/or interest in the alleged aggressor; the state of the child's dress (both outer and under garments); and the possible use of stimulants (whether just during the reported event or in general). But none of these questions directly address consent, and the only relevance of their use is in eliciting indirect associations with factors that can be expected to correlate with consensual sex.

For consenting adults, bringing a man into a state of arousal is therefore something both parties in the sex act need to avoid unless both actually seek it out. However, the legal age of consent, designed to 'protect children from themselves', should make any arousal, sexual curiosity/interest, or 'agreeing to sex' by the child completely irrelevant. In fact, as argued above, in a context where sexual activity with those under 16 is illegal, prior sexual history can only ever evidence a history of abuse and can never be used in mitigation, as evidencing 'consent'.[32] The fact that consent is taken into account in relation to those who cannot consent entails the belief that abusing a child who has been abused before is not so bad.[33]

Further to this, the police interview generally portrays child–adult sex events with a level of accuracy and detail that imbues them with a degree of 'normalcy', which will not remind those in court that all legal decisions are made by adults and not the children involved. In fact, Example (15) illustrates how the same testimony that should evidence continued abuse can be used to argue 'consent': in this case the approaches ended when her resistance became evident.

(15) Police officer, phases 2–4 (witness = girl 12 years, rape allegation)

Child: Well my dad's friend, step-dad's friend, he's called XXX and he was touching me down below and touching me up top and everything and being horrible to me when he was drunk and offering me cigarettes and beer
Yeah. How many times has that happened? [page 3]
Child: It was all through the winter and he tried it on last night, the night before that, but he didn't do anything
Right. When you say all through the winter, how many times would that be? Can you say?
Child: No
If I said to you it was once a day or once a week or
Child: He normally comes down weekends
Does he normally come down every weekend?

---

[32] <http://www.cps.gov.uk/legal/s_to_u/sentencing_manual/s5_rape_of_child_under_13/index.html>, accessed October 2011.

[33] The CPS guidelines explain that consent is intended to measure the extent of the harm caused by the abuse. However this presupposes that harm is immediately evident, and excludes psychological damage, which would be the relevant harm in cases of repeated abuse.

Child: No
No
Child: Occasionally
Would you be able to say if that was every other weekend or every month or every two months?
Child: I think it was like every other weekend or sometimes it was every weekend.
...
So that goes on for about
Child: 15–20 minutes normally
So how many times has that happened like that then? [page 5]
Child: Don't know
Has it happened just once or more than once?
Child: More than once
...
When was the last time that it happened?
Child: Well, he did try, not last night, the night before that, he tried then
OK then... You said he tried, what happened?
Child: Yeah, Well, he came into my room, woke me up and started touching me and I turned over and he just walked out.

In this case the abuse, which spanned many months, stopped as soon as the child turned away. From an adult perspective, the fact that she had not done so from the start can be indicative of 'compliance', that would likely count as mitigating consent. However, children do not have the same measure of control over stressful situations that we might imagine normal adults would have, and so their choices should not be used to mitigate illegal, adult choices, or in any way to justify the consequences of the 'autonomous testosterone' myth—i.e., a child's compliance is presumed sufficient to encourage a man's arousal; he may then be driven by his testosterone to lose control: he saw an opportunity and went for it.

Further examples of the child's conduct that may be taken by the police and/or the CPS as conveying 'consent' have been presented in several examples above, and key elements are reproduced in Example (16). In these extracts, the police officer asks about the child's state of dress (both outer and under garments) as well as her conduct during the sex acts, which, although possibly necessary to establish the full extent of the alleged crime, fail to highlight that the only person who can legally make decisions in (child) rape situations is the alleged aggressor.

(16) Police officer, phases 2–3 (witness = girl 12 years, rape allegation)

How long did that go on for then?
Child: He normally does it for 15–20 minutes
Right, during that time, do you do anything or say anything?
Child: No
Is there any reason that you don't do anything or say anything to him?
...
Right and when that was happening, what were you wearing?
Child: My nightie
Would you have anything on under your nightie, your knickers or anything?
...
When that was happening, do you just lie still or...
Child: Lie still

In effect, the content of the police interview questions show that the 'autonomous testosterone' myth is alive and well in how children are questioned in England and Wales. This is most evident in the fact that 'consent' is a mitigating factor in child rape, but it is also apparent in the need to establish the child's sexual history and state of dress to determine her contribution to the reported event. We have also revealed how sensitively questions that may serve to establish the full extent of the alleged crime need to be asked, to ensure they do not indirectly attribute blame to the questioned child (through semantic associations generated by the relevant myths discussed in this paper). Even the testimonies of under-13-year-old victims involve adult assessments of participatory roles in sexual encounters that are modelled on consenting adult choices. The factors catalogued by the police interview to measure 'consent' evidence the power of the 'autonomous testosterone' myth which, unlike the rape myth, could apply to any man and not just 'a maniac or pervert who is in the grip of an uncontrollable sexual urge'.

6. In Closing…

This paper has expanded and illustrated a range of social stereotypes that make a child's case very difficult, if not impossible. The relevant stereotypes include, first, the social perception that children lie and/or cannot be relied upon to tell the truth, and that all questioning strategies that resemble those used in cross-examination, suggesting scepticism and doubt, would resonate with this social bias against children (and, according to Stern (2010),[34] against all rape complainants in general). The second and third stereotypes are also referred to as 'myths' in that they involve characterizations of the aggressor and victim roles in rape situations that bear little resemblance to real life, but which explain the questions put to child rape/sexual violence witnesses. Social perceptions of what type of person is a true rape victim, and of what constitutes 'consent', seriously stack the cards against children in sexual assault cases in the legal system of England and Wales.

Our primary position in this paper is that the police interview should not be used in court as the child's Evidence-in-Chief. The grounds for this position include the essential position that children cannot be expected to articulate for themselves the best representation of their case to a listening jury; but more importantly, the police interviewers include a range of questions that would not be permitted in questioning 'normal' witnesses in court (such as those dealing with the victim's sexual history); furthermore, the style of questioning in the police interview has many features in common with the style of questioning during the cross-examination of witnesses in court. These questioning strategies that can convey scepticism and/or doubt would resonate with the social stereotype that 'children lie'/'don't always tell the truth', which already makes the child's case difficult for her.

Earlier literature has focused on how to encourage children to 'open up' and verbally participate, in the apparent belief that when they do, children will have a better access to the law. However quantity is not quality, and the arguments offered in this paper supplement the problems identified in earlier literature across academic disciplines (in linguistics, psychology, sociology, and criminology) pertaining to these interview phases.[35] While videoed interviews are far preferable for vulnerable children than court appearances, interviews should only be conducted by the prosecuting barrister to ensure the

---

[34] Baroness Vivien Stern, *The Stern Review* (cited in n.29); HM Government, *The Response to the Stern Review* (cited in n.29).
[35] See Aldridge and Wood, 'Telling it how it was' (cited in n.3).

questions build the best possible case for the child complainant. As early statistics have suggested a low use of videoed interviews in court, in a system where videoed interviews would typically be used there is a need to recognize that there is a general failure to protect children within the current practice.

In general, the process of obtaining true and undirected evidence from children in the first evidentiary setting (i.e., the interview with the police) has been sincere, but this objective is not the means by which children can achieve greater access to the legal process. In other words, successfully encouraging the verbal participation of children does mean they are capable of making the linguistic choices that will best further their case (this is the job of the prosecutor). Children are recognized as vulnerable precisely because they cannot make adult decisions, and making them the authors of their own testimonies requires them to accomplish for themselves what the examining barrister would ordinarily be expected to achieve for average, adult witnesses. This simply is not just, and illustrates how a greater responsibility is left to those least able to bear it. This disadvantage is further amplified by the arguments presented in this paper, showing how representations of child victims in adult terms, using adult social patterns of expectation, normalizes sex with minors and fails to remind all concerned that these people are just children who cannot give consent.

Police officers are not barristers and so the major stumbling block is not necessarily that the police do this job wrongly; but rather that they should not be expected to do it at all. The police officers' role of collecting evidence is not consistent with the subsequent use of the police interview video being shown in court as the child's Evidence-in-Chief. For all non-vulnerable witnesses, the examining barrister's primary role is to elicit their testimonies in the best and clearest way possible to emphasize the injustice done to them and that they are in fact victims. The police video testimony cannot do this because that is not its primary role.

The final issue addressed in this paper is consideration of the appropriateness of the questions used to measure the child's involvement (i.e., consent) in the reported sexual event(s). The 'rape' myth and the 'autonomous testosterone' myth deal with the same situation (i.e., rape) but differ in an important way. While the rape myth describes a male perpetrator who is a stranger, who attacks in a dark place, late at night; or a maniac or pervert who is in the grip of an uncontrollable sexual urge (i.e., someone who is distinctly different from 'normal' men), the 'autonomous testosterone' myth describes an essentially 'normal' characteristic of any man. What differentiates a rapist from a non-rapist is not the fundamental drive for sex, but the male individual's control or discretion in the situations he allows himself to be part of. Unfortunately the man's 'control' or 'likely discretion' is measured by the woman's or child's sexual history, state of dress, and/or control over the situation in which she finds herself, but none of these can evidence either 'consent' or how a man is likely to respond to her unless these factors are considered reasonable inducements to cause a 'normal' man to be swept away by his testosterone.

18

The Power of Naming: Surnames, Children, and Spouses

Jonathan Herring

Introduction

To give something or someone a name is an exercise of power.[1] This was recognized by Friedrich Nietzsche:

The lordly right of giving names extends so far that one should allow oneself to conceive the origin of language itself as an expression of power on the part of the rulers: they say 'this is this and this,' they seal every thing and event with a sound and, as it were, take possession of it.[2]

Much political control is exercised through the power to label someone a terrorist; disabled; or criminal. Universities and other institutions expect a substantial donation from someone who seeks to have a building named after them. Law is dominated by named categories and the legal consequences that flow from them. Everything in court dispute can turn on whether the words such as 'contract' or 'minor' apply to the agreement or individual before the court. According to Pierre Bourdieu, '[l]aw is the quintessential form of the symbolic power of naming that creates the things named....'[3] Much feminist writing has highlighted the ways that names and labels are used to hide women from public debate and to structure arguments or concepts in a male way.[4] The categorization used by the law can have social as well as legal results, as the current debates over same-sex marriage indicate.[5]

This chapter considers a particularly powerful example of naming in family law: spousal naming and the naming of children. In one sense it might be thought that surnames are a trivial matter. Does it really matter that much what one's name is? Yet, as we shall see shortly couples are willing to spend substantial sums of money disputing names. This is because naming is used to exercise power and control. The case law is replete with fathers seeking to reinforce a form of ownership of their children through forcing them to retain their paternal name. Further, a central theme of this chapter is that naming conveys a strong symbolic message about the family and gender relations in it. This chapter

---

[1] Justin Kaplan and Anne Bernays, *The Language of Names* (New York: Oxford University Press, 1997).

[2] Friedrich Nietzsche, *On the Genealogy of Morals*, trans. Walter Kaufmann (New York: Random House, 1989), 26.

[3] Pierre Bourdieu, *The Force of Law: Toward a Sociology of the Juridical Field* (1977) 38 *Hastings Law Journal* 805, at 817; Adrienne Rich, 'When We Dead Awaken: Writing as Re-Vision' in Sandra Gilbert and Susan Gubar (eds), *The Norton Anthology of Literature by Women*, 2nd edn (New York: WW Norton, 1996); and Dale Spender, *Man Made Language* (New York: Routledge, 1994), 183–90.

[4] e.g. Dale Spender, *Man Made Language* (cited in n.3); Robin Tolmach Lakoff, *Language And Woman's Place* (Oxford: Oxford University Press, 2004).

[5] S. Kim, 'Marital Naming/Naming Marriage: Language and Status in Family Law', *Indiana Law Journal*, forthcoming. Available at SSRN: <http://ssrn.com/abstract=1421564>.

will start by summarizing the significance of names, before briefly setting out the law and offering a critique of it.

1. Names

The significance of having a name is revealed by the fact that several international conventions express a child's right to a name.[6] In part this reflects the fact that without a name a child is likely to be subject to abuse, even sale. It ensures the child can be traced and identified by the state as an individual with rights. As Snell J put it:

> An old Roman maxim runs, 'Sine nomine homo non est' (without a name a person is nothing). One's name is a signboard to the world. It is one of the most permanent of possessions; it remains when everything else is lost; it is owned by those who possess nothing else. A name is the only efficient means to describe someone to contemporaries and to posterity. When one dies it is the only part that lives on in the world.[7]

In most developed countries it is personal identification that is nowadays the particular significance of naming. Janet Finch explains that

> personal names are a core marker of the individual.... I must provide my name—Janet Finch—in order to be able to transact even the most mundane of everyday tasks. My name has two dimensions. It marks me as a unique individual, and it also gives some indication of my location in the various social worlds which I inhabit—it encapsulates my legal persona as a British citizen, it reveals my gender and probably my ethnicity, it documents something of my family connections and, in my case, if I add my title 'professor' it states my occupation.[8]

Norbert Elias suggests that the forename can be seen as an 'I-identity' and the surname as a 'we-identity'.[9] Although the distinction between the two is far from clear cut because our identity is substantially made up from our social relationships, this still provides a helpful insight into the role played by names.

There is a lengthy history on the use of names. Long ago they were simply a marker of personal identity: referring to a characteristic of a person (Short) or the place they lived (e.g. Hill). Since these benign beginnings, names have developed as an exercise of power. Over history they have been used as a means of colonization or reinforcement of slavery;[10] or as a marker of social or economic power.[11] Malcolm X's refusal to adopt an 'orthodox' surname was a forceful statement rejecting the power exercised through surnames. Cassius Clay's change of name to Mohammed Ali was a powerful religious and cultural statement.

The traditional approach to names in Anglo-American society, namely that the wife take her husband's surname and that their children likewise take that name, has come under pressure from two directions.[12] First, there are arguments from feminists. As will

---

[6] e.g. the UN Convention on the Rights of the Child, art.7.
[7] *In re Marriage of Gulsvig*, 498 N.W.2d 725, 730 (Iowa 1994).
[8] J. Finch, 'Naming Names: Kinship, Individuality and Personal Names' (2008) 42 *Sociology* 709.
[9] Norbert Elias, *The Society of Individuals* (Oxford, 1991), 84; H. Davies, 'Sharing Surnames: Children, Family and Kinship' (2011) 45(4) *Sociology* 554.
[10] Susan Benson, 'Injurious Naming: Naming, Disavowal and Recuperation in the Contexts of Slavery and Emancipation' in Gabrielle vom Bruck and Barbara Bodenhorn (eds), *An Anthropology of Names and Naming* (Cambridge: Cambridge University Press, 2006), 178–94.
[11] Evelyn Lord, 'Given Names and Inheritance' in David Postles (ed.), *Naming, Society and Regional Identity* (Oxford: Oxford University Press, 2002), 169.
[12] Although there are historical examples of a man taking his wife's name, especially when marrying an heiress (L. Stone and J. Fawtier Stone, *An Open Elite? England 1540–1880* (Oxford: Clarendon Press, 1984)).

be argued in this chapter the current naming practices, reinforced to some extent by the law, reflect patriarchal power. It is the man's name which is generally taken to be the marker of the family: the family is 'his' and so are 'his children'. Feminists seeking to challenge such views have for decades rejected the assumptions behind these patronymic naming practices. Secondly, there are changing understandings and practices of families. Increasing rates of divorce and a broader range of families mean that family identity has become complex and certainly not reducible to one name. A single surname cannot capture our connections to the fluid family forms that are all too common in contemporary society.[13] Partners and parent figures come and go in the lives of many adults and children, giving a shifting sense of family identity. As Janet Finch notes:

> Names therefore do not act as unambiguous statements about family membership—increasingly they may not denote either household relationships or relationships formed by marriage. Indeed the variety of surnames within a household is itself an indicator that the key intimate relationships of individuals have changed over time.[14]

Further our social identities are no longer simply tied up with our families, but can reflect our place in broader kinship, racial, ethnic, religious and social groups.[15] Surnames can reflect these identities, as well as family ones. Again, showing, the difficulty in adopting a single static name as a reflection of some given identity, in the way traditional naming practices do.

Our naming practices need to reflect these changing concepts of family: families as fluid, non-patriarchal institutions; families where the doing of family life is of greater significance than the tie of blood.[16] Hence, as Hayley Davies, in an important contribution to the sociological literature, has argued, surnames are no longer a given, but reflect negotiations and creativity.[17]

2. Law of names

What follows will be only a brief summary of the law on names.[18]

What is a person's name?

English law on surnames is astonishingly unregulated. *Re T (Otherwise H) (An Infant)*[19] makes it clear that a person's surname in law is simply that by which she or he is customarily known. This does not have to be the registered name. It is possible through a deed poll to provide formal evidence of a change of surname, although that is not essential.[20]

---

[13] Davies, 'Sharing Surnames' (cited in n.9).
[14] D. R. Johnson and L. K. Scheuble, 'What Should We Call our Kids?' (2002) 39 *The Social Science Journal* 419, 428; E. Silva, 'Gender, Home and Family in Cultural Capital Theory' (2005) 56 *British Journal of Sociology* 83.
[15] R. Edwards and C. Caballero, 'What's in a Name? An Exploration of the Significance of Personal Naming of "Mixed" Children for Parents from Different Racial, Ethnic and Faith Backgrounds' (2008) 56 *The Sociological Review* 39.
[16] J. Finch, 'Displaying Families' (2007) 41 *Sociology* 65.
[17] Davies, 'Sharing Surnames' (cited in n.9).
[18] See S. Gilmore, 'The Nature, Scope, and Use of the Specific Issue Order' [2004] *Child and Family Law Quarterly* 367 for a useful discussion of the courts' approach in cases of disputes over names.
[19] [1962] 3 All ER 970.
[20] *Practice Direction (Minor: Change of Surname: Deed Poll)* [1995] 1 All ER 832.

The English position on names is remarkable in three ways. First, there is no restriction on the choice of your name. There is certainly no list of approved names. The Deed Poll Services suggests it will not accept names which are impossible to pronounce or are 'vulgar or offensive', although they are happy to accept 'ludicrous names'.[21] In fact, it seems to be the law that if you are generally known by an offensive name, that is your name, even if you cannot formalize that through a deed poll. Secondly, there is a complete lack of any requirement of formal recording of one's name or change of name. This, one might have thought, would produce all kinds of administrative difficulties for the Government. However, in practice it seems not to. In part this may be due to the use of numbers to identify people (e.g. a National Insurance number). Thirdly, even if a person does register a name formally executing a deed poll, this can be changed by common usage.[22] So, not only is there no need for a formal record of a name, even where there is a formal record this may not be the name in the eyes of the law.[23]

Spousal names

Marriage has no automatic legal effect on your name. All depends, as just indicated, on how you are generally known. If therefore on marriage a wife becomes generally known by her husband's name that becomes her name. Government offices, however, are very ready to accept that marriage has effected a change of name. The Passport Office, for example, accepts the marriage certificate or civil partnership certificate as sufficient evidence of change of name for the purposes of obtaining a new passport.[24] Other reasons for name change require much more extensive evidence.

Children's names

Registration of birth

A child's birth must be registered within 42 days[25] and the person registering the birth can declare 'the surname by which at the date of the registration of the birth it is intended that the child shall be known'.[26] Once a name has been registered it can only be changed in the case of clerical error.[27] Although it may be possible to change the name of the child later, this will not alter the name on the birth certificate. That is because the birth certificate is simply a record of the *intended* name at birth, it is not meant to be a record of the child's current name.

There is no restriction on what names parents can select. The child's surname does not need to be one of their own. Their imagination can run riot. In other countries there is far greater control over the names selected, where a forename must be chosen from an

---

[21] Deed Poll Service, 'A woman's name change rights and options upon marriage'; available at: <http://www.ukdps.co.uk>.
[22] A. Bond, 'Reconstructing Families—Changing Children's Surnames' [1998] CFLQ 17.
[23] General Register Office, 'Registering and naming your baby'; available at: <http://www.gro.gov.uk>.
[24] Passport Office, 'Changing Names and Personal Details on a Passport'; available at: <http://www.direct.gov.uk/en/TravelAndTransport/Passports/Howtochangethenameonyourpassport/index.htm>.
[25] Births and Deaths Registration Act 1953 s.2.
[26] Registration of Births and Deaths Regulations 1987 (SI 1987/2088) reg.9(3).
[27] See M Hayes, 'What's in a Name? A Child by any other Name is Surely just as Sweet?' [1999] CFLQ 423, 430 for a discussion of whether it is possible to mount a legal challenge to the registration.

approved list and there are regulations governing surnames. In most countries there is at least a discretion for the Registrar to refuse to accept a particular name.[28] This does not appear to be the case in English law.

It is, in fact, rare for a dispute over a surname to arise at the point of registration. Generally it is some time later, when the parents' relationship has broken down, that the issue arises. A typical case for a dispute involves a married couple whose children are registered at birth with the husband's surname. They divorce and the wife remarries and takes her new husband's name or reverts to her original surname. She then seeks to change the children's surname to the one she is currently using. The father objects. These are the kinds of cases that will be considered next.

Changing a name unilaterally

Where a residence order is in force the law is clear. The Children Act 1989 s.13(1) states that the written consent of every person with parental responsibility is required before a name can be changed. If consent cannot be obtained then leave of the court is required. It is notable that the consent of the child, *even if a teenager*, is not required for the change to take effect.

The Children Act 1989 provides no explicit guidance on the legal position concerning changing names where there is no residence order. The courts have drawn a distinction between cases where a person has parental responsibility and where he or she does not. Where both parents have parental responsibility it appears from the Court of Appeal decisions in *Dawson v Wearmouth*[29] and *Re T (Change of Surname)*[30] that a change of name is only permitted either if both parents agree or if the court approves it. If each parent with parental responsibility could change the name unilaterally that could lead to an absurdity because each parent could unilaterally change the name of the child repeatedly. A child could have ten names before breakfast!

Where only one parent has parental responsibility the legal position is less clear. The view with the most support in the case law is that the parent with parental responsibility does have the right unilaterally to change the name of the child.[31] However, the courts[32] have stated that this parent should consult with the other parent and that if there is no agreement the matter should be taken to court. That, however, is not a legal obligation, rather a statement of desirable practice.

In *Re H (Child's Name: First Name)*[33] it was held that the rules in relation to surnames do not apply to forenames. A court will not stop the resident parent from using whatever forename she wishes. The father had registered the child with one first name and that would remain the registered name, but for all practical purposes the mother could choose the name she wished. It was explained that children often have a number of different given names during their life. No order was necessary to allow a parent to use a different first name from the one the child was registered with.

---

[28] See, e.g., the scheme in Finland (*Johansson v Finland* [2007] 3 FCR 420).
[29] [1997] 2 FLR 629.
[30] [1998] 2 FLR 620.
[31] *Re PC (Change of Surname)* [1997] 3 FCR 544; *Re W, Re A, Re B (Change of Name)* [1999] 2 FLR 930.
[32] *Re R (A Child)* [2002] 1 FCR 170 [9].
[33] [2002] 1 FLR 973.

Court decisions where there is a dispute

If a dispute over a child's name is brought to court the Children Act 1989 s.1 requires the court to make the order which promotes the child's welfare.[34] This provides the court with a broad discretion. In *Re W; Re A; Re B (Change of Name)*[35] Butler Sloss LJ listed the following factors as relevant: which name the child was given at registration of birth; the reasons for that registration; the reasons for making the unilateral change; any change in circumstances since the registration; whether the couple were married; the degree of commitment of the father and the quality of contact. Although the registered name was an 'important consideration' it was not to be treated as 'decisive'. Much more could be said about the case law, but this chapter will focus on the broader issues.[36]

3. Discussion of the law

The power of patronymy

The naming practices of society reveal what it thinks about individual identity; the nature of families; and power relationships within families. This means that different cultures have developed different naming regimes. For example, the Himalayan Bhutanese have no surnames at all.[37] Other countries have matrilineal systems of naming children, or use systems which combine the names of both parents. As Yofi Tirosh notes of the Barriada settlements of Lima, Peru, if a married couple shared the same name that would indicate that they are brother and sister and that their relationship was incestuous.[38] So what message is sent by Anglo-American naming practices?

The current naming practices both on marriage and of children reflect and reinforce a series of views about marriage, family life, and gender relations. Surnames have been used, and continue to be used, as a way of perpetuating patriarchy.[39] As Omi Morgenstern Leissner claims:

> By the rules of patronymy ... the woman is symbolically compelled into a posture of existential derivation, dependence, and submission.'[40]

Priscilla MacDougall goes further and sees the naming of the wife and children with the husband's name as indicating ownership:

> Custom said, too, that man owned what he paid for, and could put his name on everything for which he provided money. He wrote his name more often than a little boy with chalk signs his to a fence. He put it on his land, his house, his wife and children, his slaves when he had them, and on everything that was his.[41]

These ideas need some unpacking.

---

[34] *Dawson v Wearmouth* [1999] 1 FLR 1167.
[35] [1999] 2 FLR 930, 933.
[36] See Jonathan Herring, *Family Law* (Harlow: Pearson, 2011), ch.9.
[37] L. Kelly, 'Divining the Deep and Inscrutable: Toward A Gender-Neutral, Child-Centered Approach to Child Name Change Proceedings' (1996) 99 *West Virginia Law Review* 1.
[38] Y. Tirosh, 'A Name of One's Own: Gender and Symbolic Legal Personhood in the European Court of Human Rights', Tel Aviv University Law Faculty Papers, Paper 112 (2010).
[39] Mary Daly, *Beyond the Father: Toward a Philosophy of Women's Liberation* (Boston: Beacon Press, 1973), 8–10, 47–9.
[40] O. Morgenstern Leissner, 'The Problem that has no Name' (1998) 4 *Cardozo Women's Law Journal* 321.
[41] P. MacDougall, 'The Right of Women to Name Their Children' (1985) 3 *Law & Inequality Journal* 91, 138.

Surnames and headship

The taking by the wife and children of the husband's name reflects a belief that the husband is the head of the household and the wife and children are subject to his control.[42] The wife on assuming her husband's name becomes subsumed behind his identity.[43] Patronymics reflects the well-known legal dictum that on marriage the husband and wife become one and 'the husband is that one'.[44] This headship is reflected by the use of the husband's surname as a marker for the whole family. The headship of husbands/fathers is the traditional teaching of the Christian church, although it is coming under increasing challenge even within Christianity.[45] This is most apparent in the, now admittedly less common, practice of referring to a wife as, for example, Mrs David Beckham. Priscilla Ruth MacDougall claims that a child's retention of their father's surname after divorce 'tells children that their mother's importance remains secondary to that of their fathers even after their parents are divorced'.[46] Of course there is an irony here for women who seek to break free from the tradition by selecting to keep their own names, since in doing so they often retain the names of their fathers.[47]

The change in names is an outward sign to some men of their authority in the family. It is extraordinary that although we have seen moves towards egalitarian marriage (accepted as an ideal, even if not in practice), surnames still reflect the male headship concept. In other areas of life where language and legal doctrine reflect outdated or discriminatory practice they have been abandoned. Not so, yet, in the area of family names.

The fiction of unity

Patronymy implies a loss of female identity. The taking by the wife of her husband's name is commonly regarded as a demonstration of unity.[48] A shift from being individuals to becoming a unit. Hence, there is evidence among women making naming choices that there is a degree of moral conflict; whether to prefer the individualism of retaining one's own name or to prefer the communitarianism of a joint name.[49] Women changing surname often say that they do so to keep family and unity.[50] Studies suggest a widespread perception of 'name keepers' as selfish.[51] Yet the unity argument is based on somewhat of a fiction. The wife taking the husband's name does not reflect an equal united partnership. The woman is taken to join her husband's identity, he has done no uniting with

---

[42] M. Arichi, 'Is it Radical? Women's Right to Keep their own Surnames after Marriage—Yesterday and Today' (1999) 22 *Women's Studies International Forum* 411; Johnson and Scheuble, 'What Should We Call our Kids?' (cited in n.14) 419.

[43] S. Kupper, *Surnames For Women: A Decision-Making Guide* (Jefferson, N.S.: Macfarland, 1990), 23.

[44] Sir William Blackstone, *Commentaries on the Laws of England* (Oxford: Clarendon Press, first published 1765–9, 21st edn, 1844), vol.1, 442.

[45] e.g. Adrian Thatcher, *God, Sex and Marriage* (Oxford: Oxford University Press, 2011).

[46] MacDougall, 'The Right of Women to Name Their Children' (cited in n.41) 91, 99.

[47] Omi Morgenstern Leissner, 'The Name of the Maiden' (1997) 12 *Wisconsin Women's Law Journal* 253.

[48] Sharon Lebell, *Naming Ourselves, Naming Our Children: Resolving the Last Name Dilemma* (Freedom, Calif.: Crossing Press, 1988).

[49] Colleen Nugent, 'Children's Surnames, Moral Dilemmas Accounting For The Predominance Of Fathers' Surnames For Children' (2010) 24 *Gender and Society* 499.

[50] M. Hoffnung, 'What's in a Name? Marital Name Choice Revisited' (2006) 55 *Sex Roles* 817.

[51] E. Suter, 'Tradition Never Goes out of Style: The Role of Tradition in Women's Naming Practices' (2004) 7 *Communication Review* 57.

his name. The fiction is well revealed in the following quotation from a late nineteenth-century guide to English usage and here the verb 'to marry':

> Properly speaking, a man is not married to a woman, or married with her; nor are a man and a woman married with each other. The woman is married to the man. It is her name that is lost in his, not his in hers; she becomes a member of his family, not he of hers; it is her life that is merged, or supposed to be merged, in his, not his in hers; she follows his fortunes, and takes his station, not he hers.... [W]e do not speak of tying a ship to a boat, but a boat to a ship. And so long, at least, as man is the larger, the stronger, the more individually important, as long as woman generally lives in her husband's house and bears his name—still more should she not bear his name,—it is the woman who is married to the man.[52]

The broader social significance of naming is well revealed by looking at the way lesbian couples have taken to giving surnames to children they have produced and intend to raise together. This is particularly interesting as here there is no preconceived idea of names.[53] What is notable from one leading survey is the range of surnaming practices. Of 20 couples interviewed, eight different approaches were taken. But a consistent theme was the wider social significance of their practice. One couple changed their name to a new third surname and gave their child that name too. They wanted to make it clear to society that they were starting a new family together. Many couples interviewed were attracted by versions of double-barrelled names to reflect the equal status of both parents and refute negative portrayals about lesbian motherhood. Certainly they wished to avoid the impression that one partner was the head of the family. As this shows, the decision to name cannot be made in a social vacuum. The debates between these women reflect wider debates in society over the role of surnames. Part of the reason lesbian and gay couples reject common surnames is to move away from sexist assumptions, while finding more equal ways of expressing unity.[54]

Surnames and power

In recent years we appear to have forgotten the history of surnames, which reveals the ways that names have expressed control. The Nazi regime compelled name changes for Jewish families to ensure that their identity as Jewish was marked out. Slaves were renamed by their white owners to ensure their ownership was publicly known. The connotation of name change with ownership, power, and control is well revealed in history, but too often goes unrecognized in current Anglo-American naming practices. It is revealing that the cases involving disputes over children's surnames are nearly always brought by men seeking to restrict or inhibit the decisions of mothers over the surnames for the children. As in many post-separation legal disputes, men losing power over their family on the breakdown of the relationship seek to reassert it through the law.

Surnames and identity

Naming practices may be seen as reflecting attitudes towards identity. The practice of patrimony has led some commentators to suggest that women's attitudes towards, and

---

[52] R. G. White, *Words And Their Uses* (Boston, 1886), 139–40, cited in Yofi Tirosh, 'A Name of One's Own' (cited in n.38).
[53] Kathryn Almack, 'What's in a Name? The Significance of the Choice of Surnames Given to Children Born within Lesbian-parent Families' (2005) 8 *Sexualities* 239.
[54] Almack, 'What's in a Name?' (cited in n.53).

understandings of, their names are different from those of men.[55] Women grow up realizing that they may well change their name. For many women, therefore, the surname is temporary, a symbol of their current status rather than being central to their identity. Indeed the use by women of different surnames in different contexts appears increasingly common,[56] while for men the surname will be a life-long constant, which through children may continue in history. It has therefore a sense of immutability which gives it a different context from the position of some women.

Surnames and the blood tie

The current law and practice on naming reflects the importance of blood ties over social relationships. This is an important issue and will be developed in the next section.

4. Law and patronymy

Even if one is persuaded by these arguments, it may be said that the law is not responsible for these naming practices. The law allows people to make their own decisions about names and cannot be blamed for the choices people make. There are all manner of sexist practices which reinforce patriarchy and which we might wish did not happen, but the law cannot be expected to deal with them all. Parents may raise their boys to have improper attitudes about women, but we cannot readily regulate that through the law. Education and positive encouragement are better responses to informal sexism than legal ones.

Such an argument, however, overlooks the fact that in not intervening the law allows the current status quo to be perpetuated. The claim that the current law involves the law being neutral on names, leaving it to the parties to choose their names, belies the significant pressure on people to follow patrynomic practices in Anglo-American society. Around 94 per cent of married women in the UK change their surnames on marriage to that of their husband. Around 4 per cent use both surnames and only 1 per cent keep their own surname.[57] In one American study only 6 per cent of native-born married American women did not have their husband's surname.[58] Surveys show that a large majority of the public believe that women should change their names on marriage.[59] Those women who reject the conventional form tend to be not white or to have higher educational achievement.[60] Even where the parents have different surnames the use of the father's name for children is common.[61]

Melissann Herron argues that there are strong pressures to conform:

> Keepers are viewed as unattractive, independent, feminist, poor potential wives and mothers, young, well-educated, likely to work outside the home, self-confident, outspoken, and unlikely to cook or attend church.[62]

---

[55] Leissner, 'The Name of the Maiden' (cited in n.47) 270.
[56] L. Scheuble and D. Johnson, 'Women's Situational Use of Last Names' (2005) 53 *Sex Roles* 3.
[57] M. Valetas, 'The Surnames of Married Women in the European Union' (2001) 367 *Population and Sociétés* 1.
[58] G. Gooding and R. Kreider, 'Women's Marital Naming in a Nationally Representative Sample' (2010) 31(5) *Journal of Family Issues* 681.
[59] L. Hamilton, C. Geist, and B. Powell, 'Marital Name Change as a Window into Gender Attitudes' (2011) 25 *Gender & Society* 145.
[60] Melissann L. Herron, *Patronymy as Taken-For-Granted and Enforced Patriarchal Practice? Analysis of Marital Naming Practices and Plans* (San Diego, Calif.: San Diego State University, 2010).
[61] Johnson and Scheuble, 'What Should We Call our Kids?' (cited in n.14) 419.
[62] Herron, *Patronymy as Taken-For-Granted and Enforced Patriarchal Practice?* (cited in n.60).

As this indicates, there is considerable social pressure to follow the norm. The claim that current naming practices simply reflect personal decisions needs to be treated with considerable caution.[63] Some women follow the social norm without ever making an explicit decision.[64] Many women report that even though they would have liked to keep their names, they did not want to make an issue of it.[65]

So why should the current naming practices, with their negative messages about wives and children, be permitted to continue? The Turkish Supreme Court is one of the few courts to have attempted to explain why it believes traditional naming practices should continue, arguing that they reflect social attitudes:

> The rule according to which married women bear their husband's name derives from certain social realities and is the result of the codification of certain customs that have formed over centuries in Turkish society. According to the thinking behind family law, the purpose of the rule is to protect women, who are of a more delicate nature than men, strengthen family bonds, nurture the prosperity of the marriage, and preclude bicephalous authority within the same family.[66]

This quotation lays bare what is actually being done when the law allows 'social practice' to govern an area, rather than intervene. Harmful assumptions about women and children and their role in marriage are allowed to flourish. We need to consider carefully the impact of the failure of the law to regulate or provide guidance on surnames or the names of children, and the resolution of disputes over them.

5. Arguments in favour of the current law

Triviality

Arguments can, of course, be put forward in favour of the current approach. One response to my argument is that I am greatly exaggerating the significance that is attached to surnames, which should be regarded as a relatively trivial matter. The idea that the wife is subservient to her husband is so clearly rejected that the shared name will not be said to reflect such a view. Katie Roiphe writes of the freedom that women have today:

> These days, no one is shocked when an independent-minded woman takes her husband's name, any more than one is shocked when she announces that she is staying at home with her kids. Today, the decision is one of convenience, of a kind of luxury—which name do you like the sound of? What do you feel like doing? The politics are almost incidental. Our fundamental independence is not so imperiled that we need to keep our names. The statement has, thanks to a more dogmatic generation, been made. Now we dabble in the traditional. We cobble together names. At this point—apologies to Lucy Stone, and her pioneering work in name keeping—our attitude is: Whatever works.[67]

Wilson responds to such arguments by saying that

> The feminist projects since the second wave—whether they use the term *patriarchy* or not—have elaborated on this premise by showing how many mundane, seemingly private and personal

---

[63] Katherine Franke, 'Theorizing Yes: An Essay on Feminism, Law, and Desire' (2001) 101 *Columbia Law Review* 181.
[64] S. Kline, L. Stafford, and J. Miklosovic, 'Women's Surnames: Decisions, Interpretations and Associations with Relational Qualities' (1996) 13 *Journal of Social and Personal Relationships* 593.
[65] A. Cherlin, 'Hereditary Hyphens?' (1978) *Psychology Today*, December, 4.
[66] *Unel Tekeli v Turkey*, App. No. 29865/96, ECtHR (2004).
[67] Katie Roiphe, *The Maiden Name Debate: What's Changed Since the 1970s?*, SLATE, 16 March 2004; available at: <http://www.slate.com/id/2097231/>.

experiences operated as the stratagems and tactics that underwrote and reproduced a social system of gender inequality.[68]

In other words, there are apparently minor private expressions of devaluing that combine together in an insidious way to produce the power of patriarchy.[69] The difficulty is in assessing such claims. While we may accept that current naming practices reflect patriarchal values, do they in fact play a significant role in perpetuating them? Of course we cannot know. Yet names are something used day in, day out and represent our identity to the world around us. So the prevalence of, and regularity by which, this symbol of male power is used is significant in itself.

As a society we now are committed to fighting discrimination and practices that work to restrict equality between men and women. The use of surnames to reinforce discriminatory attitudes about marriage and parenthood should be challenged.[70]

Kenneth Karst explains that 'the process by which law confers legitimacy on a structure of domination and dependency is primarily a system of symbols. For a court to add the judiciary's own special imprimatur of legitimacy on the symbolism of women's dependency is particularly destructive.'[71]

Good intentions

A second justification for current practices may be that it is wrong to assume that the selection of the taking of the man's surname either for a partner of a man or for children is a result of sexist attitudes. It may be that a couple seeking to reject sexist attitudes still choose the man's name as their family name and children's name for quite different reasons, such as: because his name is simply aesthetically more appealing; or this choice is less liable to lead to the children being ridiculed; or this choice avoids disputes with the wider family; or the wife's abuse at the hands of her father means she wishes to sever all links with him. These examples all indicate one cannot assume from a patronymic decision a sexist attitude.

In fact studies would question that view. Attitudes to surnames are closely associated with attitudes generally to gender.[72] Strong supporters of patrynomics often hold sexist views. The response to this argument is that practices may take on a social meaning which is not necessarily intended by the parties. The flying of a swastika flag or the use of a racially offensive term convey a meaning, whether the parties were in fact flying the flag because they like the design, or did not mean to use the word in 'a bad way'.[73] If therefore (and of course that is a debatable 'if') patronymy conveys a message that the father is the head of the household and that the wife's identity is subsumed within his then

---

[68] Ara Wilson, 'Patriarchy: Feminist Theory' in Cheris Kramarae and Dale Spender (eds), *Routledge International Encyclopedia of Women: Global Women's Issues and Knowledge* (New York: Routledge, 2000), 1493, 1494.

[69] Suter, 'Tradition Never Goes Out of Style' (cited in n.51) 57.

[70] D. Anthony, 'A Spouse By Any Other Name' (2010) 17 *William & Mary Journal of Women and Law* 187; H. MacClintock, 'Sexism, Surnames, And Social Progress: The Conflict Of Individual Autonomy And Government Preferences In Laws Regarding Name Changes At Marriage' (2010) 24 *Temple International and Comparative Law Journal* 277.

[71] K. Karst, 'A Discrimination So Trivial: A Note on Law and the Symbolism of Women's Dependency' (1974) 35 *Ohio State Law Journal* 546, 552.

[72] Hamilton, Geist, and Powell, 'Marital Name Change as a Window into Gender Attitudes' (cited in n.59) 145.

[73] For further discussion of social meaning see J. Herring and M. Madden Dempsey, 'Why Sexual Penetration Requires Justification' (2007) 27 *Oxford Journal of Legal Studies* 467.

that meaning cannot be defeated by the parties' intentions that it should be otherwise. Indeed in many of the cases mentioned above there would be alternative ways of naming which would not convey the negative meaning.

Privacy

A third argument in favour of the current law is that we should accept name choices as being a private issue. Julia Shear Kushner argues

> even if control over one's name is not a fundamental right, the state should restrict naming practices as little as possible because of the great importance of specific names to their bearers, compared to the minimal importance of those same names to the state, except in a minute number of circumstances. So long as names do not interfere with the public interests in identification and communication, a person's choice of name is comparatively unimportant to the state and to others. Given the value our nation places on individual rights, the better policy is to restrict matters of great importance to individuals as little as possible—an idea reflected in the strict scrutiny requirement. Therefore, although the state may not be constitutionally required to follow the strict scrutiny standard in deciding when to regulate naming, it may be best to do so where possible.[74]

Such arguments let the law off too lightly. Recall the law's historically non-interventionist approach to domestic violence. That was justified as respecting the privacy of the parties. It allowed the parties to choose whether to remain in the violent relationship or not. Yet in not intervening in domestic violence the law, in effect, allowed it to continue. We can see the same with naming. As argued earlier, by leaving naming practices unregulated, the law, in effect, reinforces the status quo. As Jean Twenge writes:

> The custom of male names appears to be well entrenched; some of the women here felt no more need to explain it than they would explain why they eat with a fork and knife.[75]

So, as argued above, non-intervention is not allowing parties to make a choice, but enables the current social norms to continue. As Suzanne Kim argues:

> Decisions about names do not arise against a blank slate of equal options, but operate within the confines of social forces that construct our options and our understanding of those options. In other words, women's name-changing operates within the structure of gender hierarchy that initially limits the options from which women are able to choose.[76]

Further, by regarding the matter as 'private' the law ignores the significant symbolic significances of names. Yet we have generally accepted that in other areas of life choice of language does matter. We should remember the power of names. Martha Minow has argued that, through naming, individuals and groups are able to inscribe their power. She writes:

> [h]uman beings use labels to describe and sort their perceptions of the world. The particular labels often chosen in American culture can carry social and moral consequences while burying the choices and responsibilities for those consequences... Language and labels play a special role in the perpetuation of prejudice about differences.[77]

---

[74] Julia Shear Kushner, 'The Right to Control One's Name' (2009) 57 *University of California Los Angeles Law Review* 313.
[75] J. Twenge, 'Mrs. His Name: Women's Preferences for Married Names' (1997) 21 *Psychology of Women Quarterly* 417.
[76] S. Kim, 'Marital Naming/Naming Marriage' (cited in n.5).
[77] Martha Minow, *Making All The Difference: Inclusion, Exclusion, And American Law* (Ithaca: Cornell University Press, 1990), 4, 6.

She notes the particular danger that the use of names can imply that certain categories and social positions are compelled by nature.[78] In this context the assumption of joint names assumes a subservience of the wife's social and legal status under her husbands. It might also be seen as a way or reinforcing claims about the uniqueness of the marriage relationship over other family forms.[79] Danielle Crittenden writes:

> The social messages are clear in either context. If a woman changes her surname to that of her husband, she is his possession; if the children bear only the father's surname, they are his possession. While some analysts of family gendering practices may perceive the surname issue as relatively unimportant, it seems to me that this is a fundamental, definitional, and ubiquitous familial gender injustice.[80]

If such claims are right then these are not private matters as they have an impact on the wider society.

Indeed, claims of state neutrality are doubtful. Special privileges do attach to families who follow the traditional model. Consider the following examples: the Passport Office provides special procedures for wives to take on their husband's name, which are not available for others seeking to change their names; many organizations simply assume that women change surnames on marriage, putting the burden of correction on who those who do not;[81] the Post Office charges one price for forwarding post where all family members share the surname, otherwise there is a charge for each surname used by a family.[82] Further, we see in the disputes over children's names that the courts have been sympathetic to the claims of fathers seeking, at least formally, that children retain their name. The courts have accepted that such a change is of such importance that it is worthy of judicial time and energy.

6. The power of blood

Many of the cases concerning disputes over surnames involve a battle over whether the child should be integrated into a new step-family by taking on the surname adopted by the mother and her new family or whether the surname should be used to retain a link between the child and the father. The courts have accepted the argument that the surname retains an important link with the birth father, but much less attention has been paid to the role that it can play in integrating the child into the step-family. In general, where there is a poor relationship between the child and the father this is seen as an argument in favour of changing the child's name from his.[83] In the case of *B* in *Re W; Re A; Re B (Change of Name)*[84] approval was given to a change of name from the father's after the father had been imprisoned. One reason for this was that there was not likely to be a meaningful relationship between the child and her father in the future. In cases involving children in care the link with the birth family provided by the name has been seen as generally important. Foster carers and special guardians are not permitted to change the

---

[78] Minow, *Making All The Difference* (cited in n.77).
[79] Kim, 'Marital Naming/Naming Marriage' (cited in n.5).
[80] Danielle Crittenden, *What Our Mothers Didn't Tell Us: Why Happiness Eludes The Modern Woman* (New York: Simon & Schuster, 1999), 453.
[81] Jane Pilcher, 'His, not Hers: Surnames and Marriage'; available at: <http://www.janepilcher.me.uk/node/15>.
[82] See <http://www2.royalmail.com/delivery/inbound-mail/redirections/prices>.
[83] *Re P (Parental Responsibility: Change of Name)* [1997] 3 FCR 739.
[84] [1999] 2 FLR 930.

child's name from that selected by the birth parents, without the leave of the court or the consent of all with parental responsibility.[85] Although, of course, on adoption the child often takes the name of the adoptive family.

The assumption in some cases that the child's link with the father should be retained through the name reflects a desire to emphasize the blood link rather than the current social relationship. This became particularly apparent in the House of Lords in *Dawson v Wearmouth*.[86] Lord Jauncey elaborated on the significance of a surname:

> A surname which is given to a child at birth is not simply a name plucked out of the air. Where the parents are married the child will normally be given the surname or patronymic of the father thereby demonstrating its relationship to him. The surname is thus a biological label which tells the world at large that the blood of the name flows in its veins. To suggest that a surname is unimportant because it may be changed at any time by deed poll when the child has attained more mature years ignores the importance of initially applying an appropriate label to that child.

This quotation is interesting for several reasons. One is that the blood in the child's body is described as 'the blood of the [father's] name', rather than being simply the child's blood or, even if one wanted to see the issue in his terms, the blood of both parents.

Nevertheless, it is clear that quite a number of people would echo Lord Jauncey's views, although none of the other Law Lords in the case did. To the non-resident parent, the change of name to that of the resident parent's new partner symbolizes the eclipse of the birth father from the child's life. It conveys the message that he is no longer the father, and never was the father. This view that names should be regarded as symbolizing the child's link with the father is one that is by no means universally held. Hale LJ states in *Re R (A Child)*[87]:

> I return to the issue of names. It is also a matter of great sadness to me that it is so often assumed, and even sometimes argued, that fathers need that outward and visible link in order to retain their relationship with, and commitment to, their child. That should not be the case. It is a poor sort of parent whose interest in and commitment to his child depends upon that child bearing his name. After all, that is a privilege which is not enjoyed by many mothers, even if they are not living with the child. They have to depend upon other more substantial things.

Bob Geldof has responded to these comments with characteristic vigour:

> judicial disapproval for a man who objected to a woman who wished to change the child's surname. 'A poor sort of parent' is what this unfortunate was called, whose child would at least know who she and her father were before the past and her identity were stripped, like a Stalinist photograph out of her family's history. He was not allowed even to give her his name. Her family name. So a man is to be stripped of even that. He is to be utterly expunged from the past.[88]

With respect, Baroness Hale's views are far more convincing. What establishes a bond of value between a parent and child is not a shared name or a blood tie, but a loving relationship. The law should do nothing to reinforce the views of those who think that being a parent is about having a name attached to the child.

As family lawyers know full well, separating parents find many things to disagree over. One of the skills of a solicitor or mediator is to encourage the parties to focus on issues

---

[85] Children Act 1989 s.14B. See further *Re L (A Child)* [2007] EWCA Civ 196; *Re D, L and LA (Care: Change of Forename)* [2003] 1 FLR 339.
[86] [1999] 2 W.L.R. 960.
[87] [2001] EWCA Civ 1344, [2001] 2 FLR 1358 [13].
[88] Bob Geldof, 'The Real Love that Dare not Speak its Name' in Andrew Bainham, Bridget Lindley, Martin Richards, and Liz Trinder (eds), *Children and their Families* (Oxford: Hart, 2003), 185.

which are important. The judiciary are not keen to hear cases on matters they regard as trivial.[89] There is not even a need for the resident parent to consult the other parent with parental responsibility over child-rearing issues unless the matter is of fundamental importance.[90] The courts have held that changing a surname is one such issue, as are issues over education, circumcision, and important medical decisions.[91] By being willing to hear these cases, often taking considerable time, the courts reinforce the notion that surnames reflect an issue of great significance, namely the blood tie. Family law has in recent years increasingly recognized that what is of value to a child is the quality of the relationships the child is in, rather than the genetic relationship between the child and the adults. An adoptive parent can be just as good a parent as a biological parent. Family law should work to reinforce and uphold the beneficial relationships which the child has, whether they be blood tied or not.[92] If changing the name reinforces the current social relationships in which the child lives, the law should support such a change.

7. The compromise solution

There have been quite a number of cases where courts have held that the child should keep the registered name (usually the father's) for formal purposes (e.g. medical records; passport), but the day-to-day name (i.e. the name the law regards as the actual name) should be the one requested by the resident parent.[93] Such a decision will often be made when the child's surname has been changed and the child has used the new name for some time before the matter is brought before the court. In such circumstances the court may easily be persuaded that it would be harmful for the child to have the name changed back to the original name.[94]

One justification for this approach is that it simply acknowledges the limits of the courts' powers. Wilson J in *Re B (Change of Surname)* accepted that, in practice, there is little the law can do to control the name by which a child is to be known on a day-to-day basis. The court can only control the name by which the child will be known in formal documents.[95] An alternative justification is that the law is respecting the rights of the resident parent. To force that parent on a daily basis to use for their child a name to which they object could be regarded as a serious invasion of their right to respect for their family life. However, if the obligation only arises on rare formal occasions the degree of interference will be much less.[96]

Despite the convenience of the approach taken by the courts, it has serious disadvantages. The occasions on which the formal name will be required: hospital appointments; meetings with educational authorities; court hearings and the like, will be fraught with tension for the child. For the child then to be called by a name with which he or she is unfamiliar or to require the child to explain any lack of continuity with names seems undesirable. At those formal times everything should be done to put the child at ease. At the very least that should mean referring to the child by the name with which s/he

---

[89] *Re P (A Minor) (Parental Responsibility Order)* [1994] 1 FLR 578.
[90] Children Act 1989 s.2(7).
[91] See Jonathan Herring, *Family Law* (Harlow: Pearson, 2011), ch.9, for a discussion of the law on this.
[92] For a recent important recognition of this see *Re B (Children)* [2009] UKSC 4.
[93] e.g. *Bucknell (formerly Hallas) v Hallas*, unreported, CA, 2 April 1990.
[94] e.g. *Re C (Change of Surname)* [1998] 2 FLR 656.
[95] [1996] 2 FCR 304.
[96] This kind of argument was influential in *Guillot v France* [1996] ECtHR 48.

is familiar. It is therefore submitted that the name the child is generally known by (i.e. their name in the eyes of the law) should be the one used on formal documents. It might be argued that this can only lead to problems with identification, although with medical documents, for example, patient numbers, rather than names, are regularly used to link documents. The 'compromise solution' favoured by the law is a solution which might leave both parents feeling they have won something, but it hardly represents a result that promotes the welfare of the child.

8. Avoiding litigation

To some the primary objective in the law should be to find a solution to disputes over names, which avoids litigation. As family lawyers know well, couples need no incentive to dispute issues. Ormrod LJ has stated:

> I am sure everyone understands that the question of the surname of a child is a matter of great emotional significance, particularly to fathers. If the name is lost, in a sense, the child is lost. That strong patrilineal feeling we all to some extent share. But this has to be kept within the bounds of common sense... what matters is whether the child identifies with the father in human terms... The one thing one should try to avoid in these cases is giving hostages to fortune, weapons to parties to quarrel with when the real issue between them is something quite other... names are really of little importance, and they only become important when they become a casus belli between the parents.'[97]

Mary Hayes[98] explains that on relationship breakdown there is often animosity and the parties will seek out issues on which to fight. She concludes 'It is surely better, therefore, to try to avoid creating the opportunity for the parents' personal hostility to be vented in litigation about their children's names if at all possible.'[99] Therefore the law should seek a rule with which to deal with these disputes, which avoids the need for them to come to court. Her proposed solution is that the law should place considerable weight on the registered name and, only if there is a very strong case not to uphold the registered name, should there be consent to depart from it.

While agreeing that it is beneficial to have a clear rule to avoid litigation, her suggestion that this be provided by the registered name is problematic. It should be recalled that all the registered name is meant to be is the name the parents intend to use for the child. If the registered name is taken to be the name that the child should have unless there are good reasons otherwise, this should be made clear to the parents at the time of registration. Further, arguing that the registered name represents the status quo is inaccurate. Where a parent has changed a child's name and the other party objects to this, the child's current name, in English law, is the name by which the child is generally known.[100] As already mentioned, the registered name is not significant in ascertaining a person's name. So the status quo is the name the child is generally known by, not their registered name. It is therefore submitted that the registered name should carry no weight when the court is resolving a dispute over names.

---

[97] *D v B (Surname: Birth Registration)* [1979] 1 All ER 92, 99–100 per Ormrod LJ.
[98] Hayes, 'What's in a Name?' (cited in n.27).
[99] Hayes, 'What's in a Name?' (cited in n.27).
[100] See Jonathan Herring, 'The Shaming of Naming: Parental Rights and Responsibilities in the Naming of Children' in Rebecca Probert, Stephen Gilmore, and Jonathan Herring (eds), *Responsible Parents and Parental Responsibility* (Oxford: Hart, 2009), 116 for debate over this.

A preferable solution is that where there is a dispute between parents over the name, a child should have two surnames, one selected by each parent.[101] So in *Dawson v Wearmouth* the child should have the surname Dawson Wearmouth.[102] This will recognize the link to both parents and does not convey a message that one parent is more important than the other.[103] It has the benefit of providing a ready solution which should leave neither side feeling it has 'lost'. There is some mild judicial support for this. In *Re R (A Child)*[104] it was suggested that using a combination of both surnames was to be encouraged because it would recognize the importance of both parents to the child.[105] It is argued here that the courts should be bolder and require a two surnames solution unless there is an extreme case where a different solution will be required (e.g. where a name change is necessary to avoid a feared abduction).[106] It might be said that double surnames are cumbersome or embarrassing or even posh. However, any harm resulting from these is arguably outweighed by the avoidance of litigation and antagonism surrounding the issue. More significantly, such an approach would represent approval by the law of the use of double surnames, a practice which recognizes that marriage should be egalitarian and marked by equality and mutual respect, rather than by ownership or domination.[107]

9. Children's rights

The child's views will be important, but not the sole consideration, when a court applies the welfare principle in a naming case. Wilson J in *Re B (Change of Surname)*[108] ordered that three children (two teenagers) keep their father's surname, despite their opposition, in order to maintain the link with their father. However, it might be thought that little more could be done to damage the relationship between a father and teenagers than forcing them to keep his name.[109] Despite this decision, it was made clear in *Re S (Change of Surname)*[110] that the views of a *Gillick*-competent child over a surname should be given careful consideration. In *Re M, T, P, K and B*[111] it was held that a court should be 'particularly loath' to refuse applications to change names which are supported by mature children. The court added, however, that such wishes are 'neither paramount nor determinative'.

The fact that children's rights to choose their names are not permitted in these cases shows how little weight the notion of children's rights actually has in UK law. This is a situation where there is an extremely strong case for allowing a competent child to choose his or her own name. The following points can be emphasized. First, the name by which

---

[101] There may be some cases where melding of the surnames of both parents would be effective.
[102] I would suggest no hyphen be used, but have no strong views on this.
[103] No doubt those desperate for a fight will want to argue about which name goes first. If a resolution is required alphabetical order or the tossing of a coin are suitably arbitrary.
[104] [2002] 1 FCR 170.
[105] One factor which may have influenced the court was that the family was moving to Spain where the use of double surnames is the normal practice.
[106] *F v M* [2007] EWHC 2543 (Fam).
[107] Elizabeth Emens, 'Changing Name Changing: Framing Rules and The Future Of Marital Names' (2007) 74 *University of Chicago Law Review* 761.
[108] *Re B (Change of Surname)* [1996] 2 FCR 304.
[109] See for further extra-judicial comment on this decision: Sir N. Wilson, 'The Ears of the Child in Family Proceedings' [2007] *Family Law* 808, 817–18.
[110] [1999] 1 FLR 672.
[111] [2000] 2 FLR 645.

a person is known is a highly personal matter affecting them with great frequency. The child's interest in what he or she is called must surely be regarded as weightier than a parent's interest in what their child is called. Secondly, this is an issue where children cannot really suffer harm, except in extreme cases.[112] Some commentators are understandably concerned about letting children make decisions for themselves where that decision will severely affect their well-being. However, a decision on a name is not an issue where that is likely to occur. Thirdly, this is an issue where views on what is best for children differ and there is no clearly correct answer. In such a case it is particularly appropriate to allow the child to make decisions for her/himself. The fact that this is not done shows that the law has a long way to go before properly acknowledging that children have rights. As it is the current law on naming reflects an attitude that children are objects for parents to control and exercise power over, rather than the attitude represented in the Children Act 1989 that children are people with rights and for whom parents have responsibilities.

10. Conclusion

When, in the latter half of the twentieth century, feminists took up the fight against the legal and social assumptions that women and children would take 'the man's name' it was assumed that in due course women would look back in horror at the past traditions. As Ellen Goodman puts it:

I guarantee you that the first generation of women who grow up without scribbling 'Mrs. Paul Newman' all over their notebooks 'just to see what it looks like' is going to think we were mad. It is a very odd and radical idea indeed that a woman would nominally disappear just because she got married.[113]

Yet, surprisingly, patronymics continues even to this day to hold considerable sway over Anglo-American naming. The law purports to respect private choice, but in fact strong social pressures mean many people do not feel the freedom to exercise that choice. A strong negative message about the nature of family life and gender relations within it is perpetuated.

What should be sought is a legal regime which avoids the sexist messages of patronymic naming; respects the right of children to change their name; and emphasizes the relationships the child is living in. I would not go so far as to compel the use of particular names, as the European Court of Human Rights has recognized that the naming of a child is an aspect of people's private and family life.[114] But the law and state should promote, encourage, and assume that couples on marriage keep their names, or if they wish for a joint name then it will be made up of both their surnames. A patronymic should be a difficult one to make. The law should recognize that once a child is competent he or she should be able to decide what name he chooses. If there is a dispute over a child's surname, the parents can choose one surname each. No longer should surnames be used as an exercise of and acknowledgement of male power. Surnames should reflect our personal and social identities, not our relationship to one man.

---

[112] e.g. where the child's name can lead to their being identified and then abducted.
[113] Ellen Goodman, 'The Name of the Game', *Boston Globe* 30 (24 September 1974), quoted in Emens 'Changing Name Changing' (cited in n.107).
[114] *Johansson v Finland* [2007] 3 FCR 420.

19

The Role of Language in Legal Contexts: A Forensic Cross-Linguistic Viewpoint

Luna Filipović

1. Introduction

Language and the law are fundamentally and intricately related though their unity is not always homogenous. Language is used to formulate laws and in turn law delimits the subset of a language that is used in such formulations, known as the notorious legalese. There is another facet to this relationship, namely when law and language go against each other, as it were. Language can open more than one possibility of interpretation in a singular legal document, the consequence of which can be the challenge of the law itself. By the same token, law regulates the use of language on a number of occasions in both its content and form to varying degrees across the world, from a complete freedom of speech in some countries (bar defamation and libel) to a very restricted or non-existent language freedom in others.

The growing interest in the complex relationship between law and language is attested among different professional groups, many of whom attended the notably successful colloquium on Law and Language, the result of which is the current volume. The work presented in this contribution is motivated by an attempt to bridge the gap between the traditional division amongst various disciplines and push for a novel view of interdisciplinarity based on the need to join forces and approach the same problems from different angles in order to find the best solutions. To this end the present paper illustrates the crucial importance of certain language contrasts for witness interviewing, interpreting, translating, remembering, and forming judgment in legally relevant contexts. The focus here is on cross-linguistic differences detected in multilingual court cases as well as language-specific impacts on the language, memory, and judgment of witnesses from different linguistic backgrounds (in this case English and Spanish).

A number of studies have addressed many relevant issues that arise in a multilingual courtroom (e.g. Berg-Seligson 1990) or other instances of multilingual interviewing (e.g. community interpreting; see Hale 2004). Numerous researchers have tackled the general problem in multilingual legal cases that stems from the extremely hard role that interpreters on occasion have to play. For instance, Berk-Seligson (1990) lists a number of features that characterize court interpreting (e.g. hedges, insertions, hesitations, etc.), which underlie the perception of witness testimony style as either powerful or powerless. A further example of cross-linguistic contrasts in translation is Hale's study (Hale 2004), which documented the difficulty of translating tag questions from English into Spanish. The most recent holistic overview of themes and methodologies in the field is given in Gibbons (2011).

The unique approach assumed in this paper (and in previous published research, e.g. Filipović 2007, 2009, 2010a, 2010b) lies in the use of both linguistic theory and linguistic evidence (corpus and experimental) in order to pin down the crucially relevant aspects of language use in legally important verbal interactions (such as police interviews and information gathering in general from witnesses and suspects) as well as other aspects of language-mediated involvement, such as witness memory and jury judgment. The languages in focus are English and Spanish, but the theory and methodology employed here are applicable to the contrasting of any language pairs. Particular emphasis is put on the features in both languages that can condition the content of witness interviews, cause difficulties in interpretation and translation and lead to serious misunderstandings of what happened, how and why, which is of central importance for the law.

The present research focus is on a subgroup of events that speakers experience and describe, namely those from two central cognitive domains (motion and causation) that are relevant for the criminal cases investigated in our research. Our first source of data for current research purposes is a database of parallel bilingual transcripts. The second is a series of experiments with monolingual speakers of either English or Spanish that probe for the effects of linguistic habits on the aspects of witnessed events stored in memory that may be impacted by language-specific patterns used to express the events. Finally, the data from mock jury experiments testify to the fundamental importance of language when it comes to the ways in which events are habitually described in different languages, where the typical means of packaging information in one language differs from that in another and when this can cause disparate judgments in two different speaker groups.

I start by introducing the theoretical backdrop for the studies discussed in this paper. The fundamental typological differences between English and Spanish are outlined in section 2. I then contrast English and Spanish with regard to the relevant typological dimensions and provide examples from the database that reflect this contrast as well as elicit different understandings of the event in the original and in the translation (section 3). I offer a detailed analysis of how motion and causation are described in the original interview texts and their translations, which makes it possible to pin down the exact points where difficulties in cross-linguistic communication are likely to occur. In section 4 I present experimental evidence in the context of witness memory and discuss what the findings imply for legal contexts. I also illustrate the ways in which mock jury judgment can be swayed along the lines of the linguistic distinctions in focus. Finally, in section 5 I comment on the transcript-making practices in different countries, I summarize the current investigation as presented in this paper, and provide an insight into possible further applications of this and similar projects.

2. Linguistic typologies and the consequences for texts and their translations

There are many ways in which languages can be classified in a linguistic typology because many different criteria can be used for such classifications. For example, languages differ in terms of whether they have complex inflectional morphology (such as verb conjugations for person, gender, and number, as in Slavonic languages), have very little of it (e.g. third person singular in English) or have no such thing as inflectional morphology (e.g. Chinese). Languages can also be classified based on the word order in a sentence. For example, English has a subject-verb-object word order (so-called *SVO* as in 'John ate an apple') while Japanese speakers put the verb at the end because their language has the subject-object-verb word order (*SOV*, e.g.

the equivalent of 'John the apple ate'). The typological classification used in this paper is not based on the presence or absence of formal features in languages and their ordering but rather stems from the different ways in which universal meanings are expressed in different languages. This approach to typology based on semantic parameters was first proposed by Len Talmy (1985, 2000), who singled out the main components (conceptual parts) of events and then analysed the means that different languages have to express them.

Motion events in particular were central in Talmy's work because motion is a universal cognitive domain and of central importance for human daily life and experience. Consequently, all languages could be expected to express the key motion event components that Talmy identified: Path, Manner, Figure, and Ground. In the sentence 'John ran into the library', the moving Figure ('John') changed location in a certain Manner ('ran'), along a certain Path ('into'), and within a certain Ground ('the library'). The core component of a motion event is that of Path because without a path there is no motion since motion is defined as a change of location which happens along a path. Languages that characteristically map this *core schema*, i.e. the Path of motion, onto the verb are said to have a framing verb and they are termed *verb-framed languages*.[1] Included among those are the following languages and language families: Romance, Semitic, Japanese, Tamil, Polynesian, most Bantu, most Mayan, Nez Perce, and Caddo. On the other hand, languages that characteristically map the core schema onto "satellites" (non-verb elements, e.g. prefixes or adverbs) are said to have a framing satellite and to be *satellite-framed languages*. This group comprises most of the languages from the Indo-European (excluding Romance) and Finno-Ugric families, as well as Chinese, Ojibwa, and Warlpiri (Talmy 1985).

The expression of motion event components is done differently in Spanish and in English. Spanish expresses Path in the verb and Manner in a non-obligatory adjunct or a subordinate clause. Most often, however, the information about Manner is not given in either spoken or written Spanish (see Slobin 2006). Spanish is a representative of the verb-framed languages in Talmy's typology. English, on the other hand, is a representative of the satellite-framed group, because the Path component in English is not habitually expressed in the verb but in 'satellites' while verbs express the Manner component. This difference is illustrated in the following example (the Path expressions are underlined):

1a) Ella salió de la casa corriendo.
She exit-3SG.PST out of house run-GERUND
'She exited the house running.'
1b) She ran out of the house.

The difference in the two typological patterns conditions the typical way of referring to motion events, the English pattern being a manner verb and a path-expressing particle (e.g. 'run out') and in Spanish, a path verb with an occasional/optional manner adjunct ('salir corriendo'—'exit running').

This difference in the way information is packaged has consequences that go further than the way information is organized on the surface. It affects native speakers' narrative habits as well the quantity and quality of information typically available in accounts of events. English speakers tend to express manner of motion almost

---

[1] The *core schema* is that of the Figure changing location, the essential component thus being the Path of motion (X moves from A to B during Time (T); X at A at T1; X at B at T2 via Path).

always and in great detail whereas Spanish speakers provide scarce reference to manner or omit it altogether (see Slobin 1996, 1997, 2000, 2003, 2006). As argued by Slobin, Spanish speakers seem to have dramatically fewer types (and consequently provide fewer tokens) of manner of motion verbs. Using complex paraphrases to translate just one English manner verb into Spanish is a particularly frequent and potentially very cumbersome task, as illustrated in the following attested translation example from Slobin (1997: 213):

2a) She rustled out of the room.
2b) Salió del cuarto, acompañada del susurro siseante de sus ropas.'
('She exited from the room, accompanied by the swishing rustle of her clothing.')

We see in (2b) that, in order to express the information that a single verb in English gives, Spanish translators need a whole adverbial phrase. Slobin's arguments are based on comprehensive data that consist of original literary texts in Spanish and English and their respective translation into English and Spanish. He found that only about a half of English manner verbs get translated into Spanish. The other half are translated by non-manner verbs or simply omitted. On the other hand, English translations of Spanish texts contain numerous additional items of Manner information that is not given in the original (see Slobin 1996, 1997). Slobin emphasizes that the contrasts between the two patterns have been confirmed in a great variety of samples from many languages. In one of his recent papers, he provides examples from numerous studies that confirm stronger Manner salience in satellite-framed languages than in verb-framed languages on the basis of lexical access, conversational use, child language acquisition, use in creative fiction and translation, metaphoric extension, mental imagery, and understanding of manner verbs (Slobin 2006). In this study I look for typological effects that go beyond the text itself in the forensic linguistic context of police interview transcripts.

A similar approach to that used in the analysis of the domain of motion is employed in the analysis of the domain of causation, where languages vary with respect to how they divide the spectrum of possible meanings to be expressed. For instance, even in a single language (e.g. English) one and the same event can be described as 'Jill broke the vase', 'The vase was broken', or 'The vase broke' depending on how much information we know or want to reveal about the event and how much agency we feel was involved. Gibbons (2003) outlines the relevant contrasts between English and Spanish in this area. He observes that the options for describing causation and the degree of agency involvement and blameworthiness for the action in Spanish are more varied than in English (see Table 1, based on Gibbons 2003).

Table 1 Degree of agency involvement and blameworthiness (in descending order from high to low)

Spanish	English
i. Rompí un vaso. (active)	vi. I broke a glass.
ii. Un vaso fue roto. (true passive)	vii. A glass was/got broken.
iii. Rompieron un vaso. (3rd person plural)	viii. A glass broke.
iv. Se me rompió un vaso. (reflexive pseudo-passive with dative of interest)	
v. Se rompió un vaso. (reflexive pseudo-passive)	

Both Spanish and English have the option either to explicitly express the agent (as in 'He broke it') or to not express it if it is unknown or if the speaker chooses not to reveal it ('It was/got broken'). However where the two languages differ significantly is the expression of the situation where the causation was *non-intentional*. Spanish has two constructions (examples iv and v in Table 1) that clearly express this meaning while English has no equivalent structure. This is the key point of contrast between the two languages and it causes a major difficulty in the context of witness descriptions of events in the two languages as well as in translation and in witness judgment (see subsection 3.2). When Spanish speakers are describing events they have to specify in their expression whether the event they saw was intentional or not. The English speakers have no such requirement in their language and can leave it unspecified, as they most frequently do. For example, 'She broke the glass' could potentially refer to an event in which the breaking of the glass was either accidental or on purpose. In Spanish, however, the two possibilities will be rendered differently in order to reflect this important distinction[2]:

3a) (Ella) rompió el vaso. ('She broke the glass intentionally.')
3b) Se le rompió el vaso. ('She broke the glass unintentionally'; lit. 'To-her-it-happened-that the glass broke.')

The construction in (3b is very frequent in Spanish. Gibbons (2003) defines it as the 'reflective pseudo-passive with dative of interest' and he stresses that this construction lies towards the very low end of his agency scale (see also Berk-Seligson 1990: 103 for similar observations). Furthermore, Pountain (2003) acknowledges the extensive use of reflexive constructions (among them the 'affective dative') in Spanish, which are 'undeniably part of the "genius" of Spanish' (Pountain 2003: 116). The same study also confirms that many structural differences between the two languages (English and Spanish) are due to different valences of 'what superficially may appear to be similar verbs', in a sense of dictionary equivalence (Pountain 2003: 78).

The difference between the presence and the frequency of use of impersonal constructions in one language (Spanish) and their absence in another (English) leads to differences in the understanding of events, depending on whether this is based on the original text or its translation in witness interviews. These differences are discussed in subsection 3.2.

3. Investigative interviewing in a cross-linguistic perspective

3.1. Describing and translating witnessed motion events

In the first original attempt to apply a linguistic typology to an analysis of forensic linguistic texts, Filipović (2007) accounts for the differences between the original and translation and addresses the consequences of these differences for the understanding and interpretation of events. This study found 457 motion event expressions in transcripts containing witness interviews in Spanish and their translation into English.[3] Out of this total of motion events in the Spanish original 21 per cent of the verbs were described with manner verbs and 79 per cent of descriptions contained only path verbs. The difference between the numbers of manner verbs and non-manner verbs

---

[2] This distinction is evident in other language groups too. For example, Slavonic languages side with Romance languages on this parameter (cf. (Serbian): 'Slomila sam čašu' (meaning 'I broke the glass either on purpose or accidentally') with 'Slomila mi se čaša' (meaning 'I broke the glass accidentally')).

[3] The data consist of over 10,000 pages of witness interview transcripts collected in different jurisdictions of the state of California, United States.

(neutral or path verbs) becomes more conspicuous if we take into consideration the fact that the events described were very dynamic, for example muggings, robberies, domestic violence, manslaughter, etc., where we could reasonably expect a variety of manners of motion. This kind of linguistic behaviour in Spanish is adequately predicted by the typology.

As in the translations of novels from Spanish into English reported in Slobin (1996, 1997, 2000), there was also a tendency to add manner of motion in the English translation of the Spanish witness interviews (see Filipović 2007):

> 4) pero...salió por la seven.
> but...exit-3SG.PST via the seven.
> Literal translation: 'But...he went onto 7th Street.'
> Transcript translation: 'The suspect ran up 7th Street'
> 5) y entró detras de mi...
> and enter-3SG.PST behind me...
> Literal translation: 'and he entered behind me...'
> Transcript translation: 'and he slipped in behind me...'

In this way, the manner of motion in Spanish is absent from the original descriptions, but present in their English translations. The consequence of this process is the image of the Figure moving in a certain manner (e.g. running), whereas the original account did not provide that piece of information. In one particular case from which Example (4) was taken, the English translation throughout the interview contains multiple uses of the verbs 'run' or 'chase' as equivalents for the Spanish witness's neutral or path verbs ('go', 'follow', etc.). No information was made available in the Spanish original on how quickly the suspect or the witnesses that followed him were moving. As a result, the situation can be interpreted as more dynamic in the English translation.

Information about the manner of motion is very important because it allows us to speculate about the suspect's physical state and location (e.g. if he was running all the time, he could be tired and hiding in the search area; he could have gone further from the crime scene if he had run than if he had limped; if he had run, it means he had not been wounded or hurt, etc.). The communicative consequence is that we could draw different conclusions about a described event from the Spanish original and its English translation.

Another issue of consequence in this context is the entrenched narrative pattern that is engendered by typological preferences. English speakers habitually describe motion events as continuous and dynamic while Spanish speakers typically provide a series of static locations (Slobin 2000). In practice this means that Spanish speakers often express where somebody was located but not *how* he/she got there. Filipović (2007) confirms this claim, citing the high frequency of expressions such as 'me metí' (lit. 'I put myself' (somewhere)) and 'se metió' (lit. 'He put himself (somewhere)'). The translation follows the typical pattern in the target language (English) and often contains additional manner verbs (Filipović 2007):

> 6) ...y se metió en el restaurante.
> ...and REFL put-3SG.PST in the restaurant.
> Literal translation: '...and put himself in the restaurant.'
> Transcript translation: '...and ran into the restaurant.'

It is clear that information about the manner of motion is of importance to police investigation and judicial enquiry. For example, the authorities trying to identify a suspect (examples (4) and (6)) may be asking questions about a person who ran into a particular restaurant. According to the Spanish original, the suspect did not run or perhaps he ran at at the beginning of the chase, but later, in order to avoid suspicion, he calmly entered the restaurant and then also walked out of it. According to the English translation of the witness interview in question, the suspect ran all the time including at the moment he entered the restaurant, which the Spanish-speaking witness did not say.

3.2. Describing and translating witnessed causation events

The difference in how causation can be expressed in different languages can have further consequences for witness interviewing and translation in this context. Filipović (2007) has shown the difficulty in interpreting what kind of situation is described by impersonal constructions such as the ones exemplified in subsection 2.2. This can have potentially profound consequences in witness interviews and their translation. This particular construction, 'se me cayó' (meaning 'to-me-it-happened-that-she-fell'; see example iv in Table 1) was used extensively by a suspect who was describing what had happened to his victim (Q = question, I = interpreter, S = suspect):

7) Q: Okay, You said before that she fell or you dropped her on the steps?
I: Usted les dijo antes de que ella se cayó o la botó en las gradas?
'You then said before that she fell, or you *dropped* her on the stairs'
S: ... sí, sí se me cayó.
'... yes, yes, to-me-it-happened-that-she-fell'
I: Yes, I *dropped* her.

We can see that the verb 'drop' was offered in both its accidental and non-accidental interpretation, while the meaning of the Spanish expression used by the suspect ('se me cayó') is unequivocally accidental. The verb 'drop' used by the interrogator was clearly referring to a non-accidental act of dropping and the answer by the suspect could be tied to his admission of guilt. The interrogator asked the same question relating to the dropping of the victim nine times during that particular interview, and by the end it was still not clear from the translation whether the suspect was stating that he had dropped the victim voluntarily or involuntarily. The suspect may have been using the non-agentive construction in order to absolve himself but then again this suspect does not seem like a particularly language-aware person, he is not choosing his words with extreme care. This is evident in Example (7), in which the verb 'botar' ('throw'—intentional) is used as an explicitly agentive verb and the equivalent of the agentive meaning of 'drop'. The suspect does not explicitly deny this accusation of voluntary involvement. In fact, he says a confused 'yes' as an answer to that potentially damaging question. The interpreter then goes on to translate 'se me cayó ('to-me-it-happened-that she fell') as 'I dropped her', which is the very phrase he/she had previously used and established as the equivalent of the explicitly agentive verb 'botar' ('throw').

What this example shows is the central importance of language contrasts in the understanding of what a suspect is or is not confessing to. Furthermore, studying patterns in language use engendered by two language types and the respective speakers' habitual preference for certain constructions can help us detect the exact points at which problems in translation may occur. In this way we can improve the focus of professionals involved in the process of collecting information that may be used as evidence. Packaging information in a language-specific way is so deeply rooted in our everyday experience and interaction with the world around us that we are often unaware that we are doing it, namely organizing information according to a certain underlying system of words and rules. In addition, if we are carrying out the extremely stressful job of interviewing and interpreting we are naturally inclined to revert to the comfort of our typical and familiar linguistic frames. By this we mean that, when under pressure, people revert to stereotypes in behaviour, including linguistic behaviour (see Mendoza-Denton 2010). The most natural and typical way of describing the situation of dropping something in English is indeed the typical English sentence, 'I dropped her'. The sequence referred to in Example (7) may not necessarily be an example of an interpreter doing a bad job. It is rather an example of doing what is most natural and in principle adequate in one's mother tongue. The fact that English speakers do not have to determine explicitly whether causation was voluntary or involuntary accounts for the fact that they do not spontaneously do so, or at least they do not do so as often and in as much detail as speakers of other languages who have this distinction explicitly ingrained in their system and their habits of language use.

Finally, suspects can use this natural ambiguity or vagueness in natural language in order to try and avoid a more serious sentence. This consequence must be borne in mind as well but it is certainly not a reason to deny people the right to adequate translation of the meaning they wish to convey.

4. Language, memory, and judgment

In this section I briefly illustrate and discuss the latest research in applied psycholinguistics that bears relevance to witness testimony and witness interviewing.

The two experiential domains in focus here are the same again, motion and causation.

4.1. Motion

If language affects what we mention in our accounts of events, both in terms of how often and in what detail, could it perhaps then also have an effect on what kind of information we remember and recall? This question has been asked many times in different contexts under the hypothesis known as *linguistic relativity*, originally inspired by the work of two anthropologists, Edward Sapir and Benjamin Lee Whorf. For present purposes, we focus on the potential of having language-specific preferences reflected in witness memory and judgment. There has been a recent renewal of interest in linguistic relativity, and numerous researchers have been re-examining the nature of the language-cognition relationship. For example, language effects have been found in colour categorization (Roberson et al., 2005, Regier and Kay, 2009), categorization of objects (Lucy and Gaskins, 2003), and spatial orientation (Levinson, 2003). Language effects on witness memory in particular have been recognized in psycholinguistics. In their seminal study, Loftus and Palmer (1974) showed that language can create false memories in eyewitnesses that are caused by the word choice in investigative questions. They demonstrated that using the verb 'crash' instead of 'collide' in mock witness interviews prompted witnesses to claim that there was a broken glass in a car crash when, in fact, there was none.

A number of studies in this area have reported a lack of effects on memory for motion events. For example, Malt et al. (2003) found language effects only on categorization after prior verbalization. English speakers grouped two motion events together if they shared the same manner even though the path in them was different. On the other hand, Spanish speakers grouped events together when they shared the same path of motion even though the manners were different. This study shows the central importance of the verb in the classification of events: it appears that in this experiment the verb is the main criterion for the grouping of events. Spanish speakers, unsurprisingly, tend to use path verbs and they classified events according to whether they contained the same path.

English speakers did the same but with manner verbs and based their judgments of similarity on shared manners in the events they witnessed. However, Malt et al. (2003) did not find any language-specific effects on memory. Similarly, Filipović (2010a, 2010b) indicated that even though Spanish and English speakers described the same events differently (the English speakers providing significantly more manner detail, while the Spanish gave hardly any), both groups of speakers performed equally well at a memory recognition task. This means that the differences in language systems and language use apparently did not impact the quantity and quality of information stored in memory.

However, language-specific effects in this domain may just be more elusive, and not necessarily non-existent. A study by Finkbeiner et al. (2002) found language effects on the memory of motion events in specific circumstances: they found that when memory load is higher, this makes speakers evoke their language-specific expression patterns as an aid to memory. The effect of memory load in eliciting language-specific effects was documented in detail in a study by Filipović (2011). It provides evidence that language can affect witnesses' memory of events under increased memory load (mimicking the additional pressure that witnesses are under when they experience events). For ethical reasons, we are not able to replicate the emotional pressure or stress levels that certainly operate in the real world and outside a laboratory setting, but the pressure in the experiments in Filipović (2011) was increased by way of the complexity of the information to be handled. The central finding of that study is that the language-specific lexical and grammatical means used to package information in the domain of motion can cause differences in how speakers of different languages remember events as well as in what kind of information they provide about them when questioned. Filipović (2011) found that, while we may not always organize our memory in accordance with our language patterns, when dealing with complex task demands, and especially when under increased pressure, we revert to the best classification system we have, namely our language. Filipović (2011) used experimental video clips that increase the memory load by depicting *complex events* in which three kinds of motion were shown in each video (e.g. limping, then swaying, and then marching). While English speakers mentioned at least two of the three manner verbs in each event they saw, Spanish speakers defined only one manner of motion (at most) of the three in each event they saw. This is illustrated in the examples below (with manner information underlined).

8a) Salió <u>despacio cojeando</u>.
'He exited slowly limping.'
8b) Caminó <u>dando pequeñitos saltos</u>.
'He walked with tiny jumps.'
8c) Cruzó el jardín <u>andando raro</u>.
'He crossed the garden going in a strange manner.'
9a) He <u>limped</u> then <u>swayed</u> across the path.
9b) He <u>leapt</u> out and <u>marched</u> across the road.
9c) He <u>emerged</u> from behind a tree, <u>smoothly walked</u> along the path then <u>skipped</u> off.

English speakers habitually used manner verbs in motion descriptions because they have multiple lexical and grammatical resources in this domain whereas Spanish speakers have fewer manner verbs as well as grammatical and stylistic restrictions that prevented them from using manner verbs or including manner descriptions elsewhere in this task. As a result of these linguistic differences monolingual speakers of English tended to provide more detailed information about the manner of motion than their Spanish peers and they also had better memory for manner. Furthermore, the task was much more taxing for Spanish speakers, who had to remember these complex motion events without labelling them efficiently with singular verbs, as English speakers did.

Filipović (2011) demonstrated that task demands and language affected memory performance: English speakers had better recognition memory in this instance than their Spanish peers. The *recognition error* (i.e. saying that the two events they saw were the same whereas in fact they differed in the manner of motion) was significantly higher for the Spanish group (68 per cent) than for the English (38 per cent). These results were also replicated in Filipović and Geva (2012).

Thus we can conclude that speakers whose languages oblige them to pay attention to an event component (e.g. manner of motion) may have an advantage in how much and how well they remember it. When witnessing an event, especially the kinds of events relevant for criminal investigation, people experience greater stress as well as a higher information and emotional load than under the normal circumstances of daily life. As we pointed out earlier, while it is harder (and unethical) to induce the same level of stress and emotional load in an experimental setting in the lab, the experimentally increased information load provided evidence that such circumstances can indeed elicit language effects in witness memory.

4.2. Causation

In a similar vein, empirical psycholinguistic research on cross-linguistic differences in the domain of causation has recently offered important insights into the role of language in witness memory and judgment. Fausey and Boroditsky (2011) examined speakers' descriptions of intentional and accidental events, and their memory for the agents of these events. English and Spanish speakers in their study described intentional events similarly, using mostly agentive language (e.g., 'She broke the vase'). However, when it came to accidental events, English speakers used the same constructions as the ones they used for non-accidental (intentional) events ('He popped a balloon'), unlike Spanish speakers, who made an explicit distinction between the two event types ('He popped the balloon' versus 'To-him-it-happened-that a balloon popped'; see subsection 2.2). Results from a non-linguistic memory task in that study mirrored the patterns in language. English and Spanish speakers remembered the agents of intentional events equally well. However, English speakers expressed and remembered the agents of accidental events better than did Spanish speakers, who did not express them. The authors conclude that it appears that patterns of language use shape how people interpret and remember causal events. Fasey and Boroditsky (2011) cautiously note, however, that their results do not show that Spanish speakers are unable to remember the individuals involved in accidental events and they emphasize that patterns in language cannot predict that. Their crucial point is that the focus on agentive language in English in descriptions of both accidental and non-accidental events may orient visual attention to the agent and make one *more likely* to represent or record details about who that agent is.

A study by Filipović (2012, in preparation) investigated another aspect of causation, namely the memory of whether the causation itself was voluntary (on purpose) or involuntary (accidental). Speakers of English and Spanish were presented with video clips depicting events where an agent was intentionally causing something (e.g. a girl pushing her Barbie doll off the bed on purpose) and those where the agents were involved in accidental causation (e.g. a woman, looking for something on a messy desk pushed a water bottle off the desk inadvertently). Speakers of both languages used similar agentive constructions to describe voluntary actions (e.g. 'The girl pushed the doll off the bed'), but they differed in the descriptions of the non-voluntary or accidental actions:

10a) The woman knocked the bottle off the table.
10b) Se le cayó la botella.

('To-her-the-bottle-fell.')
10c) The girl popped the balloon.
10d) Se le rompió el globo a la muchacha.
('To-her-the-balloon-burst to the girl.')

In these cases, the Spanish descriptions give explicit information about the action being involuntary while the English descriptions could be interpreted as either. We can expect the speakers to use language as strategy when recalling causation events since causation events are complex in themselves, as Fausey and Boroditsky (2010: 155) observe:

Observers must integrate information about the basic physics of the event (e.g., whether the person touched the balloon, whether the balloon popped, whether he touched it right before it popped) with more social cues about the individual's state of knowledge and intentions (e.g., whether he meant to touch the balloon, whether he knew the balloon was there, whether he was surprised at the outcome). The need to integrate many different types of information to construe an event may leave some events especially susceptible to linguistic and cultural influences.

We saw (in subsection 4.1) that when handling complex information stimuli in the domain of motion events, speakers relied on their preferred language patterns. Similar behaviour was detected in this memory for causation task. In this case, both English and Spanish speakers accurately recalled the clearly intentional events. However, Spanish speakers were more accurate than English speakers when it came to non-intentional (accidental) events. All events that contained accidental causation were described with an impersonal construction in Spanish (see (10b) and (10d)) and were recalled as such (100 per cent correct). The English speakers described such events ambiguously (as in (10a) and (10c)) and this result was reflected in their less accurate recall (75 per cent correct).

We can note that the within-category difference in correct responses between Spanish and English speakers is greater for complex motion events (English speakers: 68 per cent, twice as much as the Spanish speakers: 34 per cent) than that for causation events (Spanish speakers: 100 per cent compared with English speakers: 75 per cent). We can explain why that is so. The choice between accidental causation and non-accidental causation is based on a finite number of options, namely two (thus there is a 50 per cent possibility for each option in recall and consequently a smaller chance for error). On the other hand, when it comes to the unexpressed manners of motion in Spanish, the information load is higher and the number of possible candidates for labelling events (i.e. manner verbs or manner adverbials, phrases, or clauses) is potentially open-ended, or at least significantly less restricted. It was not possible for Spanish speakers to have a limited range of options for later recognition for complex motion events, while in the case of causation the task was comparatively easier for the English speakers since they have only two options to consider: accidental or non-accidental. Nevertheless, the accuracy of their recall is still lower than that of their Spanish peers in this case.

With regard to causation events it is fundamentally important to observe the following: if we read the description of an event in only one of the two languages in this case we may draw different conclusions about what happened and why. Furthermore, the amount and quality of detail that we can extract also differs, depending to an extent (as exemplified in this paper) on whether we interview a Spanish-speaking witness or an English-speaking witness. This is why both the original and the translation need to be recorded in interviews with witnesses and why interviewing personnel as well as interpreters would benefit from raised awareness about the language contrasts studied here.

4.3. Judgment

As we saw in subsections 4.1 and 4.2, there are different factors at play when it comes to how much information witnesses may remember and volunteer in their statements. When the case reaches the jury, what witnesses say is all the jury has to go by in that respect since the jury members themselves did not experience the events described at first hand. This is why it is crucial to make sure that the information available is as accurate as possible and actually reflects the meaning that is conveyed by the witness in his/her original language.

The effect of language use on jury members is well known and well illustrated in various studies, in both academic work and popular culture. An efficient argument, good presentation, and oratorical skills of persuasion in court can sway opinions. Here I cite just a few examples that illustrate how the choice of words and constructions in the domains of motion and causation can have an impact on how speakers make judgments in mock jury experiments.

A study by Trujillo (2003) explored the differences within a group of English speakers, manipulating the differential use of verbs in event descriptions, and the speakers' subsequent judgments about the observed events. The author compared accounts of the same events, some using many manner details and others without such manner detail, in order to see whether the lack of manner detail could deflect the jury from concentrating on the violence of the action because they were being manipulated into thinking the manner was unimportant. The author hypothesized that if semantically complex manner is described, people may accept it as relevant, and it will play a role in the judgments they make about the severity of punishment warranted by the actions; if manner is described in a neutral fashion, people may assume it is not important, and this may lead them to form less severe judgments because they are based less on the violent manner of the actions. The important issue here is whether manner in action is something that alters our judgments of events. The author's hypothesis has been confirmed in Trujillo's study, namely, manner information available can affect judgment.

By the same token, Fausey and Boroditsky (2010) found that English speakers who read a description of an event using agentive constructions (such as 'He broke X') judged it as warranting more severe punishment than those who read about the same event described as not explicitly agentive ('X broke'). For instance, participants in an experiment who read of the notorious 'wardrobe malfunction' (involving Justin Timberlake and Janet Jackson at the 2004 Super Bowl) in a report containing the agentive expression 'tore the bodice' not only attributed more blame to Timberlake, but also levied 53 per cent more in fines for the offence than those who read a report containing the non-agentive expression 'the bodice tore'.

Ibarretxe-Antuñano and Filipović (in press) explain how typological differences between languages can affect the understanding of events, depending on whether the readers see the original text or a translation. The material for the mock jury reported in their study comprised a selection of eight sentences expressing motion and causation taken from a bilingual on-line newspaper article available both in the Spanish original and in an English translation. The participants were asked to judge how violent the events described were, on a scale of 1 to 10 (where 1 = least violent, 10 = most violent).

There was a significant difference in the rating of violence based on the language in which the description was available. The results indicate that the speakers who read about the events in English rated the level of violence described as much higher than did those who read about it in Spanish. And when we look at the descriptions in question, we can understand more clearly why that was so. For instance, we noticed additions of manner in the translation from Spanish (11a–11d) into English (12a–12d):

11a) Me metió en su coche.
'Me he-put in his car.'
11b) Tumbaron las barricadas.
'They overturned the barricades.'
11c) Empezó a tirarme por las sposas.
'He began to pull me by the handcuffs.'
11d) Me tiró al suelo.
'He threw me on the ground.'

12a) He threw me in his car.
12b) They slammed the barricades on the floor.
12c) He started jerking me back and forth by the handcuffs.
12d) He slammed me down to the ground.

To sum up, studies based on a selected sample of motion and causation expressions and their corresponding translation illustrated the extent to which speakers can understand events differently based on the language in which they get to hear about them. And this is how we find out about events in the courtroom or how we get our knowledge about most events in life except those that we witness ourselves. It is therefore essential that we are alert to the language differences that may affect our judgment. This is especially true in contexts where it is very important to ensure that our understanding of events, and our assessment of the degree of involvement by the participants, is accurate.

5. Conclusions

The aim of this paper was to point out the potential consequences stemming from language differences in the interpretation of events and translations of witness interviews in order to make the process of evidence gathering fairer and more efficient for everybody involved. I explained why we may expect to find different accounts of the same events based on the languages in which they were given and on their respective translations. Languages engender different preferences based on the patterns available to express what we experience. Witness accounts may differ on an individual basis (e.g. some people have generally better memory than others, or they may be more focused on some aspects of what they experience than their peers), but what I presented here were robust differences based on language systems which are not driven by individual idiosyncrasies. We may expect an impact on investigative data collection in legal contexts in line with linguistic differences, and this is why further probing for information in witness interviews should reflect our knowledge that such differences may play a role. For example, we can expect an English-speaking witness to provide a more detailed and better informed account of the manner of motion and potentially to remember such detail better than a Spanish speaker. On the other hand, Spanish-speaking witnesses may be more informative than their English counterparts when it comes to describing whether an action was intentional or not. Similarly, I tried to find the limits of language effects on witness memory. Increased processing load in the domain where language as aid to memory cannot be used effectively may cause differences in the details of events remembered. This was the case with complex motion events, for which English speakers apparently had a better memory. In the causation domain, English speakers seem to have a better memory of agents than Spanish speakers since they tend to verbalize that information—regardless of whether the agent is voluntarily or involuntarily involved. Finally, when it comes to the crucial aspects of causation events, Spanish speakers are more accurate in their distinction between accidental and non-accidental causation and have better recall of this aspect than the English speakers—who tend to focus less on that component in their description, and consequently in their recall.

Raising awareness of the key point of contrasts between individual languages or language families (as is done in linguistic typologies) can help us understand what the issues are and prompt attempts to find solutions in anticipation of the greater problems that can potentially arise. This line of research also has practical applications in the domains of access to justice for non-native speakers as well as services in other contexts, such as legal, medical, employment, and education policies.

Finally, we can further improve fair treatment in the judicial and law enforcement contexts. For example, in the United States, police transcripts of witness interviews contain both the original language of a witness and the translation and the transcripts are also double checked by a control translator who provides a subsequent parallel rendering of the whole interview. This is better than the practice in the UK, where no control translation is available. In most countries however, it is hard to come by any kind of police interview transcripts; and even if they exist;, they rarely contain both the original language and the translation. Meanwhile, when it comes to court proceedings across the world, official court transcripts are normally produced only in the language of the country where the court is located.[4] There are real limitations to the provision of multilingual transcripts in general, mainly because the cost is prohibitive. Nevertheless, the option should be in place for serious cases where there is a great deal at stake and thus the practice can be revised and implemented on a case-by-case basis.

It is to be hoped that further research in this area will attract the attention of the various professionals involved, such as interpreters, interrogators, and legal representatives, to the causes and effects of the difficulties experienced by native speakers of a language different from the interview language. This approach will in turn bring to the fore the difficulties that such professionals themselves face in their work and could offer them valuable assistance. Future investigation along these lines and collaboration between researchers and practitioners (for example in sharing data and expertise) will undoubtedly lead to benefits not only for these two groups but also for the general public, to whom both academic research outcomes and informed professional support are directed.

REFERENCES

Berk-Seligson, S. (1990). *The Bilingual Courtroom: Court interpreters in the judicial process*. Chicago: University of Chicago Press.

Fausey, C. and Borditsky, L. (2010). Subtle linguistic cues influence perceived blame and financial liability. *Psychonomic Bulletin & Review*, 17(5), 644–50.

Fausey, C. and Boroditsky, L. (2011). Who dunnit? Cross-linguistic differences in eye-witness memory. *Psychonomic Bulletin & Review*, 18(1), 150–7.

Filipović, L. (2007). Language as a witness: Insights from cognitive linguistics. *International Journal of Speech, Language and the Law*, 14(2), 245–67.

Filipović, L. (2009). Motion events in semantic typology and eyewitness interviews. *Language and Linguistics Compass*, 3(1), 300–13.

---

[4] An exception may be international courts, such as the War Crimes Tribunal in The Hague.

Filipović, L. (2010a). Typology meets witness narratives and memory: Theory and practice entwined in cognitive linguistics. In E. Tabakowska, M. Choinski, and L. Wiraszka (eds), *Cognitive Linguistics in Action: Theory to Application and Back* (pp. 269–91). Berlin: Mouton de Gruyter.

Filipović, L. (2010b). Thinking and speaking about motion: Universal vs. language-specific effects. In G. Marotta, A. Lenci, L. Meini and F. Rovai (eds), *Space in Language* (pp. 235–48). Pisa: University of Pisa Press.

Filipović, L. (2011). Speaking and remembering in one or two languages: Bilingual vs. monolingual lexicalization and memory for motion events. *International Journal of Bilingualism*, 15(4), 466–85.

Filipović, L. (2012). Constructing causation: Language and memory of events in English and Spanish. University of East Anglia, ms.

Filipović, L. (in preparation). Constructing causation in language and memory: Implications for access to justice in multilingual interactions.

Filipović, L. and Geva, S. (2012). Language-specific effects on lexicalization and memory of motion events. In L. Filipović and K. Jaszczolt (eds), *Space and Time across Languages, Disciplines and Cultures: Language, Culture and Cognition* [Human Cognitive Processing Series 37] (pp. 269–82). Amsterdam: John Benjamins.

Finkbeiner, M., Nicol, J., Greth, D., and Nakamura, K. (2002). The role of language in memory for actions. *Journal of Psycholinguistic Research*, 31, 447–57.

Gibbons, J. (2003). *Forensic Linguistics*. Oxford: Blackwell.

Gibbons, J. (2011). Towards a framework of communicative evidence. *International Journal of Speech, Language and the Law*, 18(2), 233–69.

Hale, S. (2004). *The Discourse of Court Interpreting: Discourse practices of the Law, the Witness and the Interpreter*. Amsterdam: John Benjamins.

Ibarretxe-Antuñano, I. and Filipović, L. (in press). Lexicalization patterns and translation. In A. Rojo and I. Ibarretxe-Antuñano (eds), *Cognitive Llinguistics and Translation*. Berlin: Mouton de Gruyter.

Levinson, S. C. (2003). *Spatial Language and Cognition*. Cambridge: Cambridge University Press.

Loftus, E. F. and Palmer, J. C. (1974). Reconstruction of Automobile Destruction: An Example of the Interaction Between Language and Memory. *Journal of Learning and Verbal Behavior*, 13(15), 585–9.

Lucy, J. and Gaskins, S. (2003). Interaction of language type and referent type in the development of nonverbal communication. In D. Gentner and S. Goldin-Meadow (eds), *Language in Mind* (pp. 465–92). Cambridge, MA: MIT Press.

Malt, B. C., Sloman, S. A., and Gennari, S. P. (2003). Speaking versus thinking about objects and actions. In D. Gentner and S. Goldin-Meadow (eds), *Language in Mind* (pp. 81–111). Cambridge, MA: MIT Press.

Mendoza-Denton, R. (2010). Are we born racist? Inside the science of stigma, prejudice and intergroup relations. Available at: <http://www.psychologytoday.com/blog/are-we-born-racist/201012/linguistic-forensics>.

Pountain, C. (2003). *Exploring the Spanish Language*. London: Hodder Arnold.

Regier, T. and Kay, P. (2009). Language, thought, and colour: Whorf was half right. *Trends in Cognitive Sciences*, 13, 439–46.

Roberson, D., Davidoff, J., Davies, I. R. L. and Shapiro, L. R. (2005). Color Categories: Evidence for the Cultural Relativity Hypothesis. *Cognitive Psychology*, 50, 378–411.

Slobin, D. I. (1996). Two ways to travel: Verbs of motion in English and Spanish. In M. S. Shibatani and S. A. Thompson (eds), *Grammatical constructions: Their form and meaning* (pp. 195–220). Oxford: Clarendon Press.

Slobin, D. I. (1997). Mind, code, and text. In J. Bybee, J. Haiman, and S. A. Thompson, (eds), *Essays on language function and language type: Dedicated to T. Givón* (pp. 437–67). Amsterdam/Philadelphia: John Benjamins.

Slobin, D. I. (2000). Verbalized events: A dynamic approach to linguistic relativity and determinism. In S. Niemeier and R. Dirven (eds), *Evidence for linguistic relativity* (pp. 107–38). Amsterdam/Philadelphia: John Benjamins.

Slobin, D. I. (2003). Language and thought online: Cognitive consequences of linguistic relativity. In D. Gentner and S. Goldin-Meadow (eds), *Language in mind: Advances in the investigation of language and thought* (pp. 157–91). Cambridge, MA: MIT Press.

Slobin, D. I. (2006). What makes manner of motion salient? Explorations in linguistic typology, discourse, and cognition. In M. Hickmann and S. Robert (eds), *Space in languages: Linguistic systems and cognitive categories* (pp. 59–81). Amsterdam: John Benjamins.

Talmy, L. (1985). Lexicalization patterns. In T. Shopen (ed), *Language typology and syntactic description (Vol. III): Grammatical categories and the lexicon* (pp. 59–149). Cambridge: Cambridge University Press.

Talmy, L. (2000). *Toward a cognitive semantics*. Cambridge, MA: MIT Press.

Trujillo, J. (2003). The difference in resulting judgments when descriptions use high-manner versus neutral-manner verbs. Unpublished senior dissertation, University of California at Berkeley.

20

Vagueness and Power Delegation in Law: A Reply to Sorensen[†]

Hrafn Asgeirsson

In 'Vagueness has no function in law',[1] Roy Sorensen argues that it is a mistake to think that vagueness has a constructive function in law, such as delegating limited law-making power to officials[2] or eliciting certain kinds of desired behavior on the part of subjects.[3] It merely *appears* to be functional, Sorensen says, due to 'a cluster of logical and linguistic errors' about its nature. In addition, he thinks that vagueness in the law often generates serious problems, and so *cannot* have a function in the law, on the understanding that something has a function in a system if, and only if, its presence is explained by how it serves a goal of the system. Thus, for Sorensen, the issue is whether vagueness is *valuable* vis-à-vis law's aims, i.e. whether the presence of vagueness in the law does or can promote the common good.[4] The main problems he identifies are that (i) vague legislation is often used in a way contrary to the promotion of the common good,[5] and (ii) vague legal language, in *genuine* hard cases, forces serious judicial insincerity.[6] Sorensen believes, then, that he can *explain away* the evidence for the claim that vagueness has a function in law, and, further, produce evidence for the contrary claim that it has *no such function*.

One of the main aims in this paper is to examine one of Sorensen's primary claims: that vagueness in the law—properly understood—cannot be justified by appeal to the value of power-delegation. Sorensen appears to think that the delegation of power to officials is justified *only if* these officials are in a better position to discover the right answer in the relevant cases. Since vagueness proper entails that there is no answer to be discovered, power-delegation will not be justified, he says. If he is right, then he will have taken away what is traditionally thought to be the main reason for thinking that vagueness can have a constructive function in law.

In section 1, I will present Sorensen's epistemic account of vagueness, his distinction between absolute and relative borderline cases, and his argument that absolute borderline cases do not have a constructive power-delegating function in law. I should note that the examples I present are mine, except for *Brown v Board of Education*. So in case any of them are unpersuasive, Sorensen is not at fault.

In section 2, I will examine his argument, arguing that it is unsound. More specifically, I will argue that the following claim is *false*: Delegation of decision-making

---

[†] Winner of the 2011 Australian Society for Legal Philosophy Annual Essay Competition.
[1] Roy Sorensen, 'Vagueness has no function in law' (2001) 7 *Legal Theory* 385.
[2] Joseph Raz, 'Sorensen: Vagueness has no function in law' (2001) 7 *Legal Theory* 419.
[3] See Timothy A.O. Endicott and Michael J. Spence, 'Vagueness in the Scope of Copyright' (2005) 121 *Law Quarterly Review* 664, and Gillian K. Hadfield, 'Weighing the Value of Vagueness: An Economic Perspective on Precision in the Law' (1994) 82 *Calif. L. Rev.* 545.
[4] Sorensen (cited in n.1), 398.
[5] Sorensen (cited in n.1), 399.
[6] Sorensen (cited in n.1), 388–92.

authority, vis-à-vis borderline cases regarding something's being *F*, is valuable *only if* the relevant delegates are in a better position to answer the question whether *x* is *F* than those delegating the power. Delegation of decision-making authority *can* be valuable, I hope to show, *even if* the relevant delegates are *not* in a better position to answer the question whether *x* is *F*. The key to seeing why is to acknowledge that when faced with absolute borderline cases, the courts must engage with a related *normative* question—whether *x* *ought*, relative to the purposes of the law, to *count* as an *F*.

I will try to show that, under certain circumstances, it is indeed better to let the relevant delegates answer the normative question—i.e. whether *x* ought, relative to the purposes of the relevant law, to count as an *F*. If I am successful, then there are situations in which delegation of decision-making authority is valuable *even if* the relevant delegates are not in a better position to answer the question *whether x is F* than those delegating the power. That is, if I am correct, then Sorensen's argument is unsound.

1. Sorensen's view

It is standard to define vagueness with reference to *borderline cases*, in the sense that most writers on vagueness hold either that *a term is vague only if it has possible borderline cases* or that *a term is vague if, and only if, it has possible borderline cases*.[7] Since Sorensen is committed to the latter claim, and nothing in this particular paper hangs on which one of these claims is true, I will assume it here for the sake of accurately representing his argument.

The nature of borderline cases is controversial, but most theorists would accept the characterization that these are cases in which there is inherent uncertainty regarding whether or not the relevant term applies. They will vary, however, in how they think this uncertainty ought to be understood. Some will say that the appropriate explanation is fundamentally *epistemic* (i.e. concerns what we can know), others that it is *linguistic* (i.e. concerns the rules of language), and yet others that it is at bottom *ontological* (i.e. concerns the way the world is).

Sorensen thinks that the proper explanation of vagueness is primarily *epistemic*. A borderline case, unlike a clear case, is a case in which the question regarding whether a predicate '*F*' applies to an object *o* has no knowable answer. The reason that the question has no answer is that there is nothing that makes either a positive or negative answer correct. For example, in case <*F, o*> = *p* and *p* is a borderline proposition, *p* will *lack a truth-maker* (and, thus, so will ~*p*). Here, a truth-maker is something 'in the world' which makes the relevant truth true; Joe's being bald, for example, makes the proposition *that Joe is bald* a true proposition (which in turn makes the sentence 'Joe is bald' a true sentence). In general, truth-makers are also the entities via which *we come to know* the truth-values of propositions. On Sorensen's view, the borderline proposition *p* will still have a truth-value—it's either true or false—but since we cannot, via any truth-maker (*o*'s being *F*), access this truth-value we are *irremediably* in the dark as to what that

---

[7] Sorensen himself accepts the stronger claim that a term is vague *if, and only if,* it has possible borderline cases, but several authors on vagueness take the existence of borderline cases alone to be insufficient for vagueness (see e.g. Scott Soames, *Understanding Truth* (Oxford: Oxford University Press, 1999)). It is also important to distinguish between *intensional* vagueness—the possibility of having borderline cases—and *extensional* vagueness—actual borderline cases. Vagueness is properly characterized in terms of the *possibility* of borderline cases. This distinction will also play a role in determining the value of vagueness for law.

truth-value is.[8] This is what makes Sorensen's approach epistemic. Since one cannot, even in principle, justifiably believe that a borderline sentence is true (or false), it follows that one cannot, even in principle, come to know the relevant proposition. In borderline cases, then, one's lack of knowledge is irremediable.

Absolute borderline cases, relative borderline cases, and answering resources

But, says Sorensen, there are borderline cases and there are borderline cases. He distinguishes between *absolute* borderline cases—in which the ignorance really is *irremediable*—and *relative* borderline cases—in which the ignorance is *remediable*—and he thinks that confusing the two may mislead one to believe that genuine vagueness is functional in law.[9]

A term is *genuinely* vague if, and only if, it has *absolute* borderline cases, and a term has absolute borderline cases if, and only if, it has cases that are borderline given *any means* of answering 'Is x F?' That is, in principle, there exist no resources for us to answer this question with respect to genuine borderline cases. *Relative* borderline cases, on the other hand, are not evidence of vagueness proper, since the ignorance in such a case is remediable by some means or other (which may or may not be available at a given time).

Sorensen thinks that most borderline cases are relative ones.[10] Relative cases include, e.g., ignorance as the result of a 'measure-by-eye' test for whether an x falls in this or that size category, which may be resolved by a 'measure-by-ruler' test. An x may be categorized as borderline *relative to the former test* (i.e. the test doesn't, for the relevant x, return an answer to the question 'Is x F?'), while *relative to the latter* it may be categorized as a member or non-member of the relevant set (i.e. *that* test may return an answer to the question 'Is x F?'). Imagine, for example, a couple of fishermen determining by eye whether a given fish is big or not. From what they can determine by eye, the fish may be borderline big. Yet, if later measured by a ruler, it may turn out that it does fall within the category *big fish*. If so, then the case was a relative borderline case.

To take a legal example, consider the Pollution Prevention Act (1990), under which 'pollution that cannot be prevented should be recycled in an environmentally safe manner whenever feasible.'[11] Due to the complexity of environmental matters, it is clear that there are a great many possible cases that lawmakers could not categorize as safe or unsafe, but that experts nevertheless could. That is, relative to the body of information available to the average member of Congress, there may be many cases that are borderline without being borderline relative to the evolving body of information available to an agency like the Environmental Protection Agency.

Things are different when it comes to *absolute* borderline cases. Such cases include e.g. borderline patches of color in between, say, yellow and green (chartreuse). Here, arguably, the ignorance—as to whether or not a chartreuse patch is green—resulting from a 'measure-by-eye' test cannot be remedied by appeal to another test. It is not to be expected, for example, that a measurement of the spectrum of reflected light waves—or any other imaginable test—will provide us with an answer to whether or not a patch of

---

[8] Borderline cases, on Sorensen's view, therefore do not involve truth-*value* gaps, but truth-*maker* gaps.
[9] Sorensen (cited in n.1), 392–400.
[10] Roy Sorensen, *Vagueness and Contradiction* (Oxford: Oxford University Press, 2001), ch.1.
[11] 42 U.S.C. §13101–13109.

chartreuse really is green. Likewise, there will presumably be some *absolute* borderline cases of 'environmentally safe recycling.' In such cases, *no* body of information—no matter how sophisticated—can settle whether or not it is safe. Absolute cases are resistant to *any* further inquiry.

Measuring devices, bodies of information, sets of inference rules, etc. are *answering resources*—considerations capable of furnishing an answer to a question of the form 'Is x F?'[12] Such a resource may, e.g., provide a test for being F (e.g. *if condition C is satisfied, then x is F*). A test, of course, may be more or less fine-grained. Less fine-grained ones are likely to yield more borderline cases. And a case that is borderline relative to a certain answering resource may not be borderline relative to some other—perhaps more fine-grained—resource, as we have seen.[13] If there is *some* answering resource relative to which a case is *not* borderline, then the case is only *relatively* borderline. Cases in which *no* answering resource is capable of returning an answer, on the other hand, are *absolute* borderline cases.

Borderline cases and the delegation of power

Sorensen thinks that legal theorists are really interested in the functionality of *relative* borderline cases, since the relevant ignorance *can* be remedied by appeal to an appropriate answering resource. Delegation of power to administrative agencies, e.g. by means of introducing relative borderline cases into the law, is valuable, Sorensen claims, only because the relevant agencies have answering resources equipped to answer the question whether x is F. In these cases, he says, legislatures typically make it the case that certain cases are borderline relative to the answering resources *provided by law*, i.e. the law will provide no test that will, for every x, provide an answer as to whether x is F. But this doesn't mean that alternative non-legal answering resources aren't available. 'What is undecidable relative to current law,' he says, 'may be decidable with the help of supplementary premises and procedures.'[14] If I understand Sorensen correctly, I take it that, for example, the legislature may in certain cases not have the resources to answer whether or not a recycling process is 'environmentally safe'—i.e. the law does not *tell us* under which conditions such a process is safe—while scientific studies may indicate at least some such conditions. That is, it may be the case that there exists no specific regulation defining what is or is not environmentally safe, in which case an appropriate answer cannot be given by the law, yet it may be had by appealing to 'extra-legal' answering resources. The important thing is this: if such resources *are* in principle available, then the relevant case isn't an absolute borderline case—it is merely borderline *relative* to existing law.

Sorensen's own main legal example is *Brown v Board of Education*,[15] a case in which the Supreme Court ordered that school desegregation proceed 'with all deliberate speed.' The Court did not provide any explanation of what this phrase meant and there was no precedent to furnish legally clear cases of things happening with the required speed. In some cases, of course, a superficial test may suffice, e.g. if it is clear that most everybody would think that desegregation clearly had, or had not, happened with all deliberate

---

[12] Sorensen (cited in n.1), 392.

[13] Sorensen says that formal systems in which a statement which is undecidable in one but provable in another show clearly this structural relationship. Thus borderline cases are spawned by *incompleteness* of the relevant answering system: Sorensen (cited in n.10), 23.

[14] Sorensen (cited in n.1), 399. I am not sure why these additional answering resources cannot count as legal, assuming that officials are authorized to consult them, but for the sake of argument I'll go along and agree that these are somehow 'beyond the law'.

[15] 347 U.S. 483 (1954).

speed. Such a case does not call for a finer, more discriminating, test. But it may also happen that it is neither immediately clear that it hadn't happened with all deliberate speed nor that it hadn't. In this case, the courts may, e.g., appeal to explanations of what it 'really is' for something to happen with such speed. But in some cases, i.e. *genuine* borderline cases, no acceptable theory or resource of any other type will furnish an answer to the relevant question.[16] It is these sorts of cases that typically bother philosophers of logic and language. So it seems that the phrase 'with all deliberate speed' is genuinely vague.

However, the *flexibility* that this phrase was supposed to facilitate does not, Sorensen says, have to do with genuine vagueness, i.e. it does not have to do with absolute borderline cases, which exist due to the inability to answer the question whether x is F. Rather, the utility of the vague phrase has to do with *relative* borderline cases and the *ability* to furnish answers to the relevant questions. In *Brown*, the flexibility that the phrase allows is relevant to cases in which the people closest to it are in a position to say whether a *particular case* of desegregation has, or has not, happened with the required speed. That is, the decision of the Supreme Court allows the law to rely on the people who deal with the actual case to furnish the relevant answer, which is arguably better than if the Court had come up with some definition of the phrase, or used instead a more precise one. The complexity and unforeseeability of such matters as school desegregation make it the case that it is reasonable to delegate the task of finding out whether 'x is F' to those with special experience and/or who are in close proximity with the actual situation. Such individuals arguably have better discriminatory abilities—that is, they are better equipped to classify the relevant cases—and so delegating certain legal powers to them is in an important respect analogous to utilizing a more fine-grained test for F-ness. Cases that may seem borderline relative to a rather limited body of information possessed by the legislature (or the Supreme Court) may turn out not to be borderline relative to a richer body of information available to the relevant officials. So relative borderline cases may well have a valuable power-delegating function in law.

Absolute borderline cases, on the other hand, do not have any such power-delegating value, Sorensen says, since *no* answering resource is capable of providing an answer to whether the relevant xs are F. Hence, no one could ever be in a position to answer the relevant question and the delegation of power to agencies or the courts would be useless (for the purposes of settling the matter). The phrase 'endangerment to the health of persons',[17] for example, presumably has absolute borderline cases, but there is no benefit, Sorensen would say, in delegating power vis-à-vis absolute borderline cases of such endangerment, since no one can be in a better position than any other with respect to determining whether or not such a case constitutes endangerment in the relevant sense. Not even the best experts. The same goes for absolute borderline cases of 'with all deliberate speed.'

Let me conclude section 1 by summarizing Sorensen's argument:

P1. Delegation of decision-making authority, vis-à-vis borderline cases, is valuable *only if* the relevant delegates are in a better position to answer the question whether x is F than those delegating the power.

P2. When x is an *absolute* borderline case of 'F', *it is not the case* that the relevant delegates are in a better position to answer the question whether x is F than those delegating the power.

C. Therefore, when x is an *absolute* borderline case of 'F', *it is not the case* that delegation of decision making authority, vis-à-vis x, is valuable.

---

[16] Although, as Sorensen notes, Dworkin would deny this, since, on his view, *all* alleged hard cases concern relative borderline cases.

[17] See the Federal Water Pollution Control Act (1948), 33 U.S.C. §1364(a).

Sorensen's conclusion from all this, then, is that the notion of power-delegation cannot be used to show that vagueness—proper—can be a valuable feature of law.

Sorensen's distinction between absolute and relative borderline cases is quite interesting and the argument indeed threatens to take away what is traditionally taken to be the main reason for thinking that vagueness can have a constructive function in law. If the benefits of being able to delegate limited law-making power are had by introducing *relative* borderline cases into the law, rather than *absolute* ones, then power-delegation won't be a benefit due to vagueness proper. Moreover, the distinction does not depend on Sorensen's particular theory of vagueness—rather, it is one that *any* broad theory of vagueness should take seriously. More particular to our purposes here, it seems to me that P1 and P2 are jointly consistent with any viable theory of vagueness. Thus, we cannot avoid the problem posed by Sorensen's argument simply by arguing against his account of vagueness. It must be tackled some other way.

Sorensen's P2 seems safe enough. In fact, it is arguably entailed by any respectable theory of vagueness, whether epistemic, supervaluational, psychological, or indexical/contextual. As far as absolute borderline cases go, all theories will claim that for every cognizer x, every cognizer y, and every borderline proposition p, it is *never* the case that x is epistemically better situated than y vis-à-vis the truth value of p. P2 is simply a limited case of this general claim.

Now, I agree with Sorensen that the distinction between absolute and relative borderline cases is often overlooked and that, as a result, value that is appropriately associated with relative borderline cases is wrongly associated with absolute ones. Still, I think that there *are* cases in which the delegation of power—and the resulting discretion—is justified *even if* the relevant delegates are *not* in a better position to find out whether x is F. In certain cases, it may well be better to leave the *stipulation* as to whether x is F—i.e. the decision whether x ought, for the purposes of the law, to count as an F—up to competent delegates. In section 2, I try to explain some conditions under which this is the case. If I succeed, then P1 of Sorensen's argument will be false.

2. The value of vagueness

Sorensen recognizes that absolute borderline cases prompt judicial discretion, and characterizes this discretion as discretion to *substitute* the question whether x is F with the question whether *x should count as an F*. If a court is faced with a borderline case of, say, 'business establishment'—as it was in the case of *Curran v Mount Diablo Boy Scouts*[18]—the courts may relativize the concept in question to suit the purposes of the law, Sorensen says.[19] In *Curran*, for example, such relativization led to the Boy Scouts being counted as a business establishment. If I understand Sorensen correctly, he has in mind the practice of the courts to use phrases of the following sort: 'for the purposes of [such-and-such a statute], x is F'. The Boy Scouts, then, presumably counted as a business establishment *for the purposes of California's Unruh Civil Rights Act* (1959).[20] For an example in the constitutional realm, many have argued (and the Supreme Court has agreed) that *for the purposes of the First Amendment*, flag-burning counts as speech (and so is protected).[21] These, of course, are not answers to whether x is F, but to whether x should legally count

---

[18] 17 Cal. 4th 670 (1998).
[19] Sorensen (cited in n.1), 414.
[20] Cal. Civ. Code §51.
[21] See *Texas v Johnson*, 491 U.S. 397 (1989), and *U.S. v Eichman*, 496 U.S. 310 (1990).

as an *F* relative to some particular aims of the law. Thus, in absolute borderline cases, the question is—implicitly or explicitly—changed. Moreover, it is changed to one that in many cases has better prospects of being answered (i.e. a non-zero probability, unlike 'Is *x F*?').

The reason I bring this up is that I have a hard time seeing why this question-changing discretion may not be valuable. In fact, I believe that legislators often rely on this pervasive judicial response. When legislatures deliberately use vague language, they are not asking the courts to find out whether absolute borderline *F*s really are *F*s; rather, they are asking the courts to do exactly what Sorensen describes, to engage with the *normative question* whether *x* ought—relative to the purposes of the law—to count as an *F*. And I fail to see any argument in Sorensen's paper to the effect that the judicial response to this legislative 'request' cannot, under certain circumstances, be valuable. And if it can be shown that discretion to change the question *can* be valuable, then—since such discretion is *due to* absolute borderline cases—vagueness *proper* will have a constructive function in law.

One issue which may be in the back of Sorensen's mind is, I think, the following. It seems that if it is valuable to let the courts figure out whether *x* should count as an *F*, then that is because there is an answer to whether *x* should count as an *F*. And if there is an answer to whether *x* should count as an *F*, then it seems that there is a fact of the matter whether *x* is a case that ought to be regulated, on the narrow understanding that a case *c* is regulated by a rule *R* if, and only if, *c* is included in *R*'s domain of application. But, and here is the catch, if the immediate aim of the lawmakers is to regulate everything *F* and *x* is absolutely borderline *F*, then there is arguably no fact of the matter whether *x* ought or ought not to be so included. Thus, combine the relevant immediate regulatory aim with the absolute borderline status of *x* and you may have a hard time explaining how it could be valuable to let the courts decide whether or not it should be regulated. If there is a truly arbitrary distinction to be made, it seems better simply to make it at the legislative level.[22]

I suspect that the answer here lies in the question-changing element of the judicial response to absolute borderline cases. In some cases, it may be that *x* ought to be included in the relevant rule's domain of application not *simply* in virtue of its being *F*—since it is borderline—but in virtue of a *combination* of factors (of which borderline *F*-ness may be one). Even if the legislature chose vague language in order to be able to regulate everything *F* (their immediate aim), background regulatory aims or justifications may dictate that particular borderline *F*s be regulated. The background justification of the well-worn fictional 'No vehicles in the park' statute, for example, may suffice to answer the question whether a skateboard ought to count as a vehicle. In case the background justification includes, say, to minimize noise pollution in the park, then that may point in favor of skateboards counting as vehicles 'for the purposes of the statute.' If, on the other hand, the aim was to reduce exhaust pollution and/or risk of fatal accidents, then that seems to clearly count in favor of not counting them as vehicles.

---

[22] There is a potentially important general issue here regarding the question whether *x* ought to be regulated. When we ask this question, we can be asking (at least) two things: (i) ought it to be the case that there is some rule *R* such that *x* is regulated by *R*? or (ii) for some particular rule *R* and case *x*, ought it to be the case that *x* is regulated by *R*? The former question concerns whether *x* ought to be regulated by law (at all), while the latter concerns whether *x* ought to be regulated by some particular law. It is possible that, in some cases, this distinction matters—since lawmakers have an unconstrained choice of rules, while the discretion of the courts is limited to precisifications of particular (already enacted) rules—but I will not pursue these matters here.

Now, it may of course happen that the relevant background aims do not determine a verdict either way—that is, they may fail to resolve the matter. Consider the normative question once again: Ought x to count as an F? Let's semi-formalize the question in the following way ('O' here reads 'It ought to be the case that'): $O(x$ counts as an $F)$? We can then construct a complex predicate $[\lambda x\ O(x$ counts as an $F]$, which may have borderline instances, both relative and absolute—just as F, by hypothesis, does. This, however, is not a theoretical problem, and should in fact be expected. I would be highly skeptical of an account that predicted otherwise. My claim is not that looking to legislative purpose can in all borderline cases guide judicial decision—that is, I am not suggesting a uniform practical decision-procedure for all borderline cases. Nor need I suggest one in order to reply to Sorensen. I am merely pointing out that while it may be arbitrary with respect to F-ness whether x ought to count as an F, it may happen—and probably often happens—that it is not arbitrary with respect to the purposes of the law.

I should note that the law seems to embrace this question-changing resolution strategy in other varieties of hard cases too, even ones in which the particular behavior is within the *determinate anti-extension* of the relevant predicate. It seems appropriate to understand both the doctrine of *transferred intent* and the doctrine of *willful blindness* as prescriptions to treat particular cases in certain ways, *for the purposes of the law*. Take for example the case of a person A who intends to harm another person B, but who—by accident—ends up harming yet another person C. In such a case, the law often treats A as having intended to harm C. This is known as transferred intent (or transferred malice, in English law). Consider the case of *Bradshaw v Richey*,[23] in which Richey was found guilty of aggravated felony murder on the basis of this doctrine. Richey had intended to kill his ex-girlfriend and her boyfriend but ended up killing a little girl, Cynthia Collins, instead. That is, Richey's intended violation of the law failed and instead he killed a person he had no intention of killing. Still, he was found guilty of murdering the girl, a felony that requires *intent*.

The doctrine of transferred intent arguably operates on the premise that the behavior to which it applies is *just as bad as* the intended behavior. Thus, the question facing the courts is a version of the normative question: ought x—for the purposes of the law—to count as an F? The purpose, in this case, is to prevent or punish behavior that is equally as bad as intended violations of the law (assuming attempt). In *Richey*, for example, the question was whether Richey's unintentional killing of young Cynthia Collins was—given the fact that it was the result of an attempt to murder another person—equally as bad as the intended murder.

The doctrine of willful blindness operates on a similar premise: the doctrine is supposed to apply if a defendant's deliberately ignorant violation of the law is *just as bad as* a knowing violation. In *US v Jewell*,[24] for example, Jewell was convicted for knowingly transporting marijuana across the US-Mexico border in his car, despite the fact that he deliberately avoided positive knowledge of what was in the car's compartment. In this case, too, the court opted to 'change the question', from a factual one to a normative one: ought Jewell's violation—relative to the law's purpose of preventing or punishing behavior that is equally as bad as knowing violations of the law—to count as a knowing violation?

The reason I am mentioning the doctrines of transferred intent and willful blindness is that they arguably show that the question-changing strategy shows up in different sorts of hard cases. That is, it is not a strategy *particular* to borderline cases, although the particular *context* of the normative question is different because—in the typical cases where transferred intent or willful blindness are taken to apply—the relevant behavior is within the *determinate anti-extension* of the relevant predicates and the background

---

[23] 546 U.S. 74 (2005).
[24] 532 F.2d 697 (1976).

purpose is a quite particular one. In vagueness-related cases, the courts can of course also ask if the relevant behavior is just as bad as behavior that is within the determinate extension of the predicate in question, but I see no reason to suppose that the resolution of borderline cases is restricted to that particular purpose. There may be all sorts of reasons why x ought—for the purposes of the law—to count as an F.

Now that we have relieved the arbitrariness worry, by proposing a strategy grounded both in normative theory and in practice, we can ask whether the normative question is ever better left to the courts or administrative agencies. If it is, then Sorensen's argument will be unsound.

Evaluating the value of vagueness in terms of 'better than'

I want to start this section by focusing on what kind of questions it is appropriate to ask when we are considering the value of vagueness in the law. The reason is that Sorensen's framework for talking about law and vagueness can sometimes make for misleading questions. In particular, Sorensen's strict notion of function is poorly suited for asking the appropriate questions regarding the value of vagueness in the law. His criterion of function was this: something has a function in a system if, and only if, its presence is explained by how it serves a goal of the system. This prompts an unhelpful way to think about the value of vagueness, since we are in effect forced to ask whether the presence of absolute borderline cases is valuable relative to the aims of the law. It is unhelpful since it seems odd from the get-go to even entertain the thought that somehow the *presence* of a particular absolute borderline case in the law is a good thing. What value does a particular hard case promote? This way of conducting the inquiry makes claims about the value of vagueness seem dubious from the start and so should be rejected and substituted by a more sensible way of asking the relevant questions. If we don't, we run the risk of not getting to the real issues.

I propose that we evaluate the value of vagueness in law using the comparative phrase 'better than', which underlines the fact that the value of using terms that have absolute borderline cases *depends on the alternative options* available to the lawmakers. The appropriate question is, I think, whether it is *better* to leave a law vague and let the courts deal with borderline cases than to have the legislature work out a more precise alternative. Or, to put it another way: is it ever better to leave it to the courts (or administrative agencies) to answer the question whether x ought to count as an F (assuming x is a genuine borderline case)? As for Sorensen, he must think that an answer can be affirmative only if the relevant delegates are in a *better position* to answer it than the legislators. This, however, would also be a misleading way of framing the issue. *That A is in a better position than B* to answer a question does not—as the phrase seems to superficially suggest—entail that A has better *knowledge* than B. A can also be in a better position if A has better *tools* than B for finding an answer, or if A's *cost* of finding the answer is lower than B's. This latter notion of *answering cost* may be particularly helpful, I think, in understanding the benefit of letting delegates answer the question whether a borderline x ought to count as an F. And since the answering cost we are concerned with here has to do with a practical question—whether to count x as an F—we can presumably substitute it with the more familiar notion of *cost of deliberation*.[25]

---

[25] For the time being, I am including under the heading of 'cost of deliberation' the *appropriateness* of the deliberator. That is, the extent to which the deliberator is inappropriate for the task of deliberating will figure in the cost of deliberation. Ultimately, this cost should perhaps be considered separately, but I'll leave that discussion for a later occasion.

Now, in some cases it is clearly *not* better to let delegates decide whether or not particular borderline cases ought to be regulated. When it comes to drinking age, for example, it would make bad sense to formulate the law vaguely ('Only adults are permitted to purchase and publicly possess alcoholic beverages') and have the courts or law enforcement agencies deal with borderline adults, by asking whether or not this or that person should count as one. The overall cost of deliberation would be enormous. Better to avoid that mess and make a somewhat (but not totally) arbitrary cut-off point by mentioning a particular age—say, 21. That may of course be done in at least two ways, either by leaving out any mention of adults in favor of explicit age, as was done in the National Minimum Drinking Age Act (1984),[26] or by defining 'adult'.

In other cases, however, it may be better to stick with a vague formulation and let the courts change the question to whether *x* ought to count as an *F* relative to the purposes of the relevant law. Let me try out a fictional example.

The federal code concerning drive-by shooting related to major drug offenses specifies, among other things, that if one fires a weapon into a crowd '[causing] grave risk to any human life,' then one shall receive such-and-such punishment.[27] The phrase 'grave risk' here is vague, mainly in virtue of the term 'grave'. As a borderline case, we can imagine that someone, in relation to a major drug offense, fires rubber bullets into a crowd and that, given the nature of the projectiles and the circumstances of the shooting, it is indeterminate whether the shooter caused grave risk to human life. In other words, the shooting constitutes an absolute borderline case of the behavior prohibited by the statute.

Now, it seems to me that it would be a bad move for the legislature—whose aims presumably include the reduction of danger to innocent bystanders and of the public fear that drive-by shootings induce—to try to work out a precise alternative statute. In addition to the fact that it would be *very* cumbersome, it is very likely, due to the multiplicity of factors that make for the absence or presence of risk, that any attempt to come up with a formula that isn't excessively over- or underinclusive is bound to fail.[28] Also, substituting the vague law with a more precise one would mean to exclude in advance some unpredictable borderline cases and include some, thereby eliminating the possibility of determining—when they come up—whether the law has an interest, *vis-à-vis the purpose of the code*, in regulating them.

To put this point more generally, it seems to me a bad bargain, all in all, to have legislators try to deal with *intensional* vagueness instead of letting the courts deal only with *extensional* vagueness. No matter how many concrete cases end up in the courts, they will always be far fewer than even the most modest sets of possible absolute borderline cases. That is, *the cost of deliberation associated with determining in advance what to do regarding possible borderline cases will in most cases greatly exceed the cost of deliberation associated with determining what to do regarding actual borderline cases when they come up*. Although, as we saw above, sometimes the foreseeable actual borderline cases are so many that it is better to draw a *simple* bright line, as long as this 'cheaper' rule is sufficiently acceptable (with respect to the relevant legislative aims). But sometimes, such a strategy is not feasible and the better option is to leave the language vague and let the courts deal with extensional vagueness on a case-by-case basis.

If this is correct, then Sorensen's argument against the claim that vagueness proper can have power-delegating value is unsound. In particular, *it is not the case* that the delegation of limited law-making power is justified *only if* the individuals or entities to which the

---

[26] 23 U.S.C. §158.
[27] 18 U.S.C. §36(b1).
[28] I say 'excessively' since most laws are arguably both over- and underinclusive to some extent.

power is delegated are in a better position to *find out* whether *x* is *F*. Also, it seems that—at least in some cases—we can, using Sorensen's own strong notion of function, say that the occurrence of absolute borderline cases in the law is indeed explained by how they contribute to the promotion of the aims of the law. They do so *not* by delegating to the courts the task to find out whether *x* is *F*. Rather, they do so by delegating to them the task to find out whether *x* ought, relative to the purposes of the relevant law, to count as an *F*.

The above example regarding drive-by shooting is of course very limited. But there are other, more wide-ranging, cases in which similar reasoning applies. Take for example the general requirements of culpability, as defined by the Model Penal Code s.2.02. In s.2(a),[29] the vague ordinary term 'purposely' is defined partially in terms of *awareness, belief,* and *hope*. Now, there will be both relative and absolute borderline cases of persons purposely violating the law in the *ordinary* sense of 'purposely'. The definition used in the Model Penal Code is arguably a precisification vis-à-vis *relative* borderline cases, i.e. the definition supplies a somewhat helpful answering resource. But I fail to see that the definition helps eliminate absolute borderline cases in any meaningful sense. At best, it trades one set of cases for another, since 'awareness', 'belief', and 'hope' are at least as vague as 'purposely' (I'm not assuming that we have a clear theoretical way of comparing vagueness—I only mean that the following holds: If 'purposely' is vague, then so are the other terms).

The question I want to ask here is this: Which of the following options seems better?

(1) The legislature tries to preempt the occurrence of absolute borderline cases by adding further, non-circular, definitions of 'awareness', 'hope', and 'belief', *stipulating* meanings in order to eliminate absolute borderline cases of purposely violating the law.

(2) The legislature—at some fairly coarse-grained level—leaves the provision vague and gives judges the discretion to ask whether actual absolute borderline cases that reach the courts ought—relative to the purpose of the code—to be regulated and thus to be counted as being purposeful.

It seems to me that (2) is the better option. Option (1) is feasible only if the lawmakers are able to evaluate a significant number of possible borderline cases or if it makes sense to halt deliberation and opt for a cheap and simple bright-line rule. The former isn't feasible given the high cost of deliberation and limited cognitive resources of normal human beings. And the latter isn't feasible given the high likelihood of error—i.e. of drawing an unacceptable boundary, relative to the relevant regulatory aim. Better to opt for (2) and let the courts deal with borderline cases incrementally, by dealing with actual borderline cases of purposeful violations as they reach the courts.

If what I have said is correct, then Sorensen's argument against the power-delegating function of vagueness is unsound. Vagueness may indeed have such a function, and, moreover, this function seems to be significant rather than marginal. I do agree, however, that many power-delegating instances are valuable because there is hope that the delegates will in fact discover whether *x* is or is not *F*, and that we should be careful to distinguish the value of relative borderline cases from that of absolute ones.

3. Summary

In section 1, I introduced Sorensen's epistemic account of vagueness and his distinction between absolute and relative borderline cases, and explained his argument for the claim

---

[29] M.P.C. §2.02(a).

that absolute borderline cases do not have a constructive power-delegating function in law. The argument was summarized in the following way:

P1. Delegation of decision-making authority, vis-à-vis borderline cases, is valuable *only if* the relevant delegates are in a better position to answer the question whether x is F than those delegating the power.

P2. When x is an *absolute* borderline case of 'F', *it is not the case* that the relevant delegates are in a better position to answer the question whether x is F than those delegating the power.

C. Therefore, when x is an *absolute* borderline case of 'F', *it is not the case* that delegation of decision-making authority, vis-à-vis x, is valuable.

My reply, presented in section 2, was to argue that P1 is false. Delegation of decision-making authority *can* be valuable *even if* the relevant delegates are not in a better position to answer the question whether x is F than those delegating the power. The key to seeing why, I claimed, is to acknowledge that when faced with absolute borderline cases, the courts must engage with a related *normative* question—whether x *ought*, relative to the purposes of the law, to *count* as an F.

I tried to show that, under certain circumstances, it is indeed better to let the relevant delegates answer the normative question—i.e. whether x ought, relative to the purpose of the relevant law, to count as an F. It is better when both of the following options are worse: (i) lawmakers consider in advance possible borderline cases and work out a sophisticated, more precise, alternative; (ii) lawmakers halt deliberation early on and opt for a cheap and simple bright-line rule. These options are typically worse if option (i) incurs extravagant costs of deliberation and option (ii) is likely to result in a rule that is unacceptable relative to the relevant regulatory aim. If I am correct that there are situations in which neither of these options is feasible, then there are situations in which delegation of decision-making authority is valuable even if the relevant delegates are not in a better position to answer the question whether x really is F.

21

Plato's Fertility Clinic: Status and Identity Rhetoric in Parenthood Disputes

David Gurnham

Introduction

Reading legal judgments in the light of ancient metaphysical enquiries about truth and representation can sharpen our understanding of the language of modern law. A person that has been conceived by donor conception, or otherwise raised by someone other than their genetic/biological parents, may struggle to find the most appropriate linguistic framework for speaking about who their 'real' parents are. A person that is unable to trace their genetic parent may feel devalued or even orphaned by the irreparable separation of social and genetic parentage, and may come to regard the 'loss' of their genetic parent as a significant obstacle to understanding their own identity in terms of where they have come from.[1] Speaking metaphorically, words can be 'orphaned' too, by becoming cut off from their historical or etymological source. Linguists and lawyers each concern themselves with the way in which words and concepts may be legitimately interpreted, and with how meanings can be derived that are not unduly strained or glossed. The concerns of both the donor-conceived offspring and linguists and lawyers thus might be understood to meet at a conceptual level in the sense that they each involve an interest in determining identity or value in terms of knowledge of origins: essentially how '*b*' has been derived from '*a*'.

This paper examines the language of parenthood in an age of artificial reproductive technologies and increasing acceptance of 'alternative' family configurations, in which parental status and responsibility may arise in various ways. Who, if anyone, may claim to be the *natural* parents of a child when a number of disputing candidates might qualify to the exclusion of others? Derrida's reading of Plato (outlined in section 1) is used here to analyse the way that, in legal disputes about parenthood, both judges and litigants attempt to distinguish between the 'natural' or 'true' parent—the recognition of which needs no gloss—and roles that fall short of this, whose claim to parenthood may in some way be artificial and contrived. Arguing that such deployments of 'naturalness' rhetoric in law implicitly rely on metaphors of 'parenthood' and 'progeny', the paper considers in turn three types of legal claim about the definition of 'parent': genetic (section 2), social (section 3) and intentional parenthood (section 4). In each instance the discussion will focus on the rhetoric used in relevant legal disputes.

---

[1] For examples of donor-conceived offspring expressing their feelings, see D. Gollancz, 'Donor insemination: a question of rights' (2001) 4 *Human Fertility* 164–7; also the testimony of Joanna Rose in *Rose v Secretary of State for Health* [2002] EWHC 1593, discussed in section 2.

1. Parenthood as a metaphor for legitimacy: Plato and Derrida

In sketching the theoretical frame of reference for this analysis of the legal language of parenthood, I draw first upon Plato's critique of writing as a perversion of nature and of truth, and secondly upon Derrida's deconstruction of Plato insofar as the latter relies on a rhetoric that prioritizes the 'natural' over the 'artificial'. In *Phaedrus*, Plato recounts a story in which the Egyptian demigod Theuth presents to King Thamus (the king of all Egypt and thus 'father' figure for all Egyptians) a gift for which he craves the king's approval:

> ... Theuth said: 'Here, O king, is a branch of learning that will make the people of Egypt wiser and improve their memories: my discovery provides a recipe (*pharmakon*) for memory and wisdom.'[2]

Theuth's gift is writing—ideas and commands that are written down will outlive and hence remedy the fallibility of memory. Despite the obvious advantages of such an invention, the wise king is far from impressed and gives a damning judgment on the dangers of writing for the people of Egypt:

> If men learn this, it will implant forgetfulness in their souls: they will cease to exercise memory because they rely on that which is written, calling things to remembrance no longer from within themselves, but by means of external marks; what you have discovered is a recipe (*pharmakon*) not for memory, but reminder. And it is no true wisdom that you offer your disciples, but only its semblance; for by telling them of many things without teaching them you will make them seem to know much, while for the most part they no nothing.'[3]

Plato's point in recounting this story is to elucidate the nature of truth and the danger that true knowledge may become obscured in representation. Note that the Greek word that Theuth uses to describe his invention is *pharmakon*. In his deconstruction of Plato, Derrida makes much of the fact that this word is translatable from the Greek not only positively as a 'recipe' or 'remedy' but also more troublingly as 'poison', depending on the context in which the word is used.[4] *Pharmakon* itself thus signifies ambiguity, and in Plato's writing we find the word being used to describe a great many artifices that, while being apparently true or good, in fact lead astray, usurp, and degrade.[5]

In the introduction to this paper I remarked that lawyers and linguistics are concerned about the legitimacy of legal/linguistic assertions in terms of deriving them from a true and authentic source. In Plato's story, King Thamus—as 'father' of all Egyptians—represents the source of legitimate authority, which is why Theuth craves the king's approval for his invention. In Thamus's refusal to give his approval to writing, Plato signals that writing is by its nature inimical to (and thus divorced from) truth itself. In a passage that will be important for my analysis of legal language in the next sections, Derrida riffs on Plato's invocation of the metaphor of parenthood as a signifier of legitimacy, and writing as 'a desire for orphanhood':

> The specificity of writing would thus be intimately bound to the absence of the father.... The status of this orphan, whose welfare cannot be assured, ... being nobody's son at the instant it reaches

---

[2] *Plato's Phaedrus*, R. Hackforth (trans.) (Cambridge: Cambridge University Press, 1952), 157.
[3] *Plato's Phaedrus* (cited in n.2).
[4] Jaques Derrida, *Dissemination*, Barbara Johnson (trans.) (London: Athlone, 1993), 70–1.
[5] Plato describes how the virgin Orithya is blown away to her death by a wind whilst playing with *Pharmacia* (cited in n.2), which Derrida links to the story of King Thamus and Theuth etymologically: pharmacia being 'a common noun signifying the administration of the *pharmakon*, the drug: the medicine and/or poison" (cited in n.4), 70.

inscription, scarcely remains a son at all and no longer *recognizes* its origins, whether legally or morally. In contrast to writing, living *logos* is alive in that it has a living father (where-as the orphan is already half-dead), a father that is *present, standing* near it, behind it, within it, sustaining it with his rectitude, attending it in person in his own name.'[6]

Leaving aside possible gripes at the gender bias of the parental metaphor used here (mothers do not feature centrally in either Plato's or Derrida's writing), in being contrasted against truth, writing as *pharmakon* is also contrasted against the very idea of legitimacy and legitimately derived knowledge. It thus signifies uncertainty, corruption, and falsehood. I will argue that Plato's story and Derrida's analysis of it are important for an analysis of legal language in two ways. First, this association between an idea of parenthood and the ideals of truth and certainty is echoed in the legal rhetoric of judges and disputants. Secondly, critiquing judicial attempts to overcome the uncertainties as to who ought to be recognized in law as having parental status or responsibility involves uncovering and understanding the way judges create their own remedies (*pharmakon*) in the form of concepts such as 'natural parenthood'.

For Plato then, both speech and writing are the 'children' of true, living, and original thought: the difference between them is the way they stand in relation to this 'parent'. This would in itself be a basis for an interesting analysis of legal rhetoric. But deconstructing Plato's metaphors opens up still more illuminating critical possibilities. When we follow Plato's parent-child metaphor and ask in any given discourse questions such as 'Who speaks for this assertion?' or 'Who stands behind this argument?' it becomes evident that 'evidence' of legitimacy tends to be open to doubt and interpretation, making truth and authenticity fluid, slippery creatures.[7] As I try to demonstrate in this paper, hierarchies asserted in law between the 'natural' and the 'artificial' are themselves simply rhetorical devices, the persuasiveness of which depends on whether they can be deployed without becoming conspicuous. Plato wants speech to be prior because he believes that it expresses true, living thought which writing does not.[8] But if this appeal is itself rhetorical (i.e. an artful contrivance) then we might imagine that all language used to persuade, including legal language, is itself characterized by the inadequacy found by King Thamus in writing: that it has no essence of its own, providing merely the 'semblance' of wisdom.

Like much of his work, Plato's preference for speech over writing is connected to his reverence for his teacher and friend Socrates who, unlike Plato, famously left no written record of his wisdom. If there is a hint of nostalgia therefore for philosophers of Socrates' quality who had no need for 'secondary' devices for teaching and dissemination, this is also evident in modern contexts. For example the Oxford professor of Internet governance and regulation Viktor Mayer-Schönberger has produced a critique of digital memory which, like Plato, focuses on the virtuous frailties of natural memory and knowledge in the face of the seductive 'improvements' on them made possible by, for example, stored emails, mobile text messages, Google-hits, cheap hard disk storage-space, and fast data retrieval. In his award-winning book, *Delete: the Virtue of Forgetting in the Digital Age*,[9] he admits that digital memory is attractive in making possible the storage and retrieval of such quantities and quality of data as never previously imaginable.[10] But being external to

---

[6] Derrida, *Dissemination* (cited in n.4), 77, original emphasis.
[7] On this point see R. Gasché, *The Tain of The Mirror: Derrida and the Philosophy of Reflection* (Cambridge, Mass. and London: Harvard University Press, 1986), 177ff.
[8] Derrida, *Dissemination* (cited in n.4), 109.
[9] Viktor Mayer-Schönberger, *Delete: the Virtue of Forgetting in the Digital Age* (Princeton, NJ: Princeton University Press, 2009).
[10] Mayer-Schönberger, *Delete* (cited in n.9), 68.

our natural faculties brings its own limitations: The sheer volume of information accessible on the Internet may seem to be a complete picture, but being 'severed from [its] original context', it is information that carries 'the danger of misinterpretation'.[11] Mayer-Schönberger's critique of digital memory as both disconnected from and dangerous for natural memory ends up sounds uncannily similar to Plato's denunciation of writing:

> As we forget, we regain the freedom to generalize, conceptualize, and most importantly to act.... In contrast, digital memory may keep our remembering of existing knowledge so current that our ability to learn is inhibited.... We may stop trusting our own memory, and thus our own past, supplanting it not with an objective past but an artificial one. It's a past that is neither ours nor anybody else's; instead it is a synthetic past reconstructed from the limited information digital memory has stored about it, an utterly skewed patchwork devoid of time and open to manipulation in both what it contains, and what it doesn't.[12]

Plato argued that writing is opposed and external to 'truth' by drawing attention both to its inability to recall anything but 'external marks' and also to its ability to misrepresent itself as truth itself. Likewise, in this passage Mayer-Schönberger uses the same techniques for asserting the externality and dangers of digital memory with respect to *real* knowledge and memory. Like Plato, Mayer-Schönberger worries that the apparent authenticity of this artifice is so convincing that it takes considerable skill to see the fraud for what it really is. He worries that ordinary people will be fooled into thinking that their natural faculties are being straightforwardly enhanced while their ability to learn is surreptitiously eroded. Standing thus in opposition to the natural guarantor of the knowledge that it keeps (i.e. the original human source) it is thus opposed to life and the natural order itself. Like writing in the estimation of Plato, digital memory is an illegitimate remedy because in undermining those prior, original, and natural faculties, and at the same time masquerading as better than those faculties, it escapes from and exceeds its proper place as the junior assistant (or 'child') of its natural 'parent'. This turning of the natural order on its head and the consequent cutting off of the artifice from the source of true value is what brings Derrida to describe the *pharmakon* as the desire for orphanhood and parricide.[13] That Mayer-Schönberger shares with Plato this value judgment identified by Derrida is suggested in the last quoted sentence: the 'synthetic past' is so 'open to manipulation' because by standing against (and thus cutting itself off from) the natural flexibility and responsiveness of true (natural) memory and knowledge it lacks the surety and value to which it might otherwise have access.

Thus, Derrida's reading of Plato and Mayer-Schönberger's critique of digital memory speak to our own concerns about legal language on the level of the metaphors of legitimacy, origin, and identity that are intimately bound up with notions of truth and authenticity. The sections below examine this in the personal context of disputes about 'natural' parenthood that are asserted by deploying rhetorical remedies (*pharmakon*) for overcoming limitations to existing legal language. Deconstruction provides an illuminating perspective for a critique of the language of parenthood in law since 'parenthood' in its legal sense is nothing if not a site of linguistic (as well as actual) conflict and ambiguity. In English law, a woman that gives birth to a child is the legal mother.[14] Usually the man whose sperm impregnates her is the legal father, although this biological common law paternity may be displaced in favour of her partner if: a) the mother is treated with

---

[11] Mayer-Schönberger, *Delete* (cited in n.9), 90.
[12] Mayer-Schönberger, *Delete* (cited in n.9), 118–23.
[13] Derrida, *Dissemination* (cited in n.4), 100 and 109.
[14] HFE Act 1990 s.27; HFE Act 2008 s.33.

donor sperm at a fertility clinic regulated by the Human Fertilisation and Embryology Authority (hereafter HFEA) (in which case the woman's consenting partner is likely to be the second legal parent),[15] b) the mother is married and conceives non-sexually using 'unofficial'/non-regulated donor sperm, or c) the woman is married and has not used any sort of fertility treatment, and no paternity test has shown that any man other than her husband impregnated her (the common law presumption *pater est quem nuptiae demonstrant*).[16] The donor of gametes (eggs or sperm) that are used for HFEA-regulated fertility treatment for a woman or a couple according to the terms of the Human Fertilisation and Embryology Act (hereafter HFE Act) has no parental status or obligation at all. This of course leaves out of the equation those adults who actually take on parental responsibility for the child, and in *T v B*[17] Moylan J pointedly clarified that *being* a parent in law and *having* parental responsibility should not be confused. Similarly, in *Re A (a child) (joint residence: parental responsibility)*,[18] Sir Mark Potter was moved to describe as 'unfortunate'[19] the judgment of the lower court that Mr A (having care of a child but not the legal father, the mother having been impregnated by another man) 'should be referred to as 'the...Father",[20] reminding the lower court that having parental responsibility did not make someone a parent. In the case of a couple conceiving naturally or through HFEA-regulated fertility treatment, parental responsibility will follow parental status, whether by marriage/civil partnership,[21] or when an unmarried biological father registers as such when the birth is registered.[22] Disputes about parenthood arise with respect to responsibility in the context of lesbian families, having used unofficial donor sperm, where the sperm donor claims to have intended or agreed to be more than a 'mere' donor, and that he ought to be recognized as having a parental role too. Parental responsibility may be conferred on anyone by a court applying the Children Act 1989, and courts have often shown themselves prepared to accord parental responsibility to sperm donors on the basis that the best interests of a child include knowing and developing a relationship with his or her legal father.[23]

There are thus a number of legal mechanisms to account for the various possibilities for speaking about parent*hood* or parent*ing*. Is there room in this legal linguistic milieu for a notion of *natural* parenthood, the identification of which is certain and

---

[15] For formally joined couples, this applies *unless* a partner's consent to become a second parent is disproved: HFE Act 2008 s.35 (man married to woman) and s.42 (female second parent joined in civil partnership); formerly HFE Act 1990 s.28(2) (fathers—no provision for female second parent). For unmarried couples, this applies *if* the partner consents: HFE Act 2008 s.36 (unmarried male partners) and s.43 (female partners not in civil partnership). The HFE Act 1990 s.28(3) formerly required that the couple must be "treated together" for the unmarried woman's male partner to be recognized legally as the child's father. Note that, unlike married partners, the unmarried partner of a woman that conceives using donor sperm will only acquire parental status if conception took place within an HFE Authority-regulated clinic.

[16] *The father is whom the marriage vows indicate.* The cases demonstrate a fluctuating inclination on the part of the courts to order a paternity test that would displace the presumption of *pater est*. See *Re F (A minor: Paternity Tests)* [1993] 1 FLR 598; *Re H (Paternity: Blood Test)* [1996] 2 FLR 65; *Re H and A (Paternity: Blood Tests)* [2002] EWCA Civ 383; *Re J (Paternity: Welfare of Child)* [2007] 1 FLR 1064.

[17] [2010] EWHC 1444 (Fam).

[18] [2008] EWCA Civ 867; [2008] All ER (D) 421.

[19] [2008] EWCA Civ 867, para. [96].

[20] Per Adam J, 'Clarification of the final order by Recorder Adam', 10 December 2007, para. [5].

[21] Children Act 1989 s.2 (as amended). Section 3 defines parental responsibility as 'all the rights, duties, powers, responsibilities and authority which by law a parent of a child has in relation to the child and his property'.

[22] Children Act 1989 s.2(2).

[23] *Re D (contact and parental responsibility: lesbian mothers and known father)* [2006] 1 FCR 556.

unambiguous? And furthermore, what does it mean to speak of a child's 'natural' parent in contexts in which genetic, gestational, and social parenting may be separated? Plato himself did indeed anticipate the possibility of unambiguous representation, describing a discourse of 'unquestioned legitimacy' as that which is 'written in the soul', distinguishing it from that which is wasted by being written 'in water'.[24] However, as Derrida notes, Plato is here using the metaphor of uncertainty (writing) for *both* of these discourses, and thus we might justifiably wonder whether he in fact acknowledges that in representation there is nothing self-evidently or naturally true as clearly distinguished from the rhetorical or artificial, merely better or worse kinds of *pharmakon*.[25] In the remaining sections of this paper I want to demonstrate various ways in which the idea of the 'natural' parent—that is to say, an idea of parenthood of 'unquestioned legitimacy'—is deployed as a persuasive rhetorical device in legal cases. Whether used by parents or offspring or others, the language of the 'natural' serves as what deconstruction theorists call a *transcendental signified*, i.e. as a guarantor of authenticity that is itself beyond the ambiguities and contestations of argument and discourse.[26]

2. The natural parent as the genetic parent in legal rhetoric: *Re G* and *Rose*

In this section we consider two cases in which parents and offspring deploy 'natural parent' rhetoric to assert a genetic/biological idea of parenthood.

2.1. Baroness Hale on the 'natural' (genetic) parent in *Re G*

Re G (children) (residence: same-sex partner)[27] involved a dispute between two lesbian women with parental responsibility over two children regarding who should be the primary carer. One of the women (CG) was the legal mother by virtue of having given birth to both children. She was also the biological (genetic) mother, having used donor insemination. Her partner (CW), who had shared caring responsibilities equally but had no biological or gestational relationship with the children, was not a legal parent since the 1990 HFE Act did not recognize a lesbian partner as a legal parent. In the House of Lords, Baroness Hale felt that it would be useful to assess the issue of primary care according to a concept that she described as 'natural parenthood'. She explained in her judgment that there are 'at least three ways in which a person may be or become a natural parent',[28] and that these included genetic parenthood, gestational parenthood (under the HFE Act 1990 s.27), and also 'psychological parenthood: the relationship which develops through the child demanding and the parent providing for the child's needs'.[29]

The Court of Appeal in its earlier ruling on this case had taken the view that 'in the eyes of a child its natural parent might be a non-biological parent',[30] and in including 'psychological' parents as her third category of natural parents, Baroness Hale seems to

---

[24] Plato's *Phaedrus* (cited in n.2), 159.
[25] Derrida, *Dissemination* (cited in n.4), 149.
[26] Jacques Derrida, *Of Grammatology* (trans. G.C. Spivak) (Baltimore, Md.: Johns Hopkins University Press, 1997), 49.
[27] [2006] 4 All ER 241, [2006] UKHL 43.
[28] [2006] 4 All ER 241, [2006] UKHL 43 at para. [33].
[29] [2006] 4 All ER 241, [2006] UKHL 43 at para. [35].
[30] [2006] EWCA Civ 372, [2006] All ER (D) 71 at para. [44].

imply agreement with this. However, in the very next paragraph Baroness Hale muddies the water by introducing a fourth category—also called a 'natural parent'—that in being presented as a sort of *meta*-natural parent, trumps all three:

> Of course, in the great majority of cases, the natural mother combines all three. She is the genetic, gestational and psychological parent. Her contribution to the welfare of the child is unique. The natural father combines genetic and psychological parenthood. His contribution is also unique.[31]

Following the logic of giving this fourth sort of 'natural parent' priority, the House of Lords ruled that the child's primary carer ought to be the woman who, having conceived, gestated, and cared for the child, was 'both their biological and their psychological parent', rather than that woman's former partner who, having merely cared for the child, was only the child's 'psychological parent'.[32] The *most* natural parent, then, is the person that can demonstrate the most indicators of 'natural parenthood' described a paragraph earlier, which in almost all cases means giving priority to the biological mother (and Baroness Hale referred to the biological mother as 'the natural mother of these children *in every sense of the term*').[33] Subsequent cases have sought to emphasize that the House of Lords decision in *Re G* is purely a judgment about the child's best interests, and does not imply any natural or legal priority for biological over social parenting.[34] However, it is very difficult to read, say, Baroness Hale's reference to the role of the biological parent as 'unique'[35] or Lord Nicholls's view that '[a] child should not be removed from the primary care of his or her biological parents without compelling reason'[36] without a sense that status hierarchy is part of the judgment.

The rhetorical assertion that Baroness Hale wants us to accept therefore is that there is such a thing as a 'natural parent' that carries significance that convincingly resolves the conflict between two adults with parental responsibility. A biological parent is sometimes referred to as a 'natural parent', and this has particular legal significance in determining the identity of the legal parent under certain conditions. But the question for resolution in *Re G* was not legal parenthood but rather primary care, and this is a matter to be decided according to the 'best interests' of the child. If the claim in Baroness Hale's speech is the same in principle as that made by Plato on behalf of speech, or by Mayer-Schönberger on behalf of natural memory, then it implies that the idea of the 'natural parent' to be privileged is one that speaks for itself, needing no gloss or complicated interpretation, and whose origin is known and authoritative. Of course, the 'natural parent' does not speak for itself in this case. It is far from clear how its identification or its interpretation can be decisive of a child's best interests. Their Lordships' preference for the legal mother's claim on the basis of the genetic link when both women had invested equally in the raising of the child is a resolution that demands an acceptance of cultural norms about the significance of genetic parenthood. The natural parent is thus a rhetorical construct that is used by the House of Lords as a remedy (*pharmakon*) for deciding a matter on which there is no straightforward framework to be applied.

---

[31] [2006] 4 All ER 241, [2006] UKHL 43 at para. [37].
[32] [2006] 4 All ER 241, [2006] UKHL 43 at para. [38].
[33] [2006] 4 All ER 241, [2006] UKHL 43 at para. [44], emphasis added. For comment on the implications of *Re G*, and this phrase in particular, for gender and sexuality, see Jenni Millbank, 'The limits of functional family: lesbian mother litigation in the era of the eternal biological family' (2008) *IJLP & F* 22 (149), who argues that the House of Lords judgment prioritizes the biological parent.
[34] *Re A (a child) (joint residence: parental responsibility)* [2008] EWCA 867, see especially para. [91]; *Re B (a child) (residence order)* [2009] UKSC 5, see especially paras [34]–[37].
[35] [2006] 4 All ER 241, [2006] UKHL 43 at para. [36].
[36] [2006] 4 All ER 241, [2006] UKHL 43 at para. [2].

2.2. A 'natural' parent for donor-conceived offspring: the testimony of Joanna Rose

Let us now turn to a case of a much rarer type, involving an adult offspring's idea of natural parenthood, which is an idea that has nothing to do either with legal parenthood status or parental responsibility. In *Rose*, Scott-Baker J judged that Joanna Rose (an adult donor-conceived offspring) and another person (a child of 12) could successfully establish that their rights under the European Convention on Human Rights Art.8 to privacy and family life were engaged by their need and desire to know who their genetic fathers were, although the information that would have made possible the exercise of this right was either lost or unavailable due to the conditions of confidentiality surrounding its donation.[37] Joanna Rose did not claim that the adults who brought her up were in any specific way false or inadequate parents. Furthermore it was certain that the genetic father could have no legal status or responsibility as a parent. Rose's testimony is highly illuminating for the way in which the idea of natural parenthood (understood here as genetic) is invoked to sustain the legitimacy, not merely of her legal claim, but of herself as a person of value and worth:

> I feel that these genetic connections are very important to me, socially, emotionally, medically, and even spiritually.... I am angry that it has been assumed that this would not be the case, and can see no responsible logic for this... unless it is believed that if we are created artificially we will not have the natural need to know to whom we are related.[38]

The 'connections' that Rose is referring to here are of course the *biological* relation between her and her genetic father. But although there may indeed be a connection drawn on a biological family tree, there is no 'joining together' or 'relationship' that the word ordinarily implies, but rather a lack of such. Rose's relationship to her genetic father/sperm donor is (and in the circumstances can only be) one of *dis*connection. The 'natural need to know to whom we are related' that Rose refers to can only make itself felt by being lacked. It is only because the genetic 'connection' is absent in Rose's case that it takes on any shape or significance for her. The connection to the absent genetic parent is created within language itself and is thus a creature of discourse.

Rose continues:

> I feel intense grief and loss, for the fact that I do not know my genetic father and his family.... I live with the uncertainty of a reunion being possible, though unlikely, and of even unknowingly passing my biological father or siblings in the street. I wonder if we would recognize each other.[39]

The way Rose describes her feelings here conjures ghostly images of family members as spectral beings somehow perceived to be all around but never properly seen or touched. She conjures into existence a set of connections with her passionate testimony, imbuing her fantasies of chance meetings and recognition with meaning. The rhetorical appeal made in Rose's testimony mirrors Plato's sentiments about writing which seem to evoke a lost and disoriented orphan child:

> And once a thing is put in writing, the composition, whatever it may be, drifts all over the place; ... it doesn't know how to address the right people, and not to address the wrong. And when it is

---

[37] *Rose v Secretary of State for Health* [2002] EWHC 1593 (cited in n.1). All that Joanna Rose could discover about her donor/biological father was that he was 'six feet two inches tall, of medium build, has dark hair and hazel eyes and has an A positive blood group' (para. [3]).
[38] *Rose v Secretary of State for Health* [2002] EWHC 1593 at para [7], FLR 962 at 964–6.
[39] *Rose v Secretary of State for Health* [2002] EWHC 1593 at para [7], FLR 962 at 964–6.

ill-treated and unfairly abused it always needs its parent to come to its help, being unable to defend or help itself.[40]

Is this feeling—of not knowing who to address as kin and who is merely an unrelated passer-by, lacking the security and identity that one's parent would ordinarily provide—not precisely the malaise referred to by Joanna Rose? True, Rose is talking literally, and Plato metaphorically, but it must be borne in mind that Rose is not merely interested to know with whom she shares a genetic 'connection'. The significance with which she credits the genetic relation suggests that, for her, knowing where she has come from represents something crucial to her sense of self-identity and self-worth as a member of a society that places value on origins and genealogy. Riffing on Plato's text, Derrida's own description of the sad fate of writing chimes very well with Rose's language of disconnection from a secure sense of identity:

> Wandering the streets, he doesn't even know who he is, what his identity—if he has one—might be, what his name is, what his father's name is.... Not to know where one comes from or where one is going, for a discourse with no guarantor, is not to know how to speak at all, to be in a state of infancy. Uprooted, anonymous, unattached to any house or country, this almost insignificant signifier is at everyone's disposal...[41]

Until this point Rose has not explicitly referred to a 'natural' parent, but in this last passage she addresses it by way of a comparison, distinguishing between 'natural parents' that other people take for granted, and 'my parents' whose use of donor sperm to overcome their fertility problems has led to her pain:

> Other people who come from families, where they have known both of their natural parents are able to discover this through the process of time.... While I was conceived to heal the pain of others (i.e. my parents' inability to conceive children naturally), I do not feel that these are sufficient attempts to heal my pain.[42]

It is significant for our concern about legal rhetoric that Rose's reference to her 'natural parents' is closely juxtaposed with the reference to her 'pain'. Rose must have known that actually getting the information that would have enabled her to reunite with her with her 'natural' father was not possible: her birth in 1972 pre-dates even the requirement introduced by the HFE Act 1990 that clinics maintain non-identifying information, let alone information that would identify the donor many years later. Tacitly acknowledging this, Rose's reference to the need to 'heal my pain' displaces that impossible demand with a suggestion that something less might do instead—namely recognition that her Article 8 rights have been engaged by being so cut off from her 'natural' father. This focus on the symptom of the loss rather than the recovery of the thing itself is the very point of the *pharmakon* as described by Plato, because in attending to the mere symptoms of nature's faults and limitations, the recipe/remedy is only ever external to that which it attends.[43] Therefore the legal declaration that Joanna Rose sought could not of course restore her 'natural parent' to her, but it might do something to treat her feelings of loss.

If we regard Rose's testimony as an authentic account of what a 'natural parent' is, then it is likely to be because we find testimony issuing directly from the offspring herself to be a way to gain access to an unmediated truth. As this testimony is undiluted by any obvious representation or interpretation, we might consider it to be the sort of vital 'living speech' that Plato prioritizes. Of course from a deconstructive point of view, we are alert to such claims to occupy a privileged status with regard to defining 'natural

---

[40] *Plato's Phaedrus* (cited in n.2), 158.
[41] Derrida, *Dissemination* (cited in n.4), 143–4.
[42] *Rose v Secretary of State for Health* [2002] EWHC 1593 para [7], FLR 962 at 964–6.
[43] Derrida, *Dissemination* (cited in n.4), 110.

parenthood'. The idea that to testify on one's own behalf is more authoritative is itself a matter of strategic rhetorical positioning that privileges speech over writing.

3. The natural parent as the social parent and the child's voice as mark of authenticity: *Thomas S and Robyn Y* and *Re Patrick*

If we are sympathetic to the authenticity claim in Rose's testimony because we hear the voice of Joanna Rose herself as donor-conceived offspring, then it is tempting to regard with less sympathy assertions of authenticity by adults trying to establish their own status as 'natural' parents by invoking their young child's conception of parenthood. In the analysis of the cases of *Thomas S and Robyn Y*[44] and *Re Patrick*,[45] I consider the difference it makes to the efficacy of the claim about 'natural' parenthood that the very young offspring's own ideas and feelings are narrated, not by them directly, but second hand by their parents. The construction of the 'natural' is different here from that of *Re G* or *Rose* in the sense that the parents' narratives considered here assert a social (rather than a genetic) conception of parenthood.

By using informal 'self-insemination' arrangements, possibly using sperm from a male friend, women can avoid the strictures of legislation and thus maintain flexibility about the involvement of the donor in the childhood of the offspring. However as the cases we examine here show, such informality also exacerbates the potential for ambiguity about parental status and thus for legal conflict.[46] Even if an agreement between a woman or a lesbian couple and their sperm donor seems clear about the latter's role at the time of conception, people change their minds or remember things differently, and emotions may complicate things further.[47] Qualitative empirical studies have shown that women opting for this type of conception are often unable to articulate clearly a consistent view on the significance of the biological relation. For example, Fiona Kelly's research in Canada found that, despite reporting deep pessimism and anxiety about the potential disruption a sperm donor might cause if allowed to, a third of the lesbian donor-conception lesbian couples she interviewed had nevertheless voluntarily opted for a known sperm donor in order to provide a 'flexibly defined male figure', a 'symbolic father', or even a male 'parent'.[48]

As a consequence of the ambiguities of the existing linguistic framework, disputing social and genetic parents have sometimes looked to the child who, in being unschooled in the politics of parenthood or law, may be relied upon to provide a more authentic and vital testimony to the 'reality' of parenthood. Kelly criticizes the appellate division in the American case of *Thomas S and Robin Y* for reversing the view of the first instance judge that the child's own reported 'concept of family' may be decisive in determining the paternity and visitation rights of a sperm donor.[49] In that case, the views of an 11-year-old

---

[44] *Thomas S and Robyn Y* 599 NTS 2d 377 (Fam Ct 1993).
[45] *Re Patrick (an application concerning contact)* (2002) 28 Fam LR 579 (Aus).
[46] In addition to the cases discussed here, see *A.A. v B.B.* [2007] O.J. No.2 (Canada); *Re D (contact and parental responsibility: lesbian mothers and known father)* [2006] EWHC 2 (Fam); *Re B (role of biological father)* [2008] 1 FLR 1015.
[47] See Julie McCandless and Sally Sheldon, 'The human fertilisation and embryology act (2008) and the tenacity of the sexual family form' (2010) 72(2) *Modern Law Review* 175–207 at 192–3.
[48] F. Kelly, '(Re)forming Parenthood: the assignment of legal parentage within planned lesbian families' (2008–9) *Ottawa Law Rev.* 203–4.
[49] The quoted expression is from the testimony of Dr Schneider, psychiatrist for the case, *Thomas S and Robyn Y* 599 NTS 2d 377 (Fam Ct 1993), reported at 380.

child (Ry) that the donor's paternity claim was 'an attack on her positive image of herself and her family', 'selfish', and 'hurtful... to her and her family' had demonstrated to the first instance judge that a declaration of paternity for sperm donor Thomas S was not in the child's best interests.[50] Kaufman J's first instance judgment has attracted praise from feminist commentators for invoking the child's own voice in viewing the word 'parent' as a verb, rather than as a noun, leading to the conclusion that a family comprising of a mother and her female partner was not 'missing' a father figure.[51] As Kelly puts it: 'For Ry, family and parenthood were much more about functional parenthood and her lived reality.'[52] It is worth focusing on what the child's testimony is intended to do for the 'concept of family' being articulated by the disputing parties of a parenthood case. The idea, of course, is that what a child has to say about his or her 'concept' of parenthood is likely to be simple and devoid of artifice. After all, a child may be expected to know what s/he finds positive in his or her life without any overlaying of political, ethical, or legal notions about sexuality, parental rights or duties, or the cultural capital of children. But if the child's view is to have the rhetorical impact claimed for the homonuclear family in this case as naturally indicative of the meaning of parenthood, it must be shown to be self-evidently expressive, with minimum interpretive art or gloss. However, to some, the way in which the views and feelings of 11-year-old Ry as expressed in *Thomas S and Robin Y* were suspiciously loaded with political language, and the appellate division avoided having to decide how much value to place on Ry's 'concept of family' by excluding it in favour of the biological determination of paternity referred to by statute.[53] I do not take a view on this in particular, but instead would emphasize that the debate here clearly revolves around the same hierarchy of 'natural' over 'artificial' that we have discussed above, the persuasiveness of the asserted idea of parenthood depending on it being identified with the natural as opposed to an artificial (external) remedy (*pharmakon*).

In cases where the child in question is too young to communicate any sort of 'concept' of family or parenthood linguistically, the interpretive labour necessary for translating the child's feelings into a coherent legal argument may be more obviously exposed. In *Re Patrick*, the child at the centre of the proceedings was only two years old at the time of the events considered in the Australian Family Court. Patrick had been born to a woman and her lesbian partner, the former having conceived using the sperm of a friend with whom they had made an informal arrangement. A dispute soon arose regarding the precise nature of the intended relationship between the sperm donor and the child. In the ensuing litigation he claimed that the agreement had always been that he would not merely be a 'donor' but a 'father' to Patrick and a third parent alongside the mother and her female partner. The mother and her partner however fiercely denied this, claiming that the understanding was that he would be the provider of sperm and nothing more.[54] The evidence referred to in Guest J's judgment indicated contradictory 'agreements' made at different times, leading very quickly to a highly fractious situation. It provides a fascinating (if painful) example of a struggle to control the language of parenthood, central to which is an infant boy and the reflected authority of his alleged perspective.

---

[50] *Thomas S and Robyn Y* 599 NTS 2d 377 (Fam Ct 1993), at 380.

[51] Kelly, '(Re)forming Parenthood' (cited in n.48). See also Nancy D. Polikoff, 'The deliberate construction of families without fathers: is it an option for lesbian and heterosexual mothers?' (1996) 36 *Santa Clara Law Review* 375–94.

[52] F. Kelly, 'Redefining Parenthood: Gay and Lesbian Families in the Family Court—the Case of *Re Patrick*' (2002) 16 *Australian Journal of Family Law* 204.

[53] *Thomas S v Robin Y* 618 NYS 2d 356 (Appl. Div. 1994).

[54] I use the term 'father' to describe the donor/genetic father, as this is the term adopted by all parties and also the court.

In giving their evidence in court, the mother and female co-parent both testified to the 'damage' that the involvement of the father in Patrick's life would cause to their sense of being a complete and self-sufficient family.[55] In support of this, the mother and co-parent present the argument as originating not in them as adult parents but in Patrick himself. The co-parent testified that the contact with Patrick claimed by the father 'was a "*total reality shift*" for Patrick'[56] and furthermore that a proposed contact regime for the father of four hours every alternate Sunday would be 'traumatising "*for Patrick and our family*"'.[57] In an affidavit, the mother outlined 26 conditions under which she and the co-parent would tolerate contact. Condition 16 stipulated that the father must not put a 'constant focus on Patrick', and that the 'unfamiliar toys, books, music, rugs' etc. was 'contributing to Patrick and our stress'. Condition 18 required that 'the father establish a "goodbye" ritual in the last ½ hour of contact so as to avoid further confusion, stress and over-tiredness for Patrick'.[58] The mother testified that contact with the father 'transformed Patrick for over a week "'*into a different child*'", becoming "'...*scared*'" approximately 20 times per hour', particularly '[at] the sight of a red motor bike that was similar to the father's; the postman on his motor bike; men wearing a cap like the father; and eventually any mention of "the father" or even "people"'.[59]

Reading the evidence from the *Re Patrick* litigation, one gets the impression that the role of the mother and the co-parent was simply to translate the pre-linguistic wishes of the two-year old boy and thus that their own asserted view of parenthood is itself a natural one devoid of artificiality or agenda. However Guest J was not convinced by this, and dismissed it as false. He found that far from finding contact traumatizing, Patrick 'is a contented, happy child [who] enjoys contact periods with the father, ... Patrick derives both warmth and comfort when they are together'.[60]

4. Natural parent as the intentional parent: *Re R* and *Leeds Teaching Hospitals Trust*

Recall that the HFE Act allows the status of legal parent to be conferred on the partner of a woman receiving fertility treatment: if unmarried then on the condition that he or she consents,[61] and if they are married then on the less strict condition that it is not proved that the partner did *not* so consent.[62] By fulfilling these consent provisions, such a person demonstrates an intention to become (and be recognized in law as) the second parent. But are they still to be treated as a parent if what he or she consents to turns out to be in some significant way different from what is 'produced'? In such cases the concept of parenthood is up for grabs, and in a number of cases courts have become embroiled in delineating the conditions under which an intention may give rise to legal parenthood by considering what is essential and what is superfluous to the statutory provisions.

---

[55] This is an argument for the non-recognition of sperm donors as 'parents' or having 'paternity rights' that is familiar from feminist and lesbian critical commentaries. See Nancy D. Polikoff, 'Breaking the link between biology and parentall rights in planned lesbian families: when semen donors are not fathers' (2000–1) 2 *Georgetown Journal of Gender and Law* 57–90.
[56] *Re Patrick* (cited in n.45), para. [90], original emphasis, Guest J quoting testimony of the co-parent.
[57] *Re Patrick* (cited in n.45), para. [94], original emphasis.
[58] *Re Patrick* (cited in n.45), para. [101].
[59] *Re Patrick* (cited in n.45), para. [165], original emphasis, Guest J quoting evidence of the mother.
[60] *Re Patrick* (cited in n.45), para.188.
[61] HFE Act 2008 ss.36 and 43 for male and female partners respectively; formerly HFE Act 1990 s.28(3), which applied only to male partners.
[62] HFE Act 2008 ss.35 and 42 for male and female partners; formerly HFE Act 1990 s.28(2), which applied only to husbands.

In this final section, I want to demonstrate how judicial interpretations of the parenthood provisions of the HFE Act can, like the disputes considered above, be understood critically in terms of Plato's hierarchy of 'natural' over 'artificial'. How convincing any given interpretation of the statutory meaning of parenthood is depends on whether it 'naturally' gives rise to an idea of parenthood, or whether instead it is seen as an artificial stretching of the concept and thus as a *mere* contrived remedy (*pharmakon*) for the possibly detrimental limitations of the legal concepts naturally applied.

Re R[63] and *Leeds Teaching Hospitals Trust v A and others*[64] will be familiar to family and medical lawyers as they have already been the subject of considerable academic attention.[65] However, the insights these cases offer regarding the legal language of 'natural' and 'artificial' interpretations of legal parenthood have so far been unexplored and deserve critical attention. Both cases concerned men who intended to become fathers according to the parenthood provisions of the HFE Act 1990 as the partner of a woman receiving fertility treatment, but whose intended fatherhood had been thrown into doubt because the statutory conditions had not been properly fulfilled. In *Re R* the would-be father (Mr B) had consented to become the father of a child (R) with Miss D who planned to conceive using anonymous donor sperm. However, his relationship with Miss D having broken down before she conceived, doubts were raised about whether he could be said to have been 'treated together' with the mother, as required of unmarried partners by s.28(3) of the statute. The judge at first instance, Hedley J, was impressed by Mr B's sincere continued desire to take on the role of father despite having no biological connection to the child, nor any longer being the partner of the mother. He therefore found in Mr B's favour, and in terms that makes an explicit claim about the naturalness of his claim to be the father:

then in my judgment the original course of treatment continues as treatment services provided to both of them together and, if a child is conceived in the course of that, the man will be the father. This approach affords *clarity, simplicity and certainty*.'[66]

On appeal, the Court of Appeal had to decide whether Hedley J's ruling was (as Hedley J claimed) productive of a *genuine sort of parenthood*, or whether instead it artificially or unnaturally stretched the idea. Despite Hedley J's assertions about the 'clarity, simplicity and certainty' of recognizing Mr B as the father, the Court of Appeal found it all too easy to recast his approach as, not a description of parenthood itself, but a questionable remedy (*pharmakon*) for the impossibility of accommodating Mr B (despite

---

[63] *Re R (IVF: Paternity of Child)* [2005] 2 FLR 843 (HL), [2005] UKHL 33 (HL), [2005] 2 AC 621 (HL); *Re R (a child)* [2003] EWCA Civ 182 (CA); *Re R (Contact: Human Fertilisation and Embryology Act 1990)* [2001] 1 FLR 247 (Fam Div, Hedley J).

[64] [2003] All ER (D) 374, [2003] EWHC 259 (QB).

[65] On *Re R*, see S. Fovargue, '*Re R (IVF: Paternity of Child)*: assisting conception for the single infertile' (2006) 18(3) *Child and Family Law Quarterly* 423; Craig Lind, 'Case commentary—*Re R (Paternity of IVF Baby)*—Unmarried Paternity under the Human Fertilisation and Embryology Act 1990' (2003) 15(3) *Child and Family Law Quarterly* 327; Commentary, 'Assisted Conception: Parentage and Treatment "Together"' (2003) 11(1) *Medical Law Review* 128–35. On *Leeds* see Juliet Tizzard, 'Who's the Daddy?' (2003) *BioNews* 197; T. H. Murray and G. E. Kaebnick, 'Genetic ties and genetic mixups' (2003) 29 *Journal of Medical Ethics* 68–9; R. Probert, 'Families, Assisted Reproduction and the Law' (2004) 16(3) *Child and Family Law Quarterly* 273; J. Harris, 'Assisted Reproductive Technological Blunders (ARTBs)' (2003) 29 *Journal of Medical Ethics*, 205–6. On the extent to which the cases challenge traditional nuclear norms, see Sally Sheldon, 'Fragmenting Fatherhood: the regulation of reproductive technologies' (2005) 68(4) *Medical Law Review* 523–53 at 547, 546, 548: 'two [fathers] may be better than one' because in situations such as donor conception in which different men may contribute different things to a child, this could 'enrich their family situation', and 'knowledge of one's genetic paternity is not necessarily disruptive of one's social family and relationship with one's social parents'.

[66] Hedley J, *Re R* (Fam Div) (cited in n.63).

his sincerity and earnestness) within the statutory definition. First, the exteriority of Mr B's intentions from natural parenthood is arguably indicated by Hedley J's own choice of the word 'affords'. Having been conceived using anonymous donor sperm, born to a woman who had misled the fertility clinic by concealing the breakdown of her relationship with Mr B and whose new partner had shown little or no interest in taking on a parenting role, child R clearly lacked clarity and certainty as to his origins, and Hedley J saw that he had an opportunity to use the HFE Act to 'afford' this to the child. Secondly, the appellate courts, in overturning Hedley J's decision, drew attention to the fact that the judge's own sentiments (rather than a dispassionate reading of the facts and statutory clause) determined his judgment. In the Court of Appeal, Hale LJ remarked that she found the 'sympathy' shown by the first instance judge to be 'an unreliable aid to statutory construction',[67] and Lord Walker in the House of Lords agreed, warning that 'the very significant legal relationship of parenthood should not be based on a fiction (especially if the fiction involves a measure of deception by the mother)'.[68] Thirdly, in the House of Lords Peter Jackson QC alluded to the artificiality of Hedley's approach in his submission on behalf of the mother, describing it as an attempt 'to provide a doubtful remedy for an unnecessary problem'.[69]

Therefore to put the issue in the same terms used by Plato in his critique of writing, we might regard Hedley J's construction of parenthood as an offer of a remedy that *adds to* rather than simply interprets the natural meaning of parenthood under the HFE Act. The rejection of Hedley J's approach by the Court of Appeal and the House of Lords shows how, in the language of law, such a remedy is vulnerable to being received as a *poison* by being distinguished from the truth of the concept in question, and perceived to be potentially undermining of it. The opposition of 'facts' to 'fictions' in the reasoning of the appellate courts emphasizes the importance in legal reasoning of the natural/artificial opposition. To shoehorn Mr B into the status of legal father would not bring real certainty or clarity in the sense of seeing the world aright, because it would require an artificial reading of the relevant legal provision. Using the HFE Act s.28(3) in the way Hedley J wanted to might appear to be a blessing in the sense of overcoming uncertainty with respect to child R's origins, but it would also do violence to the very idea of legitimately conceived legal meaning, and in Derrida's metaphorical language would threaten to make an 'orphan' of the concept.

In *Leeds Teaching Hospitals NHS Trust v A* the problem was that Mr A (a white man) had consented to becoming the legal father of a child following treatment using his own sperm, but when his wife gave birth to mixed-race twins it became clear that there had been a mix-up between his own sperm and that of another man (Mr B—a black man, who himself had not consented to being a sperm donor). The assertion of natural parenthood made by counsel on behalf of Mr A—who still wanted to be recognized as the father despite the children not being genetically related to him—was therefore based on his unwavering intention to be recognized as the father. Butler-Sloss P in the Family Division recognized the attractiveness of interpreting the statutory provisions broadly for the sake of the children: 'If section 28 applies they would have a complete sense of belonging to Mr A. If section 28 is found not to apply then there is a period of uncertainty which is to their detriment.'[70] But would this sense of 'belonging' express a natural idea of parenthood, or would it rather be an artificial remedy (*pharmakon*) that

---

[67] *Re R (a child)* (cited in n.63), para. [9].
[68] *Re R (IVF: Paternity of Child)* [2005] 2 AC 621 at 644, para. [42] (cited in n.63).
[69] *Re R (IVF: Paternity of Child)* (cited in n.63), 628.
[70] *Leeds Teaching Hospitals NHS Trust v A* (cited in n.64), para. [55].

would come at the cost of the natural meaning of parenthood as intended for s.28(2)? Butler-Sloss P decided that it was the latter:

> Although they lose the immediate certainty of the irrebuttable presumption that Mr A is their legal father, they will remain within a loving, stable and secure home. They also retain the great advantage of preserving *the reality of their paternal identity*.[71]

As a matter of language, Butler-Sloss P's references the 'great advantage' and the 'reality' in deeming Mr B to be the father suggest a strategy of making a virtue out of the limitations of the legal and linguistic apparatus 'naturally available'. As in *Re R*, the 'affording' of paternal certainty that might have been made available through unconventional legal interpretation of the consent requirement was in the end considered to be too much of an abuse of natural linguistic meaning. In both cases, such certainty afforded for the sake of the children and intended parents would have come at the cost of allowing a mere addition to the existing legal concept of parenthood to be regarded as integral to parenthood itself. Such an outcome, while on the one hand attractive for allowing for the parents' sincere intentions to be realized, would risk sanctioning a linguistic artifice as conceptually legitimate.

Conclusion

This paper has tried to show some ways in which the disputes over the legal language of parenthood rehearse ancient anxieties about truth and representation, and as such may be approached critically through the metaphors of the parent/child relationship that figures in Plato's metaphysics and Derrida's deconstruction of Plato. Concerns about origins, legitimacy and genesis are crucial to the identification of value and meaning in the sense that assertions of where value lies tend to depend on distinguishing the 'natural' that flows directly from a legitimate source, in contrast to the 'artificial' that does not. Plato identified these states as corresponding, respectively, to speech (authenticated by a living speaker) and writing (physically separated from its author), and in a more contemporary context by Mayer-Schönberger to natural and digital memory. In this normative scheme, the first is prioritized over the second because we can be sure that it has been legitimately and directly derived from secure, true origins. The natural (e.g. speech, natural memory, natural parenthood, etc.) is the valued and reliable 'offspring' by virtue of the parent (the living speaker, etc.) that stands immediately behind it and guides it along; the artificial (writing, remedy, *pharmakon*) is the weak, homeless, directionless orphan for whom, being always external to the true, is not obviously derived from any legitimate or authoritative source. The idea behind this paper has been to analyse an area of law in these same terms of legitimate and illegitimate claims to assert truths in legal language, and to show how the metaphor of parenthood as a signifier of value in Plato's *Phaedrus* is also instructive for an understanding of the rhetorical strategies in this regard. We have seen, for example, how donor-conceived offspring Joanna Rose appealed to the personal disorientation that has resulted from her not knowing her 'natural' father; how adults disputing over who ought to be recognized as the legal parent or having primary care over a child have invoked the voice of their child as a guarantor of authenticity; how the English courts have refused to read the legal provisions under the HFE Act in order to afford a remedy for a child's obscurity of origin. In all of these examples drawn from modern law, truth, value and authenticity is identified on the basis of an original, natural or living source of authenticity.

---

[71] *Leeds Teaching Hospitals NHS Trust v A* (cited in n.64), para. [56], emphasis added.

22

Silence, Speech, and the Paradox of the Right to Remain Silent in American Police Interrogation

Janet Ainsworth

The right to remain silent has long been regarded as one of the most cherished and fundamental principles of American criminal jurisprudence, one with a venerable history stretching back centuries to the English struggle to resist the tyranny of the Star Chamber, which compelled those brought before it to answer accusations or be flogged until they did so. Colonial Americans were just as insistent as their British cousins on the importance of a right against self-incrimination; upon independence, every state constitution incorporated guarantees against compelled self-incrimination even prior to the adoption of the federal Bill of Rights.[1] In contemporary jurisprudence, the right to remain silent has been valorized as foundational to human dignity[2] and to human expressive freedom.[3] The right to remain silent is also likely the criminal law doctrine most recognized by the American general public. In fact, given the worldwide marketing of American movies and television dramas, the *Miranda* warning, beginning, "You have the right to remain silent," may well be the single most widely known principle of criminal law in the world. Little wonder that even conservative Supreme Court Chief Justice William Rehnquist—no friend to expansive constitutional protections in the criminal context—had to admit that the *Miranda* formulation of the right to remain silent had become an indelible part of the fabric of American culture.[4] Yet, despite both its deep roots in American legal history and its entrenched status in current popular culture, the right to silence as articulated in *Miranda* has in recent years been subject to a barrage of judicial limitations, qualifications, and exceptions to the point where it currently can scarcely be said to provide any meaningful constraint on police interrogation at all.

---

[1] Jan M. Rybnicek, 'Damned if You Do, Damned if You Don't?: The Absence of a Constitutional Protection Prohibiting the Admission of Post-arrest, Pre-*Miranda* Silence' (2009) 19 *George Mason University Civil Rights Law Journal* 405.
[2] Kent R. Greenawalt, 'The Right to Silence and Human Dignity' in Michael J. Meyer and William A. Parent (eds), *The Constitution of Rights: Human Dignity and American Values* (Ithaca, N.Y.: Cornell University Press, 1992), 192; Susan Easton, *The Case for the Right to Silence* (Brookfield, Vt.: Ashgate Publishing Ltd., 1998).
[3] Louis M. Seidman, *Silence and Freedom* (Stanford, Calif.: Stanford Law and Politics, 2007).
[4] *Dickerson* v. *United States*, 530 U.S. 428 (2000), at 443.

1. The origins of the *Miranda* rule

Throughout the early twentieth century, the Supreme Court struggled with the question of how to constitutionally regulate police practices that undermined civil liberties and threatened to result in the conviction of innocents. In the context of police interrogation, the Court was confronted with cases in which abusive police interrogation methods led to convictions of accused persons who were probably entirely innocent. In addition, the exposure of brutal police interrogation techniques that in effect constituted government-sanctioned torture was increasingly troubling to a nation that was coming to define its national mission as the international promotion of human rights and freedom. An early Supreme Court attempt to constrain coercive police interrogations was by applying the Fourteenth Amendment's Due Process Clause to prohibit the admission of confessions extracted as a result of beating, whipping, and partial lynching of suspects, holding that the confessions obtained in this manner were involuntary and thus inadmissible because they were the product of police violence and threats during interrogation.[5] Later on, the Court extended its due process analysis to prohibit interrogations that, while not overtly violent, nevertheless appeared to overbear the free will of the suspect through unfair and over-reaching police tactics.[6] In doing so, the Supreme Court noted that involuntary confessions carried with them the risk of unreliability, but it declared that the reason to constitutionally prohibit such interrogations went beyond mere instrumentality:

> The abhorrence of society to the use of involuntary confessions does not turn alone on their inherent untrustworthiness. It also turns on the deep-rooting feeling that the police must obey the law while enforcing the law; that in the end, life and liberty can be as much endangered from illegal methods used to convict those thought to be criminals as from the actual criminals themselves.[7]

The problem with a due-process-based voluntariness test for the admissibility of confessions, however, is that it required a case-by-case contextual analysis of both the circumstances of each interrogation and the personal characteristics of each suspect—a virtually insurmountable practical challenge for courts attempting to ensure consistent application of the constitutional voluntariness test. In addition, once the voluntariness test was expanded to prohibit over-reaching but non-violent forms of police interrogation, the context-sensitive constitutional voluntariness requirement gave little guidance to the police about what kinds of interrogation techniques might be later found to be constitutionally flawed. Clearly, a test that provided greater certainty to both the police and lower courts was imperative. After a brief flirtation with using the Sixth Amendment right to counsel to provide protections during police questioning,[8] the Supreme Court settled on a Fifth Amendment approach, based on the right against self-incrimination, in *Miranda v. Arizona*.[9]

---

[5] *Brown v. Mississippi*, 297 U.S. 278 (1936). The confessions procured from the defendants in that case were the sole evidence used to convict them of capital murder.

[6] *Spano v. New York*, 360 U.S. 315 (1959). The confession in that case resulted from an interrogation lasting nearly eight hours, in which the suspect was grilled by more than a dozen officers, including an officer who had been a friend of the suspect's in school, who lied and told Spano that if he failed to cooperate with the police, he, the friend, would lose his police job. The Court also considered the suspect's personal background—that he was foreign born, relatively uneducated, emotionally unstable, and unfamiliar with police practices. The combination of all of these factors led the Court to find his confession involuntary and thus inadmissible.

[7] *Spano v. New York* (cited in n.6), 320–1.

[8] *Escobedo v. Illinois*, 378 U.S. 478 (1964).

[9] *Miranda v. Arizona*, 384 U.S. 436 (1966).

The *Miranda* Court intended to substitute front-end protections against potentially abusive and coercive police questioning for the after-the-fact assessment of coercion required by the voluntariness test for admissibility. The Supreme Court acknowledged that physical coercion during interrogation had thankfully become rare, but it recognized that less brutal interrogation tactics designed to trick, intimidate, pressure, coax, and cajole had an equal capacity to result in potentially unreliable confessions. If the right against self-incrimination—and the attendant right to remain silent under interrogation—meant nothing more than that the police could not forcibly compel someone to answer questions, then only exceptionally strong individuals able to withstand the psychologically grueling gauntlet of protracted interrogation could meaningfully exercise that right. The *Miranda* Court fully understood that such a narrow reading of the right to remain silent would render it practically unavailable to the vast majority of people.

Rather than focusing on specific problematic aspects of individual interrogations, as the context-sensitive voluntariness test had, the *Miranda* Court examined the structural dynamics of police interrogation in the abstract. The *Miranda* majority discussed in some detail the interrogation techniques incorporated in the influential Inbau and Reid manual for law enforcement interrogation.[10] The practices recommended by Inbau and Reid were all based on a presumption that the suspect was guilty, such that the only job of the interrogator was to procure a confession rather than to objectively investigate the facts of the case. The *Miranda* majority expressed alarm at the psychologically manipulative, coercive, and deceptive interrogation techniques recommended in what had become the bible of interrogation for American law enforcement.

Understanding what it saw as the inherently coercive context of custodial interrogation, the *Miranda* Court provided what it believed to be a crucial enforcement mechanism for those who wished to avail themselves of the constitutional right to remain silent by requiring warnings prior to interrogation informing the arrestee of the right not to answer questions and providing access to legal counsel for advice on whether to exercise that right. The required warnings were intended to ensure that suspects in custody understood what rights and options they had during police questioning, and that they would therefore be in a position to make rational and informed choices about whether or not to answer police questions. Voluntariness, under this regime, could now be presumed as long as suspects in custody understood their rights and were given the ability to exercise them if desired.

In a later case interpreting the scope of the *Miranda* rule, the Supreme Court made clear that interrogation must end, at least for a period of time, whenever the suspect exercised the right to remain silent.[11] *Mosley* made explicit what *Miranda* impliedly promised—those who wanted to claim the constitutional right to remain silent could do so and thereby immediately put an end to unwanted interrogation. The *Mosley* Court called the suspect's right to cut off questioning a "critical safeguard" of the right to remain silent.[12] Abusive and coercive interrogation tactics could thus be countered whenever the suspect needed to call a halt to them.

Given this legal framework, logically there would be two ways in which someone undergoing police interrogation might attempt to exercise the right to remain silent provided under the *Miranda-Mosley* doctrine: either by not verbally responding to police questioning—literally remaining silent—or by verbally articulating their wish to

---

[10] The *Miranda* Court discussed the techniques recommended in the Inbau and Reid manual for eight full pages in their opinion: *Miranda v. Arizona* (cited in n.9), 448–56.
[11] *Mosley v. Michigan*, 423 U.S. 96 (1975).
[12] *Mosley v. Michigan* (cited in n.11), 103.

exercise the right to remain silent. As it has turned out, however, neither of these potential choices is likely to be legally efficacious in practice.

2. Remaining silent as an exercise of the right to remain silent

2.1. A linguistic consideration of the meaning of silence

Language researchers analyzing verbal communication might be thought to have little to say about silence—that is, the absence of verbal expression. After all, those analyzing meaning in written texts ordinarily concentrate on the symbols making up the text, not on the blank spaces surrounding them. Silence in communicative interaction, however, is not just the "blank space" setting off the audible elements of spoken utterances. William Samarin once compared the significance of silence within speech to the importance of zero within mathematics; neither silence nor zero should be considered as an absence without meaning, but rather as an absence with functional meaning.[13] Speech and silence mutually frame each other in discourse, with this reciprocal contextual framing giving both speech and silence their fullest meaning.[14] Within interpersonal interactions, silence can serve a multitude of communicative functions—semantic, pragmatic, and socio-pragmatic.[15] In fact, consideration of silence is so crucial to interactional analyses grounded in Conversational Analysis that its transcription conventions measure pauses to tenths of a second, with micro-silences too short to measure indicated in transcription by the use of dots.[16]

The meaning of silence, like other linguistic practices, is context-dependent, with interpretation of silence impossible without the interactional context that provides its meaning.[17] Silence only becomes a communicative act when it occurs within a communicative context—that is, within a structured interaction governed by context-dependent social norms.[18] Thus, silence can only be accorded meaning in the light of its communicative context. In that regard, one must distinguish between silence that serves to structure speech through the absence of sound—the "white space on the page between the symbols" sort of silence—and silence that has specific communicative content within the discursive context; that is, silence that can itself bear interpretive meaning.[19]

Understanding the meaning of being silent in this particular context—police interrogation—is furthered by consideration of what H. P. Grice called the rules of

---

[13] William J. Samarin, 'The Language of Silence' (1965) 12 *Practical Anthropology* 115, at 115.

[14] Penelope Eckert and Sally McConnell-Ginet, *Language and Gender* (Cambridge, UK: Cambridge University Press, 2003), 119.

[15] Muriel Saville-Troike, 'The Place of Silence in an Integrated Theory of Communication' in Deborah Tannen and Muriel Saville-Troike (eds), *Perspectives on Silence* (Norwood, N.J.: Ablex Pub. Corp., 1985), 7; Adam Jaworski, *The Power of Silence: Social and Pragmatic Perspectives* (Newbury Park, Calif.: Sage, 1993); Robin T. Lakoff, 'Cries and Whispers: The Shattering of the Silence' in Kira Hall and Mary Bucholtz (eds), *Gender Articulated: Language and the Socially Constructed Self* (New York: Routledge, 1995), 25.

[16] George Psathas, *Conversation Analysis: The Study of Talk-in-Interaction* (Thousand Oaks, Calif.: Sage, 1995), 11–13.

[17] Saville-Troike (cited in n.15), 11; Susan Gal, 'Between Speech and Silence: The Problematics of Research on Gender and Language' in Micaela di Leonardo (ed.), *Gender at the Crossroads of Knowledge: Feminist Anthropology in the Postmodern Era* (Berkeley, Calif.: University of California Press, 1991), 196; Susan Gal, 'Language, Gender, and Power: An Anthropological Review' in Alessandro Duranti (ed.), *Linguistic Anthropology: A Reader* (Malden, Mass.: John Wiley & Sons, 2001), 422–3.

[18] Peter Tiersma, 'The Language of Silence' (1995) 48 *Rutgers Law Review* 1, at 21–2.

[19] Lisa A. Mazzei, *Inhabited Silence in Qualitative Research* (New York: Peter Lang Publishing, 2007), 48.

conversational implicature.[20] The interpretive conventions identified by Grice posit that communicative interaction is a rule-governed activity, with participants interpreting each other's responses as relevant both to the context of the situation and to what has been said earlier in the interaction. For example, imagine the following exchange between friends: "Hey, I have two tickets to tonight's concert." "Oh, too bad I have to work late." On the surface, these appear to be non-sequiturs—one a statement about the possession of tickets and one about a work schedule. But, given the conventions of conversational implicature, the utterance about tickets should be construed as relevant to the hearer, and thus likely to be an indirect invitation to attend the concert with the speaker. The response is also best interpreted as relevant and responsive, that is, as ruefully declining the offer on the basis of a scheduling conflict. Interpretations like this one occur constantly in interactional discourse, generally without conscious awareness by the participants. A literal reading of the meaning of the exchange would distort the actual intended and understood meaning of the parties.

The interpretation of the meaning of silence in contexts marked by power asymmetries between the parties to the interaction must further take into account the fact that the more powerless party may be constrained in his responses and limited in his range of interactional options.[21] Police interrogation, obviously, is a context marked by extraordinary power asymmetry between the suspect and the interrogators. Alone, isolated, and unable to leave, the arrestee in police custody is physically and psychologically at the mercy of the interrogation team. Engaging in even the simplest normal human activities—eating, sleeping, smoking, using the bathroom—is now totally within the control of and at the discretion of the interrogating officers. The arrestee cannot control the timing or duration of the interrogation. Once questioning begins, its tone and tempo are set unilaterally by the interrogators, who decide what topics will be entertained and what responses will be considered satisfactory. It is difficult to conceive of a more one-sided interaction with a higher degree of power asymmetry than a custodial police interrogation. In such a situation, the range of available responses to police accusations by the arrested suspect is severely limited. Adding to this power asymmetry is the fact that the arrestee must be acutely conscious of the fact that interrogation is a high-stakes interaction in which life-changing consequences could follow from the interrogation. Therefore, appropriate interpretation of the meaning of responses of an arrestee during police interrogation must take into account both the normal contextualized processes entailed by Gricean implicature as well as special consideration of the power asymmetries inherent in the interrogation context. As will be seen, however, courts routinely fail utterly in both of these regards in assessing whether suspects invoked the right to remain silent.

3. *Berghuis* v. *Thompkins* and its consequences for the right to remain silent

Having been told that "you have the right to remain silent," an arrested person might well think that the wisest course would be to do just that—not to say anything in response to police questioning. Silence by an arrestee after being given the *Miranda* warning

---

[20] His most prominent essays articulating the function of conversational implicature are collected in H. P. Grice, *Studies in the Way of Words* (Cambridge, Mass.: Harvard University Press, 1989).
[21] Anne Graffam Walker, 'The Two Faces of Silence: The Effect of Witness Hesitancy on Lawyers' Impressions' in Deborah Tannen and Muriel Saville-Troike (eds), *Perspectives on Silence* (Norwood, N.J.: Ablex Publishing Corp., 1985), 55; Lakoff (cited in n.15), 26.

that "you have the right to remain silent and anything you say can be used against you" should logically be understood in terms of Gricean implicature as relevant and responsive to that warning. If remaining silent were so interpreted and thus legally construed as an exercise of the right to remain silent, then, under the *Miranda-Mosley* framework, interrogation would have to stop once it became clear that the arrestee did not wish to respond to questioning. Officers who continued to interrogate in the face of the claim of the right to remain silent would then be violating that asserted right, and any statements later obtained would be inadmissible.

Before 2010, appellate courts had split on the question of whether a suspect could invoke the right to silence—and thus end police questioning—simply by being consistently silent, but in that year the Supreme Court held in a 5–4 opinion that the only way in which an arrestee could exercise the *Miranda*-guaranteed right to remain silent was by affirmatively speaking and claiming that right.[22] In *Berghuis*, the defendant Thompkins was arrested on suspicion of involvement in a year-old murder case. Two officers began to interrogate him on the charge, first reading him his rights from a written *Miranda* form which they asked him to sign. Thompkins refused to do so. Although the police station where the interrogation took place had recording equipment, it was not used in this case. The interrogators did not ask Thompkins whether he wished to waive his *Miranda* rights and speak with them, but instead simply launched into an interrogation that lasted nearly three hours. Evidence of what transpired during the interrogation is sparse, based on the testimony of the interrogating officers at two court hearings held in connection with the prosecution. Both officers agreed in their testimony that Thompkins remained essentially silent during a barrage of questioning in which Thompkins was alternately accused of being the shooter, cajoled to cooperate for leniency, and warned about the dire consequences of not providing his side of the story to the police. None of these tactics got a response from Thompkins, whom the officers described in their testimony as "not verbally communicative," mainly saying nothing and sitting "with his head in his hands looking down."

Occasionally, his response to a question or accusation was to "look up and make eye contact," or to make a brief response, a "yeah" or "no" or "I don't know."[23] One of the officers candidly conceded that the interrogation was essentially "a monologue" by the officers, in which they were unable to "elicit any admissions or denials, for that matter, ... any sort of reaction" from Thompkins at all.[24] The only specific comments made during the interrogation that either officer could recall were that Thompkins declined the offer of a peppermint and at another point complained that the chair in which he was sitting was hard. Nearly three hours into this one-sided interrogation, the officers switched tactics and asked Thompkins if he believed in God and if he prayed to God. Thompkins answered both questioned in the affirmative. He was then asked if he prayed for forgiveness for shooting the victim, and he replied with the single word, "Yes." That single-word confession was admitted at trial over his objection that the interrogation had violated his *Miranda* rights by continuing for hours despite his exercise of his right to remain silent by not answering questions.

The *Berghuis* majority disagreed that Thompkins had ever effectively invoked his right to remain silent during the interrogation. His steadfast refusal to engage with the interrogating officers, no matter how long maintained, was legally insufficient to count

---

[22] *Berghuis* v. *Thompkins*, 130 S. Ct. 2250 (2010).
[23] *Berghuis* v. *Thompkins* (cited in n.22), 2267.
[24] *Thompkins* v. *Berghuis*, 547 F.3d 572, 576 (6th Cir. 2008).

as an exercise of the right to remain silent, they held. In fact, simply remaining silent under police questioning could never constitute a legally valid invocation of the constitutional right to remain silent, according to the *Berghuis* majority opinion. Despite the fact that a reasonable person, hearing the warning "You have the right to remain silent, and anything you say can be used against you" might assume that being silent in the face of police questioning would be the quintessential example of how to exercise the constitutional right to remain silent, the *Berghuis* majority instead mandated that the only legally valid way to exercise the right to remain silent is, paradoxically, to speak and invoke the right to remain silent explicitly.

4. Speaking to claim the right to remain silent

While *Berghuis* made clear that only a verbal invocation of the right to remain silent will be legally efficacious in claiming that constitutional protection during police interrogation, the *Berghuis* majority went on in its opinion to stringently prescribe the manner in which such a verbal invocation must be made in order to count as an invocation at all. According to the *Berghuis* Court, only a clear, unambiguous, and unequivocal exercise of the right to remain silent by the arrestee will count as a legally efficacious invocation. While that may sound reasonable in the abstract, in practice, courts have applied this rule[25] by using hyper-literal parsing of invocations and ignoring normal Gricean implicated meanings. As a canvassing of appellate case law will demonstrate, this cramped and narrow approach to understanding attempts to invoke rights makes it nearly impossible for suspects undergoing police interrogation to successfully exercise their rights.

When arrestees attempt to claim the right to remain silent, any linguistic features of their invocations that in any way modify or mitigate a bald assertion of the right will be seized upon by judges to disqualify the invocation and render it legally void. For example, those who soften their exercise of their constitutional rights with language like "I think" will fail to have their invocations respected:

- "I just don't think I should say anything."[26]
- "You all are scaring me, I think, yeah, I shouldn't say anymore."[27]
- "I think it's about time for me to stop talking."[28]
- When asked if he would agree to answer police questions, "Naw, I don't think so."[29]

Beginning an imperative statement with expressions like "I think" is commonly used as a way to soften the baldness of imperative demands, without in any way suggesting that the demand is equivocal.[30] For example, the restaurant patron who tells the waiter

---

[25] Prior to *Berghuis*, many state courts and federal circuits were already requiring suspects to explicitly claim the right to remain silent in an unambiguous and unequivocal manner—a doctrine that the Supreme Court has now mandated that all American courts must utilize.
[26] *Burket v. Angelone*, 208 F.3d 172 (4th Cir. 2000).
[27] *State v. Morfitt*, 956 P.2d 719 (Kan. Ct. App. 1998).
[28] *People v. Stitely*, 108 P.3d 182 (Cal. S. Ct. 2005).
[29] *People v. Patterson*, 2005 Cal. App. LEXIS 9594 (Cal. Ct. App. 21 Oct. 2005).
[30] The germinal work detailing use of language that literally appears to be hedging, but that is not intended by the speaker to be equivocal or ambiguous, but rather to express deference or politeness, is Penelope Brown and Stephen C. Levinson, *Politeness: Some Universals in Language Use* (Cambridge, UK: Cambridge University Press, 1987), 129–71. The use of hedges such as "I think" or "maybe" acts to soften the imposition on the addressee that an imperative would have in the absence of these politeness tokens.

"I think I'll have the steak" is certainly not expressing uncertainty about what she is ordering. Instead, by softening the order with the lexical hedge "I think," the customer is mitigating the aggressive edge that an unmitigated demand might otherwise entail. This avoidance of naked imperatives is particularly likely in communicative contexts marked by power asymmetry, in which an unmodified demand by the more powerless speaker would appear presumptious at best and offensive, even provocative, at worst.[31] However, appellate courts in each of the above cases held that adding the softening "I think" to the invocations here rendered them ambiguous or equivocal, and consequently legally ineffective.

Including a temporal specification was similarly fatal to the attempts by these defendants to invoke their rights:

- "I don't think I can talk. I guess I don't want to discuss it right now."[32]
- "I don't want to talk about it right now."[33]
- Officer: "Are you telling me you don't want to talk to me anymore, John?" Defendant: "Not right now. Y'all tryin' to pressure this on me."[34]

Adding any reasons to an attempt to invoke the right to remain silent doomed these defendants trying to exercise their constitutional rights:

- "I really can't say no more right now. My head is splitting. I need some rest, I really do," with police responding "Yes, you can. It's got to come out. It's going to kill you if it doesn't."[35]
- By a developmentally disabled arrestee: "I don't want to talk about it. I'm tired."[36]
- "I really don't want to talk about it. I mean, I ain't the one that did it."[37]
- "I don't even like talking about it, man... I mean, I don't even want to, you know what I'm saying, discuss no more about it, man."[38]

Preceding the invocation with an "if" clause rendered the following invocation legally void:

- "Okay, if you're implying that I've done it, I wish to not say any more. I'd like to be done with this. Cause that's just ridiculous. I wish I'd... I don't wish to answer any more questions."[39]

The *Deen* court found the invocation in that case to be equivocal because it began with the stipulation that the defendant only wanted to claim the right to remain silent under the condition that the police were insinuating his guilt. The fact that, in this case, the

---

[31] William M. O'Barr, *Linguistic Evidence: Language, Power, and Strategy in the Courtroom* (New York: Academic Press, 1982); John M. Conley and William M. O'Barr, *Just Words: Law, Language, and Power* (Chicago, Ill.: University of Chicago Press, 1998); Lawrence A. Hosman and Susan A. Siltanen, 'Powerful and Powerless Language Forms: Their Consequences for Impression Formation, Attributions of Control of Self and Control of Others, Cognitive Response, and Message Memory' (2006) 25 *Journal of Language and Social Psychology* 33.
[32] *People* v. *Peracchi*, 102 Cal. Rptr.2d 921 (Cal. Ct. App. 2001).
[33] *State* v. *Sabetta*, 680 A.2d 927 (R.I. S. Ct. 1996).
[34] *State* v. *Chesson*, 856 So.2d 166 (La. Ct. App. 2003).
[35] *Dowthitt* v. *State*, 931 S.W.2d 244 (Tex. Crim. App. 1996).
[36] *Franks* v. *State*, 90 S.W.3d 771 (Tex. Crim. App. 2002).
[37] *Davis* v. *State*, 2007 WL 858782 (Tex. Ct. App. 23 Mar. 2007).
[38] *State* v. *Jackson*, 839 N.E.2d 362 (Ohio 2006).
[39] *State* v. *Deen*, 953 So.2d 1057 (La. App. 2007).

police indeed were implying he had "done it" did not save his invocation from being disallowed as insufficiently clear and unequivocal.

Some courts interpreted attempts to invoke the right to be silent as ineffective because the arrestee phrased the invocation as unwillingness to make a statement but not separately articulating an unwillingness to answer questions:

- Officer: "Do you want to make a statement to us?" Arrestee: "Nope."[40]
- Officer: "Do you want to make a statement now?" Arrestee: "No."[41]
- "No, I do not want to declare anything. I just, I do not want to declare anything."[42]

In each of these cases, the invocations were held to be unclear—and thus legally meaningless—because the courts thought that it was possible that the suspects were saying only that they wanted to avoid making declarative statements, but that they might have agreed to answer questions. The fact that they weren't asked by the officers about answering questions, only about making statements, did not stop the appellate courts from concluding that the invocations were defective for failing to spontaneously include an objection to answering police questions as well as a refusal to make a statement.

Frequently courts have invalidated attempted invocations by characterizing them as reflecting emotional reactions of the suspects rather than crediting them with intending to put an end to interrogation by asserting the protections of the law:

- "I don't want to talk about it anymore, it hurts too much."[43]
- "I can't even talk right now."[44]
- "I can't say anything more now, because that's blowing my mind away."[45]

When people use the modal verbs "can" or "can't" in their attempts to invoke their rights, courts often disqualify these invocations as nothing more than statements about the suspects' ability to answer questions, not their affirmative intention not to do so. For example, the *Anderson* court explained its invalidation of the invocation in that case by pointing out that, by using the modal verb "can", the defendant was simply expressing his emotional inability to respond to police questions rather than articulating his desire not to respond. In another case featuring similar judicial reasoning, the defendant responded to police accusations in the following language:

- "I don't wanta say, man ... I don't wanta say that, I don't want to. NO MORE, NO MORE."[46] (emphasis in appellate record)

The court in this case ignored the plain meaning of the words of the suspect's attempts to end the questioning, and instead speculated that his invocation was only "an expression of an unwillingness to confront reality ... merely a difficult catharsis." Based on this assumption, the court felt free to hold the invocation to be legally meaningless.

---

[40] *James v. Marshall*, 322 F.3d 103 (1st Cir. 2003).
[41] *Commonwealth v. Cupp*, 2004 WL 2391944 (Va. Cir. Ct. 21 Oct. 2004).
[42] *Cuervo v. State*, 929 So.2d 640 (Fla. Dist. Ct. App. 2006).
[43] *State v. Fritschen*, 802 P.2d 558 (Kan. S. Ct. 1990).
[44] *State v. Galli*, 967 P.2d 923 (Utah S. Ct. 1998).
[45] *People v. Anderson*, 2007 WL 1429631 (Mich. Ct. App. 15 May 2007).
[46] *State v. Whipple*, 5 P.3d 478 (Idaho Ct. App. 2000).

Other courts have indulged in similar speculations to explain away what appear to be attempts to exercise the right to remain silent, thereby holding them insufficiently clear to have legal effect.

- "I'm not going to talk. That's it. I shut up."[47]

This defendant's clear assertion that he refused to talk to the police was instead characterized by the *Jennings* court as a statement of "momentary frustration and animosity, not invocation." Other defendants' invocations were dismissed as nothing more than expressions of a bad attitude or hostility to the police:

- "I ain't got shit to say to y'all."[48]
- "You can't make me say nothing."[49]
- "I'm not going to talk about nothin'."[50]

The *Sherrod* court called this clear statement of intent "as much a taunt—even a provocation—as it was an invocation of the right to remain silent." Having imagined that the defendant's words could be seen as a taunt to the police trying to interrogate him, the court concluded that the attempted invocation was therefore too ambiguous to be given legal effect.

In some cases, it is frankly impossible to tell what purported deficiency in the arrestee's invocation caused reviewing courts to find them insufficiently clear:

- "I don't have anything to say."[51]
- "I don't got nothing to say."[52]
- "I don't want to talk about it."[53]
- "I don't wanna talk no more."[54]

In one particularly perplexing case, an arrestee was asked by the officer whether he would answer police questions. He answered, "No, sir." It is hard to imagine a more clear, unambiguous, and unequivocal response claiming the right not to answer police questions. Nevertheless, the reviewing court found that the officer was justified in believing that the defendant must have misunderstood the question or misspoken, and that he was therefore allowed to "clarify" what the defendant wanted and to persuade him to talk.[55]

Cases such as these show courts avoiding giving legal effect to attempts by defendants to invoke the right to remain silent by adopting strained interpretations of the invocations, seizing upon supposed qualifications within the invocations, and inventing alternative emotional reasons other than invocation to explain away suspect refusals to answer police questions. Principles of Gricean implicature tell us that utterances ought to be interpreted contextually as responsive to the circumstances in which they are made. Yet, in these cases, courts instead take a suspect's words out of context, twist them to see if they are susceptible to any conceivable meaning other than invocation,

---

[47] *People v. Jennings*, 760 P.2d 475 (Cal. S. Ct. 1988).
[48] *Mitchell v. Commonwealth*, 518 S.E.2d 330 (Va. Ct. App. 1999).
[49] *State v. Greybull*, 579 N.W.2d 161 (N.D. S. Ct. 1998).
[50] *United States v. Sherrod*, 445 F.3d 980 (7th Cir. 2006).
[51] *State v. Hickles*, 929 P.2d 141 (Kan. S. Ct. 1996).
[52] *United States v. Banks*, 78 F.3d 1190 (7th Cir. 1996).
[53] *Owen v. State*, 862 So.2d 687 (Fla. S. Ct. 2003).
[54] *United States v. Stephenson*, 152 Fed. App'x. 904 (11th Cir. 2005).
[55] *State v. Pitts*, 936 So.2d 1111 (Fla. Dist. Ct. App. 2006).

and thereby invalidate what seem obvious attempts to claim the constitutional right to remain silent. As a result, for most arrestees in police custody, the constitutional protections of *Miranda* are, as a practical matter, beyond their reach. The right to remain silent envisioned by the *Miranda* Court as a protection against abusive police interrogation has, to all intents and purposes, vanished. True, *Miranda* rights are still routinely read to suspects in police custody, but claiming the rights articulated in the warning has become a verbal shell game in which suspects inevitably pick the wrong shell.

5. Does *Miranda* matter anymore?

Empirical research shows that the vast majority of arrested suspects fail to exercise their right to remain silent and make incriminating statements to the police, notwithstanding the near-universal police practice of reciting *Miranda* warnings.[56] Assuming that most suspects understand the rights contained in the warnings,[57] this seems puzzling. It is conceivable that the infrequency with which *Miranda* rights are claimed is because few suspects actually wish to exercise the right to remain silent. However, the stringency of the current legal regime defining legally effective invocations of the right to remain silent makes that conclusion questionable, since successfully invoking constitutional rights in interrogation is virtually impossible for anyone without a detailed understanding of the precision with which courts require invocation to be made.

The arrestee who naively attempts to exercise the right to remain silent by simply not responding gets no protection whatsoever. The arrestee who tries to verbally exercise the right to remain silent fares little better. Only the most perfect, unmitigated articulation of an invocation will count as efficacious under the hyper-technical reading of current invocation law applied by most courts. The odds that an arrestee who truly wants to exercise the right to remain silent can successfully do this are further reduced by the fact that the *Miranda* warnings themselves—likely the sole source of the suspect's information about constitutional rights—fail to inform the suspect that the precise language used to claim the right to remain silent will be legally dispositive and that any deviations from the magic formula for invocation will render it void.

One powerful data-point suggesting that the *Miranda* framework is not working at all to overcome the coercive impact of police interrogation is that, after interrogation has begun, almost no suspects ever later successfully invoke their right to remain silent and cut off interrogation.[58] Surely as an interrogation becomes more pointed and the web of inculpatory evidence tightens, suspects who understood that they could end the interrogation immediately by claiming the right to remain silent would be inclined to exercise that right. The fact that this almost never happens, no matter how coercive and accusatory the interrogation turns, strongly suggests that arrestees do not understand

---

[56] Richard A. Leo, 'Questioning the Relevance of *Miranda* in the Twenty-first Century' (2001) 99 *Michigan Law Review* 1000, at 1009.

[57] This assumption is highly questionable, however. In a recent study, jail inmates and college students were read a standard *Miranda* warning and then surveyed on their understanding of the specific rights encompassed by the warning. Both populations showed significant misperceptions about their *Miranda* rights. Richard Rogers, Jill E. Rogstad, Nathan D. Gillard, Eric Y. Drogin, Hayley L. Blackwood, and Daniel W. Shuman, 'Everybody Knows Their *Miranda* Rights: Implicit Assumptions and Countervailing Evidence' (2010) 16 *Psychology, Public Policy and Law* 300. The syntactic and lexical opacity of the warnings has been criticized by linguists as likely to lead to a lack of comprehension of the *Miranda* rights by many arrestees. See, for example, Roger W. Shuy, 'Ten Unanswered Questions About *Miranda*' (1997) 4 *International Journal of Speech, Language, and Law* 175.

[58] William Stuntz, '*Miranda*'s Mistake' (2001) 99 *Michigan Law Review* 975, at 988.

that they have the right to end the interrogation at any time, or that even when they do, they are unable to articulate their desires with sufficient hyper-precision to satisfy judicial requirements for effective invocations.

The *Miranda* framework as currently implemented fails to provide most arrestees with either the knowledge or the ability to cut off coercive questioning, contrary to the original intent of the Supreme Court in enacting *Miranda*. One might ask, what difference does it make whether current case law is faithful to the intent of the Supreme Court in enacting the *Miranda* regulatory framework? Whether *Miranda* works today does indeed matter, however, because, practically speaking, the *Miranda* framework has become the exclusive legal constraint on potentially abusive police interrogation. Under the *Miranda*-governed interrogation regime, police interrogators are permitted to conduct lengthy incommunicado interrogations in which they are free to lie to the suspect, manufacture false "evidence" of guilt, and alternately browbeat the suspect with exaggerated threats of punishment and sweet-talk him with implied promises of leniency, as long as *Miranda* warnings precede the ordeal and the right to halt interrogation is within the power of the suspect.[59] As the rules regarding invocation of constitutional rights have become increasingly stringent, however, this power has become almost entirely illusory. Far from being a bulwark against potential coercion and over-reaching in police interrogation, the empty doctrinal shell of the *Miranda* framework now acts instead primarily to shield interrogation from judicial review as to the reliability and voluntariness of statements procured.[60]

The consequences of unfettered police interrogation have begun to surface in many of the recent DNA exonerations in which innocent people were nevertheless convicted of crimes. In one large sample of these cases of erroneous conviction, one quarter of these defendants confessed under police interrogation, despite being entirely innocent of the crimes and despite having been given *Miranda* warnings.[61] It is hard for most people to believe that any innocent person would ever confess to a crime. We are all sure that we never would. And yet, the growing number of exonerated defendants—a surprising number of whom confessed to the crimes they didn't commit—ought to give the criminal justice system pause. Modern police interrogation methods are quite psychologically sophisticated, but their very sophistication inherently entails the possibility of trapping the innocent along with the guilty.[62] In particular, certain classes of suspects—the young,[63] the emotionally and mentally unsound,[64] the developmentally disabled[65]—are especially vulnerable to police pressure in police interrogation.

---

[59] Although most American courts have been quite willing to permit the police to lie and to confront suspects with false evidence during interrogation, the practice has long been criticized by scholars. See, e.g., Welsh S. White, 'Police Trickery in Inducing Confessions' (1979) 127 *University of Pennsylvania Law Review* 581; Deborah Young, 'Unnecessary Evil: Police Lying in Interrogations' (1996) 28 *Connecticut Law Review* 425; Miriam Gohara, 'A Lie for a Lie: False Confessions and the Case for Reconsidering the Legality of Deceptive Interrogation Techniques' (2006) 33 *Fordham Urban Law Journal* 79.

[60] Welsh S. White, '*Miranda*'s Failure to Restrain Pernicious Police Interrogation Practices' (2001) 99 *Michigan Law Review* 1211, at 1219–20.

[61] Steven Drizen and Richard A. Leo, 'The Problem of False Confessions in the Post-DNA World' (2004) 82 *North Carolina Law Review* 891, at 905.

[62] For a detailed description of the processes of modern American police interrogation and its tendency to construct culpability in its subjects, see Richard A. Leo, *Police Interrogation and American Justice* (Cambridge, Mass.: Harvard University Press, 2008), 165–94.

[63] Jessica Owen-Kostelnik, N. Dickson Reppucci, and Jessica R. Meyer, 'Testimony and Interrogation of Minors: Assumptions about Maturity and Morality' (2006) 4 *American Psychologist* 286.

[64] Allison Redlich, 'Mental Illness, Police Interrogations, and the Potential for False Confessions' (2004) 55 *Law and Psychiatry* 19.

[65] Morgan Cloud, George Shepherd, Alison Barkoff, and Justin Shur, 'Words Without Meaning: The Constitution, Confessions, and Mentally Retarded Suspects' (2002) 69 *University of Chicago Law Review* 495.

Certain personality types—highly suggestible individuals, acquiescent persons eager to please those in authority, those with low self-esteem, and conflict-avoiding personalities—are all disproportionately likely to agree with police accusations that are untrue.[66] Situational factors such as sleep deprivation, fatigue, and substance abuse have all been demonstrated to predispose people to falsely confessing under pressure.[67] Innocent people, too, may be at special risk because they enter the interrogation room convinced that there are no dangers there for them as a consequence of their being innocent of the crime.[68] Psychologically manipulative and coercive techniques are routinely a part of the standard police interrogation protocols, undermining the suspect's ability to resist complying with the police-desired outcome: admission of guilt.[69] The more we know about the many factors and processes that sometimes lead innocent people to falsely confess, the more it becomes clear that our folk belief—that people don't confess unless they are guilty of the offense—is a myth with dangerous consequences for justice.

Given the persistence of the myth that innocent people don't confess, however, it should not be surprising that conviction nearly always results when an admission of guilt—whether reliable or otherwise—is obtained. Once a suspect makes incriminating statements to the police, the police investigation immediately narrows in its focus to proving the guilt of the suspect. Evidence that undermines the plausibility of a confession tends to be disregarded by the police, who concentrate subsequent investigative efforts on bolstering the case against the confessing suspect.[70] Witnesses in the case who learn of a confession become more entrenched in their belief in the suspect's guilt, or may change their minds and even their testimony if they had initially doubted guilt.[71] As the case against the confessing suspect develops, all evidentiary roads come to converge on a finding of guilt.

Once formally charged with the crime by the prosecutor, the suspect who has confessed under police questioning is unlikely to be offered a plea bargain, since the prosecutor knows that the confession makes the case a strong one at trial.[72] If the suspect insists on going to trial, the odds of acquittal are small once the jurors hear the confession, even if it is recanted immediately. Even in cases in which the confession is obtained through coercive interrogation techniques and where there is strong objective evidence casting doubt on the reliability of the confession, jurors are highly likely to convict nonetheless. Studies involving mock jury trials have demonstrated the power of confessions to bias jurors in favor of guilty verdicts. In one experiment, mock trial jurors were exposed to a confession that was obtained through abusive police questioning. The jurors were

---

[66] Saul M. Kassin and Gisli Gudjonsson, 'The Psychology of Confessions: A Review of the Literature and Issues' (2004) 5 *Psychological Science in the Public Interest* 35.

[67] Mark Blagrove, 'Effects of Length of Sleep Deprivation on Interrogative Suggestibility' (1996) 2 *Journal of Experimental Psychology: Applied* 48.

[68] Saul M. Kassin, 'Does Innocence Put Innocents at Risk?' (2005) 60 *American Psychologist* 215.

[69] Richard Ofshe and Richard A. Leo, 'The Decision to Confess Falsely: Rational Choice and Irrational Action' (1997) 74 *Denver University Law Review* 979.

[70] Richard A. Leo, 'Inside the Interrogation Room' (1996) 86 *Journal of Criminal Law and Criminology* 266.

[71] For example, in one psychology experiment, some witnesses to a staged crime who had correctly identified the "perpetrator" changed their minds about their accurate eyewitness identification when told that someone else had "confessed" to the crime. They conformed their eyewitness identification to the newly learned evidence of the confession, even though the conforming identification was now wrong: Lisa E. Hasel and Saul M. Kassin, 'On the Presumption of Evidentiary Independence: Can Confessions Corrupt Eyewitness Identifications?' (2009) 20 *Psychological Sciences* 122.

[72] Richard A. Leo and Richard Ofshe, 'The Consequences of False Confessions: Deprivations of Liberty and Miscarriages of Justice in the Age of Psychological Interrogation' (1998) 88 *Journal of Criminal Law and Criminology* 429.

cautioned by the "judge" to ignore the confession. In interviews after their deliberations, jurors agreed that the confession was coerced and they reported that it had no impact on their verdict. However, those jurors were dramatically more likely to convict than were jurors hearing identical mock trial evidence minus the coerced confession.[73]

In the real world, suspects who confess under police questioning are unlikely to discover whether jurors in their cases can look beyond a confession in deciding the verdict. Their own defense lawyers will likely strongly encourage them to plead guilty once it is clear that the confession is going to be admitted at trial, knowing how powerful confession evidence is in persuading jurors of guilt. If the defendant goes to trial and is—as expected—convicted, judges routinely impose their harshest sentences on defendants who claim innocence and thereby fail to accept responsibility for the offense.[74] Thus, the consequences for a suspect of succumbing to police coercion in interrogation are drastic and, in the vast majority of cases, unredressable at any later point in the criminal process.

Despite the significant number of recent cases in which coercively obtained confessions have been conclusively shown to have resulted in innocent people being convicted of crimes they did not commit,[75] the attitude of the current US Supreme Court towards providing legal protection for suspects from abusive police interrogation has changed radically from its stance in the 1960s. Whereas the *Miranda* Court recognized the very real potential for coercion by the police during custodial interrogation, and consequently insisted that the government should have a "heavy burden" to prove that a suspect waived his right to remain silent,[76] the current *Berghuis* Court seems oblivious to the possibility of coercion that could result in unreliable confessions. Instead, they have inverted the presumption of *Miranda* that the government bears the burden of clearly showing a knowing and voluntary choice by the suspect to answer questions. The *Miranda* Court categorically rejected the notion that a waiver of constitutional rights could be proven simply by showing that the suspect at some point during interrogation responded to a police question, saying, "A valid waiver will not be presumed... simply from the fact that a confession was in fact eventually obtained."[77] In contrast, the legal rule as announced in *Berghuis* now substitutes the presumption that any utterance at any time by a suspect in custody is sufficient to demonstrate that the suspect must have intended to waive the constitutional right not to answer police questions.[78]

As Justice Sotomayor in her dissent in *Berghuis* noted, the current Supreme Court has "turned *Miranda* upside down. Criminal suspects must now unambiguously invoke their right to remain silent—which, counter-intuitively, requires them to speak," a result which she calls "inconsistent with the fair-trial principles" on which *Miranda* and its progeny are based.[79] Worse still, *Berghuis* requires that a suspect trying to invoke the right to remain silent must do so using scrupulously precise language that cannot under any stretch of the judicial imagination be interpreted to be ambiguous or equivocal.

---

[73] Saul Kassin and Holly Sukel, 'Coerced Confessions and the Jury' (1997) 21 *Law and Human Behavior* 27.
[74] See, e.g., Daniel Givelber, 'Punishing Protestations of Innocence: Denying Responsibility and its Consequences' (2000) 37 *American Criminal Law Review* 1363.
[75] Richard A. Leo, *Police Interrogation and American Justice* (Cambridge, Mass.: Harvard University Press, 2008), 240–8.
[76] *Miranda* v. *Arizona* (cited in n.9), 475.
[77] *Miranda* v. *Arizona* (cited in n.9), 475.
[78] *Berghuis* v. *Thompkins* (cited in n.22), 2262–3.
[79] *Berghuis* v. *Thompkins* (cited in n.22), 2278.

Little wonder, then, that successful exercise of the constitutional rights guaranteed by *Miranda* as protection against abusive police interrogation practices has become vanishingly rare. Unless the current Supreme Court is willing to reconsider its jurisprudence gutting *Miranda*—an unlikely eventuality—American police interrogation will continue to remain largely unconstrained, with the inevitable result being future miscarriages of justice.

23

The Consumption of Legal Language: Consuming the Law

Dr. Anthony Amatrudo*

There has been a slippage away from understanding criminal law as the domain of specialists towards a popular folk understanding of law: largely this is the outcome of the increased consumption of media. Recently academics across a range of disciplines have begun to look critically at the interplay of law and consumed media by examining legal speech and performance in a post-modern setting. This has led to an analysis of the processes involved in the way that media represents law and how this has led, in turn, to a shift away from understanding law as the domain of specialists towards an analysis of the popular understanding of the common law and legal procedure. Legal language is routinely consumed and represented to non-specialists. In the modern world there is a definite fusion of law and culture at the level of popular discourse and we find the real, and the represented, are mingled on television, radio, and film as well as in the print media and the Internet. Our notions of participation and spectatorship are also similarly confused. However, we should not be surprised at this. It is the inevitable corollary of media production and the seemingly insatiable demand for stories about law, especially criminal law, emanating from the news-consuming public; and which they act on.

We should bear in mind Lawrence Friedman's maxim that it is not law itself, but representations of it, which affect behaviour. People tend to proceed in terms of what they think the law is, rather than what it actually is.[1] Though it is important to bear in mind the point made recently by Shuy in relation to civil litigation: 'we usually don't think about our native language as we converse in it. For most adult conversation is relatively automatic and unconscious.'[2] In other words, people are not conscious of the how they are using language or, importantly, where that language came from. Persons often come to believe they understand the law, though in reality their understanding is non-technical, and largely derived from television, the cinema, newspapers and, increasingly, latterly the Internet. They consume something that they understand as knowledge of the law, though it is gained in an ad hoc, unsystematic, and partial fashion. They hold to a folk understanding of what law is. The public discuss cases and speculate about their outcomes and about the state of the law generally. The interplay of law and performance in our digitalized multimedia world has led to major changes to our treatment of legal

---

* The author acknowledges useful criticism from Professor Andrew Halpin, Professor Steven Winter, and Dr Katalin Parti.

[1] L. Friedman, 'Popular Legal Culture: Law, Lawyers and Popular Culture' (1989) 98 *Yale Law Journal* 1579–1606.

[2] R. W. Shuy, *Fighting Over Words: Language and Civil Law Cases* (Oxford: Oxford University Press, 2008), 3.

cases.³ The lives of popular celebrities highlight legal matters, in terms of specific cases, and the outcomes of these and speculation about them show that the public have a seemingly inexhaustible hunger for details of cases, for example those of Michael Barrymore, Winona Ryder, O. J. Simpson, and Anna Nicole Smith. Of course, the supply of legal information in all forms of media, notably the Internet, also feeds that public demand. There is a plethora of legal and legal-related drama on our television and here people do perceive that these have an educational function irrespective of whether they actually do. These drama series tend to be well scripted and realistically shot and aim to immerse the audience in the plot. There has been talk of this 'screening of law' through popular culture as having definite ideological aspects.⁴

We can detect a merging of popular culture and law, especially in jurisdictions which screen court cases. The discussion of legal cases in our daily lives has had an impact upon the popular perception and understanding of legal principles and ethics.⁵ Law and the popular understanding of it through our increased use of media are now fused, and confused. There has been an unprecedented change in the portrayal of law and lawyers in the media and, along with it, an attendant rise in the public's confidence that it is aware of legal statute, procedure, and precedent, as Sherwin has convincingly argued.⁶

It cannot be sustained that the general public, jurors, and witnesses come to the law *tabula rasa*: rather, it is the case that they come to the law after a lifetime of immersion in the law through an assortment of media portrayals, be they real or fictional. Moreover, all of this may be only of some minor sociological interest but for the fact that the media rely not on legal canon and procedure but on an over-simplified explanation of cases that often claims to be educative, but which in reality only flags up issues and generalities; and in doing so does not necessarily illuminate legal principle or procedure. Lucia Zedner has argued:

> Newspapers, radio and television carry reports of sentences, of judges' comments upon passing sentence, of their implications, and of reactions to and criticisms of them. Media commentary amplifies (and in amplifying may also distort) the message of the sentence, maximising its impact and inviting public debate that amplifies it further still.⁷

The notion of moral panic being fostered through media attention to issues such as mugging, mobile phone theft, and graffiti is something that academics, policymakers, and practitioners are all too aware of.⁸ In academic criminology Colin Sumner long ago argued that:

> Social censures, as negative ideological formations, are thus highly targeted, despite the universality or indeterminateness of their form of language, especially legal language. Moral language is formed and developed in social practice; its expression of unified ideological formations in censures is enabled, primarily by that unity, which itself forged in the targeting process.⁹

---

³ P. Robson, 'Lawyers and the Legal System on TV: the British Experience' (2006) 2(4) *International Journal of Law in Context* 333–62.

⁴ N. Mezey and M. Niles, 'Screening the Law: Ideology and Law in American Popular Culture' (2005) 28 *Columbia Journal of Law and the Arts* 92–186.

⁵ S. Williams, 'Moral Pluck: Legal Ethics in Popular Culture' (2001) 2 *Columbia Law Review* 421–48.

⁶ R. Sherwin, *When Law Goes Pop: the Vanishing Line between Law and Popular Culture* (Chicago: University of Chicago Press, 2000).

⁷ L. Zedner, *Criminal Justice* (Oxford: Oxford University Press, 2004), 172.

⁸ S. Cohen, *Folk Devils and Moral Panics* (Oxford: Routledge, 1980).

⁹ C. Sumner, *Censure, Politics and Criminal Justice* (Milton Keynes: Open University Press, 1990), 30–1.

1. Revisiting Sumner and ideology

Colin Sumner examined the use of language and how it impacts on the treatment of crime and criminal law in relation to censure. Sumner's ideological use of the term censure asserts the role of social structure, history, and ideology, as opposed to the normative value, of the censure.[10] In the ideological version the censure itself is problematic for it is necessarily the result, to a greater or lesser extent, of ideological determination. The censure tells us more about the power relations that give rise to its application than about its necessity in any jurisprudentially determined model. Moreover, he relates this process to traditional issues in Marxist scholarship, those of power and the state. Sumner's work on the concept of censure culminated in 1990 with the influential collection of essays *Censure, Politics and Criminal Justice* which conceived of criminal law, not in terms of a sociology of deviance or a legal canon, but in terms of the enforcement of dominant social censures by understanding the criminal justice system as being ideologically and politically constructed by dominant capitalist forces. Not only did it seek to critique the enterprise of criminal law by developing a rigorous theory of censures by drawing upon both historical and sociological research but its intention was to change the entire thrust of criminological and legal research, which it saw as inadequate.[11] As Sumner rather pithily stated:

Whether we take their abstract, discursive definitions or their practical definitions in the course of law enforcement or moral stigmatization, it is clear that the definitions of deviant behaviour, even within a single society, exclude what should be included, include what should be excluded, and generally fail to attain unambiguous, consistent and settled social meanings. To this we add massive cross-cultural differences in the meaning, enforcement and even existence of categories of deviance, and endless instances of resistance to them involving alternative categories.

Clearly, they are highly acculturated terms of moral and political judgement.[12]

In other words since there is no possibility of using the normal categories of crime and deviance in a scientific, or even consistent, fashion it is right to analyse them as moral and political discourses. Crime categories should be understood as negatively conceived ideological categories. This approach views crime categories in terms of their institutional forms and practices, that is, how and why they arise in certain places, at certain times, in relation to certain groups and how these are expressed through language.

In Marxist terms crime categories should also be understood in terms of the hegemonic function they have in signifying, denouncing, and regulating individuals and groups. Policing, the court system and other functions of the criminal justice system, Sumner argued, reflect capitalist social, economic, and political relations. The criminal justice system is in place to uphold the interests of the capitalist class. Accordingly, censures may be said not to reflect a *truth* about the extent of crime but rather 'a world-view which had not come to terms with its repressed unconscious—the fear of women, blacks, radicals, the working class and the colonized.'[13]

Following Marxist theory on class, Sumner argued that in any society dominant groups, i.e. in terms of class, gender and race, will inevitably seek to maintain their

---

[10] A. Amatrudo, *Criminology and Political Theory* (London and Los Angeles: Sage Publications, 2009).
[11] Sumner, *Censure, Politics and Criminal Justice* (cited in n.9), 23–6.
[12] Sumner, *Censure, Politics and Criminal Justice* (cited in n.9), 26.
[13] C. Sumner, *The Sociology of Deviance: an Obituary* (Buckingham: Open University Press, 1994), 310.

control through the 'capacity to assert its censures in the legal and moral discourses of the day'.[14] He argued that this involves not only the courts and police authorities but also the mass media and that it is primarily achieved through legal language. A process is set in motion which supports the discourses and practices of the state against any dissenting voices. Censures are more than labels and should be seen as 'categories of denunciation or abuse lodged within very complex, historically loaded practical conflicts and moral debates'.[15]

Sumner's theory of social censures is reliant upon earlier criminological and sociological work relating to ideology and cultural studies, notably *Policing the Crisis*, which suggested that the censure of black mugging which was expressed in the press and media and supported by the police, at the time, had no real evidential basis; but instead was the result of the political situation, then existing, and the police's focus upon blacks in the inner cities. Hall et al. suggested that the censure of blacks was, at root, an ideological phenomenon rather than a criminal justice problem per se.[16] Hall et al., like Sumner, saw the black mugger as a scapegoat for wider social and economic failures. The attention that black mugging received was no more than a deflection away from a crisis in hegemony. Sumner was concerned that scholars had both taken deviance and law-breaking to be a largely unproblematic term and overlooked the lack of consensus surrounding it. In fact, Sumner argued that deviance was being read off as a *deviation* from a dominant moral code; in other words deviance was merely a deviation from a social convention. Sumner argued that concepts of crime, deviance, and difference not only were conflated but were radically subjective terms rather than scientific categories and not up to the task of critical analysis.[17]

For Sumner, the sociology of deviance was progressive in that it focused attention away from issues of degeneracy and towards concerns around social regulation. He argued that: 'crime and deviance cannot be disentangled from the social facts of collective life' and that criminologists ought to realize the sheer complexity of the social world before venturing further in theoretical terms.[18] He suggests that 'social censures combine with forms of power and economy to provide distinct and important features of practices of domination and regulation'.[19] Sumner gives us reasons to question the censures we commonly use and to ask questions about their origin and purpose. He points us away from the immediate issues surrounding crime and towards a contextualized analysis of crime and criminalization which focused upon the role of censures; as with the analysis of Hall et al., Sumner sees censures being generated through the media in a fashion which combines with news coverage to dramatically focus moments of crisis, usually political, into a call for a more authoritarian state.

It is important to underscore the fact that most media stories about crime tend to be of a traditional cops and robbers type and the white collar criminal is largely ignored. Crime is most usually portrayed as a problem associated with the working classes and it is, moreover, usually an urban phenomenon. Following Sumner, we might ask why white collar crime is largely underrepresented in the media. The views that most people have about crime, about law and order, and about the processes of our criminal justice

---

[14] Sumner, *Censure, Politics and Criminal Justice* (cited in n.9), 27.
[15] Sumner, *Censure, Politics and Criminal Justice* (cited in n.9), 28.
[16] S. Hall, C. Critcher, T. Jefferson, J. Clarke, and B. Roberts, *Policing the Crisis* (London: Palgrave Macmillan, 1978).
[17] Sumner, *The Sociology of Deviance: an Obituary* (cited in n.13), 309–12.
[18] C. Sumner, 'The Social Nature of Crime and Deviance' in *The Blackwell Companion to Criminology* (Oxford: Blackwell, 2004), 29.
[19] Sumner, *Censure, Politics and Criminal Justice* (cited in n.9), 35.

system are garnered piecemeal through consuming various media, over time. The result of all that, of course, is that the censures we generally employ are not criticized, nor are the social conditions that gave rise to them.

In revisiting Sumner we can see how the entire language game itself is socially and politically conditioned, and contextualized, and that our language is, to some extent, always and *necessarily* polluted. As Sumner has argued: 'Now if criming cases is a very active, creative, process involving some social and legal skill, and much awareness of what magistrates and judges will accept, then presumably the fact that cases are crimed in a highly patterned and predictable way, leaving the world's prisons full of poor people, is hardly an accident.'[20]

2. Basil Bernstein: language and socialization

It will be useful for our later discussion to revisit Basil Bernstein's classic 1970 essay on cultural transmission, *Social Class, Language and Socialisation*, since it makes a number of points that bear upon the nature of the way people come to understand their world, and do so through language, which usefully bears upon media representations of the law, in its many guises. Bernstein looked back to Durkheim in terms of his analysis of the relationship between the classification and frames of symbolic order and the structuring of experience in seeing how that can lead to the 'pathological structuring of experience', i.e. a disjunction between the real and the represented.

Bernstein further tells us that the more commonality there is between persons the more likely that their language will take a specific form; in other words, that a narrower set of social relations narrows the likely range of meanings, since language is enacted against a backdrop of common assumptions, common history, common interests and that 'the unspoken assumptions underlying the relationship are not available to those outside the relationship'.[21] Bernstein here echoes Durkheim's distinction between mechanical and organic solidarity, as set out in *The Division of Labour in Society*. This is useful if one conceives of the media in these terms and re-conceives the issue of what we might call the *boundary maintenance* of the value system. The media is typically our major source of information and we can all understand its power to broaden horizons, but also its ability to narrow, or constrain, our values through its output and production values. In short, we can re-apply Bernstein's notions of boundary maintenance and substitute legitimating authority for class. In doing this we see the media as one of Bernstein's socializing agencies; and as he argued in terms of education: 'For the schools are predicated upon elaborated code and its system of social relationships. Although an elaborated code does not entail any specific value system, the value system of the middle class penetrates the texture of the very learning context itself.'[22] So as pupils imbibe the values of their school, so do viewers, readers, and listeners imbibe the values of whatever media production they are currently consuming.

3. Victims

The issue of value consumption through the media is well illustrated in the recent work of Rentschler which has shown the ways in which victims are portrayed in the news media as 'a class of citizens without rights' and who are, in turn, defended by a new class

---

[20] Sumner, *The Sociology of Deviance: an Obituary* (cited in n.13), 219.
[21] B. Bernstein, *Class, Codes and Control* (London: Routledge & Kegan Paul, 1970), 137.
[22] Bernstein, *Class, Codes and Control* (cited in n.21), 186.

of victim's rights *champions*.[23] She relates how a victim's rights discourse has come to pervade media production and contemporary journalistic practice and the public's current understanding of the law in an unbalanced and very unhelpful way through the creation of *narratives* of legal processes, rather than elucidating any established legal principle, e.g. in relation to such issues as the proper attribution of culpability and guilt and the systematic playing down of defendants' rights in terms of judicial safeguards for accused persons in criminal cases. She argues that contemporary journalistic practice encourages 'the news industry to further invest in the coverage of crime by framing crime news as a form of narrative therapy for some victim's families'.[24] Moreover, she shows how the way in which a media rights lobby propels:

victim's rights *to* and *in* the media signifies that it seeks access to and participation in media-making on crime as part of the process of re-assessing a definition of crime as interpersonal battle between offenders and their vicarious victims, the families of killed victims. In this scenario, victim's rights advocates and journalists both function as reporters of socially constructed knowledge and editors of the documentary realities of crime from the perspective of victim's rights.

While law enforcement and the court system have long been the preferred sources for crime news and other non-fiction media programming the victim's rights movement encourages reporters, and victim advocates, to direct victims' rights discourse into the news media. They teach journalists to direct victim's rights discourse into the news media. They teach journalists how to identify with the grief, anguish, and other painful feelings expressed by crime-victim families in order to give the typical law-and-order character of news a therapeutic sheen through a re-orientation of the news interview context itself. They teach advocates how to translate victim's rights into strategic calls for victim-oriented news. And they teach us that calls for a more therapeutic and hospitable news environment for news victims can mean many things, one of which signifies the links between the news media's need for crime news and the political struggles for victim's rights.[25]

I think we see all too clearly here how a diet of victim-oriented news discourse can, over time, shape the *Weltanschauung* of persons away from the rational and usher in an over-retributive focus in the general population in its wake.[26]

4. Television

Harris set out the issue of what the public *learn* from the media about the law but, more importantly, he focused academic attention upon those elements which were genuinely misleading.[27] The most important of these was the erroneous promotion of a world more violent than it actually is; promoting a belief that criminals get away with the bulk of their crimes; giving a misleadingly high standard for police clear-up rates; misrepresenting the racial profile of known victims and failing to show the complexity of legal procedure, especially in relation to the organization of court cases.

American television has had a huge influence upon the popular understanding of law and lawyers and its format and style has usually preceded development in the UK, and globally. First aired in 1957, the definitive portrayal of a lawyer on television is

---

[23] C. Rentschler, 'Victims' Rights and the Struggle over Crime in the Media' (2007) 31 *Canadian Journal of Communication* 219.
[24] Rentschler, 'Victims' Rights and the Struggle over Crime in the Media' (cited in n.23), 219.
[25] Rentschler, 'Victims' Rights and the Struggle over Crime in the Media' (cited in n.23), 235–6.
[26] M. Dubber, *Victims in the War on Crime: the Use and Abuse of Victim's Rights* (New York: New York University Press, 2002).
[27] D. Harris, 'The Appearance of Justice: Court TV, Conventional Television, and Public Understanding of the Criminal Justice System' (1993) 35 *Arizona Law Review* 785–837.

Perry Mason. The lead character was the virtuous in every way, kind-hearted, intelligent, urbane, and moral.[28] He would see above the humble lives of his clients in a never-ending search for truth. His cross-examination skills were impeccable, and Mason would get witnesses to break down and confess. Macaulay relates:

> Mason doesn't get his client acquitted by showing the prosecutor failed to carry the burden of proof. Instead, he proves his client's innocence by exposing the real killer. Surprise witnesses appear at the last minute, just before it is too late. After Mason's cross-examination, prosecution witnesses break down on the stand. As far as we can tell, Mason has never represented a guilty client or engaged in plea bargaining.[29]

In short, *Perry Mason* was the personification of all that was good about (American) legal practice; indeed in justice itself.[30]

A little later *The Fugitive* showed another side to the legal process. The plot involved a doctor, Richard Kimble, who was falsely accused of the murder of his wife. Kimble had escaped execution and become an outlaw intent on clearing his good name. It was a radical take on the law which seemed to rest on two premises, (1) that the innocent will finally prevail and (2) that the legal system needs to be guided by engaged citizens. The programme sought to actively involve viewers in Kimble's quest for justice.

Latterly, law and lawyers were, perhaps, most successfully captured in recent times with the series *L.A. Law*, which was first aired in 1986. *L.A. Law* was novel in that it was set in a leading law firm amid the affluence of 1980s America. The lawyers were all graduates of leading American Ivy League Law Schools—they wore expensive clothes, drove expensive cars, and lived in expensive houses. Their affluence was the result of their superior education, hard work, and ability, though they possessed personal character flaws too.[31] It also tended to make the work of lawyers seem more interesting than it often is by neglecting to show the more mundane aspects of legal preparation, e.g. trawling through case files and statutes, drafting letters, and so on.[32] *L.A Law* did claim to be concerned with the ethical life of lawyers and the ability of lawyers to sustain a moral professional life in the face of a legal system which was, in part, corrupted by rich and powerful individuals and corporations.[33] *L.A. Law*, even though a popular drama, did raise many real-world concerns about the ethical status of lawyers and the neutrality of the law. It is worthwhile looking at Gillers' analysis since he makes three cogent points from the perspective of a professor of law and practising attorney. Gillers' first point is that the role of lawyers is over-emphasized in *L.A. Law* in that it 'inaccurately represents the kinds of legal issues lawyers routinely address, especially lawyers in private practice'.[34] He argues that this represents a gross disjunction between how the public understand law and the legal profession and how practitioners think about their profession and about law itself. In making *L.A. Law* a successful television show, actual legal considerations will always be secondary in the production process to those of entertainment. Moreover, it is absurd to maintain that an hour of television could ever deal properly

---

[28] B. Kitei, 'The Mass Appeal of The Practice and Ally McBeal: An In-Depth Analysis of the Impact of these Television Shows on the Public's Perception of Attorneys' (1999) 7 UCLA *Entertainment Review* 169–87.

[29] S. Macaulay, 'Images of Law in Everyday Life' (1987) 21 *Law and Society Review* 198.

[30] Mezey and Niles, 'Screening the Law' (cited in n.4), 92–186.

[31] Friedman, 'Popular Legal Culture' (cited in n.1), 1579–1606.

[32] S. Gillers, 'Taking *L.A law* More Seriously' (1989) 98 *Yale Law Journal* 1607–24.

[33] W. Simon, 'Moral Luck: Legal Ethics in Popular Culture' (2001) 101 *Columbia Law Review* 428–32.

[34] Gillers, 'Taking *L.A law* More Seriously' (cited in n.32), 1607–8.

with the ambiguity and complexity of issues concerned. Gillers' second point is that *L.A. Law* does not accurately recognize or describe the ethical issues which lawyers typically face. Here Gillers acquits *L.A. Law* a little better but argues that: 'As with legal issues, the immediate ethical problems are answered because they must be, but the larger conflicts they signify are unresolved.'[35] In other words the oversimplification demanded by television is itself a distorting factor: moreover, the audience has no legal training and so largely sees the programme in terms of drama, rather than legal principle and procedure. Thirdly, Gillers points out how the work of lawyers is exaggerated and conceals the bulk of their preparation work. He shows how *L.A. Law* merely uses the law plot to tell a story, not to illuminate legal principle and procedure. He states that '*L.A. Law* makes the lawyer-storyteller, a character.'[36]

The points Gillers makes, though focused on *L.A. Law*, are applicable to the law firm genre in contemporary television in general. These reservations about the efficacy of the law became the focus of *The Practice*, which often showed its protagonists losing in court, corrupt lawyers, and a legal system in which justice does not always prevail. *The Practice* was, though, usually characterized by its characters' love of the highest ideals of the legal profession. As Mezey and Niles have argued, 'our discomfort with the existence of the morally ambiguous criminal defence attorney was assuaged by her important role in the criminal justice system, which...for all its imperfections, is mostly effective, just, and superior to the imaginable alternatives'.[37] All the lawyers in *The Practice* were streetwise and aware that deals had to be made in their professional lives; but there were definite limits to such ethical gymnastics; after all the show was made by corporate America, as Kitei has detailed.[38]

What is certain about contemporary American television portrayals of law and lawyers is that they invariably still hold to some attenuated version of *Perry Mason*; to a belief in the goodness of justice and the righteousness of a good case. Money, class, race, gender are not an obstacle to the good case winning through. American television supplies a constant stream of characters motivated by a dogged faith in the legal process. The concession to the modern world lies in its characters being more nuanced than those of yesteryear, and in the fact that the issues with which they deal are more complex too. Macaulay has argued that whilst such shows illustrate some aspects of the legal system they seldom give an accurate view of how the system typically works; nor even do they give a clue as to what happens rarely, and what typically.[39]

Ultimately, however, the way law is portrayed on American television says something about the nature of the America, it is often positivistic and naive.[40] Moreover, it may well do a disservice to justice in that it could be argued that it increases subjectivity toward the notion of culpability, in a public who are also all potential jurors.[41] More worrying still, as Stark has shown, is the very misleading conception of crime that the public derives from television, for example the over-representation of murder cases in terms of their comparatively rare occurrence in reality.[42] It also tends to see hard-fought-for

[35] Gillers, 'Taking *L.A law* More Seriously' (cited in n.32), 1618.
[36] Gillers, 'Taking *L.A law* More Seriously' (cited in n.32), 1618–20.
[37] Mezey and Niles, 'Screening the Law' (cited in n.4), 127.
[38] Kitei, 'The Mass Appeal of The Practice and Ally McBeal' (cited in n.28).
[39] Macaulay, 'Images of Law in Everyday Life' (cited in n.29), 210.
[40] P. Bergman and M. Asimow, *Reel Justice: the Courtroom Goes to the Movies*. (Kansas City: Andrews and McNeel, 1996).
[41] N. Finkel and J. Groscup, 'Crime Prototypes: Objective Versus Subjective Culpability, and a Common-sense Balance' (1997) 21 *Law and Human Behaviour* 209–30.
[42] S. Stark, 'Perry Mason meets Sonny Crockett: the History of Lawyers and the Police as Television Heroes' (1987) 42 *University of Miami Law Review* 229–82.

legal safeguards as obstacles to justice; in the American example, the *Miranda* warning.[43] The American crime drama is overwhelmingly reactionary and at the same time seems to posit that criminals tend to get their comeuppance.[44] What has been argued in the British context also serves as a general point in the American case regarding media portrayals of criminal justice: 'Even if the system changed its methods, in the public and media culture, criminal justice is still often understood as a spectacular, highly emotionally charged, drama of retribution.'[45]

There has been a great deal of discussion concerning the so-called *CSI Effect* which amounts to a concern about the exaggerated usefulness of forensic evidence and the way jurors, notably in the USA, have come to demand incredibly high standards of proof; and how this has led to a raising of the proof required to obtain a conviction.[46] An early study had claimed there was no *CSI Effect* whatsoever and that there was no evidence to support such a thing; and that claims that there was merely pointed towards deeper insecurity about justice from within: 'the psyche of the public and members of the justice system'.[47] Later studies, however, have tended to support concerns that some form of *CSI Effect* is working itself out through the American criminal justice system. It has been shown that jurors that viewed *CSI* are increasingly hesitant to believe forensic evidence presented at a criminal trial.[48] Lawson has argued that the *CSI Effect* has had a major impact in the 'realm of warping, skewing, and manipulating the realities of evidence in a way that threatens the accuracy of the verdict and the legitimacy of the criminal justice system'.[49] Lawson's major point is that:

[T]he danger that the *CSI* infection presents is not that jurors expect more forensic science, but rather that fictional entertainment will lead to misinformation about criminal investigations, prosecutions, and forensic science.

The problem is not merely a television show. The greatest threat is the inappropriate application of fictional analysis in real life cases, which in some instances has induced erroneous conclusions of fact and faulty decisions. The criminal justice system relies on laypeople, ordinary citizens untrained in the law to consider the evidence presented to them in court as neutral outsiders... The crime novels, television shows, and films depicting crimes, criminal investigations and criminal prosecutions are altered purposely for entertainment purposes, causing the line between reality and fiction to be intentionally blurred by artists to make film, novel, or television show seem real, yet still entertaining. The artists' motivation is not malicious; instead from such sources [they] may trick viewers into believing they are trained to some degree to interpret the law and science.[50]

Moreover, as Thomas has recently argued in the *Yale Law Journal*, the reasonableness, and economic sense, of using exhaustive forensic techniques in police investigations and thereafter in criminal court cases is now something that prosecutors must very much take to heart; especially since there is a growing sense among some members of the legal

---

[43] R. Rogers, K. Harrison, D. Shuman, K. Sewell, and L. Hazelwood, 'An Analysis of Miranda Warnings: Comprehension and Coverage' (2007) 31 *Law and Human Behaviour* 177–92.

[44] Robson, 'Lawyers and the Legal System on TV' (cited in n.3), 333–62.

[45] A. Doyle and R. Ericson, 'Two Realities of Police Communication' in C. Sumner (ed.), *The Blackwell Companion to Criminology* (Oxford: Blackwell, 2004).

[46] T. Tyler, 'Viewing CSI and the Threshold of Guilt: Managing Truth and Justice in Reality and Fiction' (2006) 115 *Yale Law Journal* 1050–85.

[47] K. Podlas, 'The CSI Effect: Exposing the Media Myth' (2006) 16 *Fordham Intellectual Property, Media & Entertainment Law Journal* 465.

[48] N. Schweitzer and M. Saks, 'The CSI Effect: Popular Fiction about Forensic Science Affects the Public's Expectations about Real Forensic Science' (2007) 47 *Jurimetrics Journal* 357–64.

[49] T. Lawson, 'Before the Verdict and Beyond the Verdict: The CSI Infection within Modern Jury Trials' (2009) 41 *Loyola University Chicago Law Journal* 169.

[50] Lawson, 'Before the Verdict and Beyond the Verdict' (cited in n.49), 171.

profession that jurors are more taken with forensics than with the practice and processes of the law.[51]

In terms of the use of language, Cole and Dioso-Villa have made the case that the whole *CSI Effect* debate is at another level the working out of a battle between two competing modes of language, the legal and the scientific. They point to:

[the] rising authority and prestige of science in a modern society. Science is popularly associated with such positive values as truth, certainty, goodness, enlightenment, progress, and so on... The *CSI Effect* would seem to resonate with anxieties about using law too little, and increasingly abrogating its truth-producing function to science... the *CSI Effect* would seem to give voice to fears of what we might call *hyperscientia*—too much science.[52]

In short, the *CSI Effect*, and the attention it has received from American legal scholars, represents the clearest case of a link between the consumption of television programming (and therefore language) and definite *effects* on the operation of the law, in *real-world* contexts.

A large number of the main American programmes have found their way on to British television screens. However, there is a separate genre of British, usually English, television dealing with law and lawyers, aside from the enormous number of cops and robbers shows. This English genre largely follows the American formula, though with an eye on the local production context and with its own set of foibles (i.e. eccentric characters, such as Judge John Deed, Kavanagh QC, Morse, and Rumpole of the Bailey) and conceits.[53] We should note here that in broad terms two main forms of programming are being consumed in the UK, i.e. American *and* English. The same is not true, or not to anything like the same extent, in the USA, though the accuracy of the specific legal processes represented may not matter to that audience as much as the signifiers of justice, like the clothes worn by the lawyers, the court architecture, etc.[54]

Indeed, the issue may not be so much to do with the media's ability, or otherwise, to impart *truth* concerning the law, as to do with its capacity to develop a legal consciousness and raise the level of debate generally. There may be no simple, or readily quantifiable, effects to measure at all; just an immeasurable heightening of awareness. What we might conclude, in the English example, is that the law is generally represented as a struggle for justice, which brings us back to the themes raised by Stuart Hall et al. and Colin Sumner, for as Robson has recently commented:

The justice agenda, though, dominates, TV lawyers challenge the malpractices of the system. A group of fighters for justice may legitimate the whole socio-economic system with their apparent demonstration that day in, day out, the individual has his or her day in court... The focus on the individual and the local hides what is happening at a structural level. The poor are not being enfranchised through court actions. Systemic institutional racism is not declining through the legal process. Solutions to the abuse of women are emerging from extra-legal organisations and actions like the refuge movement. Trusting in the legal system's remedies as shown on screen is comforting but involves a misplacing of trust.[55]

---

[51] A. Thomas, 'The CSI Effect: Fact or Fiction' (2006) 115 *Yale Law Journal* 70–2.
[52] S. Cole and R. Dioso-Villa, 'Investigating the "CSI Effect" Effect: Media and Litigation Crisis in Criminal Law' (2009) 61 *Stanford Law Review* 1373.
[53] Robson, 'Lawyers and the Legal System on TV' (cited in n.3), 343.
[54] S. Machura and S. Ulbrich, 'Globalizing the Hollywood Courtroom Drama' (2001) 28 *Journal of Law and Society* 117–32.
[55] Robson, 'Lawyers and the Legal System on TV' (cited in n.3), 355–6.

5. Supporting the status quo: policing and the courts

Doyle and Ericson analysed the ways in which the police communicate with the news media and try to set the news agenda themselves. They showed how the police often over-emphasize their ability to undertake successful crime control for the purposes of legitimating their role and profile.[56] They follow Hall et al. in noting the police as *primary definers* of news events and how the media are in a structurally subordinate role to primary definers.[57] They show how there is a deal of consensus on the role of the police in media coverage of news; and how media reporting tends to be skewed towards coverage of violent offenders, and what Robert Reiner has called high-status offenders and victims, and in doing this there is a tendency to make the case for a more effective police force than currently exists.[58] They argue that media coverage of the police generally supports the pre-existing, and underlying, views about policing in terms of its relationship to such variables as age, class, gender, and race and its focus on violence, high-status victims, and the heroic successes of the police. In doing this that news coverage tends to: 'reinforce one system of meaning about crime which is (already) prominent in public culture'.[59] The nature, and extent, of such news coverage tends to 'reinforce the punitive current in public media, and political discourse. The current feeds back into the system itself, fuelling alternative tendencies towards more expressive and punitive forms of criminal justice. It also justifies the elaboration of the surveillance-oriented risk-communication systems that characterize the everyday world of police work.'[60]

If we shift away from news coverage of the police to drama we see a set of processes similar to those Doyle and Ericson have discussed. Regina Rauxloh has shown how popular notions about crime are fed back to an audience, rather than challenged. Her 2005 study showed that, whatever the form of the society analysed, in this case democratic West Germany or communist East Germany, there is a general tendency to a conservative production focus. In her forensic study of the representation of policing on television in East and West Germany the police, and professionals in the wider criminal justice system, are ultimately portrayed as upholding, and reinforcing, an idealized notion of the prosecutorial process and an uncritical 'image of state and society'.[61] Her analysis shows that, although television drama can take a critical stance towards the police and the wider prosecutorial process, it rarely does so. It tends to reflect the public's pre-existing notions and rarely, if ever, looks at broader issues of criminalization.[62] In terms of the police's relationship with the prosecutorial authorities her study showed that these were unrealistic and that issues such as 'arraignments, pre-trial hearings, jury selection and plea-bargaining are rarely shown'.[63]

The portrayal of famous trials, often through reconstructed drama, has been something that BBC Radio has long since specialized in. Suzanne Shale undertook a major critical study of this genre in relation to the public understanding of law.[64] Her study

---

[56] Doyle and Ericson, 'Two Realities of Police Communication' (cited in n.45), 472.
[57] Hall et al., *Policing the Crisis* (cited in n.16), 59.
[58] R. Reiner, *The Politics of the Police* (Oxford: Oxford University Press, 2010).
[59] Doyle and Ericson, 'Two Realities of Police Communication' (cited in n.45), 474.
[60] Doyle and Ericson, 'Two Realities of Police Communication' (cited in n.45), 482.
[61] R. Rauxloh, 'Goodies and Baddies: the Presentation of German Police and Criminals in East and West Television Drama' (2005) 6 *German Law Journal* 1000.
[62] Rauxloh, 'Goodies and Baddies' (cited in n.61), 981.
[63] Rauxloh, 'Goodies and Baddies' (cited in n.61), 990.
[64] S. Shale, 'Listening to the Law: Famous Trials on BBC Radio, 1934–1969' (1996) 59 *Modern Law Review* 813–44.

showed that, perhaps inevitably, the portrayals of trials on BBC Radio were coloured by the medium that produced them. The values of the Corporation were present in all aspects of production, including selection and editing. Moreover, by concentrating on famous trials the producers presented a rather heroic view of the criminal justice system to a largely middle class audience; an audience which actively selects what it listens to. The whole enterprise did not so much elucidate legal principles as reproduce social conventions and popularly held ideas about the operation of the law. She argues that:

> The trial is a public ceremony and, in the contemporary world, the mass media determine the nature of the public for whom the ceremony is conducted. In conveying the message of the criminal trial, media do not passively represent an object to a public. On the contrary, if by legal process we mean all of the functions that law performs, the media are participants in the legal process in their role of reproducing the public ceremony... Whether or not we want to call famous trials broadcasts a form of law... they are indisputably part of something we should call popular legal culture: that constellation of attitudes, beliefs, knowledges, half-knowledges and flat misunderstandings about law that are by and large shared among members of a social group.
>
> The notion of a popular legal culture is perhaps undermined when we pose questions about the nature of the populus or social group which shares it.[65]

This is an interesting and important point to bear in mind: even if the radio production is *broad*casted it is nonetheless always received as a *narrow*cast.[66] In other words the audience for programmes is to a very large extent self-selecting. The audience for a BBC Radio broadcast on the trial process is necessarily a subset of the total listening population, which itself is made up of the aggregate number of listeners to a variety of programming.

6. Why does this matter?

The preceding discussion is not simply something that is of academic interest: it has very tangible social policy implications and affects the day-to-day workings of the criminal justice system. The issue is that regular members of the public ordinarily have no involvement in the legal process, though they all to a greater or lesser extent consume a version of it in the popular media. People tend to look, usually uncritically, to the media to furnish them with both information and entertainment, of a factual nature, about the law. The upshot of this process is that, as Gies has argued, the public's understanding of law is deeply enigmatic.[67]

On the one hand the public are increasingly aware of how to access legal services and of the content of laws through accessing the Internet and television, and on the other hand they often have a reductive, and non-technical, view of what law actually is. Moreover, Gies shows how this is mirrored in the types of material the public generally access online, which is often simplified, generic, and of little practical use in specific cases.[68] The point is that understanding law is a rather complicated enterprise which can be undertaken at a number of levels. There may be nothing false or directly misleading in any one single broadcast or piece of information discovered on the Internet but such a magpie treatment of how legal information is accumulated will always fall short of a

---

[65] Shale, 'Listening to the Law' (cited in n.64), 843–4.
[66] C. Priestman, 'Narrowcasting and the dream of radio's great global conversation' (2004) 2 *Radio Journal* 77–88.
[67] L. Gies, *Law and the Media: The Future of an Uneasy Relationship* (London: Routledge-Cavendish, 2008), 5–7.
[68] Gies, *Law and the Media* (cited in n.67), 74–91.

thorough understanding; and the last word probably rests with the legal experts anyway. Gies argues that the best way to conceive of this process is to understand that there is a real and ongoing battle at play between the law and the media's version of it and that currently the media's account of law is, perhaps unavoidably, dominant.[69]

The sociologist Gerrard Delanty put it well when he wrote that: 'contemporary society involves the proliferation of second order observations for direct observation... We are approaching a society that in perpetually experimenting with forms of communication is making the form of communication central to the experience of social content: content has become form.'[70] This pithily situates the state of play vis-à-vis the popular understanding of law through consumed media. In drawing such a comparison, however, we should note how content is in the subordinate position. Smith and Natalier have developed this sociological notion in their work and have formulated a list of areas of major concern in relation to this deficit between the consumed form and actual content. In relation to television depictions of criminal law these are the promotion of unrealistically high standards for police and forensic science specialists, in terms of their ability to assist the successful prosecution of crime; the misrepresentation of the racial basis of contemporary crime; and the reduction of the legal process to a system of formal rules. In practice they side with Friedman in seeing that people understand law in terms of how it is represented, rather than how it actually is.[71] Moreover, moving on from Friedman's insight we can see that the whole system of production, values, and the sociological enterprise of representing legal matters goes uncontested.

7. Conclusion

What we can conclude from this survey of the topic is that there has been an increase in the depiction of law and legal issues (notably of crime) in the media and that this is, in turn, consumed. What we have not established is whether this has been an empowering development or not. It would be difficult to argue that through watching their television screens and reading newspapers the bulk of people are better informed about legal principles and processes, though there is evidence that this is a generally held perception. What people may be consuming is a simulacrum of the law, as represented to them, not the law as it is. Are the public better informed about the law? They may be, but if they are then they are only in the nursery class. Law proliferates and its jurisprudence is elaborate and its procedure a matter of technical knowledge.

So if there is a heightened folk understanding of law it is at a fairly basic level. Bernstein's socio-linguistic analysis of the relationship between the classification and frames of symbolic order and the structuring of experience and how this can lead to the 'pathological structuring of experience' is very elucidating here. Bernstein argues that when there is more commonality between persons it is more likely that their language will take a specific form. In other words, that a narrow set of social relations also narrows the likely range of meanings available, since language is enacted against a backdrop of common assumptions, common history, common interests.

---

[69] Gies, *Law and the Media* (cited in n.67), 130.
[70] G. Delanty, *Modernity and Postmodernity: Knowledge, Power and the Self* (London: Sage Publications, 2000).
[71] P. Smith and K. Natalier, *Understanding Criminal Justice: Sociological Perspectives* (London: Sage Publications, 2005), 159–63.

Our current media therefore have definite hegemonic capacity and an ability to pacify. The citizenry may be falsely proud of their legal and specialist knowledge, garnered through consumption of contemporary media. The effects may be far from positive and, as noted earlier in relation to the so-called *CSI Effect*, it can result in a: 'realm of warping, skewing, and manipulating the realities of evidence in a way that threatens the accuracy of the verdict and the legitimacy of the criminal justice system.'[72] The entire process of media production can be hijacked, as in the case of victim's rights.[73] The public can only consume that which is front of them. The meta-analysis given by Colin Sumner and Stuart Hall sees censures being generated through the media in a fashion which combines with news coverage to focus moments of crisis into calls for more authoritarian state measures, as was the case for example in the Miners Strike in 1984–5.[74] Most media stories about crime tend to be of a traditional cops and robbers type and the white collar criminal is largely ignored. Crime in the media is typically portrayed as a problem associated with the urban working class. White collar crime especially is largely ignored by the media. There is never any criticism of the systems of production and the underlying socio-economic system that gave rise to it.

---

[72] Lawson, 'Before the Verdict and Beyond the Verdict' (cited in n.49), 169.
[73] Rentschler, 'Victims' Rights and the Struggle over Crime in the Media' (cited in n.23), 235–6.
[74] B. Fine and R. Millar (eds), *Policing the Miners' Strike* (London: Lawrence and Wishart, 1985).

24

(Language + Law)^2 = ?

Catrin Fflur Huws

1. Introduction

Legal texts provide a fascinating subject for the study of language. The study of two interconnected legal systems and two conceptions of the term language (as a national or cultural identifier as well as one's style of expression) brings a new dimension to this sphere of research. The nature of the devolution settlement to Wales means that Wales is now governed by a dual legal system—there has been a partial devolution of primary legislative powers to the National Assembly for Wales but extensive legislative competence remains with Westminster. Furthermore, the National Assembly for Wales has an obligation to enact legislation bilingually, with both texts having equal standing. There is therefore a linguistic as well as a legal duality. In this article, the aim is to explain the issues and challenges this situation creates, and to illustrate and evaluate the differences that exist between Welsh Assembly Measures and Acts, and Acts of the Westminster Parliament.

2. Background

Following a referendum in 1997, the National Assembly for Wales was created. The legislative system that was devised under the Government of Wales Act 1998 was one whereby the National Assembly could enact subordinate legislation on specific matters relating to Wales (s.22). The powers of the National Assembly for Wales were extended when the Government of Wales Act 2006 came into force, as s.94(1) of this Act allowed the National Assembly to pass Measures that were equivalent to primary legislation on matters listed within Sch.5 Pt 1, provided that an Order in Council was made either conferring (s.58(1)(b)) or transferring (s.58(1)(a)) legislative functions to the Welsh Ministers, the First Minister, or the Counsel General.

As a result of a further referendum in 2011, the Government of Wales Act 2006 Pt 4 came into force, which allows the National Assembly for Wales to pass primary legislation (known as Acts of the National Assembly) on the 20 matters listed in Sch.7 to the 2006 Act without any intervention from Westminster. At the time of writing, therefore, the National Assembly for Wales is able to legislate on some matters completely independently from Westminster.

2.1. Implications

This situation has a number of complex ramifications. There is considerable scope for overlap between matters that remain within Westminster's jurisdiction, and matters that fall within the jurisdiction of National Assembly for Wales. Future legislation on such issues is therefore likely to require collaboration between the Westminster Parliament and the National Assembly for Wales, in order to ensure consistency as regards both the form and content of the laws.

This need for consistency is also important because the governing law on a specific matter is likely to refer to Acts of both the National Assembly for Wales and the Westminster Parliament. For example, the current law on the legal status of the Welsh language is governed both by Westminster statutes and by Welsh Assembly Measures. The Welsh Language Act 1993 ('the 1993 Act') and to a lesser extent the Government of Wales Act 2006, along with legislation on specific areas such as education and broadcasting, are examples of legislation from Westminster that relate to the Welsh language. However, these laws operate alongside the Welsh Language (Wales) Measure 2011 ('the Measure'), a Measure of the National Assembly for Wales. There is necessarily an interrelationship between these laws and accordingly an awareness of the meaning each legislature imports into the laws it enacts is required.

While devolved matters or partly devolved matters may necessitate a consistency of meaning in texts produced by two legislatures, a further issue to consider is the fact that law uses similar terminology across a range of subject areas, with the usage sometimes being consistent, and at other times a term may have a different meaning depending on its context. For example, Mattila explains that the term civil law has three meanings in English:

> sometimes the term still refers to Roman law. In comparative law, it denotes continental law (strongly influenced by Roman law) in relation to classification of legal orders. Finally, the term refers to private law... It should be emphasised that the frontiers of 'civil law' are not necessarily quite the same from country to country. In Germany... [it] generally designates the law applied in relations between private individuals... In other countries it is understood more narrowly. For example commercial law in France is not included in civil law. (Mattila 2006: 110)

Therefore, although the drafting of a devolved issue may adopt terminology that is consistent with earlier Westminster statutes that are either being consolidated or repealed, or with Westminster statutes that will exist alongside Acts of the National Assembly for Wales, a further implication of devolution will be to consider the extent to which the laws of Wales map on to non-devolved areas of law. An example of this may be seen in the context of the term 'person'. In the Measure the term 'person' is used in such a way in s.33 that its apparent meaning (with reference to Schs 5–8) includes corporate persons in the form of public bodies, institutions, and utility providers. Nevertheless, the term person is not always narrowly defined, as Lord Wilberforce explains in *National & Grindlays Bank Ltd v Kentiles Ltd* [1966] 1 WLR 348.

Thirdly, the National Assembly for Wales has an obligation to legislate bilingually (Government of Wales Act 2006 s.111(5)), with both versions of the text having equal standing (Government of Wales Act 2006 s.156). The drafting, scrutiny, and interpretation of legislation by the courts must therefore have regard to both versions of the text. Necessarily, this will affect how the English version of texts prepared by the National Assembly for Wales will be constructed and interpreted, and it is likely to be a significant factor in the diversification between the legislative styles of Wales and Westminster, as Bush explains:

> What has happened here is that the need to express in Welsh the concept which 'shall' conveys in English has highlighted the fact that it can mean two different things; one a requirement that something be done and the other a declaration of legal effect. In Welsh these are expressed in quite

different ways to one another, and it was a natural development to use different expressions in English also, in order to convey the two different meanings thereby eliminating ambiguity from both texts. (Bush, 2004: 149)

Fourthly, a new legislature also represents an opportunity to cast aside some of the working practices that have become hardened through habit. The law is often criticized for being unnecessarily technical and obtuse (Mattila 2006: 3). There is scope therefore within a newer legislative system to move away from such habits of thought. The need to enact legislation bilingually and the different mechanisms for legislative scrutiny between Wales and Westminster are likely to be significant contributing factors in exacerbating this divergence and facilitating a move towards greater clarity in the structure and wording of legislation.

A further implication of devolution is the nature of the interrelationship between Parliament and the courts. Before 1999, the jurisdiction could be explained comparatively simply, at least as far as the requirements of this article demand. The Westminster Parliament made laws for England and Wales as a jurisdiction, and the law courts of England and Wales interpreted and applied those laws. Since 1999, and more specifically since 2011, there are two legislatures within the one jurisdiction. The draftspersons in the National Assembly for Wales must therefore take into account the need for its laws to map on to an existing forensic lexicon.

Such issues arise because of devolution and the specific form of devolution that applies to Wales. Nevertheless other, more generic factors also affect the process and the form of legislation. The cultural significance of the text, its purported readership, and the social and political context of its enactment may all affect the process of creating a new Act and its final form. What follows, therefore, is an exploration of how these aspects have influenced a specific legal text, and this is followed by a consideration of how this context will evolve in the future.

3. Case study

At the time of writing, the most recent legislation passed by the National Assembly for Wales is the Welsh Language Measure 2011. In order to illustrate the similarities and differences between the approaches of Wales and Westminster to legislative drafting, this part of the article will compare the Measure with its predecessor, the 1993 Act, according to the criteria explained in the preceding section. In addition to the advantage of its currency in terms of National Assembly drafting practice, another advantage of using this area of law as a subject of comparison is that it is an area that has been the subject of legislation from both Wales and Westminster; furthermore, it is an area of law where it is likely that both language versions of the text will be referred to with equal frequency.

3.1. The content of the two laws

a. The Welsh Language Act 1993

The 1993 Act was enacted with a view to ensuring that (according to its Long Title) 'in the conduct of public business and the administration of justice in Wales the English and Welsh languages should be treated on a basis of equality'. In order to achieve this objective, s.1 of the Act established a Welsh Language Board whose function is facilitating and promoting the use of the Welsh language and required public bodies to prepare schemes under s.5 explaining how they will give effect to the principle that Welsh and English are to be treated on a basis of equality. The 1993 Act also made miscellaneous provisions such as reiterating the right to speak Welsh in legal proceedings (s.22), and allowing Welsh forms, documents, and the titles of charities, companies, and public bodies to be recognized as valid (ss.25–33).

b. The Welsh Language Measure 2011

Section 1 of the Measure gives Welsh official status in Wales and establishes a Welsh Language Commissioner (s.2) and Tribunal (s.120). The Measure requires the Welsh Ministers to set standards regarding the expected levels of Welsh language provision (s.26). The Act also makes provision concerning the freedom to use Welsh and places restrictions on interferences with that freedom (s.113).

3.2. Overlapping jurisdiction

The relationship between the 1993 Act and the Measure is an example of Westminster and Wales having an overlapping jurisdiction. Responsibility for the Welsh language is a matter that has been devolved to the National Assembly for Wales under the Government of Wales Acts 1998 (Sch.2 para.18) and 2006 (Sch.7 para.20), with the result that it may be the subject of legislation by the National Assembly for Wales. However, according to s.107(5), the Government of Wales Act 2006 does not preclude the Westminster Parliament from legislating in relation to the Welsh language, and Sch.1 Pt 1 para.20 provides that Westminster must legislate in relation to the Welsh language in legal proceedings as this is an issue that has not been devolved. Therefore it is possible that an obligation could be imposed by Westminster as regards the use of Welsh in legal proceedings, but that a complaint about an interference with the right to speak Welsh is investigated under the Measure. A specific example may arise in connection with communication from and to Welsh-speaking prisoners, who would naturally communicate with others in Welsh but whose communications may be translated for the purposes of monitoring (Ministry of Justice 2011). As a matter relating to the Welsh language in the legal system this is something that would be regulated by Westminster, but may be actionable under the Measure as an interference with the freedom to communicate in Welsh.

Equally, the official status conferred upon the Welsh language may affect areas that have not been devolved to Wales. If Welsh has official status as s.1 of the Measure provides, then it follows that official warnings and forms of words, for example, would not be official unless provided in Welsh as well as English. If on the other hand, official status only relates to devolved areas, and does not affect the status of Welsh in other circumstances where its situation is required to be official, then there is considerable potential for Westminster law-making to undermine the impact of the law made in Wales.

Jones, Turnbull, and Williams (Jones et al. 2005) also argue that the legislation that is stated as applying to England and Wales may be problematic. Hitherto, the term 'England and Wales' has defined a single jurisdictional entity—the 'and' connector is not intended to be interpreted both jointly and severally. Although it is foreseeable that an issue such as the Welsh language will be applicable solely in relation to Wales, other areas of law may specify their application to England and Wales. Yet, Acts of the National Assembly for Wales and Acts of the Westminster Parliament that apply solely in relation to England create a dichotomy. They apply to one location: 'England' or 'Wales' but are valid in the courts of both regions. This means that the National Assembly for Wales in some senses cannot repeal laws as they apply to England and Wales. Neither can the Westminster Parliament. If the National Assembly for Wales repeals an earlier Westminster law in relation to Wales, that law must, necessarily, continue to apply in relation to Wales because courts in Wales would have to adjudicate proceedings originating in England that apply the law as it still applies in England. The converse is also true. If Westminster repeals a law in relation to England, that law may still be valid in Wales. Therefore the courts in England, and specifically the higher courts of appeal, would have to continue to apply a law, even though it has been repealed. Consequently, the overlapping nature of Wales and Westminster as legislative and forensic jurisdiction, and the disparity between the jurisdictions in terms of legislating and adjudicating, are matters that may cause considerable uncertainty, and are likely to require further clarification.

3.3. Interconnectedness

Because the Measure does not repeal the 1993 Act in its entirety, the law on the legal status of the Welsh language requires reference to both laws. Consequently, this is something to which legal draftspersons within the National Assembly for Wales must have regard—in terms of its structure and terminology, the Measure must map on to the 1993 Act. In terms of its broad structure, the Measure does this, in that Pt 2 of the Measure (the Part that establishes the role of the Welsh Language Commissioner) fulfils a similar role to the 1993 Act Pt 1 (dealing with the establishment and functions of the Welsh Language Board), and Pts IV and V of the Measure (which address the establishment of standards) map on to Pt II of the 1993 Act (relating to the form and content of Welsh Language Schemes).

In terms of the more precise detail however, the interrelationship is not as crisply defined. First, it is clear from the foregoing discussion that the relevant parts of the Act do not correspond—Pt II of the Measure for example does not map on to Pt II of the 1993 Act.

A further difficulty with the interconnectedness of the Act and the Measure is that although the Measure refers to the obligations contained in the 1993 Act this is done in an imprecise way. Section 1(3) of the Measure refers to the right to speak Welsh in legal proceedings, but does not make specific reference to the statutory origins of this entitlement. The Measure does not therefore emphasize the extent of its interconnectedness with the 1993 Act—an issue that is further demonstrated by the fact that the Measure does not specifically include Her Majesty's Courts Service within the list of persons who may be required to comply with standards, even though bilingual service delivery is crucial if the right to speak Welsh in legal proceedings is to have any meaning, and even though Her Majesty's Courts Service has an existing Welsh Language Scheme as a result of the 1993 Act. Without any specific cross-referencing it may therefore become necessary to address what will be the nature of the inter-relationship of two laws that address the same subject matter. Although the issue may not necessarily be problematic in the specific context of the 1993 Act and the Measure, the overlap of these two laws does indicate the possible difficulties that may arise where legislation is interconnected.

3.4. Audience

One of the key differences between the two laws is their intended audience. The primary focus of the 1993 Act is the Welsh Language Board and public bodies. The function of the Act therefore is to define the Welsh Language Board's role and functions, and to explain the inter-relationship between the Welsh Language Board and public bodies as regards the form, content, and approval of Welsh Language Schemes and the implications for public bodies of non-compliance with the schemes.

With the exception of provisions aimed at companies and charities regarding the recognition of the Welsh form of the organization's name, only one section of the 1993 Act confers any entitlement on the individual citizen. This is s.22, which allows a 'party, witness or other person' to use the Welsh language in legal proceedings, provided that notice is given of one's intention to do so in proceedings conducted in courts other than magistrates' courts. However, this section is also the only section that is derived from earlier legislation—the wording is identical to the wording used in the Welsh Language Act 1967 s.1.

The Measure, by contrast, has a much broader audience. First, it is to be noted that more sections of the Measure confer rights and entitlements on individuals. Part 1 of the Act provides a 'constitutional' declaration that Welsh is the official language. Further, individual entitlements are contained in Pt 6 of the Act, which allows the individual a right of complaint if it is felt that another individual has interfered with their freedom to use Welsh. Section 111(1) provides:

> (1) An individual (P) may apply to the Commissioner for the Commissioner to investigate whether a person (D) has interfered with P's freedom to undertake a Welsh communication with another individual (R) (the 'alleged interference').

Although this section does not require organizations or public bodies to communicate with an individual in his or her language of choice and does not in fact go significantly beyond what has hitherto been protected under the European Convention of Human Rights and Fundamental Freedoms Art.8, it does envisage that it will address an individual's relationship with another individual as a matter of private law, as well as the individual's relationship with the state.

The Measure also imposes duties and responsibilities on a broader range of actors, namely the Welsh Language Commissioner, the Advisory Panel to the Welsh Language Commissioner, the Welsh Language Tribunal, and the Welsh Ministers, and public bodies and other bodies who have a duty to reach the standard required by the Welsh Ministers. One notable aspect of the Measure is therefore that its intended audience consists of a broader range of public sector executive, administrative, and judicial bodies, a number of which are created by the Measure itself.

Secondly, whereas the 1993 Act conferred executive power on the Welsh Language Board, the Measure requires a greater degree of involvement on the part of the Welsh Ministers in order for many of the provisions contained in the Measure to be effective. The 1993 Act may therefore be seen to adopt a more externalist approach by devolving the responsibility for the Welsh language primarily to the Welsh Language Board, albeit reserving for the Secretary of State for Wales the power to enact subordinate legislation. However, under the Act, the Government did not envisage retaining for itself extensive decision-making powers—or, more specifically, any significant obligations.

On the other hand, the Measure confers a greater measure of power on the Government itself. The Measure views the various roles and organizations as being largely functional, with the decision-making power being reserved to the Welsh Ministers or to the First Minister. This means that the Welsh language becomes more of a political issue than an administrative issue. This means that the Welsh language has become something that must demand the time of political decision-makers within the Welsh Government and that the standards imposed may be renegotiated with each successive government. This creates the risk of destabilizing the commitments made and of not allowing new ventures to embed in a way that encourages the development of services.

Although a broader range of obligations is created by the Measure as regards public bodies and private organizations, the Measure also offers a broader range of rights and entitlements to such bodies in terms of being able to respond and object to the obligations imposed upon them. Therefore, while the 1993 Act operated on an expectation that public bodies would accept their obligations to prepare Welsh Language Schemes, albeit with scope for public bodies to object to the time limits imposed upon them for doing so under s.8, the Measure creates a more dialogic system whereby the bodies that have obligations under the Measure have greater scope to complain about the acceptability of the requirements imposed upon them as is provided in ss.54 and 55. The right of appeal against the imposition of a standard under s.58 of the Measure means that persons who object to delivering services bilingually have greater scope to have those standards reduced or set aside completely. Consequently, this may result in the Commissioner adopting more defensive practices in terms of the requirements imposed in order to reduce the scope for objection, and that fewer obligations might be imposed than might have been anticipated by campaigners.

3.5. Terminology

Given the overlapping jurisdiction between Wales and Westminster as regards the Welsh language, consistent terminology might be anticipated. It is striking therefore that the terminology employed by the two laws contains marked differences.

One particularly noteworthy aspect is the frequency with which particular terms are used within the two laws. The term 'Welsh' is used far more frequently in the Measure than in the 1993 Act. This raises a number of important consequences. Firstly the 1993 Act refers to the Welsh language in conjunction with the English language and the status and obligations as regards the Welsh language are only defined in conjunction with the obligations as regards the English language. The Measure by contrast only makes provision as regards the Welsh language, and s.1(4) specifically provides that the Measure 'does not affect the status of the English language in Wales'. Nevertheless, by legislating on the status of the Welsh language, the status of the English language is necessarily affected. If for example the Welsh language has official status in Wales, then the lack of reference to the official status of English would suggest that it is no longer 'a language used in the business of government (legislative, executive, administrative and judicial) and in the performance of the various other functions of the state' (Zall and Stein 1990: 262). Furthermore, the standards of Welsh-medium provision applicable in relation to the policy-making (s.29), operational (s.30), promotional (s.31), and record-keeping (s.32) functions of persons with a duty to comply will necessarily be defined with reference to what is required in English. Accordingly, while the emphasis on Welsh may be a means of emphasizing the extent of the National Assembly's commitment to the Welsh language, while simultaneously not acting to the detriment of the English language, it is difficult to see how the Measure will operate in practice if the commitments made in relation to Welsh are not measured against the status and opportunities offered in English.

Secondly, whereas the 1993 Act characterizes its provisions as duties and rights, the Measure places greater emphasis on expressions of expectations. Provisions such as s.3 and s.22 of the 1993 Act confer a specific obligation:

> The Board shall have the function of promoting and facilitating the use of the Welsh language.

Or a specific right:

> In any legal proceedings in Wales the Welsh language may be spoken by any party, witness or other person who desires to use it.

Furthermore, in the 1993 Act the focus is on the outcome, rather than the means of achieving that outcome, as is seen in the two sections cited above. On the other hand, the Measure focuses on nebulous concepts such as 'working towards ensuring that the Welsh language is treated no less favourably than the English language' (s.1(3)), 'the validity of the use of the Welsh language' (s.1(2)(c), 'the promotion and facilitation of the use of the Welsh language' (s.1(2)(d)), and 'the freedom of persons wishing to use the Welsh language to do so with one another' (s.1)(2)(e)). Such statements are expressions of desire, and do not give rise either to specific obligations or to measurable outcomes. This lack of precision, as Dale (1977: 12) explains, means that the meaning and the purpose of the Act is shrouded in obscurity. If the Measure is to change behaviour, then the 'constitutional' guarantee of official status must be defined more precisely.

The third striking feature of the Measure is that similar concepts are introduced but not distinguished—for example the inquiry (s.7) and the investigation (ss.61 and 71). The differences between them are not explained and neither is the function of each process. Furthermore, it is noticeable that the Measure defines each process in terms of its exceptions. For example, s.7(1) allows the Welsh Language Commissioner to conduct inquiries into any matter relating to any of the Commissioner's functions. Nevertheless, there is greater specificity within this section with regard to when an inquiry would be inappropriate:

(3) Subsection (1) does not authorise the Commissioner to conduct an inquiry in a case where he or she
   a. may or must carry out a standards investigation under Chapter 8 of Part 4
   b. undertakes (and does not discontinue) an investigation under Part 5.
(4) Subsection (1) does not authorise the Commissioner to conduct an inquiry into the failure, by one or more particular persons to comply with one or more relevant requirements.
(5) Subsection (1) does not authorise the Commissioner to conduct an inquiry into the interference, by one or more particular persons, with the freedom to communicate in Wales (but see Part 6 for power to investigate certain interference with that freedom).
(6) Subsection (4) or (5) does not prevent the Commissioner from taking the conduct of one or more particular persons into account when conducting an inquiry into—
   a. failure to comply with relevant requirements, or
   b. interference with freedom to communicate in Welsh.

What this section demonstrates is that the situations in which the Commissioner may not conduct an inquiry are more precisely defined than the situation where an inquiry would be appropriate. This is something that hinders rather than aids clarity. Terms that have a similar meaning should be defined more precisely, and as Dale (1977: 148) explains, defining a concept with reference to what it is not renders the law more inaccessible even to the professional reader.

A further difficulty is that while the wording of the 1993 Act emphasizes that the Welsh and English languages should be treated on a basis of equality, this is not reproduced in the Measure, which favours 'no less favourably' as the means of describing the interrelationship of the Welsh and English languages. Conveying the interrelationship of Welsh and English in different terminology from the 1993 Act creates further ambiguity—it is not clear whether 'treating no less favourably' is intended to be synonymous with 'on a basis of equality' or not. If so, then there may be a justification for incorporating the earlier terminology into the new Measure. If treating no less favourably has a different meaning, then this is something that must be clarified.

Yet the Measure is also the product of an ongoing agenda to make legislation more accessible. Accordingly, whereas the approach of the 1993 Act is to use longer sentences and sub-clauses, the Measure uses shorter sentences, with each sentence addressing a single issue, as is seen with the example of s.25:

> (1) A person (P) must comply with a standard of conduct specified by the Welsh Ministers in accordance with Chapter 2 if, and for as long as, the following conditions are met.
> (2) Condition 1 is that P is liable to be required to comply with standards (see Chapter 3).
> (3) Condition 2 is that the standard is potentially applicable to P (see Chapter 4).
> (4) Condition 3 is that the standard is specifically applicable to P (see Chapter 5).
> (5) Condition 4 is that the Commissioner has given a compliance notice to P (see Chapter 6).
> (6) Condition 5 is that the compliance notice requires P to comply with the standard (see Chapter 6).
> (7) Condition 6 is that the compliance notice is in force (see Chapter 6).

The consequence of this is that whereas the Act uses one section to outline a number of possible alternative situations, the Measure adopts an approach of using greater repetition to explain each alternative situation. On the one hand this may bring greater clarity in that the purpose of each section is more clearly explained. On the other hand however, it causes the drafting to be more cumbersome and repetitive, and therefore causes the Measure to be lengthier than would otherwise be necessary, as is seen from the comparison between the Act and the Measure. The Measure may provide greater accessibility but the extensive repetition, as Bowman explains, is not necessarily an aid to clarity:

> It is not always desirable to draft in short sentences. For example a long sentence may be desirable to avoid tedious repetition. This might occur where there is a list of prohibited activities, and it may be absurd to repeat the prohibition for each separate activity. (Bowman 2005: 10)

Since the 1993 Act was enacted, there has been a general development towards a more situational description of how liability is defined. For example, a party may be defined as P, with the result that in following sections and subsections, responsibility is defined as 'If P does this, then P will be liable to D'. This is an approach that is followed in the Measure, although a considerable difficulty arises from the fact that the subject of the requirement is not consistently applied—sometimes the subject is described as P (for example in s.25) whereas in some sections of the Measure the subject is described as A (for example s.30).

This characterization of liability also emphasizes a further difference between the 1993 Act and the Measure. The 1993 Act envisages corporate responsibility by conferring responsibilities either on the Welsh Language Board as an entity or on public bodies as entities. The Measure, however, envisages individual responsibility—a person is responsible rather than an organization—as is provided by s.25. On the other hand, the lists contained in Schs 5–8 identify corporate persons and institutions as being the persons upon whom a duty of compliance will be imposed. This creates considerable ambiguity. On the one hand the term person may be interpreted very broadly, with the result that the Welsh Ministers may be able to identify a specific individual within an organization who has responsibility for the provision of Welsh language services, and therefore responsibility for non-compliance is far more readily identified. On the other hand, the term person may be defined with reference to the construction of the term person, that is, essentially as a corporate person as is suggested in the Schedules. However, if this is the case then it is necessary to address the rationale for departing from the terminology used in the 1993 Act, which defines public bodies rather than persons as having the responsibility for treating the Welsh and English languages on a basis of equality.

It is also important to note, as a terminological issue, that the Welsh and English texts of the Assembly Measure cross-refer to each other. Accordingly the Welsh version of an English term appears in the English text of the Measure and vice versa. Evidently, this is not something that would be encountered in Westminster. This internal bilingualism is significant in terms of interpretation. One of the concerns with translation is that the terminology used in one language may have connotations that are not replicated in the terminology used in the other language. The cross-referencing between the two languages means that the terminology used adopts the breadth or narrowness of meaning of the other language, with the result that terms such as 'qualifying person's imposition day' in s.48 has the same breadth of meaning as '*diwrnod gosod y person neilltuedig*'. Although this may mean that 'in the legislation some of the multiple layers of meaning which certain English words have acquired over the generations will have to be sacrificed in the interests of equivalence between the two language texts' (Bush 2004: 150) it is a way of ensuring that the Welsh and English versions of legislation do not have different meanings because of the different nuances of the terminology adopted.

On the other hand, there is a danger that such an approach creates a self-referential definition. For example a 'qualifying person's imposition day' is defined as meaning '*diwrnod gosod y person neilltuedig*' which is in turn defined as a 'qualifying person's imposition day'. Such a definition does not clarify meaning because the definition refers to the thing being defined (Bowman 2005: 4). Consequently, this method of cross-referencing may have the effect of hindering rather than aiding clarity.

A particular bone of contention that the National Assembly has been keen to address has been the use of the word 'shall'. It has long been argued (Tiersma 1999: 105) that the use of the word 'shall' in legislation is ambiguous in that it could mean that A must fulfil a particular obligation, or it could mean that A will fulfil a particular obligation at some indeterminate point in the future, or it could mean that the responsibility for fulfilling a particular obligation resides with A and not B or C. Accordingly, the National Assembly for Wales has endeavoured to use 'must' whenever a clear obligation is required and to use 'may' wherever a power is conferred but with no attendant obligation. Accordingly in the Measure s.23 provides that 'The Welsh Ministers must appoint persons to be members of a panel of advisers to the Commissioner' while s.26 provides that 'The Welsh Ministers may by regulations specify...standards'. The consequence is that in the Measure there is a clearer delineation between the duties imposed and the powers conferred under the Measure. In contrast, the use of the word 'shall' in the 1993 Act gives the impression that a broader range of obligations are imposed, although the ambiguity of the word may mean that the extent of the obligations imposed may be less extensive if the word is interpreted in its more restrictive sense.

It is also striking that, unlike the 1993 Act, the Measure emphasizes a task-focused approach—the Measure is structured in such a way as to impose finite tasks on particular actors, most specifically the Welsh Ministers and the Welsh Language Commissioner. For example, s.1(3) of the Measure imposes the following expectations: a duty to adopt a strategy, create standards of conduct, create remedies, create the Welsh Language Commissioner. These are all finite responsibilities, which once fulfilled require no further obligation. On the other hand, ongoing obligations, such as the right to speak Welsh in legal proceedings, the equality of treatment of the Welsh and English languages in the proceedings of the National Assembly for Wales, and the equal standing of Acts, Measures, and subordinate legislation are described with reference to (unspecified) external legislation.

3.6. Structure

A striking difference between the 1993 Act and the Measure is in terms of its structure. The 1993 Act follows a simple linear structure, and the structure of the Act follows the structure of its long title. The Act establishes the Welsh Language Board, defines its functions, and then describes the role of the Welsh Language Schemes and the mechanisms for their creation and approval. The Act benefits from greater clarity through succinctness. Even in the long title, the Act sets out broad objectives, while also justifying why those objectives have been introduced:

> An Act to establish a Board having the function of promoting and facilitating the use of the Welsh Language, to provide for the preparation by public bodies of schemes giving effect to the principle that... the Welsh and English languages should be treated on a basis of equality.

The Measure on the other hand sets out a more detailed list of objectives, but does not justify their introduction;

> A Measure of the National Assembly for Wales to make provision about the official status of the Welsh language in Wales; to provide for a Welsh Language Partnership Council; to establish the office of Welsh Language Commissioner; to provide for an Advisory Panel to the Welsh Language Commissioner; to make provision about promoting and facilitating the use of the Welsh Language and treating the Welsh language no less favourably than the English language (including duties to comply with those standards and rights arising from the enforceability of those duties); to make provision about interference with the freedom to use the Welsh language, to establish a Welsh Language Tribunal; to abolish the Welsh Language Board and Welsh Language Schemes.

The structure of the Measure is also more complex and relies on more extensive cross-referencing between sections. This is encountered particularly in Pt 4, which begins by specifying a duty of compliance—s.25. This is followed by a list of conditions that must be fulfilled in order for the duty of compliance to be fulfilled. The conditions themselves refer to different chapters of Pt 4. Chapter 2 of Pt 4 (ss.26–27) discusses the Welsh Ministers' power to specify standards, and this is followed by a series of interpretation clauses (ss.28–31) defining the categories of standards that may be introduced. Chapter 3 defines the persons required to comply with the standards, but does so with reference to two combinations of Schedules to the Measure, as is seen in s.33:

A person (P) is liable to be required to comply with standards if P is—
a. Within Schedule 5 and also within Schedule 6, or
b. Within Schedule 7 and also within Schedule 8.

However, those included within the above Schedules are then defined more specifically in s.34:

(1) A person is within Schedule 5 if the person is within a category of persons specified in column (2) of the Schedule 5 table.
(2) A person is within Schedule 6 if the person—
 (a) is specified in column (1) of the Schedule 6 table, or
 (b) is within a category of persons specified in that column.
(3) A person is within Schedule 7 if the person is within a category of persons specified in column (2) of the Schedule 7 table.
(4) A person is within Schedule 8 if the person—
 (a) is specified in column (1) of the Schedule 8 table, or
 (b) is within a category of persons specified in that column.
(5) A change in the name of a person specified in Schedule 6 or in Schedule 8 does not affect the operation of this Measure in relation to the person.
(6) References in this Part to a person's entry in the Schedule 6 table or the Schedule 8 table are to the entry in that table which (in column (1)) specifies—
 (a) P, or
 (b) a category of persons which P is within.

What this excerpt demonstrates is that the Measure refers both to earlier and later provisions within the law and the meaning of the Measure cannot therefore be derived from a chronological reading. The consequence of this is that the nature of the obligation, and the entity upon whom it is imposed is not clearly ascertained. Rather than following Dreidger's (1957: 18) methodology of Case, Condition, Subject, Action (where X happens (case) where this is reasonable (condition), this person/organization (subject) will do this (action)), or Thornton's (1987: 23) methodology of Condition, Case, Subject, Action (if this is reasonable, where X happens, this person/organization will do this) the approach contained in the Measure is Action, Condition, Subject, Action, Subject, Condition (this will happen if these conditions are met if this entity does this, and this person or entity has to comply if these conditions are met).

For the citizen it is therefore unclear who owes a duty and whether and when a duty is breached. That being so, it becomes very difficult to identify issues of standing and liability. The consequence of this, according to Laws (2011), is that the legislation is primarily an administrative text rather than a judicial text. A particular example of this can be seen in Pt II of the Measure. This Part creates the role of the Welsh Language Commissioner. Section 3 specifies that:

> The principal aim of the Welsh Language Commissioner is to promote and facilitate the use of the Welsh language.

This is reiterated in s.4, albeit in slightly different terms as the function of promotion and facilitation are treated as two separate functions. Section 4 also indicates that the Welsh Language Commissioner has a responsibility to work towards ensuring that the Welsh language is treated no less favourably than the English language. None of these obligations creates actionable obligations, with the result that the law exists but no breach can be proved. Without the threat of sanction for non-compliance, the law is therefore little more than empty rhetoric—a document that may serve to placate the detractors, but one that is not intended to alter institutional or public behaviour.

In terms of its structure, whereas the 1993 Act includes an interpretation clause at the end of the Act, interpretation clauses in the Measure are interspersed with the substantive provisions of the Act. It may be argued that this may aid clarity in that terms are defined where they are used, thus aiding the reader's reading of the Measure:

> … the paramount consideration must be to place the definition where the casual reader is likely to either look for it or even stumble upon it. (Simamba 2007: 76)

It is easier to understand the meaning of the term in context, and the practice of interspersing interpretation clauses throughout the text is becoming increasingly common in Westminster statutes as well as in the Acts and Measures passed by the National Assembly for Wales. Nevertheless, the Westminster approach tends to favour either a single interpretation clause (as is seen in the Autism Act 2009) or an interpretation clause for each Part of the Act (as in the case of the Apprenticeships, Skills and Children Act 2009). Such a structure may also be more readily justified in the context of monolingual legislation, but the individual definition clauses that appear in the Measure are more appropriate for bilingual legislation. One difficulty with bilingual legislation is that an alphabetical list of terms will follow a different order in the two texts. Accordingly, a single interpretation clause would require the drafters to decide whether the two versions of the text should follow the same order (an issue that would be problematic in terms of their equal validity as one version would therefore be subject to the other) or whether they should both be alphabetized. The consequence of the latter approach would be that the two texts would therefore be different, and could not be compared as easily. In the context of bilingual legislation therefore, a single definition section is likely to hinder rather than aid clarity, particularly in a lengthy law such as the Measure because:

if these definitions were also placed in the main definition section, it may be rather bloated, especially in a huge Act containing many definitions. Secondly, where a word is used only in one section, it is more convenient to the reader, and understanding is better promoted, by defining the term in that one section where it is used. (Simamba 2007: 80)

Accordingly, this is an example of a situation where departing from the Westminster approach is both appropriate and necessary.

3.7. Detail

Another aspect of the two laws that merits comment is the level of detail incorporated into them. The 1993 Act takes an arm's length approach. The Act sets out a general outline of the ends to be achieved, but leaves the precise detail of implementation to the Welsh Language Board, and where appropriate to subordinate legislation. On the contrary, the Measure gives a very detailed description of the different roles and organizations that will be established under the legislation. Part 2, for example, creates the role of the Welsh Language Commissioner (s.2), but also foresees that the appointment of a Deputy Commissioner (s.12(1)(a)) and staff will also be necessary (s.12(1)(b)). Under the Westminster regime such detail would be devolved to subordinate legislation. However, in Wales, there is a greater overlap between the legislature and the administration and therefore the decision to include all the details within the primary Measure may be more readily justified.

4. The Measure and the 1993 Act; the implications for legislative drafting in Wales

4.1. The Act and the Measure as an expression of governance

A number of conclusions may be drawn from this comparative study. One key difference between the Act and the Measure is that the 1993 Act sets out a devolved but authoritarian mechanism for compliance. In essence, the Westminster Parliament laid down the standard of bilingual provision that the Act was intended to achieve—that of treating the Welsh and English languages on a basis of equality, and then conferred the power on the Welsh Language Board to ensure that this was achieved. The Board could require public bodies to prepare Welsh Language Schemes, and there was an expectation that public bodies would accept this responsibility.

The Measure, on the other hand, gives the appearance of greater democracy. The standard of bilingualism required is not statutorily defined and is left to the elected representatives to determine. Furthermore, the Measure allows the bodies that are required to comply with its requirements a means of redress if they consider that the standards that have been imposed are unduly onerous. Accordingly, it is possible that the standards adopted may vary—depending on the political hue of the Welsh Assembly Government, and on whether the Government is one that governs with a majority or one that is comprised of a coalition of parties. Furthermore, the Measure gives rise to the possibility that, unlike the situation under the 1993 Act, the standards to be applied may vary according to the region and its linguistic demography, the remit of the organization in question (for example, because of the ongoing right to speak Welsh in legal proceedings, it may be that bodies involved with the administration of justice will have higher standards imposed upon them in terms of bilingual provision), and the organization's commitment to bilingual provision. Rather than a uniform provision where all public bodies have to ensure that they treat the Welsh and English languages on a basis of equality, the impact of the Measure may therefore be to allow some organizations to make less of a commitment to bilingual services—a matter that may be compounded by the grievance procedure that exists where an organization feels that the standards that have been imposed upon it are too severe.

Accordingly, in terms of governance, what is seen from the comparison between the Act and the Measure is that the Act operates by devolving responsibility to an organization whereas the Measure envisages that the primary responsibility rests with the Government. The Act may therefore be seen as operating within a pre-devolved system where the move toward decentralizing responsibility had already begun. The Measure, on the other hand, was enacted within a context where substantive power had not long been devolved. There is a greater impetus therefore for the decision-making power to be retained by the Welsh Government. Wales is not yet ready for the devolution of its devolved powers.

4.2. The Act and the Measure as a manifestation of rights

Secondly, the differences between Wales and Westminster may be characterized by the nature of the rights conferred. Although both the Act and the Measure confer first generation and second generation rights, the emphasis within the 1993 Act is on the second generation rights—the duties imposed on the Welsh Language Board are prioritized, together with the duties that the Welsh Language Board may impose on public bodies. In contrast, the Measure imposes fewer obligations on the state, and places far greater emphasis on non-intervention with linguistic rights, as a form of first generation rights. Again there is a sense that the National Assembly for Wales is at the beginning of an evolutionary process—in order to evolve a system whereby the state provides cultural resources, it must begin by introducing non-interventionism.

4.3. The Act and the Measure and legal/cultural identity

What is encountered in this comparison of the 1993 Act and the Measure is that the National Assembly is keen to assert its own legal cultural identity—this article has demonstrated, for example, how the Measure has defined concepts and adopts a different structure from the 1993 Act, even though there is no clear indication that the terms employed (such as 'treating no less favourably' compared with 'treating on a basis of equality') have a different meaning from that in the 1993 Act. This suggests that the National Assembly for Wales is deliberately not framing its laws in the terms that have previously been employed by Westminster, and that there is therefore a desire to develop a new Welsh legal cultural identity.

Some aspects of difference are unassailable—the legislative and executive overlap in Wales means that it is less practicable to leave the technical detail of the Measure to subordinate legislation. The bilingual character of the legislation also necessitates a difference of approach both in terms of how the legislation is worded and organized and in terms of the cross-referencing between the texts.

On the other hand, the drafting techniques employed cannot be entirely divorced from Westminster, as Bush explains in the context of subordinate legislation:

Such legislation is parasitic on the relevant primary legislation. Its terminology and conceptual framework and often the basic content of its provisions are predetermined by the statute from which it springs. (Bush 2004: 148)

Although prima facie this is less of an issue as regards Acts of the National Assembly for Wales than was the case with subordinate legislation and even Measures, the way in which the National Assembly for Wales drafts legislation is nevertheless constrained both by its legislative competence under Sch.7 and the limitations on its jurisdiction under the Government of Wales Act 2006 s.108, as well as by the need for the law in Wales to map on to the existing Westminster legislative framework and the common law's body of precedent.

As has been demonstrated this continued interrelationship is particularly important in the context of the Welsh devolution settlement because of the overlapping relationship between Wales and Westminster as legislatures and as legal jurisdictions. The comparison nevertheless demonstrates very clearly that an attempt is being made to develop a legal cultural identity.

5. Considerations

This comparative study raises a number of considerations that both the National Assembly for Wales and the Westminster Parliament may need to address. First, the study demonstrates that the question of overlapping jurisdiction may need to be clarified further. The official status granted to the Welsh language means that standard forms of wording enacted in Westminster legislation may need to have regard to the status issue. What this demonstrates is that it may be difficult to maintain that Acts of the National Assembly for Wales can only apply to Wales.

Furthermore, the fact of there being an overlapping jurisdiction means that there is also a need for greater collaboration in terms of the terminology adopted. It is unclear, for example, whether terms such as 'equal standing' (in the Government of Wales Act 2006 s.156), 'treated on a basis of equality' (in the 1993 Act s.3(2)(b) and s.5(2)), and 'treated no less favourably than' and 'official status' (in the Measure s.1) are synonymous. If they are, then there may be a greater imperative to adopt consistent terminology across the legislation. If, on the other hand, there are subtle differences in their meaning, then this is something that needs specific clarification. Another issue to be considered therefore is whether terminological variations are necessary and, where such variations are adopted, what the implications of such nuanced meanings may be.

Secondly, the Measure is a salutary lesson in addressing the complexity of legislation. A number of aspects of the Measure, such as the complexity of its structure, not specifying the functions of the different actors and their interrelationship, and the self-referential definitions, do not aid clarity, and many of the provisions are not capable of adjudication because there is no clear indication of when a duty will have been breached. For example, as there is no time frame for the setting of standards by the Welsh Ministers, it may be difficult to ascertain that the individual has recourse to judicial review where no standards are set.

On the other hand, the National Assembly has seen fit to depart from the practices of Westminster in some respects, and by doing so has introduced greater clarity to the legislation. For example, defining clauses where they appear in the Measure, rather than in a single interpretation clause or an interpretation clause for each part of the Act, is one way in which the meaning of the terms employed may be rendered easier to grasp.

The third lesson that may be learned from this comparative study of the 1993 Act and the Measure is that there is a need for careful scrutiny and interpretation of Measures. Not only is there a need for scrutiny of the content of Acts, there is also a need for scrutiny of the form, the structure, and the wording of legislation. The bilingual character of the texts is one way in which this may be achieved, although, in addition to the need to be aware of the potential ambiguities that may arise, there is a need for those engaged in the drafting process to be aware of both the linguistic ambiguities (such as those that arise from the use of 'shall'), and the legal ambiguities (such as those that arise from imprecise identifiers of liability). Bates (1988) explains that greater cross-pollination between scrutiny within the legislature and the courts would be extremely beneficial, in that it would make legislative draftspersons more aware of the need to explain the purpose of the legislation, and to draft it in a way that makes it capable of adjudication by a court. It may also place greater emphasis on the need for consultation with affected parties not only on the policy behind the legislation but on the draft legislation itself. This in turn requires those who engage with the law to develop a greater awareness of the interrelationship between Wales and Westminster, as well as the increasing divergence that is likely to develop between the two corpuses of law.

6. Conclusion

What this article has sought to demonstrate therefore is that where two legislatures intersect with each other, and the additional dimension of a monolingual/bilingual drafting culture is introduced, the study of law and language is required to address cultural and structural questions that are not problematized in the same way as is encountered in the context of a single legislature drafting legislation through the medium of one language. To solve the equation of $(Law + Language)^2$ therefore necessitates an appreciation of the drafting process and the process of scrutiny and interpretation. It necessitates an understanding of the evolving legal cultures that produce the legislation, and it involves a realization that the meaning attributed to words, and the way in which legislative texts are structured, may need to be reassessed and re-evaluated. Perhaps it means that long-held assumptions may need to be cast aside. The equation is not yet solved.

REFERENCES

Primary Sources: Legislation and Cases

Apprenticeships, Skills and Children Act 2009 (2009 c.22).
Autism Act 2009 (2009 c.15).
Government of Wales Act 1998 (1998 c.38).
Government of Wales Act 2006 (2006 c.32).
National & Grindlays Bank Ltd v Kentiles Ltd [1966] 1 WLR 348.
Welsh Language Act 1967 (1967 c.66).
Welsh Language Act 1993 (1993 c.38).
Welsh Language (Wales) Measure 2011 (2011 nawm.1).

Secondary Sources

Bates, T. St J. N. 1988. 'The future of Parliamentary scrutiny of delegated legislation: some judicial perspectives.' *Statute Law Review* 19(3): 155–78.
Bowman, G. 2005. 'The art of legislative drafting.' *European Journal of Law Reform* 7: 3–18.

Bush, K. 2004. 'New Approaches to UK Legislative Drafting: the Welsh Perspective.' *Statute Law Review* 25(2): 144–150.
Dale, W. 1977. *Legislative Drafting: A New Perspective*. London: Butterworths.
Dreidger, E.A. 1957. *The Composition of Legislation*. Ottawa: Edmond Cloutier, Queen's Printer and Controller of Stationery (cited in Thornton, G.C. (1987) *Legislative Drafting* (Third edition). London: Butterworths.
Jones, T.H., Turnbull, J.H., and Williams, J.M. 2005. 'The Law of Wales or the Law of England and Wales?' *Statute Law Review* 26(3): 135–45.
Laws, S. 2011. 'Giving effect to policy in legislation: how to avoid missing the point.' *Statute Law Review* 32(1): 1–16.
Mattila, H.S. 2006 *Comparative Legal Linguistics*. Aldershot: Ashgate.
Ministry of Justice 2011. Prisoner Communications: Correspondence. Available at <http://www.justice.gov.uk/offenders/psis/prison-service-instructions-2011>, accessed 11 October 2012.
Simamba, B.H. 2007. 'The placing and other handling of definitions.' *Statute Law Review* 27(2): 75–82.
Thornton, G.C. 1987. *Legislative Drafting* (Third edition). London: Butterworths.
Tiersma, P. 1999. *Legal language*. Chicago: University of Chicago Press.
Zall, B.W. and Stein, S.M. 1990. 'Legal Background and History of the English Language Movement.' In Adams, K.L. and Brink, D.T. (eds), *Perspectives on Official English: The Campaign for English as the Official Language of the USA*. Berlin and New York: Mouton de Gruyter, 261–272.

25
MMORPGing, Law, and Lingo

*Kim Barker**

As Brian Bix states categorically, 'Language is the medium through which law acts'.[1] Law and language are therefore intertwined; law relies upon wording to regulate various aspects of our existence; the wording of contracts sets out the obligations of each party; the wording of a statutory provision lays down the intent of Parliament; questions of law hang on the interpretation and definitions given to single words and phrases by esteemed judges. Definitions appear prominently, yet are not always ready for deployment in a manner that would provide adequate and acceptable solutions to difficulties surrounding terminology and interpretation.

Whilst language is the medium, and law is the message, the message is not always assembled correctly. There are three essential elements involved in the dissemination of the legal message:

a) Language—as the medium
b) Law—as the message
c) Interpretation—as definition

1. Dissemination of the legal message

Many different areas of life have their own particular terms and language; law is no exception. Massively Multiplayer Online Role Playing Games[2] and Online Games also have their own distinct phrases, terms, and meanings. At present however, there is little cohesion between the language and terms used in online games, and acceptance or understanding of them by the legal system. Equally, gaming phraseology is still somewhat of a niche area when compared to mainstream language. Whilst the linguistic and interpretative elements of online gaming pose potential challenges to dispute resolution, a little more context clarifies the nature of the difficulties.

Typically, a virtual world resident or online game user is required to agree to a contractual agreement with the developer or platform provider of the online environment. Dannenberg highlights the all-encompassing nature of the End User License Agreement[3] used in regulating online interactive spaces:

In the landscape of the virtual world, however, life is ubiquitously but not exclusively governed by contract law. Speech, conduct and existence—in fact, everything that a virtual world [or online game] resident does or says—is supposedly constrained by a contract.[4]

---

* Thank you to all who have contributed to its formation, both before the colloquium and since.
[1] B Bix, *Law, Language and Legal Determinacy* (Clarendon Press, Oxford, 1993), 1.
[2] Hereafter MMORPGs.
[3] Hereafter EULA.
[4] R Dannenberg et al., *Computer Games and Virtual Worlds: A New Frontier in Intellectual Property Law* (ABA Publishing, Chicago, 2010), 6.

EULAs are standard-form adhesion contracts, and typically a potential user of an online game or resident of a virtual world is left with little choice as to whether or not he or she accepts the terms offered.[5] If he or she wishes to partake in the online interactive environment, he or she must accept the EULA on the terms offered. If this is not done, a user will have only limited access. Whilst this is not necessarily a legal difficulty in itself, it has provided a great deal of academic comment,[6] particularly in relation to the rights of the weaker party. More specifically, the terms of a EULA have a profound effect on the property rights and intellectual property rights that a user is entitled to benefit from. The contentious nature of these clauses suggests that disputes relating to which party benefits from certain rights are likely to occur in England and Wales, much as they have in other jurisdictions such as the USA and across Europe.[7] The use of contract law as a governing mechanism for online interactive spaces has several significant implications; not only does every aspect of online interaction and activity have to be contained within various contractual clauses but the contract has to be specific and as wide-ranging as possible whilst still being certain enough to be valid. This creates a need for medium-specific terms to be understood by the mainstream reader of the EULA. Consequently, given the lack of online-environment regulation, there is scope for disputes to reach an unprepared legal system. That being so, language and the law must work together in this area.

1.1. 'Law as communication; language as medium'[8]

Law is arguably communication in itself.[9] As a form of communication it relies—according to Bix—upon the medium of language[10] to disseminate its many—and varied—messages. However, if McLuhan's theory is applied, there are two elements to the medium adopted by law. McLuhan states that, 'in operational and practical fact, the medium is the message'.[11] Language is the medium upon which law relies; both oral and written. As McLuhan points out, in the world of electronic communication, visual media are not sufficient, 'At the high speeds of electric communication, purely visual means of apprehending the world are no longer possible; they are just too slow to be relevant or effective'.[12] Law is concerned with language, precise meanings, and interpretations of wording. Tiersma highlights the fact that law and language are interdependent on one another, 'it is utterly impossible to conceive of law without language'.[13] Nelken[14] appears to disagree with this, advocating that law is, in itself, communication. However,

---

[5] J T Kunze, 'Regulating Virtual Worlds Optimally: The Model EULA' (2008–2009) *N.W. J Tech & Intell. Prop* 102, 110.

[6] See e.g. A Jankowich, 'EULAw: The Complex Web of Corporate Rule-Making in Virtual Worlds' (2006) 8 *Tul. J Tech & Intell. Prop 2*; J J Kayser, 'The New New-World: Virtual Property and the EULA' (2006–2007) *Loy L A Ent L Rev* 60; F G Lastowka and D Hunter, 'The Laws of Virtual Worlds' [2004] 92 *Cal L Rev* 1.

[7] B Johnson, 'Virtual Theft on the Rise' (*The Guardian*, London, 20 November 2008), available online at: <http://www.guardian.co.uk/technology/2008/nov/20/theft-in-virtual-worlds> accessed 30 September 2011.

[8] K Barker, 'Medium as Message' unpublished, 2010. (Notes held on file with the author.)

[9] D Nelken (ed), *Law As Communication* (Dartmouth Publishing Company Ltd, Aldershot, 1996), 45.

[10] Bix, *Law, Language and Legal Determinacy* (cited in n.1), 1

[11] M McLuhan, *Understanding Media—The Extensions of Man* (Routledge, London 1995) 7.

[12] M McLuhan and Q Fiore, *The Medium is the Message: An Inventory of Effects* (Gingko Press, Corte Madera, Calif., 2001), 63.

[13] P Tiersma, 'What is Language and Law? And Does Anyone Care?' (2009) Loyola LA Legal Studies Paper No 11, available at: <http://ssrn.com/abstract=1352075>, 10, accessed 30 November 2010.

[14] Nelken, *Law As Communication* (cited in n.9), 45.

law cannot be communication; it deploys content and communication media to convey its messages and such methods of communicating determine the messages that different readerships receive.

The legal message is conveyed in various ways but the content will differ depending on the exact form of media that is employed. Statute is one example of a legal communication medium. The content medium will be embodied within that statute (as the communication medium) but will need analysing and interpreting. Regardless of whether the issue is one regulated by statute or precedent, there will always be a matter of interpretation. This is why the terminology used in specific areas needs to be readily accessible across all generations, and uniformly understood, especially in the growing area of online games.

1.2. Law as a message

Whilst language may prove to be the dominant medium through which law dissipates its message, the law employs various media to spread such messages. Language provides the message but media convey it, and different media place different emphases on different elements of messages. Nelken points out that it is important for law to interact with social constructs: 'The message of law in terms of law, legal doctrine and legal procedure must meet the demands of communication as a factor in general social life and in culture'.[15] In communicating, the law must ensure that the media chosen accurately reflects the kind of message and the audience that will be provided by the chosen media outlet. For example, there is no benefit in publishing, in a virtual world, information about a new regulatory framework for a precise element of life in the UK.[16]

1.3. Interpretation as definition

Law, as it rests on language, is dependent upon interpretation to accurately set precedent. Moreover, precedent needs precise application to ensure justice is delivered. This cannot fail to be important in the often changing, and constantly developing area of virtual worlds and online games. Interpretation and its precise nature have not been easy to reconcile, but this is perhaps related to the view that law and language are often treated as two distinct entities.[17] The role of interpretation and its deployment by various parties involved in the legal system has itself sparked debate.[18] Nevertheless, there is some solid agreement amongst commentators that identifies—and accepts—that there is a role to be played by interpretation in the law. As Mootz states, 'Interpretation is Janus-faced. It preserves and innovates; it recovers and projects; it acknowledges and creates. As a result, legal interpretation unavoidably is a high-wire without a safety net.'[19]

The justice system in England and Wales has developed several approaches[20] to deal with the potential pitfalls and difficulties thrown up by statutes and potential gaps in legal provisions. Those approaches reflect the ways in which the judiciary look at the

---

[15] Nelken, *Law As Communication* (cited in n.9), 57.
[16] Barker, 'Medium as Message' (cited in n.8).
[17] P Pether, 'Language' in A Sarat et al. (eds), *Law & The Humanities: An Introduction* (CUP, New York, 2010), 314.
[18] F J Mootz III, 'Interpretation' in A Sarat et al. (eds), *Law & The Humanities: An Introduction* (CUP, New York, 2010), 347.
[19] Mootz, 'Interpretation' (cited in n.18), 394.
[20] Approaches to interpretation include the literal rule, the golden rule, and the mischief rule.

wording and interpret it in situations where it is found to be problematic. The law of contract is just one area where the case law is littered with examples of judges stating that the wording in the statute is 'to be given its ordinary and natural meaning'.[21]

The judiciary is not designed to play the role of sole lawmaker; it is designed to apply the law[22] alongside the law enforcement bodies which seek to uphold the law. Nevertheless, when dealing with legal issues that refer to specific things, be it vague statutory provisions, a non-specific contractual clause, or precedent from previous cases, the judiciary has the authority and ability to examine the relevant document and consider both its meaning and the intention behind it, be that parliamentary intention or otherwise.[23] In doing so, the judiciary effectively has the power to make law: case law.[24]

Whilst judges have the authority and ability to make law, Parliament—and the government of the day—ought to fulfil their role as lawmakers.[25] Law is traditionally reactive[26] rather than proactive, and it is therefore essential for the development of online games and associated property rights that there is a specific gaming terminology. In order for the law to be applied, the law must have an idea of what it is dealing with. Given that the courts in England and Wales have just recognized for the first time that virtual property can exist,[27] it is important that there are some basic terms that are understood in a mainstream context. Courts and practitioners need to know what they are talking about to ensure that the law develops appropriately, and that cases are decided accordingly. Terminology therefore plays a pivotal role in interpretation.

2. Games

Virtual worlds and MMORPGs are the online interactive environments under consideration here.[28] The worldwide gaming industry not only is of high value, reportedly generating $50 billion annually, but is the 'largest entertainment industry in the world and continues to grow'.[29] There is a prediction that the annual revenue it generates will almost double by 2014.[30] The UK video game sector is larger and more valuable than either the film or music industry, generating £2 billion in worldwide sales in 2008,[31] with the software and electronic publishing industries making the greatest contribution to the economy of all the creative industries.[32] At present, around 70 per cent of the population

---

[21] *Fisher v Bell* [1961] 1 QB 394; *Duport Steel v Sirs* [1980] 1 All ER 529.
[22] G Slapper and D Kelly, *The English Legal System* (9th edn, Routledge Cavendish, Abingdon, 2009), 78.
[23] Slapper and Kelly, *The English Legal System* (cited in n.22), 78.
[24] M Zander, *The Law Making Process* (CUP, Cambridge, 2004), 423.
[25] Slapper and Kelly, *The English Legal System* (cited in n.22), 78.
[26] R Feldman, *The Role of Science in Law* (OUP, Oxford, 2009), 94.
[27] 'Zynga hacker faces jail for $12 million theft' (unreported) available online: <http://www.thisissouthdevon.co.uk/news/HACKER-ADMITS-STEALING-12m-POKER-CHIPS/article-3170994-detail/article.html> accessed 20 February 2011.
[28] For the purposes of this discussion, online interactive environments will be split into these categories. This is not by any means an agreed-upon split. Other commentators make distinctions in different ways: *ENISA Position Paper*, 'Virtual Worlds, Real Money—Security and Privacy in Massively Multiplayer Online Games and Social and Corporate Virtual Worlds' (November 2008), available online at: <http://www.enisa.europa.eu> accessed 1 August 2011.
[29] I Livingstone and A Hope (*Nesta*), 'Next Gen' (February 2011), 11, available online: < http://www.nesta.org.uk/publications/assets/features/next_gen>, accessed 8 October 2012.
[30] Livingstone and Hope, 'Next Gen' (cited in n.29), 11.
[31] Livingstone and Hope, 'Next Gen' (cited in n.29), 11.
[32] Department of Culture, Media and Sport, 'Creative Industries Economic Estimates—Headline Findings' (9 December 2010) available online at: <http://www.culture.gov.uk/images/research/CIEE_Headline-Findings_Dec2010.pdf> accessed 1 August 2011.

in the UK plays games.³³ The UK has enjoyed great success with creations such as *Tomb Raider* and *Grand Theft Auto*, followed more recently by *Fable* and *Runescape*.³⁴ The gaming industry is not something to be ignored, brushed aside, or taken lightly. Significant attention ought therefore to be directed to understanding the terminology it employs.

2.1. What are 'games'?

There is, as yet, no commonly agreed definition of online games or virtual worlds.³⁵ At present, each commentator sets out what he or she means by online games, and that leads to a common group of characteristics rather than a definition. Kennedy, for example, proposes that online games and virtual worlds have a number of shared characteristics including persistence.³⁶ Bell has considered this further, developing a definition, which he suggests is suitable for virtual worlds and which identifies the most dominant characteristics of online interactive spaces. According to Bell's definition, a virtual world is 'A synchronous, persistent network of people, represented as avatars, facilitated by networked computers'.³⁷ The *Virtual Worlds Review* offers a different perspective, suggesting that virtual worlds vary in style, content, and theme, but have certain characteristics in common. This adds to Bell's definition, identifying six common characteristics rather than four: a shared space with a graphical user interface, immediacy, interactivity, persistence; and socialization.³⁸ But there is still no widely used, uniform definition.

The lack of a widely accepted definition of online games and virtual worlds is indicative of their problematic nature. Difficulties in defining the entity can make it equally challenging to determine rights and responsibilities in the event of a disagreement. However, the lack of definition also highlights the fact that the terminology of online gaming can cause difficulties for mainstream bodies that need to deal with games. If experts cannot agree on a definition, those adjudicating on disputes face problems if they are unfamiliar with the entity, the elements of it, and its functionality. The definition, much like the terminology, is essential to an understanding of what exactly an online game is, and what it involves. This is especially the case when dealing with MMORPGs because simply referring to them as games is misleading. At a very basic and simple level, they are games, but they are not games in the sense that *Monopoly* or *Scrabble* are games. There are more aspects and more complexities to the function, operation, and creation of MMORPGs than to a traditional game, such as a board game. Even referring to them as computer games, whilst more accurate, still fails to convey their nature. A computer game can refer to a range of things, from a CD-ROM-based game, to a card game played on a PC, to an online game on a website such as Miniclip.com. Each of these is a computer game, but it is different from a MMORPG because each has different characteristics. Accuracy is important when dealing with MMORPGs and virtual worlds. Accuracy is not the only linguistic prerequisite when dealing with online gaming issues, but for the purposes of this discussion it is the most important. Costikyan suggests that to define what a game is, it is necessary to consider what constitutes a good game; especially, which

---

[33] Livingstone and Hope, 'Next Gen' (cited in n.29), 11.
[34] Livingstone and Hope, 'Next Gen' (cited in n.29), 11.
[35] M Bell, 'Toward a Definition of "Virtual Worlds"' (2008) 1(1) JVWResearch 2.
[36] R Kennedy, 'Virtual Rights? Property in Online Game Objects and Characters' (2008) 17(2) *Information & Communication Technology Law* 95.
[37] Bell, 'Toward a Definition of "Virtual Worlds"' (cited in n.35), 2.
[38] *Virtual Worlds Review*, 'What Is A Virtual World?', available at <http://www.virtualworldsreview.com/info/whatis.shtml> accessed 1 August 2011.

experiences a user desires and would like to repeat.[39] This is one method of defining a game and, much like the range of definitions on offer, there is a range of methods for determining them.

2.2. Types of game

The difficulties present in attempting to define a virtual world or online game are replicable when it comes to distinguishing between the types of online space. Once again, the need for accuracy is critical in determining which category a particular online entity falls into. Language has an important role to play in this, as well as in regulating game items, objects, characters, and contracts. The use of language is essential to our descriptions of items, events, and occurrences. It is therefore important to be able to distinguish between different categories of online interactive environment. In the physical world, language is used to distinguish between different leagues in sport,[40] between different degrees of relationship, between different classes of competitors, and between almost everything else that forms an essential part of life. It is much the same in the virtual environment; language is essential to distinguish one game from another, one category of online environment from another, and games from worlds.

However, unlike the language of sports leagues, degrees of relationship, and classes of competitor, the language that would distinguish different categories of game and world is not yet commonly agreed upon. Neither is it widely used or commonplace. At present, different commentators categorize different online games and worlds in different ways, and use different rationales. Reynolds, for example, splits the types of MMORPG and virtual world into four categories: civic worlds, game worlds, social worlds, and corporate worlds.[41] Sheldon, however, retains a greater degree of simplicity and divides online environments into just two categories: virtual worlds and online games.[42] Duranske appears to follow this distinction between world and game but in some specific instances appears to be undecided about how to classify a particular online environment. This is evident from the categorization of *World of Warcraft* and *EverQuest II*, which he suggests can be both worlds and games.[43] Whilst this may be true, it does appear to defeat the object of categorizing online environments and is therefore less than helpful. If, however, worlds and games can be classed as one and the same, depending on their characteristics, then terminology will be even more important when it comes to separating the categories. Terminology will also be important for explaining why a particular environment falls into a particular category.

Other commentators adapt different methods of distinction, with Alemi categorizing online games and virtual worlds according to whether they are scripted or unscripted environments.[44] Alemi explains this distinction in terms of whether or not the games require users to follow a certain pathway of levels, completing set tasks and challenges as

---

[39] G Costikyan, 'I Have No Words & I Must Design: Toward a Critical Vocabulary for Games'. Paper presented at CGDC Conference (2002), 33, available online: <http://www.digra.org/dl/db/05164.51146.pdf> accessed 1 August 2011.

[40] For example, in football and rugby, the highest league is referred to as the premiership.

[41] R Reynolds, 'The Four Worlds Theory' (August 2005) available online at: <http://terranova.blogs.com/terra_nova/2005/08/the_four_worlds.html> accessed 1 August 2011; and Livingstone and Hope, 'Next Gen' (cited in n.29), 11.

[42] D P Sheldon, 'Claiming Ownership But Getting Owned: Contractual Limitations on Asserting Property Interests in Virtual Goods' (2006–2007) 54 *UCLA L Rev* 751 at 757.

[43] B T Duranske, *Virtual Law: Navigating the Legal Landscape of Virtual Worlds* (ABA, Chicago, 2008), 6.

[44] F Alemi, 'An Avatar's Day In Court: A Proposal for Obtaining Relief and Resolving Disputes in Virtual World Games' [2007] *UCLA J.L. & Tech* 6 at [20].

they progress through the ranks in order to reach the highest level, gain the greatest gold, or defeat the final opponent to achieve the ultimate goal of the game. This distinction is based on freedom. In a scripted environment,[45] according to Alemi's distinction, a user will have very little freedom to do as he or she pleases, and will be confined to certain activities at certain times. Conversely, in an unscripted environment,[46] a user will have significantly more freedom, because there will be no set tasks, challenges, or achievements that reflect status or progress. Unscripted environments allow users to develop their online persona at a pace that suits them. They also allow users to complete various stages of their online experience in whatever order they choose (within reason). A typical unscripted environment is a virtual world such as *Second Life*, where users do not have to *do* anything other than exist and explore, if that is what they choose to do. On the basis of Alemi's categorization, a typical scripted environment is an online game such as *World of Warcraft* or *EverQuest II*, where a user is required to meet certain challenges in order to 'level up' and progress.

The categorization of online games and virtual worlds is problematic. It is possible that the categorization of games will be determined by reference to characteristics of each type of game. Costikyan believes that the meaning of a game can be determined from its arrangement, commenting that 'A game's structure creates its own meaning'.[47] This is an important point in relation to the terminology of a niche area. Whilst the language and terms in this paper have thus far been discussed in a vacuum, Costikyan highlights the fact that it is necessary to add context to the terms in order to derive meaning. He also provides the perfect example of meaning, using *Monopoly* money to demonstrate his point; giving someone *Monopoly* money outside of a game of *Monopoly* is meaningless. As soon as the gesture is repeated within the game of *Monopoly* however, it gains meaning and value. The context is arguably critical. This point is also reiterated by Steinkuehler, who suggests that language is about more than words, it is about literacy in online interactive environments.[48]

2.3. The challenges

The challenges posed by online games and virtual worlds do not relate solely to the concepts of intellectual property, virtual property, privacy, and technology. There are other issues that are related to the language and interpretation of both gaminology and gaming practices.

In complex areas of the law, such as contract, the courts tend to adopt the principle of 'ordinary and natural meaning' when interpreting statutes. Adopting the principle of 'ordinary meaning'[49] will be of limited—if any—use in gaming disputes, especially for terms such as nerfing, wizarding, and kill stealing.[50] These are not words that are used in everyday situations. Nor are they words commonly read in contracts or particulars of claim. These and other words are part of a niche language where words have specific meanings and specific connotations for behaviour and actions in games and virtual

---

[45] Alemi, 'An Avatar's Day In Court' (cited in n.44), 20.
[46] Alemi, 'An Avatar's Day In Court' (cited in n.44), 26.
[47] Costikyan, 'I Have No Words & I Must Design' (cited in n.39).
[48] C Steinkuehler, 'Massively Multiplayer Online Gaming as a Constellation of Literacy Practices' [2007] *E-Learning* 4(3) 297, 300, available online at: <http://dx.doi.org/10.2304/elea.2007.4.3.297> accessed 1 August 2011.
[49] This is discussed further in section 4, Language and law.
[50] These terms are discussed further in section 5, Terminology.

worlds. If an 'everyday ordinary meaning'[51] was given to 'wizarding', one could suppose it refers to the act of being a wizard, or the act of practising magic. In fact, in a gaming context it refers to acts of punishment and discipline that are carried out by characters of a certain rank or standing in the gaming environment.[52] The 'ordinary' meaning as interpreted in the real world bears no resemblance to the natural meaning in a game context. This sole example serves to highlight the potential dangers and difficulties that lie ahead for game-related disputes that appear before the judiciary. And this is just one of the terms.

Alongside the challenges online games pose to the traditional applications of intellectual property and property rights, online games are now beginning to challenge the long-established approaches to legal interpretation. The terminology of MMORPGing is concerned with language, law, and how it is interpreted. Law as a reactive force[53] responds to challenges or difficulties and the area of gaming is one such force for which a response is awaited. Both Parliament and the courts need to be prepared to meet the challenge and all of the aspects that present potential areas of difficulty. Reports suggest that the UK population is rapidly becoming highly involved in gaming, in terms of play, with the emphasis shifting somewhat from development to play.[54] This arguably represents a change since 2008, when the UK was one of the leading developers and producers of games; it has fallen from third to sixth in the world league table of developers.[55] Such developments will more than likely lead to a range of gaming disputes, especially if more people are becoming involved in gaming, and others have greater expectations of their rights in online environments. The shift from developer-led disputes to player-led disputes was set by South Korea and reports suggest that the UK is following suit.[56] Accordingly therefore, the courts should be prepared for the challenges facing them, and learn from South Korea rather than being caught unawares and unprepared.

3. Interpretation, gaming, and the law

One of the many concerns of the law is the interpretation of specific wording in statutes.[57] The interpretation of statutory wording is a critical function for the judiciary.[58] It is important, therefore, that the correct interpretation is made; otherwise there could potentially be disastrous results for individuals, larger groups, and even society as a whole. When judges are faced with the interpretation of, or disputes over language, they can adopt different approaches: the literal rule,[59] the golden rule,[60] or the mischief rule.[61] Each rule or approach to interpretation rests on some understanding of terminology. Attempting to interpret things which are not understood—as is the situation in online interactive environments—is a highly undesirable position for the judiciary as they are

---

[51] As in the cases cited in n.21: *Fisher v Bell* [1961] 1 QB 394; and *Duport Steel v Sirs* [1980] 1 All ER 529.
[52] This is discussed further in section 5, Terminology.
[53] As discussed in Feldman, *The Role of Science in Law* (cited in n.26).
[54] Jeremy Vine, 'Addicted to Games?' *Panorama*, BBC television programme, first broadcast, 6 December 2010.
[55] Livingstone and Hope, 'Next Gen' (cited in n.29).
[56] Jeremy Vine, 'Addicted to Games?' (cited in n.54).
[57] Slapper and Kelly, *The English Legal System* (cited in n.22), 78.
[58] Slapper and Kelly, *The English Legal System* (cited in n.22), 78.
[59] *R v Goodwin* (2005) EWCA Crim 3184.
[60] *River Wear Commissioners v Adamson* (1877) 2 App Cas 743.
[61] *Heydon's Case* (1584) 76 ER 637.

essentially giving effect to Parliamentary intent[62] and filling the gaps in that intent. By doing so, the judiciary is creating law.[63] If there are gaps in the terminology, this could lead to a body of law which is fundamentally flawed and even incompatible with that which it seeks to regulate.

Given that there are potential options open to the law to correct itself, it may not seem significant to define objects, items, and rights accurately when one has the opportunity to do so. Currently, there are no dedicated bodies of law that relate specifically to online games, gaming properties, or the protection of intangible property developed through interaction in a multi-user space. Despite this, intellectual property through copyright and trade marks does attempt to provide regulation, albeit to a limited extent. Because of this, and the novelty of gaming in the eyes of the law, it is even more important that there is a recognized—and accepted—set of definitions relating to online games and gaming terminology. Such recognition could potentially reduce the disparity of outcomes in dispute resolution and also provide a general level of understanding amongst those dealing with the issues that have recently started to arise before the courts in the UK.[64]

The distinctions between games[65] and worlds,[66] and scripted[67] and unscripted[68] environments probably mean very little to the vast majority of people. However, these terms have a significant impact upon potential property—and other—rights that may accrue to users of games and virtual worlds. The lack of a set of uniform terms in this area provides even greater challenges. There is an emerging body of literature and commentary[69] in this field that reveals the lack of an agreed uniform terminology. When the more detailed aspects of these online spaces are examined and subjected to scrutiny, the lack of standard terminology means that each commentator sets out to explain what is meant by a particular phrase or term.[70] This may seem like an insignificant point. However, given that the law is concerned with precision drafting and detailed arguments hingeing on the minutest of details—especially in contractual disputes—standard terminology is needed. This is arguably more important now, given that virtual worlds and Massively Multiplayer Online Games (MMOGs) are regulated by EULAs, which are contractual documents.

At present this may seem too much to ask in view of the fact that the law in the UK has had few dealings with virtual property disputes. However, there is a growing trend both in the West[71] and in Asia of virtual disputes reaching real world courts. In fact, the very first recognition by a UK court of a game-related virtual property occurred in February 2011—when a judge at Exeter Crown Court convicted a man of computer

---

[62] Zander, *The Law Making Process* (cited in n.24), 166.
[63] Zander, *The Law Making Process* (cited in n.24), 166.
[64] e.g. 'Zynga hacker faces jail for $12 million theft' (cited in n.27).
[65] e.g. *EverQuest II*, *World of Warcraft*, and *Lineage II* are just some of the games available.
[66] e.g. *The Sims Online*, *Habbo Hotel*, *Club Penguin*, and *Second Life* are just some of the virtual worlds available.
[67] Alemi, 'An Avatar's Day In Court' (cited in n.44), 20.
[68] Alemi, 'An Avatar's Day In Court' (cited in n.44), 20.
[69] See, e.g., G Lastowka, *Virtual Justice: The New Laws of Online Worlds* (Yale University Press, New Haven, 2010).
[70] See, e.g., S J Horowitz, 'Competing Lockean Claims to Virtual Property' (2007) 20 *Harv J.L & Tech* 443; T Westbrook, 'Owned: Finding A Place for Virtual World Property Rights' (2006) *Mich St L Rev* 779.
[71] In the USA cases concerning *Second Life* and *World of Warcraft* have been commenced: *Hernandez v Internet Gaming Entertainment*, U.S. Dist. Ct. Southern District of Florida, Case No:07-CIV-21403-COHN/SELTZER; *Blizzard Entertainment Inc. v In Game Dollar*, LLC, US Dist. Ct. Central District of California, Case No: 8:07-cv-00589-JVS-AN; *Bragg v Linden Research Inc.* (487 F.Supp 2d 593 E.D. Penn) [2007].

misuse in hacking into game accounts with the purpose of stealing virtual currency then exchanging it into real currency for his own, illegitimate benefit. The judgment expressly referred to virtual gaming property and assets for the very first time in the UK.[72] This is a significant development despite the fact that it was not a judgment by the higher courts; the UK courts have expressly recognized not only that virtual gaming property exists, but that rights can attach to it. Whilst it is true that virtual property has been recognized by statute through copyright law from its inception in the 1700s,[73] and digital property is also widely recognized through online downloads, the recognition of property in a gaming context is significant. Such a judgment is likely to be only the first of many if the example of South Korea is to be followed. South Korea not only deals with hundreds of virtual disputes each year, but even has its own dedicated team of police officers to investigate such disagreements[74] and a special committee to examine the contracts that govern online gaming.[75] This judgment is also significant because it relates to the ongoing debate concerning who has the rights to gaming property.

This all suggests that online gaming and online social spaces are proving to be more valuable to users than just an escape from reality.[76] Users are beginning to realize that they have rights in such virtual spaces, and are willing to go to court to prove this.[77] This in turn suggests that the legislature and the judiciary need to be prepared. However, this is one area where the law has the potential to be proactive so that it is not caught on the 'back foot'!

4. Language and law

The 1975 Renton Committee on the Preparation of Legislation[78] outlined four main areas of complaint about statutes, two of which were obscurity of language and over-elaborate provisions.[79] These concerns suggest that people felt that legislation was more concerned with artfulness than accuracy and user-friendliness. This report highlighted 36 years ago the problems that can arise where legislation and terminology interact without adequate mutual understanding. There seem to have been long-standing tensions between language and law, which are reflected in the tensions in the contemporary debates in law and language. It is possible to see that these complaints about statutes can be applied to online games; the language used is obscure to many who are not experts or even gamers, and is not found in mainstream terminology. In addition to this, where there is an attempt to define something accurately, there is often little or no agreement between commentators about definitions, and they therefore tend to become over-elaborate. It is easy to foresee that any statute drawn up to address issues relating to online games and virtual worlds might be in danger of being unworkable.

Whilst a statutory instrument relating solely to issues raised by online games and virtual worlds is unlikely to be produced, the dangers associated with any form of regulation

---

[72] 'Zynga hacker faces jail for $12 million theft' (cited in n.27).
[73] Statute of Anne, 1710.
[74] Ung-Gi Yoon, 'Real Money Trading in MMORPG Items From a Legal and Policy Perspective' (2008) 1 *Journal of Korean Judicature* 418.
[75] Yoon, 'Real Money Trading in MMORPG Items' (cited in n. 74), 418.
[76] D M Koo et al., 'Experimental Motives for Playing Online Games' (2007) 2(2) *Journal of Convergence Information Technology* 37, 40.
[77] As in the US cases cited in n.71.
[78] Slapper and Kelly, *The English Legal System* (cited in n.22), 75.
[79] Slapper and Kelly, *The English Legal System* (cited in n.22), 75.

remain. It is more likely that online games and virtual worlds will be dealt with through some form of independent governing body, similar to the Football Association.[80] Nevertheless, there must still be an appreciation of the problems associated with the language and terminology of online games and virtual worlds, and the potential dangers of inaccuracies.

Legislation is drafted by Parliamentary counsel.[81] Despite the numerous pressures that are placed on counsel, 'if one principle is to be pursued above all others, it is surely the need for clarity of expression and meaning'.[82] Such a conclusive statement by Slapper and Kelly reflects what the predominant aim of all legislative drafting should be, especially in technical or technological areas of the law. Clarity of expression is needed, but so too is clarity of meaning or definition. It is unlikely that there will be clarity of expression until there is also clarity of meaning. Just like law and language, clarity of expression and definitional clarity are interdependent. Of course, before drafting can begin, there needs to be a level of understanding and acceptance of terminology relating to that which is the subject of the drafting. Without accepted and accurate terminology, it is futile to draft legislation because the legislation could prove inaccurate and unworkable. If this were to be the outcome a greater burden would be placed on the judiciary, in effect to 'correct' the law, compounding the reactive nature of law. However, again, without an understanding and working knowledge of specific terms, such action would be unlikely and could even result in substantial unfairness in the law—undoubtedly an undesirable outcome.

It would therefore seem that both drafting and interpretation are critical elements for online gaming and its legal presence. It is undesirable to attempt regulation through the law until there is recognition and acceptance of how games work, and the meaning of games is expressed in everyday words. The different meanings attributed to terms employed in online gaming are a crucial part of gaming. This general principle is accepted by commentators, who recognize that legislation is a method of communication that includes language and the inherent complexities associated with language. The most complex attribute could cause a number of difficulties for the law in relation to online gaming: 'words can have more than one meaning and . . . the meaning of a word can change depending on its context'.[83]

Several approaches to statutory interpretation[84] are available to judges and the courts in England and Wales to assist them in making the correct decisions and interpreting relevant legal documents accurately. The approaches to statutory interpretation include the golden rule, the literal rule, and the mischief rule. The most alarming approach to statutory interpretation for online games would be the literal rule, largely because of the disparity in the meaning of terms in the physical non-gaming world and in the gaming sphere. The use of the literal rule could provide some interesting, if strange, judgments, which is why it is a relief that it is balanced by the golden rule where necessary.[85] The approach adopted can affect the outcome of a case. Consequently, it would be interesting to critique a particular phrase and scenario deployed in an online gaming situation and predict the likely outcome, depending on which approach to

---

[80] Credit for this example must be given to those present at the conference presentation of this primitive work.
[81] (cited in n.22), 75
[82] Slapper and Kelly, *The English Legal System* (cited in n.22), 77.
[83] Slapper and Kelly, *The English Legal System* (cited in n.22), 79.
[84] As discussed further in section 3, Interpretation, gaming, and law.
[85] Slapper and Kelly, *The English Legal System* (cited in n.22), 86.

interpretation was adopted. However, as there is no statute relating to online games in England and Wales such an exercise cannot yet be completed.

Given the potential for different outcomes, and even potentially unfair outcomes, it is apparent that there is a need to ensure the correct definition of gaming phraseology is used. Failure to do so could result in an incorrect and inaccurate approach to legal disputes over online gaming.

5. Terminology

Niche areas of interest often have their own specific terms and language. Property law, for example, uses terms such as lessee and lessor, covenant and easement. This is just one area of law that has its own distinct set of terms, as does the law of contract, and the criminal law in England and Wales. Equally, the law relating to online gaming could also benefit from acceptance of its own distinct terms. Online gaming has a host of different terms relating to specific aspects of online interaction and precise elements of interaction with a specific online space. Within the broad category of online gaming, there are various subcategories, and in addition to this, there are even platform-specific terms too: certain games or worlds have specific characteristics and therefore have specific language relating to them. It is therefore inappropriate and ill-advised to use general terms instead of the correct term when referring to such things. Referring to a game item or aspect from one game and applying that to other games could prove to be disastrous, not to mention incorrect. In an area where precision is required, accuracy is also advocated in dealing with the terminology surrounding online interactive spaces.

5.1. The problem with 'MMOG' and 'MMORPG:' distinctions between games and worlds

The use of the generic terms (or perhaps, more accurately, initialisms) MMOG (Massively Multiplayer Online Game) and MMORPG (Massively Multiplayer Online Role Playing Game) highlight the predominant issue in this emerging area of law, and exemplify the difficulties with generalizations in relation to specific terms. MMOG and MMORPG refer to a broad categorization of online spaces and interactive environments. Both terms equally fail to differentiate a particular category from others. Equally, neither term seeks distinction from virtual worlds. This in itself is difficult because there are different characteristics and implications that arise depending on which category the online space falls into. Moreover, no single initialism is applicable to all games. Different groups of games have different categories, within which different groups have distinguishing characteristics. It is important to understand the differences because they can help us to define these different groupings accurately.

The generic term 'gaming' covers a multitude of categories, the components of which all have different characteristics. That these different categories are distinct from each other is unsurprising. What is surprising is the range of differences and the attributes that apply to each of the categories. On a simplistic level, for example, there is a need to split online games into two main groups: MMOGs and virtual worlds. However, these categories can then also be further split. Each of the subcategories also have defining characteristics. These different groupings may seem somewhat trivial and minor but the characteristics relate to the terminology, and if some categories of game do not have the same characteristics as others, treating them as though they do could cause problems.

5.2. Scripted, unscripted, and scripting

Alemi points out that there are sub-categories that also need to be distinguished from the main gaming classifications. There is also a need to distinguish between scripted and unscripted environments.[86] Scripted environments refer predominantly to games. Games are said to be scripted because they require users to complete certain tasks and challenges and meet certain objectives in order to be able to progress to the next level and finish the game. Within traditional MMORPGS, which are scripted environments, there is less potential for individual users to engage in the process of scripting. Scripting refers to the activity of writing program code in order to generate objects and items within the game. Scripting is not to be confused with scripted and unscripted games; scripting is a process whereas scripted and unscripted are descriptors of game type.[87]

The use of scripted and unscripted, as terms to describe game categories, grows in complexity because the size of virtual worlds and online games provides the potential for a virtual world—which is an unscripted platform—to contain a scripted game. That is, within *Second Life* there are a number of scripted role-playing games and a number of non-role-playing games for users to interact with. Consequently, if it is accepted that virtual worlds are usually unscripted and role-playing games are usually scripted, it is entirely possible that an unscripted environment can contain scripted elements.

These distinctions may seem unimportant. However, when it is considered that the different categories of game have different EULAs and differing contractual clauses relating to property rights and intellectual property rights, the situation suddenly seems slightly less trivial. Given that most scripted environments tend to be games, the EULAs of these games tend to stipulate that the developers are the owners of all the property rights.[88] Moreover, if unscripted environments are generally virtual worlds, the EULAs of these environments tend to stipulate that users are entitled to property rights.[89] This is a crucial difference and one that could have significant implications in court disputes, which is why it is important that the correct terminology is used in a specific way.

6. Gaming terms

This paper has explored the differences between the categories of online games and virtual worlds. It has also set out why the distinction is important, and stated that there is a need to recognize that this area has its own distinct terminology. This paper does not seek to act as a dictionary for gaminology—the terms are far too varied and numerous for that to be possible. However, it is necessary to discuss a few examples to illustrate the demand for understanding and acceptance of gaming terminology and the role that this terminology will undoubtedly play in the legal system in due course.

6.1. Farming

Other terms are used to refer to specific entities within games and gaming activities. The terms used are sometimes terms used in the real world and whilst their meanings in the

---

[86] Alemi, 'An Avatar's Day In Court' (cited in n.44), 20.
[87] Second Life, 'LSL Portal' (18 March 2011), available online at: <http://wiki.secondlife.com/wiki/LSL_Portal> accessed 1 August 2011.
[88] World of Warcraft EULA, 9 December 2010, available online at: <http://us.blizzard.com/en-us/company/legal/wow_tou.html> accessed 1 August 2011.
[89] Second Life Terms of Service, Clause 7.1. 15 December 2010, available online at: <http://secondlife.com/corporate/tos.php#tos12> accessed 1 August 2011.

real and virtual world may have some similarities, the overriding meaning in cyberspace is different from that in the physical world. One example of this is 'farming'. If this phrase were to be given its ordinary meaning, most likely this would be interpreted as working on the land or caring for animals so as to generate a living.[90] However, in an online gaming context, farming refers to something with potentially similar attributes but removed from the 'manual labour' and 'living off the land' stereotypes. Farming in an online gaming context refers to the practice whereby people are employed to carry out menial tasks in a game repeatedly so as to generate amounts of game wealth. By repeatedly performing this task, people can acquire substantial reserves, which they can then sell to other users who do not wish to perform menial tasks themselves. This process is repeated around the clock to amass the greatest possible returns. 'Farming' in online games therefore refers to in-game repetitive actions rather than traditional arable or mixed farming operations.

Gold farming is a controversial aspect of online gaming enterprises, and is conducted on a far larger scale than farming. Gold farming refers to large-scale systems aimed at amassing large amounts of wealth by carrying out repetitive actions. Such activities can be carried out on a professional scale.[91] In some extreme instances, gold farming relates to a very unusual form of labour. In some Chinese prisons, prisoners are forced to engage in gold farming so as to generate a profit for their guards.[92] This controversial and contentious area of online gaming has been the subject of litigation in the USA in *Hernandez v IGE*.[93]

In *Hernandez*, the claimant alleged that *IGE* was in contravention of the EULA of *World of Warcraft* because *IGE* was engaged in collecting and selling game items and currency for real currency, thereby allowing other users to circumvent the lower levels of the game and time-consuming activities. *Hernandez* also alleged that this was devaluing the currency, as well as the efforts employed by genuine users to work through the game. A similar issue was raised in *Blizzard Entertainment Inc v In Game Dollar LLC*.[94] In this case, the developers of *World of Warcraft* (Blizzard Entertainment) issued proceedings against the defendant because the defendant was allegedly involved in assisting users to improve their level within the game in exchange for real currency. Whilst the focus of this case was ultimately on matters under fraud legislation in the USA,[95] *In Game Dollar LLC* was also involved in collecting items and currency and re-selling them to other users.

6.2. Griefing

A griefer is an avatar that sets out to cause chaos and upset throughout a game. Griefers bend the rules, cause damage and destruction, and generally disrupt ordinary game activity. Griefing is the activity carried out by a game character within a specific game.

---

[90] *Collins English Dictionary* (HarperCollins, Glasgow, 2006), 306.
[91] Discussed further in n.28, and see *ENISA Position Paper*, 'Virtual Worlds, Real Money' (cited in n.28), 3.2.3.3—Gold farming by humans.
[92] D Vincent, 'China Used Prisoners in Lucrative Internet Gaming Work' (*The Guardian*, 25 May 2011) available online at: <http://www.guardian.co.uk/world/2011/may/25/china-prisoners-internet-gaming-scam> accessed 25 May 2011.
[93] *Hernandez v Internet Gaming Entertainment*, U.S. Dist. Ct. Southern District of Florida, Case No: 07-CIV-21403-COHN/SELTZER [2007].
[94] *Blizzard Entertainment Inc v In Game Dollar LLC* (US Disc. Ct. Central District of California, Case No: 8:07-cv-00589-JVS-AN [2007].
[95] C Renaud and S F Kane, 'Virtual World Industry Outlook 2008–2009' (*Technology Intelligence Group*, 25 August 2008), available at: <http://blog.techintelgroup.com/files/virtual_world_outlook_20082009.pdf> accessed 1 August 2011.

These characters are known as griefers, and whilst they are also avatars, they receive special distinction because of their disruptive behaviour. Commentators have already highlighted the distinction between the activities of ordinary avatars and the activities of griefers.[96] Given that MMORPGs and virtual worlds rely heavily on the notion of scarcity[97]—that some items are rare creates a demand for the item and therefore interest in the game—the activities of griefers can be even more distasteful.

Foo and Koivisto have explored the idea and activity of griefing, and outline three elements to define griefing: 'The griefer's act is intentional; it causes other players to enjoy the game less; the griefer enjoys the act.'[98] This implies a significant difference in activity between griefers and ordinary 'law-abiding' virtual actors. Foo and Koivisto also suggest that this broad category of griefers can be further divided, into those who grief for the sake of griefing, and those who grief for the sake of greed, i.e. 'greed play,' which is defined as an 'act...not specifically intended to disrupt and yet the actor is the sole beneficiary, it is greed play, a subtle form of grief play'.[99]

Such activity, alongside the lack of a contractual relationship—and therefore remedy—with other users compounds the difficulties griefers pose. If users have no way of enforcing rights and there is little fairness in a game, griefers are essentially empowered to cause chaos at will without risk of punishment or reprisals. This example shows just how extreme the situation can be for users when they are required to waive their property rights and have very few methods of redress.

However, the situation with griefing in a virtual world may be different. If there is a system of griefing in a virtual world, it is entirely possible for a system of social norms to be deployed against the griefer. Equally, with the users of virtual worlds engaging in the process of scripting and setting locks on created items, the power of a griefer to disrupt may be somewhat more limited. Again though, the EULAs are the same as those for MMORPGs, and there is still no express contractual relationship between users. However, users have property rights and may use them to take action against a griefing character. One potential option would be to commence an action for something similar to nuisance in tort.

The activity of griefing is not recognized in the real world. It would simply be included under the heading of criminal activity. The everyday use of the word grief refers to upset or emotional distress.[100] Whilst the term griefing is something to do with suffering upset, it does not indicate the precise nature or extent of such activity. This therefore is another example of why there is a need for an understanding of the language of gaming.

6.3. Kill stealing

The term kill stealing has little meaning in the real world. Such a phrase could be interpreted as meaning to steal the kill of someone or something. However, even then it is of limited use. In the virtual online environment this phrase is used to describe the activity whereby the hard work of User A is stolen by User B. In a typical situation involving kill stealing, User A will have tracked down an enemy beast or some such character and will

---

[96] C Y Foo and E M I Koivisto, 'Defining Grief Play in MMORPGs: Player and Developer Perceptions' *Proceedings of the 2004 ACM SIGCHI International Conference on Advances in Computer Entertainment Technology* (ACM, New York, 2004) available online at: <http://doi.acm.org/10.1145/1067343.1067375> accessed 1 August 2011.
[97] Kennedy, 'Virtual Rights?' (cited in n.36), 95.
[98] Foo and Koivisto, 'Defining Grief Play in MMORPGs' (cited in n.96).
[99] Foo and Koivisto, 'Defining Grief Play in MMORPGs' (cited in n.96).
[100] *Collins English Dictionary* (cited in n.90), 373.

be nearing completion of killing the character. Once the kill has been completed, User A will be rewarded with experience points and perhaps even virtual gold or other such rewards.[101] However, User B will come along just before User A has finished the killing process, and User B will jump in at the last moment and finish the kill, thereby stealing both the kill and the rewards. This process is known as kill stealing.

Whilst such activity is not necessarily outlawed in the terms and conditions of games, it is generally frowned upon. It could be the type of activity that a griefer would engage in for example. In the physical world, such situations are highly unlikely to occur, and even if they did, it is highly unlikely that such a term would be used to describe the event. In this sense, the need to understand gaming terminology is critical, especially where there is no offline term that means the same thing.

6.4. Wizards[102]

Wizards are a form of avatar—the graphical representation of a game character—in the same way that griefers are avatars. Again, like griefers, wizards are avatars that perform special or distinct functions within a particular game or world. However, even within gaming circles, the term 'wizards' tends to be used in niche areas, and is not in any sense mainstream. Wizards are generally accepted to be those of high skill or respected social standing within the virtual environment. However, wizards are not present in all games and worlds. Where wizards are present, they tend to be involved in handing out community punishment demanded by their peers. This was the situation in the world of *LambdaMOO* where Mr Bungle, a *LambdaMOO* resident, was accused of committing a sexual offence. The community demanded punishment and it was carried out. After the punishment was carried out, a wizard then banished Mr Bungle from the world,[103] punishing the character twice. It is therefore apparent that wizards have specific duties to perform within online environments where they are present.

In the physical, offline world, a wizard is generally accepted to be a magical character who is capable of performing spells or magic tricks.[104] Wizards in the offline sense are commonly accepted as characters not unlike Albus Dumbledore who appears as headmaster of Hogwarts School of Witchcraft and Wizardry in the Harry Potter series written by J K Rowling.[105] It is doubtful whether the gaming definition of a wizard would be used as the most common reference to a wizard. It is therefore apparent that whilst the word wizard appears in both the physical offline and virtual online worlds, it has different connotations in each. This could prove to be problematic for legislators or courts if the gaming definition of wizards is not understood correctly.

7. Conclusion

Whilst online gaming is a mainstream form of entertainment,[106] the legal system has yet to accept that this is so. Equally, the legal system has yet to accept that there can

---

[101] WoWWiki, *Kill Steal* (*World of Warcraft* Wiki) available online: <http://www.wowwiki.com/Kill_steal> accessed 25 May 2011.
[102] Wizards tend to appear in Multi-User Dungeons (a niche form of virtual world) and the term is therefore relatively rare. Nevertheless, it serves to illustrate that a wide range of terms are used and that, regardless of where they are used, there is a need to incorporate them into mainstream understanding.
[103] J Dibbell, *My Tiny Life* (Fourth Estate Ltd, London, 1998), 21.
[104] *Collins English Dictionary* (cited in n.90), 1025.
[105] J K Rowling, The Harry Potter series of books (Bloomsbury, London, 1997–2010).
[106] L A Lievrouw and S M Livingstone, *Handbook of New Media: Social Shaping and Social Consequences of ICTs* (Sage, London, 2006), 79.

be disputes arising out of such interaction. It must do so, because once there has been recognition of the activity, there can be recognition of everything associated with it. If there are to be problems with gaming activity—as there have been in the USA, South Korea, Holland, and China to date—then the English legal system needs to accept that this challenge is en route. The area of gaming will pose challenges to the law, not just because it is something relatively new, but because it is something abstract that cannot be touched, is highly technological, and is rapidly changing. Gaming—and its associated terminology—cannot be treated as though it is part of computer software or part of information technology. Whilst it does form part of these,[107] it is more than that, and the terminology that accompanies it is also something the law needs to prepare itself to accept.

It is not just the language of online games and virtual worlds that needs to be considered. Whilst language is a critical element, it is also important to consider the impact of online gaming on literacy generally. Involvement with an online interactive space involves reading in more than one way. There is obviously the reading of commands and communications, but there is a quite different kind of reading too: the reading of the screen with which you control your contributions. The 'reading' of the screen involves a different language that very few who have never engaged with an online game or online interactive environment will be able to successfully master, interpret, or even understand.[108] It is this, alongside the precise and distinct terminology that poses potential problems for those faced with adjudicating over disputes relating to online games and virtual worlds. It is therefore necessary to appreciate that it takes a distinct linguistic ability to engage effectively with online games, and a failure to appreciate their intricacies could lead to courts missing the point of the dispute in search of an accurate definition. An understanding of the language and terminology now could prevent problems in the not too distant future.

Gaming terminology is different for a reason—as is gaming. The interpretation of specific gaming terms is also important to ensure a just outcome that is based upon an understanding of the terms in a gaming context. That means that the law needs to make accommodation for it and become familiar with its 'quirks'. It needs to accept that there is a gulf between the use of terms in the physical world and the use of the same terms in the gaming world. The issues of interpretation, whilst spread throughout the legal system are, in this instance, subject and medium specific. To date, there have been very few problems relating to gaming terminology and interpretation, but this is due to the lack of court-based disputes. An understanding of the terms is critical to an understanding of the occurrences and activities within online environments. A correct understanding and use of those terms will shed light on what could potentially be complex legal problems. Accurate language is therefore a prerequisite, and a prerequisite that should be understood in the context of virtual worlds and online games. Legal inaccuracies may be different, but just as damaging as gaming linguistic inaccuracies.

---

[107] For example, software is the platform through which games are operable, and software is protected by copyright law under the Copyright, Designs and Patents Act 1988 s.3(1)(b).

[108] Steinkuehler, 'Massively Multiplayer Online Gaming as a Constellation of Literacy Practices' (cited in n.48), 300.

26

Construing Commercial Contracts: No Need for Violence

*Paul S. Davies**

1. Introduction

Commercial parties enter into written contracts in order to define the obligations owed under the contract. But in order to determine what rights and obligations have been created, the contract needs to be 'construed'. This process of 'construction' is fraught with difficulty. Indeed, the very language of 'construction' may be liable to confuse. The 'construction' of a commercial contract has nothing to do with the *formation*, or bringing about, of a contract. Rather, it is solely concerned with ascertaining the *meaning* of the contract entered into by the parties. A judge engaged in the exercise of construction has no jurisdiction to construct an agreement for the parties, or to improve the bargain made. The judge must simply give effect to the contract reached.

Although this is clear, the term 'construction' has been used in different senses in English law. It is often considered to be synonymous with 'interpretation', so that it only covers the court's interpretation of the words used in the contract. Sometimes, however, it stretches to cover the *implication* of terms as well, in which case the judge also has to consider whether words should be added to those the parties have used. It is suggested that 'construction' should be limited to the former definition. The process of interpreting the words used by the parties should be distinct from that of supplementing the agreed written document through implying additional terms. Implying terms is more 'violent' in nature: the court might disturb the balance of the written document, and thereby impinge on the parties' freedom to contract as they choose, by adding terms. This is much more intrusive than simply stating the meaning of words present in a written document through the interpretative process. In a similar manner, the doctrine of rectification, whereby terms of the contract are altered in order to reflect the actual bargain reached by the parties,[1] wreaks controlled violence upon the written document: the language chosen by the parties is altered, albeit in order to correct a mistake.

In contrast to implication and rectification, interpretation should not be required to do violence to the language chosen by the parties. The correct interpretation of the contract logically falls to be determined prior to implication or rectification,[2] and should afford the utmost respect to the words consciously selected and agreed

---

* I am grateful to the participants at the colloquium for their comments, and to Neil Andrews and the anonymous reviewers. The usual disclaimers apply.

[1] At least in the context of common mistake rectification: this is discussed further in text to n.59 ff.
[2] Although cf. *KPMG LLP v Network Rail Infrastructure Ltd* [2007] EWCA Civ 363; [2007] Bus LR 1336, cited with approval by Lord Hoffmann in *Chartbrook Ltd v Persimmon Homes Ltd* [2009] UKHL 38; [2009] 1 AC 1101 [23].

to by both parties.³ This is important in order to uphold the fundamental principles of freedom of contract and party autonomy: the contract agreed should be given effect as concluded by the parties, and interference with the document to which both parties assented very much restricted.⁴ The best objective evidence of the parties' agreement is the written contract, and this should be given its plain and natural meaning.⁵ Only if such an interpretative process fails to reflect the bargain actually reached by the parties should the courts have recourse to the more violent doctrines of implication and rectification.

This approach to determining the content of the parties' agreement may be considered somewhat 'old-fashioned'. The modern approach is much more relaxed, favouring a 'liberal' doctrine of interpretation which does not strictly adhere to the 'plain meaning' of the text. Indeed, it has recently been said by Lord Hoffmann in *Chartbrook Ltd v Persimmon Homes Ltd* that 'there is not...a limit to the amount of red-ink or verbal rearrangement or correction which the court is allowed' in the interpretative exercise.⁶ A good example of this can be found in the leading case of *Investors Compensation Scheme Ltd v West Bromwich Building Society* (*ICS*).⁷ The decision has been seen to encapsulate the modern approach to interpretation, since it emphasized the importance of 'common sense' and the 'factual matrix' within which the agreement was reached when interpreting a contract. Such factors will be discussed in detail below, but the *result* of the case is worth highlighting at the outset.

The case concerned a large number of elderly investors who entered into 'home income plans' on the advice of a firm of independent financial advisers. This involved the investors remortgaging their homes and investing the proceeds in shares or bonds. But the investments failed, and the investors initially sought recourse against the advisers. Unfortunately, the advisers were insolvent, so the investors decided to try to seek compensation and rescission of the mortgages from West Bromwich Building Society ('West Bromwich'), which had provided the mortgages. But such a claim was not, ultimately, brought by the investors. Instead, the claim was brought by the Investors Compensation Scheme ('ICS'), who had agreed to compensate the investors from its own funds in return for an assignment of the investors' causes of action. However, in the contract of assignment between the investors and ICS the following was excluded:

Any claim (whether sounding in rescission for undue influence or otherwise) that you [the investors] have or may have against the West Bromwich Building Society in which you claim an abatement of the sums which you would otherwise have to repay to the Society....

It was accepted that the 'plain meaning' of the clause was that ICS could not sue West Bromwich for the damages suffered by the investors. This seems the natural meaning of the language used: the clause allowed the investors to retain *any claim* for damages they had against West Bromwich. Nevertheless, the majority of the House of Lords felt able to *interpret* the clause to mean:

Any claim sounding in rescission (whether for undue influence or otherwise)....

---

³ In *EE Caledonia Ltd v Orbit Valve Co Europe* [1993] 4 All ER 165, 173 (QB) Hobhouse J observed that parties have access to legal advice and 'are always able by the choice of appropriate language to draft their contract so as to produce a different effect. The choice is theirs.'

⁴ Of course, there is room for debate about whether the written document represents the bargain reached: C Mitchell, 'Contracts and Contract Law: Challenging the Distinction between the "Real" and "Paper" Deal' (2009) 29 *OJLS* 675. There is further discussion of this issue later in the text.

⁵ The term 'plain meaning' is deprecated by some, given the many nuances of language. This is considered further later in this article: e.g. in the text to nn.21–34.

⁶ [2009] UKHL 38; [2009] 1 AC 1101 [25].

⁷ [1998] 1 WLR 896 (HL).

It is apparent that this interpretation does not correspond to the obvious meaning of the words used by the parties in the written contract. Indeed, Lord Lloyd, dissenting in the House of Lords, said that:

such a construction does violence to the language. I know of no principle of construction... which would enable the court to take words from within the brackets, where they are clearly intended to underline the width of 'any claim,' and place them outside the brackets where they have the exact opposite effect. As Leggatt LJ said in the Court of Appeal, such a construction is simply not an available meaning of the words used; and it is, after all, from the words used that one must ascertain what the parties meant.[8]

Lord Loyd's dissent is forcefully expressed, and this paper aims to defend his scepticism of the majority's approach. The result of *ICS* seems to allow the court to rewrite the contract through interpreting the language used. This is difficult to accept.[9] Altering syntax should be beyond the scope of interpretation; such violence properly falls within the domain of rectification. Importantly, rectification (and implication) appears to allow some recognition of the subjective intentions of the parties, and afford some protection to third parties who rely on the objective meaning of the contract. Interpretation, by contrast, should be a purely objective exercise; rewriting the bargain when it has not been shown that the 'new' version of the language was what the parties *actually* intended is therefore both ambitious and, perhaps, speculative; after all, the best evidence of what the parties *objectively* intended is the written document itself. And if the written document is clear, there is no need for further inquiry within the realm of interpretation. Delving into the subjective intentions of the parties lies within the realm of the equitable doctrine of rectification and, to some extent, implication.[10]

The proper approach the courts should adopt with regard to interpretation has been the subject of much debate.[11] The majority of academics have welcomed a 'liberal' approach to interpretation which provides the court with more room to manoeuvre when attributing meaning to the words used in a contract.[12] The more restrictive approach of this paper therefore runs counter to the academic mainstream. However, it is not without support: important criticism of the 'liberal' approach has been voiced by practitioners[13] and judges.[14] This is unsurprising. Even if the 'liberal' mainstream may

---

[8] [1998] 1 WLR 896 (HL) 904. See too the decision of the Court of Appeal: [1997] CLC 348, 368.

[9] Extra-judicially, Sir Richard Buxton has commented that, 'Whatever the nature of the process in *ICS*, it is clear that it is not one of construing the meaning of the document... [*ICS*] confus[es] the meaning of what the parties said in their document with what they meant to say but did not say': R Buxton, '"Construction" and rectification after *Chartbrook*' (2010) *CLJ* 253, 256–7.

[10] It might be noted that, in *ICS*, the 'rewriting' of the clause favoured ICS over the investors, despite the investors being the 'weaker' party and ICS having made the mistake itself in drafting the agreement.

[11] For full-length treatments, see G McMeel, *The Construction of Contracts: Interpretation, Implication and Rectification*, 2nd edn (Oxford: Oxford University Press, 2011); K Lewison, *The interpretation of contracts*, 4th edn (London: Sweet & Maxwell, 2007); C Mitchell, *Interpretation of Contracts* (London: Routledge-Cavendish, 2007).

[12] e.g. D McLauchlan, 'Contract Interpretation: What is it about?' (2009) 31 *Sydney LR* 5; A Kramer, 'Common sense principles of contract interpretation (and how we've been using them all along)' (2003) *OJLS* 173. See also Lord Nicholls, 'My Kingdom for a Horse: the Meaning of Words' (2005) 121 *LQR* 577.

[13] A Berg, 'Thrashing through the undergrowth' (2006) 122 *LQR* 354; R Calnan, 'Construction of Commercial Contracts: A Practitioner's Perspective' in A Burrows and E Peel (eds), *Contract Terms* (Oxford: Oxford University Press, 2007) ch.2.

[14] e.g., extra-judicially, Sir C Staughton, 'How do the courts interpret commercial contracts?' (1999) 58 *CLJ* 303; J Spigelman, 'From text to context: Contemporary contractual interpretation' (2007) 81 *ALJ* 322.

be theoretically justified by emphasizing language as a tool of communication, which needs to be assessed with a generous application of 'common sense', this is bound to pose problems in practice. After all, 'common sense' itself means different things to different people.[15] It becomes unclear whether a court will depart from the 'plain meaning' of the language used in favour of a more 'common sense' interpretation about what the parties must have intended to write in their contract. And even if the courts do depart from the natural meaning of words used, it is difficult to know precisely what meaning the court will ascribe to the parties' agreement. This is unsatisfactory in the commercial context, where certainty is highly prized. Indeed, one of the reasons for entering into a formal, written contract is to enable the parties to know easily, quickly, and with certainty what their rights and duties are under the contract.[16] This is very much undermined if the parties are not able to rely upon the natural meaning of words.

Such uncertainty also makes it difficult for lawyers to provide accurate guidance with any degree of confidence; although the meaning of the words may be clear, the advice will necessarily be hedged by concerns regarding the context, or matrix, within which the contract was concluded, of which the adviser will generally know little. Ascertaining all the evidence relevant to the matrix might be a lengthy and complicated exercise, and may ultimately be of little assistance. These difficulties are often replicated in cases which advance beyond advice and reach the stage of litigation; appeals on questions of interpretation are common. Yet courts often disagree on the proper interpretation of a contract—disagreement occurring both with decisions of lower tribunals and also amongst a single panel of judges.[17] This undermines the confidence any party can have in interpreting a contract. Not only is such unpredictability problematic for the original parties to the contract, but it may also trouble third parties who have an interest in the contract: for example, third parties may have acquired rights under the contract through assignment. Practically, the 'liberal' approach poses problems. Pragmatically, a more restrictive approach to interpretation might be preferred: 'the administration of civil justice cannot sensibly be organised on the basis that time and money do not matter'.[18] Courts are concerned with the expectations of commercial parties generated by contractual language.[19]

This paper will therefore defend a more 'restrictive' approach to interpreting the meaning of the language consciously chosen by the parties.[20] This should help to further

---

[15] See e.g. *Moore Stephens (a firm) v Stone Rolls Ltd (in liquidation)* [2009] UKHL 39; [2009] 3 WLR 455 at [5] (Lord Phillips). Indeed, Ward LJ has commented that 'the higher you go [in the judiciary], the less the essential oxygen of common sense is available to you': *Oceanbulk Shipping & Trading SA v TMT Asia Ltd* [2010] EWCA Civ 79; [2010] 1 WLR 1803 at [41]; but see subsequently [2010] UKSC 44; [2011] 1 AC 662.

[16] Buxton, '"Construction" and rectification after *Chartbrook*' (cited in n.9), 256: 'The whole point of drawing up...a contractual agreement, is so that the legally binding obligations of the parties can be found in that document; which being a document can only speak through the words used in it'.

[17] *Bank of Credit and Commerce International SA (In Liquidation) v Ali (No.1)* [2001] UKHL 8; [2002] 1 AC 251; *The Starsin* [2003] UKHL 12; [2004] 1 AC 715; *Chartbrook Ltd v Persimmon Homes Ltd* [2009] UKHL 38; [2009] 1 AC 1101; *Re Sigma Finance Corp (In Administration)* [2009] UKSC 2; [2010] 1 All ER 571, and *Rainy Sky SA v Kookmin Bank* [2011] UKSC 50 have all escalated to the highest level since *ICS*, regularly disagreeing with courts below.

[18] J Steyn, 'Written Contracts: to what extent may evidence control language?' (1988) 41 *CLP* 23, 31.

[19] E Farnsworth, *Contracts*, 2nd edn (Boston: Little, Brown and Co., 1990) §7.7 observed that 'It is therefore to these expectations, rather than to the concern of the philosopher or semanticist, that we must turn in the search for the meaning of contract language'. Compare Kramer, 'Common sense principles of contract interpretation' (cited in n.12).

[20] Whereby any reference to 'context' should generally be limited to the document itself, as a whole, in order to avoid unworkable (but not unreasonable) results. This issue is discussed further at n.131 ff.

certainty in the contractual context and reduce the prevalence of appeals in this area of the law. Other doctrines, beyond interpretation, are better placed to wreak violence. Implication and rectification are very able to add to and alter the parties' bargain where appropriate, and these areas will be outlined first. But these are not aspects of interpretation, which should be limited to objectively interpreting the words chosen by the parties. The development of the courts' approach to interpretation will be highlighted; this will be followed by a critique of the current position of the law and some suggestions for how the law might develop. It will be argued that the key principles of freedom of contract and autonomy of the parties mean that the language chosen by the parties should be adhered to, and not altered, by the judges when interpreting written contracts.

The word 'violence' is provocative, but has been used judicially.[21] It emphasizes that altering the meaning of words, such that 'X' is not interpreted as meaning 'X' but rather 'Y', is a distortion of the conventional meaning of 'X'. This approach depends on the meaning of 'X' being truly unambiguous, and certainly not meaning 'Y'. Significantly, developments in the sphere of linguistics have suggested that context is crucial to the interpretation of a text.[22] Solan has contended that the notion of language having a 'plain meaning' in a legal document is a concept fraught with difficulty, particularly if the wider context within which the language is used is not known.[23] However, some care should be taken when the context is a commercial contract. Farnsworth has rightly observed that:

the language of a contract is directed not at describing experience but at controlling human behaviour, ordinarily the behaviour of the contracting parties. The concern of the court is not with the trust of this language but with the expectations that it aroused in the parties. It is therefore to these expectations, rather than to the concern of the philosopher or semanticist, that we must turn in the search for the meaning of contract language'.[24]

Indeed, in the commercial context it would appear that 'typical firms prefer courts to make interpretations on a narrow evidentiary base whose most significant component is the first written contract'.[25] Thus any context required might be restricted to the document itself.[26] Moreover, the idea that language might have a 'plain meaning' has been defended.[27] Certainly, judges appear to accept that a contract may have a 'plain meaning', even if that meaning is not given effect.[28] Lord Grabiner has recently observed:

Words are always used to convey meanings and, in the absence of contrary evidence, it is most likely that the parties intended their words to have the meaning they would convey to most people.

---

[21] See e.g. *ICS* [1998] 1 WLR 896, 904 (Lord Lloyd) and, more recently, *ING Bank NV v Ros Roca SA* [2011] EWCA Civ 353 [29] (Carnwath LJ).

[22] e.g S Pinker, *The Language Instinct—The New Science of Language and Mind* (Harmondsworth: Penguin, 1994).

[23] L Solan, *The Language of Judges* (Chicago: Chicago University Press, 1993), esp. ch.4. See too A Corbin, *Corbin on Contracts* (St Paul: West Publishing, 1960) vol.3, esp. §535 and §542.

[24] E Farnsworth, *Contracts*, 4th edn (New York: Aspen Publishers, 2004) §7.7.

[25] A Schwartz and R Scott, 'Contract theory and the limits of contract law' (2003) 113 *Yale LJ* 541, 569. This was recognized by Lord Hoffmann in *Chartbrook* (cited in n.2), [36]. See too Calnan, 'Construction of Commercial Contracts' (cited in n.13), ch.2; M Bridge, 'The Future of English Private Transactional Law' [2002] *CLP* 191, 213–14.

[26] This will be explored further later in the text: e.g. in text to n.131 ff.

[27] e.g. R Lord, *Williston on Contracts* (4th edn, 1999) §32.3. Solan, *The Language of Judges* (cited in n.23), 98, has also noted that 'there are many cases in which these interpretive difficulties do not arise'.

[28] e.g. Lord Mustill in *Charter Reinsurance Co. Ltd v Fagan* [1997] AC 313, 384. Lord Neuberger MR has recently observed that 'it is clear that there will be circumstances where the words in question are attributed a meaning which they simply cannot have as a matter of ordinary linguistic analysis, because the notional reasonable person would be satisfied that something had gone wrong in the drafting': *Pink Floyd Music Ltd v EMI Records Ltd* [2010] EWCA Civ 1429; [2011] 1 WLR 770 [18].

The natural or ordinary meaning of words exists precisely because it is the way in which most people use and understand those words and the analysis should, therefore, begin with the most likely answer. Indeed, the existence of a power to correct a mistake as a matter of construction presupposes that the analysis starts with the conventional meaning of the words used in the contract. It makes no sense to correct a mistake without first identifying a conventional meaning that is said to have been unintended.'[29]

At the very least, the plain meaning of the language used should be the starting point for the interpretative exercise.[30] And that language should not be stretched too far: that would be to wreak impermissible violence upon the document.[31] If such violence is necessary, implication and rectification should undertake the task, rather than interpretation.[32] Although such an approach has led some to lament the flaws of judges as linguists,[33] it is also unsatisfactory for judges to rely upon vague notions such as 'commercial common sense' or the 'commercial purpose' of the agreement. The warning of Neuberger LJ in *Skanska Rasleigh Weatherfoil Ltd v Somerfield Stores Ltd* should be heeded:

the court must be careful before departing from the natural meaning of the provision in the contract merely because it may conflict with its notions of commercial common sense of what the parties may must or should have thought or intended. Judges are not always the most commercially-minded, let alone the most commercially experienced, of people, and should, I think, avoid arrogating to themselves overconfidently the role of arbiter of commercial reasonableness or likelihood.[34]

2. The edges of construction: room for violence

Implication

Implication may be seen as 'violent' in the sense that it disturbs the written document concluded by the parties by supplementing it with additional terms. Terms may be implied 'at law' into all contracts of a particular type; such terms are necessary to give effect to overriding policy considerations,[35] often bearing the approval of Parliament.[36] Of more interest for the present discussion are terms implied in fact, which only apply to the particular contract in question. Intruding upon the written contract through

---

[29] Lord Grabiner, 'The iterative process of contractual interpretation' (2012) 128 *LQR* 41, 45.

[30] As Lord Hoffmann himself pointed out in *BCCI v Ali*, 'the primary source for understanding what the parties meant is their language interpreted in accordance with conventional usage': [2002] 1 AC 251; [2001] UKHL 8. See too *Estafnous v London & Leeds Business Centres Ltd* [2011] EWCA Civ 1157 [26] (Warren J).

[31] *Charter Reinsurance Co Ltd v Fagan* [1997] AC 313, 368: 'There comes a point at which the court should remind itself that the task is to discover what the parties meant from what they have said, and that to force upon the words a meaning which they cannot fairly bear is to substitute for the bargain actually made one which the court believes could better have been made. This is an illegitimate role for a court. Particularly in the field of commerce, where the parties need to know what they must do and what they can insist on not doing, it is essential for them to be confident that they can rely on the court to enforce their contract according to its terms' (Lord Mustill).

[32] See e.g. Buxton, '"Construction" and rectification after *Chartbrook*' (cited in n.9); Sir Kim Lewison, 'If it ain't broke, don't fix it' (the first memorial lecture for Jonathan Brock QC, delivered in 2008 and reproduced as an Appendix to the First Supplement (2010) to Sir Kim Lewison, *The interpretation of contracts*, 4th edn (London: Sweet & Maxwell, 2007)).

[33] e.g. Solan, *The Language of Judges* (cited in n.23), ch.2.

[34] [2006] EWCA Civ 1732; [2007] CILL 2449 [22].

[35] *Liverpool City Council v Irwin* [1977] AC 239 (HL).

[36] e.g. Sale of Goods Act 1979 ss.12–15. See further E Peden, 'Policy concerns behind implication of terms in law' (2001) 17 *LQR* 459.

adding such terms is justified on the basis either that it is necessary to ensure the 'business efficacy' of the contract,[37] or that the term corresponds with the parties' intentions. This helps to 'legitimize' the violence effected upon the written instrument: to do so is necessary to give effect to the intentions of the parties. In *Shirlaw v Southern Foundaries (1927) Ltd* MacKinnon LJ said:

Prima facie that which in any contract is left to be implied and need not be expressed is something so obvious that it goes without saying; so that, if, while the parties were making their bargain, an officious bystander were to suggest some express provision for it in their agreement, they would testily suppress him with a common 'Oh, of course!'[38]

It is important to note that *both* parties must respond with 'Oh, of course!' for this 'officious bystander test' to be satisfied. This was highlighted in *Spring v National Amalgamated Stevedores and Dockers Society (No. 2)*.[39] That case concerned a trade union dispute; it was argued that there was an implied term that members would act in conformity with the Bridlington Agreement.[40] However, the claimant, who became a member of the union, was completely unaware of the Bridlington Agreement. As a result, had he been asked by an officious bystander whether it was a term of the contract that he act in accordance with that Agreement, he would not have replied, 'Oh, of course!' but rather, 'What is that?!' Thus Sir Leonard Stone VC rightly refused to imply such a term into the agreement.

The 'violence' of implied terms might therefore be kept in check by the need for an implied term to correspond with the *actual* intentions of *both* parties.[41] Such considerations are beyond the scope of the interpretative exercise; the sole issue for the courts when interpreting a written contract is to determine the *objective* intentions of the parties, relying upon the words of the document. After all, the best evidence of what the parties objectively intended is the written contract signed by both parties. There is no room, when interpreting a contract, to ask the parties whether they would have agreed to a particular interpretation at the time the contract was made.

Despite the differences between the two doctrines,[42] there have been calls for implication to be assimilated within interpretation. Most notably, in the Privy Council decision of *Attorney-General of Belize v Belize Telecom Ltd*,[43] Lord Hoffmann deprecated the invocation of the 'officious bystander' as liable to mislead and, in contrast to the principled approach in *Spring*, expressed the view that asking how the parties would

---

[37] *The Moorcock* (1889) LR 14 PD 64, 68 (CA).
[38] [1939] 2 KB 206, 227 (CA). The origins of the 'officious bystander' can probably be found in the judgment of Scrutton LJ in *Reigate v Union Manufacturing Co (Ramsbottom) Ltd* [1918] 1 KB 592, 605 (CA).
[39] [1965] 1 WLR 585 (Ch).
[40] The Bridlington Agreement between trade unions prohibited each trade union from poaching the members of other trade unions.
[41] See further P. Davies, 'Recent developments in the law of implied terms' [2010] *LMCLQ* 140. Compare E Macdonald, 'Casting aside "officious bystanders" and "business efficacy"?' (2009) 26 *JCL* 97, who, despite *Spring*, suggests that a subjective approach is inappropriate.
[42] See further Sir Thomas Bingham MR in *Philips Electronique Grand Public SA v British Sky Broadcasting Ltd* [1995] EMLR 472, 481 (CA) (cited with approval in *Mediterranean Salvage & Towage Ltd v Seamar Trading & Commerce Inc (The Reborn)* [2009] EWCA Civ 531; [2010] 1 All ER (Comm) 1 [17]).
[43] [2009] UKPC 10; [2009] 2 All ER (Comm) 1. Although the facts concerned the articles of association of a company, Lord Hoffmann's speech makes it clear that the principles are equally applicable in the law of contract generally, and that Belizean law does not differ from English law regarding implication in fact.

have responded to the officious bystander was 'irrelevant'.[44] Lord Hoffmann preferred the following approach to implication:

There is only one question: is that what the instrument, read as a whole against the relevant background, would reasonably be understood to mean?[45]

Although his Lordship recognized that the court cannot improve upon the bargain made by the parties, or 'introduce terms to make it fairer or more reasonable',[46] this single question approach suggests that reasonableness is crucial when deciding whether to imply a term.[47] This is very similar to Lord Hoffmann's approach to interpretation in *ICS*,[48] but *Spring* suggests reasonableness alone should be insufficient for implication. Both parties must have actually agreed to the term in question: it would have been harsh to impose on the claimant in *Spring* a term to which he did not actually assent, and to which he might not have agreed, even though it might appear objectively reasonable for him to have done so. Admittedly, proving subjective intentions may be problematic, but this simply helps to restrict the circumstances in which terms will be implied. Such restrictiveness is appropriate: the intrusive jurisdiction to imply a term should be exercised rarely. Generally, the loss should simply lie where it falls, and one party should not be allowed to improve the bargain by implying a term to which the other party would not have instinctively said 'Oh, of course!'

In *Belize*, Lord Hoffmann also suggested that 'the implication of the term is not an addition to the instrument. It only spells out what the instrument means'.[49] But this might be questioned. If the contract is silent on a point, by implying a term the court is supplementing, or replacing, this silence. An implied term may give effect to what the instrument should, ideally, have expressly provided for, but not what the instrument means in the form in which it was agreed by the parties. Although it has been argued that meaning can be inferred from silence just as it can be inferred from express words,[50] this approach blurs the boundaries between seeking to ascertain the intentions of the parties from all possible evidence, and seeking to determine what intentions the parties have objectively manifested in the written document. Primacy should be given to the contract itself.[51] Moreover, silence is, generally, more ambiguous than the words expressly chosen by the parties, and it is difficult to know how the parties would have reacted if forced to consider a hypothetical term at the time of contracting; even if there would have been tentative consensus on a point, it is impossible to ascertain precisely how the relevant term would have been drafted. Interpretation and implication should remain distinct; after all, even if a term is implied, it still needs to be interpreted.[52]

---

[44] *Belize* [2009] UKPC 10 (cited in n.43), [25].
[45] *Belize* [2009] UKPC 10 (cited in n.43), [21].
[46] *Belize* [2009] UKPC 10 (cited in n.43), [16]. Lord Hoffmann also acknowledged that, usually, if a term is unexpressed it is not to be implied: *Belize* [2009] UKPC 10 (cited in n.43), [17].
[47] See e.g. Teare J in *Inta Navigation Ltd v Ranch Investments Ltd* [2009] EWHC 1216 (Comm); [2010] 1 Lloyd's Rep. 74 [43].
[48] *ICS* [1998] 1 WLR 896, 912–13 (cited in n.7).
[49] *Belize* (cited in n.43), [18].
[50] e.g. A Kramer, 'Implication in fact as an instance of contractual interpretation' (2004) 63 *CLJ* 384. See too the liberal approach to interpretation, discussed further at n.98 ff.
[51] As Sir George Jessel MR once observed, 'one must consider the meaning of the words used, not what one may guess to be the intention of the parties': *Smith v Lucas* (1881) 18 Ch D 531, 542.
[52] For example, if a term is implied such that 'reasonable' steps are taken, the meaning of 'reasonableness' still needs to be ascertained. See e.g. *Durham Tees Valley Airport Ltd v BMI Baby Ltd* [2009] EWHC 852 (Ch); [2009] 2 Lloyd's Rep. 246 (overturned on different grounds: [2010] EWCA Civ 485; [2011] 1 All ER (Comm) 731).

Undoubtedly, the 'liberal' approach to interpretation has encouraged attempts to pull implication within a wider umbrella of interpretation. If the words used can be rearranged, and even changed, through the interpretative process, why should the courts not also be able to add terms through the same mechanism? However, the foundations of such reasoning are unsatisfactory: the 'liberal' approach to interpretation is not to be welcomed.[53] Moreover, such an approach to implication undermines certainty in the commercial arena. In particular, 'reasonableness' should be of little importance when considering implication. It is useful to recall the words of Sir Thomas Bingham MR in *Philips Electronique Grand Public SA v British Sky Broadcasting Ltd*:

the court comes to the task of implication with the benefit of hindsight, and it is tempting for the court then to fashion a term which will reflect the merits of the situation as they then appear. Tempting, but wrong.[54]

In a similar vein, in *The Reborn*, the Court of Appeal adopted Lord Hoffmann's speech in *Belize*, but Sir Anthony Clarke MR was careful to state the limits of *Belize*, placed great weight on the default position being that no term should be implied,[55] and took care to 'stress the importance of the test of necessity'.[56] Subsequent cases have also emphasized the touchstone of necessity, the restrictive nature of implication, and the importance of the officious bystander.[57] This is appropriate: the intrusive nature of implication means that this doctrine should be exercised with care, and that, since the parties themselves could have included a term to cover the eventuality in question but failed to do so, the strong inference is that no term should be implied. To overcome this hurdle and interfere with the written document agreed between the parties by adding terms, the court must be satisfied that such action is necessary, either to ensure the business efficacy of the contract,[58] or to reflect the actual intentions of the parties. Violence should only be used where necessary.

Rectification

Rectification is an equitable doctrine which operates to change the words used in a contract.[59] Its purpose is to do violence to the language chosen by the parties. However, such violence is justified in order to correct a mistake in the recording of the parties' bargain. Rectification therefore helps to ensure that the 'true' agreement of the parties takes effect, rather than a mistaken 'paper record' of that agreement.

Logically, rectification should only be invoked if the true interpretation of the contract fails to accord with the agreement formed by the parties.[60] In such circumstances, Equity may intervene to rectify the error. It may be seen as something of a safety valve in order to avoid the unconscionable results which might follow from forcing the parties to comply with a document which does not reflect their true accord.[61] It is suggested that

---

[53] This issue is discussed further at n.98 ff.
[54] [1995] EMLR 472, 481.
[55] *The Reborn* (cited in n.42), [10]–[11]. Indeed, no term was implied on the facts.
[56] *The Reborn* (cited in n.42), [17]. See too Rix LJ at [48], and Carnworth LJ at [63].
[57] e.g. *Chantry Estates (South East) Ltd v Anderson* [2010] EWCA Civ 316; *Groveholt Ltd v Hughes* [2010] EWCA Civ 538. See too *Aberdeen City Council v Stewart Milne Group Ltd* [2011] UKSC 56 [38] (Lord Clarke).
[58] *The Moorcock* (1889) LR 14 PD 64, 68 (CA) (cited in n.37).
[59] Only an outline can be given here. See further J McGhee (ed.), *Snell's Equity*, 32nd edn (London: Sweet & Maxwell, 2010) ch.16.
[60] Although cf. *KPMG LLP v Network Rail Infrastructure Ltd* (cited in n.2).
[61] e.g. J Steyn, 'Interpretation: Legal Texts and their Landscape' in B S Markesinis (ed.), *The Clifford Chance Millennium Lectures; The Coming Together of the Common Law and the Civil law* (Oxford: Hart Publishing, 2000) ch.5, 80–1. Compare McMeel, *The Construction of Contracts* (cited in n.11), viii.

the subjective intentions of the parties should be paramount in this instance: if (at least one of) the parties did not actually make a mistake, there is no reason for the objectively agreed written contract to be altered.

However, the increasingly liberal approach to interpretation has subsumed, to a large extent, the role of rectification.[62] Interpretation is increasingly used to correct mistakes,[63] but the objective nature of the interpretative process means that this is achieved through employing the reasonable, detached observer, rather than the subjective intentions of the actual parties. Indeed, some judges have used the term 'common law rectification' to describe this phenomenon.[64] These developments are unsatisfactory; interpretation should not wreak violence on the language used. Rectification is better equipped to play this role, and to ensure written documents are rarely tampered with by the courts.

Rectification is generally treated as consisting of two different types: unilateral mistake rectification and common mistake rectification.[65] Ordinarily, if only one party is mistaken, then that person simply has to accept that he should not have signed the contract, and the court is powerless to intervene.[66] However, that party may still seek rectification if the non-mistaken party acted in bad faith, or unconscionably.[67]

A contract may also be rectified where the mistake in the written document is common to both parties. However, it seems sensible that in order to wreak violence upon the objectively agreed written document, it must be proved that the parties were actually mistaken, and not simply that the reasonable person would believe that they were mistaken. After all, the best evidence of the objective intentions of the parties is the written document which was signed by them. A subjective approach was traditionally preferred,[68] but since the decision in *Joscelyne v Nissen*[69] there has been some debate about whether this is still the case.

In *Joscelyne* the Court of Appeal held that it was necessary to establish not only a common intention of the parties which continued until the time of the written agreement, but also 'some outward manifestation of accord'.[70] This element, which has been frequently referred to in subsequent cases,[71] has proved troublesome. Bromley

---

[62] A Burrows, 'Construction and Rectification' in A Burrows and E Peel (eds), *Contract Terms* (Oxford: Oxford University Press, 2007); Buxton, '"Construction" and rectification after *Chartbrook*' (cited in n.9).

[63] e.g. *Mannai Investments v Eagle Star Assurance* [1997] AC 749, *ICS* (cited in n.7), *Starsin* (cited in n.17), *Chartbrook* (cited in n.2). This issue is discussed further at n.98 ff. Despite the language of 'correction of mistakes' being adopted by Lord Hoffmann, Mitchell has criticized such language in the interpretative process, since it implies that drafting was wrong rather than ambiguous: C Mitchell, 'Contract Interpretation: Pragmatism, Principle and the Prior Negotiations Rule' (2010) 26 *JCL* 134.

[64] *Holding & Barnes plc v Hill House Hammond* [2001] EWCA Civ 1334; [2002] 2 P. & C.R. 11, [47] (Nourse LJ); *Dalkia Utilities Services plc v Celtech International Ltd* [2006] EWHC 63 (Comm); [2006] 1 Lloyd's Rep 599 [107]–[120] (Christopher Clarke J).

[65] For a different view, see D McLauchlan, 'The "drastic" remedy of rectification for unilateral mistake' (2008) 124 *LQR* 608.

[66] And generally written, commercial contracts are signed, and one is bound by what one has signed: *L'Estrange v Graucob Ltd* [1934] 2 KB 394.

[67] 'Unilateral mistake rectification' generally involves deliberately exploiting and taking advantage of the other party's error: *A Roberts & Co Ltd v Leicestershire CC* [1961] Ch 555; *Thomas Bates v Wyndham's* [1981] 1 All ER 1077; *Commission for New Towns v Cooper* [1995] Ch 259. Compare D McLauchlan, 'The "drastic" remedy of rectification for unilateral mistake"' (cited in n.65). See too *Daventry District Council v Daventry & District Housing Ltd* [2011] EWCA Civ 1153; [2012] 1 WLR 1333 [173]-[178] (Toulson LJ).

[68] See generally L Bromley, 'Rectification in Equity' (1971) 87 *LQR* 532.

[69] [1970] 2 QB 86.

[70] *Joscelyne* [1970] 2 QB 86, 98.

[71] e.g. see, influentially, *The Olympic Pride* [1980] 2 Lloyds LR 67, 72–3 (Mustill J).

has suggested that this requirement is superfluous, contending that all that needs to be shown for rectification is:

> the establishment of the subjective intention of the party or of the parties to the instrument (in the latter case an identical intention). Intercommunication, however necessary in the common law of contract, properly plays no part either in the theory or in the practice of this equitable doctrine.[72]

Thus the sanctity of the written instrument is protected unless there is a very good reason for the court to interfere; that reason may be found in the actual intentions of the parties.

By contrast, Marcus Smith has criticized any reliance upon subjective intentions, partly because it would be very difficult to prove and would lead to few instances of rectification.[73] But such criticism may be misplaced: rectification should be very rare indeed.[74] Smith also appears to be concerned about the possibility of subjective intentions being pleaded without evidence or foundation, causing undue complexity and uncertainty. Yet this does not necessarily follow from a subjective approach: the threshold of proving subjective intentions is very high, and the court will not be persuaded easily. For this reason, some sort of 'outward manifestation of accord' is likely to be necessary for evidential reasons, but it need not be a substantive requirement.[75]

However, in *Chartbrook*, Lord Hoffmann, albeit *obiter*,[76] accepted the argument that 'rectification required a mistake about whether the written instrument correctly reflected the prior consensus, not whether it accorded with what the party in question believed that consensus to have been'.[77] This suggests that rectification is concerned with the *objective* agreement reached by the parties, and whether this is the same as the *actual* bargain may be irrelevant. This is a dangerous step, for the best objective evidence of the parties' intentions is the written document signed by both parties.[78] It is unclear why an earlier, objectively manifested accord should trump the later, objectively manifested agreement contained in the signed, written contract. The objective approach to rectification involves too much objectivity: objectively, a binding written contract with a particular meaning, ascertained through the process of interpretation, has been concluded.

The only reason for interfering with this must be found in the 'escape route' of the subjective intentions of the parties.[79] Objectively, if the prior consensus of the parties

---

[72] Bromley, 'Rectification in Equity' (cited in n.68).

[73] M Smith, 'Rectification of contracts for common mistake, *Joscelyne v Nissen*, and subjective states of mind' (2007) 123 *LQR* 116.

[74] Particularly in the commercial context, where parties know that the written document is important and that they are bound by what they sign.

[75] e.g. *Munt v Beasley* [2006] EWCA Civ 370; *Cambridge Antibody Technology v Abbott Biotechnology Ltd* [2004] EWHC 2974 (Pat); [2005] FSR 27.

[76] And without the benefit of full discussion regarding objectivity in rectification in the courts below (see e.g. Buxton, '"Construction" and rectification after *Chartbrook*' (cited in n.9), 261). For notes of the case, see D McLaughlin (2010) 126 *LQR* 10; J O'Sullivan (2009) 68 *CLJ* 510; P Davies [2009] *LMCLQ* 420.

[77] *Chartbrook* (cited in n.2), [57]. It is not clear whether this 'objective' approach is limited to common mistake rectification or extends to unilateral mistake rectification also.. Lord Hoffmann's approach has been applied, somewhat unsatisfactorily, in the context of common mistake rectification by the Court of Appeal in *Daventry District Council v Daventry & District Housing Ltd* [2011] EWCA Civ 1153; [2012] 1 WLR 1333. For criticism, see P Davies, 'Rectifying the course of rectification' (2012) 75 MLR 412.

[78] It suggests that parties will have to be very wary about how they communicate during the course of negotiations. A consensus on one point may be found and then apparently deemed to be continuing, despite the written contract itself providing evidence to the contrary.

[79] Lewison, 'If it ain't broke, don't fix it' (cited in n.32); Davies, 'Rectifying the course of rectification' (cited in n. 77). Note that the burden for proving rectification is high: Lord Thurlow LC demanded 'strong irrefragable evidence' in *Countess of Shelburne v Earl of Inchiquin* (1784) 1 Bro.C.C. 338, 341. See too *James Hay Pension Trustees Ltd v Kean Hird et al.* [2005] EWHC 1093 (Ch) [81].

is not represented in the final written document, it might be concluded that the agreement changed. After all, the final written contract is most likely to have been thoroughly checked in commercial situations.[80]

Rectification is rightly only available in restrictive circumstances. Violence should not be allowed free rein. It is appropriate that parties have to work hard to prove that Equity should exercise its jurisdiction to correct mistakes.[81] However, mistakes are more readily being 'corrected' through the process of interpretation, such that the scope of rectification is being squeezed. But the importance of rectification should be recognized, and interpretation must not be allowed to engulf rectification. Indeed, if interpretation adopts a more certain, restrictive approach, then there will be more room within which rectification can operate.[82] This seems particularly appropriate since rectification has developed satisfactory rules to protect the rights of third parties, whereas interpretation has not.[83] Rectification is an equitable, and therefore discretionary, remedy: relief can be withheld if to do otherwise would interfere with rights acquired in good faith by third parties. By contrast, interpretation can have a significant, and unfortunate, impact on third parties. This was recognized as a potential problem by Lord Hoffmann in *Chartbrook*, but ultimately dismissed on the basis that third parties take the risk that the contracts do not mean what they think they mean.[84] This is highly unsatisfactory: third parties should be able to rely on the plain and natural meaning of language used in the contract without having to worry about the (often unknown and difficult to ascertain) 'matrix' within which the contract was concluded. The meaning of the words chosen in the contract should only change upon the intervention of the court, and this should be through the doctrine of rectification rather than interpretation. Moreover, rectification is a question of fact not law, and it would be unfortunate if the equitable doctrine were swallowed up by interpretation whilst the latter remains a question of law: appeals on such particular points are not to be encouraged or made easier in any way.[85]

Violence: peripheral figures only

Implication and rectification are well equipped to unleash violence upon a written document agreed by the parties in appropriate circumstances. Sometimes it may be difficult to distinguish between the two: for example, if a page of a contract is missing, might that page be included through a process of implication, or rectification, or both?[86] Unlike interpretation, both doctrines are able to have regard to the subjective intentions of the parties. But for either doctrine to fulfil its natural role interpretation must not expand so

---

[80] This may not be true of any 'prior consensus', especially since the final document may not be signed by the same people who did the negotiating.

[81] Lord Thurlow LC demanded 'strong irrefragable evidence' in *Countess of Shelburne v Earl of Inchiquin* (1784) 1 Bro.C.C. 338, 341. See too *James Hay Pension Trustees Ltd. v Kean Hird et al.* [2005] EWHC (Ch) 1093 at [81].

[82] This has been advocated by Buxton, '"Construction" and rectification after *Chartbrook*' (cited in n.9).

[83] Spigelman, 'From text to context', (cited in n.14), thought it 'a significant defect in Lord Hoffmann's schema that no express provision is made in this regard'. Spigelman suggests the fact that third parties may become involved and know little about the factual matrix should limit the relevant background. Compare Thomas J in *Wholesale Distributors Ltd v Gibbons Holdings Ltd* [2007] NZSC 37 [121].

[84] *Chartbrook* (cited in n.2), [40].

[85] Compare appeals concerning interpretation, considered in n.134 ff. See P S Davies, 'Interpreting commercial contracts: back to the top' (2011) 127 *LQR* 185.

[86] Compare *The Starsin*, (cited in n.17).

broadly as to swallow up both of them. Interpretation should not be used to add to, or change, the terms of the written contract.

3. Interpretation: avoiding disturbances?

Objectivity

English contract law is not concerned with the subjective intentions of the contracting parties when deciding upon the meaning of contractual obligations. Instead, the law favours an objective approach to interpretation. Although there has been some doubt as to the exact meaning of 'objectivity', it is now reasonably clear that the objective interpretation of a contract equates to ascertaining what the words of the document would mean to the reasonable observer.[87] For example, in *Smith v Hughes*, Lord Blackburn said:

> If, whatever a man's real intention may be, he so conducts himself that a reasonable man would believe that he was assenting to the terms proposed by the other party, and that other party upon that belief enters into the contract with him, the man thus conducting himself would be equally bound as if he had intended to agree to the other party's terms.[88]

Such an objective approach may mean that in some circumstances the contract will be interpreted in a manner contrary to what the parties thought had been agreed.[89] It may, at first blush, seem surprising not to seek to give effect to the actual intentions of the parties.[90] However, especially in the commercial sphere, certainty and predictability of outcome are perhaps more important than speculating as to what the parties subjectively intended at the time of entering into the agreement. This facilitates the task of a lawyer when advising upon the meaning of a contract as it is objectively understood, whereas trying to place himself in the actual position of one of the parties would be prone to difficulties and uncertainty. An objective approach is particularly important since third parties will often rely upon the objectively plain or natural meaning of a contract when entering into business relationships with one of the contracting parties, or when taking over one of the parties' contractual rights (notably through assignment). This seems reasonable: it should be legitimate to assume that the agreement is properly recorded, and that an objective interpretation of the written contract reflects the parties' agreement. If it fails to do so, the parties should grasp the nettle of proving either that an additional term should be implied, or that the document should be rectified.

---

[87] 'Detached objectivity' *per* W Howarth, 'The Meaning of Objectivity in Contract' (1984) 100 *LQR* 265. See too W Howarth, 'A Note on the Objective of Objectivity in Contract' (1987) 103 *LQR* 527. Compare J Vorster, 'A Comment on the Meaning of Objectivity in Contract' (1987) 103 *LQR* 274; J Spencer, 'The Rule in *L'Estrange v Graucob*' (1973) 32 *CLJ* 104.

[88] *Smith v Hughes* (1871) LR 6 QB 597. See too W Gloag, *Law of Contract*, 2nd edn (Edinburgh: W.Green & Son, 1929), 7: 'The judicial task is not to discover the actual intentions of each party; it is to decide what each was reasonably entitled to conclude from the attitude of the other'. This passage has been cited on numerous occasions: e.g. *McCutcheon v David MacBrayne Ltd* [1964] 1 WLR 125, 128; *Shogun Finance Ltd v Hudson* [2004] 1 AC 919 at [183].

[89] O W Homes, 'The Path of the Law' (1897) 10 *Harvard LR* 457: 'nothing is more certain than that parties may be bound by a contract to things which neither of them intended, and when one does not know of the other's assent'.

[90] Compare civil law jurisdictions; see further Lord Hoffmann in *Chartbrook*, (cited in n.2), [39]; S Vogenauer, 'Interpretation of contracts: concluding comparative observations' in A Burrows and E Peel (eds), *Contract Terms* (Oxford: Oxford University Press, 2007).

Although the objective principle of contractual interpretation is no longer seriously opposed, understanding how a reasonable observer should read the contract remains difficult.[91] At one extreme is the 'old-fashioned' approach, which focuses almost exclusively on the words used in the document and their plain or natural meaning. At the other end of the spectrum is the modern, liberal approach, which informs the reasonable observer of all the background to the contract and allows him to make changes to the actual words used in order to decide upon the most reasonable interpretation of the agreement. A brief outline of both approaches and suggestions about how the law might develop in the future will now be given.

The old-fashioned approach: the text, the whole text, and nothing but the text

Under the traditional approach to interpretation, the court should look solely at the words used and interpret them according to their ordinary meaning. As Tindal CJ commented in *Shore v Wilson*:

> The general rule I take to be, that where the words of any written instrument are free from ambiguity in themselves... such instrument is always to be construed according to the strict, plain, common meaning of the words themselves; and that in such case evidence *dehors* the instrument, for the purposes of explaining it according to the surmised or alleged intention of the parties to the instrument is utterly inadmissible.[92]

The suggestion that extrinsic evidence should be excluded where the contract is intended to represent the entire agreement made is clearly of some merit.[93] The parties had the opportunity to read, check, and re-draft the agreement before signing it; why should the parties not be bound by the plain, ordinary meaning of what they had signed?[94]

Such a strict approach helps to preserve the natural meaning of the words chosen by the parties to be included in their written agreement. But more flexibility has always been shown where the contract itself was ambiguous,[95] or where the plain meaning would lead to an unworkable—and not just unreasonable—result.[96] Beyond this, the equitable doctrine of rectification might act as a safeguard: if the wrong words are used, or if they produce the wrong meaning,[97] one or both parties could simply seek the rectification of the contract. The rectified terms could then be interpreted in the same, objective manner.

---

[91] For interesting discussion, see D McLauchlan, 'Objectivity in Contract' (2005) 24 *UQLJ* 479; also D McLauchlan, 'Common intention and contract interpretation' [2011] *LMCLQ* 30.
[92] (1842) 9 Cl & Fin 355, 365.
[93] This rule—known as the parol evidence rule—still has some force (although it is less rigid than some criticism might suggest): see the speech of Lord Hobhouse in *Shogun Finance Ltd v Hudson* [2003] UKHL 62; [2004] 1 AC 919. See too R Stevens, 'Objectivity, Mistake and the Parol Evidence Rule' in A Burrows and E Peel (eds), *Contract Terms* (Oxford: Oxford University Press, 2007) ch.6. A more relaxed attitude concerning consumer contracts might be appropriate: J Steyn, 'The intractable problem of the interpretation of legal texts' (2003) 25 *Sydney LR* 5, 8–11.
[94] This is particularly true in the commercial context, and might be the purpose underlying entire agreement clauses: C Mitchell, 'Entire Agreement Clauses' (2006) 22 *JCL* 222.
[95] See generally Lewison, *The interpretation of contracts* (cited in n.32), ch.8.
[96] *L Schuler AG v Wickman Machine Tool Sales Ltd* [1974] AC 235. See too M Clarke, 'Interpreting contracts—the price of perspective' (2000) 59 *CLJ* 18.
[97] Accepted as a ground for rectification in *Re Butlin's Settlement Trusts* [1976] Ch 251. (Brightman J), and supported by Lord Hoffmann in *Chartbrook* (cited in n.2), [46].

The modern approach: words might not mean what you think they mean

The modern approach places great emphasis upon the context within which the contract is made. This context—also known as the 'factual matrix'[98]—may lead to the court interpreting the contract in a manner contrary to the plain, ordinary meaning of the words. This is precisely what occurred in the now famous decisions of the House of Lords in *Mannai Investments v Eagle Star Assurance*,[99] *Investors Compensation Scheme* (*ICS*),[100] *Bank of Credit and Commerce International v Ali*,[101] and *Chartbrook*.[102] In *Mannai*, the House of Lords was prepared to interpret '12 January' as '13 January'; *ICS* saw the clause 'any claim (whether sounding in rescission for undue influence or otherwise)' restricted to 'any claim for rescission (whether for undue influence or otherwise)'; a release clause was interpreted more strictly than its ordinary meaning would have suggested in *Ali*. More recently, in *Chartbrook*, the House of Lords felt able to interpret the following clause:

Additional Residential Payment ['ARP'] means 23.4% of the price achieved for each Residential Unit in excess of the Minimum Guaranteed Residential Unit Value ['MGRUV'] less the Costs and Incentives ['C&I'].

As meaning:

'ARP' means the amount (if any) by which 23.4% of the price achieved for each Residential Unit is in excess of the MGRUV less the C&I.

These decisions from the highest court signal a liberal approach to interpretation which wreaks violence upon the language chosen by the parties. It suggests that interpretation has begun to trespass upon the domain of rectification in correcting mistakes of drafting, and that the 'plain meaning' of the words used cannot be trusted, even where there is no ambiguity. This leads to uncertainty.[103] This is highlighted by the fact that the House of Lords was divided in all the above cases, with the sole exception of *Chartbrook*, although even in that case Baroness Hale was hesitant as to whether the favoured interpretation was available on the basis of the language used.[104] Moreover, the House of Lords disagreed with the Court of Appeal in all these cases apart from *Ali*, in which there was a notable dissent from Lord Hoffmann, who might be considered to be the architect of the modern approach to interpretation.[105]

Indeed, Lord Hoffmann gave a reasoned speech in all the above cases. The modern approach can perhaps be best understood through the five principles enunciated by Lord Hoffmann in *ICS*, which are worth repeating in full:[106]

> (1) Interpretation is the ascertainment of the meaning which the document would convey to a reasonable person having all the background knowledge which would reasonably

---

[98] *Prenn v Simmonds* [1971] 1 WLR 1381 at 1383 (Lord Wilberforce). See too *Reardon Smith Lines Ltd v Hansen Tangan* [1976] 1 WLR 989.
[99] *Mannai* [1997] AC 749.
[100] *ICS* [1998] 1 WLR 896 (HL) (cited in n.7).
[101] *BCCI v Ali* [2001] UKHL 8; [2002] 1 AC 251 (cited in n.17).
[102] *Chartbrook* [2009] UKHL 38; [2009] 1 AC 1101 [23] (cited in n.2).
[103] 'interpretation disputes are easy to generate and difficult to resolve with any kind of belief in conclusiveness, especially at the point of litigation': Mitchell, (cited in n.63), 146.
[104] *Chartbrook* [2009] UKHL 38; [2009] 1 AC 1101 [23] (cited in n.2), [99].
[105] This may do a disservice to Lord Wilberforce in *Prenn* and *Reardon* (cited in n.98) but the more modern impetus seems to have come from Lord Hoffmann.
[106] [1998] 1 WLR 896, 912–13.

have been available to the parties in the situation in which they were at the time of the contract.

(2) The background was famously referred to by Lord Wilberforce as the 'matrix of fact,' but this phrase is, if anything, an understated description of what the background may include. Subject to the requirement that it should have been reasonably available to the parties and to the exception to be mentioned next, it includes absolutely anything which would have affected the way in which the language of the document would have been understood by a reasonable man.

(3) The law excludes from the admissible background the previous negotiations of the parties and their declarations of subjective intent. They are admissible only in an action for rectification. The law makes this distinction for reasons of practical policy and, in this respect only, legal interpretation differs from the way we would interpret utterances in ordinary life. The boundaries of this exception are in some respects unclear. But this is not the occasion on which to explore them.

(4) The meaning which a document (or any other utterance) would convey to a reasonable man is not the same thing as the meaning of its words. The meaning of words is a matter of dictionaries and grammars; the meaning of the document is what the parties using those words against the relevant background would reasonably have been understood to mean. The background may not merely enable the reasonable man to choose between the possible meanings of words which are ambiguous but even (as occasionally happens in ordinary life) to conclude that the parties must, for whatever reason, have used the wrong words or syntax: see *Mannai Investments Co. Ltd. v Eagle Star Life Assurance Co. Ltd.* [1997] A.C. 749.

(5) The 'rule' that words should be given their 'natural and ordinary meaning' reflects the common sense proposition that we do not easily accept that people have made linguistic mistakes, particularly in formal documents. On the other hand, if one would nevertheless conclude from the background that something must have gone wrong with the language, the law does not require judges to attribute to the parties an intention which they plainly could not have had. Lord Diplock made this point more vigorously when he said in *Antaios Compania Naviera S.A. v Salen Rederierna A.B.* [1985] A.C. 191, 201:

> if detailed semantic and syntactical analysis of words in a commercial contract is going to lead to a conclusion that flouts business commonsense, it must be made to yield to business commonsense.

This contextual approach has been justified on the basis that it favours 'business commonsense in the construction of commercial documents'.[107] However, recourse to such vague notions is often unhelpful. As Lord Phillips recently observed, there is no universal meaning of 'common sense'.[108] Consequently, it is difficult to predict how the court will interpret a contract, and what weight will be given to nebulous concepts such as 'commerciality'. As Arden LJ observed in *Re Golden Key*, '[t]he line between giving weight to the commerciality of a provision and writing a provision into an agreement can become a fine one'.[109] In attempting to achieve 'commercial' interpretations, it may be that the courts are undermining what commercial parties value most—certainty.[110]

---

[107] *Antaios Compania Naviera S.A. v Salen Rederierna A.B. (The Antaios)* [1985] AC 191 at 205 (Lord Diplock).
[108] *Moore Stephens (a firm) v Stone Rolls Ltd (in liquidation)* [2009] UKHL 39; [2009] 3 WLR 455 [5] (cited in n.15).
[109] [2009] EWCA Civ 636 [29].
[110] e.g. Staughton, 'How do the courts interpret commercial contracts?' (cited in n.14); Calnan, 'Construction of Commercial Contracts' (cited in n.13). Lord Hoffmann has said that uncertainty in this area is inevitable: *Chartbrook* [2009] UKHL 38; [2009] 1 AC 1101 [23] (cited in n.2), [15].

Emphasizing context over the text itself runs the risk that courts will not really interpret the words actually used, but rather what words their Lordships considered ought to have been used.[111] It is useful to remember the warning of Lord Mustill in *Charter Reinsurance Co. Ltd v Fagan*:

> There comes a point when the court should remind itself that the task is to discover what the parties meant from what they have said, and that to force upon the words a meaning which they cannot fairly bear is to substitute for the bargain actually made one which the court believes could better have been made. This is an illegitimate role for a court. Particularly in the field of commerce, where the parties need to know what they must do and what they can insist on not doing, it is essential for them to be confident that they can rely on the court to enforce their bargain according to its terms.[112]

This is a salutary reminder that language can only be bent so far.[113] The modern approach to interpretation may afford too little respect to the language deliberately chosen by the parties in their written agreements. Although it has been suggested that Lord Hoffmann's push for a more 'common sense' approach is not as radical as may at first have been thought,[114] the fact that unambiguous terms are not given their plain and ordinary meaning does appear to represent a break from previous practice.[115] This is unsettling: it forces courts to play a more interventionist and, in a way, contract-forming role which is beyond their proper scope; courts should simply give effect to the natural meaning of the words which have been freely chosen by the parties.[116]

The way ahead: showing restraint, avoiding violence?

Lord Hoffmann has played a pre-eminent role in the modern development of the law. But, now that he is retired, it is worth contemplating the possibility that a very broad, liberal approach to interpretation may not be pursued so relentlessly. Is there scope for the courts to return to a more 'old-fashioned', sensible stance? It is suggested that there is, and that this should be welcomed in order that the faith that contracting parties, and others, are able to place in the plain meaning of the language of the written contract can be restored.

---

[111] Presciently warned against by Calnan, 'Construction of Commercial Contracts' (cited in n.13), 19: 'surely the duty of the court is to construe the words used, not those which it considers ought to have been used.'

[112] [1997] AC 313, 388. However, as McMeel has noted, some may feel that Lord Mustill's words do not sit comfortably with the conclusion he reached: McMeel, *The Construction of Contracts* (cited in n.11), para.1.133.

[113] Steyn, 'The intractable problem of the interpretation of legal texts' (cited in n.93), 7: 'But the judge's task is interpretation not interpolation. What falls beyond that range of possible contextual meanings of the text will not be a result attainable by interpretation. There is a Rubicon which judges may not cross: principles of institutional integrity forbid it.' In the Court of Appeal in *Charter Reinsurance* (cited in n.112), Staughton LJ insisted that 'There must come a time when efforts to bend meaning (or, as I would say, reverse it) have to stop'. See too Staughton, 'How do the courts interpret commercial contracts?' (cited in n.14).

[114] e.g. Chadwick LJ in *Bromarin v IMD Investments* [1999] STC 301; Lord Bingham, 'A New Thing Under the Sun: The Interpretation of Contract and the *ICS* Decision' (2008) 12 *Edinburgh Law Review* 374. In *ICS* Lord Hoffmann noted the 'fundamental change' in this area brought about by the observations of Lord Wilberforce in *Prenn* and *Reardon*.

[115] J Spigelman has extra-judicially, in 'From text to context' (cited in n.14), described this as a 'paradigm shift from text to context'.

[116] There are some exceptions to this: e.g., there may be a defect in the formation of a contract, or such inequality of bargaining power that the legislature has seen fit to intervene, but these are rarely problematic in the commercial context.

Most importantly, recourse to the 'background' or 'matrix' of the agreement should be curtailed where the objectively plain or natural meaning of the language used is straightforwardly available. Of course, it must be right that language can only be understood in a given context. But in the commercial sphere, it should suffice for the context for understanding a particular clause to be limited to the document as a whole.[117] Even then, the courts should only depart from the plain meaning of a clause if it is absurd or unworkable—not if it is merely unreasonable. It is inappropriate to strive to undermine the plain meaning of a clause by a wide examination of a broadly defined matrix, when the meaning is clear if the inquiry is limited to the document itself.

Although the principles of *ICS* are often repeated, the lower courts have not wholeheartedly accepted a wide-ranging power to interpret unambiguous clauses against their ordinary meaning. For example, in *National Bank of Sharjah v Dellborg*, Saville LJ clearly stated that:

> To my mind there is much to be said for the simple rule that where the words the parties have chosen to use have only one meaning, and that meaning (bearing in mind the aim or purpose of the agreement) is not self-evidently nonsensical, the law should take that to be their intended agreement, and should not allow the surrounding circumstances to override what (*ex hypothesi*) is clear and obvious.[118]

Such reticence of the lower courts to depart from the plain meaning of words remains common and, to a degree, unaffected by Lord Hoffmann's boldness of approach. For example, in *William Hare Ltd v Shepherd Construction Ltd*,[119] Waller LJ was 'very doubtful'[120] about whether the principles of *ICS* would apply at all to rescue a party that had mis-drafted a provision.[121] Waller LJ was unwilling to correct what a reasonable observer might have considered infelicitous drafting by doing violence to the language through the process of interpretation. Similarly, in *ING Bank NV v Ros Roca SA* the Court of Appeal allowed an appeal on an issue of interpretation, and again preferred a restrictive approach. Carnwath LJ strongly favoured an interpretation which 'does significantly less violence to the language of the clause'.[122] Rix LJ correctly pointed out that there may well have been 'errors of negotiation or commercial intuition, not errors of language in the expression of an agreement'.[123] The court must not step in to rescue a defective bargain. This approach of the Court of Appeal emphasizes that the courts will require strong evidence that something has gone wrong with the language used before refusing to give effect to the natural meaning of the contract,[124] and it sends out a helpful message to commercial parties that they need to ensure that their contracts are drafted correctly. Such judgments are not unexpected; after all, Lord Hoffmann has stated that 'we do not easily accept that people have made linguistic mistakes, particularly in formal documents'.[125] But the tenor

---

[117] Compare the discussion of *Re Sigma Finance Corp (in administration)* [2009] UKSC 2; [2010] 1 All E.R. 571 in n.127 ff and associated text. For similar reasons, this may help to justify the restriction on the admissibility of pre-contractual negotiations, affirmed in *Chartbrook* (cited in n.2).

[118] Unreported, 9 July 2007. Compare Staughton's extra-judicial comment on *ICS*: 'it is hard to imagine a ruling more calculated to perpetuate the vast cost of commercial litigation': Staughton, 'How do the courts interpret commercial contracts?' (cited in n.14), 307.

[119] *William Hare* [2010] EWCA Civ 283, [2010] BLR 358.

[120] *William Hare* [2010] EWCA Civ 283 [15]–[16].

[121] Although this seems to be the result of other leading cases, such as *Mannai, ICS,* and *Chartbrook* (discussed further at nn.99–105).

[122] *ING* [2011] EWCA Civ 353 [29].

[123] *ING* [2011] EWCA Civ 353 [80].

[124] Compare *Chartbrook* (cited in n.2), [15].

[125] This is principle (5) of *ICS*, quoted in text to n.106.

of some of the judgments of lower courts seems contrary to those of Lord Hoffmann; his Lordship seemed much more willing to find such mistakes and depart from the plain meaning of words than do the lower courts. This might explain why the House of Lords disagreed with the Court of Appeal in *Mannai*, *ICS*, and *Chartbrook*.[126]

The Supreme Court has already revisited this area after Lord Hoffmann's retirement. In *Re Sigma*, a complicated commercial trust deed included a clause about how assets were to be distributed.[127] Sales J, at first instance,[128] and the majority of the Court of Appeal,[129] held that there was a clear, plain meaning of the relevant clause in question which should be given effect by the courts. The Supreme Court, by contrast, rejected such a conclusion and once again showed a greater willingness to depart from the plain meaning of the language used. Lord Mance stated that 'the conclusion reached below attaches too much weight to what the courts perceived as the natural meaning of the words... and too little weight to the context... and to the scheme of the Security Trust Deed as a whole'.[130]

However, although the result may seem to follow the same trend as had been set by Lord Hoffmann, there is some reason to hope that the amount of time and energy that has to be spent 'thrashing through the undergrowth'[131] in order to establish the matrix and background of an agreement will be limited. For example, Lord Collins stated that:

This is not the type of case where the background or matrix of fact is or ought to be relevant, except in the most generalised way. I do not consider, therefore, that there is much assistance to be derived from the principles of interpretation re-stated by Lord Hoffmann in *Investors Compensation Scheme*... Where a security document secures a number of creditors who have advanced funds over a long period of time it would be quite wrong to take account of circumstances which are not known to all of them. In this type of case it is the wording of the instrument which is paramount. The instrument must be interpreted as a whole in the light of the commercial intention which may be inferred from the face of the instrument and from the nature of the debtor's business.[132]

Although Lord Collins agreed that the 'literal' interpretation of the courts below was not to be favoured,[133] he essentially limited the relevant 'background' to the document itself. This obviously alleviates some of the burden suffered by the parties, advisers, and the courts when interpreting a contract, but still allows the court to interfere to produce a more 'commercial' result.

Interestingly, Lord Walker dissented in *Sigma*, preferring the 'plain meaning' adopted by the lower courts. Lord Walker had previously adopted a very liberal approach to

---

[126] The Supreme Court in *Re Sigma* and *Rainy Sky SA v Kookmin Bank* (cited in n.17), also overturned the Court of Appeal.

[127] *Re Sigma Finance Corp (in administration)* [2009] UKSC 2; [2010] 1 All E.R. 571. The same *ICS* principles (cited in text to n.106) apply when interpreting the meaning of trust deeds. See the criticism of *Chartbrook* in J D Heydon, 'Implications of *Chartbrook Ltd v Persimmon Homes Ltd* for the law of trusts', Presentation at a Trusts Symposium organized by the Law Society of South Australia and the Society of Trusts and Estates Practitioners held in Adelaide on 18 February 2011.

[128] [2008] EWHC 2997 (Ch).

[129] Lord Neuberger MR dissented, but admitted that he felt comfortable with his more liberal interpretation only after the conclusion of oral argument on appeal: [2008] EWCA Civ 1303; [2009] BCC 393 [134].

[130] *Sigma* [2009] UKSC 2 (cited in n.127), [12].

[131] A Berg, 'Thrashing through the undergrowth' (2006) 122 *LQR* 354, using the language of Lightman J in *The Inntrepreneur Pub Co (GL) v East Crown Ltd* [2000] 2 Lloyd's Rep 611, [614]. Compare Thomas J in *Wholesale Distributors Ltd v Gibbons Holdings Ltd* [2007] NZSC 37 [111]–[122].

[132] *Sigma* [2009] UKSC 2 (cited in n.127), [37] (Lords Mance and Hope agreed).

[133] He thought such an approach was more appropriate to tax legislation which had undergone appropriate scrutiny: *Sigma* [2009] UKSC 2 (cited in n.127), [35].

interpreting the contract in *Chartbrook*.¹³⁴ This difference in approach may simply be because the facts of the cases were different. But this highlights the fact that the interpretation of any contract is unlikely to have much effect beyond the confines of that particular dispute.¹³⁵ It therefore seems inappropriate, if the principles of law are truly clear, for there to be so many appeals in this area. Indeed, this was also recognized by Lord Walker in *Sigma*:

> Although I was one of those who gave permission for a further appeal...I find, on closer consideration, that the case involves no issue of general public importance. There is no doubt as to the principles of construction to be applied.... The only issue is as to the interpretation of the security trust deed in the light of those principles.¹³⁶

It is surely right that appeals in this area are generally unwelcome. Parties should be able to achieve a final answer to disputes regarding interpretation quickly, rather than be encouraged to pursue an endless spiral of appeals in the hope of eventually finding a court prepared to place more or less weight on the 'commerciality' of the provision.¹³⁷ It seems far more 'commercial' for there to be a quicker, final, certain resolution to such matters.¹³⁸ Litigation is expensive, time-consuming, and, increasingly in this area, uncertain.

Moreover, if interpretation is truly now a question of 'common sense', as Lord Hoffmann stated it should be in *ICS*, then it is not clear why first instance judges cannot be trusted to apply 'common sense', and why this mysterious quality is possessed in greater abundance in the Supreme Court. Appeals should be rare, and only possible in the most egregious instances. If the principles of *ICS* are accepted, it is necessary to trust the judges to apply them sensibly. If appeals are granted regularly, as appears to happen at the moment, then this undermines the faith that can be placed in any interpretation of an agreement below the level of the Supreme Court. It also has a damaging effect upon certainty, which is clearly undesirable in the commercial context.

---

¹³⁴ *Chartbrook* (cited in n.2).
¹³⁵ With, perhaps, the exception of standard terms, although it is not clear that the 'factual matrix' is so accommodating. e.g. McMeel, *The Construction of Contracts* (cited in n.11), para.1.165; J Carter, 'Commercial Construction and Contract Doctrine' (2009) 25 *JCL* 83.
¹³⁶ *Sigma* [2009] UKSC 2 (cited in n.127), [40].
¹³⁷ This was, of course, what occurred in *Chartbrook* (cited in n.2: despite losing at first instance and in the Court of Appeal, Persimmon triumphed in the House of Lords (on what is apparently simply a matter of common sense).
¹³⁸ Staughton, 'How do the courts interpret commercial contracts?' (cited in n.14), 307 commented on *ICS*: 'It is hard to imagine a ruling more calculated to perpetuate the vast cost of commercial litigation'. Indeed, the amount of material relied upon by advocates in establishing the 'relevant background' seems to have increased substantially under the modern approach. Similarly Spigelman, 'From text to context' (cited in n.14). Sir Anthony Mason, albeit generally favouring the *ICS* approach, also admitted to the 'doubt that the Hoffmann restatement promotes cost-efficient litigation': 'Opening address' (2009) 25 *JCL* 1, 4. See also *Durham Tees Valley Airport Ltd v BMI Baby Ltd* [2009] EWHC 852 (Ch); [2009] 2 Lloyd's Rep. 246 at [3]: 'the amount of documentation put in (exceeding 15 folders) and the number of witnesses—three called on the part of the claimant and four on the part of the defendants, together with one aviation industry expert on each side—might have presaged proceedings involving claims of rectification or estoppel. But such claims are not pursued on the statements of case and were disclaimed in argument before me. Both sides also disclaimed any alternative argument of termination by reasonable notice. So the issue remains one of interpretation of the words used in the Agreements, set in context.' Lord Hoffmann, on the other hand, said in *Chartbrook* (cited in n.2) at [38]: 'I rather doubt whether the *ICS* case produced a dramatic increase in the amount of material produced by way of background for the purposes of contractual interpretation'. Similarly McMeel, *The Construction of Contracts* (cited in n.11), para.1.79 citing *Static Control Components (Europe) Ltd v Egan* [2004] EWCA Civ 392, [2004] 2 Lloyd's Rep 429 [39].

However, that such a significant number of cases have escalated to the Supreme Court in recent years, despite little being added to the principles of *ICS*, suggests that the principles of *ICS* may well be difficult to apply. It might be argued that the principles of *ICS* have done little for commercial certainty, and have proved too troublesome for the courts. It is unsatisfactory for there continually to be a split between courts and within panels of judges. Recognizing the importance of not departing from the clear meaning of language would help to limit the difficulties associated with 'common sense' and 'commerciality' to instances where there is some ambiguity inherent in the language chosen. Indeed, in *Multi-Link Leisure Developments Ltd v North Lanarkshire Council*, concerning the interpretation of a lease, Lord Hope, in the Supreme Court, held that:

> Words should not be added which are not there, and words which are there should not be changed, taken out or moved from the place in the clause where they have been put by the parties... this should not be done until it has become clear that the language the parties actually used creates an ambiguity which cannot be solved otherwise.[139]

Admittedly, *Multi-Link* was a Scottish case,[140] but Lord Hope's requirement for ambiguity does not sit well with Lord Hoffmann's approach. Nor does the judgment of Lord Rodger, giving the other leading speech, which attempts to adhere closely to the words used.[141] Moreover, the decision might not be considered to be an isolated example. In *Rainy Sky SA v Kookmin Bank*,[142] Lord Clarke, in the Supreme Court, stated that '[w]here the parties have used unambiguous language, the court must apply it'.[143] It is not clear how much should be read into this; on the facts, the term in question was ambiguous.[144] But it is possible that the Supreme Court is quietly drifting away from an application of the 'factual matrix' in the case of unambiguous clauses.

Taking a strict approach to interpretation would be a welcome return to an increased level of predictability, and would afford due respect to the language chosen by the parties. In *RTS Flexible Systems Ltd v Molkerei Alois Müller GMBH & Co. K.G. (UK Productions)* the Supreme Court sent out the clear message that 'parties should agree first and... start work later'.[145] It would be consistent for the Supreme Court now to add that commercial parties must ensure that such agreement must be accurate and precise. If claimants wish to contend that the document does not accurately reflect the agreement reached, they should make a case for rectification rather than 'creative' interpretation.

4. Conclusion

Although language often has many shades of meaning, and in some instances will be ambiguous, in many cases contractual language has an obviously plain, natural meaning. In such cases, that natural meaning should be given greater respect. This would help to further the important aims of predictability and certainty in the commercial context.

---

[139] [2010] UKSC 47; [2011] 1 All ER 175 [11].
[140] Although Lord Clarke thought that the principles applicable to interpretation were the same in Scotland and England: *Multi-Link* (cited in n.139), [45].
[141] The Scottish Law Commission, in a helpful discussion of the case, states that 'some glancing references to commercial sense possibly apart, Lord Rodger ignores the Hoffmann approach altogether': *Discussion Paper on Interpretation of Contract* (DP No 147, 2011).
[142] *Rainy Sky* [2011] UKSC 50.
[143] *Rainy Sky* [2011] UKSC 50 [23].
[144] P Davies, 'Interpreting commercial contract: a case of ambiguity?' [2012] *LMCLQ* 26.
[145] [2010] UKSC 14; [2010] 1 WLR 753 at [1].

Moreover, in many of the examples already given, the error being corrected was made by the 'stronger' party seeking to depart from the natural interpretation of words that that party proposed to the 'weaker' party.[146] This might seem inappropriate, particularly if the person signing the contract on behalf of the 'innocent' party was unaware of the 'mistake'. This may be especially important in this commercial sphere: often the people who negotiate the contract are not those who sign the final written agreement.[147] The courts should be very wary about departing from the natural meaning of the language selected by autonomous parties exercising a deliberate choice to enter into a formal, written contract. It is known that it is important thoroughly to check such documents.[148] The task for the courts should generally be straightforward: where there is no ambiguity, the objectively natural meaning should be all that is required in the interpretative exercise.

If necessary, implied terms may be added to complete an agreement, but such terms must not be inconsistent with express terms of the contract or change the bargain struck.[149] The only way to correct a mistake should be through rectification. The Supreme Court in *Oceanbulk Shipping & Trading SA v TMT Asia Ltd* has recently recognized that interpretation and rectification are 'closely related'.[150] But interpretation should not engulf rectification.[151] Rectification deserves to be the sole mechanism by which mistakes in commercial contracts should be corrected. The objectively unambiguous expression of intention through the language of a signed written document should prevail unless the actual intentions, ascertained by applying the equitable doctrine of rectification, dictate otherwise. This is particularly important since rectification will not be allowed to prejudice the rights of third parties who have acted in good faith in reliance upon the objectively plain meaning of the words of the contract. Interpretation does not grant the same level of protection to such deserving parties.[152]

Perhaps the crux of the whole debate about how commercial contracts should be interpreted is related to the tension between trying to ascertain the actual bargain struck and protecting the integrity of the paper record of the parties' bargain.[153] Clearly, giving

---

[146] Some of these examples are cited in n.121.

[147] For example, a contract may be signed by company directors, who played little part in the prior negotiations.

[148] Buxton, '"Construction" and rectification after *Chartbrook*' (cited in n.9), 256: 'The whole point of drawing up a document, and in particular a contractual agreement, is so that the legally binding obligations of the parties can be found in that document; which being a document can only speak through the words used in it'.

[149] e.g. *Holding and Management (Solitaire) Ltd v Ideal Homes North West Ltd* [2005] EWCA Civ 59.

[150] *Oceanbulk* [2010] UKSC 44; [2011] 1 AC 662, [45].

[151] Although *Chartbrook* (cited in n.2) usurps much of the role of rectification by correcting mistakes through the interpretative process, the fact that pre-contractual negotiations could not be used to aid interpretation potentially left room for rectification to operate. Note also the discussion in *Chartbrook* of *The Karen Oltmann* [1976] 2 Lloyd's Rep 708, which Lord Hoffmann explained as being a case not about interpretation, but rather about rectification.

[152] Spigelman, 'From text to context' (cited in n.14), thought it 'a significant defect in Lord Hoffmann's schema that no express provision is made in this regard', and suggests that the fact that third parties may become involved and know little about the factual matrix should limit the relevant background. But it might be suggested that this should always be the case: third parties' 'involvement' may simply be *considering* becoming involved, which may remain unknown to the courts. Compare Thomas J in *Wholesale Distributors Ltd v Gibbons Holdings Ltd* [2007] NZSC 37 at [121] and, previously, in *Yoshimoto v Canterbury Golf International Ltd* [2001] NZLR 523 at [81]. Similarly, D McLauchlan, 'Contract formation, contract interpretation and subsequent conduct' (2006) 25 *UQLJ* 77, 103 describes fears concerning third party rights as 'greatly exaggerated'. See too the concerns of Briggs J at first instance in *Chartbrook* (cited in n.2) at [111], and those expressed by the Court of Appeal, which were brushed aside by Lord Hoffmann at [40].

[153] Mitchell, 'Contracts and Contract Law' (cited in n.4), 675. See also C Mitchell, 'Leading a life of its own? The roles of reasonable expectation in contract law' [2003] *OJLS* 639.

effect to the paper record when it does not accord with the true bargain seems harsh. But rectification is the doctrine best-placed to guard against severity. And if rectification is onerous or difficult to prove, that is entirely as it should be.[154] Interpretation should not become an 'easy option' to escape the consequences of one's own error.[155] Nor should interpretation drift towards examining the subjective intentions of the parties when they formed their agreement.[156] In the commercial arena, it must be presumed that the parties realized the importance of the written document, and assented to the apparent meaning of the language used. Any other approach is inimical to certainty, and risks prejudicing others who rely on the natural meaning of words.[157] It also leads to cumbersome, lengthy, and expensive attempts to introduce a mass of extrinsic evidence in order to establish the relevant 'factual matrix' within which the contract was concluded. The uncertainty engendered by such an approach should not be allowed to continue. Language is important, and should be used appropriately. It should not be abused by distorting the words chosen by parties such that an interpretation is favoured which the contractual language cannot reasonably bear. There is simply no need for interpretation to do violence to the written contract: implication and rectification should be employed for such ends.

---

[154] The very strong presumption must be that the parties intended to be bound by the objective meaning of the document they signed.

[155] The mistake lying either in drafting the clause, or in signing the document without checking the language carefully.

[156] Staughton, 'How do the courts interpret commercial contracts?' (cited in n.14), 312–13: 'you are to find the intention of the parties, and for that purpose you look first at the wording of the contract and see what it says. You do not ask the parties to tell you what they thought it meant.'

[157] J Steyn, 'Contract law: fulfilling the reasonable expectations of honest men' [1997] *LQR* 433, 440: 'By and large the objective approach to questions of interpretation serves the needs of commerce. It tends to promote certainty in the law and predictability in dispute resolution.'

27
Why Are Non-US Contracts Written in US Legalese? Some Preliminary Thoughts and a Research Agenda

*Claire A. Hill**

1. Introduction

US/UK-style contracting[1] is spreading throughout the world. The practice has long been admired, but also reviled and ridiculed. The latter characterization is in evidence in a famous scene from the 1935 Marx Brothers movie *Night at the Opera*. Fiorello, played by Chico Marx, is an opera singer's manager; he is negotiating with Driftwood, played by Groucho, to book the singer. Driftwood gives Fiorello the proposed contract, which consists of one very long piece of paper. They begin discussing the contract, starting with the beginning, which says 'the party of the first part shall be known as the party of the first part.' After Fiorello objects to the provision, Driftwood agrees to delete it, and they tear it off. The next provision is 'the party of the second part shall be known as the party of the second part.' The same thing happens with the other provisions, including those concerning the party of the eighth and ninth part, until only a very small strip of paper is left.[2]

Many explanations exist for why US/UK-style contracting is spreading: the phenomenon is clearly overdetermined. Increasing globalization of contracting, yielding increased heterogeneity of contracting parties and more need to have a 'private law' within the contract rather than using one jurisdiction's laws, is relevant. Institutional features of US (and

---

* Thanks to participants at the Current Legal Issues Colloquium 2011 where I presented this paper, and participants at the Barbara Aronson Black Lecture at Columbia Law School, where I presented 'How Contracts On Wall Street (and Some Other Places) Do Things With Words', a related paper. Thanks also to Brian Bix, Allan Erbsen, Chris King, Dan Schwarcz, Greg Shaffer, and Larry Solan for very helpful conversations.

[1] Because the differences matter less for my purposes than the similarities, I use the term US/UK-style contracting. It should be noted, though, that there are differences, and that my arguments apply with more force to US-style contracting than to UK-style contracting.

[2] The end of the scene contains this famous dialogue:

   Fiorello: Hey, wait, wait. What does this say here, this thing here?
   Driftwood: Oh, that? Oh, that's the usual clause that's in every contract. That just says, uh, it says, uh, if any of the parties participating in this contract are shown not to be in their right mind, the entire agreement is automatically nullified.
   Fiorello: Well, I don't know...
   Driftwood: It's all right. That's, that's in every contract. That's, that's what they call a sanity clause.
   Fiorello: Ha-ha-ha-ha-ha! You can't fool me. There *ain't* no Sanity Clause!

Available at <http://en.wikipedia.org/wiki/A_Night_at_the_Opera_(film)>.

to a somewhat lesser extent UK) law practice, and the trajectory by which transaction structures have been developed and come into use also are part of the story.[3]

To some extent, what makes US/UK-style contracting admired is also what makes it reviled and ridiculed: complex and technical subject matter, addressed in detail. But the ridicule also comes from what can be considered pathologies of US/UK-style contracting: the extent of the detail, the extent of the arcane language ('legalese'), and what I have elsewhere[4] called band-aids and warring notwithstandings, multiple provisions that purport to trump all other provisions ('Notwithstanding anything else in this agreement to the contrary...'). Besides pathologies of documentation, there are also pathologies of the negotiation process, such as the excesses—excesses of time, excesses of care, vividly exemplified by middle-of-the-night arguments over the placements of semicolons—that yield the ridicule-inducing provisions and overall documentation.

This paper considers why the bad apparently comes along with the good, and makes some broader observations about the trajectory of complex business contracting. It also considers whether the trajectory is inexorable, and if not, under what circumstances we might expect some resistance to the use of US/UK-style contracting. Finally, this paper considers possible carryover effects of the use of US/UK-style contracting on lawyers and their clients—and the greater society.

2. The trajectory

I start by depicting a stylized trajectory.[5] As business globalizes, contracts in countries outside the US and the UK increasingly resemble US/UK-style contracts. The negotiation process increasingly also resembles the US/UK-style process, with its length, detail, and adversarial character. A stark contrast exists with shorter, less heavily negotiated contracts more typically used in civil law countries.

Why has this occurred? First, parties who contract with one another used to often be in homogeneous, cohesive communities. Now, parties contract with other parties who may not be in the same region, or even in the same country, who may not be in the same business, and with whom they may not share common laws, language, or culture. When parties dealt with one another repeatedly, sharing a cohesive reputational community, they could have 'thick' norms—elaborate understandings as to what constituted good and bad behavior that didn't need to be in a written agreement.[6] Within such a community, it was feasible to monitor one another's compliance with both the contract and the norms, and impose extra-legal sanctions for breach of either, including reputational sanctions. Consider in this regard the diamond industry. It has very detailed norms, and

---

[3] This discussion adapts, expands, and updates arguments I made in Claire A. Hill, 'The Trajectory of Complex Business Contracting in Latin America' (2008) 83 *Chi. Kent. L. Rev.* 197.

[4] Claire A. Hill, 'Why Contracts Are Written in Legalese' (2002) 77 *Chi. Kent. L. Rev.* 59.

[5] My discussion in this section is based on interviews with a variety of practitioners from the US, the UK, and several countries in Europe, Asia, and Latin America. See also John Flood, 'Lawyers as Sanctifiers: The Role of Elite Law Firms in International Business Transactions' (2007) 14(1) *Indiana J. Glob. Leg. Stud.* 35; and John Flood and Fabian Sosa, 'Lawyers, Law Firms and the Stabilization of Transnational Business' (2008) 28 *Northwestern J. Int'l Law & Bus.* 489. For expository ease, and because it does not affect the arguments I am making, my discussion glosses over important differences among countries.

[6] See Claire A. Hill and Christopher King, 'How German Contracts Do As Much With Fewer Words' (2004) 79 *Chi. Kent. L. Rev.* 889. See also Lisa Bernstein, 'Opting Out of the Legal System: Extralegal Contractual Relations in the Diamond Industry' (1992) 21 *Journal of Legal Studies* 115; Barak D. Richman, 'How Community Institutions Create Economic Advantage: Jewish Diamond Merchants in New York' (2006), 31 *Law & Soc. Inquiry* 383, and Robert Ellickson, *Order Without Law: How Neighbors Settle Disputes* (Cambridge, MA: Harvard University Press, 1991).

a community that allows for enforcement of those norms.[7] One author, explaining the prominence of Jewish merchants in the diamond business, argues that:

> The primary comparative advantage Jewish merchants enjoy is the ability to credibly commit to pay for the diamonds they purchase on credit. Jewish merchants owe this advantage to complementarities between the demands for governing diamond transactions and the traditional structure of Jewish communities. In short, Jewish community institutions can enforce executory contracts that are beyond the reach of public courts and thus beyond noncommunity members as well.[8]

Another community involved in the diamond business is the Palanpuri Jains, in India.[9] When asked by an interviewer what accounts for the Jains' success in the diamond industry, an industry magnate, Vijay Shah, said: 'it may be something to do with the strong work ethic of the community. This is one of many characteristics that Palanpuri Jains seem to have in common with Hasidic Jews—others are a religious orthodoxy and deep family feeling, which keeps the respective communities very close-knit.'[10]

As business globalizes, more transactions occur outside of repeat homogeneous communities. Contracting parties may be from different regions or countries; they also may be in different businesses. New parties who have not previously done business with anyone else in the community may be introduced or vouched for—for instance, a party from country A seeking to do business with a party in country B might ask its local law firm to contact a law firm in country B that might know the country B party, or the country B party might arrange such a contact itself. But the relationships within such a broader heterogenous 'community' are far more attenuated. With such attenuation, norms are apt to be far thinner, and monitoring and extra-legal enforcement will be far more difficult.

Consider, for instance, the obvious reputational sanction of 'shunning'—not dealing with an offender. In a small, repeat community, there may be a considerable consensus as to what behavior warrants shunning, and dealings with the offender may be difficult to conceal. By contrast, in a larger, less repeat community, shunning may be much more difficult, if not impossible. Some 'members' may not be aware of the sanction, some might not agree with it, and dealings with the offender may not be detected.

The foregoing account reflects more than just globalization; it also reflects the increasing sophistication of transactions. But globalization adds some important elements to the mix. First, not infrequently, parties do not have a common native language, and are not governed by the same law. They need a language that will work for both (or all) of them. English has established itself as the general 'second' language. And even if the parties do have a common language, if they anticipate that they may subsequently want to involve parties with other native languages, or English-speaking parties, they may want their documents to be in English. For instance, the documents for a financing that might be later sold in whole or in part to some US financial institutions will be in English. And transactions done by and for US or UK banks will be in English. Moreover, for many types of complex or innovative financing transactions, the documentation originally developed for the transaction is in English; later transactions, even if they do not involve one or more parties for whom English is their native language, will typically use

---

[7] See Bernstein, 'Opting Out of the Legal System' (cited in n.6); see Richman, 'How Community Institutions Create Economic Advantage' (cited in n.6).
[8] See Richman, 'How Community Institutions Create Economic Advantage' (cited in n.6), 389.
[9] See, e.g., Samyukta Bhowmick (2005), 'A peek into India's diamond trade,' *Rediff India Abroad*, available at <http://www.rediff.com/money/2005/nov/02spec.htm>.
[10] Bhowmick, 'A peek into India's diamond trade' (cited in n.9).

documentation based on that original documentation[11]—documents in English, and in the US/UK style. Other reasons why transaction documentation isn't just in English but is also of the US/UK style include the increased role the documentation must play in the relationship between the parties. With fewer and thinner norms, and less ability to monitor and enforce the use of extra-legal sanctions, more must be specified in the agreement. With no common governing law, the parties use more 'private law', detailed understandings the parties have as to their relationship that do not use or refer to a particular jurisdiction's law. Also, insofar as agreements among parties not infrequently provide for arbitration, the arbitrator may have particular need for 'private law'.[12] Finally, US firms have parlayed their connections with investment banks, their size, resources, and broad range of expertise, and their reputations, into a global presence and role as standard-setter. UK firms have played their part as well, with their history of seeking business outside the UK, which almost necessarily means in non-English speaking countries. Both the US and the UK offer LLM degrees that are quite attractive to lawyers from many other countries; these lawyers get trained in the US/UK ways, including not infrequently by spending some time employed in US or UK law firms, and bring their modes of practice back to their home countries. As John Flood notes:

Elite status is reinforced by the open recognition of many consumers of law and lawyers that of all the legal regimes in the world only two are of significant consequence in transactional work, namely English law and New York state law. The number of potential law schools able to supply graduates capable of legal work at this level is small. Other jurisdictions are significant, of course, but they are dominated by this western duopoly. I have shown elsewhere that international business lawyers often define themselves by three attributes. A mastery of the English language, which is the common language of international business and finance, an ability to draft contracts, more in the prolix Anglo-Saxon style rather than in the concise continental way, and an understanding of private dispute resolution systems, such as arbitration. On occasion another requisite is claimed, namely, admission to another jurisdiction, notably the New York Bar.[13]

---

[11] See John Flood, 'Capital Markets, Globalisation and Global Elites' in Michael B. Likosky (ed.), *Transnational Legal Processes—Globalisation And Power Disparities* (Cambridge: Butterworths, 2002), 132–3:

> It is clear that individual jurisdictions remain legitimate sources of state norms, and we have not yet arrived at the hyperglobalisers' utopia nor are we still in the sceptics' dystopia, but these, in many cases are being overridden by soft law created through contract and agreements that usually owes its "allegiance" to either New York state law or English law. Local law is in the process of becoming subsumed under highly competitive systems of law that market themselves aggressively. The result is that local law declines in importance in spite of whatever changes it may introduce to modernise itself. The Anglo-American axis is too powerful to defeat in the capital markets field. It dominates the transnational institutions such as the IMF and WTO; the prime investment banks are based in the US, and the lawyers are either in New York or London. The combination of institutional global reach, normative creativity and pluralism, and professional service flexibility and responsiveness to market changes appears impregnable.

[12] I thank Janet Ainsworth for this point.

[13] John Flood, 'Legal Education, Globalization and the New Imperialism' in F. Cownie (ed.), *The Law School—Global Issues, Local Questions* (Brookfield, VT: Ashgate, 1999), 127, 130. See Carole Silver (2002), 'The Case of the Foreign Lawyer: Internationalizing the U.S. Legal Profession' 25 *Ford. Int'l L. J.* 1039. On rival websites, Continental Europe and England are attempting to make the case for their own superiority; respectively: <http://www.fondation-droitcontinental.org/jcms/c_10442/newsletter-february-march-2011>, which includes a brochure developed jointly by French and German lawyers, touting civil law as 'global, secure, inexpensive, flexible,' and <http://www.lawsociety.org.uk/documents/downloads/jurisdiction_of_choice_brochure.pdf>, a brochure by the Law Society of England and Wales, extolling English law's benefits, including that English is the language of international business, and the transparency, predictability, and flexibility of English law. One

In a changing world, where parties are engaging in different kinds of transactions with different kinds of parties, the extent of shared norms isn't clear, and the potential role of multiple jurisdictions may lead to uncertainty, there is an important role for well-established, confident lawyers.[14] Once a typical modus operandi is established, it becomes a reputationally safe way to proceed. Doing something different is riskier: if difficulties arise, not doing 'what is typically done'—the US/UK documentation written and negotiated by US/UK lawyers—may be hard to justify. In emerging markets, doing deals the US/UK way may signal being 'in the know' and yield prestige.[15] I was told of situations where US/UK-style documentation and concepts were used even for wholly domestic transactions notwithstanding that the documentation did not 'work' under local law. I was also told of extensive negotiations on subjects that are relevant in the US but largely or even completely irrelevant in the jurisdiction where the transaction was being negotiated and done.

Another reason for the spread and persistence of US/UK-style contracting is one I proposed in an earlier article. I argued that when one party proposed to use US/UK-style contracting, the other party might have difficulty arguing against doing so.

> Once one party comes "armed" with a more complex and comprehensive contract, it is difficult for the other party to say "oh, we don't need all that extra verbiage." The countervailing arguments—this level of detail and intricacy signals distrust, this is a significant increase in paper and money without much (if any) added benefit, the poor trees are being chopped down for no good reason, and that the complexity may lead us to overlook something easy and important—are hard to advance successfully. The other side's client is getting these "protections"—surely our client needs them too.[16]

3. An explanation

The foregoing makes a case for why so much contract documentation would be in English, and of a sort familiar to US/UK parties—with considerable detail, especially as to contingencies. But it does not make a case for the pathologies and excesses of US/UK-style contracts. Indeed, an economically inclined observer might suppose that when people who typically use a different style of contracting—for instance, 'leaner' Continental contracting—encounter US/UK-style contracting, they might try to meet in the middle, taking the best of both. After all, as discussed above, there are sound reasons to have more detail in contracts among heterogeneous parties who don't share a common language or law. But the style's pathologies and excesses are apparently along for the ride: there seems to be no appreciable attempt to pare down the contracts in particular contexts. This reveals something critical about contracting—that

---

desirable and flexible feature of English law is stated to be that it allows parties to choose their own terms. By contrast in many civil law systems, more terms are provided in the applicable statute. The terms are often mandatory, but even when they are not—when parties could choose other terms—they nevertheless often use the statutory default. Whether this feature is a cost or a benefit turns in significant part on the characteristics of the contracting parties' reputational community. If thick norms and reputation will yield the desired arrangement, using the default terms or leaving quite a bit unspecified makes sense. There is far less reason to spend time in elaborate specification and customization of an agreement.

[14] See Flood, 'Lawyers as Sanctifiers' (cited in n.5), 55–7.
[15] See Hill, 'The Trajectory of Complex Business Contracting in Latin America' (cited in n.3). The lawyers I interviewed for this paper also made these observations.
[16] Hill, 'The Trajectory of Complex Business Contracting in Latin America' (cited in n.3), 180 (internal footnotes omitted).

it is importantly not just a means to the end of specifying the parties' deal to a court. Adoption of US/UK-style contracting isn't a deracinated, dispassionate, and carefully reasoned process and decision. Adoption of this style of contracting imports rituals and signals, this latter term meant both in the economic sense and in the sociological and anthropological sense.[17] Consider the mindset of the lawyers steeped in US/UK-style contracting and their clients—an ease, and self-serving 'principled' view that the process is superior and indispensable. How, they presumably think, could they serve their clients without the comprehensive forms and the detailed wrangling over language addressing any contingency that comes to any party's mind? The lawyers signal confidence and effective advocacy by proceeding as they do, starting from a detailed contract used in a previous deal and revising and adding (but almost never subtracting) elements as needed for the deal they are working on.[18] Consider, too, the mindset of those to whom the US/UK style is being introduced, and who are being called on to adopt it.

In my interviews, lawyers in European countries were sometimes depicted as being scornful and grudging, seeming to think: 'The US is the 800 pound gorilla, able to dictate what it wants by its size and influence, and by the fact that it has many investors whose participation in transactions—that is, money—is desired.' (The UK weighs in at a lesser, but still considerable, amount: maybe 500 pounds?) Lawyers in Latin American countries were more often depicted as being admiring—as wanting to be associated with doing things the way they were done in the North. My interviews of course do not provide proof—the lawyers I talked to may very well not be representative. Still, their accounts are suggestive, and the picture painted is consistent with intuition and depictions about these cultures in other contexts.

The lawyers not from the US and the UK who are trained in US and UK LLM programs can be expected generally to be ambassadors for the US/UK way. They presumably have been trained (indoctrinated?) by people with some stake in showing the merits of the US/UK way. They presumably also want to justify to themselves and others having taken the time and trouble, and incurred the expense, to study the system. Moreover, they can use their expertise in this area to distinguish themselves from their colleagues who do not have law degrees from US or UK institutions, or practiced in those countries.

4. Some questions

I argued above that contracting is importantly to be understood as a ritual. What parties are doing matters, but so does how they are doing it. Indeed, what they are doing cannot be determined without reference to context and background. Suppose that valuation of a party's interest in a venture is at issue, and the parties are considering the possibility of using expert appraisers. Assume there are two types of resolutions standard in the industry—the average of two appraisals, one from an appraiser chosen by each party, or the average of three appraisals, one chosen by each party and the third chosen by the other two. What if a party wanted four appraisers? Or a party didn't know the standard and was willing to agree to one, chosen by the other side?

---

[17] See generally Mark Suchman (2003), 'The Contract As Social Artifact' 37 *Law & Soc. Rev.* 91.
[18] I have elsewhere given an account of US-style contracting. See Hill, 'Why Contracts Are Written in Legalese', (cited in n.4) and Hill and King, 'How German Contracts Do As Much With Fewer Words' (cited in n.6).

The party requesting the four appraisers would be signaling excessive zeal or perhaps distrust; the party satisfied with one would be signaling either naivete or excessive trust. What is being signaled turns on context—there is no necessary connection between asking for four appraisers and distrust or accepting the other party's one appraiser and trust.

Another example: Imagine a contract that provides for A to make payments to B by 5 pm on a certain date each month. What have the parties agreed to with respect to performance at 5.05 pm? In my interviews, some parties said that the understanding in their communities was that B could treat the late payment as a breach without reputational consequences; others said that in their communities, B would suffer reputational consequences if it treated the late payment as a breach.

To what extent are the understandings among members of a transacting community using US/UK-style contracting imported when the contracting is used elsewhere? In other words, when US/UK-style contracting spreads, does its penumbra—of what's done, what isn't done, and the connotations thereof—spread with it? Based on my interviews, the answer would seem to be no. For instance, I was told that many practices that would be considered acceptable in a wholly US deal would be considered overreaching and unduly aggressive in deals with German parties.

Several interesting questions arise. First, consider the phenomenon of 'crowding out.'[19] An employer, trying to get the best performance from employees, can require clocking in and out with a time card. He can install a visible TV monitor to show the employees they are being watched throughout the day. But this might yield not just resentment but also a very literalist and formalist mindset, where the person does exactly what is required in order to avoid a sanction. The employee's motivation to do a good job is crowded out by the extensive monitoring. Many examples can be given in which formalism led to very bad results. Indeed, tax law is replete with examples of the dark side of formalism, with tax shelters succeeding in abiding by the letter of the law while violating its intent. In a similar vein, managers with detailed bonus formulas may 'work to bonus' rather than acting to advance what they think might be best for the business in the moderate or long term. People otherwise inclined to donate blood may be dissuaded if payment for blood becomes more common.[20]

Insofar as US/UK-style contracting involves far more detail, and far more specification, might it make the parties act in a more formalistic/legalistic manner, not only as to their compliance with their contract but also as to their relationship generally? Recall the example above about whether a payment made five minutes late could be treated as a default. Parties who know that their contracting partners will make allowances will have a different relationship than those who know that their partners will not make allowances. This issue has been raised within the US, when a contracting party not used to what I have been calling US/UK-style contracting, but which is more accurately

---

[19] See generally Ernst Fehr and Simon Gachter (2002), 'Do Incentive Contracts Crowd Out Voluntary Cooperation', IEW Working Paper No. 34.

[20] See generally Richard Titmuss, *The Gift Relationship: From Human Blood to Social Policy* (New York: Pantheon Books, 1970). The proposition is actually quite controversial, with empirical evidence offered in support and in rebuttal. Some recent work on the issue includes Joan Costa-Font, Mireia Jofre-Bonet, and Steven T. Yen (2011), 'Not All Incentives Wash Out the Warm Glow: The Case of Blood Donation Revisited', CESifo Working Paper No. 3527 (2011); C. Mellstrom and M. Johannesson, 'Crowding out in blood donation: was Titmuss right?', (2008) 6(4) *Journal of the European Economic Association* 845–63; Nicola Lacetera, Mario Macis, and Robert Slonim, 'Will There Be Blood? Incentives and Displacement Effects in Pro-Social Behavior' (2012) 4(1) *American Economic Journal: Economic Policy* 186–223.

characterized as the contracting done (domestically and internationally) by the more sophisticated and typically larger firms, contracts with a party represented by one of these firms. Indeed, the issue—the benefits of a more detailed contract versus one that specifies far less—is commonly raised in many contexts, including banking and medicine. One context is microcredit, in which relational bonds have yielded high repayment rates. Consider, too, a fanciful example, from the movie *Bedazzled*, in which a hapless short-order cook sells his soul to the Devil in exchange for seven wishes. At first, the cook expresses his wishes naively, thinking the Devil is in good faith and will simply grant them. Each time, the Devil finds a way to literally grant the wish while not giving the cook what he really wanted.[21]

A related issue concerns recent findings about the relationship between money and self-sufficiency.[22] The researchers conducted experiments which provided evidence that:

money brings about a self-sufficient orientation in which people prefer to be free of dependency and dependents. Reminders of money, relative to nonmoney reminders, led to reduced requests for help and reduced helpfulness toward others. Relative to participants primed with neutral concepts, participants primed with money preferred to play alone, work alone, and put more physical distance between themselves and a new acquaintance.[23]

The very detailed provision for and discussion of contingencies, and indeed, the intricate parsing of all language, may not only encourage literalism and crowding out; it may also operate like a money prime, insofar as it encourages articulation leading to quantification at every turn. What might be the effect of US/UK style contracting on newly developing business communities? How might the practice affect existing business communities which previously used more informal and less detailed agreements?

Another question relates to US views about government. The US has a history of hostility to government, at or near its peak at this writing: certainly, anti-government rhetoric, such as that of the Tea Party, is not rare. The inclusion of 'private law' in an agreement is in some respects opting out of government, or at least relying less on government. (Government does, of course, retain an important role in a US/UK-style contract—it may be needed to enforce agreements.) But contrast a system like that of Germany, with, as a lawyer I interviewed practicing in Germany told me, trust in the law to do a good job in interpreting contracts and filling in gaps. Might the US distrust of law as reflected in an agreement that creates a private law be contagious? Further work is needed to determine the extent to which US/UK contracting affects other aspects of parties' relationships and indeed, the greater culture.

A final set of questions: Is the trajectory of US/UK-style contracting inexorable? On the one hand, once people begin the detailed parsing and providing for contingencies— asking 'What if?'— it's hard to stop. That being said, some of my interviewees told me that they had recently experienced some resistance from clients who had previously accepted US/UK-style contracting. These interviewees were talking about deals involving Chinese and Mexican clients. Might the diminution of US prestige affect non-US parties' willingness to use the US/UK contracting style? What might this tell us about how to understand contracting?

---

[21] I discuss this issue in Hill, 'Why Contracts Are Written in Legalese' (cited in n.4), 62–70. *Bedazzled* stars Peter Cook and Dudley Moore and was released in 1967.
[22] Kathleen D. Vohs, Nicole L. Mead, and Miranda R. Goode (2006), 'The Psychological Consequences of Money' 314 *Science* 1154.
[23] Vohs et al., 'The Psychological Consequences of Money' (cited in n.22), 1154.

5. Conclusion

Contracting is not a deracinated meta-activity—a means by which parties are merely attempting to make the terms of their deal clear to a court. Rather, it is a rich phenomenon involving multiple layers of meaning. Text is embedded in, and is inextricably linked to, context. Studying the use in other countries of US/UK contracting practices offers the opportunity to illuminate more about contracting; it offers, as well, the opportunity to illuminate more about the many disparate influences on culture.

28

The Role of Parliamentary Rhetoric in Facilitating the Racial Effect of the Stop and Search Powers in Section 44 of the Terrorism Act 2000

Rachel Herron

1. Introduction

In 2010, following the judgment of the European Court of Human Rights in *Gillan v United Kingdom*, the UK government suspended, and then later repealed, the suspicion-less stop and search powers in the Terrorism Act 2000 s.44 (hereinafter s.44).[1] Whilst its judgment was based on the police's breach of Article 8 ECHR, the Court also found that the powers gave rise to a 'clear risk of arbitrariness' and that the 'discriminatory use of the powers ... [was] a very real consideration'.[2] This judicial criticism corresponded with pre-existing claims of the racially disproportionate deployment of the powers and the deleterious impact of their use on both community cohesion and effective counter-terror policing.[3]

A range of explanations have been suggested for police persistence in deploying the powers disproportionately against minority individuals, irrespective of the counter-productive impact of so doing on tackling the threat from international terrorism. The Government's then Independent Reviewer of counter-terrorism legislation, Lord Carlile, for example, suggested that an important contributing factor to the racially uneven use of s.44 was the level of police officer autonomy arising from the suspicion-less nature of the powers.[4] A further explanation has been linked to the residual effects of the types of

---

[1] Terrorism Act 2000 (c.11) ss.44(1) and (2).

[2] *Gillan and Quinton v The United Kingdom* (Application no. 4158/05), 12 January 2010, paras 83 and 85.

[3] See e.g., A. Sanders and R. Young, *Criminal Justice* (3rd edn, Oxford: Oxford University Press, 2007); B. Bowling and C. Phillips, 'Disproportionate and Discriminatory: Reviewing the evidence on police stop and search' (2007) 70(6) *Modern Law Review* 936–61; D. Moeckli, 'Stop and Search under the Terrorism Act 2000: A Comment on R (Gillan) v Police' (2007) 70(4) *Modern Law Review* 659–70; and O. De Schutter and J. Ringelheim, 'Ethnic Profiling: A Rising Challenge for European Human Rights Law' (2008) 72(3) *Modern Law Review* 358–84. Disputing such claims see P.A.J. Waddington, K. Stenson, and D. Don, 'In proportion. Race, and Police Stop and Search' (2004) 44(6) *British Journal of Criminology* 889–914; and J. Miller, 'Stop and Search in England. A Reformed Tactic or Business as Usual?' (2010) 50 *Brit. J. of Criminology* 954, 955.

[4] Lord Carlile of Berriew, *Report on the Operation in 2009 of the Terrorism Act 2000 and Part I of the Terrorism Act 2006* (July 2010), para.268.

discriminatory behaviour identified by the Macpherson Inquiry,[5] and in other studies,[6] which sustain the institutional proclivity of the police for race-based operations.[7] The antagonistic relationship between the police and minority groups is attested to by the protests and subsequent riots in London, in August 2011, which have been attributed in part to ongoing mistrust between the police and minority communities.[8] Finally, the media's reporting of the 'war on terror' has also been cited as a potentially instrumental factor in the racial effect of stop and search, through its shaping of public perceptions regarding the identity of the terrorist threat,[9] which in turn affected the way that the police deployed the highly subjective stop and search powers.[10]

Rather than focusing on the role of officer discretion, institutional bias, or the media, in fostering the racially uneven deployment of the suspicion-less stop and search powers, this paper uses s.44 as a case study through which to explore the potential role of parliamentary discourse in giving rise to this racial effect. Although pinning down the precise causative effects of parliamentary discourse is difficult, given the nature of causation, the framework of 'governmentalism' provides a means of understanding how parliamentary behaviour may have influenced the operation of the institutions of law enforcement[11] so that it was almost inevitable that police chiefs would mirror political postures.[12]

---

[5] The Stephen Lawrence Inquiry, *Report of an Inquiry by Sir William Macpherson of Cluny* Cm 4262-I (February 1999). See also J. Bourne, 'The Life and Times of Institutional Racism' (2001) 43 *Race and Class* 7–22.

[6] See Home Office, *From the Neighbourhood to the National: Policing our Communities Together* Cm 7448 (London: The Stationery Office, 2008), para.4.18. See also Simon Holdaway, *Recruiting a Multi-Racial Police Force* (London: HMSO, 1991); Simon Holdaway and Anne-Marie Barron, *Resigners? The Experience of Black and Asian Police Officers* (Basingstoke: Macmillan, 1997); E. Cashmore, 'The Experiences of Ethnic Minority Police Officers in Britain: Under Recruitment and Racial Profiling in a Performance Culture' (2001) 24(4) *Ethnic and Racial Studies* 642; and E. Cashmore, 'Behind the Window Dressing: Ethnic Minority Police Perspective on Cultural Diversity' (2002) 28(2) *Journal of Ethnic Migration Studies* 327.

[7] EHRC, *Police and Racism: What Has been Achieved 10 Years after the Stephen Lawrence Inquiry Report* (London: EHRC, 2009). See also European Commission against Racism and Intolerance, *Third Report on the United Kingdom* (15 June 2005), para.83; Janet Foster, Tim Newburn, and Anna Souhami, *Assessing the Impact of the Stephen Lawrence Inquiry* (London: The Stationery Office, 2005), 30; and S. Holdaway and M. O'Neill, 'Where has all the Racism Gone/Views of Racism within Constabularies after Macpherson' (2007) 30(3) *Ethnic and Racial Studies* 397.

[8] See Runnymede Trust, 'Tottenham—a tragedy we should have seen coming?' available at <http://www.runnymedetrust.org/blog/153/359/Tottenham—a-tragedy-we-should-have-seen-coming.html?utm_source=The+Runnymede+Trust&utm_campaign=e17d03459c-Julyupdate2011&utm_medium=email>, accessed 16.08.2011.

[9] See, e.g., F. Furedi, 'From Narrative of the Blitz to Rhetoric of Vulnerability' (2007) 1(2) *Cultural Sociology* 23; F. Furedi, 'Coping with Adversity: The Turn to the Rhetoric of Vulnerability' (2007) 20 *Security Journal* 171; and Z. Papacharissi and M. de Fatima Oliveira, 'News Frames Terrorism: A Comparative Analysis of Frames Employed in Terrorism Coverage in the US and UK Newspapers' (2008) 13 *International Journal of Press/Politics* 52.

[10] G. Mythen, S. Walklate, and F. Khan, "I'm a Muslim, but I'm not a terrorist' (2009) 49(6) *Brit. J. of Criminology* 736, 742.

[11] G. Burchell, C. Gordon, and P. Miller, *The Foucault Effect. Studies in Governmentality* (Chicago: University of Chicago Press, 1999); D. Garland, '"Governmentality" and the Problem of Crime: Foucault, Criminology, Sociology' (1997) 1(2) *Theoretical Criminology* 173; N. Rose, 'Government and Control' (2000) 40(2) *British Journal of Criminology* 321; G. Mythen and S. Walklate, 'Criminology and errorism: which thesis? Risk Society or Governmentality?' (2006) 46 *Brit. J. of Criminology* 378, 388–9.

[12] R. Lambert, 'Empowering Salafis and Islamists against al-Qaeda' 32; C. Pantazis and S. Pemberton, 'From the "Old" to the "New" Suspect Communities' (2009) 49(5) *British Journal of Criminology* 646–66; C. Pantazis and S. Pemberton, 'Restating the case for the "Suspect Community": a Reply to Greer' (2011) 61(6) *British Journal of Criminology* 1054.

Arguments as to the causative link between parliamentary discourse and police use of their stop and search powers,[13] are given further credence by the 'politicization of policing' which accelerated in the aftermath of 9/11.[14] The then Chief of Counter-terrorism of the Metropolitan Police Authority (MPA), Andy Hayman, linked the patterns of use of s.44 to a blurring of the lines between political and police objectives.[15] One indication of the increased proximity between parliamentary and police behaviour was that the police explicitly referred to governmental policy and operational aims in their use of their counter-terrorism powers.[16] This connection, coupled with the socially productive power of the parliamentary proceedings, suggests that discourses arising from within Parliament may have played a role in shaping how the police used the stop and search powers.[17]

Language is the currency of the parliamentary process[18] and contains within it top-down power to shape its legislating function; to direct executive implementation of the law; and to cultivate popular sentiment.[19] Such linguistic constructions affecting perceptions, cognition, and emotions are linked to the use of persuasive forms of language, as a means of inducing support and consensus regarding the legislative action, otherwise known as parliamentary rhetoric. Rhetoric, which comprises the art of using language to persuade,[20] is a means by which parliamentary discourse assumes its constructive nature. The power of rhetorical language to shape the framework of legislation means that it is highly susceptible to the individual and group interests within society and the relationships between them.[21] In turn, these dominant discourses have an important role in determining the way in which governance is exercised.[22] Language and discourse can, therefore, create a new social reality and the rhetoric used affects the nature of this reality.[23]

The analysis herein will focus on two distinct periods of parliamentary debate. First, this paper will demonstrate that in the debates leading up to the enactment of s.44,

---

[13] R. Reiner, *The Politics of the Police* (Oxford: Oxford University Press, 2010), 219–22.

[14] S. Poynting and V. Mason, '"Tolerance, Freedom, Justice and Peace?" Britain, Australia and anti-Muslim Racism since 11th September 2001' (2006) 27(4) *Journal of Intercultural Studies* 365, 368.

[15] A. Hayman, *The Terrorist Hunters. The Ultimate Inside Story of Britain's Fight against Terrorism* (London: Bantam Press, 2009), 119–23.

[16] MPA, *Counter-terrorism: The London Debate* (London: MPA, 2007), 67; and Joint Committee on Human Rights (JCHR), 'Demonstrating Respect for Rights? Follow-up, 22nd Report of Session 2008–09', HL141/HC522 (July 2009), para.49.

[17] J. Goldsmith and A. Vermule, 'Empirical Methodology and Legal Scholarship' (2002) 69 *U. Chi. L. Rev* 153,157.

[18] See Diana Eades, *Sociolinguistics and the Legal Process* (Bristol: Multilingual Matters, 2010).

[19] Paul Goodrich, *Legal Discourse, Studies in Linguistics, Rhetoric and Legal Analysis* (London: St. Martin's Press, 1987). Critiquing this role of language see Catherine A. MacKinnon, *Only Words* (Cambridge, Mass.: Harvard University Press, 1993); and R. Delgado, 'Norms and Normative Science: Toward a Critique of Normativity in Legal Thought' (1991) 139 *University of Pennsylvania L. Rev.* 933.

[20] This definition of rhetoric as persuasion originates from Aristotle. For a more contemporary consideration of legal rhetoric see John Hollander, 'Legal Rhetoric' in Peter Brooks and Paul Gerwitz (eds), *Law's Stories. Narrative and Rhetoric in the Law* (New Haven, Conn.: Yale University Press, 1999), 176–86.

[21] Adam Jaworski and Nikolas Coupland, 'Introduction' in Adam Jaworski and Nikolas Coupland (eds), *The Discourse Reader* (2nd edn, London: Routledge, 2004), 3. See also Michael A.K. Halliday, *Language as Social Semiotic: The Social Interpretation of Language* (London: Edward Arnold, 1978).

[22] Mythen and Walklate, 'Criminology and Terrorism: which thesis?' (cited in n.11).

[23] Richard Jackson, *Writing the War on Terrorism. Language, Politics, and Counter-terrorism* (Manchester: Manchester University Press, 2005), 23; and Ian Parker, *Discourse Dynamics: Critical for Social And Individual Psychology* (London, 1992), 5.

and its preceding statutory provisions, the socially constructive nature of parliamentary discourse operated as a tool of governance,[24] endorsing the enactment of the statutory powers, without standard safeguards against misuse, for predominantly political ends. Secondly, this paper will show that the imperative necessity of the absent statutory safeguards in preventing the misuse of s.44 was demonstrated first-hand in the febrile atmosphere post-9/11. Against the background of the terrorist attacks parliamentary imagery forged a heuristic shortcut between minority communities and the terrorist threat, creating a readily identifiable 'suspect community'.[25] Having subjected all members of such communities to a heightened level of suspicion, Parliament used vivid imagery from 9/11 to emphasise the necessity for pre-emptive police action, of a type and scale not envisaged when the powers were enacted. Descriptions of the need for the police to make full, widespread use of their counter-terrorism powers, together with the community-wide delineation of the threat, created an irresistible opportunity for the police to make high levels of pre-emptive use of the powers. Using the powers independently from any known unlawful behaviour meant that the use was in the absence of the detailed intelligence concerning the terrorist threat faced. Against this background the powers were disproportionately focused on racial minority groups, despite this not representing an operationally useful practice.[26]

2. Parliamentary rhetoric and the enactment of powers without safeguards

The enactment of the suspicion-less stop and search powers that came to constitute s.44 occurred in several stages. The power for police to stop and search pedestrians was inserted into the Prevention of Terrorism (Temporary Powers) Act 1989 by the Prevention of Terrorism (Additional Powers) Act 1996.[27] This power built on a previous amendment to the 1989 Act, made by the Criminal Justice and Public Order Act 1994, which enabled the police to stop and search vehicles and their occupants without the existence of reasonable suspicion.[28] Both powers were put on a permanent statutory footing through s.44. This section analyses the parliamentary discourse concerning the suspicion-less stop and search powers, looking first at the 1996 debate and then at the 1999/2000 debates, to demonstrate that the rationale and safeguards upon which passage of the powers was originally premised was at odds with descriptions of the nature of the powers and expectations regarding their use, set out in the later debates. The result

---

[24] M. Foucault, 'Governmentality' in J.D. Faudon (ed.) and R. Hurley (trns), *Power. The Essential Works of Foucault, 1954–1984*, vol. III (London: New Press, 1994), 206–7.

[25] P. Hillyard, *Suspect Community: Peoples' Experiences of the Prevention of Terrorism Acts* (London: Pluto Press, 1993); P. Hillyard, 'The "War on Terror": Lessons from Ireland' (2005), available at <http://www.ecln.org/essays/essay-1.pdf>, accessed 02.02.2012.

[26] Liberty, *A New Suspect Community* (October 2003), available at <http://www.liberty-human-rights.org.uk/policy/reports/a-new-suspect-community-october-2003.pdf>, accessed 26.03.2011; R. Weitzer and S.A. Tuch, 'Racially Biased Policing: Determinants of Citizen Perceptions' (2005) 83(3) *Social Forces* 1009–30; F. Gregory, 'Policing the "New Extremism" in Twenty-first Century Britain', in M. Goodwin and R. Eatwell (eds), *The "New Extremism" in Twenty-first Century Britain* (London: Routledge, 2009); Carlile, *Report on the Operation in 2009 of the Terrorism Act 2000* (cited in n.4); and Lord Carlile of Berriew, 'Terrorism, Pragmatism, Populism and Libertarianism', The Inaugural John Creaney Memorial Lecture (3 March 2010), available at <http://www.policyexchange.org.uk/modevents/item/terrorism-pragmatism-populism-and-libertarianism>, accessed 01.10.2012.

[27] Prevention of Terrorism (Additional Powers) Act 1996 (c.7), s.1.

[28] Criminal Justice and Public Order Act 1994 (c.33), s.81.

of this mismatch was that the effectiveness of safeguards originally advocated to protect against the wholly discretionary deployment of the powers was substantially diminished. At the same time, however, the expansion, renewal, and later permanent enactment of the powers were treated as an uncontroversial, even natural, progression in safeguarding the country against terrorist attack.

2.1. The Prevention of Terrorism (Temporary Powers) Act 1989

The power for police officers to stop and search pedestrians for purposes connected with the commission, preparation, or instigation of acts of terrorism passed through Parliament in a single day in 1996.[29] The decision to act with such haste was attributed to police requests for additional powers amidst fears of a terrorist attack over the Easter period.[30] Credibility was added to such claims, due to the fact that Easter marked the 80th anniversary of the Irish Republican Easter Rising in Dublin,[31] as well as the recent end to the IRA cease-fire, following the bombing of Canary Wharf in February 1996.[32] These explanations, however, do not account for the failure to introduce the powers when the Prevention of Terrorism (Temporary Provisions) Act 1989 had been renewed, only three weeks earlier.[33] One alternative explanation offered for the timing of the legislation was party political considerations, with the Government engineering an opportunity for Opposition backbenchers to rebel against their party's new policy of abstaining on national security measures.[34] Dianne Abbott, for example, described the legislation as having been 'ruthlessly promoted ... purely for the purposes of making propaganda'.[35] Such a motivation is supported by the suggestion that the police had long been requesting these powers.[36] The political opportunism behind the new powers was later endorsed in the autobiography of the then Labour Home Secretary, Roy Jenkins,[37] despite the fierce denial of such suggestions by the Home Secretary, Michael Howard.[38]

Irrespective of the motivation behind the enactment of the powers they attracted significant criticism as a result of their suspicion-less nature and because of the rapidity with which they progressed through the House.[39] In response to such criticism Michael Howard, speaking for the Government, cited several safeguards within the statutory provisions designed to ensure that their use did not infringe individual civil liberties.[40] These safeguards included the need for use of the powers to be authorised by a police officer of at least Assistant Chief Constable level. In addition the powers were geographically and temporally limited, with each authorisation being effective for no longer than 28 days. Authorisations lasting for more than 48 hours also had to be confirmed by the Secretary of State.[41] These restrictions were described as preventing the highly discretionary nature

---

[29] HC Deb 2 April 1996, cc.156–300.
[30] Michael Howard, HC Deb 1 April 1996, cc.35 and 40 and 2 April 1996 cc.214–15.
[31] e.g. Earl Russell HL Deb 3 April 1996, c.282.
[32] e.g. Tony Newton, HC Debs 2 April 1996, cc.159–60.
[33] HC Deb 14 March 1996 cc.1124–82. See also HC Deb 2 April 1996, Dennis Canavan, c.170, Max Madden, c.176.
[34] Kevin McNamara HC Deb 5 March 1996, cc.168–9.
[35] HC Deb 2 April 1996, c.297.
[36] e.g., HC Deb 5 March 1996 Alan Beith, cc.164, 198, Kevin McNamara, c.168.
[37] R. Jenkins, *A Life at the Centre* (London: Macmillan, 1991), 393–7.
[38] HC Deb 2 April 1996, cc.198–200.
[39] See, e.g., HC Debs 2 April 1996, cc.159–201.
[40] HC Debs 1 April 1996, c.35.
[41] Michael Howard HC Debs 1 April 1996, c.35 and 2 April 1996, cc.213 and 250.

of the powers from straying into misuse.[42] Indeed, the importance of the safeguards is demonstrated by one MP describing them as the only protection against the new powers effectively reviving the much-criticised 'sus laws' of the past,[43] despite other MPs rejecting this comparison.[44]

A further safeguard against misuse of the powers was the 'circumspection and sensitivity' with which the police would deploy them.[45] Statistics concerning police use of the suspicion-less powers for stopping and searching vehicles and their occupants were cited to confirm this operational restraint.[46] The powers were therefore supported on the basis that they were 'exceptional powers... that are needed exceptionally',[47] with police professionalism and training being described as 'the best guarantee that the House has that these powers will be exercised responsibly'.[48] Michael Howard offered the police 'praise and credit for the way in which they have exercised those [pre-existing] powers', adding further that 'I am certain that they will exercise the additional powers, if they are granted by Parliament, in the same way'.[49] The utility of the safeguards and the highly restrained manner in which the police were expected to deploy the suspicion-less powers were cited as key reasons behind the Opposition's support of the statutory provisions and the accelerated enactment process.[50] Despite reservations regarding the suspicion-less and discretionary nature of the powers, therefore, their passage was justified on the basis that they were subject to significant safeguards against misuse. However, in re-enacting the suspicion-less powers, on a permanent basis, parliamentary descriptions of the level of the threat and the police's role in countering it created wholly different expectations for use of the powers, as compared to those upon which their passage was premised. Such discourses helped to diminish the utility of the statutory safeguards against misuse of the powers, as will now be shown.

2.2. The Terrorism Act 2000

The debate concerning the draft Terrorism Act 2000 took place predominantly during the last quarter of 1999 and the first quarter of 2000.[51] Despite the eventual unsatisfactory impact of s.44, the debate leading to its enactment suggests that a great deal of thought went into the need to protect against police misuse of the powers,[52] with a succession of MPs affirming the importance of adhering to the country's commitments to individual rights and civil liberties.[53] Jack Straw, for example, confirmed the Government's determination to 'build safeguards into our framework of law', to ensure

---

[42] HC Debs 2 April 1996 Michael Howard, c.250, Michael Shersby, c.165, Harry Barnes, c.183, Jack Straw, cc.184, 221, David Wilshire, c.243, Timothy Kirkhope, c.276.
[43] Max Madden HC Debs 2 April 1996, c.177.
[44] See, e.g., Jack Straw, HC Debs 2 April 1996, cc.186, 223–4, Clive Soley, c.183.
[45] HC Debs 2 April 1996, Michael Howard, cc.36, 215, 253, 269, Jack Straw, c. 221.
[46] Michael Howard, HC Debs 2 April 1996, c.210.
[47] Michael Howard, HC Debs 2 April 1996, c.251.
[48] Michael Shersby, HC Debs 2 April 1996, c.252.
[49] Michael Howard, HC Debs 2 April 1996, c.253.
[50] See, e.g., HC Debs 1 and 2 April 1996 Jack Straw, cc.37–8, 184, Ann Taylor, c.161.
[51] See HC Debs 2 December 1999, c.443; 14 December 1999, cc.152–231; and 15 March 2000, cc.329–478. See also HL Debs 6 April 2000, cc.1427–90; 6 May 2000, cc.215–45; 23 May 2000, cc.728–33; and 6 June 2000, cc.1078–1103.
[52] C. Gearty, '11 September 2001, Counter-terrorism and the Human Rights Act' (2005) 32(1) *Journal of Law and Society* 18.
[53] See, e.g., HC Debs 14 December 1999, Tom King, c.179.

that counter-terrorism measures were used responsibly and proportionately.[54] Straw unequivocally announced that '[w]e are determined to strike the right balance between giving the police and other agencies the powers that they need to fight terrorism and guarding the civil liberties of people affected by the exercise of those powers'.[55] Indeed, an almost self-congratulatory tone was adopted during the debate for having identified the deficiencies of past counter-terrorism legislation and being committed to remedying them in the new statute.[56] Recognising the importance of upholding human rights whilst countering terrorism, MPs voiced concerns that the draft statute created a number of opportunities for individual rights to be infringed.[57] Particular concerns, relating to the permanence of the powers, were linked to a weakening of Parliament's ability to ensure that their deployment was within statutory parameters.[58]

Despite such comments regarding the potentially rights-infringing nature of the Terrorism Act powers the dominant parliamentary discourse maintained that the powers were essential and constituted an appropriate balance between rights and national security.[59] Jack Straw even explicitly cited the discretionary nature of the powers as demonstrating that the powers afforded the police operationally essential flexibility.[60] Similarly Ken Maginnis insisted that any effective statutory powers must be 'flexible enough to adapt to the changing nature of terrorism' and so defied tight parliamentary control.[61] Irrespective of explicit acknowledgement of the need for legislative safeguards, therefore, the Government determinedly refused to institute additional protections despite the loss of the significant safeguard against misuse which previously arose from their temporary nature. Maximum flexibility was, therefore, prioritised in favour of safeguards, amid a parliamentary desire to be seen to be taking an unyielding stand against terrorism.[62]

Regardless of reservations concerning the potential for misuse of the stop and search powers parliamentary discourse played a role in negating the effectiveness of the pre-existing statutory safeguards against such misuse. This occurred in two key ways. First, parliamentary discourse emphasised the exceptional nature of the terrorist threat against which Parliament was acting, including its global reach and the use of new, increasingly devastating, technology. Secondly, this background was then treated as necessitating both unified political support for the statutory powers and widespread police use of them. These two themes helped to mute any opposition to, or scrutiny of, the draft legislation whilst also advocating levels of police use of the powers which departed from the operational circumspection cited as safeguarding against misuse of the powers during their original enactment.[63] In the face of such parliamentary descriptions the powers

---

[54] HC Debs 14 December 1999, c.156.

[55] HC Debs 16 March 1999, c.1004.

[56] See, e.g., HC Debs 14 December 1999, Jack Straw, cc.156, 161–2; Ken Maginnis, c.195; Simon Hughes, cc.183–5.

[57] Specific references to stop and search include, e.g., HC Debs 14 December 1999, Kevin McNamara, c.176; Alan Simpson, cc.202–3; Simon Hughes, c.188; and Jeremy Corbyn, c.255; and HC Debs 15 March 2000, c.435.

[58] HC Debs 14 December 1999, Ann Widdecombe, c.171; Tom King, c.179; Fiona Mactaggart, c.181; Andrew Hunter, cc.204–5; and 15 March 2000, Simon Hughes, c.354; Richard Shepherd, c.357; Alan Simpson, c.358.

[59] Michael Ignatieff, *The Lesser Evil: Political Ethics in an Age of Terror* (Edinburgh: Edinburgh University Press, 2005).

[60] HC Debs 14 December 1999, cc.154 and 165.

[61] HC Debs 14 December 1999, c.199.

[62] D. Garland, *The Culture of Control. Crime and Social Order in Contemporary Society* (Oxford: Oxford University Press, 2001).

[63] Michael Howard, HC Debs 2 April 1996, c.37.

accommodated the potential to be used in a discretionary, even arbitrary, way without significant independent oversight.[64] Pursuant to the desire to maintain the operational independence of chief police officers, the debate concerning the counter-terrorism powers demonstrates how the threat of terrorist attack was politicised with the effect that it justified the permanent and expanded enactment of the counter-terrorism stop and search powers,[65] as will now be shown.

2.3. Exceptionalism and superlatives

The enactment of fair and even-handed legislation, which balances different, sometimes conflicting, majority and minority interests, is a key operational expectation of parliamentary law-making.[66] Despite the benefit of enacting legislation in conditions which maintain this balance, particularly legislation dealing with the sensitive subject of national security,[67] the dominant narratives in the debate concerning the Terrorism Act 2000 departed from such conditions by emphasising the novelty of the threat.[68] Jack Straw, for example, described the threat from international terrorism as 'horrific', 'considerable', and able to 'threaten the foundations of our society',[69] while other MPs described it as one of 'unmitigated horror and barbarism'[70] and 'a global activity which poses many fresh and serious challenges'.[71] The extraordinary circumstances were used to justify re-enactment of the permanent, anticipatory, counter-terrorism measures.

On top of descriptions of the present threat MPs coupled the need to support the counter-terrorism provisions with images recalling the devastation wrought by past attacks. David Lidington, for example, spoke of the IRA bombing of the Conservative Party Conference in October 1984[72] while Ken Maginnis referred to 'the terror of 3,500 people killed [and] ... 300 policemen injured'.[73] The descriptions emphasised the vulnerability of the country to terrorism and the lasting scars it had inflicted on the nation's psyche. Steve McCabe referred to the ongoing 'horror and torment' that the Birmingham bombing left amongst his constituents 25 years after the attack[74] and Simon Hughes focused on the significant sacrifices made by members of the police and armed services, who had given their lives in the fight against terrorism.[75] The past attacks were revived, shaped, and given meaning by politicians who then used them to confirm the need for the comprehensive and permanent counter-terrorism powers proposed.

Representations of the UK's experience of Irish terrorism also demonstrate the rhetorical contradictions in the parliamentary debate, which had a role in heightening the perception of the exceptional nature of the legislative context. Whilst in its own right

---

[64] *Gillan v The United Kingdom* (cited in n.2), para.83. See also Mark McGovern and Angela Tobin, *Countering Terrorism or Counter-Productive. Comparing Irish and British Muslim Experiences of Counter-insurgency Law and Policy* (Ormskirk: Edge Hill University, July 2010), para.1.3.
[65] M. Innes, 'Control Creep' (2001) 6(3) *Sociological Research Online* para.2.1.
[66] Conor Gearty and K.A. Kimbell, *Terrorism and the Rule of Law* (London: Civil Liberties Research Unit, King's College London, 1995), 14–16.
[67] F.A. Aolain and O. Gross, 'A Skeptical View of Deference to the Executive in Times of Crisis' (2008) 41 *Is. L. Rev.* 545, 546.
[68] See, e.g., Alan Simpson, HC Debs 14 December 1999, c.203.
[69] Jack Straw, HC Debs 14 December 1999, c.159.
[70] David Lidington, HC Debs 15 March 2000, c.359.
[71] Tom King, HC Debs 14 December 1999, c.177.
[72] David Lidington, HC Debs 14 December 1999, c.222.
[73] Ken Maginnis, HC Debs 14 December 1999, c.174.
[74] Steve McCabe, HC Debs 14 December 1999, c.206.
[75] Simon Hughes, HC Debs 14 December 1999, c.198.

Irish terrorism was described as horrific and scarring it was discussed in almost trivial terms when compared to the 'new' threat at which the s.44 provisions were directed. Referring specifically to the past threat from terrorism Ken Maginnis described the terrorists as having been 'most obliging' and 'like turkeys volunteering for Christmas' in their readiness to face trial.[76] By contrast, Maginnis labelled the contemporary global threat as constituting 'everything that would substitute anarchy for democracy'.[77] The contradictory descriptions of Irish terrorism, instead of revealing the fallacy of the comparison, served to emphasise the unique, almost unimaginable nature of the situation faced. The effect of these contradictory descriptions was to imbue the parliamentary debate with a sense of the very kind of emergency conditions that MPs thought were being avoided by acting outside the context of a specific terrorist threat.[78]

Parliament further emphasised the exceptional level of the threat faced through constructive narratives focusing on the technologically advanced weapons which terrorists could use. One use of such narratives was the description of the Sarin attack on the Tokyo underground system, in 1995, which had killed 13 people and injured around 50.[79] Jack Straw described the attack as 'an outrage' and used it, and the devastation it caused, as a direct justification for the expanded definition of 'terrorism' within the Act.[80] Speaking more generally, Tom King referred to the 'horrific development of [the terrorist's] technology' and described nuclear, chemical, or biological weapons as being able to 'offer new possibilities for terrorism'.[81] In using such references, Parliament focused on the most destructive forms of possible attack, without citing any grounds to suggest that they were a real probability. This prevailing discourse then treated the threat of terrorists using weapons of mass destruction as altogether real and a matter of 'common sense'.[82] The legislature's description of the law-making context, as one of abject exceptionalism, manipulated parliamentary anxiety about the terrorist threat, thereby creating a state of 'ontological hysteria' amongst MPs, who were charged with protecting the country against the next, inevitable, and devastating attack.[83] The use of danger and fear also triggered a further theme within the parliamentary discourse, namely the demands for decisive, immediate, and unified counter-terrorism law-making.

2.4. Urgency and unity

Against the 'moral panic'[84] aroused by the exceptional threat of terrorism, ever more vociferous demands were made for united support for the proposed legislative provisions. MPs, such as David Lidington and Charles Clarke, referred to a shared 'duty' to promote the strong use of the legislative powers to safeguard against the terrorist threat.[85] In response to descriptions of the exceptional threat from terrorism, Opposition politicians readily agreed that 'there should be a united front across all parties in the House in

---

[76] Ken Maginnis, HC Debs 14 December 1999, c.195 and generally cc.195–262.
[77] Ken Maginnis, HC Debs 14 December 1999, c.195.
[78] See Richard Shepherd, HC Debs 15 March 2000, c.343.
[79] Edward F. Mikolus and Susan L. Simmon, *Terrorism 1992–1995 A Chronology of Events and a Selectively Annotated Bibliography* (Westport, Conn.: Greenwood, 1997), 783–9.
[80] Jack Straw, HC Debs 14 December 1999, c.159.
[81] Tom King, HC Debs 14 December 1999, c.178.
[82] Garland, *The Culture of Control* (cited in n.62), 135.
[83] See Joseba Zulaika and William A. Douglas, *Terror and Taboo: The Follies, Fables and Faces of Terrorism* (London: Routledge, 1996).
[84] See Stanley Cohen, *Folk Devils and Moral Panics* (3rd edn, Abingdon: Routledge, 2002).
[85] See, e.g., David Lidington and Charles Clarke, HC Debs 14 December 1999, cc.222–3.

the fight against terrorism'.⁸⁶ By constructing a single identity, parliamentary discourse cultivated cross-party agreement with the Government's statutory proposals, against the exceptional nature of the terrorist threat. MPs were left with no apparent alternative but to endorse the utility of the counter-terrorism powers, or face the dire social consequences and inevitable political reprisals arising from any future terrorist attacks.⁸⁷

Against such parliamentary single-mindedness, reservations about the nature of the counter-terrorism powers were denigrated as pursuing 'a tedious path'⁸⁸ and showing an 'almost wilful misunderstanding of the Bill'.⁸⁹ Even attempts to moderate the rhetoric of acute threat were met with derision. Fiona Mactaggart, for example, cautioned against forgetting 'that the use of such [counter-terrorism] powers is itself terrorising in a sense', which was met by the retort of 'Nonsense!' after which the debate resumed the succession of supportive comments.⁹⁰ In similar vein, Jeremy Corbyn's effort to temper the emotionally charged nature of the discourse by stating that '[w]e are not in crisis at the moment, so surely it is time to do something far more rational and sane than what is proposed this evening' received the diversionary response that the measures themselves should not be seen as extraordinary so much as the situation faced.⁹¹ Not only were criticisms of the proposed legislation rebuffed but a direct link was made between a failure to support the provisions and supporting the terrorists. Ann Widdecombe, for example, stated that when 'consensus breaks down, the only people who gain any succour are those who wish to subvert democracy and the rule of law for their own ends—the terrorists themselves'.⁹² Charles Clarke described the failure to adhere to the dominant sentiment supporting the statute as 'nothing less than a betrayal of MPs' duty to their electors'.⁹³ Such accusations indicate how popular accountability was used to dissuade critics of the draft legislation from sustaining their scrutiny,⁹⁴ amid fear of a political 'counter-attack if the Government are seen to have left their people exposed'.⁹⁵

The statutory provisions, therefore, enjoyed a high level of immunity from critical scrutiny which left any recognition of the weakness of the legislative safeguards to be voiced by lone independents, or rebels at the risk of losing the party whip.⁹⁶ Concerns regarding the potentially uneven use of the powers were described as invoking 'invent[ed] hypothetical circumstances—fantastic circumstances—in which any of us...could be charged and subject to conviction'.⁹⁷ By contrast support for the proposed counter-terrorism powers was portrayed as the indisputable 'reality' of the law-making context.⁹⁸ Whilst there did not appear to be any intentional policy-making decision

---

⁸⁶ Ann Widdecombe, HC Debs 14 December 1999, c.166.
⁸⁷ M. Welch, 'Trampling Human Rights in the War on Terror: Implications to the Sociology of Denial' (2003) 12 *Critical Criminology* 1, 2.
⁸⁸ Ken Maginnis, HC Debs 14 December 1999, c.174, referring to the reservations expressed by Kevin McNamara, cc.173–4 and c.196.
⁸⁹ Jack Straw, HC Debs 14 December 1999, c.156.
⁹⁰ Fiona Mactaggart, HC Debs 14 December 1999, c.182.
⁹¹ Jeremy Corbyn, HC Debs 14 December 1999, cc.194 and 195.
⁹² Ann Widdecombe, HC Debs 14 December 1999, cc.166–7.
⁹³ Charles Clarke, HC Debs 14 December 1999, c.223.
⁹⁴ M.O. Chibundu, *'For God, For Country, For Universalism: Sovereignty as Solidarity in Our Age of Terrorism'* (2004) 56 *Fla. L. Rev* 883, 888.
⁹⁵ Tom King, HC Debs 14 December 1999, c.178.
⁹⁶ See, e.g., HC Debs 14 December 1999, Jeremy Corbyn, cc.161, 189–90, 194; Kevin McNamara, c.192; Tom King, c.178; Fiona Mactaggart, c.181; Steve McCabe, cc.206–7; and Douglas Hogg, c.214.
⁹⁷ Jack Straw, HC Debs 14 December 1999, c. 163.
⁹⁸ Ken Maginnis, HC Debs 14 December 1999, c.196.

to enact powers which facilitated uneven, discretionary use of s.44, counter-terrorism policies have always had the potential to frighten and alienate communities, regardless of arguments made concerning their desirability.[99] This potential effect developed from a contingent risk to an actual occurrence when the powers were deployed after 9/11. Accompanying these attacks, and causatively informing police use of their powers, was yet a further instrumental period of parliamentary discourse.

3. Police use of powers and parliamentary rhetoric

In the aftermath of 9/11, and aided by the lack of effective safeguards against misuse of the powers, the police were able to make widespread, pre-emptive use of the stop and search powers. Parliamentary discourse played a constructive role in shaping such use through discourses portraying the nature of the terrorist threat faced.[100] In addition, parliamentary discourses which demanded the pre-emptive use of the stop and search powers meant that the forms of particularised intelligence earlier promoted as necessary to protect against deployment on the basis of group-based stereotypes regarding the origins of the terrorist threat were not available.[101] Without the need for reasonable suspicion on which to base use of the powers, therefore, parliamentary rhetoric made the already very difficult task of avoiding ethnic profiling[102] even harder.[103] The MPA itself recognised that descriptions of the terrorist threat as 'Islamic' and as being associated with particular minority groups had affected how the police used their stop and search powers.[104] This section will show that in the aftermath of 9/11 parliamentary debate was replete with such descriptions, which were espoused alongside an emphasis on the devastation wrought by the attacks, and the imperative for those responsible for law enforcement to be freed from constraints in their deployment of counter-terrorism powers, in order that they could best protect the UK from terrorist attack.

3.1. Imagery regarding the threat

Parliamentary discourse concerning the terrorist threat helped to legitimise the police's focus on minority groups by describing the threat as not existing in particular, dangerous individuals, but within a broad, racially and religiously defined section of the population. This contributed to the 'suspect-labelling' of Asian and Arabic individuals,[105] and promotion of the idea of a 'suspect community' linked to the terrorist threat.[106] An illustration of

---

[99] Mary J. Hickman, Lyn Thomas, Sara Silvestri, and Henri Nickels, *'Suspect Communities'? Counter-terrorism Policy, the Press and the Impact on Irish and Muslim Communities in Britain. A Report for Policymakers and the General Public* (London: London Metropolitan University, 2011), 26.

[100] Hickman et al., *'Suspect Communities'?* (cited in n.100), 11.

[101] See C. Walker, 'Intelligence and Anti-Terrorism Laws in the UK' (2005) 44 *Crime, Law and Social Change* 387; and David A. Harris, *Profiles in Injustice: Why Racial Profiling Cannot Work* (New York: New Press, 2006), 11, 16.

[102] A. Blick, T. Choudhury, and S. Weir, *The Rules of the Game: Terrorism, Community and Human Rights* (York: The Joseph Rowntree Reform Trust, 2006), 40. See also B. Spalek and B. Lambert, 'Muslim Communities, Counter-terrorism and Counter-radicalisation: A Critically Reflective Approach to Engagement' (2008) 36(4) *International Journal of Law, Crime and Justice* 257.

[103] C. Walker, 'Know thine Enemy as thyself: Discerning friend from foe under anti-terrorism laws' (2008) 32 *Melbourne University Law Review* 275, 291.

[104] MPA, *The London Debate* (cited in n.16), 14.

[105] Hickman et al., *'Suspect Communities'?* (cited in n.100).

[106] Hillyard, *Suspect Community* (cited in n.25); and P. Hillyard, 'The "War on Terror": Lessons from Ireland' (cited in n.25).

the community-wide construction of the terrorist threat was Peter Mandelson's declaratory statement that to 'fight the menace of fundamental Islamic terrorism [police] recruitment has to be directed at Muslim and Arab-speaking communities', because these are where the terrorist organisations draw their own membership from.[107] Although Mandelson was referring to the recruitment of individuals to protect national security, he was effectively linking entire Muslim communities with terrorism. Such comments helped to reinforce the suspicion that all Muslims, and those perceived to be Muslim, were a legitimate target for counter-terrorism powers. Through linguistic laxness, therefore, the comments made the predominantly minority character of a place, institution, or group sufficient to place it under suspicion of involvement in international terrorism. This perceived link was reiterated by Lord Pearson, who expressed concern regarding the 'indoctrination or incitement to violence which may be taking place in our schools'.[108] Parliamentary imagery, therefore, forged a rhetorical connection between the terrorist threat and minority communities, which apparently supported the racially uneven use of the widely drafted stop and search powers by the police.[109]

The notion of the complicity of Muslim communities with terrorist attacks was also reinforced by repetition of the idea that they constituted a safe haven for terrorists. Viscount Slim, for example, warned that 'terrorists, I think, would say that Britain is a rather inviting place to come to set about their business'.[110] The idea of the UK as a safe haven was first mentioned in a pre-enactment debate concerning the Terrorism Act[111] and was effortlessly and unquestioningly adopted by various MPs and peers following 9/11.[112] Exemplifying this rhetorical theme, Baroness Cox cited five separate international terrorist attacks and linked each one to the UK through racial minority and refugee groups living in the country.[113] Baroness Cox concluded that Britain was 'viewed as the Islamist terrorist capital of the world'.[114] Such generalised connections meant that even where there was no actual evidence of support for terrorism, the veil of suspicion remained over Muslims communities on the basis that a lack of evidence 'does not mean that there are no individuals or groups who support terrorism'.[115]

Having outlined a broad, race-based suspect community, the language of the parliamentary debate also did much to exacerbate the image of their alienated and dangerous nature. The debate dehumanised the terrorists, describing them as 'faceless killers',[116] and also as 'bigoted, warped, evil people'.[117] Such imagery employed a deeply embedded tradition within political rhetoric which positions evil within specific individuals, as opposed to structural conditions or the outcome of a chain of events.[118] Through such discourse, the counter-terrorism police powers became more than simple law enforcement tools,

---

[107] Peter Mandelson, HC Debs 14 September 2001, c.627.
[108] HL Debs 14 September 2001, c.58.
[109] MPA, *The London Debate* (cited in n.16), 14.
[110] HL Debs 14 September 2001, c.83. See also Hickman et al., *'Suspect Communities'?* (cited in n.100), 14–15.
[111] HC Debs 14 December 1999, Tom King, c.165 and cc.177–8; and David Winnick, c.160.
[112] See, e.g., Michael Ancram, HC Debs 14 September 2001, c.623; and HL Debs 14 September 2001, Lord Strathclyde, c.7 and Lord Howell, c.16.
[113] Baroness Cox, HL Debs 14 September 2001, cc.37–9.
[114] Baroness Cox, HL Debs 14 September 2001, c.39.
[115] Piara S. Khabra, HC Debs 4 October 2001, c.719.
[116] Michael Howard, HC Debs 7 July 2005, c.568.
[117] John Butterfill, HC Debs 14 September 2001, c.628.
[118] R. Harriman, 'Speaking of Evil' (2003) 6(3) *Rhetoric and Public Affairs* 511, 513. See also Robert Castell, 'From Dangerousness to Risk' in Burchell et al, *The Foucault Effect* (cited in n.11), 285.

they were weapons in the battle between good and evil.[119] The representations of the terrorists and terrorist suspects also provide a clear example of the discursive construction of a monstrous 'other',[120] while evoking various religious and race-based stereotypes, to further reinforce the religious and racial identity of the threat.[121] This 'othering'[122] was also emphasised by repetition of the idea that Muslims considered events 'differently' from other people.[123] In separating 'them' from 'us'[124] Muslims were portrayed as being outside the dominant social groupings and a dangerous threat to national security.[125]

Parliament's emphasis on the religious and race-based nature of the threat was further exacerbated by the placing of narratives surrounding 9/11 within a larger meta-narrative of the conflict between civilisation and barbarism.[126] Descriptions of the terrorists as having attacked not just America but also democratic values,[127] civilised and free society,[128] and the whole of humanity,[129] turned 9/11 into a powerful semiotic: a symbol of anarchy and the dying of democracy.[130] Against such a threat, only the most uncompromising use of counter-terrorism powers, acting in accordance with 'beliefs held dear', would suffice.[131] The impact of this focus on values of paramount importance, such as democracy, liberty, and humanity, was to position the terrorists diametrically opposite to what are considered to be normative societal values and, in doing so, emphasised a powerful division between a righteous 'us' and a transgressive 'them'.[132]

The rhetorical fusion between terrorists and minority communities was given a degree of moderation by the recognition that the terrorists were a 'small number of totally unrepresentative groups and individuals'[133] and not 'those who truly follow Islam'.[134] However, following such affirmations, MPs frequently went on to reassert the damaging rhetorical connections between minority groups and the terrorist threat.[135] This tendency is demonstrated by Tony Blair who, having stated that the terrorists and terrorist suspects were separate from the 'vast majority of decent law-abiding Muslims', immediately re-emphasised the Islamic 'beliefs' of the terrorists, distinguishing them from

---

[119] HC Debs 14 September 2001, Iain Duncan Smith, c.607; Bernard Jenkin, c.662.
[120] Barbara Hudson, *Justice in a Risk Society* (London: Sage, 2003), 204.
[121] Paul Goodman, HC Debs 4 October 2001, cc.779–80.
[122] See Poynting and Mason, '"Tolerance, Freedom, Justice and Peace?"' (cited in n.14), and I.M. Porras, 'On Terrorism: Reflections on Violence and the Outlaw' (1994) *Utah L. Rev* 199.
[123] Paul Goodman, HC Debs 4 October 2001, cc.779–80.
[124] See David Blunkett, HC Debs 19 November 2001, c.25.
[125] Edward Said, *Orientalism* (New York: Random House, 1978). See also H. Vu, 'Note. Us against Them: The Path to National Security is Paved with Racism' (2002) 50 *Drake L. Rev.* 661, 663.
[126] Khaled El Fadl, 'Introduction' in Aftab A. Malik (ed.), *Shattered Illusions: Analysing the War in Collision: Terror and the Future of Global Order* (Bristol: Amal Press, 2002) and A. Hurrell, '"There are No Rules" (George W. Bush). International Order after September 11' (2002) 16(2) *International Relations* 185, 193–5.
[127] HC Debs 14 September 2001, Tony Blair, cc.604, 606; Michael Ancram, c.622; 14 November 2001, Charles Kennedy, c.853.
[128] HC Debs 14 November 2001, Jack Straw, c.618; 15 October 2001, Bridget Prentice, c.933.
[129] HC Debs 14 September 2001, Tony Blair, c.606; Iain Duncan Smith, c.607.
[130] Ian Ward, *Law, Text, Terror* (Cambridge: Cambridge University Press, 2009), 6.
[131] Tony Blair, HC Debs 14 September 2001, cc.606–7, 610–11.
[132] Hickman et al., '*Suspect Communities*'? (cited in n.100), 23. See also M.J. Hickman, 'Reconstructing, Deconstructing "race": British Political Discourses about the Irish in Britain' (1998) 21(2) *Ethnic and Racial Studies* 288, 290.
[133] Iain Duncan Smith, HC Debs 4 October 2001, c.677. See also K. Delacoura, 'Violence, September 11, and the Interpretations of Islam' (2002) 16(2) *International Relations* 269.
[134] Tony Blair, HC Debs 14 September 2001, c.612. See also Michael Ancram, HC Debs 14 September 2001, c.623.
[135] C. Pantazis and S. Pemberton, 'From the "Old" to the "New" Suspect Communities' (cited in n.12).

'our beliefs'.[136] Further, even while accepting that not all minority individuals should be considered to be terrorist suspects, they were, nevertheless, subject to dualistic treatment as compared to the rest of the population.[137] Andrew Robathan, for example, suggested that Muslims must vocally and publicly condemn terrorism to stop the attacks being associated with Islam.[138] In addition, Donald Anderson praised Muslim leaders who had spoken out but added that 'I hope they will go further... [and] say that terrorist bombing is a perversion of the Koran'.[139] The discourse, therefore, constructed Muslims as beholden to the rest of the country for the commission of the attacks and as requiring them to actively assist the police and prevent terrorism, despite these not being public duties within general criminal law.[140] As well as positioning the threat as inextricably linked to Muslim communities, parliamentary discourse also emphasised the tragic events of 9/11 to demonstrate the absolute necessity for all possible law enforcement action to be taken, as will now be shown.

3.2. The attacks and the necessary response

Against the backdrop of 9/11, and the 'desperately important' need to placate feelings of popular insecurity,[141] law enforcement operations were described as needing to be 'instinctive,'[142] 'unflinching',[143] and 'unreserved'.[144] By emphasising the safeguarding ability of the police, parliamentary discourse sought 'to feign control over the uncontrollable'[145] and reassure the public of their protection from further terrorist attacks.[146] Faced with the public expectation that they could provide complete anti-terrorism protection, the police were encouraged to make widespread, blanket use of their counter-terrorism powers in ways that would support this perception.[147] This imperative was heightened by parliamentary descriptions of the horrific events of 9/11.

Pervasive parliamentary calls for uncompromising policing and unrestrained use of counter-terrorism powers[148] were supported by the frequent repetition of media reports

---

[136] Tony Blair, HC Debs 14 September 2001, cc.606–7.

[137] B. Spalek, 'Muslim Communities Post 9/11—Citizenship, Security and Social Justice' (2008) 36 *International Journal of Law, Crime and Justice* 211.

[138] HC Debs 14 September 2001, c.656.

[139] HC Debs 4 October 2001, c.788.

[140] J. Rehman, 'Islam, "War on Terror" and the Future of Muslim Minorities in the United Kingdom, Dilemmas of Multiculturalism in the Aftermath of the London Bombings' (2007) 29 *Human Rights Quarterly* 831, 856.

[141] Tony Lloyd, HC Debs 14 September 2001, c.726.

[142] Brian Mawhinney, HC Debs 14 September 2001, c.613.

[143] Iain Duncan Smith, HC Debs 14 September 2001, c.607.

[144] Khalid Mahmood, HC Debs 14 September 2001, c.612.

[145] U. Beck, 'The Terrorist Threat: World Society Revisited' (2002) 19 *Theory, Culture and Society* 39, 41.

[146] Jackson, *Writing the War on Terrorism* (cited in n.23), 24; and Open Society Justice Initiatives, *Ethnic Profiling in the European Union: Pervasive, Ineffective and Discriminatory* (London: Open Society Foundation, 2009), 9.

[147] Home Office, *Stop and Search Action Team. Interim Guidance* (London: HMSO, 2004), para 5.1; JCHR, *Counter-terrorism Police and Human Rights: Prosecution and Pre-Charge Detention*, HL240/HC1576 (August 2006), para 8; Mythen and Walklate, 'Criminology and Terrorism: which thesis?' (cited in n.11).

[148] e.g., HC Deb 14 September 2001, Tony Blair, c. 610, Jack Straw, c.620, Michael Ancram, c.623.

on 9/11.[149] Michael Ancram, for example, referred to 'a terrible and almost unbelievable series of images and pictures', and Tony Blair alluded to the need to respond to the images seen 'daily in our newspapers and on our television screens'.[150] MPs even adopted media-like linguistic codes and rhetorical forms in their speeches. One example is the recurring image of a four-year-old child who was on one of the flights hijacked by the terrorists.[151] The theme of the loss of innocence was further developed by MPs who contrasted the imagery of 9/11 with stories from their own lives. Charles Kennedy, for example, recounted a story about his own student experiences in America and Bernard Jenkin recalled, as a tourist in New York, 'marvelling' with awe at the twin towers of the World Trade Center.[152] Such halcyon days were distinguished from images of chaos and destruction arising from the attacks, which were often compared to a horror or disaster movie.[153] Through such personal vignettes, MPs encapsulated otherwise inchoate fears arising out of the attacks and used these to shape support for the necessary law enforcement response,[154] including support for the extensive and unrestricted use of pre-existing counter-terrorism powers.[155]

The counterpart to descriptions of the destructive nature of 9/11 was the almost total loss of parliamentary debate amidst a type of 'wartime spirit, which eulogizes the term "national security," [and] produces national unity in a single cause'.[156] MPs even adopted a warlike vocabulary through the repetition of words and phrases such as 'attack',[157] 'enemy',[158] and 'war'.[159] Constructing the threat through a discourse of war helped to emphasise the exceptional nature of the context and thus the necessity of the police's full use of the counter-terrorism measures, in ways which might not have otherwise been supported.[160] The most explicit connection between war and the threat faced was made by Jack Straw, who compared the risk of the UK not making full use of national security powers with the policy of appeasement in the 1930s, which failed to stop the outbreak of the Second World War.[161] What emerges from the rhetoric, therefore, is a 'politics of fear and vengeance'[162] culminating in calls for the police to depart from circumspect use of their powers to instead pursue the most extensive programmes of deployment.[163]

---

[149] S.W. Bender, *Greasers and Gringos: Latinos, Law and the American Imagination* (New York: New York University Press, 2005), 207–8; and J. Tehranian, 'The Last Minstrel Show? Racial Profiling, the War on Terrorism, and the Mass Media' (2008–09) 41 *Connecticut Law Rev* 781–824.

[150] HC Deb 14 September 2001, c.621.

[151] Iain Paisley, HC Deb 14 September 2001, c.631. See also HC Deb 14 September 2001, c.631, David Heath, c.650, Stuart Bell, c.658, Menzies Campbell, cc.703–4; and Tony Lloyd, c.727.

[152] HC Deb 14 September 2001, cc.609 and 662.

[153] e.g., HC Deb 14 September 2001, John Battle, c.642, John Smith, c.770, and HL Deb (2001–2) 627 Lord Davies, c.55.

[154] M. Innes, 'Control Creep' (cited in n.65).

[155] e.g., HC Deb 14 September 2001, Peter Mandelson, c.626, Geoffrey Hoon, cc.665–6, Julian Lewis, c.638, David Blunkett, c.923.

[156] P.A. Thomas, 'Emergency and Anti-terrorism Power: 9/11: US and UK' (2003) 26 *Fordham International Law Journal* 1203.

[157] HC Debs 14 September 2001, Tony Blair, c.604; Iain Duncan Smith, c.608; Jack Straw, c.618; Mohammad Sarwar, c.634; Julian Lewis, c.638; Andrew Robathan, c.657; and 4 October 2001, Patsy Carlton, c.739.

[158] HC Debs 14 September 2001, Tony Blair, c.606.

[159] HC Debs 14 September 2001, Jack Straw, c.618; 4 October 2001, Iain Duncan Smith, c.677; Mike O'Brien, c.715; Jeremy Corbyn, c.734.

[160] Vivienne Jabri, *Discourses on Violence: Conflict Analysis Reconsidered* (Manchester: Manchester University Press, 1996), 6.

[161] HC Debs 14 September 2001, Tony Blair, c.618.

[162] Mythen and Walklate, 'Criminology and Terrorism' (cited in n.11), 388.

[163] C.R. Sunstein, 'Probability Neglect: Emotion, Worst Cases, and Law' (2002) 112 *Yale LJ* 61, 66.

Through Parliament's 'discourses of security',[164] 9/11 was portrayed as a single example of a broader, endemic phenomenon against which society was extremely vulnerable.[165] This mood also demanded the rejection of attempts to moderate the country's law enforcement response to the attacks. For example, Dennis Skinner's questioning of whether the UK should take a more equal role alongside America in deciding how to respond to the attacks was met with the diversionary response of 'Shame!' and dismissed by Tony Blair.[166] Acquiescence to complete cross-parliamentary cooperation was demanded as the only possible response to a 'massive tragedy... of huge and almost unparalleled historical significance',[167] and which transcended all considerations of moderating parliamentary language.[168] Debate was thus ousted in the name of public security and, in order to avoid charges of being soft on terrorism, was replaced with highly charged uncaveated calls for police use of counter-terrorism powers, including stop and search.[169] Facilitated by parliamentary rhetoric surrounding the terrorist threat, the police were implicitly encouraged to target certain minority communities, rather than serve them.[170] The result of the interaction between Parliament, popular opinion, and the police was that Parliament's construction of terrorist suspects and the nature of the terrorist threat played a role in determining how the police deployed the powers.[171]

4. Conclusion

The combination of the content of successive instances of parliamentary discourse, coupled with unforeseeable contextual developments, helped to facilitate the racially targeted use of the suspicion-less stop and search powers contained in the Terrorism Act 2000 s.44 following 9/11. The expectation of widespread police use of their powers, coupled with the assessment of risk independent of any signs, moved away from individualised suspicion, as a basis for conducting stop and search, to mere satisfaction that it was only necessary that an individual be identified as a member of a 'risky population'.[172] The antecedents for such use were, however, already an established feature of the suspicion-less powers, due to the effect of the discourse surrounding their enactment, which minimised statutory safeguards against misuse, before diminishing these still further by emphasising the need for police operational independence and the permanent renewal of the codified provisions. Whilst emotion-led responses to 9/11 are unsurprising in themselves, given the nature of the attacks, once added to Parliament's construction of the Muslim

---

[164] T. Abbas, *Muslim Britain: Communities under Pressure* (New York: Zed, 2005); and E. Poole, 'The Effects of September 11 and the War in Iraq on British Newspaper Coverage' in E. Poole and J. Richardson (eds), *Muslims and the News Media* (London: I.B. Taurus, 2006).
[165] Furedi, 'From Narrative of the Blitz to Rhetoric of Vulnerability' (cited in n.9) 235–54, Mythen and Walklate, 'Criminology and Terrorism: which thesis?' (cited in n.11); Mythen et al., '"I'm a Muslim, but I'm not a terrorist' (cited in n.10).
[166] HC Debs 14 September 2001, c.614.
[167] Jack Straw, HC Debs 14 September 2001, c.618.
[168] Blick et al., *The Rules of the Game* (cited in n.103), 66 and 68.
[169] Noel Whitty, Therese Murphy, and Stephen Livingstone, *Civil Liberties Law: the Human Rights Era* (London: Butterworths, 2003), 151.
[170] See Spalek, 'Muslim Communities Post 9/11' (cited in n.138) and Lambert, 'Empowering Salafis and Islamists against al-Qaeda' (cited in n.12).
[171] J. Miller, 'Meaning and Understanding Minority Experiences of Stop and Search in the UK' in Open Society Justice Initiative, *Justice Initiatives: Ethnic Profiling by Police in Europe* (London: Open Society Foundation, 2005); and N. Fairclough, *Critical Discourse Analysis. The Critical Study of Language* (2nd edn, Harlow: Longman, 2010), 489.
[172] Deborah Lupton, *Risk* (London: Routledge, 1999), 93.

communities as a legitimate target for counter-terrorist policing, they supported police use of their stop and search powers in a way that disproportionately targeted minority individuals. Through this process, s.44 provides a cautionary example of how unguarded parliamentary discourse can have long-term, negative effects in ways that are unforeseen at the point of their origin. Without the ability to anticipate future developments, such effects confirm that some issues of law-making should be above political point-scoring and hyperbole, whilst also adhering to normal procedural and substantive safeguards to protect against the misuse of legal powers.

29
Precedent at the Court of Justice of the European Union: The Linguistic Aspect

Karen McAuliffe*

1. Introduction

The development of a de facto precedent in EU law has recently been the subject of significant academic debate. There is no official doctrine of precedent in EU law—historically, a doctrine of binding precedent would have been entirely inappropriate in what was originally

> a court of first and last resort, many of whose decisions could only be changed by amending the Treaties... it was imperative that the Court should have the power to... depart from its previous decisions.[1]

In spite of this, however, the Court of Justice of the European Union (ECJ) does on occasion appear to regard its previous decisions as establishing law that should be applied in later disputes. For example, as noted by Komarek, the ECJ's line of cases beginning with *Brasserie du Pêcheur/Factortame III*[2] (establishing liability of the state for breach of EU obligations) changes the distinction between 'binding force' and 'legal effects' of the ECJ's judgments as drawn by Toth in 1984[3]: following this line of case law it appears that the ECJ has introduced a system of precedent and 'tied down' national courts without establishing a formal hierarchy in the strict sense.[4] Thus, in spite of the fact that the doctrine of *stare decisis* was not formally recognised by the civil law tradition of the EU's founding states, nor by international law, the ECJ 'worked assiduously to develop what is now a robust and taken-for-granted set of practices associated with precedent'.[5] While those practices may well be 'taken-for-granted' this is not to say that they are clear or uncomplicated. As Komarek points out, the EU brings together many different legal

---

* This paper is based on the results of periods of participant observation at the ECJ of the European Communities undertaken between 2002 and 2006; all comments/criticisms are welcome (k.mcauliffe@exeter.ac.uk). Unless otherwise indicated all quotes are taken from interviews with *référendaires*, judges, advocates general, and lawyer-linguists at that Court. I would like to thank Prof Robert Harmsen of the University of Luxembourg for his support and valuable comments. I would also like to thank my former colleagues at the ECJ in Luxembourg for their assistance with this research—in particular Mr Alfredo Calot-Escobar and Ms Susan Wright. Any errors are mine alone.

[1] A Arnull, 'Owning Up to Fallibility: Precedent and the Court of Justice' (1993) 30 *CMLR* 247, 248.
[2] Joined Cases C-46/93 and C-48/93.
[3] A Toth, 'The authority of judgments of the European Court of Justice: Binding force and legal effects' (1984) 4 *Yearbook of European Law* 1.
[4] J Komarek, 'Federal Elements in the Community Judicial System: Building Coherence in the Community Legal Order' (2005) 42 *CMLR* 9, 16. See, in particular, the *Köbler* and *Larsy* decisions.
[5] Alec Stone Sweet, *The Judicial Construction of Europe* (Oxford University Press, Oxford, 2004), 97–8.

orders from civil and common law traditions and the result, in terms of the status of the ECJ's decisions in EU law is somewhat puzzling.[6] On the one hand, according to the Treaty on the Functioning of the European Union (TFEU) Art.228, the decisions of the ECJ are binding only on those to whom they are addressed. On the other hand, however, in order to know how to apply the substantive law of the EU, we must consult decisions of the ECJ. Furthermore, it is in fact through those decisions that the EU legal order has developed: it is generally accepted that most of the 'constitutional law' of the EU has been developed, not in the treaties, but through the case law of the ECJ.[7] As Komarek states, this 'puzzle' of EU law is well illustrated by the major treatise on the EU judicial system which states that the 'case law—those in theory not formally binding—is often the most important source of law'.[8] Certainly, 'judicial supremacy has been a central seam in the EU legal order'.[9]

There are, of course, many different interpretations of the notion of precedent. The question of whether precedent refers to *normative implications* that a judgment may have beyond the context of a particular case or to the *strict formal binding force* of a judgment is a perennial one. In EU law, the development of 'precedent' is inextricably linked to the procedure for references for a preliminary ruling under TFEU Art.267. It is often said that national courts are 'European courts', but equally the ECJ is 'not merely a supranational court' but in the fields of 'civil, criminal and administrative law...has become part of national judicial structures'.[10] And it fulfils all of its roles in this regard through the preliminary ruling procedure. The ECJ has based much of its reasoning in relation to both the development of the principle that its decisions have binding force on all national courts as well as other authorities[11] and justifying its jurisdiction and decisions under TFEU Art.267 on the need to ensure the 'uniform application of EU law'. The question raised by commentators researching 'precedent' in EU law is thus: what exactly is meant by uniformity? It is generally agreed that 'absolute sameness' is unachievable in any legal system[12]; and Chalmers notes that more 'precedents' do not necessarily mean more uniformity.[13] According to Dyrberg, however, 'uniform application is...a sort of existential problem to which the [Union] legal order has to relate'[14]—i.e. that a presumption of uniformity is necessary for the ECJ to claim authoritative status within the EU legal order—which, as pointed out by Komarek, aims at supremacy of EU law rather than uniformity itself.[15]

It is clear that these questions surrounding the concept of precedent itself and the meaning or understanding of that concept in the EU legal order will continue to interest scholars for some time to come. There is, however, one important aspect of the development of a de

---

[6] J Komarek, 'Judicial lawmaking and precedent in supreme courts: The European Court of Justice compared to the US Supreme Court and the French Cour de cassation' (2008–09) 11 *CYELS* 399.

[7] In particular the doctrines of Supremacy and Direct Effect. cf. Case 26/62 *Van Gend en Loos v Nederlandse Administratie der Belastingen* [1963] ECR 1; Case 6/64 *Costa v ENEL* [1964] ECR 585. Over the years the parameters of those two doctrines have gradually been broadened.

[8] Komarek, 'Judicial lawmaking and precedent in supreme courts' (cited in n.6).

[9] Komarek, 'Judicial lawmaking and precedent in supreme courts' (cited in n.6).

[10] J Komarek, 'In the Court(s) We Trust? On the need for hierarchy and differentiation in the preliminary ruling procedure' (2007) *European Law Review* 467, 484.

[11] See, in particular the *Köbler* decision, which attaches the sanction of liability in the case of non-compliance with the Court's previous case law.

[12] M Dougan, *National Remedies Before the Court of Justice. Issues of Harmonisation and Differentiation* (Hart, Oxford, 2004); Komarek, 'In the Court(s) We Trust?' (cited in n.10).

[13] D Chalmers, 'The dynamics of judicial authority and the Constitutional Treaty' in *Altneuland: The EU Constitution in a Contextual Perspective*, JHH Weiler and CL Eisgruber (eds) (Jean Monnet Working Paper 5/04, 2004).

[14] P Dyrberg, 'What Should the Court of Justice be Doing?' (2001) 26 *European Law Review* 291.

[15] Komarek, 'In the Court(s) We Trust?' (cited in n.10).

facto precedent in ECJ judgments which has been thus far overlooked in the literature: the linguistic aspect. The present paper seeks to address that gap in the literature by analysing the process behind the drafting of judgments at that court.

2. Drafting judgments at the ECJ

There are 23 potential languages of procedure for actions before the ECJ.[16] For practical purposes, that court operates using a single internal working language—French.[17] The Rules of Procedure provide that judges or advocates general may request the translation of any document into the language of their choice.[18] However, the members have been obliged to forgo that choice in order not to increase the workload of the translation service and the judges must work solely in French. However, because French is rarely the mother tongue of those drafting that case law, the texts produced are often stilted and awkward. In addition, those drafting such case law are constrained in their use of language and style of writing (owing to pressures of technology and in order to reinforce the rule of law). These factors have led to the development of a 'Court French' which necessarily shapes the case law produced and has implications for its development, particularly insofar as it inevitably leads to a type of linguistic precedent in that case law.

Référendaires

Each judge and advocate general of the Court of Justice and each judge of the General Court has a *cabinet*[19]—a small team of personal legal assistants and secretaries working exclusively for him or her. Those personal legal assistants are known as *référendaires*,[20] and work very closely with 'their' judge or advocate general, carrying out preliminary research on a case, drawing up procedural documents and preparing 'first drafts' of judgments, etc. The role of the *référendaire* at the Court of Justice of the European Union has been compared with that of the *Conseiller-référendaire* of the French *Cour de Cassation* (a judge attached to that court to assist its senior members)[21] and with the law clerk of the American judicial system.[22] There are currently 62 *cabinets* at the Court of Justice of the European

---

[16] The 23 'official languages' of the EU. These are, in English alphabetical order: Bulgarian; Czech; Danish; Dutch; English; Estonian; Finnish; French; German; Greek; Hungarian; Irish; Italian; Latvian; Lithuanian; Maltese; Polish; Portuguese; Romanian; Slovakian; Slovenian; Spanish: and Swedish. The official order of these languages is to list them according to the way they are spelled each in their own language.

[17] The Rules of Procedure of the ECJ state (in Art.29(5)) that 'The President of the Court and the Presidents of Chambers in conducting oral proceedings, the Judge Rapporteur both in his preliminary report and in his report for the hearing, Judges and Advocates General in putting questions and Advocates General in delivering their opinions may use one of the [official languages] other than the language of the case'. In practice, however, the language used is French.

[18] Rules of Procedure of the ECJ Art.30.

[19] While '*cabinet*' may be translated into English as '*chambers*' the French term is used throughout this paper for two reasons: first, to avoid confusion with the use of the word '*Chamber*' for a subdivision of the Court; secondly, unlike the English word '*chambers*', '*cabinet*' in the context of the Court is used to refer both to the judge's or advocate general's suite of rooms and to the staff working there.

[20] Again, the French word *référendaire* is used throughout this paper instead of the English translation '*legal secretary*', since it is by that title that those assistants are known within the Court, the working language being French.

[21] N Brown and T Kennedy, *The Court of Justice of the European Communities* (Sweet & Maxwell, London, 2000).

[22] SJ Kenney, 'Beyond Principals and Agents: Seeing courts as organizations by comparing Référendaires at the European Court of Justice and Law Clerks at the U.S. Supreme Court' (2000) 33 *Comparative Political Studies* 593.

Union (excluding the Civil Service Tribunal): there are 27 judges' *cabinets* from both the Court of Justice and the General Court plus eight advocates general's *cabinets*.

As already mentioned, *référendaires* work exclusively for the judge or advocate general to whose *cabinet* they are attached. They are recruited by the Member him- or herself and, that being so, they are not permanent staff of the ECJ. The minimum requirement to be a *référendaire* at the Court of Justice is to be a qualified lawyer with a good knowledge of EU law and with at least a reasonable knowledge of French.[23] Almost without exception *référendaires* come from backgrounds of 'practising' lawyers—be they members of the bar of their own Member States, lawyers in large European law firms or, as is the case for many from civil law jurisdictions, law clerks for Member State courts or government agencies/organisations. When new judges or advocates general come to the Court they generally bring their own staff with them, although they sometimes keep the staff of the *cabinet* of the departing Member and they do frequently try to recruit as least one *référendaire* from the institution itself as:

it is useful to have at least one member of the cabinet who knows and understands how the institution works [judge].

Increasingly, however, lawyer-linguists from the ECJ's Translation Directorate are being seconded to *cabinets* to work as *référendaires*. Of the 13 *référendaires* interviewed for the purposes of the present paper, two had previously worked as lawyer-linguists at the Court (and are officially classed as lawyer-linguists on 'indefinite secondment'); seven had worked as 'practising lawyers' (at the bar or for law firms); three as law clerks; and one as a legal academic before coming to the Court. It is common for the *référendaires* to be of the same nationality as the judge or advocate general to whose cabinet they are attached; however this is by no means invariably the case—in fact, many judges attempt to have at least one francophone *référendaire* in their *cabinet* (since the internal working language of the Court is French and all judges' *référendaires* must work entirely in French).

The role of a *référendaire* differs to a considerable degree depending on whether he/she works for a judge, the President of the Court, or an advocate general. The present paper is concerned only with judge's *référendaires*, whose role is principally to assist the judge in drafting documents such as reports for the hearing, judgments, and, in the case of the presidents of the Court of Justice and the General Court, orders.

Judges' *référendaires* and the drafting process

In a judge's *cabinet*, *référendaires* work on cases for which 'their' judge is the judge rapporteur and on other cases that are being heard by the chamber in which their judge sits but for which he or she is not rapporteur.[24] Because of the extremely high workload at the Court, it is not possible to allocate work to *référendaires* on the basis of expertise.[25] All of the *référendaires* interviewed for the purposes of the present paper claimed that they had

---

[23] In spite of the fact that *référendaires* are required to work wholly in French they are not required to have a 'perfect' command of that language. If a *référendaire* is not sufficiently competent in the French language, however, it can cause problems for the judge in whose *cabinet* he or she works—as discussed later in this paper.

[24] For every action before the Court a 'judge rapporteur' is appointed by the President of the Court. The judge rapporteur is responsible for monitoring the progress of the case, drafting the reports at various stages of the procedure as well as the draft judgment.

[25] cf. K McAuliffe, 'Hybrid Texts and Uniform Law? The Multilingual Case Law of the Court of Justice of the European Union' (2011) 24(1) *International Journal for the Semiotics of Law*.

to be 'generalists' who are 'knowledgeable about every area of EU law'. Not only that, they also have to be able to understand and use their knowledge in French—a language that may not be (and indeed in most cases is not) their mother tongue.

Once a case has been assigned to the judge rapporteur, the *référendaire* dealing with that case will open a file and wait for the submissions to be lodged at the registry of the Court and, where necessary, be translated into French. Not until all of the documents have been translated can the *référendaire* begin to prepare the preliminary report (*rapport préalable*) and, where relevant, the report for the hearing.[26] The report for the hearing is basically a summary of the facts alleged and arguments of the parties and interveners (if any). It is drafted in French and a version of that report in the language of the case is sent to the parties and, at the hearing, it is made public, also in the language of the case.[27] Because it is a public document which is sent to the parties (who may object) the *référendaire*'s hands are tied as regards framing the facts or arguments in a particular way—the report for the hearing is therefore often largely 'cut-and-paste' from the relevant submissions.[28] The preliminary report, which is also written in French, is usually drafted in parallel with the report for the hearing. Those two documents are largely the same in their summary of the facts, law, and relevant arguments. However, the preliminary report is an internal document and it contains a section known as the 'Observations of the Judge-Rapporteur', which comprises the judge rapporteur's opinion on the case and his or her recommendations as to how the Court should rule.

Following the delivery of the advocate general's opinion, the judge rapporteur may begin to draft the judgment.[29] In reality it is the *référendaire* assigned to the case who drafts, at least the first version, of that judgment. Officially judgments are drafted, discussed, and deliberated on in French; however, it has occasionally been the case that certain General Court competition law cases, in which the language of the case was English, were dealt with entirely in that language.[30] Unofficially, a number of *référendaires* interviewed during the course of fieldwork research for the present paper reported drafting

---

[26] In reality many *cabinets* begin drafting the preliminary report, the report for the hearing, and sometimes even the judgment (as reported by a *référendaire* from one particular *cabinet*) as soon as all of the parties' submissions have been lodged, i.e. without waiting for translation of those documents.

[27] Note: until 2004 where there was no hearing in a case the report produced was known as the report of the judge rapporteur. However, the practice of producing such a report in cases that do not require an oral hearing was abolished in 2004.

[28] Note: this practice is considered 'dangerous' by the vast majority of lawyer-linguists at the Court since the documents from which the *référendaires* usually 'cut-and-paste' are in fact translations of the original submissions—aside from the accepted 'approximation' in the translation process, those translations are often rushed and frequently contain discrepancies or even errors. For this reason, many lawyer-linguists actually go back to the original submissions when translating the report for the hearing 'back' into the language of the case (cf. Karen McAuliffe, 'Law in Translation: The Production of a Multilingual Jurisprudence by the Court of Justice of the European Communities', PhD Thesis, The Queen's University of Belfast, 2006). The real danger, however, arises at the stage of translation of the judgment—if the lawyer-linguist in question does not understand the language of the case and so cannot consult either the original submissions or the translated report for the hearing but must work only from the French version, he or she may not be aware of any problems or discrepancies.

[29] Note: an opinion is not given in every case before the Court of Justice (since 2004 if a case raises no new questions of law then an advocate general's opinion is not necessary); an 'advocate general's opinion' may exceptionally be given in cases before the General Court (Rules of Procedure of the General Court Arts 17–19). However, in such an event, the opinion will be drafted by a judge of the General Court who has been designated 'advocate general' in a specific case (Rules of Procedure of the General Court Art.2).

[30] This has occurred only a handful of times, and is officially 'frowned upon' by the Court of Justice, in particular when such cases come before the Court of Justice on appeal and there are no French documents available from which that Court can work. See McAuliffe, 'Law in Translation' (cited in n.28) for commentary on the use of English at the General Court since the May 2004 enlargement.

'half in [their own mother tongue] and half in French', many working from glossaries that they had constructed themselves on the basis of 'the settled case law of the Court':

I usually know what I want to say in my own language and then I look at my glossary to find something similar that the Court has said before and use that to help me draft;

as a starting point... I scan my glossary of French terms and phrases frequently used by the Court and find something that covers the gist of what I want to say;

I will usually have a basic idea in my head of the direction I want to go in and what I want to say and then I use the set phrases that I have collated in my glossary to start me off and shape what I write .

3. Difficulties of and constraints in drafting: producing a linguistic precedent?

None of the *référendaires* interviewed for the purposes of the present paper admitted having any difficulty drafting documents in a language that is not their mother tongue (where relevant). Indeed the only *référendaires* who claimed to have such difficulties were the francophone *référendaires* who 'simply can't bear' to draft in the 'formulaic, synthetic French used at the Court'!

The mechanical French that is used at the Court is so far removed from 'proper' or 'real' French that it is almost like another language entirely;

The French used at the Court is not 'real' French but a type of 'Court French'.

Some commented that having to work in French (where it is not their mother tongue) 'slowed them down', but that, as a result of the rigid formulaic style in which they are 'required' to draft judgments:

working in 'Court French' is actually easier than drafting in your own language—provided that you don't actually want to write anything *of your own*" [interviewee's emphasis];

Judgments are time-consuming but most are easy to draft because it has all already been said by the Court—maybe once in five or six years a case will come along that might have one single paragraph saying something completely new or different;

you never get to produce anything original... you just write according to the template provided... in fact I felt little more than a report-writing machine!

When questioned about the concept of precedent in EU law, every *référendaire* interviewed acknowledged that, strictly speaking, there is no rule of precedent within the EU court system and in theory the ECJ and the General Court are not bound by their own previous decisions. In spite of that, however, it is clear that those *référendaires* feel constrained by the language used by 'the Court' and that the judgments they draft reflect their perceptions of such constraint:

We must draft using the language that has been used by the Court for over 50 years;

We are under pressure to cite 'word-for-word' when taking material from source documents... in particular from past judgments;

We work from templates, and the translators work from templates... so we cut and paste from previous judgments and the process works for everyone.

There are two main reasons for these perceived constraints: first, some argue that since the Court is building up a European case law and rule of law, it is necessary to use the same terminology constantly throughout that case law:

what you are dealing with is the rule of law in a legal system that is still developing, therefore it is important to use the same terminology and phrases all of the time, in particular because that legal system is expressed in many different languages.

In addition, it is often necessary, in judgments, orders, reports, etc., to refer to provisions of relevant EU legislation. When making such references, *référendaires* are obliged to use the same specific wording used in the provision in question.[31]

Secondly, as one *référendaire* put it: 'the pressure of computers is significant'.

With the advent and increasing use of the GTI[32] at the Court it has become important to cite entire phrases instead of merely referring to them or even paraphrasing. Then that phrase will be translated sentence-for-sentence since there is the danger that the text 'pulled up' by the GTI might not fit into the context of the case in hand unless every single word is exactly the same. There is a huge pressure for one single word to be translatable into another single word, which of course is rarely the case;

We are obliged to use the same language over and over—to 'copy-paste' from previous decisions, reports or orders so that the computer programme will pick it up for easy and quick translation. That way translation is also safer as it will not be wrong—it has already been translated and that is now the way that [the relevant concept] is in the case law. It's like a precedent [interviewee's emphasis].

On top of such perceptions of constraint as regards the language that they feel they 'should' use, *référendaires* are, for the most part, working in a language that is not their mother tongue. This has been the case since the early days of the ECJ. For that reason alone there is, and always has been, a tendency to use the same expressions over and over again:

because we are writing in a foreign language there is a tendency to do a lot of 'cutting and pasting' and so the style [in which the Court's judgments, orders, etc. are written] reproduces itself;

Working in a language that isn't your own makes you slower but it is not especially difficult because the Court has its own style that you just rigidly follow;

My French is very good, but when I am drafting judgments I will copy-paste—because I can't say it better than that way that I have read it in the settled case law.

Thus it seems that in spite of the claims of the majority of the *référendaires* that they find it relatively non-problematic to draft in French, it nonetheless has consequences. The 'Court style' of drafting by which those *référendaires* feel so constrained is shaped in a large part because of the fact that they are drafting in a language that is not their mother tongue. As one *référendaire* pointed out:

Drafting in a language that is not your mother tongue makes a big difference to the way that you write. When you write in your mother tongue it flows more naturally, it is an unconscious exercise (language-wise), words and phrases flow from associations made by your brain by drawing on a lifetime's use of the language... When you are writing in a language that is not your mother tongue you have to boil down the semantics of what you want to say into one thread, into the essential of what you want to say—then you have to put your sentences together and you end up using clumsy and clunky connections.

Three of the *référendaires* interviewed during the first stage of fieldwork research for the present paper feel that because they are 'generalists' as opposed to specialists in a particular area of European law, being thus restrained as regards drafting judgments is actually very useful as 'there is less risk of getting things wrong':

In your own language you have a huge choice of words and phrases and so there is more risk of making a mistake where you are drafting a judgment concerning an area of EU law that you may not be expert in[33];

---

[31] McAuliffe, 'Law in Translation' (cited in n.28).
[32] The GTI is a computer programme developed by the Court of Justice to aid and speed up the translation process at that Court.
[33] However, according to some lawyer-linguists such mistakes are even more likely where the *référendaire* does not fully understand the implications of the translation of their choice of wording or terminology in French—cf. McAuliffe, 'Law in Translation' (cited in n.28), 168–70.

Because of the workload we cannot specialise in a particular area of EU law, so maybe it is better that we are tied to templates... we are less likely to make a mistake this way.

However, the vast majority of those interviewed feel frustrated at the constraints under which they must draft:

it is irritating not to have control over how you can express concepts and frustrating to be tied into the 'Court style' of drafting... only a small percentage of what we draft actually shows any originality at all.

Another aspect of drafting that galls the majority of *référendaires* interviewed (13) is the 'pompous tone' of the Court's judgments. That tone seems to be based on the tone of judgments of the French *Cour de Cassation* and most *référendaires*, and indeed many members of the Court, feel that it is quite unnecessary[34]:

[the *référendaires*] only write in that stuffy way because they know that if they don't the *lecteurs d'arrêts* will return the document to the cabinet having changed its tone entirely.

Référendaires also complain that, on top of that, the *lecteurs d'arrêts*[35] read their texts with a view to whether they will be easy or difficult to translate and that they insist on reducing connecting phrases, etc. to a basic and quite simple level so that they will be easy to translate:

they push it so far, however, that [the *référendaires*] are forced to use childish links and are left with infantile simplicity in a complex text with a pompous tone!

An interesting result of *référendaires* feeling constrained in their style of drafting and bound by the language previously used by the Court is that a type of linguistic precedent is developing in judgments of the Court of Justice in spite of the fact that no such rule actually exists within the EU court system:

decisions of the Court are treated as 'stare decisis'[sic] even though, on paper, those decisions are not binding on future decisions of the Court... sometimes it seems that precedent is even more binding at the Court than it is in a common law country! [interviewee's emphasis].

Those *référendaires* interviewed who commented on that phenomenon claim that the reasons for this development of a de facto rule of precedent in Court of Justice judgments are (a) the relative inexperience of most of the *référendaires*:

who is going to change the wording or contradict something set out by the Court in a previous judgment?

and (b) since most *référendaires* are drafting in a language that is not their mother tongue and are not as confident as they would be in their own language they tend to use direct quotes and 'take entire chunks' from previous judgments. As a result:

phrases are chiselled out of the rock face of the European Court Reports and considered to be immutable—there is a de facto stare decisis.

---

[34] It must be noted that that 'pompous tone' appears to have gradually crept into the judgments of the Court of Justice. In the 1970s (when, incidentally, the President of the Court was a German, Judge Kutcher) the judgments of that Court were much lighter and 'not so stuffy'.

[35] The *lecteurs d'arrêts* are francophone lawyers who ensure that the judgments read fluently yet remain sufficiently clear and precise.

4. Collegiate judgments

A final factor that restricts how judgments are drafted and thus affects the development of the linguistic style of the Court's case law is the collegiate nature of those judgments. Those judgments are, by their very nature, often compromise documents. However, because the deliberations of the Court of Justice are secret and no dissenting opinions are published, it is impossible for anyone other than the judges involved in those deliberations to know where such compromises lie in the text. As many of the *référendaires* interviewed commented:

> you don't always know which have been the 'contentious' points in the deliberation... or how important a specific wording of a particular phrase may be... therefore it is safer just to stick with phrases that may sound awkward or badly-worded instead of changing them to sound better;

> there may be part of a judgment that took a long time for the judges to reach a compromise [on]. My judge may be able to tell me which parts are the most important without breaching the secret of the deliberations, but how can I really know? So when a part of a judgment is re-drafted in the secret deliberations I should leave the wording exactly as it is—even if it doesn't make full sense to me, it may be a sign of a compromise between the judges;

> if the judges have made a compromise in a previous judgment—how would I know? If something seems vague I can't change the wording to make it more clear because maybe the Court wanted it to be vague—the deliberations are a secret so we will never know. But to be safe we should just repeat the same language.

It seems, therefore, that there are a number of difficulties involved in the creation or drafting of the case law of the Court of Justice of the European Union. On top of having to draft that case law in a language that, in most cases, is not their mother tongue, the *référendaires* (and indeed the judges) are constrained as regards the language used and the by the fact that the judgments of the Court are collegiate in nature. Such constraints necessarily shape the linguistic development of that case law and thus the development of EU law.

5. Conclusion

It is clear that the judges and their *référendaires* at the Court of Justice seem constrained in how they can draft judgments and other documents. The question thus arises whether language is therefore a constraint on the development of EU law—i.e. does the formulaic style that constrains the *référendaires* in what they can write actually constrain the development of the case law? The members of the Court interviewed during the fieldwork research for the present paper were of the opinion that, to a certain extent, that is indeed the case:

> It is surprising how much the French language influences how the judges deliberate and draft judgments—the fact that French is used as the language of the deliberations and is the language in which the very formulaic judgments are drafted forces [the Court] to speak or rule in a certain way;

> It is often difficult to say exactly what you want to say in a judgment... often the Court will want to say X but in the very rigid French of the Court that is used in the judgments you have to get around to X by saying that it is not Y!... such use of language necessarily has implications for the way in which the case law develops.

Such constraint is perhaps most immediately obvious in the development of a linguistic precedent in the judgments of the Court. However, the vast majority of literature on the ECJ and on precedent in EU law in particular ignores the linguistic aspect of the development of a rule of law. Legal literature is generally concerned with analysing the legal logic behind the Court's rulings and discussing how that Court can affect policy changes in the EU, insofar as practice may have to change to comply with a particular ruling. Political science literature is interested in 'judicial politics', the policy dynamics that can be inferred from the Court's decisions and in examining the political context and consequences of those decisions. However, each of these bodies of literature remains predominantly focused on the decisions of the Court and on judicial reasoning and/or investigating the reasons or motivation behind those decisions. Much has been written on why the Court makes certain decisions and the effects of those decisions, particularly with regard to precedent in the EU; but there has been very little research into how its case law is produced and the role of language in the production of that case law. Even those academics interested in the actors at the Court are primarily interested in argumentation frameworks and organisation theory (courts as organisations)[36] and ignore the multilingual aspects of that institution.

This consideration of the linguistic aspect of the development of a de facto precedent at the level of the Court of Justice necessarily leads to consideration of how the synthetic construction of the Court's case law may affect the application of that law by national courts that may not be aware of the body of EU law as a synthetic construction and will be looking for clues as to its application in a national legal language.[37] This paper thus highlights a need for further research to contribute to the debate mentioned in the introduction, which aims to clarify the way in which 'precedent' may be developing in the case law of the Court of Justice and the effect that may have on the relationship between the ECJ and national courts in the context of the preliminary ruling procedure.

---

[36] Stone Sweet, *The Judicial Construction of Europe* (cited in n.5).
[37] McAuliffe, 'Hybrid Texts and Uniform Law?' (cited in n.25).

30
Law and Language(s) at the Heart of the European Project: Educating Different Kinds of Lawyers

Dr Bénédicte Sage-Fuller,
Ferdinand Prinz zur Lippe, and
Seán Ó Conaill

τὸ γὰρ κακὸν τοῦ ἀπείρου, ὡς οἱ Πυθαγόρειοι εἴκαζον, τὸ δ' ἀγαθὸν τοῦ πεπερασμένου, τὸ δὲ κατορθοῦν μοναχῶς (διὸ καὶ τὸ μὲν ῥᾴδιον τὸ δὲ χαλεπόν, ῥᾴδιον μὲν τὸ ἀποτυχεῖν τοῦ σκοποῦ, χαλεπὸν δὲ τὸ ἐπιτυχεῖν): καὶ διὰ ταῦτ' οὖν τῆς μὲν κακίας ἡ ὑπερβολὴ καὶ ἡ ἔλλειψις, τῆς δ' ἀρετῆς ἡ μεσότης ἐσθλοὶ μὲν γὰρ ἁπλῶς, παντοδαπῶς δὲ κακοί.[1]

Aristotle, *Nichomacean Ethics*, 1106b30

1. Introduction

Teaching French law through French, German law through German, and Irish law through Irish and English seems like common sense and is indeed applied in some universities in Ireland and the UK, with respect to French, Irish,[2] and German in particular. There are simple and practical reasons for this. Many academics involved in this kind of teaching are native French, Irish, or German speakers, and therefore they instinctively strive to teach through their first language. Another factor is that often the funding of certain academics through governmental or public organisations is linked to teaching programmes in a certain language.[3] Also, as students in a variety of degree programmes are required to spend a year abroad at a French or German law faculty, or on placements

---

[1] 'For evil is a form of the unlimited, as in the old Pythagorean imagery, and good of the limited, whereas success is possible in one way only (which is why it is easy to fail and difficult to succeed—easy to miss the target and difficult to hit it); so this is another reason why excess and deficiency are a mark of vice, and observance of the mean a mark of virtue: goodness is simple, badness manifold', Aristotle, *Nichomacean Ethics* (trans. H. Rackham, Cambridge, Mass.: Harvard University Press, 1934), 1106b30, available at <http://www.perseus.tufts.edu> accessed 6 January 2012.
[2] The BCL (Law and Irish) degree is unique in the world in providing an education in law and in the Irish language, including legal language.
[3] The German Academic Exchange Service (*DAAD*) currently supports 19 law lecturers as *DAAD-Fachlektoren* and their lectureships. The Higher Education Authority in Ireland supports teaching through the medium of Irish by way of the Advanced Irish Skills Initiative which is specifically aimed at increasing the number of graduates with the skill set required to facilitate the Irish language as an official EU language.

where Irish is spoken, it is necessary to give them training in linguistics and in French and German law.[4] But it is argued in this paper that there are also deeper philosophical and policy reasons why students engaged in learning the law of a country should do so directly in the language of that country. The authors argue that students need to be taught that the legal tradition of a country cannot be understood fully without mastering its language. Students need to develop their ability to reason and analyse French, Irish, and German legal principles entirely through the medium of French, Irish, or German.[5] This point is an important one for the future lawyers of Europe, from both the academic and the legal practice perspectives. Indeed, students and lawyers must be able to think rationally in order to develop and apply the laws of Europe.[6] This cannot be achieved without understanding clearly the intrinsic relationship between law and language, or to put it more precisely, between the law and the language in which it is expressed.

2. Legal traditions, justice, law, and language

The philosophical explanation that we choose to put forward is provided by Alasdair MacIntyre in Chapter 19, 'Tradition and Translation', of his book *Whose Justice? Which Rationality?*[7] In this chapter, MacIntyre explores the terms of the linguistic relationship between traditions. He argues that this relationship is one of translatability, or untranslatability. Traditions are understood as developing distinctive and rival schemes, which may be not only incompatible, but also incommensurable. Indeed, the beliefs of one tradition may involve the rejection of the beliefs of another tradition, and this means that they are not translatable from one tradition into the other, even though they may be explained. MacIntyre puts in this way:

> Yet the achievement of the understanding of one tradition by the adherents of another may have as its sequel a number of different types of outcomes: to understand may entail immediate rejection in respect of that which they are divided; or to understand may lead to the conclusion that the issues which divide the two traditions cannot be decided; and in certainly rare but crucial types of cases, ... to understand may lead to a judgment that by the standards of one's own tradition the standpoint of the other tradition offers superior resources for understanding the problems and issues which confront one's own tradition.[8]

This paper will explain MacIntyre's view of the linguistic relationship between traditions, and how this philosophy can be applied to the relationship between legal traditions. Ultimately, our aim is to show that the relationship between the legal traditions of Europe, particularly in the context of the European Union, is intrinsically dependent on the kind of legal education that is provided to law students, and in particular on the kind of understanding that law students gain of the law and language issue.

---

[4] The curriculum of Trinity College Dublin Law School's LLB (Ling. Germ.) students exceeds for such purposes the requirements of the ERASMUS guidelines of the partner universities and requires students to pass certain legal core subjects.

[5] A number of students at University College Cork undertake the study of law through the medium of three languages, English, Irish, and French.

[6] Pierre Legrand, 'Issues in the Translatability of Law' in Sara Bermann and Michael Wood (eds), *Nation, Language, and the Ethics of Translation* (Princeton, NJ: Princeton University Press, 2005), addresses the difficulties of translation facing what he calls 'comparatists-at-law' in having to understand other countries' laws, and the particular, and largely ignored, challenges that this poses for the European Union (in particular, the necessity for lawyers to place the law in its cultural context, and the impossibility of legal transplants).

[7] Alasdair MacIntyre, *Whose Justice? Which Rationality?* (London: Duckworth, 1988).

[8] MacIntyre, *Whose Justice? Which Rationality?* (cited in n.7), 370.

Writing on legal education in 1950, Lon L. Fuller tied it in with the very grave question of democracy itself: 'In my opinion, the only discipline we should seek in law school is that which sets the students' mind free, not that which makes it comfortable within a framework imposed on it from the outside.'[9] He goes on to say:

> We must come...to see law as a quest for the principles that make possible the successful living together of men. We must come again to view democracy—not as a pat formula that can be applied thoughtlessly for the cure of any kind of social disorder, nor as a system of government that by reason of historical conditioning we happen to find congenial—but as a difficult achievement, necessary for a realization of the full dignity and power of man.[10]

Like Fuller, we believe in the very difficult responsibility falling on the shoulders of law students and lawyers, particularly in the context of the European Union of the 21st century. We argue that the success of this 'difficult achievement' is inextricably dependent on the awareness and understanding that lawyers have of language issues. This is why law should be taught through the language of that law. Indeed, students, who are learning about the rationality of the Common Law, through the English language, and also about the rationality of French or German law, or of specific aspects of Irish law through respectively the French, German, and Irish languages, are at the heart of this 'difficult achievement' within the European Union. Patrick Glenn says: 'once you are thinking logically... in the Greek (or Egyptian) way, you can build things, from pyramids to temples to large philosophic or legal constructions. Using law as the instrument of reason, you can also construct a modern state, which is essentially created out of formal, written law, though resting on a transnational legal tradition supporting its existence in multiple, national forms.'[11] We can replace the words 'reason' with 'rationality', and 'logically' with 'rationally' in this quote, and agree: to construct, to defend or to maintain a modern State, the rationality of a tradition is needed. The modern State is the organisation of peoples in an effective way, in order to put their word into action. This idea requires a people sufficiently unified to form a nation (and for this, a common language is normally an essential condition).[12] This nation will have a common voice, which can be expressed through representation. For a nation to be able to express its voice and have it translated into actions is the particularity of the European law tradition. In other words, matching actions of the State with the word of the people is at the heart of European civilisation. It is the constant search for the perfect equilibrium between people and State that has characterised European civilisation in the last millennium. A breakdown of this equilibrium means ignoring the voice of the nation, and ultimately the adoption of rules, the origin of which is unknown.[13] We therefore claim that the lesson to the lawyers *en herbe*

---

[9] Lon Fuller, 'On Teaching Law' (1950) 3(1) *Stanford Law Review* 35, 38–9.
[10] Fuller, 'On Teaching Law' (cited in n.9), 46.
[11] Patrick Glenn, *Legal Traditions of the World* (4th edn, Oxford: Oxford University Press, 2010), 154.
[12] *Bunreacht na hEireann* 1937 Art.8(1), the Irish Constitution, declares that: 'The Irish language as the national language is the first official language', and Art.8(2): 'The English language is recognised as a second official language'. Before it, the 1922 Constitution of *Saorstát Éireann* Art.4 provided that: 'The national language of the Irish Free State (*Saorstát Éireann*) is the Irish language, but the English language shall be equally recognised as an official language'. Kennedy CJ in *Ó Foghludha v McClean* [1934] IR 469, [482] stated that 'The declaration by the Constitution that the national language of the Sàorstat is the Irish language is, or was at that historical moment, universally spoken by the people of the Sàorstat, which would be untrue in fact, but it did mean that it is the historic distinctive speech of the Irish people, that it is to rank as such in the nation'. The 1958 French Constitution Art.2(1) declares that: '*La langue de la République est le français*'. There are interesting parallels between France and Ireland in relation to the duties of the State and the official languages.
[13] Pierre Manent, *Les Métamorphoses de la Cité* (Paris: Flammarion, 2010), 20, author's own translation.

who are educated in multi-legal and multi-lingual programmes is not only important, but essential to Europe, albeit concerning only three of the 23 official European languages, in that it teaches them to think rationally about the law of their State, of the other State that they learn about, and of the European Union and European law. We argue that the relationship between European legal traditions is at the heart of the European Union, and is indispensable to the creation of coherent European law and effective and efficient[14] legal structures. As teachers of French, Irish, and German law, we therefore see it as critical that students learn about their tradition, and how to learn about the other tradition in their curriculum. Beyond the instinctive reasons that we have as native French, Irish, and German speakers, and trained French, Irish, and German jurists, we argue that there is a philosophical reason that justifies teaching our students the French, Irish, and German languages.

3. Multi-lingual and multi-legal education in Ireland and elsewhere

With a population of only four and a half million, and located at the most westerly point of the European continent, it is hard to imagine that Ireland could be anything more than just a small partner to large and powerful States in the European Union of 27 members and nearly 500 million people. Aside from the political, economic, financial, and even populist takes on this question, there is one discrete area where Ireland can play a meaningful role in Europe, and that is by educating lawyers with a focused training in languages, and an understanding of both the Common Law system and the continental Civil Law systems. After all, the Irish constitutional order and legal system encompass characteristics of both and so does the European Union.[15] The European Union has 23 official languages, and more than 60 regional and minority languages. It is committed to respecting these languages, as they are part of its rich cultural and linguistic diversity.[16] However, beyond the mere respect for languages, and including minority languages, the EU and the Member States need to address upfront the issue of linguistic diversity and what it means for their laws, their institutions, and their practices. There are obvious questions of drafting and translation of legislation, court decisions, administrative documents, and policy papers. The EU is currently a union based on economic cooperation, in which the law plays a fundamental role in the facilitation of a legal order, which enables citizens and economic entities to interact freely. Thus, the relationship between the legal systems and the legal professions is of crucial importance.[17] These questions

---

[14] Francis Snyder, 'The Effectiveness of European Community law: Institutions, Processes, Tools and Techniques' (1993) 56 *Modern Law Review* 19, 32.

[15] Vivian G. Curran, 'Romantic Common Law, Enlightened Civil Law: Legal Uniformity and the Homogenization of the European Union' (2001) 7 *Columbia Journal of European Law* 63.

[16] Treaty on the European Union (TEU) Art.3 para.4: '[The Union] shall respect its rich and cultural diversity, and shall ensure that Europe's cultural heritage is safeguarded and enhanced.' In the field of education, TEU Art.165(2) binds the Union to direct its action at 'developing the European dimension in education, particularly through the teaching and dissemination of the languages of the Member States'. There are various provisions throughout the TEU guaranteeing the rights of European citizens to petition, write to, and be written to in their language in their dealings with the European institutions. The Charter of Fundamental Rights of the European Union (2000/C 364/01) in its Art.21 prohibits discrimination on the ground of language.

[17] Directive 98/5/EC of the European Parliament and of the Council of 16 February 1998 to facilitate practice of the profession of lawyer on a permanent basis in a Member State other than that which the qualification was obtained, OJ L77, 14.3.1998, pp.36–43; Council Directive 89/48/EEC of 21 December 1988 on a general system for the recognition of higher-education diplomas awarded on completion of professional education and training of at least three years' duration, OJ L19, 24/01/1088,

underline the need for lawyers proficient in modern languages and able to cope with international and within-Europe legal work.[18] Ireland, we argue, is in a unique position, and therefore has an original role to play within the EU. First of all, it is one of the two main countries, with the United Kingdom, of the EU, the legal system of which belongs to the Common Law tradition.[19] In this context, there is a special task incumbent on Common Law lawyers to be involved in European legal affairs in order to protect the specificities of the Common Law amongst the overwhelming majority of Civil Law systems. Secondly, Ireland already places a special emphasis on bilingualism in its own legal system, because of the official place that the Irish language occupies in the Irish legal and constitutional order. Irish lawyers understand well how and why the Irish Common Law is different from the English Common Law because of linguistic differences and because of the nature of the formal Irish constitutional order. They are therefore already prepared to understand how the law of the EU cannot but be affected by the linguistic diversity that exists in Europe. They then can act as special connectors between the legal systems of the EU, and with EU law and institutions, both nationally and internationally. This of course can happen only if besides being proficient in English and Irish, they also master a second European language.

Three law and language degree programmes currently offered in two Irish universities are used as examples to show how these kinds of Irish lawyers are trained, primarily as Common Law lawyers, but with a true understanding of what the rich linguistic diversity of the EU means for Europe's legal institutions and practices. The degrees of BCL (Law and French) and BCL (Law and Irish) in University College Cork, and LLB (Ling. Germ.) in Trinity College Dublin primarily educate Irish law students at Common Law. They provide the basis for further legal professional training in Ireland. In addition the aforementioned degree programmes provide an extensive exposure to French, Irish, and German law respectively, through module teaching in Ireland, and a year spent studying at a French or German law university, under the Erasmus programme, or in key government or EU institutions working in the Irish language. It is important to note that these degrees do not provide a double qualification of an Irish law degree with a French or a German law degree.[20] However, they provide not only extensive legal French, Irish, or German training, but instil as well in-depth linguistic, cultural, and historical knowledge of France,[21] Ireland, and Germany. During the course of their degree, and upon graduation, students have opportunities for further study and to obtain work experience in specialised areas of French law, Irish law, German law, and EU law and practice. The study of the French, Irish, or German languages, cultures, and legal systems, alongside the study of the Irish Common Law, therefore not only broadens the horizon of these students on a personal level, but in practical terms also opens areas of opportunities that might otherwise not be easily accessible. For those students, a choice of degree, which was generally motivated by the willingness to learn about a different culture and language, evolves into a journey, through a carefully devised academic curriculum, deep into this culture that they are interested in, and embrace, but also into its legal system, its understanding of the rule of law, and its conception of law and justice.

pp.16–23; Council Directive 77/249/EEC of 22 March 1977 to facilitate the effective exercise by lawyers of freedom to provide services, OJ L78, 26/03/1977, pp.17–18.

[18] Directive 98/5/EC, reasons (2)–(5).
[19] Cyprus and Malta are mixed legal systems, with part of their law based on the Common Law too.
[20] There are a number of formal 'double degrees' offered by Irish and UK universities.
[21] In this respect it is worth noting that the BCL (Law and French) and the BCL (Law and Irish) degrees are joint honours degrees in Law and in Arts.

As teachers and directors of these three programmes, we take an approach to teaching that, while not unique, is based on the clear awareness that the law of a country cannot be taught otherwise than in the language and within the cultural context of that country. We therefore teach French, Irish, and German law through French, Irish,[22] or German to Irish law students. This approach, we claim, meets the expectations of students, raises and maintains their interest in the subject matter, and challenges them intellectually. But we also claim that this method leads future lawyers to respecting and understanding other European countries' legal traditions.[23] At a minimum, we strive to make students aware of the differences that exist between the Irish, the French, or the German legal traditions, and of the importance of being aware of these differences and thus providing them with a basis to continue their professional education and improve their qualifications later, in order to meet the requirements for legal practice across the borders of European Member States.[24] As stated and argued by other lawyers,[25] lawyer-linguists,[26] and lawyer-translators,[27] the issue of language differences in the EU is too often ignored or at least underestimated.[28]

Historically the concept of administering legal education in more than one language in Ireland is not new. Indeed the very first attempts at bilingual legal education in Ireland can be traced back to a period which predates the Common Law itself. English-language legal education and more generally an English-language-dominated legal system have been accepted since the Common Law took hold in Ireland, and is now the norm. The notion of a joint law degree or legal training in more than one language is considered to be a relatively recent innovation. However, while the current courses on offer are somewhat recent arrivals, it could be argued that they are merely picking up the baton of Irish-language legal education which was put aside when the Common Law finally vanquished the native Brehon law. The Brehon law was one of the oldest legal systems in Europe and the native early law of Ireland. It consisted of an expansive civil code with an emphasis on compensation for harm done rather than punishment. The system was administered by a class of judges known as *Breitheamh* with a separate class of academic lawyers called *Ollamh*.[29] The *Ollamh* operated law schools at various locations throughout the country where numerous manuscript texts were compiled and studied. The arrival of Christianity meant that many Brehon traditions were fused with the Canon Law to create a new bilingual legal order in Ireland, in Old Irish and in Latin. The native Irish laws were passed down orally and at a later stage recorded in Old Irish, and the Canon Law operated in the Church's lingua franca of Latin. Professor Fergus Kelly notes in his *Guide to early Irish Law*[30] that one of these early law schools was based

---

[22] Irish Common Law is taught at UCC mostly through the medium of English, but there is specialised teaching of Constitutional Law through the Irish language. In addition, BCL (Law and Irish) students complete two legal placements in Irish-speaking environments.

[23] This method also facilitates further training by students in France or Germany to access the legal professions there.

[24] See the German Federal Statute regulating the activity of European lawyers in Germany (EuRAG) para.21 I 2.

[25] e.g. Pierre Legrand, 'Antivonbar' (2005) 1(1) *Journal of Comparative Law* 13.

[26] Karen McAuliffe, 'Enlargement at the European Court of Justice: Law, Language and Translation' (2008) 14(6) *European Law Journal* 806.

[27] Simone Glanert, 'Speaking Language to Law: The Case of Europe' (2008) 28 *Legal Studies* 161.

[28] Formal participation in legal proceedings requires a sufficient knowledge of the local language; see, for Germany, German Judiciary Act (GVG) s.184, and Law regulating the activity of European lawyers in Germany (EuRAG) ss.11–16.

[29] Laurence Ginnell, *The Brehon Law: a Legal Handbook* (2nd edn, Dublin: West, 1917), 89. The terms *breitheamh* and *ollamh* survive in modern Irish, meaning judge and professor respectively.

[30] Fergus Kelly, *Guide to Early Irish Law* (Dublin: Institute for Advanced Studies, 1988), 247.

in the monastery at *Corcach*.[31] The location of that monastery is believed to be the very ground on which University College Cork stands, where the BCL (Law and French) and BCL (Law and Irish) are offered. The programmes offered at University College Cork can therefore be seen as the heirs of a long-established tradition. The motto of University College Cork, 'Where Finbar[32] Taught let Munster Learn', seems particularly apt when it comes to training lawyers in more than one language. Somewhat aptly Kelly notes that with the arrival of the Normans (and thus the Common Law) the standard of Latin used by the law schools declined as they adapted to the new languages (French and English) brought by the Normans to Ireland and the Irish legal system.[33] Adapting to changing national, international, and linguistic circumstances in addition to market demands is therefore not a new development for Irish law schools.

In more modern times the concept of bilingual legal education or legal education through a language other than the dominant language of a jurisdiction is practised in many jurisdictions throughout Europe and further afield. Key to each example is the recognition that additional challenges and opportunities exist in addition to the idea that student learning is driven by factors other than the superficial ease of translation of terminology. Canada, for example, has developed and encouraged English-French bilingual education and French-medium legal education to varying degrees. Of particular interest from a comparative point of view is the bijurial nature of Canadian legal education. Traditionally French-speaking students would have studied the civil elements of Canadian law through the medium of French and English-speaking students would have focused on the Common Law. From the 1970s onwards, however, attempts were made in particular to teach the Common Law through the medium of French. To do so a corpus of terminology was developed to allow academics, students, and practitioners to engage with the Common Law. However there was an acute recognition that terms such as these could not be borrowed from French from similar concepts in Civil Law nor could they be artificially translated from English. Instead it was recognised that Common Law terminology in French needed to evolve in the same way that Common Law terminology in English has developed, and needed to be flexible to and acceptable to the French speakers using the language.[34]

In Canada, there was a recognition that subsequent translation of laws which had been drafted in one language leads only to 'quality issues'.[35] The solution put forward, which has subsequently been adopted in Wales, was that all bilingual laws should be drafted concurrently. The English and French texts are prepared side by side, with two drafters being assigned and instructed together bilingually. Each drafter is of equal standing, one being a French speaker and one being an English speaker trained not only to understand the law in their respective languages but also to understand the importance of the precise use of language. Together the drafters produce one document which is co-edited and published. The experience in Canada (and subsequently in Wales) is that, first, the

---

[31] The modern Irish for Cork is *Corcaigh*.
[32] St Finbar is the Patron Saint of Cork and is mostly associated with the Abbey established in Cork.
[33] Kelly, *Guide to Early Irish Law* (cited in n.30), 254.
[34] National Assembly for Wales, *The Operation of a System of Law Making that in Practice Treats English and Welsh on a Basis of Equality—A Report of the Office of the Counsel General to the National Assembly for Wales* (Cardiff: National Assembly for Wales, 2006), 11.
[35] National Assembly for Wales, *Bilingual Lawmaking and Justice—A report on the lessons for Wales from the Canadian experience of bilingualism by the National Assembly for Wales* (Cardiff: National Assembly for Wales, 2006), 16, available at<http://www.assemblywales.org/bilingual-lawmaking-e.pdf> accessed 6 January 2012.

document in the second (or minority language) is of much higher quality than a document which has been merely translated without taking account of the nuances of the cultural, conceptual, and linguistic situation. Whilst there were some delays to the drafting stage the process was ultimately quicker than subsequent translation. Perhaps most crucially, however, there was a noticeable increase in the quality of the English-language drafting in Canada as a result of this process whereby two drafters rather than one examined the English text. The drafters were more likely to spot gaps and problems and were better able to deal with them when they did arise.[36]

In Cameroon the bilingual and bijurial legal system recognises that no two languages can be the same and as a result students are taught how the one legal goal is brought about differently in each language.[37] In Wales many universities have courses where students study legal Welsh and legal topics through the medium of Welsh but, as with French in Canada, the importance of developing terminology with which students can engage is crucially important.[38] Students' confidence in using the minority or second language is seen to rest upon the students' ability to engage properly with the language, understand fully the cultural context of the terminology, and grasp the differences and nuances between different language versions of laws and concepts.[39]

On the basis of these historical and contemporary examples, it is therefore clear that the making and teaching of law through the language of its tradition makes sense, is not new, and needs to continue. Lawyers are the watchdogs of democracy because they learn about its mechanisms, and how to make sure that law delivers justice. Their education should thus prepare them for this special role that they are called to play in society. We argue that the integration of linguistic issues into legal education is critical, and is supported not only by historical and contemporary evidence, but also by sound philosophical arguments.

4. Epistemology to learn law

MacIntyre's first point is to explain how the study of traditions should be undertaken. Namely, he argues that the method of epistemology should be applied. Epistemology requires a historical, ethical, and metaphysical enquiry, in order to understand the meaning of words and expressions in a tradition. In his opinion, semantics are insufficient as they are often a-historic. The interface between law and language can therefore only be grasped by students when the language element is sufficiently emphasised. Besides legal words, there is an entire context to be understood. The historical introduction to law, and language-based substantive teaching of French, Irish, and German law are necessary elements for understanding this interaction. To take a controversial yet salient example, the status of the embryo under French law can only be fully understood by reference to the Roman-law origins of French law, and the decision of the French legislator made in this context. French law, like Roman law, classifies everything into three categories:

---

[36] National Assembly for Wales, *Bilingual Lawmaking and Justice* (cited in n.35), 18.
[37] OHADA, *Uniform Act Organizing Simplified Recovery Procedures and Measures of Execution*, 3, available at <http://www.juriscope.org/infos_ohada/actseng/recovery%20procedures.pdf> accessed 6 January 2012.
[38] Glenys Williams, 'Legal Education in Welsh—An Empirical Study' (2005) 39(3) *The Law Teacher* 259, 261.
[39] Williams, 'Legal Education in Welsh' (cited in n.38), 265. Students highlighted a concern that their language choice could lead to their intentions being misinterpreted if the teacher/lecturer of the course was not entirely fluent and comfortable in the language.

actions, things, and persons. The whole set of legal rules applicable to something depends on whether it is an action, a thing, or a person. In this context, the human embryo was refused the status of person by the French legislator (in the statute on abortion and the statutes on bio-ethics).[40] The embryo can obviously not be classified as a thing, nor as an action. In legal terms, it is therefore in limbo. The debate around abortion and bio-ethics in France was therefore set in a context of complete departure from accepted legal concepts. Other legal issues related to the legal limbo of the embryo and the foetus include the refusal to consider a stillborn infant as a person if it is not born *'vivant et viable'*.[41] Among the consequences of this refusal is that it is impossible for parents to obtain a death certificate, to name, recognise, or bury their stillborn child.[42] These consequences have to be explained to Irish law students in the context of the fabric and history of French law, because their blunt and contextless reality would otherwise appear incomprehensible to those *Irish* students, considering the passionate debate surrounding the legal status of the 'unborn' in their law. To start with, there is no translation in French for 'unborn', whereas the word is used in English in *Bunreacht na hEireann* Art.40.3.3, following a 1983 constitutional amendment. The Constitution was itself co-drafted in Irish and English, but the constitutional amendments, especially the more recent ones, were drafted in English and subsequently translated into Irish. Article 40.3.3, inserted in 1983 following a referendum, says that 'The State acknowledges the right to life of the unborn'. The Irish version of Art.40.3.3 uses the expression: *beo gan breith*, which exactly means 'the living who have not been born yet'. One can immediately see the difference between the English and the Irish version of this constitutional amendment.

Bunreacht na hEireann Art.25.5.4 provides that in any conflict between the English and the Irish texts of the constitution, the Irish-language version shall prevail. This provision was particularly criticised by the late Professor J. M. Kelly, widely regarded as Ireland's foremost constitutional scholar. Kelly described the article as an 'irrational irritant'[43] as well as a 'situation pregnant with annoyance and timewasting for the Courts'.[44] In practice it is rare for such differences to exist (or at least to exist to such an extent as to have any real legal significance) and as Budd J noted in *O'Donovan v Attorney General*:

> Both texts of the Constitution are authoritative. It is not to be thought that those who framed or enacted the Constitution would knowingly do anything so absurd as to frame or enact texts with different meanings in parts. It could only happen by inadvertence... if in fact the words used are not in form really found to correspond the Irish text must prevail.[45]

It should therefore be recognised that in many instances where the English text is perhaps unclear or unsatisfactory the courts have tended to look towards the Irish text to

---

[40] Although the *Code Civil* Art.16 states that 'la loi... garantit le respect de l'être humain dès le commencement de sa vie', this provision was not interpreted as including embryos and foetuses. As a consequence, embryos and foetuses are not considered as persons under French law: Brigitte Hess-Fallon and Anne-Marie Simon, *Droit Civil* (9th edn, Paris: Sirey, 2007), 100.

[41] Meaning 'alive and viable'. See *Code Civil* Art.79–1: 'Lorsqu'un enfant est décédé avant que sa naissance ait été déclarée à l'état civil, l'officier de l'état civil établit un acte de naissance et un acte de décès sur production d'un certificat médical indiquant que l'enfant est né vivant et viable et précisant les jours et heures de sa naissance et de son décès.'

[42] The *Médiateur de la République* (French version of the Ombudsman) has brought to the attention of the public, the government, and the legislator the necessity to remedy this situation, see: Médiateur de la République, 'État civil des enfants nés sans vie', available at < http://mediateur-republique.fr/fr-citoyen-06–05–05> accessed 6 January 2012.

[43] J. M. Kelly 'The Irish Text of the Constitution' (1966) Hilary *Irish Student Law Review* 7, 10.

[44] Kelly, 'The Irish Text of the Constitution' (cited in n.43).

[45] *O'Donovan v Attorney General* [1961] IR 114, [117].

better elucidate the English text.[46] An example of application of the Irish text occurred in case law concerning the Bill of Rights portion of the Irish Constitution. In *Crowley v Ireland*[47] the Supreme Court turned to the Irish text of Art.42.4 in order to better understand the obligation the article places upon the State with regard to free primary education. The plaintiffs wanted the State to provide the special education which their son required. The Supreme Court turned to the Irish text, which contained the phrase '*socrú a dhéanamh chun*' which translates more closely as 'make provision for' rather than 'provide' as the plaintiffs had requested. A counter-example of the misapplication of Irish text includes the well-known abortion decision, the 'X Case',[48] where McCarthy J noted that there was some difference between the English and Irish text of the Constitution which could perhaps have a bearing on the right to life of the unborn but dismissed this on the basis that '[h]istorically the Irish text is a translation of that in English'. It is submitted that the learned judge erred, first, in his contention that the Irish text is a translation of the English text.[49] Secondly even if it were to be the case that the Irish text was merely a translation of the English text the provisions of Art.25.5.4 are quite clear that the text in the Irish language is to prevail in the event of a conflict. It is not the contention of this work that a different judicial approach to the Irish text of the Constitution would have resulted in a different outcome to this particular case. It does, however, follow that had there been a greater understanding of the Irish text and its status future development in relation to difficult adjudications on the law could have had a somewhat different outcome. The debates about the legal status and right to life of embryos and foetuses in Ireland are embedded in the Irish legal tradition of the late 20th and early 21st century. This is the tradition in which Irish law students learn Irish Common Law, and it is then clear that to understand the status of embryos and foetuses in French law, an epistemological enquiry is required.

This admittedly complex and controversial example shows that the first step in teaching French, Irish, or German law to Irish students is to do it through an epistemological enquiry of words, legal words, legal concepts, and legal methods. A more technical example may be the different concepts of property and ownership in Common Law and *Eigentum* and *Besitz* in the strict German (Civil) law.[50]

5. Language and tradition

The second step in MacIntyre's argument is to examine the link between language and tradition. He explains that the language of a tradition is actually the 'language as it is used in and by a particular community living at a particular time and place with particular shared beliefs, institutions and practices'.[51] In this sense, there is a very close link between beliefs, institutions, and practices of a community, and the language it uses at a given

---

[46] See generally J. M. Kelly, *The Irish Constitution* (Gerard Hogan and Gerry Whyte, eds, Dublin: Tottel, 2003), 205–11.
[47] [1980] IR 102.
[48] *Attorney General v X* [1992] IR 1.
[49] The oft-repeated claim that the Irish version of the Constitution is a mere translation of the English version has been forcefully dismissed in recent times, see generally Micheal Ó Cearúil, *Bunreacht na hÉireann—A study of the Irish text* (Dublin: Government of Ireland, 1999), available at <http://www.constitution.ie> accessed 6 January 2012.
[50] G. P. Wilson, 'Jurisprudence and the Discussion of Ownership' (1957) 15(2) *Cambridge Law Journal* 216, 229; Ugo Mattei, *Basic Principles of Property Law: A comparative legal and economic introduction* (Westport, CT: Greenwood Press, 2000) 12; German Civil Code (*BGB*) ss.854 ff., ss.903 ff.
[51] MacIntyre, *Whose Justice? Which Rationality?* (cited in n..7), 373.

time, and in a given place. The boundaries of the language are the boundaries of those beliefs, institutions, and practices. In this sense, to reject a belief will be done through linguistic transformation, at a given moment in time, or over a period of linguistic evolution. A simple example is how French criminal law in the *Nouveau Code de Procédure Pénale* of 1993 decided to reinforce the presumption of innocence, by various means. Semantically, a significant change was brought to the vocabulary relating to charging someone accused of an offence, from *inculpation* to *mise en examen* (word for word: put under examination). The two words designate the same judicial process: there are grave suspicions that someone has violated a rule of criminal law, therefore the competent authority (the *juge d'instruction*) has the power to charge that person with an offence. The process will lead to a trial, where it will be decided whether the person is guilty or not. Until the end of the trial, the person is presumed innocent. It was felt that the word *inculpation* undermined the presumption of innocence. Indeed, *inculpation* is based on the Latin root of *culpa* ('fault'), which is the same root as for *culpabilité* and *coupable*. *Mise en examen* has a more neutral tone, and therefore, since 1993, the correct legal term to designate this judicial process is no longer *inculpation* but *mise en examen*.[52] Reinforcing the change of terminology for greater value attached to the presumption of innocence in the *Code de Procédure Pénale* in 1993, the 1881 *Loi sur la liberté de la presse* (law on freedom of the press) was modified in 2000 to forbid the dissemination of images, by whatever means, of persons with handcuffs when these persons have not been convicted.[53] The obvious objective of this 2000 amendment was to remove from public life all images of a person who is *mis en examen*, to prevent the stigma attached to being caught in a criminal judicial process.[54] To Irish students reading the expression *mis en examen* for the first time, a simple word-for-word translation into 'put under examination', and even a translation into 'charged', with reference to Irish criminal legal language, would obviously truncate the meaning of the expression in the French criminal system and its recent evolution, and even in the French social fabric and language. Another example of the difficulties students face when dealing with the very abstract nature of law may be taken from the German Civil Law principles of separation and abstraction, according to which the law of obligation and the law of right *in rem* are interdependent to a certain degree.[55] Tuition in these subjects requires long explanations. Tradition also plays a strong role in

---

[52] Article 23 of Loi No 93–2 du 4 Janvier 1993 portant réforme de la procédure pénale, *Journal Officiel de la République Française* (JORF) No. 3, 4 January 1993, p.215, inserting Article 80–1 into the *Nouveau Code de Procédure Pénale*. See also Yves Amar, 'Inculpation' (*RFI*, 16 July 2008, available at <http://www.rfi.fr/lffr/articles/103/article_2476.asp> accessed 6 January 2012. The author also notes that the word *inculpation* is of course still part of the French language, even if it is no longer a legal term in French law. It is however used when referring to charging someone with an offence for example at the International Criminal Court: 'La Cour pénale internationale n'est pas liée à une langue en particulier; elle siège aux Pays-Bas. Et quand on doit traduire son action, on peut très bien utiliser ce vieux terme d'inculpation qui a tout son sens.'

[53] *Loi du 29 Juillet 1881 sur la liberté de la presse* Art.35ter, modified by *Ordonnance n. 2000–916 du 19 Septembre 2000* Art.3(V), JORF 22 September 2000: 'Lorsqu'elle est réalisée sans l'accord de l'intéressé, la diffusion, par quelque moyen que ce soit et quelle qu'en soit le support, de l'image d'une personne identifiée mise en cause à l'occasion d'une procédure pénale mais n'ayant pas fait l'objet d'un jugement de condamnation et faisant apparaître, soit que cette personne porte des menottes ou entraves, soit qu'elle est placée en détention provisoire, est punie de 15000 euros d'amende.'

[54] See, e.g. the report of Senator Charles Jolibois during the adoption process of this amendment: Charles Jolibois, 'Projet de loi sur la présomption d'innocence et propositions de loi relatives aux gardes à vue et à la détention provisoire', Sénat, Rapport 419(98–99), available at < http://www.senat.fr/rap/l98–419/l98–419.html>, accessed 6 January 2012.

[55] Hans Brox and Wolf-Dietrich Walker, *Allgemeiner Teil des BGB* (Munich: Carl Heymanns-Verlag, 2008), ref. 103–123; Nigel Foster and Satich Sule, *German Legal System and Laws* (4th edn, Oxford: Oxford University Press, 2010), 369–72.

the prominence given to the Irish language in the Irish legal system and constitutional order. Mr Justice Geoghegan in the famous case of *Ó Beoláin v Fahy*[56] which concerned Irish language rights presciently summed up the situation, noting that a constitution is a document which embodies the aspirations and emotional feelings of the people who have enacted it. An observation on the importance of tradition, made at the time of the enactment of *Bunreacht na hÉireann*, noted:

> [T]he Irish are a people to whom independence means not only political sovereignty but artistic and literary individuality as well. The emphasis upon the native tongue has been a sort of leaning over backward, a phase of the withdrawal from all things English. One of the most credible explanations of the style of James Joyce is premised upon his psychological aversion to the English vocabulary, for him 'an acquired speech'.[57]

6. Learning a second first language

Next, MacIntyre begins his demonstration of how one ought to proceed in order to understand a tradition other than one's own. He makes the strong and seemingly extreme statement that understanding a tradition requires knowing it 'as a native inhabitant knows it, and speaking hearing, writing and reading the language as a native inhabitant speaks, hears, writes and reads it'.[58] Having established the link between language and tradition, he then goes on to state that in order to fully understand a tradition, one has to acquire its language. This means 'to become a child all over again' to acquire its language as a second first language, and 'just as a child does not learn its first language by matching sentences with sentences, since it initially possesses no set of sentences of its own, so an adult who has in this way become a child again does not either'.[59]

For ancient traditions (such as those of ancient Athens, or Sparta, or Babylon, or the Rome of a particular century), acquiring the language is done by way of immersing oneself in a historical enquiry of that tradition through documents, archives, artefacts, texts, etc., so as to eventually be able to write, for example, in the Latin of the 3rd centuryAD, as someone would have written at that time. MacIntyre has already emphasised that language is the language used by a community, in a particular area, at a particular time.[60] What he says here is that in order fully to understand the tradition of that community, at that time, in that place, requires knowing the language that it speaks, or spoke. Having acquired that language, the person claiming to know the other tradition that he is studying will then be able to make the distinction between what is translatable, and what is not.

A simple example is the meaning and use of the English term *case law*. To an Irish student, case law means the body of judicial decisions which are law by virtue of the doctrine of precedent as it is defined under Irish law since 1922, which is different from precedent in the UK. Indeed, post-1922 English decisions of higher courts are

---

[56] *Ó Beoláin v Fahy* [2001] 2 IR 279 at 356.
[57] Mary Cogan-Bromage, 'Linguistic Nationalism in Éire' (1941) 3(2) *The Review of Politics*, 225, 226.
[58] MacIntyre, *Whose Justice? Which Rationality?* (cited in n.7), 374.
[59] MacIntyre, *Whose Justice? Which Rationality?* (cited in n.7), 374.
[60] Throughout ch.19 of his book, MacIntyre is careful to distinguish those types of languages (strongly tradition bound) from what he calls the internationalised languages (accessible to anyone and not particularly linked to any tradition).

not authoritative in Ireland but only persuasive in Ireland, whereas they are obviously authoritative in England. The Irish student learning French or German law will then learn that there is simply no equivalent concept in the French or German language of the 21st century.[61] This is because the doctrine of precedent does not exist in French or German law. The term 'jurisprudence' in French law means the body of judicial decisions of courts, but these decisions are not law creating. The Irish student will then have to learn about the French *Code Civil* Art.5[62] to understand the precise legal force of the judicial decisions of a French judge, detached from the English or Irish doctrine of precedent. Good teaching practice will also include a historical explanation of this article, which is rooted in the 1789 French Revolution's rejection of the powers of *parlements* as courts of law. And here is another potential pitfall: a *parlement* in 21st century French is what an Irish law student would know as *Oireachtas*,[63] or an English law student would know as 'Parliament'. But a *parlement* in 18th-century French was an institution with powers to render judicial decisions.[64]

At the end of the process of manoeuvring between French, English, and Irish, the student will have learnt the legal meaning of *case law* in English, and of *jurisprudence* in 21st-century French as it is used in France and 21st-century English as it is used in Ireland. Likewise a Law and German student will have learnt about the differences of *Kompetenz-Kompetenz*[65] and the principles of conferred powers in relation to German, Irish (and other Common Law), and European law. He will have done so, not matching word for word, but as a child would have learnt words. Significantly, however, the student will also know that neither of these words can be translated into the other's language. They can, at best, be explained.

MacIntyre pushes his point even further and says that this untranslatability may be due to the lack of linguistics and concepts in a given language, but also to the fact that a community may function on a totally different basis of beliefs, institutions, and traditions from that of another community. He says that, for this reason, the language of a tradition cannot be acquired as a second language, but as a second first language, 'or not at all'.[66]

To take the examples used above, it is obvious that *case law* and the doctrine of precedent are typical of the history of judge-made law in the Common Law. It is also obvious that this doctrine was deliberately rooted out of the French legal tradition at the 1789 Revolution, to be replaced with a system of hegemony of legislation made by elected

---

[61] In practice judicial decisions in France and in Germany are influential and tend to be followed, but strictly speaking there is no obligation on courts to apply previous decisions, or the judgments of higher courts.

[62] The *Code Civil* Art.5 reads: 'Il est défendu aux juges de prononcer par voie de disposition générale et reglementaire sur les causes qui leur sont soumises.'

[63] With the distinction that *Oireachtas* in Irish constitutional law also includes the Office of the President.

[64] The origin of the *parlement* was a meeting of the king's *curia*, or entourage, without specific judicial power, where political and financial matters were debated. By the end of the 13th century, *in parlamento domini regis* designated a section of the *Curia Regis*, where litigation took place in the absence of the king. Adjudication was done on the basis of power delegated by the king to the *parlement*: François Olivier-Martin, *Histoire du droit français, Des origines à la Révolution* (3rd edn, Paris: CNRS Éditions, 2010), 262–5.

[65] Directorate-General for Research, *The Division of Competences in the European Union, Working Paper Political Series W 26a, H. Adjudicating the Dilemma of Competences—Judicial Kompetenz-Kompetenz*, available at <http://www.europarl.europa.eu/workingpapers/poli/w26/adju_En.htm> accessed 6 January 2012.

[66] MacIntyre, *Whose Justice? Which Rationality?* (cited in n.7), 375.

representatives,[67] where judges are confined to a strict application of the law. This is why the term *jurisprudence* in French is confined to meaning judicial decisions, simply as means of adjudicating between parties.[68] A further analysis of the etymology of the word *jurisprudence* in French and in English would show that despite its origin from the late Latin *jurisprudentia*, it now has two different meanings: one in 21st-century French, as explained above, and the other in 21st-century English, where it designates the discipline of legal theory as taught in universities. In Roman law, the *jurisprudents* were a class of legal consultants who were writing opinions about abstract legal points pertinent to the resolution of litigation.[69] These opinions were written as general rules, but never with absolute authority and always with the assumption that they could be refuted by good dialectic. As Villey noted, Roman law was thus born of experience, and always submitted to the test of experience, rather than a scientific normative exercise: 'Il est une recherche, une vie.'[70] So by learning the meaning of the French word jurisprudence directly in the French language and tradition of 21st-century France, the Irish student will understand the subtle and yet important differences between the French and the Irish legal meanings of *jurisprudence*. And if the student pushes his curiosity even further and learns about *jurisprudents* in Roman law, he may even understand some traits pertaining to these systems, how they are different, and how they are similar. But we argue that the Irish law student of the 21st century cannot travel on this intellectual journey without learning the French language of 21st-century France.

7. Obstacles to translatability

What, then, are the obstacles to the translatability of words and expressions between traditions? MacIntyre argues that incommensurability and incompatibility are two such obstacles. To prove his point, he identifies three practices that languages do: naming (places and people), understanding virtues (including the virtue of justice), and the genesis of action (the psychological description of how thinking may generate action). MacIntyre explains that these three practices of languages are affected by problems of untranslatability.

Naming in a tradition, he says, is naming for the members of that community. The names therefore not only identify places or people, but also correspond to a set of beliefs peculiar to that tradition. He takes the example of the town in Northern Ireland, known in English as *Londonderry*. In Irish, the same town is known as *Doire Columcille*, which means *St Columba's Oak Grave*. There is no possible translation between *Londonderry* and *Doire Columcille*, even though they each name the same place. One names it with reference to the Unionist Protestant tradition of Northern Ireland, whereas the other is linked to the Catholic evangelisation work done in Ireland by St Columba. MacIntyre's point is strengthened by

---

[67] See *Déclaration des Droits de l'Homme et du Citoyen* Art.6: 'La loi est l'expression de la volonté générale. Tous les citoyens ont le droit de concourir personellement, ou par leurs représentants, à sa formation'. It is also generally accepted that the hegemony of legislation ('l'hégémonie de la loi') in France superseded even the supremacy of the Constitution until relatively recently; see Louis Favoreu et al., *Droit Constitutionnel* (13th edn, Paris: Dalloz, 2010), 791–2.

[68] There is a debate among French jurists as to whether *jurisprudence* in French law can be classed as a source of law. In any case, it is subordinate to legislation, but it can sometimes complement it; see, for this argument, Rémi Cabrillac, *Intoduction Générale au Droit* (7th edn, Paris: Dalloz, 2007), 129–43 and, against, Jean-Louis Aubert, *Introduction au Droit et Thèmes Fondamentaux du Droit Civil* (Paris: Armand Colin, 2000), 166–8.

[69] The collection of comments so written by *jurisprudents* was found in the Digest of Justinian's *Corpus Iuris Civilis*.

[70] 'It is a search, a life', translation by this author. Michel Villey, *Le Droit Romain* (Series, 'Que Sais-Je?' Paris: PUF, 1945), 38.

the fact that the same town is known as *Derry* to the inhabitants of the Republic of Ireland who adhere to Catholic tradition. From this example, it is also clear that the way in which places or people are named in one tradition may mean the rejection of the way of naming in another tradition. Whether Irish people use *Derry, Londonderry,* or *Doire Columcille* to name the said town may signify adherence to one tradition and rejection of another. There is therefore incompatibility between the two ways of naming the same town, with the consequence that Londonderry cannot be translated into Irish, and *Doire Columcille* cannot be translated into English (a word-for-word translation may of course be done but will not have the effect of naming the place successfully as in the other tradition).

Incommensurability occurs when words, beliefs, institutions, or practices in a tradition have no equivalent in another tradition. MacIntyre takes the example of translating Horace's Latin into 1st-century Palestine Hebrew: *Caelo tonantem credidimus Jorem regnare: praesense divus habebitur Augustus,* which in English means, 'We will have believed that Juppiter [sic] thundering reigns in the sky; Augustus will be held a present divinity'. The belief in a Roman god and divinities cannot be translated into Hebrew, as this would be seen as idolatry of evil spirits, and would amount to false and blasphemous Hebrew.

Certain words expressing a tradition's understanding of virtues, and in particular justice, are also affected by the problem of untranslatability because of incompatibility or incommensurability. The legal discipline of Equity in Common Law is a prime example of such a word being untranslatable. Equity is so distinctive of the legal system of the Common Law, having developed in parallel to the Common Law as a way of providing remedies where the latter could not grant them, that it is completely alien to the Civil Law tradition. There is simply no word in French, or in German, to designate what Equity is at law.

The word *compétence*[71] in French is fundamental to understanding the foundations of the area of public law in French law, and ultimately the relationship between the individual and the power of the State. The philosophical origins of this word are relevant, in so far as they are rooted in the notion of *État*, or State, in French law.[72] This notion of *État* was then implemented in the form of institutions in constitutional republican France, which are all defined on the basis of their *compétences*. The notion of *compétence* is at the heart of the relationship between citizens and the State.[73] It determines, for example, the conditions under which a citizen may initiate legal action against a State institution when an administrative decision allegedly infringes on the rights claimed by that citizen.[74] A tempting translation in English for this word could be *jurisdiction*, but it has a narrower meaning than *compétence*. Therefore, it is essential that students can understand the word *compétence* directly in French. To achieve this, they must learn about its origins (historical and

[71] The same applies to the German concept of *Kompetenz*, meaning the entitlement of the State to act only on the basis of a legal act which in itself is based on a foundation in constitutional law, see German Basic Law (*Grundgesetz* (GG)) Arts 30 and 70, and note on *Kompetenz-Kompetenz*.

[72] The word *État* in its modern constitutional sense dates from the theories of the Enlightenment in France and in England, particularly the writings of Montesquieu and Rousseau, see Favoreu et al., *Droit Constitutionnel* (cited in n.67), 2–9.

[73] The State and its public administration have extraordinary powers in relation to citizens, but they are submitted to the law, which defines the extent of their *compétence*: 'Toute la dialectique du droit administratif consiste à trouver un équilibre entre la nécessité de reconnaître à l'administration un certain nombre de prérogatives de puissance publique et celle de protéger le mieux possible les droits des administrés face à l'Administration': Jean Rivero and Jean Waline, *Droit Administratif* (21st edn, Paris: Dalloz, 2006), 229.

[74] There are two jurisdictional orders in French law, public and private (*ordre administratif* and *ordre judiciaire*), and the *critères de compétence* (competence criteria) are essential for determining where cases should be adjudicated. A special court (*Tribunal des Conflits*) resolves conflicts of jurisdiction, to identify cases that belong to the public law area on the basis of the criteria of public power (*critère de puissance publique*) and public service (*critère de service public*).

philosophical), and understand that it has ramifications into detailed rules. Furthermore, the notion of *compétence* is central to the allocation of powers to the European Union.[75] Therefore by understanding correctly the meaning of this word, students will also understand EU law, which is largely based on this concept of *compétence*.

This point is particularly relevant to Irish students whose legal tradition is the Common Law, where the concept does not exist, and therefore the word does not exist. Irish constitutional law deals with the issue of restraining the power of the State and its institutions towards individuals by other means, for example the non-delegation doctrine and the ultra vires doctrine.[76] The direct faithful translatability of the French legal word *compétence* into English is therefore impossible because of the incommensurability between French Civil Law and Irish Common Law on that aspect of the organisation of power in the State.[77] In the case of *compétence*, however, European Common Law countries (namely Ireland and the UK) have had to start using the English *competence* in order to describe the system of legitimacy of EU law. But *competence* in English law does not have the roots that *compétence* has in French law, and its use has had the effect of creating a new concept at law for these countries. It was therefore not a translation, but a linguistic innovation.

Another striking example is the word *rights* in English, as it is used in the expression *human rights* in Irish law, or in English law. Historically, the Common Law was not about asserting the rights of individuals against each other, and against the Crown, but more about pragmatically resolving individual conflicts, on the basis of procedures set out in writs. Glenn asserts that the concept of *rights* is completely alien to the Common Law ethos:

A law of relations, of mutual obligations, is not a law which concentrates its attention on the legal powers or interests of the individual. It is not a law of rights, and the notion of the subjective right (as they say in civilian language) played little or no role in the history of the common law in England. The existence of rights in English law was denied well into the twentieth century, and resistance in contemporary England to a bill of rights, or a right to privacy, is explained as much by unease with rights in general as it is to unease about their entrenchment or love of the reporting habits of the English press.[78]

---

[75] There are interesting differences in the translations into English of the French word *compétence* of the European institutions: *competence, power*, or *sovereignty*. See, e.g., the seminal Case 6/64, *Costa v ENEL* [1964] ECR 585, [593] which uses *compétence* in the French version, and *sovereignty* in the English version. To describe the *compétences* of the EU institutions, a French manual uses the word *compétence* consistently, and uses *pouvoirs* as being an exercise of a *compétence* (see Denys Simon, *Le Système Juridique Communautaire* (2nd edn, Paris: PUF, 1998), for example ch.2: *Les Compétences* and chs 62–63: *pouvoirs impliqués*). An English manual written by Irish and British academics uses *competence* and *power* but without explaining the relationship or distinction between the two concepts (Paul Craig and Gràinne de Búrca, *EU Law, Text, Cases and Materials* (4th edn, Oxford: Oxford University Press, 2008), 88: *Shared Competence* and 90: *Implied Powers*. Finally, a manual written in English by Belgian academics primarily uses the word *power* as being an exercise of a *competence*, see Koen Laenerts and Piet van Nuffel, *Constitutional Law of the European Union* (2nd edn, London: Thomson/Sweet & Maxwell, 2005), 86–7.

[76] See, e.g., Oran Doyle, *Constitutional Law: Text, Cases and Materials* (Dublin: Clarus Press, 2008), 321–2: 'These two restrictions (the non-delegation doctrine and the *ultra vires* doctrine) interact in a powerful way to protect individuals from the arbitrary exercise of public power.'

[77] This is not to say that there are not similarities between the Irish, the French, and the European ways of regulating the exercise of public power. The point made here is that there are significant conceptual, principled, and semantic differences between these ways, and that these differences prevent the translatability of words from one system to another.

[78] Glenn, *Legal Traditions of the World* (cited in n.11), 252–3. See also Geoffrey Samuel, '"Le Droit Subjectif" and English Law' (1987) 46(2) *Cambridge Law Journal* 264, 273: 'What the common law

Dicey also said, in the 19th century, that the Habeas Corpus Acts 'declare no principle and define no rights, but they are for practical purposes worth a hundred constitutional articles guaranteeing individual liberty'.[79] So, by becoming a signatory to the European Convention on Human Rights, the UK was effectively faced with a whole new set of beliefs, institutions, and practices, which lawyers had to integrate into the context of their own tradition of civil liberties.[80] Here again, it is argued that in legal English as it is used in the 21st century, the word *rights* is more a linguistic innovation than a translation. Ireland is in a different position, because while it is Common Law based, its *Bunreacht na hEireann* 1937 includes a large section on fundamental rights (Arts 40 to 44).

Thus becoming a signatory to the ECHR did not require such linguistic innovation in legal English as it is used in Ireland in the 21st century. There is, however, a debate among legal historians and legal philosophers on whether conceptually and historically the word *rights* can be rooted in Aquinas' *right* in his conception of natural law. Linguistically, the question is whether Aquinas used the word *ius* in a sense that could encompass the modern notion of a right, or did he only refer to the law, in the sense of justice, as in the Roman law sense of *ius*. The issue is further complicated when one considers that he also used the word *lex* to refer to the natural law.[81] For MacIntyre, 'the concept [of "a right"] lacks any means of expression in Hebrew, Greek, Latin or Arabic, classical or medieval, before about 1400, let alone in Old English, or in Japanese even as late as the mid-nineteenth century'.[82] Yet, it is undeniable that institutionally human *rights*, or *droits de l'homme*, are now part of the legal relationship between the individual and the State, and part of the dialectic of role of the individual in a community.

Interestingly, the debate on the *rights* issue has gained significant added value with the contributions of Professor Brian Tierney, a medieval historian, and the late Professor Ralph McInerny, a philosopher, both proficient in French and able to read and understand the theories on the subject matter of Michel Villey, which were formulated in French and written from a Civil Law point of view. This observation, we argue, compounds the point made throughout this paper that learning the law can only be done through the language of that law, and with the aid of epistemological enquiry. Incompatibility and incommensurability are obstacles to the translatability of words or expression from one legal language to another, be they contemporary languages, or languages separated by centuries.

---

has done is to accord to subjects strong remedies to protect certain interests. But the "actions", rather than "rights", aspect of these remedies is reflected in the fact that there is no differentiation between *ius in rem* and *ius in personam* when it comes to compensation claims: actions for compensation arising out of wrongs and actions to vindicate interferences with "rights" are both classified, as far as a civil lawyer looking at the common law is concerned, under "obligations".'

[79] A. V. Dicey, *Law of the Constitution* (10th edn, London: MacMillan and Co., 1959), 199.

[80] See, e.g., Ian Leigh and Laurence Lustgarten, 'Making Rights Real: The Courts, Remedies, and the Human Rights Act' (1999) 58(3) *Cambridge Law Journal* 509.

[81] For a compelling account of the debate among modern natural law scholars, see: Ralph McInerny, 'Natural Law and Human Rights' (1991) 36 *American Journal of Jurisprudence* 1, and 'On Natural Law and Natural Rights' (Spring 1999) *Modern Age* 174. The substance of the debate appears in Brian Tierney, 'Natural Law and Natural Rights: Old Problems and Recent Approaches' (2002) 64(3) *The Review of Politics* 389, John Finnis, 'Aquinas on ius and Hart on Rights: A Response to Tierney', (2002) 64(3) *The Review of Politics* 389, and Brian Tierney, 'Author's Rejoinder', (2002) 64(3) *The Review of Politics* 389, John Finnis, *Natural Law and Natural Rights* (Oxford: Oxford University Press, 1980), ch.8, and Michel Villey, *La Formation de la Pensée Juridique Moderne* (Paris: PUF, Quadrige, 2003), 242–68.

[82] Alasdair MacIntyre, *After Virtue* (3rd edn, London: Duckworth, 2007), 69.

8. Two further problems

MacIntyre identifies two further problems to translatability. First, he says that beliefs, institutions, and practices in a tradition shared by two persons in a dialogue allows for the understanding between them of what is said, but also of what is not said. For example, teaching the law relating to the *mesures d'ordre intérieur* (measures taken by the executive that are not judicially reviewable) in French administrative law requires explaining the concept of *Recours pour Excès de Pouvoir* (the area of judicial review of administrative decisions), and its exceptions.

It is obvious that two French lawyers talking about the former will know that they concern the exceptions to the rule of principle that all measures taken by the executive are judicially reviewable, and that these exceptions are based on the idea of *pouvoirs régaliens* of the State, that is to say the absolute prerogatives of the State. Such exceptions include for example a decision to allow American war planes to fly over French territory on their way to the scene of the second Gulf War, or the decision to carry out a round of nuclear testing in the Pacific Ocean.

The Irish law student learning about this will be taught about the *Recours pour Excès de Pouvoir* and the *mesures d'ordre intérieur* and will, like a French lawyer, understand what is said and what is unsaid when these words are uttered. He will also understand that neither of these two expressions can be translated in English as 'judicial review'. The two concepts are close, but not identical, and the exceptions to 'judicial review' in Irish law are not justified with the same reference to the *pouvoirs régaliens* of the State (which itself has no translation in English). The situation with regard to translatability in the Irish context can be further re-enforced when one looks at the Irish language term for 'judicial review', which is expressed as *athbhreithniú breithiúnacha* which would be most closely translated as 'judicial re-judging'. An Irish judge looking to interpret 'judicial review' in the Irish context would have recourse to Irish text should the English version prove problematic.

For Irish students studying the Irish constitutional position in relation to international law what is *not* said is perhaps of more importance than what is said. *Bunreacht na hÉireann* Art.29.3 states (in both official languages) that Ireland 'accepts the generally recognised principles of international law as its rule of conduct in its relations with other states'. One particular additional phrase however, which is present in the Irish text but not included in the English version, significantly changes the meaning of the provision. The Irish text includes the proviso *le bheith ina dtreoir* which would translate as 'as a guide' whereas its exclusion from the English text suggests that the generally recognised principles of international are accepted without question.

Secondly, MacIntyre argues that untranslatability is also a matter of language, not just words. So far MacIntyre's argument, and our examples, have been based on words or expressions. But learning 'how to go on and to go further' in a language, into several layers of language, is indispensable to understanding a tradition. He puts it this way:

That is to say to learn the paradigmatic uses of key expressions [in a language] at the same time and inseparably from their learning the model exemplifications of the virtues, the legitimating genealogies of their community and its key prescriptions.[83]

He says that this is what poets do in a tradition, and that a tradition is embodied in texts (or a set of texts) which constitute an authoritative basis for a philosophical

---

[83] MacIntyre, *Whose Justice? Which Rationality?* (cited in n7), 382.

enquiry into the tradition itself. He takes the very simple example of the word 'white": learning to say 'Snow is white" is simple and accessible to anyone. But going on to say 'and so are the members of the Ku Klux Klan, and white with fear is what they were in snowcovered Arkansas last Friday" requires an understanding of the meaning of the word in several layers of the English language as it is used in the USA in the 21st century.

Teaching 'how to go on and to go further" in French law is the culmination of teaching French law. It requires knowing the language, and the legal method, in order to understand the process of rationality proper to French law. In this respect, teaching Irish students how to read a decision of the *Cour de Cassation* is perhaps one of the most challenging parts of the curriculum. The recurring use of the expression *considérant que* by the court means much more than the English 'considering that", as it reflects the binding legal force of the argument being applied in a judgment and denotes in a very concise manner the reasoning followed by the judges. The German method of *subsumption* presents similar challenges to Irish law students, and yet it is key to understanding the rationality of German law. In both cases, there are of course parallels in Irish law, on which the teacher will rely to explain the French and German legal methods, but direct translation is impossible, as it would be meaningless to students.

In the Irish context, untranslatability features prominently in Ireland's bilingual Constitution with examples of differing translations and use of language. Many cultural and political influences have a strong bearing upon the use of language in the Irish text of the Irish Constitution. The term *Sacs-Bhéarla* is used in Art.8.2 of the Irish version of the Constitution to represent the word *English*. In the 1922 Constitution, in all subsequent legislation, and in any normal use in modern language the word *Béarla* is used in Irish when referring to the English language. In this instance the term *Sacs* or *Sax* precedes it. To understand such a construction one would have to understand the historical relationship between the England and Ireland, the cultural difference between the Saxon and the Gael, and the significance of the contemporary context in which the Constitution was drafted.[84] It is noted, however, that these instances, occurring in the Irish context, give rise to lesser challenges than those arising in French or German law, given that the English and Irish texts both relate to the one constitutional order rooted in the Common Law system. They contribute, nonetheless, to tainting the Irish constitutional tradition with its own unique characteristics, albeit being firmly a Common Law one.

On this final point, MacIntyre concludes that the history of linguistic and conceptual transformations and translations is inseparable from the development of beliefs, institutions, and practices in a tradition, which mark its own development. Beyond the problems of untranslatability, we therefore argue that for Irish law students to understand correctly the French, Irish, and German legal rationalities, they must do it through the French, the Irish, and the German languages and embedded in a cultural, historical, and political context. This is the only way that they can learn how 'to go on and to go further" in French law, in Irish law, and in German law.

---

[84] Ireland's 1937 Constitution sought to sever all ties with the United Kingdom which had remained in the 1922 Constitution. The use of the term '*Sacs Béarla*' was perhaps intended as a nod to Ireland's past struggles against the United Kingdom. The term was used on two occasions during the opening session of the First Dáil (a rival rebel Parliament set up during the Irish War of Independence) by Cathal Brugha, who was acting as *Ceann Comhairle* (a position which is comparable to the Speaker of the House or Chairperson).

9. Conclusion

The quotation from Aristotle at the start of this article says that what is successful is simple, and what is good is difficult. The teaching method that we are advocating is at the same time simple and difficult. It is a simple point that we develop through this paper: that the laws and legal system of a country cannot be taught and learnt successfully other than through the language of that country. The reason for this is that there are very serious obstacles of untranslatability between legal traditions. Our method is also difficult because teaching law as well as language is difficult. Yet this method ensures that Irish students learning about French or German law in our programmes are learning legal words, expressions, concepts, and systems in the contexts of the French and German legal traditions of the 21st century. They understand why translations per se are often impossible, and why words, expressions, concepts, and systems need to be explained, rather than translated. That way they also identify and avoid subtle errors or misrepresentation that could be brought about by translation, and could remain undetected. It is also a simple point to say that these law students will become lawyers better prepared to work with European or international law, because they will be sensitive to the differences that exist between the legal traditions of Europe. They will be aware of the importance of dialogue between these legal traditions in the process of European integration and creation of European law. They will understand that European integration and European law must respect European legal traditions, and can only emerge strong as a result of the dialogue between them. Joseph Weiler's Editorial in the July 2011 issue of the *European Journal of International Law* laments that 'Democracy, or rather the partial absence of which, continues to beset the Europe of 27".[85] In our paper we have explained how democracy should be seen 'as a difficult achievement, necessary for a realization of the full dignity and power of man",[86] and how we see that law students and lawyers have a special and crucial role to play in working for democracy. So while European democracy in general is a difficult enterprise, and is clearly outside the scope of our paper, it is also clear that our paper is within the scope of democracy in Europe. By paying attention to the issues relating to the linguistic diversity of Europe, by completing the difficult task of teaching French, Irish, and German law to Irish law students through the French, Irish, and German languages, we claim that our undergraduate degree programmes make a successful and good contribution in this difficult enterprise.

---

[85] Joseph Weiler, '60 Years since the First European Community—Reflections on Political Messianism' (2011) 22(2) *European Journal of International Law* 303.
[86] Fuller, 'On Teaching Law' (cited in n.9).

31

Foreign Law in Translation: If Truth Be Told...

Simone Glanert and Pierre Legrand*

What can one do but speculate, speculate, until one hits on the happy speculation?
—Beckett[1]

For the point at issue is merely the meaning of the texts, not their truth.
—Spinoza[2]

He who, in a contest of opinions, says, I have the truth, makes a claim to power.
—Arendt[3]

We take the view that, in the French philosopher Jacques Derrida's arresting formulation, '[w]e must begin *somewhere where we are*', '[s]*omewhere where we are*: within a text already where we believe that we are' (though we might want to be somewhere other than where we are).[4] One should not be surprised to find in this injunction echoes of Martin Heidegger, for Derrida often acknowledges his indebtedness to the German philosopher. He calls Heidegger his 'foreman'.[5] And he insists that Heidegger's work

---

* In principle, we use original texts and offer our own translations. When we occasionally choose to refer to a published English translation, we supply the original text parenthetically.

[1] Samuel Beckett, *The Unnamable*, in *The Grove Centenary Edition*, ed. by Paul Auster, vol. II (New York: Grove Press, 2006 [1958]), 363 ['*Que voulez-vous, il faut spéculer, spéculer, jusqu'à ce qu'on tombe sur la spéculation qui est la bonne*']. The re-writing from the French is Beckett's own.

[2] Baruch Spinoza, *Theological-Political Treatise*, 2nd edn, transl. by Samuel Shirley (Indianapolis, Ind.: Hackett, 2001 [1670]), 88 ['*De solo enim sensu-orationum, non autem de earum veritate laboramus*'].

[3] Hannah Arendt, *Denktagebuch*, ed. by Ursula Ludz and Ingeborg Nordmann, vol. II (Munich: Piper, 2002 [1963–1964]), 619 ['*Wer im Meinungskampf sagt: er habe die Wahrheit, meldet einen Herrschaftsanspruch an*'].

[4] Jacques Derrida, *De la grammatologie* (Paris: Editions de Minuit, 1967), 233 ['*Il faut commencer quelque part où nous sommes*'/'*Quelque part où nous sommes*: en un texte déjà où nous croyons être'] (emphasis original) [hereinafter *Grammatologie*]. One should not assume that the localization of one's situation is easily achieved. In fact, Derrida observes that it can be expected to induce a 'vertigo': Jacques Derrida (with Catherine Malabou), *La Contre-allée* (Paris: La Quinzaine littéraire, 1999), 147 ['*vertige*'] (hereinafter *Contre-allée*).

[5] Derrida, *Contre-allée* (cited in n.4), 57 ['*contremaître*']. The French word, which is Derrida's, connotes the idea of a 'master' (as in '*maître*') but can also, more sophisticatedly, suggest the notion of a master against whom ('*contre*') one is thinking and writing. This reading allows Derrida to assert his fidelity to Heidegger's thought while advocating his intellectual specificity, which in the very name of loyalty to Heidegger, in particular to Heideggerian contrarianism, takes the form of frequent departures from Heidegger's own ideas.

is 'extremely important', that it constitutes 'an unprecedented, irreversible advance'.[6] Indeed, he claims that 'nothing of what [he] is attempting would have been possible without the opening of Heideggerian questions'.[7] For his part, in line with his notions of 'fore-having' ('*Vorhabe*'), 'foresight' ('*Vorsicht*'), and 'fore-conception' ('*Vorgriff*'), which indicate that only within the pregiven sign-system within which one is framed does one understand, can one ascribe meaning,[8] Heidegger explains in his early correspondence that '[he] work[s] concretely and factically from [his] "I am"—from [his] spiritual and in particular factical origin—[from his] environment—[from his] life as a whole ['*Lebenszusammenhängen*'], from what is, from there, accessible [to him] as living experience, from that within which [he] live[s]'.[9] In the words of Hans-Georg Gadamer, another German philosopher (and prominent disciple of Heidegger) with whom Derrida pursued a problematic conversation over more than twenty years,[10] the idea of situatedness is such that 'one does not find oneself in front of it'.[11]

We write, then, as comparatists-at-law, that is, as academics who, as implausible as this contention may at first blush appear, attach normative value to foreign law. Our argument is not, of course, that foreign law matters because it would be binding beyond its local circumstances, but that it is valuable since it can act as persuasive authority in other settings than its own. Along with other academics who also subscribe to such deterritorialization of the law (and of the mind), we have allowed ourselves to be instituted within the field of 'comparative law'.[12] Having, with hindsight, recognizably emerged in the 1820s,[13] 'comparative law', like other academic fields, features its learned societies, journals, conferences, chairs, research institutes, courses, and postgraduate programmes.

---

[6] Jacques Derrida, *Positions* (Paris: Editions de Minuit, 1972), 73 ['*d'une extrême importance*'/'*une avancée inédite, irréversible*'] (hereinafter *Positions*).

[7] Derrida, *Positions* (cited in n.6), 18 ['*Rien de ce que je tente n'aurait été possible sans l'ouverture des questions Heideggeriennes*'].

[8] Martin Heidegger, *Being and Time*, rev'd transl. by Joan Stambaugh (Albany, NY: SUNY Press, 2010 [1927]), 145–6 [hereinafter *Being and Time*].

[9] Martin Heidegger, [Letter to Karl Löwith], in (eds), Dietrich Papenfuss and Otto Pöggeler, *Zur philosophischen Aktualität Heideggers*, vol. II (Frankfurt: V. Klostermann, 1990 [1921]), 29 ['*Ich arbeite konkret faktisch aus meinem "ich bin"—aus meiner geistigen überhaupt faktischen Herkunft—Milieu—Lebenszusammenhängen, aus dem, was mir von da zugänglich ist als lebendige Erfahrung, worin ich lebe*'].

[10] e.g. (eds), Diane P. Michelfelder and Richard E. Palmer, *Dialogue and Deconstruction: The Gadamer-Derrida Encounter* (Albany, NY: SUNY Press, 1989). For a thoughtful account of the disputation between Derrida and Gadamer, see Colin Davis, *Critical Excess* (Palo Alto, Calif.: Stanford University Press, 2010), 26–55.

[11] Hans-Georg Gadamer, *Truth and Method*, 5th edn, rev'd transl. by Joel Weinsheimer and Donald G. Marshall (New York: Continuum, 2004 [1990]), 301 ['*man sich nicht ihr gegenüber befindet*'] [hereinafter *Truth and Method*]. This statement encapsulates one of the most important epistemological commitments whereby Heidegger and his successors seek to distinguish their philosophical projects from Husserl's phenomenology regarded by them as indentured to Cartesian assumptions and as promoting the sovereignty of the subject, two features that indeed appear clearly from the phrase, 'I stand *above* the world': Edmund Husserl, *The Crisis of European Sciences and Transcendental Phenomenology*, transl. by David Carr (Evanston, Ill.: Northwestern University Press, 1970 [1937]), 152 ['*ich stehe über der Welt*'] (original emphasis in English).

[12] The label 'comparative law', though in common usage, strikes us as problematic. There is indeed no 'law' that can be said to be 'comparative'. At the very least, then, the retention of the misnomer in this paper calls for it to be held in the tweezers of quotation marks throughout.

[13] Bearing in mind how any 'origin' requires its origins to be elucidated in their turn, it seems that, in reaction to the French-initiated codification movement and what were perceived in certain academic circles as its attendant isolationist tendencies, Heidelberg professors Karl Mittermaier and Karl Zachariä took an inaugural institutional step in 1829 by launching the *Kritische Zeitschrift für Rechtswissenschaft und Gesetzgebung des Auslandes*, which lasted until 1856. For their part, Montaigne's and Montesquieu's celebrated texts offer noteworthy comparisons *avant la lettre*—of which there are, needless to add, innumerable examples.

It also boasts an orthodoxy. Indeed, in our opinion, any survey of the field is bound to reveal the ascendancy of a specific theoretical framework developed in the 1960s by Konrad Zweigert, then director of the *Max-Planck-Institut für ausländisches und internationales Privatrecht* in Hamburg, and subsequently disseminated by Hein Kötz, his disciple and, in time, his successor at the helm of the Hamburg foundation. All over the world, comparatists-at-law are well acquainted with Zweigert and Kötz's peremptory template, which has long established itself as the most influential strategy informing the study of foreign law.

Familiar phrases and sentences from Zweigert and Kötz's textbook include the enunciation of a '*præsumptio similitudinis*' as between laws,[14] the statement that laws are similar 'even as to detail',[15] the declaration about the 'immaterial[ity] of differences' to comparative research,[16] and the proclamation of the existence of a 'unitary sense of justice' across laws.[17] Zweigert and Kötz further claim that comparatists ought to aspire to 'scientific exactitude and objectivity'.[18] They stress that any examination of foreign law should be 'objective, that is, free from any critical evaluation'.[19] Not only must the comparatist avoid 'allow[ing] [his] vision to be clouded by the concepts of [his] own national system',[20] but he requires to 'cut [himself] loose from [his] own doctrinal and juridical preconceptions and liberate [himself] from [his] own cultural context'.[21] It is also for the comparatist to ensure that 'the solutions [...] [found] in the different jurisdictions [be] cut loose from their conceptual context and stripped of their national doctrinal overtones'.[22] In sum, comparative legal studies needs to operate like 'physics', 'microbiology', or 'geology'.[23] In the same manner as there is no '"German" physics', no '"British" microbiology', and no '"Canadian" geology',[24] ultimately there must be no local law. It is abidingly the task of the comparatist, to identify the generic aspect of any given law in order to allow it to surpass its localization—local accoutrements very much being apprehended as impediments on the way to a better law. Zweigert and Kötz's goal, as they themselves expressly indicate, is the kind of uniformization of laws that would allow for a return to 'the era of natural law'.[25]

---

[14] Konrad Zweigert and Hein Kötz, *Introduction to Comparative Law*, 3rd edn, transl. by Tony Weir (Oxford: Oxford University Press, 1998 [1996]), 40 [hereinafter *Introduction to Comparative Law*].

[15] Zweigert and Kötz, *Introduction to Comparative Law* (cited in n.14), 39 ['*bis in Einzelheiten hinein*'].

[16] Zweigert and Kötz, *Introduction to Comparative Law* (cited in n.14), 62 ['*(die Irrelevanz der) Unterschiede*'].

[17] Zweigert and Kötz, *Introduction to Comparative Law* (cited in n.14), 3 ['*eines einheitlichen Gerechtigkeitsgedankens*'].

[18] Zweigert and Kötz, *Introduction to Comparative Law* (cited in n.14), 45 ['*wissenschaftliche Exaktheit und Objektivität*'].

[19] Zweigert and Kötz, *Introduction to Comparative Law* (cited in n.14), 43 ['*schlicht, d.h. vor allem ohne kritische Wertung*'].

[20] Zweigert and Kötz, *Introduction to Comparative Law* (cited in n.14), 35 ['*darf (er) sich (...) den Blick durch Systembegriffe des eigenen nationalen Rechts verstellen lassen*'].

[21] Zweigert and Kötz, *Introduction to Comparative Law* (cited in n.14), 10 ['*sich (...) von seinen eigenen juristisch-dogmatischen Vorverständnissen und seinem eigenen kulturellen Umfeld lösen*'].

[22] Zweigert and Kötz, *Introduction to Comparative Law* (cited in n.14), 44 ['*Die Lösungen der untersuchten Rechtsordnungen sind von allen systematischen Begriffen dieser Rechtsordnungen zu befreien, aus ihren nur-nationalen dogmatischen Verkrustungen zu lösen*'].

[23] Zweigert and Kötz, *Introduction to Comparative Law* (cited in n.14), 15 ['*Physik*'/'*Molekularbiologie*'/'*Geologie*'].

[24] Zweigert and Kötz, *Introduction to Comparative Law* (cited in n.14), 15 ['*"deutsche" Physik*'/'*"britische" Molekularbiologie*'/'*"kanadische" Geologie*'].

[25] Zweigert and Kötz, *Introduction to Comparative Law* (cited in n.14), 45 ['*Zeit des Naturrechts*'].

Although the most recent edition of Zweigert and Kötz's textbook is dating rapidly, its predominance remains largely uncontested such that the 'Hamburg model', if we may call it that, very much continues to operate in a structuring capacity within the field, not least in the introductory courses to 'comparative law' on offer in law schools. While comparatists-at-law's allegiance to Zweigert and Kötz is at times emphatic,[26] it can also make itself more muted though no less discernible.[27] What epistemological challenges to this construction's authority have manifested themselves have thus far fallen short of fully-fledged theoretical programmes and, if for that reason alone, have accordingly enjoyed limited impact within the field of 'comparative law'.[28]

Crucially, Zweigert and Kötz's theoretical statement remains silent on the matter of translation. Yet, as interpreters seeking to ascribe meaning to foreign law's foreignness, comparatists are incessantly confronted by foreign languages, a fact that compels every student of foreign law to address issues of translation. Indeed, the extent of the challenge is much wider than might readily be expected as soon as one appreciates that even Anglophone comparatists may need to translate English—thus, 'privacy' in the UK is not 'privacy' in the USA. All the same, Zweigert and Kötz fail to address translation in any of the three editions of their text spanning a 30-year period—despite the fact that over the years their book has itself been translated from the German into various languages including English, Italian, Japanese, and Russian. Why this omission? The most charitable reconstruction of Zweigert and Kötz's organizing intuition seems to be that they did not regard translation as worthy of their attention because they deemed it, hyper-pragmatically, a non-issue. One could be forgiven, of course, for adopting the view that, on account of Zweigert and Kötz's stated ambition to make 'comparative law' into an 'international legal science',[29] to frame it as a 'universal legal science',[30] language ought to prove of the utmost significance to them. But, in the same way as James Gordley, a prominent defender of 'comparative law''s orthodoxy, claims that '[t]here [i]s nothing distinctively German, French or American about [German, French or American judicial] decisions',[31] Zweigert and Kötz can be taken to opine that there is nothing so distinctively Spanish, Dutch, or Polish about the Spanish, Dutch, or Polish languages that would get in the way of the uniformization of laws (which must remain, as far as they are concerned, 'comparative law's' abiding objective).

This improbable understanding assumes a transparency of law-texts such that they could move in unmediated fashion from language to language without undergoing any destabilization and indeed any reconstitution, that is, without the translation acting performatively in any way whatsoever or, to state the matter in slightly more dramatic terms, without the translator doing any violence to the law-text being translated or to

---

[26] e.g. Michael Bogdan, 'On the Value and Method of Rule-Comparison in Comparative Law', in (eds) Heinz-Peter Mansel et al., *Festschrift für Erik Jayme* (Munich: Sellier, 2004), 1233–42.

[27] e.g. Vicki C. Jackson, *Constitutional Engagement in a Transnational Era* (Oxford: Oxford University Press, 2010), 178, who advocates '[c]omparability in the sense of *similarity*' (emphasis original).

[28] e.g. G. Frankenberg, 'Critical Comparisons: Re-thinking Comparative Law' (1985) 26 *Harvard International L.J.* 411; P. Legrand, 'Paradoxically, Derrida: For a Comparative Legal Studies', (2005) 27 *Cardozo L.R.* 631; Richard Hyland, *Gifts* (Oxford: Oxford University Press, 2009), 63–74 and 94–113.

[29] Zweigert and Kötz, *Introduction to Comparative Law* (cited in n.14), 45 ['*internationale Rechtswissenschaft*'].

[30] Zweigert and Kötz, *Introduction to Comparative Law* (cited in n.14), 46 ['*Universalrechtswissenschaft*'].

[31] J. Gordley, 'Comparative Legal Research: Its Function in the Development of Harmonized Law' (1995) 43 *American J. Comparative L.* 555, 563.

the language into which the law-text is being translated. 'Estoppel' could be rendered in French or '*résiliation*' in English *as such*. '*Abstraktionsprinzip*' could be reproduced in Italian and '*diritti reali*' in German *as such*. In each case, there would be neither loss nor accretion—Ortega y Gasset's 'deficiencies' and 'exuberances'[32]—so that Zweigert and Kötz's indifference to language and, specifically, to the multiplicity of languages, would find itself vindicated. Indeed, why theorize translation if there is integral translatability?

We find the kind of idealized linguistic compliance being postulated by Zweigert and Kötz unwarranted. For us, in fact, linguistic compliance can only ever be partial (that is, at once incomplete and committed). The words join, but they are necessarily out of joint, and there is nothing that the assiduity of the translation can do to overcome their 'disacquaintance' for no translation can escape the semantic play that manifests itself in the configuration of meanings across languages.[33] What we have, in effect, is an articulation that is (structurally) disarticulated. If you will, translation is an experience of the same that is not the same, the point being that as any sameness postulates 'n + 1' and as, in turn, any '+ 1' assumes difference, it is the case that in order for a translation to be the same as the source word, it has to be different from it. In this sense, it is not an exaggeration to say that the relation between words across languages is also a non-relation. Translation, then, is not simple, but complicated.[34]

For us, the governing idea must be that of the debt being owed to the text, which, in the name of something like justice (though a destination we will never reach), compels the translator not to transgress the text. Perhaps the most challenging enjoinder, therefore, is for the text in translation to deploy itself so as to avoid an assimilation of the foreign text into the host language such that the foreign text's singularity would vanish along the way. As we approach the matter of translatability, the translator's aim must indeed be to preserve something of the difference of the foreign law-text on account of the recognition and of the respect that one owes it, especially as one purports to displace it across languages. For us, translation is 'a practice producing difference out of incommensurability (rather than equivalence out of difference)'.[35] Indeed, the *ference* in transference is also the *ference* in difference—or, to apply one of the many possibilities offered by the German language, any (foreign) *Wort* will either contract or expand any (local) *Ort*.[36] For example, in order to resist the attraction of seamless domestication of foreign texts, Heidegger's or Derrida's translators did not hesitate to generate an 'agrammaticality effect' thus fashioning translations that, whether through the configuration of neologisms, the modification of the usual syntactic patterns, or even the insertion of foreign words, changed current usage in the host languages.[37] In other words, these translators, as they heeded the original texts' summonses, were unwilling fully to concede to their readerships in the host languages. They were, in effect, compelling foreign readers of

---

[32] José Ortega y Gasset, 'La reviviscencia de los cuadros', in *Obras completas*, 2nd edn, vol. VIII (Madrid: Alianza Editorial, 1994 [1946]), 493 ['*Todo decir es deficiente*'/'*Todo decir es exuberante*'].

[33] Jacques Derrida and Maurizio Ferraris, *A Taste for the Secret*, ed. by Giacomo Denis and David Webb, transl. by Giacomo Denis (Cambridge: Polity, 2001 [1993]), 31.

[34] See generally Simone Glanert, *De la traductibilité du droit* (Paris: Dalloz, 2011). See also Sieglinde Pommer, *Rechtsübersetzung und Rechtsvergleichung* (Frankfurt: P. Lang, 2005).

[35] Meaghan Morris, 'Foreword', in Naoki Sakai, *Translation and Subjectivity* (Minneapolis, Minn.: University of Minnesota Press, 1997), xiii.

[36] cf. Jacques Derrida, *Sauf le nom* (Paris: Galilée, 1996), 61 and 60, respectively.

[37] Lorenzo Bonoli, *Lire les cultures* (Paris: Kimé, 2008), 98 (emphasis omitted). e.g. Heidegger, *Being and Time* (cited in n.8); Jacques Derrida, *Of Grammatology*, rev'd transl. by Gayatri C. Spivak (Baltimore, Md: Johns Hopkins University Press, 1997 [1967]).

Heidegger and Derrida to defamiliarize themselves, to make themselves aware that they were reading a *translation*, that there was a 'nonpresent' text—or that a 'nonpresent' text was not absent. These references to Heidegger and Derrida in translation show that our remarks to the effect that translation dissolves any possible unity of meaning do not call into question the necessity of the translation or indeed its possibility (we shall argue, no doubt paradoxically, that the fact that the translation is impossible does not imply that it must not be done and indeed does not mean that it cannot be done). In effect, to contend that there is necessarily a looseness in the articulation, that translation is not sheltered from semantic play, is an opportunity for the foreign law-text to have a future existence, to survive, to live on, as it becomes the object of infinite discussions and endless debates.[38]

Under conditions of identity—that is, if the word-in-translation was identical to the word being translated—the question of the 'truth' of the translation would not arise. However, given the situation as we have described it, one of the most intriguing metaphrastic questions that we must face as comparatists-at-law concerns precisely that of 'truth', which is the specific focus of the argument that follows. Indeed, this claim is very much a continuation of our prefatory observations to the effect that no word submits docilely to a translation that would carry it *as such* from one language to another: either the word-in-translation leaves behind a residue of the original idiom or it accretes meaning in the other language. Before we embark on our investigation, it seems interesting to note that, though not with specific reference to translation (which, as we have remarked, they ignore), Zweigert and Kötz express their commitment to 'truth' on more than one occasion. Thus, they call 'comparative law' an 'école de vérité'.[39] Moreover, they write that '[comparative law's] ultimate goal is [to] discove[r] the truth'.[40] And we feel confident that, had they addressed legal translation, Zweigert and Kötz, in line with the theoretical commitments that they consider must underwrite the study of foreign law, would have urged comparatists-at-law to produce true translations. Contrariwise, we want to show, making specific reference to the matter of foreign law in translation, that 'truth' has no useful contribution to make to 'comparative law'.

We begin with an influential British playwright.

∞

Harold Pinter died on Christmas Eve 2008. In the lecture that he delivered upon being awarded the Nobel prize for literature in 2005, Pinter recalled a text of his dating back nearly half a century. It concerned the matter of 'truth'. In that paper, Pinter had written as follows: 'Truth in drama is forever elusive. [. . .] [T]here never is any such thing as one truth to be found in dramatic art. There are many. These truths challenge each other, recoil from each other, reflect each other, ignore each other, tease each other, are blind

---

[38] The idea of 'survival' is a key motif in Derrida's work. e.g. Jacques Derrida, 'Living On', transl. by James Hulbert, in Harold Bloom et al., *Deconstruction and Criticism* (New York: Continuum, 2004 [1979]), 62–142. Though Derrida wrote his text in French, this English version represents its initial publication. The essay later appeared in French as Jacques Derrida, 'Survivre', in *Parages* (Paris: Galilée, 1986), 117–218. Importantly, an analogous theme, expressed as 'afterlife' ('*Fortleben*'), is present in Benjamin's seminal essay on translation: Walter Benjamin, 'The Task of the Translator', in *Selected Writings*, ed. by Marcus Bullock and Michael W. Jennings, transl. by Harry Zohn, vol. I (Cambridge, Mass.: Harvard University Press, 1973 [1923]), 256 [hereinafter 'The Task of the Translator'].

[39] Zweigert and Kötz, *Introduction to Comparative Law* (cited in n.14), 15. The unitalicized French expression is used both in the English translation and in the original German version of the book.

[40] Zweigert and Kötz, *Introduction to Comparative Law* (cited in n.14), 3 ['*(der) Zweck (der Rechtsvergleichung) ist die Erforschung der Wahrheit*'].

to each other. Sometimes you feel you have the truth of a moment in your hand, then it slips through your fingers and is lost.'[41]

We claim that what Pinter said about dramatic art also applies to foreign law in translation: '[T]here never is any such thing as one truth to be found' in translation, '[t]here are many', they 'challenge each other', and they are 'blind to each other'. Indeed, we propose to take Pinter's insight one important step further and to argue that if no comparatist-at-law can access 'one truth', if to argue for 'the true translation' concerning foreign law makes as much sense as to talk of a loud blanket or of an angry cucumber, if '[t]here is no experience of truth that is not interpretive',[42] if there would be but cognizance of '*truths*', one would do well to renounce the word 'truth' altogether—at least as far as the specific language-game of foreign law in translation is concerned.[43] In effect, there is a disturbing touch of the oxymoronic in 'truths', while a word like 'just'—there would be (relatively) 'just' translations—seems to us much more discerningly to account for the immanence that Pinter sought to capture. But we shall return to the matter of 'justness' presently.

For now, let us formulate translation's quandary for comparatists-at-law. Assume a foreign law-text. This law-text is translatable in various languages. More problematically, it is also infinitely translatable within one language. Out of this array of inter-linguistic and intra-linguistic translations, can one translation be said to disclose sufficient normative purchase on the law-text being translated so as to warrant—and indeed require—identification as the 'true' translation of it (in the sense in which it would be the unique, uniquely fixed, uniquely stable, and uniquely acknowledged translation of it)? It is this precise question that we resolutely answer in the negative, confident in the knowledge that, in such an instance, 'negativity is a *resource*'.[44] In fact, negativity epitomizes the generative, vitalistic role of a counterdiscourse—*our* counterdiscourse—positioning itself vis-à-vis an orthodoxy which, on account of the fetishism of closure that it practises through the imposition of its positivist system, purports incessantly to arrest the flow of meaning—the quest for 'truth', an imaginary goal external to the linguistic inquiry, reaching a determinate and terminating point once its aim is deemed to have been attained. We refute the idea of stasis, the view that there can ever come a moment when a foreign law-text will have been perfectly read 'in translation'. As our claim defends an interminable linguistic terminus, as it promotes 'the joyful affirmation of the play of the world',[45] rather than facile and sterile univocality, it effectuates a politics of resistance. It is, literally, an *undisciplined* gesture. It is *contrarian*.

The stakes could hardly be higher. The absence of truth-in-translation challenges one to make genuine normative choices instead of assenting to (interpretive) decisions on account of their so-called 'truth'. We are of the opinion that, rather than pander to 'truth', a comparatist-at-law must assume substantial responsibility for the normative

---

[41] Harold Pinter, *Art, Truth and Politics*, available at <http://nobelprize.org/nobel_prizes/literature/laureates/2005/pinter-lecture-e.html> [hereinafter *Art, Truth and Politics*]. The lecture was released in print by Faber and Faber in 2006.

[42] Gianni Vattimo, *A Farewell to Truth*, transl. by William McCuaig (New York: Columbia University Press, 2011 [2009]), 64.

[43] Ours is not a contention about 'truth' taken as an autonomous 'entity'. To say, as we do, that foreign law in translation can only be accessed through interpretation is not to argue that foreign law's existence is wholly subordinated to the deployment of interpretive resources by the comparatist aiming to know it. For a formulation of the distinction that we are drawing here, see B. H. Smith, 'The Chimera of Relativism' (2011) 17 *Common Knowledge* 1, 14.

[44] Jacques Derrida, *L'Ecriture et la différence* (Paris: Le Seuil, 1967), 381 ['*la négativité est une ressource*'] (emphasis original) [hereinafter *Ecriture et différence*].

[45] Derrida, *Ecriture et différence* (cited in n.44), 427 ['*l'affirmation joyeuse du jeu du monde*'].

(and fallible) elections that need to characterize the process of translation. To accept that translation is situated firmly within linguistic contingency is to begin to take responsibility for one's own perspectival apprehensions. To refuse the idea that there could be access to 'truth' is, in the end, the only way to avoid intellectual complacency—which is precisely what engulfs one when one stops thinking of a translation as a description and begins to see it as being endowed with a special quality that would somehow make it 'true'. The lack of access to 'truth' enhances agency. It forces one to select and defend one's views. Linguistic contingency is one's opportunity. Such, then, are the broad ethical parameters within which we are operating. The ethics of engagement with language that we promote wants to reach beyond established positions; it is something like an 'infinite *striving*'.[46] We claim that 'the patronising dogmas of the truth [...] [must] give way to critical theories of the particular'.[47]

Now, we find ourselves being influenced by two sets of reasons that, though hailing from very different philosophical quarters, intersect in their refusal to abide by the view that 'truth' would somehow be available in translation. To be sure, the fact that we can depend on support from two prominent philosophers located at very different points on the philosophical spectrum is not enough, in and of itself, to validate our conclusions. But, unless one is prepared to dismiss this convergence as mere coincidence—which would strike us as a jejune motion indeed—the resonance between two primordially different and deeply influential epistemes ought, at the very least, to give our sceptical readers serious pause for thought before proceeding to spurn our argument.

∞

In crucial ways, we are indebted to Jacques Derrida's views on 'truth', an idea that he castigates throughout his work as a reprehensibly 'metaphysical' concoction.[48] Whatever metaphysical thought would have us believe, Derrida claims, a focus on the operation of language shows that a text 'does not give rise, "in the final instance", to a hermeneutic deciphering, to the uncrypting of a meaning or of a truth'.[49] Derrida, then, contrasts two apprehensions of interpretation or, as he says, 'two interpretations of interpretation'.[50] Specifically, '[o]ne seeks to decipher, dreams of deciphering a truth [...] escaping the play [...] of the sign [...]. The other [...] asserts the play and attempts to move beyond [...] [the dream of] the full presence, [of the] reassuring foundation, [...] and [of] the end of play'.[51] Uncompromisingly, Derrida emphasizes that 'these two interpretations of interpretation [...] are absolutely irreconcilable'.[52] Over against any process of appeasement along the lines of a Hegelian *Aufhebung*, he situates his own work firmly in defiance of the kind of reading that assumes a text to consist of a set of grammatical propositions

---

[46] Richard Rorty, *Philosophy and the Mirror of Nature* (Princeton, NJ: Princeton University Press, 1979), 377 (emphasis original).
[47] Peter Goodrich, *Languages of Law* (London: Weidenfeld & Nicolson, 1990), 1–2.
[48] For an example of Derrida's critique of metaphysics, see Jacques Derrida, *Marges* (Paris: Editions de Minuit, 1972), 254 [hereinafter *Marges*].
[49] Derrida, *Marges* (cited in n.48), 392 ['*ne donne pas lieu "en dernière instance", à un déchiffrement herméneutique, au décryptage d'un sens ou d'une vérité*'].
[50] Derrida, *Ecriture et différence* (cited in n.44), 427 ['*deux interprétations de l'interprétation*'].
[51] Derrida, *Ecriture et différence* (cited in n.44), ['*L'une cherche à déchiffrer, rêve de déchiffrer une vérité (...) échappant au jeu (...) du signe (...). L'autre (...) affirme le jeu et tente de passer au-delà (...) (du rêve de) la présence pleine, (du) fondement rassurant (...) et (de) la fin du jeu*'].
[52] Derrida, *Ecriture et différence* (cited in n.44), ['*ces deux interprétations de l'interprétation (...) sont absolument inconciliables*'].

asserting a foundational identity, an internal coherence, a logical order, a semantic unity, a 'truth'.⁵³ While metaphysics has the text functioning as a centripetal force—ultimately, this line of interpretation features '[t]he project of returning "strategically", ideally, to an origin or to a "priority" that would be simple, intact, normal, pure, proper'⁵⁴—for Derrida the text is inescapably centrifugal. A text exists as a force of proliferation and differentiation resisting anything like 'a' meaning (as in 'this is what the text means') or 'a' truth (as in 'this is truly what the text says'). As far as Derrida is concerned, '[t]his can appear surprising or disagreeable only to those for whom things are always clear, easily decipherable, calculable, and programmable: in a word, if one wanted to be polemical, to the irresponsible'.⁵⁵ For him, two principal features inhere to any text.

First, text is language and language—within the limits set by the alphabet—is infinitely labile.⁵⁶ In Derrida's formulation, '[a] thousand possibilities will always remain open even as one understands something of that sentence that makes sense'.⁵⁷ Still in Derrida's terms, the fact is that a word or a sentence features as one of its very attributes the characteristic of being *iterable*. Using the lemma 'iter', which he claims to derive from the Sanskrit '*itara*' meaning 'other', Derrida coins 'iterability', a neologism connoting both 'reiteration' and 'alterity'.⁵⁸ *Iterability*, then, combines repeatability and differentiality. The main point is that a word or a sentence is intrinsically endowed with a force of rupture from any use to which it may have been put and to which it cannot therefore be confined. Every word or sentence is potentially repeatable and every such repetition is an othering of that word or sentence in the sense that each iteration is unique. No matter what Beckett purported to mean, for example, when he wrote *En attendant Godot* in the late 1940s, no matter how he sought to organize the specific moment of inscription of the word 'Godot', no matter how he wanted to totalize or stabilize or fixate meaning, this word is iterable such that the author's conferment of meaning can be supplemented—which is to say that the author can never *saturate* meaning,⁵⁹ that he can never completely and systematically occupy fully the 'space' of meaning so that no room would be left for anything to be added by an interpreter intervening subsequently. In other terms, meaning has a 'never-completely-achievable' quality, which, far from pertaining to occasionality, is intrinsic to it. The word or sentence never exhausts itself

---

⁵³ Note that this opposition is not direct for it would then serve to feed the Hegelian dialectical machine by reaffirming the terms of the dichotomy. Rather, it is 'an oblique movement': Jacques Derrida, *Eperons* (Paris: Flammarion, 1978), 96 ['*un mouvement oblique*'].

⁵⁴ Jacques Derrida, *Limited Inc* (Paris: Galilée, 1990), 174 ['*le projet de remonter "stratégiquement", idéalement, à une origine ou à une "priorité" simple, intacte, normale, pure, propre*'] (hereinafter *Limited*).

⁵⁵ Derrida, *Limited* (cited in n.54), 254 ['*Cela ne peut paraître surprenant ou désagréable qu'à ceux pour qui les choses sont toujours claires, facilement déchiffrables, calculables et programmables: en un mot, si l'on voulait être polémique, aux irresponsables*'].

⁵⁶ For Derrida to allow that this infinite lability is possible only from 'a finite base' such as the alphabet permits him to rebut the accusation of transcendentalism, the kind of attack that would undermine his assault on metaphysics: Christopher Johnson, *System and Writing in the Philosophy of Jacques Derrida* (Cambridge: Cambridge University Press, 1993), 152 [hereinafter *System and Writing*]. Even as it shows itself to be endlessly open, language thus frames the extent of its own possible unfolding; it reveals 'powers of coding and overcoding or, in other words, of control and self-regulation': Jacques Derrida, 'Mes chances', in *Psyché*, 2nd edn, vol. I (Paris: Galilée, 1998 [1988]), 354 ['*pouvoirs de codage ou de surcodage, autrement dit de contrôle et d'autorégulation*'] (hereinafter *Psyché*). The infinity at stake is thus 'a *finite* infinity': Johnson, *System and Writing*, 51 (emphasis original).

⁵⁷ Derrida, *Limited* (cited in n.54), 122 ['*Mille possibilités resteront toujours ouvertes, alors même qu'on comprend quelque chose de cette phrase qui fait sens*'].

⁵⁸ See Derrida, *Marges* (cited in n.48), 375.

⁵⁹ For a reference to 'empirical saturation', see Derrida, *Marges* (cited in n.48), 376 ['*saturation empirique*'].

in the moment or in the time of its inscription. Rather, it carries, as an inherent dimension of its existence as word or sentence, a 'nonpresent *remainder*',[60] that is, a sheaf of meaning that is 'nonpresent' (in the sense that it is not being presently deployed) but that is not absent either (since it is potentially present and capable of being deployed at any moment, in any hypothetical alternative set of interpretive circumstances). Using a botanical analogy, Derrida refers to a process of 'dehiscence' with a view to capturing the inherent workings of a text as it bursts open with meaning and discharges its meaningful contents.[61] Every repeated utterance or iteration alters, and thus adds 'an extra turn' to the word's or to the sentence's meaning,[62] which will then potentially haunt each successive use of it. In his writings, Derrida also mobilizes the notion of 'dissemination' so as to refer to the idea of multiplication of meaning. To the extent that he defends the view that words and sentences do not operate within closed systems of meaning as metaphysicians, and indeed as structuralists, have long maintained, Derrida's argument can fairly be regarded as counter-hegemonic.

Whilst the open-texturedness of meaning suggests the contingency of interpretation, it also points to the aleatory character of translation. As is the case with interpretation, there is 'the structure of *supplementarity* within translation'.[63] Every word or sentence being inherently iterable, the occurrence of more than one translation is, structurally so to speak, inevitable. Indeed, the problem of ascription of meaning is compounded in the case of translation—an instance of iteration squared, if you will—since the process involves more than one language: 'No matter how correct and legitimate they are, and no matter what *right* one grants them, [translations] are all maladjusted, as if unjust in the deviation that affects them: within themselves, of course, since their meaning remains necessarily equivocal, and in their relation amongst themselves and thus in their multiplicity, finally or primarily in their irreducible inadequacy to the other language and to the stroke of genius of the event that makes the law, to all the virtualities of the original.'[64]

The idea that there would exist a common semantic interface across languages allowing for unalloyed inter-linguistic correspondence is precisely the kind of metaphysical composition that Derrida has been at pains to combat.

Secondly, the process of incessant interpretation that is a feature of the text's iterability is addressed by an interpreter—say, a comparatist-at-law intervening as translator—who, as someone who is inevitably situated in place and time, can only interpret from where he is. As Derrida puts it, one must accept that '[on]e ha[s] received more than [on]e thinks [on]e know[s] from "tradition"'.[65] This claim harks back to the key Heideggerian (and anti-Cartesian) insight that we introduced early in this essay to the effect that on

---

[60] Derrida, *Marges* (cited in n.48), 378 ['restance *non-présente*'] (emphasis original).

[61] Jacques Derrida, *La Dissémination* (Paris: Le Seuil, 1972), 265 ['*déhiscence*'] (hereinafter *Dissémination*).

[62] Derrida, *Dissémination* (cited in n.61), 290 ['*(La dissémination) (...) produit une structure tropologique qui circule indéfiniment sur elle-même par le supplément incessant d'un tour de trop*'].

[63] Jacques Derrida, *Du droit à la philosophie* (Paris: Galilée, 1990), 373 ['*la structure de* supplémentarité *dans la traduction*'] (emphasis original).

[64] Jacques Derrida, *Spectres de Marx* (Paris: Galilée, 1993), 43 ['*Si correctes et légitimes qu'elles soient, et quelque* droit *qu'on leur reconnaisse, (les traductions) sont toutes désajustées, comme injustes dans l'écart qui les affecte: au-dedans d'elles-mêmes, certes, puisque leur sens reste nécessairement équivoque, puis dans leur rapport entre elles et donc dans leur multiplicité, enfin ou d'abord dans leur inadéquation irréductible à l'autre langue et au coup de génie de l'événement qui fait la loi, à toutes les virtualités de l'original*'] (emphasis original).

[65] Jacques Derrida, *Points de suspension*, ed. by Elisabeth Weber (Paris: Galilée, 1992 [1983]), 139 ['*Nous avons reçu plus que nous ne croyons savoir de la "tradition"*'].

account of one's insurmountable situatedness within tradition, one's interpretive standpoint, and therefore one's interpretation, is itself *always already* situated—the adverbial construction, Heidegger's own ('*immer schon*'), referring to the fact that interpretation is simply unimaginable otherwise than as being situated, that an interpretive stance that would be *out of situation* is simply unthinkable. In Heidegger's words, any 'unveil[ing]' is 'always done under the guidance of a perspective that fixes that with regard to which what has been understood is to be interpreted'.[66] In sum, '[t]he interpretation is grounded in a *foresight*'.[67] If you will, '[t]he interpretation has always already decided, finally or provisionally'.[68]

The Heideggerian notions, as they foreground Rudolf Bultmann's idea of 'pre-understanding' ('*Vorverständnis*') and Gadamer's conception of 'prejudice' or 'pre-judgment' ('*Vorurteil*'),[69] refer to a preliminary structure of understanding that is inherently constitutive of any understanding and, as such, that acts as a *condition* of understanding. In other words, one cannot ascribe meaning—indeed, one cannot experience anything one might want to seize as 'truth'—against a 'no-background' situation. Of course, to say that all understanding is prejudiced in that it is circumscribed by the light that the epistemological situation sheds on the interpreter is not necessarily debilitating. Neither the significance of impersonal processes in the construction of the individual nor the prominence of impersonal assumptions in the formulation of knowledge-claims detracts from the empowering character of prejudice. Thus, one can understand Marcel Duchamp's ready-mades as art because one belongs to a culture that envisages art in a certain manner, that has an idea of what art is and of what art can be. Heidegger's conclusion, then, holds: 'Whatever and however we may try to think, we think within the sphere of tradition'.[70] And this is Derrida's contention also: 'The "subject" of [interpretation] does not exist if one means by that some sovereign solitude of the [interpreter]. The subject of [interpretation] is a *system* of relations between layers: [. . .] mental, society, world'.[71] In sum, 'what one calls the [interpreting] subject is no longer he who himself or he who alone [interprets]. He comes to understand himself in an irreducible secondarity'.[72] Writing of Rousseau and his work, Derrida thus observes that '[t]here is not, strictly speaking, a text whose author or subject is Jean-Jacques Rousseau'.[73]

---

[66] Heidegger, *Being and Time* (cited in n.8), 145 ['*Enthüllung*'/'*immer unter der Führung einer Hinsicht, die das fixiert, im Hinblick worauf das Verstandene ausgelegt werden soll*'].

[67] Heidegger, *Being and Time* (cited in n.8), 145 ['*Die Auslegung gründet jeweils in einer* Vorsicht'] (emphasis original).

[68] Heidegger, *Being and Time* (cited in n.8), 146 ['*Wie immer—die Auslegung hat sich je schon endgültig oder vorbehaltlich für eine bestimmte Begrifflichkeit entschieden*'].

[69] Rudolf Bultmann, 'Das Problem der Hermeneutik', in *Glauben und Verstehen*, vol. II (Tübingen: J. C. B. Mohr, 1952), 216 [hereinafter 'Das Problem der Hermeneutik']; Gadamer, *Truth and Method* (cited in n.11), 278–306 ('Prejudices [A]s Conditions of Understanding') ['*Vorurteile als Bedingungen des Verstehens*'].

[70] Martin Heidegger, *Identity and Difference*, transl. by Joan Stambaugh (Chicago, Ill.: University of Chicago Press, 2002 [1957]), 41 ['*Was immer und wie immer wir zu denken versuchen, wir denken im Spielraum der Überlieferung*'].

[71] Derrida, *Ecriture et différence* (cited in n.44), 335 ['*Le "sujet" de l'(interprétation) n'existe pas si l'on entend par là quelque solitude souveraine de l'(interprète). Le sujet de l'(interprétation) est un système de rapports entre les couches: (...) du psychique, de la société, du monde*'] (emphasis original).

[72] Derrida, *Ecriture et différence* (cited in n.44), 265 ['*ce qu'on appelle le sujet (interprétant) n'est plus celui-là même ou celui-là seul qui (interprète). Il se découvre dans une irréductible secondarité*'].

[73] Derrida, *Grammatologie* (cited in n.4), 350 ['*Il n'y a pas, à rigoureusement parler, de texte dont l'auteur ou le sujet soit Jean-Jacques Rousseau*'].

The irreducible situatedness of interpretation and the correlative inability for an interpreter to capture alterity on its own terms (rather than on one's terms) entails that 'translation is another name for the impossible'.[74] The primordial point is this: 'Between my world, [...] what I call 'my world', [...] between my world and any other world, there is initially the space and the time of an infinite difference, of an interruption [that is] incommensurable with all the attempts at passage, at bridge, at isthmus, at communication, at translation, at trope, and at transfer that the desire for world or the lack of world, the [human] being in lack of world, will try to pose, to impose, to propose, to stabilize. There is no world, there are only islands'.[75]

Gadamer's observation is no less powerful: 'It is enough to say that we understand in a *different* way, *if we understand at all*'.[76] As if echoing both Derrida and Gadamer, Borges's question lingers, obstinately: 'You who read me—are you certain you understand my language?'[77] In his subtle way, this most cosmopolitan of writers reminds us that the abyss across languages cannot be overcome.[78] But the impossibility of translation—of any translation that could be called 'true'—cannot be allowed to detract from the paradoxical fact that translation is possible, and must be.[79] Indeed, Derrida is adamant: 'I *must* translate, transfer, transport (*übertragen*) the untranslatable in another turn where, though translated, it remains untranslatable'.[80] Derrida's demand, however, is not for the faint of heart as he asks us to accept that the impossible is possible 'not in the sense in which it would become possible, but in the more radical sense in which the impossible is possible, *as impossible*'.[81]

---

[74] Jacques Derrida, *Le Monolinguisme de l'autre* (Paris: Galilée, 1996), 103 ['*la traduction est un autre nom de l'impossible*'].

[75] Jacques Derrida, *La Bête et le souverain*, ed. by Michel Lisse, Marie-Louise Mallet, and Ginette Michaud, vol. II (Paris: Galilée, 2010 [2002]), 31 ['*Entre mon monde, (...) ce que j'appelle "mon monde", (...) entre mon monde et tout autre monde, il y a d'abord l'espace et le temps d'une différence infinie, d'une interruption incommensurable à toutes les tentatives de passage, de pont, d'isthme, de communication, de traduction, de trope et de transfert que le désir de monde ou le mal du monde, l'être en mal de monde tentera de poser, d'imposer, de proposer, de stabiliser. Il n'y a pas de monde, il n'y a que des îles*']. This text is the transcript of the last annual course of lectures that Derrida delivered at the *Ecole des hautes études en sciences sociales* in Paris in 2002–2003.

[76] Gadamer, *Truth and Method* (cited in n.11), 296 ['*Es genügt zu sagen, daß man anders versteht, wenn man überhaupt versteht*'] (emphasis original).

[77] Jorge Luis Borges, 'The Library of Babel', in *Collected Fictions*, transl. by Andrew Hurley (London: Penguin, 1998 [1941]), 118 ['*Tú, que me lees, ¿estas seguro de entender mi lenguaje?*'].

[78] cf. *Rilke Briefe*, ed. by the Rilke-Archiv in Weimar, vol. I (Frankfurt: Insel, 1950 [1902]), 41: 'And there stand those stupid languages, helpless as two bridges that go over the same river side by side but are separated from each other by an abyss. It is a mere bagatelle, an accident, and yet it separates...' ['*Und da stehen nun diese dummen Sprachen hilflos wie zwei Brücken, die nebeneinander über denselben Fluß gehen, aber durch einen Abgrund voneinander getrennt sind. Es ist nur eine Bagatelle, ein Zufall, und es trennt doch...*']. In this letter written from Paris, Rilke comments on his failure to communicate with Rodin on the occasion of his visit to him. In a letter dated 26 March 1960, the word 'abyss' also appears in Celan's correspondence with specific reference to the separation between languages: James K. Lyon, *Paul Celan and Martin Heidegger* (Baltimore, Md: Johns Hopkins University Press, 2006 [1960]), 37 ['*Abgrund*'] [hereinafter *Paul Celan and Martin Heidegger*].

[79] See Simone Glanert, 'Comparaison et traduction des droits: à l'impossible tous sont tenus', in (ed.) Pierre Legrand, *Comparer les droits, résolument* (Paris: Presses Universitaires de France, 2009), 279–311.

[80] Jacques Derrida, *Béliers* (Paris: Galilée, 2003), 77 ['*Je dois traduire, transférer, transporter (*übertragen*) l'intraduisible dans un autre tour là même où, traduit, il demeure intraduisible*'] (emphasis original).

[81] F. Raffoul, 'Derrida et l'éthique de l'im-possible' (2007) 53 *Revue de métaphysique et de morale* 73, 75 ['*non pas au sens où il deviendrait possible, mais dans le sens plus radical où l'impossible devient possible comme impossible*'] (emphasis original).

The fact that the idea of 'truth', then, is simply not suitable with respect to translation is pithily rendered by Derrida as he writes that the very word 'translation' ought to be replaced by 'transformation'. Observing that '[w]e will never have been involved and never have been involved in fact in the "transportation" of pure signifieds that the signifying instrument—or the "vehicle"—would leave intact and untouched, from one language to another',[82] he adds that 'for the notion of translation, one will have to substitute a notion of *transformation*: the regulated transformation of a language by another, of a text by another'.[83] Transformation, according to Derrida, captures untranslatability as the negative moment necessary to the recognition and to the survival of the idiomatic that exceeds one's grasp and to which one's response can therefore be neither sheer reproduction nor meaning transfer. It refers to another *economy*, to an economy of *negotiation*,[84] where '[w]hat guides [on]e is always untranslatability'.[85]

The strong assertion of the singularity of language and the related view that 'truth' cannot be an apt theoretical tool for approaching what takes place in understanding and communication—that 'the relationship between self and other can never be turned into a relationship between self and self (same and same)', that '[t]he enduring self/ other relation means that alterity can never be reduced to identity'[86]—is not, however, the exclusive province of the philosophy of deconstruction as practised by Derrida and his epigones. Specifically, we have found noteworthy reverberations between Derrida's thought and that of logician and mathematician Willard Van Orman Quine, arguably the most influential US analytical philosopher of the twentieth century.[87] And it is to this specific correspondence of outlooks that we now turn.

Quine holds a physicalist ontology—for him, 'the only things that exist are those which feature in the explanations of the most fundamental science, namely physics'— and a naturalized epistemology—'[the] investigat[ion] [of] the relationship between theory (our beliefs) and empirical evidence' requires one to proceed 'through empirical

---

[82] Derrida, *Positions* (cited in n.6), 31 ['*Nous n'aurons et n'avons en fait jamais eu affaire* à *quelque "transport" de signifiés purs que l'instrument—ou le "véhicule"—signifiant laisserait vierge et inentamé, d'une langue à l'autre*'].

[83] Derrida, *Positions* (cited in n.6), 31 ['*à la notion de traduction, il faudra substituer une notion de transformation: transformation réglée d'une langue par une autre, d'un texte par un autre*'] (emphasis original). Elsewhere, Derrida refers to a 'mutation': Jacques Derrida, 'Des tours de Babel', in *Psyché* [1985] (cited in n.56), 217 ['*mutation*'] (hereinafter 'Tours de Babel'). See also Benjamin, 'The Task of the Translator' (cited in n.38), 256: 'For in its afterlife—which could not be called that if it were not a transformation and a renewal of something living—the original undergoes a change' ['*Denn in seinem Fortleben, das so nicht heißen dürfte, wenn es nicht Wandlung und Erneuerung des Lebendigen wäre, ändert sich das Original*']. Again (see n.38), Benjamin anticipates Derrida.

[84] An apposite understanding of the word 'economy' as used by Derrida throughout his work would be 'dynamic interplay': Johnson, *System and Writing* (cited in n.56), 20. For the idea of 'negotiation', see Jacques Derrida, *Altérités* (Paris: Osiris, 1986), 85.

[85] J. Derrida, [Interview], *Magazine littéraire*, April 2004, 26 ['*Ce qui me guide, c'est toujours l'intraductibilité*'].

[86] Andrew Benjamin, *Translation and the Nature of Philosophy* (London: Routledge, 1989), 82–3.

[87] This congruence is not to hide the fact that Quine did not esteem Derrida. When the University of Cambridge chose to bestow an honorary doctorate on Derrida, Quine thus joined 18 other philosophers to oppose the decision in a scathing letter to *The Times* published on 9 May 1992. This document is reproduced in full in Jacques Derrida, *Points...*, ed. by Elisabeth Weber (Palo Alto, Calif.: Stanford University Press, 1995), 419–21. It is preceded by Derrida's reflections on the dispute: Jacques Derrida, '*Honoris Causa*: "This Is *Also* Extremely Funny"', transl. by Marian Hobson and Christopher Johnson, in *Points...* (Palo Alto, Calif.: Stanford University Press, 1995 [1992]), 399–419. Protests notwithstanding, Derrida received his distinction on 11 June 1992.

science (neurophysiology, behaviourist psychology)'.[88] For Quine, 'there is no knowledge outside science'.[89] In other terms, '[e]verything we know about the world is due to the impingement of energy on our sensory surfaces'.[90] Of course, the assumption that everything supervenes on the physical, that physics enjoys special ontological authority (which entails an assimilation of even philosophy to science),[91] is precisely the kind of metaphysical claim—'not itself a scientific finding'[92]—that Derrida chastises. But this disagreement cannot have us lose sight of significant affinities between the two philosophical projects as regards the lack of interface between translation and anything that could reasonably be called 'truth'.

With respect to translation, Quine's thesis addresses what he styles 'inscrutability of reference'.[93] But before we can say more about translation, it is necessary to take a few steps away from the topic and discuss basic aspects of Quine's philosophy. For Quine, then, ontologically speaking the only 'facts of the matter' are physical (indeed, he likens 'factuality' to 'gravitation and electric charge').[94] Meaning, however, is not part of physical reality. Since there is no fact of the matter concerning what words mean, given that '[a]scriptions of meaning cannot be reduced to physical statements',[95] physical facts cannot determine what our expressions mean. There is, therefore, a disjuncture between meaning (word) and physical reality (world). As one commentator aptly remarks, '[r]eference, for Quine, is thus not the fundamental relation that language has to the world'.[96] Observe that Quine does not say that words refer to something and that one is not in a position to ascertain what that is. For Quine, there is, more accurately, no such 'thing' as 'that which our words refer to'. To be sure, Quine falls short of arguing that words do not 'refer' in any sense of the term whatsoever. Thus, reference remains relevant for him.[97] In his view, words do 'refer', but this reference does not concern anything like the word's 'being'. All that exists is an assignment of reference to a word by its speaker. Given the ontological discrepancy between word and world, in the absence of a 'thing-like' reference, the only way for anyone to understand any language, even one's 'own' language and a fortiori another language, is therefore for one to operate on the basis of observable behaviour (verbal or non-verbal), which is the only matter that our experience allows us to speak about with a certain rigour: 'We depend strictly on overt behavior in observable situations'.[98] For example, all that we have in terms of what a speaker

---

[88] Hans-Johann Glock, *Quine and Davidson on Language, Thought and Reality* (Cambridge: Cambridge University Press, 2003), 29 [hereinafter: *Quine and Davidson*].

[89] Glock, *Quine and Davidson* (cited in n.88), 28 (emphasis omitted).

[90] Peter Hylton, 'Quine on Reference and Ontology', in (ed.) Roger F. Gibson, *The Cambridge Companion to Quine* (Cambridge: Cambridge University Press, 2004), 118 [hereinafter: 'Quine on Reference and Ontology'].

[91] For a statement to this effect, see Willard Van Orman Quine, *Word and Object* (Cambridge, Mass.: MIT Press, 1960), 22: 'What reality is like is the business of scientists, in the broadest sense, painstakingly to surmise; and what there is, what is real, is part of that question' [hereinafter *Word and Object*]. See also W. V. Quine, *Ontological Relativity and Other Essays* (New York: Columbia University Press, 1969), 84 [hereinafter *Ontological Relativity*].

[92] Glock, *Quine and Davidson* (cited in n.88), 230.

[93] See Quine, *Word and Object* (cited in n.91), 26–79. Thirty years later, Quine was taking the view that the expression '"indeterminacy of reference" would have been better': W. V. Quine, *Pursuit of Truth*, 2nd edn (Cambridge, Mass.: Harvard University Press, 1992), 50.

[94] W. V. Quine, *Theories and Things* (Cambridge, Mass.: Harvard University Press, 1981), 23 [hereinafter *Theories and Things*].

[95] Glock, *Quine and Davidson* (cited in n.88), 227.

[96] Hylton, 'Quine on Reference and Ontology' (cited in n.90), 122.

[97] Hylton, 'Quine on Reference and Ontology' (cited in n.90), 122.

[98] W. V. Quine, 'Indeterminacy of Translation Again' (1987) 84 *Journal of Philosophy* 5, 5 [hereinafter 'Indeterminacy'].

means is 'what might be implicit in his dispositions to overt behavior'.[99] And it is this dynamics that Quine has in mind as he writes that '[l]anguage is a social art'.[100]

In the absence of isomorphism between word and world, there is inevitably a process of mediation intervening between word and world with a view to specifying the word's world. And this mediation relates to the assignment of reference underlying the word, which itself is 'an obscure notion, subject to no extensional criterion of individuation and definable only in terms of other, equally obscure, intensional notions'.[101] As the assignment of reference cannot illuminate any 'thing-like' referent, as 'there is no matter of fact as to what we are *referring* to',[102] reference accordingly remains opaque or inscrutable (or indeterminate). Of course, when one speaks a familiar language—say, the 'home language', to use Quine's formulation—the matter of inscrutability does not arise as a difficulty and does not hinder language use. Thus, '"London" designates London (whatever *that* is) and "rabbit" denotes the rabbits (whatever *they* are)'; for Quine, '[i]nscrutability of reference emerges only in translation'.[103] This is the question that we now propose to address.

Assume a text and a translator purporting to offer a translation of that text. Quine emphasizes at the outset that a range of competing translations can prove equally compatible with the behaviour under examination, that is, with the empirical data. In the absence of an elucidative referent, since 'there just aren't any facts for such putative semantical statements to be about',[104] because there are 'no entities' beyond assignments of reference,[105] that is, other than as elements of a theory,[106] considering that meaning cannot be reified (or cannot be made 'thing-like'),[107] in view of the lack of any physicality assuredly correlatable with an utterance, in as much as '[r]eference itself proves behaviorally inscrutable',[108] there is no way to know which interpretation would provide the *true* interpretation of that which has been uttered. For Quine, there is no principled way of adjudicating between alternative interpretations of language such that one could be said to be (referentially) true. In other terms, with specific reference to translation, Quine's 'physicalist' claim holds that since there is no fact of the matter for the translator to be right or wrong about, since reference proves inscrutable, a range of different translations can properly entail 'the neural stimulations which would prompt speakers to assent to them', that is, the 'stimulus meaning' that would validate a particular translation, whether intensionally or extensionally,[109] in the eyes of a particular reader.[110]

---

[99] Quine, *Ontological Relativity* (cited in n.91), 27.
[100] Quine, *Word and Object* (cited in n.91), ix.
[101] Harry Deutsch, 'Extensionalism', in (eds) Jaegwon Kim and Ernest Sosa, *A Companion to Metaphysics* (Oxford: Blackwell, 1995), 160.
[102] Robert Kirk, 'Indeterminacy of Translation', in (ed.) Roger F. Gibson, *The Cambridge Companion to Quine* (Cambridge: Cambridge University Press, 2004), 165 (emphasis original).
[103] W. V. Quine, 'Reply to Paul A. Roth', in (eds) Lewis E. Hahn and Paul A. Schilpp, *The Philosophy of W. V. Quine* (LaSalle, Ill.: Open Court, 1986), 460.
[104] Roger F. Gibson, *Enlightened Empiricism* (Gainesville, Fla: University Press of Florida, 1989), 112–3 [hereinafter *Enlightened Empiricism*].
[105] Eve Gaudet, *Quine on Meaning* (New York: Continuum, 2006), 70 [hereinafter *Quine on Meaning*].
[106] '[O]bjects figure only as neutral nodes in the logical structure of our total theory of the world': W. V. Quine, 'In Praise of Observation Sentences' (1993) 90 *Journal of Philosophy* 107, 112 [hereinafter 'Observation Sentences'].
[107] W. V. Quine, 'Reply to John Woods', in (eds) Lewis E. Hahn and Paul A. Schilpp, *The Philosophy of W. V. Quine*, 2nd edn (LaSalle, Ill.: Open Court, 1999), 728.
[108] Quine, *Ontological Relativity* (cited in n.91), 35.
[109] For Quine, 'indeterminacy of translation [...] cuts across extension and intension alike': Quine, *Ontological Relativity* (cited in n.91), 35.
[110] Glock, *Quine and Davidson* (cited in n.88), 141. Quine argues that the proper way to describe the causal prompt for assent is the idea of 'neural intake': Quine, 'Observation Sentences' (cited in n.106), 108. In his view, '[n]eural intake is physical and indisputable': Quine, 'Observation Sentences' (cited in n.106), 116.

It follows that '[t]ruth is immanent'.[111] It depends on a language;[112] indeed, it is inseparable from a theory of the world for 'we can never do better than occupy the standpoint of some theory or other, the best we can muster at the time'.[113] According to Quine, 'there is no extra-theoretic truth, no higher truth than the truth we are claiming or aspiring to as we continue to tinker with our system of the world from within'.[114] Given that every translation, for example, is forced to project the ontology of a language or theory on the *interpretandum*, any 'truth' is the expression of one's epistemological stance.[115]

Importantly, despite his challenge to 'an ill-conceived notion within traditional semantics, namely, sameness of meaning',[116] Quine cannot be characterized as a semantic nihilist: 'Indeterminacy means not that there is no acceptable translation, but that there are many'.[117] In other terms, 'translations of a language can be set up in such ways that, while each is consistent with the speech dispositions of everyone concerned, they nevertheless can have different sentence-to-sentence correlations even to the point where two translations of some sentence can be correlated with sentences having opposite truth-values; *and* there is no answer to the (pseudo-) question of which translation is the *uniquely* correct one—they are *all* correct insofar as they measure up to the speech dispositions of all concerned'.[118]

While he says that all that is possible for an interpretation is the fact of practical success, Quine never claims that one cannot decide between any two interpretations. Rather, his contention is that '[i]f we transcend [the data] and decide that one of two [translations] equally in conformity to the data is better than the other, our decision will be based on mere intuition'.[119]

∞

Featuring 'startling' correlations in their philosophical projects,[120] in spite of 'quite opposite starting-points',[121] Derrida and Quine are both arguing against an 'uncritical notion of meanin[g]'.[122] And the two philosophers are both led to ascertain an abyss—a non-relation or an interruption—between language and world. They are both saying that a word (or a concatenation of words) cannot be fully present in a way that would allow it to be self-interpreting, to preclude the necessity of its being interpreted, to avoid the need to force an interpretation. For Derrida and Quine, a word as given and pure

---

[111] Quine, *Theories and Things* (cited in n.94), 21–2.
[112] See W. V. Quine, 'Reactions', in (eds) Paolo Leonardi and Marco Santambrogio, *On Quine* (Cambridge: Cambridge University Press, 1995), 353: '[S]entences are tied to languages. A string of marks is true only as a sentence of some specific language L; true in L' [hereinafter 'Reactions'].
[113] Quine, *Word and Object* (cited in n.91), 22.
[114] W. V. Quine, 'On Empirically Equivalent Systems of the World', (1975) 9 *Erkenntnis* 313, 327. This paper is reprinted in W. V. Quine, *Confessions of a Confirmed Extensionalist and Other Essays*, ed. by Dagfinn Føllesdal and Douglas B. Quine (Cambridge, Mass.: Harvard University Press, 2008). The relevant page is 242.
[115] Yet, Quine asserts that he is not a relativist. He claims that '[i]f a sentence is part of the theory that we hold, then we accept that sentence as true—not true in some relativized sense but flat-out': Hylton, 'Quine on Reference and Ontology' (cited in n.90), 132. See Quine, *Word and Object* (cited in n.91), 24–5.
[116] Quine, 'Indeterminacy' (cited in n.98), 10.
[117] Quine, 'Indeterminacy' (cited in n.98), 9.
[118] Gibson, *Enlightened Empiricism* (cited in n.104), 102.
[119] Gaudet, *Quine on Meaning* (cited in n.105), 70.
[120] Samuel C. Wheeler, *Deconstruction As Analytic Philosophy* (Palo Alto, Calif.: Stanford University Press, 2000), 3 [hereinafter *Deconstruction*].
[121] Horst Turk, 'The Question of Translatability: Benjamin, Quine, Derrida', in (eds) Harald Kittel and Armin P. Frank, *Interculturality and the Historical Study of Literary Translations* (Berlin: E. Schmidt, 1991), 120.
[122] Quine, 'Indeterminacy' (cited in n.98), 9.

meaning is an incoherent notion ('[t]he idea of a *Ding an sich* may be nonsense; the idea of a *Bedeutung an sich* is definitely nonsense on stilts').[123] Not even the 'context' can fix the reference of a word since context is not exhaustively specifiable without itself being subject to interpretation (thus, context is language-like or features language-like properties). Ultimately, all interpretation takes place via an unending regression into a sequence of what Quine calls 'background languages'.[124] There simply cannot be any interpretation beyond language or out of language. It is not, of course, that Derrida and Quine deny the existence of physical reality or anything of the kind. What they are claiming is that there is nothing semantic behind language, that one never reaches semantic bedrock. Built into interpretation, then, in the absence of the kind of 'absolute anchors' that could be supplied by the full presence of a text or a context,[125] is a 'drift',[126] which means that 'there is always a "slack" between an interpretation and the evidence for it',[127] what Derrida calls 'play'.[128] It follows that translation inevitably differs from what it is about (in that it is but an interpretation thereof) and defers what it is about (in that it calls for an interpretation of itself).[129]

The idea of 'slack' or 'play' cannot, however, be taken to embody 'unlimited polysemy'.[130] 'One does not do whatever one wants with language'.[131] Thus, a translation may be defective. Our basic argument is that a translation is a translation 'of' a text. One needs to ask, then, to what extent is a translation appropriately responding to a hidden claim of the text or illegitimately imposing itself on the text by failing to hearken to its *genius loci*. For a translation to exist as translation *of* a text, it must demonstrably engage with the claim of the text,[132] with the 'speaking-to-us' ('*Zuspruch*') of the text that is at work.[133] In other words, the translation must show itself to be hearkening to the text,[134] for 'we are compelled, as soon as we set out upon a way of thought, to give specific attention to what the word says'.[135] A translation defecting from the text—for example, on account of its absurd rendition of the text (say, 'The Fool Who Caused Trouble' for Proust's *A la recherche du temps perdu*)—could therefore be said not to be operating as a translation of the text, which means that it would be defective even as it purported to be a *translation* of the text. Through the reference to defectiveness, translational anarchism is contained—as it must be. Inevitably, borderline situations will

---

[123] Glock, *Quine and Davidson* (cited in n.88), 210.
[124] Quine, *Ontological Relativity* (cited in n.91), 49.
[125] Wheeler, *Deconstruction* (cited in n.120), 29.
[126] The word is Derrida's: *Marges* (cited in n.48), 377 ['*dérive*'].
[127] Wheeler, *Deconstruction* (cited in n.120), 29. Here is one of the various respects in which Derrida marks a break with the hermeneutic horizon.
[128] Derrida, *Ecriture et différence* (cited in n.44), 427 ['*jeu*']. The word suggests 'a kind of "looseness"' in the relations between world and world: Johnson, *System and Writing* (cited in n.56), 203 n.17.
[129] We reprise Wheeler, *Deconstruction* (cited in n.120), 28.
[130] Johnson, *System and Writing* (cited in n.56), 203 n.17.
[131] Jacques Derrida, *Apprendre à vivre enfin*, ed. by Jean Birnbaum (Paris: Galilée, 2005), 38 ['*On ne fait pas n'importe quoi avec la langue*'].
[132] Bultmann expressly advocates 'listening to the claims of the text': Bultmann, 'Das Problem der Hermeneutik' (cited in n.69), 228 ['*(den) Anspruch (des Texts) zu hören*'].
[133] For this translation from Heidegger's philosophical vocabulary, see Lyon, *Paul Celan and Martin Heidegger* (cited in n.78), 223 n.14. The reference is to Martin Heidegger, *Holzwege*, in *Gesamtausgabe*, vol. V (Frankfurt: V. Klostermann, 1977 [1950]), 369.
[134] See Martin Heidegger, *On the Way to Language*, transl. by Peter D. Hertz (New York: Harper Collins, 1971 [1959]), 124–5.
[135] Martin Heidegger, *What Is Called Thinking*, transl. by J. Glenn Gray (New York: Harper Collins, 1968 [1954]), 128 ['*sobald wir uns auf einen Weg des Denkens begeben, (sind wir) schon daran gehalten, eigens auf das Sagen des Wortes zu achten*'].

arise. Consider an anachronistic translation: does the reference to 'Cape Kennedy' in the translation of a passage from 'Homer's *Iliad* regarding Achilles's talking horses and the way in which they soar in the skies—'as in dreams, or at Cape Kennedy, they rise'[136]—pertain to defectiveness?

But the fact that certain translations can be said to be defective still does not entail that one of them need be recognized as 'true'. The idea of 'truth' traditionally connotes transcendence in the sense at least that 'truth' must exist beyond contingency. With specific reference to translation, truth classically turns on the recovery of full meaning. Neither sense of 'truth' is necessary, and one could plausibly refashion the word by contemplating other semantic extensions. However, the habitual connotations of 'truth' are sufficiently well established in philosophical, literary, and common parlance to suggest that it is by reference to them that it becomes relevant to ask whether a translation can be 'true'. And because translation is at the very minimum constrained by the language in which it is happening and by the person who is making it happen, it can never arise outside of an interpretive framework. Even assuming something like 'the text-in-itself', a translation of it cannot be 'true' in the canonical sense of the word, that is, it can never lift itself out of conjecture to reach the text 'as it is': '[T]he thing itself always slips away'.[137]

Since a translation is inherently 'maladjusted',[138] all that translation can hope to be, the best that it can expect to be, then, is (relatively) just. It can reach a point where it purports to do justice to the text through a process of incessant negotiation with it. Observe, however, that the justice at issue is not exclusively 'of' the text in the sense at least that the text's justice needs to be formulated through a process of interpretation and thus calls to be conveyed 'to' the text by the interpreter as hearkener. Yet, justice must be understood as being strictly connected to place and time, that is, as being thoroughly immanent or embedded or singular: it is of *that* text, it is being conveyed by *that* interpreter. As regards translation, justice is but the application of local interpretive knowledge in response to the claim of a specific text, a process that will itself be validated or invalidated by reference to local interpretive knowledge as deployed by a particular audience or readership.

No doubt aporetically, translation can thus be defective even as it cannot be 'true'. In translation, therefore, 'truth' cannot act as a regulative ideal. Yet translation, albeit maladjusted, can aspire to being just. It can only ever aim to be just—it can just seek justness. However, as a matter of the hearkening—of the recognition and respect—that is due to the text, it must want to be just. Indeed, 'is not a just translation hospitality itself?'[139]

∞

For Ronald Dworkin, 'a scholar who labors for years over a new reading of *Hamlet* cannot believe that his various interpretive conclusions are no more valid than the contradictory conclusions of other scholars [...]. [...] [I]f [interpreters] have come to think that one interpretation of something is best, they can also sensibly think that that interpretation meets the test of what defines success in the enterprise, even if they cannot articulate that test in much or any detail. So they can think there is objective truth in interpretation'.[140]

---

[136] Christopher Logue, *War Music: An Account of Books 1–4 and 16–19 of Homer's* Iliad (Chicago, Ill.: University of Chicago Press, 2003 [1997]), 214.

[137] Jacques Derrida, *La Voix et le phénomène* (Paris: Presses Universitaires de France, 1967), 117 ['*la chose même se dérobe toujours*'].

[138] For discussion refer to text accompanying n.64.

[139] Jacques Derrida, 'La Chance et l'hospitalité' (1999) 14/2–3 *Trois* 71, 72 [1995] ('*La traduction juste, n'est-ce pas l'hospitalité même?*').

[140] Ronald Dworkin, *Justice for Hedgehogs* (Cambridge, Mass.: Harvard University Press, 2011), 151 (emphasis original) [hereinafter *Justice for Hedgehogs*].

Elsewhere, still adverting to the matter of 'truth', Dworkin argues that although '[we] might worry that it is both arrogant and impolitic to claim absolute truth', 'we must do that'; indeed, '[w]e have no option'.[141] We disagree.

Because 'a comparative-law investigation should also concern the translation of law texts',[142] and since, as Quine's analytics makes clear, '[t]ranslation remains, and is indispensable',[143] assume a comparatist-at-law inscribing foreign law in translation. Assume further that this comparatist is acting in all earnestness and wishes to be taken seriously. Of course, one can expect this comparatist to deem her translation of foreign law more compelling than, say, her colleague's translation or than other extant translations to be found in books or journals. But this sense of achievement does not mean, need not mean, and must not mean, that this comparatist-at-law holds her interpretation to be 'true'. What this comparatist needs to think, and what others need to accept about her work, is that her translation carries a higher interpretive yield than other translations, that it is good and perhaps excellent, not that it is 'true'. 'Truth' is simply not necessary to any expression of conviction in the supremacy of one translation over others. Indeed, it is misleading for while it evokes the original text's authority, it fails to account for its vulnerability.

But we shall not-finish where we began, that is, with Pinter. In his Nobel lecture, in addition to claiming that 'there never is any such thing as one truth', that '[t]here are many', that they 'challenge each other', and that they are 'blind to each other', Pinter said that '[y]ou never quite find [truth] but the search for it is compulsive'. He added: 'The search is clearly what drives the endeavour'.[144] Although there never is any such thing as one 'truth', then, the search for it would be irresistible. This assertion is intriguing. One would be compulsively driven to search for something that never is and that never can be, such that one would find oneself locked in an impasse: 'Truth' must be abandoned, yet it cannot be jettisoned. Possibly the *idea* of 'truth' indeed remains so attractive. It may be that 'truth' continues to drive the mind despite its inexistence. And perhaps 'truth' is needed—'final belief/Must be in a fiction'[145]—an intuition that Derrida ultimately seems to accept as he writes that '*[o]ne must have* truth'.[146] Derrida's and Quine's contestations would therefore be offering 'a persistent critique of what one cannot not want'.[147] *Quaere*: Would holding that '[t]ruth in law need not extend beyond a particular culture' help to square the proverbial circle?[148] But is one then still talking of 'truth' which, by definition so to speak, cannot meaningfully be equated with local knowledge, that is, with contingency? Now, would the fact that '[t]ruth is preserved in vestigial form in the notion of error' assuage one's alleged need to believe?[149]

---

[141] Dworkin, *Justice for Hedgehogs* (cited in n.140), 338–9.

[142] Derrida, 'Tours de Babel' (cited in n.83), 228 ['*une enquête de droit comparé devrait aussi concerner la traduction des textes de droit*']. This observation must be one of Derrida's rare remarks expressly devoted to 'comparative law'.

[143] Quine, 'Indeterminacy' (cited in n.98), 9.

[144] Pinter, *Art, Truth and Politics* (cited in n.41).

[145] Wallace Stevens, 'Asides on the Oboe', in *The Collected Poems of Wallace Stevens* (New York: Vintage, 1990 [1942]), 250.

[146] Derrida, *Positions* (cited in n.6), 79–80 n.23 ['il faut *la vérité*'] (emphasis original). cf. Quine, 'Reactions' (cited in n.112), 353: 'Truth [...] looms as a haven that we keep steering for and correcting to'.

[147] Gayatri C. Spivak, 'Bonding in Difference', in (ed.) Alfred Arteaga, *An Other Tongue* (Durham, NC: Duke University Press, 1994), 285.

[148] G. P. Fletcher, 'What Law Is Like' (1997) 50 *Southern Methodist University L.R.* 1599, 1610.

[149] Barbara Johnson, *A World of Difference* (Baltimore, Md: Johns Hopkins University Press, 1987), 15.

In the course of our argument, we have wanted to focus not on whether or not there is faith in 'truth', but on whether or not there is 'truth' in translation with specific reference to foreign law. In sum, we have been asking ourselves Beckett's question: '[W]hat truth is there in all this babble?'[150] And, like Derrida and Quine, we feel able to answer that there is none, none whatsoever. Faith is quite another matter.

---

[150] Samuel Beckett, *Malone Dies*, in *The Grove Centenary Edition*, ed. by Paul Auster, vol. II (New York: Grove Press, 2006 [1951]), 229 ['*Mais je me dis tant de choses, qu'y a-t-il de vrai dans ce babil?*']. The re-writing from the French is Beckett's own. One will have recognized the biblical allusion, more apparent in the English version than in the French text.

32
First-Person Perspectives in Legal Decisions

Lorenz Kaehler

1. Introduction

A centrepiece of almost any legal theory is the judge and the role he plays in adjudication. A wide variety of legal theorists ranging from Aristotle[1] to Dworkin[2] agree that he plays the crucial role for the interpretation of the law, although they deeply disagree[3] what this role precisely consists of. If one denies Montesquieu's idea about judges as a mere mouthpiece of the law[4] it becomes decisive what they do. The reasons they find convincing govern the decisions the legislator did not reach; it is their final say that determines what the law is and which reasons are allowed to enter the legal discourse.

This central role of judges, however, is not always reflected in the language they use. This can best be seen in the way judges refer to themselves. Some courts such as the European Court of Justice and the German Supreme Court totally avoid direct reference to themselves in the first person singular or plural. For them it is a taboo to say "we" or "I" in an opinion, although its content fundamentally depends on who this "we" or " I" are. The British Supreme Court and other English courts stand in sharp contrast. The Law Lords not only issue individual opinions, but frequently refer to themselves by "I" or use expressions such as "it seems to me".[5] Justices of the US Supreme Court avoid the first person singular in joint opinions, but nevertheless use it in their individually authored opinions.[6] How, then, can one explain these differences and why is the crucial role of the judges not always reflected in the language they use?

At first glance, it might seem that some legal systems deny the crucial role of the judges because the judge is, in their view, the mouthpiece of the law and, therefore, not supposed to utter a personal expression.[7] In this perspective he is not allowed to say "I" because his personal view does not play a role. Opposite to that are legal systems which allow him to refer to his personal opinions. They appear as the enlightened ones who

---

[1] Aristotle, *Nicomachean Ethics* (Robert Bartlett and Susan Collins, transl., University of Chicago Press, Chicago, 2011), 1132a.
[2] Ronald Dworkin, *Law's Empire* (Fontana Press, London, 1986), 225.
[3] See, e.g., Hans Kelsen, *Reine Rechtslehre* (2nd edn, Verlag Oesterreich, Wien, 1960), 242; Duncan Kennedy, *A Critique of Adjudication* (Harvard University Press, Cambridge, Mass., 1997), 23; Aharon Barak, 'A Judge on Judging: The Role of a Supreme Court in a Democracy' (2002) 116 *Harvard Law Review* 16.
[4] Charles de Secondat Montesquieu, *The Spirit of Laws*, edited by David Wallace, translated by Thomas Nugent (University of California Press, Berkeley, 1977), 209.
[5] e.g. *R. v London Borough of Lambeth* [1987] 19 H.L.R. 51, 55 (Brown J).
[6] e.g. *South Central Bell Telephone Co. v Alabama* [1999] 119 S. Ct. 1180, 1182 (Breyer J). In the first version of the opinion he unintentionally slipped into "I", which was criticized as a departure from a two hundred year old tradition and later corrected, Pearl Goldman, 'Book Review of Peter M. Tiersma, Legal Language' [1999] 24 *The Legal Studies Forum* 721, 724.
[7] See, for instance, Ruth Ginsburg, 'Remarks on writing separately' [1990] 65 *Washington Law Review* 133, 134.

have overcome the illusion of deduction. The conscious use of the first person marks the role judges play. Is the avoidance of the first-person perspective hence only a remnant of a formalist ideology denying the discretion of the judge and the role of social, economic, and moral arguments in adjudication? Or is the use of "I", "me", or "we" in a legal opinion just a matter of social and linguistic convention?[8]

In this paper I try to tackle these questions. In order to do that, I will in section 1 look at some opinions using the first-person perspective and some decisions avoiding it. I will then ask whether one can transform these perspectives into each other and express the same content either by personalized or by depersonalized statements (section 2). In particular, the paper will look at some propositions which are usually expressed in the first-person perspective and which are, possibly, not transferable into impersonal ones. Among them are performative acts for which the use of the first person singular is, according to Austin, constitutive.[9] In addition, I will look at non-deductive moral arguments and propositional attitudes which are central for the role that judges play and the discretion they have. If these arguments presuppose the first-person perspective, it becomes questionable that some courts can avoid it and nevertheless use those arguments.

Section 3 will look at the limits on the transformation of personal expressions into impersonal ones. Some expressions depend on the first-person perspective and lose part of their content if they are transformed into impersonal ones. For example, sometimes it does matter whether one merely makes a statement or, in addition, says that one believes in it. The paper examines, therefore, statements in which the first-person perspective is crucial. Prominent examples are expressions of doubt and of other propositional attitudes. Only with them can one describe the difference between one's private belief and one's official opinion. When this difference is part of the legal argument the first-person perspective becomes unavoidable.

It is even more puzzling, therefore, why some legal systems use the first-person perspective and others avoid it. Why should some of them forbear using certain expressions which they need in order to express a particular idea? The last section of the paper will look more closely at these differences and try to understand the reasons for the use or avoidance of the first-person perspective. The paper concludes that there are trade-offs to be made between these uses. On the one hand, the first-person perspective best allows the expression of personal beliefs. On the other hand, it discourages the formation of general rules which can best justify legal decisions.

2. Phenomenon

Let us first look more closely at the use and avoidance of the first-person perspective. As paradigmatic examples, I will take some decisions of the U.K. Supreme Court, the German Supreme Court, and the European Court of Justice. These courts are representative of different legal cultures but are in no way exhaustive for the various legal traditions.[10]

---

[8] A similar question is whether the first-person perspective is admissible in academic work, see Norman Fairclough, *Critical Discourse Analysis* (Pearson, London, 1995), 277; Ken Hyland, *Disciplinary Discourses* (Pearson, London, 2000), 94, 125.

[9] J.L. Austin, *How to Do Things With Words* (Harvard University Press, Cambridge, Mass., 1962), 62.

[10] See for US courts: Barbara Ann Perry, *The priestly tribe: the Supreme Court's image in the American mind* (Praeger; Westport, 1999), 12–13, noting that it is mostly only dissents and concurrences that refer to the authors by the first person; for the Netherlands: Willibrord Davids, 'Judicial Reasoning and Legitimacy of the Dutch Supreme Court' in Nick Huls, Maurice Adams, and Jacco Bomhoff (eds), *The Legitimacy of Highest Courts' rulings* (TMC Asser Press, The Hague; 2009), 223, 226: "in our system... the reasoning of the judgment itself must reflect the deliberations and the debate in the conference room without referring to the names of individual judges".

(a) UK Supreme Court

When one looks from the outside at decisions of the UK Supreme Court it strikes one how extensively the Law Lords use the first-person perspective. Sentences like "my reasoning is as follows",[11] "I have come to the same conclusion",[12] or "I would dismiss this appeal"[13] are widespread. Partly, this is due to the fact that the Supreme Court delivers its decisions in individual opinions. Each judge separately states his opinion so that it seems natural to summarize the conclusion with sentences such as, "I would allow the appeal" or "I would dismiss the appeal". The individual judge speaks neither for all judges nor for the whole court. So he cannot use the first person plural and say, for instance, "we dismiss the appeal" or state objectively "appeal dismissed". Other judges might join his opinion but it still remains his. The use of the first-person perspective appears as a consequence of the judge's limited role: he can only deliver his own opinion and, consequently, has to call it "my opinion".

The use of the first-person perspective is not confined, however, to the conclusion or introduction of an opinion. English judges use it to characterize the subject matter as well. For instance, Lord Brown described the recent decision in *Child Poverty Action Group v Secretary of State for Work and Pensions*[14] with the words "I have not found this an altogether easy case... and regard the arguments as 'closely balanced'".[15] Such a statement is not necessary for the conclusion, as Lord Brown himself notes, saying that he would come to the same conclusion as the Court of Appeal.[16] Nevertheless, the expression of his hesitation helps us to understand that the legal arguments for the opposite conclusion had considerable weight and could in slightly different circumstances have justified another conclusion.

By expressing their opinions about particular questions of law in the first person, British judges also preserve the character of an oral[17] dispute. In the above-mentioned decision Brown LJ states, for instance: "I am persuaded that section 71 does indeed necessarily exclude whatever common law restitution rights the Secretary of State might otherwise have".[18] This use of the first-person perspective is not a matter of course as one could say directly, "section 71 does indeed necessarily exclude...". However, such a formulation would omit the personal point of view of the deciding judge. Words like "it seems to me that p" differ from the mere proposition p insofar as they make clear what attitude the deciding judge has. They underline that it is an individual opinion. For instance, the sentence of Lord Roger in the same decision "With some hesitation, therefore, I have come to the conclusion..."[19] could hardly be paraphrased as "I conclude as follows...".

---

[11] *Child Poverty Action Group v Secretary of State for Work and Pensions* [2010] UKSC 54, 12 (Brown LJ).
[12] *Child Poverty Action Group v Secretary of State for Work and Pensions* [2010] UKSC 54, 12 (Brown LJ).
[13] *Child Poverty Action Group v Secretary of State for Work and Pensions* [2010] UKSC 54, 36 (Dyson SCJ).
[14] [2010] UKSC 54. The issue was whether the Secretary of State could recover overpaid social security benefits on the basis of common law remedies or whether the provisions of the Social Security Act are exhaustive.
[15] *Child Poverty Action Group v Secretary of State for Work and Pensions* [2010] UKSC 54, 12 (Brown LJ).
[16] *Child Poverty Action Group v Secretary of State for Work and Pensions* [2010] UKSC 54, 12 (Brown LJ).
[17] To some extent, English decisions preserve the character of orality, see Practice Direction [1963] 1 W.L.R. 1382: "it will always be open to a Lord of Appeal, should he wish to do so, to deliver his opinion orally in the House"; Peter M. Tiersma, 'The Textualization of Precedent' (2007) 82 Notre Dame L. Rev. 1187, 1190–1204; Ross Charnock, 'Traces of Orality in Common Law Judgments' in Davide Simone Giannoni and Celina Frade (eds), *Researching Language and the Law* (Peter Lang, Berne, 2010), 113.
[18] *Child Poverty Action Group v Secretary of State for Work and Pensions* [2010] UKSC 54 [15] (Brown LJ).
[19] *Child Poverty Action Group v Secretary of State for Work and Pensions* [2010] UKSC 54 [39] (Roger SCJ).

This difference between a statement of law and a statement of personal beliefs about the law becomes even more visible when several intermingled beliefs are expressed. In *Child Poverty Action Group* the Supreme Court judge Lord Dyson dealt with arguments of the appellant by saying

> I acknowledge that such arguments might be advanced today, although I doubt that they would succeed even now after considerable developments that have taken place in recent years in this area of law. But it seems to me very unlikely… In my view….[20]

This is a personal acknowledgment constricted by two doubts which in turn are followed by a personal view. At this stage it is not only the law that has to be interpreted, but also the personal beliefs of the judges deciding the case. As we will see later, this is a crucial point, as personal beliefs are less amenable to generalization than impersonal ones.

As with the use of the first-person perspective, English decisions directly refer to opinions of other judges in previous cases instead of merely referring to a particular argument or the whole court in which these judges were acting. In *Child Poverty Action Group* Lord Dyson stated, for instance: "I do not accept the submission that the respondents have to surmount the high hurdle erected by Lord Hutton in *B (A Minor)* or Lord Hobhouse in *Morgan Greenfell.*" Tellingly, Lord Dyson did not refer to a hurdle erected by the House of Lords or a certain decision but instead to a hurdle erected by particular judges, namely Lord Hutton and Lord Hobhouse. Once again the actions of individual judges are the focus,[21] but the institutional background is not explicitly mentioned. It goes without saying that it was only this background that allowed Lord Hutton and Lord Hobhouse to erect a legally relevant hurdle.

In the same way references to the parties and their representatives focus on the person rather than on its function. So the Supreme Court does not stress the abstract role like "the appellant" but prefers a direct reference to a real name: "Mr Eadie QC disputes those conclusions".[22] From the description of the parties at the beginning of each decision one can infer that Mr Eadie in this case represented the appellant. The legal process appears as a conflict of particular persons and not an abstract exchange of ideas. Thus, the use of the first-person perspective appears as a logical consequence.

(b) German Supreme Court

German opinions stand in a sharp contrast to the English ones. Although there is no formal rule prohibiting the use of the first-person perspective,[23] it is rarely found in the opinions of German courts. The avoidance of the first person singular is not surprising, as the Supreme Court delivers a joint opinion. One of the deciding judges prepares a draft, on which all judges in turn consult. Disputes about the outcome and formulations are solved by majority vote.[24] Finally, every judge signs the opinion.[25] Thus, the opinion

---

[20] *Child Poverty Action Group v Secretary of State for Work and Pensions* [2010] UKSC 54 [21] (Dyson SCJ).
[21] Louis Blom-Cooper and Gavin Drewry, *Final Appeal* (Clarendon Press, Oxford, 1972), 79: "individuality remains the essential characteristic of the English judicial function".
[22] *Child Poverty Action Group v Secretary of State for Work and Pensions* [2010] UKSC 54 [10] (Brown LJ).
[23] The Code of Civil Procedure ("Zivilprozessordnung") para.313 s.1(6) requires that the reasons for the decision be given, but does not state how this should be done.
[24] Judicature Act ("Gerichtsverfassungsgesetz") para.194 s.2.
[25] Code of Civil Procedure ("Zivilprozessordnung") para.315; see, however, Arthur Jacobson, 'Publishing Dissent' [2005] 62 *Washington & Lee Law Review* 1607, 1609, 1633: "common law, by forcing judges to sign opinions, celebrates them as individuals".

comes from the whole court and is "per curiam", but is nevertheless neither anonymous nor necessarily unanimous.[26] Because of this joint character the judges cannot use the first person singular and say "I" or "my conclusion".

The joint character of the decisions, however, does not totally explain the avoidance of the first-person perspective. For even when judges reach a decision as an individual judge, they abstain from using the first person singular. Thus, when a single judge decides in lower courts he is likely to refrain from using "I", "me", or other personal expressions. As is the practice of the Supreme Court, he would rather talk about "the court" that has considered a case or reached a decision. Only in oral conversations at trial do judges use expressions like "I am not convinced..." or "We preliminarily think about the questions the following...". It seems awkward to say "the court" when it is, basically, just the speaker. Orally the conversation is less artificial so that judges speak in ordinary language where the first-person perspective dominates. But as soon as they formulate the decision in a written form, the first person disappears from sight.

This disappearance is the more remarkable as it would be possible to express the joint character of a decision by the use of the first person plural. Judges could, for instance, say "we think" or "we believe". By these expressions they would underline that a group of judges decides the case and that the opinion is a result of a collective decision-making process.[27] The Supreme Court of Israel, for instance, takes this approach and uses the first person plural. In *Ajuri v IDF Commander in the W. Bank* it said, for instance: "We do not replace the security considerations of the military commander's..." and "We do not adopt any position with regard to the manner in which security matters are conducted".[28] In contrast, the German Supreme Court would in such a case use the third-person perspective instead and formulate these ideas using expressions like "It is not the task of the court to replace the military commander's security considerations..." or "The court does not take any position with regard to the manner...".[29]

In order to avoid the first-person perspective German courts use a variety of linguistic devices. First, they refrain from using introductory remarks like "our reasoning is as follows",[30] "we think that..." or "we are convinced that...". Rather, they directly formulate the statement under the heading "reasoning". Personal expressions are avoided, which in part is due to the requirement to make the statement of reasoning "as short as possible".[31] It seems necessary and sufficient to state the impersonal argument, and the personal attitude towards it is regarded as superfluous. Hence it is unnecessary to stress in a first-person statement that the court believes in what it says. This requirement of brevity does not mean that judges shall not declare the reasons for their decisions fully.

---

[26] The anonymity of the decisions in "continental" courts is frequently assumed, e.g. Frank Easterbrook, 'Ways of Criticizing the Court' (1982) 95 *Harvard Law Review* 802, 810; Ginsburg, 'Remarks on writing separately' (cited in n.7), 134, 138 "anonymity and unanimity go together"; Todd Henderson, 'From Seriatim to Consensus and Back Again: A Theory of Dissent' [2007] *Supreme Court Review* 283, 291.

[27] Alternatively, the "we" might mean a collective of the judge and the reader, for instance, *Bush v Orleans Parish School Bd.* [1956] 138 F. Supp. 337, 342 (Judge Skelly Wright): "we are, all of us, freeborn Americans..."; for the importance of the "we" in building an identity see Johannes Helmbrecht, 'Grammar and Function of We' in Anna Duszak, *Us and others: social identities across languages, discourses and cultures* (John Benjamins, Amsterdam, 2002), 31, 44. Sometimes "we" is used by an individual trial judge in his opinion, e.g. *Kratz v Kratz*, [1979] 477 F. Supp. 463, 465 (Chief Justice Lord).

[28] *Ajuri et al. v IDF Commander in the W. Bank et al.* [2002] IsrLR 24, H.C. 7015/02.

[29] Similarly in opinions "of the court" in the US Supreme Court, see Barbara Ann Perry, *The Priestly Tribe: the Supreme Court's Image in the American Mind* (cited in n.10), 12, 56.

[30] As already noted in n.10.

[31] Internal Rules of Procedure of the German Supreme Court ("Geschaeftsordnung des BGH") para.13.

Indeed, they are obliged to state them.[32] Thus, opinions in complicated cases can extend to one hundred pages and more.[33] But even then, the written judgments shall entail just the reasons on which the decision rests[34] and nothing more. In this regard, the crucial point is that the reason for a decision is not the fact that the judges think in a particular way, but that there are generalizable reasons why they think so. So, the judges state these reasons without saying that it is they who think so. In this perspective it adds nothing to the argument when the courts introduce their reasons with remarks like, "Our reasoning is…" or "We think…". Such formulations are omitted for the sake of brevity.

In many cases, however, the avoidance of the first-person perspective is motivated not by brevity but rather by the attempt to state the reasons objectively. At least on a linguistic level, the courts claim that everybody should come to the same conclusion. So they say, for instance, "there is no reason"[35] instead of "we do not see a reason"; "it is not discernible"[36] instead of "we do not understand why" or "there is no evidence"[37] instead of "no evidence was presented to us…". These formulations give the impression that the decision rests not just on the opinion of the deciding judges but on objective reasons everybody must agree with. In contrast, the use of the first-person perspective appears as a humbler way to express what one thinks. It preserves the notion that, possibly, other judges would decide differently.

Especially interesting is, therefore, the avoidance of the first-person perspective in situations in which the courts have to position themselves in a controversial debate. In such circumstances, the courts cannot avoid the impression that there are several positions one could reasonably argue for. So they have to make clear which position among the competing views they take. The most natural way to do that would be to characterize their own opinion with a personal pronoun as "our opinion" or "our position". Interestingly, the German courts avoid this and prefer an institutional reference to themselves as, for instance, "according to the opinion of the panel".[38] The same holds for the citation of previous decisions. Rather than saying "as we already have decided in the case c", German courts use expressions like "as the panel has already decided in the case c". The first-person perspective is replaced by the third-person perspective, and the panel becomes the acting person. Judges formulate the decision as if they were reporting from the outside about somebody who had reached a certain decision. The use of third-person statements means that there is linguistically no difference between the courts speaking about their own position and another person describing what they did. Only the heading and the signature make clear that it is not an external report.

This avoidance of the first-person perspective is related, at least in part, to the procedural rules of decision-making. When the judges disagree about an issue and cannot reach a unanimous decision, the controversy is solved by voting.[39] In these cases only a majority of judges support the decision. Nevertheless, all judges including the dissenting ones have to sign it because all of them participated in the decision-making procedure.[40] The signatures are essential to ensure that the result announced is identical to the one

---

[32] cf. Rules of the Code of Civil Procedure ("Zivilprozessordnung") para.313 s.1(6).
[33] e.g. the decision by the German Constitutional Court in *Lissabon* [2009] *Neue Juristische Wochenschrift* 2267 (judgment of 30 June 2009, case number 2 BvE 2/08).
[34] Rules of the Code of Civil Procedure ("Zivilprozessordnung") para.313 s.3.
[35] e.g. Federal Supreme Court [2010] *Neue Juristische Wochenschrift* 3503.
[36] e.g. Federal Supreme Court [2010] *Neue Juristische Wochenschrift* 3503, 3504.
[37] e.g. Federal Supreme Court [2010] *Neue Juristische Wochenschrift* 3503, 3504.
[38] e.g. Federal Supreme Court [2004] *Neue Juristische Wochenschrift* 3188, 3189.
[39] Judicature Act ("Gerichtsverfassungsgesetz") para.194 s.2.
[40] Baumbach/Lauterbach/Albers/Hartmann, *Zivilprozessordnung* (66th edn, C.H. Beck, Munich, 2008), para.315 s.4.

reached after secret voting.[41] As the parties and the public are excluded from the consultation the signatures[42] are needed to ensure the veracity of the decision.

This requirement prevents dissenting judges from making first-person statements because, if they did, they would give the impression of unanimity among themselves. Were they to do so they would have to make a statement which they deny. This would be contrary to their constitutionally guaranteed independence.[43] They could, for instance, not say "we think" when in fact some of them do not think so. Thus, judges merely confirm by their signature that the court adopted a certain position even if they personally disagree with it. It might even happen that the judge who prepared the draft is outvoted by his colleagues. Nevertheless, after the voting he formulates the final version although he disagrees with its content. He can do so without lying by merely reporting in the third person what the court has decided. Doing so does not exclude that he thinks otherwise. The first-person perspective, however, would not be suitable for this purpose.

Theoretically it would be possible to state in such cases, "the majority of us hold the opinion...". However, this publication of internal disagreements between the judges is considered a violation of the secrecy of the consultation process,[44] and is practised only in the Constitutional Court. All other German courts publish neither dissents nor majority opinions but merely "opinions of the court". Understanding that internal dissent must be kept secret makes the use of third-person statements appear necessary. Unlike statements in the first person plural, third-person statements avoid giving a wrong impression of unanimity. They leave open the question of whether there was a dissenting minority and whether some of the signing judges voted for another outcome. For even the dissenting judges can certify by their signature that the court had a certain opinion, although it differed from their own. The opinion of German courts is hence not an explanation of what the *individual* judges believed, but rather a statement of the reasons that were *institutionally* decisive for the judgment.

This institutional character becomes even more visible when one looks at the details of the courts' reasoning. Although the statement is almost always drafted by one individual judge and adopted without major changes, all judges are involved in its final formulation. If there is a disagreement about it, the judges vote about individual parts and, sometimes, even about single sentences. The decision is hence a product of compromise and no judge must necessarily agree with every detail. Different sentences are supported by different majorities. In a panel of five judges it is, according to all mathematical permutations, possible that 16 different majorities support various parts of the decision.[45] So, at least in these cases, the reference to the "the court" instead of the personal pronoun "we" is preferable because only the court is behind the whole reasoning whereas the meaning of "we" changes from sentence to sentence. If the judges were to use "we"

---

[41] Federal Supreme Court [1993] *Neue Juristische Wochenschrift* 2603; Baumbach et al., *Zivilprozessordnung* (cited in n.40), para.315 s.4.

[42] Code of Civil Procedure ("Zivilprozessordnung") para.315 s.1 requires the signature of all judges participating in the decision (regardless of whether they agreed or dissented).

[43] Basic Law Art. 97 s.1. In England it would be regarded as a violation of the judicial oath for an individual judge to be forced to produce a single judgment: Jacobson, 'Publishing Dissent' (cited in n.25), 1607, 1609. cf. Blom-Cooper and Drewry, *Final Appeal* (cited in n.21), 82: "a submergence of his [the judge's] identity in a composite statement would be unthinkable, if not constitutionally improper".

[44] Required by the Judicature Act ("Gerichtsverfassungsgesetz") para.192 s.1. On the debate about the secrecy of the debate in courts see M. Lasser, *Judicial Deliberations* (Oxford University Press, Oxford, 2004), 325.

[45] The following combinations are possible: 1 unanimous opinion, 5 opinions with one judge dissenting, 10 (= 5 × 4 ÷ 2) opinions with two judges dissenting.

throughout the decision they would suggest that all of them supported the decision. The reference to the court instead to a collective "we" avoids this impression of unanimity.

The institutional character is especially strong in the way the Supreme Court refers to itself. Most of the time, it does so by mentioning the panel that reached the decision. It is portrayed as a person that "has already decided..."[46] or "left open"[47] a certain question or says yes and no.[48] At least on a linguistic level, the panel becomes the acting person. It draws conclusions,[49] overrules precedents,[50] and analyses arguments.[51] This personification is especially striking in references to old decisions in which none of the deciding judges participated. Even then the Supreme Court uses statements like "as the panel already decided", "in accordance with the decisions of the panel" or "in the previous decisions of the panel".[52] Nevertheless, these decisions might date back more than 50 years.[53] The panel is supposed to exist independently of the individual judges and to remain constant over time. It is hence not an abbreviated reference to the deciding judges that join or leave it but an institution independent of these people. Even when judges write in their academic work about their own decisions, they usually avoid personal references like "as I decided" or "as my senate stated". Instead they use, like most people, the impersonal third-person perspective.[54] Linguistically, they merely report on the court from the outside although it might have been they who drafted the decision.

As to the avoidance of the first-person perspective, one notable exception exists. Judges in the Constitutional Court are allowed to publish dissenting opinions and do so mostly using the first person perspective.[55] There, one finds sentences like "I would decide differently..." or "in my view...".[56] However, even this underlines the perceived irreconcilability of the first-person perspective with a legal decision. Only if a certain vote is not decisive for the result is the first-person perspective acceptable. Then the judge steps out of the court's collective announcement and becomes, on a linguistic level, a person referring to its own opinion. Despite the simultaneous publication, the dissent is not part of the decision. So, even the dissenting judge has to sign the majority opinion;[57] she or he does not agree with it, but merely confirms that the court has reached it. Once again this makes clear that the decision stems from a certain institution and is not primarily associated with particular judges.

England and Germany represent then, on a linguistic level, radically different approaches: a personal one and an institutional one. Before I come back to the advantages and disadvantages of these traditions it is worth looking at the European Court

---

[46] e.g. German Supreme Court [2010] *Neue Juristische Wochenschrift* 2573, 2575.
[47] e.g. German Supreme Court [2006] *Neue Juristische Wochenschrift* 707.
[48] e.g. German Supreme Court [2010] *Neue Juristische Wochenschrift* 3643.
[49] e.g. German Supreme Court [2011] *Neue Juristische Wochenschrift* 462, 463.
[50] e.g. German Supreme Court [2006] *Neue Juristische Online Zeitung* 1309.
[51] e.g. German Supreme Court [2011] *Neue Juristische Online Zeitung* 139.
[52] e.g. German Supreme Court [2011] *Neue Zeitschrift fuer Verwaltungsrecht* 249.
[53] e.g. the reference of the German Supreme Court, [1993] Neue Juristische Wochenschrift 2535 to a decision of the "same" panel in 1963.
[54] e.g. Karin Milger, 'Mindestanforderungen an die Betriebskostenabrechnung' [2009] *Neue Juristische Wochenschrift* 625, 628; for a contrast see the statement of Israel's Supreme Court President Barak, 'A Judge on Judging' (cited in n.3), 76: 'As I expressed in my own judgments', 91, 102, 131, 151, 162.
[55] e.g. Constitutional Court [1981] *Neue Juristische Wochenschrift* 1943, 1944 (Hirsch dissenting); Constitutional Court [1981] *Neue Juristische Wochenschrift* 1948 (Wand dissenting); Constitutional Court [2011] *Neue Juristische Wochenschrift* 1209 (Schluckebier dissenting).
[56] James Markham, 'Note: Against Individually Signed Judicial Opinions' (2006) 56 *Duke Law Journal* 923, 932 similarly observes for the USA that concurrences and dissents have a more personal nature.
[57] *Bundesverfassungsgerichtsgesetz* para.30 s.1(2). Examples are: order of the Second Senate of 6 July 2010, case number 2 BvR 2661/06 (Landau dissenting); order of the First Senate of 22 February 2011,

of Justice where judges from different backgrounds cooperate, and the various styles of decision-making clash with each other.

(c) European Court of Justice

The European Court of Justice (ECJ) delivers a joint opinion. In this regard it resembles other continental courts. The judges do not publish separate, concurring, or dissenting votes. Therefore, one cannot tell whether there was disagreement among them. The ECJ uses an abbreviated style of explanation which leaves open a detailed account of the reasons for its decisions. This can be traced in part back to the French tradition[58] which was, especially in the first years of the ECJ, dominant. In addition, the brevity of the decision is also due to the difficulties in formulating a compromise in a multilingual court. The same formulations have been used over and over again since they were agreed upon and translated into various languages. New formulations for the same idea would be regarded as too cumbersome for the multi-lingual machinery. They would have to be agreed upon and translated, and this might cause confusion, because of disparities in the way different languages use certain concepts. For these reasons the opinions of the ECJ avoid the first-person perspective.[59] Its judges do not say "we" and instead use impersonal expressions like "it must be stated",[60] "it follows",[61] "it is necessary to determine",[62] or "the question must be examined".[63] In the same way the ECJ abstains from using personal introductions like "our reasoning is as follows" and uses instead an impersonal expression like "grounds for judgment"[64] or merely "judgment".[65]

Similarly, the ECJ refers to previous decisions by citing decisions of the whole court and not by citing the opinions of particular judges. So it uses sentences like "The Court has consistently held"[66] or "the Court stated..."[67] instead of expressions like "as we said in..." or "as judges x, y, z stated in...". In this regard there is hardly any difference between the court talking about itself and somebody else talking about it. It is as if the court is unable to speak, and only somebody else can report on it. Once again the institution is the focus and not the individual judge. The published reasons are those of the whole court, whoever participated in making them. The judges discuss the reasons and vote about the wording.[68] This is done on a "point-by-point basis"[69] so that the majority

---

case number 1 BvR 699/06 (Schluckebier and Eichberger dissenting); order of 15 January 2009, case number 2 BvR 2044/07 (Vosskuhle, Osterloh, Di Fabio, and Gerhardt dissenting).

[58] Lasser, *Judicial Deliberations* (cited in n.44), 203, 315.

[59] Advocates General, however, use the first-person perspective extensively, e.g. AG Van Gerven in Case C-267/91 and C-268/91 *Keck and Mithouard* [1993] ECR I-6097; see Lasser, *Judicial Deliberations* (cited in n.44), 132.

[60] e.g. Case C-239/90 *SCP Boscher, Studer et Fromentin v. SA British Motors Wright and Others* [1991] ECR I-2034, para.10.

[61] e.g. Case C-237/02 *Freiburger Kommunalbauten GmbH Baugesellschaft & Co. KG v Ludger Hofstteller and Ulrike Hofstter* [2004] ECR I-3412, para.22.

[62] e.g. Case C-239/90 *SCP Boscher, Studer et Fromentin v. SA British Motors Wright and Others* [1991] ECR I-2034 para.17.

[63] e.g. Case 192-73 *Van Zuylen freres v Hag AG* [1974] ECR 731, para.5.

[64] e.g. Case 6/64 *Costa v Enel* [1964] ECR 585.

[65] e.g. Case C-267/91 and C-268/91 *Keck and Mithouard* [1993] ECR I-6126.

[66] e.g. Case C-239/90 *SCP Boscher, Studer et Fromentin v. SA British Motors Wright and Others* [1991] I-2034, para.14.

[67] e.g. Case C-239/90 *SCP Boscher, Studer et Fromentin v SA British Motors Wright and Others* [1991] I-2034, para.14.

[68] Alastair Sutton, 'The European Court of Justice (ECJ) after enlargement, Informal views of a new Member State judge in the ECJ', Memorandum, 01/09/2009 (on file with the author), 3.

[69] Alastair Sutton, 'The European Court of Justice (ECJ) after enlargement' (cited in n.68), 3.

can vary from sentence to sentence. As in German decisions, the use of "we" would, therefore, be misleading as the "we" in the ECJ would ignore possible dissent within the court. The "we" is not a natural entity of several persons but rather an institutional entity composed of different persons at different times.

Because of the use of this impersonal style the court appears to be an institution continuing to exist during all the decisions and not as a plurality of particular judges that come and go. In the *Keck* decision, for instance, the ECJ said, "the Court considers it necessary to re-examine and clarify its case-law".[70] It then referred[71] to its *Dassonville* judgment[72] that dated back nearly 20 years, when completely different judges made up the court. Nevertheless, the court regarded this decision as part of "its case-law". Instead of a reference by a current group of judges to the opinion of a once-existing group of judges, the court stressed that it is still the same institution as before. It would have been artificial to say "as we decided 20 years ago" because none of the judges in the *Keck* decision participated in the *Dassonville* judgment. The avoidance of the first-person perspective allows the court to treat all decisions as coming from the same institution and helps to build institutional unity over time. In this regard, the differences between the judges seem not to matter. It is no coincidence that the ECJ and not its judges are celebrated as "the engine of integration".[73] Although this is due to the actions of particular judges at certain points of time, one cannot celebrate them individually as "public heroes" as it is impossible to trace back particular important decisions to particular judges. So the whole court appears as the person one has to praise or blame. The public does not even know which judges were decisive in a certain outcome. It knows which judges participated in a decision, but not which position each of them took.

One further factor contributing to the avoidance of the first-person perspective in ECJ opinions is the lack of reference to the academic debate. As with the English decisions and in contrast to the German ones the ECJ very rarely cites scholars.[74] Its reasoning appears to be detached from the discourse outside the court. As a consequence, the ECJ does not explicitly position itself within a plurality of opinions. Its reasoning is the only one mentioned. The necessity for the use of personal pronouns in expressions like "our view" or "the position of the court" is less than if the court were to participate more directly in the public debate, for only then would it have to distinguish between its own position and various competing ones.

3. Transformations of personal and impersonal expressions

(a) Personalization and depersonalization

In view of the contrast between the UK Supreme Court and the other courts discussed earlier, the question emerges whether the use of the first person is a matter of content or a matter of style. Can one express the same legal reasons independent of whether or

---

[70] Case C-267/91 and C-268/91 *Keck and Mithouard* [1993] ECR I-6126, para.14.
[71] Case C-267/91 and C-268/91 *Keck and Mithouard* [1993] ECR I-6126., para.16.
[72] Case 8/74 *Procureur du Roi v Benoit and Gustave Dassonville* [1974] ECR 837.
[73] Mikael Rask Madsen, 'Introduction: An Ever Closer Union—An Ever Larger Market' in Hanne Petersen et al. (eds), *Paradoxes of European legal integration* (Ashgate, Aldershot, 2008), 67, 70.
[74] Lasser, *Judicial Deliberations* (cited in n.44), 107; in contrast, the Advocates General refer to this debate, e.g. the opinion of AG Van Gerven in Case C-267/91 and C-268/91 *Keck and Mithouard* [1993] ECR I-6097, n.16; see Lasser, *Judicial Deliberations* (cited in n.44), 122.

not one uses the first-person perspective? This would be the case if one could transform personal expressions in the first person into impersonal ones.

In many cases this seems to be possible. If a court utters a statement *s*, one can infer that the court thinks *s*. For the author usually implies the truth of his statement.[75] Because of this condition of truthfulness one can, in principle, infer from an impersonal statement a personal one. It is enough that a court utters it. I will call this transformation of an impersonal statement into a personal one "personalization". So even if a court avoids the first-person perspective, the statement still stems from him and can hence be understood as what, at a minimum, most of the court's judges thought. They are mentioned in the heading and sign the decision. Even if the decision is made anonymously one can attribute the statement to the court.[76] This attribution of impersonal statements to the speaker has been discussed by various philosophers for a long time. Most notably, it underlies Kant's statement, "The 'I think' must be able to accompany all my representations".[77] Kant argues that if one could not say "I think" a sentence could either not be thought at all or would, at least, not mean anything for oneself.[78] The reason for this is that there are no abstract thoughts but only the thoughts of particular persons. So if there is a thought it could be traced back to the person who had it. Similarly, one could argue that it does not make a difference at the semantic level whether one states a proposition *p* and thereby implies that one thinks *p*, or whether one explicitly uses the personal statement "I think *p*". With this transformation it appears more a matter of style than a matter of content to use the first-person perspective.

The opposite process is the transformation of personal statements into impersonal ones ("depersonalization"). Such transformation is possible for the same reasons as for the process of personalization. Propositional attitudes like "I think" or "I believe" are already implied in the fact that a certain speaker utters the statement. Hence the statement *s* of the person *p* "I think *s*" is, as far as its content is concerned, equivalent to the statement "Person *p* says: *s*". Of course, one could not deduct from this statement the fact *s*, but for the speaker it is not necessary to use the first-person perspective explicitly and to say "I think *s*" rather than "*s*". For the utterance of the statement itself makes sufficiently clear that *s* is the opinion of the speaker, although not necessarily a fact. So if the decisions of the court are to be as short as possible it seems natural to avoid personal introductions like "the issue before us is..." instead of "the issue is..." or "my reasoning is as follows"[79] instead of the mere heading "reasoning".

Some have argued that legal sentences containing a direct reference to the speaker and the audience have increasingly been replaced over time by impersonal expressions. As these are expressed in the passive voice, personal references can just be deduced from the context.[80] Direct commands from one person to another, such as "I order you to *o*"

---

[75] cf. J.L. Austin, *How to Do Things With Words* (cited in n.9), 48.
[76] Anonymity and unanimity do not necessarily go together, as Ginsburg suggests, in 'Remarks on writing separately' (cited in n.7), 138. The decisions of the German Supreme Court and Constitutional Court, for instance, are frequently unanimous but never anonymous, as discussed in n.25 and associated text.
[77] Immanuel Kant, *Kritik der reinen Vernunft*, vol. III (2nd edn, de Gruyter, Berlin, 1968; first published 1787, Akademie Textausgabe), 131.
[78] Kant, *Kritik der reinen Vernunft* (cited in n.77).
[79] e.g. *Child Poverty Action Group v Secretary of State for Work and Pensions* [2010] UKSC 54 [12] (Brown LJ).
[80] Goldman, 'Book Review of Peter M. Tiersma, Legal Language' (cited in n.6), 724; Tarja Salmi-Tolonen, 'Persuasion in Judicial Argumentation' in Helena Halmari and Tuija Virtanen (eds), *Persuasion Across Genres* (John Benjamins, Amsterdam, 2005), 59, 90; Peter von Polenz, *Deutsche Semantik* (3rd edn, de Gruyter, Berlin, 2008), 34.

became rules like "One has to *o*", which mention neither the author nor the addressee. The personal relations behind the statements vanish. In court decisions, however, the picture seems to be more complicated, and waves of more or less personalized statements in legal decisions come and go.[81] There is no reason to assume that the English approach is just a remnant from a tradition stressing the privileges of the Law Lords, and that there is no current justification. At least at first glance, the contrasts in the way opinions are formulated correspond to the different roles the judges play. The focus on the judge rather than the court corresponds to the centrality of his attitude for the outcome of the cases. But then the question emerges, why do some courts use the first-person perspective explicitly and others not? Is not the judge decisive in both cases? Are there reasons for these different traditions or is it merely a matter of style?

(b) Performative acts

A compelling reason to use the first-person perspective would be that it is necessary to express certain ideas. So it seems worthwhile to look for personal statements that cannot, without loss of content, be transformed into impersonal ones. Performative utterances are one such candidate. According to the seminal analysis of John Searle, performative utterances do not describe or report something.[82] Rather, they are part of the action.[83] Prominent examples are "I promise you...", "I baptize you...", or "I declare you wife and husband". According to Austin, verdictive sentences like "I hold..." or ""I find in favour of..."[84] in legal utterances belong to the same class. He even refers to "operative" sentences of lawyers in order to explain performative utterances in general.[85] The use of the first person singular in these sentences is not accidental. Austin claims that

> any utterance which is in fact a performative should be reducible, or expandable, or analysable into a form, or reproducible in a form, with a verb in the first person singular indicative active.[86]

His argument seems to be that a performative act presupposes an actor. If this performance is carried out by speaking, the actor must be the speaker.[87] Otherwise one would only report about somebody else's action and not perform it oneself. So, performative statements have to use the first person singular. According to this theory, legal decisions cannot contain performative statements unless they are transformable into sentences using the first person singular.

This conclusion, however, is premature. Performative statements might indeed be formulated with the first person singular. But this is not necessarily the case. One can also use the first person plural and make statements like "we hold", "we overrule", or "we confirm". Insofar as performative acts are concerned, there seems to be no difference between statements in the first person singular and those in the first person plural. If only a particular body of persons has a certain competence, then individual persons cannot perform an action which is reserved for that body. In such a case, they have to act

---

[81] See, for instance, the changes in the USA where John Marshall introduced an "opinion of the court" but the court nowadays prefers seriatim opinions, Ginsburg, 'Remarks on writing separately' (cited in n.7) 135; Henderson, 'From Seriatim to Consensus and Back Again' (cited in n.26), 283. For the Privy Council in Britain, Blom-Cooper and Drewry, *Final Appeal* (cited in n.21), 83.
[82] J.L. Austin, *How to Do Things With Words* (cited in n.9), 5.
[83] Austin, *How to Do Things With Words* (cited in n.9), 5.
[84] Austin, *How to Do Things With Words* (cited in n.9), 153.
[85] Austin, *How to Do Things With Words* (cited in n.9), 7.
[86] Austin, *How to Do Things With Words* (cited in n.9), 62.
[87] cf. Helmbrecht, 'Grammar and Function of We' (cited in n.27), 32.

on behalf of the body. For this reason, performative statements in the first person plural are not necessarily transformable into performative ones in the first person singular. The individual judge does not necessarily have the competence to say "I hold...", as this action might be preserved for the whole court. So the use of the first-person perspective depends upon whose competence it is to perform a certain action.

Moreover, the use of a first-person perspective is altogether avoidable. There is no necessity for a court to use first-person statements at all. As an institution, it cannot speak for itself but needs persons to act on its behalf. It is a matter of convention and institutional design by which individual acts are attributed to it. There is no reason why only first-person statements can be used for that purpose.[88] It is possible for performative sentences in a legal decision to be expressed in the third person, as in "the court hereby decides that...". The "hereby" is a clear sign that one is dealing with a performative utterance.[89] Nevertheless, the sentence cannot be transformed into a first-person statement as the court is by convention an institution unable to talk for itself. Its personification as an acting institution does not have to go so far as to attribute a personal voice to it. It is sufficient that individual utterances in the third person are imputed to it and that these utterances are considered as its actions. The necessary coincidence of the speech and the action is then realized not by first-person statements of the actor but by third-person statements about the court.

Ironically, some first-person statements in legal decisions are even used to avoid performative acts. Propositional attitudes in legal opinions like "I think s" or "I believe s" prevent the impression being given that the statement s is indisputably a legal rule or principle. The use of the first person stresses that s is "just" the opinion of the deciding judge and not a commonly agreed upon legal statement. Because of its formulation in the first person it has a lower precedential value than the unrestrained statement s. This necessity to restrain statements arises only because the utterance of the opinion in a legal decision is a performance that gives the uttered statements a special status. It becomes an authority to which one can later refer. This authority rests on the fact that the statement is uttered by a judge in a certain decision. Before such an occurrence in a legal decision, it is a mere opinion. In this sense any utterance in a legal decision is, in Searle's terminology, a performance through which the uttered statement changes its status. At least in precedent-based legal systems, the judge does not merely report what the law is, but rather makes a statement the law. The first-person perspective serves partially to restrict the importance of his statements.

When quoted in a latter decision, the statement preserves the notion of being a personal opinion and not a generally accepted rule. This explains why legal systems without a formal doctrine of *stare decisis* are less likely to use the first-person perspective. They do not have to confine the statements in a legal decision because these statements have no precedential authority anyway. In contrast, the widespread use of personal statements in English decisions corresponds with a comparatively strict[90] doctrine of *stare decisis*. These statements are one of many means to reduce the impact of the published opinion. Because of the expression in them of hesitations or other personal attitudes, they can hardly be generalized.[91] From the fact that a certain judge doubts proposition p_1 it does

---

[88] cf. Norman Fairclough, *Analysing discourse: textual analysis for social research* (Routledge, New York, 2003) p 117.
[89] J.L. Austin, *How to Do Things With Words* (cited in n.9), 57.
[90] cf. Neil Duxbury, *The Nature and Authority of Precedent* (Cambridge University Press, Cambridge, 2008), 31–57.
[91] Similarly, dissents are traditionally considered as being necessary to prevent precedents that are too strong, see, e.g., Thomas Jefferson, in Merrill Peterson (ed.), *The political writings of Thomas Jefferson* (University of North Carolina Press, North Carolina, 1993), 200.

not follow that he also doubts proposition p_2 although both p_1 and p_2 have the same properties.

For these reasons, performative acts in legal decisions do not require the use of the first-person perspective. They might be carried out by other means, such as third-person statements. First-person statements might even be used to avoid those performances. Hence performative acts cannot explain why the first-person perspective is used in some, but not all decisions.

(c) Non-deductive moral arguments

The avoidance of the first-person perspective in legal decisions creates, at first glance, the impression that who the deciding judges are, and what their personal beliefs are, do not play a role. The impersonal statements are reminiscent of a formalist ideology that denies the judge any discretion.[92] In contrast, decisions using the first-person perspective seem to reflect the crucial role the judges play and to make the role of their beliefs explicit. Is the first-person perspective then necessary when a legal decision cannot be reached by a simple deduction and when the judge becomes more than the "mouthpiece of the law"? Is it unavoidable if non-deductive moral arguments stand behind a judgment?

The answer to this question depends on whether non-deductive arguments might be formulated without using the first-person perspective. Most prominent among these arguments are the ones that refer either to general legal principles or to moral reasons. Although there is great dispute as to the precise nature of these principles and reasons,[93] it seems clear that this is more than the mere opinion of the speaker. For a statement can only serve as a reason for a legal proposition if it refers to something other than the fact that the speaker believes in it. Otherwise the decision becomes arbitrary. For a different opinion it would in such a case suffice that another judge thinks otherwise. There would be no reason why she or he should explain the decision. If there were no reasons for legal propositions apart from the fact that a certain judge is convinced of them, it would be a mystery why she or he would write an opinion at all and try to convince the audience. The whole point of arguing is that the speaker provides reasons that do not depend upon him- or herself. Therefore, non-deductive arguments do not presuppose the use of the first-person perspective. Their argumentative force does not rest on the speaker.

Consequently, legal arguments can in general be directly formulated without the addition that a certain judge is persuaded by them. Instead of saying, for instance, "I believe that consistency and justice require in this case that...", the judge can state "it must be accepted, on grounds of consistency and justice, that...". This is what the ECJ recently said in *Ocalan v Council of the European Union*.[94] In doing so, it used a non-deductive argument without taking the first-person perspective. The reference to justice makes clear that the ECJ judges do not act as mere mouthpieces of the law. One might still prefer the first-person perspective because of its humbler and less pretentious style. However, the argument then is not that non-deductive arguments like the

---

[92] Montesquieu, *The Spirit of Laws* (cited in n.4). Some formalists, however, stressed the discretion of Judges, e.g. Kelsen, *Reine Rechtslehre* (cited in n.3), 350.

[93] See, on the one hand, Dworkin, *Law's Empire* (cited in n.2), and, on the other, Kennedy, *A Critique of Adjudication* (cited in n.3), 135.

[94] *Osman Ocalan, on behalf of the Kurdistan Workers' Party (PKK)/Serif Vanly, on behalf of the Kurdistan National Congress (KNK) v Council of the European Union*, Case C-229/05 P [2007] ECR 2007 I-439, para.112.

reference to general principles and moral arguments can only be expressed in the first person, but rather that they could *better* be expressed in it.

Even the latter claim is far from obvious. Certainly, the impersonal style avoiding the first-person perspective *might* be used to "portray the result demanded by the law as inexorable",[95] although a different result would also be compatible with the already established legal arguments. The avoidance of the first-person perspective in passive sentences can thus be used to create an image of a rigorous implementation of norms.[96] Nevertheless, this is not the necessary consequence of impersonal statements. They might also express doubts about the outcome of a decision or a certain argument. For instance, instead of saying, as does the ECJ, "it must be accepted, on grounds of consistency and justice, that...", one could more cautiously say, "It is not clear what the law demands in this case. Consistency and justice suggest that...". In this case one would avoid the first-person perspective and still express one's doubts about the law. The avoidance of the first-person perspective is hence not necessarily connected with the claim of objectivity and necessity. The first-person perspective might even hamper the discussion of non-deductive reasons. For it presupposes that one formulates, besides the impersonal reason r, a propositional attitude such as "I think that..." or "I am convinced that...". These attitudes are superfluous, as far as the argumentative force of r is concerned. One can omit them without loss of argument. This helps one to focus on generalizable reasons justifying a decision. If there is to be a "government of law, not of men",[97] it is these reasons that are decisive and not the fact that judges are convinced of them.

The importance of impersonal reasons can also be seen in English decisions. Their first-person statements almost exclusively refer to reasons independent of the deciding judges. For instance, Lord Dyson, in the passage quoted earlier did not simply express his hesitations but also referred to the "developments that have taken place in recent years in this area of law."[98] So his personal impression was neither for the conclusion nor for the hesitations decisive. Hence, the widespread use of the first-person perspective does not correspond with justifications that merely refer to the opinion of the judges. Rather, the first-person perspective is the way in which judges express reasons independent of themselves.[99] This is also apparent when one considers the fact that judges in other courts and countries could, without loss of content, use the same reasons. If they cite an English decision without precedential weight they refer to the reasons for it and not merely to the fact that certain judges stated them. Otherwise they could not employ the same argument. The generalizability of reasons expressed in the first-person perspective shows that they can be transformed into impersonal statements.

Thus, the necessity to use non-deductive moral arguments does not require the use of the first-person perspective. They can be expressed by impersonal statements as well.

---

[95] Ginsburg, 'Remarks on writing separately' (cited in n.7), 134 for "most civil law systems".
[96] cf. von Polenz, *Deutsche Semantik* (cited in n.80), 186.
[97] For the consequence of the separation of powers, see the Constitution of the Commonwealth of Massachusetts art.XXX (1780).
[98] Passage quoted at n.20: *Child Poverty Action Group v Secretary of State for Work and Pensions* [2010] UKSC 54 [21] (Dyson SCJ).
[99] Cf. Duxbury, *The Nature and Authority of Precedent* (cited in n.90), 58; see also Barak, 'A Judge on Judging' (cited in n.3): "the judge gives expression not to his or her own beliefs but to the deep, underlying beliefs of society. The key concept is judicial objectivity."

4. The limited reducibility of the first-person perspective

(a) Expression of personal attitudes

Once it becomes clear that neither performative acts nor non-deductive moral arguments are necessarily produced in the first-person perspective, the question becomes, why is it nevertheless used in many legal decisions? Intuitively it makes a difference whether a judge states "I believe p" or whether he says p. The difference between these statements does not lie in the proposition p but in the propositional attitude of the judge formulating it. This attitude deserves closer attention.

The ordinary case of a judge's propositional attitude is that he thinks, believes, or holds a proposition p. These attitudes embrace p. Their expression is redundant, as propositions are in normal circumstances uttered under the condition of truthfulness. Therefore, transformations of personal statements into impersonal ones and vice versa are possible. However, the judge can have many other attitudes apart from thinking or believing p. He can assume p, hesitantly adopt p, suppose p, etc. These propositional attitudes are different from thinking or believing and not inferable from the statement p. Hence they contain additional information. Although one might formulate doubts in an impersonal way, as in "It is doubtful whether p", one can hardly express personal doubts by impersonal statements. There is a difference between "objective doubts" and personal doubt about p. The former is a property of p or the situation in which p is uttered, the latter a property of the speaker. Hence, there is a difference between saying "*I* doubt that p" and saying "*It is* doubtful that p". In the latter case there must be some impersonal reason why p is doubtful. On the other hand, the sentence "I doubt that p" is true if and only if the speaker doubts. He does not need to have a reason for that.[100] So one can say without contradiction that "All evidence demands the conclusion c. Nevertheless, I doubt that c". On the other hand, it would be implausible to state: "All evidence demands c. Nevertheless, c is doubtful."

This difference between a personal attitude and impersonal reasons for it is especially important for the development of the law and hence for the core activity of judges in the supreme courts. Judges often have a certain intuition but are initially unable to provide reasons for it.[101] In such cases, they might join a majority but still express a hesitation about the position adopted. This hesitation might reveal itself in later decisions and become more powerful, for newly developed reasons. Savigny even maintained that the whole of the law is based on such unconscious processes that manifest themselves in decisions, rules, and finally statutes.[102] Be that as it may, hardly anybody would claim that legal developments rest exclusively on reasons that are from the outset explicit. The very condition of innovation is that something is developed which was not there before. Some ideas and rules need time to reveal themselves; the discussion is enriched when there is room to express intuitions, doubts, inclinations, etc. It is possible that only a future judge will be able to formulate these ideas in a systematic and generalizable way. When doubts are expressed earlier on he can build on them to justify his position.

---

[100] cf. *Bernheimer v Converse* [1907] 206 U.S. 516, 535 (Justice Holmes): "under the circumstances, I shall say no more than that I doubt the result."

[101] Blom-Cooper and Drewry, *Final Appeal* (cited in n.21), 79; Frank Easterbrook, 'Ways of Criticizing the Court' (1982) 95 *Harvard Law Review* 802, 807. High justificatory burdens might, therefore, hamper debates about fairness and substantive justice: Lasser, *Judicial Deliberations* (cited in n.44), 346.

[102] Friedrich Carl von Savigny, *System des heutigen Roemischen Rechts*, Vol. 1 (Veit and Comp., Berlin, 1840), 14.

Therefore it is an advantage for judges to express their personal intuitions about a legal question without being forced to formulate them immediately in an impersonal statement and to provide generalizable reasons for them. Otherwise they would be forced either to take a stronger position than they initially believed or to abstain from stating it altogether. For instance, the statement by Lord Brown mentioned earlier, "I have not found this an altogether easy case...and regard the arguments as 'closely balanced'",[103] cannot be totally transformed into an impersonal statement. For generalizable reasons, not every case that Lord Brown considers difficult has indeed to be difficult. He does not even have to think that after careful consideration any other judge would come to the same conclusion. It suffices that in his judgment he was not sure at the time of the decision. Were he allowed to express his opinion only with impersonal statements, he would have to omit his hesitation entirely. Or he would have to say more than he maintained by making an unrestrained impersonal statement such as "This is not an altogether easy case...the arguments are 'closely balanced'". By such a statement he would characterize the case and not his personal attitude towards it. The difference can be seen when he later changes his mind and becomes more convinced of the argued-for position. In the first-person perspective he could express this change without difficulty and say, "Once I found this a not altogether easy case. Now, however, I am convinced that...". On the other hand, he could hardly describe this process by making impersonal statements. For he would have to say something like, "This is an easy case. The former position that it is a difficult one is wrong...". This would not describe the development of the judge's opinion. To account for his initial uncertainty a personal perspective is unavoidable.

It is precisely for this reason that one can find very few accounts of the personal difficulties encountered in reaching a certain conclusion in the judgments of the ECJ or the German Supreme Court.[104] The judges in these courts are not necessarily committed to another ideology than the English judges. They also have hesitations and doubts about the positions adopted. In part, they might not want these doubts to become public because they assume that this would diminish the authority and reputation of the court.[105] Most importantly, however, is the fact that the impersonal style of opinion writing does not in principle allow them to express these doubts. The judges simply lack the means to make their personal doubts public.[106] The procedural rules requiring a joint decision by the court prevent any such announcements of doubts. Although McLuhan's slogan "The Medium is the Message"[107] seems much exaggerated, the medium of impersonal legal opinions certainly has an impact on the content of these opinions.

---

[103] At n.15: *Child Poverty Action Group v Secretary of State for Work and Pensions* [2010] UKSC 54 [12] (Brown LJ).

[104] Cf. Hein Koetz, *Die Begruendung hoechstrichterlicher Urteile* (Kluwer, Deventer, 1982), 16; Tiersma, 'The Textualization of Precedent' (cited in n.17), 1252 observes that the US Supreme Court increasingly avoids references to personal attitudes like "we think" and prefers instead expressions like "we hold".

[105] For this reason John Marshall, following Edmund Pendleton, abolished the practice of writing seriatim opinions in the US Supreme Court, see Jean Edward Smith, *John Marshall: Definer of a Nation* (Henry Holt and Co., New York, 1996), 293; similarly, Justice Brandeis did not publish some of his dissents: Markham, 'Against Individually Signed Judicial Opinions' (cited in n.56), 933. See further Jacobson, 'Publishing Dissent' (cited in n.25), 1607, 1611; Vlad Perju, 'Reason and Authority in the European Court of Justice' (2009) 49 *Virginia Journal of International Law* 307, 350.

[106] Koetz, *Die Begruendung hoechstrichterlicher Urteile* (cited in n.104), 15 explains the more personal style of English decisions as deriving from the previous career of judges as lawyers and from their social prestige.

[107] Marshall McLuhan, *The Medium is the Massage* (first published 1967, Penguin Books, London, 2008).

Interestingly, this conclusion does not depend upon the much-discussed question of whether judges should be allowed to publish a dissenting vote.[108] For even if they are allowed to do so, the question remains, how does the majority formulate its position? If it has to deliver a joint opinion, personal hesitations on the part of individual judges disappear from sight. They vary from judge to judge and are not a suitable subject for collective reasoning. So one cannot know with what degree of certainty the majority adopted its position. In this regard the opinions of the European Court of Human Rights (ECtHR) do not differ from those of the ECJ. Although only the ECtHR allows dissenting votes, both have to formulate their opinions in an impersonal style. So they lack the means to express the hesitations of particular judges. On a practical level, the propositional attitudes of the judges can only be given in individual opinions. Only in theory would it be possible to report in a joint opinion the personal doubts of each of the judges, one by one. For this reason, dissents formulated in the first-person perspective can say more than the majority, which is confined to the use of impersonal statements.

(b) Differences between the judges' official and private role

When judges announce their decision they act as officials. At the same time they are citizens who have an opinion about a variety of political and social issues. These opinions are sometimes, but not always, relevant in a legal decision. If the law is clear it does not matter what the judges think about it. But even then they might want to describe the difference between their official role as judges and their private role as citizens to make clear that they act as judges and are for certain legal reasons compelled to reach a particular decision.[109] Stressing that they disagree with the law might even make their judgment more compelling because it shows that the decision does not rest exclusively on a private opinion. To describe this difference, one has as to use the first-person perspective. There are almost no other means for making it clear that a certain thought is one's private opinion and not the legal position.

This can be demonstrated with a decision of the Israeli Supreme Court denouncing the use of torture to acquire crucial information for the protection of citizens. Its president, Aharon Barak, delivered the opinion of the court and stated:

Deciding these petitions weighed heavily on this Court... We are, however, part of Israeli society. Its problems are known to us and we live its history... The possibility that this decision will hamper the ability to properly deal with terrorists and terrorism disturbs us. We are, however, judges. We must decide according to the law. This is the standard that we set for ourselves. When we sit to judge, we ourselves are judged.[110]

This quotation shows, once again, that the first-person perspective is crucial for describing propositional attitudes such as personal fears. If the court were to circumscribe them by impersonal statements the content would change. The impersonal sentence, for instance, "There is fear that the ruling will prevent the court from properly dealing

---

[108] See, e.g., Kurt Nadelmann, 'The Judicial Dissent' (1959) 8 *The American Journal of Comparative Law* 415; Blom-Cooper and Drewry, *Final Appeal* (cited in n.21), 84; William Brennan, 'In Defense of Dissents' (1986) 37 *Hastings Law Journal* 427; Perju, 'Reason and Authority' (cited in n.105), 338.

[109] For instance, *Griswold v Connecticut* [1965] 381 U.S. 479, 507 (Justice Black): "In order that there may be no room at all to doubt why I vote as I do, I feel constrained to add that the law is every bit as offensive to me as it is to my Brethren of the majority."

[110] Israeli Supreme Court, *Public Committee Against Torture v Israel* [1999] HCJ 5100/94, para.40 (Barak).

with terrorists", would differ from the personal expressions in the judgment. It would describe an impact on the court as an institution and not on its members. Only in theory could the court state in the third person, "The deciding judges fear that their ruling will hamper the ability to properly deal with terrorists...". This would sound so impersonal that it would be preferable to omit it altogether. At the very least, the rhetorical power of the argument would disappear, because of the lack of authenticity. The reference to the deciding judges would only be a hidden reintroduction of the first-person perspective in third-person statements.

The quotation also shows the difference between the official role of the judges ("we sit to judge") and the private role of citizens ("we ourselves are judged"). This difference can hardly be expressed without the first-person perspective. Only by using it can one make clear that one refers to oneself and not to an institution. To say, for instance, "the court is part of Israeli society" would be true but distinct from the sentence "we are part of Israeli society". For only in the latter case does the "we" refer to the judges as citizens and not to their institutional role as judges. If they want to describe their different roles, the first-person perspective is, as a practical matter, unavoidable. It is hence no coincidence that this quotation stems from the Israeli Supreme Court, which frequently drafts its decisions in the first person plural. Were it, like the English Supreme Court, to use the first person singular the quotation would sound overly self-confident: "When I sit to judge, I myself am judged". It would describe a property of *the* individual judge and not a general property of being *a* judge. Were the Israeli court, on the other hand, to use the third-person perspective, like the ECJ, the statement would become nonsense: "When the court sits to judge, it itself is judged". For only a person, and not an institution, can be judged. So the use of the first-person perspective impacts the possible content of the decision. It is more than a mere a matter of style.

5. Trade-offs in the avoidance or use of the first-person perspective

In view of the fact that first-person statements are mostly, but not always, reducible to impersonal statements, one must ask why the differences between the legal systems discussed in this paper are so striking. Why can one not find in every legal system some decisions using the first person singular, some using the first person plural, and some using the third person ("the court")? If every perspective is best suited to express a certain content the intent of the judges and not the established style should determine what they are able to say.

To answer these questions it is worth noting that the advantages and disadvantages of these perspectives are intermingled. One cannot accept the advantages of one perspective and avoid its disadvantages. Therefore, trade-offs in the adoption or avoidance of the first-person perspective are unavoidable. When judges use the first person singular they can best describe their inclinations, hesitations, and other personal attitudes. They might thereby give an account of how they came to a certain conclusion, thus giving hints about their future votes. Therefore, the first-person perspective is best capable of accounting for the *context of discovery*[111] of a certain decision. Moreover, the expression of these attitudes prevents a haphazard generalization of the statements. This is especially important in precedent-based systems. The first-person perspective prevents the taking

---

[111] Hans Reichenbach, *Experience and Prediction* (first published 1938, University of Notre Dame Press, Notre Dame, 2006), 7; cf. also Jacobson, 'Publishing Dissent' (cited in n.25), 1607, 1618.

of the first formulated ideas about certain issues as a ready rule for future cases.[112] On the other hand, an impersonal style and a third-person perspective are best suited to focusing on generalizable reasons and rules. For them personal attitudes do not play a role, as they are irrelevant to the argumentative force of the statement. In this regard it does not matter which judge at what moment thinks in a particular way. The only things that matter are the impersonal reasons for and against a certain position. When they are stated without personal attitudes the arguments become more visible. Therefore, the focus on generalizable reasons gives a strong incentive to describe the *context of justification*.[113] For this context, the genesis of the decision can remain open. It does not matter how the judges came to it and how they feel about it. Omitting any reference to this background and the personal attitudes accompanying it helps to make these reasons explicit. They do not become blurred by personal statements.

Similar advantages and disadvantages accompany the question of how best to predict a future decision. If one wants to base the prognosis of future outcomes on a calculation of the probable votes of the judges, it is necessary to consider how each judge thinks. For that purpose separate opinions, written in the first-person perspective, provide hints. With them, however, it becomes more difficult to predict which argument might win a majority in the court.[114] Because of the lack of a joint opinion, the majority on every issue has to be constructed from the individual opinions. This is not always possible as not every judge gives his opinion upon every issue. There is no guarantee that the judges will observe a certain structure of argumentation common in joint opinions. In this respect, joint opinions are better suited for predicting future decisions, as every sentence in them is supported by a majority.[115] The agreed-upon propositions are also the most probable common ground in future. In this way, joint opinions provide clarity as to what the majority thinks. So, in the choice between personal statements in the first-person perspective and joint impersonal statements, one must balance the clarity of the majority vote against the clarity about each judge's individual opinion. Depending on the circumstances either can be preferable. Although a decision consisting of several individual opinions provides more material and hence a deeper insight into what the judges think, many individual opinions are, at the same time, more cumbersome. Each decision takes more time and overall the court has less time to devote to other decisions. For this reason, courts allowing the first-person perspective tend to publish fewer decisions overall, but those opinions are more extensive than the decisions of courts avoiding the first-person perspective.[116]

The choice of the first-person perspective also has a considerable impact on the *incentives* for judges. When they write in the first-person perspective they are accountable for

---

[112] cf. *Cassell & Co. v Broome* [1972] A.C. 1027, 1085 (HL) (Lord Reid): "it is not the function of noble and learned Lords or indeed of any judges to frame definitions or to lay down hard and fast rules".

[113] For the difference between the context of justification and the context of discovery see Reichenbach, *Experience and Prediction* (cited in n.111).

[114] cf. Fred Bruinsma, 'A Socio-Legal Analysis of the Legitimacy of Highest Courts', in Huls et al., *The Legitimacy of Highest Courts' rulings* (cited in n.10), 61, 70.

[115] Similarly David Skeel, 'The Unanimity Norm in Delaware Corporate Law' [1997] 83 *Virginia Law Review Association* 127, 149, 170 argues that joint opinions in Delaware have a greater impact than individual opinions.

[116] In the legal year 2009/2010 the British Supreme Court heard 67 cases, available at <http://www.supremecourt.gov.uk/faqs.html#1d>, accessed 17 October 2011; the German Supreme Court in 2010 in civil cases alone made 784 judgments after a hearing, available at <http://www.bundesgerichtshof.de/DE/BGH/Statistik/statistik_node.html> accessed 17 October 2011; for a comparison between France, the USA, and the EU see Lasser, *Judicial Deliberations* (cited in n.44, 309).

their statement in public and will be blamed or honoured for their views. They thereby have the chance to be remembered not only in their function as a supreme court judge, but more specifically as the author of a particular opinion which generations of students and scholars will have to study. By doing so they become the inventors and authors of certain rules, principles, and formulations. Only in a legal system allowing them to express their individual views and to develop their own style[117] might they become "public heroes"[118] and talk to their "home crowd",[119] i.e. people with similar opinions. Thus, along with the individual opinion comes the incentive to build a certain reputation, to stick to one's own decisions,[120] and to develop original formulations. Lord Hoffmann, for instance, who is particularly praised for his style, is said to have occasionally used more time for the opening paragraph than for the rest of his entire opinion.[121]

This would hardly be the case in a system in which the majority collectively drafts a joint opinion. First, nobody in the public would know that a certain paragraph stemmed from a particular judge and could therefore honour his effort. Further, there is no guarantee that such an effort would survive the judges' meeting, as each sentence might be voted on and become an object of compromise. Even if the judge is praised by his fellows for a nice formulation, the public will not remember him. At best he can become part of a "heroic" institution. Some German judges compensate for this lack of individual publicity by undertaking academic work about the issues they deal with in their decisions. It is no coincidence that the most famous constitutional judges in Germany are almost exclusively from academia,[122] and many high court judges strive for academic credentials[123] such as an honorary professorship. As academics, they can better build a reputation independent of their work in the court. This does not, of course, mean that academics are more capable of reaching innovative decisions than judges who spend their whole carrier on the bench. But because of their individual publications, they have a better chance to make their opinions known than judges whose individual voices are drowned in collective opinions.

This lack of personal fame might under certain circumstances be an advantage. It helps in the building of an institution which is not hampered by attempts to acquire individual fame or to distinguish oneself from other judges.[124] Originality might negatively impact the consistency of formulations and hence the stability of the law. If two judges express the same rule but with different views, there might be confusion about its

---

[117] For the USA, for instance, Justice Harry Edward, 'A Judge's View on Justice, Bureaucracy, And Legal Method' (1981) 80 *Michigan Law Review* 259, 266: "Every detail of my opinions must conform to my thinking and preferred method of expression"; Lasser, *Judicial Deliberations* (cited in n.44), 312.

[118] For the USA see John Brigham, *The Cult of the Court* (Temple University Press, Philadelphia, 1987), 64: "the cult of the judge superseding the cult of the robe"; for England see Lord Hope of Craighead, *Writing Judgments* (Judicial Studies Board, London, 2005), 10: "Writing a judicial opinion is not, after all, an exercise in self advertisement... How fortunate we are however that, in our legal tradition, the character of our judges can live on through their opinions"; Lasser, *Judicial Deliberations* (cited in n.44), 312.

[119] This expression is attributed to US Justice Ginsburg, see Markham, 'Against Individually Signed Judicial Opinions' (cited in n.56), 925, who is critical of that effect.

[120] cf. Craig Lerner and Nelson Lund, 'Judicial Duty and the Supreme Court's Cult of Celebrity' (2010) 78 *George Washington Law Review* 1255, 1278.

[121] Craighead, *Writing Judgments* (cited in n.118), 6.

[122] Like Gerhard Leibholz, Ernst-Wolfgang Boeckenfoerde, Dieter Grimm, or Paul Kirchhoff.

[123] Similarly in France, see Guy Canivet, 'Formal and Informal Determinative Factors in the Legitimacy of Judicial Decisions: the Point of View of the French Court of Cassation' in Huls et al., *The Legitimacy of Highest Courts' rulings* (cited in n.10), 125, 137.

[124] cf. Skeel, 'The Unanimity Norm in Delaware Corporate Law' (cited in n.115), 162: Delaware's law "limits each justice's opportunity to develop an individual reputation"; Markham, 'Against Individually Signed Judicial Opinions' (cited in n.56), 944, arguing for anonymous decisions in the USA.

exact scope. Conversely, a judge drafting a joint opinion has an incentive to use standardized formulations used in previous decisions. These formulations are already agreed upon and the judge therefore has a better chance of obtaining enough support for his opinion among the other judges. Because nobody knows whether this judge was for or against a certain position, he is not tempted to strive for personal consistency[125] and can thus focus instead on institutional consistency.

In this regard judges writing in an impersonal style work "in the fabric of the law" and not in its art studios. They are more likely to develop standardized formulations that are used over and over again and increase the predictability of the law. For that purpose, neither the rules nor the formulations have to be original. It is enough that they are commonly agreed upon and part of a dogmatized system. If one aims at the development of a system based on generalizable rules one might, therefore, prefer such an impersonal style that removes all references to personal attitudes and prevents individual variations of the same idea. First-person statements, because of their individuality, would only hamper this process. It goes without saying that these factors might be considerably disadvantageous as well. The development of new rules and principles may be severely hampered by the necessity to stick to previous formulations. Moreover, the loss of authenticity in standardized formulations decreases the persuasiveness of a decision. The more directly a judge can express his ideas about a certain subject, the more compelling his view will become.

The use or avoidance of the first-person perspective also influences the complexity of the opinions. Collective announcements in an impersonal style further the development of an interconnected system of various decisions. For only then can one rely on each proposition being an agreed-upon statement of the whole court. This allows other decisions to build upon it, and finally a whole system of proposition and rules results. In its construction one does not have to examine which proposition is supported by a majority of the judges, and can take each sentence as a reliable stone upon which to erect a long-lasting structure. If, however, one has to take individual opinions as the basis of such a system, one must examine which proposition obtained a majority before one can build on it with further propositions.[126] This is not always possible as not every opinion addresses the same question or has the same structure.[127] The stated hesitations, doubts, and other personal attitudes make this construction of the majority opinion even more difficult. Taking propositions as an indisputable basis for a certain dogmatic position is prevented. Individual opinions are thus, in comparison with joint opinions, less capable of being used in an overall system of decisions, and hence have less *external complexity*.

On the other hand, individual opinions do not have to rely on the majority of the court and need not undergo a voting procedure. Only certain sentences and reasons survive such a procedure. The more thoroughly one tries to explain a position, the less likely one is to find a majority for it. There may often be agreement about a certain position, but not about the reasons for it. It is for this reason that joint opinions tend to become compromises between the judges, and are thus less likely to be substantiated

---

[125] For the following of 'personal' precedents see Barak, 'A Judge on Judging' (cited in n.3), 32; for serving a particular audience see Markham, 'Against Individually Signed Judicial Opinions' (cited in n.56), 944.

[126] Seriatim opinions are for this reasons sometimes criticized as providing less stability and guidance: Skeel, 'The Unanimity Norm in Delaware Corporate Law' (cited in n.115), 153; Bruinsma, 'A Socio-Legal Analysis of the Legitimacy of Highest Courts' (cited in n.114), 61, 70.

[127] For the difficulty in constructing the ratio decidendi see Rupert Cross and J.W. Harris, *Precedent in English Law* (4th edn, Clarendon Press, Oxford, 1991), 48; Duxbury, *The Nature and Authority of Precedent* (cited in n.90), 68.

by a deep and pronounced argumentation that contains more than careful formulations of common ground. Therefore, the *internal complexity* of joint opinions tends to be lower than that of first-person statements in separate opinions.[128] One can see this in the ECJ, where compromises have to be made between various judges from different legal cultures. Accordingly, the ECJ's reasoning frequently appears shallow.[129] The more an opinion becomes a matter of compromise and agreement, the less thoroughly it can be explained. Once again, the reason why impersonal opinions do not delve so deeply as individual opinions in the first-person perspective is not that the judges in such legal systems want to hide their true reasons. Rather, they are hampered by a style that hardly allows them to express personal ideas, doubts, and other views and demands severe compromises in order to reach a particular decision. Hence, in choosing between a personal and an impersonal perspective trade-offs must be made between the external complexity of all decisions and the internal complexity of the individual opinion.

Similar trade-offs appear in the choice between the first person singular and the first person plural. As the quotation from the Israeli Supreme Court shows,[130] the first person plural can unleash strong rhetorical power. A single voice is louder than a plurality of individual ones. This is a great advantage in controversial cases like those about torture.[131] However, the first person plural disguises the discrepancies between the judges. As already explained,[132] the use of the "we" can be misleading as its composition might vary from sentence to sentence. If one does not want to cover dissent between the judges, it is preferable to abstain from a collective "we" altogether and to attribute the opinion just to the court. It, as the institution, is the only one that remains constant throughout the decision.

6. Conclusion

The first-person perspective is extensively used in English decisions and is especially suitable for expressing personal attitudes like hesitations, doubts, etc. By formulating an argument in the first person one can prevent a generalization. This is preferable in a precedent-based system that has to leave room for the expression of competing ideas. The ECJ and the German Supreme Court avoid using the first-person perspective completely. This cannot be explained simply by their joint delivery of the opinions, for they could use the first person plural for that purpose. Rather, the avoidance of the first-person perspective is necessary to prevent the impression of unanimity. Dissent inside the court would otherwise be covered by the use of a "we", the composition of which changes from sentence to sentence.

Most of the time, legal arguments can, without loss of content, be formulated both with first-person statements and without them. Personal statements might be transformed

---

[128] However, majority opinions usually score higher in integrative complexity than do minority opinions, see Deborah Gruenfeld, 'Status, Ideology, and Integrative Complexity on the U.S. Supreme Court: Rethinking the Politics of Political Decision Making' (1995) 68 *Journal of Personality and Social Psychology* 5, 9.

[129] See, for instance, Case C-115/09 *Bund fuer Umwelt und Naturschutz Deutschland, Landesverband Nordrhein-Westfalen e. V. v Local Government Arnsberg* [2011] OJ C204/11 where, in a few sentences the ECJ granted non-governmental organizations the right to contest all infringements of EU environmental law in national courts; Perju, 'Reason and Authority' (cited in n.105), 339.

[130] Quoted in text at n.110.

[131] Therefore, the establishment of a court might be enhanced by such a joint opinion; see, for the US Supreme Court, Henderson, 'From Seriatim to Consensus and Back Again' (cited in n.26), 314–15; for the ECJ see Perju, 'Reason and Authority' (cited in n.105), 331.

[132] In text at n.45.

into impersonal ones, and vice versa. To abstain from the first-person perspective is not necessarily a sign of a formalist ideology denying the role of non-deductive moral arguments. The avoidance of first-person statements helps, on the one hand, to focus on the generalizable reasons for a decision, as their argumentative force does not depend upon the judges uttering them. On the other hand, the avoidance of first-person statements prevents the expression of doubts and of differences between the judge's public and private role. Therefore, in using or avoiding first-person statements trade-offs have to be made. Depending on the social, political, and historic circumstances, the first-person perspective seems preferable–or not.

33

Deaf People at the Old Bailey From the 18th Century Onwards

*Bencie Woll and Christopher Stone**

1. Introduction

Effective communication is fundamental for deaf people to access the law at all levels of legal proceedings. Without attention to the needs of a deaf person to be provided with accessible language (whether by a spoken language delivered in a way that the deaf person can understand, or by use of a sign language interpreter for those deaf people whose preferred language is a sign language) legal proceedings fail to include deaf people as witnesses, claimants, defendants or complainants, etc. Although legislation[1] now affords instruments for deaf people to ensure equality of participation in legal proceedings, until recently there has been little evidence of how deaf people accessed the legal system, what provisions existed, or the motivations behind those provisions. The Old Bailey Proceedings[2] now provide access online to records covering the years 1674 to 1913. By searching and analysing these accounts[3] we are better able to understand when and how the courts engaged with deaf people who used some form of signed communication as their preferred language choice for face-to-face communication.

2. A brief history of signing deaf people in the UK

The earliest record of some form of sign being used within a quasi-legal context in the UK is in the latter part of the 16th century in the marriage register of St. Martin's, Leicester. On 15 February 1576 Thomas Tilsye, a 'deaf and dumb' man, married Ursula Russel, with 'approbation of the Bishop, his Commissarye, the Mayor, etc'. The register notes that

the sayde Thomas, for the expression of his minde instead of words, of his own accorde used these signs: He embraced her with his arms, and took her by the hand, putt a ring upon her finger, laying his hande upon his hearte, and holdinge up his handes toward heaven. And to show his

---

* The work was supported by the Economic and Social Research Council of Great Britain (Grant RES-620-28-6002), Deafness, Cognition and Language Research Centre (DCAL).

[1] Equality Act 2010, Human Rights Act 1998, the United Nations convention on the rights of people with disabilities (UNCRPD).

[2] *Old Bailey Proceedings Online* [*OBP*], available at <http://www.oldbaileyonline.org>, version 6.0 [accessed 8 June 2011].

[3] *OBP* searched for all offences with keywords of 'deaf' and 'dumb', between 1674 and 1913.

continuance to dwell with her till his lyves ende, he did it by closing his eyes, and digging out of earth with his foote, and pulling as though he would ring a bell.[4]

A second account of the use of signing in a wedding is found in the 1618 register of St. Botolph, Aldgate. This reports how

Thomas Speller, a dumb person, by trade a Smith, of Hatfield Broadoake, in the county of Essex, and Sarah Earle, daughter to one John Earle, of Great Paringdon, in the same county, yeoman, were married by licence, granted by Dr. Edwards, Chancellor of the Diocese of London, the seventh day of November, Anno Dni 1618, which licence aforesaid was granted at the request of Sir Francis Harrington, Knight, and others of the place above-named, who by their letters certified Mr. Chancellor that the parents of either of them had given their consents to the said marriage, and the said Thomas Speller the dumb parties willingness to have the same performed, appeared, by taking the Book of Common Prayer and his licence in one hand and his bride in the other, and coming to Mr. John Briggs, our minister and preacher, and made the best signs he could to show that he was willing to be married, which was then performed accordinglie. And also the said Lord Chief Justice of the King's Bench, as Mr. Briggs was informed, was made acquainted with the said marriage before it was solemnized, and allowed to be lawful. This marriage is set down at large, because we never had the like before.[5]

Both these accounts suggest that the gestures used are communicative but do not represent a complex linguistic system and thus not a signed language. Both accounts indicate that additional permissions were required before the marriage of a 'deaf and dumb' person could take place, suggesting doubts about the status of this form of communication.

There are other references to deaf people using gestural communication in the 16th and 17th centuries. Sometimes these are instances of individuals coming together to communicate, such as Edward Bone, a deaf servant, and his friend John Kempe who, 'when they chaunced to meete, would vse such kinde embracements, such strange, often, and earnest tokenings, and such heartie laughters, and other passionate gestures, that their want of a tongue, seemed rather an hinderance to others conceiuing them, then to their conceiuing one another'.[6]

Further information from Carew's description of Edward Bone suggests that he had some level of English knowledge even though he could not speak. He was able to lipread the local preacher, by 'setting himself directly against the Preacher, looke him stedfastly in the face, while his Sermon lasted', although his preferred method of communication appears to be using 'verie effectuall signes'. His communication with hearing people is likely to have been speech accompanied by co-speech gestures, different from the communication he had with John Kempe.

Some references to deaf people can be found during the 17th century in books about signing, such as the dedication of John Bulwer's book *Philocophus* to two deaf brothers,[7] and Dalgarno's book on the nature of signs.[8] Other references, for example in Samuel

---

[4] Charles J. Cox, *The parish registers of England* (London: Methuen, 1910), 84.
[5] Available at <http://www.ebooksread.com/authors-eng/t-f-thiselton-thomas-firminger-thiselton-dyer/old-english-social-life-as-told-by-the-parish-registers-hci/page-9-old-english-social-life-as-told-by-the-parish-registers-hci.shtml>.
[6] Richard Carew, *The survey of Cornwall*, available at <http://www.archive.org/stream/thesurveyofcornw09878gut/srvcr10.txt>, 139 [accessed 7 October 2011].
[7] John Bulwer, *Philocophus, or the deaf and dumbe mans friend* (London: Humphrey Moseley, 1648).
[8] George Dalgarno, *Didascolocophus, or, The deaf and dumb mans tutor* (Oxford: At the theater, 1680).

Pepys' diary entries about the Great Fire of London, mention deaf people incidentally. Pepys describes in detail the interaction in signing between his colleague Thomas Downing and Downing's deaf servant.[9] In the 17th century there is also an account of a deaf couple in colonial New England using signs, marrying, and becoming full members of their Puritan church through sign translation and interpretation.[10]

It should be noted that before the introduction of hearing aids and effective amplification, what would now be considered as a moderate hearing impairment would have had a marked impact on a child's ability to develop speech. It was thus natural for deaf people to use gesture for communication. Where an individual deaf person was isolated from other deaf people, independent 'home sign' systems developed between that person and hearing people in his family and community.[11] Where deaf people using home signs then encounter each other, sign languages are formed.[12] From the 18th century onwards, this contributed to the development of the British Sign Language community.

These occasional references do not give the impression of a well-established regional or national sign language within the British Isles. The later establishment of Deaf educational institutions played a significant role in bringing a critical mass of deaf children together to create British Sign Language (BSL) and its regional variants within the UK.[13] The Braidwood family established the first educational institution for the 'deaf and dumb' in Edinburgh, Scotland in 1760. The school subsequently moved to Hackney, London in 1783 and then to Bermondsey, London in 1792 where it became the Asylum for the Deaf and Dumb.[14]

Other institutions were founded throughout the 19th century and these began to provide deaf people with language, education, and a community. This sense of belonging and identity can be seen as early as 1783 when the father of a deaf boy from America attending the Braidwood School, Francis Green, visited his son at the school. 'Observing that he [Green's son] was inclined in company to converse with one of his school fellows by the tacit finger language, I asked him why he did not speak to him with his mouth? To this his answer was as pertinent as it was concise: "He is deaf".'[15] Irrespective of the status of the Deaf community and/or communities in the 18th century it is clear that sign language-using deaf people met and socialized with others and in turn began to construct identities as Deaf people and members of a linguistic minority community.

3. The Old Bailey Proceedings

We searched the online Old Bailey Proceedings using the terms 'deaf and dumb'[16] and selected those which mentioned signs, motions, or interpreters. We found 11 entries

---

[9] Samuel Pepys, entry for 9 November 1666; available at <http://www.pepys.info/1666/1666nov.html>.

[10] B. Carty, S. Macready, and E. E. Sayers, '"A grave and gracious woman": Deaf people and signed language in colonial New England' (2009) 9(3) *Sign Language Studies* 287–323.

[11] Susan Goldin-Meadow, *The resilience of language: what gesture creation in deaf children can tell us about how all children learn language* (New York: Taylor & Francis, 2003).

[12] A. Senghas, S. Kita, and A. Özyürek, 'Children creating core properties of languages: evidence from an emerging sign language in Nicaragua' (2004) 305 *Science* 1779–82. Available online: search for DOI: 10.1126/science.1100199.

[13] G. Quinn, 'Schoolization: an account of the origins of regional variation in British Sign Language' (2010) 10(4) *Sign Language Studies* 476–501.

[14] Raymond Lee, *A beginner's introduction to Deaf history* (Feltham: BDHS publications, 2004).

[15] Francis Green, *Vox oculis subjecta* (London: Benjamin White, 1783), 152.

[16] As outlined in n.2.

between 1725 and 1800. In those entries where interpreters are mentioned, reference is always made to a person being sworn to interpret (the testimony of a deaf witness, complainant, or defendant) to the satisfaction of the court.

There was no obligation to ensure access for a deaf person or anyone not speaking English to court proceedings until 1916 when it was ruled that:

> When a foreigner who is ignorant of the English language is on trial on an indictment for a criminal offence, and is not defended by counsel, the evidence given at the trial must be translated to him, and compliance with this rule cannot be waived by the prisoner. If he is defended by counsel, the evidence must be translated to him unless he or his counsel express a wish to dispense with the translation and the judge thinks fit to permit the omission, but the judge should not permit it unless he is of opinion that the accused substantially understands the nature of the evidence which is going to be given against him.[17]

Of the 11 cases from 1725 to 1800 referring to deaf people, 9 involve 'dumb' or 'mute' prisoners; 1 concerns a 'dumb' witness (John Rasten)[18] and 1 a 'deaf and dumb' victim (name unknown but present in court).[19] In 8 of the cases there is explicit mention of the person being dumb/mute *by the visitation of God*. The term was used to distinguish persons with incapacities from those who were 'obstinately mute' or 'mute of malice'.[20] The court needed to determine this, as being found to be mute of malice could be taken as constructive confession.[21] The last mention of 'mute by the visitation of God' is in the case of William Burrams in 1796.[22] Being found to be 'mute by the visitation from God' also saved one prisoner from being sentenced to death by pressing (this punishment was abolished in 1772).[23]

In 6 cases within the period 1725 to 1800, interpreters are referred to. In the first of these cases, in 1725,[24] although a request was made for 'friends or family' to interpret to the satisfaction of the court no one came forward to say they were able to do so. A fellow rope maker who worked with the defendant said that although he could talk about rope making he was not able to discuss other matters. After a witness to the defendant's good character was provided, the deaf defendant was acquitted. The first case in which a person served as an interpreter was in 1771. The unnamed master/mistress of a deaf former servant, James Saytuss, known as Dumb-O-Jemmy, was 'sworn interpreter' and 'explained to him the nature of his indictment by signs'.[25] Persons were sworn as interpreters for four other prisoners in this period: Nathan Solomon,[26] Thomas Jones,[27] William Burrams,[28] and William Smith.[29] Two had family members sworn in to interpret for them (William Burrams' mother and William Smith's brother), one had a friend sworn in to interpret (a childhood friend of Nathan Solomon); Fanny Lazarus interpreted for Thomas Jones, but their relationship is unknown.

---

[17] *R v Lee Kun* (1916) 1 KB 337.
[18] *OBP* William Bartlett January 1786 (t17860111–30).
[19] *OBP* Ann Kent January 1794 (t17940430–85).
[20] Joan Colin and Ruth Morris, *Interpreters and the Legal Process* (Winchester: Waterside, 1996), 92.
[21] John Trusler, *A concise view of the common law and statute law of England, carefully collected from the statutes and best common law writers, and systematically digested* (London: W Nicholl, 1781), 370.
[22] *OBP* William Burrams January 1796 (t17960113–97).
[23] 12 Geo. III c.20, Felony and Piracy Act 1772.
[24] *OBP* George Armstrong April 1725 (t17250407–70).
[25] *OBP* James Saytuss July 1771 (t17710703–17).
[26] *OBP* Nathan Solomon April 1772 (t17720429–52).
[27] *OBP* Thomas Jones December 1773 (t17731208–23).
[28] *OBP* William Burrams January 1776 (t17760113–97).
[29] *OBP* William Smith April 1797 (t17970426–10).

In the case of a deaf defendant, Moreing (first name unknown), who had a deaf brother and sister,[30] there is mention of 'a sign made to him by a person in court'. This is the only record of any of the deaf and dumb people in the Old Bailey Proceedings having deaf family members. In the case in which an unnamed deaf victim is involved in 1794,[31] it appears that while he was in court, the deaf man was produced as evidence rather than being included in the proceedings. In summary, of the 11 cases 6 have a sworn interpreter, Moreing has a sign made in court by 'a person', an interpreter is sought but not found for George Armstrong, and there is no mention of an interpreter being sought or provided for William Truelock or James Innocent. The latter is simply categorized as 'Mute by the visitation of God' and is not tried further.

John Rasten, witness, also had a family member sworn in to interpret—his sister Martha Rasten. This case provides a detailed discussion of whether a deaf person can serve as a witness in the context of a formal objection made by Sir William Garrow, which we will look at in detail next.

4. The case of William Bartlett

This case took place in 1786,[32] only three years after the Braidwood School moved to London. It is therefore unlikely that the witness John Rasten would have had any formal education. Although there had been six previous Old Bailey cases involving deaf people, four of whom made use of interpreters of various sorts, there is still little evidence of a community of deaf people using sign language.

The defending counsel in this case is Sir William Garrow (1760–1840), who has gained a measure of fame via a BBC television series chronicling his work, and loosely based upon the Old Bailey Proceedings. Garrow is historically prominent, with the majority of his cases within the Old Bailey falling between 1783 and 1793.[33] Although holding other political and legal positions he is best renowned for his work as a barrister and was seen as 'a very great advocate' who 'reached the lead of the Old Bailey practice and domineered without a competitor at the bar'.[34]

Mr Garrow's objection to the testimony of the deaf witness is chronicled in supplementary materials to the court record.[35] To support his argument that John Rasten should not be allowed to be examined, Mr Garrow cites the authority of Lord Hale to draw Mr Justice Heath's attention to the presumption in law that there is no way to communicate with deaf and dumb people. Lord Hale 'lays it down that a man who is Surdus et Mutus etc. is in presumption an Ideot' and therefore unable to take part in court proceedings because he is incapable of distinguishing good and evil. Other accounts suggest that this view was common in relation to people who were deaf from birth or from a very young age and who had no access to education.[36]

---

[30] *OBP* Moreing April 1782 (t17820410-3).
[31] Referred to in Lee, *A beginner's introduction to Deaf history* (cited in n.14).
[32] *OBP* William Bartlett January 1786 (t17860111-30).
[33] See <http://www.oxforddnb.com/view/article/10410> [accessed 1 December 2011].
[34] (1844) 1 *Law Review*, 318–20 (cited in n.33).
[35] *OBP* William Bartlett January 1786 (o17860111-1).
[36] E. Cockayne, 'Experiences of the deaf in early modern England' (2003) 46(3) *The Historical Journal* 493–510.

Mr Justice Heath responds, 'Every body knows that there are certain signs'. This statement indicates awareness among the general public of the use of some form of gestural communication by dumb people. Lord Hale had actually ruled,

A man that is *surdus et mutus a nativitate*, is in presumption of law an ideot, and the rather, because he hath no possibility to understand, what is forbidden by law to be one, or under what penalties: but if it can appear, that he hath the use of understanding, which many of that condition discover by signs to a very great measure, then he may be tried, and suffer judgment and execution, tho great caution is to be used therein.[37]

In spite of Mr Garrow's protestations, Mr Justice Heath says there is no point of law and instructs him to sit down.

At this point Mr Justice Heath seeks to ascertain exactly how Martha Rasten will communicate the matter at hand to her brother. He asks, ' Now how is it that you would communicate the question you would ask to your brother—are they signs that you make or are they expressive of any particular words or are they expressive of letters or syllables?' to which Martha replies, 'Not letters or syllables but by motion of words.' The judge is here asking whether the communication consists of signs unrelated to English or representations of words, letters, or syllables. Martha's response indicates that John Rasten did not have access to spoken English or to the manual alphabet.

More generally the court wishes to know whether John Rasten 'knows the nature of an oath'. Here it would appear that Mr Justice Heath is trying to assess whether John Rasten's testimony is admissible, i.e. whether or not he is an 'ideot' in Hale's sense. Here Martha's response, 'So far as a short motion [i.e. a sign meaning 'oath'] he has been taught that by others not by me' suggests either that John has received some education, or that has been in the company of other signers from whom he has learnt the sign. Either way she is clear that John has a sign to express the concept of oath.

The court continues to question Martha by asking, 'Have you any doubt at all whether you can convey the meaning of this question whether he has any idea of the nature of an oath?' to which Martha simply replies, 'I have no doubt but he understands it.' In this exchange Mr Justice Heath is asking, first, whether Martha is competent to serve as an interpreter, and, secondly, whether she can swear that her brother is capable of understanding her transmission of the court's question. This question places the interpreter in the position of being not only an expert as an interpreter but also an expert in assessing her brother's competence. In this regard Mr Justice Heath takes the pragmatic view that John Rasten is witness to a crime, there is a person available who can be sworn as an interpreter, this person attests that she can interpret, the witness is capable of understanding his oath as a sworn witness, and that he understands the solemnity of the situation.

Mr Garrow as counsel for the defence takes a different position. He asks, 'Could you venture to say you are sure that he understands you?' to which Martha replies, 'I cannot pretend to swear to his thoughts but as far as motion [sign]', suggesting that she can only interpret what John says, firmly remaining within the role of interpreting from English to sign and vice versa. Mr Garrow continues with an argument along the lines that John Rasten cannot understand the seriousness of the matter. To this end his next question concerns whether John understands the consequences of perjury, to which Martha replies that he understands fully. He also asks whether John can read, to which his sister answers, 'He does not understand reading but he will look over and we explain

---

[37] Sir Matthew Hale, *Historia Placitorum Coronæ—The history of the Pleas of the Crown* Vol.1 (London: E and R Nutt, and R Gosling, 1736), 34.

to him' and that he does not write well enough to correspond in writing. Poor literacy skills among deaf people are still not unusual.[38] John's poor literacy skills require the court to rely on the interpretation of Martha Rasten, with no way of directly interacting with him.

It then becomes clear that Mr Garrow doubts the linguistic complexity of the communication used within this family. The next question Mr Garrow asks relates to a basic function of language in contrast to gesture: that one can talk about something displaced in time or space[39]:

> Mr Garrow: Suppose you was to tell him that Mr Lunardi had arisen into the Air in a Balloon, how should you communicate that Idea?
> Martha Rasten: Oh very well.
> Mr Garrow: Do you think he understands this without seeing it?
> Martha Rasten: I am sure by his motions in return.

This interaction suggests that from Martha's perspective the communication she uses with John has the features of a language. The record of Martha's interpretation definitely shows that Martha could translate John's testimony into complete and detailed English sentences, e.g. 'He shewed me he did not see it taken out of the pocket, only given behind', and that in other cases she is unable to provide detail, e.g. 'He shews me a very little way, but I cannot take upon me to say how near.'

Mr Garrow continues with his objection to accepting the witness. He states that John Rasten cannot understand the oath either through signing or on the testimony of his sister: 'the evidence does not prove that he has any idea of complex ideas; this young woman tells you that he has an idea of the Christian system. Now it is impossible my Lord that he has more ideas of that complex system than that which a common savage has who has a notion of a God'. Mr Garrow's line of argument continues to dismiss the complexity of the signing used by John Rasten and insist on his inability to understand the seriousness of the sworn oath he will take: 'Now suppose this poor creature to be aware of all the eternal sanctions that awaite on falsehood.... How can they be represented?' Notwithstanding the testimony of Martha Rasten and Mr Justice Heath's statement about common knowledge of signs, Mr Garrow maintains that communication perceived through the 'organs of vision' lacks the precision required to understand 'the vast complicated system of religion'. With no education, it might be the case that John Rasten had little knowledge of religion. However, limited knowledge of religion is not the result of using a visual language.

Coupled with Mr Garrow's argument against John Rasten understanding the oath is the argument that Martha Rasten as sworn interpreter will not be able to communicate complex concepts to him:

> Now how will these questions so complex be communicated to him? Upon your oath will you venture to swear that that man at the bar did so and so? Did you know him before? Is there any thing remarkable in his features? How are these ideas to be seperated [sic] in their communication to him? I ask again in the name of common sense how that poor woman can communicate to him that complex question?

---

[38] R. E. Mitchell and M. A. Karchmer, 'Demographic and achievement characteristics of deaf and hard-of-hearing students' in Mark Marschark and Patricia E. Spencer (eds), *The Oxford Handbook of Deaf Studies, Language and Education*, Vol.1, 2nd edn (Oxford: Oxford University Press, 2011), 18–31.

[39] C. F. Hockett, 'The origin of speech' (1960) 203 Scientific *American*, 88–96.

Mr Garrow's final line of argument appealed to the jury to disallow John Rasten's testimony:

My Lord I wish I could also address that Jury on this trial. I should be glad to ask them whether they would chuse [sic] to convict a man of felony upon the testimony of a man with whom they could not hold a conversation, who has not more rationality than an Automaton, who does not appear more competent (if I may be allowed to make such a simily [sic]) than that learned Pig which is now exhibited to the publick [sic].

Despite Mr Garrow's efforts, Mr Justice Heath decides to allow John Rasten to take the stand with his sister interpreting. Mr Justice Heath states, 'I am of Opinion that under all the circumstances of his case the Witness as a Competent Witness ought to be sworn. After he is sworn it will remain with the Jury to consider what degree of respect he ought to have'. This addresses Mr Garrow's concerns regarding the capability of John Rasten. As for his sister as interpreter, Mr Justice Heath states, 'it has been said this is as if the Man spoke an unknown language. I do not know that there is any objection to that if the language can be interpreted to the satisfaction of the Jury'. His decision was followed in subsequent cases. In answer to Mr Garrow's argument regarding holding John Rasten to account for any falsehood or perjury he may commit, Mr Justice Heath is quite clear that 'in the present case suppose the witness was to commit perjury then here is a person who could communicate to him and report the question of the prisoner to the court and jury so that a fair and full trial may be had'. In Mr Justice Heath's mind the notion of a 'deaf and dumb' person giving testimony as a witness is completely acceptable as long as there is someone present who can interpret to the satisfaction of the court and he therefore admits John Rasten as a witness 'considering him as competent and I shall leave his credit to you gentlemen and you will consider it under all the circumstances of the case'.

At that point Martha Rasten is sworn in by the court as an interpreter. Martha is asked whether she can interpret the oath to him and also as a sworn interpreter, whether she can interpret 'the questions and demands made by the Court, and also well and truly interpret the answers made to them?'[40] to which Martha Rasten replies, 'There may be some things I do not understand.' And so once again Martha indicates that if she understands a question she will be able to interpret it to John Rasten. While Mr Garrow appears to deliberately avoid using the term *interpret*, instead using terms such as *convey*, *express*, and *communicate*, Mr Justice Heath uses the term *interpret* to reinforce the legitimacy of John and Martha's presence in the courtroom and support Martha in her role by saying, 'You cannot interpret farther than you know'.

This interchange is the first extensive description of the thoughts of officers of the court with respect to deaf and dumb people using signs to communicate. It is of course always appropriate to ensure that interpreters are appropriately qualified and registered, and are able to provide interpreting at the standard required. In the 18th century, there was no means of providing interpreters for the deaf, in the absence of a London-wide signing community from whom they could be recruited. There is no evidence to suggest that John Rasten used what we would now call BSL. We can only speculate that with the establishment of the London school for deaf children awareness of signing increased, leading in turn to the acceptance of BSL.

---

[40] *OBP* William Bartlett January 1786 (t17860111–30).

5. The 19th century onwards

From 1800 onwards, a number of schools for the deaf were opened in London and other parts of the country, and the Refuge for the Deaf and Dumb (later to become the Association for the Deaf and Dumb—ADD, then the Royal Association—RADD, and finally the Royal Association for Deaf people—RAD) was established in 1841. This organization served the needs of deaf adults who used sign language and supported the development of a Deaf community in London. One of the roles for the RAD was the spiritual welfare of Deaf people and in June 1875[41] St Saviours Church for the Deaf opened on Oxford Street, remaining on this site (opposite Selfridges) until 1922. Queen Alexandra, who was herself hard of hearing, became the patron of the ADD in 1876.

Between 1801 and 1900 the Old Bailey Proceedings include 57 cases including the term 'deaf and dumb'. The last mention of 'motions' (rather than 'signs') occurs in 1808. In the 19th century, as well as signing there are also references (in 5 cases) to the use of written communication. This change is most probably related to the establishment of formal education for deaf children and the work of the RAD with deaf adults.

There are also 32 references to interpreters and thus many more cases using interpreters from 1801 to 1900 than in the century before. If we compare this to mention of interpreters in the 18th century, the figures suggest that the ratio of those cases involving deaf and dumb people with explicit mention of interpreters remained fairly constant: 6 of 11 cases (~55 per cent) in the 18th century, and 32 of 57 cases (~56 per cent) in the 19th century.

One difference is that in the 19th century there is no mention of interpreters being sworn in. The 32 cases mentioning interpreters include 7 where a sign interpreter is named, 1 where a named person interprets from gestures, and 24 unnamed interpreters. There are also 8 cases where the relationship between the person interpreting and the deaf person is given (e.g. master, brother, sister, mother). In 15 cases, there is only reference to a deaf person communicating with signs. It may be that those cases specifically mentioning interpreters are those where a person is formally sworn in as an interpreter.

Of the remaining cases, between 1800 and 1812 there were 4 where the deaf prisoner was found Not Guilty and no mention of interpreting or communication is made; in 2 of these cases (Richard Burrows[42] and William Burrows[43]) the prosecutor (complainant) did not appear, suggesting direct communication may have not been required. In 1855 David Cutler pleaded guilty with no interpreter recorded[44] and in 1886 Richard Williams was defended by a Mr Safford, at the request of the court.[45] A further 3 cases involved deaf people who gave evidence by writing and 1 prisoner who was only 'a little deaf'[46] used gestures to accompany speech. Of these 10 cases it would appear that 6 may not have needed an interpreter and so only 4 of the 57 (~7%) cases did not have an interpreter where one might have been provided.

The Old Bailey Proceedings online only provide records up to 1913. Seven cases involve deaf and dumb people between 1901 and 1913. Only 2 of these cases had an interpreter, with 1 interpreter identified as a clergyman from the church for the deaf

---

[41] <http://www.royaldeaf.org.uk/home/126.html> [accessed October 2011].
[42] *OBP* Richard Burrows July 1801 (t18010701-24).
[43] *OBP* William Burrows July 1801 (t18010701-92).
[44] *OBP* David Cutler November 1855 (t18551126-56).
[45] *OBP* Richard Williams October 1886 (t18861025-1112).
[46] *OBP* David Burrell April 1872 (18720408-358).

and dumb in Oxford Street.[47] Of the remaining 5 cases: in the first one[48] the defendant pleaded guilty. In the second[49] the 3 deaf defendants were found not guilty as the prosecution offered no evidence. In the third case[50] the defendant was deemed not fit to plead. In the fourth case,[51] the defendant was found not guilty, and in the fifth case[52] the deaf person was the complainant.

Another aspect of the presence of deaf people and interpreters within the courtroom is the role of the deaf person, be that prisoner/defendant, witness or, prosecutor/complainant. The acceptance of a deaf person as a prosecutor and especially as a witness demonstrates the court's general acceptance of deaf people who did not use spoken English and of their interpreters. From 1701 to 1800, 9 of 11 cases involved deaf prisoners, 1 involved a deaf witness (John Rasten[53] described above) and 1 a deaf victim. So deaf people's principal involvement in the legal system during the 18th century was as those arrested and charged with committing offences. From 1815 to 1900, of the 57 cases, 33 involved deaf prisoners, 21 involved deaf witnesses, and 3 involved deaf prosecutors.[54] From 1901 to 1913, of the 7 cases, 5 involved deaf prisoners and 2, deaf prosecutors. These records show that deaf and dumb people are ascribed ever-increasing legal status from 'ideots' on the authority of Hale,[55] to being able to be tried, to being able to give witness testimony to the court, and then finally to being able to lodge charges against other individuals. This increasing status of deaf and dumb people co-occurs with other developments: first, the recognition of deafblind people as witnesses; secondly, the assessment of whether a deaf and dumb defendant is fit to plead where there are concerns about his mental state (rather than his '*surdus et mudus*' status); and thirdly the fitness of a deaf and dumb witness to give evidence where there are concerns about his mental state. These will be discussed further in the following section.

6. Interpreting for Deafblind people

In the case of John Pickett 1883,[56] we have the first recorded use of the deafblind manual alphabet within the legal system anywhere in the UK. The witness/victim, Susannah Webling, had been deaf for twenty years and had then become blind, allegedly through being wounded by John Pickett. She had lost the sight of one eye two years earlier and then lost the sight of the second eye during the matter at hand (breaking the peace and wounding). The woman sworn as interpreter, Louisa Aldridge, was a nurse at the Newington Infirmary, probably part of the Newington Workhouse in Southwark. It is unclear how the nurse had learned the 'deaf and dumb alphabet' although from the description given in the records: 'each letter being indicated by pressure of the witness' finger' it appears to be the deafblind manual alphabet used today. There are no further remarks regarding interpreting and the testimony is described in full so one can presume that other than noting that the interpreter was present and sworn this was considered

---

[47] *OBP* Lawrence Ernest Smith July 1906 (t19060723–18).
[48] *OBP* Charles Randall July 1901 (t19010722–534).
[49] *OBP* Charles Roberts, Thomas Randall, Daniel Brittain March 1903 (t19030309–263).
[50] *OBP* Henry Pays, Willian Jones November 1904 (t19041114–59).
[51] *OBP* William Frankland, Francis Best March 1905 (t19050306–295).
[52] *OBP* Charles Birch October 1908 (t19081020–47).
[53] *OBP* William Burrams January 1776 (cited in n.28).
[54] *OBP* Emma Stachley February 1815 (t18150215–120).
[55] Hale, *Historia Placitorum Coronæ* (cited in n.37).
[56] *OBP* John Pickett July 1883 (t18830730–758).

unremarkable. The acceptance of additional forms of language within the legal system permits the examination of deaf people according to their ability to communicate effectively via court-appointed interpreters.

7. Unfitness to plead

Although there are several cases exploring whether deaf people 'mute by the visitation of God' can be tried,[57] the case of George Birch in 1838[58] appears to be the first example of a deaf and dumb person being judged unfit to plead. In this case the prisoner's mother interpreted the case but it is noted that the prisoner did not appear to understand. This recognition of communication difficulties can be understood within the context of schools for the deaf and dumb having been established in London since 1783. With a history of 55 years of deaf education it became possible to identify differences between deaf people who had language and could effectively engage with the legal system and those who were unable to understand court proceedings. In the early 18th century, in contrast, there is little evidence that within the jurisdiction of the Old Bailey there was a signing deaf community. Instead deaf people used home sign to communicate within their immediate family and friends. In 1853 there is a second example of a deaf and dumb prisoner being deemed unfit to plead.[59] Here the defendant refused to reply even though there was an interpreter present. Both the surgeon who dealt with the case (Mr Bishop) and the surgeon of Newgate prison (Mr McMurdo) stated that in their opinion the prison was not of sound mind. In both these cases the defendants were found not guilty on the grounds of being unfit to plead, because of their inability to communicate with the court via an interpreter.

In the early 20th century two further cases are reported where the prisoners are not deemed competent. In 1904, William Jones[60] is deemed not to be 'in a condition to give proper instructions for his defence or to defend himself'. The jury was discharged from giving a verdict; William Jones was detained on the evidence of Dr James Scott.

In 1906, Lawrence Ernest Smith had an interpreter (a clergyman from the church in Oxford Street, i.e. RADD) and also provided a hand-written statement,[61] from which we can infer that Lawrence was educated. The clergyman had known Lawrence 'for years' and he said he was always of the opinion that Lawrence was not in his right mind, and that that was still his opinion.

Unlike the cases discussed above, here an expert with experience in working professionally with deaf people states his opinion. His expert view that Lawrence was not in his right mind, although neither a medical nor a psychiatric expert opinion, takes into account the norms of behaviour within the Deaf congregation of the Oxford Street church. Lawrence pleaded guilty and was sentenced to imprisonment involving penal servitude for life. The judgment also indicated that he would be observed and if deemed 'really insane he would be removed to an asylum'. Irrespective of the expert opinion being provided by the court-sanctioned interpreter undertaking this dual role, the sentence means that Lawrence would have been imprisoned in an environment where he

---

[57] *OBP* Elizabeth Steel May and October 1787 (o17870523–1; t17871024–15) and *R v Pritchard* (1836) 173 E.R. 135.
[58] *OBP* George Birch January 1838 (t18380129–634).
[59] *OBP* James Evans October 1853 (t18531024–1084).
[60] *OBP* William Jones November 1904 (t19041114–59).
[61] *OBP* Lawrence Ernest Smith July 1906 (t19060723–18).

would not have been able to communicate with any of his fellow inmates or prison wardens; this situation remains today for deaf people using sign language.

8. Unfit witnesses

In the case which involved the witness William Knight in 1892,[62] the interpreter, Dr Stainer, explained that the witness 'did not understand the deaf and dumb alphabet'. This may have indicated that William had a low level of literacy, but not that William had no functional language. It may be a reflection on the abilities of Dr Stainer as an *interpreter*; it is conceivable that Dr Stainer knew only fingerspelling and did not know sign language (BSL). Nevertheless, 'Mr Justice Collins held that owing to the questions being necessarily leading, the evidence was not wholly reliable'. In this case there is no challenge from counsel as to the appropriateness of a deaf person giving evidence, just the qualification that due care should be used when considering the evidence.

One further example of the status of a deaf witness's evidence being queried is in the case involving Walter Bovington.[63] It is noted that the deaf witness, William Joyce, is uneducated. While in the 18th century this would have been the status quo, by the end of the 19th century this was not the norm[64] and this is the only case where the lack of education is noted. As someone who was uneducated it is probable that he did not fully acquire a sign language and that he used 'home sign'. This case is somewhat similar to the trial of Jean Campbell in Scotland in 1817 for infanticide, which was reported in the *Caledonian Mercury*.[65] Jean Campbell lived in Glasgow and at that time the only school for deaf children in Scotland was in Edinburgh. Her counsel, Mr McNeil, 'stated an objection against her going to trial, on the grounds of her being deaf and dumb from infancy, and that he was totally unable to get any information from her to conduct her defence'. Mr Drummond, the counsel for the Crown, called Thomas Sibbald, keeper of the jail, to describe how Jean Campbell had interacted and behaved during her two months in the Edinburgh jail.

Her communication is described in some detail and indicates that she communicated with gestures rather than with sign language. The headmaster of the Edinburgh school for the deaf, Mr Kinniburgh, attended both jail and court as interpreter and interpreted using home signs to the best of his ability. He stated that he 'had communication with her by means of signs; in general he understood her, but in particular instances he did not' and also that 'she seemed to understand him about as much as he understood her'. It is also of interest that when Mr Kinniburgh was asked about whether Jean Campbell 'could be made to understand the question, whether she is guilty or not guilty', his response was, 'that from the way in which he would put it, by asking her by signs whether she threw her child over the bridge or not, he thinks she could plead not guilty by signs... and this is the only way that he can put the question to her'. As to other matters concerning the trial and the circumstances of the event, Mr Kinniburgh 'has no idea, abstractly speaking, that she knows what a trial is, but that she knows she is brought into Court about her child; That she has no idea of religion, although he has seen her point as if to a Supreme Being above, and communicates merely by natural signs and not upon

---

[62] *OBP* Giuseppe Zoller September 1892 (t18920912–856).
[63] *OBP* Walter Bovington November 1897 (t18971122–35).
[64] Education Act 1880.
[65] *Caledonian Mercury* (Edinburgh, Scotland), 3 July 1817, issue 14916.

any system'. Similar issues were raised in *R v Pritchard* in 1836[66] and formed the basis of subsequent decisions regarding whether deaf persons were fit to plead.

9. The interpreters

In the Old Bailey Proceedings online, the term 'interpreter' (for deaf people) is mentioned 37 times in total, with Fanny Lazarus the first interpreter to be named, in 1773.[67] In total 10 interpreters are named with a further 10 instances when the interpreter's relationship to the deaf and dumb person or their profession was noted. Two of the interpreters were former masters (employers), 3 were friends, 6 were family members, and 9 were from the asylum (school), with the first mention of the asylum being made in 1808.[68] In this first case, the interpreter is described as an assistant teacher at the asylum where the prisoner, William Rawlins, had been under his instruction. It also says that William communicated his evidence not only by 'motions' but also by writing, indicating a degree of literacy.

As discussed earlier, in the 18th century the interpreters are sworn whereas in the 19th century the interpreters are 'allowed'. As the communication of deaf people becomes more sophisticated and related to what is now known as BSL, there are greater moves to the use of 'impartial' interpreters, with the last reference to a family member interpreting for a deaf and dumb person in 1848.[69] The role of the interpreter, however, continued not only to provide the court with access to the evidence of the deaf person, but also to act as a character witness and often to assist the court in deciding whether or not the deaf person was fit to plead.

10. Conclusions

The Old Bailey Proceedings provide evidence that from 1725 onwards it was recognized that deaf people could participate in legal proceedings. This participation was not restricted to defendants but also to witnesses, victims, and deaf people bringing allegations against others. The interpreters ensured that the court and jury had access to the evidence, rather than providing communication support to enable the deaf person to participate fully. Because it is unlikely that deaf people in the 18th century had access to a full language such as BSL, home signs or 'natural signs' were acceptable to the court.

In the 21st century it is possible, although rare, to find 'language isolates' like Jean Campbell. Neonatal screening can identify deafness within 48 hours of birth and all deaf children receive intervention from the point of diagnosis to the completion of their schooling. Nevertheless some deaf children are failed by the system and ineffective education is often only recognized in late pre-teen years.[70] Although such children can acquire effective face-to-face communication they may in some cases not acquire a full first language. There are also a small number of deaf people who arrive in the UK as immigrants or asylum-seekers, who have not had formal access to education; these individuals may only be able to communicate by means of gesture or home sign. Such people may find

---

[66] (1836) 173 E.R. 135.
[67] *OBP* Thomas Jones December 1773 (cited in n.27).
[68] *OBP* William Rawlins January 1808 (t18080113–67).
[69] *OBP* Rachel Levy January 1848 (t18480103–444).
[70] Mitchell and Karchmer, 'Demographic and achievement characteristics of deaf and hard-of-hearing students' (cited in n.38).

it difficult to fully understand the subtleties of language use within a courtroom. Often qualified deaf interpreters are best able to communicate with these individuals and may work alongside hearing interpreters to ensure optimum access.

Even though the treatment of deaf people improved throughout the 19th century there is no evidence that proceedings were interpreted for defendants. In some ways this is unremarkable: deaf defendants were treated no differently from those who spoke a foreign language and did not understand the proceedings. It is not until 1916[71] that a ruling was made requiring non-English-speaking defendants to have access to court proceedings. More recently (1995)[72] anti-discrimination legislation has placed deaf people within a disability context, requiring reasonable adjustments such as the provision of sign language interpreters. The Human Rights Act 1998 places special emphasis on verifying the competence of an interpreter and the European Convention on Human Rights Art.6 requires an interpreter in criminal proceedings to be fully competent in the scope of the assigned task.

There is explicit mention in the Police and Criminal Evidence Act 1984 of using interpreters from the register of sign language interpreters. This Act brought about a national agreement[73] specifying the use of registered interpreters for police and court proceedings[74] (the relevant register for sign language interpreters being the NRCPD, previously CACDP), and for spoken language interpreters, NRPSI). Current agreements by the Ministry of Justice still require that only sign language interpreters registered with the NRCPD be used; this register now includes both deaf and hearing interpreters working between English and BSL, and in addition interpreters working between different sign languages. These provisions will enable deaf European citizens to gain access to legal proceedings.

Looking to the future, it will be interesting to see whether new legislation will allow court proceedings to be video- or audio-recorded. This will enable a more fine-grained analysis of the types of decisions, both linguistic and communicative, which interpreters make in British courtrooms, and how officers of the court interact during interpreter-mediated court proceedings. Such developments will lead to improved verification of the competence of interpreters, and in turn to ensuring deaf people's human rights.

---

[71] *R v Lee Kun* (1916) 1 KB 337. See <http://www.ruth-morris.info/wp-content/uploads/2010/03/Historical-Aspects-of-Court-InterpretingFINAL.pdf> for a full historic analysis of court interpreting.
[72] See the Equality Act 2010 which subsumed the Disability Discrimination Act 1995.
[73] <http://www.justice.gov.uk/downloads/guidance/courts-and-tribunals/courts/interpreters/National_Agreement_on_Use_of_Interpreters-August_2008.pdf>.
[74] This was revised in 2007; see <http://www.cps.gov.uk/legal/h_to_k/interpreters/>.

34

Rule of the Root: Proto-Indo-European Domination of Legal Language

Gary Watt

When Jonathan Swift had Captain Lemuel Gulliver remark upon the "peculiar cant and jargon" that is current amongst lawyers, it is very doubtful that the author appreciated quite how peculiar, and how much like an oft-repeated incantation, legal language is.[1] Swift is not the only cynic to have observed that there is a certain distinctive and technical quality to the language of law which seems more or less designed to exclude the uninitiated, but what is not generally appreciated is that even the everyday language of the law—from "court", to "statute", to "case", to "law" itself—derives from language which has its roots in prehistoric, specifically Proto-Indo-European, society. This paper will correct that oversight, but it aims to do more than simply reveal the hidden roots of legal language; it also seeks to explore the implications of, and to suggest a response to, the discovery that modern legal language is subject to the ongoing dominion of the Proto-Indo-European lexicon and the realization that it is arguably, therefore, subject to the ongoing influence of Proto-Indo-European thought.

Etymology isn't what it used to be. In earlier ages, when scholars were routinely educated in the classical languages, there was naturally a tendency to look to etymology to elucidate the meaning of words. Likewise, when bar and bench had Latin and a little Greek, judges engaged in etymological deliberations more frequently than they do now. Some crude statistical evidence for this is a search for the word "etymology" in UK cases on the Westlaw legal database, which reveals that, despite a proliferation of law reporting during the last century, most of the references appear in cases that are now more (sometimes much more) than a hundred years old.[2] Within the cases in which the authority of etymology is discussed, we are frequently cautioned to resist its allure.[3] The etymology of

---

[1] Jonathan Swift, *Gulliver's Travels* (1726) pt IV 'A Voyage to The Country of The Houyhnhnms' ch 5 (London: Penguin Popular Classics, 1994), 276.
[2] Searched 25 October 2011.
[3] See, e.g., *Meriel Tresham's Case* (1612) 9 Coke Reports 108a at 110b; *Benyon v Evelyn* (1660) Bridgman, O. 621 at 631; *Forbes v Forbes* (1854) Kay 341, 352. In one case we are cautioned that "meal" need not connote food stuff that has been ground down in a mill (*Parsons v Gillespie* [1898] A.C. 239, PC). In fact, the etymology of "meal" is actually rather more sophisticated than any law report is likely to reveal. The rhythmic and grinding aspects of processing grain appear to have evolved along two different lines to produce two distinct senses—one indicating something like "periodic routine" and the other indicating "grinding down of grain". Both senses are combined in the idea of "meal time". (Unless otherwise stated, all etymological proofs are taken from R K Barnhart (ed.), *Chambers Dictionary of Etymology* (London: H Wilson and Company, 1988)). For a rare judicial call to respect etymology, albeit in the narrow context of the construction of wills, see *Blamford v Blamford* (1615) 3 Bulstrode 98; 81 E.R. 84 at 93.

"etymology" suggests that it was once considered to be a study of the "truth" of words,[4] but this is another sense in which etymology isn't what it used to be. In one Victorian case, an exasperated Sir John Wickens VC opined that "etymology is a very unsafe guide to meaning".[5] And even during Shakespeare's lifetime, when the renaissance of classical rhetoric was in full bloom and the *figura etymologica* was a popular rhetorical trope,[6] Coke's report of *Calvin's Case* warns that "arguments drawn from Etymologies, are too weak and too light for Judges to build their judgments upon".[7] The message from the reports is clear—it is not that scholars should be deterred from mining for the deep meaning of words or that advocates should be prohibited from buttressing a winning argument with etymology,[8] only that none of us should expect judges to be persuaded by the authority of etymology.

In this paper I am not concerned with ornamental etymology. I am not concerned with the sort of etymological authority that barristers consciously choose to invoke and judges choose to reject. My concern is with the sort of etymological authority that is so deeply rooted in our legal language that it seems impossible to undermine. My hypothesis is that legal thought is dominated by legal language and that legal language, being deeply conservative, is still dominated by its ancient roots and hence by ancient thought. It is telling, for instance, that the jurist just cited said that "arguments drawn from etymologies are too weak and too light for Judges to *build* their judgments upon" (emphasis added). He instinctively used the metaphor of construction to describe the judicial process, thereby alluding to an ideal of social stability, structure, and regulation—the architectural ideal—which, as this paper will show, has been fundamental to legal language and legal thought since ancient times.

Sir William Jones, an English colonial judge in India, and, more significantly, an exceptionally gifted hyperpolyglot and philologist, was the first person to postulate the language which today we call Proto-Indo-European. In 1786, in a celebrated lecture to the Asiatic Society which he had founded, he observed that:

> The Sanscrit language, whatever be its antiquity, is of a wonderful structure; more perfect than the Greek, more copious than the Latin, and more exquisitely refined than either, yet bearing to both of them a stronger affinity, both in the roots of verbs and the forms of grammar, than could possibly have been produced by accident; so strong indeed, that no philologer could examine them all three, without believing them to have sprung from some common source, which, perhaps, no longer exists; there is a similar reason, though not quite so forcible, for supposing that both the Gothic and the Celtic, though blended with a very different idiom, had the same origin with the Sanscrit; and the old Persian might be added to the same family.[9]

---

[4] Marcus Tullius Cicero considered, but decided against, coining "*veriloquium*" as a Latin neologism for the Greek "*etymologia*" (Frederick M Rener, *"Interpretatio": Language and Translation from Cicero to Tytler (Approaches to Translation Studies)* (Amsterdam: Editions Rodopi B.V., 2009), 105.

[5] This observation, made at first instance, is recorded in the report of the decision on appeal to the Court of Appeal in Chancery (*Hext v Gill* (1871–72) L.R. 7 Ch. App. 699).

[6] Shakespeare's own lines frequently exemplify this trope, in which, in its purest form, distinct words sharing the same etymological root are juxtaposed in speech or text. Witness, for instance, the following example from Sonnet 129, which the reader will discover is loaded with legal and Proto-Indo-European interest: "Had, having, and in quest to have, extreme;/A bliss in proof, and proved, a very woe".

[7] *Calvin's Case, or the Case of the Postnati* (1608) 7 Coke Reports 1a at 27b; 77 E.R. 379 at 411, in the Court of King's Bench, heard in the Exchequer by the Chancellor and all the Judges of England. This quote is immediately followed in the report by the cautionary maxim *Saepenumero ubi proprietas verborum attenditur, sensus veritatis amittitur* ("Where attention is paid to the precise properties of words, their true meaning is lost").

[8] See, e.g., *Knowles v Attorney-General* [1951] P 54 at 60.

[9] 2 February 1786 (published in the first volume of *Asiatick Researches* (1788) 415–31).

It is notable that Sir William attached such significance to grammar, even at the dawn of the discipline of Proto-Indo-European studies, for what we know of the Proto-Indo-Europeans and their language is attributable more to grammatical resemblance than to similarity in vocabulary. Grammatical structures are not casually borrowed between cultures in the way that vocabulary may be. That said, similarities in vocabulary can at the very least add strength to theories based on grammar.

In addition to its other aims, the present paper seeks to remedy a surprising and enduring ignorance amongst jurists of the significant historical connections between the discipline of law and the discipline of etymology, for as the origins of modern etymological scholarship can be traced to an English colonial judge, so its development owes a great deal to the German jurist and philologist Jacob Ludwig Carl Grimm (1785–1863), more generally famous as one of the brothers Grimm of fairy-tale renown. Jacob Grimm postulated the fundamental rules which govern differences in the pronunciation of consonants between the Indo-European and Proto-Germanic languages. These rules are known collectively as "Grimm's Law".[10] That title indicates that the discipline of law is linked to the early development of the discipline of etymology by something more than the identity of individual scholars. The essential regularity of linguistic development—its obedience to certain "laws" of change—is in some respects paralleled in the way in which juridical laws, if they are worthy of that name, must maintain a certain stability and predictability even as they keep pace with social and cultural change. A mind attuned to appreciate the development of law is thus a mind attuned to appreciate etymology and the development of language.

The remainder of this paper is directed to proving the survival in modern legal language of some of the essential features of Proto-Indo-European thought; and, secondly, which is the most important issue going forward, to identify an appropriate practical response to its ongoing influence.

1. The archaic nature of legal language

From century to century the essentials of legal language remain to a remarkable degree unchanged. Warren Cowgill writes of "the abundantly documented conservative character of legal language in all or most societies",[11] and Calvert Watkins, another specialist in Proto-Indo-European etymology, writes in the same vein that "[t]he conservatism of legal language in the various Indo-European linguistic traditions (modern as well as ancient) has long been recognized, and scarcely needs comment".[12] It perhaps needs little comment amongst etymologists, but the peculiarly archaic nature of modern legal language, as compared with other branches of our current lexicon (with the possible exception of the religious lexicon), is a fact that has been almost universally overlooked by lawyers, and its implications have, until this paper, received no sustained consideration by a legal

---

[10] Also known as the "Rask's-Grimm's rule" or the "First Germanic Sound Shift" or the "Germanic Consonant Shift". An example of Grimm's Law is the rule that the Indo-European voiced stops "b", "d", and "g" become, respectively, the voiceless stops "p", "t", and "k" in Proto-Germanic.

[11] Warren Cowgill, "Two Further Notes on the Origin of The Insular Celtic Absolute and Conjunct Verb Endings" (1975) 26 *Ériu* 27 at 32.

[12] Calvert Watkins, "Studies in Indo-European Legal language, Institutions, and Mythology" in G Cardona, H M Hoenigswald, and A Senn (eds), *Indo-European and Indo-Europeans: Papers Presented at the Third Indo-European Conference at the University of Pennsylvania* (Philadephia: University of Pennsylvania Press, 1970) 321–54 at 321.

scholar. No doubt the conservatism of legal language has been confirmed throughout history by the need to keep written records of laws and legal affairs, but it must also be significant that law by its nature, and for its authority, depends upon a certain reputation of permanence and stability. Law is precedented; law is law-abiding. It should hardly surprise us, then, that legal language is conventional. How many neologisms have been admitted into the inner sanctum of the law? The answer is very few. What is the latest thing in law-speak amongst practitioners: is it "human rights", or "arbitration", or "dispute resolution", or "regulatory reform"? Most of these words are almost nakedly Latin, and that makes them, in essence, far more ancient than the Romans, for as Michael Weiss has observed: "[t]he Latin lexicon, especially in the religious and legal spheres, shows some notable agreements with Indo-Iranian that are undoubtedly archaic":[13] The law contains few neologisms, few root-less words. Law is not a domain in which to hunt for Jabberwocks. In preparing this paper, I found a neologism (albeit nothing much like a Jabberwock) on the website of one of the world's largest law firms, Herbert Smith Freehills. The website was advertising a "webinar". This is not legal language, of course, but lawyers have appropriated it, and that seems as good a tactic as any by which to convince clients that their advisers are in all respects "bang up-to-date". Except that the title of this particular webinar rather gives the game away: "The changing face of UK financial services regulatory architecture".[14] This short phrase contains several of the most ancient, fundamental, and deeply rooted linguistic expressions of legal thought. The "face" of the law recalls the fact that the artificial construct we call the legal "person" derives from "*persona*", which is the Latin word for the ancient Greek-style dramatic mask.[15] The word "regulatory" derives from the Proto-Indo-European (PIE) root **reg-*, which has yielded a whole set of words associated with legal and political order, including regina, rex, royal, director, right, and rule.[16] Maine argues that our current conception of a legal right is not ancient,[17] but even if that is true, it cannot be denied that the notion of social regulation being "rectilinear" and "level" and in some way equivalent to the direction of a "straight path" is truly archaic, as Maine himself acknowledges elsewhere.[18] One might add that the language that we use to describe the infringement of legal rights has been dominated since time immemorial by the idea of "wrong" and "tort", which as every first-year law student is taught, connotes the physical twisting of something which ought to be straight.[19] Next in the title of the law firm's webinar is "architecture". This describes the art of the "master builder", which, as has already been mentioned, and as the word-set

---

[13] Michael Weiss, "Indo-European Languages" in M Gagarin and E Fantham (eds), *The Oxford Encyclopedia of Ancient Greece & Rome* (Oxford: Oxford University Press, 2010), 61–3 at 63.
[14] <http://hsf-fsrandcorpcrimenotes.com/webinars/> (accessed 11 October 2012).
[15] The *Chambers Dictionary of Etymology* (cited in n.3) records that the Latin *persona* may be "borrowed from the Etruscan *phersu* mask". It might also be connected to a sense of sound passing through (*per-sono*).
[16] The asterisk symbol which frequently appears in a PIE root, such as **reg-*, indicates a conjectured reconstruction.
[17] Sir Henry S Maine, *Dissertations on Early Law and Custom* (London: John Murray, 1914) 390: "[t]he clear conception of a legal right is not ancient, or even Roman, but... it belongs distinctively to the modern world".
[18] Maine, *Ancient Law* (cited in n.52). See also W Cesarini-Sforza, *"ius" e "directum". Note sull'origine storica dell'idea di diritto* (Bologna: Stab. poligr. riuniti, 1930) (I am grateful to my colleague Professor Emanuele Conte of the Law School at the Università Degli Studi Roma Tre for bringing this source to my attention).
[19] "Wrong" is cognate with the Old Icelandic *rangr*, meaning crooked or awry, and the Proto-Indian **wrengh-* ("to turn"). The synonymous "Tort" comes to us from the PIE base **twork-/*twerk* ("twist") via the Latin *tortus* ("twisted").

of *reg- confirms, was a paradigm for social order and regulation even before Aristotle offered the famous metaphor which likened equitable judgment to building using a flexible rule.[20] Sometimes the survival of an archaic expression is exact. For instance, it is still the law of England that an easement acquired by prescription must be acquired "*nec vi, nec clam, nec precario*" (without force, without stealth, without permission). The negation "*nec*" is, as Calvert Watkins observes, "ancient".[21] His point is that it was ancient even to the Romans who used it. From our perspective it is truly archaic. Modern legal language is not merely conservative; in many of its aspects it is prehistoric, it is primal.

2. Proto-Indo-Europeans

"...etymology is usually indicative of some kind of historical connection. The question is whether the connection is essential or contingent".[22]

Etymology is a discipline in which it is rarely safe to make categorical claims, especially with regard to the cultural origins of a language; more especially when one is digging down as deep as the Proto-Indo-European. Language is always changing, so it is inconceivable that our current version of the reconstructed Proto-Indo-European lexicon was ever actually spoken by a certain people at a certain time. We can only speculate that an early people group in the course of its development from generation to generation cultivated a language which at some time or other established the roots for the languages which would later be used in the various branches (including Latin and Greek) of the Indo-European family of people groups. Thus the Proto-Indo-European lexicon was probably formed around the period 4500–4000 BCE and had undergone major dispersal by around 2300–1600 BCE, which is approximately when the speakers of Greek are thought to have arrived in the territory of Greece.[23] Modern English, formed as it is for the most part by an unusual combination of Germanic and Italic influences,[24] with contributions from Greek, Celtic, and others, represents a particularly rich intertwining—in some sense a "re-joining"—of several major branches of the Indo-European family of languages.

Scholars cannot agree as to the geographical origins of the people whom we call "Proto-Indo-European". In the words of Professor James Mallory, one can only ask of the specialists: "[w]here do they put it now?"[25] It is, he adds, a "Never-Ending Story".[26] If I, an outsider (blindfolded by the fact that my first discipline is law) were to pin a tail

---

[20] Aristotle, *The Nicomachean Ethics*, Book V ch.10.
[21] Calvert Watkins, "'In the interstices of procedure': Indo-European legal language and comparative law" (1986) 13(1) *Historiographia Linguistica* 27–42 at 35.
[22] John Lyons, "Linguistics and law: the legacy of Maine" in Alan Diamond (ed.), *The Victorian Achievement of Sir Henry Maine: A Centennial Reappraisal* (Cambridge: Cambridge University Press, 1991) 337.
[23] Martin E Huld, "Indo-Europeans" in Gagarin and Fantham, *The Oxford Encyclopedia of Ancient Greece & Rome* (cited in n.13) 63–5.
[24] W. Rothwell, "The Missing Link in English Etymology: Anglo-French" (1991) 60 *Medium Aevum* 173.
[25] J P Mallory, *In Search of the Indo-Europeans: Language, Archaeology, and Myth* (London: Thames & Hudson, 1989) 143; J P Mallory and D Q Adams, *The Oxford Introduction to Proto-Indo-European and the Proto-Indo-European World* (Oxford: Oxford University Press, 2006) 460. See also J P Mallory, "The homelands of the Indo-Europeans" in R Blench and M Spriggs (eds), *Archaeology and Language I: Theoretical and Methodological Orientations* (London: Routledge, 1997); C Renfrew, *Archaeology and Language: The Puzzle of Indo-European Origins* (London: Jonathan Cape, 1987).
[26] Mallory and Adams, *The Oxford Introduction to Proto-Indo-European* (cited in n.25) 442.

on the donkey based only on what the majority of expert etymologists seem to be saying on one side and the other, I would put the pin in the steppe land which lies to the north of the Black Sea and the Caspian Sea. The reconstructed Proto-Indo-European lexicon provides clues to locate its speakers in a temperate zone where snow is found but sun-baked bricks are not.[27] It is hard enough to pin the tail on a static donkey, but presumably the Proto-Indo-Europeans did not stand still during the hundreds of years in which their language achieved the wide lexicon which is attributed to it today. There is bound to be a margin of error in identifying the homeland of a prehistoric people, and very likely a wide one.

If there is chronic disagreement about the geographical homeland of the Proto-Indo-Europeans, there is also ongoing controversy concerning the nature of their culture. Perhaps the Proto-Indo-Europeans inhabited an agrarian idyll in which they worshipped their gods, administered justice amongst their people, and kept themselves to themselves. For a people who achieved such linguistic imperium over the rest of the world, that image cannot tell the whole truth. Did a language ever achieve significant territorial dominion without militaristic expansion? (Witness the linguistic imperium of Chinese, English, French, Greek, Latin, and Spanish.) Whatever the Proto-Indo-Europeans might have been to begin with, the ones responsible for taking their language abroad had a well-developed language of conflict. Their language is agrarian, but it is also aggressive. Mallory and Adams observe that within the reconstructed Proto-Indo-European lexicon:

> the vocabulary of strife...is fairly extensive (at least twenty-seven verbs) and while a number may be dismissed as purely expressions of the general application of physical force, e.g. striking an object, others such as *seĝh- "hold fast, conquer" certainly make better sense in a military context.[28]

A most striking and revealing feature of Indo-European language is the abundance of words for taking and seizing and the relative scarcity of words for donation.[29] The Proto-Indo-European instinct was to have and to hold. There was the instinct to *have* in the sense of "heave" or "grasp",[30] and there was the instinct to *hold* in the sense of "keep a settled hold of". The latter sense derives from the Latin *habere* and produces such modern English words as "landholding" and "habitat". The Latin *habere* can ultimately be traced back to the PIE base *ghabh-, which is not without a sense of the PIE root *kap- ("seize" or "grab") but also indicates a holding so settled that it can be given away (the Indo-European *ghabh- is also the root of "give"). The close connection between "have" (as in holding) and "give" that the root *ghabh- implies survives in the maxim of English law "nobody can give that which they do not have", which we still express in the Latin *nemo*

---

[27] "In short, the evidence for architectural terms in Proto-Indo-European is most consistent with an architectural tradition somewhere in temperate Eurasia where houses were exclusively built of timber rather than brick" (Mallory and Adams, *Oxford Introduction to Proto-Indo-European* (cited in n.25) 228). There is an intriguing theory, widely accepted by geologists, that the Black Sea was deluged from the Mediterranean around 5600 BC, causing it to expand greatly to the north-west. Underwater excavation has apparently discovered rectangular settlement architecture at the pre-deluge shoreline, and one can speculate that the original shore-dwellers, who might well have been forebears of the Proto-Indo-Europeans, were driven north by the flood. The spread of the Proto-Indo-Europeans has frequently been attributed to a range of climatic and geophysical factors as well as the more straightforward factor of territorial acquisition by conquest.

[28] Mallory and Adams, *Oxford Introduction to Proto-Indo-European* (cited in n.25) 284.
[29] Mallory and Adams, *Oxford Introduction to Proto-Indo-European* (cited in n.25) 270.
[30] From the Proto-Germanic *haben- from PIE *kap- "to grasp".

dat quod non habet. Likewise, the so-called "*habendum*" clause" in a lease or other deed of transfer often begins with the words "to have and to hold" even though it describes the asset that is being given away. These survivors support the view that in Proto-Indo-European society conquest, to whatever extent it existed, was closely accompanied by settlement. The Proto-Indo-Europeans were probably aggressive, but they were certainly agrarian; we know that livestock held a significant place in their society (in later societies "heads" of livestock eventually produced the language of "capital" and "chattels" from the Latin "*capita*").[31] In Proto-Indo-European society it is likely that young men of the tribe constituted a distinct warrior caste and that older members of the society who were settled in agrarian routines resented any call to military service. In Ancient Greece we know that "the absence of a citizen farmer on a military campaign, normally fought in the summer, might threaten the very survival of his family at home".[32] Similar tensions between care for one's own and conquest of the other must have existed in Proto-Indo-European society.

The plough or plow is a material key to Indo-European culture. The root **arə* "to plough" is attested in Celtic, Italic, Germanic, Balto-Slavic, and Greek,[33] and the idea of driving animals "underlies all of the cognates".[34] Agrarian culture is plough culture. To plough you need to clear ground of trees. This is the job of an axe; which therefore becomes a symbol of both the aggressive and the agrarian aspects of Proto-Indo-European society.[35] Trees not used for fuel are used to form utensils, ornaments, and, most significant in terms of settlement, fences and houses and communal buildings. One of the prime material indicators of Roman authority was the *fasces*—a bundle of sticks bound together with an axe. The fasces, with its connotations of communal, agrarian order defended by military force, epitomizes Aryan and other Indo-European culture. In the mid-20th century the atrocities perpetuated by the Nazis and their self-styled "fascist" allies perverted long-standing cultural associations of the words "fasces" and "Aryan", but even today the symbol of the bundle of sticks survives, albeit frequently absent the axe, in the architectural rhetoric of such celebrated modern monuments to the rule of law as the US House of Representatives, the Lincoln Memorial, and the statues guarding the main stairway to the entrance of the US Supreme Court building in Washington (the pediment of the front face of the building even contains the relief image of a Roman lictor complete with fasces). The vestige of Proto-Indo-European thought has routinely been overlooked in modern legal architecture, and the argument of this paper is that it has likewise been routinely overlooked in modern legal language.

---

[31] The word "hold" derives from the Proto-Germanic **haldanan* and originally indicated to keep and watch over livestock. It will not surprise us that the older form "holden" is now all but extinct except in legal vernacular. The law reports are replete with references to meetings of courts, trade unions, churches that were "holden" at some time or other. Even today Peers are summoned to attend a "a certain Parliament to be holden at Our City of Westminster" (see *Lord Mayhew of Twysden's Motion* [2002] 1 A.C. 109 at 115 (House of Lords)).

[32] Joint Association of Classical Teachers, *The World of Athens: An Introduction to Classical Athenian Culture* (Cambridge: Cambridge University Press, 1984) 69.

[33] Warren Cowgill, "A comment on Bernard Wailes, 'Origins of Settled Farming in Temperate Europe'" in Cardona et al, *Indo-European and Indo-Europeans* (cited in n.12) 279–305 at 301. Mallory and Adams, *Oxford Introduction to Proto-Indo-European* (cited in n.25) 242–3 identify the root in the complex code of the specialist etymologist as $h_2\acute{e}rh_3yelo$.

[34] Barnhart, *Chambers Dictionary of Etymology* (cited in n.3).

[35] Barnhart, *Chambers Dictionary of Etymology* (cited in n.3).

Stones, like trees, must be cleared before the plough, and would have been piled as boundary markers. Numerous ancient texts, including legal texts, attest to the significance of boundary markers; and antique marble stones (*horoi*) can still be seen today at the site of the ancient *Agora* of Athens where they marked out the boundary of the market place half a millennium before Christ. Enclosure and plough culture are almost symbiotically connected—agriculture produces stone and wood boundaries; boundaries of stone and wood protect cultivated plots. The significance of this for present purposes is that enclosure remains a hard habit of legal thought in Europe and in jurisdictions established after European influence or example. That legal ideas of enclosure and privatization are not an inevitable fact of human relations to the natural environment is brought most clearly to light by land disputes between non-enclosure cultures, such as the aboriginal inhabitants of Australia, and jurisdictions of the European (we might say Indo-European) type.[36] Milner S Ball devotes his book *Lying Down Together* to exposing and critiquing the image of law as defensive wall which he identifies to be the self-image most powerfully promoted and perpetuated by European-type legal systems. He convincingly argues that "[l]aw as bulwark, or something very like it, is the present, predominate conception of law".[37] Describing the position in the USA in terms which apply as well to England and to Europe as far back as the Indo-Europeans, he writes that, even though "[b]oundaries and fences now figure not so much in conquest as in ownership. The conceptual differences are not great. The bulwark is evident in the exhibition and defence of property holdings."[38] Earlier on the same page he had noted that "[r]ock walls were an import from Europe, the symbol of a life-style, a reinforcement of conquest ideology, and so a realization of bulwark thought and practice".[39] All of this might explain why the infringement of a legal duty has, since at least as far back as the Laws of Cnut (*c*.1025), been described using the same word—"breach" (from the PIE **bhreg*-)—that came to describe the infraction of a defensive barrier.[40]

The possibility of a gap in the legal defensive bulwark is regarded with the sort of disdain with which military defenders once regarded weaknesses in the castle wall. We frequently talk of legal "loopholes", but do we appreciate that a "loophole" denotes an arrow slit—a narrow point of vulnerability in a castle wall—and do we stop to consider what this might say about our image of the law? The very fact that the *inter*-disciplinary work in which some legal scholars specialize is sometimes considered to be "beyond the pale" by the main camps of legal practice and doctrinal scholarship is in itself a small proof of law's ongoing habit of raising its drawbridge against the wider world.

Plough culture of the sort that was central to Proto-Indo-European society shapes legal thought in another respect. It has been observed that "small ploughed fields are most economically of square or rectangular shape, particularly when adjoining to form a 'field system'".[41] Ploughing prefers straight lines and it prefers enclosures to be quadrilateral. Tim Ingold, in his study of the history of lines, attributes writing in straight lines to

---

[36] See, generally, Graeme J Neate, "Legal Language Across Cultures: Finding the Traditional Aboriginal Owners of Land" (1981) 12 Fed L Rev 207.

[37] Milner S Ball, *Lying Down Together: Law Metaphor and Theology* (Madison: The University of Wisconsin Press, 1985) 36.

[38] Ball, *Lying Down Together* (cited in n.37) 97.

[39] Ball, *Lying Down Together* (cited in n.37) 97.

[40] Hence Shakespeare's famous lines: "Once more unto the breach, dear friends, once more,/Or close the wall up with our English dead." *Henry V* (3.1.1–2) in J Bate and E Rasmussen (eds), *The RSC Shakespeare: Complete Works* (London: Macmillan, 2007).

[41] Bernard Wailes, "Origins of Settled Farming in Temperate Europe" in Cardona et al., *Indo-European and Indo-Europeans* (cited in n.12) 279–305, 283.

the ancient practice of weaving threads into textiles and to the practice of plotting land with threads.[42] If the latter explanation holds good, then it may be just another way of saying that writing in lines is a feature that follows the furrows of the plough. Some of the earliest species of writing were actually set out in exact plough-form, known by the Greek *boustrophedon* ("as the ox turns"), with alternate lines reading left to right then right to left along the tablet. The rectilinear frames of Proto-Indo-European thought which produced rectilinear regulation with strict (that is "straight") law might have its origins in the practical economies of ploughing in straight lines.

People of the plough need stable shelter for their animals and for themselves. Such "stability"—a word derived from the Proto-Indo-European base **stā-* or *stə-* or *sth-*. ("to stand")—is the origin of the political state. Legal language would not exist as we know it if embedded metaphors of stasis and standing were removed. As you read the following paragraph, make a note of the words which are ultimately derived from the PIE root **stā- (stə-/sth-)*. You will no doubt be surprised to discover the pervasive influence of this one root in modern legal language and thought.

Cases and statutes are the two key components of the corpus of common law, and both are underpinned by the constitutional authority of the State. One may initiate litigation provided that one has standing to appear. In court, one will present one's case as statements (made on a form drawn up by the law stationer). Having heard the case stated, the judge decides the matter bearing in mind the need to "stand by" precedents established in the past, in accordance with the doctrine of *"stare decisis"* ("stand by the thing decided"). Precedents may be departed from in certain circumstances, one of which is where the precedent can be shown to have become obsolete because it was decided *rebus sic stantibus* ("as matters then stood"). Having decided the case, the judge may stay execution. One of the key causes of judicial business is the legal estate (freehold or lease), and it is significant how closely social status (station in life) is aligned with a great landed estate... This is all supposing that the matter is a civil matter. If it is a criminal matter it will all start at the police station with a police constable.[43]

Another legal idea, a Roman one as it happens, which is thoroughly indebted to the PIE root **stā-* is "restitution", which denotes the process by which assets or funds are reinstated or, which is often the same thing, by which persons are returned to the position— the "*status quo ante*" (another legal **stā-* phrase)—in which they stood prior to some legally relevant action or occurrence.

There was an archaic form of *lis* ("lawsuit") spelled STLIS in inscriptions.[44] Lionel S Joseph observes that "[b]y the end of the Republican period, the forms in *stl-* are restricted almost entirely to the fixed phrase DECEMVIR STLITIBVS IVDICANDIS 'decemvir for judging lawsuits'".[45] He adds that the spelling with the prefix *stl-* was retained only by the jurists; in other literary language from Plautus onwards, *lis* appears in its more usual simplified form. Joseph acknowledges the argument that the additional "ST" may be a cognate of *stare* to stand,[46] but thinks that this is unconvincing semantically. Nevertheless, it seems to this author to be at least plausible to suppose that the dominance of **stā-* in legal language might have turned *lis* into STLIS with something

---

[42] Tim Ingold, *Lines: A Brief History* (Abingdon: Routledge, 2008) 159.
[43] A solution can be found in G Watt, *Equity Stirring: The Story of Justice Beyond Law* (Oxford: Hart Publishing, 2009) 185, where a similar text is set out with the relevant **stā-* words underlined.
[44] Lionel S Joseph, "A Survival from the Italo-Celtic Legal Vocabulary" (1986) 37 *Ériu* 119–25, 121.
[45] Joseph, "A Survival from the Italo-Celtic Legal Vocabulary" (cited in n.44) 121.
[46] Joseph, "A Survival from the Italo-Celtic Legal Vocabulary" (cited in n.44) 122 n.7.

like the root for standing in mind, especially when one considers that in this context we are talking about the inscription of legal language on one of the most ancient sites of legal text—a stele or standing stone. Admittedly, it is puzzling that in the later Roman period STLIS seems occasionally to have become, for no apparent reason, SCLIS, but this can perhaps be put down to error caused by the shorthand or abbreviated nature of stone-inscribed text, through which original meanings were liable to be forgotten. Whatever its origin, the fact that ST was exclusively retained in legal terminology confirms what was claimed at the outset of this paper—that legal language is peculiarly conservative. Further evidence in support of that view appears from the Celtic, where the prefix "es" appears in non-legal language but does not appear in formulaic legal language. The absence of "es" in this context has been attributed to the fact that the legal terminology was settled before "es" entered everyday language:

> the absence of *(e)s in such legal formulaic utterances as *atmu* "I grant", *aicdiu* "I invoke as surety"... is in all probability pure archaism: these formulae would have become fixed already before *(e)s had become a necessary component of all statements that were not replies to questions.[47]

Let us now go very deep; deeper even than the Proto-Indo-Europeans, to the first root of who we are—to our physically being human. Before language was written it was spoken and before it was speech it was only the sound of throat, tooth, palette, lip, and tongue. The very word "language" still recalls the last of these. Might it be that the "st" sound, which even today so dominates legal language, is a primitive example of "sound symbolism"?[48] The sound itself, like the metaphor of physical standing and stability which it expresses, has an arresting quality. The swift flow of breath is stopped by tongue on tooth. The moving becomes still. The moving sound of the "s" is terminated by the "t" and the resulting "st" becomes a perfectly efficient expression of the very thing it stands for—which is movement coming to a standstill.[49] Society becomes state. Justice becomes statute. Culture becomes constitution. Watkins observes similar sound symbolism in the fact that:

> a final labial stop or nasal is extremely characteristic of words meaning "take, seize, hold" and the like in a variety of languages. Cf. Lat. *rap-iō, cap-iō, carp-ō*, Gk. *harpázo*, Skt. *grabh-*, Russ. *xap-at'*, Hitt. *ep-zi*, OIr. *gaib-id*, or Eng. *grab, cop, clasp, nab*.[50]

In these examples, the physical enclosure of the lips signifies the conceptual enclosure expressed by the sense of the words.

According to Mallory and Adams, "it seems fairly clear that the Proto-Indo-Europeans occupied substantial houses rather than flimsy shelters".[51] For this one needs level ground, and perhaps a fabricated foundation, all of which ties in with the earliest metaphors for legal social order. As Maine observed, "the earliest notion of order doubtless involved straight lines, even surfaces, and measured distances".[52] Mallory and Adams

---

[47] Cowgill, "Two Further Notes" (cited in n.11) 27–32, 32. The author of this article suggests that *(e)s had as its original function "that of an asseverative particle, etymologically *esti '(it) is (s)' used in statements of fact".

[48] On sound symbolism generally see, e.g., David Reid, *Sound Symbolism* (Edinburgh: T & A Constable Ltd, 1967); Roman Jakobson and Linda R Waugh, *The Sound Shape of Language* (Bloomington: Indiana University Press, 1979); Leanne Hinton, Johanna Nichols, and John J Ohala (eds), *Sound Symbolism* (Cambridge: Cambridge University Press, 1994).

[49] cf. Raymond W Gibbs, Jr., Dinara A Beitel, Michael Harrington, and Paul E Sanders, "Taking a Stand on the Meanings of *Stand*: Bodily Experience as Motivation for Polysemy" (1994) 11 *Journal of Semantics* 231–51.

[50] Watkins, "Studies in Indo-European Legal language" (cited in n.12) 328.

[51] Mallory and Adams, *Oxford Introduction to Proto-Indo-European* (cited in n.25) 227.

[52] Sir Henry S Maine, *Ancient Law* (London: John Murray, 1861) (London: Dent ('Everyman' edn), 1917) 34.

add that with regard to "actual house structure, it is certainly easiest to imagine some form of timber-built structure given the abundance of words for post... and perhaps the word for floor (*$telh_x$-om)".[53] As further evidence for this, the authors cite PIE words for wattle and daub. The authors also provide evidence of internal compartmentalization, with reference to the large number of root words for "chambers" (note the ongoing significance in modern law of cells, judicial chambers, and hearings *in camera*) which they say "suggests the presence of either multi-room constructions or specialized outbuildings for storage and other purposes".[54] They observe, further, that "[t]he reconstructed lexicon also indicates some form of nucleated settlement, i.e. a group of houses" and "[w]e have a series of words for some form of enclosure".[55] The first root word which the authors list in the "enclosure" series is *ghórdhos*, which derives from *gherdh- ("to gird"). The PIE root *ghórdhos became *chórtus* (farmyard) in Greek, *hortus* (enclosed garden) in Latin and later *court* in French and English.[56] It is sobering to think that even today when a police constable takes a prisoner from court to the cells of the police station, the prisoner is feeling at first hand the fearful life of captives in a Proto-Indo-European settlement. The long arm of the law stretches across millennia.

So far I have portrayed Proto-Indo-European architectural and agricultural settlement as a process designed to dominate nature by capture and exclusion. In a similar critical vein, Linda Mulcahy sees the evolution of legal architecture in terms of a gradual enclosure of space and exclusion of free access to that space.[57] There is clearly much truth in that view, especially when one bears in mind (as Mulcahy invites us to bear in mind) that the first courts met in the open air beneath trees. There is, however, an alternative and more hopeful, perhaps too optimistic, way of reading the development of courtrooms and judicial spaces. The "multi-room constructions", which Mallory and Adams attribute to Proto-Indo-European society, developed in some early European civilizations to produce vast building complexes; of which the Palace of Knossos in Crete is an impressive early example. In the Palace of Knossos a labyrinthine network of rooms was grouped around a central court. In the days before effective artificial lighting, large architectural developments required open courts to admit natural light into the heart of the structure.[58] Courts, in the judicial sense, can therefore be regarded as an attempt to bring the lights of natural justice into the artificial confines of legal regulation and compartmentalization. Close critical examination of our received habits of legal language and legal thought reveals the possibility of cultivating a new language from the roots of the old. It cannot be denied that "court" is the etymological cousin of "gird" and "yard", with all the connotations of capture, exclusion, and measurement those words imply, but "court" is even more closely related to "garden" and the garden of the law, which

---

[53] Mallory and Adams, *Oxford Introduction to Proto-Indo-European* (cited in n.25) 228. Even at a very early date some buildings were laid out on the rectangular plan that is ubiquitous in "Western" architecture today (Mallory and Adams, (at n.27 and n.58)).

[54] Mallory and Adams, *Oxford Introduction to Proto-Indo-European* (cited in n.25) 228.

[55] Mallory and Adams, *Oxford Introduction to Proto-Indo-European* (cited in n.25) 227.

[56] Mallory and Adams, *Oxford Introduction to Proto-Indo-European* (cited in n.25) 221, 232.

[57] Linda Mulcahy, *Legal Architecture: Justice, Due Process and the Place of Law* (Oxford: Routledge, 2011).

[58] William Bell Dinsmoor, *The Architecture of Ancient Greece: An Account of its Historic Development* 3rd rev. edn (London: B T Batsford Ltd, 1950) 4. This author observes that "[o]n the Greek mainland...the normal form of the earliest houses was the circular hut common to all nomadic peoples.... The gradual straightening of the walls until the sides become parallel, with a façade wall at right angles containing the doorway, marks the beginning of the rectangular plan" (5–6). The Palace of Knossos was built, over hundreds of years, in the middle of the second millennium BC.

we are accustomed to regard as a site of seclusion and exclusion but which might, if we imagine a different history, be considered a site of openness and light.

If the Proto-Indo-European world seems to us to have been a darkly primitive world of warfare and servitude to fixed categories of social status, it was nevertheless a world in which, in theory at least, justice was conceived in terms of striving to attain and maintain an order sanctioned as much by spiritual as by secular powers.[59] Mallory and Adams write that:

> Our recovery of legal institutions, at least on the basis of the reconstructed lexicon, is meager. There seems to be an acceptance of a concept of *$h_2értus$ "what is fitting", i.e. the cosmic order that must be maintained. This should be done by adhering to *$dhéh_1mi$-/men- "what is established, law", here generally taken (on the basis of Greek and Indo-Iranian comparative studies) to be the law that has been established ($dhéh_1$) by the gods for humans.[60]

The Latin *jus*, which produces "justice" and our words for speaking justice (including "judge", "adjudication", and "jurisdiction") is of unknown origin, but it might well derive from the PIE base *$yewes$- via the Old Latin *ious*, which connotes a process of ritual purification (this is the sense of the Avestan *yaozda*, and the same sense is retained, for example, in the Christian doctrine of spiritual "justification" through faith). If you assault me and break my bone, we say that I have suffered an injury, but it may be more accurate, etymologically speaking, to say that you have inflicted an injury on yourself. Etymologically, "injury" seems to fit better as a description of the perpetrator's taint than as a description of the victim's harm.

We can summarize this part, and preface the next, with the words of Calvert Watkins who observes that the tripartite characterization of Indo-European society as "a society of priests, warriors, and farmers—can be applied with profit to aspects of Indo-European law".[61]

3. Legal language

There is no statistically reliable method of delineating the content of legal language in any modern jurisdiction. In the spirit of experiment (and with no pretence to having carried out a scientific survey) I have conducted a statistical analysis of the lexicon used in one recent case decided by the Supreme Court of the United Kingdom. The case title is an efficient epitome of legal jargon:

> Hilary Term
> [2011] UKSC 10
> On appeal from: [2009] EWCA Civ 1159;
> [2009] EWCA Civ 1211
> JUDGMENT
> Sienkiewicz (Administratrix of the Estate of Enid
> Costello Deceased) (Respondent) v Greif (UK)
> Limited (Appellant)
> Knowsley Metropolitan Borough Council
> (Appellant) v Willmore (Respondent)

---

[59] Mallory and Adams, *Oxford Introduction to Proto-Indo-European* (cited in n.25) 285.
[60] Mallory and Adams, *Oxford Introduction to Proto-Indo-European* (cited in n.25) 276.
[61] Watkins, "'In the interstices of procedure'" (cited in n.21) 29.

The vernacular of this case heading, with its modern abbreviations and Latin terms of art, must be virtually impenetrable to the uninitiated. Even seemingly familiar words appear in unfamiliar form. For example, there is no "e" in the middle of the "judgment" because the word is being used here in a judicial context. This is a shibboleth for the identification of non-lawyers so subtle that there is not so much as a clue in the sound of the word to tell whether the middle "e" is present or not. Marginally less subtle is the letter "v" which connects the parties in the title of the case. In the jurisdiction of England and Wales it is proper form for lawyers to pronounce this "and"; preferably not "versus", and certainly never "vee".

So much for the heading of the report. Turning to the substance, we discover that the case concerns the liability of defendants who were the sole known source of the claimants' occupational exposure to asbestos dust. Cases in different fields of law produce somewhat different lexical distributions. There is naturally a difference in the legal lexicon when one moves from, say, the context of tortious litigation to property disputes to family cases to crime—but close attention to any case reveals something of the general nature of legal linguistic usage. In the present case of *Sienkiewicz* v *Greif*, when one removes general non-technical English words such as "the, be, to, of" and "and",[62] and such narrowly fact-specific words as "exposure", "mesothelioma", "epidemiological", "dust" and "dermatitis", the most common words which have a specific technical signification in law are as follows (the number in parenthesis indicates the frequency of references to the word):

caused[167] causation[137] cause[81] causes[33]
case[179] cases[138]
risk[250]
prove[61] proved[36] proof[33] probability [93]
defendant[118] defendants[54]
evidence[155]
Lord[85] Lords[30] LJ (i.e. Lord Justice)[38]
claimant[145]
materially[61] material[49]
appeal[69] appeals[30]
balance[98]
injury [90]
court [88]
apply [30] applied [43]
victim [72]
v (i.e. "versus") [72]
rule [69]
law [61]
fact [59]
judge [58]
duty[58]
liable[55]
breach[51]

---

[62] These happen to be, in that order, the first most common words in practical use in the English language: <http://www.oxforddictionaries.com/page/oecfactslanguage/the-oec-facts-about-the-language> (accessed 11 October 2012).

The preceding list includes all "legal" words, which, with their inflections and close variations (e.g. prove and proved), receive more than 50 mentions in the report of the case. Let us suppose, which seems reasonable to suppose, that the high incidence of words denoting "causation" and "risk" should be demoted, because such concepts are unusually pertinent to the particular issue in dispute in this case (that is, the issue of liability for causing disease through exposure to asbestos dust). We are then left with a revealing top rank of words. First on the list is the word "case", which, if the reader will excuse the pun, we will consider as a special case towards the end of this paper. That word is followed, in rough order of precedence, by the categories of persons involved ("defendant", "claimant", "law lord", "victim"); by an extensive set of words concerned with the trial of fact ("evidence", "balance", "proof", and so forth); and then, in quick succession, by the words "injury", "court", and "rule" (whose Proto-Indo-European credentials have already been outlined in this paper). The concerns and content of the language as one continues down the list are revealed to be wholly contemporary and yet entirely archaic. We will now briefly consider each of the two major word sets—the status of persons and the trial of fact—in turn. Before we do so, it may be reassuring to point out that the example of *Sienkiewicz v Greif*, though it was chosen somewhat arbitrarily, nevertheless appears to be fairly representative. I conducted a survey of the lexicon in another recent decision of the UK Supreme Court, a case chosen at random, that of *Roberts v Gill & Co Solicitors*,[63] and found that it was similarly replete with frequent references to the status of relevant persons and the process of trial.[64] This is, of course, precisely what we would expect to find in a report of litigation that has reached the highest court in the land. We might expect to find a rather different distribution if we were to examine other varieties of documentary repositories of legal language, such as a statute, a law review article, a legal dictionary, or even documents (such as a will or a commercial lease) which are drafted to meet the particular needs of named individuals. As was said earlier, it is not within the scope or purpose of this paper to present a statistically comprehensive survey of the lexical distribution of legal terminology, still less to attempt the foolishly ambitious task of drawing up a definitive dictionary of modern legal language in most frequent use. It will suffice to observe that legal language employed in the perennial social context of judicial dispute resolution appears still to address timeless concerns using language which for the greater part continues to hark back to origins in Proto-Indo-European culture and thought.

The status of persons

Steven L Winter argues that the legal metaphor of standing originates in the physical act of standing near the seat of judgment and that the related idea of status indicates a physical state of standing in proximity to the seat of judgment.[65] At the seat of judgment we find the king or lord, who in the present case appears in the figure of the "law lord". "Lord" is a word heavily loaded with significations going back to the Proto-Indo-European. The PIE root

---

[63] [2010] UKSC 22, UKSC 2009/0071.

[64] The top-50 ranked words having distinctly legal significance in this case are as follows (the frequency of the occurrence of each word is indicated in parenthesis): action[179]; claim[169]; party[117]; court[116]; v (i.e. "versus")[110]; case[88]; lord[85]; limitation[81]; circumstances[67]; capacity[66]; derivative[65]; proceedings[59]; estate[59]; beneficiary[59]; administrator[56]; section[52]; rule[52]; CPR (i.e. "Civil Procedure Rule(s)")[52]; trustees[51].

[65] S L Winter, "The Metaphor of Standing and the Problem of Self-Governance" (1988) 40(6) *Stanford Law Review* 1371–1516, 1383 n.63.

wordhā means "guard" or "warden" from whose remuneration we derive one of the earliest instances of an "award" or "reward". The law lord, and by extension even inferior judges, can therefore be regarded as a sort of guardian. The precise derivation of "lord" indicates a "loaf ward", which is to say a keeper of the stores of grain or bread.[66] If we wear optimistic spectacles a judge can therefore be seen to be a guardian of the commonwealth and the protector of citizens' goods and welfare; although, through a more critical lens, the judge may be considered to occupy the uppermost place in a hierarchy that ensures its own reward through monopolistic control of access to basic communal benefits. One does not have to move far along the more critical path to discover that the etymological distinction between lord and lady enshrines a curious gender distinction which almost certainly establishes a further level of social hierarchy in favour of the lord and at the very least establishes a peculiar functional distinction between the man who is perceived to guard the goods and the woman who, as "lady" or *læfdige* (Middle English), was the one tasked with kneading the dough.

"Claimant" is another word worthy of critical attention from the etymological point of view. The claimant is the one who clamours or calls out for justice (from the Old French *clamer*, which in turn derives from the Latin *clamare* "to cry out"). Ultimately, the word is etymologically and onomatopoeically derived from the cockerel's "cock-a-doodle-do", so a legal claim is, and has been since the earliest times of domesticated society, a sort of wake-up call.[67] As such, it is rarely welcome or sweet-sounding. A legal claim that resonates beautifully on the ear must be as rare and fantastic as Chaucer's cockerel Chauntecleer, who was said to sing with a voice "merier than the mery organ".[68] The word "appeal", which also appears high up the rankings in *Sienkiewicz* v *Greif* might seem at first sight to have an exclamatory connotation not dissimilar to that of "claim". Such are the perils of untested etymological assumptions. In fact, the word "appeal" is closer in signification to the word "propel". An "appeal" connotes a process of pushing or driving on.

The description "defendant" sounds passive, but it is actually, in its etymology, more active than the current sense of the word would suggest. The party who actively raises a defence, as much as the party who pursues a claim, ensures the continuation of litigation. One might almost say that the person who sets up a fortified position commits as socially damaging an act as the one who would seek to tear a barrier down. There is arguably a certain active violence inherent in the seemingly submissive act of setting up a fence, even if the fence is erected in self-defence of one's own territory. Tangible evidence for this is seen in political *pali* (Latin "fences") from the Great Wall of China and Hadrian's Wall to the Anglo-Irish "Pale" and more recent examples such as the partition walls of Berlin, Belfast, and Gaza. Etymology attests to the violence inherent in defence. The Latin *defendere* derives from *fendere* "to strike, push" and ultimately from the PIE base **gwhen-* which means "to strike" or "to kill".

So far as the descriptions of the interested parties are concerned, the most haunting of all the echoes of the ancient world may be those that resonate around the word "victim". The word derives from the PIE root **weik-* and indicates one who is spiritually and socially set apart, much as a living creature might be set apart for sacrifice.[69] The word is imbued with a strong sense of taboo and social taint. Witches, or self-styled "Wicca", are etymologically associated with victims through the PIE root **weik-*. Historically

---

[66] From the Middle English "*laverd*" or "*loverd*" from the Old English "*hlaford*" and even earlier "*hlafweard*".
[67] The PIE root **kele-* which means "to call" is onomatopoeic for a cockerel's "dawn-calling". (Note that the Sanskrit and Middle Irish words for "cock" are, respectively, "*usakala*" and "*cailech*".)
[68] Geoffrey Chaucer, *The Nonnes Preestes Tale*.
[69] Mallory and Adams, *Oxford Introduction to Proto-Indo-European* (cited in n.25) 412.

speaking it is undoubtedly true that witches were set apart from society and, whether or not they sacrificed innocent victims to their craft, it is clear that they have long been victims of judicial process. Thus in the Laws of Ælfred we find the following edict set down: "*Ða fæmnan þe gewuniað onfon gealdorcræftigan & scinlæcan & wiccan, ne læt þu ða libban*" ("Women who practice in enchantment and sorcery and witchcraft, you should not allow to live"). Earlier in this paper we observed that the consequence of a harm is to taint the perpetrator with an injury that sets him apart from society, but now we can see that there is a cultural sense in which harm also sets the innocent victim apart from the group. This sense is powerfully expressed by Antonio, the title character of Shakespeare's *The Merchant of Venice*, who, as he sits constrained in the Ducal court anticipating Shylock's blade, describes himself as a "tainted wether of the flock,/Meetest for death".[70] Although arguably it is even more graphically expressed in the fate of Shylock himself, who is truly ostracized by the action of the play and may be considered the real victim of the trial.

The process of trial

A set of words pertaining to the process of trial appears high up the ranking of the legal lexicon in *Sienkiewicz* v *Greif*. When those words are considered closely one discovers that they are all clearly and directly derived from metaphors that express basic aspects of material life, many of which would have directly concerned our ancient ancestors. The relevant group of words includes, in ranking order: [prove[61], proved[36], proof[33], probability[93]], evidence[155], [materially[61], material[49]], [appeal[69], appeals[30]], balance[98], [apply[30] applied[43]].

The meaning of "appeal" was considered earlier, as was the link between "balance" and bodily stability which we saw adds a material dimension to that word that goes beyond its traditional and well-known association with the set of scales or balances that have been used in just trade, and images of justice, since ancient times.[71] The word "apply" deserves a brief mention. It means to "lay on" (from the Latin: *ap-* "on" and *plicare* "to lay fold, twist") and in its earliest origins described the laying on of threads in the process of plaiting (from the PIE base **plek-* "to plait, twist"). The word "apply" still serves very well, therefore, as a metaphor of the lawyer's art of laying down the law to fit upon a factual base. The words "materially" and "material" that appear in the "process of trial" set of words are perhaps not so distinctively "legal" that they deserve a place in the lexicon, but they have been included to emphasize the point made earlier—that the law's concern with evidential matters is dominated by metaphors directly derived from the material world. The remaining words in the set very clearly bear this out. The word "evidence" is concerned with visual appearance, and the group of "proof" words (prove[61], proved[36], proof [33], probability[93]) derive from the closely related metaphor of probing the materials of surface appearance.[72] The word "evidence" is also evidence of

---

[70] William Shakespeare, *The Merchant of Venice* (4.1.113–14) (this text is from J Drakakis (ed.), *The Merchant of Venice*, The Arden Shakespeare Third Series (London: Methuen Drama, 2011)).

[71] e.g. the Egyptian goddess Maat, a goddess of law and order, was sometimes depicted with a set of balances. See, generally, J Resnik and D Curtis (eds), *Representing Justice: Invention, Controversy, and Rights in City-States and Democratic Courtrooms* (New Haven and London: Yale University Press, 2011) ch.2.

[72] The equivalence of "probing" and "proving" is of uncertain antiquity, but dates back at least as far as the Middle Ages. On cultural connections between processes of probing material externalities and processes of proving evidence, see G Watt, *Dress, Law and Naked Truth: A Cultural Study of Fashion and Form* (London: Bloomsbury Academic, 2013). In its oldest etymological origins "probe" and "prove" suggest a strong sense of appearance or "front" (literally "being before" or "*pro-be*" from the PIE *probhows*).

the dominance of visual metaphors in legal thought.[73] Justice, it is said, must not only be done but must be seen to be done. The original etymology of vision indicated something more than physical sensory perception; it also indicated insight.[74] Primitive societies revered those who, by means of unusual capacities, were able to see (even to foresee) what others did not. These seers were called the "wise" (the etymological synonym of "visionary"); a virtue which we still like to associate with our judiciary.

4. "...the case is altered"[75]

Excepting the set of words concerned with "cause" and "causation", the top-ranked word in the lexicon in *Sienkiewicz* v *Greif* is "case". If you were asked to sketch the first thing that comes into your mind at the mention of the word "case", it is almost certain that you would draw an enclosed container of some sort; probably something like a briefcase. How many of us would draw a waterfall? Etymologically speaking, that is what we ought to draw. A legal case is not a box; it is a thing that falls. Its etymological cousins are not the casement or casket but the chase of water or cascade. The word derives from the Latin *casus* which denotes an event that befalls someone, and *casus* derives from *cas-* which is a stem of the verb *cadere* ("to fall"). Latin words from this stem describe, not only events that befall individuals, but also great changes of state (such as the fall of Troy) and, most tantalizing of all from a legal perspective, the falling into place—that is, the ordering or settlement—of the heavenly spheres. The latter sense is a survivor of the PIE base **kad-* which signifies, amongst other things, to "lay out, fall or make fall". The word "law" itself denotes a layer (from the PIE root **legh-*),[76] and even today we talk of "laying down" the law.[77] The sense that law is a thing laid down sits well with the idea that a case is a thing that falls down or is handed down, and of course it is still commonplace to regard written law as a deposited or posited thing. The idea of "case" as a falling thing might have its prehistoric source in the fall from the firmament of such stuff as rain or hail.[78] For a prehistoric society, what greater symbol for the dispensation of divine justice or the positing of divine law can one imagine than the regular falling into place of the heavenly spheres and the life-changing fall of water from the heavens to the earth? The fall of rain, with the associated blessing (or, in extremity, curse) of swift-flowing rivers and waterfalls, speaks of provision from an unseen powerful source. There is also a certain sense of justice inherent in the physical properties of water, given its natural predisposition to humble itself by falling to the lowest place it can find and there to find a perfectly straight level free of all unevenness and bias. All in all, we can say that, anthropologically, even psychologically, there is a stronger natural sense of justice in the notion that a case is something that falls from the facts of social life than there is in the jaundiced view that a case is something that lawyers capture and contain. At this juncture it is interesting to recall that the words which came first in the frequency rankings in our statistical survey of legal language in *Sienkiewicz* v *Greif* were those in the set of words concerned with "cause" and "causation". The medieval word "cause" clearly derives from the Latin "*causa*", which was frequently used to describe a reason for action, and not least a reason

---

[73] Bernard J Hibbits, "Making Sense of Metaphors: Visuality, Aurality and the Reconfiguration of American Legal Discourse" (1994) 16 *Cardozo Law Review* 229.
[74] Latin *videre* "to see" from PIE base **weid-* "to know, to see".
[75] The Earl of Warwick in William Shakespeare, *III Henry VI* (4.3.33).
[76] Mallory and Adams, *Oxford Introduction to Proto-Indo-European* (cited in n.25) 277.
[77] Daniel Greenberg, *Laying Down the Law* (London: Sweet & Maxwell, 2011).
[78] The modern Irish word for "shower" is *casair*.

for legal action. The idea of a legal "cause" is sometimes used in effect as a synonym for legal "case", and although there is no clear support for an etymological connection between the two words, it can be observed that the various senses of the words "cause" and "causation" are connected by the sense that one thing "flows from" another. This, one can speculate, might suggest an early etymological association between "case" and "cause". The sound symbolism of both words might be informative. Whereas the sound of the legal staple "st" in "statute", "constitution", and so forth stops the flow of breath, "cas" has the opposite effect of releasing the flow of breath from a state of capture.

The purpose of this close examination of the word "case" is to demonstrate that we are prejudiced to regard law as a rectilinear domain of capture, compartmentalization, containment, and exclusion. We have seen that much of this prejudice is culturally ingrained in our legal language and thought and has been since the days of the Proto-Indo-Europeans. In the case of "case", we have inadvertently suppressed the original PIE sense of a moving, flowing, judicial process under a closed and contained concept that might itself have been cultivated in us by Proto-Indo-European language and thought. The hope is that, being alert to the subtle influences of etymology we will be able to critique them and resist them and reform them where necessary. Let us return, briefly, to "statute". Is the great pillar of legal thought—the stele or standing stone—as immovable as it seems? Not if it can be persuaded to move through an imaginative engagement with legal language. The PIE root *stā-, which gives us "statute" and "statute", also gives us *stasis*. All these words connote unmoving states, but we often overlook the fact that *stasis* connotes a state that is only *temporarily* unmoving. In rhetoric, *stasis* denotes a fixed or stubborn truth-claim on which one takes a stand; but stasis can only be temporary in the context of an art which is designed to move hearts and minds.[79] In medicine, stasis indicates an interruption in the normal flow of blood. The root *stā-, which indicates standing, has been too readily and too completely associated with unmoving states. We have tended to ignore the fact that a standing thing is only a moving thing paused or that, even in the apparently motionless state of bodily standing, a great deal of muscular tension and constant adjustment is devoted to keeping the appearance of balance and poise.[80] One has only to consider Stonehenge to witness that even when great stones are set up to stand for all time, they remain moving things—they are moved over long distances to their standing spots but their motion does not end there—eventually they topple down. Installation is only stalled motion. Statues fall down. Ozymandias fell. Statutes too are movable things. Every lawyer knows that texts are to a large degree open to interpretation, but this paper has shown that an imaginative engagement with legal language has the power to move even the settled meaning of an individual word, and as it were to bring a dead letter back to life.

5. Conclusion

The scholarly study of Proto-Indo-European language and culture is deeply dependent upon legal materials and indeed indebted for its very existence to the philological work of an English judge, and yet legal scholarship has so far been at best indifferent to, and

---

[79] See, generally, H F Plett, T O Sloane, and P L Oesterreich (eds), *Rhetorica Movet: Studies in Historical and Modern Rhetoric in Honour of Heinrich F. Plett* (Leiden: Brill Academic, 1999).

[80] R W Gibbs, JR, D A Beitel, M Harrington and P E Sanders (eds), "Taking a Stand on the Meanings of Stand: Bodily Experience as Motivation for Polysemy" (1994) 11 *Journal of Semantics* 231–51 at 250.

at worst ignorant of, the ongoing domination of Proto-Indo-European language and the ongoing influence of Proto-Indo-European thought upon modern legal language and thought. A search for the term "Proto-Indo-European" within the "Combined World Journals" on Westlaw—a compendious collection of legal journals throughout the Anglo-American and British Commonwealth traditions—produces just seven hits.[81] If this is ignorance then it is ignorance of a potentially dangerous sort, for Proto-Indo-European thought is potentially a dangerous species of thought. Of course, the neglect of etymology in law and legal scholarship is only partly because of ignorance; it is also attributable to pragmatic resignation. Proto-Indo-European is our language and it is our thought. By what means can we speak other than by *our* speech? By what means might we think other than by *our* thought? We might as well object to the fact that we stand on two legs as to object to the essence of our linguistic structures. And yet, even if we cannot uproot the roots of who we are, we nevertheless have the power to resist them and irritate them. And resist we must, for lawyers who purport to play with words without respect for the original power of words will find to their cost that the words are playing with them.

Respect for etymology and appropriate resistance to the historical force of words can form part of a wider project of speaking in a way that is living rather than dead. For James Boyd White, "living speech" is the key to resisting what he calls the "Empire of Force".[82] What this paper has sought to show is that one source of the forces that form our modern habits of thought is the Proto-Indo-European lexicon and, with it, the cultural vestiges of Proto-Indo-European society. In a similar spirit, Milner S Ball offers the following call to future progress based on a critical appreciation of ongoing historical influences:

> unearthing law rocks—the stone tablets, steles, codes, regulations, rules, principles, reports of opinions, and casebooks—may be fruitful survival work if turning them up leads us to find something of the *corpus juris* or our own buried life. And laying down the law may prove promising if the law laid down is not like rocks for a dam in opposition to life, but like stones on a creek bank along the axis of revolutionary movement. The end is not stasis but circulation.[83]

If we cultivate what James Boyd White referred to as "the legal imagination"[84] we will come to appreciate that statutes need not stand still, that courts need not enclose and exclude, and that cases need not be shut up. Our legal thought often takes linguistic form in conflict, conquest, and exclusion—too much either of having or of holding. Looking back we can blame the Proto-Indo-Europeans for giving us the linguistic tools that frame those thoughts; looking forward we have only ourselves to blame for what we make of them.

---

[81] As at 11 October 2012.
[82] J B White, *Living Speech: Resisting the Empire of Force* (Princeton: Princeton University Press, 2006).
[83] Ball, *Lying Down Together* (cited in n.37) 33.
[84] J B White, *The Legal Imagination* (Boston: Little, Brown, 1973).

35

Necessary Violence? Inscribing the Subject of Law

*Penelope Pether**

> We empiricists hold dear to our hearts the idea that objective factual investigation can resolve honest disagreements and focus debate on core values.[1]
>
> Definitions [belong] to the definers—not the defined.[2]
>
> [L]ooking forward as though into unmarked space upon which history will be created results in recreating history.[3]

1. Introduction

In 2004, a law professor at UCLA with a Ph.D. in Economics as well as a law degree[4] (both) from Northwestern University,[5] whose law school has been one of the breeding grounds for the "empirical move" that has increasingly marked the rhetoric of scholarly

---

* This article is dedicated to Tiri Smarr, and Jarid Smith, in awe, and to Professor J. Amy Dillard, for making a difference. Thanks are due to Andrew M. Rein, Villanova University School of Law Class of 2012, and David Salazar, Villanova University School of Law Class of 2013, for the research that made the writing of this article possible, to Brian J. Boyle, Villanova University School of Law Class of 2013 and Susan Rexford, for editing and logistical assistance, and to Associate Dean for Faculty Research Steven M. Chanenson, for research support. Professor Peter Goodrich of Benjamin N. Cardozo School of Law at Yeshiva University provided helpful comments on a draft of this article and, together with Professor Michael Freeman, Professor of English Law at University College, London, and Professor Mitu Gulati of Duke Law School, urged me on. Professor Steven Lamos of the Program for Writing and Rhetoric and the English Department, and Faculty Director of the Writing Center at the University of Colorado-Boulder provided invaluable guidance to the scholarship on critical race pedagogy in Rhetoric and Composition Studies. And, as always, Professor David S. Caudill had my back.

[1] Richard H. Sander, "Comment in Reply" (1997) 47 J. Legal Educ. 512, 512.
[2] Toni Morrison, *Beloved* (Plume, 1988) 190.
[3] Nan Seuffert, *Jurisprudence of National Identity: Kaleidoscopes of Imperialism and Globalisation from Aotearoa New Zealand* (Ashgate, 2006) 138.
[4] "Faculty Website Biography" (*U.C.L.A. Law*), available at <http://www2.law.ucla.edu/sander/Bio_CV/Bio.htm> accessed 24 Aug. 2011.
[5] A recent deconal departure at Northwestern has unleashed a trenchant critique in the blogosphere from a senior member of Northwestern's faculty about the institution's shift to numbers understood as truths able to save law from its contingency, see Brian Leiter, "Reflections on the Van Zandt Era at Northwestern" (*Brian Leiter's Law School Reports*, 21 Mar. 2011), available at <http://leiterlawschool.typepad.com/leiter/2011/03/reflections-on-the-van-zandt-era-at-northwestern-an-interview-with-ronald-j-allen.html> accessed 25 Oct. 2011. All of which is to say, paraphrasing Santayana, that those who forget history, in this case the legacies of legal realism, are condemned to repeating it.

value in the U.S. legal academy over the past decade,[6] and who had been a player in the move to get the legal academy and profession to undertake empirical analysis of what they were actually doing as they went about the business of lawyer formation,[7] got his big scholarly break.

He published an article in the *Stanford Law Review*[8] with the deceptively bland title "A Systemic Analysis of Affirmative Action in U.S. Law Schools."[9] As far as I can glean from his Internet-published curriculum vitae,[10] his "best placement" before that date on the U.S.'s remarkable hit parade of law review publishing had been a work published in Northwestern's *Law Review* while he was a student there;[11] and a co-authored piece in Georgetown's "main"—and thus most intra-institutionally elite[12]—law journal in 1993.[13] There were also a number of pieces in journals like *Law and Social Inquiry*,[14] the *Journal of Legal Education*,[15] and *Law and Contemporary Problems*;[16] and a lot of

---

[6] As reflected, for example, in the theme for the American Association of Law Schools' 2006 Annual meeting; see "Empirical Scholarship: What Should We Study and How Should We Study It? Program of the 2006 Annual Meeting" (*American Association of Law Schools*, 3 Jan. 2006). <http://www.aals.org/am2006/program/finalprogrammain2006.pdf> accessed 25 Oct. 2011.

[7] Professor Sander was a Member of the Oversight and Steering Committees of "After the JD," a longitudinal study of the careers of young lawyers, funded by the American Bar Foundation, the National Science Foundation, NALP, LSAC, and the Soros Foundation, 1999–present; and has been its Co-Chair since 2001.

[8] The *Washington & Lee Law Review* ranking system gives *Stanford Law Review* a "1" ranking.

[9] Richard H. Sander, "A Systemic Analysis of Affirmative Action in American Law Schools" (2004) 57 Stan. L. Rev. 367.

[10] Richard H. Sander, "Bibliography" (*U.C.L.A. Law*), available at <http://www2.law.ucla.edu/sander/Bio_CV/CV.htm #Bibliography> accessed 24 August 2011.

[11] Richard Sander, "Individual Rights and Demographic Realities: The Problem of Fair Housing" (1988) 82 Nw. U. L. Rev. 874.

[12] Georgetown's "main" law journal, in the parlance of U.S. legal journal publishing, is the *Georgetown Law Journal*. Students at Georgetown, as is common in law schools across the country, also establish with faculty approval other law journals, albeit lower status ones (called "specialist" journals), but in the vigorous competition among first year law students to either "grade on" or in institutions where this is permitted "write on" in a writing competition whose timing and rules frequently seem like an elaborate (and, given the low number of places in competition, low return) hazing ritual, no one who is offered a place on the staff of *Georgetown Law Journal* would turn it down for a place on the *Georgetown Immigration Law Journal*, *Georgetown International Environmental Law Review*, *Georgetown Journal of Gender and the Law*, *Georgetown Journal of Legal Ethics*, *Georgetown Journal on Poverty Law and Policy*, or the *Georgetown Journal of Law and Public Policy*, unless they had managed to resist the culture of hierarchy that characterizes U.S. legal education. Faculty members seeking to place articles would make the same decision unless they, too, were out of touch with what functions as "reality."

[13] Richard Sander and E. Douglass Williams, "The Prospects for 'Putting America to Work' in the Inner City" (1993) 81 Geo. L.J. 2003.

[14] Richard Sander, "Why Are There So Many Lawyers? Perspectives on a Turbulent Market" (1989) 14 Law & Soc. Inquiry 431; Richard Sander, "A Little Theorizing about the Big Law Firm: Galanter, Palay, and the Economics of Growth" (1992) 17 Law & Soc. Inquiry 391; Richard Sander, "Elevating the Debate on Lawyers & Economic Growth" (1992) 17 Law & Soc. Inquiry 659; Richard Sander, "The Tributaries to the River" (2000) 25 Law & Soc. Inquiry 557.

[15] Richard Sander, "Book Review" (1994) 44 J. Legal Educ. 143 (reviewing Nancy A. Denton and Douglas S. Massey, *American Apartheid* (Harvard University Press, 1993)); Kristine S. Knaplund and Richard Sander, "The Art and Science of Academic Support" (1995) 45 J. Legal Educ. 157; Richard Sander, "Experimenting With Class-Based Affirmative Action" (1997) 47 J. Legal Educ. 472; Richard Sander, "Comment in Reply" (1997) 47 J. Legal Educ. 512; Richard Sander et al., "The Happy Charade: An Empirical Examination of the Third Year of Law School" (2001) 51 J. Legal Educ. 235.

[16] Carrie Menkel-Meadow and Richard Sander, "The 'Infusion' Method at UCLA: Teaching Ethics Pervasively" (1995) 58 Law & Contemp. Probs. 129.

published reports on fair housing and the minimum wage,[17] his early professional specialties. This was solid, respectable, but distinctly unsexy stuff.

Two pieces of context are in order at this point for my non-American audience. U.S. legal scholarly journal publication is, as (Stanford Law Professor) Michele Landis Dauber notes in her coruscating response to Sander, the only place *anywhere* in the scholarly journal publishing world where expert, often so-called "blind" peer-reviewing isn't the metric for decisions about what to publish.[18] A point which might be added to this part of Dauber's critique is not only that law reviews are the only scholarly journals that do not peer review, but that law journals in other common law countries do peer review.[19]

With a few exceptions,[20] in the U.S., law students choose what they'll publish.[21] "Impact" is one of the things which drives them. Thus controversial pieces which are written and framed in such a way that they are both accessible and attractive to law students, start out with an advantage. The eliteness of the author is, however, critical.[22]

Studies show, for example, that the *identical* article gets more offers if it's submitted under the letterhead of an elite school than if it comes from someone using the stationery

---

[17] Richard Sander, "Process for a Housing Policy: A Report to the Mayor of Chicago" (1983) report for the Chicago Mayoral Transition Team, available at <http://www2.law.ucla.edu/sander/Bio_CV/CV.htm>; Richard Sander, "Fair Housing Policy in Southern California: Achieving the Goals" in Allen J. Scott (ed.), *Policy Options for Southern California* (UCLA, Lewis Center for Regional Policy Studies, 1993); Richard Sander, "Fair Housing in Los Angeles County: An Assessment of Progress and Challenges, 1970–1995" (1996), report for the City and County of Los Angeles, available at <http://www2.law.ucla.edu/sander/Bio_CV/CV.htm>; Richard Sander and E. Douglass Williams, "An Empirical Analysis of the Proposed Los Angeles Living Wage Ordinance" (1997), report commissioned and published by the City of Los Angeles, available at <http://www2.law.ucla.edu/sander/Bio_CV/CV.htm>; Richard Sander and Joseph Doherty, "An Economic Analysis of the Proposed Santa Monica Living Wage" (2000), report by the UCLA Empirical Research Group; Richard Sander, "Fair Housing in Santa Clara County: An Assessment of Conditions and Programs, 2000–2002" (2002), report commissioned and published by the County of Santa Clara and six cities in Santa Clara County; Richard Sander, "Fair Housing in Oxnard: An Assessment of Conditions in 2001" (2002), report commissioned and published by the City of Oxnard 2002; Richard Sander, Joseph Doherty, and E. Douglass Williams, "The Economic and Distributional Consequences of the Santa Monica Minimum Wage Ordinance" (2002), report for the Employment Policy Institute, available at <http://epionline.org/studies/sander_10–2002.pdf> accessed 25 Oct. 2011.
[18] Michele Landis Dauber, "The Big Muddy" (2005) 57 Stan. L. Rev. 1899, 1910.
[19] I am regularly called upon, for example, to review submissions to two of the top-ranked (by an independent government accrediting body) Australian law school-based law reviews, *Melbourne Law Review* and *Griffith Law Review*.
[20] At some schools influential faculty may have some screening role in what gets published; there are some specialist peer-reviewed journals, such as the *Journal of Legal Education* and *Law and Social Inquiry*, and some other specialist journals do some measure of peer-reviewing, like the *Administrative Law Review*, published under the auspices of the ABA but out of American University Washington College of Law with student editors, which, while not undertaking full-scale peer-reviewing, has submissions reviewed by faculty members with some level of expertise in their subject matter during the editorial process.
[21] I am told that at Harvard at least one faculty member reviews each piece that its *Law Review* publishes, and that at USC a list of submissions is circulated to faculty members inviting comment. This is not necessarily a benign practice: a colleague at another school, a prolific scholar on the verge of tenure, was recently informed by a law review Editor-in-Chief who wanted to publish her submission that a non-tenure track faculty member, with only one publication to his name, which publication my colleague's article was critical of, summarily killed the possibility of the law review publishing her submission.
[22] See Penelope Pether, "Negotiating the Structures of Violence; or, On Not Inventing 'The Sullivans'" (2005) 15 Soc. Semiotics 6, 13–14 and sources cited there; Penelope Pether, "Discipline and Punish: Dispatches from the Citation Manual Wars and Other (Literally) Unspeakable Stories" (2001) 10 Griffith L. Rev. 101, 103–4 and sources cited there.

of a less elite school.[23] Law review editors also often ask for curricula vitae to be submitted with articles[24] (thus obviating the possibility that you're really a big dog whom they are too provincial to have heard about or who is too junior to have the markers of a legal academic Crufts winner). The context that makes this frenzied replication of eliteness of salience to my argument in this Article: "[M]inority students are substantially underrepresented on law reviews around the country."[25]

The second piece of context is this: in 2003 the U.S. Supreme Court handed down its decision in *Grutter v. Bollinger*, a case brought by Barbara Grutter, "a white Michigan resident who applied to the [elite University of Michigan] Law School in 1996 with a 3.8 grade point average and 161 LSAT [Law School Admissions Test, hereafter LSAT] score," and didn't get in, challenging its admissions process. That admissions process, in seeking to promote "diversity" in its law student cohort, had advanced the law school's "longstanding commitment" to "'racial and ethnic diversity with special reference to the inclusion of students from groups which have been historically discriminated against, like African-Americans,... who without this commitment might not be represented in [Michigan Law School's] student body in meaningful numbers."[26]

The case, like the admissions policy it cleared of an unconstitutionality challenge on the grounds that it breached the Equal Protection Clause of the U.S. Constitution's Fourteenth Amendment, was superbly lawyered by Michigan.[27] Successive Directors of Admissions at Michigan testified that they sought to enroll a "critical mass" of underrepresented minority students in each entering Michigan Law class, and that this required consideration of the race of such students "because a critical mass of underrepresented minority students could not be enrolled if admissions decisions were based primarily on undergraduate GPAs [Undergraduate Grade Point Averages, hereinafter UGPAs] and LSAT scores."[28]

Translation: the (rough and often unreliable) predictors of law school academic success that are constructed as the markers of "academic merit" that get you admitted to a high status—and indeed more or less any—law school are as a practical matter race-biased, specifically against African-Americans and other members of socioeconomically and educationally disadvantaged racial minority groups.[29] While there is a voluminous

---

[23] See Dan Subotnick and Glen Lazar, "Deconstructing the Rejection Letter: A Look at Elitism in Article Selection" (1999) 49 J. Legal Educ. 601.

[24] Including, for example, *Arizona Law Review*, *Boston College Law Review*, and the *University of Denver Law Review*. The *Florida Law Review* asks for "a short list of your recently published scholarly work."

[25] Mark A. Godsey, "Educational Inequities, the Myth of Meritocracy, and the Silencing of Minority Voices: The Need for Diversity of America's Law Reviews" (1995) 12 Harv. J. on Racial & Ethnic Just. 59, 61.

[26] *Grutter v. Bollinger* 539 US 306, 316 (2003).

[27] At this stage in the development of U.S. Constitutional jurisprudence, Equal Protection can be breached by denying whites—who benefit from what is likely to be a presently constitutionally-sanctioned but may be constitutionally vulnerable (an issue beyond the scope of this article, but which I will explore in a future one) group-based legal educational advantage in public law school admissions—what counts as the equal protection of the law.

[28] *Grutter v. Bollinger* (cited in n.26) 317.

[29] Such as Native Americans and non-white Hispanics. See Linda F. Wightman, "The Threat to Diversity in Legal Education: An Empirical Analysis of the Consequences of Abandoning Race as a Factor in Law School Admission Decisions" (1997) 72 N.Y.U. L. Rev. 1, 15, 19. There is also evidence that economically disadvantaged white students experience difficulty securing admission to elite higher education; the bar passage literature is also beginning to register non-English-speaking background as a risk for bar examination failure. See Jane Yakowitz, "Marooned: An Empirical Investigation of Law School Graduates Who Fail the Bar Exam" (2010) 60 J. Legal Educ. 21.

literature seeking to explain that race bias away, a prominent African-American apologist for the race neutrality of the LSAT and a former chair of the LSAC, which currently administers the test, concedes that "African-Americans... score approximately one standard deviation [on the LSAT] below that of similarly situated whites."[30]

The race neutrality of the LSAT (and indeed of UGPAs) is thus, as might be imagined, a contested claim. The stakes of that contestedness are signaled by this: the LSAT generally outranks undergraduate UGPA in significance in the numerical markers[31] which, absent race-conscious affirmative action for "underrepresented minority" students, as for some of their most privileged and well-connected white "peers,"[32] effectively determine who gets into what U.S. law school.[33]

The LSAT is produced by the Law School Admission Council (LSAC), which in turn is "'owned' by the American Bar Association accredited law schools."[34] At most U.S. law schools, decisions about who gets a place are based on the combination of LSAT and UGPA.[35] This combination "exhibits only a modest correlation with first year law school grades".[36] However, they "do not predict... anywhere close to precisely... how students will perform in the first year of law school";[37] and indeed, while in the words of the aforementioned apologist for the LSAT's race neutrality, "it is well known that LSAT and UGPA, when combined together, provide some predictive ability for correlating first year and ultimately cumulative Law School Grade Point Averages (LGPA).... The LSAC research has concluded repeatedly that there is a variance in outcomes that does not correlate to these two variables—that there is a roughly 0.43 correlation between these two variables and first year law school grades (which in lay person's terms means that these two variable[s]—grades and LSAT—account for approximately 25% of what goes into achieving that first year grade point average).[38]

---

[30] Alex M. Johnson, Jr., "Knots in the Law School Pipeline for Students of Color: The LSAT Is Not the Problem and Affirmative Action Is Not the Answer" (2008) University of Virginia Law School Working Paper No. 103, 27, available at <http://law.bepress.com/cgi/viewcontent.cgi?article=1161&context=uvalwps&sei-redir=1#search=%22Knots%20Pipeline%20Prospective%20Lawyers%20Color%3A%20LSAT%20Not%20Problem%20Affirmative%20Action%20Not%20Answer%22>. "Similar situatedeness" in this context means "controlling for socio-economic status and undergraduate grade point average[, even though] African-Americans do have UGPA that are less than [those of] whites on average"; Johnson, "Knots in the Law School Pipeline" n.71. Such a claim of controlling for socioeconomic status merits closer investigation. If it is based on income, it is fatally flawed given the poor proxy for actual socioeconomic status income is for blacks. See Deborah C. Malamud, "Assessing Class-Based Affirmative Action" (1997) 47 J. Legal Educ. 452, 477.

[31] While Johnson notes that schools can choose to weight UGPA more highly than LSAT scores in calculating their admissions "number," see Alex M. Johnson, Jr., "The Destruction of the Holistic Approach to Admissions: the Pernicious Effects of Rankings" (2006) 81 Ind. L.J. 309, 349, he acknowledges that "[t]he fact that there is an almost perfect correlation between a school's median LSAT score and the U.S. News ranking provides a strong incentive for deans to increase their median LSAT score by all legal means."

[32] Johnson, "The Destruction of the Holistic Approach to Admissions" (cited in n.31) n.12; Thomas D. Russell, "From the Trenches and Towers: The Shape of the Michigan River as Viewed from the Land of Sweatt v. Painter and Hopwood" (2000) 25 Law & Soc. Inquiry 507, 517.

[33] See Timothy T. Clydesdale, "A Forked River Runs Through Law School: Toward Understanding Race, Gender, Age, and Related Gaps in Law School Performance and Bar Passage" (2004) 29 Law & Soc. Inquiry 711, 737; Johnson, "Knots in the Law School Pipeline" (cited in n.30) 40–3.

[34] Clydesdale, "A Forked River Runs Through Law School" (cited in n.33).

[35] Johnson, "The Destruction of the Holistic Approach to Admissions" (cited in n.31).

[36] Johnson, "The Destruction of the Holistic Approach to Admissions" (cited in n.31) 313.

[37] Johnson, "The Destruction of the Holistic Approach to Admissions" (cited in n.31) 347.

[38] Johnson, "Knots in the Law School Pipeline" (cited in n.30) n.93. Johnson, a very successful African-American legal academic, former Dean of the elite University of Minnesota Law School and a member of the faculty of the University of Virginia Law School, is both an apologist for the LSAT, having had a string of institutional roles within the LSAC, which administers that LSAT, including a term as its Chair,

Guinier et al.'s study of performance of law students at the University of Pennsylvania Law School "confirm[ed] that the LSAT alone is not a very good predictor of performance for all students, not just women or minorities. Some women underperform compared to their scores on the LSAT. Many males overperform compared to their LSAT scores. But *very few students actually performed in ways predicted by the LSAT*. LSAT 'explains' at most 21% of performance at Penn Law School in the third year. For students in their first and second years, the LSAT explains even less."[39]

The essence of what I have just written is this: those U.S. law schools accredited by the ABA own a standardized testing operation which administers a test that they use to save them time and money in deciding whom they will admit; they know that test is an unreliable predictor of the construction of merit[40] principally used to justify it, prediction of law school grades. And they also know, manifesting denials of seeing the monarch naked that are located somewhere on the scale from cynical sophistry to willfully constructing a parallel universe to that of the rational one which the legal scholar might be expected to inhabit, that that test is racially biased against African-Americans.

The nation's legal educators also know that so far as places in elite public law schools are concerned, the LSAT plus UGPA without a race-conscious affirmative action admissions model used, for example, at the elite University of Texas, is (nonmeritocratically, if the combination of UGPA and LSAT score is imagined to be the marker of merit)[41]

---

while also a strong critic of the view that the LSAT discriminates against African-American students, even though he concedes that "African-Americans...score approximately one standard deviation below that of similarly situated whites," (Johnson, "Knots in the Law School Pipeline" (cited in n.30) 27). I note that Professor Johnson, having previously written that the correlation between LSAT scores and first year law school grades is modest, goes on to add that "it is beyond cavil that there is a strong correlation [between UGPA and LSAT scores and first year law school grades] and the greater the difference between the LSAT scores the more likely the disparity between first year grades" (n.93). However, I have regularly seen students whom I have taught graduate, for example with honors, high honors, or indeed summa cum laude and at the top of their class, or become Editor-in-Chief or achieve other high office in the relevant institution's main law review (with no prizes for guessing that, absent some traumatic life experience over the bar preparation period, these students pass the bar without difficulty). This is despite their initial low (in terms of their incoming class cohort) LSAT scores. I can also acknowledge, having from 2006 to 2011 chaired a task force at my current institution, that students with low LSATs at this institution are at significantly elevated risk of not passing the bar examination, although our strongest predictor of risk is low LSGPA. This task force significantly raised our students' bar passage rates (well above what their incoming indicators would predict, for those like Professor Johnson who characterized legal education as a pipeline which would deliver equal educational opportunity regardless of race were it not for the places at which it "leaks"). What makes the difference between students with low LSATs who succeed and those who do not is the rate at which they participate in what the NSSE Study of law student engagement calls "educationally meaningful activities," and how seriously the institution takes matters including the issue of inculcating disciplinary literacy, mitigating academic risk as soon as it manifests itself.

[39] Lani Guinier, Michelle Fine, Jane Balin, *Becoming Gentlemen: Women, Law School, and Institutional Change* (Beacon Press, 1997) 8.

[40] To Professor Johnson's credit, he clearly understands merit as a constructed and not neutral category, see Johnson, "The Destruction of the Holistic Approach to Admissions" (cited in n.31), 333. Patricia Williams has made an incisive critique of the construction of merit in elite law schools, see Patricia A. Williams, *The Alchemy of Race and Rights* (Harvard University Press, 1991) 99. Daria Roithmayr has historicized the race-based construction of merit in which contemporary law school admissions standards developed, see "Deconstructing the Distinction between Bias and Merit" (1997) 85 Calif. L. Rev. 1449.

[41] For critiques of this construction of merit, see Richard Delgado, "Rodrigo's Tenth Chronicle: Merit and Affirmative Action" (1995) 83 Geo. L.J. 1711; Richard Delgado, "Rodrigo's Chronicle" (1992) 101 Yale L.J. 1357, 1364; Robert L. Hayman, Jr. and Nancy Levit, "The Tales of White Folk: Doctrine, Narrative and the Reconstruction of Racial Reality" (1996) 84 Calif. L. Rev. 377, 403; Duncan Kennedy, "A Cultural Pluralist Case for Affirmative Action in Legal Academia" (1990) 1990 Duke L.J. 705; Gary Peller, "Race Consciousness" (1990) 1990 Duke L.J. 758, 803–7.

biased *in favor* of in-state students, most of whom will be white because whites (especially white men)[42] score better on the LSAT than blacks, at the expense of out-of-state students with better numerical entering credentials.[43] And one more point should be briefly raised here, once again emanating from the pen of the aforementioned former head of the LSAC, and LSAT race bias-denier, this last despite the contextually poignant fact that he has acknowledged that "I took the [LSAT] once and only once in 1975. And although I graduated magna cum laude from Claremont Men's College in the top 5% of my class, my LSAT score, which I refuse to divulge, was clearly not in the top 5% of all test-takers. Nevertheless, it was good enough to secure my admission to my first choice law school, UCLA"[44]:

> [the] focus [of law schools in making admissions decisions] on the LSAT score, [which is] to maintain or improve the Law School's rankings in the all important *U.S. News and World Report* annual rankings, leads to the rejection of the holistic or whole person approach in admissions and gives impermissible weight to the LSAT.[45]

The ABA—and in the case of AALS member schools, a Reporter who travels with the ABA accreditation team—does indeed accredit U.S. law schools, but those accreditation systems as they presently operate have no capacity to let intending law students or legal employers know anything meaningful about the quality of the legal education delivered to students at different schools.[46] Not only is the ABA currently the subject of criticism for noncompliance with Department of Education standards for educational accrediting bodies,[47] but, having served on ABA accreditation fact-finding teams, I have considerable doubts about the validity of its metrics for educational quality. An accreditation system that (in the informational digital age) specifies a "no-brainer" list of hard copy library holdings as an accreditation standard[48] while not requiring professors to provide syllabi for their courses as relevant to accreditation[49] strikes me as meriting a re-examination of its own priorities.

That it has a relatively relaxed attitude to lax law school ethics in relation to what I will call the fiduciary obligation of those who make comfortable livings off high law school tuition to disclose to law students things like their bar failure risk, as Jane Yakowitz has

---

[42] Russell, "From the Trenches and Towers" (cited in n.32).
[43] Russell, "From the Trenches and Towers" (cited in n.32) 510–11, 516.
[44] Johnson, "The Destruction of the Holistic Approach to Admissions" (cited in n.31) 335 n.98.
[45] Johnson, "Knots in the Law School Pipeline" (cited in n.30), 40.
[46] See Law School Admission Council, "LSAC Official Guide to Accredited Law Schools", available at<https://officialguide.lsac.org/release/OfficialGuide_Default.aspx> accessed 8 September 2011.
[47] "A recent Department of Education review of the ABA's accreditation work found that the agency does not demand schools keep loan default rates below a certain level, as required. The ABA has also failed to set minimum standards for postgraduate employment rates and show that it has a transparent and public accreditation process, a department review panel found in a June hearing. The panel found that the ABA unit fell short on meeting 17 federal standards required of accreditation agencies." Catherine Ho, "ABA Faces Scrutiny as Job Prospects, Debt Levels for Law School Grads Worsen" *Washington Post* (Washington, D.C., 24 July 2011). Available at <http://www.washingtonpost.com/business/capital-business/aba-faces-scrutiny-as-job-prospects-debt-levels-for-law-school-grads-worsen/2011/07/21/gIQAjDJ3WI_story.html>.
[48] See *American Bar Association Section on Legal Education and Admissions to the Bar, Standards and Rules of Procedure for Approval of Law Schools 2009–2010*, Interpretation 606–5.
[49] There is no accreditation Standard or Interpretation that requires professors to provide syllabi for courses, as I was tartly reminded by the Dean of a law school for which I served as a member of an ABA sabbatical site inspection team and in the team's standard terminal meeting with the Dean informed him that a significant number of students had complained about courses without syllabi.

argued,[50] or the low statistical likelihood of retaining a scholarship beyond the first year of a law school that has lured a student with desirable entering indicators to enroll on the basis of that scholarship, rather than take those LSAT and UGPA scores somewhere else, is evident from the recent response by the director of the ABA's law school accreditation operation when asked by a *New York Times* journalist why law schools should not publish to intending law students offered scholarships the statistics on how many students lose them after the first year. His reply: "[t]hat is a good question, a legitimate question.... It hasn't been an issue brought to our attention. Nobody has written us, contacted us, to say 'This needs to be put on the table.'"[51]

Let me bring this slightly closer to home: I was the hapless faculty member who stumbled across, and with two colleagues initially investigated, and with one of them reported to the Dean of my present law school that it appeared the school had been falsifying admissions data for years[52]: systematically and significantly over-representing LSAT and UGPA 25 and 75 percentiles and medians to both the ABA and *U.S. News*,[53] which verifies LSAT data provided to it by law schools through the ABA.[54] That fraud was significantly enabled by the fact that the ABA reaccreditation process as it then stood only checked the law-school-provided data for one year: for the incoming class in the year the sabbatical reaccreditation site visit will occur.[55] One last reflection here on Johnson's LSAT race-bias denial, before I move on to Sander and the tournament of (fatally conceptually flawed)[56] empiricism that has followed "A Systemic Analysis" through this

---

[50] Johnson, "Knots in the Law School Pipeline" (cited in n.30) 3, 40 (concluding that "[l]aw schools owe it to their most at-risk prospective students to provide candid information about the probability and costs of failing the bar examination").

[51] David Segal, "Law Students Lose the Grant Game as Schools Win" *N.Y. Times* (New York, May 1, 2011) BU1.

[52] See Council of The Section of Legal Education and Admissions to the Bar of the American Bar Association, "Public Censure of Villanova University School of Law" August 12, 2011; Jack Crittenden, "A New Low in the Rankings Arms Race" *Nat'l Jurist* (San Diego, March 2011) 4, 6. I was the Chair of the Bar Passage Task Force described in that censure who discovered and reported apparent "inaccuracies in the admissions data concerning LSAT and undergraduate GPA that had been reported to the ABA for the classes entering in fall 2008 and 2009."

[53] Letter from John Y. Gotanda, Dean, Villanova University School of Law, to Robert J. Morse, Director of Data Research, *U.S. News & World Report* (Feb. 10, 2011), available at <http://static.usnews.com/documents/education/villanova-letter-us-news.pdf>.

[54] Johnson, "The Destruction of the Holistic Approach to Admissions" (cited in n.31) 355.

[55] This is because (until procedural changes made as a result of the discovery of the fraud) as part of the material provided for the site visit held as part of the ABA's sabbatical accreditation process, the school was required to produce a list of all students with GPA and LSAT next to their names. On the annual questionnaire, by contrast, the school is only asked to report its median, 75th and 25th UGPAs and LSATs without verifiable data supporting the claims.

[56] I use the term "fatally flawed" because, regardless of political investments of the authors, which in each case can be read clearly from the way they interpret data that is presented as speaking for itself, none acknowledges awareness of the legal historian Thomas D. Russell's much more sophisticated (and alternative disciplinary empiricist's) insight into the study by Lempert et al. (Richard O. Lempert, David L. Chambers, and Terry K. Adams, "Michigan's Minority Graduates in Practice: The River Runs Through Law School" (2000) 25 Law & Soc. Inquiry 395): "Lempert and his coauthors have a more focused, parallel goal with their study [than Bowen and Bok's "Shape of the River"]: examination of how well Michigan Law School's students, particularly students of color, fared as law students and also how successful they have been with their subsequent careers. That is the neutral, social-scientific description of their research aim, but there is no reason to be coy about the study really being a defense of the University of Michigan Law School's use of face as a criterion of admissions": Russell, "From the Trenches and Towers" (cited in n.32) 509. All of this is to say that for any sophisticated historian, or indeed any sophisticated social scientist, the conceit that dataset accumulation does not have a purpose, like the claim that data is intersubjectively interpretable to yield identical results, as suggested by Professor Sander in the second epigraph to this article, is a nonsense. One more note is in order here:

nation's elite law reviews. First, UCLA Law School was among the leaders of elite law schools in institutionalizing affirmative action in admission in the late 1960s and early 1970s;[57] however, the explosion in law school applications that occurred over the course of the 1970s produced the rise of the LSAT as the most significant factor in law school admissions.[58] 1976 marked the beginning of the era when "[w]hite [law school] applicants consistently had higher admissions rates than African Americans among those with [high] UGPAs... [and] the depressed admissions rates for African American 'high achievers' [was] most likely attributable to law schools giving the greatest weight to precisely the criterion that disadvantages students of color most: the LSAT."[59] Ergo, given that at the point Johnson was seeking admission to law school the LSAT was operating to disadvantage black students with high UGPAs as against white students with equal college-level achievement, one wonders whether his story might be differently inflected if his first choice law school had been Yale.

2. The professor's project

Sander's self-proclaimed project in "A Systemic Analysis" was to interject into the (at that stage, in numerical terms relatively modest) scholarly endeavors to quantify the success of affirmative action in higher education, whose results had been positive,[60]

Professor Russell was a tenured Professor of Law at the University of Texas. He opened 2000's "From the Trenches to the Towers" thus: "[t]here are 5 African Americans among the 433 students in the University of Texas School of Law's class of 2000. There are 7 in the class of 2001, and 7 in the class of 2002 [following the decision of the Fifth Circuit in Hopwood v. Texas that the law school had to practice race-blind admissions and the broadening of the impact of the decision by the then Texas Attorney General] as a result of the decision. With 1,387 students, the UT School of Law is big. The 19 African American students comprise 1.4% of the total....And has been lower than in the fall of 1950, the first year UT admitted African Americans to the law school [as a result of the decision in *Sweatt v. Painter*, which forced integration of UT Law School]" (Russell, "Trenches and Towers" 507). In the same article he wrote that his "personal view is that most of the law school's faculty are fully committed to the theoretical proposition that the university and law school's use of race in admissions is constitutionally permissible" but that his "personal view is also that the UT law faculty are less committed to the practice of admitting African American and Latino law students than they were to the constitutional theory that would support such a practice" (Russell, "Trenches and Towers"508). He joined the law faculty at the University of Denver Sturm School of Law in 2001, the year after "From the Trenches and the Towers" was published, departing from UT, so a former colleague of his recently informed me, with his tenure barely intact. His historical research in his last semester at Texas had led to his authoring a paper establishing that a new hall of residence at the University of Texas had been named after a prominent Klansman, which led to the renaming of the relevant edifice. See Thomas D. Russell, "Op-Ed: Professor's Paper Targets Klan Reference on University of Texas Dorm...And Gets Action" *The Huffington Post* (Online, July 18, 2010), available at <http://papers.ssrn.com/sol3/papers.cfm?abstract_id=1644822>. See also Thomas D. Russell, "Keep Negroes Out of Most Classes Where There are a Large Number of Girls: The Unseen Power of the Ku Klux Klan and Standardized Testing at the University of Texas, 1899–1999" in Robert M. Gordon and Morton J. Horwitz (eds), *Law, Society, and History: Themes in the Legal Sociology and Legal History of Lawrence M. Friedman* (Cambridge University Press, 2011) 309.

[57] William C. Kidder, "The Struggle for Access from 'Sweatt' to 'Grutter': A History of the African American, Latino, and American Indian Law School Admissions, 1950–2000" (2003) 19 Harv. J. on Racial & Ethnic Just. 1, 16–19. Kidder notes (at 17) that in the period between 1970 and 1975, numbers of law school applications increased exponentially, and the sheer logistical press of dealing with admissions numbers "led to the LSAT becoming the centerpiece of the admissions process".

[58] Kidder, "The Struggle for Access from 'Sweatt' to 'Grutter'" (cited in n.57) 26–7.

[59] Kidder, "The Struggle for Access from 'Sweatt' to 'Grutter'"(cited in n.57) 27.

[60] See William G. Bowen and Derek Bok, *The Shape of the River: Long-Term Consequences of Considering Race in College and University Admissions* (Princeton University Press, 1998); (referred to in n.56). Note that the latter study was produced for the purposes of providing "a defense of the University of Michigan Law School's use of race as a criterion in admissions" for the purposes of the *Grutter* litigation. See

"a comprehensive attempt to assess the relative costs and benefits of racial preferences"[61] in U.S legal education, in particular as to "the effects racial preferences in admissions have on the largest class of intended beneficiaries: black applicants to law school."[62] His conclusion:

> [the] system of racial preferences[in the interests of affirmative action in U.S. law school admissions] produces more harms than benefits for its putative beneficiaries.... [M]ost black law applicants end up at schools where they will struggle academically and fail at higher rates than they would in the absence of preferences. The net trade-off of higher prestige but weaker academic performance substantially harms black performance on bar exams and harms most new black lawyers on the job market.... [A] strong case can be made that in the legal educational system as a whole, racial preferences end up producing fewer black lawyers each year than would be produced by a race-blind system. Affirmative action as currently practiced by the nation's law schools does not, therefore, pass even the easiest test one can set. In systemic, objective terms, it hurts the group it is most designed to help.[63]

Let me say something about Sander's self-presentation in the article, its discourse, and its inclusions and exclusions, how it tells the story it tells while occluding others, even while registering Sander's awareness of them *en passant*,[64] before I go on briefly to document and critique and then make practical use of the tournament of empiricists which emerged in its wake. First, he makes a point of non-racist self-representation:

> much of my adult career has revolved around issues of racial justice. Immediately after college, I worked as a community organizer on Chicago's South Side. As a graduate student, I studied housing segregation and concluded that selective race conscious strategies were critical, in most cities, to breaking up patterns of housing resegregation. In the 1990s, I cofounded a civil rights group that evolved into the principal enforcer (through litigation) of fair housing rights in Southern California.[65]

He also establishes his credentials as one who has worked in the trenches at UCLA to attempt to ensure those "mismatched" black students would succeed: "[a]s a young member of the UCLA School of Law faculty, I was deeply impressed by the remarkable diversity and sense of community the school fostered, and one of my first research efforts was an extensive and sympathetic analysis of academic support as a method of helping the beneficiaries of affirmative action succeed in law school."[66]

What made him turn? The ground for the explicit answer surfaces in some more of Sander's self-presented biodata in "A Systemic Analysis": he is white;[67] he attended a public high school;[68] he received his undergraduate education at Harvard College.[69]

Russell, "From the Trenches and Towers" (cited in n.32) 509. See also David B. Wilkins, "Rollin' on the River: Race, Elite Schools, and the Equality Paradox" (2000) 25 Law & Soc. Inquiry 527.

[61] Sander, "A Systemic Analysis of Affirmative Action in American Law Schools" (cited in n.9) 368.
[62] Sander, "A Systemic Analysis of Affirmative Action in American Law Schools" (cited in n.9) 369.
[63] Sander, "A Systemic Analysis of Affirmative Action in American Law Schools" (cited in n.9) 371–2.
[64] See Sander, "A Systemic Analysis of Affirmative Action in American Law Schools" (cited in n.9) 360, where Sander notes that he is not going to consider "[t]he 'costs' to blacks that flow from racial preferences [that] are often thought of, in the affirmative action literature, as rather subtle matters, such as the stigma and stereotypes that might result from differential admissions standards. These effects are interesting and important, but I give them short shrift for the most part because they are hard to measure and there is not enough data available that is thorough and objective enough for my purposes."
[65] Sander, "A Systemic Analysis of Affirmative Action in American Law Schools" (cited in n.9) 370.
[66] Sander, "A Systemic Analysis of Affirmative Action in American Law Schools" (cited in n.9) 370.
[67] Sander, "A Systemic Analysis of Affirmative Action in American Law Schools" (cited in n.9) 370.
[68] Sander, "A Systemic Analysis of Affirmative Action in American Law Schools" (cited in n.9) 449.
[69] Sander, "A Systemic Analysis of Affirmative Action in American Law Schools" (cited in n.9) 449.

And he went to law school at Northwestern. As to the straw that broke the camel's back, his early sympathetic labors for nonwhite students admitted to UCLA law school under its affirmative action program was, he writes, undermined by his research, which "suggested that UCLA's diversity programs had produced little socioeconomic variety; students of all races were predominantly upper crust."[70] Indeed, in 1997 Sander had published "Experimenting with Class-Based Affirmative Action,"[71] which documented a pilot class-based affirmative action program of which he had been a principal architect at UCLA Law School in the wake of the University of California Regents' 1995 decision banning the use of race in admissions.

His conclusion about that pilot program was that it meant that more poor students got seats at this elite public law school,[72] that it had very little effect on circumventing the whitening of the UCLA law student body, which saw "[t]he enrollment of Blacks and American Indians [falling] by more than 70 percent from levels typically achieved under the old race-based preference system."[73] He also makes it clear that one attractive aspect of the class-based admissions program was that it cost UCLA very little in terms of imperiling its *U.S. News* entering qualification data,[74] and that the institution dodged the bullet that admitting more low(ish) socioeconomic status students might have cost it in financial aid terms by "scal[ing] down its grant levels enough to offset the higher burdens."[75]

A detailed account of Deborah Malamud's critique of Sander's campaign for class-based affirmative action[76] is beyond the scope of this article. Let me register, however, that there is ample evidence that LSAT scores are positively influenced by family income,[77] regardless of whether the test-taker is black or white,[78] as is performance on standardized tests that get U.S. students into college.[79] First year LSGPAs are positively influenced by elevated socioeconomic status,[80] as are bar passage rates.[81] Next, it is difficult to disentangle race and class.[82] While "lower economic status correlates with lower scores on typical standardized tests not just for the poor, but for everyone, at every step in the economic hierarchy,"[83] black Americans are disproportionately poorer than whites[84] and "at all economic levels, the black middle class is systematically worse off than the white middle

---

[70] Sander, "A Systemic Analysis of Affirmative Action in American Law Schools" (cited in n.9) 371.
[71] Sander, "Experimenting With Class-Based Affirmative Action" (cited in n.15). See also Richard H. Sander, "Class in American Legal Education" (2011) 88 Denv. U. L. Rev. 631 (extending the argument to the national context without addressing Malamud's critique).
[72] Sander, "A Systemic Analysis of Affirmative Action in American Law Schools" (cited in n.9) 473.
[73] Sander, "A Systemic Analysis of Affirmative Action in American Law Schools" (cited in n.9) 473.
[74] Sander, "A Systemic Analysis of Affirmative Action in American Law Schools" (cited in n.9) 496–8.
[75] Sander, "A Systemic Analysis of Affirmative Action in American Law Schools" (cited in n.9) 499.
[76] Deborah C. Malamud, "Assessing Class-Based Affirmative Action" (1997) 47 J. Legal Educ. 452; Deborah C. Malamud, "A Response to Professor Sander" (1997) 47 J. Legal Educ. 504.
[77] See David Oppenheimer and Kristen Holmquist, "Predictors for Successful Lawyering: Rethinking Law School Admissions" (2011) New York Law School *Future Ed* Paper, available at <http://dotank.nyls.edu/futureed/2011proposals/07pfsl.pdf> accessed 25 October 2011; Richard Delgado, "Official Elitism or Institutional Self-Interest? 10 Reasons Why the U.C. Davis Should Abandon the LSAT (and Why Other Good Law Schools Should Follow Suit)" (2001) 34 U.C. Davis L. Rev. 593, 600–2.
[78] Clydesdale, "A Forked River Runs Through Law School" (cited in n.33) n.170.
[79] Clydesdale, "A Forked River Runs Through Law School" (cited in n.33) n.170. See also Richard D. Kahlenberg, *The Remedy: Class, Race, and Affirmative Action* (New York: Basic Books, 1996) 99.
[80] Clydesdale, "A Forked River Runs Through Law School" (cited in n.33) 737.
[81] Clydesdale, "A Forked River Runs Through Law School" (cited in n.33) 749.
[82] Malamud, "Assessing Class-Based Affirmative Action" (cited in n.76) 452.
[83] Malamud, "Assessing Class-Based Affirmative Action" (cited in n.76) 461.
[84] Malamud, "Assessing Class-Based Affirmative Action" (cited in n.76) 465.

class with respect to housing, occupational advancement, income and income security, wealth, educational opportunity, the intergenerational transmission of middle-class status, and the enjoyment of the public dignity that customarily defines and accompanies membership in the middle class."[85] Malamud also intuits what Sander conceded happened at UCLA: the unlikelihood that those most socioeconomically disadvantaged will benefit from class-based affirmative action policies, because of the likelihood that they will have lower test scores and thus "cost" the admitting institution too much in terms of rankings to admit them.[86] Indeed, while "high-SES blacks had been eligible for affirmative action consideration…[under the class-based system at UCLA]…a large majority of academically qualified blacks were deemed too well-off to be eligible for affirmative action,"[87] in part because UCLA raised "*its minimum entrance requirements at the same time that it switched from race-based to class-based affirmative action.*"[88] The families of those students admitted under UCLA's class-based admissions program "were not the typical poor: they had higher educational levels than one generally finds among the poor."[89]

Sander's response to Malamud conceded that "the black/white [socioeconomic status] gap increases, and does indeed *approach or even exceed the test-score gap.*"[90]

3. Truth and consequences

Seven years later the fruits of Sander's sea-change were evident in "A Systemic Analysis," although others had made his case before him in 1998,[91] and before that 1970,[92] albeit in both cases framing the mismatch effect as what Beverley Moran[93] outs as making "[t]he case for black inferiority" more[94] or less[95] explicitly, rather than confining themselves to handwringing about the damage it does to blacks. One more thing that should not be overlooked about that *Stanford* publication is this: Sander was off to the races professionally. Not only did he get yet another *Stanford* publication shortly thereafter,[96] responding to his critics, but his response to a critique of his analysis by a Yale law student, Daniel Ho,[97] also got him published in the *Yale Law Journal*.[98] His claims got him

---

[85] Malamud, "Assessing Class-Based Affirmative Action" (cited in n.76) 467.
[86] Malamud, "Assessing Class-Based Affirmative Action" (cited in n.76) 455–6.
[87] Malamud, "A Response to Professor Sander" (cited in n.76) 505.
[88] Malamud, "A Response to Professor Sander" (cited in n.76) 506 (emphasis added).
[89] Malamud, "A Response to Professor Sander" (cited in n.76) 510.
[90] Sander, "Comment in Reply" (cited in n.1) 513 (emphasis added).
[91] Stephan Thernstrom, "Diversity in Legal Education: A Critical Evaluation of Linda F. Wightman's 'The Threat to Diversity in Legal Education'" (1998) 15 Const. Comment. 11.
[92] Clyde W. Summers, "Preferential Admissions: An Unreal Solution to a Real Problem" (1970) 2 U. Tol. L. Rev. 377.
[93] Beverley I. Moran, "The Case for Black Inferiority? What Must Be True If Professor Sander Is Right? A Response to 'A Systemic Analysis of Affirmative Action in American Law Schools'" (2005) 5 Conn. Public Interest L.J. 42.
[94] Thernstrom, "Diversity in Legal Education" (cited in n.91).
[95] Summers, "Preferential Admissions" (cited in n.92) 395–6. Summers does some performative handwringing about the "harm" done by race-conscious admissions programs, to be sure, but the article is a period piece in the way it performs its racism.
[96] Richard H. Sander, "A Reply to Critics" (2005) 57 Stan. L. Rev. 1963, 1964.
[97] Daniel E. Ho, "Why Affirmative Action Does Not Cause Black Students to Fail the Bar" (2005) 114 Yale L.J. 1997.
[98] Richard H. Sander, "Mismeasuring the Mismatch: A Response to Ho" (2005) 114 Yale L.J. 2005. Ho in turn got to reply to Sander, see Daniel E. Ho, "Affirmative Action's Affirmative Actions: A Reply to Sander" (2005) 114 Yale L.J. 2011.

attention from CNN.com, the *Wall Street Journal*, the *New York Times*, the *Chronicle of Higher Education, The Rocky Mountain News*, the *Los Angeles Times*, the *Legal Times*, and *Newsweek*.[99]

He also appeared on Fox News's *Hannity & Colmes*,[100] and as Dauber notes, to "present... his claims at a meeting of the Board of Regents at the University of California at the invitation of anti-affirmative action activist Ward Connerly."[101]

He was offered "a contract for a book on affirmative action (and an advance)" by "[a] major university press,"[102] which he evidently thought bolstered the integrity of his statistics and their interpretation against his numerous critics: he noted that major university presses "of course rely on outside reviewers in evaluating books."[103] On this article of faith, let me just note that while OUP, say, is not driven by the same economic pressures as commercial publishing houses, it, like other university presses, generally needs to stay solvent rather than transforming itself into an economic sinkhole. Additionally, both my law professor spouse and I[104] are frequently asked to peer-review book proposals for academic presses including university presses. While one endeavors to be both intellectually honest and constructive, this is not the kind of peer-reviewing that gets you published in *Nature*. Indeed, peer-reviewers for university presses are often those suggested by the contract-seeking author herself.

Stanford's law student elite clearly knew they had a hit on their hands, devoting the next issue of the *Law Review* to responses to Sander's article, after either inviting or receiving a slew of offers to take Sander on;[105] and including a response from Sander to those four selected responses in the same number. With what might strike the legal academic status realist as an unwonted ingratitude, Sander introduced that response, titled "A Reply to Critics,"[106] thus:

[a]lthough the public and academic reaction to A Systemic Analysis of Affirmative Action in American Law Schools... has been predominantly favorable, many of my most sympathetic readers predicted a fierce reaction from what they often called "the affirmative action establishment." And although the four responses published in this issue are not the first outpourings of critical reaction, they are certainly the most concerted. When the Stanford Law Review editors sifted through the stack of prospective contributions to this issue they specifically tried to select those who would offer the strongest critiques, bypassing several more sympathetic proposals.[107]

One more thing to note at this point. If Sander was right in his data-crunching, which assumes that the current criteria for assessing "merit" in the U.S. law school admissions context are "accurate" indexes of whatever merit is constructed to be,[108] black intending

---

[99] Dauber, "The Big Muddy" (cited in n.18) n.59.
[100] On January 5, 2005, see Dauber, "The Big Muddy" (cited in n.18) nn.56, 60.
[101] Dauber, "The Big Muddy" (cited in n.18) 1911.
[102] See Sander, "A Reply to Critics" (cited in n.96) 1982.
[103] Sander, "A Reply to Critics" (cited in n.96) 1982.
[104] Both of whom hold research-based Ph.Ds as well as law degrees.
[105] Sander, "A Reply to Critics" (cited in n.96) 1964. It also seems possible that the reaction of some Stanford faculty members to the *Law Review*'s publication of "A Systemic Analysis" was responsible for the reprise, given the demolition job done by Professor Dauber in "The Big Muddy"(cited in n.18) both to Sander's method and to the law review publication system that got the piece an outing in the big league, and those Stanford faculty members she thanks in its star footnote.
[106] Sander, "A Reply to Critics" (cited in n.96).
[107] Sander, "A Reply to Critics" (cited in n.96) 1964.
[108] For the voluminous earlier critique of this assumption, see Delgado, "Rodrigo's Tenth Chronicle" (cited in n.41) 1711; Delgado, "Rodrigo's Chronicle" (cited in n.41) 1364; Hayman and Levit, "The Tales of White Folk" (cited in n.41) 403; Kennedy, "A Cultural Pluralist Case for Affirmative Action in

law students were, sooner or later, on their way to the back of the bus, or the end of the lunch counter, or at least to the third or fourth tier law schools where their entering "credentials," undergraduate GPA and LSAT, would "naturally" place them, because it would be fair to them, good for them. Why?

Because, as Johnson and many others have noted before me, the crazy system that really matters in assessing the *status* (affirmatively not delivered educational *quality* measured in any credible way) of U.S. law schools is one devised and published by *The U.S. News and World Repo*rt, a conservative wannabe *Time* or *Newsweek*, owned since 1984 by Mort Zuckerman, who also owns *The New York Daily News* (the moral equivalent of the British tabloid *The Daily Mirror* on the side of the Atlantic where I presently make my home and living, and indeed modeled on that organ of the Press). Zuckerman purchased *U.S. News* from its staff, who the year before the purchase had made it an attractive acquisition for someone like Zuckerman by starting to publish the nation's higher education league tables, which in the case at least of law schools effectively rank schools principally based on institutional wealth, haphazardly and unreliably gathered reputational factors, and incoming student LSAT.

What that ratings system does is replicate hierarchy: one of the two highest percentage items on that 0–100 scale is "student selectivity," at 25%, with LSAT (at 12.5%) and UGPA (at 10%) the biggest components of that number. Another significant number is the 10% allotted "[institutional] resources per student," i.e. how rich the institution is, and the 25% allotted to "academic reputation," as judged by the results of a remarkable self-fulfilling prophesy clothed as a survey mailed out annually to some faculty members at law schools around the country.[109]

And the current ferocious scholarship bidding wars between U.S. law schools for students, as the national pool of applicants shrinks, are mopping up money (often money provided in steep tuition fees paid by students whom law schools really don't want, because their indicators will drive the institution's status down not up, and who are often the most academically at risk), to buy the students with the credentials that will improve the school's status.

That money, absent the brainless and expensive replication of hierarchy driven by *U.S. News* and what I will delicately call ethical insensitivity on the part of many in legal education, could be spent on making law schools in the U.S. more educationally functional. Doing that would include taking steps to ensure that law schools mitigate the academic and bar passage risk of students whom those law schools admit while either actually knowing (or having an obligation to know, if they reviewed their student performance data responsibly) that they are at academic and bar failure risk as soon as they produce that information, which a system that almost exclusively produces first year LGPA by end-of-semester terminal examination does far too late.

They would do so, first, as I will go on to argue, by inculcating disciplinary literacy effectively, and secondly, by mitigating bar failure risk as soon as it is detected. This may in practice be, as Sander's theory implies, as early as the point of admission, once our most predictive bar failure indicator (in my institution, for example, low law school GPA) has been identified and addressed for the students whose bar failure risk factors are most readily remediable.

Legal Academia" (cited in n.41) 705; Peller, "Race Consciousness" (cited in n.41) 803–7; and Russell, "From the Trenches and Towers" (cited in n.32).

[109] Other high scorers are placement in employment three months after graduation, at 14% and reputation among lawyers and judges, at 15%.

Let me make a few brief points before returning to Sander, and adding some context to his analysis. If

- law schools are able to manipulate the *U.S. News* 75/25 percentile and median (rather than mean) admissions academic indicators rankings to admit students, often but not always students of color from disadvantaged racial minority groups (you also tend to find children of big (often alumni) donors with low scores here) with "low indicators" in their bottom quartile while minimizing institutional status threat; and if

- the performative or actually egalitarian imperative for law schools to present themselves as "diverse" means, as appears likely, that the only students in that bottom quartile who are getting sizeable scholarships are students of color;[110] then if

- the empiricist *du jour* tells you that you're hurting those among those students who are black; and

- freeing up scholarship money is a real temptation, because it helps you buy students with better scores;[111] and

- the law school applicant pool is shrinking (in particular in the recent past the numbers of women applying to law schools have dropped considerably);

- the Supreme Court said in 2003 that the need for affirmative action in the elite public law school context will have likely run its course by 2028; then why on earth, unless something more than institutional status as evaluated by the *U.S. News* was important to you, would you seek to address the visible legacies of centuries of structural subordination of African-Americans as you ran your law school admissions process?

And that empiricist *du jour* was indeed telling the readership of *Stanford Law Review* and organs of the press that affirmative action in law school admissions was hurting black law students, badly, adding:

(a) law school admissions offices rely primarily on academic indices in selecting their students;

(b) because the number of blacks with high indices is small, elite law schools achieve something close to proportional representation either by maintaining separate

---

[110] Because higher-ranked schools are using scholarship money to "buy" black students whose indicators would otherwise put them squarely in your admissions pool.

[111] See Segal, "Law Students Lose the Grant Game as Schools Win" (cited in n.51, which exposed the apparently calculated way in which Golden Gate Law School had allegedly used scholarship money to enroll law students who had very little chance of retaining scholarships past the first year, saying that "American law schools have quietly gone on a giveaway binge in the last decade. In 2009, the most recent year for which the American Bar Association has data, 38,000 of 145,000 law school students—more than one in four—were on merit scholarships. The total tab for all schools in three years: more than $500 million." In a "related" sidebar to Segal's article, Jerry Organ, a Professor at the University of St. Thomas law school, was quoted as saying what to any professor in the current U.S. legal academy with a pulse would fall within the Monty Python category of the "bleeding obvious": "many schools use merit grant programs to climb the ranking in U.S. News & World Report." A follow-up article the next day noted that "more than one in four [law students nationally]...were on merit scholarships" and underscores how critical raising median LSAT is if a school wants to rise in or even hold steady in the U.S. News ranking. See Paul L. Caron, "Law Schools Award Merit Scholarships To Recruit Students (and Goose U.S. News Ranking), And Then Take Them Away With Rigid Grading Curves" (*TaxProf Blog*, 1 May 2011), available at <http://taxprof.typepad.com/taxprof_blog/2011/05/ny-times-law-school.html> accessed Aug. 26, 2011.

black and white admissions tracks or by giving black applicants large numerical boosts; and

(c) the use of these preferences by elite schools gives nearly all other law schools little choice but to follow suit. The result is a game of musical chairs where blacks are consistently being bumped up several seats in the law school admissions hierarchy, producing a large black-white gap in the academic credentials of students at nearly all law schools.[112]

Suffice it to say here that the various critics of Sander's data (and its analysis in that blockbuster legal education affirmative action fight issue of *Stanford Law Review*) and the high-status legal academic periodical publications that joined the fray crunch his data rather differently; some also provide some (relatively thin) context.

Before I go on to discuss them, however, let me just ask and answer the following question. Why spend more time on Sander? After all, Beverley Moran[113] has delivered a blistering critique of Sander's "weav[ing] together a seemingly empirical story that supports his claims."[114] After a brisk review of the flaws disclosed by other scholars in Sander's methodology and data interpretation,[115] she lays out the "six truths" about black inferiority that Sander's theory about the mismatch effect relies on.[116] The two most salient for my purposes here are, first, that:

Professor Sander is explicit... [that a]ffirmative action helps white students by providing them with less competition. By forcing blacks to fill the bottom of each law school class, affirmative action allows every white student to think he or she is above average. According to Professor Sander [who wrote in "A Systemic Analysis" that race-based affirmative action means that "whites probably have higher grades, graduation rates and bar passage than they would in a system totally lacking racial preferences]",[117] white students could not maintain this superior self-perception if they were actually forced to compete against their true peers.[118]

And second, that Sander's repeated claims that the black-white law student performance gap has nothing to do with race per se equate to a claim the UGPA and LSAT race gaps "[a]re [e]xplained by [b]ad [b]lack [p]arenting"[119] as is evident from his reasoning that

[r]esearchers have made great strides over the past generation in accounting for the black-white gap in measured cognitive skills. The dominant consensus is that: (a) the gap is real, and shows up under many types of measurement; (b) the gap is not genetic, i.e. black infants raised in white households tend to have the same or higher cognitive skills as whites raised in the same conditions; and (c) there are a variety of cultural and parenting differences between American blacks and whites (e.g. time children spend reading or watching television) that substantially contribute to measured skill gaps).[120]

---

[112] Sander, "A Systemic Analysis of Affirmative Action in American Law Schools" (cited in n.9), 418–19.
[113] Moran, "The Case for Black Inferiority?" (cited in n.93).
[114] Moran, "The Case for Black Inferiority?" (cited in n.93) 43.
[115] Moran, "The Case for Black Inferiority?" (cited in n.93) 44–8.
[116] Moran, "The Case for Black Inferiority?" (cited in n.93) 48–57.
[117] Sander, "A Systemic Analysis of Affirmative Action in American Law Schools" (cited in n.9) n.6.
[118] Moran, "The Case for Black Inferiority?" (cited in n.93) 53.
[119] Moran, "The Case for Black Inferiority?" (cited in n.93) 50.
[120] Sander, "Experimenting With Class-Based Affirmative Action" (cited in n.15), 472 n.175. See also Sander, "Experimenting With Class-Based Affirmative Action" (cited in n.15) n.16, citing "data suggesting that a combination of family SES, childrearing practices, and neighborhood characteristics explains over half black/white differences in test performance."

Let me note two things at this point. First, Sander does not acknowledge that there might be a connection, say, between poverty and the time a parent reads to a child or allows her to watch television; nor that if the parent has poor literacy skills or is illiterate, both factors themselves correlated with poverty and dysfunctional and often violent public school education in a system with funding based in significant part on local property taxes, and cannot afford books or lives in a neighborhood without access to a public library or which is so plagued by violence that accessing a nearby public library is dangerous, this no doubt has an impact on how much reading to a child a parent does.

Next, as Moran so aptly puts it, "according to Professor Sander, the only factor that seems to help black students rise above the credentials gap between blacks and whites is removal from black parents and placement in a white household."[121] Indeed, I am reminded of the experience of a highly qualified African-American colleague who, like her (eminent) mother, is a high-achieving legal scholar and teacher. During the interviewing process she went through while seeking a position as a law professor, after telling an interviewing panel from a law school that will remain unnamed that her interest in being a law professor resulted in part from her mother's profession, she was asked by a white law professor on the panel, "Are you adopted?"

It is the brute reality that I have just laid out,[122] and the utter blindness of all those involved in the tournament of empiricists to how law schools in particular, in combination with the structural race-based educational disadvantage from preschool to OneL which causes the black-white law school achievement gap, that makes spending time on Sander imperative. As I will demonstrate in the final part of this article, law schools know or should know how they can change legal education so it offers a fair balance of access and merit,[123] and most of them fail to do so.

So too does the fact that law schools continue to use an admissions test that they know to be race-biased, and that is generated in their own laboratory. They only get themselves into constitutional trouble when attempts are made to redress the pro-white male economically privileged bias of that test. There are indeed alternative models of admissions-testing that might measure something that indeed can be defensibly constructed in context as race-neutral merit, for example the Shultz-Zedek test, designed to admit students based on accurate prediction of "eventual success as a lawyer."[124]

4. The tournament of empiricists

My Ph.D. is in literary studies, not statistics, so I do not propose to spend time on evaluating who gets the best of the fight over the numbers; in part to do so would be *de trop*, given the time and energy Sander has spent responding to his critics and adjusting his data as a result.[125] In any event, all the participants in the tournament of empiricists end with the same dispiriting conclusion (which I would read as an insistent ethical challenge

---

[121] Moran, "The Case for Black Inferiority?" (cited in n.93) 52.

[122] Of Sander's failure to recognize the persisting transhistorical effects of slavery and Jim Crow on life opportunities for black Americans.

[123] Thanks to Professor Steven Lamos of the Program for Writing and Rhetoric and the English Department, and Faculty Director of the Writing Center at the University of Colorado-Boulder, for his insights on this question.

[124] William P. Lapiana, "Merit and Diversity: The Origins of the Law School Admissions Test" (2004) 48 St. Louis L.J. 955.

[125] Richard Sander, "Supplemental Analyses for Reply to Critics" (*U.C.L.A. Law*), available at <http://www2.law.ucla.edu/sander/Systemic/SuppCritic.htm> accessed 26 August 2011.

to the nation's legal educators, law schools, the ABA, the AALS, and the LSAC), that whites significantly outperform blacks on the LSAT, at law school, and on the bar examination. And they all conclude that we should really be doing something about it, if we just knew what to do.

What I am trained to do (other than to be a lawyer) is to read texts critically, so I will offer a brief critical reading of some of the most prominent quantitative empirical responses to Sander, and seek to lay bare the story that they, too, tell. To the extent that the participants in the tournament of empiricists fight over datasets, and the "truth" of what they mean, my point is precisely that decontextualized quantitative empiricism gets us not very far, especially if we are as naïve about the "truth" of social science as the epigraph to this article quoting Sander suggests he is. I will then go on to present what is hiding in plain view, by outlining exactly what we already know can be done to fix the problem, and where we should go elsewhere in the university to enrich that knowledge.

Ian Ayres and Richard Brooks, for example, in *Does Affirmative Action Reduce the Number of Black Lawyers?* register the stark facts about black/white inequality in U.S. law schools:

[w]ith the exception of the traditionally black law schools (where blacks still make up 43.8% of the student body), the median black law school grade point average is at the 6.7th percentile of white law students. This means that only 6.7% of whites have lower grades than 50% of blacks. One finds a similar result at the other end of the distribution—as only 7.5% of blacks have grades that are higher than the white median.... In the LSAC data, 83.2% of whites graduated and passed the bar within 5 years of entering law school, while only 57.5 % of blacks entering law school became lawyers.[126]

But their conclusion is that "even more affirmative action would have been likely to produce more black lawyers,"[127] that "[b]lack law students attending the white median tier schools are substantially less likely to become lawyers than white students with the same index score attending the same tier,"[128] and that "[b]lack students have a higher probability of becoming lawyers when they attend higher-quality tiers."[129] Ayres and Brooks speculate that "they do better because... [they are] pulled along, inspired, or pushed to success by the greater resources and stronger academic environment at more selective law schools."[130]

Or perhaps—my suggestion, although not a novel one—if the studies suggesting undergraduate GPA and LSAT are race-biased are correct, black law students at elite schools may do better in a context where so many black Americans still disproportionately experience impoverishment and substandard access to basic school education for another reason. Maybe those successful black students at Harvard and Yale and the Universities of Michigan and Virginia are just more intellectually able, more meritorious occupants of those highly contested seats in elite law schools than are their economically and race-privileged white peers.

---

[126] Ian Ayres and Richard Brooks, "Does Affirmative Action Reduce the Number of Black Lawyers?" (2005) 57 Stan. L. Rev. 1807, 1808.
[127] Ayres and Brooks, "Does Affirmative Action Reduce the Number of Black Lawyers?" (cited in n.126) 1853–4.
[128] Ayres and Brooks, "Does Affirmative Action Reduce the Number of Black Lawyers?" (cited in n.126) 1816.
[129] Ayres and Brooks, "Does Affirmative Action Reduce the Number of Black Lawyers?" (cited in n.126) 1853–4.
[130] Ayres and Brooks, "Does Affirmative Action Reduce the Number of Black Lawyers?" (cited in n.126) 1854.

Chambers et al. "agree with Sander that the high rate at which African-American students fail to graduate and fail to pass the bar is alarming."[131] However, in addition to criticizing aspects of his methodology,[132] they conclude, *contra* Sander, that ending affirmative action in law school admissions would significantly reduce the number of African-Americans attending "at the great majority of the nation's fifty to eighty most selective law schools."[133] Supporting the contention of Ayres and Brooks, they show that "African Americans at first-tier schools graduate and pass the bar at higher rates than African Americans with the same credentials at schools in the lower tiers."[134]

They note that a significant number of African-American students at highly ranked schools with race-conscious admissions programs cite the relatively high proportions of black law students at those schools as a factor in deciding to attend, thus leading to the conclusion that the few black students who would secure admission to elite schools without affirmative action may decide not to apply to them because they will be members of a tiny and highly visible minority.[135] They also suggest, correctly in my view, that the relative poverty of African-Americans is likely to mean that they will conclude that the financial and other costs undertaken in traveling out of state to attend an elite law school are worth it, but that doing so to attend a low-ranked school are not, and indeed that Sander's assumption that absent affirmative action African-American students are likely to be *able* to attend a lower-tier local school lacks support.[136] Once again, like Ayres and Brooks,[137] they acknowledge that the "high rate of dropout and bar failure by black law students is a very serious problem,"[138] but seemingly have no sense of how it might be remedied.

Rothstein and Yoon's analysis reaches similar conclusions to the work of Chambers et al., finding that "[e]liminating affirmative action would dramatically reduce the number of law students, particularly at the most selective schools"[139] where their numbers would fall "to nearly zero."[140] They also conclude that the "mismatch effect" is much less significant than Sander contends, and even then is "concentrated among the students with the weakest entering credentials."[141] Their failure to address the literature that might explain

---

[131] David L. Chambers, Timothy T. Clydesdale, William C. Kidder, and Richard O. Lempert, "The Real Impact of Eliminating Affirmative Action in American Law Schools: An Empirical Critique of Richard Sander's Study" (2004) 57 Stan. L. Rev. 1855, 1857.

[132] Such as his choice of a dataset from 2001, a year of especially low numbers of white law school applications, Chambers et al., "The Real Impact of Eliminating Affirmative Action in American Law Schools" (cited in n.131) 1860.

[133] Chambers et al., "The Real Impact of Eliminating Affirmative Action in American Law Schools" (cited in n.131) 1858.

[134] Chambers et al., "The Real Impact of Eliminating Affirmative Action in American Law Schools" (cited in n.131) 1897.

[135] Chambers et al., "The Real Impact of Eliminating Affirmative Action in American Law Schools" (cited in n.131) 1864.

[136] Chambers et al., "The Real Impact of Eliminating Affirmative Action in American Law Schools" (cited in n.131) 1865–7.

[137] Ayres and Brooks, "Does Affirmative Action Reduce the Number of Black Lawyers?" (cited in n.126) 1651.

[138] Chambers et al., "The Real Impact of Eliminating Affirmative Action in American Law Schools" (cited in n.131) 1898.

[139] Jesse Rothstein and Albert H. Yoon, "Affirmative Action in Law School Admissions: What do Racial Preferences Do?" (2008)75 Univ. Chicago L. Rev. 649, 652.

[140] Rothstein and Yoon, "Affirmative Action in Law School Admissions" (cited in n.139) 676.

[141] Rothstein and Yoon, "Affirmative Action in Law School Admissions" (cited in n.139) 652.

what to do about the gaps between black and white law school outcomes is especially marked, as is the discourse of detachment of science from ethics:

> [w]e treat law schools as "black boxes," where the inputs are applicants for admission and the outputs are lawyers. We examine the effects of the quality of the inputs, but do not explore the cultural, pedagogic, or other features of the law school environment that account for these effects. While our estimates here are clearly relevant to any normative evaluation, we leave to others the task of applying them to policy and the law.[142]

Nonetheless, they also concede that "it is incontrovertible that average outcomes for black law students are worse than those for white law students. Ninety-two percent of white matriculants graduate from law school, but only 81 percent of black matriculants do. Eighty-seven percent of white graduates and 64 percent of black graduates pass the bar exam within one year."[143] Why then do they say Sander overstates the responsibility of the mismatch effect for this achievement gap? Because his data combines black students who would gain admission to a school at a particular level without affirmative action and those who wouldn't.[144] And they emphasize that it is at the lowest-ranked law schools where black students substantially underperform whites: further up the law school food chain, "black students graduate at approximately the same rates as whites."[145]

Ho criticizes Sander's statistical method, claiming he "misapplies basic principles of causal inference, which enjoy virtually universal acceptance in the scientific community," and that "[a]s a result, the study draws internally inconsistent and empirically invalid conclusions about the effects of affirmative action."[146] His conclusion? "Correcting the assumptions and testing the hypothesis directly shows that for similarly qualified black students, attending a higher-tier law school has no detectable effect on bar passage rates"[147] (although Ho concedes this is not the case when law school grades are considered).[148] Unfortunately, this does not take redressing the black-white achievement gap very far: blacks significantly underperform whites on both LSAT and UGPA.

Finally, Sander's response to his critics yields a claim of salience to the critique which follows. Engaging with part of the argument generated by Ayres and Brooks, he analyzes the relative performance of graduation rates and bar passage at the first attempt of three groups of students: whites, blacks who, although admitted to a higher-ranked school, chose to attend a school that was lower-ranked, and all other black law students. Black students in the former group significantly outperform other black students. The graduation rate for whites is 92.2%, for blacks passing up their first choice school 89.5%, for other black law students 81.1%. As to first-time bar passage, the rates are 92.1%, 80.3%, and 59.6% respectively.[149] Sander registers that "the LSAC-BPS data does suggest that black second-choice students are somewhat less affluent and that they were relatively

---

[142] Rothstein and Yoon, "Affirmative Action in Law School Admissions" (cited in n.139) 653; Rothstein and Yoon, "Affirmative Action in Law School Admissions" (cited in n.139) 661–2 (speculating about how law schools might harm the chances of black law students); Rothstein and Yoon, "Affirmative Action in Law School Admissions" (cited in n.139) 711 (showing that half of black underperformance at law school and on the bar examination is not attributable to the credentials gap).
[143] Rothstein and Yoon, "Affirmative Action in Law School Admissions" (cited in n.139) 677.
[144] Rothstein and Yoon, "Affirmative Action in Law School Admissions" (cited in n.139) 677.
[145] Rothstein and Yoon, "Affirmative Action in Law School Admissions" (cited in n.139) 689.
[146] Ho, "Why Affirmative Action Does Not Cause Black Students to Fail the Bar" (cited in n.97) 1997.
[147] Ho, "Why Affirmative Action Does Not Cause Black Students to Fail the Bar" (cited in n.97) 1997.
[148] Ho, "Affirmative Action's Affirmative Actions: A Reply to Sander" (cited in n.98) 2014.
[149] Sander, "A Reply to Critics" (cited in n.96) 1974 (Table 2).

more concerned about cost... in choosing a law school."[150] This makes sense. Economic insecurity is a known contributor to bar failure.[151] Law students who are distracted by the need to do paid work during the school year to cope financially tend, in my observation, to do relatively poorly academically, and we know already that socioeconomic status has an impact on LSGPA as well as on bar passage. Finally, to the extent that I (like many others) regularly see students with low LSATs wildly outperform what it would predict of them, those students are always participants in "educationally meaningful activities"[152] at a high level. This suggests a kind of situational common sense about how to do well academically, a situational common sense that might equally explain black students who choose a less elite law school knowing that doing so will put them under less economic stress.[153]

One of the oddest gaps in Sander's account of his empirical study and his interpretive reading of it, given his stated aim to "analyze legal education as a complete interlocking system"[154] is that he (and except for the odd footnote or aside here or there, the critics who follow him through a tournament of data-crunching and data-analysis in elite law reviews from Stanford to Yale to Chicago over the latter part of the first decade of the current century)[155] treat U.S. legal education like a piece of PVC pipe[156] delivering educational social Darwinism. Sander does, in a short section of "A Systemic Analysis," cast some perfunctory statistical doubt on the long-articulated claims that LSAT and UGPA are poor predictors of law school performance and bar passage; and that they are racially biased. As he makes clear, however, he has little stomach to tangle with this type of what I will call "thick" critique, nuanced, particularistic, observational, and experiential, as exemplified, for example, by David Wilkins,[157] of what legal educational institutions and discourses in the U.S. do to black law students:

[t]he battlefield staked out by these two critiques is bloody and littered with corpses. For the most part, my approach... is to sidestep the field by presenting new, real, and systematic data on the actual consequences of affirmative action.... If we actually know black-white differences in law school grades, retention rates, and bar passage, theoretical arguments about predictive indices

---

[150] Sander, "A Reply to Critics" (cited in n.96) 1976.
[151] See Denise Riebe and Michael Hunter Schwartz, *Pass the Bar!* (Carolina Academic Press, 2006) 7.
[152] A phrase used by the *National Survey of Student Engagement* (NSSE).
[153] Indeed one of the great contributions of David Wilkins' response to Sander is that he chronicles the reduced likelihood that black law students will have acquired the kind of knowledge about how to thrive in a white-dominated culture largely blind to white privilege that will enable them to thrive in elite law practice, see David Wilkins, "A Systematic Response to Systemic Disadvantage: A Response to Sander" (2004) 57 Stan. L. Rev. 1915, 1934, nn.71–72.
[154] Sander, "A Systemic Analysis of Affirmative Action in American Law Schools" (cited in n.9) 369.
[155] Ayres and Brooks, for example, while directing some brief attention in their conclusion to identifying what law schools do that means that black and white law students with the same credential entering the same level school perform significantly differentially poorly, suggest that "better information about the risk of the undertaking [of legal education for black law students] might reduce their 'supply.'" See Ayres and Brooks, "Does Affirmative Action Reduce the Number of Black Lawyers?" (cited in n.126) 1809.
[156] A metaphor also used by Professor Johnson. Indeed the literature on black-white gaps in law school performance is flooded with effluvial metaphors.
[157] For two studies that do this work well in the field of black performance in legal practice, which are beyond the scope of this article, see James E. Coleman, Jr. and Mitu Gulati, "A Response To Professor Sander: Is It Really All About the Grades?" (2005) 84 N.C. L. Rev. 1823;; and David Wilkins, "A Systematic Response to Systemic Disadvantage: A Response to Sander" (2004) 57 Stan. L. Rev. 1915, 1934, nn.71–72.

become in some sense moot. However, since...the arguments...are so widely believed, and so often repeated, and have gained so much apparent legitimacy,[158] that he needs to give them some cursory statistical bludgeoning.[159]

However, Sander seems to be completely unaware of the historical literature on the rise of the use of the LSAT as a—or at present the—principal metric for law school admissions, in spite of what it does to the chances of black students. Daria Roithmayr's searching 1997 critical history of the racially exclusionary context in which the standards of merit which both the LSAT and the Bar Examination construct were developed[160] significantly predates "A Systemic Analysis." And her work in turn synthesizes that of scholars of American legal and legal educational history including Jerrold Auerbach,[161] Richard Delgado,[162] Paul Finkelman,[163] and Robert Stevens[164] dating from 1976, 1994, 1995, and 1983 respectively.[165]

Let me return at this point to Johnson. There are two things to raise here that undermine Johnson's claims for the race neutrality of the LSAT. First, given that it tests "[l]ogical [r]easoning, [a]nalytical [r]easoning and [r]eading comprehension,"[166] he himself cites elsewhere excerpts from the mass of educational research showing that African Americans from fourth grade on score systematically below whites on reading comprehension, and that African Americans wildly underperform whites on the analytic component of the GRE.[167]

His data also rings a (dissonant) chord with Sander's sheeting home the achievement gap on the LSAT to bad black parenting and I and many others would sheet home to poverty and impoverished school education. African-American children score much lower on vocabulary tests than their white peers.[168] Mertz's critical analysis of scholarship of language in classrooms from grade school on shows how the inculcation of literacy is a practice of power that silences children who are not socialized like their teachers, nor in the way that dominant group literacy normalizes.[169] She also registers that research into elementary school teaching shows that "[s]o-called low ability reading classes are typically more characterized [by a reading pedagogy that is 'fragmented' and 'focused on the pragmatics of pronunciation'] where the more empowering pedagogy in high-ranked reading classes pushes children to move beyond merely pronouncing the text correctly, to discussing and extracting its content."[170]

---

[158] Sander, "A Systemic Analysis of Affirmative Action in American Law Schools" (cited in n.9) 420.
[159] Sander, "A Systemic Analysis of Affirmative Action in American Law Schools" (cited in n.9) 420–3.
[160] D. Roithmayr, "Deconstructing the Distinction between Bias and Merit" (cited in n.40).
[161] Jerold S. Auerbach, *Unequal Justice: Lawyers and Social Change in Modern America* (Oxford, 1976).
[162] Delgado, "Rodrigo's Tenth Chronicle" (cited in n.51) 1740–1.
[163] Paul Finkelman, "Not Only the Judge's Robes Were Black: African-American Lawyers as Social Engineers" (1994) 47 Stan. L. Rev. 161.
[164] Robert Stevens, *Law School: Legal education in America from the 1850s to the 1980s* (University of North Carolina Press, 1983).
[165] Roithmayr, "Deconstructing the Distinction between Bias and Merit" (cited in n.40) 1476.
[166] Johnson, "Knots in the Law School Pipeline" (cited in n.30) 39.
[167] Johnson, "The Destruction of the Holistic Approach to Admissions" (cited in n.31) 341–2 and accompanying notes.
[168] Johnson, "The Destruction of the Holistic Approach to Admissions" (cited in n.31) 341.
[169] Elizabeth Mertz, *The Language of Law School: Learning to "Think Like a Lawyer"* (Oxford, 2007) 22–5.
[170] Mertz, *The Language of Law School* (cited in n.169) 50. See also Jacqueline Jordan Irvine, *Black Students and School Failure: Policies, Practices and Prescriptions* (Praeger, 1990) 9–12.

5. Hidden in plain view

Sander is also quite wrong about at least one critical assumption of "A Systemic Analysis"[171]: that bar examination failure has to do with what he comprehends from his own observation of black students who perform poorly in his classes: that they fall behind on acquiring the "vocabulary" of the specific doctrinal subject being taught and that on the exam "many C students seem to have missed fundamentals" of the course in question.[172] (Rothstein and Yoon make slightly different but similarly incorrect assumptions about what causes bar failure and why black students from elite law schools fail the bar.)[173] Let's leave aside for now what it must feel like to be a black student in the class of a professor who is making his name by making the case that you really don't belong at a law school as elite as UCLA's, and how the scholarly literature including Mertz's *The Language of Law School* shows that institutional and classroom environment really matter in how well black students perform.

The scholarship on what causes bar failure is clear: it is not gaps in doctrinal knowledge that lead to failure, but deficiencies in legal disciplinary literacy.[174] And let me add some critical context here: one thing the U.S. legal academy seems blithely unaware of is that the fit between educational fairness and differential levels of entering-level tertiary literacy and differential rates of development of legal disciplinary literacy is not assisted by the fact that in most first year law school classes assessment is by means of a final written examination, while interim informal performance assessment in classroom exchange is almost always confined to assessment of oral performance. There is almost zero comprehension in the industry of what the basic literature on good quality education practice will tell you: that skilling in the assessment *mode* is as critical as enabling effective learning of "content" if your aim is to maximize all students' competence, to be educationally equitable.[175]

In addition to her basic conclusions about what legal subject formation in the U.S. as a generalizeable matter does to students, Mertz finds "differential effects of race and gender on inclusion in first year classrooms,"[176] and produces a good deal of fine-grained empirical and analytical indications of what might compromise the chances of academic success of black students in law school, such as her conclusion that "two classes taught by professors of color ... [in her study] at elite schools were characterized by high par-

---

[171] He is also wrong, as indicated above, about the assumption that black and white students with equal numerical indicators admitted to the same law school would perform as their indicators would suggest. In fact black students in this scenario would underperform their white classmates, see Cheryl I. Harris and William C. Kidder, "The Black Student Mismatch Myth in Legal Education: The Systemic Flaws in Richard Sander's Affirmative Action Study" (Winter 2004/2005) J. of Blacks in Higher Educ., 104.

[172] Sander, "A Systemic Analysis of Affirmative Action in American Law Schools" (cited in n.9) 450.

[173] Rothstein and Yoon, "Affirmative Action in Law School Admissions" (cited in n.139) 661.

[174] See Lorenzo A. Trujillo, "The Relationship Between Law School and the Bar Exam: A Look at Assessment and Student Success" (2007) 78 U. Colo. L. Rev. 69 (noting for example at p. 85 that *proponents* of the current bar examination system argue that "[legal] analysis" and "effective writ[ing of] an answer in the language of the law are more important in passing the bar examination than knowing the doctrinal rules involved").

[175] See Roy Stuckey et al., "Best Practices for Legal Education: A Vision and A Road Map" (CLEA, 2007) 236–9.

[176] Mertz, *The Language of Law School* (cited in n.169)) 197.

ticipation rates on the part of students of color, a result apparently unaffected by status of school."[177]

There are two good studies, one produced on academic support programs at the elite UCLA Law School,[178] ironically in context co-written by none other than Sander, and a more recent one dealing with an academic support program at the non-elite St. Thomas.[179] These studies show how law schools can intervene effectively in a range of ways to increase the chances of academic success of students who have markers of academic and bar failure risk, in the first case; or in the second, raise GPAs of students such that they outperform their entering numerical indicators, if they participate in the first year of law school in a well-designed academic support program designed to inculcate active learning.[180] Indeed, Sander himself acknowledges that the UCLA academic support program (for students with weak entering numerical indicators admitted under a race-conscious affirmative action plan at UCLA law school) in which he worked, and which he and Kristine Knaplund documented, increased graduation and bar passage:

[a]lthough the academic credentials (undergraduate grades and LSATs) of black, Latino, and American Indian admits were, on average, significantly lower than those of whites, the school pioneered effective academic support programs for students who needed them, and the rate at which matriculants graduated from the school and passed the bar examination was quite high.[181]

What else is invisible to Sander and his fellow empiricists? It is that looking solely at the forest that is the total national performance of black and white students on the bar examination shows complete ignorance about the institutional and programmatic trees that buck national trends and predictions based on them. I've designed and implemented two foundational legal literacy courses at two U.S. law schools at different eliteness levels. A collateral effect of those programs has been to substantially increase bar passage rates.[182] At my current institution I've spearheaded an effort specifically to

---

[177] Mertz, *The Language of Law School* (cited in n.169) 196.

[178] Kristine S. Knaplund and Richard H. Sander, "The Art and Science of Academic Support" (1995) 45 J. Legal Educ. 157.

[179] Patricia W. Hatamyar and Todd P. Sullivan, "The Impact of Active Learning on Law School Performance" (2007) 3(2) J. Multidisciplinary Research 67.

[180] I am bracketing for now the question about curve-based assessment that characterizes U.S. law schools, and alternative forms of assessment, such as competency-based assessment. The point of the St. Thomas study by Hatamayar and Sullivan, on my reading (given that at my law school, like many, low LSGPA is our most reliable indicator of bar examination failure), is that even if a student ends, because of curved grading, near the bottom of his class, if his fundamental legal literacy and law school learning skills are enhanced, his bar passage rates are also likely to be improved. However, the St. Thomas program, which fits with what we know about the improved law school performance of students who participate at high rates in "educationally meaningful activities," depends on students to participate voluntarily. Those who tend to perform as Sander and his ilk would contend they inevitably do, characteristically behave in maladaptive ways to a pedagogical context that puts them for one or more reasons, including institutional inclusiveness tone, at academic risk. They are also less likely to participate voluntarily in such a program than their (actually if not statistically) less "at risk" peers. Professor Knaplund has told me that one effect of UCLA's pre-orientation program that is not documented in article she and Sander co-authored is that participation in it increased uptake in academic support services during law school.

[181] Sander, "Experimenting With Class-Based Affirmative Action" (cited in n.15), 474.

[182] In the year before the first Southern Illinois University School of Law student cohort to take the Lawyering Skills course I designed, administered, and taught in sat the bar examination, the school's Illinois bar passage rate for first-time takers was 69.4%. For the two years in which SIU students taking the bar had taken my course in their first year (2001 and 2002), the school's Illinois bar passage rate was 84.3% and 85.2%. For the subsequent 2003 cohort (after I had left SIU for American University Washington College of Law) the SIU bar passage rate in Illinois dropped to 77.8%. At American, the Maryland bar passage rate for WLS students the last year before the new Legal Rhetoric course I

address lagging bar passage rates; our students as a cohort now significantly outperform what their incoming numerical indicators would predict of them if Sander were correct about how predictive LSAT scores were as predictors of bar passage.[183]

There are other innovative approaches to enhancing law school and bar passage success by students with low entering indicators. The non-elite Nova Southeastern Law School developed a summer pre-admission program which would enable them to predict which students at the bottom of their entering indicators pool would be likely to succeed and which wouldn't. Only the former were in fact admitted to the law school, and when I visited and spoke with law school administrators there about it, relatively early in its existence, they indicated that those "marginal" admits routinely academically outperformed their peers with higher admissions indicators, and passed the bar, and that the program enabled them to include a more significant number of "minority" students in their admitted cohort than they had been able to achieve without it.

And there's also what those of us who do bar passage work know: there are frequent wild anomalies in schools' bar passage rates, where cohorts strikingly underperform or overperform their admissions indicators, suggesting that it is what is happening to students in law schools, not just or even mostly the indicators that Sander reduces them to, that make bar passage easier or harder. Take, for example, non-elite Northern Illinois University School of Law, which had the third-best pass rate of schools reporting in that state, outperforming schools with students with much higher admissions indicators, like the very elite University of Chicago, for first-time takers of the Illinois July Bar Examination for 2008: nearly 95%. Last year in the Virginia July Bar Examination Washington and Lee, a top-tier law school, and within recent memory a top 20 school nationally, had a bar passage rate of 72.7%, under the Virginia state pass rate of 75.2%. Anyone who works in legal literacy inculcation in general and bar passage support in particular will tell you that these aren't anomalies: they are the result of schools taking seriously or not the question of inculcation of all aspects of legal literacy and their student cohorts' bar failure risks, and educating accordingly.

Addressing the latter doesn't require "teaching to the bar," as is so often dismissively said of low-tier law schools who work effectively to enable their graduates to get the

---

designed, directed, and taught in was 72.7%. The first year of the program was difficult, in terms of institutional politics, faculty and student buy-in, and staffing, and the Maryland first-time taker passage rate of that cohort of OneLs was 70%. In the subsequent years it lifted to 84.9%, 80.3%, 81.4% (all in Maryland); and 88% (in New York, in which WCL began to report bar passage in New York; schools report bar passage to the ABA and *U.S. News* for the jurisdiction in which the largest number of its graduates sit the bar). In the year after I left WCL for Villanova, when the Associate Director of the Program I had directed, Professor Amy Dillard, now of the University of Baltimore School of Law, took over the Acting Directorship, WCL's New York bar passage rate was 92% for the cohort who took the course that year.

[183] I joined the Villanova faculty in 2004. That year the school's first-time taker pass rate in Pennsylvania was 78.89%, under the state average of 80.78%. The Dean appointed me head of a Bar Passage Task Force to address our students' underperformance on the bar examination. Over subsequent years, the task force incrementally developed and backed in from the third year to the first programming based on the literature on best practices in legal education and evidence-based bar passage enhancement programs that were directed at improving student performance in law school rather than "teaching to the bar." In the last three years, with most of the planks of the program in place, VLS first time takers passed the Pennsylvania Bar at 91.89% (2008), 90.57% (2009) and 89.87% (2010). It is also worth noting that the (second-tier) Temple Law School Pennsylvania bar passage rates for 2009 and 2010, 95.57% and 92.34%, are almost identical to those of the elite University of Pennsylvania (96.08% and 92.86%). For obvious reasons, information about how Temple is achieving what it is achieving is not easy to come by. If I had to speculate, I would suggest that the fact that its foundational legal literacy faculty are tenured or tenure-track has a significant role in its students' performance.

critical credential they need to practice law. A Washington and Lee student cohort (and institutional context) likely needs different approaches to that at a fourth-tier school, to be sure, but fundamental disciplinary literacy is what's critical.

6. Conclusion: Willful ignorance

Let me close with how Virginia Woolf's "snail's eye" view—in this case of those who do what under present conditions is usually the hard women's work of inculcating legal disciplinary literacy—might provide "thick" contexts that would destabilize Sander's theory more profoundly than the empyrean struggle over numbers by (mostly) male academics, and to gesture towards another question about race and disciplinary literacy pedagogy.

A major similarity between Sander's and Mertz's studies is that they privilege oral evidence of competency in disciplinary literacy and more or less completely disregard its read and written components. David Wilkins notes in his critique of Sander's commentary about black student underperformance in legal writing classes, that

> Sander points to evidence from two data sources that the black-white gap in legal writing courses is equal to, if not larger than, the gap for courses using traditional exams.... As he concedes, however, the sample size for both data sources is tiny ands the samples are arguably quite skewed. Moreover, as he notes but then dismisses, legal writing classes are not graded anonymously. Although I tend to agree with Sander that professors—or, more likely, the recent graduates or adjuncts who actually grade student papers in these courses—are not likely to be consciously biased against blacks, as my interviews have revealed time and time again, the stereotype that "blacks can't write" is so pervasive in our culture that it is quite possible that it often penetrates at a subconscious level the highly discretionary subjective judgments that those grading these exercises often employ.[184]

Further, if as Mertz shows, *professorial race matters* in the oral disciplinary literacy competency black students manifest in the first year doctrinal law school classroom, the fact that the legal writing professoriate is overwhelmingly white and female[185] may have an impact on black student learning in this context. More significantly, as is shown by (a) the critical race literature on school- and college-level literacy teaching and learning that I will touch on; (b) Johnson's and Mertz's evidence (about how black students' reading comprehension and analytical ability is negatively affected by the contexts and practices of their disciplinary literacy training and by blacks' disproportionate poverty); and (c) Moran's work on black children's likelihood of living in neighborhoods with underfunded schools, transgenerational poverty, and poor schooling; these circumstances are, from the very beginning, likely to negatively impact the written "tertiary literacy" competence with which black law students enter law school.

Laurel Currie Oates has demonstrated how entering law students with low indicators in fact performed across the spectrum of law school success, and established that it is teachable student reading practices that separate the students with low entering indicators who do very well academically and those who perform as their indicators would "predict."[186] And in a world where, as Mertz registers, most first year courses in most law

---

[184] Wilkins, "A Systematic Response to Systemic Disadvantage: A Response to Sander" (cited in n.153) 1949 n.127.

[185] See Pamela Edwards, "Teaching Legal Writing as Women's Work: Life on the Fringes of the Academy" (1997) 4 Cardozo Women's L.J. 75; Christine Haight Farley, "Confronting Expectations: Women in the Legal Academy" (1996) 8 Yale J. L. & Feminism 333.

[186] Laurel Currie Oates, "Beating the Odds: Reading Strategies of Law Students Admitted Through Alternative Admissions Programs" (1997) 83 Iowa L. Rev. 139.

schools are assessed exclusively by a terminal written examination, there is the written legal literacy issue which is more or less invisible to most of those who teach in the U.S. legal academy.

As I have already indicated, students need to be taught not just course content, but how to perform effectively in course assessment mode if they are all to be given an equitable chance to succeed; not to do this is to reinforce educational social Darwinism. Some law students just "get" how to prepare for and to write a classic issue-spotter law school exam. Many do so after a while. Some "get it" only if it's explicitly taught.[187]

Then there is the rhetoric and composition scholarship which takes a critical race theory approach to the inculcation of tertiary literacy in the undergraduate education context, and how race matters there.[188] As a placeholder for my discussion of what legal education might learn from that body of work, just let me gesture towards three things. First, continuing black and white economic disparities matter in educational outcomes from grade school to law school, and the intersection of race and class and the association of socioeconomic status with tertiary educational outcomes for students in the U.S. ought also to be part of thinking about how to address what law schools do to black students which hampers their chances of success. Next, Mertz notes the different ways in which students perceived as dull and bright in the school education context are taught to read; reading that work against Oates's, for example, should suggest that entering law students' educational background ought routinely to be assessed in determining how to educate them equitably at the legal disciplinary literacy acquisition stage. And then this: consider the complex relationships with legal literacy that people whose forebears were classed as property by the texts, institutions, and practices of the law might be reasonably expected to have, especially given that for them education, and the acquisition of literacy in particular, was circumscribed in many ways, but most obviously by the statutes that criminalized teaching slaves to read. This history deserves reading by legal educators with an additional awareness of the literature on how high educational performance became stigmatized as "acting white" in significant parts of contemporary African-American society.

Finally, let me say this: I come to the praxis of the inculcation of legal disciplinary literacy as a Foucaultian and a Bourdian, and thus, as I have touched on here and written about elsewhere, I come to this aspect of what I will call in this context the civil rights struggle with the understanding that legal education, and perhaps especially the inculcation of its specific legal literacy, are paradigmatic of what Foucault understood

---

[187] The first year "Legal Writing" course taught in U.S. law schools can have an impact on such literacy, depending on how it is taught and by whom. But it does not teach students how to perform effectively in a three-hour timed examination; nor does it always take the risks and make the investments necessary to do even its job properly. Where the course is taught, as it usually is, by women whose markers of institutional status makes it clear to students that what they teach is institutionally constructed as marginal, in a world where Mertz notes, (tenured or tenure-track) white men teach most doctrinal first year classes, and where, as the literature on student assessment of teaching suggests, giving students interim grades has a negative effect on teaching evaluations, then there is a significant incentive for legal writing programs only to assess "for grade" the terminal piece of work product, with predictable results for students academically at risk.

[188] See Tom Fox, *Defending Access: A Critique of Standards in Higher Education* (Boynton/Cook, 1999); Jennifer S. Trainor, *Rethinking Racism: Emotion, Persuasion, and Literacy Education in an All-White High School* (Southern Illinois University Press, 2008); and the considerable bodies of work by Gloria Ladson-Billings on the way race impacts the inculcation of literacy; by Catherine Prendergast on literacy and racial justice; by Geneva Smitherman on race, language, and rights; and by Victor Villanueva on the interconnectedness among rhetoric, ideology, and racism, and their manifestation in literacy and literacy practices.

as the violence of the disciplines. And as we teach students out of the legal educational paradigm that was formed around the bodies of privileged white men, which at the foundational stage in the U.S. has changed very little indeed since the late nineteenth century, we teach our students how to take for granted and thus to make in their turn what it is we teach them. Nonetheless, the philosopher and Deleuze scholar Paul Patton has acutely identified how power, including disciplinary violence, might be reconceived: as "the idea of capacity to act [rather] than ... the normative notion of action which adversely affects the capacity of others to act."[189]

Or perhaps it partakes of aspects of both. If so, acknowledging this and exploring what it might enable us to learn about teaching legal disciplinary literacy in the U.S. law school, we might convert that metaphorical PVC pipe into a vector for delivering racial justice, surely an obligation of those of us who practice and teach the law that made all the injustice possible.

---

[189] Paul Patton, *Deleuze and the Political* (Routledge, 2000) 2.

Subject Index

Alice's Adventures in Wonderland, 164
Arabic language, 187, 188, 190, 192, 509
Assisted reproduction, 357, 359–361
Authority, claims of legal, Ch. 6, passim
    character of authorities' claims, 81–86
    claims as expressions of intention, 97–99
    claims as speech acts, 83–88
Authority, law as, 123
Autonomous testosterone myth, 305–308, 309

Babel, Tower of, 1, 525
Berghuis v Thompkins, 375–377
Bernstein, Basil
    language and socialization, 390–391
Blood tie, surname and, 318, 322–324
Borderline cases, 346–347
    and delegation of power, 347–349
Brown v Board of Education, 239, 347–348

Canada, 499, 500
Canons of Construction, Ch. 2, passim
Case, meaning of, 587–588
    case is altered, 587–589
Children
    naming of, Ch. 18, passim
    rights over name, 326–327
    video testimonies and, Ch. 17, passim
Claimant, 585
Codification, 1, 197
Common law reasoning, 37–39
Comparative law, Ch. 31, passim
Confessions, 6
Constitutional law, 4–5
Constructive interpretation, 37
Contract
    construing commercial, Ch. 26, passim
    use of US legalise, Ch. 27, passim
Conversational implicature
    Grice and, 5
Core and penumbra
    Hart on, 115
Criminal law, 4
    the deaf and, Ch. 33, passim
    sexual offences, Ch.1, passim
    terrorism, 469–482

Deaf persons
    in court, Ch. 33, passim
    interpreters for, 549
    unfitness to plead, 567–568
Deaf/Blind persons, 566–567
Defamation, law of, 182–183
Deontic logic, 2
Dictionary
    law and the, 115
Discourse analysis, 5, 6
Domestic violence, 236

Donoghue v Stevenson, 129

East India Act (Charter Act), 187, 189–190, 191, 193, 194, 196
Education, legal, Ch. 30, passim
    epistemology, 500–502
Equity, law of, 160–162
European Union, Court of Justice of, Ch. 29, passim
    drafting judgments in, 485–488
    joint opinions in, 501–502

Farming, 429–430
Fiction, universality of, 166–175
Film
    Lawyer, Lawyer Ch. 15
Forensic linguistics, 6
Frame–based meaning, 297

Games, 420–423
    challenges, 423–424
    world's and, 428
German Supreme Court, 536–541
God, 183, 184
Griefing, 430–431
Gulliver's Travels, 571, 581

Hamlet, Ch. 13, passim
Hansard, 195–197
Henry V, 214
Henry V I, Part Two, 203–208
Holocaust denial, 182
Hong Kong, Ch. 15, passim

Ideology
    Sumner and, 388–390
Iliad, 530
In Cold Blood, 180
India
    Macaulay and, 187–189
    Macaulay versus Prinsep, 190–192
    Penal Code, 198, 200
    religion in, 192–194
Internal aspect of rules, 121—122
    H. L. A. Hart on, 116, 123, 124
Interpretation
    as definition, 419–420
    contracts, of, Ch. 26, passim
    in language and the law, Ch. 9, passim
Ireland, 496—500
Israel Supreme Court, 537

Jaffa Cakes, 125
Jews, 135
Judges
    official and private roles, 550–551
Judgments

Subject Index

first person in, Ch. 32, passim
Julius Caesar, 181
Juries
  understanding of narratives, 234–235
Justice
  law and language and, 494–496

Kill stealing, 431–432

Language
  memory and judgment, 335–337
Law and Film, Ch. 15, passim
Law and literature, 2-3, Ch.13, passim, Ch.14
Law as institutional fact, 37
Law as normative system, 37
Law, Shakespeare and, Ch 13, passim
Le Rouge et Le Noir, 180
Legal education
  minority students and, Ch.35, passim
Legal language
  archaic nature of, 570–575
  consumption of, Ch. 23, passim
  Hamlet, in, Ch. 13, passim
  interpretation of, 16–34
  Proto-Indo-European domination of, Ch. 34, passim
Legislative history, 189
Linguistic meaning, role of, 43–44
Linguistic pragmatics, 5
Linguistic typologies, 329–331
Literal rule, 138
Lord, 584–585
  as authority, 120, 123
  as moral imperative, 123
  as social identity, 123, 124
  as social mechanism, 123
  as social obligation, 123, 124
  as strategic goal, 123

Madame Bovary, 180, 181
Magic, law as, 2
Marx Brothers, 457
Measure for Measure, 206
Medium, language as, 418–419
Merchant of Venice, 208, 246–247, 250–254, 586
Message, language as, 417-418, 419
Miners' Strike, 399
Miranda Rule
  Does it matter today? 381–385
  origins, 372–374
Mistake, legal, 39–42
Moll Flanders, 180
Mona Lisa, 164
Multi–lingual court, Ch. 19, passim

Names, law of, 312–313
  changing a name, 314
  children's names, 313–314
  disputes over, 315
  headship and, 316
  identity and, 317–319
  special, 313

Natural Born Killers, 182
Natural law, 39, 41–42
Night at the Opera, 457
Nuremberg Trials, 37

Old Bailey, 180
  trials of deaf persons, Ch. 33
O. J. Simpson trial, 5–6
Open justice, principle of, 178, 179
Open texture of law, 20–23, 130, 131–133, 137
Originalism, 270–273
Overruling, 145–146

Parents, Ch. 21, passim
  children's views as to, 365–367
Parliamentary discourse, 467–469
  power without safeguards, 469–470
Performative acts, 2, 544–546
Plea bargaining, 235
Pluralism, legal, Ch. 7, passim
Police and Criminal Evidence Act 1984, 570
Power, Foucault and, 205, 215–216
  of naming, Ch.18, passim
  of patronymy, 315–316, 318—319
Practical knowledge, 88–97
Pragmatics
  nature of, 9–13
  maxims/hermeneutics, 13–16
Precedent, 38, 246, 248–250, 254–258, 288
  in Court of Justice of European Union, Ch. 29, passim
Proto–Indo–Europeans, 575–582

Race
  legal education and, Ch. 35, passim
Radbruch's Formula, 39
Rape myths, 300–301
Rectification of contracts, 442–445
Relevance theory, 227–32, 273–280, 280–286, 289–290, 2
Richard II, 206
Right answer
  Dworkin and, 35
Roman law, 401
Rule-following, 142–144
Rule scepticism, 143

Sanskrit, 187, 188, 190, 192, 572
Scandinavian Realism, 2
Semiotics, 6
Sign language, 557–558, 570
Silence
  meaning of, 374–375
  right of, Ch.22, passim
Sociolinguistics, 5
Speech act theory, 6
Speech, freedom of, 4–5
Star Chamber, 371
State surveillance, 208–212
Statutory interpretation, 5, 427–428
Stories in law, Ch. 14, passim

Television
 and law, 391–395
Terrorism
 imagery, 476–479
Terrorism Act 2000, 406, 411–413
Textualist/Orientalist debate, 23–27
Tradition
 language and, 502–504
Translation
 obstacles to, 506–511
Truth
 children and lying, 294–295
Truth, legal, 34–35, 39, 44, 45–61, 62–78
 threshold questions, 36–37

Unity, fiction of, 316, 317
Useful knowledge, 192, 193

Vagueness, Ch. 20, passim
 value of, 349–354
Verfremdung [alienation]
 Brecht and, 205, 207
Video-recorded testimonies, Ch. 17,
 passim
Violence, 1, 2, 438, 439–442, 443–446,
 450, 454
 Cover and, 1, 2
 necessary, Ch. 35, passim
Virtue
 in law and literature, Ch. 10, passim
Vulnerable witnesses, 293–294

Wales, Ch. 24, passim, 500
Welsh language, Ch. 24, passim
Wizards, 432

Name Index

Abrams, M. H., 287
Ainsworth, J, 4
Alexy, R, 84, 85
Almack, K, 307
Anscombe, E, 80, 81, 87, 88, 89, 90, 92, 93
Aquinas, St T, 509
Aristomodou, M, 236, 237, 242, 247
Aristotle, 87, 96, 161, 170, 171, 184, 534
Austin, J, 6
Austin, J. L., 2, 85–87, 116, 130, 137, 543, 544, 545
Ayres, I, 607, 609

Ball, M, 578, 589
Barak, A, 547, 550
Barthes, R, 170, 228
Beckett, S, 532
Bell, D, 243
Benjamin, W, 518
Bentham, J, 6
Bernstein, B, 390
Bernstein, L, 455, 456
Blackstone, Sir W, 316
Borges, J, L, 514
Bourdieu, P, 311, 616
Bowman, G, 408
Brookes, R, 607, 609
Bruner, J, 229
Bultmann, R, 525, 529
Bulwer, J, 558
Bush, K, 401–402, 414

Capote, T, 180
Carroll, L, 264
Carston, R, 136, 275, 278
Celan, P, 524
Chaucer, G, 585
Cicero, M. T., 572
Cole, S, 595
Conley, J. M, 6
Cordozzi, M, 227, 228
Cotterill, J, 5
Coulshard, M, 6

Daly, M, 315
Davies, H, 311, 312
Davis, E. M, 265, 269, 283
Defoe, D, 180
Delanty, G, 398
Delgado, R, 234, 238–239
Dennett, D, 274
Derrida, J, 133, 357, 358, 359, 361, 364, 370, 514, 517, 518, 520, 521, 522, 523, 524, 525, 528, 529, 532
Dickens, C, 152, 153, 154, 155
Dioso-Villa, R, 395
Donne, J, 174

Doyle, A, 395
Duchamp, M, 523
Durkheim, E, 390
Duxbury, N, 284, 285, 547
Dworkin, R, 67, 77, 116, 118, 123, 124, 125, 126, 260, 267, 268, 280, 285, 530, 534, 546

Eades, D, 6
Eagleton, T, 252, 257
Ehrlich, S, 6, 294, 301
Ekins, R, 267–268
Eliot, G, 152–153
Emeens, E, 326
Endicott, T, 90
Ericson, R, 396
Eskridge, W, 260, 267, 271, 280, 287, 288
Evans, G, 90
Ewick, S, 244–245

Filipović, L, 329, 336, 337
Fillmore, C, 116, 117, 141
Finbar, J, 499
Finch, J, 312
Finnis, J, 77
Fish, S, 257
Flaubert, G, 180
Flood, J, 460, 461
Foucault, M, 616
Franke, K, 319
Frege, G, 150
Fuller, L, 495, 512

Gadamer, H-G, 114
Gardner, J, 83, 84
Garfinkel, H, 232
Gaskell, E, 153, 155
Geldof, B, 363
Gewirth, P, 224
Gibbons, J, 378
Gies, L, 397–398
Glenn, P, 508
Goodman, E, 327
Goodrich, P, 3–4, 520
Gordley, J, 516
Greenawalt, K, 260, 284
Greimas, A. J., 6
Grice, H, 5, 374–375, 377
Grimm, J. L. C., 573
Guinier, L, 595
Gurnham, D, 236

Hagerstrom, A, 2
Hale, M, 562
Harris, S, 225
Hart, H. L. A., 2, 6, 78, 90, 115, 116, 124, 148–150, 272

Herron, M, 318
Ho, D, 601, 609
Holmes, O. W., 6, 122, 123
Husserl, E, 514
Hylton, P, 526

Jackson, B, 6, 225, 226
Jefferson, G, 230
Johnson, A, 514, 515, 595
Jones, Sir W, 502, 503
Joyce, J, 167

Kahn, P, 260, 274
Kant, I, 543
Karst, K, 320
Kelly, F, 365, 366
Kelsen, H, 534, 546
Kennedy, D, 67, 546
Kim, S, 320, 322
King, M, 107, 109
Kotz, H, 516, 517, 518
Kripke, O, 102, 103
Kurzon, D, 6
Kushner, J. S., 323

Labov, W, 224, 227, 244
Lacan, J, 6
Lawson, T, 394
Legrand, P, 498
Leisner, O. M., 315, 316
Levinson, S, 261, 279, 285, 286
Lewis, D, 147
Llewellyn, K, 124
Luhmann, N, 103, 104, 107, 111

Mac Cormick, N, 65
MacIntyre, A, 494, 502, 504, 505, 506, 510–511
MacKinnon, C, 243
Macaulay, S, 393
Maine, Sir H, 574, 580
Malory, T, 155
Marmor, A, 143
Matosian, G, 6
Mattila, H. S., 401
Maynard, D. W., 235
McDougall, P. R, 316
Mertz, E, 612, 614, 615, 616
Mezey, N, 393
Milton, J, 157
Minow, M, 321—322
Montesquieu, C, 534, 546
Moore, S. F., 113
Moorhead, R, 135
Moran, B, 601, 605–606
Morris, W, 156, 157
Mulcahy, L, 583

Natalier, K, 398
Nelson, C, 263, 264
Nietzsche, F, 311
Nises, J, 393

O'Barr, W, 6, 225, 235, 240, 308
Olivecrona, K, 2

Patton, P, 617
Pether, P, 4
Pinter, H, 518–519
Plato, 96, 167, 170, 171, 357, 358, 359, 362, 364, 370
Putnam, H, 132, 134, 135

Quine, W, 525–529, 531, 532

Racine, J, 165
Rawls, J, 154
Raz, J, 73, 81–82, 84, 85
Reissman, C. K., 227
Renschler, C, 390, 391
Robson, P, 395
Roiphe, K, 317
Rorty, R, 520
Rose, G, 159
Ryave, A, 230

Samarin, W, 374
Sander, R. H., 590–591, 599–606, 609, 610, 611, 612
Sapir, E, 335
Sarat, A, 3
Saussure, F de, 106
Savigny, F. C. von, 548
Scary, E, 226
Schauer, F, 2
Scheppele, K, 233
Searle, J, 86, 87, 273
Shakespeare, W, 107, 111, 572
Sherwin, R, 234, 243, 244
Siegel, J, 263, 264, 283
Simmonds, N, 98
Sinclair, M. B. W., 5
Singer, J, W, 240
Slaughter, J, 152
Slobin, D, 330, 331
Smith, P, 398
Smith, S, 270
Solan, L, 4, 5, 6
Sperber, D, 273, 274, 275, 276, 277, 281, 282, 286
Sumner, C, 387–388, 389, 399

Talmy, L, 330
Tasioulas, J, 161–162
Tennyson, Lord A, 152, 157, 158, 161, 162
Teubner, G, 101, 102
Thomas,, A, 394–395
Tiersma, P, 4, 6
Tirosh, Y, 315
Titmuss, R, 463
Tribe, L, 265, 271
Twining, W. L., 126, 325

Vermeule, A, 266
Villey, M, 509

Waismann, F, 131–133
Watkins, D, 241, 243
Watt, G, 160–161, 579
Weiler, J, 512
Weisberg, R, 2–3
Wesley-Smith, P, 249
West, R, 3

White, J. B., 2–3, 587
Wilkins, D, 610–611
Winter, S, 5, 243, 584

Zedner, L, 387
Zweigert, K, 516, 517, 518